Economics and Financial Statement Analysis

LEVEL I

2006

CFA PROGRAM CURRICULUM • VOLUME II

CFA INSTITUTE

PEARSON
Custom Publishing

Printed in the United States of America

10 9 8 7 6 5 4 3

ISBN 0-536-91836-8

2004160639

BK/JS

Please visit our web site at *www.pearsoncustom.com*

PEARSON CUSTOM PUBLISHING
75 Arlington Street, Suite 300, Boston, MA 02116
A Pearson Education Company

CONTENTS

Preparing to Study the CFA Curriculum Materials on Economics

Before beginning the Reading Assignments for Study Sessions 4 through 6, candidates should have a basic mastery of the concepts typically presented in introductory college-level economics courses. The primary source of Reading Assignments in the CFA Curriculum is *Economics: Private and Public Choice,* Tenth edition, by Gwartney, Stroup, Sobel, and Macpherson.

Reading Assignments assume candidates are already knowledgeable in economics, and understand the following important subjects:

- using national income, output, and price measures to track the performance of national economies
- economic terms and definitions
- factors affecting aggregate demand and supply, and how markets adjust to changes in these factors
- major theoretical and practical considerations of macroeconomic models
- the laws of supply and demand, and factors causing shifts in or movements along the supply and demand curves
- price determination, market equilibrium, and the behavior of market participants
- the operation of market forces in resource and funds markets
- effects on economic activity of price controls and taxes

If you have not taken an introductory economics course during the past few years, we strongly encourage you to consider additional study of introductory course material. Although examination questions are drawn only from the Reading Assignments, studying the additional introductory material will strengthen candidates' understanding of the required concepts. CFA Institute's book distributor offers the textbook used for the Reading Assignments, *Economics: Private and Public Choice,* Tenth edition, by Gwartney, Stroup, Sobel, and Macpherson. At a minimum, we recommend that you study the following chapters:

- Chapter 3—Supply, Demand and the Market Process
- Chapter 4—Supply and Demand: Applications and Extensions
- Chapter 7—Taking the Nation's Economic Pulse
- Chapter 10—Working with Our Basic Aggregate Demand/Aggregate Supply Model
- Chapter 11—Keynesian Foundations of Modern Macroeconomics

Many economics textbooks and courses provide similar coverage and will enable you to master the concepts and principles discussed in the Gwartney text.

If you do not have a strong background in economics, please take some extra time before you begin your study program to review economics concepts and principles.

ECONOMICS

The candidate should be able to demonstrate a thorough knowledge of macroeconomic and microeconomic principles, including the key components of economic activity, macroeconomic theory and policy, international trade, and exchange rates.

STUDY SESSION 4 ECONOMICS: MACRO-ECONOMIC ANALYSIS

READING ASSIGNMENTS

Reading 14 Economic Fluctuations, Unemployment, and Inflation
Reading 15 Fiscal Policy
Reading 16 Money and the Banking System
Reading 17 Modern Macroeconomics: Monetary Policy
Reading 18 Stabilization Policy, Output, and Employment

LEARNING OUTCOMES

Reading 14: Economic Fluctuations, Unemployment, and Inflation

The candidate should be able to:

a. explain the phases of the business cycle;
b. discuss the problems in measuring unemployment and describe the three types of unemployment;
c. explain full employment and the natural rate of unemployment;
d. define inflation, discuss its causes, distinguish between anticipated and unanticipated inflation, and discuss the harmful effects of both on economic activity.

Reading 15: Fiscal Policy

The candidate should be able to:

a. explain the process by which, according to the Keynesian view, fiscal policy affects aggregate demand and aggregate supply;
b. explain the importance of the timing of changes in fiscal policy and the difficulties in achieving proper timing;
c. discuss the impact of expansionary and restrictive fiscal policies based on the basic Keynesian model, the crowding-out model, the new classical model and supply-side model;
d. identify automatic stabilizers and explain how such stabilizers work.

Reading 16: Money and the Banking System

The candidate should be able to:

a. explain the relationship among the required reserve ratio, the potential deposit expansion multiplier, and the deposit expansion multiplier;

b. describe the role of a country's central bank and the tools that a central bank can use to control the money supply, and explain how a central bank can use monetary tools to implement monetary policy;

c. discuss potential problems in measuring an economy's money supply.

Reading 17: Modern Macroeconomics: Monetary Policy

The candidate should be able to:

a. discuss the determinants of money demand and supply

b. discuss how anticipation of the effects of monetary policy can influence the policy's effectiveness;

c. identify the components of the equation of exchange, discuss the implications of the equation for monetary policy, describe the quantity theory of money, and discuss its implications for the determination of inflation;

d. compare and contrast the impact of anticipated and unanticipated monetary policy on the inflation rate, real output and employment, and interest rates.

Reading 18: Stabilization Policy, Output, and Employment

The candidate should be able to:

a. describe the composition and use of the index of leading economic indicators;

b. discuss the time lags that may influence the performance of discretionary monetary and fiscal policy;

c. contrast the adaptive expectations hypothesis to the rational expectations hypothesis, and discuss implications on prices and output under the two hypotheses when there are changes in macroeconomic policies;

d. distinguish between an activist and a non-activist strategy for stabilization policy.

ECONOMIC FLUCTUATIONS, UNEMPLOYMENT, AND INFLATION

READING 14

LEARNING OUTCOMES

The candidate should be able to:

a. explain the phases of the business cycle;

b. discuss the problems in measuring unemployment and describe the three types of unemployment;

c. explain full employment and the natural rate of unemployment;

d. define inflation, discuss the causes, distinguish between anticipated and unanticipated inflation, and discuss the harmful effects of both on economic activity.

INTRODUCTION 1

Prosperity is when the prices of the things that you sell are rising; inflation is when the prices of the things that you buy are rising. Recession is when other people are unemployed; depression is when you are unemployed.

—Anonymous

The performance of the economy influences our job opportunities, income levels, and quality of life. Thus, key indicators of economic performance, such as growth of real GDP, the rate of unemployment, and the inflation rate, are closely watched by investors, politicians, and the media. This reading focuses on how several key economic indicators are derived and explains how changes in these measures influence our lives.

The primary objectives of macroeconomic policy are rapid growth of output, a high level of employment, and stability in the general level of prices. There is widespread agreement concerning the desirability of these goals. However, there is considerable controversy with regard to how they can be achieved. As we proceed, the causes of economic instability and the potential of government policy as a stabilizing force will be analyzed in detail.

2 SWINGS IN THE ECONOMIC PENDULUM

During this century, the annual growth rate of real GDP in the United States has averaged approximately 3 percent. The rate of growth, however, has not been steady. During the Great Depression of the 1930s, economic growth plunged. Real GDP declined by 7.5 percent or more each year from 1930 to 1932. In 1933 it was almost 30 percent less than it was in 1929. The 1929 level of real GDP was not reached again until 1939. The Second World War was characterized by a rapid expansion of GDP, which was followed by a decline after the war. Real GDP did not reach its 1944 level again until 1953, although the output of consumer goods did increase significantly in the years immediately following the war.

As Exhibit 14-1 illustrates, real GDP has continued to grow at an annual rate of approximately 3 percent from 1960 to 2001. Economic ups and downs have also continued. Real GDP grew rapidly throughout most of the 1960s, 1972–1973, 1976–1977, 1983–1988, and most of the 1990s. Since 1960, however, there have also been seven periods (1960, 1970, 1974–1975, 1980, 1982, 1991, and 2001) of falling real GDP. Compared to the first half of this century, the growth of real GDP has been more stable during the last four decades. During this period, the annual fluctuations in real GDP have fallen within the range of *minus* 2 percent to *plus* 6 percent. This is a definite improvement. Figures on GDP and related data can be obtained from the Bureau of Economic Analysis on the Internet at www.bea.doc.gov.

A Hypothetical Business Cycle

The economic record of the United States and other modern economies is characterized by both growth of real GDP and an instability in the pattern of that growth. Periods of economic expansion do not last forever. Inevitably, growth of

EXHIBIT 14-1 Instability in the Growth of Real GDP

While real GDP in the United States fluctuates substantially, periods of positive growth outweigh the periods of declining real income. Since 1960, the U.S. growth rate of real GDP has averaged approximately 3.0 percent annually. Economists refer to periods of declining real GDP as recessions. The recessionary periods are shaded.

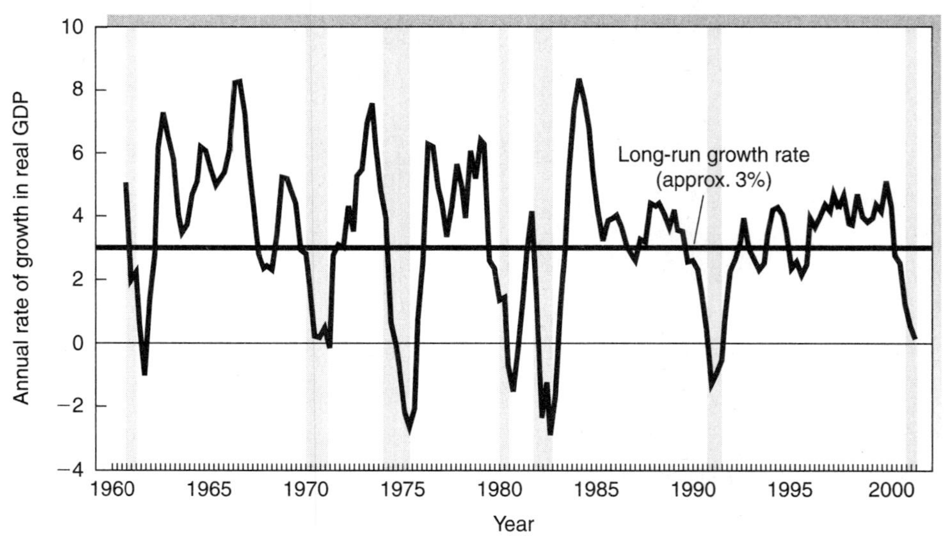

Source: Economic Report of the President, various issues.

EXHIBIT 14-2 Business Cycle

In the past, ups and downs have often characterized aggregate business activity. Despite these fluctuations there has been an upward trend in real GDP in the United States and other industrial nations.

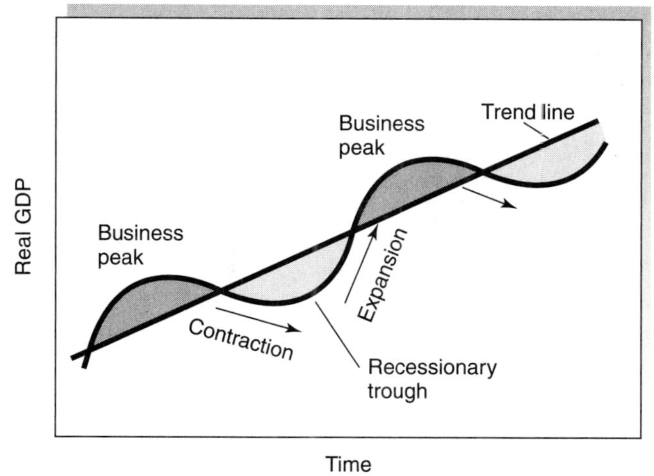

real GDP has been followed by economic slowdown and contraction. Economists refer to these swings in the rate of output as the **business cycle**. Periods of growth in real output and other aggregate measures of economic activity followed by periods of decline are the distinguishing characteristics of business cycles.

Business cycle
Fluctuations in the general level of economic activity as measured by such variables as the rate of unemployment and changes in real GDP.

Exhibit 14-2 illustrates a hypothetical business cycle. When most businesses are operating at capacity level and real GDP is growing rapidly, a *business peak*, or boom, is present. As aggregate business conditions slow, the economy begins the *contraction*, or recessionary, phase of a business cycle. During the contraction, the sales of most businesses fall, real GDP grows at a slow rate or perhaps declines, and unemployment in the aggregate labor market increases.

The bottom of the contraction phase is referred to as the *recessionary trough.* After the downturn reaches bottom, and economic conditions begin to improve, the economy enters the *expansion* phase of the cycle. Here business sales rise, GDP grows rapidly, and the rate of unemployment declines. The expansion eventually blossoms into another business peak. The peak, however, peters out and turns into a contraction, beginning the cycle anew.

Recession
A downturn in economic activity characterized by declining real GDP and rising unemployment. In an effort to be more precise, many economists define a recession as two consecutive quarters in which there is a decline in real GDP.

The term **recession** is widely used to describe conditions during the contraction and recessionary trough phases of the business cycle—that is, a period during which real GDP declines. Many economists specify that a recession means a decline in real GDP for two or more successive quarters.[1] When a recession is prolonged and characterized by a sharp decline in economic activity, it is called a **depression**.

Depression
A prolonged and very severe recession.

In one important respect, the term *business cycle* is misleading. *Cycle* generally implies that there is some regularity—like that indicated by the hypothetical business cycle of Exhibit 14-2—in the timing and duration of the activity. In the

[1] See Geoffrey H. Moore, "Recessions," in *The Fortune Encyclopedia of Economics,* edited by David R. Henderson (New York: Time Warner Inc., 1993), for additional information on recessions in the United States. Also see "Symposium on Business Cycles." *Journal of Economic Perspectives,* Spring 1999, pp. 19–90.

real world, as Exhibit 14-1 illustrates, this is not the case. The expansions and contractions last varying lengths of time, and the swings differ in terms of their magnitude. For example, the recessions of 1961, 1982, and 1990 were followed by eight years or more of uninterrupted growth of output. In contrast, the recession of 1980 was followed by an expansion that lasted only 12 months. The expansionary phase following the recessions of 1970 and 1974–1975 fell between these two extremes. *In the real world, the observed fluctuations in real output are irregular and unpredictable.*

How can one know where an economy is on the business cycle? Of course, changes in real GDP would provide the answer, but they are only available quarterly and it is usually 4 to 6 weeks after the quarter is over before reliable figures are released. Various indicators that are available monthly or more often can provide clues. For example, auto sales, new housing starts, new factory orders, and even the stock market will generally increase during an expansion and decline when the economy dips into a recession. Thus, these indicators are monitored carefully by those most interested in business cycle conditions.

3 ECONOMIC FLUCTUATIONS AND THE LABOR MARKET

Civilian labor force
The number of persons 16 years of age and over who are either employed or unemployed. In order to be classified as unemployed, one must be looking for a job.

Unemployed
The term used to describe a person not currently employed who is either (1) actively seeking employment or (2) waiting to begin or return to a job.

Labor force participation rate
The number of persons in the civilian labor force 16 years of age or over who are either employed or actively seeking employment as a percentage of the total civilian population 16 years of age and over.

Fluctuations in real GDP influence the demand for labor and employment. In our modern world, people are busy with jobs, household work, school, and other activities. Exhibit 14-3 illustrates how economists classify these activities in relation to the **civilian labor force**, defined as the number of persons age 16 years and over who are either employed or seeking employment. The noninstitutional civilian adult population is grouped into two broad categories: (1) persons not in the labor force and (2) persons in the labor force. There are a variety of reasons why individuals may not currently be in the labor force. Some are retired. Others may be working in their own household or attending school. Still others may not be working as a result of illness or disability. Although many of these people are quite busy, their activities are outside the market labor force.

As Exhibit 14-3 illustrates, **unemployed** workers who are seeking work are included in the labor force along with employed workers. The **labor force participation rate** is the number of persons in the civilian labor force (including both the employed and the unemployed) as a percentage of the civilian population 16 years of age and over. In 2001, the population (16 years of age and over) of the United States was 211.9 million, 141.8 million of whom were in the labor force. Thus, the U.S. labor force participation rate was 66.9 percent (141.8 million divided by 211.9 million).

The labor force participation rate varies substantially across countries. For example, in 2000 the labor force participation rate was 67.2 percent in the United States, 77.4 percent in Canada, and 76.2 in Sweden. In contrast, the labor force participation rate was only 56.3 percent in Mexico and 60.0 percent in Italy. The percent of married women in the labor force is generally smaller in countries like Italy and Mexico that have a low labor force participation rate.

In the United States, one of the most interesting labor force developments of the post-World War II era is the dramatic increase in the labor force participation rate of women. Exhibit 14-4 illustrates this point. In 2001, 60.1 percent of adult women worked outside the home, up from 32.7 percent in 1948. Married women accounted for most of this increase. More than half of all married women now are in the labor force, compared to only 20 percent immediately following the Second World War. While the labor force participation of women rose, the rate for men fell. In 2001, the labor force participation rate of men was

EXHIBIT 14-3 Population, Employment, and Unemployment, 2001

The accompanying diagram illustrates the alternative participation-status categories for the adult population.

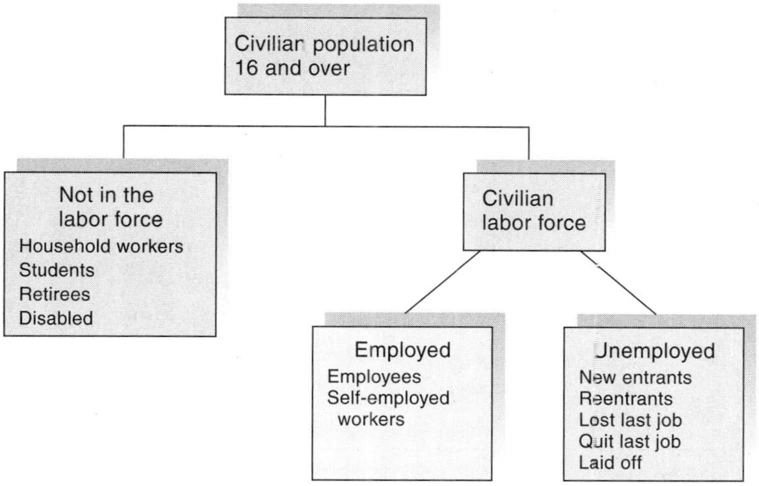

	Number of Persons, 2001
Noninstitutional civilian population (age 16 and over)	211.9
Not in labor force	70.1
Total civilian labor force	141.8
Employed	135.1
Unemployed	6.7
Rate of labor force participation	66.9%
Employment/population ratio	63.8%
Rate of unemployment	4.8%

*Data are measured in millions, except those expressed as percentages.
Source: www.bls.gov.

74.4 percent, down from 83.3 percent in 1960 and 86.6 percent in 1948. Clearly, the composition of workforce participation within the family has changed substantially during the past five decades.

Rate of unemployment The percentage of persons in the labor force who are unemployed. Mathematically, it is equal to number of persons unemployed/ number of persons in the labor force × 100.

The **rate of unemployment** is a key barometer of conditions in the aggregate labor market. This notwithstanding, the term is often misunderstood. At the most basic level, it is important to note that unemployment is different from not working. As we have already indicated, there are several reasons—including household work, school attendance, retirement, and illness or disability—why a person may be neither employed nor looking for a job. These people, though not employed, are not counted in the unemployment tally.

Moreover, persons must either be employed or unemployed before they are counted as part of the labor force. Part-time as well as full-time workers are counted as employed members of the labor force. The rate of unemployment is the number of persons unemployed expressed as a percentage of the labor force. In 2001 the rate of unemployment in the United States was 4.8 percent

EXHIBIT 14-4 Labor Force Participation of Men and Women, 1948–2001

As the chart illustrates, the labor force participation rate for women has been steadily increasing for several decades, while the rate for men has been declining.

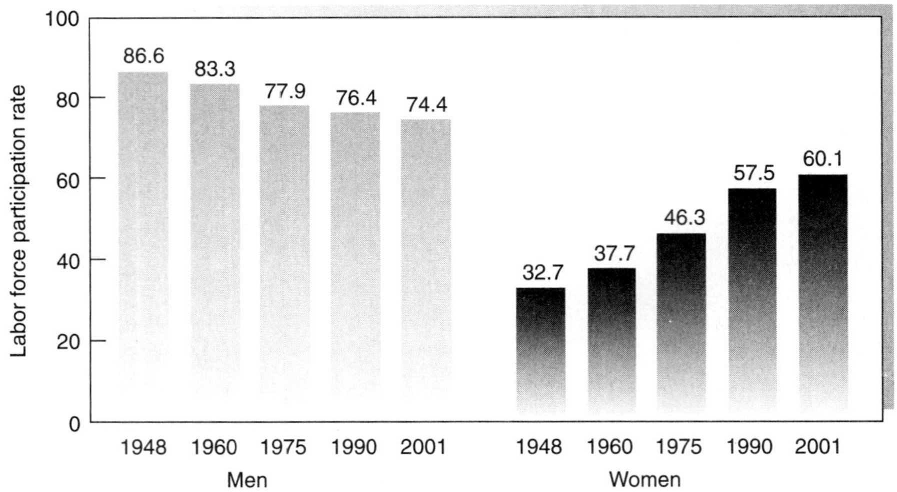

Source: www.bls.gov.

Employment/population ratio
The number of persons 16 years of age and over employed as civilians divided by the total civilian population 16 years of age and over. The ratio is expressed as a percentage.

(6.7 million out of a labor force of 141.8 million). (See the Applications in Economics box for information on how the Bureau of Labor Statistics derives the unemployment rate.)

In addition to the rate of unemployment, many economists also use the **employment/population ratio**—the number of persons employed expressed as a percentage of the population 16 years and over—to monitor labor market conditions. This ratio will tend to rise during an expansion and fall during a recession. Both the number employed and the population age 16 and over are well

APPLICATIONS IN ECONOMICS

Deriving the Unemployment Rate

Each month, the Bureau of Labor Statistics (BLS) contacts a sample of 50,000 households that reflects the population characteristics of the United States. Specially trained interviewers pose identical questions designed to determine whether each of the approximately 90,000 adults in these households is employed, unemployed, or not in the labor force. Persons aged 16 years and over are considered employed if they (1) worked at all (even as little as one hour) for pay or profit during the survey week, (2) worked 15 hours or more without pay in a family-operated enterprise during the survey week, or (3) have a job at which they did not work during the survey week because of illness, vacation, industrial disputes, bad weather, time off, or personal reasons.

People are considered unemployed if they (1) do not have a job, (2) are available for work, and (3) have actively looked for work during the past four weeks. Looking for work may involve any of the following activities: (1) registration at a public or private employment office, (2) meeting with prospective employers, (3) checking with friends or relatives, (4) placing or answering advertisements, (5) writing letters of application, or (6) being in a union or on a professional register. In addition, those not working are classified as unemployed if they are either waiting to start a new job within 30 days or waiting to be recalled from a layoff.

The BLS uses its survey data to calculate the unemployment rate and other employment-related statistics each month. States use the BLS survey and employment figures from industries covered by unemployment insurance to construct state and area employment statistics. These labor market figures are published by the U.S. Department of Labor in the *Monthly Labor Review* and on the Internet at www.bls.gov.

defined and readily measurable. Their measurement does not require a subjective judgment as to whether a person is actually "available for work" or "actively seeking employment." Thus, some believe that the employment/population ratio is a more objective indicator of job availability than the rate of unemployment. The employment/population ratio was 63.8 percent in 2001. The accompanying Thumbnail Sketch provides the formulas that can be used to calculate the major indicators of conditions in labor markets.

THUMBNAIL SKETCH

Formulas for Key Labor Market Indicators

1. **Labor force** = Employed + Unemployed
2. **Labor force participation rate** = number in labor force/population (age 16 and over)
3. **Rate of unemployment** = number unemployed/number in labor force
4. **Employment/population ratio** = number employed/population (age 16 and over)

Reasons for Unemployment

Not all people who are unemployed lost their last job. A dynamic economy will be characterized by considerable labor mobility as workers move (1) from contracting to expanding industries and (2) into and out of the labor force. Spells of unemployment often accompany such changes.

The Department of Labor indicates five reasons why workers may experience unemployment. Exhibit 14-5 indicates the share of unemployed workers in each of these five categories in 2001. Interestingly, 6.7 percent of the unemployed workers were first-time entrants into the work force and 30.1 percent were reentering after exiting for additional schooling, household work, or other

EXHIBIT 14-5 Composition of the Unemployed by Reason

This chart indicates the various reasons why persons were unemployed in 2001. Slightly more than one-third (35.3 percent) of the persons unemployed were dismissed from their last job. More than one-third (36.8 percent) of the unemployed workers were either new entrants or reentrants into the labor force.

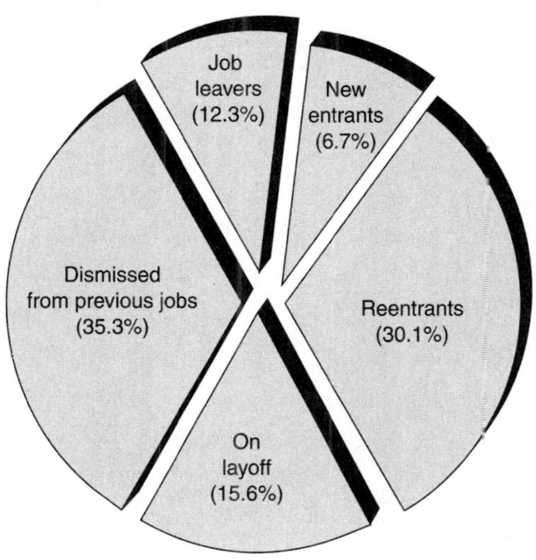

Source: www.bls.gov.

reasons. Thus, 36.8 percent of the unemployed workers were experiencing unemployment as the result of entry or reentry into the labor force. One out of every eight (12.3 percent) of the unemployed quit their last job. People laid off and waiting to return to their previous positions contributed 15.6 percent to the total. Workers dismissed from their job accounted for slightly more than one-third (35.3 percent) of the unemployed workers.

In a dynamic world where information, like most other things, is scarce and people are free to choose among jobs, some unemployment is inevitable. As new products are introduced and new technologies developed, some firms are expanding while others are contracting. Still other firms may be going out of business. This process results in the creation of new jobs and the disappearance of old ones. Similarly, at any point in time potential workers are switching from school (or nonwork) to the labor force, while others are retiring or taking a leave from the labor force. Workers are mobile as they voluntarily quit and search for better opportunities, or reallocate work responsibilities within the family; some unemployment will always be present.

There is a positive side to job search and unemployment: It generally permits individuals to better match their skills and preferences with the requirements of a job. Such job moves enhance both employee productivity and earnings.

Young workers often switch jobs and move between schooling and the labor force as they search for a career path that best fits their abilities and preferences. As the result of this job switching, the unemployment rate of younger workers is substantially higher than that for more established workers. As Exhibit 14-6 shows, in 2001 the unemployment rate of workers 20–24 years of age was more than twice the rate for their counterparts aged 25 years and over. The unemployment rate for teenagers was approximately four times the rate of older workers.

4 THREE TYPES OF UNEMPLOYMENT

Although some unemployment is perfectly consistent with economic efficiency, this is not always the case. Abnormally high rates of unemployment generally reflect weak demand conditions for labor, counterproductive policies, and/or the inability or lack of incentive on the part of potential workers and potential

EXHIBIT 14-6 Unemployment Rate by Age and Gender, 2001

Group	Civilian Rate of Unemployment, 2001 (percent)
Total, all workers	4.8
Men, Total	4.8
Ages 16–19	15.9
Ages 20–24	8.9
Ages 25 and over	3.6
Women, Total	4.7
Ages 16–19	13.4
Ages 20–24	7.5
Ages 25 and over	3.7

Source: www.bls.gov.

employers to arrive at mutually advantageous agreements. To clarify matters, economists divide unemployment into three categories: frictional, structural, and cyclical. Let us take a closer look at each of these three classifications.

Frictional Unemployment

Unemployment that is caused by constant changes in the labor market is called **frictional unemployment**. It occurs because (a) employers are not fully aware of all available workers and their job qualifications and (b) available workers are not fully aware of the jobs being offered by employers. In other words, the main cause of frictional unemployment is imperfect information. The number of job vacancies may match the number of persons seeking employment. The qualifications of the job seekers may even meet those required by firms seeking employees. Nonetheless, frictional unemployment will still occur because persons seeking jobs and firms hiring employees with the qualifications of the job seekers do not know about each other. Seeking to improve their options, both employers and employees will search for better alternatives.

Frictional unemployment Unemployment due to constant changes in the economy that prevent qualified unemployed workers from being immediately matched up with existing job openings. It results from the scarcity of information and the search activities of both employers and employees for information that will help them make better employment choices.

Employers looking for a new worker seldom hire the first applicant who walks into their employment office. They want to find the "best available" worker to fill the opening. It is costly to hire workers who perform poorly. It is sometimes even costly to terminate their employment. So, employers search—they expend time and resources screening applicants in an effort to find the best qualified workers willing to accept their wage and employment conditions.

Similarly, job seekers search for their best option among the potential alternatives. They make telephone calls, search newspaper ads and Internet sites, submit to job interviews, use employment services, and so on. Pursuit of personal gain—the landing of a job that is more attractive than the current options of which they are aware—motivates job seekers to engage in job search activities.

As a job searcher finds out about more and more potential job opportunities, it becomes less likely that *additional search* will uncover a more attractive option. Therefore, the *marginal benefit* derived from job search declines with time spent searching for a job, because it becomes less likely that additional search will lead to a better position. The primary cost of job search is generally the opportunity cost of wages forgone as the result of failure to accept one's best current alternative. This cost will increase as better alternatives are found. Thus, the *marginal cost* of job search will rise with the length of one's job search time, primarily because still more search means forgoing wages on more attractive jobs discovered by prior search.

As the marginal benefit from additional search declines and marginal costs rise, eventually the rational job seeker will conclude that potential gain from additional search is not worth the cost. The best alternative resulting from the search process will be accepted. However, this process takes time, and during this time the job seeker is contributing to the frictional unemployment of the economy. It is important to note that, even though frictional unemployment is a side effect, the job search process typically leads to improved economic efficiency and a higher real income for employees (see the Myths of Economics box on the next page).

Changes that affect the costs and benefits of job search influence the level of unemployment. It is interesting to reflect on the potential impact of the Internet on the job search process. Increasingly, both employers and employees are using Internet sites as a means of communicating with each other. Employers provide information about job openings in various skill and occupational categories, while employees supply information about their education, skills, and experience. This electronic job search process reduces information costs and makes it possible for both employers and employees to consider quickly a wide range of alternatives. As this method of employment search becomes more widespread, it will tend to shorten the job search process and improve the match between

MYTHS OF ECONOMICS

"Unemployed resources would not exist if the economy were operating efficiently."

Nobody likes unemployment. Certainly, extended unemployment can be a very painful experience. Job search, however, performs an important labor market function: It leads to improvement in the match between worker skills and the requirements of jobs.

In a world of imperfect information, prospective employees will engage in a job search in order to acquire information about employment opportunities and job requirements. In essence, job searchers are "shopping"—they are searching for information about the job opportunity that best fits their skills, earning capabilities, and preferences. Similarly, employers shop when they are seeking labor services. They, too, acquire information about available workers that will help them select employees whose skills and preferences match the demands of the job.

This shopping results in some unemployment, but it also provides both employees and employers with information that will help them make better choices. If the resources of an economy are going to be used effectively, the skills of workers must be matched with the jobs of employers. Waste will result if, for example, a person with high-level computer skills ends up working as a janitor while someone else with minimal computer skills is employed as a computer programmer. Job search improves the match between the skills and preferences of employees and the demands of various jobs. As workers search to find jobs for which their skills are well suited, they achieve higher wage rates and the economy is able to generate a larger output.

Perhaps thinking about the housing market will help the reader better understand why search time can be both beneficial and productive. As with the employment market, the housing market is characterized by both imperfect information and dynamic change. New housing structures are brought into the market; older structures depreciate and wear out. Families move from one community to another. In this dynamic world, it makes sense for renters from time to time to shop among the available accommodations, seeking the housing quality, price, and location that best fit their preferences and budgets. Similarly, landlords search among renters, seeking to rent their accommodations to those who value them most highly. Housing vacancies, a type of "frictional unemployment," occur. Is this indicative of inefficiency? No. It is the result of imperfect information and the search for a more efficient match on the part of both landlords and renters.

Of course, some types of unemployment, particularly cyclical unemployment, are indicative of inefficiency. However, this is not the case with frictional unemployment. The job searching (as well as the frictional unemployment that accompanies it) helps both job seekers and employers make better choices, and it leads to a more efficient match of applicants with job openings than would otherwise be possible. It is perfectly consistent with economic efficiency.

employee qualifications and the skills required for high-productivity job performance. Thus, frictional unemployment may well be lower in the future.

On the other hand, a change that makes it cheaper to reject available opportunities and continue searching will encourage employees to lengthen their periods of search. For example, an increase in unemployment benefits would make it less costly to continue looking for a preferred job. As a result, job seekers will expand the length of their search time and the unemployment rate will rise.

Structural Unemployment

Structural unemployment Unemployment due to the structural characteristics of the economy that make it difficult for job seekers to find employment and for employers to hire workers. Although job openings are available, they generally require skills that differ from those of the unemployed workers.

In the case of **structural unemployment**, changes in the basic characteristics of the economy prevent the "matching up" of available jobs with available workers. It is not always easy to distinguish between frictional and structural unemployment. In each case, job openings and potential workers searching for jobs are present. The crucial difference between the two is that, with frictional unemployment, workers possess the requisite skills to fill the job openings; with structural unemployment, they do not. Essentially, the primary skills of a structurally unemployed worker have been rendered obsolete by changing market conditions and technology. Realistically, the structurally unemployed worker faces the prospect of either a career change or prolonged unemployment. For older workers in particular, these are bleak alternatives.

There are many causes of structural unemployment. Technological change is of course at the top of the list. The introduction of new products and production technologies can substantially later the relative demand for workers with various skills. Changes of this type can affect the job opportunities of even highly skilled workers, particularly if their skills are not easily transferable to other industries and occupations. The "computer revolution" has dramatically changed the job opportunities of many workers. The alternatives available to workers with the skills required to operate and maintain high-tech equipment have improved substantially, while the prospects of those without such skills have, in some cases, deteriorated drastically.

Shifts in public sector priorities can also cause structural unemployment. For example, environmental regulations designed to improve air quality led to a reduction in the demand for coal during the 1990s. As a result many coal miners in West Virginia, Kentucky, and other coal mining states lost their jobs. Unfortunately, the skills of many of the job losers were ill-suited for employment in expanding industries. Structural unemployment was the result.

Institutional factors may also make it difficult for some workers to find jobs. For example, minimum wage legislation may push the wages of low-skill workers above their productivity and thereby severely retard the job opportunities that are available to them. Structural unemployment would increase as a result.

Cyclical Unemployment

Cyclical unemployment Unemployment due to recessionary business conditions and inadequate aggregate demand for labor.

When there is a general downturn in business activity, **cyclical unemployment** arises. Because fewer goods are being produced, fewer workers are required to produce them. Employers lay off workers and cut back employment.

Unexpected reductions in the general level of demand for goods and services are the major cause of cyclical unemployment. In a world of imperfect information, adjustments to unexpected declines in demand are often painful. When the demand for labor declines generally, workers will at first not know whether they are being laid off because of a specific shift in demand away from their previous employer or because of a general decline in demand. Similarly, they will not be sure whether their current bleak employment prospects are temporary or long-term. Workers will search for employment, hoping to find a job at or near their old wage rate. If their situation was merely the result of shifts among employers in demand, or if the downturn is brief, workers dismissed by employers cutting back output will generally be able to find jobs with employers who are expanding and hiring additional workers. The situation is different, however, when there is a general decline in demand. Many employers will be laying off workers and few will be hiring. Under these circumstances, most workers' search efforts will be fruitless and the duration of their unemployment will be abnormally long.

With time, unemployed workers will lower their expectations and many will be willing to accept employment at a lower wage. This adjustment process, however, will take time. During the adjustment period, an increase in the rate of unemployment is the expected result. As we proceed, we will investigate potential sources of cyclical unemployment and consider policy alternatives to reduce it.

EMPLOYMENT FLUCTUATIONS—THE HISTORICAL RECORD 5

Employment and output are closely linked over the business cycle. If we are going to produce more goods and services, we must either increase the number of workers or increase the output per worker. Although productivity, or output per worker, is the primary source of long-term economic growth, it changes slowly from year to year. Thus, rapid increases in output, such as those that occur during a strong business expansion, generally require an increase in employment.

EXHIBIT 14-7 Unemployment Rate, 1960–2001

Here we illustrate the rate of unemployment during the 1960–2001 period. As expected, the unemployment rate rose rapidly during each of the seven recessions (the shaded years indicate periods of recession). In contrast, soon after each recession ended, the unemployment rate began to decline as the economy moved to an expansionary phase of the business cycle. Also note that the actual rate of unemployment was substantially greater than the natural rate during and immediately following the recessions.

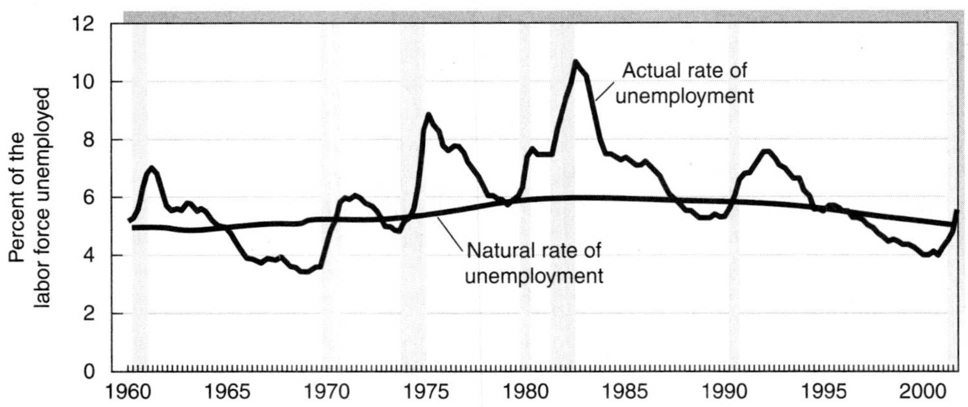

Source: www.bls.gov and Robert J. Gordon, *Macroeconomics* (Boston: Little Brown, 1990).

As a result, output and employment tend to be positively related. Correspondingly, there is an inverse relationship between growth of output and the rate of unemployment.

The empirical evidence is consistent with this view. As **Exhibit 14-7** shows, the unemployment rate generally increases during a recession (indicated by shading), and declines during periods of expansion in output. During the recession of 1960–1961, the rate of unemployment rose to approximately 7 percent. In contrast, it declined throughout the economic boom of the 1960s, only to rise again during the recession of 1970. During the recession of 1974–1975, the unemployment rate jumped to more than 9 percent. Similarly, it soared to nearly 11 percent during the severe recession of 1982 and to 7.6 percent during the aftermath of the 1991 recession. Conversely, it declined substantially during the strong expansions of 1983–1989 and 1992–2000.

Full employment
The level of employment that results from the efficient use of the labor force after allowance is made for the normal (natural) rate of unemployment due to information cost, dynamic changes, and the structural conditions of the economy. For the United States, full employment is thought to exist when approximately 95 percent of the labor force is employed.

Natural rate of unemployment
The long-run average unemployment rate due to frictional and structural conditions of labor markets. This rate is affected both by dynamic change and by public policy. It is sustainable into the future. The current natural rate of unemployment in the United States is thought to be approximately 5 percent.

Full Employment and the Natural Rate of Unemployment

Full employment, a term widely used by economists and public officials alike, does not mean zero unemployment. As we have noted, in a world of imperfect information, both employees and employers will "shop" before they agree to accept a job or hire a new worker. Much of this shopping is efficient, since it leads to a better match between the skills of employees and the skills necessary to carry out productive tasks. Some unemployment is thus entirely consistent with the efficient operation of a dynamic labor market. ***Consequently, economists define full employment as the level of employment that results when the rate of unemployment is normal, considering both frictional and structural factors. In the United States, full employment is currently believed to be approximately 95 percent of the labor force.***

Closely related to the concept of full employment is the **natural rate of unemployment**, the amount of unemployment reflected by job shopping and imperfect information. ***The natural rate of unemployment is not a temporary high or low; it is a rate that is sustainable into the future. Economists sometimes refer to it as the unemployment rate accompanying the economy's "maximum sustainable" rate of output.***

When unemployment is at its natural rate, full employment is present and the economy is achieving the highest rate of output that it can sustain.

The natural rate of unemployment, however, is not immutably fixed. It is influenced both by the structure of the labor force and by changes in public policy. Over time, changes in the demographic composition of the labor force will influence the natural rate. The natural rate of unemployment generally increases when youthful workers expand as a proportion of the workforce. Because youthful workers change jobs and move in and out of the labor force often, they experience high rates of unemployment (refer to Exhibit 14-6). Therefore the overall rate is pushed upward as they become a larger share of the labor force. This is precisely what happened during the 1960s and 1970s. In 1958 youthful workers (ages 16 to 24) constituted only 15.6 percent of the labor force. As the postwar "baby boom" generation entered the labor market, youthful workers as a share of the labor force rose dramatically. By 1980 one out of every four workers was in the youthful-worker grouping. In contrast, prime-age workers (over age 25) declined from 84.4 percent of the U.S. workforce in 1958 to only 75.3 percent in 1980. As a result of these demographic changes, studies indicate that the natural rate of unemployment rose from approximately 5 percent in the late 1950s to over 6 percent in 1980.

During the last two decades, the situation has reversed. The natural rate of unemployment has receded as the baby boomers moved into their prime working years and youthful workers declined as a share of the labor force. Today, most researchers estimate that the natural rate is once again near the 5 percent level, about the same as during the late 1950s.

Public policy also affects the natural rate of unemployment. When public policy makes it more costly to employ workers and/or less costly for persons to remain unemployed, it increases the natural rate of unemployment. The large European economies illustrate the importance of public policy. The economies of France, Germany, Italy, and Spain are characterized by high unemployment benefits and regulations that both increase the cost of dismissing workers and mandate uniform wages nationwide. Regulations of this type reduce the flexibility of labor markets and make it more costly to hire and employ workers. Thus, they lead to persistently high rates of unemployment.

As Exhibit 14-8 shows, the unemployment rates of the major European economies were substantially higher during the last decade than the comparable

EXHIBIT 14-8 Average Unemployment Rate for Major Economies, 1990–1999

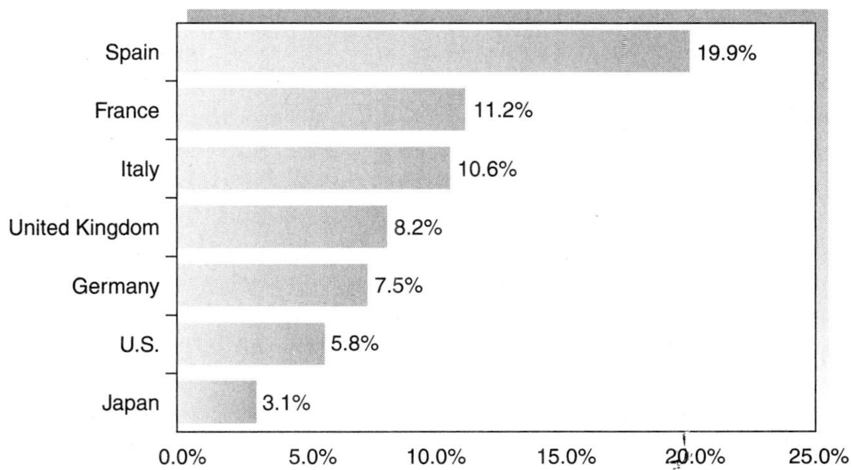

Source: Economic Outlook, OECD (Dec. 2000).

figures for the United States and Japan, for example. High unemployment rates over such a lengthy time period are indicative of structural rather than cyclical factors. They are also reflective of the adverse impact of public policy on the natural rate of unemployment. See the Special Topic "Labor Markets and Unemployment: A Cross-Country Analysis," for additional information on this topic.

Exhibit 14-7 illustrates the relationship between the *actual* unemployment rate and the *natural* unemployment rate for the United States during the past four decades. The actual unemployment rate fluctuates around the natural rate, in response to cyclical economic conditions. The actual rate generally rises above the natural rate during a recession and falls below the natural rate when the economy is in the midst of an economic boom. For example, the actual rate of unemployment was substantially above the natural rate during the recessions of 1974–1975 and 1982, while the reverse was the case during the economic booms of the 1960s and 1990s. As we proceed, we will often compare the actual and natural rates of unemployment. In a very real sense, macroeconomics studies why the actual and natural rates differ and attempts to discern the factors that cause the natural rate to change with the passage of time.

Without detracting from the importance of full employment—in the sense of maximum sustainable employment—we must not overlook another vital point. Employment is a means to an end. We use employment to produce desired goods and services. Full employment is an empty concept if it means employment at unproductive jobs. It is a meaningful concept only if it refers to productive employment that will generate goods and services desired by consumers at the lowest possible cost.

6 ACTUAL AND POTENTIAL GDP

If an economy is going to realize its potential, full employment is essential. When the actual rate of unemployment exceeds the natural rate, the actual output of the economy will fall below its potential. Some resources that could be productively employed will be underutilized.

Potential output
The level of output that can be achieved and sustained into the future, given the size of the labor force, expected productivity of labor, and natural rate of unemployment consistent with the efficient operation of the labor market. For periods of time, the actual output may differ from the economy's potential.

The Council of Economic Advisers defines the **potential output** as: "The amount of output that could be expected at full employment . . . It does not represent the absolute maximum level of production that could be generated by wartime or other abnormal levels of aggregate demand, but rather that which would be expected from high utilization rates obtainable under more normal circumstances."

The concept of potential output encompasses two important ideas: (1) full utilization of resources, including labor, and (2) the potential output is constrained. Potential output might properly be thought of as the maximum *sustainable* output level consistent with the economy's resource base, given its institutional arrangements. Estimates of the potential output level involve three major elements: the size of the labor force, the quality (productivity) of labor, and the natural rate of unemployment. Because these factors cannot be estimated with certainty, some variation exists in the estimated values of the potential rate of output for the U.S. economy. Relying on the projections of potential output developed by the Council of Economic Advisers, Exhibit 14-9 illustrates the relationship between the actual and potential output of the United States since 1960.

The relationship between actual and potential GDP reflects the business cycle. Note the similarity in the pattern of the actual real GDP data of Exhibit 14-9 and the hypothetical data of an idealized business cycle of Exhibit 14-2. Although the actual data of Exhibit 14-9 are irregular compared to the hypothetical data,

EXHIBIT 14-9 Actual and Potential GDP

Here we illustrate both the actual and potential GDP. Note the gap (shaded area) between the actual and potential GDP during periods of recession.

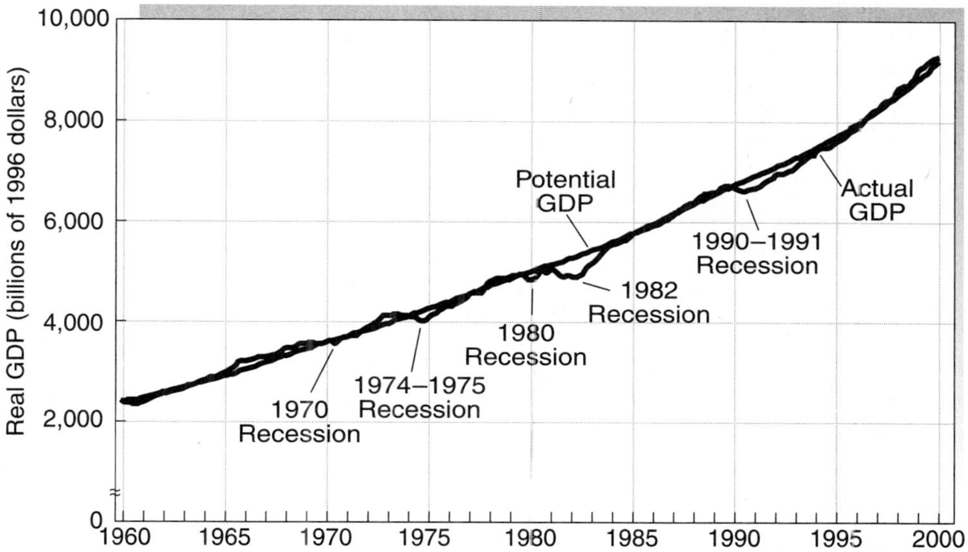

Source: U.S. Department of Commerce, Bureau of Economic Analysis.

periods of expansion and economic boom followed by contraction and recession are clearly observable. During the boom phase, actual output expands rapidly and may temporarily exceed the économy's long-run potential. In contrast, recessions are characterized by an actual real GDP that is less than its potential. As we proceed, we will focus on how we can achieve the maximum potential output while minimizing economic instability.

EFFECTS OF INFLATION: AN OVERVIEW

7

Inflation
A continuing rise in the general level of prices of goods and services. The purchasing power of the monetary unit, such as the dollar, declines when inflation is present.

Inflation is a continuing rise in the general level of prices such that it costs more to purchase the typical bundle of goods and services that is produced or consumed or both. Of course, even when the general level of prices is stable, some prices will be rising and others will be falling. During a period of inflation, however, the impact of the rising prices will outweigh that of falling prices. Because of the higher prices (on average), a dollar will purchase less than it did previously. Inflation, therefore, might also be defined as a decline in the value (the purchasing power) of the monetary unit.

How do we determine whether prices, in general, are rising or falling? Essentially, we answered that question in the preceding chapter when we indicated how a price index is constructed. When the general level of prices is rising, the price index will also rise. The annual inflation rate is simply the percent change in the price index (PI) from one year to the next. Mathematically, the inflation rate can be written as:

$$\text{inflation rate} = \frac{\text{This year's PI} - \text{Last year's PI}}{\text{Last year's PI}} \times 100$$

EXHIBIT 14-10 The Inflation Rate, 1953–2001

Here we present the annual rate of inflation for the last five decades. Between 1953 and 1965, prices increased at an annual rate of only 1.3 percent. In contrast, the inflation rate averaged 9.2 percent during the 1973–1981 era, reaching double-digit rates during several years. Since 1982, the rate of inflation has been lower (the average annual rate was 3.2 percent during 1983–2001) and more stable.

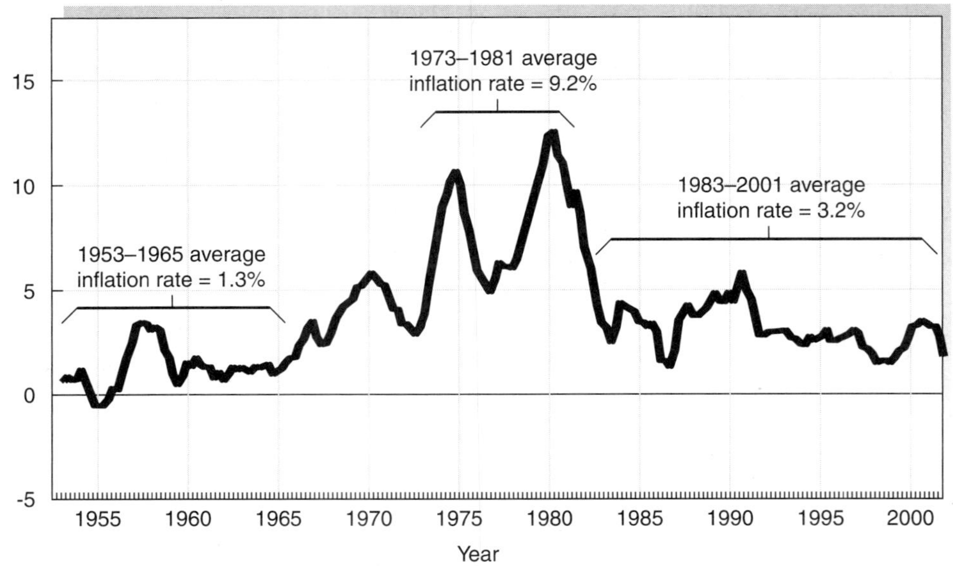

Source: Derived from computerized data supplied by FAME ECONOMICS. Also see *Economic Report of the President* (published annually).

If the price index this year was 220, compared to 200 last year, the inflation rate would equal 10 percent:

$$\frac{220 - 200}{200} \times 100 = 10$$

The consumer price index (CPI) and the GDP deflator are the price indexes most widely used to measure the inflation rate in the United States. As we discussed in the preceding chapter, these two measures of the rate of inflation tend to follow a similar path. How rapidly has the general level of prices risen in the United States? Using the annual rate of change in the CPI, Exhibit 14-10 presents a picture of the U.S. inflation rate since the early 1950s. During the 1950s and into the mid-1960s, the annual inflation rate was generally low. The average inflation rate during the 1953–1965 period was 1.3 percent. Beginning in the latter half of the 1960s, inflation began to accelerate upward, jumping to 12 percent or more during 1974, 1979, and 1980. During the 1973–1981 period, the inflation rate averaged 9.2 percent. Price increases moderated again in the mid-1980s, as the inflation rate averaged 3.4 percent during 1983–2001. Additional details on inflation and related measures can be obtained on the Internet at www.bls.gov.

The rate of inflation varies widely among countries. Exhibit 14-11 provides data on the annual inflation rates during 1994–2000 for Canada, Germany, Japan, Singapore, and the United States—five countries with low rates of inflation. The annual inflation rate of these countries was generally less than 4 percent during this period; moreover, the year-to-year variation was relatively small. The inflation rate of these countries seldom changed by more than 1 or 2 percent from one year to the next.

EXHIBIT 14-11 Variation in the Annual Inflation Rate of Selected Countries, 1994–2000

Country	1994	1995	1996	1997	1998	1999	2000
Low Inflation							
Canada	0.2	2.1	1.6	1.6	1.0	1.7	2.7
Germany	2.7	1.7	1.4	1.9	1.0	0.6	2.0
Japan	0.7	−0.1	0.1	1.7	0.7	−0.3	−0.7
Singapore	3.0	1.7	1.4	2.0	−0.3	0.1	1.4
United States	2.6	2.8	2.9	2.3	1.6	2.1	3.4
High Inflation							
Brazil	2050.0	66.1	15.8	6.9	3.2	4.9	7.1
Bulgaria	95.9	62.1	121.6	1058.4	18.7	2.6	10.4
Ecuador	27.4	22.9	24.4	30.6	36.1	52.3	96.1
Romania	137.0	32.3	38.8	154.8	59.1	45.8	45.7
Turkey	106.2	88.0	80.3	85.8	84.6	64.9	54.9
Venezuela	60.7	60.0	99.9	50.0	35.8	23.6	16.2

Source: International Monetary Fund, *International Financial Statistics* (April 2001, February 2001). The consumer price index was used to measure the inflation rate of each country.

Exhibit 14-11 also presents parallel inflation rate data for six high-inflation countries: Brazil, Bulgaria, Ecuador, Romania, Turkey, and Venezuela. In contrast with the low-inflation countries, the inflation rate of the high-inflation countries was not only higher, it varied substantially more from one year to another. For example, consider the data for Romania. The inflation rate of Romania jumped from 121.6 percent in 1996 to 1,058.4 percent in 1997 and receded to 18.7 percent in 1998 and eventually to 10.4 percent in 2000. (*Note:* An annual inflation rate of 1,000 percent indicates that the general level of prices is 10 times the level of just one year earlier!) The other countries in the high-inflation group also experienced wide fluctuations in the annual rate of inflation. The data of Exhibit 14-11 reflect a general pattern. ***High rates of inflation are almost always associated with substantial year-to-year swings in the inflation rate.***

Anticipated and Unanticipated Inflation

Before examining the effects of inflation, it is important that we distinguish between unanticipated and anticipated inflation. **Unanticipated inflation** is an increase in the price level that comes as a surprise, at least to most individuals. For example, suppose that, based on the recent past, most people anticipate an inflation rate of 3 percent. If the actual inflation rate turns out to be 10 percent, it will catch people off-guard. When the rate of inflation is high and variable, like the rates for the high-inflation countries of Exhibit 14-11, it will be virtually impossible for decision makers to anticipate future rates accurately, and long-range planning will be extremely difficult.

Unanticipated inflation
An increase in the general level of prices that was not expected by most decision makers.

Anticipated inflation is a change in the price level that is widely expected. Decision makers are generally able to anticipate slow steady rates of inflation—such as those present in Canada, Germany, Japan, Singapore, and the United States during 1994–2000—with a high degree of accuracy.

Anticipated inflation
An increase in the general level of prices that was expected by most decision makers.

Contrary to the satirical statement presented in the opening quote, inflation will affect the prices of things we sell as well as the prices of goods we buy. Both resource and product prices are influenced by inflation. Before we become too upset about inflation "robbing us of the purchasing power of our paychecks," we should recognize that inflation influences the size of those paychecks. The weekly earnings of employees would not have risen at an annual rate of 7 percent during the 1970s if the rate of inflation had not increased rapidly during that period. Wages are a price, also. Inflation raises both wages and prices.

Harmful Effects of Inflation

Simply because money income initially tends to rise with prices, it does not follow that there is no need to be concerned about inflation, particularly high rates of inflation. Inflation causes problems! Our modern living standard is the result of gains from specialization, division of labor, and mass-production processes. Realization of gains from these sources is dependent upon trade and a smooth-functioning system of exchange. High and variable rates of inflation will generate uncertainty and weaken the link between income and productive activity. There are three major reasons why inflation will have a harmful impact on the economy.

1. ***Because unanticipated inflation alters the outcomes of long-term projects, such as the purchase of a machine or an investment in a business, it will increase the risks and retard the level of such productive activities.*** When the price level rises 15 percent one year, 40 percent the next year, and then increases again by 20 or 25 percent the following year, no one knows what to expect. Unanticipated changes of even 5 percent or 10 percent in the rate of inflation can often turn an otherwise profitable project into a personal economic disaster. Given the uncertainty that it creates, many decision makers will simply forgo capital investments and other transactions involving long-term commitments when the rate of inflation is highly variable and therefore unpredictable. As a result, mutually advantageous gains from trade will be lost and the efficiency of markets reduced.
2. ***Inflation distorts the information delivered by prices.*** Prices communicate important information concerning the relative scarcity of goods and resources. Some prices can be easily and regularly changed. But this will not be true for others—particularly those set by long-term contracts. For example, time delays will occur before the prices accompanying rental lease agreements, items sold in catalogs, mortgage interest rates, and collective bargaining contracts can be changed. Because some prices will respond quickly to inflationary policies while others will change more slowly, an unanticipated change in the rate of inflation will change *relative prices* as well as the *general price level.* The distorted relative prices will be a less reliable indicator of relative scarcity. As a result of these unreliable price signals, producers and resource suppliers will often make choices that they will later regret, and the allocation of resources will be less efficient than would be the case if the general level of prices was more stable.
3. ***People will respond to high and variable rates of inflation by spending less time producing and more time trying to protect themselves from inflation.*** Since the failure to anticipate accurately the rate of inflation can have a substantial effect on one's wealth, individuals will divert scarce resources from the production of desired goods and services to the acquisition of information on the future rate of inflation and methods to cope with it. The ability of business decision makers to forecast and deal with changes in prices becomes

> more valuable relative to their ability as managers and organizers of production. Speculative practices are encouraged as people try to outguess one another with regard to the future direction of prices. Funds flow into speculative investments, such as gold, silver, and art objects, rather than into productive investments (buildings, machines, and technological research) that expand the investor's ability to produce goods and services. Such practices are socially counterproductive. They reduce our production possibilities.

Low and stable rates of inflation will exert a positive impact on real output and the level of prosperity. The U.S. experience illustrates this point. During the 1983–2000 period, inflation in the United States was low and relatively stable. This period was characterized by strong growth and only 8 months of recession. In contrast, when the inflation rate was high and variable during the 1970s, the United States experienced two recessions (1974–1975 and 1979–1980) and sluggish growth of real GDP.

What Causes Inflation?

We must acquire some additional tools before we can answer the question of what causes inflation in detail, but at this point we can outline a couple of theories. First, economists emphasize the link between aggregate demand and supply. If aggregate demand rises more rapidly than supply, prices will rise. Second, nearly all economists believe that a rapid expansion in a nation's stock of money causes inflation. The old saying is that prices will rise because "there is too much money chasing too few goods." The hyperinflation experienced by South American countries and, more recently, the countries of the former Soviet Union has mainly been the result of monetary expansion. Once we develop additional knowledge about the operation of our economy, we will consider this issue in more detail.

8 SUMMARY

- During the past century, real GDP in the United States has grown at an average annual rate of approximately 3 percent.
- Real GDP has also been characterized by cyclical movements. The four phases of the business cycle are *expansion, peak (or boom), contraction,* and *recessionary trough.*
- A recession is defined as two successive quarters of declining real GDP. If a recession is quite severe, it is called a depression.
- There are three types of unemployment: (a) frictional unemployment, (b) structural unemployment, and (c) cyclical unemployment. In a world of imperfect information and dynamic change, some unemployment is inevitable.
- Full employment is the employment level consistent with the economy's natural rate of unemployment. Both full employment and the natural rate of unemployment are associated with the economy's maximum sustainable rate of output.
- The concept of potential output encompasses two important ideas: (a) full utilization of resources and (b) a supply constraint that limits our ability to produce desired goods and services. Potential output is the maximum *sustainable* output level consistent with the economy's resource base and current institutional arrangements.
- Inflation is a general rise in the level of prices. It is important to distinguish between anticipated and unanticipated inflation. Unanticipated changes in the rate of inflation often alter the intended terms of long-term agreements and cause people to make choices that they will later regret.
- Inflation, particularly unanticipated inflation, has harmful effects. These include: (a) additional uncertainty accompanying time-dimension contracts, (b) distortion of relative prices, and (c) the shift of resources into activities designed to prevent inflation from eroding one's wealth.

FISCAL POLICY

READING 15

LEARNING OUTCOMES

The candidate should be able to:

a. explain the process by which, according to the Keynesian view, fiscal policy affects aggregate demand and aggregate supply;

b. explain the importance of the timing of changes in fiscal policy and the difficulties in achieving proper timing;

c. discuss the impact of expansionary and restrictive fiscal policies based on the basic Keynesian model, the crowding-out model, the new classical model, and supply-side model;

d. identify automatic stabilizers and explain how such stabilizers work.

In the early stages of the Keynesian revolution, macroeconomists emphasized fiscal policy as the most powerful and balanced remedy for demand management. Gradually, shortcomings of fiscal policy became apparent. The shortcomings stem from timing, politics, macroeconomic theory, and the deficit itself.[1]

—Paul Samuelson, Nobel Laureate

INTRODUCTION 1

As we indicated previously, fiscal policy involves the use of the government's spending and taxing authority. Until now, we have assumed that the government's fiscal policy remained unchanged. We are now ready to relax this assumption and investigate the impact of fiscal policy on output, prices, and employment.

There is some disagreement among economists with regard to both how fiscal policy works and its potential to improve the performance of a market economy. In fact, views on this topic have changed in recent decades. This reading will cover four alternative fiscal policy models—the Keynesian, crowding-out, new classical, and supply-side. We will consider how and why views toward these

[1] Paul A. Samuelson and William D. Nordhaus, *Economics*, 15th ed. (New York: McGraw-Hill, 1995), p. 644.

models have changed in recent decades. The basic *AD/AS* macroeconomic model will be used to illustrate each of the fiscal policy perspectives.

Because we want to isolate the impact of changes in fiscal policy from changes in monetary policy, we will continue to assume that the monetary authorities maintain a constant supply of money. We will begin our analysis of monetary policy in the following reading.

2 BUDGET DEFICITS AND SURPLUSES

OPTIONAL SEGMENT

Balanced budget
A situation in which current government revenue from taxes, fees, and other sources is just equal to current government expenditures.

Budget deficit
A situation in which total government spending exceeds total government revenue during a specific time period, usually one year.

Budget surplus
A situation in which total government spending is less than total government revenue during a time period, usually a year.

Discretionary fiscal policy
A change in laws or appropriation levels that alters government revenues and/or expenditures.

Fiscal policy is reflected through the government's spending, taxing, and borrowing policies. It is one of the major tools that might be used to help promote the goals of full employment, price stability, and rapid economic growth. When the supply of money is constant, government expenditures must be financed with either: (1) taxes and other revenues derived from the sale of services or assets or (2) borrowing. When government revenues from taxes and sales are equal to government expenditures (including both purchases of goods and services and transfer payments), the government has a **balanced budget**. The budget need not be in balance, however. A **budget deficit** is present when total government spending exceeds total government revenue from all sources. When a budget deficit is present, the government must borrow funds to finance the excess of its spending relative to revenue. It borrows by issuing interest-bearing bonds that become part of what we call the national debt, the total amount of outstanding government bonds. Conversely, a **budget surplus** is present when the government's revenues exceed its total expenditures. The surplus allows the government to reduce its outstanding debt.

The federal budget is much more than a mere revenue and expenditure statement of a large organization. Of course, its sheer size means that it exerts a substantial influence on the economy. Its importance, though, stems from its position as a policy variable. The federal budget is the primary tool of fiscal policy. In contrast with private organizations that are directed by the pursuit of income and profit, the federal government can alter its budget with an eye toward influencing the future direction of the economy.

Changes in the size of the federal deficit or surplus are often used to gauge whether fiscal policy is adding additional demand stimulus or imposing additional demand restraint. It is important to note, however, that changes in the size of the deficit or surplus may arise from two different sources. ***First, changes in the size of the deficit or surplus may merely reflect the state of the economy.*** During a recession, tax revenues generally fall and expenditures on transfer programs increase as the result of the weak economic conditions. This will shift the budget toward a deficit even if there is no change in fiscal policy. Just the opposite will happen during the expansion phase of the business cycle. Tax revenue will increase and transfer payments decline as the result of the rapid growth of income. This will shift the budget toward a surplus (or smaller deficit) during a strong economic expansion. ***Second, changes in the deficit or surplus may reflect* discretionary fiscal policy.** Policymakers may institute deliberate changes in tax laws or spending on government programs in order to alter the size of the budget deficit (or surplus). When we speak of "changes in fiscal policy," we are referring to changes of this type—deliberate changes in government expenditures or tax policy or both that are designed to affect the size of the budget deficit or surplus.

OPTIONAL SEGMENT ENDS

KEYNESIAN VIEW OF FISCAL POLICY 3

Prior to the 1960s, the desirability of a balanced federal budget was widely accepted among business and political leaders. Keynesian economists, though, were highly critical of this view. Keynesians argued that the federal budget should be used to promote a level of aggregate demand consistent with the full employment rate of output.

How might policy makers use the budget to stimulate aggregate demand? First, an increase in government purchases of goods and services will directly increase aggregate demands. As the government spends more on highways, flood control projects, education, and national defense, for example, these expenditures will increase demand in the goods and services market. Second, changes in tax policy will also influence aggregate demand. For example, a reduction in personal taxes will increase the current disposable income of households. As their after-tax income rises, individuals will spend more on consumption. In turn, this increase in consumption will stimulate aggregate demand. Similarly, a reduction in business taxes increases after-tax profitability, which will stimulate both business investment and aggregate demand.

When an economy is operating below its potential capacity, the Keynesian model suggests that government should institute **expansionary fiscal policy**. In other words, the government should either increase its purchases of goods and services or cut taxes or both. Of course, this policy will increase the government's budget deficit. In order to finance the enlarged budget deficit, the government will have to borrow from either private domestic sources or foreigners.[2]

Expansionary fiscal policy
An increase in government expenditures and/or a reduction in tax rates such that the expected size of the budget deficit expands.

Exhibit 15-1 illustrates the case for expansionary fiscal policy when an economy is experiencing abnormally high unemployment caused by deficient aggregate demand. Initially, the economy is operating at e_1. Output is below potential capacity, Y_F, and unemployment exceeds its natural rate. As we discussed previously, if there is no change in policy, abnormally high unemployment and excess supply in the resource market would eventually reduce real wages and other resource prices. The accompanying lower costs would increase aggregate supply (shift to $SRAS_3$) and guide the economy to a full employment equilibrium (E_3) at a lower price level (P_3). In addition, lower real interest rates resulting from weak business demand for investment funds may help stimulate aggregate demand and restore full employment.

As we noted previously, Keynesians believe that wages and prices are inflexible—particularly in a downward direction. Thus, they have little confidence in the ability of lower wages and falling interest rates to restore full employment in the midst of a recession. Keynesians recommend government action—a shift to a more expansionary fiscal policy in order to speed up the movement toward full employment equilibrium. Keynesians advocate more government spending or a reduction in taxes or both—that is, a deliberate increase in the budget deficit—as a means of stimulating aggregate demand. Furthermore, they argue that the multiplier process will magnify the initial increase in spending. Suppose that the government holds taxes constant and increases its spending on highways and school construction by $20 billion. The additional spending will enhance the incomes of those undertaking the construction by $20 billion. As these individuals use a portion of this income to buy consumer goods, this will provide

[2] Alternatively, the government could borrow from its central bank—the Federal Reserve Bank in the United States. However, as we will see in the following reading, this method of financing a budget deficit would expand the money supply. Since we want to differentiate between fiscal and monetary effects, we must hold the supply of money constant. So for now, we assume that the government deficit must be financed by borrowing from private sources.

EXHIBIT 15-1 Expansionary Fiscal Policy to Promote Full Employment

Here we illustrate an economy operating in the short run at Y_1, below its potential capacity of Y_F. There are two routes to a long-run full employment equilibrium. First, policy makers could wait for lower wages and resource prices to reduce costs, increase supply to $SRAS_3$, and restore equilibrium at E_3. Keynesians believe this market-adjustment method will be slow and uncertain. Alternatively, expansionary fiscal policy could stimulate aggregate demand (shift to AD_2) and guide the economy to E_2.

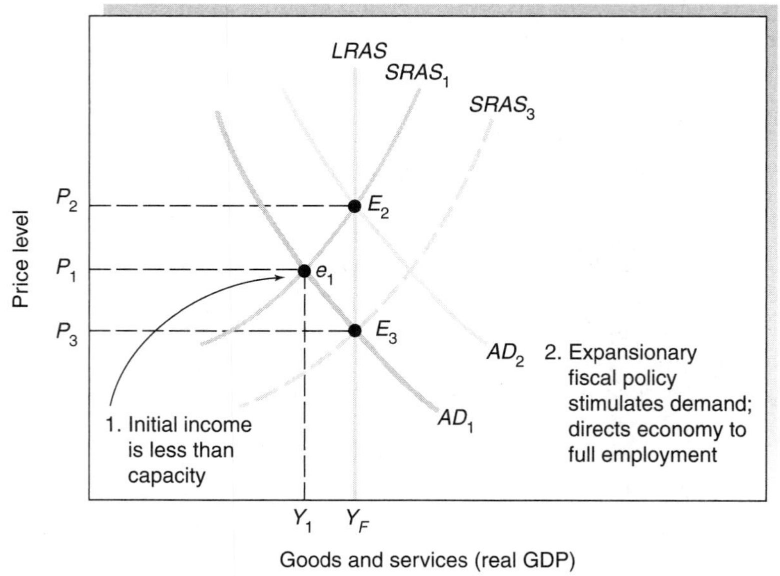

additional demand stimulus. Thus, Keynesians expect that the total increase in aggregate demand will be substantially greater than the initial \$20 billion increase in government purchases.

When an economy is operating below its potential capacity, the Keynesian prescription calls for expansionary fiscal policy—a deliberate change in expenditures and/or taxes that will increase the size of the government's budget deficit. An appropriate dose of expansionary fiscal policy, if timed properly, would stimulate aggregate demand (shift the curve to AD_2 in Exhibit 15-1) and guide the economy to full employment equilibrium (E_2).

The Keynesian view also provides a fiscal policy remedy for inflation. Suppose that an economy is experiencing an inflationary economic boom as the result of excessive aggregate demand. As Exhibit 15-2 illustrates, in the absence of a change in policy, the strong demand (AD_1) would push up wages and other resource prices. In time, the higher resource prices would increase costs, reduce aggregate supply (from $SRAS_1$ to $SRAS_3$), and lead to a higher price level (P_3). The basic Keynesian model, however, indicates that **restrictive fiscal policy** could be used to reduce aggregate demand (shift to AD_2) and guide the economy to a noninflationary equilibrium (E_2). A reduced level of government purchases would diminish aggregate demand directly. Alternatively, higher taxes on households and businesses could be used to dampen consumption and private investment. The restrictive fiscal policy—a spending reduction and/or an increase in taxes—would shift the government budget toward a surplus (or smaller deficit). ***The Keynesian analysis suggests that a shift toward a more restrictive fiscal policy is the proper prescription with which to combat inflation generated by excessive aggregate demand.***

Restrictive fiscal policy
A reduction in government expenditures and/or an increase in tax rates such that the expected size of the budget deficit declines (or the budget surplus increases).

EXHIBIT 15-2 Restrictive Fiscal Policy to Combat Inflation

Strong demand such as AD_1 will temporarily lead to an output rate beyond the economy's long-run potential (Y_F). If maintained, the high level of demand will lead to long-run equilibrium (E_3) at a higher price level. However, restrictive fiscal policy could restrain demand to AD_2 (or better still, prevent demand from expanding to AD_1 in the first place) and thereby guide the economy to a noninflationary equilibrium (E_2).

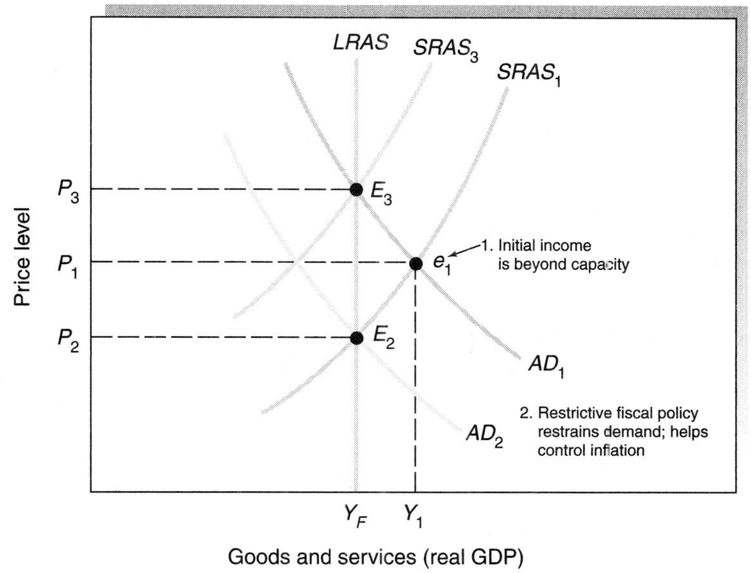

Outstanding Economist

Paul Samuelson (1915–)

The first American to win the Nobel Prize in Economics, Paul Samuelson played a central role in the development and acceptance of Keynesian economics in the 1950s and 1960s. Through the years, his views regarding the effectiveness of fiscal policy have gradually changed (see the quotation at the beginning of this reading). A professor of economics at MIT for more than four decades, Samuelson's *Collected Scientific Papers* encompass five lengthy volumes.[1]

[1]Paul Samuelson, *Collected Papers of Paul Samuelson* (Cambridge: MIT Press, 1966).

The Keynesian revolution challenged the view that a responsible government should constrain spending within the bounds of its revenues. Rather than balancing the budget annually, the Keynesian view stressed the importance of* countercyclical policy, *that is, policy designed to "counter" or offset fluctuations in aggregate demand. When an economy is threatened by a recession, the government should shift to a more expansionary fiscal policy, increasing spending or reducing taxes in a manner that will increase the size of the budget deficit. On the other hand, fiscal policy should become more restrictive—the budget should be shifted toward a smaller deficit or larger surplus—in response to a threat of inflation. According to the Keynesian view, fluctuations in aggregate demand are the major source of economic disturbances. Moreover, wise use of fiscal policy can help stabilize and maintain demand at or near the full employment rate of output.

Countercyclical policy
A policy that tends to move the economy in an opposite direction from the forces of the business cycle. Such a policy would stimulate demand during the contraction phase of the business cycle and restrain demand during the expansion phase.

4 FISCAL POLICY AND THE CROWDING-OUT EFFECT

By the early 1960s, the Keynesian view was widely accepted both by economists and by policy makers. At that time, it was generally believed that changes in the size of the budget deficit exerted a powerful impact on aggregate demand and output. More recently, however, economists have noted that there are secondary effects that tend to weaken the potency of fiscal policy.

When the government borrows funds to finance an enlarged deficit, typically it will do so by issuing additional bonds. As we previously discussed, issuing bonds is simply a means of demanding loanable funds. The total demand for loanable funds will increase as government borrowing competes with private borrowing for the available supply of funds. Thus, the additional government borrowing to finance a larger deficit will increase the demand for loanable funds and thereby place upward pressure on the real interest rate.

What impact will a higher real interest rate have on private spending? Consumers will reduce their purchases of interest-sensitive goods, such as automobiles and consumer durables. More important, a higher interest rate will increase the opportunity cost of investment projects. Businesses will postpone spending on plant expansions, heavy equipment, and capital improvements. Residential housing construction and sales will also be hurt. Thus, the higher real interest rates caused by the larger deficit will retard private spending. Economists refer to this squeezing out of private spending by a deficit-induced increase in the real interest rate as the **crowding-out effect**.

Crowding-out effect
A reduction in private spending as a result of higher interest rates generated by budget deficits that are financed by borrowing in the private loanable funds market.

The crowding-out effect suggests that budget deficits will exert less impact on aggregate demand than the basic Keynesian model implies. Because financing the deficit pushes up interest rates, budget deficits will tend to retard private spending, particularly spending on investment. This reduction in private spending as the result of higher interest rates will at least partially offset additional spending emanating from the deficit. Thus, the crowding-out effect implies that expansionary fiscal policy will exert little, if any, impact on demand, output, and employment.

Furthermore, the crowding-out effect indicates that the budget deficit will change the composition of aggregate demand. As the higher interest rates accompanying the deficits crowd out private investment, the output of capital goods will decline. As a result, the future stock of capital (for example, heavy equipment, other machines, and buildings) will be smaller than would otherwise have been the case. To the extent that budget deficits crowd out private investment, they will reduce the supply of capital available to future workers and thereby reduce their productivity and income.

Many Keynesians argue that, while crowding-out may occur when an economy is at or near full employment, it is unlikely to be very important during a recession, particularly a serious one. When widespread unemployment is present during a serious recession, an increase in government purchases may well exert a substantial multiplier effect on output, employment, and real income. If the incomes of households increase, they will save more, which will permit the government to finance its enlarged deficit without much upward pressure on interest rates. In addition, when applied during a recession, the demand stimulus may improve business profit expectations and thereby stimulate additional private investment.

The implications of the crowding-out analysis are symmetrical. Restrictive fiscal policy will "crowd in" private spending. If the government increases taxes and/or reduces its spending, the budget will shift toward a surplus (or smaller deficit). As a result, the government's demand for loanable funds will decrease, placing downward pressure on the real interest rate. The lower real interest rate will stimulate additional private investment and consumption. So the fiscal policy restraint will be at least partially offset by an expansion in private spending. ***As the result of this crowding in, restrictive fiscal policy may not be very effective as a weapon against inflation.***

The Crowding-Out Effect in a World of Global Financial Markets

Today, financial capital can rapidly move into and out of countries. How does the global nature of financial markets influence the crowding-out effect? Suppose that the budget deficit of the United States increased and that the additional borrowing of the Treasury pushed real interest rates upward just as the crowding-out theory implies. Think how investors will respond to this situation. The higher real interest yields on bonds and other financial assets will attract funds from abroad. In turn, this inflow of financial capital will increase the supply of loanable funds and thereby moderate the rise in real interest rates in the United States.[3]

At first glance, the crowding-out effect would appear to be weakened because the inflow of funds will moderate the upward pressure on domestic interest rates. Closer inspection, though, reveals this will not be the case. Foreigners cannot buy more U.S. bonds and financial assets without "buying" more dollars. Thus, additional bond purchases will increase the demand for U.S. dollars (and supply of foreign currencies) in the foreign exchange market—the market that coordinates exchanges of the various national currencies. As foreigners demand more dollars in order to increase their financial investments in the United States, their actions will cause an appreciation in the foreign exchange value of the dollar. The appreciation of the dollar will make imports cheaper for Americans. Simultaneously, it will make U.S. exports more expensive for foreigners. Predictably, the United States will import more and export less. Thus, net exports will decline (or net imports increase), causing a reduction in aggregate demand. Therefore, while the inflow of capital from abroad will moderate the increase in the interest rate and the crowding out of private domestic investment, it will also reduce net exports and thereby retard aggregate demand.

Exhibit 15-3 summarizes the crowding-out view of budget deficits in an open economy. The additional government borrowing triggered by the budget deficits will cause interest rates to rise and this will lead to two secondary effects that will dampen the stimulus impact of the deficits. First, the higher interest rates will reduce private investment, which will directly restrain aggregate demand. Second, the higher interest returns will also attract an inflow of foreign capital. While the capital inflow will moderate both the rise in real interest rates and the reduction in domestic private investment, it will also cause the dollar to appreciate in the foreign exchange market. In turn, the appreciation of the dollar will reduce both net exports and aggregate demand. ***According to the crowding-out theory, these two factors will largely, if not entirely, offset the stimulus effects of a larger budget deficit.***

[3] For students who are unsure about the demand for and supply of loanable funds, this would be a good time to review the topic within the framework of our basic macro model outlined in Chapter 9. Household saving and the inflow of financial capital from abroad supply loanable funds. In turn, private investment and borrowing by the government to finance budget deficits generate the demand for these funds.

EXHIBIT 15-3 Visual Presentation of the Crowding-Out Effect in an Open Economy

An increase in government borrowing to finance an enlarged budget deficit will place upward pressure on real interest rates. This will retard private investment and thereby aggregate demand. In an open economy, the higher interest rates will also increase the inflow of capital from abroad, which will cause the dollar to appreciate and net exports to decline. Thus, the higher interest rates will trigger reductions in both private investment and net exports, which will weaken the expansionary impact of a budget deficit.

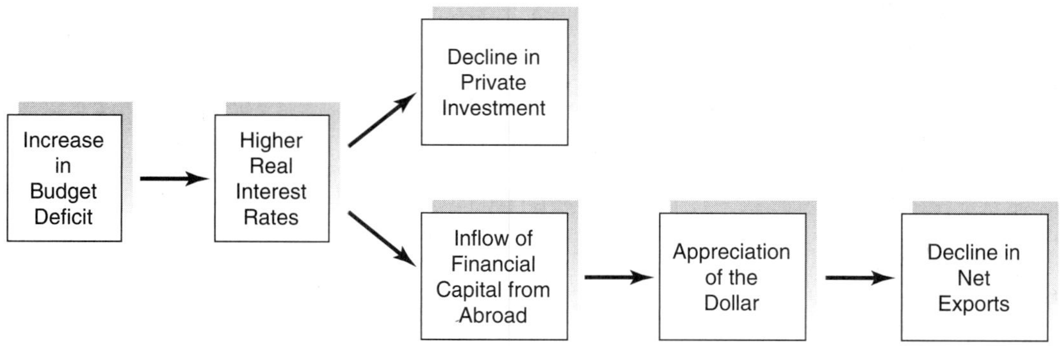

5 NEW CLASSICAL VIEW OF FISCAL POLICY

Some economists stress still another possible offsetting secondary effect that may weaken the impact of budget deficits on aggregate demand. Rather than spending more, households may save more so they will be better able to pay the higher future taxes implied by the larger outstanding debt. Until now, we have implicitly assumed that the current saving decisions of taxpayers are unaffected by the higher future taxes implied by budget deficits. Some economists argue that this is an unrealistic view. Robert Lucas (University of Chicago), the 1995 Nobel laureate, Thomas Sargent (University of Minnesota), and Robert Barro (Harvard University) have been leaders among a group of economists arguing that taxpayers will reduce their current consumption and increase their saving in anticipation of the higher future taxes implied by the debt financing. Because this position has its foundation in classical economics, these economists and their followers are referred to as **new classical economists**.

New classical economists Economists who believe there are strong forces pushing a market economy toward full employment equilibrium and that macroeconomic policy is an ineffective tool with which to reduce economic instability.

In the basic Keynesian model, a reduction in current taxes financed by borrowing increases the current disposable income of households. Given their additional disposable income, households increase their current consumption. New classical economists argue that this analysis is incorrect because it ignores the impact of the higher future tax liability implied by the budget deficit and the interest payments required to service the additional debt. ***New classical economists stress that debt financing simply substitutes higher future taxes for lower current taxes. Thus, budget deficits affect the timing of the taxes, but not their magnitude.***

A mere change in the timing of taxes will not alter the wealth of households. Therefore, there is no reason to believe that current consumption will change when current taxes are cut and government debt and future taxes are increased by an equivalent amount. According to the new classical view, households will reduce their current consumption in response to additional government debt (and the higher taxes that the debt implies) just as surely as if the equivalent amount of current taxes had been levied. In essence, households will simply save the reduction in their current taxes so they will have the funds with which to pay the higher future taxes implied by the additional government debt. In turn, the increase in saving will allow the government to finance its deficit without an increase in the interest rate. Thus, the substitution of debt for taxes will leave private consumption, aggregate demand, and real interest rates unchanged. This view that taxes and debt financing are essentially equivalent is known as **Ricardian equivalence**, after the nineteenth-century economist, David Ricardo, who initially developed the idea.

Ricardian equivalence
The view that a tax reduction financed with government debt will exert no impact on current consumption and aggregate demand because people will fully recognize the higher future taxes implied by the additional debt.

Perhaps an illustration will help explain the underlying logic of the new classical view. Consider the following alternative methods of paying a $2,000 tax liability: (1) a one-time payment of $2,000 or (2) payments of $200 each year in the future. When the interest rate is 10 percent, the opportunity cost of a $200 liability each year is $2,000. Therefore, just as the first option reduces current wealth by $2,000, so, too, does the second.

Now let us consider the impact of the two options on future income. If you dip into your savings to make a one-time $2,000 payment, your future interest income will be reduced by $200 each year in the future (assuming a 10 percent interest rate). Just as the second option reduces your future net income by $200 each year, so, too, does the first. In both cases, current wealth is reduced by $2,000. Similarly, in both cases the flow of future net income is reduced by $200 each year. Because of this, the new classical economists believe the two options are essentially the same.

Exhibit 15-4 illustrates the implications of the new classical view as to the potency of fiscal policy. Suppose the fiscal authorities issue $50 billion of additional debt in order to cut taxes by an equal amount. The government borrowing increases the demand for loanable funds (D_1 shifts to D_2 in part b of Exhibit 15-4) by $50 billion. If the taxpayers did not recognize the higher future taxes implied by the debt, they would expand consumption in response to the lower taxes and the increase in their current disposable income. Under such circumstances, aggregate demand in the goods and services market would expand to AD_2 (part a). In the new classical model, though, this will not be the case. Recognizing the

EXHIBIT 15-4 New Classical View—Higher Expected Future Taxes Crowd Out Private Spending

New classical economists emphasize that budget deficits merely substitute future taxes for current taxes. If households did not anticipate the higher future taxes, aggregate demand would increase to AD_2. However, demand remains unchanged at AD_1 when households fully anticipate the future increase in taxes (a). Simultaneously, the additional saving to meet the higher future taxes will increase the supply of loanable funds to S_2 and permit the government to borrow the funds to finance its deficit without pushing up the real interest rate (b). In this model, fiscal policy exerts no effect. The real interest rate, real GDP, and level of employment all remain unchanged.

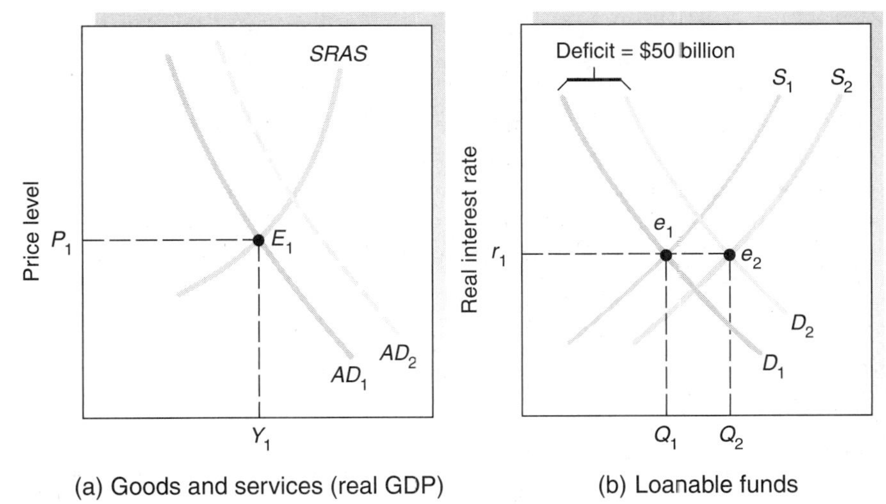

higher future taxes, taxpayers will maintain their initial level of consumption spending and use the tax cut to increase their savings in order to generate the additional income required to pay the future taxes implied by the $50 billion of additional debt. Because consumption is unchanged, aggregate demand also remainds constant (at AD_1). At the same time, the additional saving (to pay the implied increase in future taxes) allows the government to finance its deficit without an increase in the real interest rate. In this polar case, fiscal policy exerts no demand stimulus. In fact, it does not change much of anything. Output, employment, the price level, and even the real interest rate all remain constant.

The new classical view might be summarized as follows: The substitution of government debt for current taxes will fail to alter either the wealth or permanent income of the taxpaying households. Households will continue to maintain the same level of consumption even if the government cuts taxes and increases its outstanding debt. Thus, budget deficits will not stimulate aggregate demand. Neither will they affect output and employment. Similarly, the real interest rate is unaffected by deficits since people will save more in order to pay the higher future taxes. According to the new classical view, fiscal policy is completely impotent.

This new classical theory of fiscal policy is controversial.[4] Critics argue that it is unrealistic to expect that taxpayers will anticipate all or even most of the future taxes implied by additional government debt. In addition, even if people did anticipate the higher future taxes, in our world of limited life spans, many would recognize that they will not be around to pay, at least not in full, the future tax liability implied by debt financing. Many economists reject the new classical view of fiscal policy, at least in its pure form. Nonetheless, the significance of the new classical theory and its implications with regard to fiscal policy continue to provide one of the lively topics of debate in modern macroeconomics.

6 FISCAL POLICY: PROBLEMS OF PROPER TIMING

If fiscal policy is going to reduce economic instability, changes in policy must inject stimulus during a recession and restraint during an inflationary boom. But proper timing of fiscal policy is not an easy task. Because forecasting a forthcoming recession or boom is a highly imperfect science, there is usually a time lag between when a change in policy is needed and when its need is widely recognized by policymakers.

In addition, there is generally a lag between the time when the need for a fiscal policy change is recognized and the time when it is actually instituted. Discretionary fiscal policy requires changes in tax laws and government expenditure programs. The time required for such changes is likely to be quite lengthy. This will be particularly true for a political structure like that of the United States, with a number of checks and balances built into the system.[5] Congressional committees must meet, hear testimony, and draft legislation. Key legislators may choose to delay action if they can use their positions to obtain special favors for their constituencies. A majority of the lawmakers must be convinced that a proposed action is in the interest of the country, and the details of the policy must be arranged such that they will also believe that their own districts and supporters will not be disadvantaged. All these things take time.

---

[4] See Robert J. Barro, "The Ricardian Approach to Budget Deficits," *Journal of Economic Perspectives* (spring 1989): pp. 37–44; and John J. Seater, "Ricardian Equivalence," *Journal of Economic Literature* (March 1993): pp. 142–190.

[5] The time required for the institution of a change in fiscal policy may be shorter under a parliamentary political system, such as that of Canada or the United Kingdom. This is highly likely to be the case if a single party has a parliamentary majority.

An excellent example of the delays involved in conducting discretionary fiscal policy is the 2001 tax cut. The legislation to implement the tax decrease moved slowly through Congress in 2001 due to a debate about who would get their taxes cut. In particular, the argument centered on how much of the tax cut would be directed to high-income families relative to low-income families. While policymakers debated, conditions deteriorated and the economy fell into a recession.

Finally, still another factor adds to the complexity of fiscal policy making: Even after a policy is adopted, it may be six to twelve months before its major impact is felt. If government expenditures are going to be increased, time will be required for competitive bids to be submitted and new contracts granted. Contractors may be unable to begin work right away. Although a tax reduction will generally exert demand stimulus more quickly, it will take time for these effects to work their way through the economy.

Macroeconomic policymaking is a little bit like lobbing a ball at a moving target that sometimes changes directions unpredictably. In order to institute fiscal policy in a manner that will help stabilize the economy, policymakers need to know what economic conditions are going to be six, twelve, or eighteen months in the future. Unfortunately, our ability to forecast future economic conditions is limited. Therefore, in a world characterized by dynamic change and unpredictable events, some policy errors are inevitable.

Exhibit 15-5 illustrates the implications of the difficulties involved in the proper timing of fiscal policy. Suppose that policymakers attempt to use expansionary fiscal policy to stimulate aggregate demand during an economic downturn. If inability to forecast a recession and delays accompanying the adoption of a policy change take a substantial period, the economy's self-corrective mechanism may already have restored full employment by the time the fiscal stimulus begins to exert its primary impact. If so, the fiscal stimulus may well create excessive demand that will soon lead to inflation. Similarly, restrictive fiscal policy to cool an overheated economy may cause a recession if aggregate demand declines prior to the fiscal restraint.

In the real world, a discretionary change in fiscal policy is like a two-edged sword—it has the potential to do harm as well as good. If timed correctly, it will reduce economic instability. If timed incorrectly, however, the fiscal change will increase rather than reduce economic instability.

Automatic Stabilizers

Fortunately, there are a few fiscal programs that tend automatically to apply demand stimulus during a recession and demand restraint during an economic boom. Programs of this type are called **automatic stabilizers**. They are automatic in that, without any new legislative action, they tend to increase the budget deficit (or reduce the surplus) during a recession and increase the surplus (or reduce the deficit) during an economic boom.

Automatic stabilizers Built-in features that tend automatically to promote a budget deficit during a recession and a budget surplus during an inflationary boom, even without a change in policy.

The major advantage of automatic stabilizers is that they institute countercyclical fiscal policy without the delays associated with policy changes that require legislative action. Thus, they minimize the problem of proper timing. When unemployment is rising and business conditions are slow, these stabilizers automatically reduce taxes and increase government expenditures, giving the economy a shot in the arm. On the other hand, automatic stabilizers help to apply the brakes to an economic boom, increasing tax revenues and decreasing government spending. Three of these built-in stabilizers deserve specific mention: unemployment compensation, corporate profit tax, and progressive income tax.

EXHIBIT 15-5 Why Proper Timing of Fiscal Policy Is Difficult

Here we consider an economy that experiences shifts in AD that are not easy to forecast. Initially, the economy is in long-run equilibrium (E_0) at price level P_0 and at output Y_0. At this output, only the natural rate of unemployment is present. However, an investment slump and business pessimism result in an unanticipated decline in aggregate demand (to AD_1). Output falls and unemployment increases. After a time, policymakers institute expansionary fiscal policy seeking to shift aggregate demand back to AD_0. By the time fiscal policy begins to exert its primary effect, though, private investment has recovered and decision makers have become increasingly optimistic about the future. So aggregate demand is already, on its own accord, shifting back to AD_0. Thus, the expansionary fiscal policy overshifts aggregate demand to AD_2 rather than AD_0. Prices rise as the economy is now overheated. Unless the expansionary fiscal policy is reversed, wages and other resource prices will eventually increase, shifting *SRAS* to the left, thus pushing the price level still higher to (P_3). Alternatively, suppose an investment boom disrupts the equilibrium. The increase in investment shifts aggregate demand to AD_2, placing upward pressure on prices. Policymakers respond by increasing taxes and cutting government expenditures. By the time the restrictive fiscal policy exerts its primary impact, though, investment returns to its normal rate. As a result, the restrictive fiscal policy overshifts aggregate demand to AD_1 and throws the economy into a recession. Since fiscal policy does not work instantaneously, and since dynamic factors are constantly influencing private demand, proper timing of fiscal policy is not an easy task.

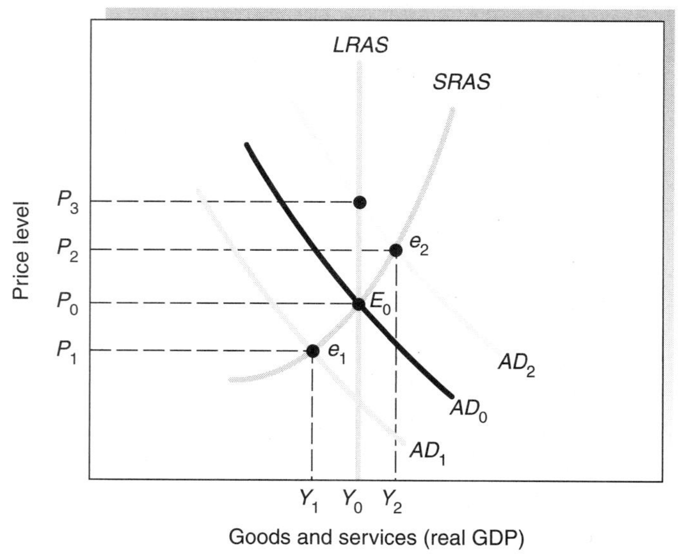

Unemployment Compensation

When an economy begins to dip into a recession, government payments for unemployment benefits will increase as the number of laid-off and unemployed workers expands. Simultaneously, the receipts from the employment tax that finances the system will decline because employment falls during a recession. Therefore, this program will automatically run a deficit during a business slowdown. In contrast, during an economic boom, the tax receipts from the program will increase because more people are now working, and the amount paid out in benefits will decline since fewer people are unemployed. Thus, the program will automatically tend to run a surplus during good times. So without any change in policy, the unemployment compensation program has the desired countercyclical effect on aggregate demand.[6]

[6] Although unemployment compensation has the desired countercyclical effect on demand, it also reduces the incentive to accept available employment opportunities. Research in this area indicates that the existing unemployment compensation system increases the length of job search by unemployed workers and thereby increases the long-run natural (normal) unemployment rate.

Corporate Profit Tax

Tax studies show that the corporate profit tax is the most countercyclical of all the automatic stabilizers. This results because corporate profits are highly sensitive to cyclical conditions. During a recession, corporate profits decline sharply, and so too do corporate tax payments. In turn, the decline in tax revenues will enlarge the size of the budget deficit. In contrast, when the economy is expanding, corporate profits typically increase much more rapidly than wages, income, or consumption. This increase in corporate profits will result in a rapid increase in the "tax take" from the business sector during the expansion phase of the business cycle. Thus, corporate tax payments will go up during an expansion and fall rapidly during a contraction, even though no new legislative action has been instituted.

Progressive Income Tax

When income grows rapidly, the average personal income tax liability of individuals and families increases. With rising incomes, more people will find their income above the "no tax due" cutoff. Others will be pushed into a higher tax bracket. Therefore, during an economic expansion, revenue from the personal income tax increases more rapidly than income. Other things constant, the budget moves toward a surplus (or smaller deficit), even though the economy's tax rate structure is unchanged. On the other hand, when income declines, many individuals will be taxed at a lower rate or not at all. Income tax revenues will fall more rapidly than income, automatically enlarging the size of the budget deficit during a recession.

FISCAL POLICY AS A STABILIZATION TOOL: A MODERN SYNTHESIS 7

During the 1960s the basic Keynesian view was widely accepted. Fiscal policy was thought to be highly potent. Furthermore, it was widely believed that political decision makers, with the assistance of their economic advisors, were fully capable of instituting discretionary fiscal policy changes in a manner that would help stabilize the economy. During the 1970s and 1980s, both the operation of fiscal policy and its efficacy as a stabilization tool were analyzed and hotly debated among professional economists. A synthesis view has emerged from that debate. Most macroeconomists—both Keynesian and non-Keynesian—now accept the following three elements of the modern synthesis view.

1. ***Proper timing of discretionary fiscal policy is both difficult to achieve and of crucial importance.*** Given our limited ability to forecast turns in the business cycle and the political delays that inevitably accompany a change in fiscal policy, the effectiveness of discretionary fiscal policy as a stabilization tool is highly questionable. Therefore, most macroeconomists now place less emphasis on fiscal policy. (*Note:* The quotation at the beginning of this reading from Paul Samuelson, a long-time Keynesian, highlights this point.)
2. ***Automatic stabilizers reduce the fluctuation of aggregate demand and help to direct the economy toward full employment.*** Since they are not dependent on legislative action, automatic stabilizers are able consistently to shift the budget toward a deficit during a recession and toward a surplus during an economic boom. Thus, they add needed stimulus during the recession and act as a restraining force during an inflationary boom. Although some question their potency, most all would agree that they exert a stabilizing influence.

3. ***Fiscal policy is much less potent than the early Keynesian view implied.*** The current debate among macroeconomists concerning the impact of fiscal policy during normal times is not whether crowding out takes place, but rather how it takes place. The crowding-out and new classical models highlight this point. Both models indicate that there are side effects of budget deficits that will substantially, if not entirely, offset their impact on aggregate demand. In the crowding-out model, higher real interest rates and a decline in net exports as the result of currency appreciation reduce private demand and offset the expansionary effects of budget deficits. In the new classical model, higher anticipated future taxes lead to the same result. Both models indicate that fiscal policy will exert little, if any, impact on current aggregate demand, employment, and real output during normal economic times.

8 SUPPLY-SIDE EFFECTS OF FISCAL POLICY

Supply-side economists Modern economists who believe that changes in marginal tax rates exert important effects on aggregate supply.

Thus far, we have focused on the potential demand-side effects of fiscal policy. However, when fiscal changes alter tax rates, they influence the incentive of people to work, invest, and use resources efficiently. Thus, tax changes may also influence aggregate supply. Prior to 1980, macroeconomists generally ignored the supply-side effects of changes in tax rates, thinking they were of little importance. **Supply-side economists** challenged this view. The supply-side argument was central to the tax rate reductions of the 1980s and it also played a role in the structure of the tax legislation passed in 2001.

From a supply-side viewpoint, the marginal tax rate is of crucial importance. As we discussed previously, the marginal tax rate determines the breakdown of one's additional income between tax payments on the one hand and personal income on the other. A reduction in marginal tax rates increases the reward derived from added work, investment, saving, and other activities that become less heavily taxed. People shift into these activities away from leisure (and leisure-intensive activities), tax shelters, consumption of tax-deductible goods, and other forms of tax avoidance. Supply-side economists believe that these substitutions both enlarge the effective resource base and improve the efficiency with which the resources are applied.

The source of the supply-side effects accompanying a change in tax rates is fundamentally different from the source of the demand-side effects. A change in tax policy affects aggregate demand through its impact on disposable income and the flow of expenditures. ***In contrast, changes in tax rates, particularly marginal tax rates, will affect aggregate supply through their impact on the relative attractiveness of productive activity in comparison to leisure and tax avoidance.***

Exhibit 15-6 graphically depicts the impact of a supply-side tax cut, one that reduces marginal tax rates. The lower marginal tax rates increase aggregate supply as the new incentive structure encourages taxpayers to earn additional income and use resources more efficiently. If the tax change is perceived as long-term, both long- and short-run aggregate supply (*LRAS* and *SRAS*) will increase. Real output and income expand. As real income expands, aggregate demand will also increase (shift to AD_2). If the lower marginal rates are financed by a budget deficit, aggregate demand may increase by a larger amount than aggregate supply, placing upward pressure on the price level.

Supply-side economics should not be viewed as a short-run countercyclical tool. It will take time for changing market incentives to move resources out of tax-motivated investments and into higher-yield activities. The full positive effects of lower marginal tax rates will not be observed until labor and capital markets have time to adjust fully to the new incentive structure. ***Clearly, supply-side economics is a long-run, growth-oriented strategy.***

EXHIBIT 15-6 Tax Rate Effects and Supply-Side Economics

Here we illustrate the supply-side effects of a reduction in marginal tax rates. The lower marginal tax rates increase the incentive to earn and use resources efficiently. Since these effects are long-run as well as short-run, both *LRAS* and *SRAS* increase (shift to the right). Real output expands. In turn, the higher income levels accompanying the expansion in real output will stimulate aggregate demand (shift to AD_2).

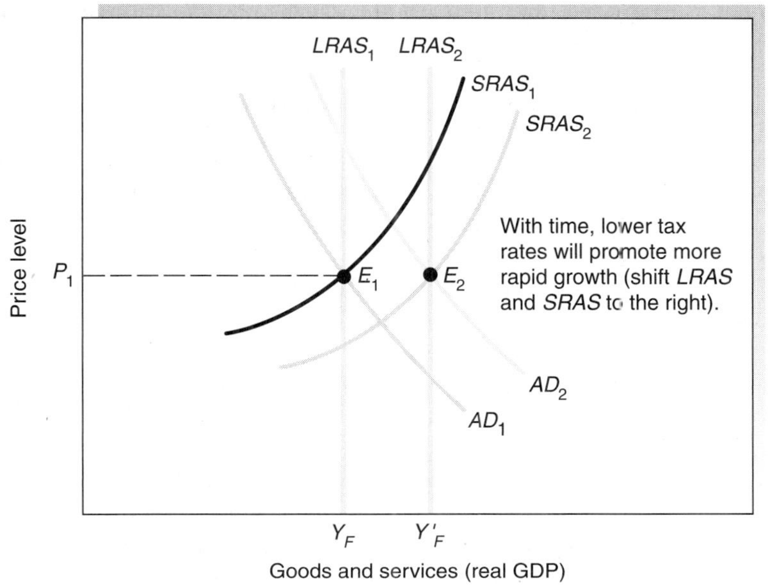

Why High Tax Rates Tend to Retard Output

There are three major reasons why high tax rates are likely to retard the growth of output. First, high marginal tax rates discourage work effort and reduce the productive efficiency of labor. When marginal tax rates soar to 55 percent or 60 percent, individuals get to keep less than half of what they earn—and when the payoff from working declines, people tend to work less. Some (for example, those with a working spouse) will drop out of the labor force. Others will simply work fewer hours. Still others will decide to take more lengthy vacations, forgo overtime opportunities, retire earlier, or forget about pursuing that promising but risky business venture. In some cases, high tax rates will even drive highly productive citizens to other countries where taxes are lower. High tax rates will also result in inefficient utilization of labor. Some individuals will substitute less-productive activities that are not taxed (for example, do-it-yourself projects) for work opportunities yielding taxable income.

Second, high tax rates will adversely affect the rate of capital formation and the efficiency of its use. When tax rates are high, foreign investment will be repelled and domestic investors will search for investment projects abroad where taxes are lower. In addition, domestic investors will direct more of their time and effort into hobby businesses (for example, collecting antiques, raising horses, or giving golf lessons) that provide both enjoyable activities and tax-shelter benefits. This process will divert investment resources away from projects with a higher rate of return but fewer tax-avoidance benefits. As the result of the tax-shelter benefits, individuals will often be able to gain even though the "investments" reduce the value of resources. Scarce capital is wasted and resources are channeled away from their most productive uses.

Third, high marginal tax rates encourage individuals to substitute less-desired tax-deductible goods for more-desired nondeductible goods. Here the inefficiency stems from the fact that individuals do not bear the full cost of tax-deductible purchases.

High marginal tax rates make tax-deductible expenditures cheap for persons in high tax brackets. Since the personal cost, but not the cost to society, is cheap, taxpayers confronting high marginal tax rates will spend more money on pleasurable, tax-deductible items, such as plush offices, professional conferences held in favorite vacation spots, and various fringe benefits (for example, a company luxury automobile, business entertainment, and a company retirement plan). Because such tax-deductible purchases reduce their taxes, people will often buy such goods even though they do not value them as much as the cost of producing them.

How Important Are Supply-Side Effects?

There is division among economists with regard to the strength of the supply-side incentive effects. Critics of supply-side economics stress that the rate reductions of the 1980s were associated with a modest growth rate of output, a significant reduction in the real tax revenue of the federal government, and large budget deficits. These outcomes do not indicate that the supply-side effects are highly potent. Defenders of the supply-side position respond by noting that the rate reductions of both the 1960s and the 1980s resulted in impressive growth and lengthy economic expansions. They also stress that the supply-side response in the top brackets—where lower rates have the largest incentive effects—is particularly strong.[7]

It is interesting to view the supply-side perspective within the framework of the Laffer Curve analysis. The Laffer Curve indicates that the revenues collected from a tax will expand as tax rates are increased. Eventually, however, higher and higher rates will lead to a revenue maximum point and rate increases beyond this level will actually reduce the revenue collected. It is also important to note that tax rates at or near the revenue maximum point are highly inefficient because in that range the high rates are eliminating a substantial amount of beneficial economic activity without raising much additional revenue. Tax rates on the backward bending portion of the Laffer Curve involve a double barrel negative impact: productive economic activity is eliminated and the government loses revenue by imposing such high rates.

During the last four decades, there has been a substantial reduction in the personal income tax rates applicable to those with high incomes. As the top marginal rates have fallen, the share of income tax revenue derived from those in the upper brackets has increased. Exhibit 15-7 on the next page presents data on the share of the personal income tax derived from the top one-half percent of income recipients since 1960. When the top marginal tax rate was sliced from 91 percent to 70 percent by the Kennedy-Johnson tax cut of 1964, the share of the personal income tax paid by the top half percent rose from 16 percent to 18 percent. In contrast, as inflation pushed more and more taxpayers into higher brackets during the 1970s, the share paid by the top half percent declined. When the tax cuts of the 1980s once again reduced the top rates, the share paid by the top half percent climbed to more than 20 percent of the total. As the top marginal rate was increased in 1991 and again in 1993, there was little change in the share of taxes paid by the top group. Beginning in 1997, the tax rate on income from capital gains was cut from 28 percent to 20 percent. This rate reduction was

[7] The incentive effects are greater in the upper brackets because a similar percentage rate reduction will have a greater impact on take-home pay in this area. For example, if a 70 percent marginal tax rate is cut to 50 percent, take-home pay per additional dollar of earnings will increase from 30 cents to 50 cents, a 67 percent increase in the incentive to earn. On the other hand, if a 14 percent marginal rate is reduced to 10 percent, take-home pay per dollar of additional earnings will increase from 86 cents to 90 cents, only a 5 percent increase in the incentive to earn.

EXHIBIT 15-7 How Have Changes in Marginal Tax Rates Affected the Share of Taxes Paid by the Rich?

The accompanying graph indicates the share of the personal income tax paid by the top one-half percent of earners during 1960–1998. There were four major reductions in marginal tax rates during this period. First, the Kennedy-Johnson tax cut reduced the top rate from 91 percent in 1963 to 70 percent in 1965. During the Reagan years, the top rate was reduced from 70 percent in 1980 to 50 percent in 1982 and in 1986 it was sliced again to approximately 30 percent. Most recently, the capital gains tax rate was sliced from 28 to 20 percent in 1997. Interestingly, the share of the tax bill paid by these "super-rich" earners increased following each of these tax cuts. These findings suggest that, at least for this group of high-income recipients, strong supply-side effects accompanied the rate cuts. Perhaps surprising to some, these high-income taxpayers paid a larger portion of the tax bill when the top marginal rate was less than 40 percent (1986–1998) than was true during the 1960s and 1970s when the top marginal rate was 70 percent or more.

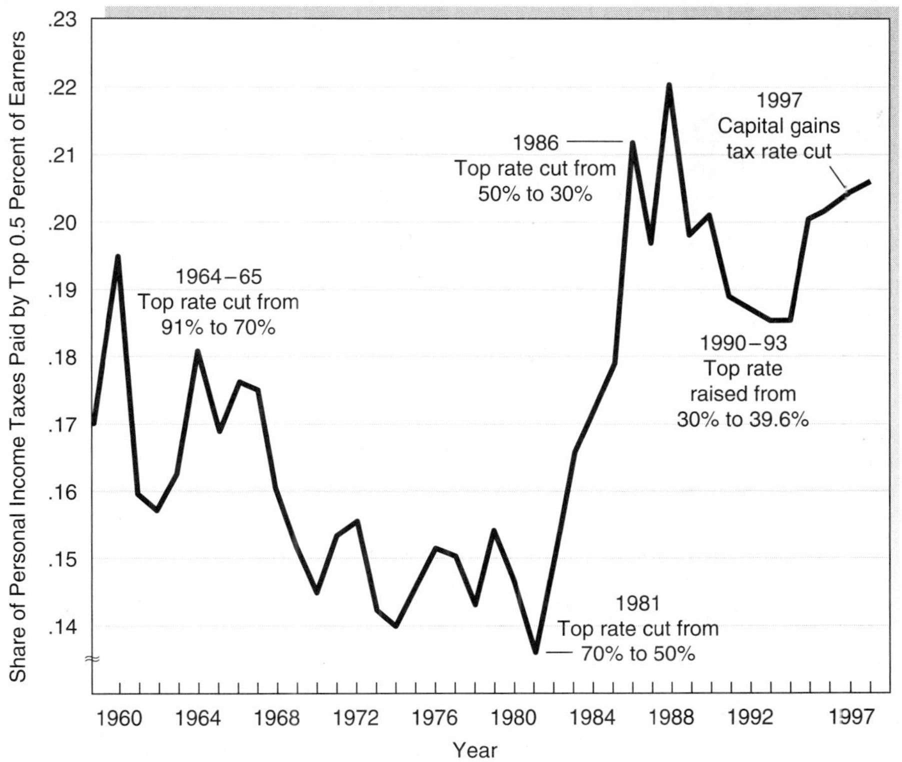

accompanied by a substantial increase in revenues derived from the taxation of capital gains and an increase in the share of the personal income tax collected from high-income taxpayers.[8]

Supply-side economists argue that findings like these illustrate that economic activity is quite sensitive to changes in tax rates, particularly the highest marginal rates. They also indicate that high marginal tax rates, like those of the 1960s and 1970s are counterproductive; they reduce productive activity without raising any appreciable revenue. Since 1986 the top marginal personal income tax rate has been less than 40 percent compared to 70 percent or more prior to 1981. Nonetheless, those with high incomes are now paying more. For example, 25.7 percent of the personal income tax was collected from the top half percent of earners in 1998, up from the 16 to 18 percent range of the early 1960s. Perhaps the supply-siders have found a way to "soak the rich"—keep their marginal tax rates relatively low.

[8] In 1996, capital gains income was $261 billion, which yielded tax revenues of $66 billion. By 2000, income due to capital gains had risen to $652 billion, with corresponding tax revenues of $129 billion.

Gradual rate reductions are an integral part of the tax legislation passed in 2001. This bill will reduce the top marginal rate to 35 percent in 2006, down from 39.6 percent in 2000. The 28%, 31% and 36% rates of 2000 will be phased downward to 25%, 28% and 33% by 2006. The proponents of this legislation believe that it will improve supply-side incentives and thereby enhance long-run economic growth. In the years immediately ahead, it will be interesting to track both the level of economic activity and the revenues collected from those with high incomes.

In today's global economy, tax policy is not conducted in a vacuum. Taxes can influence the choices of both business and labor. Ireland provides a vivid illustration of this point. During the last 15 years, Ireland has significantly reduced both personal and corporate income taxes. The lower tax rates help it attract foreign business, expand employment, and promote economic growth. During the 1990s, Ireland had the highest growth rate in Europe and many Irish immigrants who had moved abroad to find work returned to their homeland.

On the other hand, high taxes can drive both business and labor elsewhere.[9] Taxes are generally higher in Europe than the United States, and many believe that this has contributed to Europe's sluggish growth. Several high-tax European countries—including Belgium, Denmark, France, Germany, The Netherlands, and Sweden—confront a "brain drain" problem, an exodus of high-skill (and therefore high-income) business and professional workers. While supply-side effects of this type do not dramatically alter year-to-year growth rates, they can exert a significant impact on income levels with the passage of time.

9 THE FISCAL POLICY OF THE UNITED STATES

OPTIONAL SEGMENT

The accompanying Thumbnail Sketch summarizes the major implications of the alternative theories with regard to the impact of expansionary fiscal policy. In general, the effects of restrictive fiscal policy would be just the opposite. As we previously mentioned, economists use changes in the size of the deficit or sur-

THUMBNAIL SKETCH

Impact of Expansionary Fiscal Policy—A Summary of Four Models

1. **Basic Keynesian model:** An increase in government spending and/or a reduction in taxes will be magnified by the multiplier process and lead to a substantial increase in aggregate demand. When an economy is operating below capacity, real output and employment will also increase substantially.
2. **Crowding-out model:** Expansionary fiscal policy will exert little or no impact on aggregate demand and employment because borrowing to finance the budget deficit will push up interest rates and crowd out private spending, particularly investment. In an open economy, the higher interest rates will lead to an inflow of capital, a currency appreciation, and a decline in net exports.
3. **New classical model:** Expansionary fiscal policy will exert little or no impact on aggregate demand and employment because households will anticipate the higher future taxes implied by the debt and reduce their spending (and increase their saving) in order to pay them. Like current taxes, debt (future taxes) will crowd out private spending.
4. **Supply-side model:** A reduction in marginal tax rates will increase the incentive to earn (produce) and improve the efficiency of resource use, leading to an increase in aggregate supply (real output) in the long run.

[9] See Fabio Padovano and Emma Galli, "Tax Rates and Economic Growth in the OECD Countries," *Economic Inquiry* (January 2001): pp. 44–57, for evidence on the relationship between taxes and growth.

plus, rather than the absolute amount, to determine whether fiscal policy is shifting toward expansion or restriction. Movement toward a larger deficit (or a smaller surplus) relative to GDP indicates that fiscal policy is becoming more expansionary. Conversely, a reduction in the deficit as a share of GDP (or increase in the surplus) would imply a more restrictive fiscal policy.

Exhibit 15-8 presents data on federal expenditures and revenues as a share of GDP during the last four decades. While deficits were present throughout most of the 1960s and 1970s, they were small relative to the size of the economy except during the recessions of 1970 and 1974–1975. Budget deficits have generally increased during recessions (indicated by the shaded bars) and shrunk during expansions. However, the changes in the size of the deficit over the business cycle have been primarily the result of automatic stabilizers rather than discretionary use of fiscal policy. Major discretionary changes motivated by business conditions have generally been too late to have much countercyclical impact. For example, this was the case with the 1968 tax increase to combat inflation during the Vietnam War and the anti-recession tax rebate of 1975.

Business cycle conditions are not the only factor underlying fiscal policy. Sometimes changes in external conditions (the threat of war) or demographic factors (like a change in the number of retirees or prime-age workers) exert a strong impact on expenditure and revenue levels. This was true during the last two decades. Fiscal policy during the first half of the 1980s was driven by a supply-side tax cut and expansion in defense expenditures. These two factors along with the severe recession of 1982 pushed the federal deficit to peacetime highs in the

EXHIBIT 15-8 Federal Government Expenditures and Revenues as a Percentage of GDP, 1960–2000

Except during recessions (indicated by shaded bars), budget deficits were small as a share of the economy prior to 1980. After a period of persistently large deficits during the 1980s, the federal deficit shrank and by the late 1990s a surplus was present. Revenue increases propelled by a strong economy and spending reductions on defense (see the following exhibit) were the primary factors underlying the shift from deficits to surpluses.

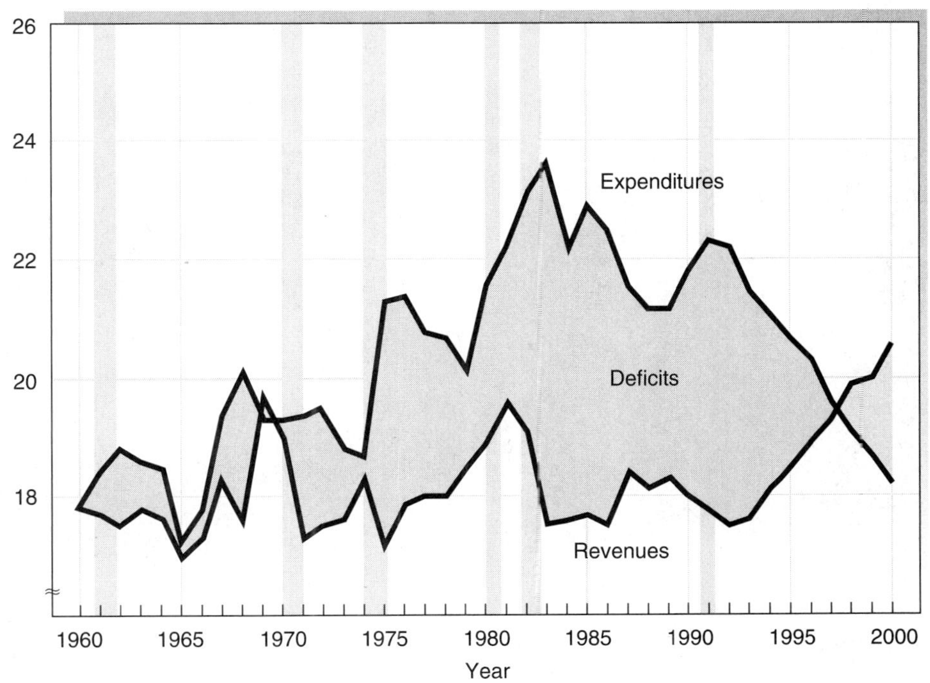

Source: Economic Report of the President, 2001, tables B-1 and B-79.

mid-1980s. The deficit declined as the economy grew rapidly during the latter half of the 1980s, but increased once again during the recession and sluggish growth of the early 1990s.

How Were the Deficits Transformed into Surpluses?

Several factors played a role in the transformation of the federal budget from deficit to surplus during the 1990s. While modest tax increases were passed in both 1990 and 1993, strong growth of the economy propelled revenues in the latter half of the decade. The growth of real income within the framework of a progressive tax structure increases effective tax rates. As real income expands, more and more income is pushed into higher tax brackets, which automatically increases both average tax rates and tax revenues as a share of income. As Exhibit 15-8 shows, federal tax revenues rose from 17.5 percent of GDP in 1992 to a post–World War II high of 20.6 percent in 2000.

While increases in defense spending expanded the deficit during the 1980s, defense cuts helped shrink it in the 1990s. Exhibit 15-9 illustrates this point. During the mid-1980s, real defense expenditures (4-year moving average) grew at an annual rate of almost 8 percent. This rapid growth pushed up federal expenditures as a share of the economy and contributed to the large deficits of the decade. In the aftermath of the Cold War, however, defense expenditures plunged. By the mid-1990s, real defense expenditures were declining at an annual rate of 4 percent. Real defense spending continued to decline throughout the 1990s, slowing the growth of total federal expenditures. During 1996–2000, real federal spending grew at an annual rate of only 1 percent, the slowest rate of any 5-year period since the end of World War II. This combination of factors—

As a share of GDP, government expenditures fell and tax revenues increased in the 1990s. This combination substantially reduced the budget deficit (see Exhibit 15-8). Reduction in national defense spending from 5.2 percent to 3.0 percent of GDP between 1990 and 2000 was the primary reason for the lower expenditures, while the higher average tax rates accompanying the growth of income was primarily responsible for the increase in revenues.

EXHIBIT 15-9 Growth Rate of Real Federal Government and Defense Expenditures, 1980–2000

The growth rates of both total and defense spending adjusted for inflation are shown here. During the 1980s, rapid growth of defense spending pushed total federal expenditures upward and contributed substantially to the large deficits of the decade. During the 1990s, defense cuts in the aftermath of the Cold War retarded the growth of federal spending and thereby contributed substantially to the recent surpluses.

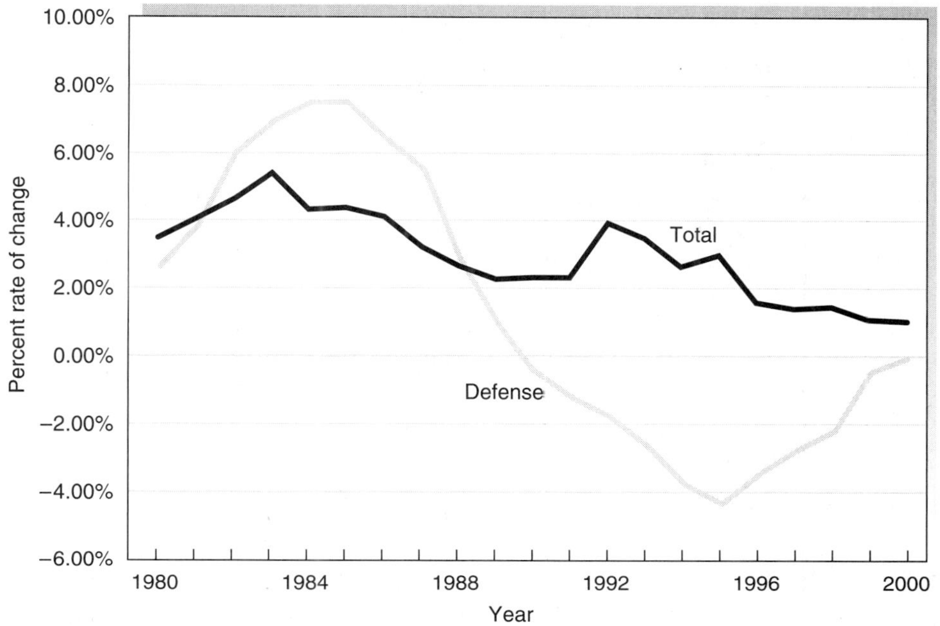

Source: Bureau of Economic Analysis, website http://www.bea.doc.gov. The growth rates are calculated as a four-year moving average of the annual rates in order to reduce the impact of the business cycle on changes in expenditures.

rapid expansion in revenues propelled by both economic growth and higher average tax rates and slow growth of spending due to defense cuts—eliminated the federal deficit in the late 1990s.

Demographic factors smoothed the path for deficit reduction. The huge baby boom generation (persons born between 1946 and 1960) moved into their prime earning years during the 1990s. By 1999, persons age 35–54 comprised 48.3 percent of the labor force, up from 41.6 percent at the beginning of the decade. This increase in prime-age earners contributed to the strong growth of both personal income and federal tax revenues in the 1990s. On the other hand, most of those retiring during the 1990s were born during the 1930s. Because the birthrate was low during these Great Depression years, the growth of retirees during the 1990s was low. This made it easier to control expenditures on Social Security and Medicare, two of the largest federal programs.

While fiscal policy was highly expansionary during the 1980s, the inflation rate fell from the double-digit levels of 1979–1980 to 4 percent in 1983. The economy grew rapidly throughout the remainder of the decade and inflation remained in check. In contrast with the 1980s, fiscal policy was highly restrictive in the 1990s. Nonetheless, the economy grew rapidly and inflation remained at a low level. Even though fiscal policy was quite expansionary during the 1980s and quite restrictive during the 1990s, both decades were characterized by strong growth and low rates of inflation. These results do not indicate that fiscal policy—either expansionary or restrictive—exerts a strong impact on aggregate demand. Thus, they are more consistent with the crowding out and new classical theories than the Keynesian view.

The Future

As the budget surplus soared to more than 2 percent of GDP during 2000, large surpluses were projected for several years into the future. This was true even after the effects of the 2001 tax cut were taken into account. However, all of this changed with the September 11 attacks and the War on Terrorism. Federal expenditures increased in several areas including national defense, intelligence gathering, domestic security (a new cabinet level office was established), airport security, and subsidies to the airline industry. The spending increases along with the adverse impact of the recession quickly dissipated the budget surplus.

What is likely to happen to the budget when the economy recovers and growth returns? The answer to this question is dependent on factors that are very difficult to forecast, things like the cost of the War on Terrorism and the perceived likelihood of future terrorist attacks. If the War on Terrorism is relatively short and the related long-term spending increases on national defense and domestic security are small, budget surpluses might well reemerge. Even if this is the case, however, there is reason to question their political viability. Public choice analysis indicates that vote-maximizing politicians have an incentive to increase spending on their constituents, particularly if they can do so without having to raise taxes. The presence of surpluses would make it tempting for political decision makers to undertake new spending projects. Thus, the occurrence of persistent budget surpluses over a lengthy period of time seems unlikely.

The demographics will continue to exert a favorable budgetary impact through the first decade of the twenty-first century. A large share of the labor force will remain in the prime-earning age categories, while the number of new retirees will grow slowly. However, all of this will change dramatically once the baby boomers begin to retire around 2010. Approximately one-third of the federal budget is devoted to spending on the elderly through Medicare and Social Security. The retirement of the baby boomers will push spending on these programs up substantially. As this happens, an era of large deficits is likely to return.

SUMMARY

10

- The federal budget is the primary tool of fiscal policy. Discretionary fiscal policy encompasses deliberate changes in the government's spending and tax policies designed to alter the size of the budget deficit and thereby influence the overall level of economic activity.
- According to the Keynesian view, fluctuations in aggregate demand are the major source of economic instability. Policies that help to maintain aggregate demand at a level consistent with the economy's full employment capacity will reduce economic instability.
- Rather than balancing the budget annually, Keynesian analysis indicates that fiscal policy should reflect business cycle conditions. During a recession, fiscal policy should become more expansionary (a larger deficit should be planned). During an inflationary boom, fiscal policy should become more restrictive (shift toward a budget surplus).
- The crowding-out model indicates that expansionary fiscal policy will lead to higher real interest rates and less private spending, particularly for investment. In an open economy, the higher interest rates will also lead to an inflow of capital, appreciation of the dollar, and a reduction in net exports. The crowding-out theory implies that these secondary effects will largely offset the demand stimulus effects of expansionary fiscal policy. The secondary effects of restrictive fiscal policy will also render it impotent.
- The new classical model stresses that substitution of debt for tax financing changes the timing, but not the level, of taxes. According to this view, the higher expected future taxes implied by the bond financing of the deficit will lead to more saving and less private spending, which will offset the expansionary effects of the deficit.
- Changes in fiscal policy must be timed properly if they are going to exert a stabilizing influence on an economy. The ability of policymakers to time fiscal policy changes in a countercyclical manner is reduced by (a) our limited ability to forecast future macroeconomic conditions, (b) predictable delays in the institution of policy changes, and (c) a time lag between when a policy change is instituted and when it will exert its primary impact.
- The problem of proper timing is reduced in the case of automatic stabilizers—programs that apply stimulus during a recession and restraint during a boom even though no legislative action has been taken.
- A modern synthesis concerning the impact of fiscal policy as a stabilization tool has emerged. The major points of the synthesis view are: (1) Proper timing of discretionary fiscal policy is both difficult to achieve and crucially important; (2) automatic stabilizers reduce the fluctuation of aggregate demand and thereby help to promote economic stability; and (3) fiscal policy is much less potent than the early Keynesian view implied.
- When fiscal policy changes marginal tax rates, it influences aggregate supply by altering the relative attractiveness of productive activity compared to leisure and tax avoidance. Other things constant, lower marginal tax rates will increase aggregate supply. Supply-side economics should be viewed as a long-run strategy, not a countercyclical tool.
- The United States ran large budget deficits throughout the 1980s, but the deficits were eliminated and transformed into surpluses in the late 1990s. Rapid growth of tax revenues during the expansion of the 1990s and slow growth of expenditures resulting from a plunge in defense

spending were the primary factors underlying the shift from deficits to surpluses.

- Demographic factors—rapid growth of prime-age earners and slow growth of retirees—enhanced revenues and made it easier to control spending growth during the 1990s. These factors will exert the opposite impact once the baby boomers begin retiring during the years following 2010.

MONEY AND THE BANKING SYSTEM

READING

16

LEARNING OUTCOMES

The candidate should be able to:

a. explain the relationship among the required reserve ratio, the potential deposit expansion multiplier, and the deposit expansion multiplier;

b. describe the role of a country's central bank and the tools that a central bank can use to control the money supply, and explain how a central bank can use monetary tools to implement monetary policy;

c. discuss potential problems in measuring an economy's money supply.

Money is whatever is generally accepted in exchange for goods and services—accepted not as an object to be consumed but as an object that represents a temporary abode of purchasing power to be used for buying still other goods and services.

—Milton Friedman[1]

INTRODUCTION 1

The simple macroeconomic model we have developed thus far has four major markets: (1) goods and services, (2) resources, (3) loanable funds, and (4) foreign exchange. When people make exchanges in any of these markets, they generally use money. Money is used to purchase all types of goods, services, physical assets such as houses, and financial assets such as stocks and bonds.

This reading focuses on the nature of money, how the banking system works, and how the **central bank**—the Federal Reserve System in the United States—controls the supply of money. Money and monetary policy play an important role in the operation of an economy. Reflecting this importance, the next two readings will focus primarily on how monetary policy works and the impact that it has on the level of prices, output, employment, and the business cycle.

Central bank
An institution that regulates the banking system and controls the supply of money of a country.

[1] Milton Friedman, *Money Mischief: Episodes in Monetary History* (New York: Harcourt Brace Jovanovich, 1992), p. 16.

2 WHAT IS MONEY?

Money is the item that is commonly used as a means of payment for goods, services, assets, and outstanding debt. (See the opening quotation of Professor Friedman on the previous page.) Paradoxically, most modern money has no intrinsic worth. Nonetheless, most of us would like to have more of it. Why? Because money is an asset that performs three basic functions: It serves as a medium of exchange, it provides a means of storing value for future use, and it is used as an accounting unit.

Medium of Exchange

Medium of exchange
An asset that is used to buy and sell goods or services.

Money is one of the most important inventions in human history because of its role as a **medium of exchange**. Money simplifies and reduces the costs of transactions. This reduction in transaction cost permits us to realize the enormous gains from specialization, division of labor, and mass-production processes that underlie our modern standard of living. Without money, exchange would be complicated, time-consuming, and enormously costly. Think what it would be like to live in a barter economy—one without money, where goods were traded for goods. If you wanted to buy a pair of jeans, for example, you would have to first find someone willing to sell you the jeans who was also willing to purchase your labor services or something else you were willing to supply. Such an economy would be highly inefficient.

Money oils the wheels of trade and makes it possible for each of us to specialize in the supply of those things that we do best while purchasing (and consuming) a broad cross-section of goods and services consistent with our individual preferences. People simply sell their productive services or assets for money and, in turn, use the money to buy the goods and services they want. For example, if a farmer wants to exchange a cow for electricity and medical services, the cow is sold for money, which is then used to buy the electricity and the medical services. Money permits a society to escape cumbersome barter procedures.

Store of Value

Store of value
An asset that will allow people to transfer purchasing power from one period to the next.

Liquid asset
An asset that can be easily and quickly converted to purchasing power without loss of value.

Money is a financial asset—a method of storing value and moving purchasing power from one time period to another. There are some disadvantages of money as a **store of value**. Many methods of holding money do not yield an interest return. During a time of inflation, the purchasing power of money will decline, imposing a cost on those who are holding wealth in the form of money.

Money is not the only way of storing value. Other assets, such as food products, land, houses, stocks, or bonds, might be used to store value for the future. *Money, however, has one big advantage—because of its use as a medium of exchange, money is the most* ***liquid*** *of all assets.* It can be easily and quickly transformed into other goods at a low transaction cost and without an appreciable loss in its nominal value. In contrast, it will take time to locate an acceptable buyer for a house, a plot of land, or an office building. Thus, these assets are illiquid. While stocks and bonds are quite liquid—they can usually be sold quickly for only a small commission—they are not readily acceptable as a direct means of payment. Money provides readily available purchasing power for dealing with an uncertain future. Thus, most people hold some of their wealth in the form of money.

Unit of Account

Unit of account
The units of measurement used by people to post prices and keep track of revenues and costs.

Money also serves as a **unit of account**. Just as we use yards or meters to measure distance, units of money are used to measure the exchange value and costs of goods, services, assets, and resources. The value (and cost) of movie tickets, personal computers, labor services, automobiles, houses, and numerous other items is measured in units of money. Money serves as a common denominator for the expression of both costs and value. If consumers are going to spend their income wisely, they must be able to compare the costs of a vast array of goods and services. Prices measured in units of money help them make such comparisons. Similarly, sound business decisions require cost and revenue comparisons among vastly different productive services. Resource prices and accounting procedures measured in money units facilitate this task.

WHY IS MONEY VALUABLE? 3

At various times in the past, societies have used gold, silver, beads, seashells, cigarettes, precious stones, and other commodities as money. When commodities are used as money, people will employ scarce resources—resources that could be used to produce valuable goods and services—trying to produce more of the thing that is used as money. Because of this, the opportunity cost of commodity-based money is high.

If a society uses something as money that costs little or nothing to produce, more scarce resources are available for the production of desired goods and services. Thus, most modern nations use **fiat money**, money that has little or no intrinsic value. A dollar bill is just a piece of paper. Checking account deposits are nothing more than accounting numbers. Coins have some intrinsic value as metal, but in most cases this value is considerably less than their value as money.

Fiat money
Money that has neither intrinsic value nor the backing of a commodity with intrinsic value; paper currency is an example.

Why is fiat money valuable? To a degree, its value is based on the confidence of the people who use it. People are willing to accept fiat money because they know it can be used to purchase real goods and services. Governments issuing fiat money often designate it as "legal tender," meaning it is acceptable for payment of debts.

Money is the item commonly used to buy and sell things. During the Second World War, prisoners of war used cigarettes as money in POW camps.

The main thing that makes money valuable, however, is the same thing that generates value for other commodities: Demand relative to supply. People demand money because it reduces the cost of exchange. When the supply of money is limited relative to the demand, money will be valuable.

The value of a unit of money—a dollar, for example—is measured in terms of what it will buy. Its value, therefore, is inversely related to the level of prices. An increase in the level of prices and a decline in the purchasing power of a unit of money are the same thing. If the purchasing power of money is to remain stable over time, the supply of money must be controlled. Assuming a constant rate of use, if the supply of money grows more rapidly than the real output of goods and services, prices will rise. In layman's terms, there is "too much money chasing too few goods."

When government authorities rapidly expand the supply of money, it becomes less valuable in exchange and is virtually useless as a store of value. The rapid growth in the supply of money in Germany following the First World War provides a dramatic illustration of this point. During the period 1922–1923, the supply of German marks increased by 250 percent *per month* for a time. The German government was printing money almost as fast as the printing presses would run. Since money became substantially more plentiful in relation to goods and services, it quickly lost its value. As a result, an egg cost 80 billion marks and a loaf of bread 200 billion. Workers picked up their wages in suitcases. Shops closed at the lunch hour to change price tags. The value of money had eroded. More recently (in the 1980s and 1990s), Argentina, Bolivia, Brazil, Israel, Yugoslavia, Russia, and Ukraine (and several other countries of the former Soviet Union) have experienced this same cycle of rapid growth in the money supply (to pay for government expenditures) and hyperinflation.

M1 (money supply)
The sum of (1) currency in circulation (including coins), (2) checkable deposits maintained in depository institutions, and (3) traveler's checks.

4 THE SUPPLY OF MONEY

How is the supply of money defined? There is no straightforward, single answer to this question. Economists and policy makers have developed several alternative measures. We will briefly describe the two most widely used of these money supply measures.

The M1 Money Supply

Transaction accounts
Accounts, including demand deposits and interest-earning checkable deposits, against which the account holder is permitted to transfer funds for the purpose of making payment to a third party.

Demand deposits
Non-interest-earning checking deposits that can be either withdrawn or made payable on demand to a third party. Like currency, these deposits are widely used as a means of payment.

Other checkable deposits
Interest-earning deposits that are also available for checking.

Above all else, money is a medium of exchange. The narrowest definition of the money supply, **M1**, focuses on this function. Based on its role as a medium of exchange, it is clear that currency (including both coins and paper bills) and checkable deposits should be included in the supply of money. Deposits that can be drawn from by writing a check are called **transaction accounts**. There are two general categories of transaction accounts. First, there are **demand deposits**, non-interest-earning deposits with banking institutions that are available for withdrawal ("on demand") at any time without restrictions. Demand deposits are usually withdrawn by writing a check. Second, there are **other checkable deposits** that earn interest but carry some restrictions on their transferability. Interest-earning checkable deposits generally either limit the number of checks written each month or require the depositor to maintain a substantial minimum balance ($1,000, for example). Like currency and demand deposits, interest-earning checkable deposits are available for use as a medium of exchange. Traveler's checks are also a means of payment. They can be freely converted to cash at parity (equal value). ***Thus, the M1 money supply comprises (1) currency in circulation, (2) checkable deposits (both demand deposits and interest-earning checkable deposits), and (3) traveler's checks.***

As Exhibit 16-1 shows, the total M1 money supply in the United States was $1,203 billion at year-end 2001. Demand and other checkable deposits accounted for approximately two-thirds of the M1 money supply. This large share reflects the fact that most of the nation's business is conducted by check.

The Broader M2 Money Supply

In modern economies, several financial assets can easily be converted into checking deposits or currency; therefore, the line between money and "near monies" is often blurred. Broader definitions of the money supply include various assets that can be easily converted to checking account funds and cash. The most common broad definition of the money supply is **M2**. It includes all the items included in M1 plus (1) savings deposits (including money market deposit accounts), (2) time deposits of less than $100,000 at all **depository institutions**, and (3) money market mutual funds.

Although the non-M1 components of the M2 money supply are not generally used as a means of making payment, they can be easily and quickly converted to currency or checking deposits for such use. For example, if you maintain funds in a savings account, you can easily transfer them to your checking account for use as a means of payment. **Money market mutual funds** are interest-earning accounts offered by brokerage firms that pool depositors' funds and invest them in highly liquid short-term securities. Because these securities can be quickly converted to cash, depositors are permitted to write checks (which reduce their share holdings) against these accounts.

M2 (money supply)
Equal to M1 plus (1) savings deposits, (2) time deposits (accounts of less than $100,000) held in depository institutions, and (3) money market mutual fund shares.

Depository institutions
Businesses that accept checking and savings deposits and use a portion of them to extend loans and make investments. Banks, savings and loan associations, and credit unions are examples.

Money market mutual funds
Interest-earning accounts offered by brokerage firms that pool depositors' funds and invest them in highly liquid short-term securities. Since these securities can be quickly converted to cash, depositors are permitted to write checks (which reduce their share holdings) against their accounts.

EXHIBIT 16-1 Composition of Money Supply in the United States

The size and composition (as of December 2001) of the two most widely used measures of the money supply are shown. M1, the narrowest definition of the money supply, is comprised of currency, checking deposits, and traveler's checks. M2, which contains M1 plus the various savings components indicated, is approximately four times the size of M1.

Money Supply, M1 (in billions)	
Currency (in circulation)	$586
Demand deposits	347
Other checkable deposits	262
Traveler's checks	8
Total, M1	$1,203

Money Supply, M2 (in billions)	
M1	$1,203
Savings deposits[a]	2,312
Small time deposits	970
Money market mutual funds (retail)	995
Total, M2	$5,480

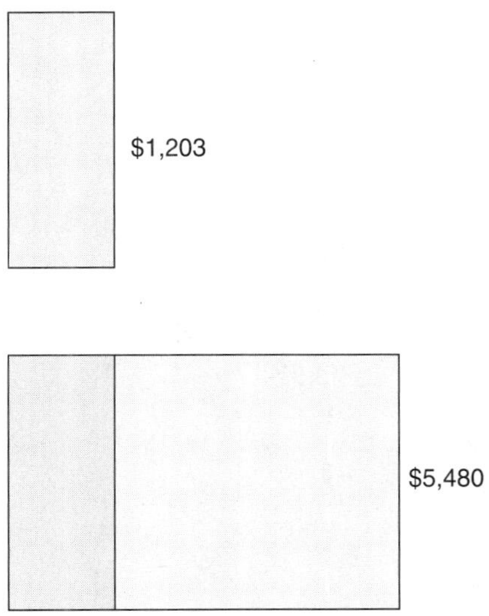

[a] Including money market deposit accounts.
Source: www.federalreserve.gov

Many economists—particularly those who stress the store-of-value function of money—prefer the broader M2 definition of the money supply to the narrower M1 concept. As Exhibit 1 shows, at year-end 2001 the M2 money supply was $5,480 billion, approximately four times the M1 money supply. Other definitions of the money supply have been developed for specialized purposes, but the M1 and M2 definitions are the most important and most widely used.

Credit Cards Versus Money

Credit
Funds acquired by borrowing.

It is important to distinguish between money and credit. Money is a financial asset that provides the holder with future purchasing power. **Credit** is a liability acquired when one borrows funds. This distinction sheds light on a question students frequently ask: "Because credit cards are often used to make purchases, why aren't credit card expenditures part of the money supply?" In contrast with money, credit cards are not purchasing power. They are merely a convenient means of arranging a loan. When you use your Visa or MasterCard to buy a DVD player, for example, you are not really paying for the player. Instead, you are taking out a loan from the institution issuing your card, and that institution is paying for the player. Payment is not made by you until you write a check to settle your credit card bill and thereby reduce your money balances. Thus, credit card purchases are not money; they are not an asset representing future purchasing power.

Although credit cards are not money, their use will influence the amount of money people will want to hold. Credit cards make it possible for people to buy things throughout the month and then pay for them with a single transaction at the end of the month. This makes it possible for people to conduct their regular business affairs with less money than would otherwise be needed. Thus, widespread use of credit cards will tend to reduce the average quantity of money people hold.

Money is an asset; it is part of the wealth of the people who hold it. In contrast, credit card purchases create a liability. They are merely a convenient method of arranging a short-term loan.

THE BUSINESS OF BANKING 5

We must understand a few things about the business of banking before we can explain the factors that influence the supply of money. The banking industry in the United States operates under the jurisdiction of the **Federal Reserve System**, the nation's central bank. Not all banks belong to the Federal Reserve, but under legislation enacted in 1980, only a nominal difference exists between member and nonmember banks. We will discuss the Federal Reserve System in detail later in this reading.

Federal Reserve System
The central bank of the United States; it carries out banking regulatory policies and is responsible for the conduct of monetary policy.

The banking system is an important component of the capital market. Like other private businesses, banks are profit-seeking operations. Banks provide services (for example, safekeeping of funds and checking-account services) and pay interest in order to attract both checking and savings depositors. ***They help to bring together people who want to save for the future with those who want to borrow in order to undertake investment projects.*** Income derived from loans in support of investment projects is the primary source of revenue for banks.

When deciding whether to fund a project, bankers have a strong incentive to judge both the project's expected profitability and the borrower's creditworthiness. Borrowers may be unable to repay their loans if the funds are channeled into unprofitable investments. In turn, lenders who finance business failures may lose all or part of their funds. Efficient allocation of investment funds is an important source of economic growth. Profitable business projects increase the value of resources and promote economic growth; unprofitable projects have the opposite effect. An efficiently operating capital market, of which the banking system is an integral part, will extend loans and provide financial support for projects that are more likely to be winners—that is, profitable rather than unprofitable.

Savings and loan associations
Financial institutions that accept deposits in exchange for shares that pay dividends. Historically, these funds have been channeled into residential mortgage loans. Under banking legislation adopted in 1980, S&Ls are permitted to offer a broad range of services similar to those of commercial banks.

In the United States, the banking system consists of savings and loan institutions, credit unions, and commercial banks. **Savings and loan associations** accept deposits in exchange for shares that pay dividends. **Credit unions** are cooperative financial organizations of individuals with a common affiliation (such as an employer) that accept deposits, pay interest (or dividends) on them, and generate earnings primarily through the extension of loans to members. **Commercial banks** offer a wide range of services—including checking and savings accounts and extension of loans—and are owned by stockholders. Under legislation passed in 1980, all these depository institutions are authorized to offer both checking and savings accounts and to extend a wide variety of loans to customers.

Credit unions
Financial cooperative organizations of individuals with a common affiliation (such as an employer or a labor union). They accept deposits, including checkable deposits, pay interest (or dividends) on them out of earnings, and channel funds primarily into loans to members.

All these depository institutions are now under the jurisdiction of the Federal Reserve System, which applies similar regulations and offers similar services (for example, check clearing and access to borrowing from the Fed) to each. ***Therefore, when we speak of the banking industry, we are referring to not only commercial banks, but savings and loan associations and credit unions as well.***

The consolidated balance sheet of commercial banking institutions (Exhibit 16-2) illustrates the major banking functions. It shows that the major liabilities of banks are transaction (checking), savings, and time deposits. *From the viewpoint of a bank*, these are liabilities because they represent an obligation of the bank to its depositors. Outstanding interest-earning loans comprise the major class of banking assets. In addition, most banks own sizable amounts of interest-earning securities—bonds issued by either governments or private corporations.

Commercial banks
Financial institutions that offer a wide range of services (for example, checking accounts, savings accounts, and extension of loans) to their customers. Commercial banks are owned by stockholders and seek to operate at a profit.

Banking differs from most businesses in that a large portion of the liabilities are payable on demand. However, even though it would be possible for all depositors to demand the money in their checking accounts on the same day, the probability of this occurring is generally quite remote. Typically, while some individuals are making withdrawals, others are making deposits. These transactions tend to balance out, eliminating sudden changes in demand deposits.

EXHIBIT 16-2 Functions of Commercial Banking Institutions

Banks provide services and pay interest to attract transaction (checking), savings, and time deposits (liabilities). Most of the deposits are invested and loaned out, providing interest income for the bank. Banks hold a portion of their assets as reserves (either cash or deposits with the Fed) to meet their daily obligations toward their depositors.

Consolidated Balance Sheet of Commercial Banking Institutions, Year-end 2001 (billions of dollars)

Assets		Liabilities	
Vault cash	$ 32	Transaction deposits	$ 665
Reserves at the Fed	9	Savings and time deposits	3,596
Loans outstanding	3,964	Borrowings	1,241
U.S. government securities	832	Other liabilities	515
Other securities	648	Net worth	453
Other assets	985		
Total	$6,470		$6,470

Source: www.federalreserve.gov

Bank reserves
Vault cash plus deposits of the bank with Federal Reserve banks.

Thus, banks maintain only a fraction of their assets in reserves to meet the requirements of depositors. As Exhibit 16-2 illustrates, **bank reserves**—vault cash plus reserve deposits with the Federal Reserve—were only $41 billion at year-end 2001, compared to transaction (checking) deposits of $665 billion. Thus, on average, banks were maintaining less than 10 percent of their assets in reserve against the checking deposits of their customers.

Fractional Reserve Goldsmithing

Economists often like to draw an analogy between our current banking system and the goldsmiths of the past. In the past, gold was used as the means of making payments. It was money. People would store their money with a goldsmith for safekeeping, just as many of us open a checking account for safety reasons. Gold owners received a certificate granting them the right to withdraw their gold anytime they wished. If they wanted to buy something, they would go to the goldsmith, withdraw gold, and use it as a means of making a payment. Thus, the money supply was equal to the amount of gold in circulation plus the gold deposited with goldsmiths.

The day-to-day deposits of and requests for gold were always only a fraction of the total amount of gold deposited. A major portion of the gold simply "lay idle in the goldsmiths' vaults." Taking notice of this fact, goldsmiths soon began loaning gold to local merchants. After a time, the merchants would pay back the gold, plus pay interest for its use. What happened to the money supply when a goldsmith extended loans to local merchants? The deposits of persons who initially brought their gold to the goldsmith were not reduced. Depositors could still withdraw their gold anytime they wished (as long as they did not all try to do so at once). In addition, the merchants were now able to use the gold they borrowed from the goldsmith as a means of payment. ***As goldsmiths lent gold, they increased the amount of gold in circulation, thereby increasing the money supply.***

It was inconvenient to make a trip to the goldsmith every time one wanted to buy something. Because the certificates were redeemable in gold, they began to circulate as a means of payment. The depositors were pleased with this arrangement because it eliminated the need for a trip to the goldsmith every time something was exchanged for gold. As long as they had confidence in the goldsmith, sellers were glad to accept the certificates as payment.

As gold certificates began to circulate, the daily withdrawals and deposits with goldsmiths declined even more. Local goldsmiths would keep about 20 percent of the total gold deposited with them so they could meet the current requests to redeem the gold certificates in circulation. The remaining 80 percent of their gold deposits would be loaned out to merchants, traders, and other citizens. Therefore, 100 percent of the gold certificates was circulating as money. That portion of gold that had been loaned out, 80 percent of the total deposits, was also circulating as money. The total money supply, gold certificates plus gold, was now 1.8 times the amount of gold that had been originally deposited with the goldsmith. Because the goldsmiths issued loans and kept only a fraction of the total gold deposited with them, they were able to increase the money supply.

As long as the goldsmiths held enough reserves to meet the current requests of the depositors, everything went along smoothly. Most gold depositors probably did not even realize that the goldsmiths did not have their actual gold and that of other depositors, precisely designated as such, sitting in the "vaults."

Goldsmiths derived income from loaning gold. The more gold they loaned, the greater their total income. Some goldsmiths, trying to increase their income by extending more and more interest-earning loans, depleted the gold in their vaults to imprudently low levels. If an unexpectedly large number of depositors wanted their gold, these imprudent goldsmiths would be unable to meet their requests. As this happened, the system of fractional reserve goldsmithing would tend to break down.

Fractional Reserve Banking

In principle, our modern banking system is very similar to goldsmithing. The United States has a **fractional reserve banking** system. Banks are required to maintain only a fraction of their deposits in the form of cash and other reserves. Just as the early goldsmiths did not have enough gold to pay all their depositors simultaneously, neither do our banks have enough reserves (vault cash and deposits with Federal Reserve banks) to pay all their depositors simultaneously. (*Note:* As Exhibit 16-2 illustrates, the vault cash plus the reserves held with the Federal Reserve are less than 10 percent of the transaction—that is, checking—deposits of commercial banks.) The early goldsmiths expanded the money supply by issuing loans. So do present-day bankers. The amount of gold held in reserve to meet the requirements of depositors limited the ability of the goldsmiths to expand the money supply. The amount of cash and other **required reserves** limits the ability of present-day banks to expand the money supply.

Fractional reserve banking
A system that permits banks to hold reserves of less than 100 percent against their deposits.

Required reserves
The minimum amount of reserves that a bank is required by law to keep on hand to back up its deposits. Thus, if reserve requirements were 15 percent, banks would be required to keep $150,000 in reserves against each $1 million of deposits.

However, there are also important differences between modern banking and early goldsmithing. Today, the actions of individual banks are regulated by a central bank. The central bank is supposed to follow policies designed to promote a healthy economy. It also acts as a lender of last resort. If all depositors in a specific bank suddenly attempted to withdraw their funds simultaneously, the central bank would intervene and supply the bank with enough funds to meet the demand.

6

BANK RUNS, BANK FAILURES, AND DEPOSIT INSURANCE

Compared to other businesses, banks are more vulnerable to failure (and abuse), and the consequences of failure exert a larger impact on the economy. The vulnerability of banks reflects the fact that their liabilities to depositors are current, while many of their assets are illiquid. This means that if a significant share of depositors lose confidence and withdraw their funds, it will quickly lead to problems. In turn, when a bank fails, it affects not only the owners and employees, but the depositors as well. These secondary effects can undermine the operation of an economy.

The U.S. economy has had its share of banking problems. Between 1922 and 1933, more than 10,000 banks (one-third of the total) failed. Most of these failures were the result of "bank runs," panic withdrawals as people lost confidence in the banking system. Remember, under a fractional reserve system, banks do not have a sufficient amount of reserves to redeem the funds of all (or even most) depositors seeking to withdraw their funds at the same time.

Federal Deposit Insurance Corporation (FDIC)
A federally chartered corporation that insures the deposits held by commercial banks and thrift institutions.

The bank failures of the 1920s and 1930s led to the establishment of the **Federal Deposit Insurance Corporation** (**FDIC**) in 1934. The FDIC guarantees the deposits of banking customers up to some limit—currently $100,000 per account. Even if the bank should fail, the depositors will be able to get their money (up to the $100,000 limit). Member banks pay an insurance premium to the FDIC for each dollar on deposit, and the FDIC uses these premiums to reimburse depositors with funds in a bank that fails. The FDIC restored confidence in the banking system and brought bank runs to a halt. As a result, bank failures are extremely rare now.

7

HOW BANKS CREATE MONEY BY EXTENDING LOANS

Required reserve ratio
A percentage of a specified liability category (for example, transaction accounts) that banking institutions are required to hold as reserves against that type of liability.

Excess reserves
Actual reserves that exceed the legal requirement.

Under a fractional reserve system, an increase in reserves will permit banks to extend additional loans and thereby create additional transaction (checking) deposits. Since transaction deposits are money, the extension of the additional loans expands the supply of money. To enhance our understanding of this process, let us consider a banking system without a central bank, one in which only currency acts as a reserve against deposits. Initially, we will assume that all banks are required by law to maintain vault cash equal to at least 20 percent of the checking accounts of their depositors. This proportion of the percent of reserves that must be maintained against checkable transaction deposits is called the **required reserve ratio**. The required reserve ratio in our example is 20 percent.

Suppose you found $1,000 that your long-deceased uncle had apparently hidden in the basement of his house. How much would this newly found $1,000 of currency expand the money supply? You take the bills to the First National Bank, open a checking account of $1,000, and deposit the cash with the banker. First National is now required to keep an additional $200 in vault cash, 20 percent of your deposit. However, it received $1,000 of additional cash, so after placing $200 in the bank vault, First National has $800 of **excess reserves**, reserves over and above the amount it is required by law to maintain. Given its current excess reserves, First National can now extend an $800 loan. Suppose it loans $800 to a local citizen to help pay for a car. At the time the loan is extended, the money supply will increase by $800 as the bank adds the funds to the checking account of the borrower. No one else has less money. You still have your $1,000 checking account, and the borrower has $800 for a new car.

When the borrower buys a new car, the seller accepts a check and deposits the $800 in a bank, Citizen's State Bank. What happens when the check clears? The temporary excess reserves of the First National Bank will be eliminated when it pays $800 to the Citizen's State Bank. But when Citizen's State Bank receives $800 in currency, it will now have excess reserves. It must keep 20 percent, an additional $160, as required reserves against the $800 checking account deposit of the automobile seller.

The remaining $640 could be loaned out. Because Citizen's State, like other banks, is in business to make money, it will be quite happy to "extend a helping hand" to a borrower. When the second bank loans out its excess reserves, the deposits of the person borrowing the money will increase by $640. Another $640 has now been added to the money supply. You still have your $1,000, the automobile seller has an additional $800, and the new borrower has just received an additional $640. Because you found the $1,000 and deposited it in the bank, the money supply has increased by $1,440 ($800+$640).

Of course, the process can continue. Exhibit 16-3 follows the potential creation of money resulting from the initial $1,000 through several additional stages. When the reserve requirement is 20 percent, the money supply can expand to a maximum of $5,000, the initial $1,000 plus an additional $4,000 in demand deposits that can be created by extending new loans.

The multiple by which new reserves increase the stock of money is referred to as the **deposit expansion multiplier**. The amount by which additional reserves can increase the supply of money is determined by the ratio of required reserves to deposits. In fact, the **potential deposit expansion multiplier** is merely the reciprocal of the required reserve ratio (r). Mathematically, the potential deposit expansion multiplier is equal to $1/r$. In our example, the required reserves are 20 percent, or one-fifth of the total deposits. So the potential deposit expansion multiplier is 5. If only 10 percent reserves were required, the potential deposit expansion multiplier would be 10, the reciprocal of one-tenth. ***The lower the percentage of the reserve requirement, the greater is the potential expansion in the money supply resulting from the creation of new reserves. The fractional reserve requirement places a ceiling on potential money creation from new reserves.***

Deposit expansion multiplier
The multiple by which an increase (decrease) in reserves will increase (decrease) the money supply. It is inversely related to the required reserve ratio.

Potential deposit expansion multiplier
The maximum potential increase in the money supply as a ratio of the new reserves injected into the banking system. It is equal to the inverse of the required reserve ratio.

EXHIBIT 16-3 Creating Money from New Reserves

When banks are required to maintain 20 percent reserves against demand deposits, the creation of $1,000 of new reserves will potentially increase the supply of money by $5,000.

Bank	New Cash Deposits: Actual Reserves	New Required Reserves	Potential Demand Deposits Created by Extending New Loans
Initial deposit (Bank A)	$1,000.00	$ 200.00	$ 800.00
Second stage (Bank B)	800.00	160.00	640.00
Third stage (Bank C)	640.00	128.00	512.00
Fourth stage (Bank D)	512.00	102.40	409.60
Fifth stage (Bank E)	409.60	81.92	327.68
Sixth stage (Bank F)	327.68	65.54	262.14
Seventh stage (Bank G)	262.14	52.43	209.71
All others (other banks)	1,048.58	209.71	838.87
Total	$5,000.00	$1,000.00	$4,000.00

The Actual Deposit Multiplier

Will the introduction of new currency reserves necessarily have a full deposit expansion multiplier effect? The answer is no. The actual deposit multiplier will generally be less than the potential for two reasons.

First, the deposit expansion multiplier will be reduced if some persons decide to hold the currency rather than deposit it in a bank. For example, suppose the person who borrowed the $800 in the preceding example spends only $700 and stashes the remaining $100 away for a possible emergency. Only $700 can then end up as a deposit in the second stage and contribute to the excess reserves necessary for expansion. The potential of new loans in the second stage and in all subsequent stages will be reduced proportionally. When currency remains in circulation, outside the banks, it reduces the size of the deposit expansion multiplier.

Second, the actual deposit multiplier will be less than its maximum potential when banks fail to use all the new excess reserves to extend loans. Banks, though, have a strong incentive to loan out or invest most of their new excess reserves. Idle excess reserves do not earn interest. Because banks are in business to earn income, they will maintain only a very small portion of their assets—mostly currency needed for daily transactions—in the form of excess reserves. In recent years, excess reserves have accounted for less than 1 percent of the total reserves of banks.

Currency leakages and idle excess bank reserves will result in a deposit expansion multiplier that is less than its potential maximum. However, because people generally keep most of their money in bank deposits (rather than currency) and the excess reserves of banks are typically small, the injection of new reserves into the system can be counted on to expand the supply of money by a multiple of the additional reserves.

8 THE FEDERAL RESERVE SYSTEM

Most countries have a central banking authority that controls the money supply and conducts monetary policy. As we previously noted, the central bank of the United States is the Federal Reserve System. In the United Kingdom, the central bank is the Bank of England; in Canada, it is the Bank of Canada; in Japan, it is the Bank of Japan. Central banks are responsible for the conduct of their nation's monetary policy.

Structure of the Fed

The major purpose of the Federal Reserve System (and other central banks) is to regulate the money supply and provide a monetary climate that is in the best interest of the entire economy. Congress has instructed the Federal Reserve, or the Fed, as it is often called, to conduct monetary policy in a manner that promotes both full employment and price stability. Unlike commercial banks, the Federal Reserve is not a profit-making institution. The earnings of the Fed, over and above its expenses, belong to the Treasury.

Exhibit 16-4 illustrates the structure of the Fed. There are three major centers of decision making within the Federal Reserve: (1) the Board of Governors, (2) the district and regional banks, and (3) the Federal Open Market Operations Committee.

Board of Governors

The Board of Governors is the decision-making center of the Fed. This powerful board consists of seven members, each appointed to a staggered 14-year term by the president with the advice and consent of the Senate. The president designates

EXHIBIT 16-4 Structure of Federal Reserve System

The Board of Governors of the Federal Reserve System is at the center of the banking system in the United States. The board sets the rules and regulations for all depository institutions. The seven members of the Board of Governors also serve on the Federal Open Market Committee, a 12-member board that establishes Fed policy with regard to the buying and selling of government securities, the primary mechanism used to control the money supply in the United States.

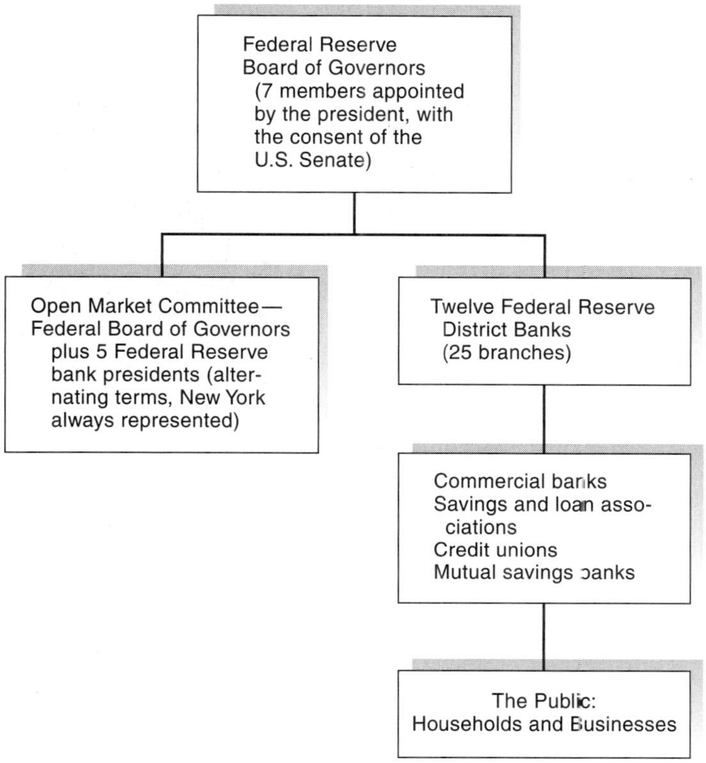

one of the seven members as chair for a four-year term. (See the Outstanding Economist box on Alan Greenspan on the next page.) The Board of Governors establishes the rules and regulations applicable to all depository institutions. It sets the reserve requirements and regulates the composition of the asset holdings of depository institutions. The board is the rule maker, and often the umpire, of the banking industry.

Federal Reserve District Banks

There are 12 Federal Reserve District banks with 25 regional branches spread throughout the nation. Exhibit 16-5 shows the regions covered by each of the 12 district banks. These district and regional banks operate under the supervision of the Board of Governors. Federal Reserve banks are bankers' banks; they provide banking services for commercial banks. Private citizens and corporations do not bank with the Fed.

The district banks are primarily responsible for the monitoring of the commercial banks in their region. They audit the books of depository institutions regularly in order to assure their compliance with reserve requirements and other regulations of the Fed. The district banks also play an important role in the clearing of checks through the banking system. Most depository institutions, regardless of their Fed membership status, maintain deposits with Federal

EXHIBIT 16-5 The Twelve Federal Reserve Districts

The map indicates the 12 Federal Reserve districts and the city in which the district bank is located. These district banks monitor the commercial banks in their region and assist them with the clearing of checks. If you look at any dollar bill, it will identify the Federal Reserve district bank that initially issued the currency. The Board of Governors of the Fed is located in Washington, D.C.

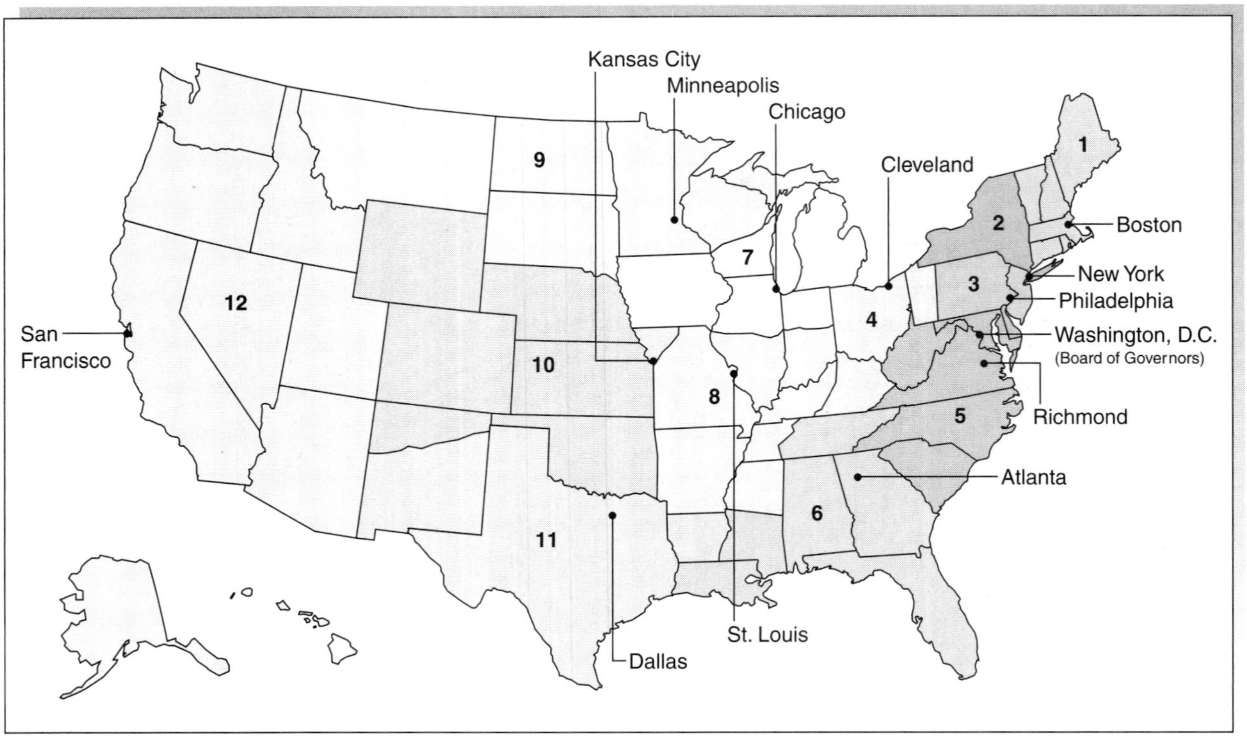

Outstanding Economist

Alan Greenspan

From 1954 to 1974, Greenspan ran a very successful economic consulting firm in New York City. After serving as the chair of the Council of Economic Advisers (1974–1977) during the Ford administration, he returned to his consulting firm for the following ten years. During this period, he also served as Chairman of the National Commission on Social Security Reform and as a board member of many corporations. In 1987, President Reagan appointed him to a four-year term as chairman of the Fed's Board of Governors. Later, he was reappointed to that position by both Presidents Bush and Clinton. The Fed chairman directs the staff, presides over Board meetings, and testifies frequently before Congress. Because of the importance of monetary policy and the power of the position, the Fed chairman is often said to be the second most influential person—next to the president—in the United States. As the result of the low rate of inflation and the lengthy economic expansion of the 1990s Greenspan is given high marks for his tenure as chairman.

Reserve Banks. As a result, the clearing of checks through the Federal Reserve System becomes merely an accounting transaction. The district and regional banks handle approximately 85 percent of all check-clearing services of the banking system.

Federal Open Market Committee (FOMC)

The **Federal Open Market Committee** is a powerful committee that determines the Fed's policy with respect to the purchase and sale of government bonds. As we shall soon see, this is the Fed's most frequently used method of controlling the money supply in the United States. This important policy-making arm of the Fed is made up of (1) the seven members of the Board of Governors, (2) the president of the New York District Bank, and (3) four (of the remaining eleven) additional presidents of the Fed's District Banks, who rotate on the committee. Although they do not always have a vote, all 12 Federal Reserve district bank presidents participate in the FOMC meetings, held every five to eight weeks.

Federal Open Market Committee (FOMC)
A 12-member board that establishes Fed policy with regard to the buying and selling of government securities, the primary mechanism used to control the money supply in the United States.

The Independence of the Fed

Like the Supreme Court, the Federal Reserve operates with considerable independence from both Congress and the executive branch of government. Several factors contribute to this independence. The lengthy terms—14 years—protect the seven members of the Fed's Board of Governors from political pressures. Because their terms are staggered—a new governor is appointed only every two years—even two-term presidents are well into their second term before they are able to appoint a majority of the Fed's governing board. The Fed's earnings on its financial assets, mostly government bonds, provide it with substantially more funding than is needed to cover its operating costs. Thus, it is not dependent on Congress for funding allocations. The Fed does not even have to undergo audits from the General Accounting Office, a government agency that audits the books of most government operations. This independence of the Fed is designed to reduce the likelihood that political pressures will adversely affect its ability to follow a stable, noninflationary monetary policy.

Does the independence of a central bank affect policy? There is considerable variation in the independence of central banks. Like the Fed, the German Bundesbank was largely insulated from the political authorities. (*Note:* With the development of a European currency, the Bundesbank has been replaced by the European central bank.) In other instances, central banks are directly beholden to political officials. The central banks of many Latin American countries fit into this category. Studies of this topic indicate that when a country's central bank is strongly influenced by political considerations, the bank is more likely to follow inflationary policies.

How the Fed Controls the Money Supply

The Fed has three major means of controlling the money stock: (1) establishing reserve requirements for depository institutions, (2) buying and selling U.S. government securities in the open market, and (3) setting the interest rate at which it will loan funds to commercial banks and other depository institutions. We will analyze in detail how each of these tools can be used to regulate the amount of money in circulation.

Reserve Requirements

The Federal Reserve System requires banking institutions (including credit unions and savings and loan associations) to maintain reserves against the demand deposits of their customers. The reserves of banking institutions are composed of (1) currency held by the bank (vault cash) and (2) deposits of the bank with the Federal Reserve System. A bank can always obtain additional currency by drawing on its deposits with the Federal Reserve. So both cash-on-hand and the bank's deposits with the Fed can be used to meet the demands of depositors. Both therefore count as reserves.

Exhibit 16-6 indicates the required reserve ratio—the percentage of each deposit category that banks are required to keep in reserve (that is, in the form of either vault cash or deposits with the Fed). As of December 2001, the reserve requirement for transaction accounts was set at 3 percent for amounts above \$5.7 million and up to \$41.3 million and 10 percent for amounts in excess of \$41.3 million. Currently, banks are not required to keep reserves against their savings and time deposits or on the first \$5.7 million of transactions deposits.

Why are commercial banks required to maintain assets in the form of reserves? One reason is to prevent imprudent bankers from overextending loans and thereby placing themselves in a poor position to deal with any sudden increase in withdrawals by depositors. The quantity of reserves needed to meet such emergencies is not left totally to the judgment of individual bankers. The Fed sets the rules.

The Fed's control over reserve requirements, however, is important for another reason. By altering reserve requirements, the Fed can alter the money supply. The law does not prevent commercial banks from holding reserves over and above those required by the Fed, but, as we previously noted, banking institutions will want to hold interest-earning assets (like loans to customers and bonds) rather than excess reserves. Because reserves draw no interest, profit-seeking banks will shave their excess reserves to a low level. As a result, an increase in reserve requirements will typically force banks to reduce their outstanding loans and investments. As the volume of loans (and other forms of credit) extended by banks declines, so, too, will the money supply. ***Thus, an increase in the reserve requirements will reduce the supply of money.***

EXHIBIT 16-6 Required Reserve Ratio of Banking Institutions

Banking institutions are required to maintain 3 percent reserves against transaction-account deposits of over \$5.7 million and up to \$41.3 million and 10 percent reserves for transaction deposits over \$41.3 million (in effect December 2001).

	Transaction Accounts[a]		
	\$0–\$5.7 million	\$5.7–\$41.3 million	Over \$41.3 million
Required reserves as a percent of deposits	0%	3%	10%

[a] The dividing points are adjusted each year to reflect changes in total transaction-account deposits in all banking institutions.

Source: www.federalreserve.gov

A reduction in reserve requirements will have the opposite impact. When the Fed reduces the reserve requirements, it creates additional excess reserves for banks. Predictably, profit-seeking banks will use a large portion of these newly created excess reserves to extend additional loans and undertake other investments. As they do so, their actions will expand the supply of money. ***Thus, lower reserve requirements increase the capacity of banks to lend and, as they extend additional loans, the money supply increases.***

In recent years, the Fed has seldom used its regulatory power over reserve requirements to alter the supply of money. Why? For one thing, changes in reserve requirements can be disruptive of banking operations. An increase in the required reserve ratio may force many banks to sell securities quickly or call in loans even if there has been no change in the level of their deposits. Furthermore, reserve requirement changes are a blunt instrument—small changes in reserve requirements can sometimes lead to large changes in the money supply. The magnitude and timing of a change in the money stock resulting from a change in reserve requirements are difficult to predict with precision. For these reasons, the Fed has usually preferred to use other monetary tools.

Open Market Operations

Open market operations The buying and selling of U.S. government securities in the open market by the Federal Reserve.

The most common tool used by the Fed to alter the money supply is **open market operations**—the buying and selling of U.S. securities on the open market. As we indicated earlier, Fed policy in this area is conducted by the Federal Open Market Committee (FOMC). This committee meets every few weeks to map out the Fed's policy. Open market operations can be undertaken easily and quietly. Because they influence the money supply either directly or through their impact on bank deposits, open market operations are less disruptive than changes in reserve requirements.

Unlike individuals, businesses, and even other government agencies, the Fed can write a check without funds in its account. When the Fed buys things, it creates money. The primary thing that the Fed buys is the national debt bonds that were originally issued by the U.S. Treasury and sold to private parties in order to finance budget deficits.

If the Fed wanted to expand the money supply, it would merely instruct its bond traders at the New York Federal Reserve Bank to buy bonds. (*Note:* Because of its location near major financial markets, the New York bank handles the Fed's bond trading.) ***When the Fed purchases U.S. securities, it injects "new money" into the economy in the form of additional currency in circulation and deposits with commercial banks.***

Let us consider a hypothetical case. Suppose the Fed purchases $10,000 of U.S. securities from Maria Valdez. The Fed receives the securities and Valdez receives a check for $10,000. If she merely cashes the check drawn on the Federal Reserve, the amount of currency in circulation would expand by $10,000, increasing the money supply by that amount. If, as is more likely to be the case, she deposits the funds in her checking account at City Bank, the supply of checking-account money will increase by $10,000 and new bank reserves are created. City Bank is required to maintain additional reserves of only a fraction of Valdez's $10,000 deposit. Assuming a 10 percent required reserve ratio, City Bank can now extend new loans of up to $9,000 while maintaining its initial reserve position. As the new loans are extended, they too will contribute to a further expansion in the money supply. Part of the new loans will eventually be deposited in other banks, and they also will be able to extend additional loans. As the process continues, the money supply expands by a multiple of the securities purchased by the Fed.

Open market operations can also be used to reduce the money stock. ***If the Fed wants to reduce the money stock, it sells some of its current holdings of government***

securities. When the Fed sells securities, the buyer pays for them with a check drawn on a commercial bank. As the check clears, both the buyer's checking deposits and the reserves of the bank on which the check was written will decline. Thus, the action will reduce the money supply both directly (by reducing checking deposits) and indirectly (by reducing the quantity of reserves available to the banking system).

Monetary base
The sum of currency in circulation plus bank reserves (vault cash and reserves with the Fed). It reflects the stock of U.S. securities held by the Fed.

The Fed's purchase and sale of U.S. securities influence the size of the **monetary base**. The monetary base is equal to the reserves of commercial banks (vault cash and reserve deposits with the Fed) plus the currency in circulation. As Exhibit 16-7 illustrates, the monetary base provides the foundation for the money supply of the United States. Of course, the currency in circulation ($594 billion in December 2001) contributes directly to the money supply. In turn, the bank reserves ($41 billion in December 2001) underpin the checking deposits ($609 billion). Fed purchases of U.S. securities increase the monetary base. Some of the proceeds (received by those selling bonds to the Fed) will circulate as currency. Each new dollar of currency in circulation will increase the money supply by exactly $1. In addition, many of those receiving proceeds from bond sales to the Fed will deposit the funds in a bank. When this happens, bank reserves increase and most of the additional reserves will be used to extend loans, causing additional expansion in the money supply.

By how much will the money supply change as the Fed injects and withdraws reserves through open market operations? Given the reserve requirements present in the early 2000s (see Exhibit 16-6), an increase in the monetary base could potentially expand the money supply (M1) by a multiple of 10 or more. However, leakages in the form of additional currency in circulation and increases in excess bank reserves will result in an actual deposit expansion multiplier that is substantially less than the potential. Exhibit 16-7 shows that the M1 money supply was approximately twice the size of the monetary base in 2001. This suggests that changes in the monetary base as the result of the Fed's open market operations will change the M1 money supply by about $2 for every $1 change in the monetary base.

EXHIBIT 16-7 Monetary Base and Money Supply (Year-end 2001)

The monetary base (currency plus bank reserves) provides the foundation for the money supply. The currency in circulation contributes directly to the money supply, while the bank reserves provide the underpinnings for checking deposits. Fed actions that alter the monetary base will affect the money supply (all figures are in billions).

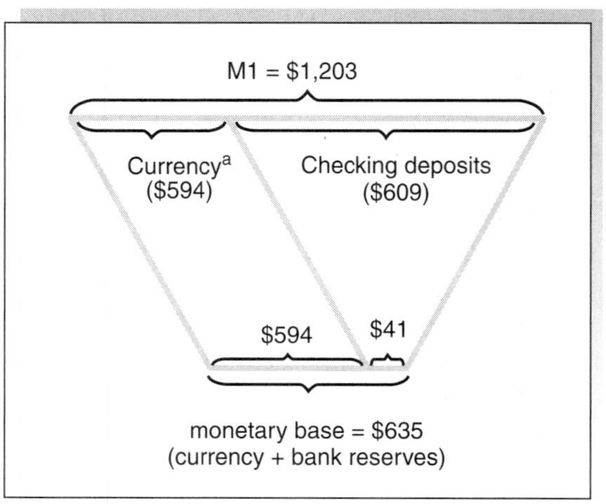

[a] Traveler's checks are included in this category.

Discount Rate—The Cost of Borrowing from the Fed

When banking institutions borrow from the Federal Reserve, they must pay interest on the loan. The interest rate that banks pay on loans from the Federal Reserve is called the **discount rate**. Borrowing from the Fed is a privilege, not a right. The Fed does not have to loan funds to banking institutions. Banks borrow from the Fed primarily to meet temporary shortages of reserves. They are most likely to borrow from the Fed for a brief period of time while they are making other adjustments in their loan and investment portfolios that will permit them to meet their reserve requirement.

Discount rate
The interest rate the Federal Reserve charges banking institutions for borrowing funds.

An increase in the discount rate makes it more expensive for banking institutions to borrow from the Fed. Borrowing is discouraged, and banks are more likely to build up their reserves to ensure that they will not have to borrow from the Fed. ***An increase in the discount rate is thus restrictive. It tends to discourage banks from shaving their excess reserves to a low level.***

In contrast, a reduction in the discount rate is expansionary. At the lower interest rate, it costs banks less if they have to turn to the Fed to meet a temporary emergency. Therefore, as the cost of borrowing from the Fed declines, banks are more likely to reduce their excess reserves to a minimum, extending more loans and increasing the money supply.

The general public has a tendency to overestimate the importance of a change in the discount rate. Many people think an increase in the discount rate means their local banker will (or must) charge them a higher interest rate for a loan.[2] This is not necessarily so. Reserves acquired through transaction and time deposits are the major source of loanable funds for commercial banks. Borrowing from the Fed amounts to less than one-tenth of 1 percent of the available loanable funds of commercial banks. Since borrowing from the Fed is such a negligible source of funds, a 0.5 percent change in the discount rate has something less than a profound impact on the availability of credit and the supply of money. Certainly, it does not necessarily mean that your local bank will alter the rate at which it will lend to you.

The Federal Funds Interest Rate

If a bank has to borrow to meet its reserve requirements, it need not turn to the Fed. Instead, it can go to the **federal funds market**. In this market, banks with excess reserves extend short-term (sometimes for as little as a day) loans to other banks seeking additional reserves. If the interest rate in the federal funds market is lower or approximately the same as the discount rate, banks seeking additional reserves will generally borrow from the federal funds market rather than the Fed. The federal funds rate and the discount rate tend to move together. If the federal funds rate is significantly higher than the discount rate, banks will attempt to borrow heavily from the Fed. Typically, when this happens, the Fed will raise its discount rate, removing the incentive for banks to borrow from it rather than from the federal funds market.

Federal funds market
A loanable funds market in which banks seeking additional reserves borrow short-term (generally for seven days or less) funds from banks with excess reserves. The interest rate in this market is called the federal funds rate.

In recent years, the announcements of the Fed regarding monetary policy have focused on its target for the federal funds rate. This does not conflict with the earlier statement that open market operations are the primary tool used by the Federal Reserve to control the supply of money. The Fed uses open market operations to control the federal funds rate. If the Fed wants to lower the federal

[2] The discount rate is also sometimes confused with the prime interest rate, the rate at which banks loan money to low-risk customers. The two rates are different. A change in the discount rate will not necessarily affect the prime interest rate.

funds interest rate, it will purchase government securities and thereby inject additional reserves into the banking system. This will both reduce the federal funds rate and expand the supply of money.

Conversely, if the Fed wants to increase the federal funds rate, it will sell some of its bond holdings and thereby drain reserves from the system. In turn, the reduction in the supply of reserves will both push the federal funds rate upward and reduce the supply of money. The relationship between the money supply and interest rate will be discussed in more detail in Reading 17.

Controlling the Money Supply—A Summary

Exhibit 16-8 summarizes the monetary tools of the Federal Reserve. ***If the Fed wants to follow an expansionary policy, it can decrease reserve requirements, purchase additional U.S. securities, and/or lower the discount rate.*** If it wants to reduce the money stock, it can increase the reserve requirements, sell U.S. securities, and/or raise the discount rate. Because the Fed typically seeks only small changes in the money stock (or its rate of increase), it typically uses only one or two of these tools at a time to accomplish a desired objective.

The Fed and the Treasury

Many students have a tendency to confuse the Federal Reserve with the U.S. Treasury, probably because both sound like monetary agencies. The Treasury is a budgetary agency. If there is a budgetary deficit, the Treasury will issue U.S. securities as a method of financing the deficit. Newly issued U.S. securities are almost always sold to private investors (or government trust funds). Bonds issued by the Treasury to finance a budget deficit are seldom purchased directly by the Fed. In any case, the Treasury is primarily interested in obtaining funds so it can pay

EXHIBIT 16-8 Summary of Monetary Tools of the Federal Reserve

Federal Reserve Policy	Expansionary Monetary Policy	Restrictive Monetary Policy
1. Reserve requirements	*Reduce reserve requirements,* because this will create additional excess reserves and induce banks to extend additional loans, which will expand the money supply.	*Raise reserve requirements,* because this will reduce the excess reserves of banks, causing them to make fewer loans; as the outstanding loans of banks decline, the money stock will be reduced.
2. Open market operations	*Purchase additional U.S. securities,* which will expand the money stock directly, and increase the reserves of banks, inducing bankers in turn to extend more loans; this will expand the money stock indirectly.	*Sell previously purchased U.S. securities,* which will reduce both the money stock and excess reserves; the decline in excess reserves will indirectly lead to an additional reduction in the money supply.
3. Discount rate	*Lower the discount rate,* which will encourage more borrowing from the Fed; banks will tend to reduce their reserves and extend more loans because of the lower cost of borrowing from the Fed if they temporarily run short on reserves.	*Raise the discount rate,* thereby discouraging borrowing from the Fed; banks will tend to extend fewer loans and build up their reserves so they will not have to borrow from the Fed.

Frank and Ernest® by Bob Thaves

Source: Frank and Ernest reprinted by permission of Newspaper Enterprise Association, Inc.

Uncle Sam's bills. Except for nominal amounts, mostly coins, the Treasury does not issue money. Borrowing—the public sale of new U.S. securities—is the primary method used by the Treasury to cover any excess of expenditures in relation to revenues from taxes and other sources.

Whereas the Treasury is concerned with the revenues and expenditures of the government, the Fed is concerned primarily with the availability of money and credit for the entire economy. The Fed does not issue U.S. securities. It merely purchases and sells government securities issued by the Treasury as a means of controlling the economy's money supply. Unlike the Treasury, the Fed can purchase government bonds by writing a check on itself without having deposits, gold, or anything else to back it up. In doing so, the Fed creates money out of thin air. The Treasury does not have this power. The Fed does not have an obligation to meet the financial responsibilities of the U.S. government. That is the domain of the Treasury. Although the two agencies cooperate with each other, they are distinctly different institutions established for different purposes (see the Thumbnail Sketch on the next page).

It is important to recognize that the buying and selling of bonds by the Treasury and by the Fed have different effects on the supply of money. The key point here is that the Treasury and the Fed handle revenues collected from the selling of bonds in a different manner. When the Treasury issues and sells bonds, it does so to pay for federal government expenditures. After all, the Treasury issues the bonds in order to generate the required revenue for its spending. The people who buy the bonds from the Treasury have less money, but when the Treasury spends, the recipients of its spending will have more money. Thus, Treasury borrowing and spending does not change the supply of money.

In contrast, when the Fed sells bonds, it, in effect, takes the revenues and holds them, keeping them out of circulation. Because this money is out of circulation and can no longer be used for the purchase of goods and services, the money supply shrinks. On the other hand, if the Fed later wishes to increase the money supply, it can buy bonds, which will increase the availability of bank reserves and the money supply.

AMBIGUITIES IN THE MEANING AND MEASUREMENT OF THE MONEY SUPPLY 9

In the past, economists have generally used the *growth rate* of the money supply (either M1 or M2) to gauge the direction of monetary policy. A rapid growth rate of the money supply was indicative of expansionary monetary policy—a policy

THUMBNAIL SKETCH

What Are the Differences between the U.S. Treasury and the Federal Reserve Banking System?

U.S. Treasury

1. Concerned with the finances of the federal government
2. Issues bonds to the general public to finance the budget deficits of the federal government
3. Does not determine the money supply

Federal Reserve

1. Concerned with the monetary climate for the economy
2. Does not issue bonds
3. Determines the money supply—primarily through its buying and selling of bonds issued by the U.S. Treasury

that was adding stimulus to the economy. Conversely, slow growth, or a decline, in the money stock implied a more restrictive monetary policy.

Both the history of money and recent developments in financial markets are causing many economists to reconsider the significance of growth rate figures. Historically, major shifts in the nature of money (for example, the shift from precious metals to a fiat currency) have substantially influenced the lives of people. Financial innovations continue to affect our methods of payment and the meaning of the various money supply measures.

Throughout most of the 1970s, M1 was comprised almost entirely of currency and demand deposits. At the time, regulations virtually prohibited banks from offering their customers interest-earning checking accounts. Increased competition from mutual funds led to the repeal of the regulatory restraints in 1980, and, as Exhibit 16-9 illustrates, this repeal was followed by rapid growth of interest-earning checking deposits. In turn, growth of these deposits pushed up the growth rate of the M1 money supply. The growth of M1 during the 1980s, however, was deceptive. To a degree, it reflected a change in the nature of the M1 money supply. Interest-earning checking accounts are less costly to hold than currency and demand deposits. In essence, interest-earning checking accounts are partly medium-of-exchange money and partly savings. As a result, the M1 money supply of the 1980s is not precisely comparable with the figures for earlier years.

Another innovation influenced the M1 money supply in the 1990s. Beginning in 1994, a number of banks began to encourage customers to move deposits from interest-earning checking accounts into money market deposit accounts. Each of these accounts provides customers with similar services. However,

EXHIBIT 16-9 The Changing Nature of the M1 Money Supply

As a result of deregulation during the 1980s, interest-earning checkable deposits grew rapidly and they now account for approximately one-quarter of the M1 money supply. Since the opportunity cost of holding these other checkable deposits is less than for other forms of money, strictly speaking, the money supply today is not exactly comparable to the money supply prior to 1980.

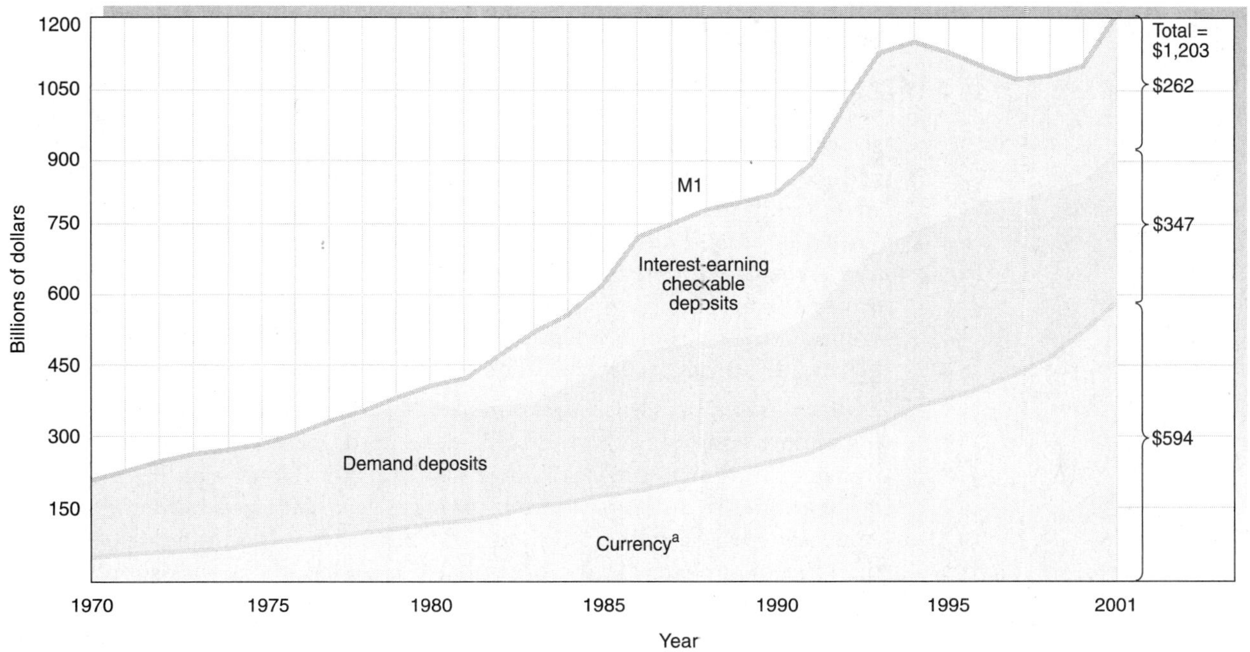

[a] Traveler's checks are included in this category.
Source: http://www.federalreserve.gov

because interest-earning checking deposits are included in M1 but money market deposits are not, this shift reduced the size of the M1 money supply figures. It was largely responsible for the decline in the M1 money supply during the period 1995–1997 (see Exhibit 16-9). As with the introduction of interest-earning checking during the 1980s, these shifts distorted the M1 money supply statistics and reduced their comparability across time periods.

Other structural changes and financial innovations—some of which are already present and others of which are likely to develop in the near future—are altering the nature of money, and therefore the usefulness of money growth figures (both M1 and M2), as an indicator of monetary policy. Let's consider three of these factors.

1. ***Widespread use of the U.S. dollar outside the United States.*** The U.S. dollar is widely used in other countries. To a degree, this has been true for a long time. However, a number of countries have recently relaxed legal restraints limiting the domestic use of foreign currencies (and the maintenance of foreign currency bank accounts).[3] As noted earlier, the currency

[3] The number of countries where it is legal for citizens to maintain a foreign currency bank account rose from 38 in 1985 to 62 in 1995. See James Gwartney, Robert Lawson, and Walter Block, *Economic Freedom of the World: 1975–1995* (Washington, D.C.: Cato Institute, 1996), p. 81.

component of the M1 money supply was approximately $586 billion at year-end 2001. According to a recent study by the Federal Reserve, more than one-half and perhaps as much as two-thirds of this currency is held overseas. The movement of these funds abroad (and our inability to measure it with any degree of precision) substantially reduces the reliability of the M1 money supply figures. (*Note:* There is also some impact on M2. However, since the currency component is a much smaller proportion of M2 than M1, the distortion of M2 is less severe.)

2. ***The increasing availability of low-fee stock and bond mutual funds.*** Until recently, financial investors were generally required to pay a substantial start-up, or load, fee when purchasing stock and bond mutual funds. This reduced their attractiveness relative to the various savings instruments included in the M2 money supply. No-load stock and bond mutual funds—that is, funds without an initial fee—are now increasingly available. Because stock and bond mutual fund investments are not counted in any of the monetary aggregates, movement of funds from various M2 components (money market mutual funds, for example) will distort the M2 money supply figures.[4]

3. ***Debit cards and electronic money.*** Financial innovators are currently developing a more convenient and versatile debit card. A card of this type would transfer funds from the cardholder's bank account to that of the seller. If more and more businesses accept payment via debit cards in the future, Americans will have less reason to hold currency. As less money is held in the form of currency (and more as bank deposits), the money supply will grow rapidly unless the Fed takes offsetting actions. Like other changes in the nature of money, innovations in this area will reduce the future reliability of the money supply data, particularly the M1 figures, as indicators of monetary policy.

   Finally, there is the expected development of electronic money. It is difficult to forecast the nature of changes in this area. However, if individuals and businesses can economically and safely use electronic cash, instead of checking deposits and currency, it will clearly change the nature of money and the meaning of the monetary aggregates. If, as is anticipated, these electronic deposits can safely be maintained outside the banking system, they may also change the major functions of the banking system.

Exhibit 16-10 presents data on the annual growth rates of both M1 and M2. Reflecting the factors we have just discussed, the M1 money supply has recently shown more variability than the M2 figures. When using money supply growth rates as an indicator of monetary policy, most analysts now rely on M2 (rather than M1). We will follow this convention. However, we should keep in mind that future innovative changes are likely to alter the nature of money and therefore the reliability of the money supply figures (including those for M2) as an indicator of monetary policy.

---

[4] For additional information on this topic, see Sean Collins and Cheryl L. Edwards, "Redefining M2 to Include Bond and Equity Mutual Funds," Federal Reserve Bank of St. Louis *Review*, November/December 1994, pp. 7–30; Kenneth N. Daniels and Neil B. Murphy. "The Impact of Technological Change on the Currency Behavior of Households: An Empirical Cross-Section Study," *Journal of Money, Credit, and Banking* 26 (November 1994): 867–874; and John V. Duca, "Should Bond Funds Be Included in M2?" *Journal of Banking and Finance* 19 (April 1995): 131–152.

EXHIBIT 16-10 The Growth Rate of the M1 and M2 Money Supply: 1970–2001

Here we present the annual growth rates for both the M1 and M2 money supply figures. Since the mid-1980s, the variability of the M1 supply has been much greater than that for M2. To a large degree, the greater variability of M1 reflects regulatory changes and innovations in financial markets that have changed the nature of M1.

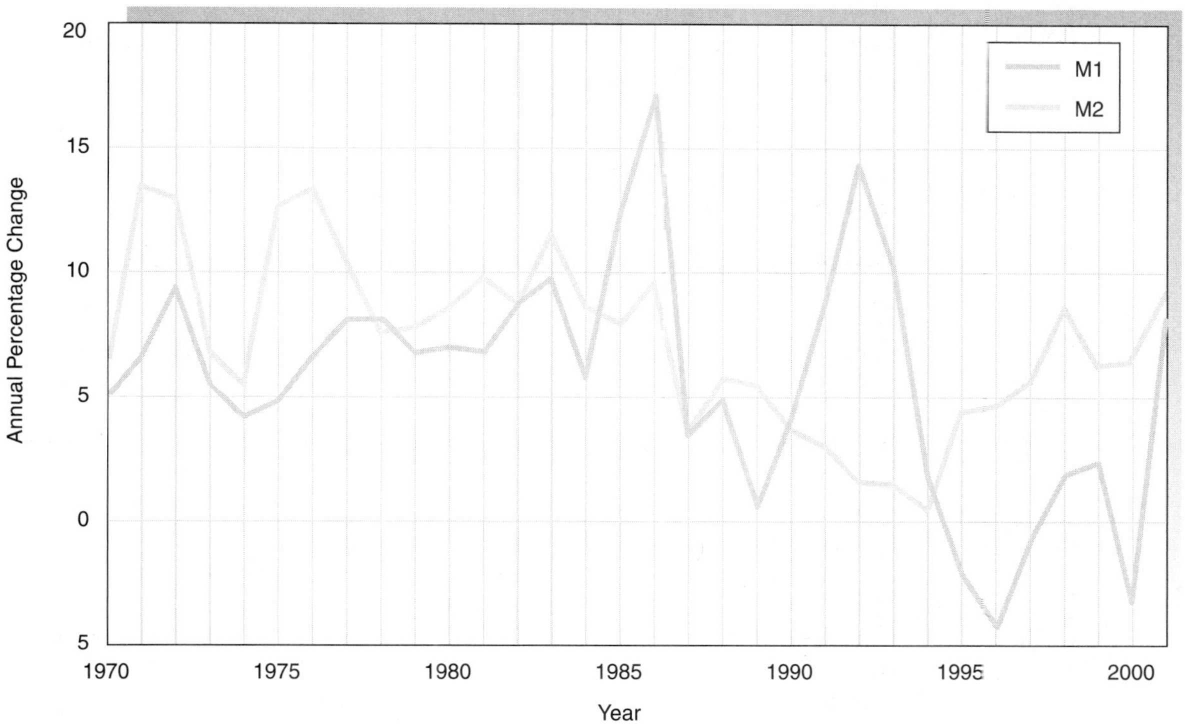

Source: http://www.federalreserve.gov

THE FUTURE OF MONEY 10

Technological Changes

Will electronic money alter your future? Consider a world where your "paycheck" is deposited in an electronic cash account accessible through your personal computer, but protected with a personal code. With the touch of a few computer keys, you can transfer funds to pay your monthly utility bill, mortgage and auto loan payments, and other regular expenditures. You can also shop on the Internet and use your deposits to pay for magazines, financial advice, and numerous consumer goods. Your funds can also be used to purchase stocks, bonds, mutual funds, and other financial investments. Like your paycheck, earnings from (or future sales of) these investments can be automatically deposited into your electronic cash account. If you want to withdraw some electronic cash, you merely insert a card and load it with transferable purchasing power, which is widely accepted by restaurants, recreation facilities, retail stores, and other business establishments. If you want to give or receive funds from family or friends, you simply merge their "cash cards" with yours and funds can be added to one card and subtracted from another. In effect, your electronic money allows you to do anything you can currently do with currency or checking deposits—and you can do it faster, safer, and more conveniently.

Many think that this world, or something very much like it, is only a few years away. Already at over 40 colleges and universities such as Colby College, Florida State University, and Pennsylvania State University, student identification cards have become so-called Smart Cards. Students can store money on these Smart Cards, which can be used to make purchases at retail stores as well as pay university fees such as parking tickets and tuition. Technological innovations such as these will certainly alter the nature of money and reduce the importance of the banking system. They may even limit the ability of central banks to conduct monetary policy.

Institutional Changes

Introduction of a New Currency—The Euro

If you have ever traveled in Europe in the past, you know that as you went from country to country, you had to exchange currencies in order to do business. Starting in January 2002, this was no longer necessary. Twelve European nations (Austria, Belgium, Finland, France, Germany, Greece, Ireland, Italy, Luxembourg, Netherlands, Portugal, and Spain) now use a single European currency, the euro. This new currency is managed by a new central bank, the European Central Bank (ECB).

The relationship between the ECB and the former central banks of the 12 countries is much like that between the Board of Governors of the Fed and the District Federal Reserve banks. The ECB sets policy; the national central banks are expected to carry it out. The ECB, located in the Eurotower in Frankfurt, is directed by a 6-member executive committee and a 18-member council comprised of the six executive committee members plus the central bank governor from each of the 12 euro countries. On paper, the ECB is largely independent of political forces—some have called it the world's most independent central bank. Its prime objective laid out in the Maastricht Treaty is price stability. The current target rate of inflation is 2 percent or less. The euro is expected not only to reduce transactions costs within the monetary union, but also to challenge the dollar and the yen for use in international markets. It will be interesting to follow the development of this new currency. One thing is certain—credibility is an important element influencing the choice of currency. Thus, it will be vitally important for the euro to get off to a good start to begin establishing a record of price stability along with sound economic growth.

Movement Toward Fewer Currencies

The number of independent currencies in the world is shrinking. Smaller countries have been linking their currencies to those of larger countries. For example, Hong Kong ties its domestic currency—the Hong Kong dollar—to the U.S. dollar at a 7.7-to-one rate. Other countries adopting a similar strategy include Lithuania, Bosnia, Bulgaria, and Estonia. When a country ties its currency to a strong foreign currency and backs each unit with assets denominated in the foreign currency, people are more likely to be persuaded that the currency will maintain its future value. This increased credibility is an important benefit, particularly for countries with a long history of hyperinflation and monetary instability.

Another factor reducing the number of currencies has been the informal use or outright adoption of a strong foreign currency as a means of payment. The U.S. dollar has been formally adopted as the official currency in Panama, El Salvador, and Ecuador. Currently, dollars are also widely held and, in some cases, used as a means of exchange in Russia (and several other countries of the former

Soviet Union), Argentina, Bolivia, Mexico, and other Latin American countries. As we previously noted, an estimated $300 billion of U.S. currency—more than half of the total—is held abroad.

There are three distinct advantages for foreign countries to use U.S. dollars or another strong currency as the means of payment. First, it increases trade as their citizens can buy and sell with more people without converting into another currency. Second, the U.S. dollar and several other currencies have a history of relatively stable value and thus are a more reliable store of value. Third, increased foreign investment is likely since investors won't have to worry as much about exchange rate risk.

How do these holdings of dollars by foreigners affect the U.S. economy? Foreigners acquired the dollars by providing goods and services to Americans. In effect, Americans got valuable goods and services by simply issuing pieces of paper—dollar bills. The dollars held abroad are very much like an interest-free loan to the U.S. government and, indirectly, the taxpayers of the United States. If foreigners were not willing to hold these dollars at a zero interest rate, the U.S. Treasury would have to issue more bonds (perhaps as much as $300 billion more) and pay interest to the bondholders. As a result, the annual interest costs of the federal government would be about $15 billion higher.

What does the future hold? The U.S. dollar is likely to become the dominant currency in the Americas. If the euro gains credibility, then European countries which do not belong to the European Union are likely to adopt the euro or link their currency to it. Likewise, the Japanese yen may emerge as the primary currency in Asia. Therefore, in the relatively near future, most of the world's trade—both domestic and foreign—may well be conducted with only three or four currencies.

11 SUMMARY

- Money is a financial asset that is widely accepted as a medium of exchange. It also provides a means of storing purchasing power into the future and is used as a unit of account. Without money, exchange would be both costly and tedious. Money derives its value from its scarcity (supply) relative to its usefulness (demand).
- Economists use alternative measures of the money supply to judge the conduct of monetary policy. The narrowest definition of the money supply (M1) includes only (a) currency in the hands of the public, (b) checkable deposits (both demand and interest-earning) held in depository institutions, and (c) traveler's checks.
- The broader M2 money supply includes M1 plus (a) savings deposits, (b) time deposits (of less than $100,000), and (c) money market mutual fund shares.
- Banking is a business. Banks provide their depositors with safekeeping of money, check-clearing services on demand deposits, and interest payments on time deposits. Banks derive most of their income from the extension of loans and investments in interest-earning securities.
- Under legislation adopted in 1980, savings and loan associations and credit unions are permitted to provide essentially the same services as commercial banks. The Federal Reserve System imposes similar regulation on all these depository institutions. In essence, they are all part of an integrated banking system.
- Under a fractional reserve banking system, banks are required to maintain only a fraction of their deposits in the form of reserves (vault cash or deposits with the Fed). Excess reserves may be invested or loaned to customers. When banks extend additional loans, they create additional deposits and thereby expand the money supply.
- The Federal Reserve System is a central banking authority designed to provide a stable monetary framework for the entire economy. The Fed is a banker's bank. The structure of the Fed is designed to insulate it from political pressures so that it will have greater freedom to follow policies more consistent with economic stability.

  The Fed has three major tools with which to control the money supply.

  A. ***Establishment of the required reserve ratio.*** When the Fed lowers the required reserve ratio, it creates excess reserves and allows banks to extend additional loans, expanding the money supply. Raising the reserve requirements has the opposite effect.

  B. ***Open market operations.*** When the Fed buys U.S. securities, the money supply will expand because bond buyers will acquire money and bank reserves will increase, placing banks in a position to expand the money supply through the extension of additional loans. When the Fed sells securities, the money supply will contract because bond buyers are giving up money in exchange for securities and the reserves available to banks will decline (causing them to extend fewer loans).

  C. ***The discount rate.*** An increase in the discount rate is restrictive because it discourages banks from borrowing from the Fed to extend new loans. A reduction in the discount rate is expansionary because it makes borrowing from the Fed less costly.

- The Federal Reserve and the U.S. Treasury are distinct agencies. The Fed is concerned primarily with the money supply and the establishment of a stable monetary climate, while the Treasury focuses on budgetary matters—tax revenues, government expenditures, and the financing of government debt.
- Historically, the rate of change of the money supply has been used to judge the direction and intensity of monetary policy. However, recent financial innovations and other structural changes (for example, the widespread use of U.S. currency in other countries) have blurred the meaning of money and reduced the reliability of the various money supply measures. In the computer age, continued change in this area is likely.

MODERN MACROECONOMICS: MONETARY POLICY

READING 17

LEARNING OUTCOMES

The candidate should be able to:

a. discuss the determinants of money demand and supply;

b. discuss how anticipation of the effects of monetary policy can influence the policy's effectiveness;

c. identify the components of the equation of exchange, discuss the implications of the equation for monetary policy, describe the quantity theory of money, and discuss its implications for the determination of inflation;

d. compare and contrast the impact of anticipated and unanticipated monetary policy on the inflation rate, real output and employment, and interest rates.

The conventional wisdom once held that money doesn't matter. Now there is wide agreement that monetary policy can significantly affect real economic activity in the short run, though only price level in the long run.

—Daniel L. Thornton and David C. Wheelock[1]

INTRODUCTION 1

In the preceding reading we noted that many consider the chairman of the Federal Reserve System to be the second most important person—next to the president—in the United States. Why is this so? Along with other members of the Fed's Board of Governors and Federal Open Market Committee, the Fed chairman is in charge of monetary policy. Monetary policy exerts a powerful impact on the economy. The central objective of monetary policy is the establishment of a stable environment so the economy can achieve high levels of both output and employment. Price stability—a persistently low rate of inflation—is crucial for the achievement of this objective. When conducted appropriately,

---

[1] Daniel L. Thornton and David C. Wheelock, "Editor's Introduction," *Federal Reserve Bank of St. Louis: Review* (May/June 1995): vii.

monetary policy provides the foundation for economic prosperity. In contrast, the consequences of inappropriate monetary policy are often disastrous.

As we have used the aggregate demand/aggregate supply model up to this point, we have assumed that the supply of money was constant. We will now relax this assumption. The previous reading outlined the tools the Fed has to alter the supply of money. This reading will focus on how monetary policy works—how changes in the supply of money affect interest rates, output, and prices.

2 IMPACT OF MONETARY POLICY

Like the modern view of fiscal policy, the modern view of monetary policy is the product of an evolutionary process. In the aftermath of the Great Depression and Keynesian Revolution, there was a great debate concerning the importance of monetary policy. During the 1950s and 1960s, most Keynesians argued that monetary policy could be used to control inflation, but that it was often ineffective as a means of stimulating aggregate demand. It was popular to draw an analogy between monetary policy and the workings of a string. Like a string, monetary policy could be used to pull (hold back) price increases and thereby control inflation. However, just as one cannot push with a string, according to this popular view, monetary policy could not be used to push (stimulate) aggregate demand.

Monetarists
A group of economists who believe that (1) monetary instability is the major cause of fluctuations in real GDP and (2) rapid growth of the money supply is the major cause of inflation.

Beginning in the late 1950s, this position was hotly contested by Milton Friedman, later a Nobel laureate, and a group of economists, subsequently called **monetarists**. In contrast with the Keynesians of that era, the monetarists argued that changes in the stock of money exerted a powerful influence on output (in the short run), as well as prices (in the long run). Indeed, the monetarists charged that erratic monetary policy was the primary source of both business instability and inflation. Milton Friedman summarized the monetarist position in his 1967 presidential address to the American Economic Association when he stated,

> Every major contraction in this country has been either produced by monetary disorder or greatly exacerbated by monetary disorder. Every major inflation has been produced by monetary expansion.[2]

A modern view of monetary policy emerged from this debate. While minor disagreements remain, both modern Keynesians and monetarists now agree that monetary policy produces an important impact on our economy.[3] The following sections present the modern consensus view with regard to how monetary policy affects the economy.

Demand and Supply of Money

Why do individuals and businesses want to hold cash and checking-account money rather than bonds, stocks, automobiles, buildings, and consumer durables? When considering this question, one must not confuse (1) the desire to

---

[2] Milton Friedman. "The Role of Monetary Policy," *American Economic Review* (March 1968): 12.

[3] The evolution of the views of Paul Samuelson, who might properly be regarded as the father of American Keynesian economics, best illustrates the change in the Keynesian view with regard to the relative importance of monetary and fiscal policy. Commenting on the 12th edition of his classic text in 1985. Samuelson stated: "In the early editions of the book, fiscal policy was top banana. In later editions that emphasis changed to equality. In this edition we've taken a stand that monetary policy is most important."

Outstanding Economist

Milton Friedman (1912–)

The 1976 recipient of the Nobel Prize, Friedman is widely regarded as the most influential spokesman for a free market economy in the twentieth century. With the assistance of other monetarists, he eventually convinced even his critics that monetary policy exerts a strong impact on the economy. Friedman maintains that business fluctuations are the result of monetary instability. His popular books *Capitalism and Freedom* (1962) and *Free to Choose* (1980), coauthored with his wife, Rose, are classical treatises in support of economic freedom. After spending years at the University of Chicago, he is currently on the faculty at Stanford University. Now in his nineties, he continues to be an active scholar and writer.

hold money balances with (2) the desire for more wealth (or income). Of course, all of us would like to have more wealth, but we may be perfectly satisfied with our holdings of money in relation to our holdings of other goods, *given our current level of wealth.* When we say people want to hold more (or less) money, we mean that they want to restructure their wealth toward larger (smaller) money balances.

People hold money for a variety of reasons. As we discussed in the previous reading, money provides us with instant purchasing power. At the most basic level, we hold money so we can conduct transactions. Households hold money balances so they can pay for the weekly groceries, the monthly house payment, gasoline for the car, lunch for the kids, and other items purchased regularly. Businesses demand money so they can meet the weekly payroll, pay the utility bills, purchase supplies, and conduct other transactions. Most individuals also hold money so they will be in a better position to deal with the uncertainties of the real world—an unexpected repair bill, an accident, or a medical emergency, for example. Economists refer to this as the *precautionary motive* for holding money. In addition, money is an asset—a means of storing value. Some may hold money as a method of storing purchasing power for future use.

Higher interest rates make it more costly to hold money. Consider the cost of holding $1,000 in the form of currency and demand deposits (which do not earn interest) rather than in interest-earning bonds, for example. If the interest rate is 10 percent, it will cost you $100 per year to hold an additional $1,000 of noninterest-earning money. In contrast, if the interest rate is 1 percent, the annual cost of holding the $1,000 money balance will be only $10. Even if you maintain money balances in an interest-earning checking account, higher interest returns are generally available if you are willing to tie up the funds in a bond or some other less liquid form of savings. Thus, the opportunity cost of holding money is directly related to the nominal interest rate.

A curve that outlines the relationship between the interest rate (measured on the y-axis) and the quantity of money (measured on the x-axis) is called the* demand for money. *As part a of* Exhibit 17-1 *illustrates, there is an inverse relationship between the interest rate and the quantity of money demanded. This inverse relationship reflects the fact that higher interest rates make it more costly to hold money instead of interest-earning assets like bonds. Therefore, as interest rates rise, individuals and businesses will try to manage their affairs with smaller money balances.

Demand for money
A curve that indicates the relationship between the interest rate and the quantity of money people want to hold. Because higher interest rates increase the opportunity cost of holding money, the quantity demanded of money will be inversely related to the interest rate.

Like other demand curves, the demand curve for money is constructed holding other things constant. The demand for money balances will generally increase with the nominal value of transactions. If wages and prices increase, more money will be required by households to purchase the costlier weekly market basket, and more money will be required by businesses to pay the larger wage bill. Similarly, if prices remain constant, while the quantity of goods bought and

EXHIBIT 17-1 Demand and Supply of Money

The demand for money is inversely related to the money interest rate (a). The supply of money is determined by the monetary authorities (the Fed) through their open market operations, discount-rate policy, and reserve requirements (b).

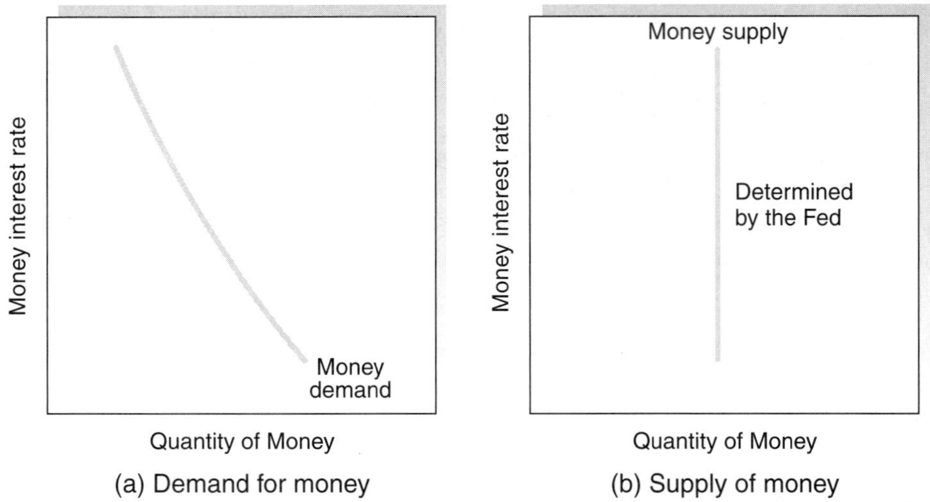

sold increases, larger money balances will be required to conduct the larger volume of business. In essence, as nominal GDP increases as the result of either higher prices or the growth of real output, the demand for money balances will also increase—that is, the entire demand for money schedule will shift to the right. Conversely, a decline in nominal GDP will decrease the demand for money, shifting the schedule to the left.

With the passage of time, changes in institutional factors will also influence the demand schedule for money. Both evidence and logic indicate that changes in institutional arrangements have reduced the demand for money in recent years. The widespread use of general purpose credit cards makes it easier for households to reconcile their bills with their receipt of income. Readily available short-term loans have reduced the need to maintain substantial cash balances for emergencies. These changes have gradually reduced the demand for money (shifting the entire schedule to the left).

As we discussed in the previous reading, the quantity of money available to the economy is determined by the monetary authorities, the Fed in the case of the United States. The Fed can use its control over reserve requirements, the discount rate, and especially open market operations to set the supply of money at whatever level it wants. Changes in the interest rate do not alter the Fed's ability to determine the supply of money. Therefore, as Exhibit 17-1 (part b) illustrates, the money supply schedule is vertical. The vertical supply curve reflects that the quantity of money is determined by Fed policy and it is not affected by changes in the interest rate.

Equilibrium Between Money Demand and Money Supply

Exhibit 17-2 brings the money demand and money supply together and illustrates how they determine the equilibrium rate of interest. The money interest rate will move toward i_e, where the quantity of money demanded by households and businesses is just equal to the quantity supplied by the Fed. At the equilibrium interest rate, people are willing to hold the stock of money the Fed has supplied to the economy.

EXHIBIT 17-2 Money Supply, Money Demand, and Equilibrium

The money interest rate will tend to gravitate toward equilibrium, i_e, where the quantity of money demanded by households and businesses will equal the quantity of money supplied by the Fed.

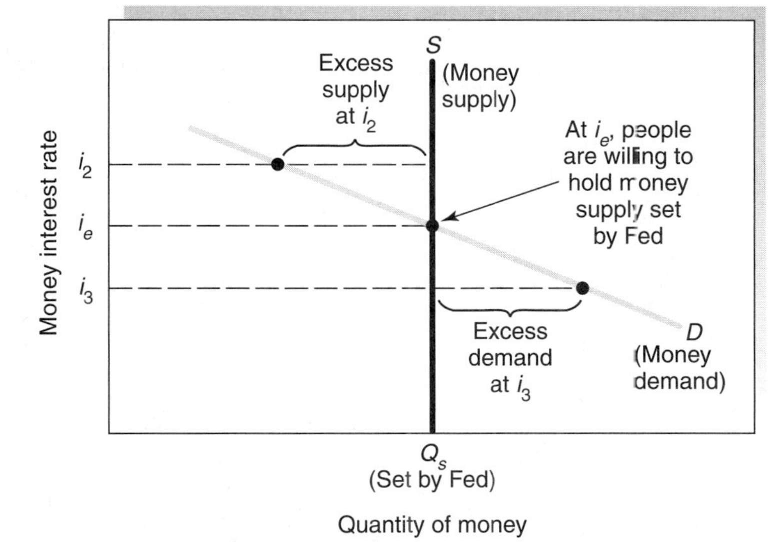

At an above equilibrium interest rate, i_2 for example, people would not want to hold as much money as the Fed has supplied. Accordingly, they would try to reduce their money balances. They might do so by using some of their money balances to buy bonds. This increase in demand for bonds would drive bond prices up and interest rates down. (*Remember:* Higher bond prices imply lower interest rates.) As a result, the money interest rate would move toward the i_e equilibrium. On the other hand, at a below equilibrium money interest rate, i_3 for example, an excess demand for money would be present. Excess money demand indicates that people would like to hold a larger quantity of money than the Fed has supplied. Under these circumstances, they might sell bonds in an effort to get their hands on more money. In turn, their sale of bonds would reduce bond prices and place upward pressure on interest rates, causing them to move toward i_e. Therefore, only the equilibrium interest rate i_e would tend to persist into the future.

Transmission of Monetary Policy

How will a change in the money supply affect the economy? As we previously noted, the Fed typically uses open market operations to control the supply of money. If the Fed wants to shift to a more **expansionary monetary policy**, it will buy bonds. Exhibit 17-3 illustrates the impact on the economy. Initially, we consider the situation where the money interest rate (i_1 in the money balances market) is equal to the real interest rate (r_1 in the loanable funds market). This indicates that the expected rate of inflation is zero. When the Fed purchases bonds in order to increase the money supply (shift from S_1 to S_2 in part a), it bids up bond prices and injects additional reserves into the banking system. Profit-seeking banks will not let the additional reserves lie idle; they will seek to attract additional loan customers so that the available reserves can be fully invested in interest-earning assets. This combination of factors—higher bond prices and additional reserves that the banks will use to extend loans—will increase the supply of loanable funds (shift to S_2 as shown in part b of Exhibit 17-3). In the short run, the real interest rate will fall to r_2.

Expansionary monetary policy
A shift in monetary policy designed to stimulate aggregate demand. Bond purchases, creation of additional bank reserves, and an increase in the growth rate of the money supply are generally indicative of a shift to a more expansionary monetary policy.

EXHIBIT 17-3 Transmission of Monetary Policy

When the Fed shifts to a more expansionary monetary policy, it will generally buy additional bonds. This will supply the banking system with additional reserves. Both the Fed's bond purchases and the banks' use of the additional reserves to extend new loans will increase the supply of loanable funds (shift from S_1 to S_2, part b) and place downward pressure on the real rate of interest. As the real interest rate falls (to r_2), aggregate demand increases (to AD_2 in part c). Since the effects of the monetary expansion were unanticipated, the expansion in AD leads to both an increase in current output (to Y_2) and higher prices (inflation) in the short run.

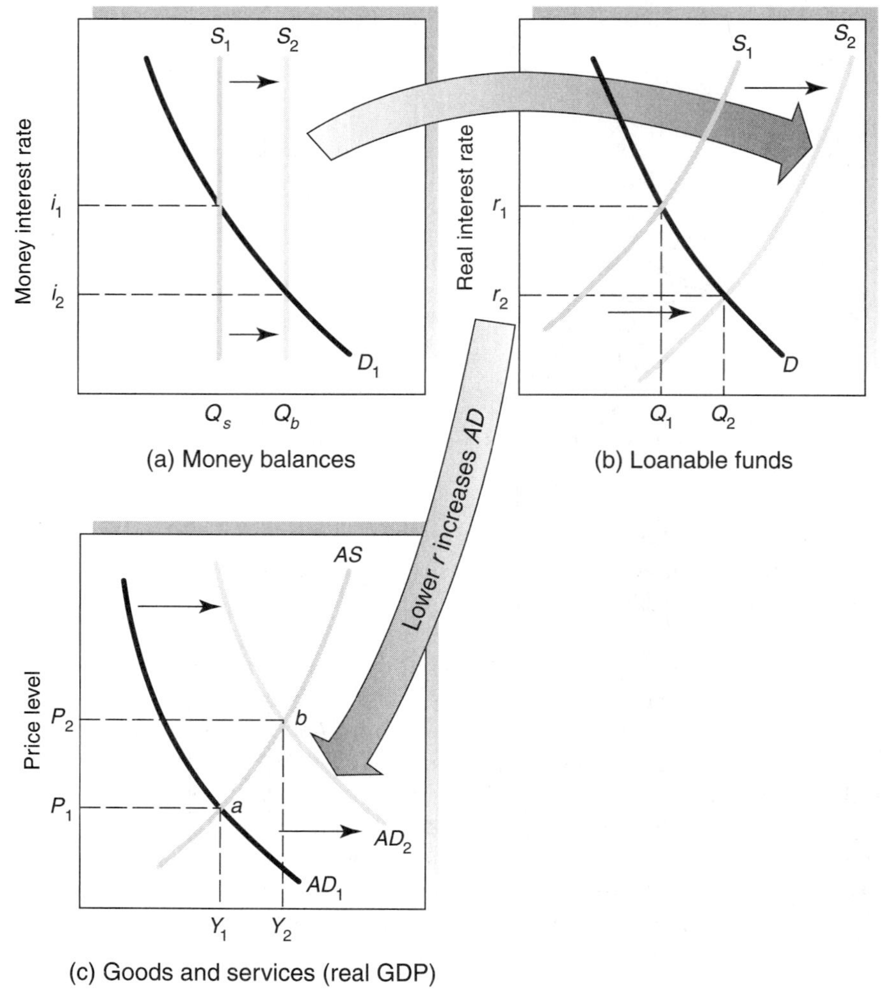

How will the Fed's bond purchases, creation of additional bank reserves, and lower real interest rate influence the demand for goods and services? As part c of Exhibit 17-3 illustrates, aggregate demand will increase (shift from AD_1 to AD_2). Economists stress the importance of three factors that contribute to this increase in aggregate demand.[4]

1. ***The lower real interest rate will make current investment and consumption cheaper relative to future spending.*** At the lower interest rate, entrepreneurs will undertake some investment projects they otherwise would have forgone. Spending by firms on structures and equipment will increase. Similarly,

---

[4] See the *Federal Reserve Bank of St. Louis: Review* (May/June 1995) and the *Journal of Economic Perspectives* (Fall 1995) for additional details on how changes in monetary policy affect aggregate demand.

consumers will decide to expand their purchases of automobiles and consumer durables, which can now be enjoyed with smaller monthly payments.

2. ***The lower interest rate may also lead to an outflow of capital, which will cause the dollar to depreciate and thereby stimulate the net export component of aggregate demand.*** As domestic interest rates fall, both domestic and foreign investors will shift some of their financial investments to other countries where rates of return are more attractive. As investors shift funds abroad, they will supply dollars and demand foreign currencies in the foreign exchange market. This will cause the dollar to depreciate. In turn, the depreciation in the exchange-rate value of the dollar will make imports more expensive for Americans and U.S. exports cheaper for foreigners. As a result, U.S. imports will decline and exports will expand. This increase in net exports will also stimulate aggregate demand.
3. ***The lower interest rates will tend to increase asset prices—for example, the prices of stocks, houses, and other structures—which will also stimulate current demand.*** As the prices of real and financial assets rise, household wealth increases, which will stimulate additional consumption. Perhaps more important, the higher prices of houses and other physical assets will make new construction of these assets more profitable. The increased profitability will induce entrepreneurs to undertake additional construction in these areas, which will expand both investment and aggregate demand.

The Thumbnail Sketch on page 86 outlines the complex sequence of events through which Fed bond purchases expand the money supply and stimulate aggregate demand. This sequence is sometimes referred to as the interest rate transmission mechanism of monetary policy.[5]

Unanticipated Expansionary Monetary Policy

As we have previously discussed, modern macroeconomic analysis stresses the importance of whether a change is anticipated or unanticipated. If people do not anticipate the increase in aggregate demand accompanying an expansionary monetary policy, costs will rise less than prices in the short run. Profit margins will improve. Businesses will respond with an expansion in the output of goods and services (as illustrated by the increase in real output from Y_1 to Y_2 in part c of Exhibit 17-3).

Modern analysis indicates that an unexpected increase in the supply of money will reduce the real rate of interest, thereby triggering an increase in the demand for goods and services. In turn, the increase in aggregate demand will expand real output and employment in the short run.

Part a of Exhibit 17-4 illustrates the potential of expansionary monetary policy to direct a recessionary economy to full employment. Consider an economy initially at output Y_1, below full employment capacity (Y_F). Expansionary monetary policy will increase aggregate demand (to AD_2). Real output will expand (to Y_F). In essence, the expansionary monetary policy provides an alternative to the economy's self-corrective mechanism. In the absence of demand stimulus,

---

[5] There is also a more direct route through which expansionary monetary policy may stimulate aggregate demand. When the Fed expands the supply of money, it will create an "excess supply of money" *at the initial money interest rate.* People may respond by directly increasing their purchases of goods and services in an effort to reduce their money balances to desired levels. Obviously, this will increase aggregate demand. This direct path is most relevant when the government expands the supply of money by paying its bills with newly created currency. Because the money supply of the United States is generally expanded via open market operations, we have focused on the transmission of monetary policy through the interest rate. The implications of both the direct and indirect paths are identical—both indicate that expansionary monetary policy will stimulate aggregate demand.

THUMBNAIL SKETCH

Transmission of Monetary Policy—A Summary

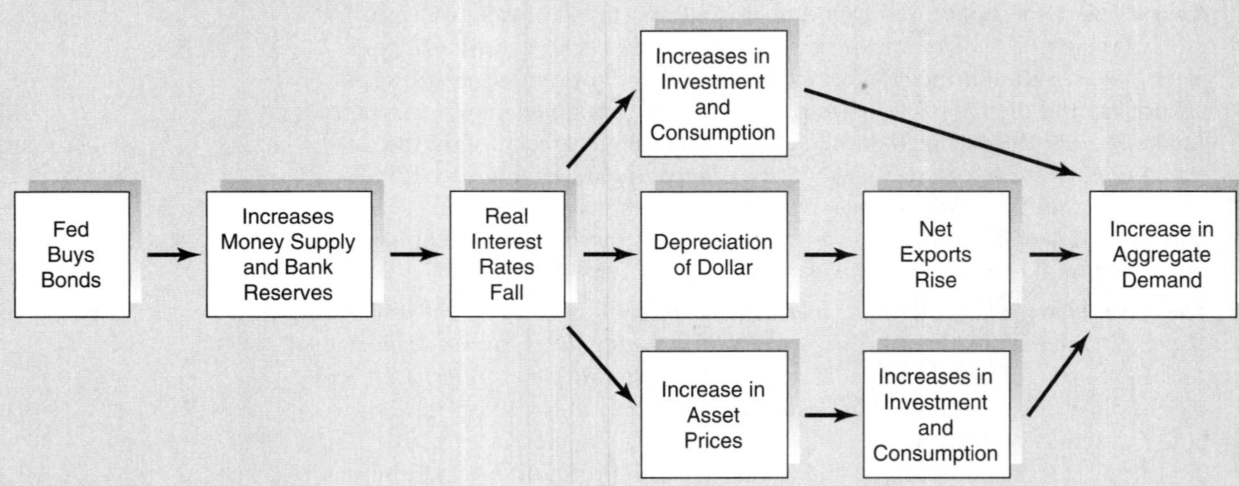

EXHIBIT 17-4 Effects of Expansionary Monetary Policy

If the impact of an increase in aggregate demand accompanying expansionary monetary policy is felt when the economy is operating below capacity, the policy will help direct the economy to a long-run full-employment equilibrium (a). In this case, the increase in output from Y_1 to Y_F will be long term. In contrast, if the demand-stimulus effects are imposed on an economy already at full employment (b), they will lead to excess demand and higher product prices. Output will temporarily increase (to Y_2). However, in the long run, the strong demand will push up resource prices, shifting short-run aggregate supply to $SRAS_2$. The price level will rise to P_3 and output will recede (to Y_F) from its temporary high.

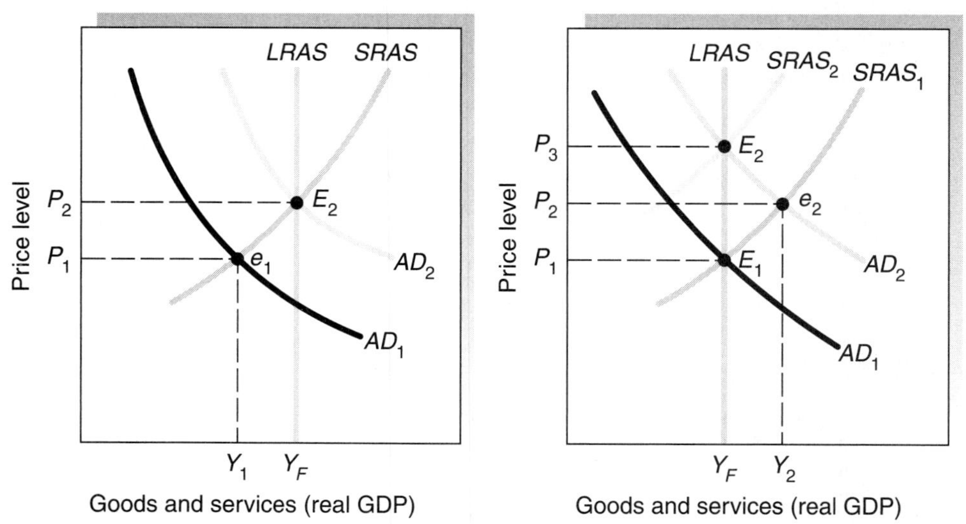

(a) Output is initially at less than full employment

(b) Output is initially at full employment

declining resource prices and real interest rates will eventually restore full employment. But many economists believe that expansionary monetary policy can hasten the return to full-employment equilibrium.

How would a shift to expansionary monetary policy influence output and the price level if the economy were already at full employment? Although this is generally not a desirable strategy, nonetheless it is interesting to analyze the outcome. As part b of Exhibit 17-4 illustrates, the monetary expansion will increase aggregate demand, causing product prices to rise relative to costs, important components of which are temporarily fixed by long-term contracts. The shift in demand will *temporarily* push real output to Y_2, beyond the economy's long-run capacity of Y_F. Output and employment will expand. However, the high rates of output (Y_2) and employment will not be sustainable. Eventually, long-term contracts based on the previously weaker demand (AD_1) will expire. New agreements will reflect the stronger demand. Resource prices will rise, shifting *SRAS* upward to the left. Eventually, long-run equilibrium (E_2) will result at a higher price level (P_3). Output will recede to Y_F. Thus, when an economy is already at full employment, an unexpected shift to a more expansionary monetary policy will temporarily increase output, but in the long run it merely leads to higher prices. Hence, the wisdom of such a shift is highly questionable.

Restrictive monetary policy
A shift in monetary policy designed to reduce aggregate demand and place downward pressure on the general level of prices (or the rate of inflation). Bond sales by the Fed, a decline in bank reserves, and a reduction in the growth rate of the money supply are generally indicative of a restrictive monetary policy.

Unanticipated Restrictive Monetary Policy

Suppose the Fed moves toward a more **restrictive monetary policy**. It would generally do so by selling bonds to the general public, which will reduce both the supply of money and the reserves of banks. Exhibit 17-5 illustrates the impact of the more restrictive monetary policy on the loanable funds and goods and services markets. The Fed's sale of bonds reduces bond prices and drains reserves from the banking system (reducing the ability of banks to extend loans). As a result, the supply of loanable funds will decline, causing the real interest rate to rise (from r_1 to r_2 in frame a of Exhibit 17-5). The higher real interest rates will

EXHIBIT 17-5 Short-run Effects of a More Restrictive Monetary Policy

When the Fed shifts to a more restrictive policy, it sells bonds, which reduces the reserves available to banks, decreases the supply of loanable funds, and places upward pressure on interest rates (a). The higher interest rates will decrease aggregate demand (shift to AD_2 in b). When the reduction in aggregate demand is unanticipated, real output will decline (to Y_2) and downward pressure on prices will result.

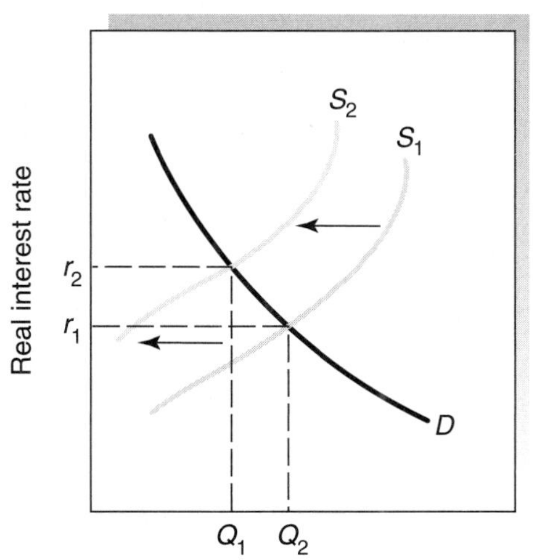

(a) Loanable funds market

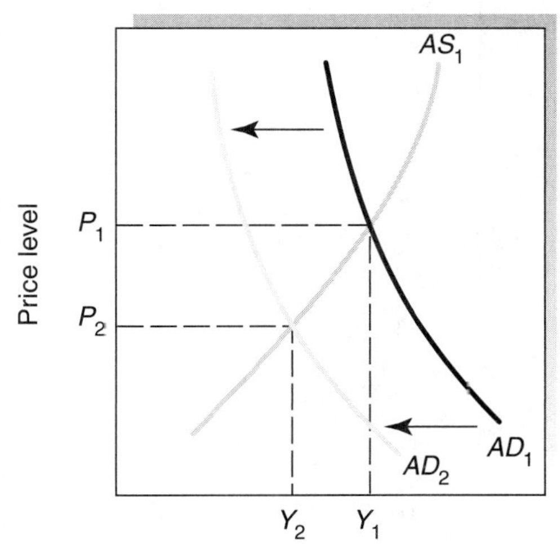

(b) Goods and services (real GDP)

tend to reduce current spending on both investment and consumer durables. They are also likely to cause an inflow of capital and appreciation in the exchange-rate value of the dollar. In turn, this appreciation of the dollar will encourage imports and discourage exports, leading to a reduction in net exports (and aggregate demand). The higher interest rates may also reduce the prices of housing and other assets, thereby discouraging new construction. All these factors will tend to reduce aggregate demand in the goods and services market (shift from AD_1 to AD_2 in part b of Exhibit 17-5).

The unexpected decline in the demand for goods and services will place downward pressures on prices, squeeze profit margins, and reduce output in the goods and services market. As part b of Exhibit 17-5 illustrates, the price level will decline (to P_2) and output will fall (to Y_2) as the result of the restrictive monetary policy.

The appropriateness of a restrictive policy depends on the initial state of the economy. Exhibit 17-6 illustrates this point. When an economy is experiencing upward pressure on prices as the result of strong demand, restrictive policy is an effective weapon against inflation. Suppose that, as illustrated by part a of Exhibit 17-6, an economy is temporarily operating at e_1 and Y_1, beyond its full employment real GDP of Y_F. Strong aggregate demand is placing upward pressure on prices. The problem is inflation, not recession. Under these circumstances, restrictive policy makes good sense. It would help control the inflation. If the proper dosage is timed correctly, restrictive policy would retard aggregate demand (to AD_2) and direct the economy to a noninflationary, long-run equilibrium at P_2 and Y_F (that is, E_2).

As part b of Exhibit 17-6 illustrates, however, an unanticipated shift to restrictive policy would be damaging if applied to an economy in full-employment equilibrium. If the output of an economy is at full employment (or worse still, at less than full employment), a shift to restrictive policy would reduce aggregate

EXHIBIT 17-6 Effects of Restrictive Monetary Policy

The stabilization effects of restrictive monetary policy depend on the state of the economy when the policy exerts its primary impact. Restrictive monetary policy will reduce aggregate demand. If the demand restraint comes during a period of strong demand and an overheated economy, then it will limit or even prevent the occurrence of an inflationary boom (a). In contrast, if the reduction in aggregate demand takes place when the economy is at full employment, then it will disrupt long-run equilibrium, reduce output, and result in a recession (b).

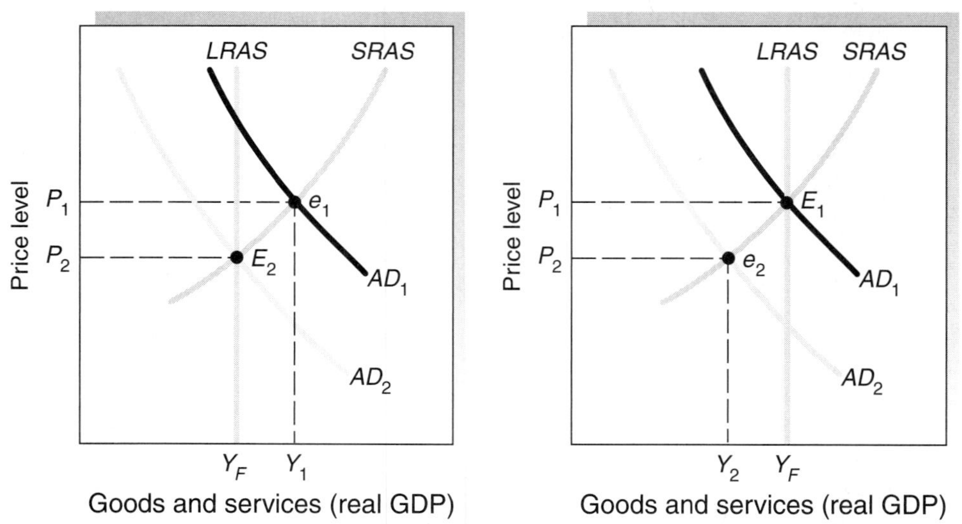

(a) Restrictive policy to control inflation

(b) Restrictive policy that causes a recession

demand (shift to AD_2) and throw the economy into a recession. Real GDP would decline from Y_F to Y_2. Output would fall below the economy's full employment capacity, and unemployment would rise above the natural rate of unemployment.

Proper Timing

As with fiscal policy, monetary policy must be properly timed if it is to help stabilize an economy. Exhibits 17-4 and 17-6 highlight this point. When an economy is operating below its long-run capacity, expansionary monetary policy can stimulate demand and push the output of the economy to its sustainable potential (part a of Exhibit 17-4). Similarly, if properly timed, restrictive monetary policy can help control (or prevent) inflation (part a of Exhibit 17-6).

If it is timed improperly, however, monetary policy can be destabilizing. Expansionary monetary policy is a source of inflation if the effects of the policy are felt when the economy is already at or beyond its capacity (part b of Exhibit 17-4). Similarly, if the effects of a restrictive policy come when an economy is operating at its potential GDP, recession is the likely outcome (part b of Exhibit 17-6). Worse still, the impact of restrictive policy may be disastrous if imposed on an economy already in the midst of a recession.

Proper timing of monetary policy is not an easy task. While the Fed can institute policy changes rapidly, there may be a substantial time lag before the change in policy will exert a significant impact on aggregate demand. Economists who have studied this issue estimate that this impact lag will be five or six months at a minimum. Some economists, particularly monetarists, estimate that the primary impact of a change in monetary policy on output and employment is often as much as 12 to 18 months after the change is instituted. In terms of its impact on the price level and rate of inflation, the estimated impact lag is even longer, perhaps as much as 36 months. Given our limited ability to forecast the future, such lengthy time lags clearly reduce the potential effectiveness of discretionary monetary policy as a stabilization tool.

MONETARY POLICY IN THE LONG RUN 3

Since the middle of the eighteenth century, economists have argued that excessive money growth leads to inflation. Nearly a hundred years ago, Englishman Alfred Marshall and American Irving Fisher formalized the **quantity theory of money** in support of this view. ***The quantity theory indicates that an increase in the supply of money will cause a proportional increase in the price level.***

Quantity theory of money
A theory that hypothesizes that a change in the money supply will cause a proportional change in the price level because velocity and real output are unaffected by the quantity of money.

The quantity theory of money can be more easily understood once we recognize that there are two ways of viewing GDP. As the *AD/AS* model shows, nominal GDP is the sum of the price, P, times the output, Y, of each final-product good purchased during the period. In aggregate, P represents the economy's price level, while Y indicates real income or real GDP. There is also a second way of visualizing GDP. When the existing money stock, M, is multiplied by the number of times, V, that money is used to buy final products, this, too, yields the economy's nominal GDP. Therefore,

$$PY = \text{GDP} = MV$$

The **velocity of money** (V) is simply the average number of times a dollar is used to purchase a final product or service during a year. Velocity is equal to nominal GDP divided by the size of the money stock. For example, in 2000 GDP was equal to $9,963 billion, while the M1 money supply was $1,088 billion. On average, each dollar in the M1 money supply was used 9.2 times to purchase

Velocity of money
The average number of times a dollar is used to purchase final goods and services during a year. It is equal to GDP divided by the stock of money.

final-product goods and services included in GDP. The velocity of the M1 money stock therefore was 9.2. The velocity of the M2 money stock can be derived in a similar manner. In 2000, the M2 money stock was $4,945 billion. Thus, the velocity of M2 was 2.0 ($9,963 billion divided by $4,945 billion).

The concept of velocity is closely related to the demand for money. When decision makers conduct a specific amount of business with a smaller amount of money, their demand for money balances is reduced. Each dollar, though, is being used more often—the velocity of money has increased. Thus, for a given income level, when the demand for money declines, the velocity of money increases. Correspondingly, an increase in the demand for money is a reflection of a reduction in velocity.

When considering the behavior of prices, output, money, and velocity over time, we can write the quantity theory equation in terms of growth rates:

Rate of inflation + Growth rate of real output = Growth rate of the money supply + Growth rate of velocity

Equation of exchange $MV = PY$, where M is the money supply, V is the velocity of money, P is the price level, and Y is the output of goods and services produced.

The $MV = PY$ relationship is simply an identity, or a tautology. Economists refer to it as the **equation of exchange**, because it reflects both the monetary and real sides of each final-product exchange. The quantity theory of money, though, postulates that Y and V are determined by factors other than the amount of money in circulation. Classical economists believed that real output Y was determined by such factors as technology, the size of the economy's resource base, and the skill of the labor force. These factors were thought to be insensitive to changes in the money supply. Similarly, the velocity of money was thought to be determined primarily by institutional factors, such as the organization of banking and credit, the frequency of income payments, the rapidity of transportation, and the communication system. These factors would change quite slowly. Thus, classical economists thought that, for all practical purposes, both Y and V were constant (or changed only by small amounts) over periods of two, three, or four years. If both Y and V are constant, then the $MV = PY$ relationship indicates that an increase in the money supply will lead to a proportional increase in the price level. Correspondingly, an increase in the growth rate of the money supply can be expected to cause a similar increase in the rate of inflation.

Long-Run Implications of Modern Analysis

What does modern analysis indicate with regard to the validity of the quantity theory of money? In addressing this question, it will be helpful to focus on the dynamic long-run implications of the *AD/AS* model. Thus far, we have used comparative statics to analyze monetary policy. Within this framework, an increase in the supply of money is reflective of more expansionary policy. In the real world, however, shifts in monetary policy generally involve changes in the *growth rate* of the money supply. An increase in money growth suggests a move toward a more expansionary monetary policy, while a reduction in the growth rate of the money supply implies a shift to a more restrictive policy. Similarly, in a comparative static framework, an increase in the price level implies inflation. However, inflation is a dynamic concept—a rate of increase in prices, not a once-and-for-all movement to a higher price level.

In order to both add realism and analyze the long-run implications more fully, this section will recast the prior static analysis into a dynamic framework. We will begin with a simple dynamic case. Suppose that the real GDP of an economy is growing at a 3 percent annual rate and that the monetary authorities are expanding the money supply by 3 percent each year. In addition, let's assume that the velocity of money is constant. This would imply that the 3 percent annual increase in output would lead to a 3 percent annual increase in the demand

EXHIBIT 17-7 Long-run Effects of More Rapid Expansion in the Money Supply—Goods and Services Market

Here we illustrate the long-term impact of an increase in the annual growth rate of the money supply from 3 to 8 percent. Initially, prices are stable (P_{100}) when the money supply is expanding by 3 percent annually. The acceleration in the growth rate of the money supply increases aggregate demand (shift to AD_2). At first, real output may expand beyond the economy's potential (Y_F). However, abnormally low unemployment and strong demand conditions will create upward pressure on wages and other resource prices, shifting aggregate supply to AS_2. Output will return to its long-run potential and the price level will increase to P_{105} (E_2). If the more rapid monetary growth continues in subsequent periods, AD and AS will continue to shift upward, leading to still higher prices (E_3 and periods beyond). The net result of the process is sustained inflation.

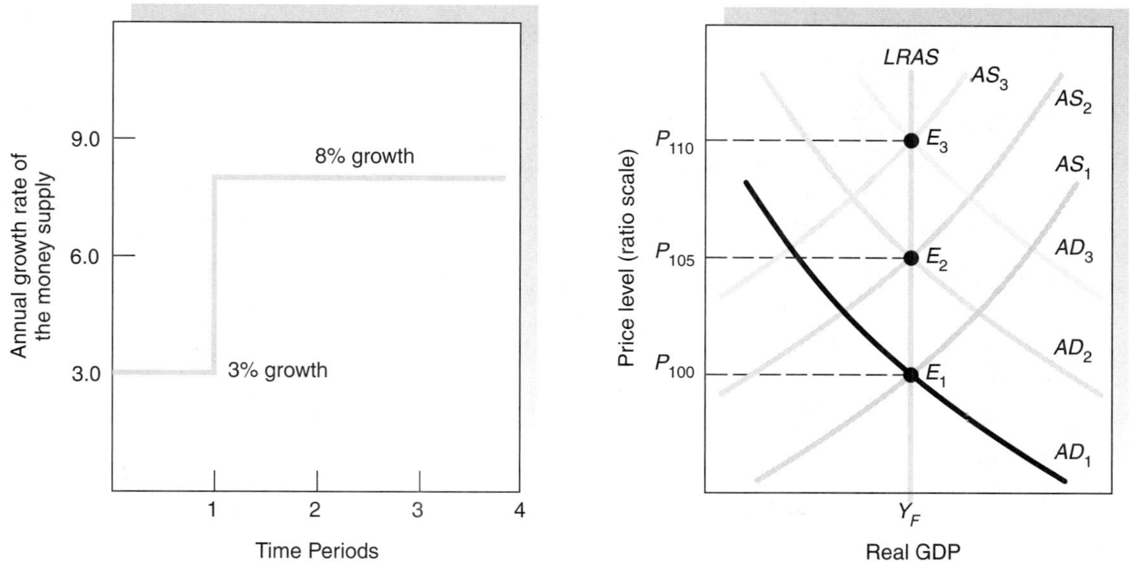

(a) Growth rate of the money supply

(b) Impact in the goods and services market

for money. Under these circumstances, the 3 percent monetary growth would be consistent with stable prices (zero inflation). Initially, we will assume that the economy's real interest rate is 4 percent. Because the inflation rate is zero, the nominal rate of interest is also equal to 4 percent. Exhibits 17-7 and 17-8 illustrate an economy initially (Period 1) characterized by these conditions.

What will happen if the monetary authorities permanently increase the growth rate of the money supply from 3 percent to 8 percent annually (see part a of Exhibit 17-7, beginning in Period 2)?[6] In the short run, the expansionary monetary policy will reduce the real interest rate and stimulate aggregate demand (shift to AD_2 in part b of Exhibit 17-7), just as we previously explained (Exhibits 17-3 and 17-4). For a time, real output may exceed the economy's potential. However, as they confront strong demand conditions, many resource suppliers (who previously committed to long-term agreements) will want to modify these agreements in light of the strong demand conditions. With the passage of time, more and more resource suppliers (including labor represented by union officials) will have the opportunity to alter their prior contracts. As this happens, wages and other resource prices will increase. As they do, costs will rise

[6] In the preceding reading, we noted the difficulties involved in the measurement of the money supply (both M1 and M2). Changes in the growth rate of the money supply may not always be indicative of a shift in monetary policy. More generally, the example presented here assumes that the Fed has shifted to a more expansionary monetary policy—one that will lead to an increase in the rate of inflation—regardless of whether the monetary aggregates as currently measured reflect this shift.

EXHIBIT 17-8 Long-run Effects of More Rapid Expansion in the Money Supply—Loanable Funds Market

When prices are stable, supply and demand in the loanable funds market are in balance at a real and nominal interest rate of 4 percent. If more rapid monetary expansion leads to a long-term 5 percent inflation rate (see Exhibit 17-7), borrowers and lenders will build the higher inflation rate into their decision making. As a result, the nominal interest rate (i) will rise to 9 percent—the 4 percent real rate plus a 5 percent inflationary premium.

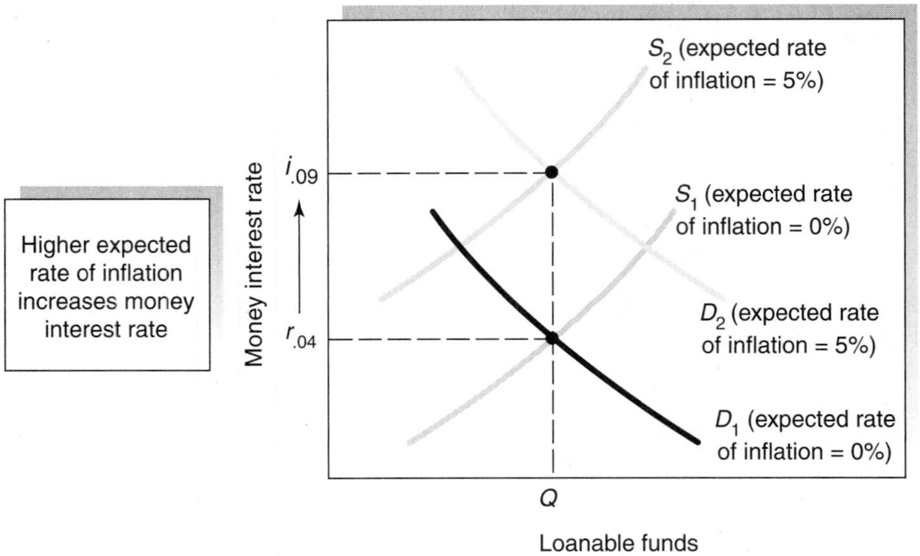

and profit margins will recede to normal levels. The higher costs will reduce aggregate supply (shift to AS_2). As the rapid monetary growth continues in subsequent periods (periods 3, 4, and so on), both *AD* and *AS* will shift upward. The price level will rise to P_{105}, P_{110}, and on to still higher levels as the money supply continues to grow more rapidly than the monetary growth rate consistent with stable prices. The continuation of the expansionary monetary policy leads to a higher and higher price level—that is, a sustained inflation.

Suppose an inflation rate of 5 percent eventually emerges from the more rapid growth rate (8 percent rather than 3 percent) of the money supply. With the passage of time, more and more people will adjust their decision making in light of the persistent 5 percent inflation. In the resource market, both buyers and sellers will eventually incorporate the expectation of the 5 percent inflation rate into long-term contracts, such as collective bargaining agreements. Once this happens, resource prices and costs will rise as rapidly as prices in the goods and services market. ***When the inflation rate is anticipated fully, it will fail to either reduce real wages or improve profit margins. Unemployment will return to its natural rate.***

Exhibit 17-8 illustrates the adjustments in the loanable funds market once borrowers and lenders expect the 5 percent inflation rate. When lenders anticipate a 5 percent annual increase in the price level, a 9 percent interest rate will be necessary to provide them with as much incentive to supply loanable funds as 4 percent interest provided *when stable prices were expected.* Thus, the supply of loanable funds will shift vertically by the 5 percent expected rate of inflation. Simultaneously, borrowers who were willing to pay 4 percent interest on loans when they expected stable prices will be willing to pay 9 percent when they expect prices to increase by 5 percent annually. The demand for loanable funds will therefore also increase (shift vertically) by the expected rate of inflation. Once borrowers and lenders anticipate the higher (5 percent) inflation rate, the equilibrium money interest rate will rise to 9 percent. Of course, the real interest rate is equal to the money interest rate (9 percent) minus the expected rate of inflation (5 percent). In the long run, a 4 percent real interest rate will emerge with inflation, just as it did with stable prices.[7] Inflation, then, will fail to reduce the real interest rate in the long run.

The long-run implications of modern analysis are consistent with those of the earlier quantity theory of money. ***In the long run, the major consequence of rapid money growth is inflation. While an unanticipated shift to a more expansionary policy may exert a positive impact on output and employment in the short run, this will not be the case in the long run. Rapid monetary growth will neither reduce unemployment nor stimulate real output in the long run.***

MONETARY POLICY WHEN EFFECTS ARE ANTICIPATED 4

Thus far, we have assumed that decision makers come to anticipate the effects of monetary policy only after they begin to occur. For example, we assumed that borrowers and lenders began to anticipate a higher inflation rate only after prices began to rise more rapidly. Similarly, resource suppliers anticipated the inflation only after it had begun.

What if enough decision makers in the market catch on to the link between expansionary monetary policy and an increase in the inflation rate? Suppose borrowers and lenders start paying attention to the money supply figures and other monetary policy indicators. Observing a shift toward a more expansionary monetary policy, they revise upward their expectation of the future inflation rate. Lenders become more reluctant to supply loanable funds. Simultaneously, borrowers increase their demand for loanable funds at existing rates of interest because they also anticipate a higher rate of future inflation and they want to buy now before prices rise. Under these circumstances, a reduction in supply and an increase in demand for loanable funds will quickly push up the money interest rate. If borrowers and lenders quickly and accurately forecast the future rate of inflation accompanying the monetary expansion, the real interest rate will decline for only a short period of time, if at all.

If buyers and sellers in the goods and services market also anticipate a shift to a more expansionary monetary policy, they too may anticipate its inflationary consequences. As buyers anticipate future price increases, many will buy now rather than later. Current aggregate demand will rise. Similarly, expecting an acceleration in the inflation rate, sellers will be reluctant to sell except at premium prices. Current aggregate supply will fall. This combination of factors will quickly push prices of goods and services upward.

Simultaneously, if buyers and sellers in the resource market believe that more rapid monetary growth will lead to a higher rate of inflation, they too will build this view into long-run contracts. Union officials will demand and employers will pay an inflationary premium for future money wages, based on their expectation of inflation. Alternatively, they may write an **escalator clause** (sometimes called cost-of-living adjustments) into their collective bargaining agreements. Such provisions will automatically raise money wages when the inflation transpires. If decision makers in the resource market correctly anticipate the inflation, real resource prices will not decline once prices accelerate upward.

Escalator clause
A contractual agreement that periodically and automatically adjusts money wage rates upward as the price level rises. They are sometimes referred to as cost-of-living adjustments or COLAs.

[7] Higher rates of inflation are generally associated with an increase in the variability of the inflation rate. Thus, greater risk (the possibility of either a substantial gain or loss associated with a sharp change in the inflation rate) accompanies exchange in the loanable funds market when inflation rates are high. This additional risk may result in higher real interest rates than would prevail at lower rates of inflation. The text discussion does not introduce this consideration.

EXHIBIT 17-9 Short-Run Effects of Anticipated Monetary Expansion

When decision makers fully anticipate the effects of monetary expansion, the expansion does not alter real output even in the short run. Suppliers, including resource suppliers, build the expected price rise into their decisions. The anticipated inflation leads to a rise in nominal costs (including wages), causing aggregate supply to decline (shift to $SRAS_2$). While nominal wages, prices, and interest rates rise, their real counterparts are unchanged. The result: inflation without any change in real output (Y_1).

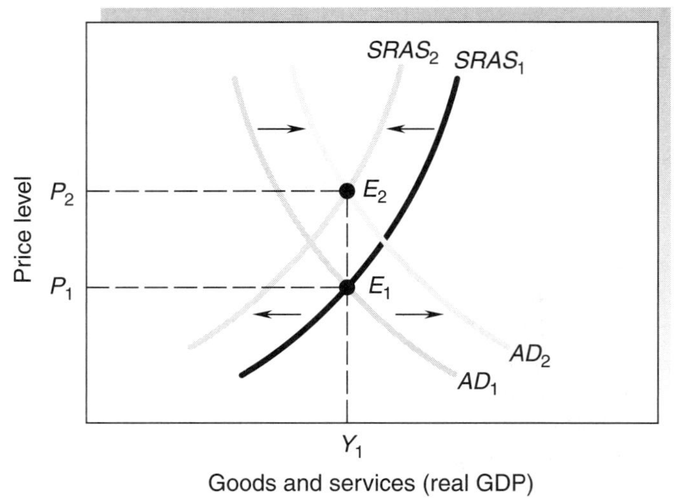

As Exhibit 17-9 illustrates, when individuals correctly anticipate the effects of expansionary monetary policy *prior to their occurrence*, the short-run impact of monetary policy is much like its impact in the long run. The price level will increase, pushing up money income (P_2 Y_1), but real income (Y_1) will be unchanged. Nominal interest rates will rise, but real interest rates will be unchanged. Thus, when the effects of expansionary monetary policy are fully anticipated, they exert little impact on real economic activity.

Are people likely to anticipate the effects of monetary policy? This is a topic of hot debate among economists, and we will consider it in more detail in the next reading. Because the effects of monetary policy differ substantially depending on whether they are anticipated, the question is clearly a very important one.

5 INTEREST RATES AND MONETARY POLICY

Can the Fed control interest rates? How quickly will a shift in monetary policy exert a significant impact on output and prices in the goods and services market? These two questions are linked. Let us begin with the interest rate question. In order to simplify matters, we have proceeded as if there were only a single interest rate in the loanable funds market. In the real world loanable funds market, of course, there are numerous interest rates reflecting loans of differing risk and time length. For example, there are short-term interest rates, such as those for federal funds, Treasury bills, and savings deposits. In addition, there are longer-term rates, such as those for home mortgages and long-term bonds.

When the Fed moves toward a more expansionary policy for example, when it purchases bonds and injects additional reserves into the system, there is an immediate impact on short-term interest rates, like the rate in the federal funds market—the market where banks with excess reserves extend short-term loans to banks with insufficient reserves. As the federal funds rate declines, so too will other short-term interest rates—for example, the rates on savings deposits, three-month Treasury bills, and bank certificates of deposit (CDs).

However, the impact of the expansionary monetary policy on long-term interest rates, such as home mortgages and ten-year bonds, will be more modest and less predictable. There are two reasons for this: First, the long-term rates are influenced more by real factors, such as the demand for investment funds, than by monetary factors. Second, to the extent that monetary factors influence long-term interest rates, they operate primarily through their impact on the expected rate of inflation. The expected long-term future rate of inflation is an important component of long-term nominal interest rates. If people expect a higher future rate of inflation as the result of the shift to a more expansionary policy, long-term rates may rise rather than fall. Thus, although a shift in Fed policy is able to exert a substantial impact on short-term interest rates rather quickly, its impact on longer-term rates is both less certain and likely to occur with a substantially longer time lag. Because long- and medium-term rates are most relevant for the investment decisions of businesses and households, the ambiguity concerning the impact of monetary policy on these rates is particularly important.

Short-Term Interest Rates, Velocity of Money, and Time Lag of Monetary Policy

Furthermore, the impact of the change in short-term nominal interest rates on the velocity of money adds an additional complication. A reduction in the short-term rates will reduce the opportunity cost of holding money balances. Predictably, the velocity of money will decline, which will tend to dampen the initial stimulus effects of the monetary expansion. Of course, if the more expansionary monetary policy persists, a combination of lower real interest rates—particularly short-term rates—and more readily available credit will eventually stimulate aggregate demand (see Exhibit 17-3). With time, the additional demand will place upward pressure on prices, which will also serve to increase both the expected rate of inflation and nominal interest rates, including short-term nominal rates. When this happens—and several quarters may pass before it does—the higher short-term nominal interest rates will increase the velocity of money and amplify the demand-stimulus effects of the policy. It is at this point in time that the primary effects of the expansionary monetary policy will be most potent.

The same forces are also present in the case of a shift to a more restrictive monetary policy. When the Fed shifts to a more restrictive policy, it typically drains reserves from the banking system, which will quickly place upward pressure on the federal funds rate and other short-term interest rates. The restrictive policy, however, will generally exert less impact on longer-term interest rates. If people perceive that inflation is a smaller threat as the result of the more restrictive monetary policy, this factor will place downward pressure on long-term interest rates, which will at least partially offset the restraining effects emanating from the increase in the short-term rates.

At the same time, the higher short-term rates will increase the opportunity cost of holding money and, as a result, its velocity. This increase in the velocity of money will promote additional spending, which will, *for a time*, tend to dampen the restrictive effects of the policy. Of course, the restrictive policy, if continued, will eventually begin to retard inflation and lower nominal interest rates (including short-term rates), which will reduce the velocity of money. Once this happens, and many months may pass before it does, the restrictive policy will be highly potent—it will substantially reduce aggregate demand, output, and prices.

All these factors suggest that the linkage between a change in monetary policy and a change in output and prices is likely to be both lengthy and variable. When there is a shift in monetary policy, the potency of the short-run effects may differ substantially from the potency of the policy shift over a longer period of time. Obviously, these factors will complicate the job of monetary policy makers and make it more difficult for them to institute changes in a manner that will exert a stabilizing influence on the economy.

Money Supply and the Federal Funds Rate

Throughout, we have used shifts in the money supply to indicate the direction of changes in monetary policy. In recent years, however, the Fed has often used interest rates—particularly the federal funds rate—as a means of instituting changes in monetary policy. If the Fed wants to shift toward a more expansionary policy, it may announce that it is reducing its target for the federal funds interest rate. The Fed controls this rate through its open market operations. In order to achieve the lower rate, it will buy more bonds and thereby inject additional reserves into the system, which will place downward pressure on the federal funds rate. Of course, the Fed's buying of bonds will also increase the money supply. Therefore, even though the news media and others may highlight the change in the federal funds rate, the impact on the economy will be the same as for an increase in the money supply. On the other hand, when the Fed shifts to a more restrictive policy, it may seek to increase the federal funds rate. However, the Fed achieves this objective through its sale of bonds, which will reduce the reserves available to the banking system. Again, the result will be the same as for a reduction in the money supply.

Dangers of Using Interest Rates as an Indicator of Monetary Policy

Are interest rates indicative of Fed policy? For example, do low interest rates indicate that the Fed is following an expansionary policy? Here, it is vitally important to distinguish between the short run and the long run. When the Fed shifts to a more expansionary policy, it generally injects additional reserves into the banking system. In the short run, this will place downward pressure on interest rates—particularly for short-term rates. However, think what would happen if the Fed continued on a highly expansionary course, seeking to push interest rates down over a long period of time. In the long run, the monetary expansion will lead to inflation. As people come to expect the inflation, nominal interest rates will rise instead of fall. Once the inflation is anticipated fully, even real interest rates will return to their normal level.

Paradoxically, while expansionary monetary policy can reduce interest rates in the short run, in the long run the result will be just the opposite. A persistent expansionary monetary policy will lead to inflation and higher nominal interest rates. Similarly, a shift to a more restrictive policy will increase interest rates in the short run. But when pursued over a lengthy time period, restrictive policy will lead to deflation (falling prices) and low interest rates.

Thus, interest rates are often a misleading gauge of monetary policy. In the United States, interest rates were high during the 1970s, a period of expansionary monetary policy and inflation. On the other hand, interest rates were relatively low during the 1960s and 1990s, periods of more restrictive monetary policy. During the Great Depression, interest rates fell to less than 1 percent. But this was not indicative of expansionary monetary policy. To the contrary, it was reflective of a highly restrictive monetary policy that was causing deflation and the expectation of a falling price level. Internationally, the picture is the same. The highest interest rates in the world are found in countries experiencing hyperinflation—Argentina and Brazil in the 1980s and Russia in the 1990s, for example. In the late 1990s, several interest rates in Japan fell below 1 percent. Like the United States during the Great Depression, the low Japanese interest rates are reflective of a highly restrictive monetary policy, one that has led to a falling price level and the expectation of deflation.

EFFECTS OF MONETARY POLICY—A SUMMARY 6

The accompanying Thumbnail Sketch summarizes the theoretical implications of our analysis. The impact of monetary policy on major economic variables is indicated for three alternatives: (1) the short run when the effects are unanticipated, (2) the short run when the effects are anticipated, and (3) the long run. Note that the impact of monetary policy in the latter two cases is the same. When decision makers quickly anticipate the effects of monetary policy, the adjustment process speeds up, and therefore the short-run effects are identical to the long-run effects. Under these circumstances, only nominal variables (money interest

THUMBNAIL SKETCH

What Is the Impact of Monetary Policy?

	Short-Run Effects When Policy Is Unanticipated (1)	Short-Run Effects When Policy Is Anticipated[a] (2)	Long-Run Effects (3)
Impact of Expansionary Monetary Policy on			
Inflation rate	Only a small increase, particularly if excess capacity is present	Increase	
Real output and employment	Increase, particularly if excess capacity is present	No change	
Money interest rate	Short-term rates will probably decline	Increase	
Real interest rate	Decrease	No change	
Impact of Restrictive Monetary Policy on			
Inflation rate	Only a small decrease	Decrease	
Real output and employment	Decrease, particularly if economy at less than capacity	No change	
Money interest rate	Short-term rates will probably increase	Decrease	
Real interest rate	Increase	No change	

[a] Beginning from long-run equilibrium

(Entries in columns (2) and (3) are bracketed together and apply to both.)

rates and the inflation rate) are affected. Real variables (real GDP, employment, and the real interest rate) are unaffected.

Five major predictions flow from our analysis:

1. ***An unanticipated shift to a more expansionary (restrictive) monetary policy will temporarily stimulate (retard) output and employment.*** As Exhibits 17-3 and 17-4 illustrate, an increase in aggregate demand emanating from an unanticipated increase in the money supply will lead to a short-run expansion in real output and employment. Conversely, as Exhibit 17-5 shows, an unanticipated move toward a more restrictive monetary policy reduces aggregate demand and retards real output.
2. ***The stabilizing effects of a change in monetary policy are dependent upon the state of the economy when the effects of the policy change are observed.*** If the effects of an expansionary policy come when the economy is operating at less than capacity, then the demand stimulus will push the economy toward full employment. However, if the demand stimulus comes when the economy is operating at or beyond capacity, it will contribute to an acceleration in the inflation rate. Correspondingly, restrictive policy will help to control inflation if the demand-restraining effects are felt when output is beyond the economy's long-run capacity. On the other hand, restrictive policy will result in recession if the reduction in demand comes when the economy is at or below long-run capacity.
3. ***Persistent growth of the money supply at a rapid rate will cause inflation.*** Although the short-run effects of expansionary monetary policy may be primarily on output, particularly if excess capacity is present, a persistent expansion in the money supply at a rate greater than the growth of real output will cause inflation. The more rapid the sustained growth rate of the money supply (relative to real output), the higher the accompanying rate of inflation.
4. ***Money interest rates and the inflation rate will be directly related.*** As the inflation rate rises, money interest rates will eventually increase because both borrowers and lenders will begin to expect the higher rate of inflation and build it into their decision making. Conversely, as the inflation rate declines, a reduction in the expected rate of inflation will eventually lead to lower money interest rates. Therefore, when monetary expansion leads to an acceleration in the inflation rate, it will also result in an increase in nominal interest rates.
5. ***There will be only a loose year-to-year relationship between shifts in monetary policy and changes in output and prices.*** It takes time for markets to adjust to changing demand conditions. Some prices in both product and resource markets are set by long-term contracts. Obviously price responses in these markets will take time. In some cases, people may anticipate the effects of a policy change and adjust quickly; in others, the reaction to a policy change may take more time. Differences in this area will weaken the year-to-year relationship between monetary indicators and important economic variables.

In addition, a monetary policy shift will initially exert a far greater impact on short-term interest rates than on longer-term rates. Movements in the short-term nominal rates are likely to cause changes in the velocity of money that will tend to dampen the initial effects of a monetary policy shift. This, too, will tend to weaken the year-to-year link between changes in monetary policy and changes in output and prices. Therefore, even though our analysis indicates that monetary policy does influence output and prices, the year-to-year relationships are likely to be weak.

TESTING THE MAJOR IMPLICATIONS OF MONETARY THEORY

7

Is the real world consistent with our analysis? The next four exhibits provide evidence on this topic. Our analysis indicates that a shift to a more expansionary monetary policy will initially stimulate output, while a shift to monetary restriction will retard it. Exhibit 17-10 shows the relationship between changes in the growth rate of the money supply and real output since 1960 for the United States. In order to smooth the temporary quarterly fluctuations, the annual rates for both figures are for a 4-quarter moving average. Because the introduction of interest-earning checking accounts dramatically changed the nature of M1 (and affected its growth rate) during the 1980s, the M2 money-supply measure is used here. Of course, changes in the growth rate of M2 may not always accurately reflect the direction of monetary policy and other factors such as supply shocks and fiscal policy changes will also influence the growth of output. Thus, the relationship between changes in the money supply and the growth of real GDP will probably be fairly loose. However, close inspection of the data reveals that periods of sharp acceleration in the growth rate of the money supply were generally associated with an acceleration in the growth rate of real GDP. For example, an acceleration in the growth rate of the money supply during 1961–1964, 1971–1972, 1976, and 1983 was associated with an increase in the growth rate of real GDP.

EXHIBIT 17-10 Monetary Policy and Real GDP

Sharp declines in the growth rate of the money supply, such as those of 1968–1969, 1973–1974, 1977–1978, 1988–1991, and 1999–2000 have generally preceded reductions in real GDP and periods of recession (indicated by shading). Conversely, periods of sharp acceleration in the growth rate of the money supply, such as 1971–1972 and 1976, have often been followed by a rapid growth in GDP. The monetary authorities have generally increased the growth rate of the money supply during recessions. Note that the growth rate of the money supply has been slower and more stable in the last decade.

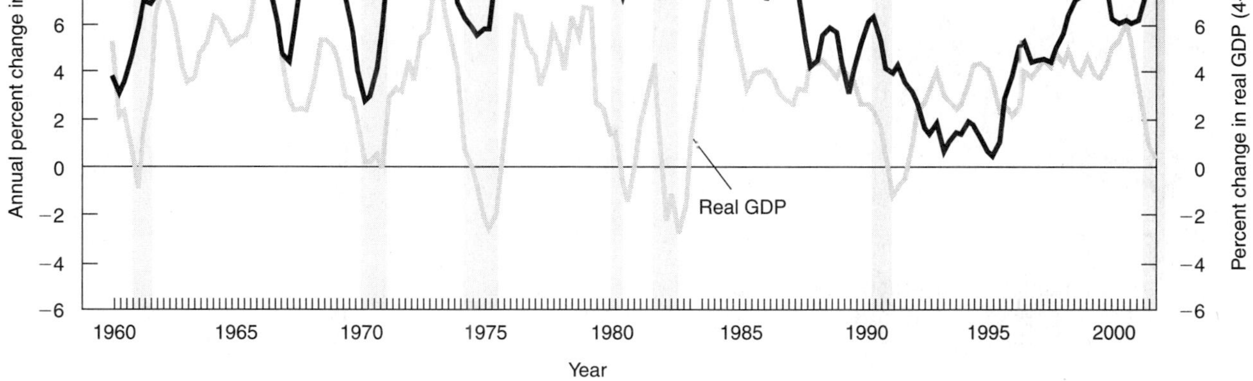

Source: Federal Reserve Bank of St. Louis, http://www.stls.frb.org. Also see *Economic Report of the President* (published annually).

The converse was also true: Periods of sharp deceleration in the growth rate of the money supply were generally associated with (or followed by) economic recession. A decline in the growth rate of the money supply preceded the recessions of 1960, 1970, and 1974–1975. Similarly, a sharp decline in the growth rate of the money stock from 13 percent in 1976–1977 to less than 8 percent in 1978–1979 preceded the back-to-back recessions and sluggish growth of 1979–1982. Prior to the 1990 recession, the growth rate (4-quarter moving average) of the money supply fell from 9.3 percent in 1987 (first quarter) to only 2.6 percent in 1989 (fourth quarter). After increasing at an annual rate of less than 5 percent throughout the 1990s, the money growth rate jumped to more than 8 percent during 1998–1999 before receding to 6 percent at year-end 2000. Between October 1999 and July 2000, the Fed increased its discount rate and target federal funds rate five times. The more restrictive monetary policy of 2000 contributed to the recession of 2001. Just as our theory predicts, there does appear to be a relationship between shifts in monetary policy and changes in real GDP.

Exhibit 17-11 presents a graphic picture of the relationship between monetary policy and the inflation rate for the United States. Although our theory indicates that persistent, long-term growth of the money supply will be closely associated with inflation, it also indicates that time is required for a monetary expansion (or contraction) to alter demand relationships and impact prices. Most economists believe that the time lag between shifts in monetary policy and observable changes in the level of prices is often two or three years. Reflecting these views, Exhibit 17-11 compares the current money supply (M2) data with the

EXHIBIT 17-11 Effect of Changes in Money Supply on Inflation

Here we illustrate the relationship between the rate of growth of the money supply (M2) and the annual inflation rate three years later. While the two are not perfectly correlated, the data do indicate that periods of monetary acceleration (for example: 1971–1972 and 1975–1976) tend to be associated with an increase in the inflation rate about three years later. Similarly, a slower growth rate of the money supply, like that of the 1990s, is generally associated with a reduction in the rate of inflation.

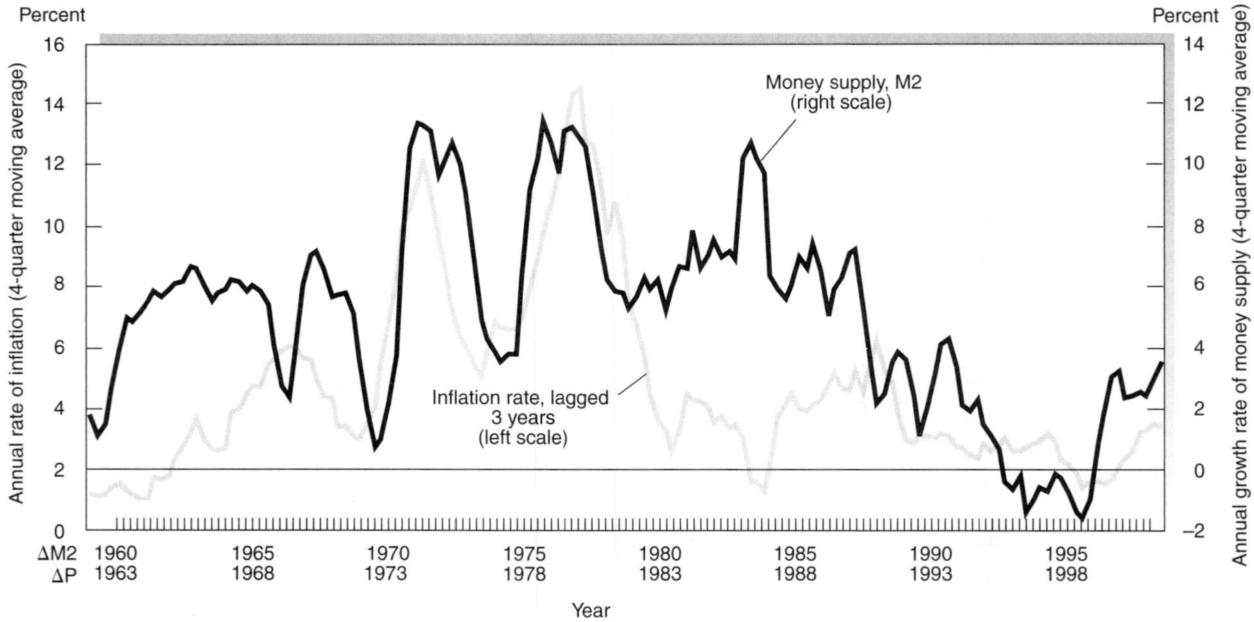

Source: Federal Reserve Bank of St. Louis, http://www.stls.frb.org. Also see *Economic Report of the President* (published annually). The consumer price index was used to measure the rate of inflation.

inflation rate three years in the future. Once again, though the linkage is far from tight, it definitely exists. Most noticeably, the rapid monetary acceleration during 1971–1972 was followed by a similar acceleration in the inflation rate during 1973–1974. Similarly, the sharp monetary contraction of 1973–1974 was accompanied by not only the recession of 1974–1975, but also a substantial reduction in the inflation rate during 1975–1976. However, as monetary policy again shifted toward expansion in 1976–1977, the double-digit inflation rates of 1979–1980 were soon to follow.

During the 1980–1986 period, the linkage between monetary growth and the inflation rate a few years later appeared to weaken. To some degree this may reflect the financial innovations and changing nature of money during this period. There is some evidence that the relationship is once again becoming more predictable now that the transition period to interest-earning checking accounts has been completed. During the 1987–1993 period, the annual growth rate of the money supply (M2) decelerated from more than 8 percent to less than 2 percent. With a lag, the inflation rate followed a similar path. Furthermore, the low rate of money growth during the 1990s—the money growth rate averaged approximately 3 percent during this period—has been associated with low rates of inflation.

Exhibit 17-12 shows the relationship between the inflation rate (change in CPI) and the nominal interest rate. Because our measure of inflation is the rate of change in the price level during the last year, we will compare it with a short-term nominal interest rate—the three-month Treasury bill rate. Our theory implies that nominal interest rates will tend to rise with the rate of inflation. The empirical evidence indicates that is indeed the case. As the inflation rate rose significantly during the late 1960s, so also did the nominal rate of interest. During the 1970s, sharp increases in the inflation rate, particularly during

EXHIBIT 17-12 Inflation Rate and the Money Interest Rate

The expectation of inflation (a) reduces the supply and (b) increases the demand for loanable funds, causing money interest rates to rise (see Exhibit 17-8). Note how the short-term money rate of interest has tended to increase when the inflation rate accelerates (and decline as the inflation rate falls).

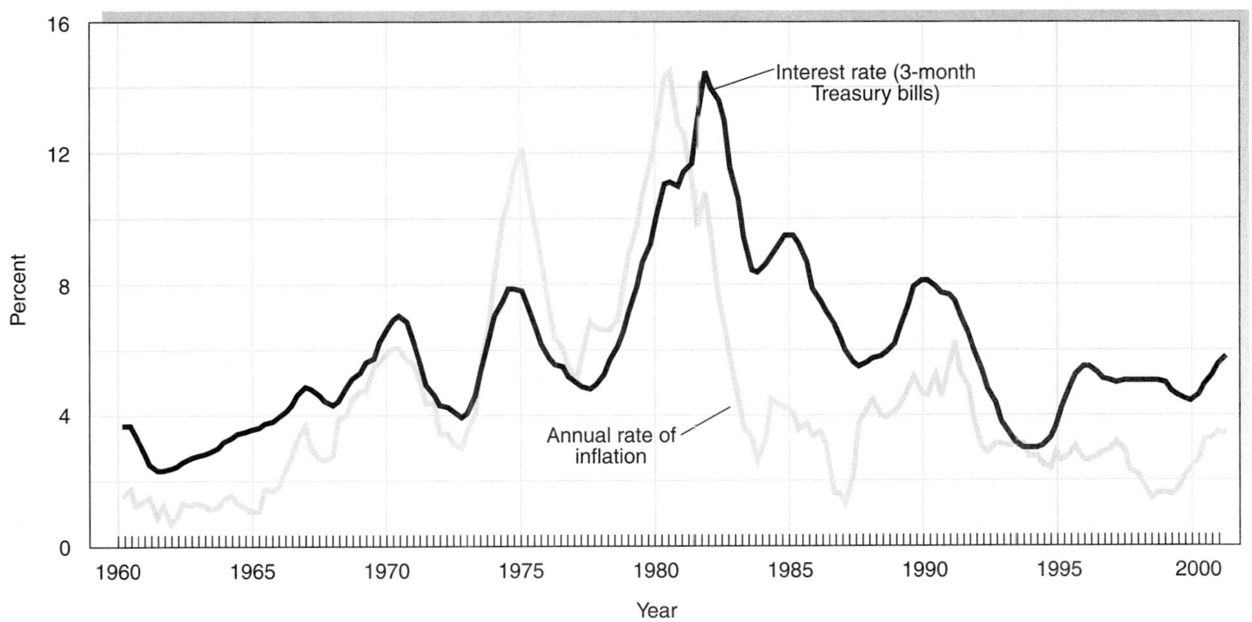

Source: Federal Reserve Bank of St. Louis, http://www.stls.frb.org. Also see *Economic Report of the President* (published annually). The consumer price index was used to measure the rate of inflation.

1977–1980, were accompanied by substantial increases in the nominal interest rate. Similarly, as the inflation rate decelerated from the double-digit levels of the late 1970s, the money interest rate also plunged during 1981–1987. Later, a modest increase in the inflation rate during 1988–1990 resulted in a similar modest increase in short-term interest rates. Finally, as the inflation rate hovered around 3 percent during 1994–2000, the short-term nominal interest rate fluctuated near the 5 percent range. These data provide strong evidence that, just as our theory predicts, the choices of borrowers and lenders are strongly influenced by the inflation rate and expectations concerning its path in the future.

A major implication of our analysis is that rapid growth rates in the money supply over long periods of time will be associated with high rates of inflation. Exhibit 17-13 presents data on the annual growth rate of the money supply (adjusted for the growth rate of the nation's output) and the rate of inflation for

EXHIBIT 17-13 Money and Inflation—An International Comparison, 1980–1999

The relationship between the average annual growth rate of the money supply and the rate of inflation is shown here for the 1980–1999 period. Clearly, there is a close relationship between the two. Higher rates of money growth lead to higher rates of inflation.

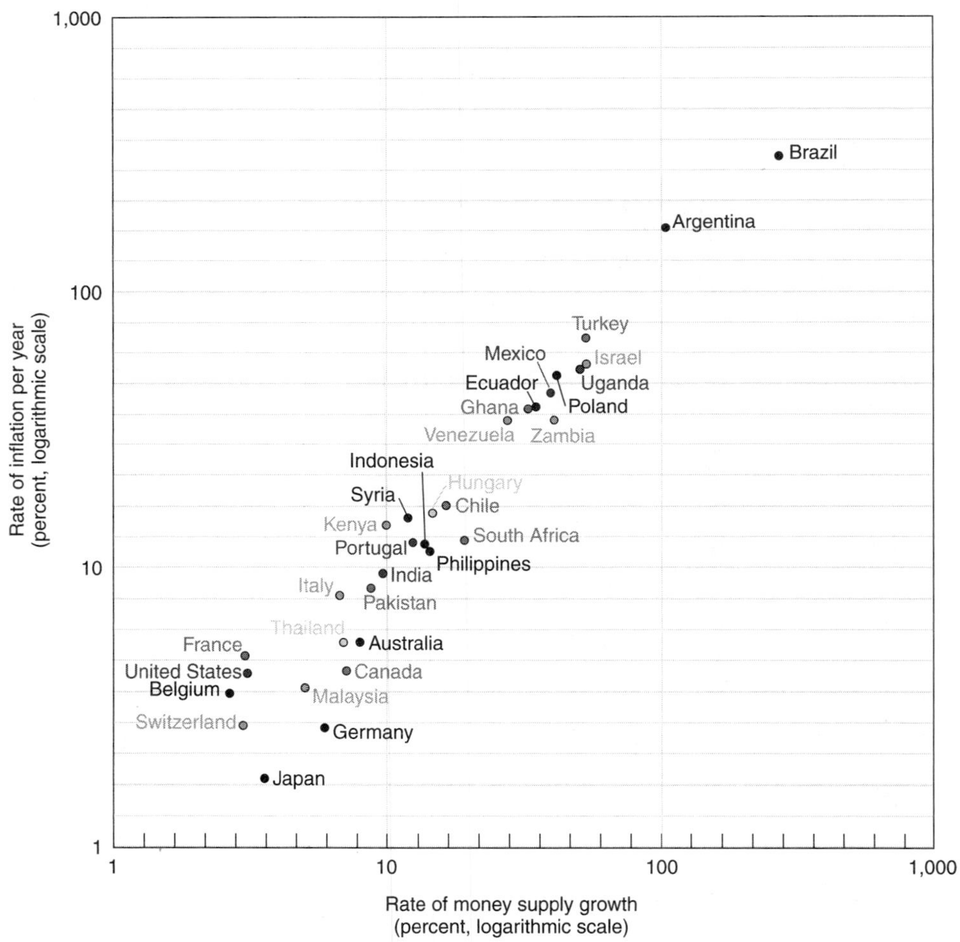

Note: The money supply data are the actual growth rate of the money supply minus the growth rate of real GDP. Data for members of the European Monetary Union are for 1980–1998.

Source: International Monetary Fund, *International Financial Statistics Yearbook;* 1993, 1997, 2001. *Penn World Tables;* and The World Bank, *World Development Indicators,* 2001.

a diverse set of countries during the 1980–1999 period. The results clearly illustrate the linkage between monetary policy and inflation. Countries with single-digit rates of money growth—for example, Belgium, Japan, Malaysia, Switzerland, and the United States—experienced single-digit rates of inflation. Similarly, countries with rates of money growth in the 10 percent to 20 percent range experienced rates of inflation in this same range. The data for the Philippines, South Africa, Kenya, Hungary, and Chile illustrate this point. Countries like Mexico, Ghana, and Poland with money growth rates in the 30 percent to 50 percent range had inflation rates within this same range. Finally, look at the data for Argentina and Brazil. The average annual rate of money growth of these two countries exceeded 100 percent during this period. So too did their average inflation rate. Most of the money growth of Argentina and Brazil occurred during the 1980s. Predictably, the substantially lower rates of money growth during the 1990s resulted in substantially lower rates of inflation.

When considered over a lengthy time period, the linkage between money growth and inflation is one of the most consistent relationships in all of economics. Inflation is a monetary phenomenon. Persistently low rates of money growth lead to low rates of inflation. Similarly, high rates of money growth lead to high rates of inflation.

8 SUMMARY

- The quantity of money people want to hold is inversely related to the money rate of interest, because higher interest rates make it more costly to hold money instead of interest-earning assets like bonds. The supply of money is vertical because it is determined by the Fed. The money interest rate will gravitate toward the rate where the quantity of money people want to hold is just equal to the stock of money the Fed has supplied.
- The impact of a shift in monetary policy is generally transmitted through interest rates, exchange rates, and asset prices.
- When instituting a more expansionary monetary policy, the Fed generally buys bonds, which will both increase bond prices and create additional bank reserves, placing downward pressure on real interest rates. In the short run, an *unanticipated* shift to a more expansionary policy will stimulate aggregate demand and thereby increase output and employment.
- When instituting a more restrictive monetary policy, the Fed sells bonds, which will depress bond prices and drain reserves from the banking system. An unanticipated shift to a more restrictive monetary policy will increase real interest rates and reduce aggregate demand, output, and employment in the short run.
- The quantity theory of money postulates that the velocity of money is constant (or approximately so) and that real output is independent of monetary factors. When these assumptions hold, an increase in the stock of money will lead to a proportional increase in the price level.
- In the long run, the primary impact of monetary policy will be on prices rather than on real output. When expansionary monetary policy leads to rising prices, decision makers eventually anticipate the higher inflation rate and build it into their choices. As this happens, money interest rates, wages, and incomes will reflect the expectation of inflation, so real interest rates, wages, and output will return to their long-run normal levels.
- When the effects of expansionary monetary policy are anticipated prior to their occurrence, the short-run impact of an increase in the money supply is similar to its impact in the long run. Nominal prices and interest rates rise, but real output remains unchanged.
- While the Fed can strongly influence short-term interest rates, its impact on long-term rates is much more limited. Interest rates can be a misleading indicator of monetary policy. In the long run, expansionary monetary policy leads to inflation and high interest rates, rather than low interest rates. Similarly, restrictive monetary policy when pursued over a lengthy time period leads to low inflation and low interest rates.
- The empirical evidence indicates that changes in monetary policy influence real GDP in the short run.
- Both the U.S. experience and international comparisons strongly indicate that persistent, rapid growth in the money supply is closely linked with inflation. Countries with low (high) rates of growth in the money supply tend to experience low (high) rates of inflation.

STABILIZATION POLICY, OUTPUT, AND EMPLOYMENT

READING 18

LEARNING OUTCOMES

The candidate should be able to:

a. describe the composition and use of the index of leading economic indicators;

b. discuss the time lags that may influence the performance of discretionary monetary and fiscal policy;

c. contrast the adaptive expectations hypothesis to the rational expectations hypothesis, and discuss implications on prices and output under the two hypotheses when there are changes in macroeconomic policies;

d. distinguish between an activist and a nonactivist strategy for stabilization policy.

Unfortunately, policymakers cannot act as if the economy is an automobile that can quickly be steered back and forth. Rather, the procedure of changing aggregate demand is much closer to that of a captain navigating a giant supertanker. Even if he gives a signal for a hard turn, it takes a mile before he can see a change, and ten miles before the ship makes the turn.

—Robert J. Gordon[1]

INTRODUCTION 1

In previous readings we have analyzed the impact of both fiscal and monetary policy on output, employment, and prices. We have also noted that the initial impact of policy changes often differs from the impact over a more lengthy time period. We now want to consider the potential of macro policy as a stabilization tool. Can active management of fiscal and/or monetary policy reduce economic instability? What types of fiscal and monetary policy are best for the economy? This reading will focus on the tools that enhance and the factors that limit the achievement of a stable economic environment. We will also consider alternative theories about how expectations are formed and investigate their implications with regard to how macroeconomic policy works. We will begin by taking a look at the magnitude of economic fluctuations during this century.

---

[1] Robert J. Gordon, *Macroeconomics* (Boston: Little, Brown, 1978), p. 334.

2 ECONOMIC FLUCTUATIONS—THE HISTORICAL RECORD

OPTIONAL SEGMENT

Wide fluctuations in the general level of business activity—in income, employment, and the price level—make personal economic planning extremely difficult. Such changes can cause even well-devised investment plans to go awry. The tragic stories of unemployed workers begging for food and newly impoverished investors jumping out of windows during the Great Depression vividly portray the enormous personal and social costs of economic instability and the uncertainty that it generates.

Historically, substantial fluctuations in real output have occurred. Exhibit 18-1 illustrates the growth record of real GDP in the United States during the past 90 years. Prior to the Second World War, double-digit swings in real GDP during a single year were not uncommon. Real GDP rose by more than 10 percent annually during the First World War, during an economic boom in 1922, during a

EXHIBIT 18-1 Post-Second World War Decline in Economic Instability

Prior to the conclusion of the Second World War, the United States experienced double-digit increases in real GDP in 1918, 1922, 1935–1936, and 1941–1943. In contrast, real output fell by 5 percent or more in 1920–1921, 1930–1932, 1938, and 1946. As illustrated here, fluctuations in real GDP have moderated during the last five decades. Most economists believe that more appropriate macro policy—particularly monetary policy—deserves much of the credit (see Exhibit 18-2).

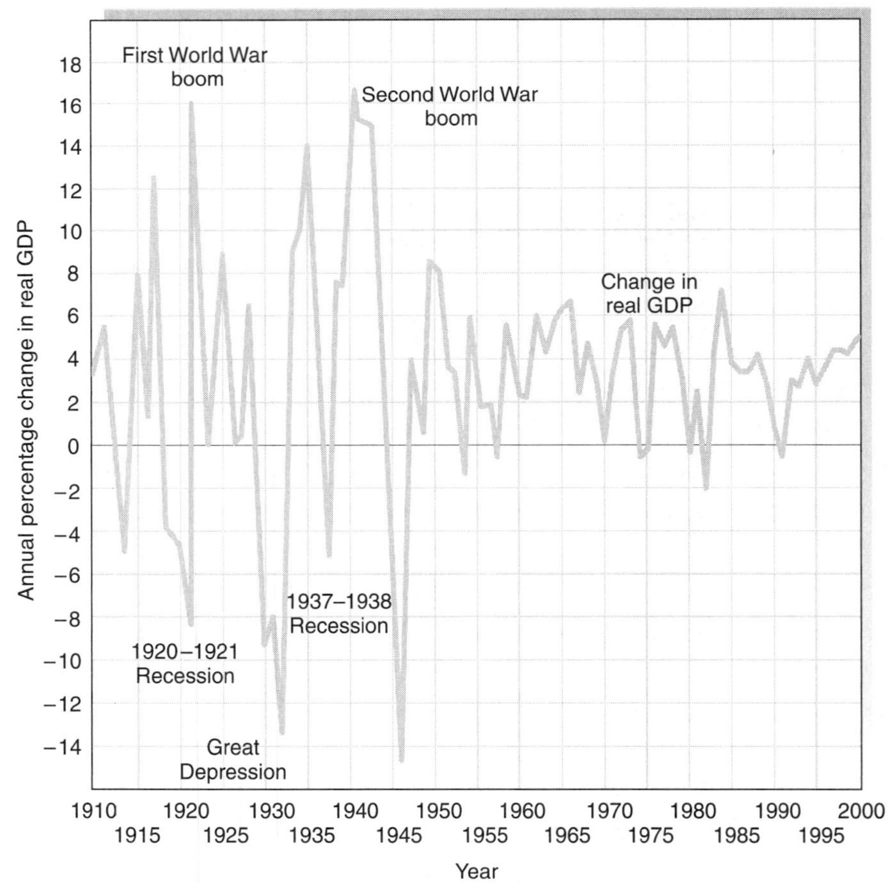

Sources: Historical Statistics of the United States, p. 224; and Bureau of Economic Analysis, www.bea.doc.gov

mid-1930s recovery, and again during the Second World War. In contrast, output fell at an annual rate of 5 percent or more during the 1920–1921 recession, in the depression years of 1930–1932 and 1938, and again following the Second World War. Since 1950, economic ups and downs have been more moderate. Nevertheless, substantial fluctuations are still observable.

OPTIONAL ENDS SEGMENT

PROMOTING ECONOMIC STABILITY—ACTIVIST AND NONACTIVIST VIEWS

3

There is widespread agreement concerning the goals of macroeconomic policy. Economists of almost all persuasions believe that the performance of a market economy would be improved if economic fluctuations were minimal, the general level of prices stable, and employment maintained at a high level (unemployment at the natural rate).

How to achieve these goals is, however, a hot topic of debate among macroeconomists. Many economists argue that the major macroeconomic goals can best be achieved through the active use of discretionary monetary and fiscal policy. The proponents of an **activist strategy** believe that macro policy can be used successfully to speed the adjustment process and reduce the swings of the business cycle. Activists often argue that the economy's self-corrective mechanism works slowly. Therefore, when economic shocks disrupt equilibrium, activists believe that policymakers will be able to manage demand in a manner that will keep the economy on track and minimize the adverse consequences of disruptions.

Activist strategy
Deliberate changes in monetary and fiscal policy in order to inject demand stimulus during a recession and apply restraint during an inflationary boom and thereby, it is hoped, minimize economic instability.

In contrast, advocates for a **nonactivist strategy** argue that discretionary use of monetary and fiscal policy in response to changing economic conditions is likely to do more harm than good. According to the nonactivist view, the economy's self-corrective mechanism, if not stifled by perverse macro policy, will prevent prolonged periods of economic decline and high unemployment. Nonactivists charge that erratic policy, particularly the instability of monetary policy, is a major source of economic fluctuations. They note that the really serious cases of economic instability, such as the Great Depression of the 1930s and the inflation of the 1970s, were primarily the result of policy errors. Rather than altering macro policy in a discretionary manner, nonactivists believe that economic stability can best be achieved by following rules and guidelines that will provide for stable monetary and fiscal policy.

Nonactivist strategy
The maintenance of a steady monetary and fiscal policy during all phases of the business cycle. According to this view, adjusting macro policy in response to current cyclical conditions is likely to increase, rather than reduce, instability.

There are points of agreement between activists and nonactivists. Both recognize that policy errors have contributed to economic instability. Prior to the Keynesian revolution, governments often raised taxes to balance the budget when revenue declined during a recession. Of course, modern analysis implies that such a policy may add to the severity of a recession. Both activists and nonactivists recognize the potential dangers of monetary instability. As Exhibit 18-2 illustrates, extreme gyrations in the money supply characterized monetary policy prior to the Second World War. Sharp contractions in the money supply often accompanied major recessions, while double-digit money growth was observed during the inflationary periods of the First and Second World Wars. Activists and nonactivists agree that erratic policy changes, particularly those in the monetary area, have contributed to economic instability. (See Applications in Economics, "Perverse Macroeconomic Policy and the Great Depression," on page 110 for evidence on the tragic role of policy during the 1930s.)

As Exhibit 18-2 shows, swings in monetary policy have moderated considerably since the end of the Second World War. So too have business cycle fluctuations. Activists and nonactivists agree that the link between the more stable monetary policy and moderation of the business cycle is no coincidence. We now turn to an analysis of how macroeconomic policy might be actively used to smooth the

EXHIBIT 18-2 Post-Second World War Decline in Monetary Instability

Prior to 1950, monetary policy was characterized by wide swings. Huge increases (15 percent or more) in the supply of money (M2) were often followed by sharp monetary contractions. Since the end of the Second World War, the fluctuations in the supply of money have declined, as the monetary authorities followed a more stable course. As the prior exhibit illustrates, the more stable monetary policy has been associated with a more stable economy.

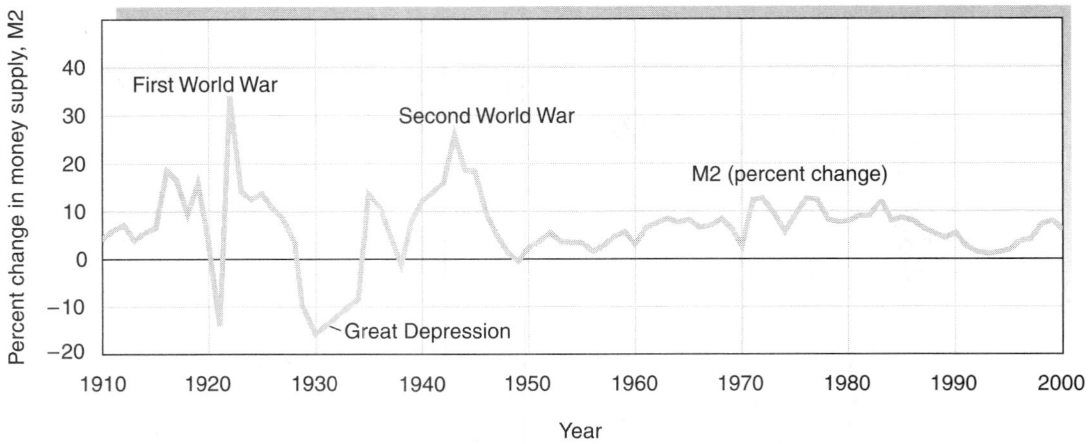

Sources: Federal Reserve, www.federalreserve.gov; and Robert J. Gordon, *Macroeconomics* (Glenview, Ill: Scott Foresman, 1990).

ups and downs of the business cycle. As we proceed, we will consider some of the limitations of this strategy. Later, we will also present the nonactivist view of macroeconomic policy.

4

THE CONDUCT OF DISCRETIONARY STABILIZATION POLICY

Macroeconomic policy reduces instability only if it injects stimulus and applies restraint at the proper phase of the business cycle. Proper timing is the key to effective stabilization policy. But how can policymakers know whether they should be stimulating aggregate demand or applying the economic brake?

Of course, economic indicators, such as the growth of real GDP and the rate of unemployment, provide policymakers with information on the current state of the economy. However, this is not exactly what policymakers need. Because it takes time for macroeconomic policy to work, policymakers really need to know about the future—where the economy is going to be six to twelve months from now. They need to know whether a business recession or an inflationary boom is around the corner. If they do not know where the economy is going, a policy change may fail to exert its primary impact quickly enough to offset a downturn or restrain future inflation.

How can policymakers find out where the economy is going in the future and when a turn in the macroeconomic road is about to occur? The two most widely used sources of information on the future direction of the economy are the index of leading economic indicators and economic forecasting models.

Index of leading indicators An index of economic variables that historically has tended to turn down prior to the beginning of a recession and turn up prior to the beginning of a business expansion.

Index of Leading Indicators

The **index of leading indicators** is a composite statistic based on 10 key variables that generally turn down prior to a recession and turn up before the beginning of a business expansion (see Measures of Economic Activity, "Index of Leading

Indicators" on page 114). Exhibit 18-3 illustrates the path of the index during the 1959–2000 period. Three consecutive monthly declines in the index are considered a warning that the economy is about to dip into a recession. This index has forecast each of the seven recessions since 1959. On four occasions, the downturn occurred eight to eleven months prior to a recession, providing policymakers with sufficient lead time to modify policy, particularly monetary policy. In other instances it has been quite lengthy, as when it turned down 18 months prior to the 1990–1991 recession.

A downturn in the index is not always an accurate indicator of the future. On five occasions (1962, 1966, 1984, 1987, and 1995), a decline in the index of leading indicators forecast a future recession that did not materialize. This has given rise to the quip that the index has accurately forecast twelve of the last seven recessions.

Forecasting Models

Economists have developed highly complex econometric (statistical) models to improve the accuracy of macroeconomic forecasts. In essence, these models use past data on economic interrelationships to project how currently observed changes will influence the future path of key economic variables, such as real GDP, employment, and the price level. The most elaborate of these models use hundreds of variables and equations to simulate the various sectors and macroeconomic markets. Powerful, high-speed computers are employed to analyze the effects of various policy alternatives and attempt to predict the future.

EXHIBIT 18-3 Index of Leading Indicators

The shaded periods represent recessions. The index of leading indicators forecast each of the seven recessions during the 1959–2001 period. As the arrows show, however, the time lag between when the index turned down and when the economy fell into a recession varied. In addition, on five occasions (1962, 1966, 1984, 1987, and 1995), the index forecast a recession that did not occur.

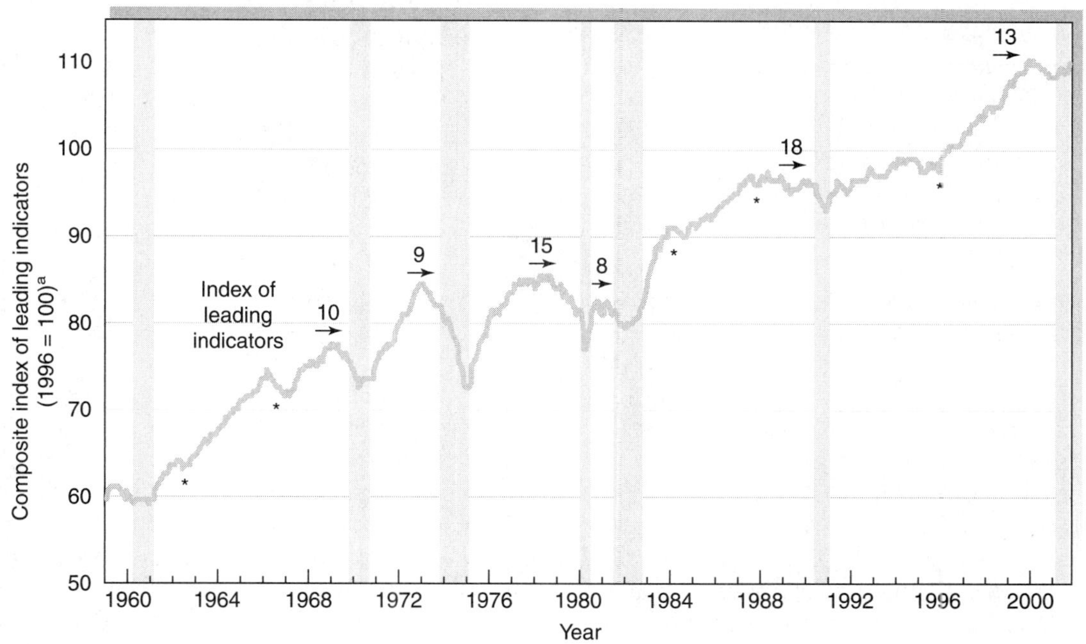

[a] The arrows indicate the number of months that the downturn in the index preceded a recession. An asterisk (*) indicates a false signal of a recession.

Source: Conference Board, www.globalindicators.org

APPLICATIONS IN ECONOMICS

Perverse Macroeconomic Policy and the Great Depression

As we previously discussed, the Great Depression exerted an enormous impact both on economic thought and on economic institutions. Table 18-1 presents data that illustrate both the severity and length of the economic contraction. For four successive years (1930–1933), real output fell. Unemployment soared to nearly one-quarter of the workforce in 1932 and 1933. Although recovery did take place during 1934–1937, the economy again fell into the depth of depression in 1938. Ten years after the catastrophe began, real GDP was virtually the same as it had been in 1929.[1]

Armed with knowledge of how monetary and fiscal policies work, one can clearly see that at least the severity of the calamity was the result of perverse macroeconomic policy. Three important factors contributed to the economic collapse of the 1930s.

Perhaps the most catastrophic example of inappropriate stabilization policy was that of the Great Depression. A sharp reduction in the supply of money, a huge tax increase, and protectionist trade policies turned a recession into the worst depression in U.S. history.

1. ***A sharp reduction in the supply of money during 1930–1933 reduced aggregate demand and real output.*** The supply of money expanded slowly but steadily throughout the 1920s.[2] As Table 18-1 shows, monetary policy suddenly shifted in 1930. The money supply fell by 6.9 percent during 1930, by 10.9 percent in 1931, and by 4.7 percent in 1932. As banks failed and the money supply collapsed, the Fed failed to inject new reserves into the system. Neither did it act as a lender of last resort. The quantity of money in 1933 was 27 percent less than in 1929! A sudden shift to a restrictive monetary policy will reduce both aggregate demand and real output. Our analysis indicates that a drastic reduction in the money supply, such as that of the early 1930s, will almost surely result in a drastic reduction in output. This is precisely what happened. Real output plunged. By 1933, real GDP was 29 percent lower than the 1929 level.
2. ***A large tax increase in the midst of a severe recession made a bad situation worse.*** Prior to the Keynesian revolution, the dominant view was that the federal budget should be balanced. Reflecting the ongoing economic downturn, the federal budget ran a deficit in 1931, and an even larger deficit was shaping up for 1932. Assisted by the newly elected Democratic majority in the House of Representatives, the Republican Hoover administration passed the largest peacetime tax rate increase in the history of the United States. At the bottom of the income scale, marginal tax rates were raised from 1.5 percent to 4 percent in 1932. At the top of the scale, tax rates were raised from 25 percent to 63 percent. As our prior analysis of fiscal policy suggests, a huge tax increase in the midst of a severe recession will further reduce aggregate demand and the incentive to earn. Table 18-1 shows the degree to which this happened. As tax rates were increased in 1932, real GDP fell by 13.3 percent. Unemployment rose from 15.9 percent in 1931 to 23.6 percent in 1932.
3. ***Tariff increases retarded international exchange.*** Concerned about low agricultural prices, an influx of imports, rising unemployment, and declining tax revenues, Congress adopted various trade restraints. Tariffs (taxes on imported goods) on a wide range of products were increased substantially in early 1930.[3] Other countries promptly responded by increasing their tariffs, further reducing the volume of trade between nations. As the flow of trade diminished, so too did the mutual gains trading partners derive from specialization and exchange.

When discussing the Great Depression, historians often stress the role of the 1929 stock market crash. Since the stock market crash diminished the wealth of many, it was a contributing factor to the reduction in aggregate demand and output. However, the severity of the Great Depression was the result of disastrous macroeconomic policy, not an inevitable consequence of a stock market crash. The experience following the October 1987 crash illustrates this point. In just a few days, the stock market lost a third of its value

Table 18-1 The Economic Record of the Great Depression

Year	Real GDP in 1989 Dollars (billions)	Implicit GDP Deflator (1929 = 100)	Unemployment Rate	Percent Change in the Money Supply (M1)
1929	821.8	100.0	3.2	+1.0
1930	748.9	96.8	8.7	−6.9
1931	691.3	88.0	15.9	−10.9
1932	599.7	77.6	23.6	−4.7
1933	587.1	76.0	24.9	−2.9
1934	632.6	82.4	21.7	+10.0
1935	681.3	84.8	20.1	+18.2
1936	777.9	84.8	16.9	+13.9
1937	811.4	89.6	14.3	+4.7
1938	778.9	87.2	19.0	−1.3
1939	840.7	86.4	17.2	+12.1

Source: Economic Report of the President: 1993 (Washington, D.C.: U.S. Government Printing Office, 1993); and Bureau of the Census, *The Statistical History of the United States from Colonial Times to the Present* (New York, Basic Books, 1976).

in 1987, just as it did in 1929. But that is where the parallel ends. In contrast with the response to the 1929 crash, in 1987 the Fed moved quickly to supply reserves to the banking system. The money supply did not fall. Tax rates were not increased. And even though there was a lot of political rhetoric about "the need to protect American businesses," trade barriers were not raised. In short, sensible policies were followed subsequent to the crash of 1987. Continued growth and stability were the result. Inadvertently, perverse macroeconomic policies were followed subsequent to the crash of 1929. Economic disaster was the result.

[1] See Robert J. Samuelson, "Great Depression," in *The Fortune Encyclopedia of Economics*, ed. David R. Henderson (New York: Warner Books, 1993), for an interesting and informative commentary on this time period.

[2] From 1921 through 1929, the money stock expanded at an annual rate of 2.7 percent, slightly less rapidly than the growth in the output of goods and services. Thus, the 1920s were a decade of price stability, even of slight deflation.

[3] The high-tariff policy was ineffective as a revenue measure. Even though the taxes on imported goods were increased by approximately 50 percent, imports declined so sharply that tariff revenues fell from $602 million in 1929 to $328 million in 1932.

To date, the record of computer forecasting models is mixed. When economic conditions are relatively stable (for example, when the growth of real GDP and the rate of inflation follow a steady trend), the models have generally provided accurate forecasts for both aggregate economic variables and important subcomponents of the economy. Unfortunately, however, they have generally missed the major turns in the economic road. For example, none of the major computer models forecast the recessions of 1990 and 2001.

Many economists maintain that accurate forecasts are beyond the reach of economics. Two major factors underlie this view. First, business cycle conditions often reflect economic shocks and unforeseen events—for example, an unexpected policy change, discovery of a new resource or technology, abnormal weather, or political upheaval in an important oil-exporting nation. There is no reason to believe that economists or anyone else will be able to predict such changes accurately and consistently. Thus, while economic theory helps to predict the implications of unforeseen events, it cannot foretell what those events

MEASURES OF ECONOMIC ACTIVITY

Index of Leading Indicators

History indicates that no single indicator is able to forecast accurately the future direction of the economy. However, several economic variables do tend to reach a high or low prior to the peak of a business expansion or the trough of an economic recession. Such variables are called leading economic indicators.

To provide more reliable information on the future direction of the economy, economists have devised an index of 10 such indicators:

1. Length of the average workweek in hours
2. Initial weekly claims for unemployment compensation
3. New orders placed with manufacturers
4. Percentage of companies receiving slower deliveries from suppliers
5. Contracts and orders for new plants and equipment
6. Permits for new housing starts
7. Interest rate spread, 10-year Treasury bonds less fed funds rate
8. Index of consumer expectations
9. Change in the index of stock prices (500 common stocks)
10. Change in the money supply (M2)

The variables included in the index were chosen both because of their tendency to lead (or predict) turns in the business cycle and because they are available frequently and promptly. In some cases, it is easy to see why a change in an economic indicator precedes a change in general economic activity. Consider the indicator of "new orders placed with manufacturers" (measured in constant dollars). An expansion in the volume of orders is generally followed by an expansion in manufacturing output. Similarly, manufacturers will tend to scale back their future production when a decline in new orders signals the probability of weak future demand for their products. The index of leading indicators is published by the Conference Board in *Business Cycle Indicators*.

will be and when they might occur. Second, the critics of forecasting models argue that the future will differ from the past because people will often make different choices as the result of what they learned from previous events. Therefore, forecasting models based on past relationships—including elaborate computer models—will never be able to generate consistently accurate predictions.

Market Signals and Discretionary Monetary Policy

Some economists believe that information supplied by certain markets can also provide policymakers with an early warning of the need to institute a change in policy. For example, since they fluctuate daily and are determined in auction markets, changes in commodity prices often foretell future changes in the general price level. An increase in a broad index of commodity prices implies that money is plentiful (relative to demand). This suggests the Fed should shift toward a more restrictive policy in order to offset future inflation. In contrast, falling commodity prices indicate that deflation is a potential future danger, in which case the Fed might want to shift toward a more expansionary policy.

Exchange rates also provide policymakers with information about the relative scarcity of money and fear of inflation. Because exchange rates, to a degree, reflect the willingness of foreigners to hold U.S. dollars, a decline in the exchange rate value of the dollar (the value of the dollar relative to other currencies) often implies a fear of higher inflation and a reluctance to hold dollars. This would signal the need to shift to a more restrictive policy. Conversely, an increase in the exchange rate value of the dollar is a strong vote of confidence in the future purchasing power of the dollar. This provides the Fed with some leeway to move toward a more expansionary policy.

Commodity prices, exchange rates, and other market signals can help us judge the early effects and likely future impact of current policies. They are best used as a supplement to, rather than as a substitute for, other economic indicators and forecasting devices.

Discretionary Policy—The Activist View

Activists recognize that it is difficult to institute countercyclical macroeconomic policy. However, they believe that the index of leading indicators, forecasting models, sensitive market variables, and other economic indicators provide policymakers with an early warning system. Thus, they are able to alter policy in a manner that will smooth business ups and downs. Responding to the early signals, policy makers can initially undertake moderate changes. With the passage of time, more substantial changes can be instituted if more comprehensive information indicates they are needed.

The following scenario outlines the essentials of the activist view. Suppose the economy were about to dip into a recession. Prior to the recession, the index of leading indicators would almost surely alert policymakers to the possibility of a downturn. This would permit them to shift toward macroeconomic stimulus, expanding the money supply more rapidly. Initially, the shift toward macroeconomic stimulus could be applied in moderate doses, which could easily be reversed in the future if necessary. On the other hand, if the signs of a downturn became more pronounced and current business conditions actually weakened, additional stimulus could be injected. Perhaps a tax reduction or a speedup in government expenditures might be used to supplement the more expansionary monetary policy.

Policymakers can constantly monitor the situation, adjusting their actions as additional information becomes available. If the weakness persists, the expansionary policy can be continued. Conversely, when the signs point to a strong recovery, policymakers can move toward restraint and thereby head off potential inflationary pressure. According to the activist view, policymakers are more likely to keep the economy on track when they are free to apply stimulus or restraint based on forecasting devices and current economic indicators.

Lags and the Problem of Timing

Discretionary changes in both monetary and fiscal policy must be timed appropriately if they are going to exert a stabilizing influence on the economy. There are three time lags that make proper timing difficult. First, there is the **recognition lag**, the time period between a change in economic conditions and recognition of the change by policymakers. It generally takes a few months to gather and tabulate reliable information on the recent performance of the economy in order to determine whether it has dipped into a recession or whether the inflation rate has accelerated, and so forth.

Recognition lag
The time period after a policy change is needed from a stabilization standpoint but before the need is recognized by policymakers.

Second, even after the need for a policy change is recognized, there is generally an additional time period before the policy change is instituted. Economists refer to this delay as administrative lag. In the case of monetary policy, the **administrative lag** is generally quite short. The Federal Open Market Committee meets every few weeks and is in a position to institute a change in monetary policy quickly. This is a major advantage of monetary policy. For discretionary fiscal policy, the administrative lag is likely to be much longer. Congressional committees must meet. Legislation must be proposed and debated. Congress must act, and the president must consent. Each of these steps takes time.

Administrative lag
The time period after the need for a policy change is recognized but before the policy is actually implemented.

Finally, there is the **impact lag**, the time period between the implementation of a macro policy change and when the change exerts its primary impact on the

Impact lag
The time period after a policy change is implemented but before the change begins to exert its primary effects.

economy. Although the impact of a change in tax rates is generally felt quickly, the expansionary effects of an increase in government expenditures are usually much less rapid. It will take time for the submission of competitive bids and the letting of new contracts. Several months may pass before work on a new project actually begins. The impact lag in the case of monetary policy is likely to be even longer. The time period between a shift in monetary policy, a change in interest rates, and, in turn, a change in the level of spending may be quite lengthy.

Economists who have studied this topic, including Milton Friedman and Robert Gordon, conclude that the combined duration of these time lags is generally 12 to 18 months in the case of monetary policy, and even longer in the case of fiscal policy. This means that, if a policy is going to exert the desired effect at the proper time, policymakers cannot wait until a problem develops before they act. Rather, they must correctly forecast the future direction of the economy and act before there is a contraction in real GDP or an observable increase in the rate of inflation. Given our ability to forecast the future, nonactivists argue that proper timing of discretionary policy changes is unrealistic. Furthermore, even if forecasting were a more precise science, the time lags accompanying changes in monetary and fiscal policies are long and variable. This also reduces the viability of discretionary policy as a stabilization tool.

Exhibit 18-4 presents a graphic illustration of the difference between the views of the activists and nonactivists. When the economy begins to dip into a recession, activists argue that policymakers can reasonably be expected to recognize the danger and shift to a more expansionary policy at point *B*. If the demand-stimulus effects are felt quickly (before the economy gets to point *C*), the shift to the more expansionary macro policy will help to minimize the decline in output accompanying the business downturn.

EXHIBIT 18-4 Time Lags and Effects of Discretionary Policy

Beginning with *A*, we illustrate the path of a hypothetical business cycle. If a forthcoming recession can be recognized quickly and a more expansionary policy instituted at point *B*, the policy may add stimulus at point *C* and help to minimize the magnitude of the downturn. Activists believe that discretionary policy is likely to achieve this outcome. However, if delays result in the adoption of the expansionary policy at *C* and if it does not exert its major impact until *D*, the demand stimulus will exacerbate the inflationary boom. In turn, an anti-inflationary strategy instituted at *E* may exert its primary effects at *F*, just in time to increase the severity of a recession beyond *F*. Nonactivists fear that improper timing of discretionary macro policy will exert such destabilizing effects.

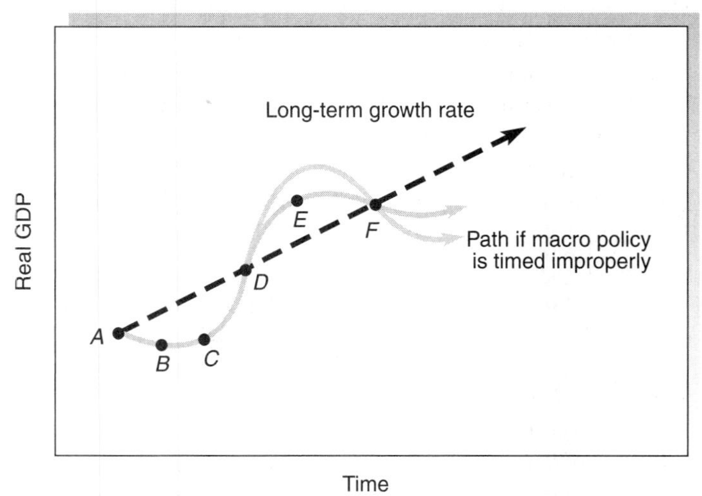

In contrast, nonactivists believe that policymakers are unlikely to act so quickly, and, even if they did, the time lags accompanying changes in monetary and fiscal policies are likely to make their actions ineffective. The shift to the more expansionary policy will not come until point *C*, according to this reasoning, and its effects will not be significant until point *D*. In this case, the expansionary policy will contribute to the severity of the inflationary boom (beyond point *D*). Similarly, a subsequent shift to an anti-inflationary policy may begin to exert its major impact at point *F*, just in time to make an oncoming recession worse (beyond point *F*). Therefore, nonactivists believe that discretionary policy shifts are likely to be destabilizing rather than stabilizing.

HOW ARE EXPECTATIONS FORMED? 5

Throughout this text, we have carefully differentiated between anticipated and unanticipated changes. A change may exert a very different impact, depending on whether it is widely expected or catches people by surprise. Given the importance of expectations, we need to analyze how they are formed. There are two general theories in this area. Let us outline the essentials of each.

Adaptive Expectations

The simplest theory concerning the formation of expectations is that people rely on the past to predict future trends. According to this theory, which economists call the **adaptive-expectations hypothesis**, decision makers believe that the best indicator of the future is what has happened in the recent past. For example, individuals would expect the price level to be stable next year if stable prices had been present during the past two or three years. Similarly, if prices had risen at an annual rate of 4 or 5 percent during the past several years, people would expect similar increases next year.

Adaptive-expectations hypothesis
The hypothesis that economic decision makers base their future expectations on actual outcomes observed during recent periods. For example, according to this view, the rate of inflation actually experienced during the past two or three years would be the major determinant of the rate of inflation expected for the next year.

Exhibit 18-5 presents a graphic illustration of the adaptive-expectations hypothesis. In period 1, prices were stable (part a). Therefore, on the basis of the experience of period 1, decision makers assume that prices will be stable in period 2 (part b). However, the actual rate of inflation in period 2 jumps to 4 percent. Continuation of the 4 percent inflation rate throughout period 2 (the periods may range from six months to two or three years in length) causes decision makers to change their expectations. Relying on the experience of period 2, they anticipate 4 percent inflation in period 3. When their expectations turn out to be incorrect (the actual rate of inflation during period 3 is 8 percent), they again alter their expectations accordingly. Then, during period 4, the actual rate of inflation declines to 4 percent, less than the expected rate. Again, decision makers adjust their expectations as to the rate of inflation in period 5.

Of course, one would not expect the precise mechanical link between past occurrences and future expectations outlined in Exhibit 18-5. Rather than simply using the inflation rate of the immediate past period, people may use a weighted average of recent inflation rates when forming their expectations. It is the structure, however, that is important. With adaptive expectations, decision makers will always expect the next period to be pretty much like the recent past.

Rational-expectations hypothesis
The hypothesis that economic decision makers weigh all available evidence, including information concerning the probable effects of current and future economic policy, when they form their expectations about future economic events (such as the probable future inflation rate).

Rational Expectations

The idea that people form their expectations about the future on the basis of all available information, including knowledge about policy changes and how they affect the economy, is called the **rational-expectations hypothesis**. According to this view, rather than merely assuming the future will be pretty much like the

EXHIBIT 18-5 Adaptive-Expectations Hypothesis

According to the adaptive-expectations hypothesis, the actual occurrence during the most recent period (or set of periods) determines people's future expectations. Thus, the expected future rate of inflation (b) lags behind the actual rate of inflation (a) by one period as expectations are altered over time.

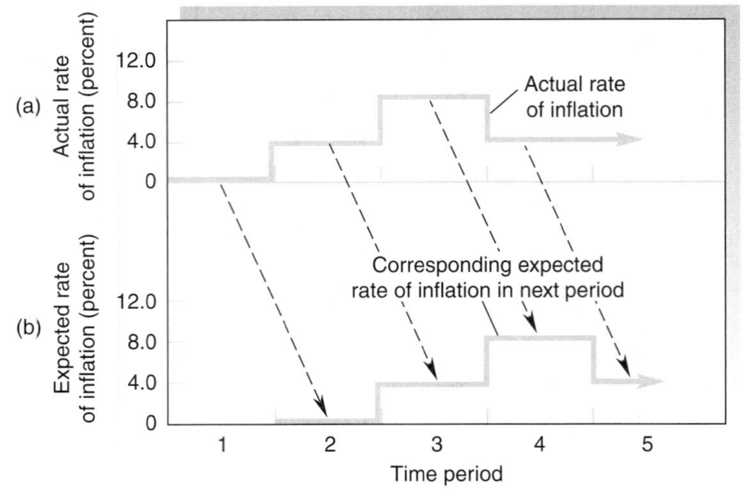

immediate past, people also consider the expected effects of changes in policy. Based on their understanding of economic policy, people alter their expectations with regard to the future when the government, for example, runs a larger deficit or expands the supply of money more rapidly.

Perhaps an example will help clarify the rational-expectations hypothesis. Suppose prices had increased at an annual rate of 3 percent during each of the past three years. In addition, assume that decision makers believe there is a relationship between the growth rate of the money supply and rising prices. They note that the money stock has expanded at a 12 percent annual rate during the last nine months, up from the 4 percent rate of the past several years. According to the rational-expectations hypothesis, they will integrate the recent monetary acceleration into their forecast of the future inflation rate. Thus, they may project an increase in the inflation rate, perhaps to the 6 to 10 percent range. In other words, they will expect the future inflation rate to respond to the more rapid growth of the money supply. In contrast, the adaptive-expectations hypothesis implies that people would expect the inflation rate for the next period to be the same as that for the last period (or the last several periods).

The rational-expectations hypothesis does not assume that forecasts will always be correct. We live in a world of uncertainty. Even rational decision mak-

Outstanding Economist

Robert Lucas (1937–)

The 1995 Nobel laureate, Robert Lucas is generally given credit for the introduction of the rational-expectations theory into macroeconomics. His technical work in this area has substantially altered the way economists think about macroeconomic policy. He is a longtime professor of economics at the University of Chicago.

ers will err. But they will learn from their past mistakes; they will not continue to make the same types of errors. Thus, the rational-expectations hypothesis assumes that the errors of decision makers will tend to be random. For example, sometimes decision makers may overestimate the increase in the inflation rate caused by monetary expansion, and at other times they may underestimate it. But because they learn from prior experience, people will not continue to make systematic errors year after year.

Recent technological innovations have increased the availability of low-cost information. For example, information on economic matters is now readily available through both the Internet and a proliferation of finance-related networks and programs. As a result, ordinary Americans may now be better prepared to develop well informed forecasts about the future direction of the economy. If so, this will tend to enhance both the relevance and validity of the rational expectations hypothesis.

Major Differences Between Adaptive and Rational Expectations

The adaptive- and rational-expectations theories differ in two major respects: (1) how quickly people adjust to a change and (2) the likelihood of systematic forecasting errors. If the adaptive-expectations theory is correct, people will adjust more slowly. When a more expansionary policy leads to inflation, for example, there will be a significant time lag before people come to expect the inflation and incorporate it into their decision making. In contrast, the rational-expectations theory implies that people will begin to anticipate more inflation as soon as they observe a move toward a more expansionary policy, perhaps even before there is an actual increase in the rate of inflation. Therefore, with rational expectations, the time lag between a shift in policy and a change in expectations is likely to be brief.

Systematic errors will occur with adaptive expectations. For example, when the inflation rate is rising, decision makers will systematically tend to underestimate the future rate of inflation. In contrast, when the rate of inflation is falling, individuals will tend systematically to overestimate its future rate. With rational expectations, the errors will be random. People will be as likely to overestimate as to underestimate the future rate of inflation.

HOW MACRO POLICY WORKS: THE IMPLICATIONS OF ADAPTIVE AND RATIONAL EXPECTATIONS 6

From the viewpoint of macro policy, does it make any difference how quickly people alter their expectations and whether errors are random or systematic? The *AD/AS* model can be used to address this question. Suppose that there is a shift to a more expansionary macro policy—an increase in the money growth rate, for example. As part a of Exhibit 18-6 illustrates, the policy shift will stimulate aggregate demand and place upward pressure on the price level (or the inflation rate in the dynamic case). Under adaptive expectations, people will initially fail to anticipate the higher prices. Therefore, as we have previously discussed, output will temporarily increase to Y_2, beyond the economy's long-run potential. Correspondingly, employment will expand and unemployment will recede below the economy's natural rate. When the effects of expansionary policy are unanticipated, both output and employment increase in the short run. Of

EXHIBIT 18-6 Expectations and the Short-run Effects of Demand Stimulus

Under adaptive expectations, anticipation of inflation will lag behind its actual occurrence. As a result, a shift to a more expansionary policy will increase aggregate demand and lead to a temporary increase in real GDP from Y_F to Y_2, (a). In contrast, under rational expectations, decision makers will quickly anticipate the inflationary impact of a demand-stimulus policy. Thus, resource prices and production costs will rise as rapidly as prices. While aggregate demand shifts upward, so too will short-run aggregate supply (shift to $SRAS_2$) (b). With rational expectations, the demand-stimulus policy will increase prices without altering real output even in the short run.

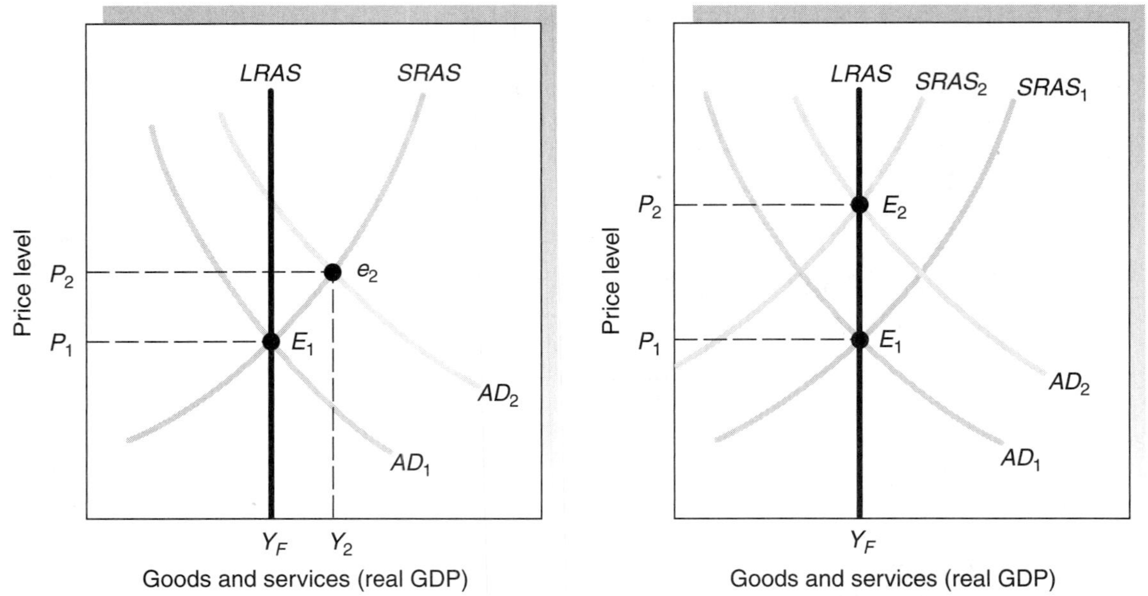

(a) Expansionary policy under adaptive expectations

(b) Expansionary policy under rational expectations

course, the output rate beyond the economy's capacity will be unsustainable. Eventually, strong demand for resources and the expectation of a higher price level (or rate of inflation) will push resource prices up also. Thus, the high level of output and employment will only be temporary. When decision makers adjust slowly, however, it may be possible to maintain the higher rate of output for a year or two, perhaps even a little longer.

Part b of Exhibit 18-6 illustrates the impact of expansionary macroeconomic policy under rational expectations. Remember with rational expectations, decision makers will quickly begin to anticipate the probable effects of the more expansionary policy—stronger demand and a rising rate of inflation, for example—and alter their choices accordingly. Agreements specifying future wage rates and resource prices will quickly make allowance for an expected increase in the price level. These agreements may even incorporate escalator clauses providing for automatic increases in nominal wages as the general price level rises. When buyers and sellers in the resource market anticipate fully and adjust quickly to the effects of the demand-stimulus policies, wage rates and resource prices will rise as rapidly as product prices. Hence, the short-run aggregate supply curve will shift upward (to $SRAS_2$) as rapidly as the aggregate demand curve. When people quickly and accurately anticipate the inflationary effects of the more expansionary policy, the result will merely be an increase in the general level of prices (move from E_1 to E_2 in part b of Exhibit 18-6). Neither real output nor employment will expand.

The implications are symmetrical for restrictive policy. Under adaptive expectations a shift to a more restrictive policy will reduce both aggregate demand and real output. Under rational expectations, however, the weaker demand and lower prices will be anticipated quickly. Thus, there will also be downward pressure on resource prices and costs, which will make it possible to maintain the initial level of output, even though the general price level has fallen.

The proponents of rational expectations believe that the effects of a change in policy will be widely and quickly anticipated by decision makers. Once this occurs, the policy will fail to exert a systematic impact on real output and employment. Economists refer to this phenomenon as the **policy-ineffectiveness theorem**.

Policy-ineffectiveness theorem
The proposition that any systematic policy will be rendered ineffective once decision makers figure out the policy pattern and adjust their decision making in light of its expected effects. The theorem is a corollary of the theory of rational expectations.

As we noted, rational-expectations theory does not imply that forecasts will always be correct. But the errors will be random. This means that, for example, when there is a shift to a more expansionary macro policy, people will be as likely to overestimate the inflationary side effects as to underestimate them. If people underestimate the future rate of inflation, product prices will rise relative to costs (resource prices) leading to a temporary increase in output. However, if decision makers overestimate the inflationary side effects, costs will increase relative to product prices and output will fall. As we noted, when the increase in inflation accompanying a more expansionary policy is accurately forecast, real output will remain unchanged. Thus, the theory of rational expectations implies that the impact of a shift in monetary and/or fiscal policy on output is unpredictable. A shift in macro policy is as likely to cause a reduction in output as an increase. This unpredictability explains why proponents of rational expectations argue that macro policy should follow a steady course and focus on long-range objectives.

Policy Implications: A Summary

Thus, the adaptive- and rational-expectations theories have quite different implications with regard to the likely short-run effects of changes in macroeconomic policy. ***With adaptive expectations, there will be a time lag before people anticipate the eventual effects of a shift to a more expansionary policy. Therefore, policies that stimulate demand and place upward pressure on the general level of prices will temporarily increase output and employment. In contrast, when the inflationary side effects of expansionary policies are anticipated quickly, as the rational-expectations theory implies, the primary impact of the demand stimulus will be an increase in the price level.***

While the implications of the two expectations theories differ with regard to the short-run effects of policy changes, their long-run implications are identical. Like rational expectations, the adaptive-expectations theory indicates that decision makers will eventually anticipate the long-run effects of more expansionary policy. As this happens, output will recede to the economy's long-run potential. Therefore, both theories imply that the long-run effects of a more expansionary macro policy will be inflation, rather than sustainable increases in output. The Thumbnail Sketch on page 122 summarizes the implications of both adaptive and rational expectations regarding how a change in macro policy will impact the price level (inflation) and real output in both the long and short runs.

NONACTIVIST STABILIZATION POLICY 7

Timing problems, the public choice perspective, and the theory of rational expectations provide the foundation for the nonactivist view of macro policy. While nonactivists often arrive at their position from different paths, they have two major points in common. They believe that (1) discretionary policy changes will increase rather than reduce economic instability and (2) greater stability would result if stable, predictable policies based on predetermined rules or guidelines were followed.

Nonactivists recommend that policymakers choose a long-run policy path (for example, a low, stable rate of inflation and no change in tax rates or real

THUMBNAIL SKETCH

Expectations and the Impact of Shifts in Macro Policy

	Under Adaptive Expectations (1)	Under Rational Expectations (2)		Under Adaptive Expectations (1)	Under Rational Expectations (2)
Impact in the Short Run			**Impact in the Long Run**		
Shift to a More Expansionary Policy	Higher prices (inflation); increase in output	Higher prices (inflation); no change in output	Shift to a More Expansionary Policy	Higher prices (inflation); no change in output	Higher prices (inflation); no change in output
Shift to a More Restrictive Policy	Lower prices (deflation); reduction in output	Lower prices (deflation) no change in output	Shift to a More Restrictive Policy	Lower prices (deflation); no change in output	Lower prices (deflation) no change in output

Note: Price stability was initially assumed to be present. If inflation was initially present, the shift to a more restrictive policy would reduce the rate of inflation rather than lead to deflation.

government expenditures) and inform the public of this choice. This course should then be pursued regardless of cyclical ups and downs. As policymakers stay on course, they will gain credibility. The public will develop confidence in the future stability of the policy. Uncertainty will be reduced, thereby increasing the efficiency of private decision making. Nonactivists are confident this strategy would result both in less instability and in more rapid growth than Western economies have experienced in the past.

Nonactivist Monetary Policy

Suppose we are going to adopt a nonactivist strategy. What rules or guidelines would we choose? Nonactivists believe that monetary policy should focus on achieving either (1) a stable growth rate of the money supply or (2) a stable price level.

Monetary Growth Rule

Many nonactivists favor the constant money growth rule long championed by Milton Friedman. Under this plan, the money supply would be expanded continuously at an annual rate (3 percent, for example) that approximates the long-run growth of the U.S. economy. When real output is growing rapidly (for example, 5 percent annually), the supply of money would decline relative to real GDP. Thus, monetary policy would automatically exert a restraining influence during a period of rapid growth. In contrast, during a recession, the constant money growth rate would exceed the growth of real output, offsetting any tendency toward a downward spiral.

Nonactivists note that monetary policy has often followed a stop-and-go pattern. Many times, after expanding the money supply and causing inflation, policymakers have slammed on the monetary brakes and thrown the economy into a recession (see Exhibit 18-1). The nonactivists believe that monetary instability is the major source of economic instability. Rather than responding to forecasts and current economic indicators, the Fed, they say, would be a more stabilizing force if it simply increased the supply of money, month after month, at a low (noninflationary) constant rate.

The experience of the 1980s highlighted a potential drawback of the monetary rule approach. The introduction of interest-earning checking deposits drastically changed the nature of the M1 money supply during the 1980s. As the interest-earning checking accounts were legalized and more people began using them, the M1 money supply grew rapidly and fluctuated substantially. But this growth was not indicative of a highly expansionary monetary policy. The inflation rate declined sharply during the early 1980s and was relatively constant during the remainder of the decade. When the nature of money is changing, steady money growth may fail to yield monetary and price stability.

Furthermore, as people shift their savings among financial instruments, the shifts influence the growth of the various money supply measures. This can result in conflicting signals. For example, the M1 money supply contracted at a −0.4 percent annual rate during 1999–2000, suggesting that monetary policy was quite restrictive. During the same period, the annual growth of the M2 money supply was 6.2 percent, indicating that monetary policy was moderately expansionary. Technological developments in the financial sector have substantially reduced the usefulness of the money supply figures as an indicator of monetary policy. In a dynamic world, changes in this area are almost sure to continue. (Some of these changes were discussed in Reading 16 in the sections on measurement problems and the future of money.)[2]

Price Level Rule

The shortcomings of money supply figures as an indicator of monetary policy have enhanced the attractiveness of price level targeting. Under this approach, the monetary authorities would directly target a broad price index, such as the GDP deflator or consumer price index. The advocates of a price level rule argue that, in the long run, monetary policy cannot determine real output, employment, interest rates, or other real variables. What it can and does determine is the level of prices. Therefore, why not require that the monetary authorities maintain a persistently low rate of inflation and hold them accountable for their actions? Under this plan, if the general price index were rising, the monetary authorities would have an incentive to institute more restraint. Conversely, if the price level were falling, a move toward expansion would be in order. The proponents of this rule argue that it would reduce both instability arising from monetary sources and the uncertainty of time-dimension transactions (for example, loan agreements and other long-term contracts).

New Zealand adopted a price level rule in 1990. Although the Central Bank of New Zealand is fully responsible for monetary policy, it is legally required to maintain the inflation rate within a narrow range, currently between zero and 2 percent. If the central bank fails to meet this target, the bank's governor is subject to dismissal. This structure requires the central bank to focus on a well-defined target (a

[2] In recent years, economists have generally placed more confidence in the M2 money supply figures. But there are no assurances that future financial innovations will not also alter the nature of M2 and undermine its use as a gauge of monetary policy. In fact, evidence of such changes is already present. In response to recent reductions in the start-up cost of stock and bond mutual funds, many individuals shifted funds from various savings instruments that are part of the M2 money supply to the mutual funds, which are not. These shifts reduced both the growth rate of the M2 money supply during 1994–1995 and the reliability of these figures as an indicator of monetary policy.

low rate of inflation) that is achievable with monetary policy and holds it accountable for failure to meet the objective. To date, the policy has been highly successful. Prior to 1990, New Zealand had the highest and most variable inflation rate among the high-income industrial nations. In contrast, its rate of inflation has been low (between 0.1 percent and 2.7 percent) since the legislation took effect. Other countries appear to be moving in this direction. The new European Central Bank has committed itself to the achievement of price stability. Several other central banks have also set targets and designated price stability as their primary objective.

Nonactivist Fiscal Policy

In the area of fiscal policy, the simplest rule would require that the budget be balanced annually. Because revenues and expenditures fluctuate over the business cycle, however, a balanced budget rule would require tax increases and/or expenditure reductions during a recession. The opposite changes would be required during a period of rapid growth. Such changes are inconsistent with the nonactivist pursuit of stable (unchanged) policies.

In theory, the proper nonactivist fiscal strategy is a balanced budget *over the business cycle*. Under this plan, the same tax rates and expenditure policies would remain in effect during both booms and recessions. Surpluses would result during periods of prosperity while deficits would accrue during recessions. Unfortunately, this rule is an elastic band constraint. At any point in time, it is difficult to assess if current tax and expenditure policy will balance the budget over the cycle. Thus, nonactivists, particularly those of a public choice persuasion, recognize that a "balance the budget over the business cycle" rule is unlikely to impose a steady course on policymakers.

Some nonactivists believe that a constitutional amendment limiting both government spending and budget deficits is a necessary ingredient for stable fiscal policy. Pressure from special interest groups and the short time horizon of political officials elected for limited terms biases the political process toward expansionary fiscal policy (increased spending and debt). Because of this, some nonactivists argue that a supramajority (for example, 60 percent) should be required for congressional approval for either (1) deficit-financed government spending or (2) rapid increases (more rapid than the growth of national income) in federal spending.

It is one thing to favor a general strategy and another to develop a workable program for implementation. Clearly, the nonactivists have not yet arrived at a detailed fiscal policy program that would command wide acceptance among even the proponents of nonactivism.

8 ROLE OF MONETARY POLICY: A CONSENSUS VIEW

OPTIONAL SEGMENT

Price stability
When monetary policymakers consistently achieve price stability, they are providing the foundation for both economic stability and the efficient operation of markets.

A modern consensus view has developed with regard to the proper role of monetary policy. ***Economists of almost all persuasions now believe that monetary policy should focus on* price stability—*the attainment of persistently low rates of inflation.*** Achievement of this objective will promote economic stability and provide the framework for healthy long-term economic growth.

The high standard of living that Americans enjoy is the result of gains from specialization, divisions of labor, and mass production processes. Price stability and the smooth operation of the pricing system will help individuals more fully realize the potential gains from these sources. In contrast, high and variable rates of inflation create uncertainty, distort relative prices, and reduce the efficiency of a market economy.

There is no conflict between price stability and full employment. When the general level of prices is approximately stable, the uncertainties of time dimension activities like investment will be reduced. This will help promote both full employment (low unemployment) and strong economic growth. When price stability is achieved and maintained, monetary policymakers have done their job well.

EMERGING CONSENSUS ON OTHER MATTERS 9

Monetary policy is not the only area where a consensus is emerging. There is also substantial agreement in three other areas of stabilization policy.

1. ***Demand stimulus policies cannot reduce the rate of unemployment below the natural level—at least not for long.***
   In the 1960s and 1970s, many economists thought that there was a trade-off between inflation and unemployment. While recognizing demand stimulus policies would lead to some inflation, many believed that they would also reduce the unemployment rate. Expectations theories highlight the error of this view. Once people come to expect inflation, the inflation–unemployment trade-off dissipates. While the adaptive-expectations theory implies that an unanticipated shift to a more expansionary policy can temporarily reduce the unemployment rate, the rational-expectations theory indicates that even the temporary reduction is questionable. Given the uncertainty of the short-run trade-off and clear absence of a long-lasting trade-off, most economists now believe that stimulating inflation in an effort to reduce unemployment is both destabilizing and shortsighted.
2. ***Wide swings in both monetary and fiscal policy should be avoided.***
   Given our limited forecasting ability and knowledge about how quickly changes in monetary and fiscal policy impact the economy, policymakers should not attempt to respond to every turn in the economic road. Major changes in tax policy, budget deficits, and the money supply *in response to business cycle conditions* are likely to increase rather than reduce instability. More stability will result if the policymakers adopt a long-range strategy and stick with it.
3. ***Use of discretionary fiscal policy as an effective stabilization tool is impractical, particularly in countries like the United States.***
   Proper timing is essential for the effective use of stabilization policy. Given the checks and balances built into the U.S. political structure, it is unrealistic to expect speedy changes in fiscal policy. The crowding-out effect creates additional uncertainty with regard to the potency of fiscal policy. These shortcomings have caused even longtime Keynesians like Paul Samuelson to conclude that fiscal policy is an impractical stabilization tool.

STABILIZATION POLICY AND THE U.S. ECONOMY 10

The focus of stabilization policy has changed dramatically during the last four decades. In the 1960s, it was widely believed that macro policy—particularly fiscal policy—could be effectively used both to smooth the ups and downs of the business cycle and to promote a high level of employment. Both the integration of expectations into macro models and the instability of the 1970s dampened the earlier enthusiasm for fine-tuning policies.

Rather than trying to control output and employment, the focus shifted to the achievement of price stability during the 1980s and 1990s. Paradoxically, this shift and the accompanying low and more stable rates of inflation were associated with a reduction in economic fluctuations. Exhibit 18-7 illustrates this point. From 1910 to 1959, the U.S. economy was in recession 32.8 percent of the time. Between 1960 and 1982, recession was present 22.8 percent of the time. By way of comparison, 1983–2000 was an unprecedented period of economic stability. Over this 216-month period, the economy was in recession only eight months—3.7 percent of the time.

What accounts for the recent stability? The public tends to credit as well as blame the president for the state of the economy. Though the president has the power of the veto and can initiate legislative proposals, he is only one player in the formulation of policy. Members of Congress, particularly party leaders and chairmen of key committees, also play an important role in the development of fiscal and regulatory policy.

Furthermore, economists—particularly proponents of the crowding-out and new classical theories—are increasingly skeptical about the potency of fiscal policy. During the 1980s, taxes were cut and increases in defense expenditures pushed the overall level of federal spending upward. The federal government ran large budget deficits, indicating that fiscal policy was highly expansionary. Nonetheless, the inflation receded from the double-digit levels of the 1970s. This suggests that the demand-side effects of the expansionary fiscal policy were relatively weak. During the 1990s, fiscal policy was far more restrictive. Defense expenditures were cut, federal spending declined as a share of the economy, and the federal budget shifted to a surplus. Once again, there was little evidence that

EXHIBIT 18-7 Reduction in the Incidence of Recession

The U.S. economy was in recession 32.8 percent of the time during the 1910–1959 period and 22.8 percent of the time between 1960 and 1982, but only 3.7 percent of the time during 1983–2000.

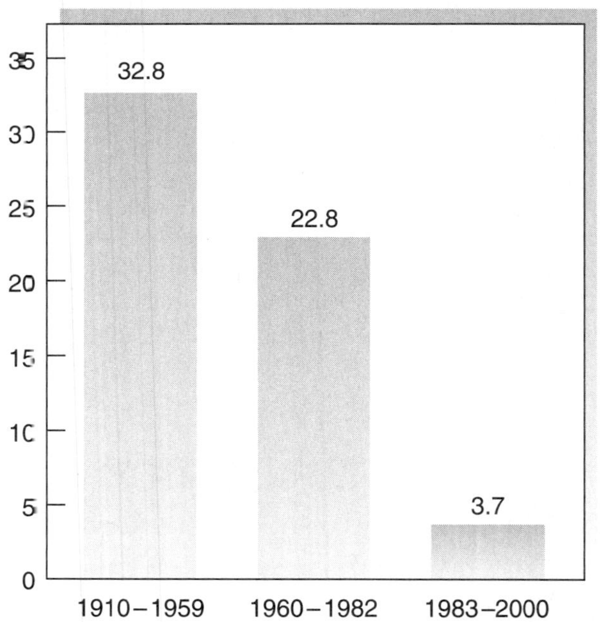

Sources: R.E. Lipsey and D. Preston, *Source Book of Statistics Relating to Construction* (1966); and National Bureau of Economic Research, www.nber.org

the fiscal policy changes exerted much impact. Growth continued at a brisk pace, while the inflation rate remained under control.

The experience of Japan during the 1990s also raises doubts about the potency of fiscal policy. Between 1991 and 2000, the Japanese economy grew at an annual rate of only 1.2 percent, far below its growth of more than 4 percent during the prior decade. The Japanese shunned expansionary monetary policy. The broad money supply (comparable to M2) grew at an annual rate of only 2.6 percent during 1991–2000 compared to 9.9 percent during 1975–1990. Instead, the Japanese shifted to a highly expansionary fiscal policy in an effort to stimulate the economy. Measured as a share of the economy, government expenditures rose from 30.9 percent in 1991 to 38.1 percent in 1999. During the same period, government revenues declined from 33.8 percent of GDP to 31.1 percent.[3] The budget of the Japanese government went from a surplus of 2.9 percent of GDP in 1991 to a deficit of 7 percent of GDP in 1999. (By way of comparison, the largest general government deficit in the United States during the last 50 years was the 1986 deficit of 5.3 percent of GDP.) In spite of this highly expansionary fiscal policy, demand stagnated and the Japanese economy continued to struggle.

Economists now believe that fiscal policy is far less potent than was thought to be the case during the 1960s. Thus, most would give the more stable policies of the Federal Reserve the primary credit for the economic stability in the United States during the last two decades. Under the leadership of first Paul Volcker and later Alan Greenspan, the Fed avoided wide swings in the rate of inflation. During the entire 1983–2000 period, the inflation rate (as measured by the GDP deflator) remained in a narrow range between 1.1 percent and 4.3 percent. Even more impressive, the year-to-year change in the inflation rate never exceeded 1.2 percent. In essence, the Fed followed policies consistent with a low and stable rate of inflation, and these policies resulted in both economic stability and strong growth.

The Future

Even though the economic record of the 1980s and 1990s was highly impressive, clouds began to appear on the horizon during 2000. The price of crude oil rose from $12 to $32 per barrel during 1999–2000, pushing gasoline and other petroleum-based products sharply higher. The growth of the late 1990s moved more and more income into higher tax brackets and, as a result, federal taxes as a share of national income rose to the highest levels since World War II. Fed policy was also restrictive during the first half of 2000, and stock prices collapsed during the second half of the year. This combination of shocks—sharply higher oil prices, high taxes, restrictive monetary policy, and sharp reduction in stock values—slowed the economy and eventually led to recession beginning in March of 2001. As real GDP declined, the unemployment rate rose from 4.0 percent in December 2000 to nearly 6 percent a year later.

The Federal Reserve reversed its earlier policy and moved aggressively to combat the recession. The Fed supplied additional reserves and lowered key short-term interest rates just about every month during 2001. Congress and the Bush Administration cut taxes and sent $600 tax rebate checks to millions of taxpayers. But it takes time for monetary policy to work and the potency of fiscal policy is questionable. (See prior discussion of the Japanese experience during the 1990s.)

---

[3] See Robert H. Rasche and Daniel L. Thornton, "The Monetary/Fiscal Policy Debate: A Controlled Experiment," *Monetary Trends*, Federal Reserve Bank of St. Louis, page 1. Oct. 2001 for additional details on this topic.

In September of 2001, a U.S. economy that was already in recession was hit with another shock: A terrorist attack on the World Trade Center and the Pentagon that killed nearly 4,000. This led to a military build up and a War on Terrorism. These events, along with anthrax attacks through the postal system, created uncertainty and shook the confidence of many Americans. Airlines, hotels, and other transportation sectors of the economy were hit particularly hard.

Will the actions of the Fed stimulate recovery? Will fiscal policy actions be helpful or harmful? Will the War on Terrorism be lengthy and expensive? Policymakers are now dealing with these questions, and the future stability of the U.S. economy is dependent upon the answers that emerge.

SUMMARY

- Historically, the United States has experienced substantial swings in real output. Prior to the Second World War, year-to-year changes in real GDP of 5 to 10 percent were experienced on several occasions. During the last five decades, the fluctuations of real output have been more moderate.
- While stable growth, price level stability, and full employment are widely recognized as desirable, there is considerable disagreement concerning how these objectives can be achieved. Activists believe that discretionary use of macro policy can contribute to the achievement of these goals, while nonactivists argue that steady, more passive policies are better.
- After a change in policy has been undertaken, there will be a time lag before it exerts a major impact on economic activity. This means the policymakers need to forecast economic conditions several months in the future in order to institute policy changes effectively.
- The index of leading indicators and other forecasting tools provide policymakers with information about the likely future economic conditions. Activists argue that policymakers can initially respond with caution to signals indicating the need for a policy change and then act more aggressively if the situation merits it. Activists are confident that discretionary monetary and fiscal policy can be used effectively to promote economic stability.
- Nonactivists believe that a market economy's self-corrective mechanism works quite well if it is not short-circuited by perverse macroeconomic policy. Furthermore, they argue that the problems of proper timing and political considerations undermine the effectiveness of discretionary macro policy as a stabilization tool. Rather than reacting to cyclical conditions, nonactivists favor steady, predictable policies.
- There are two major theories as to how expectations are formed. According to the adaptive-expectations hypothesis, individuals form their expectations about the future on the basis of data from the recent past. The rational-expectations hypothesis assumes that people use all pertinent information, including data on the conduct of current policy, in forming their expectations about the future.
- With adaptive expectations, an unanticipated shift to a more expansionary policy will temporarily stimulate output and employment. In contrast, with rational expectations, expansionary policy will fail, even temporarily, to systematically increase output. Both expectations theories indicate that sustained expansionary policies will lead to inflation without permanently increasing output and employment.
- Analysis of the Great Depression indicates that the severity and length of the economic plunge, if not its onset, were the result of perverse macroeconomic policy—a sharp contraction in the money supply, a huge tax increase, and a sharp rise in tariff rates.
- While debate about macro policy continues, most economists now believe that monetary policy consistent with approximate price stability is the key ingredient of effective stabilization policy. In contrast with the 1960s, use of fiscal policy as an effective stabilization tool is now thought to be impractical.

STUDY SESSION 5 ECONOMICS: MICRO-ECONOMIC ANALYSIS

READING ASSIGNMENTS

LEARNING OUTCOMES

Reading 19: Demand and Consumer Choice

The candidate should be able to:

a. explain the fundamental principles of consumer choice and discuss marginal utility, marginal benefit, and the demand curve;

b. distinguish between the income effect and the substitution effect;

c. discuss the determinants of price and income elasticity of demand and explain the concepts of price and income elasticity of supply;

d. calculate and interpret price and income elasticity of demand and explain why the price elasticity of demand tends to increase in the long run;

e. discuss the characteristics of consumer indifference curves, the role of the consumption-opportunity constraint, and the budget constraint in indifference curve analysis.

Reading 20: Costs and the Supply of Goods

The candidate should be able to:

a. describe the principal-agent problem of the firm, distinguish among the types of business firms, and discuss the major factors promoting cost efficiency and consumer service;

b. distinguish between 1) explicit costs and implicit costs, 2) economic profit and accounting profit, and 3) the short run and the long run in production;

c. define and identify opportunity costs, fixed costs, variable costs, marginal costs, average costs, and sunk costs and differentiate between economic costs and accounting costs;

d. state the law of diminishing returns, and explain its impact on a company's costs;

e. describe the shapes of the short-run marginal cost, average variable cost, average fixed cost, and average total cost curves;

f. define economies and diseconomies of scale, explain how each is possible, and relate each to shapes of long-run average total cost curves;

g. describe both the factors that cause cost curves to shift and the economic way of thinking about costs.

Reading 21: Price Takers and the Competitive Process

The candidate should be able to:

a. discuss the conditions that characterize pure competition (price taker) market and explain how and why price takers maximize profits at the quantity for which marginal cost, price, and marginal revenue are equal;

b. calculate and interpret the total revenue and the marginal revenue for a price taker and explain the relationship between total revenue, total costs, price, marginal revenue, marginals costs, and the profit maximizing output level;

c. explain the decision by price takers to continue to operate, temporarily shut down, or go out of business when faced with price below average total cost;

d. describe the short-run supply curves for a company and for a competitive market;

e. explain the impact on prices and output of increases or decreases in demand in a competitive market;

f. contrast the role of constant-cost, increasing-cost, and decreasing-cost industries in determining the shape of a long-run market supply curve;

g. explain the impact of time on the elasticity of market supply and discuss the role of profits and losses in a purely competitive market.

Reading 22: Price-Searcher Markets with Low Entry Barriers

The candidate should be able to:

a. describe the conditions that characterize monopolistic competition (a competitive price-searcher market);

b. explain how firms choose price and output combinations in a monopolistic competition;

c. summarize the debate about the allocative efficiency of monopolistic competition with low barriers to entry, including the implications of contestable markets and entrepreneurship;

d. discuss the principle of price discrimination and illustrate how a firm might apply this principle to gain from such a practice.

Reading 23: Price-Searcher Markets with High Entry Barriers

The candidate should be able to:

a. discuss entry barriers that may protect companies against competition from potential market entrants;

b. differentiate between a monopoly and an oligopoly;
c. describe how a profit-maximizing monopolist sets prices and determines output and discuss price and output under oligopoly, with and without collusion;
d. discuss why oligopolists have a strong incentive to collude and to cheat on collusive agreements and discuss the obstacles to collusion among oligopolistic companies;
e. describe the different defects that can occur in a market with high entry barriers;
f. describe government policy alternatives that are intended to reduce the problems stemming from high barriers to entry.
g. contrast the pricing and output decisions of a firm in pure competition, monopolistic competition, oligopoly, and monopoly with reference to quantity produced, price, marginal revenue, marginal cost, demand, and average total cost.

Reading 24: The Supply of and Demand for Productive Resources

The candidate should be able to:

a. explain the relationship between the price of a resource and the quantity demanded of that resource with reference to supply, demand, and derived demand;
b. identify and describe three factors that may cause shifts in the demand curve for a resource;
c. define marginal product, marginal revenue, value of marginal product (VMP), the marginal revenue product (MRP) of a resource, and explain the relation between MRD and demand for that resource;
d. explain the necessary conditions to achieve the cost-minimizing employment levels for two or more variable resources;
e. discuss the factors that influence resource supply and demand in the short run and long run.

Reading 25: The Financial Environment: Markets, Institutions, and Interest Rates

The candidate should be able to:

a. identify and explain the factors that influence the cost of capital;
b. describe the role of interest rates in allocating capital;
c. explain how the supply of and demand for funds determine interest rates;
d. discuss the factors that cause the supply and demand curves for funds to shift;
e. distinguish between the real and the nominal risk-free rate of interest;
f. discuss economic conditions that can change the real risk-free rate of interest;
g. explain the effect of inflation on the real rate of return earned by financial securities and by physical assets;
h. describe default risk, liquidity risk, and maturity risk premiums;
i. explain interest rate risk and reinvestment rate risk;
j. explain how inflation-indexed bonds can protect investors from inflation and maturity risk.

DEMAND AND CONSUMER CHOICE

READING 19

LEARNING OUTCOMES

The candidate should be able to:

a. explain the fundamental principles of consumer choice and discuss marginal utility, marginal benefit, and the demand curve;

b. distinguish between the income effect and the substitution effect;

c. discuss the determinants of price and income elasticity of demand and explain the concepts of price and income elasticity of supply;

d. calculate and interpret price and income elasticity of demand and explain why the price elasticity of demand tends to increase in the long run;

e. discuss the characteristics of consumer indifference curves, discuss the role of the consumption-opportunity constraint and the budget constraint, in indifference curve analysis.

The most famous law in economics, and the one economists are most sure of, is the law of demand. On this law is built almost the whole edifice of economics.

—David R. Henderson[1]

A thing is worth whatever a buyer will pay for it.

—Publilius Syrus, first century B.C.[2]

INTRODUCTION 1

The statement of David Henderson highlights the central position of the law of demand in economics. As Publilius Syrus noted more than 2,000 years ago, demand reflects the willingness of individuals to pay for what is offered in the market. In this reading, we begin our examination of microeconomic markets for specific products with an analysis of the demand side of markets. In essence we will be going "behind" the market demand curve to see how it is made up of individual consumer demands, and what factors determine the choices of individual consumers.[3]

---

[1] David R. Henderson, "Demand," in *The Concise Encyclopedia of Economics*, ed. David R. Henderson www.econlib.org/library/CEE.html

[2] Quoted in Michael Jackman, ed., *Macmillan Book of Business and Economic Quotations* (New York: Macmillan, 1984), p. 150.

[3] You may want to review the section on demand in Chapter 3 before proceeding with this reading.

2 THE FUNDAMENTALS OF CONSUMER CHOICE

Each of us must decide how to allocate our limited income among the many possible things we could purchase. The prices of goods, *relative to each other*, are very important determining factors. If your favorite cereal doubled in price, would you switch to a different brand? Would your decision be different if all cereals, not just yours, doubled in price? Your choice *between* brands of cereal will be affected only by the change in relative prices. If all cereal prices rose, you might quit purchasing cereal, but this would not give you a strong reason to switch to a different brand. Relative prices measure opportunity cost. If cereal is $5 per box when movie tickets are $10, you must give up two boxes of cereal to purchase a movie ticket.

There have been some substantial changes during the past few decades in the way American consumers allocate their income. For example, as a share of total consumption, spending on food (including beverages and tobacco) fell from 26 percent in 1963 to 15 percent in 1999. Out of each food dollar, spending on food away from home and snacks rose from 34 cents in 1970 to 42 cents in 1999. Between 1950 and 1999, spending on housing, excluding utilities and similar items, slightly more than doubled as a share of total consumption. During the last 15 years, spending on clothing has been relatively stable.

Several fundamental principles of consumer behavior account for these changes, as well as for consumer choice more generally.

1. ***Limited income necessitates choice.***
Because of scarcity we all have limited incomes. The limited nature of our income requires us to make choices about which goods we will and will not purchase. When more of one good or service is purchased, we must purchase less of some other goods if we are to stay within our budget. This is the meaning of the "cost" of purchasing something.
2. ***Consumers make decisions purposefully.***
The goals that underpin consumer choice can usually be met in alternative ways. If two products have an equal cost, a consumer would choose to purchase the one expected to have the higher benefit. On the other hand, if two products yield equal benefits, the consumer would choose to purchase the cheaper one. Fundamentally, we assume that consumers are rational—they are able to weigh the costs and benefits of alternative choices.
3. ***One good can be substituted for another.***
Consumers can achieve *utility*—that is, satisfaction—from many different alternatives. Either a hamburger or a taco might satisfy your hunger, while going either to a movie or to a football game might satisfy your desire for entertainment. With $600, you might either buy a new TV set or take a short vacation. No single good is so precious that some of it will not be given up in exchange for a large enough quantity of other goods. There are many competing wants, and each can be satisfied in alternative ways.

   We have been discussing "wants," but how about our "need" for basic commodities such as water or energy? The need of a person for an item is closely related to its cost—what must be given up to obtain the item. Do southern California residents need water from the north? More expensive water leads individual residents to plant cactus instead of grass, pay a plumber to fix leaking faucets, and use flow constrictors on shower heads. Each of these reduces the need for water, illustrating that need depends on cost to the user. People living in Montana, where household electricity in recent years cost nearly twice as much as in nearby Washington, used about half as much electricity per household. Other factors besides the price of electricity enter their decisions, but Montanans clearly were able to reduce their "need" for electricity by substituting gas, fuel oil, insulation, and wool sweaters for the relatively more expensive electricity. Each of the things we purchase has substitutes.

4. ***Consumers must make decisions without perfect information, but knowledge and past experience will help.***
Information is costly to acquire. Asking family and friends, searching through magazines such as *Consumer Reports*, and contacting the local Better Business Bureau are all ways of gathering information about products and potential sellers. The likelihood that a consumer will spend the necessary time, effort, and money to gather this information is directly related to its value to the consumer. Many people will collect this information when deciding on the purchase of a new automobile, but very few would do the same for a purchase of a pencil or a roll of paper towels. When even a bad decision will not be very costly, consumers will rationally remain less informed.

    No human being has perfect foresight. Consumers will not always correctly anticipate the consequences of their choices. They will, however, have a good chance of doing so in areas of common knowledge and experience. You have a pretty good idea of what to expect when you buy a cup of coffee, five gallons of gasoline, or a box of your favorite cereal. Why? Because you have learned from experience—your own and that of others. Your expectations may not always be fulfilled precisely (for example, the coffee may be stronger than expected or the gasoline may make your car's engine knock), but even then, you will gain valuable information that will help you project the outcome of future choices more accurately. Being a good consumer includes learning through previous choices.

5. ***The law of diminishing marginal utility applies: As the rate of consumption increases, the marginal utility derived from consuming additional units of a good will decline.***
Utility is a term economists use to describe the subjective personal benefits that result from an action. The **law of diminishing marginal utility** states that the **marginal** (or additional) **utility** derived from consuming successive units of a product will eventually decline as the rate of consumption increases. For example, the law says that even though you might like ice cream, your marginal satisfaction from additional ice cream will eventually decline. Ice cream at lunchtime might be great. An additional helping for dinner might also be good. However, after you have had it for lunch and dinner, another serving as a midnight snack will be less attractive. When the law of diminishing marginal utility sets in, the additional utility derived from still more units of ice cream declines.

    The law of diminishing marginal utility explains why, even if you really like a certain product, you will not spend your entire budget on it. Consumers would be unlikely to stop purchasing a good if an additional unit yielded more satisfaction than the previous one. Failure to purchase an additional unit indicates that the buyer has reached the point where additional units provide less and less marginal utility. Utility-seeking buyers will not operate in the range of increasing marginal utility, but in the range where their marginal utility is declining.

Law of diminishing marginal utility
The basic economic principle that, as the consumption of a commodity increases, the marginal utility derived from consuming more of the commodity (per unit of time) will eventually decline.

Marginal utility
The additional utility received from the consumption of an additional unit of a good.

Marginal Utility, Marginal Benefit, and the Demand Curve

The law of diminishing marginal utility helps us to understand the law of demand and the shape of the demand curve. The height of an individual's demand curve at any specific unit is equal to the maximum price the consumer

Marginal benefit
The maximum price a consumer would be willing to pay for an additional unit. It is the dollar value of the consumer's marginal utility from the additional unit, and thus falls as consumption increases.

would be willing to pay for that unit—its **marginal benefit** to the consumer—given the number of units already purchased. Although marginal benefit is measured in dollars, it reflects the opportunity cost of the unit, in terms of other goods forgone. If a consumer is willing to pay, at most, $5 for an additional unit of the product, this indicates a willingness to give up, at most, $5 worth of other goods. ***Because a consumer's willingness to pay for a unit of a good is directly related to the utility derived from consuming the unit, the law of diminishing marginal utility implies that a consumer's marginal benefit, and thus the height of the demand curve, falls with the rate of consumption.***

Exhibit 19-1 shows this relationship for a hypothetical consumer Jones, relative to her weekly consumption of frozen pizza. The law of diminishing marginal utility applies—each additional pizza consumed per week will generate less marginal utility for Jones than the previous pizza. For this reason, Jones's maximum willingness to pay—her marginal benefit—will fall as the quantity consumed increases. In addition, the steepness of Jones's demand curve, or its responsiveness to a change in price—its elasticity—is a reflection of how rapidly marginal utility diminishes with additional consumption. An individual's demand curve for a good whose marginal value declines more rapidly will be steeper.

Given knowledge about a consumer's maximum willingness to pay for additional units of a good, we are now in a position to discuss the choice of how many units a consumer will choose to purchase. ***At any given price, consumers will purchase all units of a good for which their maximum willingness to pay—their marginal benefit—is greater than the price.*** They will stop at the point where the next unit's marginal benefit would be less than the price. Although there are some problems with divisibility (it is hard to purchase half a car), we can generally say that

EXHIBIT 19-1 Diminishing Marginal Utility and the Individual's Demand Curve

An individual's demand curve, Jones's demand for frozen personal pizzas in this case, reflects the law of diminishing marginal utility. Because marginal utility (*MU*) falls with increased consumption, so does the consumer's maximum willingness to pay—marginal benefit (*MB*). A consumer will purchase until *MB* = *Price*, so at $2.50 Jones would purchase 3 pizzas and receive a consumer surplus shown by the shaded triangle.

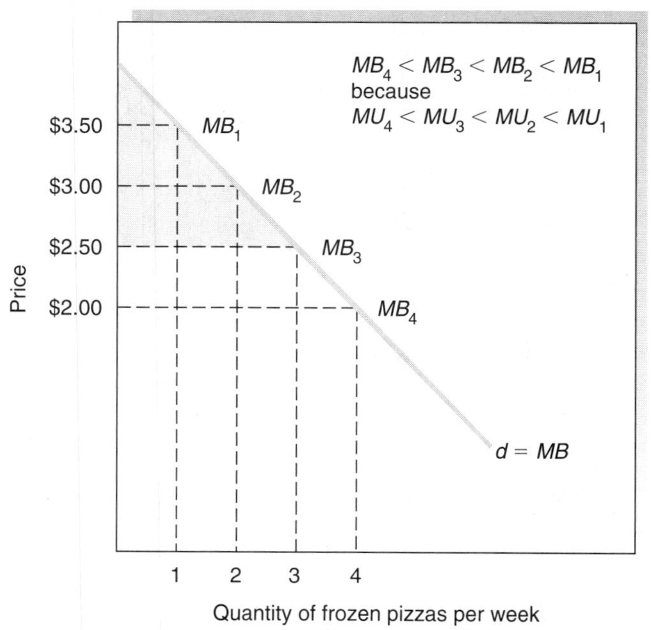

a consumer will purchase all units of a good up to the point where the marginal benefit equals the price of the good ($MB = P$).

Returning to Exhibit 19-1, if the price of frozen pizza were $2.50, Jones would purchase three frozen pizzas per week.[4] Remember that consumer surplus is defined as the difference between the maximum price the consumer would be willing to pay and the price actually paid. Jones's maximum willingness to pay for the first unit is $3.50, which, at a price of $2.50, generates $1.00 of consumer surplus for Jones. When a consumer has purchased all units to the point where $MB = P$, total consumer surplus is the total triangular area under the demand curve, but above the price. Total consumer surplus for Jones is shown as the shaded area in Exhibit 19-1.

Within this framework, how would a consumer respond to a decline in the price of a good? Answer: Purchases will be increased to the point where marginal benefit diminishes to the level of the new lower price. If marginal utility declines rapidly with consumption, the consumer will expand purchases only slightly. If marginal utility declines less rapidly, it will take a larger expansion in purchases to reach this point. If the price were to rise, the consumer would cut back purchases, eliminating those for which marginal benefit was now less than the price. It is through this linkage of marginal benefit with maximum willingness to pay that the law of diminishing marginal utility underlies an individual demand curve.

Consumer Equilibrium with Many Goods

The last time you were at the mall, you probably saw something, perhaps a nice billfold, that you liked. After all, there are many things we would like—many different alternatives that would give us utility. Next, you looked at the price tag: "$50, wow! That's too much." What you were really saying was "I like the billfold, but not as much as the $50 worth of other goods that I would have to give up." Consumer choice is a constant comparison of value relative to price. Consider another example—you may prefer steak to less costly hamburger. Nonetheless, your happiness may be better served by buying the hamburger, and saving the extra money to spend on something else.

The idea that choices across goods are based upon a relative comparison of marginal utility (MU) to price (P) can be expressed more precisely. If a consumer is spending a limited income across products so as to maximize total utility, the following relationship will be present:

$$\frac{MU_A}{P_A} = \frac{MU_B}{P_B} = \ldots = \frac{MU_n}{P_n}$$

Here MU represents the marginal utility derived from the last unit of a product, and P represents the price of the good. The subscripts $_{A, B, \ldots, n}$ indicate the different products available to the consumer. ***In the continuous case, this expression implies that the consumer will maximize his or her satisfaction (or total utility) by ensuring that the last dollar spent on each commodity yields an equal degree of marginal utility. Alternatively stated, the last unit of each commodity purchased should provide the same marginal utility per dollar spent on it.*** Thus, if the price of a gallon of ice cream is twice as high as the price of a liter of Coke, a consumer will purchase

[4] Jones would certainly purchase the second unit because $MB > P$. For the third unit, $MB = P$, so Jones would be indifferent between buying the unit and not purchasing it. For a good that is easily divisible, say, pounds of roast beef, the consumer would continue purchasing up to 2.9999 pounds. Thus, economists are comfortable with simply concluding that the consumer will purchase this final unit, implying that Jones will purchase three frozen pizzas.

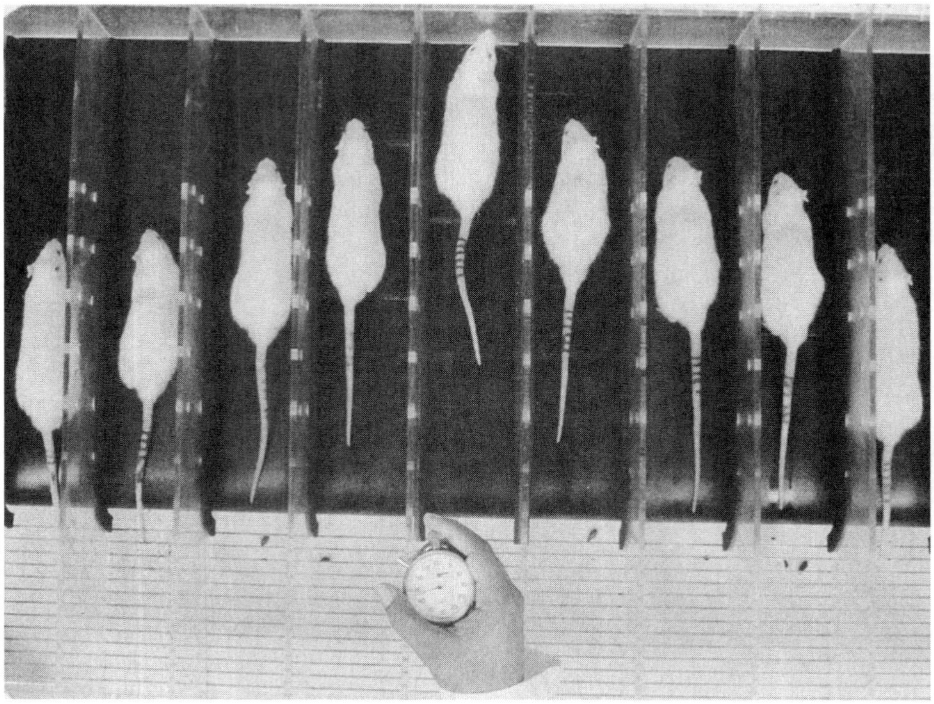

Using experimental methods, researchers have found that the economic fundamentals of consumer choice theory can even explain the consumption choices of rats and other animals. Other economists have found that these theories can also be used to explain such things as a family's choice concerning how many children to have and a criminal's decision regarding the commission of crimes.

these items to the point where the marginal utility of the last gallon of ice cream is twice as high as the marginal utility of the last liter of Coke.

Perhaps the best way to grasp this point is to think about what happens when your ratios of marginal utility to price are not equal for two goods. Suppose that you are at a local restaurant eating buffalo chicken wings and drinking Coke. For simplicity, assume that a large Coke and an order of wings each costs \$2. With your \$10 budget, you decide to purchase four orders of wings, and one large Coke. When you finish your Coke, there are still lots of wings left. You have already eaten so many wings that those remaining do not look as attractive. You could get more utility with fewer wings and another Coke, but it is too late. You have not spent your \$10 in a way that gets the most for your money. Instead of satisfying the above condition, you find that the marginal utility of wings is lower than the marginal utility of a Coke, and because they both have the same price (\$2), this implies

$$\frac{MU_{wings}}{P_{wings}} < \frac{MU_{Coke}}{P_{Coke}}$$

If you had purchased fewer wings and more Coke, your total utility would be higher. Spending more on Coke would decrease its marginal utility, lowering the value of the right side of the equation. Simultaneously, spending less on wings would raise the marginal utility of wings, increasing the value of the left side of the equation. You will maximize your utility—and get the most "bang for the buck" from your budget—when you make these values (the ratios) equal.

The equation can also be used to derive the law of demand. Beginning from a situation where the two sides were equal, suppose the price of wings increased. It would lower the value of *MU/P* for wings below the *MU/P* for Coke. In response you would reallocate your budget, purchasing fewer of the more costly wings and more Coke. Thus we have the law of demand—as the price of wings rises you will purchase less. When people try to spend their money in a way that gives them the greatest amount of satisfaction, the consumer decision-making theory outlined here is difficult to question. In the next section, we take the theory a little farther.

Price Changes and Consumer Choice

The demand curve or schedule shows the amount of a product that consumers would be willing to purchase at alternative prices during a specific time period. The law of demand states that the amount of a product purchased is inversely related to its price. We have seen how the law of demand can be derived from fundamental principles of consumer behavior. Now, we go farther and distinguish two different phenomena underlying a consumer's response to a price change. First, as the price of a product declines, the lower opportunity cost will induce consumers to buy more of it—even if they have to give up other products. Economists refer to this tendency to substitute a product that has become cheaper for goods that are now relatively more expensive as the **substitution effect** of a price change.

Substitution effect
That part of an increase (decrease) in amount consumed that is the result of a good being cheaper (more expensive) in relation to other goods because of a reduction (increase) in price.

Second, with a fixed money income, a reduction in the price of a product will increase a consumer's real income—the amount of goods and services consumers are able to purchase with their fixed amount of money income. A rent or mortgage payment decline by $100 per month would allow you to buy more of numerous other goods. This increase in your real income has the same effect as if the rent had remained the same, but your income had risen by $100 per month. Because of this equivalence, this second way in which a price change affects consumption is referred to as the **income effect**. Typically, consumers will respond by purchasing more of the cheaper product and other products as well, because they can now better afford to do so. (Both the income and substitution effects are derived graphically in the addendum to this reading, titled "Consumer Choice and Indifference Curves.") The substitution and income effects will generally work in the same direction, causing consumers to purchase more as the price falls and less as the price rises.[5]

Income effect
That part of an increase (decrease) in amount consumed that is the result of the consumer's real income (the consumption possibilities available to the consumer) being expanded (contracted) by a reduction (rise) in the price of a good.

Time Cost and Consumer Choice

You may have heard the saying that "time is money." It is certainly true that time has value, and this value can sometimes be measured in dollars. For example we might ask how much a person would be willing to pay to save an hour (perhaps for a nonstop airline flight that takes one hour less travel time, or for a house with a shorter commute to work). Another measure of the value people place on their time is their wage rate, the price at which they are selling an hour of their time.

The monetary price of a good is not always a complete measure of its cost to the consumer. Consumption of most goods requires time as well as money; and time, like money, is scarce to the consumer. So a lower time cost, like a lower money price, will make a product more attractive. For example, patients in a dentist's office would prefer a shorter wait before receiving care. One study showed that dental patients are willing to pay more than $5 per minute saved, to shorten their times in the waiting room.[6] The rise in expenditures on fast foods, mentioned above, is another

[5] The substitution effect will always work in this direction. The income effect, however, may work in the reverse direction for some types of goods known as inferior goods. These will be addressed later in this reading.

[6] Rexford E. Santerre and Stephen P. Neun, *Health Economics: Theories, Insights and Industry Studies* (Orlando: Harcourt, 2000), p. 113.

illustration. Indeed, commodities such as automatic dishwashers, prepared foods, air travel, and taxi service are demanded mainly for the time savings they offer. People are often willing to pay relatively high money prices for such goods.

Time costs, unlike money prices for goods, differ among individuals. They are higher for persons with higher wage rates, for example. Other things being equal, high-wage consumers choose fewer time-intensive (and more time-saving) commodities than persons with a lower time cost. High-wage consumers are overrepresented among air and taxicab passengers but underrepresented among television watchers, chess players, and long-distance bus travelers. Can you explain why? You can, if you understand how both money and time costs influence the choices of consumers.

Failure to account for time costs can lead to bad decisions. For example, which is cheaper for consumers: (a) waiting in line three hours to purchase a $25 concert ticket or (b) buying the same ticket for $40 without standing in line? A consumer whose time is worth more than $5 per hour will find that $40 without the wait in line is less costly. Time costs matter. For example, when government-imposed price ceilings create shortages, rationing by waiting in line is frequently used. In many cases, the benefit of the lower price to consumers will be largely, if not entirely, offset by their increased time cost.

3 MARKET DEMAND REFLECTS THE DEMAND OF INDIVIDUAL CONSUMERS

The market demand schedule is the relationship between the market price of a good and the amount demanded by all the individuals in the market area. Because individual consumers purchase less at higher prices, the amount demanded in a market area as a total is also inversely related to price.

Exhibit 19-2 illustrates the relationship between individual demand and market demand for a hypothetical two-person market. The individual demand curves for both Jones and Smith are shown. Jones and Smith each consume three frozen pizzas per week at a price of $2.50. The amount demanded in the two-person

EXHIBIT 19-2 Individual and Market Demand Curves

The market demand curve is merely the horizontal sum of the individual demand curves. It will slope downward to the right just as the individual demand curves do.

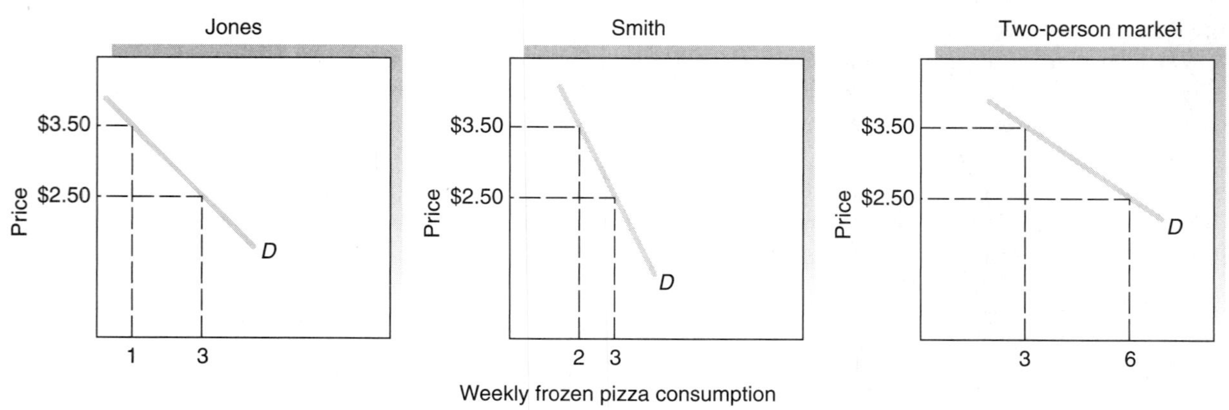

market is six pizzas. If the price rises to $3.50 per pizza, the amount demanded in the market will fall to three pizzas, one demanded by Jones and two by Smith. ***The market demand is simply the horizontal sum of the individual demand curves.***

Market demand reflects individual demand. Individuals buy less as price increases. Therefore, the total amount demanded in the market declines as price increases. That is not difficult to understand, when we think about it. Comparing market prices of different goods, however, can introduce a puzzle.

Nothing is more useful than water; but it will purchase scarce anything. . . . A diamond, on the contrary, has scarce any value in use; but a very great quantity of other goods may frequently be had in exchange for it.

—Adam Smith[7]

Total Versus Marginal Value

The classical economists, including Adam Smith, were puzzled that water, which is necessary for life, sells so cheaply, while diamonds have a far greater price. Does this mean that people value diamonds more than water? This same confusion can be found in everyday life. For example, a spouse or good friend might inquire, "You are going out to play golf? Is golf more important to you than I am?"

A century after Smith's time, economists solved this puzzle when they discovered the importance of the marginal analysis we have been discussing. The total value of a good includes consumer surplus for all units consumed; thus, total value can be quite large even though the price (which reflects the marginal value) is quite low. These factors provide the explanation for why market price has so little to do with the total contribution that a good makes to the welfare of users.

It is possible for something to have a large total value, but a very small marginal value, and also for something with high marginal value to have a low total value. Spending time with a spouse or friend can be more valuable in total than playing golf, but it can simultaneously be true that one *additional* hour spent with that person is less valuable than an *additional* hour of golf.

The willingness to pay for additional units depends on one's valuation of the marginal unit, not on the value of all units taken together. While, in total, water is far more valuable to you than diamonds, you may well value an additional cup of diamonds more than an additional cup of water. If you had no diamonds and no water, you would certainly value the first cup of water more than the first cup of diamonds. But this is not where you are. You consume hundreds of gallons of water per year, but you may only have one or two diamonds.

Items available at a low cost will be consumed until their marginal value is low enough to match the low cost. Because the supply of water is large, water has a low price. At this low price people use water for frequent showers, fish tanks, and many other low-valued uses. If diamonds were as plentiful as water, and sold for only pennies per pound, we might use them for gravel in the bottom of our fish tanks. On the other hand, if water became significantly less abundant, its price would be very high and we might quit taking showers because each costs $1,000 worth of water.

---

[7] Adam Smith, *An Inquiry into the Nature and Causes of the Wealth of Nations*, 1776, ed. Edwin Cannan (Chicago: University of Chicago Press, 1976), p. 33.

4 DETERMINANTS OF SPECIFIC PREFERENCES: WHY CONSUMERS BUY WHAT THEY BUY

Did you ever wonder why a friend spent hard-earned money on something that you would not want even if it were free? People have different tastes and preferences, but what determines these preferences? Economists have not been able to say very much on this topic. Without a theory of preferences, the best strategy has generally been to take preferences as given, using price and other demand-related factors to explain and predict human behavior. Still, several observations about what influences consumer preferences have been made:

1. ***The determining factors in consumer preferences are frequently complex.*** People looking for a house want far more than just a shelter: They want an attractive setting, a convenient location, higher-quality public services, and a great many other things. Moreover, each person may evaluate the same housing attribute differently. For example, living near a school may be a high priority for a family with children but a nuisance to a retired couple.
2. ***Consumer preferences are shaped by attitudes toward time and risk.*** A consumer would nearly always prefer to receive a good now rather than later. The degree of this difference, however, differs across consumers. Those with a higher rate of time preference will be willing to pay extra (perhaps by taking out a loan and paying interest) to make goods available earlier, while others will save and let their money grow in the bank with interest until they can make their desired purchase. This interest is the reward earned for delaying current consumption.

   In addition to time preference, consumers also differ in the degree of risk they are willing to take (or more precisely how much they are willing to pay to reduce risk). Would you prefer to pay $20 more for a brand name product, or take a gamble on an unknown product that costs less? A risk taker may choose the cheaper product. Buying insurance is another way to reduce risk. Some consumers will decide to purchase flood insurance for their homes, or dental insurance, while others will not. They will prefer to save the money from the premiums and pay out-of-pocket for any expenses incurred.

   With regard to risk preference, a person may be either *risk loving, risk neutral,* or *risk averse.* Suppose you could have either $50 cash or a chance to flip a fair coin where heads wins $100 and tails wins nothing. Which would you choose—the certain $50 or the 50 percent chance at winning $100? A risk-loving person would prefer to take the gamble at winning $100, a risk-averse person would take the cash, and a risk-neutral person would be indifferent between the two alternatives.
3. ***Advertising influences consumer choice and preferences.*** Advertisers would not spend more than $100 billion in the United States each year if they did not get results. But exactly how does advertising affect consumers? Does it simply provide valuable information about product quality, price, and availability? Or does it use repetition and misleading information to manipulate consumers? Economists are not of one opinion. Let us take a closer look at this important issue.

Advertising—Is It Useful to Consumers?

Advertising revenues reduce the purchase price of newspapers and magazines, and make broadcast television free to viewers. But since the consumers of the advertised products indirectly pay for these benefits, advertising cannot be defended solely on the basis of its sponsorship role.

Advertising does convey information about product price, quality, and availability. New firms or those with new products, new hours, new locations, or new services can use advertising to keep consumers informed, thus facilitating more efficient trading. After all, people who do not know the advantages of the newly available product or service, and how and where to get it, are not likely to become customers.

Is Advertising Wasteful?

Some repetitious commercials offer little or no new information, but rather seek to take customers from competitors or promote their brand name. A multimillion-dollar media campaign by a soft drink or automobile manufacturer designed to capture a larger market share may be offset by a similar campaign waged by a competitor. The consumers of these products end up paying the costs of these battles for their attention and their dollars. Consumers, though, are under no obligation to purchase advertised products. If advertising results in higher prices with no compensating benefits, consumers can turn to cheaper, unadvertised products. Many, however, buy the advertised brand names. How can brand names, especially those created by competing advertising campaigns, possibly benefit consumers?

A brand name in which people have confidence, even one established by advertising, has a function beyond gaining the attention of consumers. It is an asset at risk for the seller. People value buying from sellers in whom they have confidence, and will pay a premium to do so. That premium makes a brand name valuable. If something happens to damage the reputation of a brand name, the willingness of consumers to purchase the product falls. In a very real sense, the brand name is hostage to consumer satisfaction.

When brand names are not allowed, as in the case of alcoholic beverages during Prohibition, consumers often suffer. For example, with no brand name reputations to protect, anonymous moonshiners sometimes were careless and allowed dangerous impurities into the brew. Some consumers were blinded, and others died. Today the situation is different. Those who buy Johnnie Walker scotch know that the distiller has an enormous sum of money tied up in the brand—about $3 billion by one estimate.[8] The Guinness Corporation, owner of the brand, would spend a large amount of money to avoid even one death from an impure batch. And this brand's value is dwarfed by many others. The estimated value of the brand name for Microsoft is more than $56 billion, and for Coca-Cola, more than $83 billion. Alternative brands of software and soft drinks compete with these two giants, and do far less advertising. Is a brand name, promoted by costly advertising, worthwhile to the customer? In a market, each buyer decides.

Is Advertising Misleading and Manipulative?

Unfair and deceptive advertising—including false promises, whether spoken privately by a seller or packaged by an advertising agency—is illegal; and a publicly advertised false claim is easier to prosecute than the same words spoken in private.

What about ads that are not fraudulent, but simply attempt to manipulate, or shape the preferences of people? In evaluating the manipulative effect

---

[8] *Financial World* magazine estimated the Johnnie Walker Red brand name to be worth $3.2 billion (expressed in year 2000 dollars).

of advertising, two things should be kept in mind. First, business decision makers are likely to choose the simplest route to economic gain. Generally, it is easier for business firms to cater to the actual desires of consumers than to attempt to reshape their preferences or persuade them to purchase an undesired product. Second, when advertising influences preferences, does it follow that this is bad? College classes in music and art appreciation, for example, may also change preferences for various forms of art and music. Does this make them bad? Economic theory is neutral. It neither condemns nor defends advertising—or college classes—as they try to change the tastes of target audiences.

From market demand and the preferences that lie behind it, we turn now to the measurement of buyer and seller responsiveness to market changes. Intelligent pricing decisions for businesses, universities, and individuals depend on the ability of decision makers to understand this responsiveness and even in some cases to look for measures of buyer responses. The same is true for government decision makers considering tax changes.

5 ELASTICITY OF DEMAND

Buyers will predictably demand fewer units when the price rises. If a university raises tuition, fewer students will enroll. How many fewer? That depends on a number of factors, including the available substitutes, the cost of change, and the time available to make the change. Entering freshmen may be more responsive to the price change than seniors who would have trouble transferring credits to another school. Students wanting a specific program that is unavailable other places may also be less responsive to the tuition change.

Similarly, when electricity prices rise, as they recently did in California, consumers will buy less. Per-person consumption of electricity there is already the lowest in the nation, but much more conservation is possible. How responsive will consumers be to a specific change in the price of electricity? Again, many factors will enter, from the options available to consumers to the period of time we want to consider. Consumer response to a specific price increase will be greater over a five-year period than a five-week period. Over time, users can gradually replace appliances, lighting fixtures, and water heaters with energy-saving models, learn the habit of switching off unused lights and computers, or switch from electric to gas heat, all in response to the higher electricity price. Estimating short- and long-run responses to a change in price is crucial for government regulators and for electric utility managers.

To learn about and describe buyer responsiveness to price change, economists have developed a concept called *elasticity.* The responsiveness of buyers to a change in price is measured by the **price elasticity of demand**, defined as:

Price elasticity of demand The percent change in the quantity of a product demanded divided by the percent change in the price causing the change in quantity. Price elasticity of demand indicates the degree of consumer response to variation in price.

$$\text{Price elasticity of demand} = \frac{\text{Percentage change in quantity demanded}}{\text{Percentage change in price}} = \frac{\%\Delta Q}{\%\Delta P}$$

This ratio is often called the *elasticity coefficient.* To express it more briefly, we use the notation $\%\Delta Q$ to represent percent change in quantity and $\%\Delta P$ to represent percent change in price. (The Greek letter delta (Δ) means "change in.") The law of demand states that an increase in price lowers quantity purchased, while a decrease in price raises it. Because a change in price causes the quantity demanded to change in the opposite direction, the price elasticity coefficient is always negative, although economists often ignore the sign and simply use the absolute value of the coefficient.

To see how the concept of elasticity works, suppose that the price of the Ford Taurus rose 10 percent, while other prices remained the same. Ford could expect Taurus sales to fall substantially—perhaps 30 percent—as car buyers responded by switching to the many competing cars whose price had not changed. The strong responsiveness of buyers means that the demand for the Taurus is elastic.

Now consider a different situation. Suppose that because of a new tax, the price of not only the Taurus *but all new cars* rises 10 percent. Consumer options in responding to *this* price increase are much more limited. They can't simply switch to a cheaper close substitute, as they could if the price of the Taurus alone rose. They might either simply pay the extra money for a new car or settle for a used car instead. The 10 percent rise in the price of all new cars will lead to a smaller response, perhaps a 5 percent decline in sales of new cars.

To calculate the elasticity coefficient for the Taurus in our example above, we begin with the 30 percent decline in quantity demanded, and divide by the 10 percent rise in the price that caused the decline. Thus, the elasticity of demand for the Taurus would be:

$$\frac{\%\Delta\text{Quantity}}{\%\Delta\text{Price}} = \frac{-30\%}{+10\%} = -3$$

(or 3.0 if we ignore the minus sign), implying that the percentage change in quantity demanded is three times the percentage change in price.

To calculate the demand elasticity for *all* cars (our second example), we see that the percentage change in quantity, 5 percent, divided by the percentage change in price, 10 percent, gives us $-\frac{1}{2}$, or -0.5. The price elasticity of demand for all cars implies that the percentage change in quantity is half the percentage change in price, using our hypothetical numbers.

To calculate elasticity, we usually begin with the quantities purchased at different prices and first compute the percentage changes. Suppose we begin with a price change from P_0 to P_1, which causes a change in quantity demanded, from Q_0 to Q_1. The change in quantity demanded is $Q_0 - Q_1$. To calculate the percentage change in quantity we divide the actual change by the midpoint (or average) of the two quantities.[9] Although it is often easy to find the midpoint without a formula (halfway between \$4 and \$6 is \$5), it can also be found as $(Q_0 + Q_1)/2$. Finally, because 0.05 is simply 5 percent, we multiply by 100. Thus, we may express the percentage change in quantity demanded as:

$$\frac{Q_0 - Q_1}{(Q_0 + Q_1)/2} \times 100$$

Similarly, when the change in price is $P_0 - P_1$, the *percentage* change in price is

$$\frac{P_0 - P_1}{(P_0 + P_1)/2} \times 100$$

Dividing the resulting percentage change in quantity by the percentage change in price gives the elasticity.

Using these expressions for the percentage changes suggests a more direct method of computing elasticity from the numbers. Dividing the percentage change in quantity by the percentage change in price and simplifying gives

[9] This formula uses the average of the starting point and the ending point of the change so that it will give the same result whether we start from the lower or the higher price. This arc elasticity formula is not the only way to calculate elasticity, but it is the most frequently used.

$$\frac{(Q_0 - Q_1)/(Q_0 + Q_1)}{(P_0 - P_1)/(P_0 + P_1)}$$

(Because each term is multiplied by 100 and the denominator of each term contains a 2, these factors cancel out of the final expression.)

A numerical example may help to illustrate. Suppose that Trina's Cakes can sell 50 specialty cakes per week at $7 each, or 70 of the cakes at $6 each. The percentage difference in quantity is the difference in the quantity ($50 - 70 = -20$), divided by the midpoint (60), times 100. The result is a -33.33 percent change in quantity ($-20 \div 60 \times 100 = -33.33$). The percentage change in price is the difference in price ($7 – $6 = $1) divided by the midpoint price ($6.50) times 100, or a 15.38 percent change in price ($1 \div 6.5 \times 100 = 15.38$). Dividing the percentage change in quantity by the percentage change in price ($-33.33 \div 15.38$) gives an elasticity coefficient of -2.17. Alternatively, we could have expressed this directly as:

$$\frac{[(50 - 70)/(50 + 70)]}{[(7 - 6)/(7 + 6)]} = \frac{-20/120}{1/13} = \frac{-1/6}{1/13} = \frac{-13}{6} = -2.17$$

The same result is obtained either way. The elasticity of -2.17 indicates that the percentage change in quantity is just over twice the percentage change in price.

The elasticity coefficient lets us make a precise distinction between elastic and inelastic. When the elasticity coefficient is greater than 1 (ignoring the sign), as it was for the demand for Trina's Cakes, demand is elastic. When it is less than 1, demand is inelastic. Demand is said to be of *unitary elasticity* if the price elasticity is exactly 1.

Graphic Representation of Price Elasticity of Demand

Exhibit 19-3 presents demand curves of varying elasticity. A demand curve that is completely vertical is termed *perfectly inelastic.* In the real world, such a demand is nonexistent. The substitutes for a good become more attractive as the price of that good rises, and since the income effect is also present, we should expect that a higher price will always reduce quantity demanded, other things remaining the same. Still, the (mythical) perfectly inelastic demand curve is shown in part a of Exhibit 19-3.

The more inelastic the demand, the steeper the demand curve *over any specific price range.* Inspection of the demand for cigarettes (part b of Exhibit 19-3), which is highly inelastic, and the demand for apples (part d), which is relatively elastic, indicates this. When demand elasticity is unitary, as part c illustrates, a demand curve that is convex to the origin will result. When a demand curve is completely horizontal, an economist would say that it is *perfectly elastic.* Demand for the wheat marketed by a single wheat farmer, for example, would approximate perfect elasticity (part e).

Because elasticity is a relative concept, the elasticity of a straight line demand curve will differ at each point along the demand curve. As **Exhibit 19-4** illustrates, the elasticity of a straight line demand curve (one with a constant slope) will range from highly elastic to highly inelastic. Here, when the price rises from $10 to $11, sales decline from 20 to 10. According to the formula, the price elasticity of demand is -7.0. Demand is very elastic in this region. In contrast, demand is quite inelastic in the $1 to $2 price range. As the price increases from $1 to $2, the amount demanded declines from 110 to 100. The 10-unit change in quantity is the same, but it is a smaller *percentage* change. And the $1 change in price is the same, but it is now a larger *percentage* change. The elasticity of demand in this range is only -0.14; demand here is highly inelastic.

It is clear now that elasticity is more than just the slope of the demand curve. This is important because unlike the slope, elasticities are independent of the

EXHIBIT 19-3 Elasticity of Demand

a) Perfectly inelastic: Despite an increase in price, consumers still purchase the same amount. In fact, the substitution and income effects prevent this from happening in the real world.

b) Relatively inelastic: A percent increase in price results in a smaller percent reduction in sales. The demand for cigarettes has been estimated to be highly inelastic.

c) Unitary elastic: The percent change in quantity demanded is equal to the percent change in price. A curve of decreasing slope results. Sales revenue (price times quantity sold) is constant.

d) Relatively elastic: A percentage increase in price leads to a larger percent reduction in purchases. When good substitutes are available for a product (as in the case of apples), the amount purchased will be highly sensitive to a change in price.

e) Perfectly elastic: Consumers will buy all of Farmer Jones's wheat at the market price, but none will be sold above the market price.

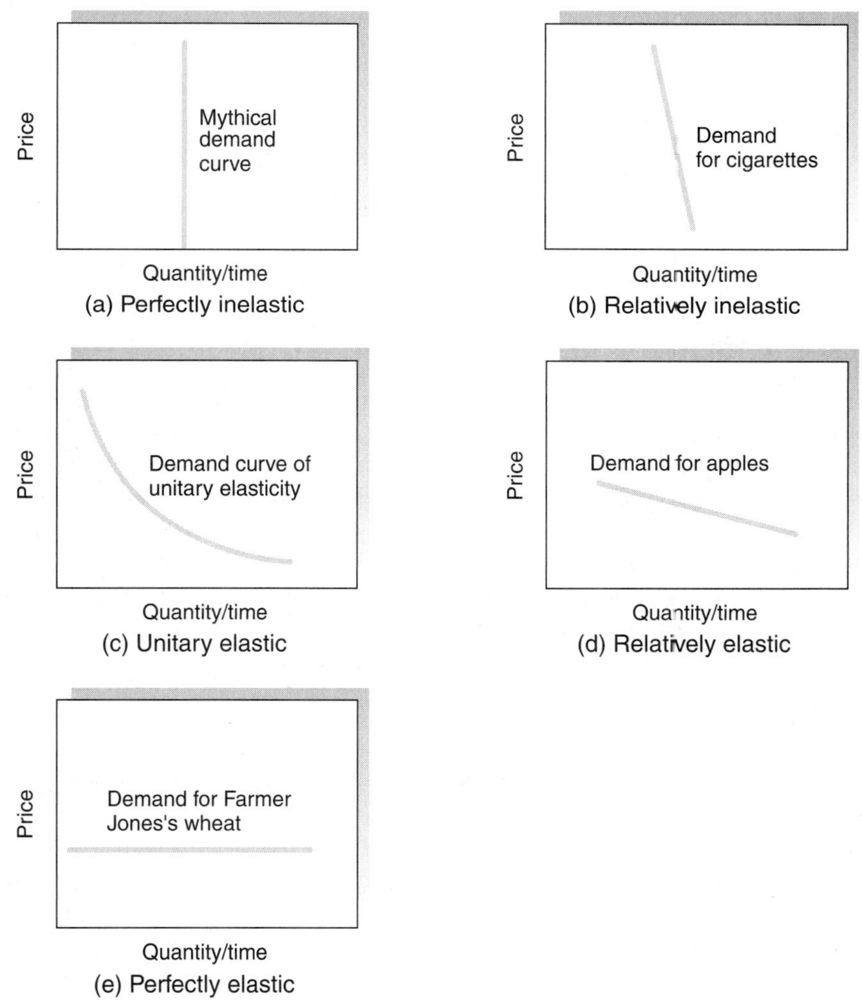

units of measure. The elasticity is the same whether we talk about dollars per gallon or cents per liter, even though the slope changes. Elasticity is the appropriate measure, because people do not care what units of measurement are used; their response depends on the actual terms of exchange.

How large is the price elasticity of demand for various goods? What determines those elasticities? The next section reports some estimates and steps back to explain them.

EXHIBIT 19-4 Slope of Demand Curve Versus Price Elasticity

With this straight line (constant slope) demand curve, demand is more elastic in the high price range. The formula for arc elasticity shows that, when price rises from $1 to $2 and quantity falls from 110 to 100, demand is inelastic. A price rise of the same magnitude (but of a smaller percentage), from $10 to $11, leads to a decline in quantity of the same size (but of a larger percentage), so that elasticity is much greater. (Price elasticities are negative, but economists often ignore the sign and look only at the absolute value.)

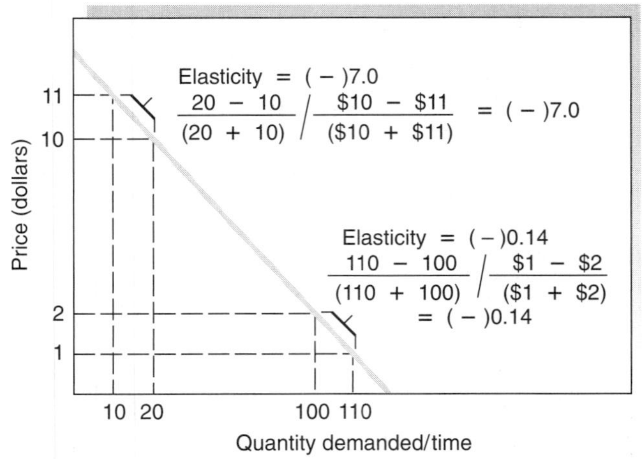

Price Elasticities and Their Determinants

Economists have estimated the price elasticity of demand for many products. As Exhibit 19-5 illustrates, the elasticity of demand varies substantially among products. The demand is highly inelastic for several products—salt, toothpicks, matches, light bulbs, and newspapers, for example—in their normal price range. On the other hand, the demand curves for fresh tomatoes, Chevrolet automobiles, and fresh green peas are highly elastic. The primary factors explaining this variation are the availability of good substitutes and to some extent the share of the typical consumer's total budget expended on a product.

Availability of Substitutes

The most important determinant of the price elasticity of demand is the availability of substitutes. When good substitutes for a product are available, a price rise induces many consumers to switch to other products. Demand is elastic. For example, if the price of felt tip pens increased, many consumers would simply switch to pencils, ballpoint pens, or (for children) crayons. If the price of apples increased, consumers might substitute oranges, bananas, peaches, or pears.

When good substitutes are unavailable, the demand for a product tends to be inelastic. Medical services are an example. When we are sick, most of us find witch doctors, faith healers, palm readers, and aspirin to be highly imperfect substitutes for the services of a physician. Not surprisingly, the demand for physician services is inelastic.

The availability of substitutes increases as the product class becomes more specific, thus increasing price elasticity. For example, as Exhibit 19-5 shows, the price elasticity of Chevrolets, a narrow product class, exceeds that of the broad class of automobiles in general. If the price of Chevrolets alone rises, many substitute cars are available. But if the prices of all automobiles rise together, consumers have fewer good substitutes.

EXHIBIT 19-5 Estimated Price Elasticity of Demand for Selected Products

Inelastic	
Salt	−0.1
Matches	−0.1
Toothpicks	−0.1
Airline travel, short run	−0.1
Gasoline, short run	−0.2
Gasoline, long run	−0.7
Residential natural gas, short run	−0.1
Residential natural gas, long run	−0.5
Coffee	−0.25
Fish (cod), consumed at home	−0.5
Tobacco products, short run	−0.45
Legal services, short run	−0.4
Physician services	−0.6
Dental services	−0.7
Taxi, short run	−0.6
Automobiles, long run	−0.2

Approximately unitary elasticity	
Movies	−0.9
Housing, owner occupied, long run	−1.2
Shellfish, consumed at home	−0.9
Oysters, consumed at home	−1.1
Private education	−1.1
Tires, short run	−0.9
Tires, long run	−1.2
Radio and television receivers	−1.2

Elastic	
Restaurant meals	−2.3
Foreign travel, long run	−4.0
Airline travel, long run	−2.4
Fresh green peas	−2.8
Automobiles, short run	−1.2–1.5
Chevrolet automobiles	−4.0
Fresh tomatoes	−4.6

Sources: Hendrick S. Houthakker and Lester D. Taylor, *Consumer Demand in the United States, 1929–1970* (Cambridge: Harvard University Press, 1966, 1970); Douglas R. Bohi, *Analyzing Demand Behavior* (Baltimore: Johns Hopkins University Press, 1981); Hsaing-tai Cheng and Oral Capps Jr., "Demand for Fish," *American Journal of Agricultural Economics*, August 1988; U.S. Department of Agriculture; and Rexford E. Santerre and Stephen P. Neun, *Health Economics: Theories, Insights and Industry Studies* (Orlando: Harcourt, 2000).

Share of Total Budget Expended on Product

If the expenditures on a product are quite small relative to the consumer's budget, the income effect will be small even if there is a substantial increase in the price of the product. This will make demand less elastic. Compared to one's total budget, expenditures on some commodities are almost inconsequential. Matches, toothpicks, and salt are good examples. Most consumers spend only $1 or $2 per year on each of these items. A doubling of their price would exert little influence on the family budget. Therefore, even if the price of such a product were to rise sharply, consumers would still not find it in their interest to spend much time and effort looking for substitutes.

Exhibit 19-6 provides a graphic illustration of both elastic and inelastic demand curves. In part a, the demand curve for ballpoint pens is elastic, because there are good substitutes—for example, pencils and felt tip pens. Therefore, when the price of the pens increases from $1.00 to $1.50, the quantity purchased declines sharply from 100,000 to only 25,000. The calculated price elasticity equals −3.0. The fact that the absolute value of the coefficient is greater than 1 confirms that the demand for ballpoint pens is elastic over the price range illustrated.

EXHIBIT 19-6 Inelastic and Elastic Demand

As the price of ballpoint pens (a) rose from $1.00 to $1.50, the quantity purchased plunged from 100,000 to 25,000. The percent reduction in quantity is larger than the percent increase in price. Thus, the demand for the pens is elastic. In contrast, an increase in the price of cigarettes from $1.00 to $1.50 results in only a small reduction in the number purchased (b). Reflecting the inelasticity of demand for cigarettes, the percent reduction in quantity is smaller than the percent increase in price.

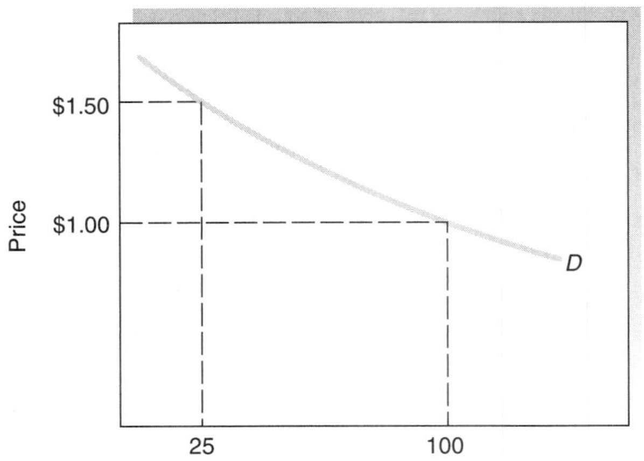

(a) Ballpoint pens per week (in thousands)

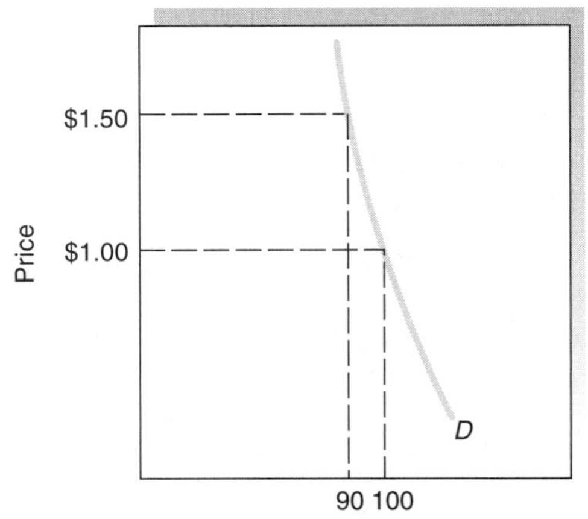

(b) Cigarette packs per week (in millions)

Part b of Exhibit 19-6 illustrates the demand curve for cigarettes. Because most smokers do not find other products to be a good substitute, the demand for cigarettes is highly inelastic. If a unit of six cigarettes is worth a dollar, a substantial (from $1.00 to $1.50) increase in price leads to only a small reduction in quantity demanded. The price elasticity coefficient is −0.26, substantially less in absolute value than 1, confirming that the demand for cigarettes is inelastic. (*Exercise:* Use the price elasticity formula to verify the values of these elasticity coefficients.)

Time and Demand Elasticity

As changing market conditions raise or lower the price of a product, both consumers and producers will respond. However, their response will not be instantaneous, and it is likely to become larger over time. ***In general, when the price of a product increases, consumers will reduce their consumption by a larger amount in the long run than in the short run. Thus, the demand for most products will be more elastic in the long run than in the short run. This relationship between the elasticity coefficient and the length of the adjustment period is sometimes referred to as the second law of demand.***

The first law of demand says that buyers will respond predictably to a price change, purchasing more when the price is lower than when the price is higher, if other things remain the same. The second law of demand says that the buyers' response will be greater after they have had time to adjust more fully to a price change.

6 TOTAL EXPENDITURE, TOTAL REVENUE, AND THE PRICE ELASTICITY OF DEMAND

In this section we examine the relationship between the price elasticity of demand and the total expenditure on an item (or revenue derived from its sale). Demand elasticity can be used to determine changes in total consumer expenditures at three levels: (1) for an individual's total spending on a product using the demand elasticity from an individual's demand curve for the product, (2) for the total combined expenditures of all consumers on a product using the elasticity from the total market demand curve for a product, or (3) for total consumer expenditures on the product of an individual business firm using the demand curve facing that firm.

If the price of a product rises, total consumer expenditures on it can either rise, fall, or stay the same, depending on the elasticity of demand. According to the law of demand, as the price rises the quantity purchased will fall, and as price falls the quantity purchased will rise:

Total Expenditures	=	Price	×	Quantity
?	=	↑	×	↓
?	=	↓	×	↑

Because total expenditures are equal to price times quantity, and because price and quantity move in opposite directions, the net effect on total expenditures depends upon whether the (percent) price change or the (percent) quantity change is greater. When demand is inelastic, the price elasticity coefficient is less than one. This means that the percentage change in price is greater. ***Therefore, when demand is inelastic, a change in price will cause total expenditures to change in the same direction.***

When demand is elastic, the effect of the change in quantity will be greater than the effect of the change in price. ***Therefore, a change in price will cause total expenditures to move in the opposite direction when demand is elastic.***

When demand elasticity is unitary, the change in quantity will be equal in magnitude to the change in price. With regard to their impact on total expenditures, these two effects will exactly offset each other. ***Thus, when price elasticity of demand is equal to one, total expenditures will remain unchanged as price changes.***

The demand curves shown in Exhibit 19-6 can be used to illustrate the linkage between elasticity of demand and changes in total revenue. In the case of cigarettes (part b), the price elasticity of demand for the price increase from $1.00 to $1.50 is 0.26, indicating that demand is inelastic. This increase in cigarette prices leads to an increase in expenditures on the product from $100 million ($1.00 × 100 million units) to $135 million ($1.50 × 90 million units). If the change had occurred in the opposite direction, with the price falling from $1.50 to $1.00, total expenditures would have declined.

The price elasticity of demand for ballpoint pens for a price increase from $1.00 to $1.50 (part a of Exhibit 19-6) is 3.0, indicating that demand is elastic. This increase in the price of ballpoint pens leads to a reduction in total consumer expenditures from $100,000 ($1.00 × 100,000 pens) to $37,500 ($1.50 × 25,000 pens). If the change had occurred in the opposite direction, with the price falling from $1.50 to $1.00, total expenditures would have risen.

Exhibit 19-7 summarizes the relationship between changes in price and total expenditures for products with demands of varying elasticity. The (inelastic) demand for cigarettes implies that a price increase will result in higher total consumer expenditures on them. But a price increase for ballpoint pens, with their elastic demand, would lead to lower total expenditures on that item.

This same analysis can be performed using a particular firm's demand curve, rather than the total market demand curve for the product. Here, total consumer expenditures are, from the firm's perspective, the firm's total revenues—the price per unit times the quantity sold. As we discussed earlier in this chapter, the demand curve facing one specific firm in an industry will be substantially more elastic than the demand curve for the entire market. (Remember the demand elasticity comparison between the Ford Taurus and all automobiles.)

Depending on the relationship between price and quantity sold, a firm's total revenue can rise, fall, or stay the same in response to a change in price. Again, the outcome is determined by price elasticity of demand. When demand

EXHIBIT 19-7 Demand Elasticity and How Changes in Price Affect Total Consumer Expenditures or a Firm's Total Revenue

Price Elasticity of Demand	Numerical Elasticity Coefficient (in absolute value)	Impact of Raising Price on Total Consumer Expenditures or a Firm's Total Revenue	Impact of Lowering Price on Total Consumer Expenditures or a Firm's Total Revenue
Elastic	1 to ∞	decrease	increase
Unitary Elastic	1	unchanged	unchanged
Inelastic	0 to 1	increase	decrease

for the firm's product is inelastic, its total revenues will rise if it increases its price, or fall if it lowers its price. When demand is elastic, however, revenue will fall if price is increased, and will rise if price is reduced. When demand elasticity is unitary, a change in price will leave total revenue unaffected. Exhibit 19-8 gives a numerical example to illustrate this point.

Part a of the exhibit shows how a firm's total revenue is calculated from data on price and quantity sold. In addition, the price elasticity has been computed using the formula. These same data are shown graphically along with the

EXHIBIT 19-8 Demand Elasticity and a Firm's Total Revenue

(a) The Firm's Price, Quantity Sold, Total Revenue, and Price Elasticity[a]

Price		Quantity Sold		Total Revenue	Price Elasticity of Demand
$9	×	0	=	$0	
					((0−1)/(0+1)) / ((9−8)/(9+8)) = 17.00
$8	×	1	=	$8	
					((1−2)/(1+2)) / ((8−7)/(8+7)) = 5.00
$7	×	2	=	$14	
					((2−3)/(2+3)) / ((7−6)/(7+6)) = 2.60
$6	×	3	=	$18	
					((3−4)/(3+4)) / ((6−5)/(6+5)) = 1.57
$5	×	4	=	$20	
					((4−5)/(4+5)) / ((5−4)/(5+4)) = 1.00
$4	×	5	=	$20	
					((5−6)/(5+6)) / ((4−3)/(4+3)) = 0.64
$3	×	6	=	$18	
					((6−7)/(6+7)) / ((3−2)/(3+2)) = 0.38
$2	×	7	=	$14	
					((7−8)/(7+8)) / ((2−1)/(2+1)) = 0.20
$1	×	8	=	$8	
					((8−9)/(8+9)) / ((1−0)/(1+0)) = 0.06
$0	×	9	=	$0	

(b) The Firm's Demand Curve, Total Revenue, and Elasticity[a]

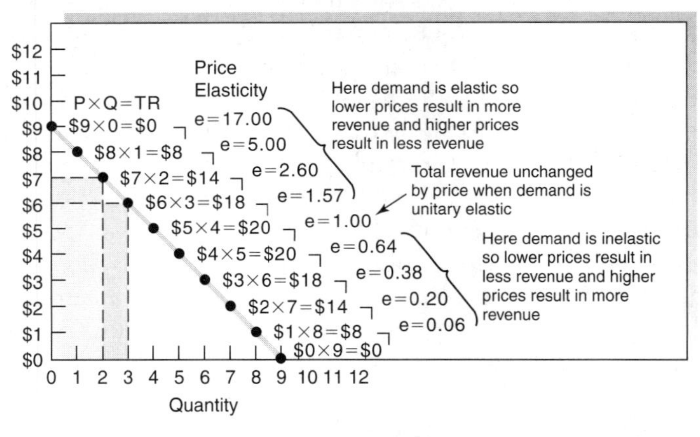

(c) Price versus Total Revenue

(d) Quantity versus Total Revenue

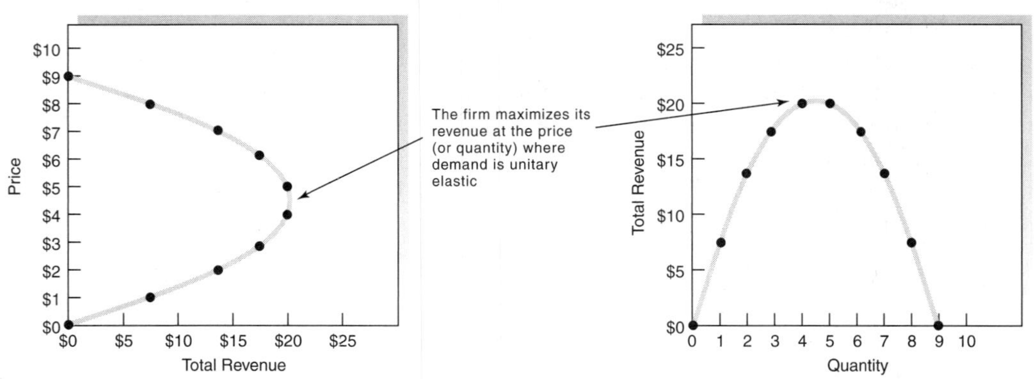

[a] The sign of all elasticity coefficients is negative.

firm's demand curve in part b of the exhibit. As the firm lowers its price from $9 to $8 to $7, the firm's revenues expand from $0 to $8 to $14. In this range, the firm's demand curve is elastic, so total revenue is rising as price falls. Intuitively, as the firm lowers its price, it is losing revenue from customers who would have paid more for some units but it is gaining revenue from customers, including new ones, who are buying more at the lower price. When demand is elastic, the expansion in revenue from additional sales is more than enough to offset the reductions in revenue on some units due to the lower price. An example of this is shown by the shaded areas in part b of the exhibit. At a price of $7, the firm sells 2 units. Total revenue is $14, which is shown by the red shaded area. When price is lowered to $6, sales increase to 3 units, and total revenue is $18, shown by the shorter rectangle that includes the blue shaded area. The small part of the red shaded area above the blue area is lost revenue on existing sales, while the small part of the blue area to the right of the red area is the gain in revenue on new sales. Because the gain is greater than the loss, revenue increases.

This process continues until demand reaches unitary elasticity between a price of $4 and $5. In this range total revenue is unchanged at $20 regardless of whether price is $4 or $5. Here, as price is lowered, the revenue from new sales exactly offsets the loss in revenue from existing sales.

As price falls further from $4 to $3 to $2, the firm's total revenues begin to fall. Here, price reductions result in lower revenue because the lower part of the demand curve is inelastic. The revenue from the new sales is not enough to offset the losses in revenue due to the lowered price.

Of course, this example could be viewed in reverse. As the firm raises its price up from $1, revenues expand until demand is unit elastic, and, above this, revenues fall with further price increases as demand becomes elastic. The issue is whether the higher revenue from the sales that remain is sufficient to offset the lower revenue from the lost sales.

This relationship between the firm's total revenue and its price is shown in part c of the exhibit. Alternatively, we may view this as a relationship between the quantity and the total revenue, as shown in part d. The firm maximizes its revenue at the price (or quantity) where demand is unit elastic.[10] We might notice a similarity between the graph shown in part c of the exhibit and the Laffer curve between tax rates and total tax revenue from Chapter 4. It is indeed the elasticity of the tax base to a tax rate change that underlies the Laffer curve in a similar manner.

Firms attempt to maximize profit, not revenue. Profit is total revenue *minus total cost.* The price or output where demand is unit elastic and revenue is maximized is not the same as the one where total profit is maximized—unless output can be increased at zero cost. They will be close, however, for some types of firms whose costs are mostly upfront (or "fixed") with little marginal cost of producing additional units. For a concert or sporting event, most of the cost is of this type, and there is very little additional cost of allowing more people into the event.

Suppose that the exhibit shown is for the price, quantity (in thousands), and total revenue (also in thousands) for a firm selling tickets to a concert. Can you explain why even if the capacity of the stadium was 10 thousand, the firm might decide to set the ticket price at a level that does not sell out the stadium? Alternatively, suppose the exhibit was the relationship between a university's tuition (in thousands) and its enrollment (also in thousands). If current tuition was $6 thousand, can you explain why the university could get more tuition revenue by

---

[10] An astute student might note that total revenue is really maximized at a price of $4.50 and a quantity of 4.5 (if possible, say, 4.5 pounds of roast beef). Here total revenue is $20.25. Because the elasticity formula uses the midpoint as a basis, the elasticity shown for the price change from $4 to $5 is really the elasticity at the midpoint between these two prices, or $4.50

lowering its tuition? If you can, you understand the importance of price elasticity of demand for decision makers in the business firm.

Beyond the price elasticity of demand, two other elasticity relationships are important in any given market. We end this reading with a brief discussion of income elasticity of demand and of price elasticity of supply.

7 INCOME ELASTICITY

Income elasticity
The percentage change in the quantity of a product demanded divided by the percentage change in consumer income causing the change in quantity demanded. It measures the responsiveness of the demand for a good to a change in income.

Normal good
A good that has a positive income elasticity, so that, as consumer income rises, demand for that good rises also.

Increases in consumer income will increase the demand (the quantity demanded at each price) for most goods. Income elasticity indicates the responsiveness of the demand for a product to a change in income. **Income elasticity** is defined as:

$$\text{Income Elasticity} = \frac{\text{Percentage change in quantity demanded}}{\text{Percentage change in income}}$$

As Exhibit 19-9 shows, although the income elasticity coefficients for products vary from one good to another, they are normally positive. In fact, the term **normal good** refers to any good with a positive income elasticity of demand. Some normal goods have lower income elasticities than others, however. In general, goods that people regard as "necessities" will have low income elasticities (between 0 and 1). Significant quantities are purchased even at low incomes, and, as income increases, spending on these items will increase by less than a proportional amount. It is understandable that such items as fuel, electricity, bread, tobacco, economy clothing, and potatoes have a low income elasticity.

Goods that consumers regard as "luxuries" generally have a high (greater than 1) income elasticity. For example, private education, new automobiles, recreational activities, donations to environmental groups, swimming pools, and vacation air travel are all highly income elastic. As income increases, the demand for these goods expands even more rapidly, and therefore spending on these items increases as a proportion of income.

EXHIBIT 19-9 Estimated Income Elasticity of Demand for Selected Products

Low income elasticity		High income elasticity	
Margarine	−0.20	Private education	2.46
Fuel	0.38	New cars	2.45
Electricity	0.20	Recreation and amusements	1.57
Fish (haddock)	0.46	Alcohol	1.54
Food	0.51		
Tobacco	0.64		
Hospital care	0.69		

Sources: Hendrick S. Houthakker and Lester D. Taylor, *Consumer Demand in the United States, 1929–1970* (Cambridge: Harvard University Press, 1966); L. Taylor, "The Demand for Electricity: A Survey," *Bell Journal of Economics* (Spring 1975); F. W. Bell, "The Pope and the Price of Fish," *American Economic Review 58* (December 1968); and Rexford E. Santerre and Stephen P. Neun, *Health Economics: Theories, Insights, and Industry Studies* (Orlando: Harcourt, 2000).

A few commodities, such as margarine, low-quality meat cuts, and bus travel, actually have a negative income elasticity. Economists refer to goods with a negative income elasticity as **inferior goods**. As income expands, the demand for inferior goods will decline. Conversely, as income declines, the demand for inferior goods will increase.

Inferior goods
Good that have a negative income elasticity, so that, as consumer income rises, the demand for those goods falls.

PRICE ELASTICITY OF SUPPLY

8

We may also define the **price elasticity of supply**, which is the percentage change in quantity supplied, divided by the percentage change in the price causing the supply response. Because this measures the responsiveness of sellers to a change in price, it is analogous to the price elasticity of demand. However, the price elasticity of supply will be positive because the quantity producers are willing to supply is directly related to price. As in the case of demand elasticity, time plays a role. Supply elasticities will be greater when suppliers have a longer time to respond to a price change. In the next two chapters we will discuss more fully the factors that determine supply elasticity. For now, it is important simply to recognize the concept of supply elasticity and the fact that suppliers (like buyers) will be more responsive to a price change when they have had more time to adjust to it.

Price elasticity of supply
The percentage change in quantity supplied, divided by the percentage change in the price causing the change in quantity supplied.

Demand, Choice, and Price-Responsive Consumers

In today's market economies, consumers face complex choices. Substitutes are everywhere, so the demand curve for any one product slopes downward to the right. Movies, sports, camping, TV, swimming, and bowling are all substitutes for one another, for many people. Time is the individual's unique constraint; not the supplier's action or price. Further, the demand for the product of any one firm is generally elastic, reflecting the large range of choices among goods competing for the dollars of consumers. Is there only one movie theater in town? Substitutes for a movie at the theater nonetheless abound, from competing activities like those above, to rental movies on tape or DVD. The price elasticity of demand at the theater is thus likely to be large, even when other local theaters are unavailable. This fact is important for policymakers as well as consumers, as we will see in later readings.

9 SUMMARY

- Consumer choice is a process of allocating limited income among a multitude of goods and services in a way that maximizes utility. The role of relative prices, information, preferences for risk and time, and the law of diminishing marginal utility help explain these choices. These ideas underlie the position and shape of an individual's demand curve for a product.
- The market demand curve reflects the demand of individuals. It is simply the horizontal sum of the demand curves of individuals for the product.
- A good with high total value can have low marginal value, and vice versa. Because market price reflects marginal valuations, it has little relationship to the total value of the good.
- The advertising budgets of profit-seeking business firms indicate that advertising influences the choices of consumers. Advertising can reduce the search time of consumers, help them make more informed choices and, through brand names, provide assurances with regard to quality.
- Price elasticity reveals the responsiveness of the amount purchased to a change in price. When there are good substitutes available and the item forms a sizable component of the consumer's budget, its demand will tend to be more elastic. Typically, the price elasticity of a product will increase as more time is allowed for consumers to adjust to a change in price. This direct relationship between size of the elasticity coefficient and the length of the adjustment period is often referred to as the *second law of demand.*
- The concept of elasticity is useful in determining how a change in price will affect total consumer expenditures on an item or a firm's total revenue. An increase in price will lower total revenue (or expenditure) when demand is elastic, but increase it when demand is inelastic. A decrease in price will raise total revenue (or expenditure) when demand is elastic, but decrease it when demand is inelastic. When demand is of unitary elasticity, total revenue (or expenditure) is unaffected by a change in price.
- The concept of elasticity can also be applied to consumer income (income elasticity of demand) and supply (the price elasticity of supply).

ADDENDUM: CONSUMER CHOICE AND INDIFFERENCE CURVES

Advanced Material

In the text of this reading, we used marginal utility analysis to develop the demand curve of an individual. In developing the theory of consumer choice, economists usually rely on a more formal technique—*indifference curve* analysis. Because this technique is widely used at a more advanced level, many instructors like to include it in their introductory course. In this addendum, we use indifference curve analysis to develop the theory of demand in a more formal—some would say more elegant—manner.

What are indifference curves?

There are two elements in every choice: (1) preferences (the desirability of various goods) and (2) opportunities (the attainability of various goods). The **indifference curve** relates to the former: the preferences of an individual. It separates better (more preferred by this individual) bundles of goods from inferior (less preferred) bundles, providing a diagrammatic picture of how an individual ranks alternative consumption bundles.

To illustrate indifference curves, we begin with the title character from the classic *Robinson Crusoe*, by Daniel Defoe, published in 1719 and thought to be the first English novel. Crusoe was shipwrecked on a desert island. In Exhibit 19-A1, we assume that he is initially consuming 8 fish and 8 breadfruit per week (point *A*). This initial bundle provides him with a certain level of satisfaction (utility). He would, however, be willing to trade this initial bundle for certain other consumption alternatives if the opportunity presented itself. Since he likes both fish and breadfruit, he would especially like to obtain bundles to the northeast of point *A* in the diagram, since they represent more of both goods. However, he would also be willing to give up some breadfruit if in return he received a compensatory amount of fish. Similarly, if the terms of trade were right, he would be willing to exchange fish for breadfruit. The trade-offs he is just willing to make—those that would make him no better and no worse off—lie *along* the indifference curve. Of course, he is happy to move to any bundle on a higher indifference curve.

Starting from point *A* (8 fish and 8 breadfruit), we ask Crusoe if he is willing to trade that bundle for various other bundles. He answers "Yes" (*Y*), "No" (*N*), or "I do not care" (*i*). Exhibit 19-A1 illustrates the pattern of his responses. Crusoe's "I do not care" answers indicate that the original bundle (point *A*) and each alternative indicated by an *i* are valued equally by Crusoe. These *i* points, when connected, form the indifference curve. This line separates the preferred bundles of fish and breadfruit from the less-valued combinations. Note that such a curve is likely to be entirely different for any two people. The preferences of individuals vary widely.

We can establish a new indifference curve for the individual by starting from any point not on the original curve and following the same procedure. If we start with a point (a consumption bundle) to the northeast of the original indifference curve, all points on the new curve will have a higher level of satisfaction for Crusoe than any on the old

EXHIBIT 19-A1 The Indifference Curve of Robinson Crusoe

The curve generated by connecting Crusoe's "I do not care" answers separates the combinations of fish and breadfruit that he prefers to the bundle *A* from those that he judges to be inferior to *A*. The *i* points map out an indifference curve.

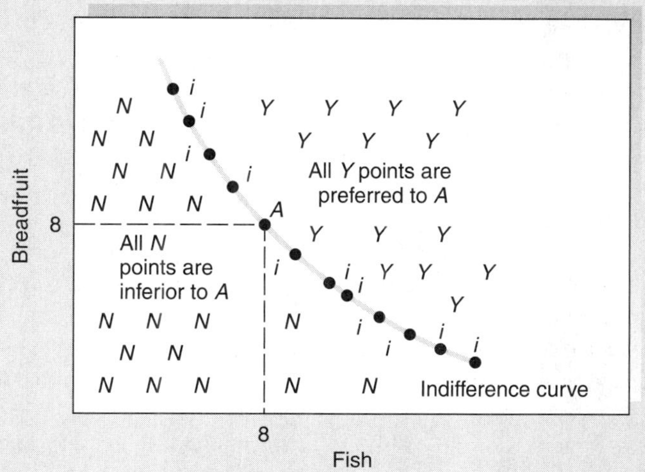

curve. The new curve will probably have about the same shape as the original.

Characteristics of Indifference Curves

In developing consumer theory, economists assume that the preferences of consumers exhibit certain properties. These properties enable us to make statements about the general pattern of indifference curves. What are these properties, and what do they imply about the characteristics of indifference curves?

1. ***More goods are preferable to fewer goods—thus, bundles on indifference curves lying farthest to the northeast of a diagram are always preferred.*** Assuming the consumption of only two commodities that are both desired, the individual will always prefer a bundle with more of one good (without loss of the other) to the original bundle. This means that combinations to the northeast of a point on the diagram will always be preferred to points lying to the southwest.
2. ***Goods are substitutable—therefore, indifference curves slope downward to the right.*** As we indicated in the text of this reading, individuals are willing to substitute one good for another. Crusoe will be willing to give up some breadfruit if he is compensated with enough fish. Stated another way, there will be some amount of additional fish such that Crusoe will stay on the same indifference curve, even though his consumption of breadfruit has declined. However, in order to remain on the same indifference curve, Crusoe must always acquire more of one good to compensate for the loss of the other. The indifference curve for goods thus will always slope downward to the right (run northwest to southeast).
3. ***The valuation of a good declines as it is consumed more intensively—therefore, indifference curves are always convex when viewed from below.*** The slope of the indifference curve represents the willingness of the individual to substitute one good for the other. Economists refer to the amount of one good that is just sufficient to compensate the consumer for the loss of a unit of the other good as the **marginal rate of substitution**. It is equal to the slope of the indifference curve. Reflecting the principle of diminishing marginal utility, the marginal rate of substitution of a good will decline as the good is consumed more intensively relative to other goods. Suppose Crusoe remains on the same indifference curve while continuing to expand his consumption of fish relative to breadfruit. As his consumption of fish increases (and his consumption of breadfruit declines), his valuation of fish relative to breadfruit will decline. It will take more and more units of fish to compensate for the loss of still another unit of breadfruit. The indifference curve will become flatter, reflecting the decline in the marginal rate of substitution of fish for breadfruit as Crusoe consumes more fish relative to breadfruit.

   Of course, just the opposite will happen if Crusoe's consumption of breadfruit increases relative to that of fish—if he moves northwest along the same indifference curve. In this case, as breadfruit is consumed more intensively, Crusoe's valuation of it will decline relative to that of fish, and the marginal rate of substitution of fish for breadfruit will rise (the indifference curve will become steeper and steeper). Therefore, since the valuation of each good declines as it is consumed more intensively, indifference curves must be convex when viewed from the origin.
4. ***Indifference curves are everywhere dense.*** We can construct an indifference curve starting from any point on the diagram. This simply means that any two bundles of goods can be compared by the individual.
5. ***Indifference curves cannot cross—if they did, rational ordering would be violated.*** If indifference curves crossed, our postulate that more goods are better than fewer goods would be violated. Exhibit 19-A2 illustrates this point. The crossing of the indifference curves implies that points *Y* and *Z* are equally preferred, since they both are on the same indifference curve as *X*. Consumption bundle *Y*, though, represents more of both fish and breadfruit than bundle *Z*, so *Y* must be preferred to *Z*. Whenever indifference curves cross, this type of internal inconsistency (irrational ranking) will arise. So, the indifference curves of an individual must not cross.

The Consumer's Preferred Bundle

Used together with the opportunity constraint of the individual, indifference curves can be used to indicate the most preferred consumption alternatives available to an individual. The **consumption opportunity constraint** separates consumption bundles that are attainable from those that are unattainable.

Assuming that Crusoe could produce only for himself, his consumption opportunity constraint would look like the production possibilities curves discussed in Chapter 2. What would happen if natives from another island visited Crusoe and offered to make exchanges with him? If a barter market existed that permitted Crusoe to exchange fish for breadfruit at a specified exchange rate, his options would resemble those of the market constraint illustrated by Exhibit 19-A3. First, let us consider the case where Crusoe inhabits a barter economy in which the current market exchange rate is 2 fish to 1 breadfruit. Suppose as a result

EXHIBIT 19-A2 Indifference Curves Cannot Cross

If the indifference curves of an individual crossed, it would lead to the inconsistency pictured here. Points *X* and *Y* must be equally valued, since they are both on the same indifference curve (i_1). Similarly, points *X* and *Z* must be equally preferred, since they are both on the indifference curve (i_2). If this is true, *Y* and *Z* must also be equally preferred, since they are both equally preferred to *X*. However, point *Y* represents more of both goods than *Z*, so *Y* has to be preferred to *Z*. When indifference curves cross, this type of internal inconsistency always arises.

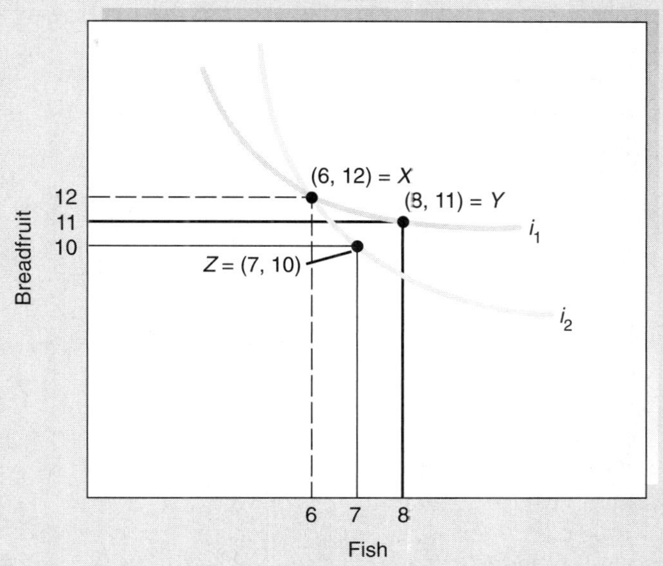

EXHIBIT 19-A3 Consumer Maximization—Barter Economy

Suppose that the set of indifference curves shown here outlines Crusoe's preferences. The slope of the market (or budget) constraint indicates that 2 fish trade for 1 breadfruit in this barter economy. If Crusoe produces 16 fish per week, he will trade 8 fish for 4 breadfruit in order to move to the consumption bundle (8 fish and 4 breadfruit) that maximizes his level of satisfaction.

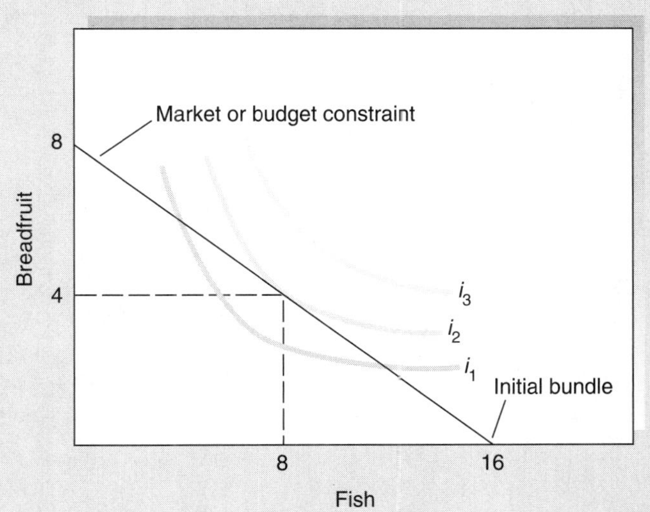

of his expertise as a fisherman, Crusoe specializes in this activity and is able to bring 16 fish to the market per week. What consumption alternatives will be open to him? Since 2 fish can be bartered in the market for 1 breadfruit, Crusoe will be able to consume 16 fish, or 8 breadfruit, or any combination on the market constraint indicated by the line between these two points. For example, if he trades 2 of his 16 fish for 1 breadfruit, he will be able to consume a bundle consisting of 14 fish and 1 breadfruit. Assuming that the set of indifference curves of Exhibit 19-A3 outlines Crusoe's preferences, he will choose to consume 8 fish and 4 breadfruit. Of course, it will be possible for Crusoe to choose many other combinations of breadfruit and fish, but none of the other attainable combinations would enable him to reach as high a level of satisfaction. Because he is able to bring only 16 fish to the market, it would be impossible for him to attain an indifference curve higher than i_2.

Crusoe's indifference curve and the market constraint curve will coincide (they will be tangent) at the point at which his attainable level of satisfaction is maximized. At that point (8 fish and 4 breadfruit), the rate at which Crusoe is willing to exchange fish for breadfruit (as indicated by the slope of the indifference curve) will be just equal to the rate at which the market will *permit* him to exchange the two (the slope of the market constraint). If the two slopes differ at a point, Crusoe will always be able to find an attainable combination that will permit him to reach a *higher* indifference curve. He will always move down the market constraint when it is flatter than his indifference curve, and up if the market constraint is steeper.

Crusoe In a Money Economy

As far as the condition for maximization of consumer satisfaction is concerned, moving from a barter economy to a money income economy changes little. Exhibit 19-A4 illustrates this point. Initially, the price of fish is $1, and the price of breadfruit is $2. The market therefore permits an exchange of 2 fish for 1 breadfruit, just as was the case in Exhibit 19-A3. In Exhibit 19-A4, we assume that Crusoe has a fixed money income of $16. At this level of income, he confronts the same market constraint (usually called a **budget constraint** in an economy with money) as in Exhibit 19-A3. Given the product prices and his income, Crusoe can choose to consume 16 fish, or 8 breadfruit, or any combination indicated by a line (the budget constraint) connecting these two points. Given his preferences, Crusoe will again choose the combination of 8 fish and 4 breadfruit if he wishes to maximize his level of satisfaction. As was true for the barter economy, when Crusoe maximizes his satisfaction (moves to the highest attainable indifference curve), the rate at which he is willing to exchange fish for breadfruit will just equal the rate at which the market will permit him to exchange the two goods. Stated in more technical terms, when his level of sat-

EXHIBIT 19-A4 Consumer Maximization—Money = Income Economy

Suppose that Crusoe's income is $16 per day, the price of fish (P_F) is $1, and the price of breadfruit (P_b) is $2. Thus, Crusoe confronts exactly the same price ratio and budget constraint as in Exhibit 19-A3. Assuming that his preferences are unchanged, he will again maximize his satisfaction by choosing to consume 8 fish and 4 breadfruit. What will happen if the price of fish rises to $2? Crusoe's consumption opportunities will be reduced. His budget constraint will turn clockwise around point *A*, reflecting the higher price of fish. His fish consumption will decline to 5 units. (*Note:* Because Crusoe's real income has been reduced, his consumption of breadfruit will also decline.)

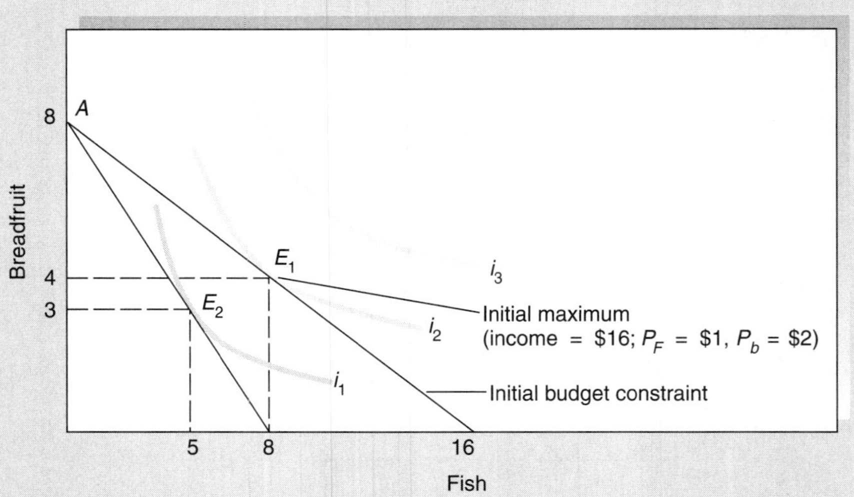

isfaction is at a maximum, Crusoe's marginal rate of substitution of fish for breadfruit, as indicated by the slope of the indifference curve at E_1, will just equal the price ratio (P_F/P_b, which is also the slope of the budget constraint).

What will happen if the price of fish increases? Exhibit 19-A4 also answers this question. Since the price of breadfruit and Crusoe's *money* income are constant, a higher fish price will have two effects. First, it will make Crusoe poorer, even though his money income will be unchanged. His budget constraint will turn clockwise around point *A*, illustrating that his consumption options are now more limited—that is, his real income has declined. Second, the budget line will be steeper, indicating that a larger number of breadfruit must now be sacrificed to obtain an additional unit of fish. It will no longer be possible for Crusoe to attain indifference curve i_2. The best he can do is indifference curve i_1, which he can attain by choosing the bundle of 5 fish and 3 breadfruit.

Using the information supplied by Exhibit 19-A4, we can now locate two points on Crusoe's demand curve for fish. When the price of fish was $1, Crusoe chose 8 fish; when the price rose to $2, Crusoe reduced his consumption to 5 (see Exhibit 19-A5). Of course, other points on Crusoe's demand curve could also be located if we considered other prices for fish.

The demand curve of Exhibit 19-A5 is constructed on the assumption that the price of breadfruit remains $2 and that Crusoe's money income remains constant at $16. If either of these factors were to change, the entire demand curve for fish, illustrated by Exhibit 19-A5, would shift.

The indifference curve is a useful way to illustrate how a person with a fixed budget chooses between two goods. In the real world, of course, people have hundreds, or even thousands, of goods to choose from, and the doubling of only one price usually has a small impact on a person's overall consumption and satisfaction possibilities. In our simple example, the twofold increase in the price of fish makes Crusoe much worse off, because he spends a large portion of his budget on the item.

The Income and Substitution Effects

In the text, we indicated that, when the price of a product rises, the amount consumed will change as a result of both an *income effect* and a *substitution effect*. Indifference curve analysis can be used to separate these two effects. Exhibit 19-A6 is similar to Exhibit 19-A4. Both exhibits illustrate Crusoe's response to an increase in the price of fish from $1 to $2 when money income ($16) and the price of breadfruit ($2) are held constant. Exhibit 19-A6, however breaks down his total response into the substitution effect and the income effect. The reduction in the consumption of fish solely because of the substitution (price) effect, holding Crusoe's real income (level of utility) constant, can

EXHIBIT 19-A5 Crusoe's Demand for Fish

As Exhibit 19-A4 illustrates, when the price of fish is $1, Crusoe chooses 8 units. When the price of fish increases to $2, he reduces his consumption to 5 units. This gives us two points on Crusoe's demand curve for fish. Other points on the demand curve could be derived by confronting Crusoe with still other prices of fish. (*Note:* Crusoe's money income [$16] and the price of breadfruit [$2] are unchanged in this analysis.)

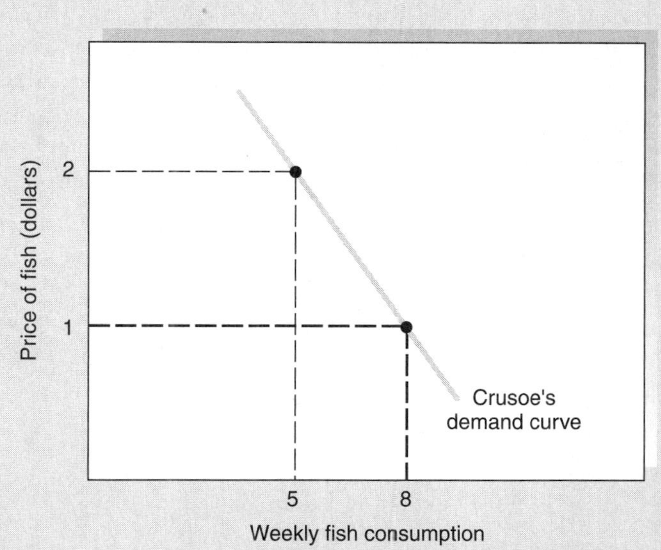

EXHIBIT 19-A6 The Income and Substitution Effects

Here we break down Crusoe's response to the rise in the price of fish from \$1 to \$2 (see Exhibit 19-A4) into the substitution and income effects. The move from E_1 to F illustrates the substitution effect, whereas the move from F to E_2 reflects the income effect.

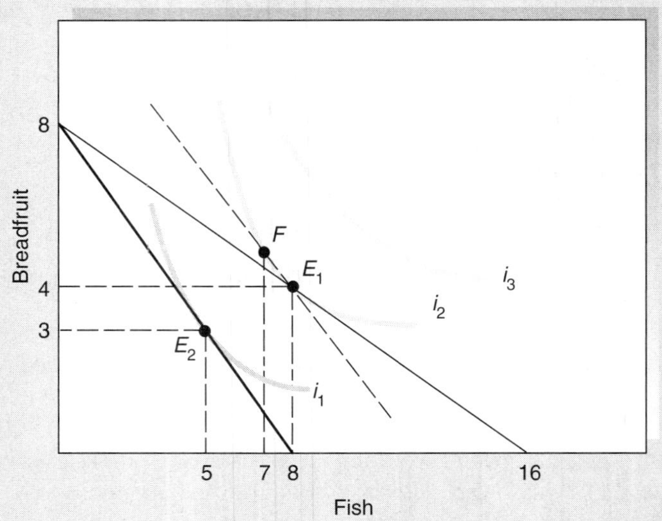

be found by constructing a line tangent to Crusoe's original indifference curve (i_2), and having a slope indicating the higher price of fish. This line (the broken line in Exhibit 19-A6), which is parallel to Crusoe's actual budget constraint (the line containing point E_2), reflects the higher price of fish. It is tangent to the original indifference curve i_2, so Crusoe's real income is held constant. As this line indicates, Crusoe's consumption of fish would fall from 8 to 7, due strictly to the fact that fish are now more expensive. This move from E_1 to F is a pure substitution effect.

Real income, though, has actually been reduced. As a result, Crusoe will be unable to attain point F on indifference curve i_2. The best he can attain is point E_2, which decreases his consumption of fish by another 2 units to 5. Since the broken line containing F and the budget constraint containing E_2 are parallel, the relative price of fish and breadfruit is held constant as Crusoe moves from F to E_2. This move from F to E_2 is thus a pure income effect. (*Note:* Because the consumption of both goods drops in this move, when income falls but the prices do not change, both goods must be normal goods.) This reduction in the consumption of fish (and breadfruit) in the move from F to E_2 is due entirely to the decline in Crusoe's real income.

Indifference curve analysis highlights the assumptions and considerations that enter into consumer decisions. The logic of the proof that there is an inverse relationship between the price and the amount demanded is both elegant and reassuring. It is elegant because of the internal consistency of the logic and the precision of the analysis. It is reassuring because it conforms with our expectations, which are based on the central postulate of economics—that incentives matter in a predictable way.

COSTS AND THE SUPPLY OF GOODS

READING 20

LEARNING OUTCOMES

The candidate should be able to:

a. describe the principal-agent problem of the firm, distinguish among the types of business firms and discuss the major factors promoting cost efficiency and consumer service;

b. distinguish between 1) explicit costs and implicit costs, 2) economic profit and accounting profit, and 3) the short run and the long run in production;

c. define and identify opportunity costs, fixed costs, variable costs, marginal costs, average costs, and sunk costs and differentiate between economic costs and accounting costs;

d. state the law of diminishing returns, and explain its impact on a company's costs;

e. describe the shapes of the short-run marginal cost, average variable cost, average fixed cost, and average total cost curves;

f. define economies and diseconomies of scale, explain how each is possible, and relate each to shapes of long-run average total cost curves;

g. describe both the factors that cause cost curves to shift and the economic way of thinking about costs.

INTRODUCTION 1

From the standpoint of society as a whole, the "cost" of anything is the value that it has in alternative uses.

—Thomas Sowell[1]

Demand and supply interact to determine the market price of a product. In the preceding reading, we illustrated that the demand for a product reflects the strength of consumer desire for that product. In this reading, we focus on the cost of production. The resources needed to produce one good could be used to produce other goods instead. As Thomas Sowell points out in the quotation that begins this reading, the cost to society of anything is the value that it has in

[1] Thomas Sowell, *Basic Economics* (New York: Basic Books, 2000), p. 10.

alternative uses. The market for resources makes that cost clear to producers: The maker of soccer balls, for example, must compete against producers of other goods in purchasing the machines, materials, and labor needed to produce the balls. The producer passes that cost message along to consumers. The firm must gain sufficient revenue from selling the product to cover the cost of the resources, and thus the cost of the balls. The cost of a good in the product market reflects the value in alternate uses of the resources needed to produce it.

Costs carry an important message to producers from the rest of society. If the cost of producing a good exceeds its price, the market is signaling that, although the good may be desired, there is an even greater desire for other goods that could be produced with the same resources. The message comes with an important incentive attached. Producers suffer losses when the per-unit cost of a good exceeds the price they can get for it. In a market economy, they are unlikely to continue supplying the good under such conditions. Thus, supply and cost of production are closely linked. For example, a producer who faces a cost of $1,500 to produce a high quality TV set is unlikely to continue supplying the sets for very long if their market price is $1,000. In the long run, sets that cost $1,500 will be supplied only if their market price is at least that amount.

In this reading, we lay the foundation for a detailed investigation of the links between costs, business output, and market supply. What do economists mean by costs? How do costs guide the owners and managers of firms in a market economy? Why are costs important to managers, even when they personally do not pay them? We discuss these and related questions in this reading.

2 ORGANIZATION OF THE BUSINESS FIRM

The business firm is an entity designed to organize raw materials, labor, and machines with the goal of producing goods and/or services. Firms (1) purchase productive resources from households and other firms, (2) transform them into a different commodity, and (3) sell the transformed product or service to consumers.

Economies differ in the amount of freedom they allow business decision makers and also in the incentive structure used to stimulate and guide business activity. Yet every society relies on business firms to organize resources and transform them into products. In market economies, most business firms choose their own price, output level, and methods of production. They reap the benefits of sales revenues, but they also pay the costs necessary to earn those revenues. In socialist countries, government policy often sets the selling price and constrains the actions of business firms in various other ways. Firms typically do not pay all their bills from their revenues, and they are often not allowed to keep revenues that exceed costs. In any case, the business firm is the entity used to organize production in capitalist and socialist economies alike. In this reading we focus on the organization and behavior of firms in a market economy.

Incentives, Cooperation, and the Nature of the Firm

In capitalist countries, most firms are privately owned. Owners risk their wealth on the success of the business. If the firm is successful and earns profits, these financial gains go to the owners. Conversely, if the firm suffers losses, the owners must bear the consequences. Because the owners receive what remains after the revenue of the firm is used to pay the contractual costs, they are called **residual claimants**.

Residual claimants
Individuals who personally receive the excess, if any, of revenues over costs. Residual claimants gain if the firm's costs are reduced or revenues increased.

In a market economy, the property right of owners to the residual income of the firm plays a very important role: It provides owners with a strong incentive to organize and structure their business in a manner that will keep their cost of producing output low (relative to the value of the output). The wealth of these residual claimants is directly influenced by the success or failure of the firm. Thus, they have both the authority and a strong incentive to see that resources under their direction are used efficiently and directed toward production of goods that are valued more highly than their costs.

There are two ways of organizing productive activity: contracting and **team production**, in which workers are hired by a firm to work together under the supervision of the owner, or the owner's representative—a manager. Most business firms use both contracting and team production.

Team production
A process of production wherein employees work together under the supervision of the owner or the owner's representative.

In principle, all production could be accomplished solely through contracting. For example, a builder might have a house built by contracting with one person to pour the concrete, another to construct the wooden part of the house, a third to install the roofing, a fourth to do the electrical wiring, and so on. No employees would have to be involved in such a project. More commonly though, goods and services are produced with some combination of contracting and the use of team production by employees of a firm.

Why do firms use team production? If contracting alone is used to produce something, the producer must, for each project (1) determine what is required to produce the desired result in the best way, given the circumstances and the current technology and prices, (2) search out reliable suppliers, and (3) negotiate and enforce the contracts. The entrepreneur who wants to produce by this method must have specialized knowledge in a variety of areas and must devote a great deal of time and effort to the planning and contracting processes. Not many people have the expertise or the time to perform all these tasks by themselves except on a small scale. Team production for certain tasks may be more practical and less costly.

Accordingly, a builder is likely to hire knowledgeable, experienced workers to plan the construction process, to purchase materials, and to build such structures as houses and office buildings. The firm itself will then contract with others to obtain materials and specialized labor services.

A firm, then, is a business organization that may use team production to reduce many of the transaction costs associated with contracting. Team production, however, raises another set of problems. Team members—that is, the employees working for the firm—must be monitored and given incentives to avoid shirking, or working at less than a normal rate of productivity. Taking long work breaks, paying more attention to their own convenience than to work results, and wasting time when diligence is called for are examples of **shirking**. A worker will shirk more when the costs of doing so are shifted to other team members, including the owners of the firm. Hired managers, even including those at the top, must be monitored and provided with the incentive to avoid shirking.

Shirking
Working at less than a normal rate of productivity, thus reducing output. Shirking is more likely when workers are not monitored, so that the cost of lower output falls on others.

When team production is utilized, the problem of imperfect monitoring and imperfect incentives is always present. It is part of a larger class of what economists call **principal-agent problems**. Any person taking a car to an auto mechanic experiences such a problem. The mechanic wants to get the job done quickly and to make as much money on it as possible. The car owner wants to get the job done quickly also, but in a way that permanently fixes the problem, at the lowest possible cost. Because the mechanic typically knows far more about the job than the customer, it is hard for the customer to monitor the mechanic's work. There is a possibility, therefore, that the mechanic may charge a large amount for a "quick fix" that will not last.

Principal-agent problem
The incentive problem arising when the purchaser of services (the principal) lacks full information about the circumstances faced by the seller (the agent) and thus cannot know how well the agent performs the purchased services. The agent may to some extent work toward objectives other than those sought by the principal paying for the service.

The owner of a firm is in a similar situation. It is often difficult to monitor the performance of individual employees and provide them with an incentive structure that will encourage high productivity. Nonetheless, the ability of the firm to use resources effectively, and to succeed in a competitive market, depends crucially upon resolving these problems. To keep costs low and the value of output high, a firm must discover and use an incentive structure that motivates managers and workers, and discourages shirking. The problem extends all the way to the top.

Even top-level executives hired to manage a firm do not have the same objectives as owners—primarily profit maximization—unless, of course, the managers are the owners. So the judgments of executives, too, are influenced by what is in their personal best interests. They want perks, personal job security, and other benefits that may not be consistent with profit maximization for the firm. The problem becomes more serious as firms grow larger and acquire more managers and employees. Ultimately it is the job of the owners, as residual claimants, to develop an incentive structure that minimizes the principal-agent problem. For the owner, the saying "the buck stops here" always applies.

Three Types of Business Firms

Business firms can be organized in one of three ways: as a proprietorship, a partnership, or a corporation. The structure chosen determines how the owners share the risks and liabilities of the firm and how they participate in the making of decisions.

Proprietorship
A business firm owned by an individual who possesses the ownership right to the firm's profits and is personally liable for the firm's debts.

A **proprietorship** is a business firm that is owned by a single individual who is fully liable for the debts of the firm. In addition to assuming the responsibilities of ownership, the proprietor often works directly for the firm, providing managerial and other labor services. Many small businesses, including neighborhood grocery stores, barbershops, and farms, are business proprietorships. As Exhibit 20-1 shows, proprietorships account for 73 percent of the business firms in the United States. Because most proprietorships are small, however, they account for only 7 percent of all business revenues.

EXHIBIT 20-1 How Business Firms Are Organized

Nearly three out of every four firms are proprietorships, but only 6 percent of all business revenue is generated by proprietorships. Corporations account for only one out of every five firms, but generate 88 percent of all revenues.

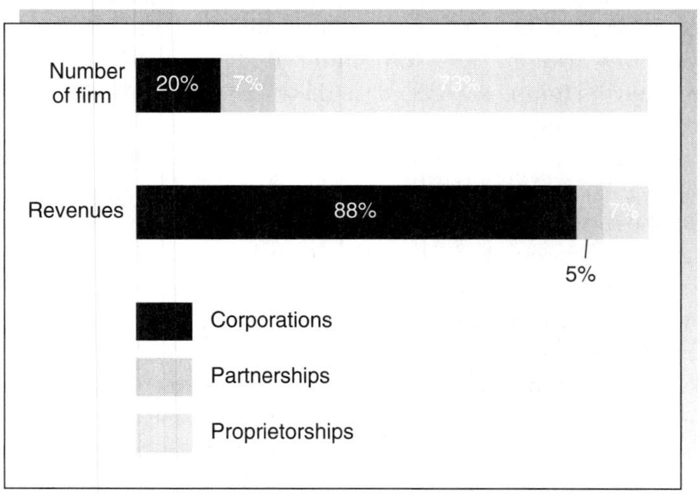

Source: Statistical Abstract of the United States, 2000, Table 855. (Data are for 1997.)

A **partnership** consists of two or more persons acting as co-owners of a business firm. The partners share risks and responsibilities in some prearranged manner. There is no difference between a proprietorship and a partnership in terms of owner liability. In both cases, the owners are fully liable for all business debts incurred by the firm. Many law, medical, and accounting firms are organized along partnership lines. This form of business structure accounts for only 7 percent of the total number of firms and 5 percent of all business revenues.

Partnership
A business firm owned by two or more individuals who possess ownership rights to the firm's profits and are personally liable for the debts of the firm.

The business firms that are **corporations** account for 88 percent of total business revenue, even though they comprise only 20 percent of all firms. What accounts for the attractiveness of the corporate structure? First, although the stockholders of the corporation are the legal owners, their liability is limited to the extent of their explicit investment. If a corporation owes you money, you cannot directly sue the stockholders. Of course, you can sue the corporation. However, if a corporation goes bankrupt, you and others to whom the firm owes money may simply be out of luck. This limited liability makes it possible for corporations to attract investment funds from a large number of "owners" who do not participate in the day-to-day management of the firm.

Corporation
A business firm owned by shareholders who possess ownership rights to the firm's profits, but whose liability is limited to the amount of their investment in the firm.

Second, ownership can easily be transferred under the corporate structure. The shares, or ownership rights, of an owner who dies can be sold by the heirs to another owner without disrupting the business firm. Because of this, the corporation is an ongoing concern. Similarly, stockholders who become unhappy with the way a corporation is run can bail out merely by selling their stock.

The stockholders of large corporations, through their elected board of directors, usually hire managers—trained experts—to operate the firm. Will the managers operate the firm efficiently and satisfy customers? Offering consumers value at a low cost is the ticket to profitability. In an owner-managed firm, the owner's property right to the residual income provides a strong incentive both to reduce costs and to please consumers.

For a large corporation with many stockholders—millions in some cases—the situation is more complex. Although the stockholders own the residual income, professional managers operate the firm. The objectives of managers may conflict with those of stockholders. For example, managers may prefer high salaries, large offices, first-class travel, and other cost-raising benefits for themselves. They may also prefer the power and prestige of business expansion, even if it reduces profitability. Can the stockholders control the actions of managers and direct them toward the pursuit of profitability? Direct control is unlikely. Stockholders elect a board of directors, which in turn appoints high-level managers, but few individual stockholders own enough shares to give them either the incentive or the information to exercise direct control. Most find it too expensive even to attend the annual shareholder's meeting. As the following section describes, however, all is not lost. Internal corporate policies and market activities originating outside the firm both reduce this important form of the principal-agent problem.

COSTS, CONSUMERS, AND CORPORATIONS 3

Three major factors promote cost efficiency and customer service within the corporation, thus limiting the power of corporate managers. Let us consider each.

1. ***Competition for Investment Funds and Customers***
   Even without the ability to exercise direct control of the corporation, stockholders (and the investment advisors, pension fund managers, and others hired to help them) have an incentive to monitor the corporation's management in order to anticipate problems and direct constructive changes. Investors who are the first to spot a good, new management strategy can

buy stock early, before others realize the opportunity and bid the price up. A rising stock price is both a signal of approval to good managers and an incentive to manage well. In the case of decisions that are interpreted to be against the interest of stockholders, the opposite occurs. Stockholders who are the first to spot a problem can bail out by selling their stock before others see the problem and dump their stock, thus depressing the price. So managers get constant feedback via stock price changes, which can be just as important as current profits to stockholders and boards of directors.

Similarly, consumers have an incentive to monitor the quality and price of the firm's output. No one forces them to buy the corporation's product; so, if other firms supply superior products or offer a lower price, consumers can take their business to rival firms. Thus, the corporation's need to meet the competition limits the ability of managers to pursue their personal objectives at the expense of either stockholders or customers.

2. ***Compensation and Management Incentives***
The compensation of managers can be structured in a manner that will bring the interests of managers into harmony with those of shareholders. Corporations usually tie the compensation of managers to the market success of the business. Salary increases and bonuses of most high level managers are directly related to the firm's profitability and the price of its shares. How important are these incentives? In 2001, a survey of 200 large U.S. corporations showed that nearly 60 percent of the chief executives' compensation was in the form of stock options-to-buy.[2] These options are extremely valuable if the market value of the firm's shares rises over time, but may become worthless if it falls. Only 9 percent of these executives' pay was in salary. Such policies encourage corporate managers to maximize the flow of the firm's profits (and the value of the shares), reducing the conflict between the interests of managers and shareholders. Further encouragement comes from the fact that managers often change jobs. More than 21 percent of the chief executives of the top 200 corporations left those firms in 2000. Managers with a record of adding value to the firms they serve earn greater job security and an obvious advantage in finding better positions.

3. ***Threat of Corporate Takeover***
Managers who do not serve the interests of their shareholders are vulnerable to a takeover, a move by an outside person or group to gain control of the firm. As we previously noted, shareholders who lose confidence in management can exit the arrangement by selling their shares. When a significant number of shareholders follow this course of action, the market value of the firm's stock will decline. This will increase the attractiveness of the firm to takeover specialists shopping for a poorly run business, the value of which could be substantially increased by a new management team.

Consider a firm currently earning $1.50 per share. Reflecting current earnings that are expected to continue, the market value of the firm's stock might be $15 per share (assuming a 10 percent interest rate). If the earnings of the firm are low because the current management team is pursuing its own objectives at the expense of profitability, then a corporate takeover could lead to substantial gain. Suppose some outside persons believe that they could restructure the firm, improve the management, and thereby increase the firm's earnings to $3 per share. Therefore, they tender a takeover bid—an offer to buy the firm's stock from shareholders (or they make the offer directly to the board, in a "bear hug" that tries to use stock-

---

[2] Study of top 200 U.S. industrial and service companies, online at http://www.execpay.com/trends2001.htm#Intro

Competition for investment funds and for consumers, management compensation in the form of stock options, and the threat of a takeover increase the incentive of corporate managers to serve the interests of customers and stockholders.

holder pressure to force the board to sell) at $20 per share. If the takeover team gains control, improves the firm's performance, and it increases its earnings to $3 per share, then the stock value of the firm will rise accordingly (to $30 per share).

Of course, the current management has an incentive to resist the takeover. After all, they are likely to lose their jobs if the potential new owners are successful. Managers seldom give such outsiders a warm welcome. Shareholders or their board of directors, however, will decide whether to accept the outsiders' offer. In any case, the presence of large inefficiencies is a powerful attraction for an effective takeover. The mere potential of the takeover reduces the likelihood that managers will stray too far from the profit maximization strategy.

Corporations: Controlling Costs and Serving Customers

How well does the corporate business structure serve consumers and investors? Perhaps history provides the best answer. If the corporate structure were not an effective form of business organization, it would not have continued to survive, nor would it be so prevalent. Rival forms of business organization, including proprietorships, partnerships, consumer cooperatives, employee ownership, and mutually owned companies can and do compete in the marketplace for investment funds and in the product market for customers. In certain industries, some of these alternative forms of business organization are dominant. Nonetheless, in most industries, the corporate structure is the dominant form of business organization (see Exhibit 20-1). This is strong evidence that, despite its defects, it is generally a cost-efficient, consumer-sensitive form of organization.

4 ECONOMIC ROLE OF COSTS

Consumers would like to have more economic goods, but resources to produce them are scarce. How much of each desired good should be produced? Every economic system must balance consumers' competing desires. When decisions are made in the political arena, the budget process performs this balancing function. Congress (or the central committee, or the king) decides which goods will be purchased or produced and which will be forgone. Taxes and budgets are set accordingly.

In a market economy, consumer demand and cost of production are central to the performance of this balancing function. ***The demand for a product represents the voice of consumers instructing firms to produce a good, while costs of production represent the desire of consumers for other items that could be produced instead, with the same resources.*** A profit-seeking firm will try to produce only those units of output for which buyers are willing to pay the full cost. Proper measurement and interpretation of costs by the firm are critical both to the firm's profitability and the efficient use of resources.

Calculating Economic Costs and Profits

Business firms, regardless of their size, are primarily concerned with profit. Profit, of course, is the firm's total revenue minus its total costs. But to state profit correctly, costs must be measured properly. Most people, including some who are in business, think of costs as amounts paid for raw materials, labor, machines, and similar inputs. However this concept of cost, which stems from accounting procedures, may exclude some important components of the firm's costs. When cost is miscalculated, so, too, is profit because it is merely revenue minus cost. Bad economic decisions may result from a miscalculation of cost and profit.

Explicit costs
Payments by a firm to purchase the services of productive resources.

Implicit costs
The opportunity costs associated with a firm's use of resources that it owns. These costs do not involve a direct money payment. Examples include wage income and interest forgone by the owner of a firm who also provides labor services and equity capital to the firm.

Total cost
The costs, both explicit and implicit, of all the resources used by the firm. Total cost includes an imputed normal rate of return for the firm's equity capital.

The key to understanding the economist's concept of profit is remembering the idea of *opportunity cost*—the highest valued alternative foregone by the resource owner when the resource is used. These costs may either be explicit or implicit. **Explicit costs** result when the firm makes a monetary payment to resource owners. Money wages, interest, and rental payments are a measure of what the firm gives up to employ the services of labor and capital resources. Firms may also incur **implicit costs**—those associated with the use of resources owned by the firm. Since implicit costs do not involve a direct money or contractual payment, they are sometimes excluded from accounting statements. For example, the owners of small proprietorships often work for their own business. There is an opportunity cost associated with the use of this resource (the owner's labor services); other opportunities for the owner's time have to be given up because of the time spent in the operation of the business. The highest valued alternative forgone is the opportunity cost of the labor service provided by the owner. The **total cost** of production is the sum of the explicit and implicit costs incurred by the employment of all resources involved in the production process.

Accounting statements generally omit the implicit cost of equity capital—the cost of funds supplied by owners. If a firm borrows financial capital from a bank or other private source, it will have to pay interest. Accountants properly record this interest expense as a cost. In contrast, when the firm acquires financial capital through the issuance of stock, accountants make no allowance for the cost of this financial capital. Regardless of whether it is acquired by borrowing or stock (equity capital), the use of financial capital involves an opportunity cost. Persons who supply equity capital to a firm expect to earn at least a normal rate of return—a return comparable to what they could earn if they chose other investment opportunities (including bonds). If they do not earn this normal rate of return, investors will not continue to supply financial capital to the business.

When calculating costs, economists use the normal return on financial capital as a basis for determining the implicit **opportunity cost of equity capital**. If the normal rate of return on financial capital is 10 percent, equity investors will refuse funds to firms that persistently fail to earn a 10 percent rate of return on capital assets.

Opportunity cost of equity capital
The implicit rate of return that must be earned by investors to induce them to continue to supply financial capital to the firm.

Accounting Profit and Economic Profit

Because economists seek to measure the opportunities lost due to the production of a good or service—the cost to society of that production—they include both explicit and implicit costs in total cost. **Economic profit** is equal to total revenues minus total costs, including both the explicit and implicit cost components. Economic profits will be positive only if the earnings of the business exceed the opportunity cost of all resources used by the firm, including *the opportunity cost of the assets owned by the firm.* Zero economic profit, then, includes just the market wage for the unpaid work of owners, and the normal or competitive rate of return (in investments of similar risk) for their capital. In contrast, economic losses result when the earnings of the firm are insufficient to cover explicit and implicit costs. That is why the **normal profit rate** is zero economic profit, providing just the competitive rate of return on the capital (and labor) of owners. A higher rate will draw more entry into the market, while a lower rate will cause an exit of investors and capital.

Remember that zero economic profits do not imply that the firm is about to go out of business. On the contrary, they indicate that the owners are receiving exactly the normal profit rate, or the competitive market rate of return on their investment (the value of the assets owned by the firm).

Economic profit
The difference between the firm's total revenues and its total costs, including both the explicit and implicit cost components.

Normal profit rate
Zero economic profit, providing just the competitive rate of return on the capital (and labor) of owners. An above-normal profit rate will draw more entry into the market, while a below-normal rate will cause an exit of investors and capital.

Because accounting procedures often omit implicit costs, such as those associated with owner-provided labor services or capital assets, the accounting costs of the firm generally understate the opportunity costs of production. This understatement of cost leads to an overstatement of profits. Therefore, the **accounting profits** of a firm are generally greater than the firm's economic profits (see the Applications in Economics box on accounting costs on the next page). When the omission of the costs of owner-provided services is unimportant, as is the case for most large corporations, accounting profits approximate the returns to the firm's equity capital. High accounting profits (measured as a rate of return on a firm's assets), relative to the average for other firms, suggest that a firm is earning an economic profit. Correspondingly, a low rate of accounting profit implies economic losses. Either positive or negative economic profits, of course, call for a change in output. Such a change will take time.

Accounting profits
The sales revenues minus the expenses of a firm over a designated time period, usually one year. Accounting profits typically make allowances for changes in the firm's inventories and depreciation of its assets. No allowance is made, however, for the opportunity cost of the equity capital of the firm's owners, or other implicit costs.

SHORT RUN AND LONG RUN

5

A firm cannot instantaneously adjust its output. Time plays an important role in the production process. All of a firm's resources can be expanded (or contracted) over time, but for specialized or heavy equipment, expanding (and contracting) availability quickly may be very expensive or even impossible. Economists often speak of the **short run** as a time period so short that the firm is unable to alter its present plant size. In the short run, the firm is "stuck" with its existing plant and heavy equipment. They are "fixed" for a given time period. The firm can alter

Short run (in production)
A time period so short that a firm is unable to vary some of its factors of production. The firm's plant size typically cannot be altered in the short run.

APPLICATIONS IN ECONOMICS

Economic and Accounting Costs: A Hypothetical Example

The revenue-cost statement for a corner grocery store owned and operated by Terry Smith is presented here.

Terry works full-time as the manager, chief cashier, and janitor. Terry has $140,000 worth of refrigeration and other equipment invested in the store. Last year, Terry's total sales were $170,000; suppliers and employees were paid $100,000. Terry's revenues exceeded explicit costs by $70,000.

Did Terry make a profit last year? The accounting statement for the store will probably show a net profit of $70,000. However, if Terry did not have a $140,000 personal investment in equipment, these funds could be earning 5 percent interest. Thus, Terry is forgoing $7,000 of interest each year. Similarly, if the building that Terry owns was not being used as a grocery store, it could be rented to someone else for $1,500 per month. Rental income thus forgone is $18,000 per year. In addition, since Terry is tied up working in the grocery store, a $50,000 managerial position with the local Safeway is forgone. Considering the interest, rental, and salary income that Terry had to forgo in order to operate the grocery store last year, Terry's implicit costs were $75,000. The total costs were $175,000. The total revenue of Terry's grocery store was less than the opportunity cost of the resources utilized. As a result, Terry incurred an economic loss of $5,000, despite the accounting profit of $70,000.

TOTAL REVENUE	
Sales (groceries)	$170,000
Costs (explicit)	
Groceries, wholesale	$ 76,000
Utilities	4,000
Taxes	6,000
Advertising	2,000
Labor services (employees)	12,000
Total (explicit) costs	$100,000
Net (accounting) profit	$ 70,000
Additional (implicit) costs	
Interest (personal investment)	$ 7,000
Rent (Terry's building)	18,000
Salary (Terry's labor)	50,000
Total (implicit) costs	$ 75,000
TOTAL EXPLICIT AND IMPLICIT COSTS	$175,000
ECONOMIC PROFIT (TOTAL REVENUE MINUS EXPLICIT AND IMPLICIT COSTS)	−$ 5,000

output, however, by applying larger or smaller amounts of "variable" resources, such as labor and raw materials. Existing plant capacity can thus be used more or less intensively in the short run.

In sum, we can say that the short run is that period of time during which at least one factor of production, usually the size of the firm's plant, cannot be varied. How long is the short run? The length varies from industry to industry. A trucking firm might be able to hire more drivers and buy or rent more trucks, and double its hauling capacity in a few months. In other industries, particularly those that use assembly lines and mass production techniques (for example, the automotive factory supplying trucks), increasing production capacity might take a year or even several years.

Long run (in production) A time period long enough to allow the firm to vary all factors of production.

The **long run** is a time period of sufficient length to allow a firm the opportunity to alter its plant size and capacity and all other factors of production. All resources of the firm are variable in the long run. In the long run, from the viewpoint of an entire industry, new firms may be established and enter the industry; other firms may dissolve and leave the industry. Thus, the short run may be alternatively viewed as a time period during which the number of firms in the industry is fixed.

Perhaps an example will help to clarify the distinction between the short- and long-run time periods. If a battery manufacturer hired 200 additional workers and ordered more raw materials to squeeze a larger output from the existing plant, it would be making a short-run adjustment. In contrast, if the manufacturer built an additional plant (or expanded the size of its current facility) and installed additional heavy equipment, it would be undertaking a long-run adjustment.

CATEGORIES OF COSTS 6

To describe various aspects of the firm's costs and the relationship of those costs to the level of output, even without detailed knowledge of the production process, we need some definitions. We have emphasized that in the short run some of a firm's factors of production, such as the size of the plant, will be fixed. Other productive resources will be variable. In the short run, then, we can break the firm's costs into these two categories—fixed and variable. Examining how each category of costs behaves, and seeing that behavior graphically, will illustrate characteristics of the profit-maximizing level of output for a firm. It will be important to distinguish between a firm's total costs and its per-unit costs, which will be called "average" costs.

Each of the firm's fixed costs, and their sum, **total fixed cost** (***TFC***), will remain unchanged when output is altered in the short run. For example, a firm's insurance premiums, its property taxes, and, most significantly, the opportunity cost of using its fixed assets will be present whether the firm produces a large or small rate of output. These costs will not vary with output. They are "fixed" as long as the firm remains in business. Fixed costs will be present at all levels of output, including zero. They can be avoided only if the firm goes out of business.

What will happen to **average fixed cost** (***AFC***), fixed costs per unit, as output expands? Remember that the firm's fixed cost will be the same whether output is 1, 100, or 1,000. The *AFC* is simply fixed cost divided by output. As output increases, *AFC* declines because the fixed cost will be spread over more and more units (see part a of Exhibit 20-2).

Some costs vary with output. For example, additional output can usually be produced by hiring more workers and buying more raw materials. The sum of those and other costs that rise as output increases comprise the firm's **total variable cost** (***TVC***). At any given level of output, the firm's **average variable cost** (***AVC***) is the total variable cost divided by output.

Total fixed cost
The sum of the costs that do not vary with output. They will be incurred as long as a firm continues in business and the assets have alternative uses.

Average fixed cost
Total fixed cost divided by the number of units produced. It always declines as output increases.

Total variable cost
The sum of those costs that rise as output increases. Examples of variable costs are wages paid to workers and payments for raw materials.

Average variable cost
The total variable cost divided by the number of units produced.

EXHIBIT 20-2 General Characteristics of Short-Run Cost Curves

Average fixed costs (a) will be high for small rates of output, but they will always decline as output expands. Marginal cost (b) will rise sharply as the plant's production capacity *q* is approached. As graph (c) illustrates, *ATC* will be a U-shaped curve, since *AFC* will be high for small rates of output and *MC* will be high as the plant's production capacity is approached.

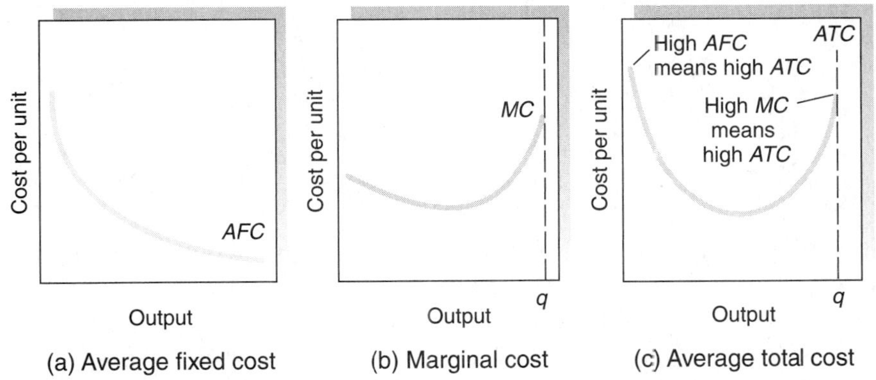

We have noted that total cost (*TC*) includes explicit and implicit costs. The total cost of producing a good is also the sum of the fixed and variable costs at each output level. At zero output, total cost will equal total fixed cost. As output expands from zero, variable cost and fixed cost must be added to obtain total cost. **Average total cost** (***ATC***), sometimes referred to as unit cost, can be found by dividing total cost by the total number of units produced. *ATC* is also equal to the sum of the average fixed and average variable costs. It indicates the amount per unit of output that must be gained in revenue if total cost is to be covered.

Average total cost
Total cost divided by the number of units produced. It is sometimes called per-unit cost.

The economic way of thinking emphasizes the importance of what happens "at the margin." How much does it cost to produce an additional unit? **Marginal cost** (***MC***) is the change in total cost that results from the production of one additional unit. The profit-conscious decision maker recognizes *MC* as the addition to cost that must be covered by additional revenue if producing the marginal unit is to be profitable. In the short run, as illustrated by Exhibit 20-2b, *MC* will generally decline if output is increased, reach a minimum, and then increase. The rising *MC* simply reflects the fact that it becomes increasingly difficult to squeeze additional output from a plant as the facility's maximum capacity (the dotted line of part b of Exhibit 20-2) is approached. The Thumbnail Sketch summarizes the interrelationships among a firm's various costs.

Marginal cost
The change in total cost required to produce an additional unit of output.

7 OUTPUT AND COSTS IN THE SHORT RUN

As a firm alters its rate of output in the short run, how will unit cost be affected? First, let us look at this question intuitively. In the short run, the firm can vary output by using its fixed plant size more (or less) intensively. As Exhibit 20-2 illus-

THUMBNAIL SKETCH

Compact Glossary on Cost

Term	Symbol	Equation	Definition
Fixed cost			Cost that is independent of the output level
Variable cost			Cost that varies with the output level
Total fixed cost	*TFC*		Cost of the fixed inputs (equals sum of quantity times unit price for each fixed input)
Total variable cost	*TVC*		Cost of the variable inputs (equals sum of quantity times unit price for each variable input)
Total cost	*TC*	$TC = TFC + TVC$	Cost of all inputs (equals fixed costs plus variable costs)
Marginal cost	*MC*	$MC = \Delta TC \div \Delta q$	Change in total cost resulting from a one-unit rise in output (q) [equals the *change* in total cost divided by the *change* in output]
Average fixed cost	*AFC*	$AFC = TFC \div q$	Total fixed cost per unit of output (equals total fixed cost divided by total output)
Average variable cost	*AVC*	$AVC = TVC \div q$	Total variable cost per unit of output (equals total variable cost divided by total output)
Average total cost	*ATC*	$ATC = AFC + AVC$	Total cost per unit of output (equals average fixed cost plus average variable cost)

trates, there are two extreme situations that will result in a high unit cost of output. First, when the output rate of a plant is small relative to its capacity, it is obviously being underutilized. Under these circumstances, *AFC* will be high, and therefore *ATC* will also be high. It will be costly and inefficient to operate a large plant substantially below its production capacity. At the other extreme, overutilization can also result in high unit cost. An overutilized plant will mean congestion, time spent by workers waiting for machines, and similar costly delays. As output approaches the maximum capacity of a plant, overutilization will lead to high *MC* and therefore to high *ATC*.

Thus, the* ATC *curve will be U-shaped, as pictured in part c of Exhibit 20-2.* ATC *will be high for both an underutilized plant (because* AFC *is high) and an overutilized plant (because* MC *is high).

Diminishing Returns and Production in the Short Run

Our analysis of the changes in unit cost as the output rate rises reflects a long-established economic law. This **law of diminishing returns** states that, as more and more units of a variable factor are applied to a fixed amount of other resources, output will eventually increase by smaller and smaller amounts. Therefore, in terms of their impact on output, the returns to the variable factor will diminish. The impact on costs is clear: When the returns to the variable factor are rising, marginal costs (the additions to total variable cost from adding a unit of output) are falling. Similarly, when the returns to the variable factor are falling, marginal cost is increasing.

Law of diminishing returns
The postulate that, as more and more units of a variable resource are combined with a fixed amount of other resources, employment of additional units of the variable resource will eventually increase output only at a decreasing rate. Once diminishing returns are reached, it will take successively larger amounts of the variable factor to expand output by one unit.

The law of diminishing returns is as famous in economics as the law of gravity is in physics. It is based on common sense and real-life observation. Have you ever noticed that, as you apply a single resource more intensively, the resource eventually tends to accomplish less and less? Consider a wheat farmer who applies fertilizer (a resource) more and more intensively to an acre of land (a fixed factor). At some point, the application of additional 100-pound units of fertilizer will expand the wheat yield by successively smaller amounts.

Essentially, the law of diminishing returns is a constraint imposed by nature. If it were not valid, it would be possible to raise all the world's food on an acre of the best land, or even in a flowerpot. Logically, then, there would be no point in cultivating any of the less-fertile land. We would be able to increase output simply by applying another unit of labor and fertilizer to the world's most fertile flowerpot! In the real world, of course, this is not the case; the law of diminishing returns is valid and it restricts our options.

Total product
The total output of a good that is associated with alternative utilization rates of a variable input.

Exhibit 20-3 illustrates the law of diminishing returns numerically. Column 1 indicates the quantity of the variable resource, labor in this example, that is combined with a specified amount of the fixed resource. Column 2 shows the **total product** that will result as the utilization rate of labor increases. Column 3 provides data on the **marginal product**, the change in total output associated with each additional unit of labor. Without the application of labor, output would be zero. As additional units of labor are applied, total product (output) expands. As the first three units of labor are applied, total product increases by successively larger amounts (8, then 12, then 14). Beginning with the fourth unit, however, diminishing returns are confronted. When the fourth unit is added, marginal product—the change in the total product—declines to 12 (down from 14, when the third unit was applied). As additional units of labor are applied, marginal product continues to decline. It is increasingly difficult to squeeze a larger total product from the fixed resources (for example, plant size and equipment). Eventually, marginal product becomes negative (beginning with the tenth unit).

Marginal product
The increase in the total product resulting from a unit increase in the employment of a variable input. Mathematically, it is the ratio of the change in total product to the change in the quantity of the variable input.

Average product
The total product (output) divided by the number of units of the variable input required to produce that output level.

Column 4 of Exhibit 20-3 provides data for the **average product** of labor, which is simply the total product divided by the units of labor applied. Note the

EXHIBIT 20-3 Law of Diminishing Returns (Hypothetical Data)

(1) Units of the Variable Resource, Labor (per day)	(2) Total Product (output)	(3) Marginal Product	(4) Average Product
0	0		—
		8	
1	8		8.0
		12	
2	20		10.0
		14	
3	34		11.3
		12	
4	46		11.5
		10	
5	56		11.2
		8	
6	64		10.7
		6	
7	70		10.0
		4	
8	74		9.3
		1	
9	75		8.3
		−2	
10	73		7.3

average product increases as long as the marginal product is greater than the average product. Whenever the marginal unit's contribution is greater than the average, it must cause the average to rise. Here, this is true through the first four units. The marginal product of the fifth unit of labor, though, is 10, less than the average product for the first four units of labor (11.5). Therefore, beginning with the fifth unit, the average product declines as additional labor is applied. When marginal productivity is below the average, it brings down the average product.

Using the data from Exhibit 20-3, Exhibit 20-4 illustrates the law of diminishing returns graphically. Initially, the total product curve (part a) increases quite rapidly. As diminishing marginal returns are confronted (beginning with the fourth unit of labor), total product increases more slowly. Eventually, a maximum output (75) is reached with the application of the ninth unit of labor. The marginal product curve (part b) reflects the total product curve. Geometrically, marginal product is the slope—the rate of increase—of the total product curve. That slope, the marginal product, reaches its maximum with the application of three units of labor. Beyond three units, diminishing returns are present. Eventually, at ten units of labor, the marginal product becomes negative. When marginal product becomes negative, total product is necessarily declining. The average product curve rises as long as the marginal product curve is above it, since each added unit of labor is raising the average. The average product reaches its maximum at four units of labor. Beyond that, each additional unit of labor brings down the average product, and the curve declines.

Diminishing Returns and Cost Curves

What impact will diminishing returns have on a firm's costs? Once a firm confronts diminishing returns, larger and larger additions of the variable factor are required to expand output by one unit. This will cause marginal costs **(MC)** ***to rise. As*** **MC** ***continues to increase, eventually it will exceed average total cost. Until that point,*** **MC** ***is below***

EXHIBIT 20-4 Law of Diminishing Returns

As units of variable input (labor) are added to a fixed input, total product will increase, first at an increasing rate and then at a declining rate (a). This will cause both marginal and average product curves (b) to rise at first and then decline. Note that the marginal product curve intersects the average product curve at its maximum (when 4 units of labor are used). The smooth curves indicate that labor can be increased by amounts of less than a single unit.

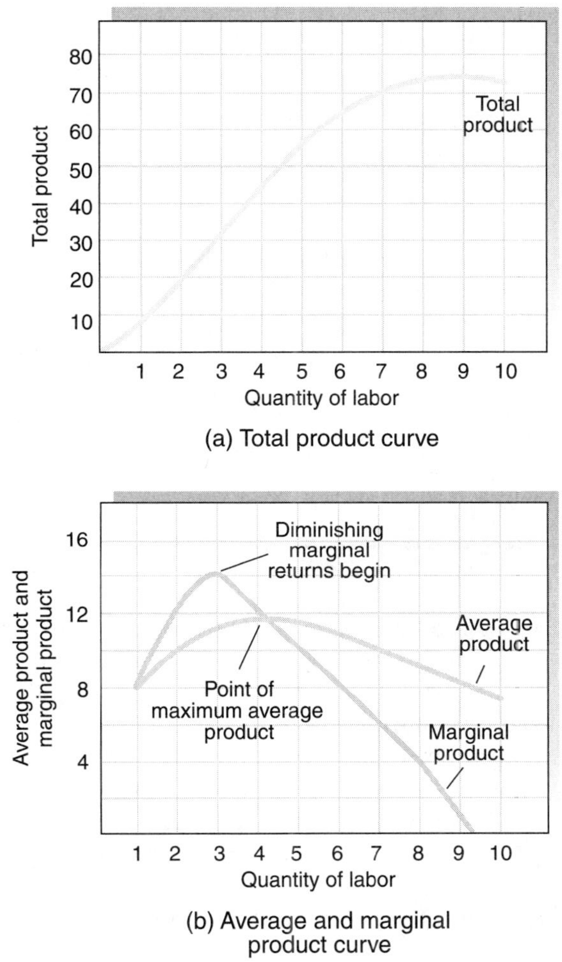

ATC, *bringing* ATC *down. When* MC *is greater than* ATC, *the additional units cost more than the average, and* ATC *must increase.* To make the point clear, consider a similar case in another setting. What happens when you make an additional exam grade above your current class average? Your class average goes up. What happens if a unit of above-average cost is added to output? Average total cost rises. The firm's MC curve therefore crosses the ATC curve at the ATC's lowest point. For output rates beyond the minimum ATC, the rising MC causes ATC to increase.

Exhibit 20-5 numerically illustrates the implications of the law of diminishing returns for a firm's short-run cost curve. Here, we assume that Royal Roller Blades, Inc., combines units of a variable input with a fixed factor to produce units of output (pairs of inline skates). Columns 2, 3, and 4 indicate how the total cost schedules vary as output is expanded. Total fixed costs (*TFC*), representing the opportunity cost of the fixed factors of production, are $50 per day at all levels of output. For the first four units of output, total variable costs (*TVC*)

EXHIBIT 20-5 Numerical Short-Run Cost Schedules of Royal Roller Blades, Inc.

Total Cost Data (per day)				Average/Marginal Cost Data (per day)			
(1) Output per Day	(2) *TFC*	(3) *TVC*	(4) *TC* (2) + (3)	(5) *AFC* (2) ÷ (1)	(6) *AVC* (3) ÷ (1)	(7) *ATC* (4) ÷ (1)	(8) *MC* Δ(4) ÷ Δ(1)
0	$50	$ 0	$ 50	—	—	—	—
1	50	15	65	$50.00	$15.00	$65.00	$15
2	50	25	75	25.00	12.50	37.50	10
3	50	34	84	16.67	11.33	28.00	9
4	50	42	92	12.50	10.50	23.00	8
5	50	52	102	10.00	10.40	20.40	10
6	50	64	114	8.33	10.67	19.00	12
7	50	79	129	7.14	11.29	18.43	15
8	50	98	148	6.25	12.25	18.50	19
9	50	122	172	5.56	13.56	19.11	24
10	50	152	202	5.00	15.20	20.20	30
11	50	202	252	4.55	18.36	22.91	50

increase at a decreasing rate. Why? In this range, there are increasing returns to the variable input. Beginning with the fifth unit of output, however, diminishing marginal returns are present. From this point on, *TVC* and *TC* increase by successively larger amounts as output is expanded.

Columns 5 through 8 of Exhibit 20-5 reveal the average and marginal cost schedules. For small output rates, the *ATC* of producing roller blades is high, primarily because of the high *AFC*. Initially, *MC* is less than *ATC*, so *ATC* is falling. When diminishing returns set in for output rates beginning with five units, however, *MC* rises. Beginning with the sixth unit of output, *MC* exceeds *AVC*, causing *AVC* to rise. Beginning with the eighth unit of output, *MC* exceeds *ATC*, causing it also to rise. *ATC* thus reaches its minimum at seven units of output. Look carefully at the data of Exhibit 20-5 to be sure that you fully understand the relationships among the various cost curves. Do you understand how columns 4 to 8 are derived from columns 1 to 3?

Using the numeric data of Exhibit 20-5, Exhibit 20-6 graphically illustrates the total, the average, and the marginal cost curves. Note that the *MC* curve intersects both the *AVC* and *ATC* curves at their minimum points (part b). As *MC*, driven up by diminishing returns, continues to rise above *ATC*, unit costs rise higher and higher as output increases beyond seven units.

In sum, the firm's short-run cost curves reflect the law of diminishing marginal returns. Assuming that the price of the variable resource is constant, *MC* declines so long as the marginal product of the variable input is rising. This results because, in this range, smaller and smaller additions of the variable input are required to produce each extra unit of output. The situation is reversed, however, when diminishing returns are confronted. Once diminishing returns set in, more and more units of the variable factor are required to generate each additional unit of output. *MC* will rise, because the marginal product of the variable resource is declining. Eventually, *MC* exceeds *AVC* and *ATC*, causing these costs also to rise. A U-shaped short-run average total cost curve results.

EXHIBIT 20-6 Costs in the Short Run

Using data from Exhibit 20-5, this exhibit illustrates the general shape of the firm's short-run total cost curves (a), and average and marginal cost curves (b). Note that when output is small (for example, 2 units), *ATC* will be high because the *AFC* is so high. Similarly, when output is large (for example, 11 units), per-unit cost *(ATC)* will be high because it is extremely costly to produce the marginal units. Thus, the short-run *ATC* curve will be U-shaped.

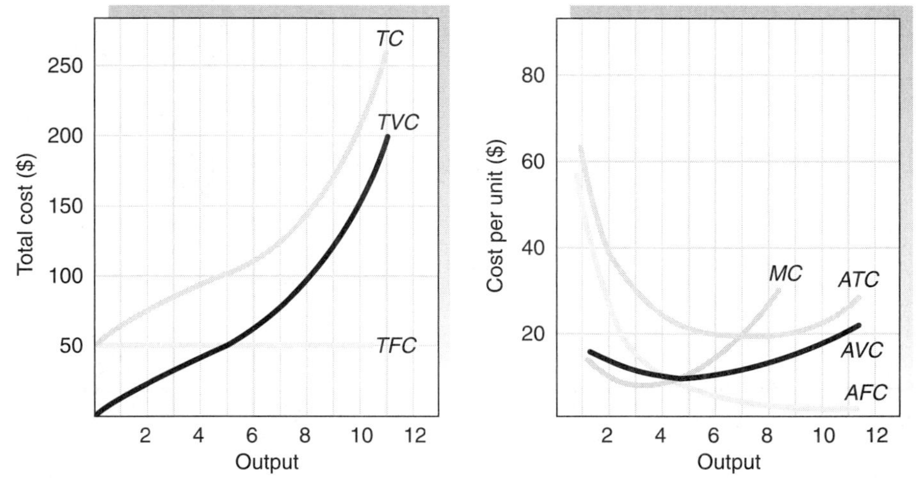

(a) Total cost data

(b) Average and marginal cost data

OUTPUT AND COSTS IN THE LONG RUN 8

The short-run analysis relates costs to output *for a specific size of plant.* Firms, though, are not committed forever to their existing plant. In the long run, a firm can alter its plant size and all other factors of production. All resources used by the firm are variable in the long run. Thus, there are no fixed and variable cost categories in the long run.

How will the firm's choice of plant size affect per unit production costs? Exhibit 20-7 illustrates the short-run *ATC* curves for three different plant sizes, ranging from small to large. If these three plant sizes were the only possible choices, which one should be chosen, as the firm plans for the future? The answer depends on the rate of output the firm expects to produce from the plant to be built. The smallest plant would have the lowest cost if an output rate of less than q_1 were produced. The medium-sized plant would provide the least-cost method of producing output rates between q_1 and q_2. For any output level greater than q_2, the largest plant would be the most cost-efficient.

The long-run ATC curve shows the minimum average cost of producing each output level when the firm is free to choose among all possible plant sizes. It can best be thought of as a planning curve, because it reflects the expected per-unit cost of producing alternative rates of output while plants are still in the blueprint stage.

Exhibit 20-7 illustrates the long-run *ATC* curve when only three plant sizes are possible, and the planning curve *ABCD* is thus mapped out. Of course, given sufficient time, firms can usually choose among many plants of various sizes. Exhibit 20-8 presents the long-run planning curve under these circumstances. It is a smooth curve, with each short-run *ATC* curve tangent to it.

It is important to keep in mind that no single plant size could produce the alternative output rates at the costs indicated by the planning curve* LRATC *in Exhibit 20-8. Any of

EXHIBIT 20-7 Long-run Average Total Cost

The short-run average total cost curves are shown for three alternative plant sizes. If these three were the only possible plant sizes, the long-run average total cost curve would be *ABCD.*

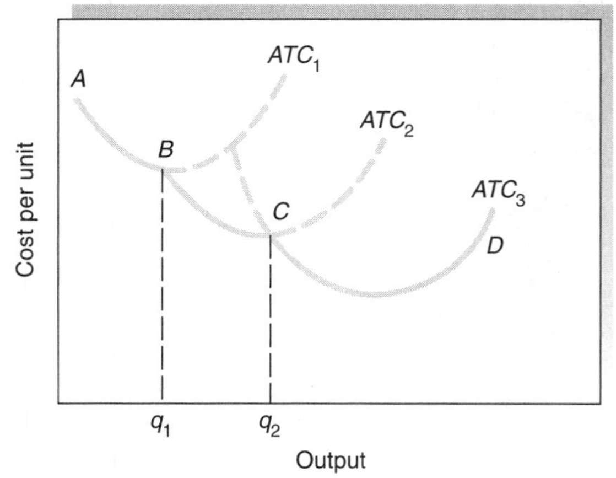

the planning curve options are available before a plant size is chosen and the plant is built; however, although the firm can plan for the long run, choosing among many options, it can *operate* only in the short run. The *LRATC* curve outlines the possibilities available in the planning stage, indicating the expected average total costs of production for each of a large number of plants, which differ in size.

Economies and Diseconomies of Scale

Do larger firms have lower minimum unit costs than smaller ones? The answer to this question depends on which industries are being considered. There is a sound basis, though, for expecting some initial reductions in per-unit cost from large-scale production methods. Why? Large firms typically produce a large total vol-

EXHIBIT 20-8 Planning Curve (*LRATC*)

When many alternative plant sizes are possible, the long-run average total cost curve (*LRATC*) is mapped out.

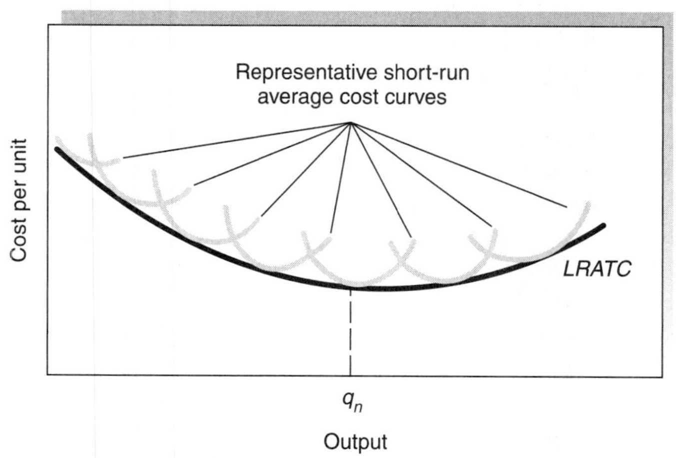

When firms are able to plan large volumes of output, the use of mass-production methods will generally lead to lower per-unit costs. This helps explain why the *LRATC* has a downward-sloping portion.

ume of output.[3] Volume of output denotes the total number of units of a product that the firm expects to produce.[4] There are three major reasons why planning a larger volume generally reduces, at least initially, unit costs: (1) economies accompanying the use of mass-production methods, (2) higher productivity as a result of specialization and "learning by doing," and (3) economies in promotion and purchasing. Let us consider each of these factors.

Mass-production techniques usually are economical only when large volumes of output are planned, since they tend to involve large development and setup costs. Once the production methods are established, though, marginal costs are low. For example, the use of molds, dies, and assembly line production methods reduce the per-unit cost of automobiles only when the planned volume

---

[3] Throughout this section, we assume that firms with larger plants necessarily plan a larger volume of output than do their smaller counterparts. Reality approximates these conditions. Firms choose large plants because they are planning to produce a large volume.

[4] Note the distinction between rate and volume of output. Rate of output is the number of units produced during a specific period (for example, the next six months). Volume is the total number of units produced during all time periods. For example, Boeing might produce two 777 airplanes per month (rate of output) while planning to produce a volume of two hundred 777s during the expected life of the model. Increasing the rate (reducing the time period during which a given output is produced) tends to raise costs, whereas increasing the volume (total amount produced) tends to lower costs.

is in the millions. High-volume methods, although cheaper to use for high rates of output and high volumes, will typically require high fixed costs, and therefore will cause unit costs to be far higher for low volumes of production.

Large-scale operation also permits specialized use of labor and machines. In a giant auto plant, hundreds of different jobs must be done, and many of them require a training period for each worker. In a small plant, the same worker might do 10 or 20 of these jobs, so each worker would have a much longer, more costly training period. Even then, the worker doing so many tasks might never fully develop the same level of proficiency of the more specialized worker. Baseball players improve by playing baseball, and pianists by playing the piano. Similarly, the employees of a firm improve their skills as they experience "learning by doing" in their jobs. Even better, concentration on a narrower range of tasks may help workers discover or develop cost-reducing techniques. The result of greater size and specialization is often more output per unit of labor.

Large firms may also be able to achieve lower costs by spreading fixed costs (such as the costs of advertising, developing specialized equipment, and searching out or negotiating better input prices) over many more units. For example, both McDonalds and General Motors are able to spread these costs over a large number of stores and volume of sales. The cost advantages of scale come in many forms.

Economies of scale
Reductions in the firm's per-unit costs that are associated with the use of large plants to produce a large volume of output.

Economic theory explains why, at least initially, larger firms have lower unit costs than comparable smaller firms. Declining unit costs mean that **economies of scale** are present over the initial range of outputs. The long-run *ATC* curve is falling.

What about *dis*economies of scale? As output continues to expand, is there reason to believe that larger firms will eventually have higher average total costs than smaller ones? The underlying causes of diseconomies of scale are less obvious, but they do occur. As a firm gets bigger and bigger, beyond some point, bureaucratic inefficiencies *may* result. Code-book procedures tend to replace managerial genius and innovation is more difficult. Motivating the workforce and carrying out managerial directives are also more complex when the firm is larger, and principal-agent problems grow as the number of employees increases and more levels of monitoring need to be done.

Circumstances vary, so diseconomies of scale set in earlier for some kinds of firms than for others. For example, the firms in the fast food industry can be very large and remain efficient; economies of scale apparently outweigh the diseconomies even for giants like McDonalds. Yet in the fine dining portion of the restaurant industry, the best restaurants seem to be small. In those firms, customers demand individual attention, and a constantly changing and innovative menu is important. Diseconomies seem to set in at a much smaller size for that portion of the industry.

The bottom line for diseconomies of scale is this: For some firms, bureaucratic inefficiencies, principal-agent problems, difficulties with innovation, and similar problems cause long-run average total costs to rise beyond some output level in the firm. However, there is considerable variation among industries and even among firms in the same industry concerning the precise output level at which diseconomies of scale begin to occur.

It is important to note that scale economies and diseconomies stem from sources different from those of increasing and diminishing returns. ***Economies and diseconomies of scale are long-run concepts. They relate to conditions of production when all factors are variable. In contrast, increasing and diminishing returns are short-run concepts, applicable only when the firm has a fixed factor of production.***

Alternative Shapes of the LRATC

Exhibit 20-9 outlines three different long-run average total cost (*LRATC*) curves, each describing real-world conditions in differing industries. For a firm described by the cost curve in part a, both economies and diseconomies of scale are present.

EXHIBIT 20-9 Three Different Types of Long-run Average Total Cost Curves

For one type of *LRATC* curve, economies of scale are present for output levels less than q, but immediately beyond q, diseconomies of scale dominate (a). In another instance, economies of scale are important until some minimum output level (q_1) is attained. Once the minimum has been attained, there is a wide range of output levels (q_1 to q_2) that are consistent with the minimum *ATC* for the industry (b). In a third situation, economies of scale exist for all relevant output levels (c). As we will see later, this type of *LRATC* curve has important implications for the structure of the industry.

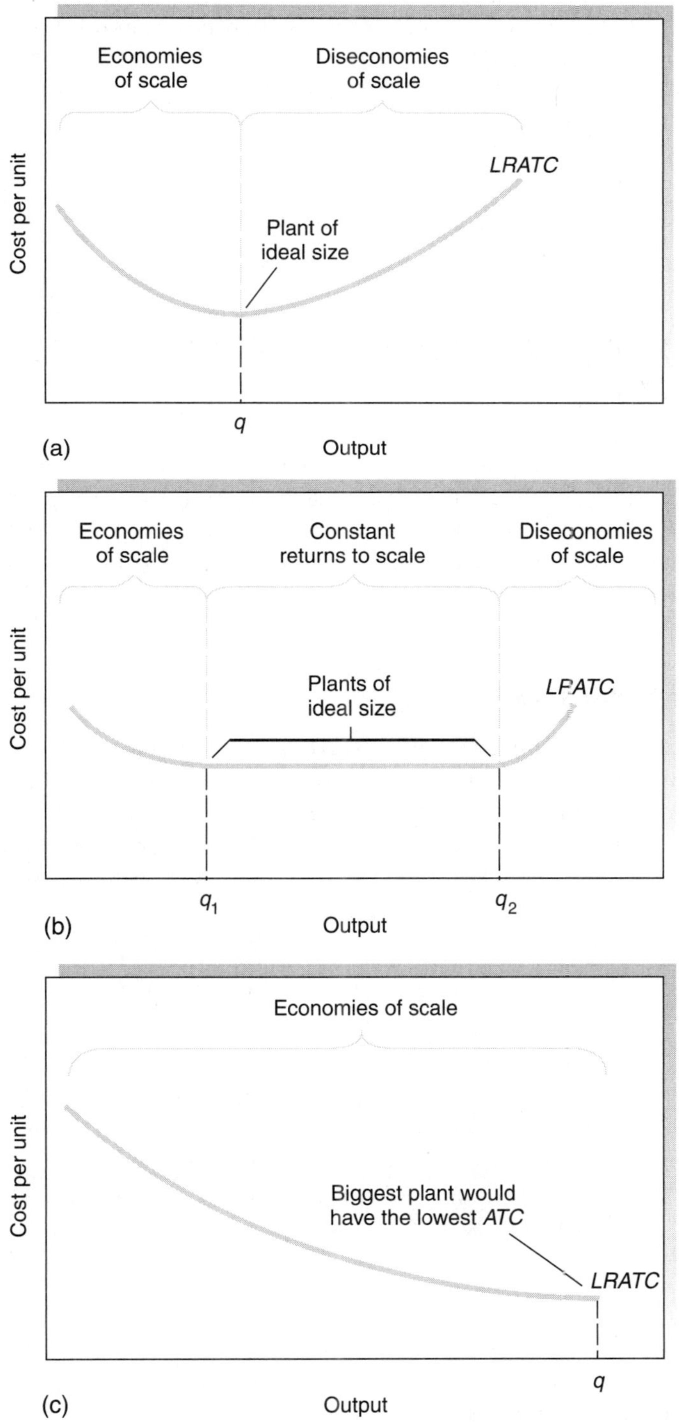

Higher per-unit costs will result if the firm chooses a plant size other than the one that minimizes the cost of producing output q. If each firm in an industry faces the same cost conditions, we can generalize and say that all plants larger or smaller than this ideal size will experience higher unit costs. A very narrow range of plant sizes would be expected in industries with the *LRATC* depicted by part a. Some lines of retail sales and agriculture might approximate these conditions.

Part b demonstrates the general shape of the *LRATC* that economists believe is present in most industries. Initially, economies of scale exist, but once a minimum efficient scale is reached, wide variation in firm size is possible. Firms smaller than the minimum efficient size would have higher per-unit costs, but firms larger than that would not gain a cost advantage. **Constant returns to scale** are present for a broad range of output rates (between q_1 and q_2). This situation is consistent with real-world conditions in many industries. For example, small firms can be as efficient as larger ones in such industries as apparel, lumber, publishing, and several lines of retailing.

Constant returns to scale Unit costs that are constant as the scale of the firm is altered. Neither economies nor diseconomies of scale are present.

In part c of Exhibit 20-9, economies of scale exist for all relevant output levels. The larger the firm size, the lower the per-unit cost. The *LRATC* in the local telephone service industry may approximate the curve shown here.

9 WHAT FACTORS CAUSE COST CURVES TO SHIFT?

In outlining the general shapes of a firm's cost curves in both the long run and short run, we assumed that certain other factors—resource prices, taxes, regulations, and technology—remained constant as the firm altered its rate of output. Let us now consider how these other factors would affect production costs if they did not remain constant.

Prices of Resources

If the price of resources used should rise, the firm's cost curves will shift upward, as Exhibit 20-10 illustrates. Higher resource prices will increase the cost of producing each alternative output level. For example, what happens to the cost of producing automobiles when the price of steel rises? The cost of producing automobiles also rises. Conversely, lower resource prices will result in cost reductions. Thus, the cost curves for any specific plant size will shift downward.

Taxes

Taxes are a component of a firm's cost. Suppose that an excise tax of 20 cents were levied on the seller for each gallon of gasoline sold. What would happen to the seller's costs? They would increase, just as they did in Exhibit 20-10. The firm's average total and marginal cost curves would shift upward by the amount of the tax. If the tax were an annual business license fee instead, it would raise the average cost, but not the variable cost.

Regulations

The government often imposes health, safety, environmental, and production regulations on business firms. Regulations may require businesses to provide a certain number of water fountains and restrooms for customers and workers.

EXHIBIT 20-10 Higher Resource Prices and Cost

An increase in resource prices will cause the firm's cost curves to shift upward.

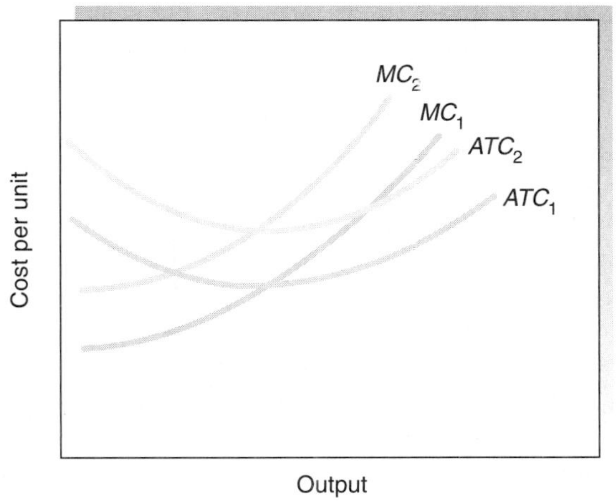

The Americans With Disabilities Act forces many firms to make their facilities accessible for persons in wheelchairs. Regulations may force firms to include certain features in a product (for example, strong bumpers and air bags for automobiles). Although regulations yield benefits, they are also costly. Merely processing the required paperwork for submission to regulators is costly, and so are the other requirements. Like tax increases, increases in regulatory compliance costs will shift cost curves upward. In some cases, only fixed costs will be affected, while in other instances variable costs will be altered as well. In both cases, the firm's *ATC* will be higher.

"OF COURSE YOU MAY REGISTER A COMPLAINT ABOUT ALL THE GOVERNMENT PAPERWORK, SIR... BUT IT HAS TO BE IN WRITING."

Technology

Technological improvements often make it possible to produce a specific output with fewer resources. For example, computers and robots have reduced costs in many industries. The rapid expansion through the Internet of business-to-business or "B2B" services has made it easier to locate and contract for shared services, ranging from building maintenance, computer, and bookkeeping services to important components for manufacturing processes. Small firms can gain from specialization without being large themselves, and even large firms are participating. Federated Department stores, owners of Bloomingdales, Macy's, Burdines, and the Bon Marché, among others, recently contracted with a specialty firm to manage all of its building facilities worldwide. Federated expects to save $150 million per year from the change.[5] The *Wall Street Journal* reported that Micropub Systems of Rochester, N.Y., can install an entire brewery in 96 square feet, allowing the premium local brews to be made and delivered at lower cost than those currently available from the largest national brewers.[6] As Exhibit 20-11 shows, a technological improvement will shift the firm's cost curves downward, reflecting the reduction in the amount of resources used to produce alternative levels of output.

EXHIBIT 20-11 Egg-Production Costs and Technological Change

Suppose that an egg producer discovers (or develops) a "super" mineral water that makes it possible to get more eggs from the same number of chickens. Because of this technological improvement, various output levels of eggs can now be produced with less feed, space, water, and labor. Costs will be reduced. The egg producer's *ATC* and *MC* curves will shift downward.

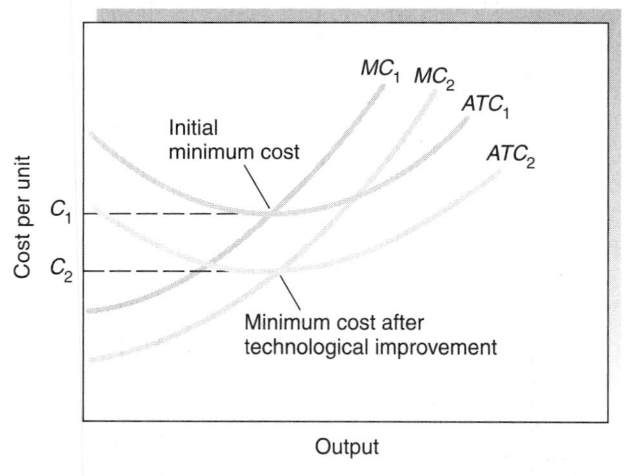

[5] "Economies of Scale: Spend to Save," *Chain Store Age*, Vol. 76, Issue 2, Feb. 2000, p. 2B.

[6] Thomas Petzinger, Jr., "The Rise of the Small and Other Trends to Watch This Year," *Wall Street Journal*, Jan. 9, 1998, p. B1.

ECONOMIC WAY OF THINKING ABOUT COSTS

10

When analyzing the firm's costs, economists often present a highly mechanical—some would say unrealistic—view. The role of personal choice in a world of uncertainty is often glossed over.

It is important to keep in mind that costs are incurred when choices are made. When business decision makers choose to purchase raw materials, hire new employees, or renew the lease on a plant, they incur costs. All these decisions, like other choices, must be made under conditions of uncertainty. Of course, past experience can help business decision makers to anticipate the likely costs of various decisions. But the world is constantly changing; the future may differ substantially from the past.

Opportunity costs are expected costs—they represent the highest valued option that the decision maker expects to give up as the result of a choice. Think for a moment of what the cost curves developed in this chapter really mean. The firm's short-run *MC* curve represents the opportunity cost of expanding output, *given the firm's current plant size.* The firm's long-run *ATC* curve represents the opportunity cost per-unit of output associated with varying plant sizes and rates of output, *given that the alternative plants are still on the drawing boards.* Opportunity costs look forward, reflecting expectations as to what will be forgone as a result of current decisions. At the time decisions must be made, neither the short-run MC nor the long-run *ATC* can be determined from accounting records, since accounting costs look backward. Accounting figures yield valuable information about historical costs, but, as the following section illustrates, they must be interpreted carefully when forecasting future costs.

Sunk Costs

Sunk costs
Costs that have already been incurred as a result of past decisions. They are sometimes referred to as historical costs.

Sunk costs are historical costs associated with past decisions that cannot be reversed. While sunk costs provide knowledge relevant to current decisions, the specific costs themselves are no longer relevant. When past choices cannot be reversed, money that has been spent is gone for good. Current choices must be based on the costs and benefits expected in relation to *current and future* market conditions, if mistakes are to be avoided (see the Myths of Economics box on the next page).

If they are to minimize costs, business decision makers must recognize the irrelevance of sunk costs. Let us consider a simple example that emphasizes this point. Suppose that the firm of Exhibit 20-5 pays $100,000 to purchase and install a roller blade producing machine. The machine is expected to last ten years. The company's books record the cost of the machine as $10,000 each year under the heading of depreciation. The machine can be used only to make roller blades. Since dismantling and reinstallation costs are high, it cannot be leased or sold to another firm. Also, it has no scrap value. In other words, there are no alternative uses for the machine. The machine's annual production of roller blades will generate $50,000 of revenues for the firm when it is employed with raw materials and other factors of production that cost $46,000. Thus, the net revenue generated by the machine is $4,000.

Should the firm continue to use the machine? Its annual depreciation cost suggests that the machine cost the firm $10,000, compared to the $4,000 of net revenue it generates. Thus, the accounting records indicate that the machine reduces the firm's profit by $6,000 annually. The machine's depreciation cost, however, is a sunk cost. It was incurred when the machine was installed. The current opportunity cost of the machine is precisely zero. The firm is not giving up anything by continuing to use it. Since use of the machine generates $4,000 of additional net revenue, the firm can gain from its continued operation. Of

MYTHS OF ECONOMICS

"A good business decision maker will never sell a product for less than its production costs."

This statement contains a grain of truth. A profit-seeking entrepreneur would not undertake a project knowing that the costs could not be covered. However, this view fails to emphasize (1) the time dimension of the production process and (2) the uncertainty associated with business decisions. The production process takes time. Raw materials must be purchased, employees hired, and plants equipped. Retailers must contract with suppliers. As these decisions are made, costs result. Many of the firm's costs of production are incurred long before the product is ready for marketing.

Even a good business decision maker is not always able to predict the future. Market conditions may change in an unexpected manner. At the time the product is ready for sale, buyers may be unwilling to pay a price that will cover the seller's past costs of production. These past costs, however, are now sunk costs and no longer relevant. Current decisions must be made on the basis of current cost and revenue considerations.

Should a grocer refuse to sell oranges that are about to spoil because their wholesale cost cannot be covered? The grocer's current opportunity cost of selling the oranges may be nearly zero. The alternative may be to throw them in the garbage next week. Almost any price, even one far below past costs, would be better than letting the oranges spoil.

Consider another example. Suppose a couple who own a house plan to relocate temporarily. Should they refuse to rent their house for $500 (if this is the best offer available) because their monthly house payment is $800? Of course not. The house payment will go on, regardless of whether they rent the house. If the homeowners can cover their opportunity costs (perhaps wear and tear plus a $60 monthly fee for a property management service), they will gain by renting rather than leaving the house vacant.

Past mistakes provide useful lessons for the future, but they cannot be reversed. Bygones are bygones, even if they resulted in business loss. There is no need to fret over spilt milk, burnt toast, or yesterday's business losses.

course, if current market conditions are not expected to improve, the firm will not purchase a similar machine or replace the machine when it wears out, but this should not influence the decision of whether to continue operating the current one. The irrelevance of sunk costs helps explain why it often makes sense to continue using older equipment (it has a low opportunity cost), even though it may not be wise to purchase similar equipment again.

Cost and Supply

Economists are interested in cost because they seek to explain the supply decisions of firms. A strictly profit-maximizing firm will compare the expected revenues derived from a decision or a course of action with the expected costs. If the expected revenues exceed costs, the course of action will be chosen because it will expand profits (or reduce losses).

In the short run, when making supply decisions, the marginal cost of producing additional units is the relevant cost consideration. A profit-maximizing decision maker will compare the expected marginal costs with the expected additional revenue from larger sales. If the latter exceeds the former, output (the quantity supplied) will be expanded.

Whereas marginal costs are central to the choice of short-run output, the expected average total cost is vital to a firm's long-run supply decision. *Before entering an industry* (or purchasing capital assets for expansion or replacement), a profit-maximizing decision maker will compare the expected market price with the expected long-run average total cost. Profit-seeking potential entrants will supply the product if, and only if, they expect the market price to exceed their long-run average total cost. Similarly, existing firms will continue to supply a product only if they expect that the market price will enable them at least to cover their long-run average total cost.

SUMMARY

- The business firm is used to organize productive resources and transform them into goods and services. There are three major types of business structure—proprietorships, partnerships, and corporations.
- To solve the principal-agent problem, which tends to reduce worker efficiency in team production, every firm must provide work incentives and monitoring.
- The demand for a product indicates the intensity of consumers' desires for the item. The (opportunity) cost of producing the item indicates the intensity of consumer desires for other goods that could have been produced instead, with the same resources.
- In economics, total cost includes not only explicit payments for resources employed by the firm, but also the implicit costs associated with the use of productive resources owned by the firm (such as the opportunity cost of the firm's equity capital or owner-provided services).
- Because accounting methods omit the cost of equity capital (and sometimes other implicit costs), they generally understate the opportunity cost of producing a good and overstate the firm's economic profit.
- Economic profit (loss) results when a firm's sales revenues exceed (are less than) its total costs, both explicit and implicit. Firms that are making the market (or "normal") rate of return on their assets will therefore make zero economic profit.
- The firm's short-run average total cost (*ATC*) curve will tend to be U-shaped.
- The law of diminishing returns explains why a firm's short-run marginal and average total costs will eventually rise. When diminishing marginal returns are present, successively larger amounts of the variable input will be required to increase output by one more unit.
- The long-run *ATC* (*LRATC*) reflects the costs of production for plants of various sizes. When economies of scale are present, *LRATC* will decline. When constant returns to scale are experienced, *LRATC* will be constant. When diseconomies of scale are present, *LRATC* will rise.
- Changes in (a) resource prices, (b) taxes, (c) regulations, and (d) technology will cause the cost curves of a firm to shift.
- Sunk costs are costs that have already been incurred and cannot be recovered. While they may provide information helpful for future decisions, sunk costs are no longer directly relevant for decision making.

PRICE TAKERS AND THE COMPETITIVE PROCESS

READING 21

LEARNING OUTCOMES

The candidate should be able to:

a. discuss the conditions that characterize pure competition (price taker) market and explain how and why price takers maximize profits at the quantity for which marginal cost, price, and marginal revenue are equal;

b. calculate and interpret the total revenue and the marginal revenue for a price taker and explain the relationship between total revenue, total costs, price, marginal revenue, marginal costs, and the profit maximizing output level;

c. explain the decision by price takers with economic losses to continue to operate, temporarily shut down, or go out of business when faced with price below average total cost;

d. describe the short-run supply curves for a company and for a competitive market;

e. explain the impact on prices and output of increases or decreases in demand in a competitive market;

f. contrast the role of constant-cost, increasing-cost, and decreasing-cost industries in determining the shape of a long-run market supply curve;

g. explain the impact of time on the elasticity of market supply and discuss the role of profits and losses in a purely competitive market.

Competition means decentralized planning by many separate persons.

—*Friedrich A. von Hayek*[1]

[I]t is competition that drives down costs and prices, induces firms to produce the goods consumers want, and spurs innovation and the expansion of new markets . . .

—*President's Council of Economic Advisers*[2]

INTRODUCTION 1

In the previous readings we saw how firms make production decisions and how costs affect those decisions. In this and the next two readings, we take a closer look at how the product prices and profit levels that emerge from market trading will influence production. How much will be produced in a given market? What

[1] F. A. Hayek, "The Use of Knowledge in Society," *American Economic Review* 35 (September 1945): 521.

[2] President's Council of Economic Advisers, *Economic Report of the President, 1996* (Washington, D.C.: U.S. Government Printing Office, 1996), p. 155.

determines the profitability of firms, and how does the level of profit influence market supply over time? When goods and services are allocated by markets, will resources be allocated efficiently? Is there any reason to believe that there will be a linkage between market allocation and economic prosperity? These are the major questions that we will address in the next several readings.

2 PRICE TAKERS AND PRICE SEARCHERS

Price takers
Sellers who must take the market price in order to sell their product. Because each price taker's output is small relative to the total market, price takers can sell all their output at the market price, but they are unable to sell any of their output at a price higher than the market price.

This reading will focus on markets where the firms are **price takers**: They simply take the price that is determined in the market. ***In a price-taker market, the firms all produce identical products (for example, wheat, eggs, or regular unleaded gasoline) and each seller is small relative to the total market. Thus, the output supplied by any single firm exerts little or no effect on the market price. Each firm can sell all its output at the market price, but it is unable to sell any of its output at a price higher than the market price.*** When a firm is a price taker, there is no price decision to be made. Price takers will merely attempt to choose the output level that will maximize profit, given their costs and the price determined by the market.

Price takers are assumed to seek profits, like all other firms. They need to be sensitive to cost, in order to thrive, or even to survive in a competitive environment. However, price-taker markets and price-searcher markets have differing degrees of competition, ease of entry, and perhaps differing scale economies as well. Competition for consumer business requires each firm to provide a high level of delivered benefits per dollar, compared to what consumers can find elsewhere. No firm can force consumers to purchase its product, and all products have many substitutes. Successful firms are those that stay ahead of competitors and potential competitors.

Price searchers
Firms that face a downward sloping demand curve for their product. The amount that the firm is able to sell is inversely related to the price that it charges.

In the real world, most firms are not price takers. If the firm lowers its price, it will generally attract additional customers. Correspondingly, firms are usually able to increase their price, at least a little, without losing all their customers. For example, if Nike increased the price of its athletic shoes by 10 percent, the number of shoes sold would decline, but it would not fall to zero. Firms like Nike are **price searchers**: They choose the price they will charge for their product, but the quantity that they are able to sell is very much related to that price. As price searchers seek maximum profit, they must not only decide how much to produce, but also what price to charge. We will examine markets where the firms are price searchers in the following two readings.

Competition as a dynamic process
A term that denotes rivalry or competitiveness between or among parties (for example, producers or input suppliers), each of which seeks to deliver a better deal to buyers when quality, price, and product information are all considered. Competition implies a lack of collusion among sellers.

If most real-world firms are price searchers rather than price takers, why take the time to analyze the latter? There are several reasons to do so. First, although most firms are not price takers, there are a number of important markets, particularly in agriculture, where the firms do essentially take the price determined in the market. Second, the price-taker model helps clarify the relationship between the decision making of individual firms and market supply in both price-taker and price-searcher markets. Finally, and perhaps most important, the study of markets where firms are price takers enhances our knowledge of **competition as a dynamic process**. Understanding how the competitive process works when firms are price takers will also contribute to our understanding of the process as it applies to many price searchers.

Pure competition
A market structure characterized by a large number of small firms producing an identical product in an industry (market area) that permits complete freedom of entry and exit. Also called price-taker markets.

Historically, the term **pure competition** has been used when referring to markets where firms are price takers. However, these markets are increasingly referred to as "price-taker markets" because this expression is more descriptive. Furthermore, this label avoids the implication that competitive forces are necessarily less pure or less intense in price-searcher markets. Often this is not the case. Many price searchers use a broad array of competitive weapons—for exam-

APPLICATIONS IN ECONOMICS

The Aalsmeer Flower Auction: An Illustration of a Competitive Market

The Aalsmeer Flower Auction, located near Amsterdam, illustrates a highly competitive market with a large number of both buyers and sellers. Approximately 5,000 growers from the Netherlands and other countries such as Israel, Kenya, and Zambia supply their products to this market. On a typical day, several thousand buyers representing wholesale florists from around the world participate in the auction. More than 18 million flowers and 2 million plants are sold each day from a building equal in size to 125 football fields.

The 50,000 daily transactions are made possible by the Dutch auction system. Under this system, a clock runs backward from the highest to the lowest price per unit. The buyer pushes a button indicating a willingness to purchase when the clock reaches an acceptable per unit-price. The purchaser is the first buyer to push the button. Flowers and plants auctioned in the morning at Aalsmeer will be available in shops around the world within 24 hours.

ple, quality of product, style, convenient location, advertising, and price—all in an effort to attract consumers. When **barriers to entry** are low, the competitive process is just as important in price-searcher markets as it is when the firms are price takers.

Barriers to entry
Obstacles that limit the freedom of potential rivals to enter and compete in an industry or market.

Nonetheless, it should be noted that price-taker markets and purely competitive markets are merely alternative names for the same thing. Thus, if you hear someone speak of pure competition or a purely competitive market, the person is referring to markets that have characteristics like those analyzed in this reading.

MARKETS WHEN FIRMS ARE PRICE TAKERS 3

Consider the situation of Les Parrot, a Texas cattle rancher. As Parrot consults the financial pages of the local newspaper, he finds that the current market price of quality steers is 88 cents per pound. Even if his ranch is quite large, there is little that Parrot can do to change the market price of beef cattle. After all, there are tens of thousands of farmers who raise cattle. Thus, Parrot supplies only a small portion of the total cattle market. The amount that he sells will exert little or no impact on the market price of cattle. Parrot is a price taker.

The firms in a market will be price takers when the following four conditions are met:

1. All the firms in the market are producing an identical product (for example, beef cattle of a given grade).
2. A large number of firms exist in the market.
3. Each firm supplies only a very small portion of the total amount supplied to the market.
4. No barriers limit the entry or exit of firms in the market.

When these conditions are met, the firms in the market must accept the market price. This is why they are called price takers. Exhibit 21-1 illustrates the

EXHIBIT 21-1 Price Taker's Demand Curve

The market forces of supply and demand determine price (b). Price takers have no control over price. Thus, the demand for the product of the firm is perfectly elastic (a).

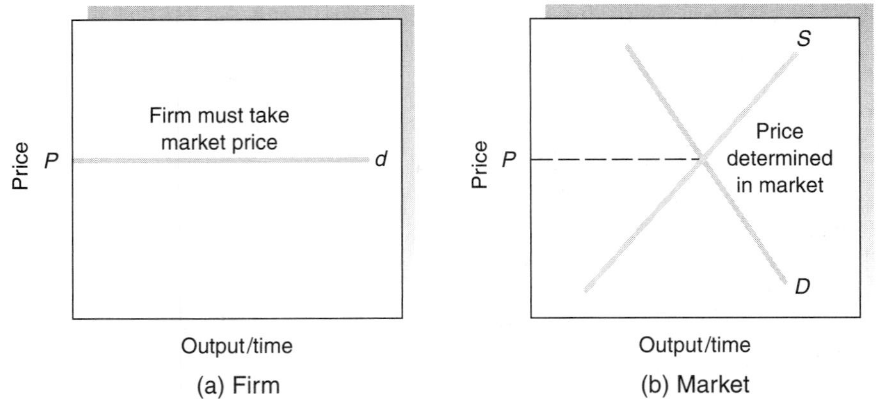

relationship between the market forces (part *b*) and the demand curve facing the price-taking firm (part *a*). If the firm sets a price above the market level, consumers will simply buy from other sellers. Why pay the higher price when the identical good is available elsewhere at a lower price? For example, if the price of wheat were $5.00 per bushel, a farmer would be unable to find buyers for wheat at $5.50 per bushel. A firm could set its price below the market level. However, since one firm is small relative to the total market, the firm can already sell as much as it wants at the market price. A price reduction would merely reduce revenues. A firm that is a price taker thus confronts a perfectly elastic demand for its product. (Note in the exhibit, that a lower case *d* is used to denote the demand curve faced by the *firm* while a capital *D* indicates the *market* demand curve.)

4 OUTPUT IN THE SHORT RUN

The firm's output decision is based on comparison of benefits with costs. If a firm produces at all, it will expand output as long as the benefits (additional revenues) from the production and sales of the additional units exceed their mar-

Producers in the wheat farming and beef cattle markets are price takers. If they are going to sell their output, they must do so at the price determined by the market. Because individual producers are small relative to the total market, they can sell as many units as they like at the market price.

ginal costs. How will changes in output influence the firm's costs? In a previous reading, we discovered that the firm's short-run marginal costs will eventually increase as the firm expands its output by working its fixed plant facilities more intensively. The law of diminishing marginal returns assures us that this will be the case. Eventually, both the firm's short-run marginal and average total cost curves will turn upward.

What about the benefits or additional revenues from output expansion? **Marginal revenue (*MR*)** is the change in the firm's total revenue per unit of output. It is the additional revenue derived from the sale of an additional unit of output. Mathematically,

Marginal revenue *(MR)* The incremental change in total revenue derived from the sale of one additional unit of a product.

$$MR = \text{Change in total revenue}/\text{Change in output}$$

The price taker sells all units at the same price; therefore, its marginal revenue will be equal to the market price.

In the short run, the price taker will expand output until marginal revenue (its price) is just equal to marginal cost. This decision-making rule will maximize the firm's profits (or minimize its losses).

Exhibit 21-2 helps explain why. Since the firm can sell as many units as it would like at the market price, the sale of one additional unit will increase revenue by the price of the product. Does the firm gain by producing an extra unit? The answer is yes, as long as the marginal revenue (price, for the price taker) is greater than or equal to the marginal cost of that unit. Profit is simply the difference between total revenue and total cost. Profit will increase as long as production and sale of a unit add more to revenue than to cost. Thus, the firm will gain from an increase in output as long as marginal revenue exceeds marginal cost. Eventually, however, as the firm produces a larger and larger quantity from its fixed size of plant, marginal costs will rise and exceed price and marginal revenue. When production of an additional unit adds more to cost than it adds to revenue, profit will be reduced if the unit is produced. Thus, the profit of the price taker is maximized at the output rate where $P = MR = MC$. In Exhibit 21-2, this occurs at output level q.

A profit-maximizing firm with the cost curves indicated by Exhibit 21-2 would produce exactly q. The total revenue of the firm would be the sales price P multiplied by output sold q. Geometrically, the firm's total revenues would be $P0qB$. The firm's total cost would be found by multiplying the average total cost

EXHIBIT 21-2 Profit Maximization When the Firm Is a Price Taker

The price taker would maximize profits by producing the output level q, where $P = MC$.

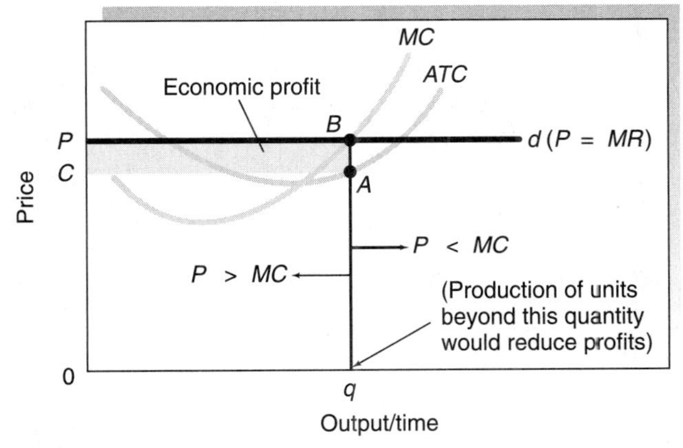

(ATC) by the output level. Geometrically, total costs are represented by $COqA$. The firm's total revenues exceed total costs, and the firm is making short-run economic profit (the shaded area).

In the real world, of course, decisions are not made by entrepreneurs who spend time drawing demand and marginal cost curves. Many have not even heard of these concepts. A business decision maker who has never heard of the $P = MR = MC$ rule for profit maximization, however, probably has another rule that yields approximately the same outcome. For example, the rule might be to produce those units, and only those units, that add more to revenue than to cost. This ensures maximum profit (or minimum loss). It also takes the firm to the point at which $P = MR = MC$. Why? To stop short of that point would mean not producing some profitable units that would add more to revenue than to cost. Similarly, the decision maker would not go beyond that point because production of such units would add more to cost than to revenue. This commonsense rule thus leads to the same outcome as our model, even when the decision maker knows none of the technical jargon of economics. No wonder economics is sometimes thought of as "organized common sense."

Just how accurate is the price taker's competitive model in predicting behavior in real markets? Do other models, which assume that sellers collude to eliminate competition, yield better predictions? Direct scientific evidence bearing on such questions is highly desirable. As the Applications in Economics box on the significance of competition indicates, such evidence has been produced repeat-

APPLICATIONS IN ECONOMICS

Experimental Economics: The Significance of Competition

Do individual decision makers, without any economics training, behave as if they understand marginal costs? Do they act as price takers, even though not all the assumptions of that model are satisfied? Or, when there are only a few sellers, do they collude successfully so as to raise price above marginal cost?

A normal economic event that we can observe may be the result of more than one cause; therefore, the economist seeking to isolate the impact of one causal factor must try to be sure that other factors influencing the outcome do not vary, or else try to take them into account in the analysis. This is not an easy task. In other disciplines, scientists use carefully designed laboratory experiments to test and verify the basic principles on which their science is built.

Beginning about the middle of the twentieth century, economists also began to conduct laboratory experiments. A good many experiments have been conducted to investigate the predictive power of the price-taker model. In one of the earliest, conducted in 1956 by leading experimental economist Vernon Smith of the University of Arizona, individuals were brought into a laboratory setting and arbitrarily assigned roles as buyers and sellers, in a game-like setting. Each buyer was given a different "limit price" (that is, a maximum price he or she was allowed to pay) for a paper asset. Any buyer who could purchase the paper commodity for less than the limit price received a cash payment equal to the difference between the limit price and the amount actually paid. Therefore, as in other markets, each buyer gained financially by purchasing at lower prices. The sellers were treated in a parallel fashion. Each had a "limit price" (a minimum selling price) and received in cash any extra revenue above that price.

Buyers and sellers were free to make verbal offers to buy or sell. How did markets develop? Did the outcomes resemble a market where sellers compete, or did sellers collude, controlling the market price for their own benefit and controlling entry into the market?

The price-taker model predicts that all mutually advantageous trades among buyers and sellers will occur and that the price of the good will converge toward a single price—the market price. Prior to the work in experimental economics, many economists thought this model was relevant only under highly restrictive conditions. By changing the number of sellers, the type of trading rules, and so on, experimental researchers have generated similar results under a wide variety of conditions. Their findings suggest that outcomes approximating those of the price-taker model often emerge even when the strict assumptions of the model are absent. For example, even if the number of sellers is relatively small, say ten to fifteen, outcomes similar to those predicted by the price-taker model generally occur.

Participants in these experiments are often startled to discover that their competitive trading generated the largest possible joint income gain and, furthermore, that the competitive model presented in this chapter predicted this occurrence. Vernon Smith cites cases where, after the experiment, participants describe the experimental market as "unorganized, unstable, chaotic, and confused." Generally, they are amazed when shown that their actions (trades) achieved the maximum income for the group, and that a sealed envelope, given to them prior to the experiment, predicted the approximate amount of their (maximum) joint gain.

Smith himself was at first surprised at the efficient outcomes resulting from economic experiments. He had not been prepared to believe Adam Smith's principle that markets cause individual traders to reach efficient outcomes, even though this is not their intention. These results are achieved even when the individual participants are far from proficient traders. After numerous experiments, the modern Smith stated:

> In many experimental markets, poorly informed, error-prone, and uncomprehending human agents interact through the trading rules to produce social algorithms which demonstrably approximate the wealth maximizing outcomes traditionally thought to require complete information and cognitively rational actors.[1]

Experimental economics has confirmed that Adam Smith was right in 1776 when he described the invisible hand of the market at work. It has also established that the invisible hand does not require very much beyond the desire of each individual to better his or her own situation. Perfect information, perfect traders, and perfect markets are not necessary for traders to reach efficient solutions, when they can trade freely.

Experimental economics has researched many additional economic questions. Vernon Smith and his colleague Arlington Williams, another leading researcher in this area, summarize the findings of their work in the following manner:

> Experimental market research has provided an empirical foundation for tenets of economic theory that were already well established, and it has also yielded insight into the details of how particular rules affect the outcome of the trading process. Thirty years of experiments have also brought good news: under most circumstances, markets are extremely efficient in facilitating the movement of goods from the lowest-cost producers to the consumers who place the highest value on them. Organized exchange thus effectively advances human welfare.[2]

[1] Vernon L. Smith, "Economics in the Laboratory," *Journal of Economic Perspectives* 8, no. 1 (winter, 1994): 118.

[2] Vernon L. Smith and Arlington W. Williams, "Experimental Market Economics," *Scientific American* 267 (December 1992): 121. See also Smith, "Economics in the Laboratory," 113–32.

edly in recent decades by the relatively new subdiscipline of experimental economics. The evidence indicates that the general implications of the price-taker model are valid under a variety of circumstances.

Profit Maximizing—A Numeric Example

Exhibit 21-3 uses numeric data to illustrate profit-maximizing decision making for a firm that is a price taker. Put yourself in the place of the owner of this firm. Your short-run total and marginal cost schedules have the general characteristics we discussed in the previous chapter. Since the firm confronts a market price of \$5 per unit, its marginal revenue is \$5. Total revenue thus increases by \$5 per additional unit of output produced and sold. You will maximize your profit when you supply an output of 15 units.

There are two ways of viewing this profit-maximizing output rate. First, profit is equal to the difference between total revenue and total cost. Thus, profit will be maximized at the output rate at which this difference (*TR* minus *TC*) is greatest. Column 6 of Exhibit 21-3 provides this information. For small output rates (less than 11), you and your firm would actually experience losses. But at 15 units of output, an \$11 profit is earned (\$75 total revenue minus \$64 total cost). A look at the profit figures of column 6 indicates that it would be impossible to earn a profit larger than \$11 at any other rate of output.

EXHIBIT 21-3 Profit Maximization for a Price Taker: A Numeric Illustration

(1) Output (per day)	(2) Total Revenue (*TR*)	(3) Total Cost (*TC*)	(4) Marginal Revenue (*MR*)	(5) Marginal Cost (*MC*)	(6) Profit (*TR* − *TC*)
0	$ 0.00	$ 25.00	$0.00	$ 0.00	$−25.00
1	5.00	29.80	5.00	4.80	−24.80
2	10.00	33.75	5.00	3.95	−23.75
3	15.00	37.25	5.00	3.50	−22.25
4	20.00	40.25	5.00	3.00	−20.25
5	25.00	42.75	5.00	2.50	−17.75
6	30.00	44.75	5.00	2.00	−14.75
7	35.00	46.50	5.00	1.75	−11.50
8	40.00	48.00	5.00	1.50	− 8.00
9	45.00	49.25	5.00	1.25	− 4.25
10	50.00	50.25	5.00	1.00	− 0.25
11	55.00	51.50	5.00	1.25	3.50
12	60.00	53.25	5.00	1.75	6.75
13	65.00	55.75	5.00	2.50	9.25
14	70.00	59.25	5.00	3.50	10.75
15	75.00	64.00	5.00	4.75	11.00
16	80.00	70.00	5.00	6.00	10.00
17	85.00	77.25	5.00	7.25	7.75
18	90.00	85.50	5.00	8.25	4.50
19	95.00	95.00	5.00	9.50	0.00
20	100.00	108.00	5.00	13.00	− 8.00
21	105.00	125.00	5.00	17.00	−20.00

Exhibit 21-4 presents in part a the total revenue and total cost approach in graph form. (However, the curves are drawn smoothly, as though output could be increased by tiny amounts, not just in whole-unit increments as shown in Exhibit 21-3.) Profits will be greatest when the total revenue line exceeds the total cost curve by the largest vertical amount. That takes place, of course, at 15 units of output.

You can also use the marginal approach to determine the profit-maximizing rate of output for this competitive firm. Remember, as long as price (marginal revenue) exceeds marginal cost, production and sale of additional units will add to the firm's profit (or reduce its losses). A look at columns 4 and 5 of Exhibit 21-3 reveals that *MR* is greater than *MC* for the first 15 units of output. Producing these units will expand the firm's profit. In contrast, producing any unit beyond 15 adds more to cost than to revenue. Profit will therefore decline if you expand output beyond 15 units. Given the firm's cost and revenue schedule, you will maximize profit by producing 15, and only 15, units per day.

EXHIBIT 21-4 Profit Maximization—The Total and Marginal Approaches

Using the data of Exhibit 21-3, here we provide two ways of viewing profit maximization. In the first, the profits of the price taker are maximized at the output level at which total revenue exceeds total cost by the maximum amount (a). In the second, the maximum-profit output is identified by comparing marginal revenue and marginal cost (b).

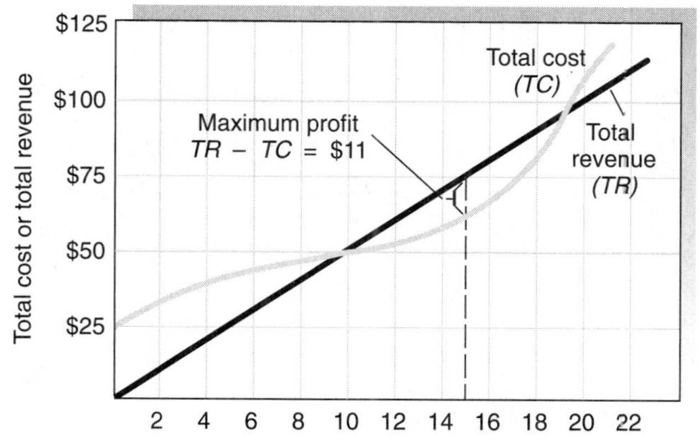

(a) Total revenue/total cost approach

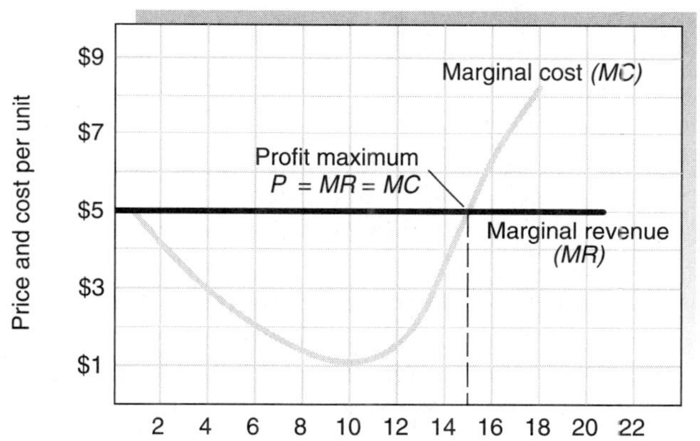

(b) Marginal revenue/marginal cost approach

Part b of Exhibit 21-4 graphically illustrates the marginal approach. Note here that the output rate (15 units) at which the marginal cost and marginal revenue curves intersect coincides with the output rate in part a at which the total revenue curve exceeds the total cost curve by the largest amount. Beyond that output rate, *MR* is less than *MC*, so profit must decline.

Losses and Going Out of Business

Suppose changes take place in the market that depress the price below a firm's average total cost. How will a profit maximizer (or loss minimizer) respond to this situation? The answer to this question depends both on the firm's current sales revenues relative to its variable cost and on its expectations about the future. The firm's owner has three options: (1) continue to operate in the short run, (2) shut down temporarily, or (3) go out of business.

EXHIBIT 21-5 Operating with Short-Run Losses

A firm making losses will operate in the short run if it (1) can cover its variable costs now and (2) expects price to be high enough in the future to cover all its costs.

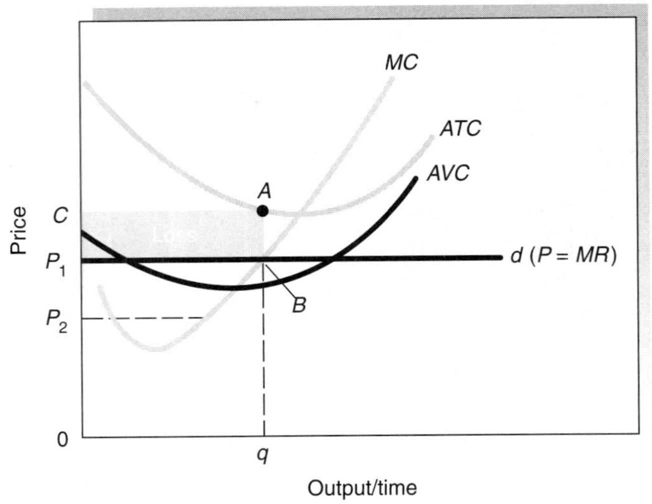

If the firm anticipates that the lower market price is temporary, it may want to continue operating in the short run as long as it can cover its variable cost.[3] Exhibit 21-5 illustrates why. The firm shown in this exhibit would minimize its loss at output level q, where $P = MR = MC$. But at q, total revenues ($OqBP_1$) are less than total costs ($OqAC$). The firm faces short-run economic losses. Even if it shuts down completely, it will still incur fixed costs, *unless the firm goes out of business.* If it anticipates that the market price will increase enough that the firm will be able to cover its average total costs in the future, it may not want to terminate operations and sell its assets. It may choose to produce q units in the short run, even though losses are incurred. At price P_1, production of output q is clearly more advantageous than shutting down, because the firm is able to cover its variable costs and pay some of its fixed costs. If it were to shut down, *but not sell out,* the firm would lose the entire amount of its fixed cost.

Shutdown
A temporary halt in the operation of a business firm. Because the firm anticipates returning to the market in the future, it does not sell its assets and go out of business. The firm's variable cost is eliminated by the shutdown, but its fixed costs continue.

What if the market price declines below the firm's average variable cost (for example, P_2)? Under these circumstances, a temporary **shutdown** is preferable to short-run operation. Continuing to operate in the short run would add more to cost than to revenue, so operating losses merely add to losses resulting from the firm's fixed costs. Therefore, even if the firm's owner expects the market price to increase later, enabling it to survive and prosper in the future, shutting down in the short run will reduce losses when the market price falls below the firm's average variable cost (AVC). Temporary shutdowns are actually planned on a regular basis in some markets. For example, many ski resorts, golf courses, hotels, and restaurants in vacation areas plan to shut down in slow seasons, operating only when tourists or other seasonal purchasers provide enough demand. The price-

[3] Keep in mind the opportunity-cost concept. The firm's fixed costs are opportunity costs that do not vary with the level of output. They can be avoided if, and only if, the firm goes out of business. To specify fixed costs, we need to know (1) how much the firm's fixed assets would bring if they were sold or rented to others and (2) any other costs, such as operating license fees and debts, that could be avoided if the firm declared bankruptcy and/or went out of business. Since fixed costs can be avoided if the firm goes out of business, the firm will foresee greater losses from operating even in the short run if it does not expect conditions to improve.

This ice cream store in Morgantown, West Virginia, closes for several months each winter and reopens during the summer. During these short-run shutdowns, the store still pays fixed costs, such as rent, taxes, and insurance. Only variable costs are avoided during the winter months.

taker model predicts that these firms will operate only when they expect to cover at least their variable costs.

The firm's third option is **going out of business** immediately. Since a cost that cannot be avoided by closing the business is not a cost of operating the business, even the losses resulting from the firm's fixed costs can be avoided if the firm sells out. When market conditions are not expected to change for the better, going out of business is the preferred option.

Going out of business The sale of a firm's assets and its permanent exit from the market. By going out of business, a firm is able to avoid fixed costs, which would continue during a shutdown.

Firm's Short-run Supply Curve

The price taker that intends to stay in business will maximize profits (or minimize losses) when it produces the output level at which P = MR = MC and variable costs are covered. Therefore, the portion of the firm's short-run marginal cost curve that lies above its average variable cost is the short-run supply curve of the firm.

Part a of Exhibit 21-6 illustrates that, as the market price increases, the firm will expand output along its *MC* curve. If the market price were less than P_1, the firm would shut down immediately because it would be unable to cover even its variable costs. If the market price is P_1, however, a price equal to the firm's average variable cost, the firm may supply output q_1 in the short run. Economic losses will result, but the firm would incur similar losses if it shut down completely. As the market price increases to P_2, the firm will happily expand output along its

EXHIBIT 21-6 Short-run Supply Curve for the Firm and the Market

As price increases, firms will expand output along their *MC* curve. Thus, the firm's *MC* curve is also its supply curve (a). When resource prices are constant, the short-run market supply is merely the sum of the supply produced by all the firms in the market area (b).

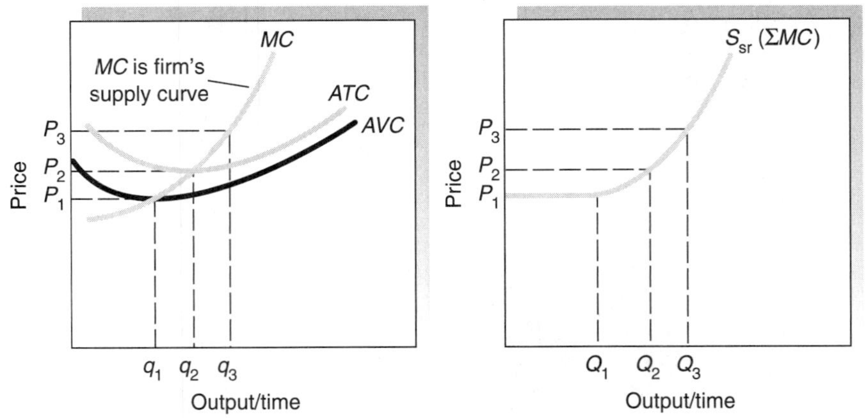

(a) Representative firm

(b) Market

MC curve to q_2. At P_2, price is also equal to average total costs. The firm is making a "normal rate of return," or zero economic profits. Higher prices will result in a still larger short-run output. The firm will supply q_3 units at market price P_3. At this price, economic profits will result. At still higher prices, output will be expanded even more. As long as price exceeds average variable cost, higher prices will cause the firm to expand output along its *MC* curve, which therefore becomes the firm's short-run supply curve.

Short-run Market Supply Curve

The short-run market supply curve corresponds to the total amount supplied by all the firms in the market. ***When the firms are price takers, the short-run market supply curve is the horizontal summation of the marginal cost curves (above the level of average variable cost) for all firms in the market. Since individual firms will supply a larger amount at a higher price, the short-run market supply curve will slope upward to the right.***

Part b of Exhibit 21-6 illustrates this relationship. As the price of the product rises from P_1 to P_2 to P_3, the individual firms expand their output along their marginal cost curves. Since the individual firms supply a larger output as the market price increases, the total amount supplied to the market also expands.

Our construction of the short-run market supply curve assumes that the prices of the resources used by the industry are constant. When the entire industry (rather than just a single firm) expands output, resource prices may rise. If so, the short-run market supply curve (reflecting the higher prices of purchased inputs) will be slightly more inelastic (steeper) than the sum of the supply curves of the individual firms. The reason, of course, is that when just one firm expands, it has a minuscule effect on the market for resources, but when the entire industry expands output, the rise in resource demand is larger, so resource prices are more likely to rise.

The short-run market supply curve, together with the demand curve for the industry's product, will determine the market price. At the short-run equilibrium market price, each firm will have expanded output until marginal costs have risen to the market price. Firms will have no desire to change output, *given their current size of plant.*

OUTPUT ADJUSTMENTS IN THE LONG RUN

5

In the long run, firms have the opportunity to alter their plant size and enter or exit an industry. As long-run adjustments are made, output in the whole industry may either expand or contract.

Long-Run Equilibrium

In addition to the balance between quantity supplied and quantity demanded necessary for short-run equilibrium, firms that are price takers must earn the normal rate of return, and only the normal rate, before long-run equilibrium can be attained. ***If economic profit is present, new firms will enter the industry, and the current producers will have an incentive to expand the scale of their operations. This increase in supply will place downward pressure on prices. In contrast, if firms in the industry are suffering economic losses, they will leave the market. This decrease in supply will place upward pressure on prices.***

Therefore, as Exhibit 21-7 illustrates, when a price-taker market is in long-run equilibrium (1) the quantity supplied and the quantity demanded will be equal at the market price, and (2) each firm in the industry will be earning normal (zero) economic profit (that is, its minimum *ATC* will just equal the market price).

EXHIBIT 21-7 Long-Run Equilibrium in a Price-Taker Market

The two conditions necessary for equilibrium in a price-taker market are depicted here. First, quantity supplied and quantity demanded must be equal in the market (b). Second, the firms in the industry must earn zero economic profit (that is, the "normal rate of return") at the established market price (a).

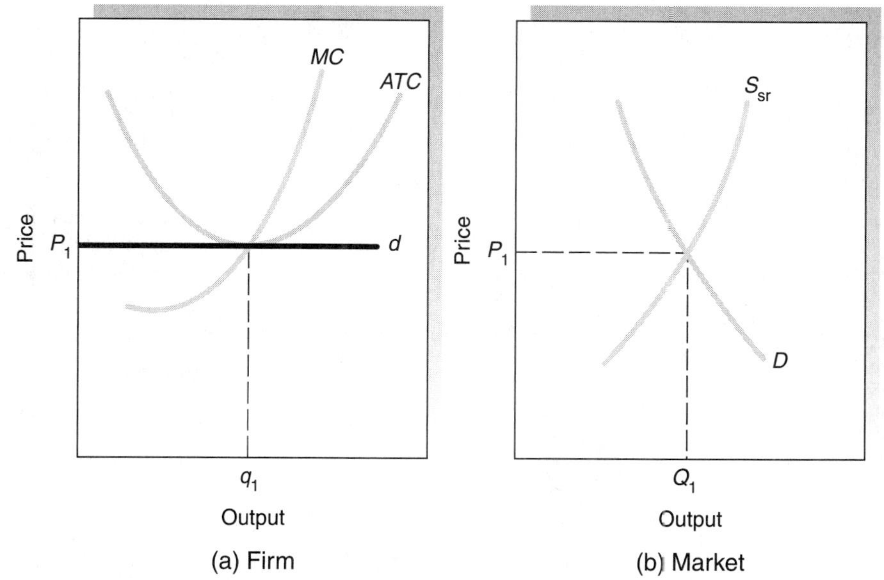

Adjusting to an Expansion in Demand

Suppose a price-taker market is in equilibrium. What will happen if there is an increase in demand? Exhibit 21-8 presents an example. An entrepreneur introduces a fantastic new candy product. Consumers go wild over it. However, since it sticks to one's teeth, the market demand for toothpicks increases from D_1 to D_2. The price of toothpicks rises from P_1 to P_2. What impact will the higher market price have on the output level of toothpick-producing firms? It will increase (from q_1 to q_2 in part a of the exhibit) as the firms expand output along their *MC* curves. In the short run, the toothpick producers will make economic profits. The profits will attract new toothpick producers to the industry and cause the existing firms to expand the scale of their plants. Hence, the market supply will increase (shift from S_1 to S_2) and eventually eliminate the short-run profits. If the prices of resources supplied to the industry are unchanged, the market price for toothpicks will return to its initial level, even though output has expanded to Q_3.

Adjusting to a Decline in Demand

Economic profits attract new firms to an industry. In contrast, economic losses (when they are expected to continue) encourage capital and entrepreneurship to move out of the industry and into other areas where the profitability potential is more favorable. Economic losses mean that the owners of capital in the industry (or firms that purchase the services of the capital) are earning less than the market rate of return. The opportunity cost of continuing in the industry exceeds the gain.

Exhibit 21-9 illustrates how market forces react to economic losses. Initially, assume that an equilibrium price exists in the industry. The firms are able to cover their average costs of production. Now suppose there is a reduction in con-

EXHIBIT 21-8 Market Response to Increased Demand

The introduction of a new candy product that sticks to one's teeth causes the demand for toothpicks to increase to D_2(b). Toothpick prices rise to P_2, inducing firms to expand output. Toothpick firms make short-run profits (a), which draw new competitors into the industry. Thus, the toothpick supply expands (shifts from S_1 to S_2). If cost conditions are unchanged, the expansion in supply will continue until the market price of toothpicks has declined to its initial level of P_1.

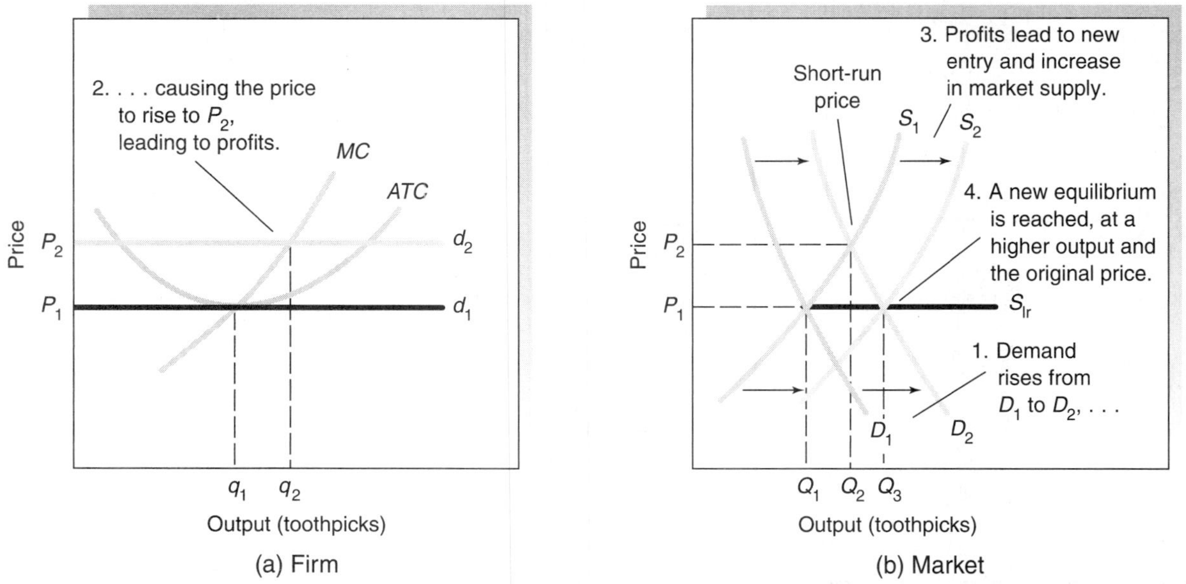

EXHIBIT 21-9 Impact of Decline in Demand

A reduction in market demand will cause price to fall and short-run losses to occur. The losses will cause some firms to go out of business and others to reduce their scale. In the long run, the market supply will fall, causing the market price to rise. The supply will continue to decline and price will continue to rise until the short-run losses have been eliminated.

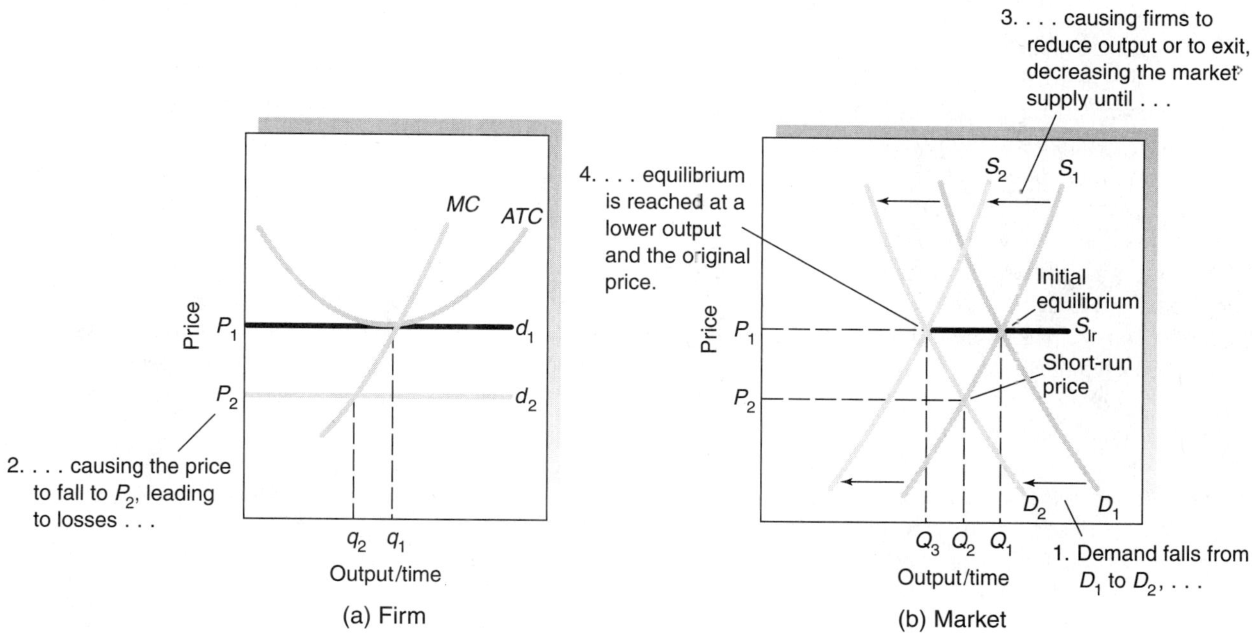

sumer income, causing the market demand for the product to decrease and the market price to decline. At the new, lower price, firms in the industry will not be able to cover their costs of production. In the short run, they will reduce output along their *MC* curve. This reduction in output by the individual firms results in a reduction in the quantity supplied in the market. For an example of how firms react to changes in market price, see the Applications in Economics feature on coffee production in a price-taker market on the next page.

In the face of short-run losses, the inflow of capital will decline and the industry's capital assets will shrink as firms fail to replace equipment when it wears out. Some firms will leave the industry as their fixed costs become variable and they are no longer able to cover their variable costs at the prevailing price. Others will reduce the scale of their operations, producing only those units for which the new, lower revenues can still justify the production costs. These factors will cause the industry supply to decline, indicated by the shift from S_1 to S_2. What impact will this have on price? It will rise. Over time, given no other shifts in demand, the short-run market supply curve will decline—will continue shifting to the left—until the price rises sufficiently to permit the firms remaining in the industry to earn once again "normal profits." At that point, long-run equilibrium is reached.

Long-Run Supply

The *long-run market supply curve* indicates the minimum price at which firms will supply various market output levels, given sufficient time both to adjust plant size (or other fixed factors) and to enter or exit from the industry. The shape of the curve depends on what happens to the cost of production as the *industry's* output

APPLICATIONS IN ECONOMICS

Coffee Production in a Price-Taker Market

Sellers to the world's coffee market are price takers. Hundreds of thousands of farmers produce coffee beans, and no grower has a significant impact on the world price. Each grower takes the price as given, and is free to respond to any price change. Changes can be dramatic in the coffee market. The market price rose from less than $1 per pound on average to more than $2 during the 1990s.

As growing coffee became more profitable, coffee production around the world expanded. For example, Vietnam growers more than quadrupled their coffee production, from 92,000 tons in 1990 to 487,000 tons in 1999. By 2000, Vietnam had became the world's second largest coffee-producing nation after Brazil.

But the expanded production proved to be more than consumers were willing to pay for. The market price fell. The price decline began in 1998; by August of 2001, coffee bean prices were averaging below $.60 per pound. Many coffee plantations could not cover their costs at such low prices, and growers began to shift some of these crop lands to other uses. Some landowners in Indonesia, for example, planted rice. Others, especially in Central and Latin America, moved toward planting shade-grown coffee (in the shade of larger trees), organic, and other specialty coffee requiring special expertise and supervision, with lower yields but offering higher prices. Still other producers, including some in Vietnam, simply abandoned the least profitable plantations, at least temporarily. In Mexico, more than 300,000 farmers are estimated to have left their coffee farms to seek other opportunities, unable to cover even their variable costs.

The world coffee market illustrates very clearly how producers in price-taker markets can quickly expand production when rising prices are seen or expected, but can also contract production in response to falling prices and profits.

Source: The information presented is from Howard LaFranchi, "Economic Upheaval over Coffee," Christian Science Monitor, Aug. 15, 2001, p. 1, and from London's BBC Website at http://www.bbc.co.uk/worldservice/business/story_fdh200301.shtml, downloaded Sept. 17, 2001.

is altered. Three possibilities emerge, although one is far more likely than the other two.

Constant-Cost Industries

Constant-cost industry An industry for which factor prices and costs of production remain constant as market output is expanded. Thus, the long-run market supply curve is horizontal.

If resource prices remain unchanged, the long-run market supply curve will be perfectly elastic. In terms of economics, this describes a **constant-cost industry**. Exhibits 21-8 and 21-9 both picture constant-cost industries. As Exhibit 21-8 illustrates, an expansion in demand causes prices to increase *temporarily*. With time, however, the higher prices and profits will stimulate expansion and additional production, which will push the market price down to its initial level (and profitability to its normal rate). In the long run, the larger supply will not require a permanent price increase. Similarly, Exhibit 21-9 illustrates the impact of a decline in demand in a constant-cost industry. The *long-run supply curve* (S_{lr}) is perfectly elastic, reflecting the basically unchanged cost at the lower rate of industry output.

A constant-cost industry is most likely to arise when the industry's demand for resource inputs is quite small relative to the total demand for these resources. For example, the demand of the matches industry for wood, chemicals, and labor is very small relative to the total demand for these resources. Thus, doubling the output of matches would exert very little impact on the price of the resources used by this industry. Matches therefore approximate a constant-cost industry.

Increasing-cost industry An industry for which costs of production rise as output is expanded. Thus, even in the long run, higher market prices will be required to induce the firms to expand the total output in such industries. The long-run market supply curve in such industries will slope upward to the right.

Increasing-Cost Industries

In most industries, an increase in market demand and *industry* output will lead to higher per-unit production costs for all the firms in the industry. Economists refer to such industries as **increasing-cost industries**. The rising output and expanded resource demand in such industries result in higher prices for at least some resources, causing the firms' cost curves to shift upward. For example, a rising demand for housing places upward pressure on the prices of lumber, window frames, building sites, and construction labor, causing the cost of housing to rise. Similarly, an increase in demand (and market output) for beef may cause the prices of feed grains, hay, and grazing land to rise. Thus, the production costs of beef rise as more of it is produced.

For an increasing-cost industry, an expansion in market demand will bid up resource prices, causing the per-unit cost of the firms to rise. As a result, a larger market output will be forthcoming only at a higher price. The long-run market supply curve for the product will therefore slope upward.

Exhibit 21-10 depicts an increasing-cost industry. Greater demand causes higher prices and a larger market output. As the industry expands, the price of resources (factors of production) rises so that costs increase. What happens to the firm's cost curves? Both the average and marginal cost curves rise (shift to ATC_2 and MC_2). Greater production cost necessitates a higher long-run price (P_2), so the long-run supply curve slopes upward to the right.

Decreasing-Cost Industries

Sometimes, factor prices will decline when the market output of a product is expanded. The lower resource prices will reduce the unit costs of the firms, placing them in a position to supply a larger market output at a lower price. In such **decreasing-cost industries**, the long-run (but not the short-run) market supply curve will slope downward to the right. For example, as the electronics industry expands, suppliers of certain components may be able to adopt large-scale production techniques that will lead to lower component prices. If rising electronics demand leads to reduced component cost (and if other resource prices do not rise to offset the reductions), then the cost curves of the electronics firms will

Decreasing-cost industry
An industry for which costs of production decline as the industry expands. The market supply is therefore inversely related to price. Such industries are atypical.

In central areas of large cities, the supply of parking spaces can be expanded only by using higher-cost space and higher-cost techniques, such as taller parking garages that use a large portion of the building for access ramps. As a result, the unit cost of parking spaces increases as the total number is expanded. Thus, provision of parking space is an increasing-cost industry.

EXHIBIT 21-10 Increasing Costs and Long-run Supply

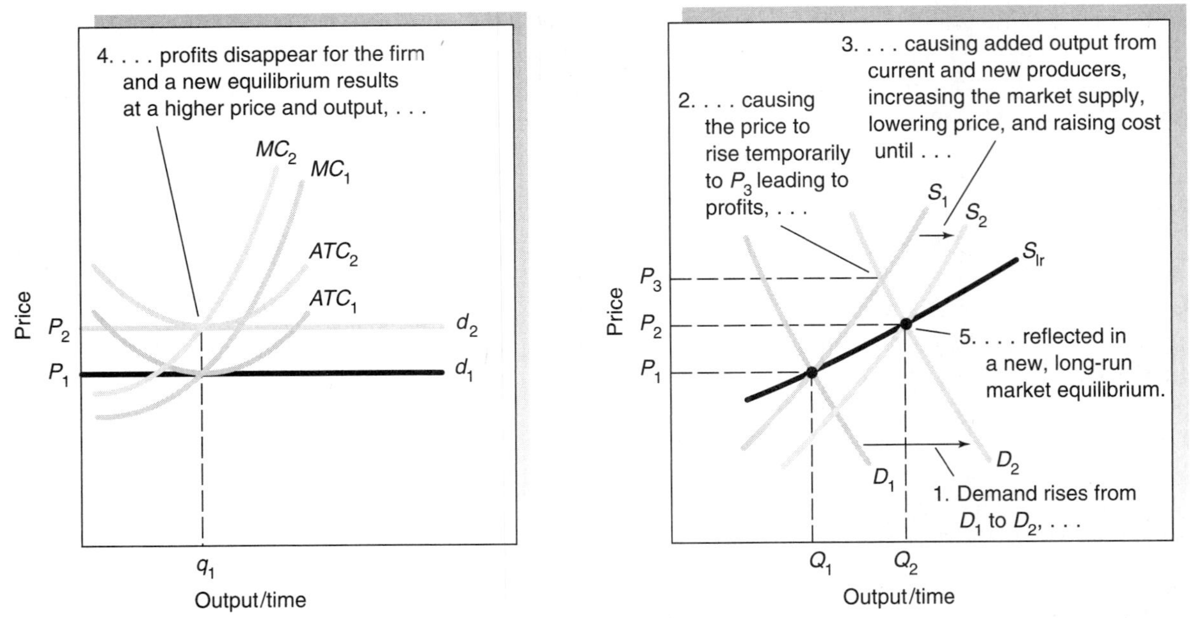

(a) Firm (b) Market

shift downward. Under these circumstances, the industry supply curve for electronics products—reflecting the lower cost—will slope downward to the right.

In most industries, however, increases in demand and expansion in market output cause higher rather than lower input prices. Thus, increasing-cost industries are the norm, and decreasing-cost industries are quite rare.

Supply Elasticity and the Role of Time

It takes time for firms to adjust to a change in the price of a product. In the short run, firms are stuck with the existing size of their plant. If price increases in the short run, they can expand output only by utilizing their existing plant more intensely. Thus, their output response will be limited. In the long run, however, they will have time to build new plants. This will allow them to expand output by a larger amount in response to an increase in price. Thus, the market supply curve will be more elastic in the long run than in the short run.

The short- and long-run distinction offers a convenient two-stage analysis, but in the real world there are many intermediate production "runs." The delivery rates for some factors that could not be easily increased in a one-week time period can be increased over a two-week period. It might take two weeks, for example, to hire reliable workers for jobs requiring no specialized skill. Economical expansion of other factors might require a month, and still others, six months. Ordering a new custom-made machine tool at Boeing, or hiring a competent new manager to expand an eastern Montana ranch operation might take a year. To be more precise, the cost penalty for quicker availability is greater for some productive resources than for others. In any case, a faster expansion usually means that greater cost penalties are necessary to provide for an earlier availability of resources needed for production.

When a firm has a longer time period to plan output and adjust all its productive inputs to the desired utilization levels, it will be able to produce any spe-

EXHIBIT 21-11 Time and Elasticity of Supply

The elasticity of the market supply curve usually increases as more time is allowed for adjustment to a change in price.

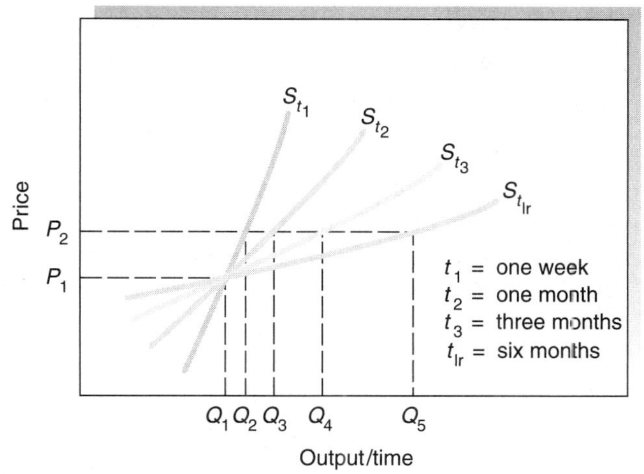

cific new rate of output at a lower cost. ***Because it is less costly to expand output slowly in response to a demand increase, the expansion of output by firms will increase with time, as long as price exceeds cost. Therefore, the elasticity of the market supply curve will be greater when more time is allowed for firms to adjust output.***

Exhibit 21-11 illustrates the impact of time on the response by producers to an increase in price resulting from an expansion in demand. When the price of a product increases from P_1 to P_2, the immediate supply response of the firms is small, reflecting the high cost of hasty expansion. After one week, firms are willing to expand output only from Q_1 to Q_2. After one month, because of cost reductions made possible by the longer production planning period, firms are willing to offer Q_3 units at the price P_2. After three months, the rate of output expands to Q_4. In the long run, when it is possible to adjust all inputs to the desired utilization levels (after a six-month time period, for example), firms are willing to supply Q_5 units of output at the market price of P_2. The supply curve for products is typically more elastic over a longer time period than over a shorter period.

ROLE OF PROFITS AND LOSSES 6

The price-taker model highlights the role of profits and losses: They are signals sent to producers by consumers. Economic profits will be largest in those areas where the value of additional units to consumers is highest relative to their production costs. Profit-seeking entrepreneurs will guide additional resources into these areas. Supply will increase, driving prices down and eliminating the profits. ***Free entry and the competitive process will protect the consumer from arbitrarily high prices. In the long run, competitive prices will reflect costs of production.***

Economic profits result because a firm or an entrepreneur acts to increase the value of resources. Business firms purchase resources and use them to produce a product or service that is sold to consumers. Costs are incurred as the business pays workers and other resource owners for their services. If the sales of the business firm exceed the costs of employing all the resources required to produce the firm's output, then the firm will make a profit. ***In essence, profit is a reward that business owners will earn if they produce a good that consumers value more (as measured by their willingness to pay) than the resources required for the good's production (as measured by the cost of bidding the resources away from their alternative employment possibilities).***

For example, suppose that it costs a shirt manufacturer $20,000 per month to lease a building, rent the required machines, and purchase the labor, cloth, buttons, and other materials necessary to produce and market 1,000 shirts per month. Thus, the average cost of the shirts is $20 (the $20,000 monthly cost divided by the 1,000 monthly output). If the manufacturer sells the 1,000 shirts for $22 each, its actions create wealth. Consumers value the shirts more than they value the resources required for their production. The manufacturer's $2 profit per shirt is a reward received for increasing the value of the resources.

In contrast, losses are a penalty imposed on businesses that reduce the value of resources. Losses indicate that the value of the resources used (as measured by their cost) by the firm exceeds the price consumers are willing to pay for the product supplied. Losses, along with bankruptcies, are the market's way of bringing such wasteful activities to a halt.

We live in a world of changing tastes and technology, imperfect knowledge, and uncertainty. Business decision makers cannot be sure of either future market prices or costs of production. Their decisions must be based on expectations. Nonetheless, the reward-penalty structure of a market economy is clear. ***Firms that anticipate correctly the products and services for which future demand will be most urgent (relative to production cost), and produce and market them efficiently will make economic profits. Those that are inefficient and allocate resources incorrectly into areas of weak demand (relative to cost) will be penalized with losses.***

The firms most adept at giving consumers value for money thrive and expand, while those less successful in doing so tend to shrink or even to disappear from the market. When entry barriers are low, small firms are sometimes able to challenge and compete successfully against rivals that are much larger. Michael Dell's success in the personal computer market provides a vivid illustration of this point. In 1984 Dell began producing and marketing personal computers while he was still a student at the University of Texas. At the age of 19, he began operations from his dormitory room with an investment of $1000.[4] Then as now, Dell took orders for PCs, bought component parts from competing sellers, and custom-built the machines almost immediately to fill each order for quick delivery directly to consumers. His firm has very low cost partly because it keeps on hand only 4 days' inventory. This lean operation also allows him to offer and build in the latest technical innovations as soon as they are available. In contrast, IBM, Compaq, and Apple, the dominant firms at the time Dell entered the market, built PCs equipped in one specific way by the thousands and marketed them through retailers.

Dell passes on the firm's low costs, including the constantly falling prices of computer chips and other components. And it contracts with local computer service firms to provide dependable warranty service. Dell's business plan helped the firm build volume year after year until it became the industry leader. By the year 2000, Dell was selling $32 billion worth of computers and related equipment. Michael Dell's stock had made him a billionaire. By 2001, losses had caused IBM to exit the PC market, Compaq was struggling in the PC market and turning its attention to other products, and Apple had a much smaller share of the market than before.

---

[4] These and other facts about Dell are from Michael Dell and Andrew Fisher. "It's Crunch Time for Your Competitors," *Financial Times* (London), Sept. 5, 2001, p. 10.

Outstanding Economist

Friedrich A. von Hayek (1899–1992)

Remarkably, the writings of this 1974 Nobel Prize recipient spanned seven decades. His work on knowledge and markets both enhanced our understanding of the competitive process and highlighted the fatal defects of central planning. He also made major contributions in areas as diverse as monetary theory, law and economics, business cycles, and capital theory.

Dell is not truly a price taker, since it does lower price in order to sell more PCs. However, the same low barriers to entry that allowed it to enter and succeed will stop it from raising its price much above the lowest achievable cost, even if its low prices drive other competitors out of business. Many firms, large and small, can quickly enter and expand production of PCs, if Dell raises its prices. A higher price would be an open invitation for others to step in and lure away Dell's customers, just as Dell earlier took customers from the largest firms in the industry. And even if he does not raise his price, there are many college students with $1000, some of them no doubt seeking an even better way to make PCs, or better machines than PCs, standing ready to displace Michael Dell as the top producer in this easy-to-enter business.

COMPETITION AND PROSPERITY 7

Competition
Competition provides businesses with a strong incentive to produce efficiently, cater to the views of consumers, and search for innovative improvements.

The price-taker model highlights the importance of the competitive process. Competition places pressure on producers to operate efficiently and use resources wisely. Each business firm will have a strong tendency to produce its output as cheaply as possible. Holding quality constant, pursuit of profit will encourage each firm to minimize the cost of production—to use the least valued set of resources needed to produce the desired output.

Correspondingly, firms in competitive markets will have a strong incentive to discover and produce goods that are valued more highly than the resources required for their production. Thus, resources are drawn to those uses where they are most productive, as judged by the consumers' willingness to pay. The ability of firms freely to expand or contract their businesses, and to enter or exit the market, means that resources that could be more valuable elsewhere will not be trapped unproductively in a particular industry. Resource owners can move them to where they are most highly valued in production.

Competition weeds out inefficient producers—those who are unable to produce goods and services as economically as their rivals in the marketplace. It also keeps producers on their toes in other areas. The production techniques and product offerings that lead to success today will not necessarily pass the competitive market test tomorrow. Producers who survive in a competitive environment cannot be complacent. As this reading's opening quotation from the President's Council of Economic Advisers indicates, competition forces firms to be forward-looking and innovative. They must be willing to experiment and quick to adopt improved methods.

In competitive markets, business firms must serve the interests of consumers. As Adam Smith noted more than 200 years ago, competition harnesses personal self-interest and puts it to work, elevating our standard of living and directing our resources toward the production of those goods that we desire most intensely relative to their cost. Smith stated:

> It is not from the benevolence of the butcher, the brewer, or the baker, that we expect our dinner, but from their regard to their own self-interest. We address ourselves, not to their humanity but to their self-love, and never talk to them of our own necessities, but of their advantages.[5]

In a competitive environment, even self-interested individuals and profit-seeking business firms have a strong incentive to recognize and serve the interests of others, and to supply products that are valued more highly than the resources required for their production. This is the path to greater income and larger profits. Paradoxical as it may seem, personal self-interest—a characteristic many view as less than admirable—is a powerful source of economic progress when it is directed by competition.

---

[5] Adam Smith, *An Inquiry into the Nature and Causes of the Wealth of Nations* (1776; Cannan's ed., Chicago: University of Chicago Press, 1976), p. 18.

SUMMARY

8

- A firm that confronts a perfectly elastic demand for its product is a price taker. A firm that can raise its price without losing all its customers (and which must lower its price in order to sell more units) is a price searcher.
- To maximize profit, a price taker will expand output as long as the sale of additional units adds more to revenues than to costs. Therefore, the profit-maximizing price taker will produce the output level at which marginal revenue (and price) equals marginal cost.
- The price taker's short-run marginal cost curve (above its average variable cost) is its supply curve. The short-run market supply curve is the horizontal summation of the marginal cost curves (above *AVC*) of the firms in the industry.
- A firm experiencing losses, but anticipating that it will be able to cover its costs in the long run, will operate in the short run if it can cover its average variable costs. Conversely, the firm will shut down if it cannot cover average variable cost. A firm that does not anticipate being able to cover its average total cost even in the long run will minimize losses by immediately going out of business.
- When price exceeds average total cost, a firm will make economic profit. When entry barriers are absent, profits will attract new firms into the industry and stimulate the existing firms to expand. This increasing market supply continues and puts downward pressure on price until it reaches the level of average total cost, eliminating the economic profit.
- When the market price is less than the firm's average total cost, the resulting losses imply that the resources could be used to produce more value elsewhere. Losses will cause firms to leave the industry or to reduce the scale of their operations. This declining market supply continues and puts upward pressure on price until the firms remaining in the market are able to earn normal returns (zero economic profit).
- As the output of an industry expands, marginal costs will increase in the short run, causing the short-run market supply curve to slope upward to the right. Normally, as industry output expands, rising factor prices will push the costs of each firm upward, causing the long-run market supply curve to slope upward to the right.
- In the short run, "fixed" resources like the size of the firm's plant will limit the ability of firms to expand output quickly. In the long run, firms can alter the size of their plants and other resources that are fixed in the short run. As a result, the market supply curve will generally be more elastic in the long run.
- Firms earn economic profit by producing goods that can be sold for more than the cost of the resources required for their production. Profit is a reward for actions that increase the value of resources. Conversely, losses are a penalty imposed on those who use resources in a way that reduces their value.
- The competitive process provides strong pressure for producers to operate efficiently and heed the views of consumers. Competition and the market process harness self-interest and use it to direct producers toward wealth-creating activities.

PRICE-SEARCHER MARKETS WITH LOW ENTRY BARRIERS

READING 22

LEARNING OUTCOMES

The candidate should be able to:

a. describe the conditions that characterize monopolistic competition (a competitive price-searcher market;

b. explain how firms choose price and output combinations in a monopolistic competition;

c. summarize the debate about the allocative efficiency of monopolistic competition with low barriers to entry, including the implications of contestable markets and entrepreneurship;

d. discuss the principle of price discrimination and illustrate how a firm might apply this principle to gain from such a practice.

[T]he price to the price-searcher is not determined for him as if by some impersonal market mechanism. Instead he must search out the optimal (wealth-maximizing) price. And, not knowing the demand schedule exactly, he will have to resort to retrial-and-error search processes.

—Armen A. Alchian and William R. Allen[1]

INTRODUCTION 1

In the previous reading we learned that price takers must accept the market price. They merely adjust their output to supply more units if they expect the cost of the additional units to be less than the market price. Price searchers have a more complex set of decisions to make in their search for profit. (See this reading's opening quotation from Professors Alchian and Allen.) In this reading we consider the choices facing price searchers in markets where entry barriers are low. Low entry barriers are the key to competitive markets. When the restraints limiting entry are minimal, any opportunity for profit will attract competitors. Markets with low entry barriers, but where firms can raise their prices without losing all their customers, are described as **competitive price-searcher markets**.

Competitive price-searcher market
A market where the firms have a downward-sloping demand curve, and entry into and exit from the market are relatively easy.

---

[1] Armen A. Alchian and William R. Allen, *University Economics*, 2d ed. (Belmont, Calif.: Wadsworth Publishing Co., 1967), p. 113.

2 COMPETITIVE PRICE-SEARCHER MARKETS

Differentiated products Products distinguished from similar products by such characteristics as quality, design, location, and method of promotion.

Monopolistic competition Term often used by economists to describe markets characterized by a large number of sellers that supply differentiated products to a market with low barriers to entry. Essentially, it is an alternative term for a competitive price-searcher market.

Competitive price-searcher markets are characterized by (1) low entry barriers and (2) *firms* that face a downward-sloping demand curve.[2] In contrast with price-taker markets where the firms produce identical products, price searchers produce **differentiated products**. The products supplied by the alternative sellers may differ in their design, dependability, location, ease of purchase, and a multitude of other factors. Sometimes economists use the term **monopolistic competition** to describe markets quite similar to those of the competitive price-searcher model. Since there is nothing "monopolistic" about these markets, we believe that this term is misleading. *Competitive price searcher* is much more descriptive of conditions in these markets. However, students should be aware that the expression "monopolistic competition" is often used to describe markets very much like those analyzed in this reading.

Product differentiation explains why firms in price-searcher markets confront a downward-sloping demand curve. Ice cream from Häagen-Dazs is not identical to ice cream from Ben and Jerry's, Breyers, or Baskin-Robbins. Since some consumers are willing to pay more in order to get the specific product they like best, the *firm* will not lose all its customers to rivals if it raises its price. Rival firms, however, supply products that are quite similar to those supplied by the price searcher, so as the firm raises its price, some of its consumers will switch to the substitutes. ***Thus, the demand curve faced by the firm in a competitive price-searcher market will be highly elastic, because good substitutes for its output are readily available from other suppliers.***

The price searcher must choose between lower prices with larger quantities sold, and higher prices with smaller sales. ***Although a price searcher can set the price for its products, market forces will determine the quantity sold at alternative prices.*** In trying to find the profit-maximizing price and quantity combination, therefore, price searchers must try to estimate not just one market price, but how buyers will respond to the various prices that might be charged. In effect, price searchers must estimate the relationship between price and quantity demanded for their product. And the complexity does not end there.

Demand is not simply a given, to be discovered by the price searcher. The firm, by changing product quality, location, and service (among many other factors), and by advertising, can alter the demand for its products. It can increase demand by drawing customers from rivals if it can convince consumers that its products provide more value. When an airline adopts a more generous frequent-flier program or a soap manufacturer provides "cents-off" coupons, each is trying to make its product a little more attractive than rival products, for certain potential customers. The precise effects of such decisions cannot easily be predicted, but they can make the difference between profit and loss for the firm. In the real world, most firms occupy this complex and risky territory of the price searcher.

Sellers in competitive price-searcher markets face competition both from firms already producing in the market and from potential new entrants into the market. If profits are present, firms can expect that new rivals will be attracted. Because of the low entry barriers, competitive forces will be strong in price-searcher markets.

Price and Output in Competitive Price-Searcher Markets

How does a price searcher decide what price to charge and what level of output to produce? For the price searcher, reducing price in order to expand output and sales has two conflicting influences on total revenue. As Exhibit 22-1 illustrates,

---

[2] It is important to distinguish between the demand curve faced by the firm and the market demand curve. The competitive price-searcher model focuses on the *firm's* demand curve.

In the highly competitive market for custom-fitted golf clubs, firms use style, variable length and flexibility of club shaft, swingweight, advertising, and celebrity endorsements as competitive weapons. Firms in this market are price searchers.

the increase in sales (from q_1 to q_2) due to the lower price will, by itself, add to the revenue of the price searcher. The price reduction, however, also applies to units *that would otherwise have been sold at a higher price* (P_1, rather than the lower price, P_2). This factor by itself will cause a reduction in total revenue. As price is reduced in order to sell additional units, these two conflicting forces will result in marginal revenue—that is, change in total revenue—that is less than the sales price of the additional units. Since the price of units that could have been sold at the higher price must also be reduced, the price searcher's marginal revenue will be less than price. As Exhibit 22-1 shows, the marginal revenue curve of the price searcher will always lie below the firm's demand curve.[3] (Remember, the lowercase d is used when the reference is to the *firm's* demand curve.)

Any firm can increase profits by expanding output as long as marginal revenue exceeds marginal cost. Therefore, a price searcher will lower price and expand output until marginal revenue is equal to marginal cost.

Exhibit 22-2 illustrates the profit-maximizing price and output. The price searcher will increase profit by expanding output to q, where marginal revenue is equal to marginal cost and price P can be charged. Beyond q, the price reduction required for the sale of additional output would reduce the firm's profit. For any output level less than q (for example, R), a price reduction and sales expansion will add more to total revenues than to total costs. At output R, marginal revenues exceed marginal costs. Thus, profits will be greater if price is reduced

[3] For a straight-line demand curve, the marginal revenue curve will bisect any line parallel to the x-axis. For example, the MR curve will divide the line P_2F into two equal parts, P_2E and EF.

EXHIBIT 22-1 Marginal Revenue of a Price Searcher

When a firm faces a downward-sloping demand curve, a price reduction that increases sales will exert two conflicting influences on total revenue. First, total revenue will rise because of an increase in the number of units sold (from q_1 to q_2). However, revenue losses from the lower price (P_2) on units that could have been sold at a higher price (P_1) will at least partially offset the additional revenues from increased sales. Therefore, the marginal revenue curve will lie inside the firm's demand curve.

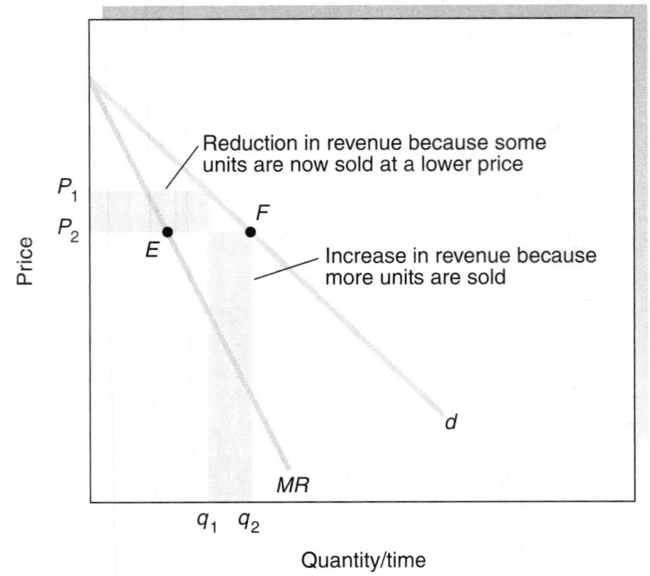

EXHIBIT 22-2 The Price Searcher's Price and Output

A price searcher maximizes profits by producing output *q*, for which *MR* = *MC*, and charging price *P*. The firm is making economic profits. What impact will they have if this is a typical firm?

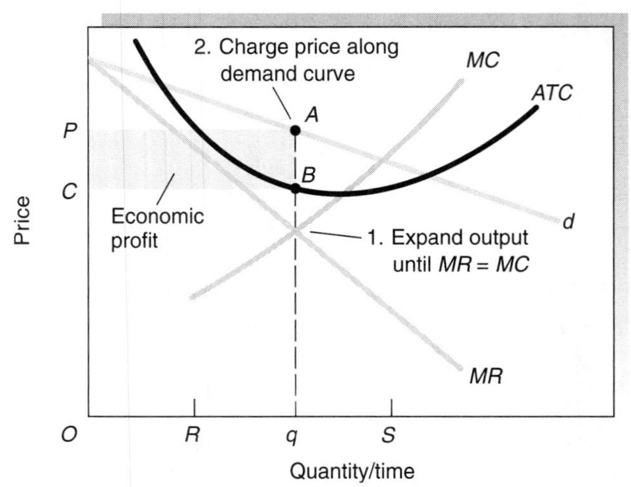

so output can be expanded. On the other hand, if output exceeds *q* (for example, *S*), sale of additional units beyond *q* will add more to costs (*MC*) than to revenues (*MR*). The firm will therefore gain by raising the price to *P*, even though the price rise will result in the loss of some customers. Profits will be maximized by charging price *P* and producing the output level *q*, where *MC* = *MR*.

The firm pictured in Exhibit 22-2 is making an economic profit. Total revenues *PAqO* exceed the firm's total costs *CBqO* at the profit-maximizing output level. Given the low barriers to entry, profits will attract rivals. Other firms will enter the market and attempt to produce a similar product (or service).

What will the entry of new rivals do to the demand for the products of the firms already in the market? These new rivals will draw customers away from existing firms and thereby reduce the demand for their output. As long as new entrants expect to make economic profits, additional competitors will be attracted to the market. This entry of new firms into the market will continue until competition among rivals shifts the demand curve in far enough to eliminate the economic profit. As Exhibit 22-3 illustrates, when long-run equilibrium is present in a price-searcher market, price will equal per-unit cost. The firms will produce at the *MR* = *MC* output level, but they will be unable to earn economic profit because competitive pressures will force the price down to the level of per-unit costs.

If losses are present in a specific market, with time, some of the firms in the market will go out of business. As firms leave, some of their previous customers will buy from other firms. The demand curve facing the remaining firms in the industry will be shifted outward by this process until the economic losses are eliminated and the long-run, zero-profit equilibrium illustrated by Exhibit 22-3 is restored.

Whenever firms can freely enter and exit a market, profits and losses play an important role in determining the size of the industry. Economic profits will attract new competitors to the market. The increased availability of the product (and similar products) will drive the price down until the profits are eliminated. Conversely, economic losses will cause competitors to exit from the market. The decline in the availability of the product (supply) will allow the price to rise until firms are once again able to cover their average total costs.

EXHIBIT 22-3 Competitive Price Searcher and Long-run Normal Profit

Since entry and exit are free, competition will eventually drive prices down to the level of average total cost for the representative price searcher.

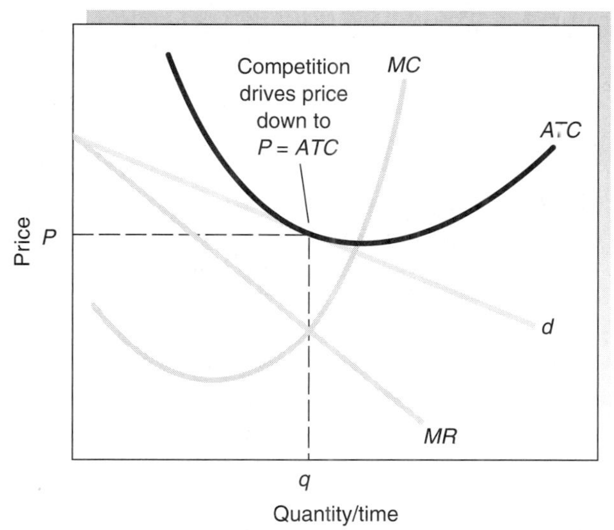

Firms in competitive price-searcher markets may make either economic profits or losses in the short run. After long-run adjustments have been made, however, only a normal profit (that is, zero economic profit) will be possible because of the competitive conditions caused by freedom of entry.

Business Failures, the Competitive Process, and Economic Progress

Business failures and cutbacks in output and employment are generally reported under the heading of negative news about the economy. Clearly, they are often painful for the parties directly involved. Owners often lose a substantial amount of their wealth and employees are forced to search for alternative job opportunities. From the standpoint of the entire economy, however, business failures play an important role that is often overlooked: they release resources so they can be employed more productively elsewhere. The assets and workers of firms that fail become available for use by others supplying goods that consumers value more relative to costs. Without this release of resources, the expansion of both profitable firms and the entire economy would be slowed.

Business failures may occur for a variety of reasons, but the introduction of improved products and adoption of lower-cost production techniques *by rivals* is clearly one of the more important sources. Suppose that an innovative firm figures out how to supply an improved product at a lower cost. The introduction of this product at an attractive price will reduce the demand for the goods supplied by competitors. Facing intense competition from the innovator, some of the existing firms will experience losses and eventually be driven out of business. Viewed from this perspective, business failure is merely the flip side of innovative actions that improved products and reduced costs.

The great Austrian economist Joseph Schumpeter referred to competition arising from the development of new products, new technologies, and superior forms of organization as "creative destruction." This competitive result is both widespread and highly important in price-searcher markets. Such dynamic competition will lead to the expansion of some firms and contraction of others. Examples abound. In early 2001, Lucent, a high-technology firm, announced that its sales had fallen 28 percent, while rival Nortel Networks had experienced a 34 percent increase. Lucent's failure to adopt a new generation of optical technology production quickly forced it to announce the elimination of 16,000 jobs.

Important changes were also taking place in the retail sector. J. C. Penney announced that it would shut 47 stores, 11 months after it had closed 45 others. In 2002, Kmart filed for bankruptcy. Meanwhile, Wal-Mart, Costco, and Target were rapidly expanding across the United States, "the way the Huns blew into Europe," as one news report put it.[4]

In the 1990s, the demand for computer services rose dramatically, as they became more productive and less expensive. Employment in the computer service and data processing industry more than doubled, rising from 736,000 in 1989 to 1,831,000 in 1999. In that same period, however, the demand for guided missiles and space-related equipment fell substantially, as the federal government changed its spending priorities. Employment in that industry fell by more than half, from 194,000 to only 88,000.

Numerous businesses come and go. Each year, newly incorporated businesses account for about 10 percent of the total. Approximately 1 percent of businesses file for bankruptcy during a typical year. In addition, many others close their doors or sell their assets to other, more successful (or more optimistic) operators.

---

[4] Steve Syre and Charles Stein, "Capitalism's Messy Ways Still Come Up Rosy." *Boston Globe*, Jan. 26, 2001, p. C1.

It is important to recognize that business failures do not destroy either the assets owned by the firm or the talents of its workers. Instead, they release these resources for use by other firms that will employ them more productively. The losses underlying the failures indicate that consumers are unwilling to pay enough to cover the cost of the items supplied by these firms. A larger output could be achieved if the resources were released for use by profitable firms supplying goods and services that are more highly valued relative to their cost. It would be a mistake to continue with the operation of the loss-making firms. Thus, even though business failures are painful for the parties involved, they are necessary for the reallocation of resources toward higher-valued uses and the economic progress that this reallocation helps to promote.

CONTESTABLE MARKETS AND THE COMPETITIVE PROCESS

3

If firms can easily enter and exit a market and there is little risk that entry will result in substantial loss of wealth, competitive pressures may be strong even if there are few firms currently operating in the market. Economists refer to such markets as **contestable markets**.[5] Entry into a contestable market may require substantial amounts of financial capital, but so long as it is largely recoverable, the large capital requirement is not a major deterrent (barrier) to entry. If entry into a contestable market is later judged to be a mistake, exit is relatively easy because large components of the capital costs are recoverable.

Contestable market
A market in which the costs of entry and exit are low, so a firm risks little by entering. Efficient production and zero economic profits should prevail in a contestable market. A market can be contestable even if capital requirements are high.

When there are no legal barriers restricting entry, an airline route provides a classic example of a contestable market. Consider the case of the airline route between Salt Lake City, Utah, and Albuquerque, New Mexico. Only Delta Airlines provides nonstop service on this route, since it has so little traffic. Further, there would seem to be high barriers to entry, since it takes multimillion-dollar airplanes to compete, as well as facilities for reservations, ticketing, baggage handling, and so on. One might expect Delta, as the only provider of nonstop service, to charge a high price, substantially above its cost. But a deterrent to doing so is the fact that abnormal profits would probably attract direct competitors from the other airlines that are free to enter its nonstop market. Delta is well aware of its rivalry with competitors, some of whom already serve both Salt Lake City and Albuquerque, and in fact provide service between the two, via connecting flights from other cities.

To compete on an airline route may require millions of dollars in equipment, but if there is no problem with renting access to airport facilities, then the barriers to entry are much lower than equipment costs suggest. The nonstop Salt Lake City–Albuquerque market, for example, can be entered simply by shifting aircraft, personnel, and equipment from other routes and locations. Airlines often rent or lease their aircraft in any case. By the same token, if a new entrant (or an established firm) later wants to leave that market, nearly all the invested capital values can be recovered through shifting the aircraft and other capital equipment to other routes or leasing them to other firms.

In a contestable market, potential competition, as well as actual entry, can discipline firms selling in the market. When entry and exit are not expensive, even a single seller in a market faces the serious prospect of competition. Contestable markets yield two important results: (1) prices will not for long be higher than the level necessary to achieve zero economic profits, and (2) minimum cost of production will occur. This is true because both prices above costs

[5] The classic article on this topic is William J. Baumol's "Contestable Markets: An Uprising in the Theory of Industry Structure," *American Economic Review* 72 (March 1982): 1–15.

Airliners are extremely expensive and their cost might be a barrier to entry. But airplanes can be leased and are highly mobile among markets, as are pilots, flight attendants, and office workers. These highly mobile resources allow firms to enter into a given air transport market, and to leave it, with relative ease. Such a market is contestable.

and inefficiency in production present a profitable opportunity to new entrants. Potential competitors who see an opportunity for economic profit can be expected to enter and drive the price down to the level of per-unit costs.

These results do have a policy implication: If policy makers are concerned that a market is not sufficiently competitive, they should consider what might be done to make the market in question contestable. Much of the enthusiasm of economists for deregulation can be traced to the fact that regulation often is the primary restraint to entry. Many economists believe that deregulation permitting new entry can make many markets contestable, achieving lower prices and more efficiency than can direct regulation of producers.

4 COMPLEX DECISION MAKING AND THE ENTREPRENEUR

To help us understand facts and make predictions, a scientific model must simplify what it describes and draw attention to the most important relationships. Economic models are no exception. The price-taker and competitive price-searcher models highlight the choices common to all firms in these markets. But these models leave out some important elements of the business decision-making process. Furthermore, they gloss over the complexity of other decisions that must be made by real-world entrepreneurs.

Would profits increase if prices were raised, or would lower prices lead to larger profits? Real-world decision makers cannot go into the back room and look at their demand-cost diagram to answer these questions. They must search for clues, experiment with actual price changes, and interpret what they see, often using a great deal of "seat-of-the-pants" judgment. The successful entrepreneur will search and find (or at least approximate) the profit-maximizing price—the $MR = MC$ price-and-output combination that our model shows so simply.

The competitive price-searcher model indicates how entrepreneurs will react to profit and loss in a specific market and explains why their reactions will tend to direct the market toward equilibrium. It does not, however, explain how and when new products will be developed or new production techniques applied. How will consumers react to a potential new product? Can it be produced profitably? Would a new production process or alternative technology reduce cost? Could per-unit costs be reduced if the firm offered a different combination of products and services? Here, as in other areas of profit maximization, the marginal principle applies. If the change adds more to revenue than to cost, it should be made. How much of a change? Up to the point where $MC = MR$! But identifying that point for each potential change is difficult. Such decisions generally involve an important variable that is omitted from our economic models: entrepreneurship.

The Left Out Variable: Entrepreneurship

Entrepreneurial judgment is necessary when there is no decision rule that can be applied using only information that is freely available. For this reason, we are unable to incorporate fully the function of the entrepreneur into economic models. There simply is no way to model these complex decisions that involve uncertainty, discovery, and business judgment. All we can do is note the importance of entrepreneurial judgment and recognize that our models are limited because they are unable to capture this critical element of both business success and economic progress.

If we cannot put entrepreneurship into our models, what can we say about its function? One way to answer this question is to consider a generalized job description for an entrepreneurial position. An investor who lacks the desire, or perhaps the skill, to be an entrepreneur, but nonetheless wants to be in business, may seek someone to act as the business entrepreneur, while the investor provides some of the capital. A newspaper ad to find such a person (though perhaps not the usual way for the investor to search) might read as follows:

> *Wanted: Entrepreneur.* Diverse skills required. Must be (1) alert to new business opportunities and to new problems before they become obvious; (2) willing to back judgments with investments of hard work and creative effort before others recognize correctness of judgments; (3) able to make correct decisions and to convince others of their validity, so as to attract additional financial backing; and (4) able to recognize own inevitable mistakes and to back away from incorrect decisions without wasting additional resources. Exciting, exhausting, high-risk position. Pay will be very good for success, and very poor for failure.

Entrepreneurship
The entrepreneurial discovery and development of improved products and production processes is a central element of economic progress.

Entrepreneurship is not for the fainthearted or the lazy. Entrepreneurs are at the center of the action in the real world, even if they do not have a place in most economic models.[6]

ENTREPRENEURSHIP AND ECONOMIC PROGRESS

5

Discovery and development of improved products and production methods propel economic progress. Think of the new products that have been introduced during the last 50 years: microwave ovens, videocassette recorders, color television sets, personal computers, compact disc players, fax machines, cellular telephone service, and coronary artery bypass techniques come to mind. Innovations like these and many others exert an enormous impact on our lives.

---

[6] For a more complete overview of entrepreneurship and references on the topic, see Mark Crosson, "Entrepreneurship," in *The New Palgrave: A Dictionary of Economics*, ed. John Eatwell et al. (New York: Stockton Press, 1987), pp. 151–153.

APPLICATIONS IN ECONOMICS

Entrepreneurs at the Helm of Some Bizarre Occupations

These innovative people see a need and find a niche in the market

By David Young
(CHICAGO TRIBUNE)

Mike Turk lost a coin toss and wound up with a thousand teak trophy bases he couldn't get rid of. So he bolted Army surplus hand grenades to them and sold them for $15 apiece as desk ornaments. Joseph Tokarski, a postal worker contemplating a post-retirement business, found something of an aftermarket cleaning up Canada goose droppings.

"There are two important dimensions to being an entrepreneur: The first is risk and the second is innovation," said Sumaria Mohan-Neill, professor of entrepreneurship at Roosevelt University's College of Business Administration. "To succeed, a person has to be innovative. Some would call it bizarre," she added.

Turk and Tokarski are among what may be scores of entrepreneurs around Chicago who have found unusual business niches and somehow make their living at bizarre occupations. They manufacture odd products, they provide unusual services and some sell the grotesque. Sometimes these entrepreneurs accidentally find their callings; sometimes out of desperation they gravitate to odd occupations after losing their regular jobs; and in some cases, they are able to turn their hobbies into going business concerns.

"People leverage their knowledge," said Steven C. Michael, business administration professor at the University of Illinois' College of Commerce in Urbana. According to Michael, entrepreneurs have a vision of their mission and are able to sell that to other people, but they also have to be flexible enough to change course.

"Entrepreneurs don't spot markets. They spot needs and assemble the skills to fill them," says Michael, and that's the genesis of Magic Mound Mover, Joseph Tokarski's business. Tokarski said he developed a vacuum system to clean up the backyard scat from his own dogs because no one else in the family would do the chore. The device worked so well that he decided to mount it on a golf cart and go after a problem common in Midwestern open spaces: Canada goose droppings. A little advertising in local newspapers and by word of mouth has resulted in jobs with apartment complexes, park districts and school systems cleaning up after the ubiquitous geese.

"Complaint Department: Take a number." (Pull the pin of the hand grenade.)

Similarly, coming up with a clever idea to solve a problem played a big role for Turk, who was working in the family-owned surplus business Surplus Trading Corp. in Benton Harbor, Mich. Only for Turk, the problem was what to do with 1,000 teak trophy bases he acquired on the toss of coin that determined their price. "We have all kinds of ways of doing deals in the surplus business," concedes Turk, who over the years has bought and sold 85 dozen women's panties from Victoria's Secret, 60 cases of olive oil and 500 pounds of hard candy. But he couldn't unload the teak at any price, so he decided to turn them into novelty items. He bolted Army surplus hand grenades to the bases and attached plaques that read, "Complaint Department: Take a number." The number is attached to the detonating pin. He has sold hundreds of them.

Turk and Tokarski are the lucky ones; the failure rate for entrepreneurs is high, possibly as much as 70 to 80 percent, according to business scholars.

APPLICATIONS IN ECONOMICS

Four Entrepreneurs Who Have Changed Our Lives

Unlike movie stars and athletes, business entrepreneurs seldom command great respect in our society. Often, their contributions are either overlooked or misunderstood. In a competitive economy, entrepreneurs get ahead by discovering better ways of doing things, such as new production techniques that reduce cost or new products that are highly valued (relative to their cost). An interesting aspect of entrepreneurship is that it often comes from unusual sources—people who have an ability to think about and institute unconventional ideas.

Of course, highly successful entrepreneurs make a lot of money. Remember, however, that trade helps both the buyer and the seller. To be successful, entrepreneurs must provide their customers with value—a better deal than they can get elsewhere. Thus, they are an important source of economic progress. Highly successful entrepreneurs often exert enormous impact on our lives, far more than most of us realize. Consider how four key entrepreneurs of our age have affected our lives.

Fred Smith (1944–)

When he was in college in the 1960s, Fred Smith foresaw that computers were going to become a major part of people's lives. And he predicted a logical consequence: If computers were going to replace people for many tasks, the computers would have to be in good working order every day. If something went wrong, they had to be fixed immediately, and parts had to be available right away. As Smith describes it now, computer companies needed a "logistics system that provided the parts and pieces wherever that computer was located whenever it was needed."

Smith developed the idea and described the system in a paper for a business strategy course while studying in the MBA program at Yale. Perhaps because it seemed far-fetched at the time, the professor gave him a "gentleman's C." In the following decade, however, Smith founded Federal Express and created the express delivery system outlined in his paper. Beginning in 1973, FedEx created a giant network of airplane and truck transportation capable of providing overnight delivery around the world. Smith's chief innovation was the development of a transportation system with a "central switch" or "central junction." For FedEx, that was Memphis, Tennessee. When one looks at moving an item from Detroit to Minneapolis via Memphis, it seems inefficient, says Smith. "But when you take all of the transactions on the network together, it's tremendously efficient."

FedEx has revolutionized the express mail and package delivery system. The company has consistently earned a profit and annual revenue now exceeds $20 billion. Furthermore, FedEx has forced competitors, from the U.S. Post Office to United Parcel Service, to become more efficient and make major changes in their operations. Smith has transformed the lives of millions of customers, who use the term FedEx as a verb and know they can get a package anywhere "absolutely positively overnight"—to quote one of the company's past advertising slogans. Smith can take great pride in the fact that the market gave him a much higher grade than his old MBA professor.

For more detail, see "Fred Smith," *Forbes Great Minds of Business*, Gretchen Morgenson ed. (New York: John Wiley & Sons, 1997), 35–71.

Pleasant Rowland

Even though she had never run a business nor studied in an MBA program, Pleasant Rowland used her life savings to start a company. Today, the Pleasant Company is a $250 million-a-year business that sells a popular line of dolls and books known as The American Girl. Rowland was motivated by a mission: the desire for girls age 7 to 12 to experience the love of dolls and the fun of reading that she remembered from her childhood. Rowland's idea began to take shape one Christmas season when she tried to find some dolls for her nieces, then ages 8 and 10. The dolls she found—Cabbage Patch babies and Barbie dolls—seemed of mediocre quality, and they failed to evoke "what it meant to be a girl growing up in America." She had already been thinking about American history. While visiting Colonial Williamsburg, Virginia, she fell in love with the historic buildings and streets. She began to wonder, "Isn't there some way that I can make the magic of this historic place come alive for little girls?"

Her idea was a subtle one, creating a distinctive line of dolls that reflect authentic American history and serve as appealing role models. She had to find designers and craftspeople who could create dolls that captured the imagination and love of young girls, dolls with often poignant stories—a girl who pioneered in the West or one who escaped slavery in the South. Rowland shaped her products as she went along, drawing on all her talents and not being swayed by those who thought she was on the wrong track. She had been a teacher and a writer, so she knew how to communicate with children. She knew that her kind of doll wasn't suited for garish Saturday morning television commercials, where she would be battling against giant companies like Hasbro and Mattel—and she didn't have enough money, anyway. So she marketed her dolls through a catalog, writing her own copy in a "softer" voice.

She was right; there was a void, and her dolls helped fill it. Books and a magazine, *The American Girl*, were natural follow-ons. Rowland says today: "I don't think I'm in the doll business or the book business or the direct mail business. I'm in the little girl business." By following her convictions, Rowland found an audience ready to purchase what she wanted to provide. "The great joy of finding this enormous audience hungry for our values, our quality, our perspective on girlhood has been very, very heartening."

For more detail, see "Pleasant Rowland," in *Forbes Great Minds of Business*, Gretchen Morgenson ed., New York: John Wiley and Sons, 1998. 121–155.

Ted Turner (1938–)

Rejected by Harvard, Ted Turner went to Brown University. Originally enrolled as a humanities major, he eventually shifted his major to economics. His studies in economics, however, did not occupy enough of his time to keep him out of trouble while in college. After being thrown out of his fraternity, Kappa Sigma, he was later expelled from college during his senior year.

After his failed attempt at college, Turner worked in his father's outdoor billboard business and eventually took over the company. In 1970 he risked his assets in the billboard business to acquire an unprofitable TV station, WTCG, in Atlanta. He renamed the station WTBS, the "Superstation," and managed to get it on many of the local cable systems around the country. The station offered mostly movies and major league baseball after Turner purchased the Atlanta Braves.

In 1980, Turner risked all his assets and arranged for additional financing through the "junk bond" market in order to launch a 24-hour news network, a network that is now known to the world as CNN (Cable News Network). Most experts in the TV industry predicted the venture would fail. Prior to his final decision to start CNN, Turner's own employees gave him the following message: "Please, Ted! Don't do this to us! If you commit to a venture of this size, you'll sink the whole company!"

Of course, risk taking is an integral part of entrepreneurship. Few, however, have risked so much on an idea so widely viewed as a long shot. Propelled by Turner's determination and confidence concerning what TV viewers wanted, the venture succeeded. The market verified his judgment. By 1991 Turner's cable TV operations (WTBS, CNN, TNT, and Headline News) attracted one-third of the cable TV listening audience. Turner's news stations are now widely viewed around the world. In 1995, he sold his broadcasting businesses to media giant Time Warner, receiving $7.5 billion in the bargain and becoming vice chairman of that firm. In 2001, *Forbes* magazine estimated his net worth at more than $6 billion, despite his prior gifts to the United Nations that had amounted to hundreds of millions of dollars. Who would have thought a college dropout who obtained his business experience in billboard advertising would change the way the world watches television, and become a billionaire in the process?

For more detail, see Gene N. Landrum, *Profiles of Genius* (Buffalo: Prometheus Books, 1993); and Robert F. Hartley, *Management Mistakes and Successes* (New York: John Wiley and Sons, Inc., 1994).

William "Bill" Gates III (1955–)

Even as a child, Bill Gates loved computers. At the early age of 15 he earned $20,000 by writing a computer program to help manage traffic. He entered Harvard at the age of 17, and while still an undergraduate, developed BASIC for the first microcomputer, the MITS Altair. Convinced that eventually most offices and homes would have a microcomputer, Gates, along with his friend Paul Allen, created Microsoft in 1975. The focus of the business was the development of software designed to make microcomputers both more useful and more user friendly.

Gates quickly earned a reputation as a programming genius. When IBM decided to enter the personal computer (PC) market in 1980, they contracted with Gates to provide the basic operating software for their computers, a system now known as MS-DOS. Gates reserved the rights to sell his MS-DOS software to other firms. As IBM (and IBM clones) grew to dominate the PC market during the 1980s, Gates's fortune rose as well. Microsoft developed into the dominant firm in the computer software industry. Gates's programs are now used to run more than 90 percent of the world's computers. Gates's MS-DOS–based software program, Windows 98, along with Windows 2000 and the newer Windows XP, are among the most popular in the world. Doing good for society in this way paid him well. Near the end of 2001, Bill Gates's personal fortune was estimated at more than $50 billion. This was after giving $21 billion to his charitable foundation, and losing more than $9 billion in the falling stock market that year.

Gates attributes his success to his workaholic nature. He continues to work long hours and is still actively involved in the operation and strategic decision making of Microsoft. If you have ever used a computer, you have almost certainly benefitted from programs that Gates created. His remarkable programming genius has changed the way we use personal computers both at home and in the workplace.

For more detail, see Gene N. Landrum, *Profiles of Genius* (Buffalo: Prometheus Books, 1993); and Robert F. Hartley, *Management Mistakes and Successes* (New York: John Wiley and Sons, Inc., 1994).

But no one knows what the next innovative breakthrough will be or precisely which production techniques will minimize per-unit costs. Better ways of doing things do not just happen; they must be discovered and developed by entrepreneurs. While the potential for financial reward is enormous, entrepreneurial activities are also risky. Is that new visionary idea the greatest thing since the development of the fast-food chain? Or is it simply another dream that will soon turn to vapor?

In a market economy, it is relatively easy to try new business ideas. One only needs to win the support of a few investors willing to finance the innovative new product or production technology. However, competition holds entrepreneurs and the investors who support them accountable: Their ideas must face a "reality check" imposed by production cost and consumer willingness to pay. Consumers are the ultimate judge and jury. If they do not value an innovative new product or service enough to cover its cost, it will not survive in the marketplace.

Furthermore, today's successful product may not pass tomorrow's competitive test. Thus, entrepreneurs must be good at anticipating, identifying, and quickly adopting improved ideas, whether their own or others'. The ongoing reality of dynamic change in a competitive world must constantly be confronted.

Entrepreneurial Decision Making and the Structure, Size, and Scope of Firms

Entrepreneurs must also discover the type of business structure, scale of operation, and scope of activities that best keeps the per-unit cost of their product or service low. Pursuit of profit provides them with a strong incentive to do so.

Unlike other economic systems, a market economy does not mandate or limit the types of firms that are permitted to compete. Any form of business organization is permissible. An owner-operated firm, a partnership, a corporation, an employee-owned firm, a consumer cooperative, a commune, or any other form of business is free to enter the market. In order to be successful, however, a business structure must be cost-effective. A form of business organization that results in high per-unit cost will be driven from a competitive market by lower-cost rivals.

The same is true for the size of a firm. For some products, a business must be quite large to take full advantage of economies of scale. When per-unit costs decline as output increases, small businesses tend to have higher production costs (and therefore higher prices) than their larger counterparts. When this is the case, consumers interested in maximum value for their money will tend to buy from the lower-priced larger firm. In contrast, when personalized service and individualized products are valued highly by consumers, small firms, often organized as individual proprietorships or partnerships, are likely to be more cost-effective. It is up to the entrepreneur to discover the scale of operation that best fits the circumstances of each market.

The scope of a business is another variable requiring entrepreneurial decision making. Should a gasoline station stand alone, or should its scope be expanded to include auto repair services? Or should it instead be combined with a convenience store, or would a different combination create more value relative to cost? Numerous alternative combinations of business activities are possible. Differences in locations and other circumstances will often influence how well each is received. A new and better combination of products and services in the right place can generate a profit, at least temporarily until others catch on and provide close substitutes. In contrast, a business choosing the wrong scope of operation for the situation will earn less and it could be driven from the market by rivals offering a more appropriate scope of activities. Once again, consumer choices and market forces will determine the scope of operation that best fits the circumstances.

Because of the vast array of decisions to be made in price-searcher markets, the role of the entrepreneur is particularly important here. In price-searcher markets, entrepreneurs may use a variety of weapons—quality of product, style, service, convenience of location, advertising, and price to compete with rival firms. But financial success is still dependent on the dollar votes of consumers. ***In order to be successful, entrepreneurs must consistently offer consumers at least as much value for their dollar as can be obtained elsewhere. Put another way, they must figure out how to supply consumers with goods and services that are valued highly relative to their costs. As they do so, their actions create wealth and increase the value of resources. Even though many of their activities are omitted from our basic economic models, the vitally important role of entrepreneurs as agents of economic progress is nonetheless abundantly clear.***

6 AN EVALUATION OF COMPETITIVE PRICE-SEARCHER MARKETS

As we saw earlier, determination of price and output for price searchers is in some ways similar to that for price takers. Because the long-run, equilibrium conditions in price-taker markets are consistent with ideal economic efficiency, it is useful to compare and contrast them with conditions in price-searcher markets when entry barriers are low. There are both similarities and differences.

When barriers to entry are low, businesses must compete for the loyalty of customers. Neither price takers nor price searchers in markets with low entry barriers will be able to earn long-run economic profit. Competing firms drawn by economic profits—that is, returns greater than opportunity costs—will enter until, in the long run, competition has driven the market price down to the level of average total cost. Entrepreneurs in both price-taker and price-searcher markets have a strong incentive to manage and operate their businesses efficiently. Inefficient operation will lead to higher costs, losses, and forced exit from the market. Similarly, price takers and competitive price searchers alike will be motivated to develop and adopt new cost-reducing procedures and techniques because lower costs will mean higher short-run profits (or at least smaller losses).

The response to changing demand conditions in price-taker and price-searcher markets with low entry barriers is also similar. In both cases, an increase in market demand leads to higher prices, short-run profits, expansion of the existing producers, and the entry of new firms. With the entry of new producers, and the concurrent expansion of existing firms, the market supply will increase, placing downward pressure on price. The process will continue until the market price falls to the level of average total cost, squeezing out all economic profit.

Correspondingly, a reduction in demand will lead to lower prices and short-run losses, causing output to fall and some firms to exit. As the market supply declines, prices will rise and eventually the short-run losses will be eliminated and the firms remaining in the industry will once again be able to cover their costs. Regardless of whether the firms are price takers or price searchers, profits and losses will direct their output decisions when barriers to entry are low.

As Exhibit 22-4 illustrates, while the price taker confronts a horizontal demand curve, the demand curve faced by a price searcher is downward sloping. This is important because it means that the marginal revenue of the price searcher will be less than, rather than equal to, the price charged for the quantity sold. So, when the profit-maximizing price searcher expands output until $MR = MC$, price will still exceed marginal cost (panel b). In contrast, the price charged by a profit-maximizing price taker will equal marginal cost (panel a). In addition,

EXHIBIT 22-4 Comparing Price-Taker and Price-Searcher Markets

Here we illustrate the long-run equilibrium conditions of a price taker and a price searcher when entry barriers are low. In both cases, price is equal to average total cost, and economic profit is zero. However, since the price searcher confronts a downward-sloping demand curve for its product, its profit-maximizing price exceeds marginal cost, and output is not large enough to minimize average total cost when the market is in long-run equilibrium. For identical cost conditions, the price of the product in a price-searcher market will be slightly higher than in a price-taker market. This slightly higher price is considered by some to be indicative of inefficiency, while others perceive it to be the premium a society pays for variety and convenience (price differentiation).

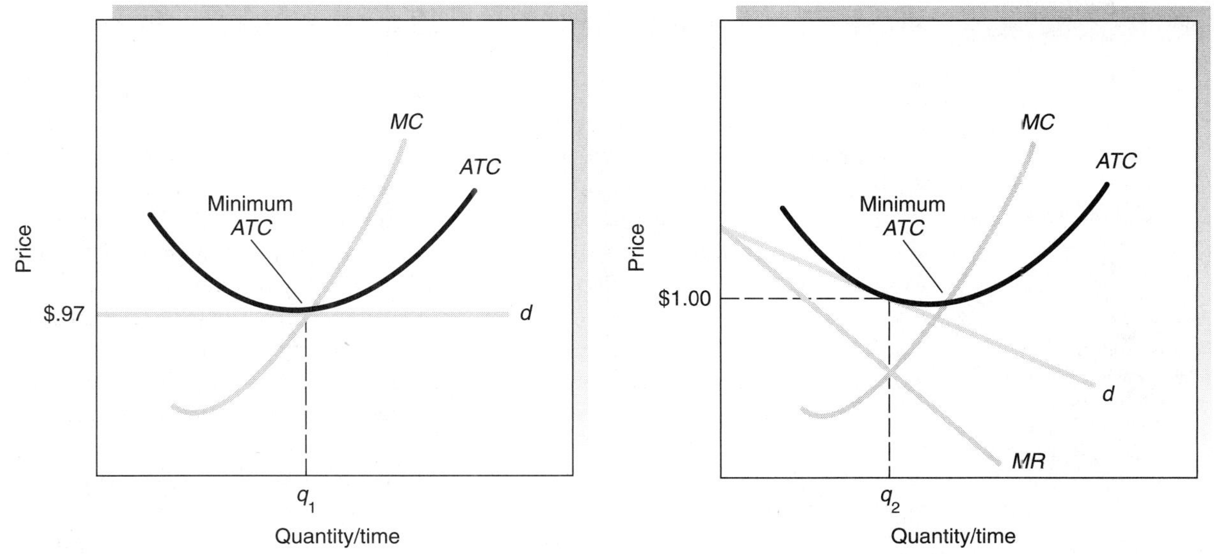

(a) Price taker

(b) Price searcher

when a price searcher is in long-run equilibrium, the firm's output rate will be less than the rate that would minimize average total cost. The price searcher would have a lower per-unit cost (97 cents rather than $1) if a larger output were produced.

Is the higher cost and price and the greater variety found in the price-searcher market less efficient than the slightly lower price and cost in the price-taker market with less variety? It is impossible to say, since the products in the price-searcher market are substitutes for one another, but they are not quite the same. Thus the output is, for consumers, at least slightly different between the two markets.

Price-searcher firms advertise, but price takers do not. Advertising is costly, and in the long run, consumers cover this cost in the form of higher prices. Do advertised products provide enough information and variety to justify the higher cost from the consumer viewpoint? We cannot know for certain. However, we observe that producers are always free to use low-priced, more uniform and less-advertised products in order to lure buyers away from firms that advertise and provide variety at a higher price. Some firms do, and sometimes the strategy works; yet many consumers choose to buy advertised goods and pay the higher prices. This result suggests that many customers do find that advertised products and greater variety are worth more.

Are resources allocated efficiently in a price-searcher market with low barriers to entry? This question is difficult to answer with certainty. **Allocative efficiency** is achieved when the goods and services most desired by consumers are produced at the lowest possible cost. Clearly, price-taker markets allocate resources efficiently. In a price-searcher market, however, the greater variety of products involves a cost. Therefore, some argue that this is a deviation from ideal

Allocative efficiency
The allocation of resources to the production of goods and services most desired by consumers, at the lowest possible cost.

allocative efficiency. But a broader range of choices also provides benefits. The greater variety makes it possible for a wider range of consumers to obtain the quality, style, and accompanying service that best fits their preferences. Perhaps most importantly, competitive price-searcher markets provide entrepreneurs with a strong incentive to innovate and discover better ways of doing things. In a dynamic setting, this is vitally important for the efficient use of resources.

7 A SPECIAL CASE: PRICE DISCRIMINATION

Price discrimination
A practice whereby a seller charges different consumers different prices for the same product or service.

Thus far, we have assumed that all sellers of a product will charge each customer the same price. Sometimes, though, price searchers can increase their revenues (and profits) by charging different prices to different groups of consumers. Such businesses as hotels, restaurants, and drugstores often charge senior citizens less than other customers. Students and children are often given discounts at movie theaters and athletic events. Grocery stores commonly give discounts to customers who clip "cents off" coupons from newspapers or magazines. Colleges often give financial aid (reduced tuition) to students from less-wealthy families. These practices are called **price discrimination.** ***To gain from such a practice, price searchers must be able to do two things: (1) identify and separate at least two groups with differing elasticities of demand, and (2) prevent those who buy at the low price from reselling to the customers charged higher prices.***

Let us take a closer look at why sellers may find price discrimination advantageous. Suppose that a seller has two groups of customers: one with an inelastic demand for its product and the other with an elastic demand. An increase in the price charged the first group will increase the total revenue derived from that group. On the other hand, a reduction in price will increase revenues derived from the latter. Thus, a seller may be able to increase total revenue and profit by charging the first group a higher price than the second.

The pricing of airline tickets illustrates the potential of price discrimination. The airline industry has found that the demand of business fliers is substantially more inelastic than the demand of vacationers, students, and other travelers. Thus, airlines usually charge high fares to persons who are unwilling to stay over a weekend, who spend only a day or two at their destination, and who make reservations a short time before their flight. These high fares fall primarily on business travelers who are less sensitive to price. In contrast, discount fares are offered to fliers willing to make reservations well in advance, travel during off-peak hours, and stay at their destinations over a weekend before returning home. Such travelers are likely to be vacationers and students, who are highly sensitive to price.

Exhibit 22-5 illustrates the logic of this policy. Panel a shows what would happen if a single price were charged to all customers. Given the demand, the profit-maximizing firm expands output to 100, where *MR* equals *MC*. The profit-maximizing price on coast-to-coast flights is $400, which generates $40,000 of revenue per flight. Since the marginal cost per passenger is $100, this provides the airline with net operating revenue of $30,000 with which to cover other costs.

However, as panel b shows, although the market demand schedule is unchanged, the airline can do even better if it uses price discrimination. When it charges business travelers $500, most of these passengers continue to travel since their demand is highly inelastic. On the other hand, a $100 price cut generates substantial additional ticket sales from vacationers, students, and others whose demands are more elastic. Therefore, with price discrimination, the airline can sell 60 tickets (primarily to business travelers) at $500 and 60 additional tickets to others at $300. Total revenue jumps to $48,000 and leaves the airline with $36,000 ($48,000 minus 120 times the $100 marginal cost per passenger) of rev-

EXHIBIT 22-5 Price Discrimination

As panel a illustrates, a $400 ticket price will maximize profits on coast-to-coast flights if an airline charges a single price. However, the airline can do still better if it raises the price to $500 for passengers (business travelers) with a highly inelastic demand and reduces the price to $300 for travelers (for example, students and vacationers) with a more elastic demand. When sellers can segment their market, they can gain by (a) charging a higher price to consumers with a less elastic demand and (b) offering discounts to customers whose demand is more elastic.

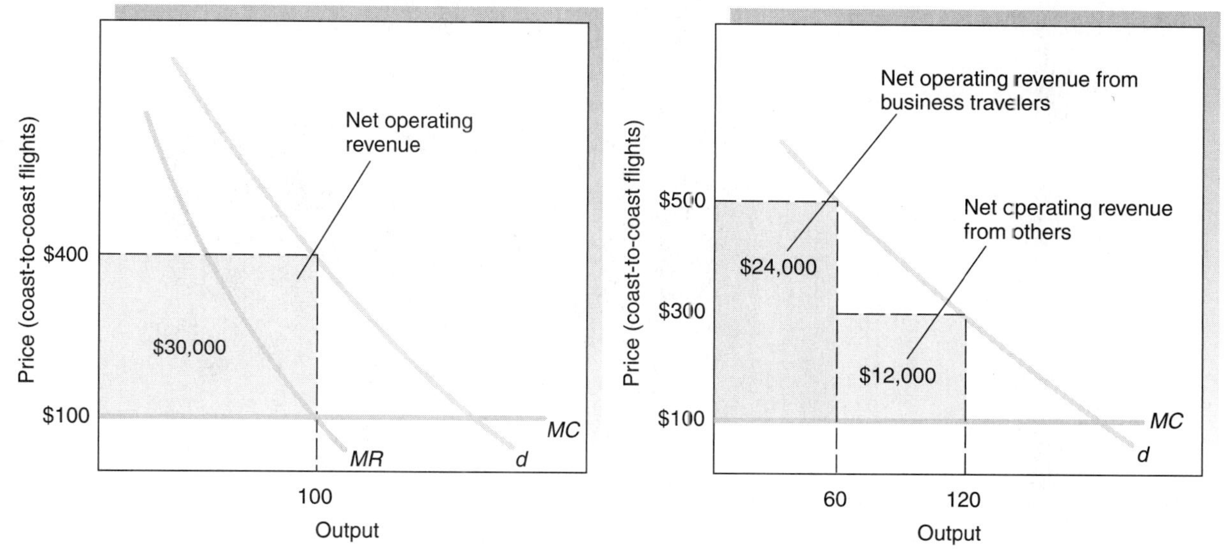

(a) Seller charges a single price

(b) Seller uses price discrimination

enue in excess of variable cost. Compared to the single-price outcome (panel a), the price discrimination strategy expands profit by $6,000.

When sellers can segment their market (at a low cost) into groups with differing price elasticities of demand, price discrimination can increase profits. For *each group*, the seller will maximize profit by equating marginal cost and marginal revenue. This rule will lead to higher prices for groups with more inelastic demand and lower prices for groups with more elastic demand. Compared to the single-price situation, price discrimination increases profitability because a higher price increases the net revenue from groups with an inelastic demand, while a lower price increases the net revenue from price-sensitive customers. With price discrimination, the number of units sold also increases (compare panel a with panel b) because the discounts provided to price-sensitive groups increase the quantity sold more than the higher prices charged the less price-sensitive groups reduce sales.

Sometimes price discrimination is subtle. Colleges engage in price discrimination by charging a high standard tuition to get additional revenue from high-income students with a more inelastic demand, while providing low-income students with scholarships based on need (tuition "discounts"). Recently at the University of Maine, for example, tuition at the undergraduate level ran between $12,998 and $20,738, depending on the degree. Financial aid, however, amounted to 54 percent of tuition for students from low-income families, while for high-income students, it was only 17 percent of tuition. Partial-tuition scholarships given to students whose parents are less wealthy enable a school to attract students who have a more elastic demand. Low-income students thus are not so often priced out of the market by the high standard tuition.

How do buyers fare when a seller can price discriminate? Some buyers pay more than they would if a single intermediate price were offered. They purchase

Giving financial aid, in the form of lower tuition charges, to students from families with lower incomes and who thus are likely to be more price-sensitive allows a college to practice price discrimination, charging a higher tuition price to those who are expected to be less price-sensitive.

fewer units, and they are worse off. In contrast, those for whom the price discrimination process lowers the price are better off. Of course, with some products, such as airline transportation, a single buyer might be better off with some purchases and worse off with others.

On balance, however, we can expect that output will be greater with price discrimination than it would be with a single price. The market is not as understocked as it would have been in the absence of the price discrimination. Thus, from an allocative standpoint, price discrimination gets high marks; it allows more trades, reducing the allocative inefficiency due to price being set above marginal cost. Some of the gains that would accrue to consumers with an inelastic demand are transferred to the price searcher as increased revenue, but additional gains from trade are created by the increased output of goods that would be lost if the price searcher did not (or could not) price discriminate.

In some markets, there is an additional gain emanating from price discrimination: Production may occur that would be lost entirely if only a single price could be charged. With price discrimination, some otherwise unprofitable firms may be able to generate enough additional revenue to operate successfully in the marketplace. For example, some small towns in Montana might not provide enough revenue at a single price to enable a local physician to cover her opportunity costs. However, if she is able to discriminate on the basis of income, charging higher-income patients more than normal rates and lower-income patients less, the resulting revenues from practice in the small town may enable the physician to stay in the community. In this case, all residents of the town may be better off as the result of the price discrimination, because it makes it possible for them to access a local physician. After all, even those being charged the highest prices are not disadvantaged if the price discrimination keeps the physician in town. They are just as able to seek physician services elsewhere as they would have been in the absence of the price-discriminating local doctor. With or without price discrimination, access to competing sellers (or buyers) protects market participants from unfair treatment.

In summary, if potential customers can be segmented into groups with different elasticities of demand and retrading can be controlled at a low cost, sellers can often gain by charging higher prices to those with the more inelastic demand (and lower prices to those with an elastic demand). Price discrimination can also increase the total gains from trade and thereby reduce allocative inefficiency. Sometimes it even allows production where none would have otherwise occurred.

8 SUMMARY

- Firms in price-searcher markets with low barriers to entry face a downward-sloping demand curve. They are free to set the prices for the products that they sell, but face strong competitive pressure from existing and potential rivals.
- The mark of the price-searcher market with low barriers to entry is product differentiation. Price searchers use product quality, style, convenience of location, advertising, and price as competitive weapons. Because each firm competes with rivals offering similar products, each confronts a highly elastic demand curve for its products.
- A profit-maximizing price searcher will expand output as long as marginal revenue exceeds marginal cost, lowering its price in the process, until $MR = MC$. The price charged by the profit-maximizing price searcher will be greater than its marginal cost.
- If firms in a price-searcher market with low barriers to entry are making economic profits, rival firms will be attracted to the market. Their entry will expand the supply of the product (and similar products), lowering price and enticing some customers away from established firms. The demand curve faced by each firm will fall (shift inward) until the economic profits have been eliminated.
- Economic losses will cause price searchers to exit from the market, raising the demand for each remaining firm (shifting it outward) until the losses have been eliminated, ending the incentive to exit.
- When barriers to entry are low, firms in a market will make only normal profits in the long run. In the short run, they may make either economic profits or losses, depending on market conditions.
- Competition can come from potential as well as actual rivals. If entry and exit can be arranged at low cost, and if there are no legal barriers to entry, the theory of contestable markets indicates that competitive results will be approximated even if there are only a few firms actually in the market.
- Although standard economic models do not include the central role of entrepreneurial decision making in a world of uncertainty, economists recognize its importance. Entrepreneurs who discover and introduce lower-cost production methods and new products that are highly valued relative to cost promote economic progress. Entrepreneurs also have a strong incentive to discover the type of business structure, size of firm, and scope of operation that can best keep the per-unit cost of products or services low.
- Competitive price-searcher markets provide more variety but may raise costs, relative to price-taker markets because (a) price exceeds marginal cost at the profit-maximizing output level; (b) long-run average cost is not minimized; and (c) advertising is costly. When barriers to entry are low, however, price searchers have an incentive to (a) produce efficiently; (b) undertake production if and only if their actions will increase the value of resources used; and (c) be innovative in offering new product options.
- When a price searcher can (a) identify groups of customers that have different price elasticities of demand and (b) prevent customers from retrading the product, price discrimination may emerge. Sellers may be able to gain by charging higher prices to groups with a more inelastic demand and lower prices to those with a more elastic demand. The practice generally leads to a larger output and more gains from trade than would otherwise occur.

PRICE-SEARCHER MARKETS WITH HIGH ENTRY BARRIERS

READING 23

LEARNING OUTCOME

The candidate should be able to:

a. discuss entry barriers that may protect companies against competition from potential market entrants;

b. differentiate between a monopoly and an oligopoly;

c. describe how a profit-maximizing monopolist sets prices and determines output and discuss price and output under oligopoly, with and without collusion;

d. discuss why oligopolists have a strong incentive to collude and to cheat on collusive agreements and discuss the obstacles to collusion among oligopolistic companies;

e. describe the different defects that can occur in a market with high entry barriers;

f. describe government policy alternatives that are intended to reduce the problems stemming from high barriers to entry.

g. contrast the pricing and output decisions of a firm in pure competition, monopolistic competition, oligopoly, and monopoly with reference to quantity produced, price, marginal revenue, marginal cost, demand, and average total cost.

INTRODUCTION 1

If there are economies of scale throughout the region of possible industry outputs, only one or a few firms may be able to exist in the industry.

—George Stigler[1]

In the previous two readings, we analyzed the way firms behave in competitive markets, characterized by low barriers to entry. We now turn to the analysis of firm behavior when entry barriers are high and there are few, if any, rival firms offering the same or similar products. This reading focuses on factors that increase the difficulty of entry into a market and analyzes how they influence the ability of markets to discipline business firms. The potential of various policy alternatives that might improve the efficiency of resource allocation in these markets will also be considered.

---

[1] George J. Stigler, *The Theory of Price* (New York: Macmillan, 1987), p. 204.

2 WHY ARE ENTRY BARRIERS SOMETIMES HIGH?

What makes it difficult for potential competitors to enter a market? Four factors can be important: economies of scale, government licensing, patents, and control over an essential resource.

Economies of Scale

In some industries, firms experience declining average total costs over the full range of output that consumers are willing to buy. When this is the case, the larger firm will always have lower unit costs. Because the unit costs of smaller firms are higher than those of their larger rivals, it will be difficult for small firms to enter the market, build a reputation, and compete effectively. Under these circumstances, a single firm will tend to emerge in the industry, and the cost advantage resulting from its size will provide the firm with protection from potential rivals.

Government Licensing

Legal barriers are the oldest and most effective method of protecting a business firm from potential competitors. Kings once granted exclusive business rights to favored citizens or groups. Today, governments continue to establish barriers, restricting the right to buy and sell goods. To compete in certain parts of the communications industry in the United States (for example, to operate a radio or television station), one must obtain a government franchise. Similarly, local governments often grant exclusive franchises for the operation of cable television systems.

Licensing
A requirement that one obtain permission from the government in order to perform certain business activities or work in various occupations.

Licensing limits entry. States and cities often require operators of liquor stores, hair styling shops, taxicabs, funeral homes, drugstores, and many other businesses, to obtain a license. Sometimes these licenses cost little and are designed to ensure certain minimum standards. In other cases, they are expensive and designed primarily to limit competition.

Patents

Most countries have patent laws to give inventors a property right to their inventions. A patent grants the owner the exclusive legal right to the commercial use of a newly invented product or process for a limited period of time, 17 years in the United States. Others are not allowed to copy the product or procedure without the permission of the patent holder. For example, when a pharmaceutical company is granted a patent for a newly developed drug, other potential suppliers must obtain permission from the patent holder before producing and selling the product. Others might be able to supply the drug more economically. If they want to do so, however, they will have to purchase the production and marketing rights from the originating firm as long as the patent is in effect.

Costs, as well as benefits, come with a patent system. The entry barrier created by the grant of a patent generally leads to higher consumer prices for products that have already been developed. On the positive side, however, patents increase the potential returns to inventive activity, thus encouraging scientific research and technological improvements. It typically costs $200 million to develop and test a new drug, for example. Without the profit potential from patents on new drugs, less research would be undertaken by drug firms. Eliminating patent protection might well slow the pace of technological innovation.

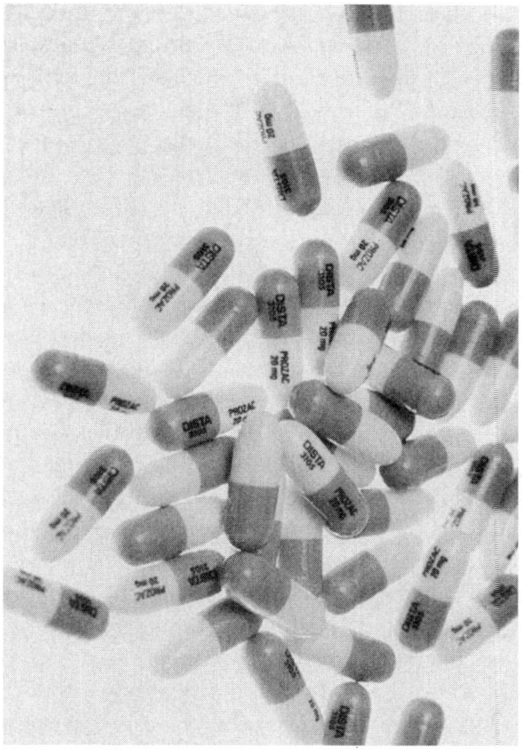

A firm that develops a new drug can use patent protection to restrain production by others for 17 years. Although consumers will pay higher prices than if open competition were permitted, they may benefit from additional investment in research and more rapid development of new products than would be the case in the absence of patent protection.

Control Over an Essential Resource

A single firm with sole control over a resource essential for entry into an industry is free from direct competitors. An example often cited is the Aluminum Company of America, which before World War II controlled the known supply of bauxite conveniently available to American firms. Without this critical raw material, potential competitors could not produce aluminum. With time, however, other supplies of bauxite were found, and this source of monopoly was lost to the company. As this case illustrates, resource monopolies are seldom complete. Profit opportunities provide challengers with an incentive to search for mineral deposits, new technologies, and substitute resources. Over time, they are usually found.

Barriers to entry are often temporary, but they do exist. Let us move on to see what happens when, at least temporarily, there is a barrier to entry high enough to limit the market to only one seller.

Monopoly
A market structure characterized by (1) a single seller of a well-defined product for which there are no good substitutes and (2) high barriers to the entry of any other firms into the market for that product.

THE CASE OF MONOPOLY 3

The word *monopoly*, derived from two Greek words, means "single seller." We will define **monopoly** as a market characterized by (1) high barriers to entry and (2) a single seller of a well-defined product for which there are no good substitutes. Even this definition is ambiguous, because "high barriers" and "good substitutes" are both relative terms. Are the barriers to entry into the automobile or steel industries high? Many observers would argue that they are. After all, economies of scale are important in these industries and it would take a great deal of financial capital to operate at the least-cost scale of output. However, there are no *physical* or *legal* restraints that prevent an entrepreneur from producing automobiles or steel. If price is well above cost and profit potential is present in these industries, it should not be too difficult to find the necessary investment capital. Thus, some would argue that entry barriers into these industries are not particularly high.

"Good substitute" is also a subjective term. There is always some substitutability among products, even those produced by a single seller. Is a letter a good substitute for a telephone or e-mail message? For some purposes—correspondence between law firms, for example—a letter delivered by mail is a very good substitute. In other cases, when the speed of communication and immediacy of response are important, telephone and e-mail communication are far superior. Are there any good substitutes for electricity? Most of the known substitutes for electric lighting (candles, oil lamps, and battery lights, for example) are inferior to electric lights in most uses. Natural gas, fuel oil, and wood, though, are often excellent substitutes for electric heating. Also, electric utilities have found that many of their largest industrial customers can generate their own electricity, sometimes at low cost, in conjunction with other fuel-burning operations.

Monopoly, then, is always a matter of degree. Only a small fraction of all markets are served by only one seller. Nevertheless, there are two reasons why it is important to understand how such markets work. First, the monopoly model will help us understand markets in which there are few sellers and little active rivalry. When there are only two or three producers in a market, firms may seek to collude rather than compete, and thus together behave like a monopoly. Second, in a few important industries there is by law often only a single producer in each market. Local telephone and electricity services are examples. The monopoly model will illuminate the operation of such markets.

Price and Output Under Monopoly

Suppose you invent, patent, and produce a microwave device that locks the hammer of any firearm in the immediate area. This fabulous invention can be used to immobilize potential hijackers or armed robbers. Since you own the exclusive patent right to the firearm lock device, you are not concerned about a competitive supplier in the foreseeable future. Although other products are competitive with your invention, they are poor substitutes. In short, you are a monopolist.

What price should you charge for your product? Because you are the only seller of this device, the demand for your product is also the market demand curve. It will be downward sloping because consumers will cut back on their purchases as the price of the firearm lock increases. Like other price searchers, you will have to search to determine the most profitable price to charge. An expansion in output will increase profit as long as the production and sale of additional units add more to revenue than to cost. ***Like other price searchers, the monopolist will expand output until marginal revenue equals marginal cost. This profit-maximizing output rate can be sold at a price indicated on the firm's demand curve.***

Exhibit 23-1 graphically illustrates how a monopolist derives the profit-maximizing output rate.[2] The firm will continue to expand output as long as

[2] In this reading we assume that firms are unable to use price discrimination to increase their revenues. If they could, the analysis of price discrimination from the previous reading would help to describe their decisions.

EXHIBIT 23-1 Short-Run Price and Output of a Monopolist

The monopolist will reduce price and expand output as long as *MR* exceeds *MC.* Output *Q* will result. When price exceeds average total cost at any output level, profit will accrue at that output level.

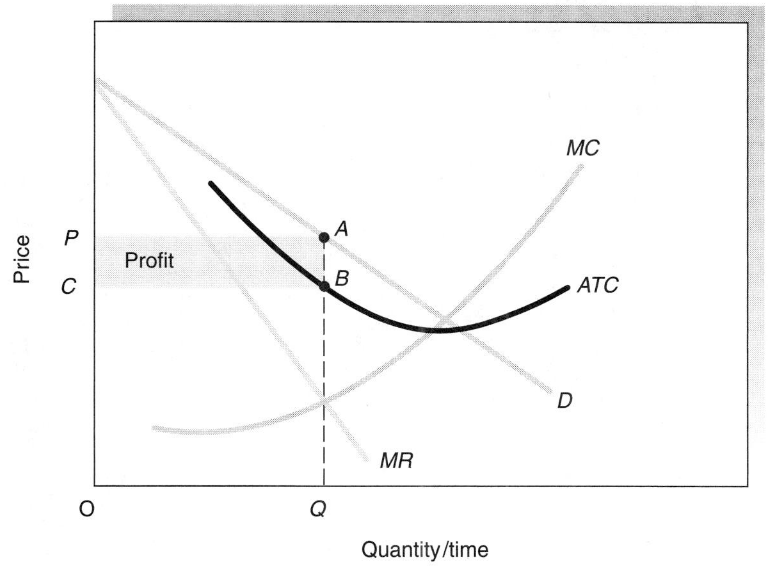

marginal revenue exceeds marginal cost. Therefore, output will be expanded to *Q,* where *MR* = *MC.* The monopolist will be able to sell the profit-maximizing output *Q* at price *P,* the height of the demand curve at *Q.* At any output less than *Q,* the benefits (marginal revenue) of producing the *additional* units will exceed their costs. In this range, the monopolist will gain by reducing price and expanding output toward *Q.* For any output greater than *Q,* the monopolist's costs of producing additional units will be greater than the benefits (marginal revenue). Production of such units would reduce profits. Thus, output rate *Q* and price *P* will maximize the firm's profit.

Exhibit 23-1 also depicts the profits of a monopolist. At output *Q* and price *P* the firm's total revenue is equal to *PAQO,* the price times the number of units sold. The firm's total cost would be *CBQO,* the average per-unit cost multiplied by the number of units sold. The firm's profits are merely total revenue less total cost, the shaded area of Exhibit 23-1.

Exhibit 23-2 provides a numeric illustration of profit-maximizing decision making. At low output rates, marginal revenue exceeds marginal cost. The monopolist will continue expanding output as long as *MR* is greater than *MC.* Thus, an output rate of eight units per day will be chosen. (*Note:* If tiny portions of a unit could be produced and sold, then production would increase to where *MR* = *MC.*) Given the demand for the product, the monopolist can sell eight units at a price of $17.25 each. Total revenue will be $138, compared to a total cost of $108.50. The monopolist will make a profit of $29.50. The profit rate will be smaller at all other output rates. For example, if the monopolist reduces the price to $16 in order to sell nine units per day, revenue will increase by $6. However, the marginal cost of producing the ninth unit is $6.25. Since the cost of producing the ninth unit is greater than the revenue it brings in, profits will decline.

When high barriers to entry are present, they will insulate the monopolist from direct competition with rival firms producing a similar product. In markets with high

EXHIBIT 23-2 Profit Maximization for a Monopolist

Rate of Output (per day) (1)	Price (per unit) (2)	Total Revenue (1) × (2) (3)	Total Cost (per day) (4)	Profit (3) − (4) (5)	Marginal Cost (6)	Marginal Revenue (7)
0	—	—	$ 50.00	$−50.00	—	—
1	$25.00	$ 25.00	60.00	−35.00	$10.00	$25.00
2	24.00	48.00	69.00	−21.00	9.00	23.00
3	23.00	69.00	77.00	−8.00	8.00	21.00
4	22.00	88.00	84.00	4.00	7.00	19.00
5	21.00	105.00	90.50	14.50	6.50	17.00
6	19.75	118.50	96.75	21.75	6.25	13.50
7	18.50	129.50	102.75	26.75	6.00	11.00
8	17.25	138.00	108.50	29.50	5.75	8.50
9	16.00	144.00	114.75	29.25	6.25	6.00
10	14.75	147.50	121.25	26.25	6.50	3.50
11	13.50	148.50	128.00	20.50	6.75	1.00
12	12.25	147.00	135.00	12.00	7.00	−1.50
13	11.00	143.00	142.25	.75	7.25	−4.00

entry barriers, monopoly profits will not attract—at least not quickly—rivals who will expand supply, cut prices, and spoil the seller's market.

Protected by high entry barriers, a monopolist may be able to continue earning a profit, even in the long run. Does this mean that monopolists can charge as high a price as they want? Monopolists are often accused of price gouging. In evaluating this charge, however, it is important to recognize that, like other sellers, monopolists will seek to maximize *profit,* not *price.* Consumers will buy less as price increases. Thus, a higher price is not always best for monopolists. Exhibit 23-2 illustrates this point. What would happen to the profit of the monopolist if price were increased from $17.25 to $18.50? At the higher price, only seven units would be sold, and total revenue would equal $129.50. The cost of producing seven units would be $102.75. Thus, when price is $18.50 and output seven units, profit is only $26.75, less than could be attained at the lower price ($17.25) and larger output (eight units). The highest price is not always the best price for the monopolist. Sometimes a price reduction will increase the firm's total revenue more than its total cost.

Will a monopolist always be able to make an economic profit? The profitability of a monopolist is limited by the demand for the product that it produces. In some cases, a monopolist—even one protected by high barriers to entry—may be unable to sell for a profit. For example, there are thousands of clever, patented items that are never produced because demand-cost conditions are not favorable. Exhibit 23-3 illustrates this possibility. Here, the monopolist's average total cost curve is above its demand curve at every level of output. Even when operating at the $MR = MC$ rate of output, economic losses (shaded area) will occur. While output Q could be sold at price P, this price is too low to cover the per-unit cost of the monopolist. Under these circumstances, not even a monopolist would want to operate, at least not for long.

EXHIBIT 23-3 When a Monopolist Incurs Losses

Even a monopolist will incur losses if the average total cost curve lies above the demand curve.

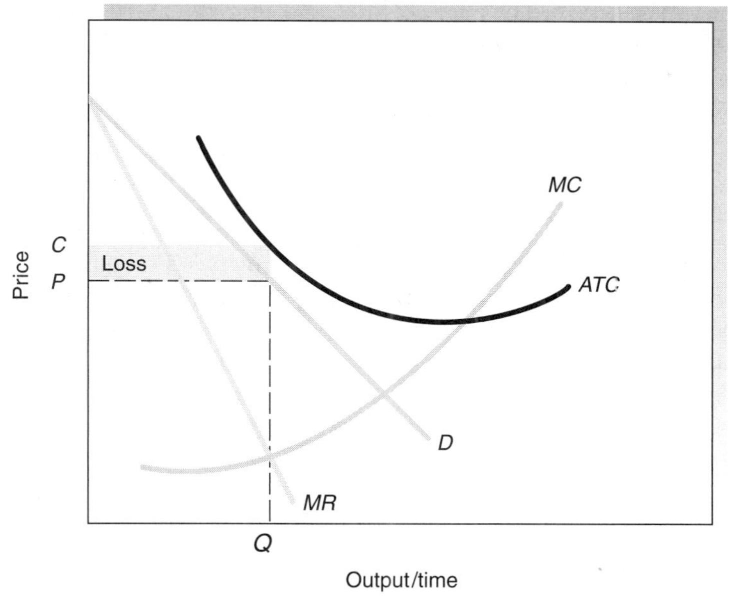

The Monopoly Model and Decision Making in the Real World

Until now, we have proceeded as if monopolists always knew exactly what their revenue and cost curves looked like. Of course, this is not true in the real world. Like other price searchers, a monopolist cannot be sure of the demand conditions for a product. Demand curves frequently shift, and choices must be made without the benefit of perfect knowledge. How many sales will be lost if the price is raised? How many sales will be added if the price is lowered? Like other price searchers, monopolists often experiment with price changes, attempting to find the price at which profit will be maximized. Price will be set on the basis of what the price-searching monopolist expects to happen when price is changed. Thus, the revenue and cost data illustrated in Exhibits 23-1, 23-2, and 23-3 represent *expected* revenues and costs associated with various output levels. To complicate matters further in real life, quality changes of various sorts can be undertaken by the monopolist searching for additional profits. Buyer reactions to potential quality changes, and resulting shifts in demand and cost, must also be considered by the profit-seeking monopolist.

A monopolist, like other business decision makers, seldom calculates what we have called demand, marginal revenue, and cost curves. Given imperfect information, the profit-maximizing price may be only approximated. Like other price searchers, however, the monopolist has a strong incentive to find the profit-maximizing price and output rate and, when it does, the outcome will be as if the $MR = MC$ rule had been used to maximize profit.

It is difficult for a monopolist to predict demand conditions and consumer response to quality and price changes. But life is even more complex for the next class of price searchers we consider: large firms with few rivals in a market protected by high barriers to entry.

4 CHARACTERISTICS OF OLIGOPOLY

Oligopoly
A market situation in which a small number of sellers compose the entire industry. It is competition among the few.

In the United States, the great majority of output in such industries as automobiles, cigarettes, and aircraft is produced by five or fewer dominant firms. These industries are characterized by **oligopoly**. *Oligopoly* means "few sellers." ***The distinguishing characteristics of an oligopolistic market are (1) a small number of rival firms, (2) interdependence among the sellers because each is large relative to the size of the market, (3) substantial economies of scale, and (4) high entry barriers into the market.***

Interdependence Among Oligopolistic Firms

Since the number of sellers in an oligopolistic industry is small, the decisions of one firm will influence the demand, price, and profit of rivals. This adds to the complexity of the firm's decision making. A firm that is deciding what price to charge, output to produce, or quality of product to offer, must consider the potential reactions of rivals. After all, the demand for its own output depends on the available substitutes offered by rival firms. The business decisions of each firm depend on the policies it expects its major rivals to follow.

Substantial Economies of Scale

In an oligopolistic industry, large-scale production (relative to the total market) is generally required to achieve minimum per-unit cost. Economies of scale are present, so a small number of large-scale firms can produce the entire market demand for the product. Using the automobile industry as an example, Exhibit 23-4 illustrates the importance of economies of scale as a source of oligopoly. It has been estimated that each firm must produce approximately 1 million automobiles annually before its per-unit cost of production is minimized. However, when the selling price of automobiles is barely sufficient to cover costs, the total quantity demanded from these producers is only 6 million. To minimize costs, then, each firm must produce at least one-sixth (1 mil-

EXHIBIT 23-4 Economies of Scale and Oligopoly

Oligopoly exists in the automobile industry because firms do not fully realize the cost reductions from large-scale output until they produce approximately one-sixth of the total market.

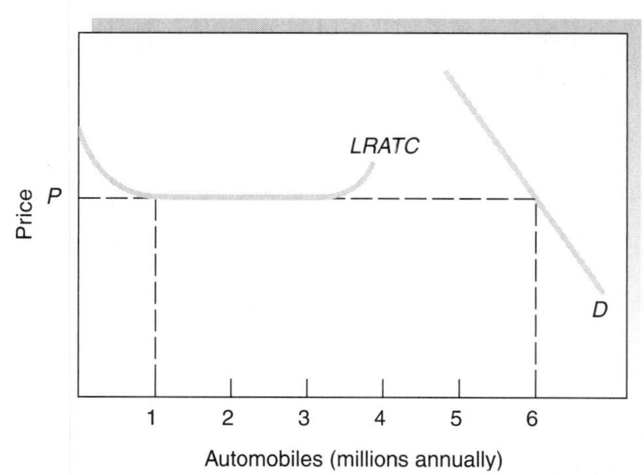

lion of the 6 million) of the output demanded. In other words, the industry can support no more than five or six domestic firms of cost-efficient size.

Significant Barriers to Entry

As with monopoly, barriers to entry limit the ability of new firms to compete effectively in oligopolistic industries. Economies of scale are probably the most significant entry barrier protecting firms in an oligopolistic industry.[3] A potential competitor may be unable to start out small and gradually grow to the optimal size, since it must gain a large share of the market before it can minimize per-unit cost. The manufacture of refrigerators and diesel engines, as well as automobile production, seems to fall into this category. Other factors, including patent rights, control over an essential resource, and government-imposed entry restraints, may also prevent new competitors from entering profitable oligopolistic industries. The presence of high entry barriers is what distinguishes oligopoly from a competitive price-searcher market.

Products May Be Either Identical or Differentiated

The products of sellers in an oligopolistic industry may be either similar or differentiated. When firms produce identical products, such as milk or gasoline, there is less opportunity for nonprice competition. On the other hand, rival firms producing differentiated products are more likely to use style, quality, and advertising as competitive weapons.

PRICE AND OUTPUT IN THE CASE OF OLIGOPOLY 5

Unlike a monopolist or a price taker, an oligopolist cannot determine the product price that will deliver maximum profit simply by estimating its own costs and the *existing* market demand. The demand facing an oligopolistic firm depends also on the pricing behavior of close rivals. Suppose, for example, that General Motors is considering how to price next year's new Chevrolet model when it comes on the market. The number of Chevrolets it can sell at each price will depend not only on buyer preferences, but also on the prices (and quality) of substitutes available from Ford, Toyota, and other GM rivals. What pricing strategy will each rival use if GM puts a low price on its new model? How would each rival firm react to a higher GM price?

Economics cannot predict these complex interactions among rivals, without making some strong, simplifying assumptions about how each firm reacts when one firm makes a change in price or quality. These simplifying assumptions will not be realistic for the general case, and therefore the precise price and output that will emerge under oligopoly cannot be uniquely determined. Economics does, however, indicate a potential range of prices and the factors that will determine whether prices in the industry will be high or low relative to costs of production.

---

[3] Economies of scale will not be a barrier to entry in the industry, of course, if resources can be freely moved into and out of the industry at a low cost. Such resource mobility would render the market contestable, a market structure that we discussed in the previous reading.

Consider a typical oligopolistic industry in which seven or eight rival firms produce the entire market output because substantial economies of scale are present. The firms produce nearly identical products and have similar costs of production. Exhibit 23-5 depicts the market demand conditions and long-run costs of production of the individual firms for such an industry.

What price will prevail? We can answer this question for two extreme cases. First, suppose that each firm sets its price independently of the other firms. There is no collusion (no agreement among the firms to limit output and keep the price high), so each competitive firm is free to seek additional customers and profits by offering buyers a slightly better deal than its rivals. Under these conditions, the market price would be driven down to P_c. Firms would be just able to cover their per-unit costs of production. If a single firm raised its price, its customers would switch to rival firms, which would now expand to accommodate the new customers. The firm that raised its price would lose out. It would be self-defeating for any one firm to raise its price if the other firms did not raise theirs.

What happens if the current price is greater than P_c, perhaps because the market has not yet adjusted fully to a recent reduction in resource prices that lowered production costs? As a result, price is above per-unit cost and the firms are making economic profit. However, any *individual firm* that reduces its price slightly, by 1 or 2 percent, for example, will gain numerous customers if the other firms maintain the higher price. The price-cutting firm will attract some new buyers to the market, but more important, it will also lure many buyers away from rival firms charging higher prices. Thus, if the rival sellers act independently, each will have a strong incentive to reduce price in order to increase sales and gain a larger share of the total market. But what happens when each firm attempts to undercut its rivals? Price is driven down to P_c, and the economic profit of the firms is eliminated.

When rival oligopolists compete (on the basis of price) with one another, they drive the market price down to the level of costs of production. They do not

EXHIBIT 23-5 Range of Price and Output Under Oligopoly

If oligopolists were to act independently and compete with one another, price cutting would drive price down to P_c. In contrast, perfect cooperation among firms would lead to a higher price of P_m and a smaller output (Q_m rather than Q_c). The shaded area shows profit if firms collude. Demand here is the market demand.

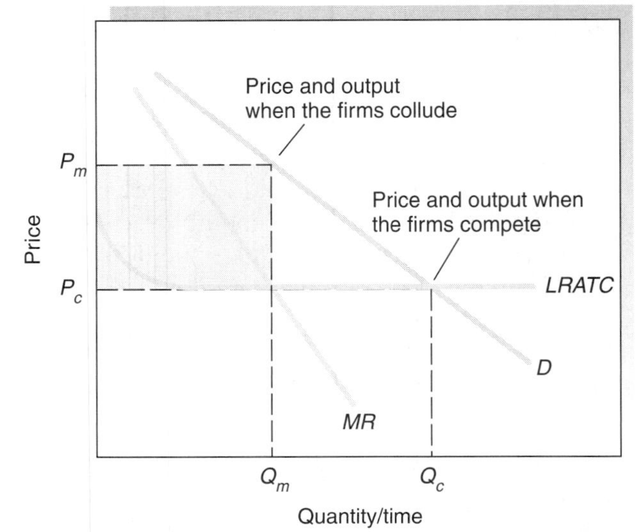

always compete, however. There is a strong incentive for oligopolists to collude, agreeing to raise prices and to restrict output.

Suppose the oligopolists, recognizing their interdependence, acted cooperatively to maximize their joint profit. They might form a **cartel** to accomplish this objective. Probably the world's best-known cartel is the Organization of Petroleum Exporting Countries (OPEC), a group of oil-producing nations formed in 1960 to limit their combined production and thus raise world oil prices. From the beginning, different goals among members caused problems. Members like Saudi Arabia and Kuwait, with few people and large oil reserves, wanted moderately higher prices that would limit the incentives for long-term development of new oil substitutes and new oilfields. Other member nations such as Algeria and Libya, with smaller reserves and more people, wanted much higher prices, to gain more revenue from their limited reserves more quickly. Despite these disagreements, by 1973 OPEC had settled on a production strategy, with quotas for each producer. They succeeded in limiting their output enough to raise oil prices.

Cartel
An organization of sellers designed to coordinate supply decisions so that the joint profits of the members will be maximized. A cartel will seek to create a monopoly in the market.

Higher oil prices, however, encouraged energy conservation and the greater use of coal, nuclear energy, and other oil substitutes. The higher prices also increased incentives for individual OPEC members to exceed their cartel quotas, and for non-OPEC producers to find and bring to market new oil and to produce more from marginal oilfields. Since the mid-1980s, these factors together have reduced OPEC's ability to keep world oil prices high. OPEC nations control 80 percent of the world's known oil reserves, including those from which oil can be produced most cheaply. Yet in 2001, their production was less than 40 percent of the world's oil output. Cartel agreements are difficult to arrange and to enforce. It is also difficult to protect the cartel market from nonmember producers, who will sell more if the cartel pushes the price up.

Instead of forming a cartel, oligopolists might collude without the aid of a formal organization. Under federal antitrust laws in the United States, collusive action to raise price and expand the joint profit of the firms would be illegal. Nevertheless, let us see what would happen if oligopolists followed this course. Exhibit 23-5 shows the marginal revenue curve that would accompany the market demand D for the product. Under perfect cooperation, the oligopolists would refuse to produce units for which marginal revenue to the group was less than marginal cost. Thus, they would restrict joint output to Q_m where $MR = MC$. Market price would rise to P_m. With collusion, substantial joint profits (the shaded area of Exhibit 23-5) could thus be attained. The case of perfect cooperation would be identical with the outcome under monopoly.

In the real world, the outcome is likely to be between the two polar case extremes of price competition and perfect cooperation. Oligopolists generally recognize their interdependence and try to avoid vigorous price competition, which would drive price down to the level of per-unit costs. But there are also obstacles to collusion, which is why prices in oligopolistic industries are unlikely to rise to the monopoly level. ***Thus, oligopolistic prices are typically above per-unit cost but below those a monopolist would set.***

Collusion
Agreement among firms to avoid various competitive practices, particularly price reductions. It may involve either formal agreements or merely tacit recognition that competitive practices will be self-defeating in the long run. Tacit collusion is difficult to detect. In the United States, antitrust laws prohibit collusion and conspiracies to restrain trade.

The Incentive to Collude and to Cheat

Collusion is the opposite of competition. It involves cooperative actions by sellers to turn the terms of trade in their favor and against buyers. Oligopolists as a group can profit by colluding to restrict output and raise price, giving them a strong incentive to do so. To accomplish this, however, the firms must also agree on production shares for each firm, or a division of the market so that production is limited to the level that will be purchased at the chosen cartel price.

Collusive agreements among oligopolists and cartels like OPEC are difficult to maintain because any individual cartel member would be better off if it could cheat on the agreement and charge a slightly lower price, if other members do not.

Each individual oligopolist also has an incentive to cheat on collusive agreements. Exhibit 23-6 explains why. An undetected price cut will enable a firm to attract (1) customers who would not buy from any firm at the higher price and (2) those who would normally buy from other firms. Thus, the demand facing each *individual firm* will be considerably more elastic than the market demand curve. As Exhibit 23-6 shows, the price P_i that maximizes the industry's profits will be higher than the price P_F that is best for a single oligopolist when the others stay with the higher price. If a firm can use secret rebates or other ways to undercut the price set by the collusive agreement, while other sellers maintain the higher price, the firm's expanded sales (beyond the level agreed upon by the cartel) will more than make up for the reduction in per-unit profit margin.

In oligopolistic industries, there are two conflicting tendencies. An oligopolistic firm has a strong incentive to cooperate with its rivals so that joint profit can be maximized. However, it also has a strong incentive to cheat secretly on any collusive agreement in order to increase its share of the joint profit. Oligopolistic agreements, therefore, tend to be unstable. This instability exists whether the cooperative behavior is formal, as in the case of a cartel, or informal.

Obstacles to Collusion

There are certain situations in which it is more difficult for oligopolists to collude. Five major obstacles limit collusive behavior.

1. ***As the number of firms in an oligopolistic market increases, the likelihood of effective collusion declines.***

   Other things constant, an increase in the number of major firms in an industry will make it more difficult for the oligopolists to communicate, negotiate, and enforce agreements among themselves. In addition, the greater the number of firms, the more likely it is that the objectives of individual firms will conflict with those of the industry. Each firm will want a

EXHIBIT 23-6 Gaining from Cheating

The industry demand (D_i) and marginal revenue (MR_i) curves show that the joint profits of oligopolists would be maximized at Q_i where $MR_i = MC$. Price P_i would be best for the industry as a whole (a). However, the demand curve (d_F) facing each firm (under the assumption that no other firms cheat) would be much more elastic than D_i. Given the greater elasticity of its demand curve, an individual firm (b) would maximize its profit by cutting its price to P_F and expanding output to q_F, where $MR_F = MC$. Thus, individual oligopolists could gain by secretly shaving price and cheating on the collusive agreement.

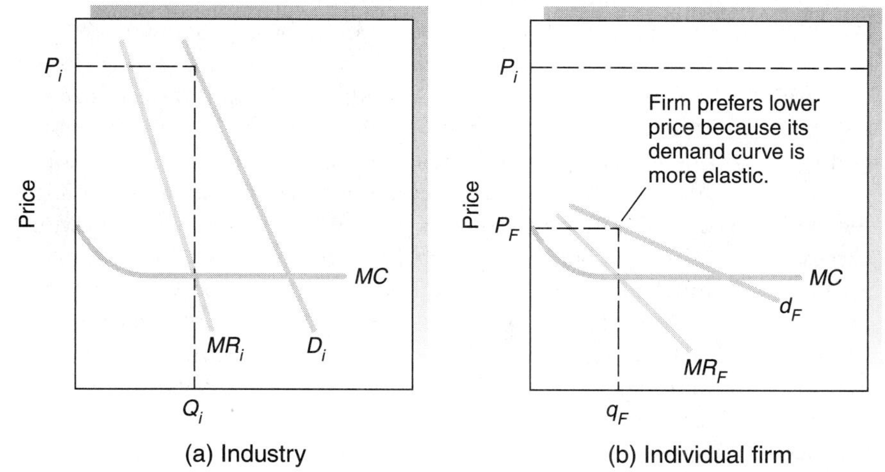

bigger slice of the pie. Opinions about the best collusive price arrangement will differ because marginal costs, unused plant capacity, and estimates of market demand elasticity are likely to differ among firms. Aggressive, less mature firms may be especially interested in expanding their share of total output. Exactly these problems have reduced the ability of OPEC to maintain high oil prices, as we noted previously. Conflicting interests will always make it more difficult to reach a collusive agreement and will contribute to the breakdown of any agreement that is made.

2. ***When it is difficult to detect and eliminate price cuts, collusion is less attractive.*** Unless a firm has a way of policing the pricing activities of rivals, it may be the "sucker" in a collusive agreement. Firms that secretly cut prices may gain a larger share of the market, while those maintaining higher prices are losing customers and profits. OPEC illustrates the explanatory power of the theory. Cheating by members on production and sales quota agreements has been a persistent problem for the cartel.

   Price cutting can sometimes be accomplished in ways that are difficult for the other firms to identify. For example, a firm might provide better credit terms, faster delivery, and other related services "free" to improve slightly the package offered to the buyer. In industries where differentiated products are supplied, oligopolists can hold money prices constant and still use improvements in quality and style to provide consumers with more value. "Price cuts" like this are particularly attractive to oligopolists because they cannot be easily and quickly duplicated by rivals. Competitors can quickly match a reduction in money price, but it will take time for them to match an improvement in quality. Collusive agreements on price are of limited value in situations where quality and style are important competitive weapons. The bottom line is this: When cheating (price cutting) is profitable and difficult for rivals to detect and police, collusive agreements—both formal and informal—will be difficult to maintain.

3. ***Low entry barriers are an obstacle to collusion.***

   Unless potential new rivals can be excluded, oligopolists will be unable to sustain economic profits. Profitable collusion will merely attract competitors into the industry until the profits drawing the entrants are eliminated. Once again, OPEC illustrates the point. OPEC's member nations produced more than half the world's oil in 1973, when they began to reduce output and raise oil prices. But higher prices led firms in other nations to seek, find, and produce more oil. By 1985, OPEC had cut its production by 12 percent, driving world oil prices up to more than triple their 1973 level. As prices rose, however, the output of non-OPEC members expanded by approximately 30 percent and OPEC's share of the market shrank from 55 percent to only 30 percent. OPEC changed its course, expanding output in order to recapture a larger share of the world oil market. Prices quickly fell by about half, as more and more production came onto the market. Non-OPEC production stopped growing with the lower price, but corrected for inflation, the price of oil in the 1990s was only about one-third of its peak in the early 1980s. Even with successful collusion, the benefits to sellers of higher prices must be shared with new entrants, unless entry into the industry can be blocked. Otherwise, entry will continue until falling prices drive economic profits to zero.[4]

   Local markets are sometimes dominated by a few firms. For example, many communities have only a small number of ready-mix concrete producers, bowling alleys, accounting firms, and furniture stores. In the absence of government restrictions, however, entry barriers into these markets are generally low. The threat of potential rivals reduces the gains from collusive behavior under these conditions. Even if the number of rival firms is small, the firms will be unable to maintain above-normal profit rates when entry barriers are low. Under these circumstances, the competitive price-searcher model, rather than oligopoly, is more applicable.

4. ***Unstable demand conditions are an obstacle to collusion.***

   Demand instability leads to honest differences of opinion among oligopolists about what is best for the industry. One firm may want to expand because it anticipates a sharp increase in future demand, while a more pessimistic rival may want to hold the line on existing industrial capacity. The larger the differences in expectations about future demand, the greater the potential for conflict among oligopolistic firms. Successful collusion is more likely when demand is relatively stable.

5. ***Vigorous antitrust action increases the cost of collusion.***

   Under existing antitrust laws, collusive behavior is prohibited. Secret agreements are, of course, possible. Simple informal cooperation might be conducted without discussions or collusive agreements. However, like other illegal behavior, such agreements are not legally enforceable by any firm. Vigorous antitrust action can discourage firms from making such illegal agreements. As the threat of getting caught increases, participants will be less likely to attempt collusive behavior.

Uncertainty and Oligopoly

Uncertainty and imprecision characterize the theory of oligopoly. We know that firms will gain if they successfully restrict output and raise prices. However, collusion is fraught with conflicts and difficulties. In some industries, these difficulties

---

[4] We are speaking here of profit from operating the firm. Ownership of a resource, such as an oilfield, does not involve an economic profit or a loss. The market value of the resource (e.g., the oilfield) represents the opportunity cost of using it in production, and the benefit of owning it—the owner could get that value in cash by selling the resource to an oil company, for example. It does not provide profit to the oil producer.

are so great that the **market power** of the oligopolists is relatively small. In other industries, oligopolistic cooperation, although not perfect, may raise prices significantly, indicating a higher degree of market power, which is, in effect, a degree of monopoly power. Analysis of the costs and benefits of collusive behavior, under varying degrees of cooperation and conflict, has become an important part of economics over the last two decades. (See the Applications in Economics feature on **game theory**.) Although this developing field of economics does not yield precise predictions on oligopoly pricing and output, it does suggest the conditions that make it more likely that an oligopolist will face discipline from competitive pressures.

Market power
The ability of a firm that is not a pure monopolist to earn unusually large profits, indicating that it has some monopoly power. Because the firm has few (or weak) competitors, it has a degree of freedom from the discipline of vigorous competition.

MARKET POWER AND PROFIT—THE EARLY BIRD CATCHES THE WORM

6

Game theory
Analyzes the strategic choices made by competitors in a conflict situation, such as decisions made by members of an oligopoly.

Our analysis of both monopoly and oligopoly indicates that because entry barriers into these markets are often high, firms may be able to earn economic profit over lengthy periods of time. Suppose a well-established firm, such as Disney or IBM, was able to use its market power to persistently earn above-normal returns. Would the current stockholders gain? Surprisingly, the answer is no. The ownership value of a share of corporate stock for such corporations would long ago have begun to reflect their market power and expected future profitability. Many of the present stockholders would have paid high prices for their stock because they expected these firms to be highly profitable. In other words, they paid for any above-normal economic profits that the firm was expected to earn because of its market power.

Do not expect to get rich buying the stock of monopolistic or oligopolistic firms known to be highly profitable. You are already too late. The early bird catches the worm. Those who owned the stock when these firms initially developed their market position have already captured the gain. The value of their stock increased at that time. After a firm's future prospects are widely recognized, subsequent stockholders fail to gain a higher-than-normal rate of return on their financial investment.

Monopolists, by keeping the market constantly understocked, by never fully supplying the effectual demand, sell their commodities much above the natural price, and raise their emoluments, whether they consist of wages or profit, greatly above their natural rate.

—Adam Smith[5]

DEFECTS OF MARKETS WITH HIGH ENTRY BARRIERS

7

What types of problems arise when entry barriers limit the number of firms in an industry to a single monopolist or a small group of oligopolists? From Adam Smith's time to the present, economists have generally considered monopoly a necessary evil at best. The attitude toward markets with only a few sellers and

[5] Adam Smith, *An Inquiry into the Nature and Causes of the Wealth of Nations* (1776; Cannan's ed., Chicago: University of Chicago Press, 1976), p. 69.

APPLICATIONS IN ECONOMICS

Oligopolistic Decision Making, Game Theory, and the Prisoner's Dilemma

In an oligopoly, a few firms compete by selling into the same market, and the actions of each influence the demand faced by rival sellers. Because they sell similar products and compete for the same customers, the interests of each firm are in conflict with the interests of the others. One firm can gain customers at the expense of the others by reducing its price or increasing its advertising. But if the other firms react competitively by doing the same, then all the firms may lose. Yet if rivals cut price or take other steps to offer consumers a better deal, firms that fail to follow suit will lose customers to their more aggressive competitors. Thus, each firm finds itself on the horns of a dilemma—in this case a variant of the classic "prisoner's dilemma."

Economists have increasingly used game theory, as in the analysis of the prisoner's dilemma, to analyze strategic choices made by competitors in a conflict situation, such as members of an oligopoly. Such choices depend on the anticipated actions of others.

To understand the prisoner's dilemma, consider the hypothetical case of Al and Bob, two touring Americans who just met at a train station in a small foreign country. They are taken prisoner and hauled into the local police station to be questioned separately. They are suspected of being the two men who robbed a local merchant, and each is told that if he makes the job of the police easier by confessing immediately, he will get only a 6-month sentence. But each is also told that if he says nothing while the other confesses, then the one who did not confess immediately will get a 12-month sentence. If neither confesses, both will be held for 3 months while the investigation continues. Al and Bob will not be allowed to communicate with each other. Will they confess?

To analyze such situations, the game theorist begins by laying out the alternative outcomes and showing how they are related to choices made by the players of the game, as we do in Exhibit 23-7. For each man individually, in this version of the dilemma, the box reveals that the best choice depends on what the other does. If Al confesses, then Bob can save 6 months of jail time by also confessing. The same holds for Al, if he thinks Bob will confess. But if neither confesses, both serve only three months in jail.[1] The proper strategy for each prisoner depends heavily on his estimate of the likelihood that the other will confess. The problem becomes more complex if we consider prisoners who face a series of such decisions over time, each prisoner learning the other's previous choice before the next set of choices must be made.

Firms in an oligopoly must make decisions somewhat like those of the prisoners: Should a firm cut its price, luring more customers, some from competitors, or should it keep its price high and risk losing customers to competitors who cut prices? If all firms keep the price high, then as a group they will reap more profit. If all cut prices, then as a group they will reap less profit. But the firm that fails to cut price when others do so will lose many customers to the other competing firms. The decision about whether to spend large amounts on advertising has similar characteristics.

For example, consider the pricing policy or advertising strategy of large automakers, such as Ford, General Motors, and Chrysler. Suppose the profit rate of each would be 15 percent if all the major automobile producers raised their prices (or cut their advertising expenditures) by a similar amount. In contrast, each would have a profit rate of only 10 percent if intense competition leads to lower prices and/or larger advertising expenditures. Industry profits are highest when all firms decide to charge high prices. However, if one automaker reduces its price or advertises more heavily, it will be able to win customers away from rivals and increase its profit rate to 20 percent. Thus, if the firm thinks its rivals will continue to charge higher prices (or fail to match its advertising expenditures), it will be able to gain from cutting its prices (and increasing its advertising). If the other firms follow a similar course, however, this strategy will backfire and the profit rate of all the firms in the industry will be less than the level that would have

EXHIBIT 23-7 The Prisoner's Dilemma

		Al's Choice	
		Confess	Not Confess
Bob's Choice	Confess	6 months each	Al: 12 months Bob: 6 months
	Not Confess	Al: 6 months Bob: 12 months	3 months each

Al and Bob must each decide, without communicating with each other, whether to confess. Al knows that if Bob does not confess, then Al can either confess and spend 6 months in jail, or not confess and spend 3 months. But if Bob does confess, then Al's failure to confess would cost him an additional 6 months in jail. Bob is in a similar situation, facing the same options under the same assumptions about whether Al confesses. Each has the incentive to confess if he thinks the other one will, but to not confess if he thinks the other will also remain silent.

been achieved had they all charged higher prices (or spent less on advertising).

While our simplified analysis highlights the interdependence among the firms and the importance of probability estimates concerning the strategy of rivals, the real world is much more complex. The choices of the rival firms will be repeated over and over again, although often in modified forms. A prior strategy may be modified in light of previous reactions on the part of rivals. The attractiveness of a strategy will be influenced by the likelihood it will be detected by rivals and the speed with which they might be able to react effectively. In addition, the strategies of oligopolistic firms will be influenced by market conditions and the threat of foreign competition, factors that change with the passage of time. Within the framework of game theory models, additional assumptions must be made in order to account for these and other complex factors—factors that often change in the real world. In turn, if the assumptions incorporated into game theory models are not consistent with real-world conditions, the implications of the game theory analysis may well be invalid.

Economists have used game theory extensively to show how results change when the "rules of the game" change for the firms in an oligopolistic market, as well as for auction-bidding markets and other business decision-making situations. When the rules of the game are carefully defined and enforced, as in the case of economic experiments in laboratories, game theory has yielded interesting and important testable conclusions. But in open markets in the real world, empirical work using game theory has been less successful. The use of models is always difficult when the problem to be solved is complex, and human expectations about the changing strategy choices of other human beings must be taken into account. There is no question, however, that game theory can be useful for scholars and business practitioners alike, in helping them to frame the issues involved in strategic decision making.[2]

---

[1]If the numbers were slightly different from those in the accompanying chart, both Al and Bob would have an incentive to confess regardless of what they thought the other would do. For example, if each were told that he would get only a 1-month sentence if he confessed and the other party did not, then confession would become the dominant strategy for both Bob and Al. Under these circumstances, if Bob thought Al would remain silent, then Bob would spend only 1 month in jail if he confessed (compared to 3 months if he also remained silent). Al would be in a similar situation if he believed Bob would remain silent. On the other hand, if Bob thought Al would confess, then Bob's best option would be to also confess since confession would lead to only a 6-month sentence while silence would result in a 12-month jail term. The same would also be true for Al if he thought Bob would confess. Thus, in this classic prisoner's dilemma case, both have an incentive to confess even though confession leads to more jail time for both of them—6 months rather than 3 months. What is best for the individual (or firm) does not always lead to the best outcome from the viewpoint of the group (or industry).

[2]For a further explanation of game theory and the prisoner's dilemma, see Avinash Dixit and Barry Nalebuff, "Game Theory," in David R. Henderson, ed., *The Concise Encyclopedia of Economics*, www.econlib.org/library/CEE.html.

high entry barriers is only slightly more tolerant. Open competition, unfettered by high barriers to entry, has been recognized as a key form of market discipline restraining the behavior of producers and encouraging innovation. There are three major reasons for this view.

1. ***When entry barriers are high and there are few, if any, alternative suppliers, the discipline of market forces is weakened.***

When entry barriers are low, consumers are well equipped to direct the behavior of suppliers. Producers have little choice but to serve the interest of consumers. The choices of consumers will drive firms from the market if they charge high prices, supply unattractive goods, or otherwise fail to serve the interest of consumers. If you do not like the food at a local restaurant, you eat elsewhere. If you think prices are high and the selection poor at a department store, you patronize rival firms. But consider your alternatives if you do not like the local cable television service. The entry of competitors is typically forbidden in that market. What can you do when the service is bad? You can voice a complaint to the company or your legislative representative, but unlike a competitive situation, you have no exit option other than sacrificing your cable service, perhaps to rely instead on satellite dish service. Cable and satellite service are imperfect substitutes, each with its own disadvantages. When consumers do not have good exit options—when they must either take what the seller offers or do without—their ability to discipline sellers is greatly reduced.

2. ***Reduced competition results in allocative inefficiency.***
   Allocative efficiency requires that additional units be produced when they are valued more highly than what it costs to produce them. When barriers to entry are low, production of each good will be expanded until its price is driven down to the level of per-unit costs. With high barriers to entry, however, this will not generally be the case. A monopolist or cartel that does not have to worry about rivals entering the market can often gain by restricting output and raising price. That is, output may not be produced even though consumers value it more than its costs of production. Prices may exceed not only marginal costs, but also average total cost for a long period of time when entry barriers into a market are high. As Adam Smith noted more than 200 years ago, monopolists (and cartels) will understock the market and charge a higher price than would prevail if the producers were disciplined by independent rivals and the threat of new entrants.

3. ***Government grants of monopoly power will encourage rent seeking; resources will be wasted by firms attempting to secure and maintain grants of market protection.***
   Grants of special favor by the government will lead to costly activities seeking those favors. As we noted in Chapter 6, economists refer to such activities as rent seeking. When government licenses or the imposition of other entry barriers enhance profitability and provide protection from the rigors of market competition, people will expend scarce resources attempting to secure and maintain these political favors. From an efficiency standpoint, such rent-seeking activities are wasteful; they consume valuable resources without contributing to output. In aggregate, output is reduced as the result of these wasteful activities. These rent-seeking costs from grants of monopoly power add to the welfare losses resulting from the allocative inefficiency mentioned previously.

   By way of illustration, suppose the government issues a license providing a seller with the exclusive right to sell liquor in a specific market. If this grant of monopoly power permits the licensee to earn monopoly profit, potential suppliers will expend resources trying to convince government officials that they should be granted the license. The potential monopolists will lobby government officials, make political contributions, hire representatives to do consulting studies, and undertake other actions designed to convince politicians and their appointees that they can best "serve the public interest" as a monopoly supplier. Any firm that expects its rent-seeking activities to be successful will be willing to spend up to the present value of the future expected monopoly profits, if necessary, to obtain the monopoly protection. Other suppliers, of course, may also be willing to invest in rent-seeking activities. When several suppliers believe they can win, the total expenditures of all firms on rent-seeking activities may actually consume resources worth more than the economic profit expected from the monopoly enterprise.

8 POLICY ALTERNATIVES WHEN ENTRY BARRIERS ARE HIGH

What government policies might be used to counteract the problems that result from high barriers to entry? Economists suggest four policy options:

1. Control the structure of the industry in order to assure the presence of rival firms.
2. Reduce artificial barriers that limit competition.

3. Regulate the price and output of firms in the market.
4. Supply the market with goods produced by a government firm.

Each of these policies has been used to either reduce entry barriers or to counteract their negative results. We will briefly consider each of them and analyze both their potential and limitations as tools with which to improve the efficiency of resource use.

Antitrust Policy and Controlling the Structure of an Industry

The major problems raised by high barriers to entry and monopoly power are avoided when rival sellers are present. A firm will be unable to restrict output and raise price when it confronts rivals producing the same product or close substitutes. The United States, to a greater degree than most Western countries, has adopted antitrust laws designed to prevent monopoly and promote competition. Antitrust legislation began in 1890 with the passage of the Sherman Antitrust Act. Additional legislation, including the Clayton Act and the Federal Trade Commission Act of 1914, has buttressed policy in this area.

Antitrust laws provide the U.S. Department of Justice (DOJ) with the power to prosecute firms engaging in collusive behavior or other actions designed to create a monopoly or cartel. They also provide the government with the power to break up an existing monopoly and prevent mergers that significantly reduce competition. The Federal Trade Commission (FTC) is allowed to bring charges under the Sherman Act. Private firms can also bring suits charging antitrust violations by a rival under the Sherman and Clayton acts, and may collect up to three times any actual damages caused by the rival firm. Each year, far more cases are brought by private firms against their competitors than by the two federal agencies. Rival firms can also ask that the two agencies step in to bring antitrust cases against successful competitors who may have, or threaten to gain, monopoly power.

Economists are not in total agreement on the usefulness of strong antitrust laws. Those who support aggressive antitrust policy believe that only by preserving numerous competitors in a market can we be confident that monopoly has been controlled. Opponents point to the danger of protecting high-cost firms at the expense both of consumers and the more aggressive and successful firm(s) in the market. Protection of less efficient firms from successful competitors, they say, is all too common in the actual practice of antitrust policy. Economists on both sides of this lively debate in economics have provided commentary during and after the highly publicized case brought by DOJ against Microsoft Corporation. (See the Applications in Economics feature on "Antitrust, Monopoly and Competition: The Microsoft Case on page 256.)

When analyzing the attractiveness of antitrust actions designed to maintain or increase the number of firms in an industry, the potential importance of economies of scale must also be considered. If economies of scale are unimportant, maintaining and/or expanding the number of rivals in an industry can be a good strategy. However, when substantial economies of scale are present, larger firms will have lower per-unit cost than smaller ones. Sometimes economies of scale are so important that per-unit cost of production will be lowest when the entire output of the industry is produced by a few firms (an oligopoly) or even a single firm (a monopoly). In the latter case, the "natural" tendency will be toward a **natural monopoly**—the situation where economies of scale are such that unit cost will be minimized only if the entire industry output is produced by a single firm.

Natural monopoly
A market situation in which the average costs of production continually decline with increased output. Therefore, average costs of production will be lowest when a single, large firm produces the entire output demanded.

In the natural monopoly case, breaking up a large firm in order to increase the number of rivals in the industry is clearly a counter-productive strategy.

APPLICATIONS IN ECONOMICS

Antitrust, Monopoly, and Competition: The Microsoft Case

In 1998, the Justice Department filed a highly publicized antitrust case against Microsoft, the software giant. Microsoft's rivals lobbied for this lawsuit. They charged that Microsoft had a monopoly in the market for computer operating systems, and was using its power in that market to give other Microsoft products, and especially its Internet Explorer Web browser, an unfair market advantage. For example, Microsoft had added its Internet Explorer browser to every copy of Windows, its operating system, and thus was giving the browser away free. Critics worried that Microsoft was trying to extend its monopoly on operating systems into the browser market. Several months earlier, IBM had begun to bundle a browser with its OS/2 operating system, but IBM had a much smaller market share. Microsoft's action forced the leading seller of browsers, Netscape, to lower its price to zero also. Like billboard space along a busy road, space on the browser's opening screen is valuable for advertising. Therefore, opportunity for profit was still present, even at a zero price, because a firm with the sizable share of the browser market could promote products and websites for itself and for others.

When Microsoft introduced its Internet Explorer in 1995, Netscape's Navigator dominated the browser market. Within a couple of years, Netscape's dominant position in the browser market was eroded and its revenues from browser sales virtually eliminated. Netscape argued that Microsoft's packaging of its browser within its operating system was an unfair competitive tactic. It also retained the services of Robert Bork, one of the nation's leading antitrust lawyers, in an effort to convince the general public and the Department of Justice that antitrust law should be used to protect the future of the Internet. Other rivals of Microsoft joined in the battle. Novell, a Microsoft rival located in Utah, enlisted the help of Utah Senator Orrin Hatch, chairman of the Senate Judiciary Committee. Senator Hatch held hearings to advance the case against Microsoft.

In May 1998, the Justice Department brought a case charging Microsoft with violating antitrust law. There were two primary allegations: (1) Microsoft was compelling computer manufacturers who installed its operating system, Windows, to also license and install Microsoft's Web browser, the Internet Explorer, in an attempt to monopolize the browser market, and (2) Microsoft made contracts that excluded rivals. In addition, Microsoft was charged with various forms of predatory conduct in order to force competitors from the market.

Supporters of the antitrust case against Microsoft argued that a firm with substantial market power cannot be allowed to leverage that power by tying other products to the one that it dominates. Neither can it be allowed to use its market power to bludgeon independent manufacturers not to deal with its competitors, or impose a pricing system that accomplishes the same result. The Justice Department also argued that Microsoft's Windows operating system imposed a serious barrier to entry. A new operating system, such as Linux, faces the problem that far fewer programs are written to be compatible with it, so users are hesitant to adopt it. This enhances Microsoft's market share, and according to the DOJ, justifies judicial intervention.[1]

Opponents of the strong stand taken by the Justice Department argue that antitrust policy is being used to reverse competitive outcomes at the expense of consumers. According to this view, the success of Microsoft's browser had little to do with its Windows operating system. Microsoft defenders buttress their case with evidence from published magazine reviews indicating that Netscape Navigator "was clearly considered the higher quality browser until late 1996, when Explorer became the superior product."[2] After that—and only then—was there a rapid increase in its market share.

More broadly, critics of the antitrust action argue that consumers have benefited from the pricing policies of Microsoft. When Microsoft has entered software markets, prices have consistently fallen, and stayed low. Data for 1988–1995 show that software in markets with direct Microsoft competition fell in price by nearly 60 percent; in markets without a direct Microsoft entrant, prices fell only 15 percent. Critics of the antitrust action stress that, far from restricting output and raising price, as a monopolist would do, Microsoft has substantially lowered the price of software products. In short, the DOJ critics argue that Microsoft's presence has benefited consumers and that most of the restraints that "trust busters" would place on Microsoft would harm consumers, and unfairly harm Microsoft.

The trial judge ruled that Microsoft had maintained its operating system as a monopoly by anticompetitive means and had attempted to establish a monopoly in the browser market by unlawfully bundling Internet Explorer with its Windows operating system. He ordered that Microsoft be split into two firms and established restrictions on the firm's business practices prior to that time.

Microsoft appealed. The appeals court upheld the trial court's ruling on several antitrust violations, but reversed the judge's breakup order and removed him from the case, citing "serious judicial misconduct" regarding his derogatory comments about the company. It ordered that another judge find a remedy that would restore competition and prevent further monopolization of the industry. The new judge encouraged Microsoft and the DOJ to settle the case themselves. The agreement they reached (pending approval from the court as this is written) restrained Microsoft from retaliation against firms that install software from rivals on Microsoft Windows operating systems. It also forced Microsoft to share key parts of its Windows programming codes with its competitors, helping them to design application software to run more smoothly with Windows.

[1] For additional details, see Irwin Stelzer, *Microsoft and the Antitrust Laws: Old-Fashioned Problems and a New Economy*, AEI-Brookings Joint Center for Regulatory Studies, Policy Matters 01–09. March 2001.

[2] For this quote and more evidence on the position of those opposing the antitrust action against Microsoft, see Stan J. Liebowitz and Stephen E. Margolis, *Winners, Losers and Microsoft*, (Independent Institute: Oakland, CA, 1999) and Albert Nichols *Getting the Facts Straight on Microsoft*, AEI-Brookings Joint Center for Regulatory Studies, Policy Matters 01–13, May 2001.

Expanding the number of firms would lead to higher unit costs of production. Because of their higher costs, the prices charged by the smaller firms might even exceed those of a monopolist. Furthermore, it will be difficult to maintain the larger number of rivals because the firms will have a strong incentive to grow and/or merge in order to achieve the lower unit costs accompanying a larger scale of operation. Thus, use of antitrust laws to expand the number of firms is not an attractive option when an industry is a natural monopoly.

Reduce Artificial Barriers to Trade

Government-imposed restraints such as licensing requirements, tariffs, and quotas often reduce the competitiveness of markets. For example, local governments often require potential entrants into the taxicab business to prove that "additional capacity is needed to serve the market." Hearings must be held to address this issue and existing firms are allowed to explain why the new entrant is not needed. Governments also restrain entry into various occupations through the use of substantial licensing fees, complex examinations, and lengthy training requirements. When government-imposed restrictions are the source of the monopoly power, the appropriate policy action is straightforward: remove the restraints. Of course, this is often easier said than done. The restraints generally reflect the power of special interest groups—the producers currently in the industry—who have a vested interest in restricting competition and keeping prices high.

If a product is traded in international markets, foreign suppliers can enhance the competitiveness of a domestic market. When the domestic market is dominated by a small number of firms, removal of tarriffs, quotas, and other obstacles that limit competition from abroad is particularly important. The competition of foreign rivals will help assure that the domestic firms improve quality and keep their costs low.

The U.S. automobile industry illustrates the importance of this approach. Profits for U.S. producers in the highly competitive automobile segment of the industry have been low. The 2.5 percent tariff on imported autos has had only a small impact. In contrast, there is a 25 percent tariff on imported trucks (placed there in 1963 in response to foreign treatment of U.S. frozen chicken exports). The higher tariff protects the same U.S. producers in the truck segment of the industry. There, profits per vehicle are much higher. When General Motors began selling its newly designed line of full-sized pickups in 1998 (the first full updating of those models in 10 years), the profit on a well-equipped $30,000 unit was reported to be $8,000. The tariff keeps the price of foreign imports high, so the level of competition is lower in the U.S. market for new trucks than in the market for cars. Clearly, the competition from abroad has helped keep domestic auto producers on their toes. As a result, most observers believe that the quality of automobiles available to the American consumer, including those produced by domestic manufacturers, is higher than would have been the case in the absence of the competition from abroad.

As in the case of domestically imposed entry restraints, political considerations often make it difficult to remove obstacles that retard competition from abroad. Trade restraints that limit competition from foreign suppliers are generally a special interest issue. The beneficiaries of the restraints—primarily the owners, managers, and workers in the protected industries—are highly concentrated and generally well organized. In contrast, the costs of the restraints are nearly always thinly spread among poorly organized consumers. The better organized, concentrated interests are likely to prevail. Therefore, even when lower trade barriers are needed to increase the competitiveness of an industry, political factors may reduce the likelihood they will be adopted.

Regulate the Protected Producer

Can government regulation improve the allocative efficiency of a monopoly or an oligopoly? In theory, the answer to this question is clearly yes. Exhibit 23-8 illustrates why ideal government price regulation, in the case of a monopolist, would improve resource allocation. Note, the firm illustrated here is a natural monopoly. Its LRATC falls over the entire relevant range of output. Thus, antitrust action that divided the firm into several smaller rivals would be ineffective because the unit cost of the smaller firms would be higher than if the output was produced by a monopolist. Nonetheless, the profit-maximizing monopolist will produce an output that is too small and charge a price that is too high from the viewpoint of allocative efficiency. It will set price at P_0 and produce output Q_0, where $MR = MC$. Consumers, however, would value additional units more than the opportunity cost. Let us consider the potential of two regulatory options and also analyze some of their real-world limitations.

EXHIBIT 23-8 Regulation of a Monopolist

If unregulated, a profit-maximizing monopolist with the costs indicated here would produce Q_0 units and charge P_0. If a regulatory agency forced the monopolist to reduce price to P_1, the monopolist would expand output to Q_1. Ideally, we would like output to be expanded to Q_2, where $P = MC$, but regulatory agencies usually do not attempt to keep prices as low as P_2. Can you explain why?

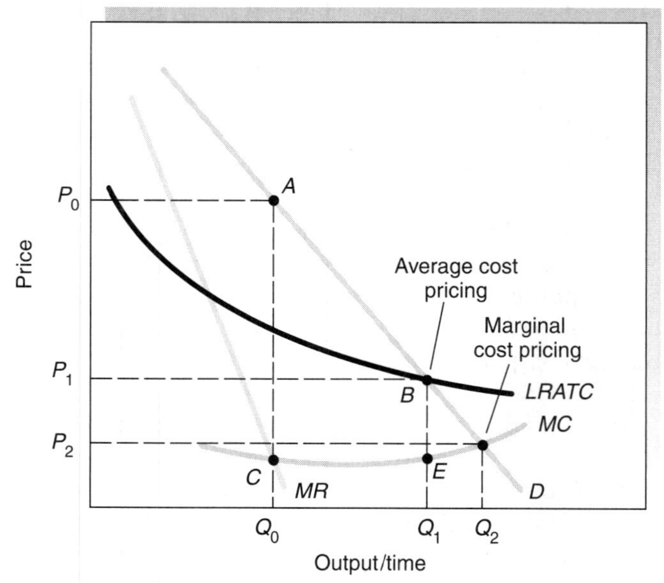

Average Cost Pricing

If a regulatory agency forces the firm in Exhibit 23-8 to reduce price to P_1, at which the *ATC* curve intersects with the market (and firm) demand curve, the firm will expand output to Q_1. Since it cannot charge a price above P_1, the firm cannot increase revenues by selling a smaller output at a higher price. Once the price ceiling is instituted, the firm can increase revenues by P_1, and by only P_1, for each unit it sells. The regulated firm's *MR* is constant at P_1 for all units sold until output is increased to Q_1. Since the firm's *MC* is less than P_1 (and therefore less than *MR*), the profit-maximizing regulated firm shown here will expand output from Q_0 to Q_1. The benefits from the consumption of these units (ABQ_1Q_0) clearly exceed their costs (CEQ_1Q_0). Social welfare has improved as a result of the regulatory action (we will ignore the impact on the distribution of income). At that output level, revenues are sufficient to cover costs. The firm is making zero economic profit (or "normal" accounting profit).

Marginal Cost Pricing

Even at the Q_1 output level, marginal cost is still less than price. Additional welfare gains could be achieved if output were increased to Q_2. However, if a regulatory agency forced the monopolist to reduce price to P_2 (so that price would equal marginal cost at the output level Q_2), economic losses would result. Even a monopolist, unless subsidized, would not undertake production if the regulatory agency set the price at P_2 or any price below P_1. Usually, problems associated with determining and allocating the necessary subsidy would make this option unfeasible.

Problems with Regulation

Even though government regulation of monopoly seems capable of improving market results, as in the preceding average cost pricing example, both economic analysis and history of regulation suggest that regulation will usually not be an ideal solution. Why is regulation an imperfect solution? Four factors tend to reduce both the effectiveness of regulation and the probability that the regulators will act on behalf of all citizens to control monopoly. Let us look at each of these factors.

1. ***Lack of Information.*** In discussing ideal regulation, we assumed that we knew what the firm's *ATC, MC,* and demand curves looked like. In reality, of course, this would not be the case. The firms themselves have difficulty knowing their costs, and especially their demand curves, with any precision. Furthermore, both supply and demand will vary with time and place. The market for electricity is an excellent example. Because electricity cannot be stored for later use, the highly variable supply and demand conditions in that market cause the opportunity cost of power to change dramatically from one day, or even one hour, to the next. California utilities experienced that problem early in the summer of 2001, as low rainfall reduced hydropower generation, rising natural gas prices increased thermal generation costs, and some hot weather early in the summer added to an already growing demand. These factors combined to sharply raise the marginal cost of delivering electric power. The regulated retail power rates were far too low to cover costs in this situation. Later in the summer, these demand and supply factors had shifted back toward their previous levels, and the marginal cost of power had declined substantially. Meanwhile, however, the resulting power outages and utility revenue shortfalls caused serious problems.

   Because estimates of demand and marginal costs are difficult to obtain, regulatory agencies usually use profits (or rate of return) as a gauge to determine whether the regulated price is too high or too low. The regulatory agency, guarding the public interest, seeks to impose a "fair" or "normal" rate of return on the firm. If the firm is making profits (that is, an abnormally high rate of return), the regulated price must be higher than P_1 of Exhibit 23-8 and therefore that price should be lowered. Alternatively, if the firm is incurring losses (less than the fair or normal rate of return), this indicates that the regulated price is less than P_1, and therefore the firm should be permitted to charge a higher price.

The actual existence of profits, though, is not easily identified. Accounting profit is not the same as economic profit, which focuses on opportunity cost. In addition, regulated firms have a strong incentive to adopt reporting techniques and accounting methods that conceal profits. This will make it difficult for a regulatory agency to identify and impose a price consistent with allocative efficiency.

2. ***Cost Shifting.*** Regulation changes incentives, and therefore it can affect costs. As long as demand is sufficient, the owners of the regulated firm can expect the long-run rate of profit to be essentially fixed, regardless of whether efficient management reduces costs or inefficient management allows costs to increase. If costs decrease, the "fair return" rule imposed by the regulatory agency will force a price reduction; if costs increase, the "fair return" rule will allow a price increase. Compared to the managers of unregulated firms, managers of regulated firms have more freedom to pursue personal objectives and less incentive to seek lower costs. Predictably, they will often fly first-class, entertain lavishly at company expense, grant unwarranted wage increases, and so on. Actions like these will make managerial life more comfortable, but they will also lead to higher unit cost. As the result of the firm's monopoly position, consumers are unable to switch to substitute products (and rival firms) and thereby help to control managerial inefficiency. Normally, wasteful activities would be policed by the owners, but since the firm's rate of return is set by the regulatory agency, the owners have little incentive to be concerned. Prices will be adjusted by regulators to reflect costs as they are. Thus, to a large degree, the incentive structure accompanying price regulation is inconsistent with the minimization of production cost.

3. ***Special-Interest Influence.*** The difficulties of government regulation discussed thus far are practical limitations that a regulatory agency would confront in seeking to perform its duties efficiently. But, in the political arena, regulatory authorities cannot necessarily be expected to pursue only efficiency. Regulated firms have a strong incentive to see that "friendly," "reasonable" people serve as regulators, and they will invest political and economic resources to this end. Just as rent-seeking activities designed to gain monopoly privileges can be expected, so can activities to influence regulatory decisions.

Each competing segment of a regulated industry will try to use the regulatory mechanism for its own competitive advantage. What services and specialized programming should a regulated cable television firm be allowed to offer, at each price? Alternative providers of TV services, such as satellite companies, will work to see that regulated prices and services of the cable firms are set to minimize the ability of cable firms to compete with the providers of satellite video services.

Consumer interests, in contrast to those of industry, are widely dispersed and disorganized. Ordinarily, consumers cannot be expected to invest the time and resources required to understand regulatory policy and the political contributions that are often necessary to influence its direction. The firms that are regulated can, however, be expected to influence regulators by making such investments. Even though the initial stimulus for regulatory action often comes from consumer interests, economic theory suggests that, with time, regulatory commissions are likely to reflect the views of the business and labor interests they were designed to regulate.

4. ***Slow Response to Changing Conditions.*** In a time of rapid change, lack of detailed knowledge and understanding of the industry can reduce the rate at which regulators adjust prices. When costs are falling, "regulatory lag" contributes to suppliers' profits. When costs rise, adjustment is also slower.

Tardiness in the adjustment to changing conditions was a major factor underlying the electricity crisis of California during 2000–2001. Sharply higher crude oil and natural gas prices substantially increased the cost of generating electricity during 2000. Because of its heavy dependence on electricity generated from these sources, these price increases were particularly important in California. While the regulatory commission deliberated, various consumer groups lobbied against rate increases and the regulated retail rates remained well below cost for several months. As time passed, one of California's two largest utility companies, Pacific Gas and Electric, was driven into bankruptcy. The other, Southern California Edison, suffered huge losses and was unable to borrow in the credit market. At the low regulated price, consumers had little incentive to reduce their power use or invest in power-saving appliances, computers, and other capital items. These circumstances combined to yield several months of brown-outs and rotating blackouts in areas of California where the regulated rates applied. Eventually, the regulated utilities were permitted to raise their rates and, in order the deal with the shortfall, the state of California entered into long-term contracts for the import of electricity from other regions. As it turned out, the state's long-term contracts for the import of electricity were negotiated at a time when electricity prices were exceedingly high. Electricity and other energy prices fell substantially as the economy weakened in 2001. Thus, the taxpayers of California are now stuck with an estimated bill of $20 billion to cover the cost of these high-priced electricity imports. As the California case illustrates, while regulation has the potential to improve resource allocation, it is not a magic cure.

Supply Market with Government Production

Government-operated firms—socialized firms such as the U.S. Postal Service, the Tennessee Valley Authority, and many local public utilities—present an alternative to both private monopoly and regulation. However, both theory and experience indicate that socialized firms will fail to counteract fully the problems that stem from high barriers to entry. The same perverse managerial incentives—incentives to ignore efficiency and pursue personal or professional objectives at the firm's expense—that regulated firms confront also tend to plague government-operated firms. In addition, the rational ignorance effect comes into play here. Individual voters have little incentive to acquire information about the operation of government firms because their choices will not be decisive. Predictably, the "owners" of a socialized firm (voters) will be uninformed about how well the firm is run, or how it might be run better. This is especially true when there are no direct competitors against which the firm's performance might easily be compared.

Government-operated firms do not provide an environment that rewards efficient management and reductions in cost. Unlike investors in the private sector, no small group of voters normally is in a position to gain substantial wealth by taking over the socialized firm and improving its management. Even more than with monopoly or oligopoly in the private sector, customers of the socialized monopoly (voter-taxpayers) cannot easily switch their business to other sellers. Even those voter-taxpayers who do not consume the product often have to pay taxes to support its provision. When the government operates a business—particularly one with monopoly power—there is typically less investor scrutiny, less reward for efficiency, and less penalty for inefficiency. Higher costs are an expected result.

Government ownership, like unregulated monopoly and government regulation, is a less than ideal solution. Thus, it should not be surprising that those who denounce monopoly in, for instance, the telephone industry seldom point to a government-operated monopoly—such as the postal service—as an example of how an industry should be run.

Pulling It Together

The policy implications that can legitimately be drawn from an analysis of high barriers to entry are less than fully satisfying. We may not like the reduction in competition or its effects, but economic analysis suggests important qualifications to the "solutions" usually put forth.

Most of the policy alternatives are not terribly attractive. Economies of scale often reduce the attractiveness of antitrust actions. When larger firms have lower per-unit costs, restructuring the industry to increase the number of firms will be both costly and difficult to maintain. Antitrust policy can also be used by rivals to increase the cost of successful firms that have simply given consumers a better deal, and taken a large market share from their competitors in the process. Policy actions to stop or to punish such progress is counterproductive for customers. Government measures, such as tariff reductions and removal of entry barriers into markets, are perhaps the surest recommendation for increasing competition. Such policies, however, will certainly face political opposition, primarily from owners and workers in protected industries.

Regulation is also a less than ideal solution. Regulators do not possess the information necessary to impose an efficient outcome, and they may be susceptible to manipulation by industrial and labor interests. Moreover, since public-sector managers are likely to pursue political objectives at the expense of economic efficiency, public ownership also has shortcomings. Thus, economic theory indicates that there are no ideal solutions when substantial economies of scale are present. Policy choices are made among imperfect alternatives. In this imperfect world, however, consumers have many choices.

9 THE COMPETITIVE PROCESS IN THE REAL WORLD

How competitive are markets? In a very real sense, every firm competes with every other firm for the consumer's additional dollar of spending. Firms in markets that appear to be unrelated often compete with each other. Sellers of compact discs, for example, compete with the bookstore and the local restaurant for our entertainment budgets. The suppliers of swimming pools compete with airlines, hotels, casinos, and automobile rental companies for the vacation and leisure time expenditures of consumers.

Competition to provide better, lower cost goods and services is everywhere. Innovation and nonprice competition on product quality, design, convenience, and other factors is used constantly by firms seeking greater market share and profitability. Like price reductions, improvements in product quality provide consumers with more value per dollar of expenditure. Competition of this type makes collusion more difficult to agree upon and enforce, and it erodes profits even in industries with few rival firms. Patents and technological innovations may temporarily provide firms a measure of protection from rivals. But there is also a positive side to market power of this type: it encourages innovations that improve products and reduce costs.

The pervasiveness of the competitive process helps explain why profit levels, even in manufacturing industries, are considerably lower than many people think. A national sample poll of adults conducted by Opinion Research of Princeton found that the average person thought profits comprised 29 percent of every dollar of sales in manufacturing. In reality, the after-tax accounting profits of manufacturing corporations are about 4 cents to 5 cents per dollar of sales. Competition among manufacturers is generally strong.

The competitiveness of markets is complex and difficult to measure directly. However, economists generally agree that the U.S. economy has become more competitive over the past several decades. Reductions in transport costs, improvements in communications, the development of the Internet, increased competition from imports, and deregulation of several key markets have all tended to enhance the competitiveness of markets in the United States.

10 SUMMARY

- The four major barriers to entry into a market are economies of scale, government licensing, patents, and control of an essential resource.
- Monopoly is present when there is a single seller of a well-defined product for which there are no good substitutes and the entry barriers into the market are high. While there are only a few markets for which the entire output is supplied by a single seller, the monopoly model also helps one better understand the operation of markets dominated by a small number of firms.
- The market demand curve is also the monopolist's demand curve. Like other price searchers, a profit-maximizing monopolist will lower price and expand output as long as marginal revenue exceeds marginal cost. At the maximum-profit output, *MR* will equal *MC*. The monopolist will charge the price on its demand curve consistent with that output.
- If profit is present, high barriers to entry will shield a monopolist from direct competition, and in such cases, monopolists can earn long-run economic profits. Sometimes demand and cost conditions will be such that even a monopolist will be unable to earn economic profit.
- An oligopolistic market is characterized by (1) a small number of rival firms, (2) interdependence among the sellers, (3) substantial economies of scale, and (4) high entry barriers into the market.
- There is no general theory of equilibrium price and output for oligopolistic markets. If rival oligopolists acted totally independent of their competitors, they would drive price down to the per-unit cost of production. Alternatively, if they colluded perfectly, price would rise to the level a monopolist would charge. The actual outcome will generally fall between these two extremes.
- Oligopolists have a strong incentive to collude and raise their prices. However, each firm will be able to gain if it can cut its price (or raise the quality of its product) because the demand curve confronted by the firm is more elastic than the industry demand curve. This introduces a conflict between the interests of individual firms and the industry as a whole. This conflict makes collusive agreements difficult to maintain.
- Oligopolistic firms are less likely to collude successfully against the interests of consumers if (a) the number of rival firms is large; (b) it is costly to prohibit competitors from offering secret price cuts (or quality improvements) to customers; (c) entry barriers are low; (d) market demand conditions tend to be unstable; and/or (e) the threat of antitrust action is present.
- Economists criticize high barriers to market entry because (a) the ability of consumers to discipline producers is weakened, (b) the unregulated monopolist or oligopolist can often gain by restricting output and raising price, and (c) legal barriers to entry will encourage firms to "invest" resources in seeking additional protective barriers and maintaining existing ones.
- A natural monopoly exists when long-run average total costs continue to decline as firm size increases, over the entire range of market demand. Thus, a larger firm always has lower costs.
- When entry barriers are high and competition among rival firms weak, the major policy alternatives are: (a) antitrust action designed to maintain or increase the number of firms in the industry, (b) relaxation of regulations that limit entry and trade, (c) price regulation, and (d) provision of output by government firms. When feasible, option (b) is the most attractive alternative. Under most circumstances, all the other options have shortcomings.
- Competitive forces are present even in markets with high barriers to entry. Quality competition is an important element of the competitive process. Profitability and high prices encourage the development of new technologies and substitute products.

THE SUPPLY OF AND DEMAND FOR PRODUCTIVE RESOURCES

READING 24

LEARNING OUTCOMES

The candidate should be able to:

a. explain the relationship between the price of a resource and the quantity demanded of that resource with reference to supply, demand, and derived demand;

b. identify and describe three factors that may cause shifts in the demand curve for a resource;

c. define the marginal product, marginal revenue, value of marginal product (VMP), marginal revenue product (MRP) of a resource, and explain the relation between MRD and demand for that resource;

d. explain the necessary conditions to achieve the cost-minimizing employment levels for two or more variable resources;

e. discuss the factors that influence resource supply and demand in the short run and long run.

It is . . . necessary to attach price tags to the various factors of production . . . in order to guide those who have the day-to-day decisions to make as to what is plentiful and what is scarce.

—Professor James Meade[1]

INTRODUCTION 1

Recent readings have focused on product markets, markets where consumers purchase goods and services supplied by business firms. Our analysis now shifts to **resource markets**, markets where firms hire productive resources such as machines and workers and use them to produce goods and services. (*Note*: Because resources are also referred to as *factors or inputs*, these markets are also known as *factor markets* or *input markets*.)

Resource markets
Markets in which business firms demand factors of production (for example, labor, capital, and natural resources) from household suppliers. The resources are then used to produce goods and services. These markets are sometimes called factor markets or input markets.

Just as in product markets, the forces of supply and demand combine to determine price in resource markets. The buyers and sellers in resource markets are just the reverse of what they are in product markets. In resource markets,

[1] James E. Meade was a longtime professor of economics at Cambridge University.

business firms are the purchasers; they demand resources that are used to produce goods and services. Households are the sellers; they (and firms they own) supply resources in exchange for income. The income derived from supplying productive resources, such as the wages received from the sale of labor services, provides the major source of income for most of us. Prices in resource markets coordinate the choices of buyers and sellers and bring the amount of each resource demanded into harmony with the amount supplied. Resource prices also help to allocate factors of production efficiently and channel them into the areas in which they are most productive. This enables us to have higher incomes and a larger supply of consumer goods than would otherwise be the case.

As the circular flow diagram of Exhibit 24-1 illustrates, there is a close relationship between product and resource markets. Households earn income by selling factors of production—for example, the services of their labor and capital—to business firms. Their offers to sell form the supply curve in resource markets (bottom loop). The income households derive from the sale of resources provides them with the buying power required to purchase goods and services in product markets. These household expenditures for products generate revenues that provide business firms with the incentive to produce goods and services (top loop). In turn, the business firms demand resources because they contribute to the production of goods and services that can be sold in product markets.

2 HUMAN AND NONHUMAN RESOURCES

Nonhuman resources
The durable, nonhuman inputs that can be used to produce both current and future output. Machines, buildings, land, and raw materials are examples. Investment can increase the supply of nonhuman resources. Economists often use the term physical capital when referring to nonhuman resources.

Broadly speaking, there are two different types of productive inputs, nonhuman and human. **Nonhuman resources** can be further broken down into the categories of physical capital, land, and natural resources. *Physical capital* consists of human-made resources, such as tools, machines, and buildings, that are used to produce other things.

Net investment can increase the supply of nonhuman resources. Investment, however, involves a cost. Resources that are used to produce machines, upgrade the quality of land, or discover natural resources could be used directly to produce goods and services for current consumption. Why take the roundabout path? The answer is that sometimes indirect methods of producing goods are less costly in the long run. For example, Robinson Crusoe found he could catch more fish by taking some time off from hand-fishing to build a net. Even though his initial investment of time in making the net reduced his current catch, once the net was completed he was able to more than make up for this loss. Benefits and costs will influence investment choices ranging from fishing nets to complex machines. These investments will be undertaken only when decision makers expect the benefits of a larger future output to more than offset the current reduction in the production of consumption goods. Just as the supply of machines can be increased, so, too, can wise land development and soil-conservation practices be used to upgrade both the quantity and quality of land. Similarly, the supply of natural resources can be increased (within limits) by the application of more resources to discovery and development.

Human resources
The abilities, skills, and health of human beings that can contribute to the production of both current and future output. Investment in training and education can increase the supply of human resources.

Human resources are composed of the skills and knowledge of workers. Investment in such things as education, training, health, and experience can enhance the skill, ability, and ingenuity of individuals, and thereby increase their

EXHIBIT 24-1 The Market for Resources

Until now, we have focused on product markets, where households demand goods and services that are supplied by firms (upper loop). We now turn to resource markets, where firms demand factors of production—human capital (for example, skills and knowledge of workers) and physical capital (for example, machines, buildings, and land)—which are supplied by households in exchange for income (bottom loop). In resource markets, firms are buyers and households are sellers, just the reverse of the case for product markets.

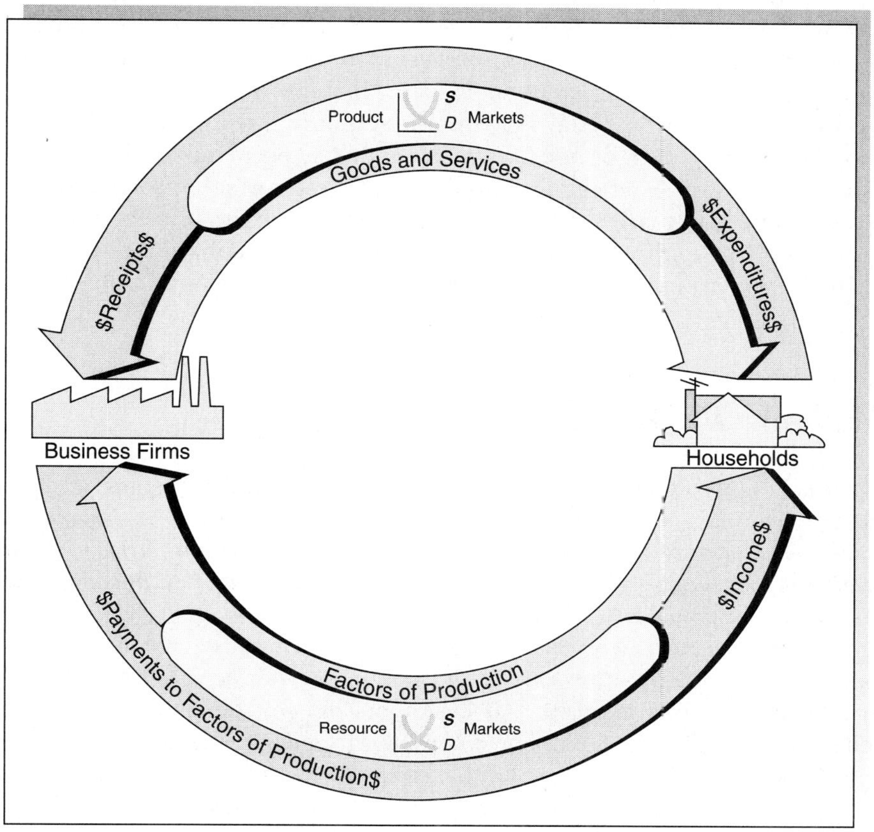

productivity. Economists refer to such activities as **investment in human capital**.[2] Like physical capital, human capital also depreciates (human skills decline with age or lack of use). During any given year, education and training will add to the stock of human capital while depreciation detracts from it.

Investment in human capital
Expenditures on training, education, skill development, and health designed to increase human capital and the productivity of an individual.

Decisions to invest in human capital involve all the basic ingredients of other investment decisions. Consider the decision of whether to go to college. As you know, an investment in a college education requires the sacrifice of current earnings as well as payments for direct expenses, such as tuition and books. The investment is expected to lead to a better job (when both monetary and nonmonetary aspects are considered) and other benefits. The rational investor will

[2] The contributions of T. W. Schultz and Gary Becker to the literature on human capital have been particularly significant. See Ronald G. Ehrenberg and Robert S. Smith, *Modern Labor Economics: Theory and Public Policy*, Seventh Edition (Reading, MA: Addison Wesley, 2000), Chapter 9, for additional detail on human capital theory.

weigh the current costs against the expected future benefits. College will be chosen only if the benefits outweigh the costs.

Human resources differ from nonhuman resources in two important respects. First, human capital is embodied in the individual. Individuals cannot be separated from their knowledge, skills, and health conditions in the same way that they can be separated from physical capital, such as buildings or machines that they might own. As a result, choices concerning the use of human resources are vitally affected by working conditions, location, job prestige, and similar nonpecuniary factors. Although monetary factors influence human capital decisions, individuals will often choose to trade off some money income for better working conditions.

Second, human resources cannot be bought and sold in nonslave societies. Workers sell only the *services* of their labor, not the ownership to the human resource itself. Individuals have the option of quitting, selling their labor services to another employer, or using them in an alternative manner. Thus, we usually speak of the worker as selling (and the firm as buying) labor services.

In competitive markets, the price of resources, like the price of products, is determined by supply and demand. We will begin our analysis of resource markets by focusing on the demand for resources, both human and nonhuman.

3 DEMAND FOR RESOURCES

Profit-seeking producers employ laborers, machines, raw materials, and other resources because they help produce goods and services. ***The demand for a resource exists because there is a demand for goods that the resource helps to produce. The demand for each resource is thus a*** **derived demand*****; it is derived from the demand of consumers for products.***

Derived demand
The demand for a resource; it stems from the demand for the final good the resource helps to produce.

For example, a service station hires mechanics because customers demand repair service, not because the service station owner receives benefits simply from having mechanics around. If customers did not demand repair service, mechanics would not be employed for long. Similarly, the demand for such inputs as carpenters, plumbers, lumber, and glass windows is derived from the demand of consumers for houses and other consumer products these resources help to make. Most resources contribute to the production of numerous goods. For example, glass is used to produce windows, ornaments, dishes, light bulbs, and mirrors, among other things. The total demand for a resource is the sum of the derived demands for it in each of its uses.

Outstanding Economist

Gary Becker (1930–)

This 1992 Nobel Prize recipient is best known for his role in the development of human capital theory and his innovative application of that theory to areas as diverse as employment discrimination, family development, and crime. In his widely acclaimed book *Human Capital,** he developed the theoretical foundation for human investment decisions in education, on-the-job training, migration, and health. Becker is a past president of the American Economic Association and a longtime professor at the University of Chicago.

* Gary Becker, *Human Capital* (New York: Columbia University Press, 1964).

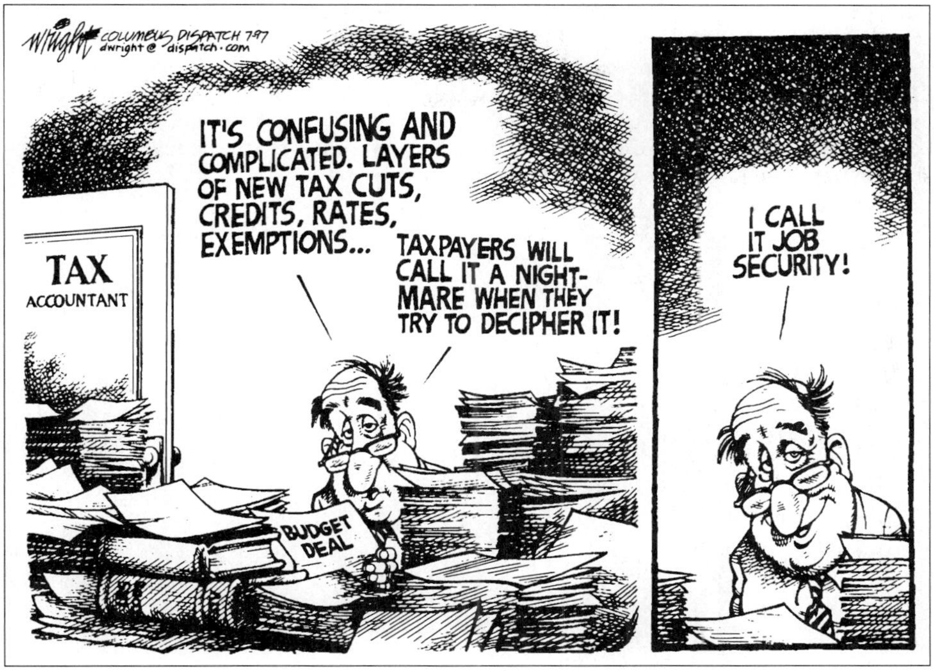

The demand for resources is a derived demand. A more complex tax code would increase the demand for (and thus the wages of) accountants, while a simpler tax code would lower the demand for (and wages of) accountants.

The demand curve for a resource shows the amount of the resource that will be used at different prices. As Exhibit 24-2 illustrates, there will be an inverse relationship between the price of a resource and the amount demanded of it. There are two major reasons why less of a resource will be demanded as its price increases: (1) producers will turn to substitute resources and (2) consumers will buy less of goods that become more expensive as the result of higher resource costs. Let us take a closer look at each of these factors.

Substitution in Production

Firms will use the input combination that minimizes their cost. When the price of a resource goes up, firms will turn to lower-cost substitute inputs and cut back on their use of the more expensive resource.

Typically, there are many ways producers can reduce their use of a more expensive resource. For example, if the price of oak lumber increases, furniture manufacturers will use other wood varieties, metals, and plastics more intensely. Similarly, if the price of copper tubing increases, construction firms and plumbers will substitute plastic pipe for the more expensive tubing. Sometimes producers will alter the style and dimensions of a product in order to conserve on the use of a more expensive resource. In other cases, a shift in location may play a role in the substitution process. For example, if prices of office space and land increase in the downtown area of a large city, firms may move to the suburbs in order to cut back on their use of the more expensive resource.

The degree to which firms will be able to reduce their use of a more expensive resource will vary. The easier it is to turn to substitute factors, the more elastic the demand for a resource. ***Other things constant, the more (and better) substitute resources that are available, the more elastic the demand for the resource.***

EXHIBIT 24-2 The Demand Curve for a Resource

As the price of a resource increases, producers that use the resource intensely will (1) turn to substitute resources and (2) face higher costs, which will lead to higher prices and a reduction in output. At the lower rate of output, producers will use less of the resource that increased in price. Both of these factors contribute to the inverse relationship between the price and amount demanded of a resource.

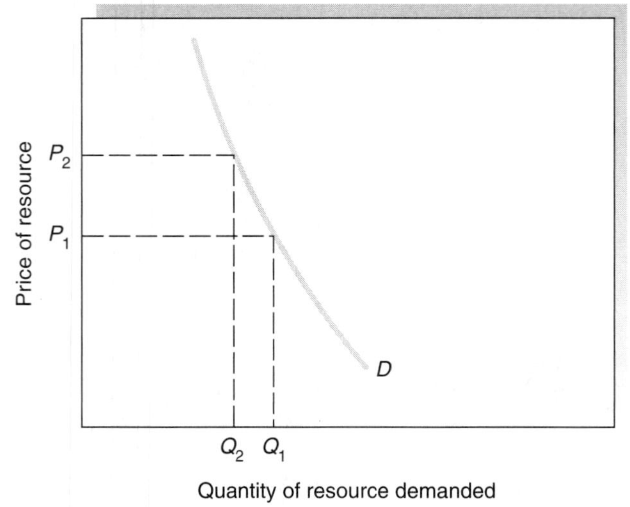

Substitution in Consumption

An increase in the price of a resource will lead to higher costs of production and thus higher prices for the products that the input helps to produce. Faced with these higher prices, *consumers* will turn to substitute products and cut back on their purchases of the more expensive products. In turn, a smaller quantity of resources (including less of the one that rose in price) will be required to produce the smaller amount demanded by consumers at the now higher price.

The experience of the U.S. auto industry in the early 1980s vividly illustrates the importance of the substitution-in-consumption effect. Substantial wage increases pushed the costs of American automakers upward during this period. As the prices of domestically produced autos rose, many consumers switched to substitutes, particularly automobiles produced abroad. The sales of American producers fell sharply, causing a reduction in the quantity of labor demanded (and employment) in the U.S. automobile industry.

Other things constant, the more elastic the demand for the product, the more elastic the demand for the resource. This relationship stems from the derived nature of resource demand. An increase in the price of a product for which consumer demand is highly elastic will cause a sharp reduction in the sales of the good. There will thus also be a relatively sharp decline in the demand for the resources used to produce the good.

In summary, the demand elasticity of a resource will vary with the ease of substitution in both production and consumption. The demand for a resource will tend to be elastic when it is easy to substitute other resources for it in production and when the resource helps produce goods for which demand is relatively elastic. Conversely, the demand for a resource will tend to be inelastic when it is difficult to find good substitutes in production and when the resource is used to produce products for which demand is more inelastic.

Time and the Demand for Resources

The elasticity of resource demand is also influenced by the length of the time period under consideration. It takes time for producers to adjust fully to a change in the price of a resource. Typically, a producer will be unable to alter a production process or the design of a product immediately in order to conserve on the use of a more expensive input or to make better use of an input whose price has declined. Consumers may also find it difficult to alter their consumption patterns quickly in response to price changes. Thus, the demand for a resource generally becomes more elastic with the passage of time.

Exhibit 24-3 illustrates the impact of time on the elasticity of resource demand. Because it is generally difficult to substitute quickly away from a more expensive resource, demand is relatively inelastic in the short run. Thus, an increase in price from P_1 to P_2 will lead to only a small reduction in quantity of the resource used (from Q_1 to Q_2). Given more time, however, producers will be able to make a larger substitution away from the more expensive resource. Therefore, the P_2 price increase elicits a larger reduction in quantity demanded (to Q_3) with the passage of time. In the long run, the demand for a resource is nearly always more elastic than in the short run.

Shifts in the Demand for Resources

Like the demand schedule for a product, the entire demand curve for a resource may shift. There are three reasons why this may occur.

1. ***A change in the demand for a product will cause a similar change in the demand for the resources used to make the product.*** Anything that increases the demand for a consumer good simultaneously increases the demand for resources required to make it. Conversely, a decline in product demand will reduce the demand for resources embodied in the product.

EXHIBIT 24-3 Time and the Demand Elasticity of Resources

The demand for a resource will be more elastic (1) the easier it is for firms to switch to substitute inputs and (2) the more elastic the consumer demand for the products the resource helps to produce. As we illustrate here, demand for a resource in the long run (D_{lr}) is nearly always more elastic than demand in the short run (D_{sr}).

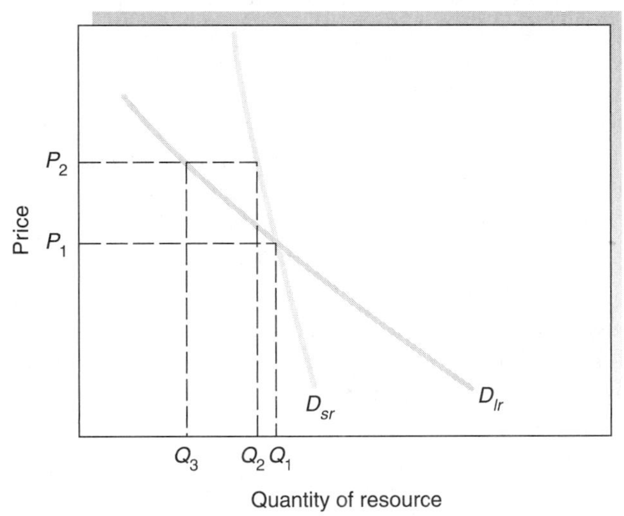

Changes in the music recording industry provide a good example of the linkage between product and resource demand. During the late 1980s and early 1990s, the demand for compact discs increased sharply, driven by the rapidly falling prices of compact disc players. This increase in demand for compact discs led to an increase in demand for workers to produce them. Employment at plants producing the laser optic encoding devices and the types of plastics and metals used to produce the discs expanded rapidly. Similarly, the higher consumer demand for compact discs meant falling demand for vinyl records and tapes. Workers were being laid off at plants producing raw vinyl and related items, such as diamond record player needles. Reflecting the changing demand in product markets, employment in industries related to compact discs expanded, while employment in industries related to records and tapes fell. This reallocation of resources is a natural and integral part of how markets respond to changing consumer demands.

2. ***Changes in the productivity of a resource will alter demand—the higher the productivity of a resource, the greater will be the demand for it.*** As the productivity of a resource increases so does its value to potential employers. Improvements in the quality or skill level of a resource will increase productivity and therefore the demand for the resource. As workers obtain valuable new knowledge and/or upgrade their skills through investments in human capital, they enhance their productivity. In essence, such workers move into a different skill category, one where demand is greater.

   The productivity of a resource will also depend on the amount of other resources with which it is working. In general, additional capital will tend to increase the productivity of labor. For example, someone with a dump truck can haul more material than the same person with a wheelbarrow. The quantity and quality of the tools with which we work significantly affect our productivity.

   This helps to explain why technological advances, like automation or computer technology, do not have a large negative impact on labor employment. While the substitution that occurs in the production process toward the new capital equipment and away from labor lowers the demand for labor, the technology itself makes labor more productive, which tends to increase the demand for labor. This second effect will partially, and sometimes more than completely, offset the first effect. Improvements in the word-processing equipment have enhanced the productivity of secretaries, journalists, lawyers, and writers. Similarly, computers have substantially increased the productivity of typesetters, telephone operators, scientific researchers, and workers in many other occupations.

   These factors help explain why wage rates in the United States, Canada, Western Europe, and Japan are higher than in most other areas of the world. Given the skill level of workers, the technology, and the capital equipment with which they work, individuals in these countries produce more goods and services per hour of labor than workers in most other countries. In turn, the demand for their labor (relative to supply) is greater because of their high productivity. Essentially, the workers' greater productivity leads to their higher wage rates.

3. ***A change in the price of a related resource will affect the demand for the original resource.*** A rise in the price of a resource will cause the demand for substitute resources to expand. For example, when the price of lumber increases, the demand for bricks will increase as home builders switch to building more brick homes and fewer wood homes. Conversely, an increase in the price of a resource that is a *complement* to a given resource will decrease the demand for the given resource. Higher prices for lumber would most likely cause the demand for nails, which are used to hold wood in place, to fall.

MARGINAL PRODUCTIVITY AND THE FIRM'S HIRING DECISION

4

How does a producer decide whether to employ additional units of a resource? Like other decisions, the marginal benefit relative to the marginal cost is the determining factor. Because firms are mostly price takers in resource markets (meaning they can hire as many units of the resource as they wish without affecting the market price of the resource), the marginal cost of hiring one more worker is simply the relevant wage cost, while the marginal cost of purchasing a machine is its price. These represent the increase in the firm's costs that results from employing one more unit of the resource. But what about the marginal benefit of the resource to the firm? It is measured by the increase in the firm's revenue that results from employing one more unit of the resource, the resource's **marginal revenue product** (*MRP*). A profit-maximizing firm will hire an additional unit of the resource only if the marginal revenue product exceeds the cost of employing the resource.

Marginal revenue product *(MRP)*
The change in the total revenue of a firm that results from the employment of one additional unit of a resource. The marginal revenue product of an input is equal to its marginal product multiplied by the marginal revenue of the good or service produced.

Suppose a retail store was considering hiring a security guard at a wage rate of $25 per hour to help reduce shoplifting. If the security guard could prevent $20 worth of shoplifting per hour, should the profit-maximizing firm hire the guard? Because the marginal cost of employing the security guard (the wage of $25) is higher than the guard's marginal revenue product (the $20 reduction in shoplifting per hour), the wise decision is for the firm not to hire the security guard. Hiring the guard would result in a reduction in the firm's profit of $5 per hour. The guard would be employed only if the reduction in shoplifting would exceed the wage cost. In most situations, the direct impact of hiring an additional resource on a firm's revenue is not as clear, so let's take a closer look at the firm's decision and how marginal revenue product is determined.

Employment of a Variable Resource with a Fixed Resource

When an additional unit of the resource is employed relative to a fixed amount of other resources, the direct result is that the firm's output will increase by an amount equal to the resource's **marginal product** (*MP*). Because this is measured in units of physical output, it is sometimes referred to as marginal physical product. How much additional revenue can the firm derive from the employment of the resource? Recall that **marginal revenue** (*MR*) is the increase in the firm's revenue that results from the sale of each additional unit of output. Thus, a resource's marginal revenue product is equal to the marginal product of the resource multiplied by the marginal revenue of the good or service produced. ***Because of the law of diminishing returns, the marginal product of a resource will fall as employment of the resource expands, and thus the marginal revenue product of a resource will also fall as employment expands.***

Marginal product *(MP)*
The change in total output that results from the employment of one additional unit of a resource, one workday of skilled labor for example.

Marginal revenue *(MR)*
The change in a firm's total revenue that results from the production and sale of one additional unit of output.

The relationship between the marginal revenue a firm derives from selling an additional unit of output and the price for which it is sold is different for *price taker* firms than for *price searcher* firms, however. Because a price taker firm sells all units produced at the same price, the price taker's marginal revenue will be equal to the market price of the product. The price searcher, however, must reduce price (for all units) in order to expand the number of units sold. Thus, the price searcher's marginal revenue will be less than the sales price of the units. The marginal product of a resource multiplied by the selling price of the product is called the resource's **value marginal product** (*VMP*). ***For a price taker firm, the* MRP *of a resource is equal to its* VMP *because price and marginal revenue are equal. For a price searcher firm, however, the* MRP *of a resource will be lower than its* VMP *because marginal revenue is less than price.***

Value marginal product *(VMP)*
The marginal product of a resource multiplied by the selling price of the product it helps to produce. For a price taker firm, marginal revenue product (*MRP*) will be equal to the value marginal product (*VMP*).

EXHIBIT 24-4 Short-Run Demand Schedule of a Firm

Compute-Accounting, Inc., uses computer technology and data-entry operators to provide accounting services in a competitive market. For each accounting statement processed, the firm receives a $200 fee (column 4). Given the firm's current fixed capital, column 2 shows how total output changes as additional data-entry operators are hired. The marginal revenue product (*MRP*) schedule (column 6) indicates how hiring an additional operator affects the total revenue of the firm. Since a profit-maximizing firm will hire an additional employee if, and only if, the employee adds more to revenues than to costs, the marginal revenue product curve is the firm's short-run demand curve for the resource (see Exhibit 24-5).

Units of Variable Factor (data-entry operators) (1)	Total Output (accounting statements processed per week) (2)	Marginal Product (change in column 2 divided by change in column 1) (3)	Sales Price per Statement (4)	Total Revenue (2) × (4) (5)	MRP (3) × (4) (6)
0	0.0	—	$200	$ 0	—
1	5.0	5.0	200	1,000	1,000
2	9.0	4.0	200	1,800	800
3	12.0	3.0	200	2,400	600
4	14.0	2.0	200	2,800	400
5	15.5	1.5	200	3,100	300
6	16.5	1.0	200	3,300	200
7	17.0	0.5	200	3,400	100

Using these measures, Exhibit 24-4 illustrates how a firm decides how much of a resource to employ. Compute-Accounting, Inc., uses computer equipment and data entry operators to supply clients with monthly accounting statements. The firm is a price taker: It sells its service in a competitive market for $200 per statement. Given the fixed quantity of computer equipment owned by Compute-Accounting, column 2 relates the employment of data entry operators to the expected total output (quantity of accounting statements). One data entry operator can process five statements per week. When two operators are employed, nine statements can be completed. Column 2 indicates how total output is expected to change as additional data entry operators are employed. Column 3 presents the marginal product schedule for data entry operators. Column 6, the *MRP* schedule, shows how the employment of each additional operator affects total revenue. Both fall as additional operators are employed due to the law of diminishing returns.

Because Compute-Accounting is a price taker, the marginal revenue product and the value marginal product of labor are equal. Thus, the marginal revenue product of labor (column 6) can be calculated by multiplying the marginal product (column 3) times the sales price of an accounting statement (column 4).

How does Compute-Accounting decide how many operators to employ? Answer: it analyzes benefits relative to costs. As additional operators are employed, the output of processed statements (column 2) will increase, which will expand total revenue (column 5). Employment of additional operators, though, will also add to production costs because the operators must be paid. Applying the profit-maximization rule, Compute-Accounting will hire additional operators as long as their employment adds more to revenues than to costs. This will be the case as long as the *MRP* (column 6) of the data-entry operators exceeds their wage rate. At a weekly wage of $1,000, Compute-Accounting would hire only one operator. If the weekly wage dropped to $800, two operators would be hired. At still lower wage rates, additional operators would be hired.

Profit-maximizing firms will expand their employment of each variable resource until the* MRP *of the resource (the firm's additional revenue generated by the resource) is just equal to the price of the resource (the firm's marginal cost of employing the resource). This profit-maximization rule applies to all firms, price takers and price searchers alike.

MRP and the Firm's Demand Curve for a Resource

Using the data in Exhibit 24-4, one can construct Compute-Accounting's demand curve for data entry operators. Recall that the height of a demand curve shows the maximum price (here the wage) the buyer (here the firm) would be willing to pay for the unit. Because the marginal revenue product of the first data entry operator is $1,000, the firm would be willing to hire this worker only up to a maximum price of $1,000. Because of this relationship, as Exhibit 24-5 illustrates, a firm's short-run demand curve for a resource is precisely the *MRP* curve for the resource.[3] Using this demand curve yields the identical solutions as the table. At a weekly wage of $1,000, Compute-Accounting would hire only one operator. If the weekly wage dropped to $800, two operators would be hired. At

EXHIBIT 24-5 The Firm's Demand Curve for a Resource

The firm's demand curve for a resource will reflect the marginal revenue product (*MRP*) of the resource. In the short run, it will slope downward because the marginal product of the resource will fall as more of it is used with a fixed amount of other resources. The location of the *MRP* curve will depend on (1) the price of the product, (2) the productivity of the resource, and (3) the quantity of other factors working with the resource.

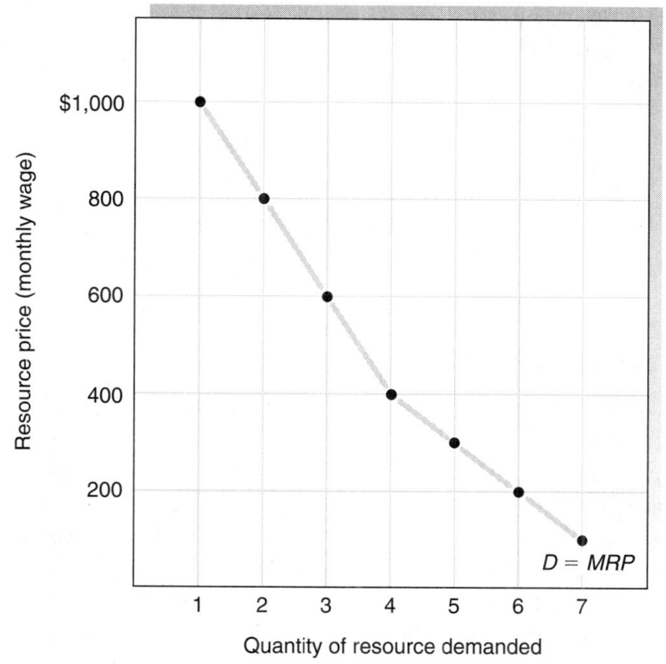

[3] Strictly speaking, this is true only for a variable resource that is employed with a fixed amount of another factor.

still lower wage rates, additional operators would be hired. Underlying the downward-sloping demand curve is the law of diminishing returns causing *MP*, and thus *MRP*, to fall as employment of the resource expands.

The location of the firm's *MRP* curve depends on (1) the price of the product, (2) the productivity of the resource, and (3) the amount of other resources with which the resource is working. Changes in any one of these three factors will cause the *MRP* curve to shift. For example, if Compute-Accounting obtained additional computer equipment that made it possible for the operators to complete more statements each week, the *MRP* curve for labor would increase (shift outward). This increase in the quantity of the other resources working with labor would increase labor's productivity.

Employment Levels When There Are Numerous Factors of Production

Thus far, we have analyzed the firm's hiring decision assuming that it employed one variable resource (labor) and one fixed resource. Production, though, usually involves the use of many resources. How should these resources be combined to produce the product? We can answer this question by considering either the conditions for profit maximization or the conditions for cost minimization.

Profit Maximization When Multiple Resources Are Employed

The same decision-making considerations apply when the firm employs several factors of production. The profit-maximizing firm will expand its employment of a resource as long as the *MRP* of the resource exceeds its employment cost. If we assume that resources are perfectly divisible, the profit-maximizing decision rule implies that, in equilibrium, the *MRP* of each resource will be equal to the price of the resource. Therefore, the following conditions will exist for the profit-maximizing firm:

MRP of skilled labor = Price (wage rate) of skilled labor

MRP of unskilled labor = Price (wage rate) of unskilled labor

MRP of machine A = Price (explicit or implicit rental price) of machine A

and so on, for all other factors.

Cost Minimization When Multiple Resources Are Employed

If the firm is maximizing profits, clearly it must produce the profit-maximizing output at the least possible cost. If the firm is minimizing costs, the marginal dollar expenditure for each resource will have the same impact on output as every other marginal resource expenditure. ***Factors of production will be employed such that the marginal product per last dollar spent on each factor is the same for all factors.***

To see why, consider a situation in which a \$100 expenditure on labor caused output to rise by ten units, whereas an additional \$100 expenditure on machines generated only a five-unit expansion in output. Under these circumstances, five more units of output (at no added cost) would result if the firm spent \$100 less on machines and \$100 more on labor. The firm's *per-unit* cost would be reduced if it substituted labor for machines.

If the marginal dollar spent on one resource increases output by a larger amount than a dollar expenditure on other resources, costs can always be reduced by substituting resources with a high marginal product per dollar expenditure for those with a low one. Substitution will continue to reduce unit costs (and add to profit) until the marginal product per dollar expenditure on each resource is equalized. This will occur because as additional units of a resource are hired, their marginal product will fall. Thus, the proportional relationship between the price of each resource and its marginal product will eventually be achieved.

Therefore, the following condition exists when per unit costs are minimized:

$$\frac{\textbf{MP } \textit{of skilled labor}}{\textit{Price of skilled labor}} = \frac{\textbf{MP } \textit{of unskilled labor}}{\textit{Price of unskilled labor}} = \frac{\textbf{MP } \textit{of machine A}}{\textit{Price (rental value) of machine A}}$$

This relationship, which will be present if a firm is minimizing its per-unit cost of production, indicates why wage differences across skill categories will tend to reflect productivity differences. If skilled workers are twice as productive as unskilled workers, their wage rates will tend toward twice the wage rates of unskilled workers. For example, suppose that a construction firm hiring workers to hang doors is choosing among skilled and unskilled workers. If skilled door hangers can complete four doors per hour, while unskilled workers can hang only two doors per hour, a cost-minimizing firm would hire only skilled workers—as long as their wages are less than twice the wages of unskilled workers. On the other hand, only unskilled workers would be hired if the wages of skilled workers are more than twice that of unskilled workers. With competition, wages across skill categories will tend to mirror productivity differences.

Low wages do not necessarily mean low cost; it is not always cheaper to hire the lowest wage workers. It is not just wages, but rather wages *relative to productivity* that matter. If the wages of skilled workers are twice those of unskilled workers, it will still be cheaper to hire additional skilled workers if their marginal productivity (output per hour) is more than twice that of the unskilled workers.

The importance of wages relative to productivity explains why relatively few firms moved to Mexico following the passage of the North American Free Trade Agreement (NAFTA). Remember the forecast by some of a "giant sucking sound" indicating the movement of both firms and jobs to Mexico? Why didn't the low wages of Mexico cause firms to relocate? *Answer:* While wages are low in Mexico, so, too, is productivity. Given this factor, many firms are able to achieve lower production costs in the high-wage United States than in low-wage Mexico. Suppose that the average wage rate of a U.S. worker is $12 per hour and average hourly productivity is 36 units, while the average wage is $4 per

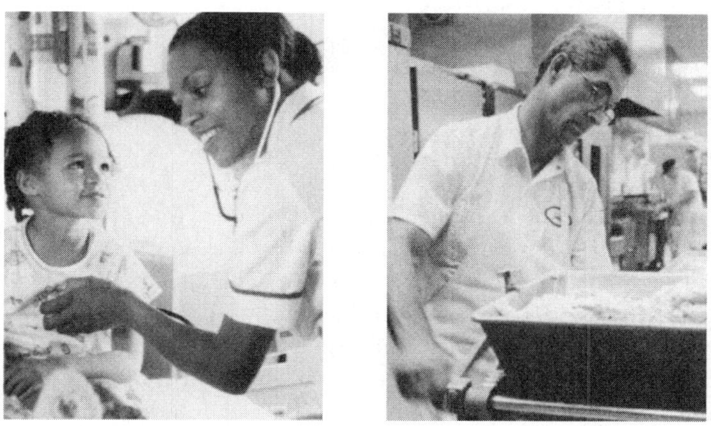

Workers in occupations like nursing that require substantial skill and education will generally earn higher wages than those in occupations requiring little training or experience.

hour in Mexico and average productivity is 8 units. To maximize profits (or minimize costs) a firm should locate wherever *MP/P* is greatest. In the United States the firm would get 3 units of output (36/12) per dollar spent on labor. In Mexico, the firm would get only 2 units of output (8/4) per dollar spent on labor. Thus, a cost-minimizing firm would want to locate in the United States despite the higher wages, because the productivity difference more than makes up for the wage difference. Although U.S. wages are 3 times higher, U.S. productivity is 4.5 times higher. The higher productivity more than compensates for the higher wage cost.

The Central Proposition of the Marginal Productivity Theory of Employment

The central proposition of the marginal productivity theory of resource employment is that firms minimize their per-unit costs of production when they hire additional units of each resource as long as the units' marginal productivity generates revenues in excess of costs. Firms that minimize per-unit costs and maximize profit will never pay more for a unit of input, whether it is skilled labor, a machine, or an acre of land, than the input is worth to them. The worth of a unit of input to the firm is determined by how much additional revenue (marginal revenue product) is expected from its employment.

In the real world, it is sometimes difficult to measure the marginal product of a factor. And, as we have indicated, the marginal product of a resource is influenced by the other factors with which it is employed. Production is a team effort involving interdependent use of resources. We do not mean to imply that business decision makers will necessarily think in terms of equating the marginal product/price ratio (*MP/P*) for each factor of production. Their thought process may well be something like this: "Can we reduce costs by using more of one resource and less of another?" Real-world business decision makers may use experience, trial and error, and intuitive rules as they seek to minimize costs.

Regardless of the methods and procedures used, however, when a firm maximizes profits and minimizes costs, the marginal product/price ratio will be equal for all factors of production. The results will be *as if* the firms had followed the cost-minimization decision-making rules presented earlier. Furthermore, competitive forces will more or less force firms to approximate these minimum cost conditions. Firms that fail to do so will be unable to compete successfully with rivals achieving lower per-unit costs.

The marginal-productivity theory explains the conditions underlying the demand for resources. Of course, resource prices will also be influenced by the supply of resources. We now turn to that topic.

5 SUPPLY OF RESOURCES

In essence, our analysis of resource demand concludes that employers will hire a resource so long as they can gain by doing so. The same basic postulate also applies to resource suppliers. Resource owners will supply their services to an employer only if they perceive that the benefits of doing so exceed their costs (the value of the other things they could do with their time or resources). Thus, in order to attract factors of production, employers must offer resource owners at least as good a deal as they can get elsewhere. For example, if an employer does not offer a potential employee a package of income payments and working conditions that is as good as or better than the worker can get elsewhere, the employer will be unable to attract that worker.

Resource owners will supply their services to those who offer them the best employment alternative, all factors considered. Other things constant, as the price of a specific resource (for example, engineering services, craft labor, or wheat farmland) increases, the incentive of potential suppliers to provide the resource increases.

An increase in the price of a resource will attract potential resource suppliers into the market. A decrease will cause them to shift into other activities. Therefore, as Exhibit 24-6 illustrates, the supply curve for a specific resource will slope upward to the right.[4]

Short-Run Versus Long-Run Resource Supply

As in the case of demand, the supply response in resource markets may vary between the short run and long run. If the wage rate for CPAs rose, for example, we would expect more workers supplying their services as CPAs. But where do these additional CPAs come from? In the short run, the additional supply must come from individuals who possess the necessary skills, but are currently doing other things. The higher wages might induce some college accounting professors and some stay-at-home spouses with accounting credentials to move into employment as CPAs. In the short run, there is insufficient time to alter the availability of a resource through investment in human and physical capital. In contrast, in the long run, resource suppliers have time to adjust their investment

EXHIBIT 24-6 The Supply of a Resource

As the price of a resource increases, individuals have a greater incentive to supply it. Therefore, a direct relationship will exist between the price of a resource and the quantity supplied.

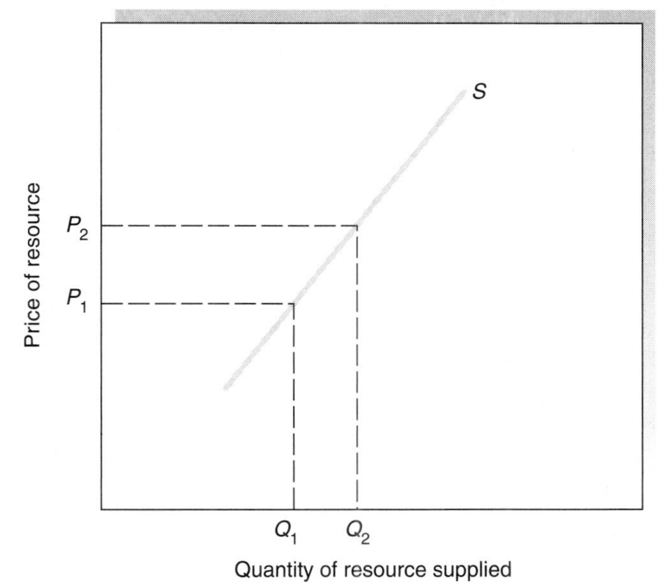

[4] Although the supply for nonhuman resources will always slope upward, the supply of labor at very high wage rates can become backward bending. As wages rise, individuals will substitute toward more work, but simultaneously the higher income will cause them to desire more leisure. At very high wage rates the income effect might dominate, causing a negative relationship between wage rates and quantity of labor supplied in this range. For example, at a wage of $10,000 per hour, many individuals would probably supply fewer hours of work than at $500 per hour!

choices in response to a change in resource prices. With time, the higher wages for CPAs would cause more students to major in accounting, and others to pursue the necessary additional courses to become CPAs. Higher resource prices will increase the quantity supplied in both the short run and the long run, but the response will be greater in the long run. Therefore, as Exhibit 24-7 illustrates, the long-run supply of resources will be more elastic than the short-run supply.

Short-Run Supply

Resource mobility
The ease with which factors of production are able to move among alternative uses. Resources that can easily be transferred to a different use or location are said to be highly mobile. Resources with few alternative uses are immobile.

The short-run supply response to a change in price is determined by how easily the resource can be transferred from one use to another—that is, **resource mobility**. The supply of resources with high resource mobility will be relatively elastic even in the short run. Resources that have few alternative uses (or are not easily transferable) are said to be immobile. The short-run supply of immobile resources will be highly inelastic.

Consider the mobility of labor. Within a skill category (for example, plumber, store manager, accountant, or secretary), labor will be highly mobile within the same geographic area. Movements between geographic areas and from one skill category to another are more costly to accomplish. Labor will thus be less mobile for movements of this variety. In addition, because it is easier for a high-skilled person to perform effectively in a lower-skill position than vice versa, short-run mobility will tend to decline as the skill level of the occupation rises. Thus, the short-run supply curve in high-skill occupations like architect, mechanical engineer, and medical surgeon is usually quite inelastic.

What about the mobility of land? Land is highly mobile among uses when location does not matter. For example, the same land can often be used to raise corn, wheat, soybeans, or oats. Thus, the supply of land allocated to production of each of these commodities will be highly responsive to changes in their relative prices. Undeveloped land on the outskirts of cities is particularly mobile

EXHIBIT 24-7 Time and the Elasticity of Supply for Resources

The supply of certified public accountant (CPA) services and other resources that require a substantial period of time between current investment and expansion in the future quantity supplied will be more elastic in the long run than in the short run.

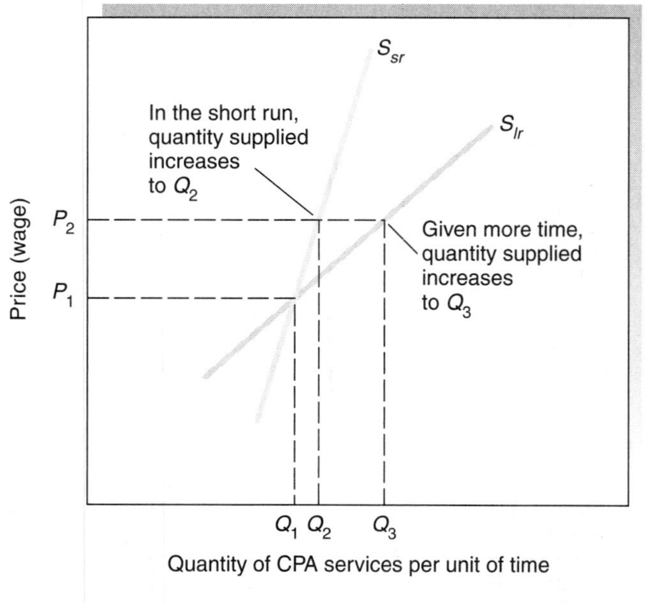

among uses. In addition to its value in agriculture, such land might be quickly subdivided and used for a housing development or a shopping center. Because land is totally immobile physically, one might think that its supply is unresponsive to changes in price that reflect the desirability of a location. However, the supply of usable space at a specific location can be expanded through the construction of multiple-story buildings. As the demand for a given location increases, higher and higher multilevel construction will be justified. This is why tall buildings are generally located in city centers and major satellite areas, the locations with the strongest demand for space.

Machines are typically not very mobile among uses. A machine developed to produce airplane wings is seldom of much use in the production of automobiles, appliances, or other products. Steel mills cannot easily be converted to produce aluminum. There are, of course, some exceptions. Trucks can typically be used to haul a variety of products. Building space can often be converted from one use to another. In the short run, however, immobility and inelasticity of supply characterize much of our physical capital.

Long-Run Supply

In the long run, the supply of resources can change substantially. Machines wear out, human skills depreciate, and even the fertility of land declines with use and erosion. These factors reduce the supply of resources. On the other hand, investment can expand the supply of productive resources. Additional resources can be used to expand the stock of machines, buildings, and durable assets. Correspondingly, investments in training and education can develop and improve the skills of future labor force participants. Thus, the supply of both physical and human resources in the long run is determined primarily by investment and depreciation.

As the price of a resource increases, more and more people will make the investments necessary to supply the resource. This will be true for human as well

The supply curve for truck drivers will be considerably more elastic than the supply of doctors. Can you explain why?

as physical resources. Examples abound. As the spread of the computer revolution pushed the salaries of programmers, systems analysts, and computer technicians upward during the early 1990s, there was a sharp increase in the number of students training for jobs in these areas. In the late 1990s, attractive salaries for physical therapists led to both new programs and expanded enrollments. Higher salaries for lawyers stimulate law school enrollments. According to Harvard University economist Richard Freeman, a 1 percent increase in starting law salaries causes enrollment in the first year of law school to rise by 2 percent.

The long run, of course, is not a specified length of time. Investment can increase the availability of some resources fairly quickly. For example, it does not take very long to train additional over-the-road truck drivers. However, it takes a long time to train physicians, dentists, lawyers, and pharmacists. Higher earnings in these occupations may have only a small impact on their current availability. Additional investment will go into these areas, but it will typically be several years before there is a substantial increase in the quantity supplied in response to higher earnings for these resources.

6 SUPPLY, DEMAND, AND RESOURCE PRICES

In a market economy, resource prices will be determined by the forces of supply and demand. When factor prices are free to vary, resource prices will bring the choices of buyers and sellers into line with each other. Exhibit 24-8 illustrates how the forces of supply and demand push the market wage rates of engineers toward equilibrium, where quantity demanded and quantity supplied are equal. Equilibrium is achieved when the price (wage rate) for engineering services is P_1. Given the market conditions illustrated by Exhibit 24-8, an excess supply is present if the price of engineering services exceeds P_1. Some engi-

EXHIBIT 24-8 Equilibrium in a Resource Market

The market demand for a resource, such as engineering services, is a downward-sloping curve, reflecting the declining *MRP* of the resource. The market supply curve slopes upward because higher resource prices (wage rates) will induce individuals to supply more of the resource. Market price will move toward equilibrium (P_1), where the quantity demanded and quantity supplied are in balance.

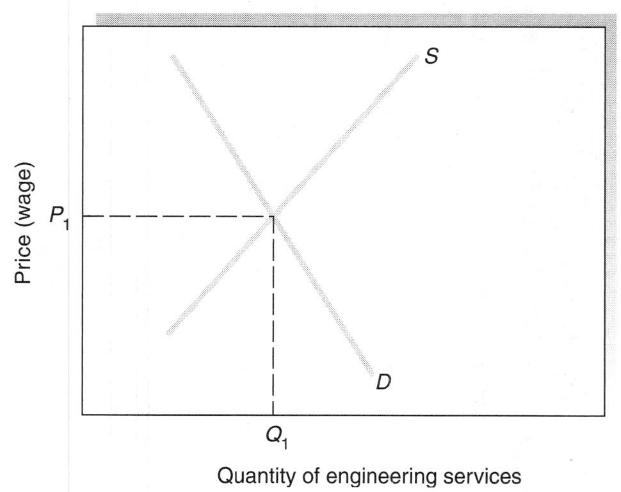

neers will be unable to find jobs at the above-equilibrium wage. This excess supply of engineers will cause the wage rate for engineers to fall, thereby pushing the market toward equilibrium. In contrast, if the resource price is less than P_1, excess demand is present. Employers are unable to obtain the desired amount of engineering services at a below-equilibrium resource price. Rather than doing without the resource, employers will attempt to hire engineers away from other firms by bidding the price up to P_1 and thereby eliminating the excess demand.

How will a resource market adjust to an unexpected change in market conditions? Suppose that there is a sharp increase in the demand for houses, apartments, and office buildings. The increase in demand for these products will also increase the demand for resources required for their construction. Thus, the demand for such resources as steel, lumber, brick, and the labor services of carpenters, architects, and construction engineers will increase. Exhibit 24-9 provides a graphic illustration of both the increase in demand for new houses and buildings (part a) and the accompanying increase in demand for construction engineers. The market demand for the services of construction engineers increases from D_1 to D_2 (part b) and initially there is a sharp rise in their wages (price increases from P_1 to P_2). The higher wages will induce additional people to undertake the education and training necessary to become a construction engineer. With the passage of time, the entry of the newly trained construction engineers will increase the elasticity of the resource supply curve. As these new construction engineers eventually enter the occupation, the supply curve will become more elastic (S_{lr} rather than S_{sr}), which will place downward pressure on wages in the occupation (the move from b to c). Therefore, as part b of

EXHIBIT 24-9 Adjusting to Dynamic Change

An increase in the demand for housing and commercial buildings (part a) will lead to an increase in demand for the services of construction engineers (part b) and other resources used in the construction industry. Initially, the increase in the resource price will be substantial (move from a to b), particularly if the supply of the resource is highly inelastic in the short run. The higher resource price will attract additional human capital investment and, with time, the resource supply curve will become more elastic, which will moderate the price (or wage) increase of the resource (move from b to c).

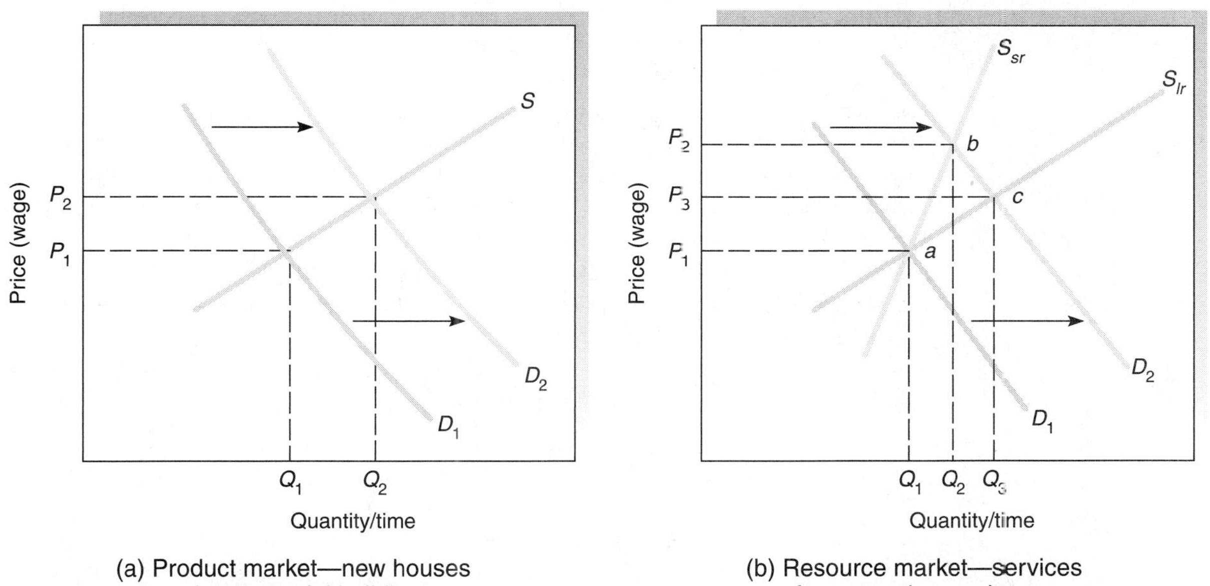

(a) Product market—new houses and commercial buildings

(b) Resource market—services of construction engineers

Exhibit 24-9 illustrates, the long-run price increase (to P_3) will be less than the short-run increase (to P_2).

The supply response and market adjustment for other resources—physical as well as human—will be similar. For example, an unexpected construction boom will generally cause sharp initial increases in the prices of lumber, bricks, and other building materials. With time, however, additional investment will increase the availability of these resources and moderate the increase in their price, just as additional investment in human capital eventually moderated the wage increases of the construction engineers.

The market adjustment to an unexpected reduction in demand for a resource is the same. The price falls farther in the short run than in the long run. At the lower price, some resource suppliers will use their talents in other areas, and the incentive for potential new suppliers to offer the resource will be reduced. Thus, with time, the quantity of the resource supplied will decline, moderating the reduction in price. Those with the poorest alternatives (that is, lowest opportunity cost) will continue to provide the resource at the lower prices. Those with better alternatives will move to other areas.

Pulling things together, our analysis indicates that prices in resource markets play a vitally important role. These prices coordinate the actions of the firms demanding factors of production and the households supplying them. Resource prices provide users with both information on scarcity and the incentive to economize on resource use when producing output. They also provide suppliers with an incentive to learn skills and provide resources—particularly those that are intensely demanded by users. Without the use of resource markets and the price incentives they provide, efficient use and wise conservation of resources would be extremely difficult to achieve.[5]

The Coordinating Function of Resource Prices

Throughout this text we have stressed that profit is a reward earned by producers who increase the value of resources, while loss is a punishment imposed on producers who reduce the value of resources to society. The key links in this process are the prices of the products being sold and the prices of the resources used in production. A firm's profits are its revenues (which are determined by the product price) minus its costs (which are determined by the prices of the resources it uses). The price of the product measures the value that consumers place on that product. The price of the resources, however, measures the value that consumers place on *other products* that could be produced with those same resources. Let us explore the importance of this linkage in a little more detail.

As we have shown, the price of a resource will equal the resource's marginal revenue product when the resource market is in equilibrium. The resource's marginal revenue product depends upon the price consumers are willing to pay for (and thus their value of) the output produced by the resource. When a firm wishes to hire a resource, it must offer that resource a payment at least as attractive as the resource could have earned elsewhere—that is, the resource's *MRP* in its next best alternative employment. Thus, the price a firm pays for a resource is equal to the resource's value (as measured by consumer valuation) in the alternative use. If the output the firm produces with that resource can be sold at a higher price than the price of the alternative outputs, then and only then will the

---

[5] Analysis of energy consumption under central planning illustrates this point. The centrally planned economies both used more energy per unit of output and their energy consumption was less responsive to changes in price than was true for economies that used markets to allocate energy. For evidence on these points, see Mikhail S. Bernstam, *The Wealth of Nations and the Environment* (London: Institute of Economic Affairs, 1991).

firm earn a profit. Thus, profit is a reward to those entrepreneurs who are able to see and act on opportunities to put resources to higher-valued uses. Because consumer tastes and preferences continuously change, so do product and resource prices, and thus these opportunities are created and destroyed on a daily basis in a dynamic market economy.

The ability of resource prices to adjust is essential for a properly functioning market system. They determine the reallocations of resources between industries that allow an economy to satisfy the changing preferences of consumers. The way in which market prices provide an incentive for resources to flow continuously to their highest-valued social uses is indeed the essence of Adam Smith's *invisible hand principle.*

7 SUMMARY

- Productive assets and services are bought and sold in resource markets. These markets help to determine what is produced, how it is produced, and the distribution of income. There are two broad classes of productive resources: (1) nonhuman capital and (2) human capital.
- The demand for resources is derived from the demand for products that the resources help to produce. The quantity of a resource demanded is inversely related to its price because of substitutions made by both producers and consumers.
- The demand curve for a resource, like the demand for a product, may shift. The major factors that can increase the demand for a resource are (a) an increase in demand for products that use the resource, (b) an increase in the productivity of the resource, and (c) an increase in the price of substitute resources.
- Profit-maximizing firms will hire additional units of a resource up to the point where the marginal revenue product (*MRP*) of the resource equals its price. With multiple inputs, firms will expand their usage of each until marginal product divided by price (*MP/P*) is equal across all inputs. When real-world decision makers minimize per-unit costs, the outcome will be as if they had followed these mathematical procedures, even though they may not consciously do so.
- The amount of a resource supplied will be directly related to its price. The supply of a resource will be more elastic in the long run than in the short run. In the long run, investment can increase the supply of both physical and human resources.
- The prices of resources are determined by supply and demand. Changes in the market prices of resources will influence the decisions of both users and suppliers. Higher resource prices give users a greater incentive to turn to substitutes and suppliers a greater incentive to provide more of the resource.
- Changes in resource prices in response to changing market conditions are essential for the efficient allocation of resources in a dynamic world. Profit is a reward to the entrepreneur who is able to see and act on opportunities to put resources to higher-valued uses.

THE FINANCIAL ENVIRONMENT: MARKETS, INSTITUTIONS, AND INTEREST RATES

READING 25

LEARNING OUTCOMES

The candidate should be able to:

a. identify and explain the factors that influence the cost of capital;
b. describe the role of interest rates in allocating capital;
c. explain how the supply of and demand for funds determine interest rates;
d. discuss the factors that cause the supply and demand curves for funds to shift;
e. distinguish between the real and the nominal risk-free rate of interest;
f. discuss economic conditions that can change the real risk-free rate of interest;
g. explain the effect of inflation on the real rate of return earned by financial securities and by physical assets;
h. describe default risk, liquidity risk, and maturity risk premiums;
i. explain interest rate risk and reinvestment rate risk;
j. explain how inflation-indexed bonds can protect investors from inflation and maturity risk.

CITIGROUP BUILT TO COMPETE IN A CHANGING ENVIRONMENT 1

Financial managers and investors don't operate in a vacuum—they make decisions within a large and complex financial environment. This environment includes financial markets and institutions, tax and regulatory policies, and the state of the economy. The environment both defines the available financial alternatives and affects the outcomes of various decisions. Therefore, it is crucial that financial managers and investors have a good understanding of the environment in which they operate.

Good financial decisions require good estimates of movements in the economy, interest rates, and the stock market, but figuring out what's likely to happen is no trivial matter. Throughout most of the 1990s the financial environment was extraordinarily favorable: The stock market registered impressive gains, the economy was strong, and both interest rates and inflation were low. More recently, though, the economy has slowed and the stock market has declined, and accurately predicting the next moves is difficult.

The underlying financial environment has been undergoing tremendous changes, including breakthroughs in technology, increased globalization, and shifts in the regulatory environment. All of these factors have presented financial managers and investors with opportunities, but opportunities accompanied by substantial risks.

Consider the case of Citigroup Inc. which was created in 1998 when Citicorp and Travelers Group (which included the investment firm Salomon Smith Barney) merged. Citigroup today operates in 100 countries, has roughly 200 million customers and 230,000 employees, and holds more than a trillion dollars (that's a thousand billion!) worth of assets.

Citigroup was created because of three important trends: (1) A regulatory change made it possible for a U.S. corporation to be engaged in commercial banking, investment banking, and insurance. (2) Increased globalization made it desirable to follow their clients and operate in many countries. (3) Changing technology led to increased economies of scale and scope, both of which helped spur a rapid consolidation of the financial services industry.

The same forces that are transforming the financial services industry have affected other industries. In particular, the growth of the Internet has provided many companies with increased opportunities, but it has also created additional competition and additional risk. For example, it has altered the way millions of consumers purchase airline tickets, hotel rooms, books, and automobiles. Consequently, financial managers must understand today's technological environment and be ready to change operations as the environment evolves.

PUTTING THINGS IN PERSPECTIVE 2

In earlier readings we discussed financial statements and showed how financial managers and others analyze them to see where their firms have been and are headed. Financial managers also need to understand the environment and markets within which businesses operate. Therefore, this reading describes the markets where capital is raised, securities are traded, and stock prices are established, as well as the institutions that operate in these markets. In the process, we also explore the principal factors that determine the level of interest rates.

THE FINANCIAL MARKETS

3

OPTIONAL SEGMENT

Businesses, individuals, and governments often need to raise capital. For example, suppose Carolina Power & Light (CP&L) forecasts an increase in the demand for electricity in North Carolina, and the company decides to build a new power plant. Because CP&L almost certainly will not have the $1 billion or so necessary to pay for the plant, the company will have to raise this capital in the financial markets. Or suppose Mr. Fong, the proprietor of a San Francisco hardware store, decides to expand into appliances. Where will he get the money to buy the initial inventory of TV sets, washers, and freezers? Similarly, if the Johnson family wants to buy a home that costs $100,000, but they have only $20,000 in savings, how can they raise the additional $80,000? If the city of New York wants to borrow $200 million to finance a new sewer plant, or the federal government needs money to meet its needs, they too need access to the capital markets.

On the other hand, some individuals and firms have incomes that are greater than their current expenditures, so they have funds available to invest. For example, Carol Hawk has an income of $36,000, but her expenses are only $30,000, and in 2001 Ford Motor Company had accumulated roughly $18 billion of cash and marketal securities, which it has available for future investments.

Types of Markets

People and organizations wanting to borrow money are brought together with those having surplus funds in the *financial markets.* Note that "markets" is plural—there are a great many different financial markets in a developed economy such as ours. Each market deals with a somewhat different type of instrument in terms of the instrument's maturity and the assets backing it. Also, different markets serve different types of customers, or operate in different parts of the country. For these reasons it is often useful to classify markets along various dimensions:

1. **Physical asset vs. Financial asset markets.** *Physical asset markets* (also called "tangible" or "real" asset markets) are those for such products as wheat, autos, real estate, computers, and machinery. *Financial asset markets,* on the other hand, deal with stocks, bonds, notes, mortgages, and other *claims on real assets,* as well as with *derivative securities* whose values are *derived* from changes in the prices of other assets.
2. **Spot vs. Futures markets. Spot markets** are markets in which assets are bought or sold for "on-the-spot" delivery (literally, within a few days). **Futures markets** are markets in which participants agree today to buy or sell an asset at some future date. For example, a farmer may enter into a futures contract in which he agrees today to sell 5,000 bushels of soybeans six months from now at a price of $5 a bushel. In contrast, an international food producer looking to buy soybeans in the future may enter into a futures contract in which it agrees to buy soybeans three months from now.
3. **Money vs. Capital markets. Money markets** are the markets for short-term, highly liquid debt securities. The New York, London, and Tokyo money markets are among the world's largest. **Capital markets** are the markets for intermediate- or long-term debt and corporate stocks. The New York Stock Exchange, where the stocks of the largest U.S. corporations are traded, is a prime example of a capital market. There is no hard and fast rule on this, but when describing debt markets, "short term" generally means less than one year, "intermediate term" means one to five years, and "long term" means more than five years.

Spot markets
The markets in which assets are bought or sold for "on-the-spot" delivery.

Futures markets
The markets in which participants agree today to buy or sell an asset at some future date.

Money markets
The financial markets in which funds are borrowed or loaned for short periods (less than one year).

Capital markets
The financial markets for stocks and for intermediate- or long-term debt (one year or longer).

Primary markets
Markets in which corporations raise capital by issuing new securities.

Secondary markets
Markets in which securities and other financial assets are traded among investors after they have been issued by corporations.

Initial public offering (IPO) market
The market in which firms "go public" by offering shares to the public.

Private markets
Markets in which transactions are worked out directly between two parties.

Public markets
Markets in which standardized contracts are traded on organized exchanges.

4. **Primary vs. Secondary markets. Primary markets** are the markets in which corporations raise new capital. If Microsoft were to sell a new issue of common stock to raise capital, this would be a primary market transaction. The corporation selling the newly created stock receives the proceeds from the sale in a primary market transaction. **Secondary markets** are markets in which existing, already outstanding, securities are traded among investors. Thus, if Jane Doe decided to buy 1,000 shares of AT&T stock, the purchase would occur in the secondary market. The New York Stock Exchange is a secondary market, since it deals in outstanding, as opposed to newly issued, stocks and bonds. Secondary markets also exist for mortgages, various other types of loans, and other financial assets. The corporation whose securities are being traded is not involved in a secondary market transaction and, thus, does not receive any funds from such a sale.

   The **initial public offering (IPO) market** is a subset of the primary market. Here firms "go public" by offering shares to the public for the first time. Microsoft had its IPO in 1986. Previously, Bill Gates and other insiders owned all the shares. In many IPOs, the insiders sell some of their shares plus the company sells new shares to raise additional capital. We discuss IPOs in more detail in Chapter 8.
5. **Private vs. Public markets. Private markets,** where transactions are worked out directly between two parties, are differentiated from **public markets**, where standardized contracts are traded on organized exchanges. Bank loans and private placements of debt with insurance companies are examples of private market transactions. Since these transactions are private, they may be structured in any manner that appeals to the two parties. By contrast, securities that are issued in public markets (e.g., common stock and corporate bonds) are ultimately held by a large number of individuals. Public securities must have fairly standardized contractual features, both to appeal to a broad range of investors and also because public investors cannot afford the time to study unique, nonstandardized contracts. Their diverse ownership also ensures that public securities are relatively liquid. Private market securities are, therefore, more tailor-made but less liquid, whereas public market securities are more liquid but subject to greater standardization.

Other classifications could be made, but this breakdown is sufficient to show that there are many types of financial markets. Also, note that the distinctions among markets are often blurred and unimportant, except as a general point of reference. For example, it makes little difference if a firm borrows for 11, 12, or 13 months, hence, whether we have a "money" or "capital" market transaction. You should recognize the big differences among types of markets, but don't get hung up trying to distinguish them at the boundaries.

A healthy economy is dependent on efficient transfers of funds from people who are net savers to firms and individuals who need capital. Without efficient transfers, the economy simply could not function: Carolina Power & Light could not raise capital, so Raleigh's citizens would have no electricity; the Johnson family would not have adequate housing; Carol Hawk would have no place to invest her savings; and so on. Obviously, the level of employment and productivity, hence our standard of living, would be much lower. Therefore, it is absolutely essential that our financial markets function efficiently—not only quickly, but also at a low cost.[1]

[1] As the countries of the former Soviet Union and other Eastern European nations move toward capitalism, just as much attention must be paid to the establishment of cost-efficient financial markets as to electrical power, transportation, communications, and other infrastructure systems. Economic efficiency is simply impossible without a good system for allocating capital within the economy.

Table 25-1 gives a listing of the most important instruments traded in the various financial markets. The instruments are arranged from top to bottom in ascending order of typical length of maturity. As we go through the book, we will look in much more detail at many of the instruments listed in Table 25-1. For example, we will see that there are many varieties of corporate bonds, ranging from "plain vanilla" bonds to bonds that are convertible into common stocks to bonds whose interest payments vary depending on the inflation rate. Still, the table gives an idea of the characteristics and costs of the instruments traded in the major financial markets.

Students can access current and historical interest rates and economic data as well as regional economic data for the states of Arkansas, Illinois, Indiana, Kentucky, Mississippi, Missouri, and Tennessee from the Federal Reserve Economic Data (FRED) site at **http://research.stlouisfed.org/fred/**.

Recent Trends

Financial markets have experienced many changes during the last two decades. Technological advances in computers and telecommunications, along with the globalization of banking and commerce, have led to deregulation, and this has increased competition throughout the world. The result is a much more efficient, internationally linked market, but one that is far more complex than existed a few years ago. While these developments have been largely positive, they have also created problems for policy makers. At a recent conference, Federal Reserve Board Chairman Alan Greenspan stated that modern financial markets "expose national economies to shocks from new and unexpected sources, and with little if any lag." He went on to say that central banks must develop new ways to evaluate and limit risks to the financial system. Large amounts of capital move quickly around the world in response to changes in interest and exchange rates, and these movements can disrupt local institutions and economies.

With globalization has come the need for greater cooperation among regulators at the international level. Various committees are currently working to improve coordination, but the task is not easy. Factors that complicate coordination include (1) the differing structures among nations' banking and securities industries, (2) the trend in Europe toward financial service conglomerates, and (3) a reluctance on the part of individual countries to give up control over their national monetary policies. Still, regulators are unanimous about the need to close the gaps in the supervision of worldwide markets.

Another important trend in recent years has been the increased use of **derivatives**. A derivative is any security whose value is *derived* from the price of some other "underlying" asset. An option to buy IBM stock is a derivative, as is a contract to buy Japanese yen six months from now. The value of the IBM option depends on the price of IBM's stock, and the value of the Japanese yen "future" depends on the exchange rate between yen and dollars. The market for derivatives has grown faster than any other market in recent years, providing corporations with new opportunities but also exposing them to new risks.

Derivative
Any financial asset whose value is derived from the value of some other "underlying" asset.

Derivatives can be used either to reduce risks or to speculate. Suppose an importer's net income tends to fall whenever the dollar falls relative to the yen. That company could reduce its risk by purchasing derivatives that increase in value whenever the dollar declines. This would be called a *hedging operation,* and its purpose is to reduce risk exposure. Speculation, on the other hand, is done in the hope of high returns, but it raises risk exposure. For example, in the late 1990s, Procter & Gamble disclosed that it lost $150 million on derivative investments, and Orange County (California) went bankrupt as a result of its treasurer's speculation in derivatives.

The size and complexity of derivatives transactions concern regulators, academics, and members of Congress. Fed Chairman Greenspan noted that, in theory, derivatives should allow companies to manage risk better, but that it is not clear whether recent innovations have "increased or decreased the inherent stability of the financial system."

Table 25-1 Summary of Major Market Instruments, Market Participants, and Security Characteristics

			Security Characteristics		
Instrument (1)	Market (2)	Major Participants (3)	Riskiness (4)	Original Maturity (5)	Interest Rate on 4/12/02[a] (6)
U.S. Treasury bills	Money	Sold by U.S. Treasury to finance federal expenditures	Default-free	91 days to 1 year	1.68%
Bankers' acceptances	Money	A firm's promise to pay, guaranteed by a bank	Low degree of risk if guaranteed by a strong bank	Up to 180 days	1.90
Dealer commercial paper	Money	Issued by financially secure firms to large investors	Low default risk	Up to 270 days	1.86
Negotiable certificates of deposit (CDs)	Money	Issued by major money-center commercial banks to large investors	Default risk depends on the strength of the issuing bank	Up to 1 year	1.86
Money market mutual funds	Money	Invest in Treasury bills, CDs, and commercial paper; held by individuals and businesses	Low degree of risk	No specific maturity (instant liquidity)	1.56
Eurodollar market time deposits	Money	Issued by banks outside U.S.	Default risk depends on the strength of the issuing bank	Up to 1 year	1.88
Consumer credit loans	Money	Issued by banks/ credit unions/ finance companies to individuals	Risk is variable	Variable	Variable
U.S. Treasury notes and bonds	Capital	Issued by U.S. government	No default risk, but price will decline if interest rates rise	2 to 30 years	5.65

[a] The yields reported (except for the corporate and municipal bonds) are from *The Wall Street Journal.* Money market rates assume a 3-month maturity. The corporate and municipal bond rates are for 30-year AAA-rated bonds; quotes are from **http://www.bondsonline.com**.

Self-Test Questions

Distinguish between physical asset and financial asset markets.

What is the difference between spot and futures markets?

Distinguish between money and capital markets.

What is the difference between primary and secondary markets?

Differentiate between private and public markets.

Why are financial markets essential for a healthy economy?

What is a derivative, and how is its value related to that of an "underlying asset"?

Table 25-1 continued

Instrument (1)	Market (2)	Major Participants (3)	Security Characteristics: Riskiness (4)	Original Maturity (5)	Interest Rate on 4/12/02[a] (6)
Mortgages	Capital	Borrowings from commercial banks and S&Ls by individuals and businesses	Risk is variable	Up to 30 years	6.53%
State and local government bonds	Capital	Issued by state and local governments to individuals and institutional investors	Riskier than U.S. government securities, but exempt from most taxes	Up to 30 years	5.22
Corporate bonds	Capital	Issued by corporations to individuals and institutional investors	Riskier than U.S. government securities, but less risky than preferred and common stocks; varying degree of risk within bonds depending on strength of issuer	Up to 40 years[b]	6.79
Leases	Capital	Similiar to debt in that firms can lease assets rather than borrow and then buy the assets	Risk similar to corporate bonds	Generally 3 to 20 years	Similar to bond yields
Preferred stocks	Capital	Issued by corporations to individuals and institutional investors	Riskier than corporate bonds, but less risky than common stock	Unlimited	7 to 9%
Common stocks[c]	Capital	Issued by corporations to individuals and institutional investors	Risky	Unlimited	NA

[b] Just recently, a few corporations have issued 100-year bonds; however, the majority have issued bonds with maturities less than 40 years.

[c] While common stocks do not pay interest, they are expected to provide a "return" in the form of dividends and capital gains. As you will see in Chapter 5, historical stock returns have averaged between 10 and 15 percent a year. Of course, if you buy a stock, your *actual* return may be considerably higher or lower than these historical averages.

FINANCIAL INSTITUTIONS 4

Transfers of capital between savers and those who need capital take place in the three different ways diagrammed in Figure 25-1:

1. *Direct transfers* of money and securities, as shown in the top section, occur when a business sells its stocks or bonds directly to savers, without going through any type of financial institution. The business delivers its securities to savers, who in turn give the firm the money it needs.

FIGURE 25-1 Diagram of the Capital Formation Process

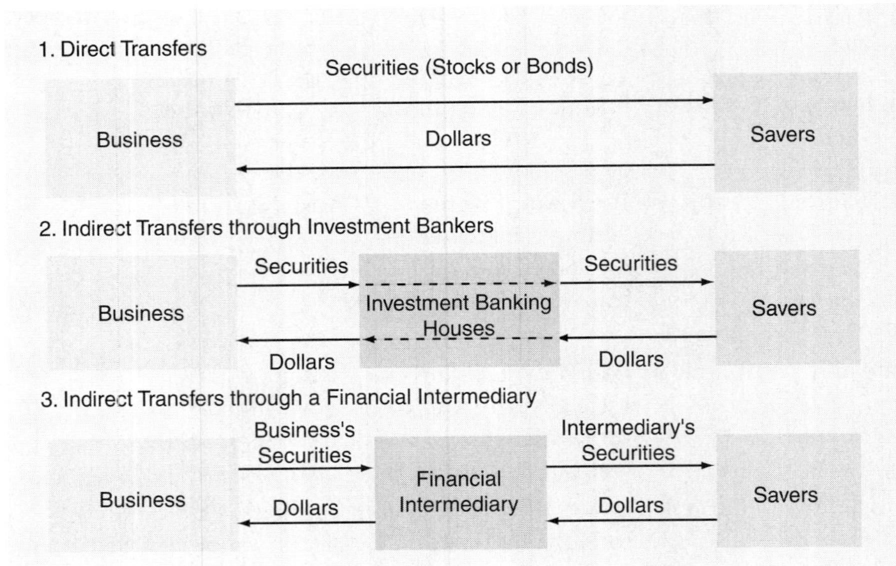

2. As shown in the middle section, transfers may also go through an *investment banking house* such as Merrill Lynch, which *underwrites* the issue. An underwriter serves as a middleman and facilitates the issuance of securities. The company sells its stocks or bonds to the investment bank, which in turn sells these same securities to savers. The businesses' securities and the savers' money merely "pass through" the investment banking house. However, the investment bank does buy and hold the securities for a period of time, so it is taking a risk—it may not be able to resell them to savers for as much as it paid. Because new securities are involved and the corporation receives the proceeds of the sale, this is a primary market transaction.
3. Transfers can also be made through a *financial intermediary* such as a bank or mutual fund. Here the intermediary obtains funds from savers in exchange for its own securities. The intermediary then uses this money to purchase and then hold businesses' securities. For example, a saver might give dollars to a bank, receiving from it a certificate of deposit, and then the bank might lend the money to a small business in the form of a mortgage loan. Thus, intermediaries literally create new forms of capital—in this case, certificates of deposit, which are both safer and more liquid than mortgages and thus are better securities for most savers to hold. The existence of intermediaries greatly increases the efficiency of money and capital markets.

In our example, we assume that the entity needing capital is a business, and specifically a corporation, but it is easy to visualize the demander of capital as a home purchaser, a government unit, and so on.

Investment banking house
An organization that underwrites and distributes new investment securities and helps businesses obtain financing.

Direct transfers of funds from savers to businesses are possible and do occur on occasion, but it is generally more efficient for a business to enlist the services of an **investment banking house** such as Merrill Lynch, Salomon Smith Barney, Morgan Stanley Dean Witter, or Goldman Sachs. Such organizations (1) help corporations design securities with features that are currently attractive to investors, (2) then buy these securities from the corporation, and (3) resell them to savers. Although the securities are sold twice, this process is really one primary market transaction, with the investment banker acting as a facilitator to help transfer capital from savers to businesses.

Financial intermediaries Specialized financial firms that facilitate the transfer of funds from savers to demanders of capital.

The **financial intermediaries** shown in the third section of Figure 25-1 do more than simply transfer money and securities between firms and savers—they literally create new financial products. Since the intermediaries are generally large, they gain economies of scale in analyzing the creditworthiness of potential borrowers, in processing and collecting loans, and in pooling risks and thus helping individual savers diversify, that is, "not putting all their financial eggs in one basket." Further, a system of specialized intermediaries can enable savings to do more than just draw interest. For example, individuals can put money into banks and get both interest income and a convenient way of making payments (checking), or put money into life insurance companies and get both interest income and protection for their beneficiaries.

In the United States and other developed nations, a set of specialized, highly efficient financial intermediaries has evolved. The situation is changing rapidly, however, and different types of institutions are performing services that were formerly reserved for others, causing institutional distinctions to become blurred. Still, there is a degree of institutional identity, and here are the major classes of intermediaries:

1. *Commercial banks,* the traditional "department stores of finance," serve a wide variety of savers and borrowers. Historically, commercial banks were the major institutions that handled checking accounts and through which the Federal Reserve System expanded or contracted the money supply. Today, however, several other institutions also provide checking services and significantly influence the money supply. Conversely, commercial banks are providing an ever-widening range of services, including stock brokerage services and insurance.
2. *Savings and loan associations (S&Ls),* which have traditionally served individual savers and residential and commercial mortgage borrowers, take the funds of many small savers and then lend this money to home buyers and other types of borrowers. In the 1980s, the S&L industry experienced severe problems when (a) short-term interest rates paid on savings accounts rose well above the returns being earned on the existing mortgages held by S&Ls and (b) commercial real estate suffered a severe slump, resulting in high mortgage default rates. Together, these events forced many S&Ls to either merge with stronger institutions or close their doors.
3. *Mutual savings banks,* which are similar to S&Ls, operate primarily in the northeastern states, accept savings primarily from individuals, and lend mainly on a long-term basis to home buyers and consumers.
4. *Credit unions* are cooperative associations whose members are supposed to have a common bond, such as being employees of the same firm. Members' savings are loaned only to other members, generally for auto purchases, home improvement loans, and home mortgages. Credit unions are often the cheapest source of funds available to individual borrowers.
5. *Pension funds* are retirement plans funded by corporations or government agencies for their workers and administered primarily by the trust departments of commercial banks or by life insurance companies. Pension funds invest primarily in bonds, stocks, mortgages, and real estate.
6. *Life insurance companies* take savings in the form of annual premiums; invest these funds in stocks, bonds, real estate, and mortgages; and finally make payments to the beneficiaries of the insured parties. In recent years, life insurance companies have also offered a variety of tax-deferred savings plans designed to provide benefits to the participants when they retire.

7. *Mutual funds* are corporations that accept money from savers and then use these funds to buy stocks, long-term bonds, or short-term debt instruments issued by businesses or government units. These organizations pool funds and thus reduce risks by diversification. They also achieve economies of scale in analyzing securities, managing portfolios, and buying and selling securities. Different funds are designed to meet the objectives of different types of savers. Hence, there are bond funds for those who desire safety, stock funds for savers who are willing to accept significant risks in the hope of higher returns, and still other funds that are used as interest-bearing checking accounts (the **money market funds**). There are literally thousands of different mutual funds with dozens of different goals and purposes.

Money market fund A mutual fund that invests in short-term, low-risk securities and allows investors to write checks against their accounts.

Mutual funds have grown more rapidly than any other institution in recent years, in large part because of a change in the way corporations provide for employees' retirement. Before the 1980s, most corporations said, in effect, "Come work for us, and when you retire, we will give you a retirement income based on the salary you were earning during the last five years before you retired." The company was then responsible for setting aside funds each year to make sure that it had the money available to pay the agreed-upon retirement benefits. That situation is changing rapidly. Today, new employees are likely to be told, "Come work for us, and we will give you some money each payday that you can invest for your future retirement. You can't get the money until you retire (without paying a huge tax penalty), but if you invest wisely, you can retire in comfort." Most workers know they don't know how to invest wisely, so they turn their retirement funds over to a mutual fund. Hence, mutual funds are growing rapidly. Excellent information on the objectives and past performances of the various funds are provided in publications such as *Value Line Investment Survey* and *Morningstar Mutual Funds,* which are available in most libraries.

Financial institutions have historically been heavily regulated, with the primary purpose of this regulation being to ensure the safety of the institutions and thus to protect investors. However, these regulations—which have taken the form of prohibitions on nationwide branch banking, restrictions on the types of assets the institutions can buy, ceilings on the interest rates they can pay, and limitations on the types of services they can provide—have tended to impede the free flow of capital and thus have hurt the efficiency of our capital markets. Recognizing this fact, Congress has authorized some major changes, and more are on the horizon.

The result of the ongoing regulatory changes has been a blurring of the distinctions between the different types of institutions. Indeed, the trend in the United States today is toward huge **financial service corporations**, which own banks, S&Ls, investment banking houses, insurance companies, pension plan operations, and mutual funds, and which have branches across the country and around the world. Examples of financial service corporations, most of which started in one area but have now diversified to cover most of the financial spectrum, include Merrill Lynch, American Express, Citigroup, Fidelity, and Prudential.

Financial service corporation A firm that offers a wide range of financial services, including investment banking, brokerage operations, insurance, and commercial banking.

Panel a of Table 25-2 lists the 10 largest U.S. bank and thrift holding companies, and panel b shows the leading world banking companies. Among the world's 10 largest, only two (Citigroup and J. P. Morgan Chase) are from the United States. While U.S. banks have grown dramatically as a result of recent mergers, they are still small by global standards. Panel c of the table lists the 10 leading underwriters in terms of dollar volume of new issues. Six of the top underwriters are also major commercial banks or are part of bank holding companies, which confirms the continued blurring of distinctions among different types of financial institutions.

Table 25-2 10 Largest U.S. Bank and Thrift Holding Companies and World Banking Companies and Top 10 Leading Underwriters

Panel A U.S. Bank and Thrift Holding Companies[a]	Panel B World Banking Companies[b]	Panel C Leading Global Underwriters[c]
Citigroup Inc.	Mizuho Holdings (Tokyo)	Citigroup/Salomon Smith Barney
J. P. Morgan Chase & Co.	Citigroup Inc. (New York)	Merrill Lynch
Bank of America Corp.	Sumitomo Mitsui Banking Corp. (Tokyo)	Credit Suisse First Boston
Wachovia Corp.	Mitsubishi Tokyo Financial Group (Tokyo)	J. P. Morgan Chase & Co.
Wells Fargo & Co.	Deutsche Bank (Frankfurt)	Goldman Sachs
Bank One Corp.	Allianz AG (Munich)	Morgan Stanley Dean Witter
MetLife Inc.	UBS AG (Zurich)	Lehman Brothers
Taunus Corp.	BNP Paribas (Paris)	UBS Warburg
Washington Mutual Inc.	HSBC Holdings PLC (London)	Deutsche Bank
FleetBoston Financial Corp.	J. P. Morgan Chase & Co. (New York)	Banc of America Securities

NOTES:

[a] Ranked by total assets as of December 31, 2001. SOURCE: "Top 150 Bank and SL Holding Companies by Yearend '01 Assets," AmericanBanker.com, June 11, 2002.

[b] Ranked by total assets as of December 31, 2001. SOURCE: "World's Top Banking Companies by Assets," AmericanBanker.com, July 12, 2002.

[c] Ranked by dollar amount raised through new issues in 2001. For this ranking, the lead underwriter (manager) is given credit for the entire issue.

Source: Adapted from *The Wall Street Journal,* January 2, 2002, R19.

Self-Test Questions

Identify three different ways capital is transferred between savers and borrowers.

What is the difference between a commercial bank and an investment bank?

Distinguish between investment banking houses and financial intermediaries.

List the major types of intermediaries and briefly describe the primary function of each.

THE STOCK MARKET 5

As noted earlier, secondary markets are those in which outstanding, previously issued securities are traded. By far the most active secondary market, and the most important one to financial managers, is the *stock market,* where the prices of firms' stocks are established. Since the primary goal of financial management is to maximize the firm's stock price, a knowledge of the stock market is important to anyone involved in managing a business.

While the two leading stock markets today are the New York Stock Exchange and the Nasdaq stock market, stocks are actually traded using a variety of market procedures. However, there are just two basic types of stock markets: (1) *physical location exchanges,* which include the New York Stock Exchange (NYSE), the American Stock Exchange (AMEX), and several regional stock exchanges, and (2) electronic dealer-based markets that include the Nasdaq stock market, the less formal over-the-counter market, and the recently developed electronic communications networks (ECNs). (See the Technology Matters box entitled, "Online Trading Systems" on the next page.) Because the physical location exchanges are easier to describe and understand, we consider them first.

The Physical Location Stock Exchanges

Physical location exchanges
Formal organizations having tangible physical locations that conduct auction markets in designated ("listed") securities.

The **physical location exchanges** are tangible physical entities. Each of the larger ones occupies its own building, has a limited number of members, and has an elected governing body—its board of governors. Members are said to have "seats" on the exchange, although everybody stands up. These seats, which are bought and sold, give the holder the right to trade on the exchange. There are currently 1,366 seats on the New York Stock Exchange, and on February 19, 2002, two seats on the NYSE sold for $2.5 million and $2.475 million each, which was down from the previous high of $2.65 million.

Most of the larger investment banking houses operate *brokerage departments,* and they own seats on the exchanges and designate one or more of their officers as members. The exchanges are open on all normal working days, with the members meeting in a large room equipped with telephones and other electronic equipment that enable each member to communicate with his or her firm's offices throughout the country.

You can access the home pages of the major U.S. stock markets by typing http://www.nyse.com or http://www.nasdaq.com. These sites provide background information as well as the opportunity to obtain individual stock quotes.

Like other markets, security exchanges facilitate communication between buyers and sellers. For example, Merrill Lynch (the second largest brokerage firm) might receive an order in its Atlanta office from a customer who wants to buy shares of AT&T stock. Simultaneously, Morgan Stanley Dean Witter's Denver office might receive an order from a customer wishing to sell shares of AT&T. Each broker communicates electronically with the firm's representative on the NYSE. Other brokers throughout the country are also communicating with their own exchange members. The exchange members with *sell orders* offer the shares for sale, and they are bid for by the members with *buy orders.* Thus, the exchanges operate as *auction markets.*[2]

---

[2] The NYSE is actually a modified auction market, wherein people (through their brokers) bid for stocks. Originally—about 200 years ago—brokers would literally shout, "I have 100 shares of Erie for sale; how much am I offered?" and then sell to the highest bidder. If a broker had a buy order, he or she would shout, "I want to buy 100 shares of Erie; who'll sell at the best price?" The same general situation still exists, although the exchanges now have members known as *specialists* who facilitate the trading process by keeping an inventory of shares of the stocks in which they specialize. If a buy order comes in at a time when no sell order arrives, the specialist will sell off some inventory. Similarly, if a sell order comes in, the specialist will buy and add to inventory. The specialist sets a *bid price* (the price the specialist will pay for the stock) and an *asked price* (the price at which shares will be sold out of inventory). The bid and asked prices are set at levels designed to keep the inventory in balance. If many buy orders start coming in because of favorable developments or sell orders come in because of unfavorable events, the specialist will raise or lower prices to keep supply and demand in balance. Bid prices are somewhat lower than asked prices, with the difference, or *spread,* representing the specialist's profit margin.

Special facilities are available to help institutional investors such as mutual funds or pension funds sell large blocks of stock without depressing their prices. In essence, brokerage houses that cater to institutional clients will purchase blocks (defined as 10,000 or more shares) and then resell the stock to other institutions or individuals. Also, when a firm has a major announcement that is likely to cause its stock price to change sharply, it will ask the exchanges to halt trading in its stock until the announcement has been made and digested by investors.

TECHNOLOGY MATTERS

Online Trading Systems

The forces described in the vignette that have spurred the consolidation of the financial services industry have also promoted online trading systems that bypass the traditional exchanges. These systems, known as Electronic Communications Networks (ECNs), use technology to bring buyers and sellers together electronically. ECNs have already captured about 30 percent of Nasdaq's trading volume, and the vast majority of these transactions are conducted by three firms: Instinet, Island, and the recently merged firm of Archipelago and Redibook. In mid-2002, Instinet had also begun talks to explore buying Island ECN. If that merger is consumated, the two firms will have about 22 percent of Nasdaq's trading volume, which will provide more liquidity and the ability to spread the cost of new technology over more trades. If this transaction is completed, the combined company would pose an even more significant threat to Nasdaq.

In either event, ECNs will accelerate the move toward 24-hour trading. Large clients who want to trade after the other markets have closed may utilize an ECN, bypassing the NYSE and Nasdaq. The move toward faster, cheaper, and continuous trading obviously benefits investors, but it does present regulators, who try to ensure that all investors have access to a "level playing field," with a number of headaches.

Because of the threat from ECNs and the need to raise capital and increase flexibility, both the NYSE and Nasdaq plan to convert from privately held, member-owned businesses to stockholder-owned, for-profit corporations. This suggests that the financial landscape will continue to undergo dramatic changes in the upcoming years.

Sources: Katrina Brooker, "Online Investing: It's Not Just for Geeks Anymore," *Fortune,* December 21, 1998, 89–98; 'Fidelity, Schwab Part of Deal to Create Nasdaq Challenger," *The Milwaukee Journal Sentinel,* July 22, 1999, 1; and "Instinet Group Is Holding Talks to Buy Island ECN," *The Wall Street Journal,* May 16, 2002, C1.

The Over-the-Counter and the Nasdaq Stock Markets

While the stocks of most large companies trade on the NYSE, a larger number of stocks trade off the exchange in what has traditionally been referred to as the **over-the-counter market (OTC)**. An explanation of the term "over-the-counter" will help clarify how this term arose. As noted earlier, the exchanges operate as auction markets—buy and sell orders come in more or less simultaneously, and exchange members match these orders. If a stock is traded infrequently, perhaps because the firm is new or small, few buy and sell orders come in, and matching them within a reasonable amount of time would be difficult. To avoid this problem, some brokerage firms maintain an inventory of such stocks and stand prepared to make a market for these stocks. These "dealers" buy when individual investors want to sell, and then sell part of their inventory when investors want to buy. At one time, the inventory of securities was kept in a safe, and the stocks, when bought and sold, were literally passed over the counter.

Over-the-counter market (OTC)
A large collection of brokers and dealers, connected electronically by telephones and computers, that provides for trading in unlisted securities.

Today, these markets are often referred to as **dealer markets**. A dealer market is defined to include all facilities that are needed to conduct security transactions not made on the physical location exchanges. These facilities include (1) the relatively few *dealers* who hold inventories of these securities and who are said to "make a market" in these securities; (2) the thousands of brokers who act as *agents* in bringing the dealers together with investors; and (3) the computers, terminals, and electronic networks that provide a communication link between dealers and brokers. The dealers who make a market in a particular stock quote the price at which they will pay for the stock (the *bid price*) and the price at which they will sell shares (the *ask price*). Each dealer's prices, which are adjusted as supply and demand conditions change, can be read off computer screens all across the world. The *bid-ask spread,* which is the difference between bid and ask prices, represents the dealer's markup, or profit. The dealer's risk increases if the stock is more volatile, or if the stock trades infrequently. Generally, we would expect

Dealer market
Includes all facilities that are needed to conduct security transactions not conducted on the physical location exchanges.

volatile, infrequently traded stocks to have wider spreads in order to compensate the dealers for assuming the risk of holding them in inventory.

Brokers and dealers who participate in the over-the-counter market are members of a self-regulatory body known as the *National Association of Securities Dealers (NASD)*, which licenses brokers and oversees trading practices. The computerized network used by the NASD is known as the NASD Automated Quotation System.

Nasdaq started as just a quotation system, but it has grown to become an organized securities market with its own listing requirements. Over the past decade the competition between the NYSE and Nasdaq has become increasingly fierce. In an effort to become more competitive with the NYSE and with international markets, the Nasdaq and the AMEX merged in 1998 to form the Nasdaq-Amex Market Group, which might best be referred to as an *organized investment network*. This investment network is often referred to as Nasdaq, but stocks continue to be traded and reported separately on the two markets. Increased competition among global stock markets assuredly will result in similar alliances among other exchanges and markets in the future.

Since most of the largest companies trade on the NYSE, the market capitalization of NYSE-traded stocks is much higher than for stocks traded on Nasdaq ($11.7 trillion compared with $2.9 trillion at year-end 2001). However, reported volume (number of shares traded) is often larger on Nasdaq, and more companies are listed on Nasdaq.[3]

Interestingly, many high-tech companies such as Microsoft and Intel have remained on Nasdaq even though they easily meet the listing requirements of the NYSE. At the same time, however, other high-tech companies such as Gateway 2000, America Online, and Iomega have left Nasdaq for the NYSE. Despite these defections, Nasdaq's growth over the past decade has been impressive. In the years ahead, the competition will no doubt remain fierce.

Self-Test Questions

What are the differences between the physical location exchanges and the Nasdaq stock market?

What is the bid-ask spread?

OPTIONAL ENDS SEGMENT

6 THE COST OF MONEY

Production opportunities
The returns available within an economy from investments in productive (cash-generating) assets.

Time preferences for consumption
The preferences of consumers for current consumption as opposed to saving for future consumption.

Capital in a free economy is allocated through the price system. *The interest rate is the price paid to borrow debt capital. With equity capital, investors expect to receive dividends and capital gains, whose sum is the cost of equity money.* The factors that affect supply of and demand for investment capital, hence the cost of money, are discussed in this section.

The four most fundamental factors affecting the cost of money are (1) **production opportunities**, (2) **time preferences for consumption**, (3) **risk**, and (4) **inflation**. To see how these factors operate, visualize an isolated island community where the people live on fish. They have a stock of fishing gear that per-

---

[3] One transaction on Nasdaq generally shows up as two separate trades (the buy and the sell). This "double counting" makes it difficult to compare the volume between stock markets.

mits them to survive reasonably well, but they would like to have more fish. Now suppose Mr. Crusoe had a bright idea for a new type of fishnet that would enable him to double his daily catch. However, it would take him a year to perfect his design, to build his net, and to learn how to use it efficiently, and Mr. Crusoe would probably starve before he could put his new net into operation. Therefore, he might suggest to Ms. Robinson, Mr. Friday, and several others that if they would give him one fish each day for a year, he would return two fish a day during all of the next year. If someone accepted the offer, then the fish that Ms. Robinson or one of the others gave to Mr. Crusoe would constitute *savings;* these savings would be *invested* in the fishnet; and the extra fish the net produced would constitute a *return on the investment.*

Risk
In a financial market context, the chance that an investment will provide a low or negative return.

Inflation
The amount by which prices increase over time.

Obviously, the more productive Mr. Crusoe thought the new fishnet would be, the more he could afford to offer potential investors for their savings. In this example, we assume that Mr. Crusoe thought he would be able to pay, and thus he offered, a 100 percent rate of return—he offered to give back two fish for every one he received. He might have tried to attract savings for less—for example, he might have decided to offer only 1.5 fish next year for every one he received this year, which would represent a 50 percent rate of return to Ms. Robinson and the other potential savers.

How attractive Mr. Crusoe's offer appeared to a potential saver would depend in large part on the saver's *time preference for consumption.* For example, Ms. Robinson might be thinking of retirement, and she might be willing to trade fish today for fish in the future on a one-for-one basis. On the other hand, Mr. Friday might have a wife and several young children and need his current fish, so he might be unwilling to "lend" a fish today for anything less than three fish next year. Mr. Friday would be said to have a high time preference for current consumption and Ms. Robinson a low time preference. Note also that if the entire population were living right at the subsistence level, time preferences for current consumption would necessarily be high, aggregate savings would be low, interest rates would be high, and capital formation would be difficult.

The *risk* inherent in the fishnet project, and thus in Mr. Crusoe's ability to repay the loan, would also affect the return investors would require: the higher the perceived risk, the higher the required rate of return. Also, in a more complex society there are many businesses like Mr. Crusoe's, many goods other than fish, and many savers like Ms. Robinson and Mr. Friday. Therefore, people use money as a medium of exchange rather than barter with fish. When money is used, its value in the future, which is affected by *inflation,* comes into play: the higher the expected rate of inflation, the larger the required return. We discuss this point in detail later in the reading.

Thus, we see that the interest rate paid to savers depends in a basic way (1) on the rate of return producers expect to earn on invested capital, (2) on savers' time preferences for current versus future consumption, (3) on the riskiness of the loan, and (4) on the expected future rate of inflation. Producers' expected returns on their business investments set an upper limit on how much they can pay for savings, while consumers' time preferences for consumption establish how much consumption they are willing to defer, hence how much they will save at different rates of interest offered by producers.[4] Higher risk and higher inflation also lead to higher interest rates.

---

[4] The term "producers" is really too narrow. A better word might be "borrowers," which would include corporations, home purchasers, people borrowing to go to college, or even people borrowing to buy autos or to pay for vacations. Also, the wealth of a society and its demographics influence its people's ability to save and thus their time preferences for current versus future consumption.

Self-Test Questions

What is the price paid to borrow money called?

What are the two items whose sum is the "price" of equity capital?

What four fundamental factors affect the cost of money?

7 INTEREST RATE LEVELS

Capital is allocated among borrowers by interest rates: Firms with the most profitable investment opportunities are willing and able to pay the most for capital, so they tend to attract it away from inefficient firms or from those whose products are not in demand. Of course, our economy is not completely free in the sense of being influenced only by market forces. Thus, the federal government has agencies that help designated individuals or groups obtain credit on favorable terms. Among those eligible for this kind of assistance are small businesses, certain minorities, and firms willing to build plants in areas with high unemployment. Still, most capital in the U.S. economy is allocated through the price system.

Figure 25–2 shows how supply and demand interact to determine interest rates in two capital markets. Markets A and B represent two of the many capital markets in existence. The going interest rate, which can be designated as either k or i, but for purposes of our discussion is designated as k, is initially 10 percent for the low-risk securities in Market A.[5] Borrowers whose credit is strong enough to borrow in this market can obtain funds at a cost of 10 percent, and investors who want to put their money to work without much risk can obtain a 10 percent return. Riskier borrowers must obtain higher-cost funds in Market B. Investors who are more willing to take risks invest in Market B, expecting to earn a 12 percent return but also realizing that they might actually receive much less.

If the demand for funds declines, as it typically does during business recessions, the demand curves will shift to the left, as shown in Curve D_2 in Market A. The market-clearing, or equilibrium, interest rate in this example declines to 8 percent. Similarly, you should be able to visualize what would happen if the Federal Reserve tightened credit: The supply curve, S_1, would shift to the left, and this would raise interest rates and lower the level of borrowing in the economy.

Capital markets are interdependent. For example, if Markets A and B were in equilibrium before the demand shift to D_2 in Market A, then investors were willing to accept the higher risk in Market B in exchange for a *risk premium* of $12\% - 10\% = 2\%$. After the shift to D_2, the risk premium would initially increase to $12\% - 8\% = 4\%$. Immediately, though, this much larger premium would induce some of the lenders in Market A to shift to Market B, which would, in turn, cause the supply curve in Market A to shift to the left (or up) and that in Market B to shift to the right. The transfer of capital between markets would raise the interest rate in Market A and lower it in Market B, thus bringing the risk premium back closer to the original 2 percent.

There are many capital markets in the United States. U.S. firms also invest and raise capital throughout the world, and foreigners both borrow and lend in the United States. There are markets for home loans; farm loans; business loans;

---

[5] The letter "k" is the traditional symbol for interest rates and the cost of equity, but "i" is used frequently today because this term corresponds to the interest rate key on financial calculators. Therefore, in Chapter 6, when we discuss calculators, the term "i" will be used for the interest rate.

FIGURE 25-2 Interest Rates as a Function of Supply and Demand for Funds

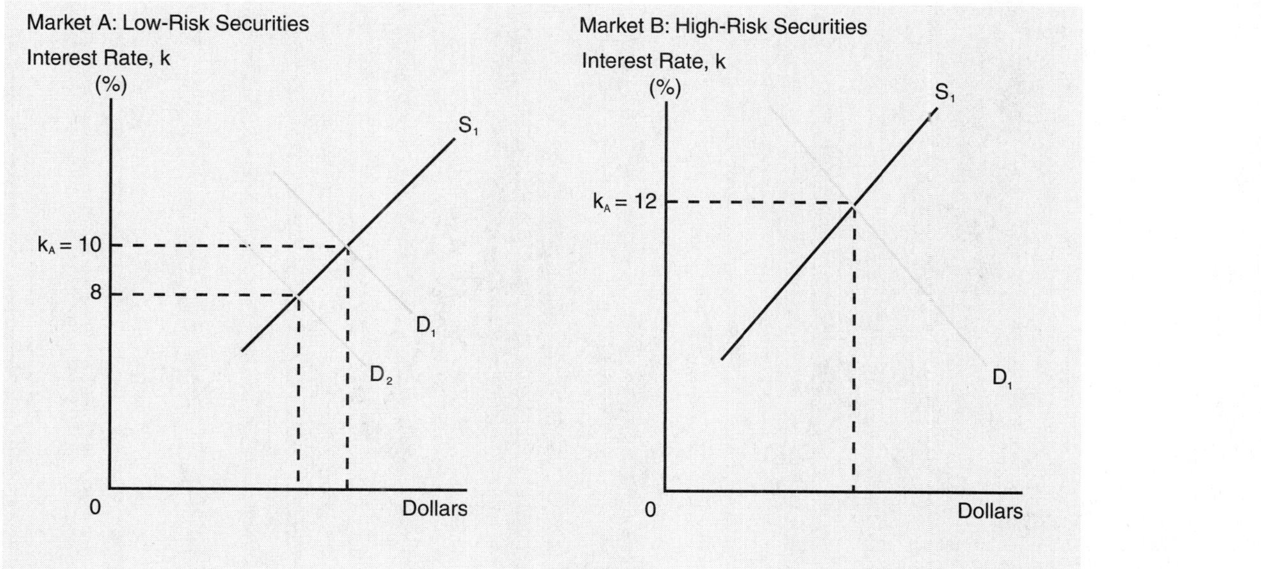

federal, state, and local government loans; and consumer loans. Within each category, there are regional markets as well as different types of submarkets. For example, in real estate there are separate markets for first and second mortgages and for loans on single-family homes, apartments, office buildings, shopping centers, vacant land, and so on. Within the business sector there are dozens of types of debt and also several different markets for common stocks.

There is a price for each type of capital, and these prices change over time as shifts occur in supply and demand conditions. Figure 25-3 shows how long- and short-term interest rates to business borrowers have varied since the early 1960s. Notice that short-term interest rates are especially prone to rise during booms and then fall during recessions. (The shaded areas of the chart indicate recessions.) When the economy is expanding, firms need capital, and this demand for capital pushes rates up. Also, inflationary pressures are strongest during business booms, and that also exerts upward pressure on rates. Conditions are reversed during recessions such as the one that began in March 2001. Slack business reduces the demand for credit, the rate of inflation falls, and the result is a drop in interest rates. Furthermore, the Federal Reserve deliberately lowers rates during recessions to help stimulate the economy.

These tendencies do not hold exactly—the period after 1984 is a case in point. The price of oil fell dramatically in 1985 and 1986, reducing inflationary pressures on other prices and easing fears of serious long-term inflation. Earlier, these fears had pushed interest rates to record levels. The economy from 1984 to 1987 was strong, but the declining fears of inflation more than offset the normal tendency of interest rates to rise during good economic times, and the net result was lower interest rates.[6]

---

[6] Short-term rates are responsive to current economic conditions, whereas long-term rates primarily reflect long-run expectations for inflation. As a result, short-term rates are sometimes above and sometimes below long-term rates. The relationship between long-term and short-term rates is called the *term structure of interest rates,* and it is discussed later in the reading.

FIGURE 25-3 Long- and Short-Term Interest Rates, 1961–2001

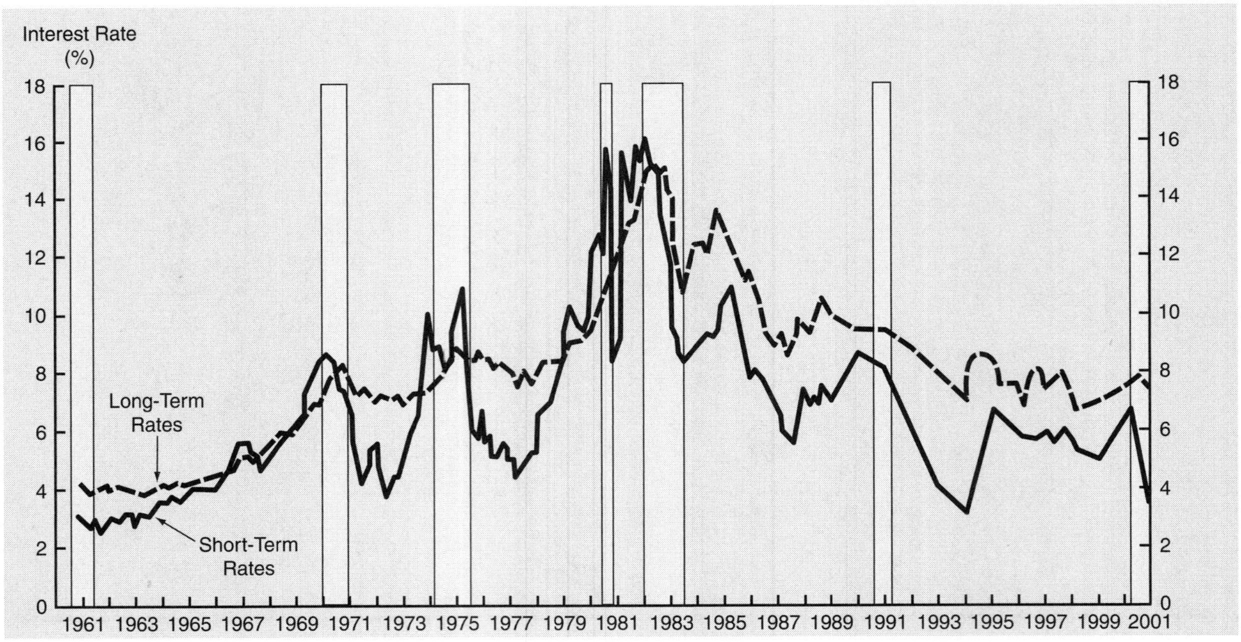

NOTES:

a. The shaded areas designate business recessions.

b. Short-term rates are measured by three- to six-month loans to very large, strong corporations, and long-term rates are measured by AAA corporate bonds.

Source: Adapted from *Federal Reserve Bulletin; Federal Reserve Statistical Release.*

The relationship between inflation and long-term interest rates is highlighted in Figure 25-4, which plots rates of inflation along with long-term interest rates. In the early 1960s, inflation averaged 1 percent per year, and interest rates on high-quality, long-term bonds averaged 4 percent. Then the Vietnam War heated up, leading to an increase in inflation, and interest rates began an upward climb. When the war ended in the early 1970s, inflation dipped a bit, but then the 1973 Arab oil embargo led to rising oil prices, much higher inflation rates, and sharply higher interest rates.

Inflation peaked at about 13 percent in 1980, but interest rates continued to increase into 1981 and 1982, and they remained quite high until 1985, because people were afraid inflation would start to climb again. Thus, the "inflationary psychology" created during the 1970s persisted to the mid-1980s.

Gradually, though, people began to realize that the Federal Reserve was serious about keeping inflation down, that global competition was keeping U.S. auto producers and other corporations from raising prices as they had in the past, and that constraints on corporate price increases were diminishing labor unions' ability to push through cost-increasing wage hikes. As these realizations set in, interest rates declined.

The gap between the current interest rate and the current inflation rate is defined as the "current real rate of interest." It is called the "real rate" because it shows how much investors really earned after taking out the effects of inflation.

FIGURE 25-4 Relationship between Annual Inflation Rates and Long-Term Interest Rates, 1961–2001

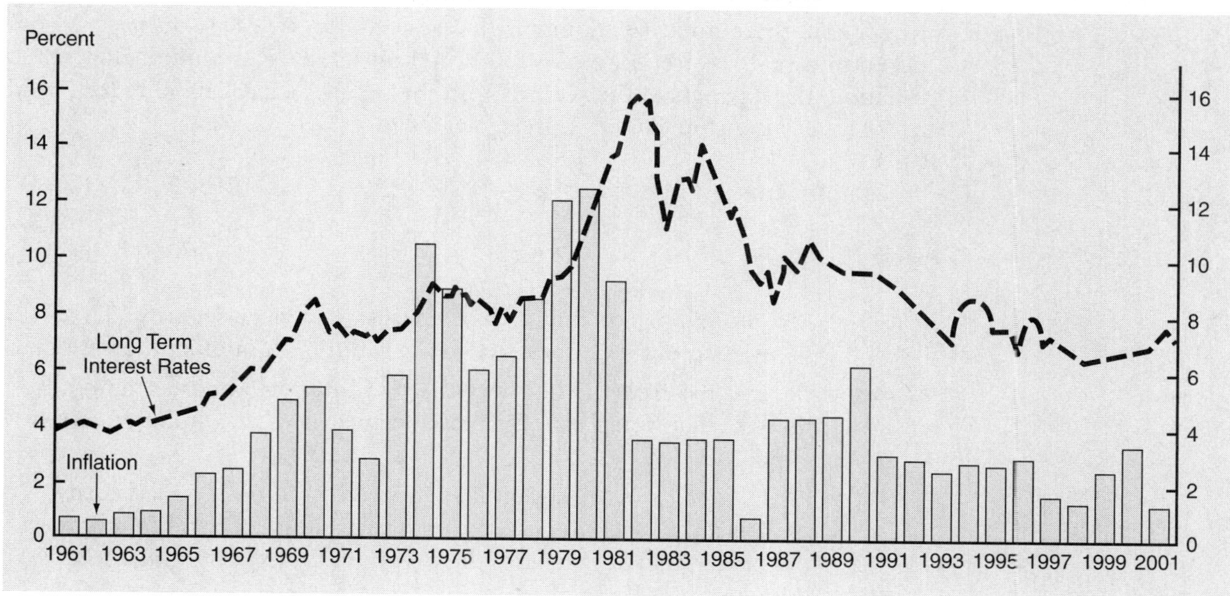

NOTES:

a. Interest rates are those on AAA long-term corporate bonds.

b. Inflation is measured as the annual rate of change in the Consumer Price Index (CPI).

Sources: Adapted from *Federal Reserve Bulletin; Federal Reserve Statistical Release.*

The real rate was extremely high during the mid-1980s, but it averaged about 4 percent during the 1990s.

In recent years, inflation has been running at about 2.5 percent a year. However, long-term interest rates have been volatile, because investors are not sure if inflation is truly under control or is getting ready to jump back to the higher levels of the 1980s. In the years ahead, we can be sure that the level of interest rates will vary (1) with changes in the current rate of inflation and (2) with changes in expectations about future inflation.

Self-Test Questions

How are interest rates used to allocate capital among firms?

What happens to market-clearing, or equilibrium, interest rates in a capital market when the demand for funds declines? What happens when inflation increases or decreases?

Why does the price of capital change during booms and recessions?

How does risk affect interest rates?

8 THE DETERMINANTS OF MARKET INTEREST RATES

In general, the quoted (or nominal) interest rate on a debt security, k, is composed of a real risk-free rate of interest, k*, plus several premiums that reflect inflation, the riskiness of the security, and the security's marketability (or liquidity). This relationship can be expressed as follows:

$$\text{Quoted interest rate} = k = k^* + IP + DRP + LP + MRP. \quad \textbf{(25-1)}$$

Here

k = the quoted, or nominal, rate of interest on a given security.[7] There are many different securities, hence many different quoted interest rates.

k* = the real risk-free rate of interest. k* is pronounced "k-star," and it is the rate that would exist on a riskless security if zero inflation were expected.

k_{RF} = k* + IP, and it is the quoted risk-free rate of interest on a security such as a U.S. Treasury bill, which is very liquid and also free of most risks. Note that k_{RF} includes the premium for expected inflation, because $k_{RF} = k^* + IP$.

IP = inflation premium. IP is equal to the average expected inflation rate over the life of the security. The expected future inflation rate is not necessarily equal to the current inflation rate, so IP is not necessarily equal to current inflation as reported in Figure 25-4.

DRP = default risk premium. This premium reflects the possibility that the issuer will not pay interest or principal at the stated time and in the stated amount. DRP is zero for U.S. Treasury securities, but it rises as the riskiness of issuers increases.

LP = liquidity, or marketability, premium. This is a premium charged by lenders to reflect the fact that some securities cannot be converted to cash on short notice at a "reasonable" price. LP is very low for Treasury securities and for securities issued by large, strong firms, but it is relatively high on securities issued by very small firms.

MRP = maturity risk premium. As we will explain later, longer-term bonds, even Treasury bonds, are exposed to a significant risk of price declines, and a maturity risk premium is charged by lenders to reflect this risk.

As noted above, since $k_{RF} = k^* + IP$, we can rewrite Equation 25-1 as follows:

$$\text{Nominal, or quoted, rate} = k = k_{RF} + DRP + LP + MRP.$$

We discuss the components whose sum makes up the quoted, or nominal, rate on a given security in the following sections.

---

[7] The term *nominal* as it is used here means the *stated* rate as opposed to the *real* rate, which is adjusted to remove inflation effects. If you had bought a 10-year Treasury bond in April 2002, the quoted, or nominal, rate would be about 5.2 percent, but if inflation averages 2.5 percent over the next 10 years, the real rate would be about 5.2% − 2.5% = 2.7%.

The Real Risk-Free Rate of Interest, k*

The **real risk-free rate of interest, k***, is defined as the interest rate that would exist on a riskless security if no inflation were expected, and it may be thought of as the rate of interest on *short-term* U.S. Treasury securities in an inflation-free world. The real risk-free rate is not static—it changes over time depending on economic conditions, especially (1) on the rate of return corporations and other borrowers expect to earn on productive assets and (2) on people's time preferences for current versus future consumption. Borrowers' expected returns on real asset investments set an upper limit on how much they can afford to pay for borrowed funds, while savers' time preferences for consumption establish how much consumption they are willing to defer, hence the amount of funds they will lend at different interest rates. It is difficult to measure the real risk-free rate precisely, but most experts think that k* has fluctuated in the range of 1 to 5 percent in recent years.[8] The best estimate of k* is the rate of return on indexed Treasury bonds, which are discussed in a box later in the reading.

Real risk-free rate of interest, k*
The rate of interest that would exist on default-free U.S. Treasury securities if no inflation were expected.

The Nominal, or Quoted, Risk-Free Rate of Interest, k_{RF}

The **nominal,** or **quoted, risk-free rate, k_{RF},** is the real risk-free rate plus a premium for expected inflation: $k_{RF} = k^* + IP$. To be strictly correct, the risk-free rate should mean the interest rate on a totally risk-free security—one that has no risk of default, no maturity risk, no liquidity risk, no risk of loss if inflation increases, and no risk of any other type. There is no such security, hence there is no observable truly risk-free rate. However, there is one security that is free of most risks—an indexed U.S. Treasury security. These securities are free of default, maturity, and liquidity risks, and also of risk due to changes in the general level of interest rates.[9]

Nominal (quoted) risk-free rate, k_{RF}
The rate of interest on a security that is free of all risk; k_{RF} is proxied by the T-bill rate or the T-bond rate. k_{RF} includes an inflation premium.

If the term "risk-free rate" is used without either the modifier "real" or the modifier "nominal," people generally mean the quoted (nominal) rate, and we will follow that convention in this book. Therefore, when we use the term risk-free rate, k_{RF}, we mean the nominal risk-free rate, which includes an inflation premium equal to the average expected inflation rate over the life of the security. In general, we use the T-bill rate to approximate the short-term risk-free rate, and the T-bond rate to approximate the long-term risk-free rate. So, whenever you see the term "risk-free rate," assume that we are referring either to the quoted U.S. T-bill rate or to the quoted T-bond rate.

[8] The real rate of interest as discussed here is different from the *current* real rate as discussed in connection with Figure 25-4. The current real rate is the current interest rate minus the current (or latest past) inflation rate, while the real rate, without the word "current," is the current interest rate minus the *expected future* inflation rate over the life of the security. For example, suppose the current quoted rate for a one-year Treasury bill is 5 percent, inflation during the latest year was 2 percent, and inflation expected for the coming year is 4 percent. Then the *current* real rate would be 5% − 2% = 3%, but the *expected* real rate would be 5% − 4% = 1%. The rate on a 10-year bond would be related to the expected inflation rate over the next 10 years, and so on. In the press, the term "real rate" generally means the current real rate, but in economics and finance, hence in this book unless otherwise noted, the real rate means the one based on *expected* inflation rates.

[9] Indexed Treasury securities are the closest thing we have to a riskless security, but even they are not totally riskless, because k* itself can change and cause a decline in the prices of these securities. For example, between October 1998 and January 2000, the price of one indexed Treasury security declined from 98 to 89, or by almost 10 percent. The cause was an increase in the real rate on long-term securities from 3.7 percent to 4.4 percent. Two years later, the real rate on long-term securities has dropped to 3.375 percent.

Inflation Premium (IP)

Inflation has a major impact on interest rates because it erodes the purchasing power of the dollar and lowers the real rate of return on investments. To illustrate, suppose you saved $1,000 and invested it in a Treasury bill that matures in one year and pays a 5 percent interest rate. At the end of the year, you will receive $1,050—your original $1,000 plus $50 of interest. Now suppose the inflation rate during the year is 10 percent, and it affects all items equally. If gas had cost $1 per gallon at the beginning of the year, it would cost $1.10 at the end of the year. Therefore, your $1,000 would have bought $1,000/$1 = 1,000 gallons at the beginning of the year, but only $1,050/$1.10 = 955 gallons at the end. In *real terms,* you would be worse off—you would receive $50 of interest, but it would not be sufficient to offset inflation. You would thus be better off buying 1,000 gallons of gas (or some other storable asset such as land, timber, apartment buildings, wheat, or gold) than buying the Treasury bill.

Inflation premium (IP) A premium equal to expected inflation that investors add to the real risk-free rate of return.

Investors are well aware of all this, so when they lend money, they build in an **inflation premium** (**IP**) equal to the average expected inflation rate over the life of the security. As discussed previously, for a short-term, default-free U.S. Treasury bill, the actual interest rate charged, $k_{\text{T-bill}}$, would be the real risk-free rate, k^*, plus the inflation premium (IP):

$$k_{\text{T-bill}} = k_{RF} = k^* + IP.$$

Therefore, if the real risk-free rate of interest were $k^* = 2.8\%$, and if inflation were expected to be 2 percent (and hence IP = 2%) during the next year, then the quoted rate of interest on one-year T-bills would be 2.8% + 2% = 4.8%.

It is important to note that the inflation rate built into interest rates is the *inflation rate expected in the future,* not the rate experienced in the past. Thus, the latest reported figures might show an annual inflation rate of 3.3 percent, but that is for the *past* year. If people on the average expect a 6 percent inflation rate in the future, then 6 percent would be built into the current interest rate. Note also that the inflation rate reflected in the quoted interest rate on any security is the *average rate of inflation expected over the security's life.* Thus, the inflation rate built into a one-year bond is the expected inflation rate for the next year, but the inflation rate built into a 30-year bond is the average rate of inflation expected over the next 30 years.[10]

Expectations for future inflation are closely, but not perfectly, correlated with rates experienced in the recent past. Therefore, if the inflation rate reported for last month increased, people would tend to raise their expectations for future inflation, and this change in expectations would cause an increase in interest rates.

Note that Germany, Japan, and Switzerland have over the past several years had lower inflation rates than the United States, hence their interest rates have generally been lower than ours. Italy and most South American countries have experienced high inflation, and that is reflected in their interest rates.

---

[10] To be theoretically precise, we should use a *geometric average.* Also, since millions of investors are active in the market, it is impossible to determine exactly the consensus expected inflation rate. Survey data are available, however, which give us a reasonably good idea of what investors expect over the next few years. For example, in 1980 the University of Michigan's Survey Research Center reported that people expected inflation during the next year to be 11.9 percent and that the average rate of inflation expected over the next 5 to 10 years was 10.5 percent. Those expectations led to record-high interest rates. However, the economy cooled in 1981 and 1982, and, as Figure 25-4 showed, actual inflation dropped sharply after 1980. This led to gradual reductions in the *expected future* inflation rate. As inflationary expectations change, so do quoted market interest rates.

Default Risk Premium (DRP)

The risk that a borrower will *default* on a loan, which means not pay the interest or the principal, also affects the market interest rate on a security: the greater the default risk, the higher the interest rate. Treasury securities have no default risk, hence they carry the lowest interest rates on taxable securities in the United States. For corporate bonds, the higher the bond's rating, the lower its default risk, and, consequently, the lower its interest rate.[11] Here are some representative interest rates on long-term bonds during February 2002:

	Rate	DRP
U.S. Treasury	5.4%	—
AAA	6.5	1.1%
AA	7.0	1.6
A	7.4	2.0
BBB	7.9	2.5

The difference between the quoted interest rate on a T-bond and that on a corporate bond with similar maturity, liquidity, and other features is the **default risk premium (DRP)**. Therefore, if the bonds listed above were otherwise similar, the default risk premium would be DRP = 6.5% − 5.4% = 1.1 percentage points for AAA corporate bonds, 7.0% − 5.4% = 1.6 percentage points for AA, 7.4% − 5.4% = 2.0 percentage points for A corporate bonds, and so forth. Default risk premiums vary somewhat over time, but the February 2002 figures are representative of levels in recent years.

Default risk premium (DRP)
The difference between the interest rate on a U.S. Treasury bond and a corporate bond of equal maturity and marketability.

Liquidity Premium (LP)

A "liquid" asset can be converted to cash quickly and at a "fair market value." Financial assets are generally more liquid than real assets. Because liquidity is important, investors include **liquidity premiums (LPs)** when market rates of securities are established. Although it is difficult to accurately measure liquidity premiums, a differential of at least two and probably four or five percentage points exists between the least liquid and the most liquid financial assets of similar default risk and maturity.

Liquidity premium (LP)
A premium added to the equilibrium interest rate on a security if that security cannot be converted to cash on short notice and at close to "fair market value."

Maturity Risk Premium (MRP)

U.S. Treasury securities are free of default risk in the sense that one can be virtually certain that the federal government will pay interest on its bonds and will also pay them off when they mature. Therefore, the default risk premium on Treasury securities is essentially zero. Further, active markets exist for Treasury securities, so their liquidity premiums are also close to zero. Thus, as a first approximation, the rate of interest on a Treasury bond should be the risk-free rate, k_{RF}, which is equal to the real risk-free rate, k*, plus an inflation premium,

[11] Bond ratings, and bonds' riskiness in general, are discussed in detail in Chapter 7. For now, merely note that bonds rated AAA are judged to have less default risk than bonds rated AA, while AA bonds are less risky than A bonds, and so on. Ratings are designated AAA or Aaa, AA or Aa, and so forth, depending on the rating agency. In this book, the designations are used interchangeably.

INDUSTRY PRACTICE

An Almost Riskless Treasury Bond

Investors who purchase bonds must constantly worry about inflation. If inflation turns out to be greater than expected, bonds will provide a lower-than-expected real return. To protect themselves against expected increases in inflation, investors build an inflation risk premium into their required rate of return. This raises borrowers' costs.

In order to provide investors with an inflation-protected bond, and also to reduce the cost of debt to the government, on January 29, 1997, the U.S. Treasury issued \$7 billion of 10-year inflation-indexed bonds. These initial bonds paid an interest rate of 3.375 percent plus an additional amount to offset inflation. At the end of each six-month period, the principal (originally set at par, or \$1,000) is adjusted by the inflation rate. For example, during the first six-month interest period, inflation (as measured by the CPI) was 1.085 percent. The inflation-adjusted principal was then calculated as \$1,000(1 + inflation) = \$1,000 × 1.01085 = \$1,010.85. So, on July 15, 1997, each bond paid interest of 0.03375/2 × \$1,010.85 = \$17.06. Note that the interest rate is divided by two because interest is paid twice a year.

By January 15, 1998, a bit more inflation had occurred, and the inflation-adjusted principal was up to \$1,019.69, so on January 15, 1998, each bond paid interest of 0.03375/2 × \$1,019.69 = \$17.21. Thus, the total return during the first year consisted of \$17.06 + \$17.21 = \$34.27 of interest and \$1,019.69 − \$1,000.00 = \$19.69 of "capital gains," or \$34.27 + \$19.69 = \$53.96 in total. Thus, the total return was \$53.96/\$1,000 = 5.396%.

This same adjustment process will continue each year until the bonds mature on January 15, 2007, at which time they will pay the adjusted maturity value. Thus, the cash income provided by the bonds rises by exactly enough to cover inflation, producing a real, inflation-adjusted rate of 3.375 percent. Further, since the principal also rises by the inflation rate, it too is protected from inflation. The accompanying table gives the inflation-adjusted principal and interest paid during the life of these 3⅜ percent coupon, 10-year, inflation-indexed bonds:

Date	Inflation-Adjusted Principal	Interest Paid
7/15/97	\$1,010.85	\$17.06
1/15/98	1,019.69	17.21
7/15/98	1,026.51	17.32
1/15/99	1,035.12	17.47
7/15/99	1,049.01	17.70
1/15/00	1,061.92	17.92
7/15/00	1,080.85	18.24
1/15/01	1,098.52	18.54
7/15/01	1,118.82	18.88
1/15/02	1,120.74	18.91

Source: Bureau of the Public Debt's Online, Historical Reference CPI Numbers and Daily Index Ratios for 3⅜%, 10-year note due January 15, 2007, at **http://www.publicdebt.treas.gov/of/ofhiscpi.htm**.

The Treasury regularly conducts auctions to issue indexed bonds. The 3.375 percent rate was based on the relative supply and demand for the issue, and it will remain constant over the life of the bond. However, new bonds are issued periodically, and their "coupon" real rates depend on the market at the time the bond is auctioned. In

Interest rate risk
The risk of capital losses to which investors are exposed because of changing interest rates.

Maturity risk premium (MRP)
A premium that reflects interest rate risk.

IP. However, an adjustment is needed for long-term Treasury bonds. The prices of long-term bonds decline sharply whenever interest rates rise, and since interest rates can and do occasionally rise, all long-term bonds, even Treasury bonds, have an element of risk called **interest rate risk.** As a general rule, the bonds of any organization, from the U.S. government to Continental Airlines, have more interest rate risk the longer the maturity of the bond.[12] Therefore, a **maturity risk premium (MRP)**, which is higher the longer the years to maturity, must be included in the required interest rate.

---

[12] For example, if someone had bought a 30-year Treasury bond for \$1,000 in 1998, when the long-term interest rate was 5.25 percent, and held it until April 2002, when long-term T-bond rates were about 5.7 percent, the value of the bond would have declined to about \$936. That would represent a loss of 6.4 percent, and it demonstrates that long-term bonds, even U.S. Treasury bonds, are not riskless. However, had the investor purchased short-term T-bills in 1998 and subsequently reinvested the principal each time the bills matured, he or she would still have had \$1,000. This point will be discussed in detail in Reading 7.

INDUSTRY PRACTICE (continued)

January 2002, 10-year indexed securities had a real rate of 3.375 percent.

Federal Reserve Board Chairman Greenspan lobbied in favor of the indexed bonds on the grounds that they would help him and the Fed make better estimates of investors' expectations about inflation. He did not explain his reasoning (to our knowledge), but it might have gone something like this:

> We know that interest rates in general are determined as follows:
>
> $$k = k^* + IP + MRP + DRP + LP.$$
>
> For Treasury bonds, DRP and LP are essentially zero, so for a 10-year bond the rate is
>
> $$k_{RF} = k^* + IP + MRP.$$

The reason the MRP is not zero is that if inflation increases, interest rates will rise and the price of the bonds will decline. Therefore, "regular" 10-year bonds are exposed to maturity risk, hence a maturity risk premium is built into their market interest rate.

> The indexed bonds are protected against inflation—if inflation increases, then so will their dollar returns, and as a result, their price will not decline in real terms. Therefore, indexed bonds should have no MRP, hence their market return is
>
> $$k_{RF} = k^* + 0 + 0 = k^*.$$

In other words, the market rate on indexed bonds is the real rate.

> The difference between the yield on a regular 10-year bond and that on an indexed bond is the sum of the 10-year bonds' IP and MRP. In 1997, the yield on regular 10-year bonds was 6.80 percent when the first indexed bonds were issued, and the indexed bonds' yield was 3.375 percent. The difference, 3.425 percent, is the average expected inflation rate over the next 10 years plus the MRP for 10-year bonds.

> The 10-year MRP is about 1.0 percent, and it has been relatively stable in recent years. Therefore, the expected rate of inflation in January 1997 was about 2.425 percent (3.425% − 1.00% = 2.425%).

The interest received and the increase in principal are taxed each year as interest income, even though cash from the appreciation will not be received until the bond matures. Therefore, these bonds are especially suitable for individual retirement accounts (IRAs), which are not taxed until funds are withdrawn.

Keep in mind, though, that despite their protection against inflation, indexed bonds are not completely riskless. The real rate of interest can change, and if k* rises, the price of the indexed bonds will decline. This just confirms one more time that there is no such thing as a free lunch or a riskless security!

Sources: "Inflation Notes Will Offer Fed Forecast Tool," *The Wall Street Journal,* February 3, 1997, C1; and *The Wall Street Journal,* January 6, 2000, C21.

The effect of maturity risk premiums is to raise interest rates on long-term bonds relative to those on short-term bonds. This premium, like the others, is difficult to measure, but (1) it varies somewhat over time, rising when interest rates are more volatile and uncertain, then falling when interest rates are more stable, and (2) in recent years, the maturity risk premium on 30-year T-bonds appears to have generally been in the range of one or two percentage points.[13]

We should mention that although long-term bonds are heavily exposed to interest rate risk, short-term bills are heavily exposed to **reinvestment rate risk.** When short-term bills mature and the funds are reinvested, or "rolled over," a decline in interest rates would necessitate reinvestment at a lower rate, and this would result in a decline in interest income. To illustrate, suppose you had $100,000 invested in one-year T-bills, and you lived on the income. In 1981, short-

Reinvestment rate risk
The risk that a decline in interest rates will lead to lower income when bonds mature and funds are reinvested.

[13] The MRP for long-term bonds has averaged 1.3 percent over the last 76 years. See *Stocks, Bonds, Bills, and Inflation: (Valuation Edition) 2002 Yearbook* (Chicago: Ibbotson Associates, 2002).

term rates were about 15 percent, so your income would have been about \$15,000. However, your income would have declined to about \$9,000 by 1983, and to just \$2,370 by 2002. Had you invested your money in long-term T-bonds, your income (but not the value of the principal) would have been stable.[14] Thus, although "investing short" preserves one's principal, the interest income provided by short-term T-bills is less stable than the interest income on long-term bonds.

Self-Test Questions

Write out an equation for the nominal interest rate on any debt security.

Distinguish between the *real* risk-free rate of interest, k*, and the *nominal*, or *quoted*, risk-free rate of interest, k_{RF}.

How is inflation dealt with when interest rates are determined by investors in the financial markets?

Does the interest rate on a T-bond include a default risk premium? Explain.

Distinguish between liquid and illiquid assets, and identify some assets that are liquid and some that are illiquid.

Briefly explain the following statement: "Although long-term bonds are heavily exposed to interest rate risk, short-term bills are heavily exposed to reinvestment rate risk. The maturity risk premium reflects the net effects of these two opposing forces."

9 THE TERM STRUCTURE OF INTEREST RATES

OPTIONAL SEGMENT

Term structure of interest rates
The relationship between bond yields and maturities.

Yield curve
A graph showing the relationship between bond yields and maturities.

Students can find current U.S. Treasury yield curve graphs and other global and domestic interest rate information at Bloomberg markets' site at **http://www.bloomberg.com/markets/index.html**.

The **term structure of interest rates** describes the relationship between long- and short-term rates. The term structure is important to corporate treasurers who must decide whether to borrow by issuing long- or short-term debt and to investors who must decide whether to buy long- or short-term bonds. Thus, it is important to understand (1) how long- and short-term rates relate to each other and (2) what causes shifts in their relative positions.

Interest rates for bonds with different maturities can be found in a variety of publications, including *The Wall Street Journal* and the *Federal Reserve Bulletin,* and on a number of websites, including Bloomberg, Yahoo, and CNN Financial. From interest rate data obtained from these sources, we can construct the term structure at a given point in time. For example, the tabular section below Figure 25-5 presents interest rates for different maturities on three different dates. The set of data for a given date, when plotted on a graph such as that in Figure 25-5 is called the **yield curve** for that date.

The yield curve changes both in position and in slope over time. In March 1980, all rates were relatively high, and since short-term rates were higher than long-term rates, the yield curve was *downward sloping.* However, by February 2000, all rates were lower, and the yield curve had become *humped*—medium-term rates were higher than both short- and long-term rates. Roughly two years later,

[14] Long-term bonds also have some reinvestment rate risk. If one is saving and investing for some future purpose, say, to buy a house or for retirement, then to actually earn the quoted rate on a long-term bond, the interest payments must be reinvested at the quoted rate. However, if interest rates fall, the interest payments must be reinvested at a lower rate; thus, the realized return would be less than the quoted rate. Note, though, that reinvestment rate risk is lower on a long-term bond than on a short-term bond because only the interest payments (rather than interest plus principal) on the long-term bond are exposed to reinvestment rate risk. Zero coupon bonds, which are discussed in Reading 7, are completely free of reinvestment rate risk during their life.

FIGURE 25-5 U.S. Treasury Bond Interest Rates on Different Dates

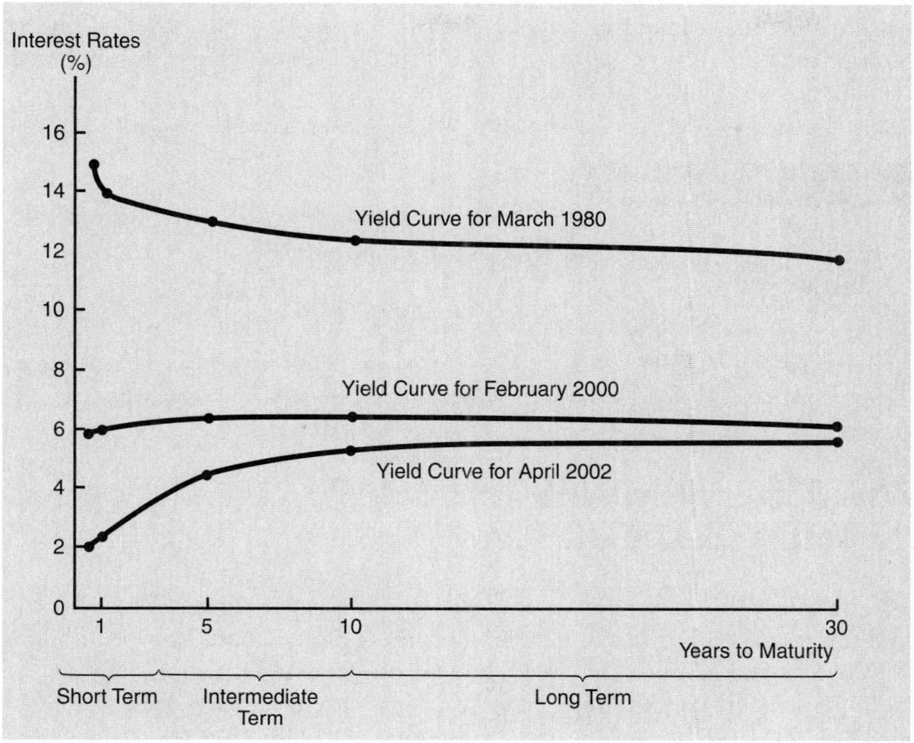

	Interest Rate		
Term to Maturity	**March 1980**	**February 2000**	**April 2002**
6 months	15.0%	6.0%	2.0%
1 year	14.0	6.2	2.3
5 years	13.5	6.7	4.5
10 years	12.8	6.7	5.2
30 years	12.3	6.3	5.7

all rates had fallen below the 2000 levels, and because short-term rates were lower than long-term rates, the yield curve was *upward sloping.*

Figure 25-5 shows yield curves for U.S. Treasury securities, but we could have constructed curves for corporate bonds issued by AT&T, IBM, Delta Airlines, or any other company that borrows money over a range of maturities. Had we constructed corporate curves and plotted them on Figure 25-5, they would have been above those for Treasury securities because corporate yields include default risk premiums. However, the corporate yield curves would have had the same general shape as the Treasury curves. Also, the riskier the corporation, the higher its yield curve, so Delta Airlines, which has a lower bond rating than either AT&T or IBM, would have a higher yield curve than those of AT&T and IBM.

Historically, in most years long-term rates have been above short-term rates, so the yield curve usually slopes upward. For this reason, people often call an upward-sloping yield curve a **"normal" yield curve** and a yield curve that slopes downward an **inverted,** or **"abnormal" yield curve**. Thus, in Figure 25-5 the yield curve for March 1980 was inverted, while the yield curve in April 2002 was normal. However,

"Normal" yield curve
An upward-sloping yield curve.

Inverted ("abnormal") yield curve
A downward-sloping yield curve.

Humped yield curve
A yield curve where interest rates on medium-term maturities are higher than rates on both short- and long-term maturities.

the February 2000 curve was a **humped yield curve**, which means that interest rates on medium-term maturities were higher than rates on both short- and long-term maturities. We explain in detail in the next section why an upward slope is the normal situation, but briefly, the reason is that short-term securities have less interest rate risk than longer-term securities, hence smaller MRPs. Therefore, short-term rates are normally lower than long-term rates.

Self-Test Questions

What is a yield curve, and what information would you need to draw this curve?

Distinguish among the shapes of a "normal" yield curve, an "abnormal" curve, and a "humped" curve.

10 WHAT DETERMINES THE SHAPE OF THE YIELD CURVE?

Since maturity risk premiums are positive, then if other things were held constant, long-term bonds would have higher interest rates than short-term bonds. However, market interest rates also depend on expected inflation, default risk, and liquidity, and each of these factors can vary with maturity.

Expected inflation has an especially important effect on the yield curve's shape. To see why, consider U.S. Treasury securities. Because Treasuries have essentially no default or liquidity risk, the yield on a Treasury bond that matures in t years can be expressed as follows:

$$k^*_t + IP_t + MRP_t.$$

While the real risk-free rate, k*, may vary somewhat over time because of changes in the economy and demographics, these changes are random rather than predictable, so it is reasonable to assume that k* will remain constant. However, the inflation premium, IP, does vary significantly over time, and in a somewhat predictable manner. Recall that the inflation premium is simply the average level of expected inflation over the life of the bond. Thus, if the market expects inflation to increase in the future, the inflation premium will be higher the longer the bond's maturity. On the other hand, if the market expects inflation to decline in the future, long-term bonds will have a smaller inflation premium than short-term bonds. Finally, if investors consider long-term bonds riskier than short-term bonds, the maturity risk premium will increase with maturity.

Panel a of Figure 25-6 shows the yield curve when inflation is expected to increase. Here long-term bonds have higher yields for two reasons: (1) Inflation is expected to be higher in the future, and (2) there is a positive maturity risk premium. Panel b of Figure 25-6 shows the yield curve when inflation is expected to decline, causing the yield curve to be downward sloping. Downward sloping yield curves often fore-shadow an economic downturn, because weaker economic conditions tend to be correlated with declining inflation, which in turn leads to lower long-term rates.

Now let's consider the yield curve for corporate bonds. Recall that corporate bonds include a default-risk premium (DRP) and a liquidity premium (LP). Therefore, the yield on a corporate bond that matures in t years can be expressed as follows:

$$k^*_t + IP_t + MRP_t + DRP_t + LP_t.$$

FIGURE 25-6 Illustrative Treasury Yield Curves

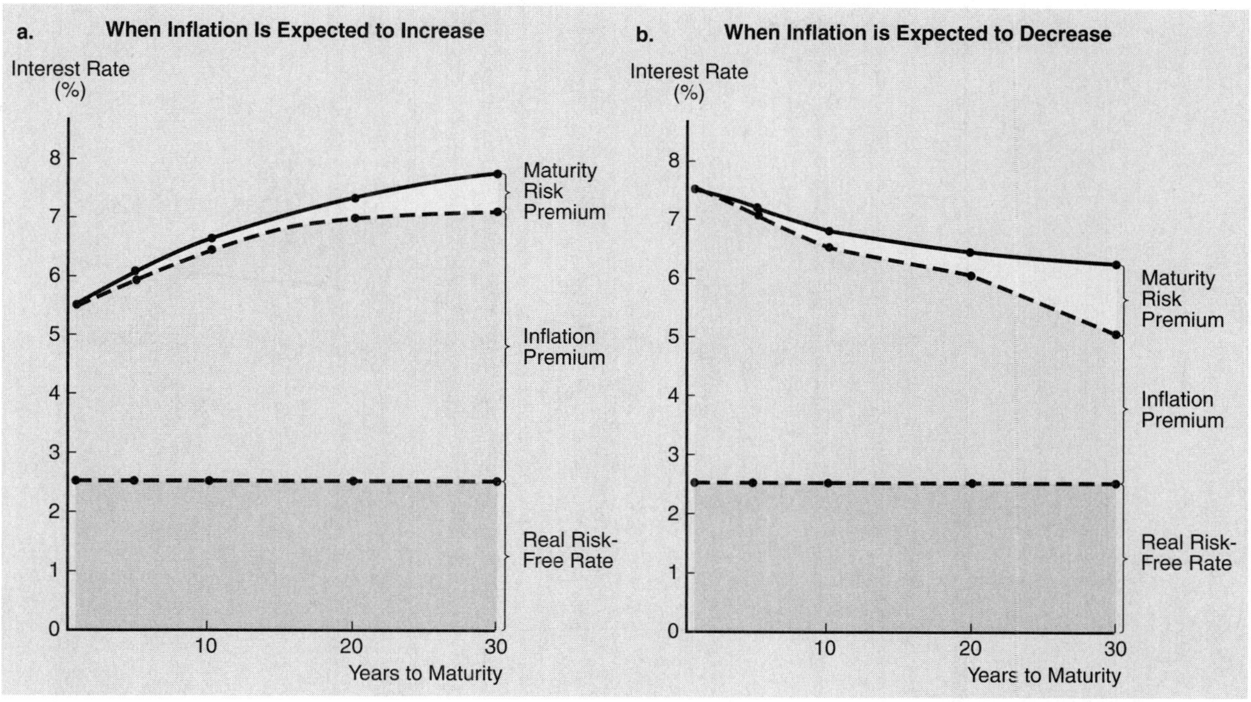

With Increasing Expected Inflation

Maturity	k*	IP	MRP	Yield
1 year	2.50%	3.00%	0.00%	5.50%
5 years	2.50	3.40	0.18	6.08
10 years	2.50	4.00	0.28	6.78
20 years	2.50	4.50	0.42	7.42
30 years	2.50	4.67	0.53	7.70

With Decreasing Expected Inflation

Maturity	k*	IP	MRP	Yield
1 year	2.50%	5.00%	0.00%	7.50%
5 years	2.50	4.60	0.18	7.28
10 years	2.50	4.00	0.28	6.78
20 years	2.50	3.50	0.42	6.42
30 years	2.50	3.33	0.53	6.36

A corporate bond's default and liquidity risks are affected by its maturity. For example, the default risk on Coca-Cola's short-term debt is very small, since there is almost no chance that Coca-Cola will go bankrupt over the next few years. However, Coke has some 100-year bonds, and while the odds of Coke defaulting on these bonds still might not be that high, the default risk on these bonds is considerably higher than that on its short-term debt.

Longer-term corporate bonds are also less liquid than shorter-term debt, hence the liquidity premium rises as maturity lengthens. The primary reason for this is that, for the reasons discussed earlier, short-term debt has less default risk, so a buyer can buy short-term debt without having to do as much credit checking as would be necessary for long-term debt. Thus, people can move into and out of short-term corporate debt much more rapidly than long-term debt. The end result is that short-term corporate debt is more liquid, hence has a smaller liquidity premium than the same company's long-term debt.

Figure 25-7 shows yield curves for two hypothetical corporate bonds, an AA-rated bond with minimal default risk and a BBB-rated bond with more default risk, along with the yield curve for Treasury securities as taken from

FIGURE 25-7 Corporate and Treasury Yield Curves

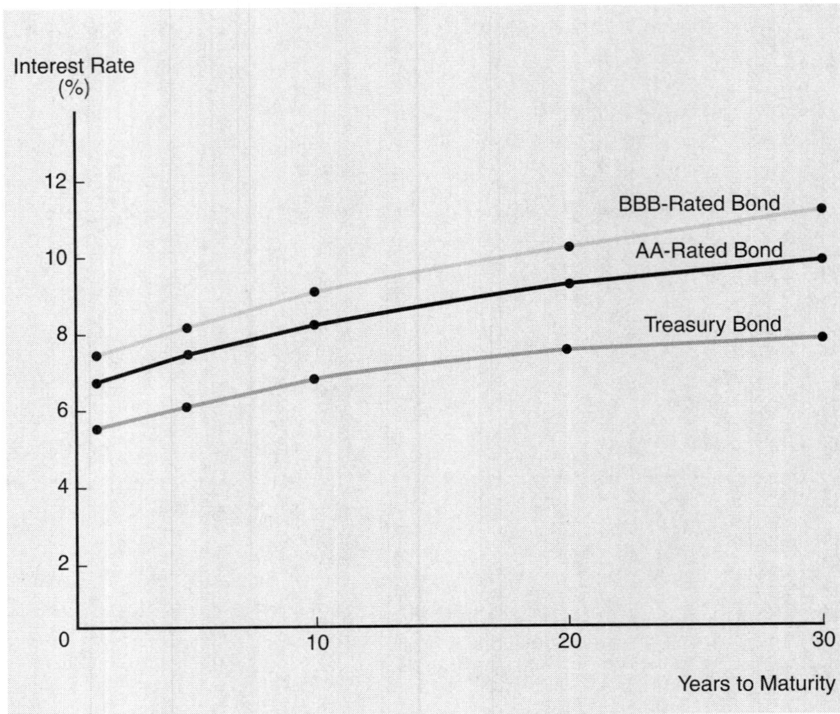

Term to Maturity	Interest Rate		
	Treasury Bond	AA-Rated Bond	BBB-Rated Bond
1 year	5.5%	6.7%	7.4%
5 years	6.1	7.4	8.1
10 years	6.8	8.2	9.1
20 years	7.4	9.2	10.2
30 years	7.7	9.8	11.1

panel a of Figure 25-6. Here we assume that inflation is expected to increase, so the Treasury yield curve is upward sloping. Because of their additional default and liquidity risk, corporate bonds always trade at a higher yield than Treasury bonds with the same maturity, and BBB-rated bonds trade at higher yields than AA-rated bonds. Finally, note that the yield spread between corporate bonds and Treasury bonds is larger the longer the maturity. This occurs because longer-term corporate bonds have more default and liquidity risk than shorter-term bonds, and both of these premiums are absent in Treasury bonds.

Self-Test Questions

How do maturity risk premiums affect the yield curve?

If the rate of inflation is expected to increase, would this increase or decrease the slope of the yield curve?

If the rate of inflation is expected to remain constant in the future, would the yield curve slope up, down, or be horizontal?

Explain why corporate bonds' default and liquidity premiums are likely to increase with maturity.

Explain why corporate bonds always trade at higher yields than Treasury bonds and why BBB-rated bonds always trade at higher yields than AA-rated bonds.

USING THE YIELD CURVE TO ESTIMATE FUTURE INTEREST RATES[15]

11

In the last section we saw that the shape of the yield curve depends primarily on two factors: (1) expectations about future inflation and (2) the relative riskiness of securities with different maturities. We also saw how to calculate the yield curve, given inflation and maturity-related risks. In practice, this process often works in reverse: Investors and analysts plot the yield curve and then use information embedded in it to estimate the market's expectations regarding future inflation and risk.

This process of using the yield curve to estimate future expected interest rates is straightforward, provided (1) we focus on Treasury securities, and (2) we assume that all Treasury securities have the same risk; that is, there is no maturity risk premium. Some academics and practitioners contend that this second assumption is reasonable, at least as an approximation. They argue that the market is dominated by large bond traders who buy and sell securities of different maturities each day, that these traders focus only on short-term returns, and that they are not concerned with risk. According to this view, a bond trader is just as willing to buy a 30-year bond to pick up a short-term profit as he would be to buy a three-month security. Strict proponents of this view argue that the shape of the yield curve is therefore determined only by market expectations about future interest rates, thus their position has been called the *pure expectations theory* of the term structure of interest rates.

The pure **expectations theory** (which is sometimes simply referred to as the "expectations theory") assumes that investors establish bond prices and interest rates strictly on the basis of expectations for interest rates. This means that they are indifferent with respect to maturity in the sense that they do not view long-term bonds as being riskier than short-term bonds. If this were true, then the maturity risk premium (MRP) would be zero, and long-term interest rates would simply be a weighted average of current and expected future short-term interest rates. For example, if 1-year Treasury bills currently yield 7 percent, but 1-year bills were expected to yield 7.5 percent a year from now, investors would expect to earn an average of 7.25 percent over the next two years.[16]

Expectations theory
A theory which states that the shape of the yield curve depends on investors' expectations about future interest rates.

$$\frac{7\% + 7.5\%}{2} = 7.25\%.$$

[15] This section is relatively technical, but instructors can omit it without loss of continuity.

[16] Technically, we should be using geometric averages rather than arithmetic averages, but the differences are not material in this example. For a discussion of this point, see Robert C. Radcliffe, *Investment: Concepts, Analysis, and Strategy,* 5th ed. (Reading, MA: Addison-Wesley, 1997), Chapter 5.

According to the expectations theory, this implies that a 2-year Treasury note purchased today should also yield 7.25 percent. Similarly, if 10-year bonds yield 9 percent today, and if 5-year bonds are expected to yield 7.5 percent 10 years from now, then investors should expect to earn 9 percent for 10 years and 7.5 percent for 5 years, for an average return of 8.5 percent over the next 15 years:

$$\frac{9\% + 9\% + \cdots + 9\% + 7.5\% + \cdots + 7.5\%}{15} = \frac{10(9\%) + 5(7.5\%)}{15} = 8.5\%.$$

Consequently, a 15-year bond should yield this same return, 8.5 percent.

To understand the logic behind this averaging process, ask yourself what would happen if long-term yields were *not* an average of expected short-term yields. For example, suppose 2-year bonds yielded only 7 percent, not the 7.25 percent calculated above. Bond traders would be able to earn a profit by adopting the following trading strategy:

1. Borrow money for two years at a cost of 7 percent.
2. Invest the money in a series of 1-year bonds. The expected return over the 2-year period would be $(7.0 + 7.5)/2 = 7.25\%$.

In this case, bond traders would rush to borrow money (demand funds) in the 2-year market and invest (or supply funds) in the 1-year market. Recall from Figure 25-2 that an increase in the demand for funds raises interest rates, whereas an increase in the supply of funds reduces interest rates. Therefore, bond traders' actions would push up the 2-year yield but reduce the yield on 1-year bonds. The next effect would be to bring about a market equilibrium in which 2-year rates were a weighted average of expected future 1-year rates.

Under these assumptions, we can "back out" of the yield curve the bond market's best guess about future interest rates. If, for example, you observe that Treasury securities with 1- and 2-year maturities yield 7 percent and 8 percent, respectively, this information can be used to calculate the market's forecast of what 1-year rates will yield one year from now. If the pure expectations theory is correct, the rate on 2-year bonds is the average of the current 1-year rate and the 1-year rate expected a year from now. Since the current 1-year rate is 7 percent, this implies that the 1-year rate one year from now is expected to be 9 percent:

$$\text{2-year yield} = 8\% = \frac{7\% + X\%}{2}$$

$$X = 16\% - 7\% = 9\% = \text{1-year yield expected next year.}$$

The preceding analysis was based on the assumption that the maturity risk premium is zero. However, most evidence suggests that there is a positive maturity risk premium, so the MRP should be taken into account.

For example, assume once again that 1- and 2-year maturities yield 7 percent and 8 percent, respectively, but now assume that the maturity risk premium on the 2-year bond is 0.5 percent. This maturity risk premium implies that the expected return on 2-year bonds (8 percent) is 0.5 percent higher than the expected returns from buying a series of 1-year bonds (7.5 percent). With this background, we can use the following two-step procedure to back out X, the expected 1-year rate one year from now:

Step 1: 2-year yield − MRP on 2-year bond = 8.0% − 0.5% = 7.5%.
Step 2: 7.5% = (7.0% + X%)/2
X = 15.0% − 7.0% = 8.0%.

Therefore, the yield next year on a 1-year T-bond should be 8 percent, up from 7 percent this year.

Self-Test Questions

What key assumption underlies the pure expectations theory?

Assuming that the pure expectations theory is correct, how are long-term interest rates calculated?

According to the pure expectations theory, what would happen if long-term rates were *not* an average of expected short-term rates?

INVESTING OVERSEAS 12

Investors should consider additional risk factors before investing overseas. First there is **country risk,** which refers to the risk that arises from investing or doing business in a particular country. This risk depends on the country's economic, political, and social environment. Countries with stable economic, social, political, and regulatory systems provide a safer climate for investment, and therefore less country risk, than less stable nations. Examples of country risk include the risk associated with changes in tax rates, regulations, currency conversion, and exchange rates. Country risk also includes the risk that property will be expropriated without adequate compensation, as well as new host country stipulations about local production, sourcing or hiring practices, and damage or destruction of facilities due to internal strife.

Country risk
The risk that arises from investing or doing business in a particular country.

A second point to keep in mind when investing overseas is that more often than not the security will be denominated in a currency other than the dollar, which means that the value of your investment will depend on what happens to exchange rates. This is known as **exchange rate risk.** For example, if a U.S. investor purchases a Japanese bond, interest will probably be paid in Japanese yen, which must then be converted into dollars if the investor wants to spend his or her money in the United States. If the yen weakens relative to the dollar, then it will buy fewer dollars, hence the investor will receive fewer dollars when it comes time to convert. Alternatively, if the yen strengthens relative to the dollar, the investor will earn higher dollar returns. It therefore follows that the effective rate of return on a foreign investment will depend on both the performance of the foreign security and on what happens to exchange rates over the life of the investment.

Exchange rate risk
The risk that exchange rate changes will reduce the number of dollars provided by a given amount of a foreign currency.

Self-Test Questions

What is country risk?

What is exchange rate risk?

13

OTHER FACTORS THAT INFLUENCE INTEREST RATE LEVELS

In addition to inflationary expectations, other factors also influence both the general level of interest rates and the shape of the yield curve. The four most important factors are (1) Federal Reserve policy; (2) the federal budget deficit or surplus; (3) international factors, including the foreign trade balance and interest rates in other countries; and (4) the level of business activity.

Federal Reserve Policy

The home page for the Board of Governors of the Federal Reserve System can be found at http://www.federalreserve.gov/. You can access general information about the Federal Reserve, including press releases, speeches, and monetary policy.

As you probably learned in your economics courses, (1) the money supply has a major effect on both the level of economic activity and the inflation rate, and (2) in the United States, the Federal Reserve Board controls the money supply. If the Fed wants to stimulate the economy, as it did in 1995, it increases growth in the money supply. The initial effect of such an action is to cause interest rates to decline. However, a larger money supply may also lead to an increase in the expected inflation rate, which, in turn, could push interest rates up. The reverse holds if the Fed tightens the money supply.

To illustrate, in 1981 inflation was quite high, so the Fed tightened up the money supply. The Fed deals primarily in the short-term end of the market, so this tightening had the direct effect of pushing short-term rates up sharply. At the same time, the very fact that the Fed was taking strong action to reduce inflation led to a decline in expectations for long-run inflation, which led to a decline in long-term bond yields.

In 1991, the situation was just the reverse. To combat the recession, the Fed took steps to reduce interest rates. Short-term rates fell, and long-term rates also dropped, but not as sharply. These lower rates benefited heavily indebted businesses and individual borrowers, and home mortgage refinancings put additional billions of dollars into consumers' pockets. Savers, of course, lost out, but the net effect of lower interest rates was a stronger economy. Lower rates encourage businesses to borrow for investment, stimulate the housing market, and bring down the value of the dollar relative to other currencies, which helps U.S. exporters and thus lowers the trade deficit.

During periods when the Fed is actively intervening in the markets, the yield curve may be temporarily distorted. Short-term rates will be temporarily "too low" if the Fed is easing credit, and "too high" if it is tightening credit. Long-term rates are not affected as much by Fed intervention. For example, the fear of rising inflation led the Federal Reserve to increase short-term interest rates six times during 1994. While short-term rates rose by nearly 4 percentage points, long-term rates increased by only 1.5 percentage points.

Budget Deficits or Surpluses

If the federal government spends more than it takes in from tax revenues, it runs a deficit, and that deficit must be covered either by borrowing or by printing money (increasing the money supply). If the government borrows, this added demand for funds pushes up interest rates. If it prints money, this increases expectations for future inflation, which also drives up interest rates. Thus, the larger the federal deficit, other things held constant, the higher the level of interest rates. Whether long- or short-term rates are more affected depends on how the deficit is financed, so we cannot state, in general, how deficits will affect the slope of the yield curve.

GLOBAL PERSPECTIVES

Measuring Country Risk

Various forecasting services measure the level of country risk in different countries and provide indexes that measure factors such as each country's expected economic performance, access to world capital markets, political stability, and level of internal conflict. Country risk analysts use sophisticated models to measure it, thus providing corporate managers and overseas investors with a way to judge both the relative and absolute risk of investing in a given country. A sample of recent country risk estimates compiled by *Institutional Investor* is presented in the following table. The higher the country's score, the lower its estimated country risk. The maximum possible score is 100.

The countries with the least amount of country risk all have strong, market-based economies, ready access to worldwide capital markets, relatively little social unrest, and a stable political climate. Switzerland's top ranking may surprise you, but that country's ranking is the result of its strong economic performance. You may also be surprised that the United States was not ranked in the top five—it is ranked seventh.

Arguably, there are fewer surprises when looking at the bottom five. Each of these countries has considerable social and political unrest, and none has embraced a market-based economic system. Clearly, an investment in any of these countries is a risky proposition.

Top Five Countries (Least Amount of Country Risk)

Rank	Country	Total Score (Maximum Possible = 100)
1	Switzerland	95.6
2	Luxembourg	94.2
3	Germany	94.1
4	Netherlands	93.8
5	United Kingdom	93.7

Bottom Five Countries (Greatest Amount of Country Risk)

Rank	Country	Total Score (Minimum Possible = 0)
147	North Korea	8.8
148	Democratic Republic of Congo	8.4
149	Sierra Leone	8.3
150	Liberia	8.0
151	Afganistan	4.5

Source: Adapted from Harvey D. Shapiro, "Looking Up," *Institutional Investor,* March 2002, 165–167.

Students can access the home page of *Institutional Investor* magazine by typing http://www.institutionalinvestoronline.com. Although the site requires users to register, the site is free to use. (Some data sets and articles are available only to subscribers.)

Over the past several decades, the federal government routinely ran large budget deficits. However, in 1999, for the first time in recent memory, the government had a budget surplus, and further surpluses are projected on into the future. As a result, the government is buying back some of the outstanding Treasury securities. If these surpluses become a reality, the government would become a net supplier of funds rather than a net borrower of funds. All else equal, this would tend to reduce interest rates.

International Factors

Businesses and individuals in the United States buy from and sell to people and firms in other countries. If we buy more than we sell (that is, if we import more than we export), we are said to be running a *foreign trade deficit.* When trade deficits occur, they must be financed, and the main source of financing is debt. In other words, if we import $200 billion of goods but export only $100 billion, we run a trade deficit of $100 billion, and we would probably borrow the $100 billion.[17] Therefore, the larger our trade deficit, the more we must borrow, and as we increase our borrowing, this drives up interest rates. Also, foreigners are willing to hold U.S. debt if and only if the rate paid on this debt is competitive with interest rates in other countries. Therefore, if the Federal Reserve attempts to lower interest rates in the United States, causing our rates to fall below rates abroad, then foreigners will sell U.S. bonds, those sales will depress bond prices, and the result will be higher U.S. rates. Thus, if the trade deficit is large relative to the size of the overall economy, it may hinder the Fed's ability to combat a recession by lowering interest rates.

The United States has been running annual trade deficits since the mid-1970s, and the cumulative effect of these deficits is that the United States has become the largest debtor nation of all time. As a result, our interest rates are very much influenced by interest rates in other countries around the world (higher rates abroad lead to higher U.S. rates). Because of all this, U.S. corporate treasurers—and anyone else who is affected by interest rates—must keep up with developments in the world economy.

Business Activity

Figure 25-3, presented earlier, can be examined to see how business conditions influence interest rates. Here are the key points revealed by the graph:

1. Because inflation increased from 1961 to 1981, the general tendency during that period was toward higher interest rates. However, since the 1981 peak, the trend has generally been downward.
2. Until 1966, short-term rates were almost always below long-term rates. Thus, in those years the yield curve was almost always "normal" in the sense that it was upward sloping.
3. The shaded areas in the graph represent recessions, during which (1) both the demand for money and the rate of inflation tend to fall and (2) the Federal Reserve tends to increase the money supply in an effort to stimulate the economy. As a result, there is a tendency for interest rates to decline during recessions. For example, the economy began to slow down in 2000, and we entered a mild recession in 2001. In response to this economic weakness, the Federal Reserve cut interest rates. Now, in mid-2002, there are some tentative signs that the economy has begun to rebound, so the Fed has stopped cutting short-term rates, and is poised to raise rates once it is sure the economy has truly regained its strength.
4. During recessions, short-term rates decline more sharply than long-term rates. This occurs because (1) the Fed operates mainly in the short-term sector, so its intervention has the strongest effect there, and (2) long-term rates reflect the average expected inflation rate over the next 20 to 30 years, and

---

[17] The deficit could also be financed by selling assets, including gold, corporate stocks, entire companies, and real estate. The United States has financed its massive trade deficits by all of these means in recent years, but the primary method has been by borrowing from foreigners.

this expectation generally does not change much, even when the current inflation rate is low because of a recession or high because of a boom. So, short-term rates are more volatile than long-term rates. Taking another look at Figure 25-3, we indeed see that short-term rates have declined much more than long-term rates have during the most recent economic decline in 2001.

Self-Test Questions

Other than inflationary expectations, name some additional factors that influence interest rates, and explain the effects of each.

How does the Fed stimulate the economy? How does the Fed affect interest rates?

Does the Fed have complete control over U.S. interest rates; that is, can it set rates at any level it chooses?

INTEREST RATES AND BUSINESS DECISIONS 14

The yield curve for April 2002, shown earlier in Figure 25-5, indicates how much the U.S. government had to pay in 2002 to borrow money for one year, five years, ten years, and so on. A business borrower would have had to pay somewhat more, but assume for the moment that we are back in April 2002 and that the yield curve for that year also applies to your company. Now suppose your company has decided (1) to build a new plant with a 30-year life that will cost $1 million and (2) to raise the $1 million by selling an issue of debt (or borrowing) rather than by selling stock. If you borrowed in 2002 on a short-term basis—say, for one year—your interest cost for that year would be only 2.3 percent, or $23,000. On the other hand, if you used long-term (30-year) financing, your cost would be 5.7 percent, or $57,000. Therefore, at first glance, it would seem that you should use short-term debt.

However, this could prove to be a horrible mistake. If you use short-term debt, you will have to renew your loan every year, and the rate charged on each new loan will reflect the then-current short-term rate. Interest rates could return to their previous highs, in which case you would be paying 14 percent, or $140,000, per year. Those high interest payments would cut into, and perhaps eliminate, your profits. Your reduced profitability could easily increase your firm's risk to the point where its bond rating would be lowered, causing lenders to increase the risk premium built into the interest rate they charge. That would force you to pay an even higher rate, which would further reduce your profitability, worrying lenders even more, and making them reluctant to renew your loan. If your lenders refused to renew the loan and demanded its repayment, as they would have every right to do, you might have to sell assets at a loss, which could lead to bankruptcy.

On the other hand, if you used long-term financing in 2002, your interest costs would remain constant at $57,000 per year, so an increase in interest rates in the economy would not hurt you. You might even be able to buy up some of your bankrupt competitors at bargain prices—bankruptcies increase dramatically when interest rates rise, primarily because many firms do use too much short-term debt.

Does all this suggest that firms should always avoid short-term debt? Not necessarily. If inflation falls over the next few years, so will interest rates. If you had borrowed on a long-term basis for 5.7 percent in April 2002, your company would be at a major disadvantage if it were locked into 5.7 percent debt while its competitors (who used short-term debt in 2002 and thus rode interest rates down in subsequent years) had a borrowing cost of only 3 or 4 percent.

Financing decisions would be easy if we could make accurate forecasts of future interest rates. Unfortunately, predicting interest rates with consistent accuracy is somewhere between difficult and impossible—people who make a living by selling interest rate forecasts say it is difficult, but many others say it is impossible.

Even if it is difficult to predict future interest rate *levels*, it is easy to predict that interest rates will *fluctuate*—they always have, and they always will. This being the case, sound financial policy calls for using a mix of long- and short-term debt, as well as equity, to position the firm so that it can survive in any interest rate environment. Further, the optimal financial policy depends in an important way on the nature of the firm's assets—the easier it is to sell off assets to generate cash, the more feasible it is to use large amounts of short-term debt. This makes it more feasible for a firm to finance its current assets such as inventories than its fixed assets such as buildings with short-term debt. We will return to this issue later in the book, when we discuss working capital policy.

Changes in interest rates also have implications for savers. For example, if you had a 401(k) plan—and someday you almost certainly will—you would probably want to invest some of your money in a bond mutual fund. You could choose a fund that had an average maturity of 25 years, 20 years, and so on, down to only a few months (a money market fund). How would your choice affect your investment results, hence your retirement income? First, your annual interest income would be affected. For example, if the yield curve were upward sloping, as it normally is, you would earn more interest if you choose a fund that held long-term bonds. Note, though, that if you choose a long-term fund and interest rates then rose, the market value of the bonds in the fund would decline. For example, as we will see in Reading 7, if you had $100,000 in a fund whose average bond had a maturity of 25 years and a coupon rate of 6 percent, and if interest rates then rose from 6 percent to 10 percent, the market value of your fund would decline from $100,000 to about $64,000. On the other hand, if rates declined, your fund would increase in value. In any event, your choice of maturity would have a major effect on your investment performance, hence your future income.

Self-Test Questions

If short-term interest rates are lower than long-term rates, why might a borrower still choose to finance with long-term debt?

Explain the following statement: "The optimal financial policy depends in an important way on the nature of the firm's assets."

OPTIONAL SEGMENT ENDS

SUMMARY 15

In this reading, we discussed the nature of financial markets, the types of institutions that operate in these markets, how interest rates are determined, and some of the ways interest rates affect business decisions. In later readings we will use this information to help value different investments, and to better understand corporate financing and investing decisions. The key concepts covered are listed below.

- There are many different types of **financial markets.** Each market serves a different region or deals with a different type of security.
- **Physical asset markets,** also called tangible or real asset markets, are those for such products as wheat, autos, and real estate.
- **Financial asset markets** deal with stocks, bonds, notes, mortgages, and other claims on real assets.
- **Spot markets** and **futures markets** are terms that refer to whether the assets are bought or sold for "on-the-spot" delivery or for delivery at some future date.
- **Money markets** are the markets for debt securities with maturities of less than one year.
- **Capital markets** are the markets for long-term debt and corporate stocks.
- **Primary markets** are the markets in which corporations raise new capital.
- **Secondary markets** are markets in which existing, already outstanding, securities are traded among investors.
- A **derivative** is a security whose value is derived from the price of some other "underlying" asset.
- Transfers of capital between borrowers and savers take place (1) by **direct transfers** of money and securities; (2) by transfers through **investment banking houses,** which act as middlemen; and (3) by transfers through **financial intermediaries,** which create new securities.
- Among the major classes of intermediaries are **commercial banks, savings and loan associations, mutual savings banks, credit unions, pension funds, life insurance companies,** and **mutual funds.**
- One result of ongoing regulatory changes has been a blurring of the distinctions between the different financial institutions. The trend in the United States has been toward **financial service corporations** that offer a wide range of financial services, including investment banking, brokerage operations, insurance, and commercial banking.
- The **stock market** is an especially important market because this is where stock prices (which are used to "grade" managers' performances) are established.
- There are two basic types of stock markets—the **physical location exchanges** (like the NYSE) and the **electronic dealer-based markets** (that include the Nasdaq and the over-the-counter market).
- Capital is allocated through the price system—a price must be paid to "rent" money. Lenders charge **interest** on funds they lend, while equity investors receive **dividends and capital gains** in return for letting firms use their money.
- Four fundamental factors affect the cost of money: (1) **production opportunities,** (2) **time preferences for consumption,** (3) **risk,** and (4) **inflation.**
- The **risk-free rate of interest, k_{RF},** is defined as the real risk-free rate, k^*, plus an inflation premium, IP, hence $k_{RF} = k^* + IP$.

- The **nominal** (or **quoted**) **interest rate** on a debt security, **k,** is composed of the real risk-free rate, k*, plus premiums that reflect inflation (IP), default risk (DRP), liquidity (LP), and maturity risk (MRP):

  $$k = k^* + IP + DRP + LP + MRP.$$

- If the **real risk-free rate of interest and the various premiums were constant over time,** interest rates would be stable. However, both the real rate and the premiums—especially the premium for expected inflation—**do change over time, causing market interest rates to change.** Also, Federal Reserve intervention to increase or decrease the money supply, as well as international currency flows, leads to fluctuations in interest rates.
- The relationship between the yields on securities and the securities' maturities is known as the **term structure of interest rates,** and the **yield curve** is a graph of this relationship.
- The shape of the yield curve depends on two key factors: (1) **expectations about future inflation** and (2) **perceptions about the relative riskiness of securities with different maturities.**
- The yield curve is normally **upward sloping**—this is called a **normal yield curve.** However, the curve can slope downward (an **inverted yield curve**) if the inflation rate is expected to decline. The yield curve can also be **humped,** which means that interest rates on medium-term maturities are higher than rates on both short- and long-term maturities.
- Because interest rate levels are difficult if not impossible to predict, **sound financial policy** calls for using a mix of short- and long-term debt, and also for positioning the firm to survive in any future interest rate environment.

STUDY SESSION 6 ECONOMICS: GLOBAL ECONOMIC ANALYSIS

READING ASSIGNMENTS

Reading 26 Gaining from International Trade
Reading 27 Foreign Exchange
Reading 28 Foreign Exchange Parity Relations

LEARNING OUTCOMES

Note:
Candidates are responsible for the problems listed after the readings. Solutions to the problems are found in Appendix A.

Reading 26: Gaining from International Trade

The candidate should be able to:

a. state the conditions under which a nation can gain from international trade in the context of both comparative and absolute advantage, and describe the benefits of international trade;

b. discuss the effects of international trade on domestic supply and demand;

c. distinguish between commonly used trade-restricting devices, including tariffs, quotas, voluntary export restraints, and exchange-rate controls, and explain their impact on the domestic economy;

d. identify who benefits and loses from the imposition of a tariff;

e. discuss the three arguments to adopt trade restrictions and discuss the popular fallacies related to trade restrictions.

Reading 27: Foreign Exchange

The candidate should be able to:

a. define direct and indirect methods of foreign exchange quotations and calculate and interpret the spread on a foreign currency quotation, and convert direct (indirect) foreign exchange quotations into indirect (direct) foreign exchange quotations;

b. explain how spreads on foreign currency quotations can differ as a result of market conditions, bank/dealer positions, and trading volume;

c. calculate and interpret currency cross rates, given two spot exchange quotations involving three currencies;

d. distinguish between the spot and forward markets for foreign exchange;

e. calculate the spread on a forward foreign currency quotation and explain how spreads on forward foreign currency quotations can differ as a result of market conditions, bank/dealer positions, trading volume, and maturity/length of contract;

f. calculate and interpret a forward discount or premium and express it as an annualized rate;

g. explain interest rate parity and illustrate covered interest arbitrage.

Reading 28: Foreign Exchange Parity Relations

The candidate should be able to:

a. explain how exchange rates are determined in a flexible or floating exchange rate system;

b. explain the role of each component of the balance-of-payments accounts;

c. explain how current account deficits or surpluses and financial account deficits or surpluses affect an economy;

d. describe the factors that cause a nation's currency to appreciate or depreciate;

e. explain how monetary and fiscal policies affect the exchange rate and balance-of-payments components;

f. describe a fixed exchange rate and a pegged exchange rate system;

g. discuss absolute purchasing power parity and relative purchasing power parity.

GAINING FROM INTERNATIONAL TRADE

READING 26

LEARNING OUTCOMES

The candidate should be able to:

a. state the conditions under which a nation can gain from international trade in the context of both comparative and absolute advantage, and describe the benefits of international trade;

b. discuss the effects of international trade on domestic supply and demand;

c. distinguish between commonly used trade-restricting devices, including tariffs, quotas, voluntary export restraints, and exchange-rate controls, and explain their impact on the domestic economy;

d. identify who benefits and loses from the imposition of a tariff;

e. discuss the three arguments to adopt trade restrictions and discuss the popular fallacies related to trade restrictions.

The evidence is overwhelmingly persuasive that the massive increase in world competition—a consequence of broadening trade flows—has fostered markedly higher standards of living for almost all countries who have participated in cross-border trade. I include most especially the United States.

—Alan Greenspan[1]

INTRODUCTION 1

We live in a shrinking world. The breakfast of many Americans includes bananas from Honduras, coffee from Brazil, or hot chocolate made from Nigerian cocoa beans. Americans often drive a car produced by a Japanese or European manufacturer that consumes gasoline refined from petroleum extracted in Saudi Arabia or Venezuela. Similarly, many Americans work for companies that sell a substantial amount of their products to foreigners. Spurred by cost reductions in transportation and communications, the volume of international trade has grown rapidly in recent decades. Approximately 21 percent of the world's total output is now sold

[1] Speech before the Alliance for the Commonwealth Conference on International Business, Boston, Massachusetts, on June 2, 1999.

in a country other than that in which it was produced—double the figure of four decades ago.

Perhaps surprising to some, most international trade is not between the governments of the nations involved but rather between individuals and business firms that happen to be located in different countries. Why do people engage in international trade? The expectation of gain provides the answer. Domestic producers are often able to sell their products to foreigners at attractive prices, while domestic consumers sometimes find that the best deals are available from foreign suppliers. Like other voluntary exchange, international trade results because both the buyer and the seller expect to gain and generally do. If both parties did not expect to gain, they would not agree to the exchange.

2 CROSS COUNTRY DIFFERENCES IN THE SIZE OF THE TRADE SECTOR

The size of the trade sector varies substantially among nations. Some of the difference is due to size of country. For industries in which economies of scale are important, the domestic market of a less-populated country may not be large enough to support cost-efficient firms. Therefore, in small countries, firms in such industries will tend to export a larger share of their output, and consumers will be more likely to purchase goods produced abroad. As a result, the size of the trade sector as a share of the economy tends to be inversely related to the population of the country.

Even among countries of similar size, there is considerable variation in the size of the trade sector. Among the countries with a large population (120 million or more), the trade sector is largest in Indonesia. In 1999, exports accounted for 35 percent of GDP in Indonesia, about three times the figure for Japan, Brazil, and the United States. Among the mid-size countries (population between 40 million and 65 million), the trade sectors of Thailand, Philippines, and South Korea are quite large, while those of Egypt and Turkey are small. As a share of domestic output, Singapore and Hong Kong have the largest international trade sectors in the world. Both import large quantities of raw materials and unfinished goods and manufacture them into products that are often exported abroad. Therefore, the gross exports of these two vibrant trade centers actually exceed their gross domestic product.

3 THE TRADE SECTOR OF THE UNITED STATES

As Exhibit 26-1 illustrates, the size of the trade sector of the United States has grown rapidly during the last several decades. In 1960, total exports of goods and services accounted for 4.8 percent of the U.S. economy, while imports summed to 4.3 percent. By 1975, both exports and imports were approximately 7.5 percent of the economy. Since 1975 the size of the trade sector as a *share of the economy* has nearly doubled. In 2000, exports accounted for 11.2 percent of total output, while imports summed to 14.9 percent.

Who are the major trading partners of Americans? Canada, Japan, and Mexico head the list. In 1999, approximately 45 percent of U.S. exports were sold to

EXHIBIT 26-1 The Growth of the Trade Sector in the United States: 1960–2000

During the past several decades, international trade has persistently risen as a share of GDP. Imports rose from 7.5 percent of GDP in 1975 to 14.9 percent in 2000. During the same period, exports rose from 8.2 percent to 11.2 percent of GDP.

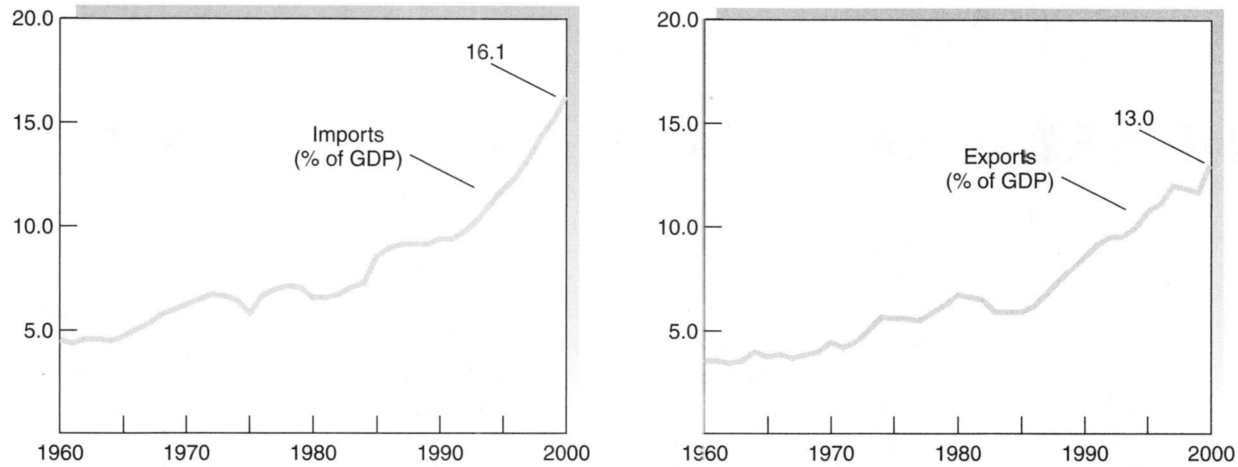

(a) Imports as a Share of GDP

(b) Exports as a Share of GDP

Source: Economic Report of the President, 2001, Table B-2. The figures are based on data for real imports, exports, and GDP.

NOTE: The values shown for 2000 in panel (a) and panel (b) are not consistent with the values cited in the narrative. The intent of the graph is to show that the U.S. trade sector has grown from 1960 to 2000. Candidates are not responsible for the numerical values.

purchasers in these three countries. Canadians purchased 24 percent of U.S. exports, while Mexicans purchased 13 percent, and the Japanese 8 percent. These three countries also supplied approximately 43 percent of the U.S. imports—19 percent by Canadians, 13 percent by Japanese, and 11 percent by Mexicans. The nations of the European Union (particularly Germany, the United Kingdom, France, and Italy), China (including Hong Kong), and several other smaller Asian countries (Taiwan, South Korea, Singapore, and Malaysia) are also major trading partners of the United States.

What are the leading imports and exports of the United States? The United States both imports and exports a substantial quantity of capital goods, such as automobiles, computers, semiconductors, telecommunications equipment, and industrial machines. The markets for these items are worldwide. Producers in the United States sell substantial quantities abroad, while, at the same time, many U.S. consumers purchase these goods from foreign manufacturers. Civilian aircraft, electrical equipment, chemicals, and plastics are also among the leading export products of the United States, while crude oil, textiles, toys, sporting goods, and pharmaceutical products are major imports.

Clearly, the impact of international trade differs across industries. In some industries, domestic producers find it very difficult to compete with their rivals abroad. For example, approximately 90 percent of the shoes purchased by Americans and nearly two-thirds of the radio and television sets, watches, and motorcycles are produced abroad. Imports also supply a high percentage of the clothing and textile products, paper, cut diamonds, and VCRs consumed in the United States. On the other hand, a large proportion of the aircraft, power-generating equipment, scientific instruments, construction equipment, and fertilizers produced in the United States is exported to purchasers abroad.

If a foreign country can supply us with a commodity cheaper than we ourselves can make it, [we had] better buy it of them with some part of our own industry, employed in a way in which we have some advantage.

—Adam Smith[2]

4 GAINS FROM SPECIALIZATION AND TRADE

Comparative advantage
The ability to produce a good at a lower opportunity cost than others can produce it. Relative costs determine comparative advantage.

As we discussed in Chapter 2, the law of **comparative advantage** explains why a group of individuals, regions, or nations can gain from specialization and exchange. ***International trade leads to mutual gain because it allows the residents of each country to: (1) specialize more fully in the production of those things that they do best, and (2) import goods when foreigners are willing to supply them at a lower cost than domestic producers.*** Labor-force skills and resource endowments differ substantially across countries. These differences influence costs. Therefore, a good that is quite costly to produce in one country may be economically produced in another. For example, the warm, moist climate of Brazil, Colombia, and Guatemala enhances the economical production of coffee. Countries like Saudi Arabia and Venezuela with rich oil fields can produce petroleum cheaply. Countries with an abundance of fertile land, like Canada and Australia, are able to produce products like wheat, feed grains, and beef at a low cost. In contrast, land is scarce in Japan, a nation with a highly skilled labor force. The Japanese, therefore, specialize in manufacturing, using their comparative advantage to produce cameras, automobiles, and electronic products for export. With international trade, the residents of each country can gain by specializing in the production of goods that they can produce economically and using the proceeds to import goods that would be expensive to produce domestically.

Because failure to comprehend the principle of mutual gains from trade is often a source of "fuzzy thinking," we will take the time to illustrate the principle in detail. To keep things simple, we will consider a case involving only two countries, the United States and Japan, and two products, food and clothing. Furthermore, we will assume that labor is the only resource used to produce these products. In addition, since we want to illustrate that gains from trade are nearly always possible, we are going to assume that Japan has an **absolute advantage**—that the Japanese workers are more efficient than the Americans—in the production of both commodities. Exhibit 26-2 illustrates this situation. Perhaps due to their prior experience or higher skill level, Japanese workers can produce three units of food per day, compared with only two units per day for U.S. workers. Similarly, Japanese workers are able to produce nine units of clothing per day, compared to one unit of clothing per day for U.S. workers.

Absolute advantage
A situation in which a nation, as the result of its previous experience and/or natural endowments, can produce more of a good (with the same amount of resources) than another nation.

Let us consider the following question: Can two countries gain from trade if one of them can produce both goods with fewer resources? Perhaps surprising to some, the answer is yes. As long as *relative* production costs of the two goods differ between Japan and the United States, gains from trade will be possible. Consider what would happen if the United States shifted three workers from the clothing industry to the food industry. This reallocation of labor would allow the United States to expand its food output by six units (two units per worker), while clothing output would decline by three units (one unit per worker). Suppose

[2] Adam Smith, *An Inquiry into the Nature and Causes of the Wealth of Nations* (1776; Cannan's ed., Chicago: University of Chicago Press, 1976), pp. 478–479.

EXHIBIT 26-2 Gains from Specialization and Trade

Columns 1 and 2 indicate the daily output of either food or clothing of each worker in the United States and Japan. If the United States moves 3 workers from the clothing industry to the food industry, it can produce 6 more units of food and 3 fewer units of clothing. Similarly, if Japan moves 1 worker from food to clothing, clothing output will increase by 9 units while food output will decline by 3 units. With this reallocation of labor, the United States and Japan are able to increase their aggregate output of both food (3 additional units) and clothing (6 additional units).

	Output per Worker Day		Potential Change in Output[a]	
Country	**Food (1)**	**Clothing (2)**	**Food (3)**	**Clothing (4)**
United States	2	1	+6	−3
Japan	3	9	−3	+9
Change in Total Output			+3	+6

[a]Change in output if the United States shifts three workers from the clothing to the food industry and if Japan shifts one worker from the food to the clothing industry.

Japan reallocates labor in the opposite direction. When Japan moves one worker from the food industry to the clothing industry, Japanese clothing production expands by nine units while food output declines by three units. Exhibit 26-2 shows that this reallocation of labor *within* the two countries has increased their joint output by three units of food and six units of clothing.

The source of this increase in output is straightforward: Aggregate output expands because the reallocation of labor permits each country to specialize more fully in the production of those goods that it can produce at a *relatively* low cost. Our old friend, the opportunity-cost concept, reveals the low-cost producer of each good. If Japanese workers produce one additional unit of food, they sacrifice the production of three units of clothing. Therefore, in Japan the opportunity cost of one unit of food is three units of clothing. On the other hand, one unit of food in the United States can be produced at an opportunity cost of only one-half unit of clothing. American workers are therefore the low-opportunity-cost producers of food, even though they cannot produce as much food per day as the Japanese workers. Simultaneously, Japan is the low-opportunity-cost producer of clothing. The opportunity cost of producing a unit of clothing in Japan is only one-third unit of food, compared to two units of food in the United States. The reallocation of labor illustrated in Exhibit 26-2 expanded joint output because it moved resources in both countries toward areas where they had a comparative advantage.

As long as the relative costs of producing the two goods differ in the two countries, gains from specialization and trade will be possible. When this is the case, each country will find it cheaper to trade for goods that can be produced only at a high opportunity cost. For example, both countries can gain if the United States trades food to Japan for clothing at a trading ratio greater than one unit of food equals one-half unit of clothing (the U.S. opportunity cost of food) but less than one unit of food equals three units of clothing (the Japanese opportunity cost of food). Any trading ratio between these two extremes will permit the United States to acquire clothing more cheaply than it could be produced within the country and simultaneously permit Japan to acquire food more cheaply than it could be produced domestically.

How Trade Expands Consumption Possibilities

Because trade permits nations to expand their joint output, it also allows each nation to expand its consumption possibilities. The production-possibilities concept can be used to illustrate this point. Suppose that there were 200 million workers in the United States and 50 million in Japan. Given these figures and the productivity of workers indicated in Exhibit 26-2, the production-possibilities curves for the two countries are presented in Exhibit 26-3. If the United States used all of its 200 million workers in the food industry, it could produce 400 million units of food per day—two units per worker—and zero units of clothing (point *N*). Alternatively, if the United States used all its workers to produce clothing, daily output would be 200 million units of clothing and no food (point *M*). Intermediate output combinations along the production-possibilities line (*MN*) intersecting these two extreme points also could be achievable. For example, the United States could produce 150 million units of clothing and 100 million units of food (point US_1).

Part b of Exhibit 26-3 illustrates the production possibilities of the 50 million Japanese workers. Japan could produce 450 million units of clothing and no food (*R*), 150 million units of food and no clothing (*S*), or various intermediate combinations, like 225 million units of clothing and 75 million units of food (J_1). The slope of the production-possibilities constraint reflects the opportunity cost of food relative to clothing. Because Japan is the high-opportunity-cost producer of food, its production-possibilities constraint is steeper than the constraint for the United States.

In the absence of trade, the consumption of each country is constrained by the country's production possibilities. Trade, however, expands the consumption

EXHIBIT 26-3 Production Possibilities of the United States and Japan Before Specialization and Trade

Here we illustrate the daily production possibilities of a U.S. labor force of 200 million workers and a Japanese labor force of 50 million workers, given the cost of producing food and clothing presented in Exhibit 26-2. In the absence of trade, consumption possibilities will be restricted to points such as US_1 in the United States and J_1 in Japan along the production possibilities curve of each country.

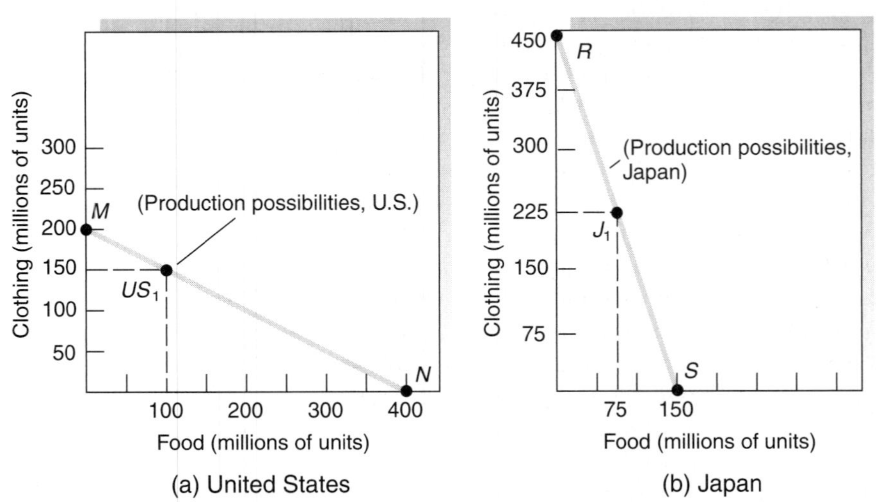

EXHIBIT 26-4 Consumption Possibilities with Trade

With specialization and trade, the consumption possibilities of a country can be expanded. If the United States can trade one unit of clothing for one unit of food, it can specialize in the production of food and consume along the *ON* line (rather than its original production-possibilities constraint, *MN*). Similarly, when Japan is able to trade one unit of clothing for one unit of food, it can specialize in the production of clothing and consume any combination along the line *RT*. For example, with specialization and trade, the United States could increase its consumption from US_1 to US_2, gaining 50 million units of clothing and 100 million units of food. Simultaneously, Japan could increase consumption from J_1 to J_2, a gain of 125 million units of food and 25 million units of clothing.

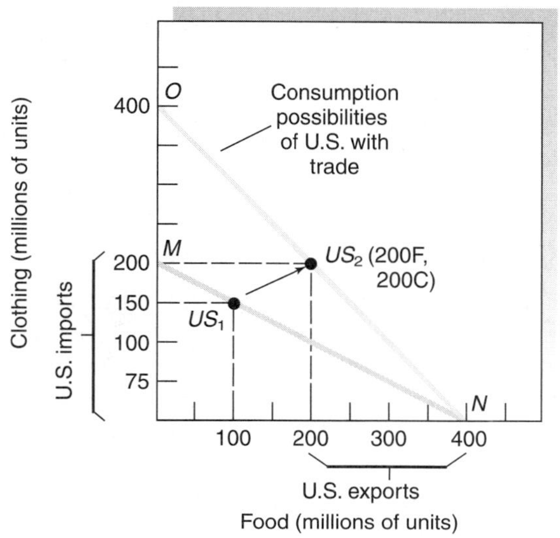

(a) United States

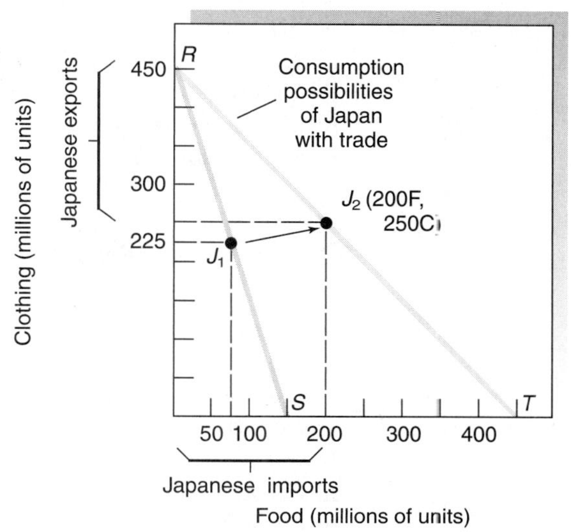

(b) Japan

possibilities of both. As we previously indicated, both countries can gain from specialization if the United States trades food to Japan at a price greater than one unit of food equals one-half unit of clothing but less than one unit of food equals three units of clothing. Suppose that they agree on an intermediate price of one unit of food equals one unit of clothing. As part a of Exhibit 26-4 illustrates, when the United States specializes in the production of food (where it has a comparative advantage) and trades food for clothing (at the price ratio where one unit of food equals one unit of clothing), it can consume along the line *ON*. If the United States insisted on self-sufficiency, it would be restricted to consumption possibilities like US_1 (100 million units of food and 150 million units of clothing) along its production-possibilities constraint of *MN*. With trade, however, the United States can achieve such combinations as US_2 (200 million units of food and 200 million units of clothing) along the line *ON*. Trade permits the United States to expand its consumption of both goods.

Simultaneously, Japan is able to expand its consumption of both goods when it is able to trade clothing for food at the one-to-one price ratio. As part b of Exhibit 26-4 illustrates, Japan can specialize in the production of clothing and consume along the constraint *RT* when it can trade one unit of clothing for one unit of food. Without trade, consumption in Japan would be limited to points like J_1 (75 million units of food and 225 million units of clothing) along the line *RS*. With trade, however, it is able to consume combinations like J_2 (200 million units of food and 250 million units of clothing) along the constraint *RT*.

Look what happens when Japan specializes in clothing and the United States specializes in food. Japan can produce 450 million units of clothing, export 200 million to the United States (for 200 million units of food), and still have 250 million units of clothing remaining for domestic consumption. Simultaneously, the United States can produce 400 million units of food, export 200 million to Japan (for 200 million units of clothing), and still have 200 million units of food left for domestic consumption. After specialization and trade, the United States is able to consume at the point of US_2 and Japan at point J_2, consumption levels that would be unattainable without trade. Specialization and exchange permit the two countries to expand their joint output, and, as a result, both countries can increase their consumption of both commodities.

The implications of the law of comparative advantage are clear: Trade between nations will lead to an expansion in total output and mutual gain for each trading partner when each country specializes in the production of goods it can produce at a relatively low cost and uses the proceeds to buy goods that it could produce only at a high cost. It is comparative advantage that matters. As long as there is some variation in the relative opportunity cost of goods across countries, each country will always have a comparative advantage in the production of some goods.

Some Real-World Considerations

In order to keep things simple, we ignored the potential importance of transportation costs, which, of course, reduce the potential gains from trade. Sometimes transportation and other transaction costs, both real and artificially imposed, exceed the potential for mutual gain. In this case, exchange does not occur.

We also assumed that the cost of producing each good was constant in each country. This is seldom the case. Beyond some level of production, the opportunity cost of producing a good will often increase as a country produces more and more of it. Rising marginal costs as the output of a good expands will limit the degree to which a country will specialize in the production of a good. This situation would be depicted by a production-possibilities curve that was convex, or bowed out from the origin. In cases of increasing cost there will still be gains from trade but there need not be complete specialization.

Trade Openness, Income, and Living Standards

International trade
When people are permitted to engage freely in international trade, they are able to achieve higher income levels and living standards than would otherwise be possible.

Most of us specialize in a relatively few productive activities and use the income from these activities to purchase most of the goods and services that we consume. Of course, the domestic market of our country provides opportunity for gains from specialization and trade. This is particularly true for those who live in a country such as the United States with a large domestic market. International trade makes it possible for individuals to buy from and sell to an even larger market. Thus, it expands the opportunity for gains from trade.

Specialization and comparative advantage provide the foundation for gains from international trade. As we have just explained, trade makes it possible for the residents of each nation to trade for those things for which they are a high opportunity cost producer and, at the same time, focus more of their resources on things they do well. When trading partners use more of their time and resources producing things they do best, they are able to produce a larger output and consume a larger, more diverse bundle of goods than would otherwise be attainable. In addition to these benefits, other gains are also derived from trade openness. We will briefly discuss three of them.

Greater Realization of Gains from Large-scale Production

International trade allows both domestic producers and consumers to gain from reductions in per-unit costs that often accompany large-scale production, marketing, and distribution. Trade expands the potential size of the market available to both domestic and foreign firms. When economies of scale are important in an industry, successful domestic firms will be able to produce larger outputs and achieve lower costs than would be possible if they were unable to sell abroad.

This point is particularly important for small countries. For example, textile manufacturers in Malaysia, Taiwan, and South Korea would have much higher costs if they could not sell abroad. The domestic textile markets of these countries are too small to support large, low-cost firms in this industry. With international trade, however, textile firms in these countries operate at a large scale and compete quite effectively in the world market.

International trade also benefits domestic consumers by permitting them to purchase from large-scale producers abroad. The aircraft industry provides a vivid illustration of this point. Given the huge design and engineering costs, the domestic market of almost all countries would be substantially less than the quantity required for the efficient production of jet planes. With international trade, however, consumers around the world are able to purchase planes economically from large-scale producers like Boeing.

Gains from More Competitive Markets

Openness to international trade promotes competition and thereby encourages both innovative and efficient production. At the same time, it provides consumers with a much broader array of goods than would be available in the absence of trade. The competition from abroad helps keep domestic producers on their toes and provides them with a strong incentive to improve the quality of their products. The experience of the U.S. auto industry illustrates this point. Faced with stiff competition from Japanese firms during the 1980s, U.S. auto makers worked hard to improve the quality of their vehicles. As a result, the reliability of the automobiles and light trucks available to American consumers—including those produced by domestic manufacturers—is almost certainly higher than would have been the case in the absence of international competition.

Brain power and innovation are important sources of economic growth. Trade across national boundaries will lead to greater awareness of technologies and innovative ideas employed elsewhere. In many cases, local entrepreneurs will emulate procedures and products that have been successful in other countries. They may also introduce modifications that make products more suitable for the local market. Dynamic competition of this type is an important source of growth and prosperity, particularly for less developed countries.

Gains from the Adoption of Better Institutions and Policies

Not only do firms of an open economy face more intense competition, so too does government. Openness provides political officials with a strong incentive to establish sound institutions and follow constructive policies. If they do not, both labor and capital will move toward a more favorable environment. For example, neither domestic nor foreign investors will want to place their funds in countries characterized by hostility toward business, monetary instability, legal uncertainty, high taxes and low-quality public services. When labor and capital are free to move elsewhere, policies that penalize success and undermine productive activities become more costly. Even though this indirect effect is generally overlooked, it may well be one of the most beneficial attributes of an open economy.

5 EXPORT-IMPORT LINK

Doubts about the merits of international trade often result from a failure to consider all the consequences. Why are other nations willing to export their goods to the United States? So they can obtain dollars. Yes, but why do they want dollars? Would foreigners be willing to continue exporting oil, televisions, watches, cameras, automobiles, and thousands of other valuable products to Americans in exchange for pieces of paper? If so, Americans could all be semi-retired, spending only an occasional workday at the dollar printing-press office! Of course, foreigners are not so naive. They trade goods for dollars so they can use the dollars to buy U.S. goods and purchase ownership rights to U.S. assets.

Exports, broadly perceived to include goods, services, and assets, provide the buying power that makes it possible for a nation to import.[3] If a nation did not export, it would not have the foreign currency that is required for the purchase of imports. Similarly, if a nation did not import, foreigners would not have the purchasing power to buy that nation's export items. Therefore, if imports decline, so will the demand for the nation's exports. Exports and imports are closely linked.

6 SUPPLY, DEMAND, AND INTERNATIONAL TRADE

International trade can also be analyzed within the framework of supply and demand. This approach highlights how trade influences price and output in domestic markets. Given our modern transportation and communication networks, the market for many commodities is worldwide. When a product can be transported long distances at a low cost (relative to its value), the domestic price of the product is in effect determined by the forces of supply and demand in the world market.

Consider the market for a good that U.S. producers are able to supply at a low cost. Using soybeans as an example, Exhibit 26-5 illustrates the relationship between the domestic and world markets. The price of soybeans is determined by the forces of supply and demand in the world market. In an open economy, domestic producers are free to sell and domestic consumers are free to buy the product at the world market price (P_w). At this price, U.S. producers will supply Q_p, while U.S. consumers will purchase Q_c. Reflecting their low cost (comparative advantage), U.S. soybean producers will export $Q_p - Q_c$ units at the world market price.

Let us compare the open-economy outcome with the situation in the absence of trade. If U.S. producers were not allowed to export soybeans, the domestic price would be determined by the domestic supply (S_d) and demand (D_d) only. A lower "no-trade" price (P_n) would emerge. Who are the winners and losers as the result of free trade in soybeans? Clearly, soybean producers gain. Free trade allows domestic producers to sell a larger quantity (Q_p rather than Q_n). As a result, the net revenues of soybean producers will rise by P_wbcP_n. On the other hand, domestic consumers of soybeans will have to pay a higher price under free trade. Soybean consumers will lose (1) because they have to pay P_w rather than P_n for the Q_c units they purchase, and (2) because they lose the con-

[3] The data of Exhibit 26-1 indicate that imports have exceeded exports in recent years. These data are for goods and services only; they omit the purchase and sale of assets. In the following reading, we will illustrate that once the asset transactions with foreigners are also included, the equality between imports and exports is indeed present.

EXHIBIT 26-5 Producer Benefits from Exports

The price of soybeans and other internationally traded commodities is determined by the forces of supply and demand in the world market (b). If U.S. soybean producers were prohibited from selling to foreigners, the domestic price would be P_n (a). Free trade permits the U.S. soybean producers to sell Q_p units at the higher world price (P_w). The quantity $Q_p - Q_c$ is exported abroad. Compared to the no-trade situation, the producers' gain from the higher price (P_wbcP_n) exceeds the cost imposed on domestic consumers (P_wacP_n) by the triangle *abc*.

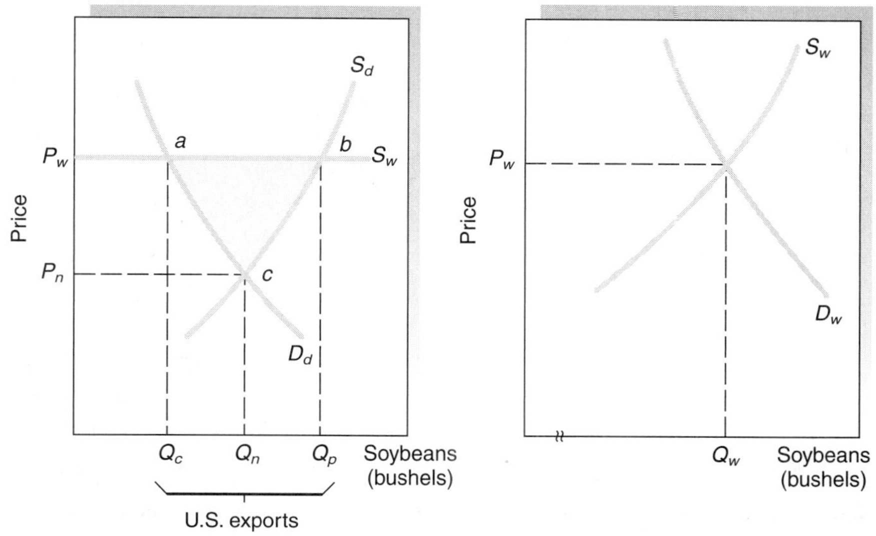

(a) U.S. market for soybeans

(b) World market for soybeans

sumer surplus on the $Q_n - Q_c$ units now purchased at the higher price. Thus, free trade imposes a net cost of P_w acP_n on consumers. As can be seen in Exhibit 26-5, however, the gains of soybean producers outweigh the losses to the consumers by the triangle *abc*. Free trade leads to a net welfare gain.

When one focuses only on an export product, it appears that free trade benefits producers relative to consumers—but this ignores the secondary effects. How will foreigners generate the dollars they need to purchase the export products of the United States? If foreigners do not sell goods to Americans, they will not have the purchasing power necessary to purchase goods from Americans. U.S. imports—that is, the purchase of goods from low-cost foreign producers—provide foreigners with the dollar purchasing power necessary to buy U.S. exports. In turn, the lower prices in the import-competitive markets will benefit the U.S. consumers who appeared at first glance to be harmed by the higher prices (compared to the no-trade situation) in export markets.

Using shoes as an example, Exhibit 26-6 illustrates the situation when the United States is a net importer. In the absence of trade, the price of shoes in the domestic market would be P_n, the intersection of the domestic supply and demand curves. However, the world price of shoes is P_w. In an open economy, many U.S. consumers would take advantage of the low shoe prices available from foreign producers. At the lower world price, U.S. consumers would purchase Q_c units of shoes, importing $Q_c - Q_p$ from foreign producers.

Compared to the no-trade situation, free trade in shoes results in lower prices and an expansion in domestic consumption. The lower prices lead to a net consumer gain of P_nabP_w. Domestic producers lose P_nacP_w in the form of lower sales prices and reductions in output. However, the net gain of the shoe consumers exceeds the net loss of producers by *abc*.

EXHIBIT 26-6 Consumer Benefits from Imports

In the absence of trade, the domestic price of shoes would be P_n. Since many foreign producers have a comparative advantage in the production of shoes, international trade leads to lower prices. At the world price P_w, U.S. consumers will demand Q_c units, of which $Q_c - Q_p$ are imported. Compared to the no-trade situation, consumers gain P_nabP_w, while domestic producers lose P_nacP_w. A net gain of *abc* results.

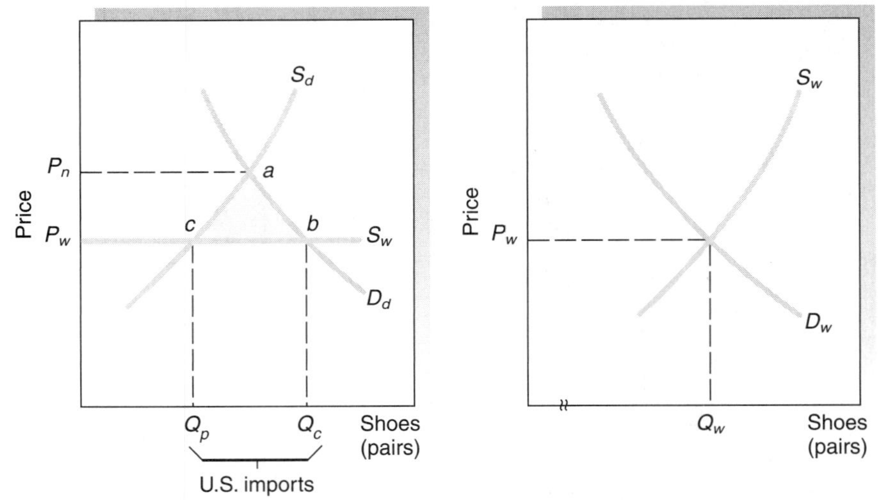

(a) U.S. market for shoes

(b) World market for shoes

International competition will direct resources toward their area of comparative advantage. If domestic producers have a comparative advantage in the production of a good, they will be able to compete effectively in the world market and profit from the export of goods to foreigners. In turn, the exports will generate the purchasing power necessary to buy goods that foreigners can supply more economically.

As supply and demand analysis shows, trade makes it possible for the people of a nation to (a) sell goods they can produce cheaply at higher prices and (b) buy items that would be costly to produce at lower prices. Gain is derived from both the high prices received for exports and the lower prices paid for imports. Furthermore, trade permits the residents of each nation to concentrate on the things they do best (produce at a low cost), while trading for those they do least well. The result is an expansion in both output and consumption compared to what could be achieved in the absence of trade.

The pattern of U.S. exports and imports is consistent with this view. The United States is a nation with a technically skilled labor force, fertile farmland, and substantial capital formation. Thus, we export computers, aircraft, power-generating equipment, scientific instruments, and land-intensive agricultural products—items we are able to produce at a comparatively low cost. Simultaneously, we import substantial amounts of petroleum, textile (clothing) products, shoes, coffee, and diamonds—goods costly for us to produce. Clearly, trade permits us to gain by specializing in those areas in which our comparative advantage is greatest.

7 ECONOMICS OF TRADE RESTRICTIONS

Despite the potential benefits from free trade, almost all nations have erected trade barriers. Tariffs, quotas, and exchange-rate controls are the most commonly used trade-restricting devices. Let us consider how various types of trade restrictions influence the economy.

Economics of Tariffs

Tariff
A tax levied on goods imported into a country.

A **tariff** is nothing more than a tax on imports from foreign countries. As Exhibit 26-7 shows, average tariff rates of between 30 percent and 50 percent of product value were often levied prior to 1945. The notorious Smoot-Hawley trade bill of 1930 pushed the average tariff rate upward to 60 percent. Many economists believe that this legislation was a major contributing factor to the length and severity of the Great Depression. During the past 50 years, the tariff rates of the United States have declined substantially. In 1999, the average tariff rate on imported goods was only 4 percent.

Exhibit 26-8 illustrates the impact of a tariff on automobiles. In the absence of a tariff, the world market price of P_w would prevail in the domestic market. At that price, U.S. consumers purchase Q_1 units. Domestic producers supply Q_{d1}, while foreigners supply $Q_1 - Q_{d1}$ units to the U.S. market. When the United States levies a tariff, t, on automobiles, Americans can no longer buy cars at the world price. U.S. consumers now have to pay $P_w + t$ to purchase an automobile from foreigners. At that price, domestic consumers demand Q_2 units (Q_{d2} supplied by domestic producers and $Q_2 - Q_{d2}$ supplied by foreigners). The tariff results in a higher price and lower level of domestic consumption.

The tariff benefits domestic producers and the government at the expense of consumers. Since they do not pay the tariff, domestic producers will expand their output in response to the higher (protected) market price. In effect, the tariff acts as a subsidy to domestic producers. Domestic producers gain the area S (Exhibit 26-8) in the form of additional net revenues. The tariff raises revenues equal to the area T for the government. The areas U and V represent costs imposed on consumers that do not benefit either producers or the government. Simply put, U and V represent *deadweight losses* in the form of reductions in the consumer surplus that buyers would have derived if the tariff had not been imposed.

As a result of the tariff, resources that could have been used to produce goods that U.S. firms produce efficiently (compared to producers abroad) are diverted into the production of automobiles. Thus, we end up producing less in areas where we have a comparative advantage and more in areas where we are a high-cost producer. Potential gains from specialization and trade go unrealized.

EXHIBIT 26-7 How High Are U.S. Tariffs?

Tariff rates in the United States fell sharply during the period from 1935 to 1950. Subsequently, after rising slightly during the 1950s, they have trended downward since 1960. In 1999, the average tariff rate on merchandise imports was 4.0 percent.

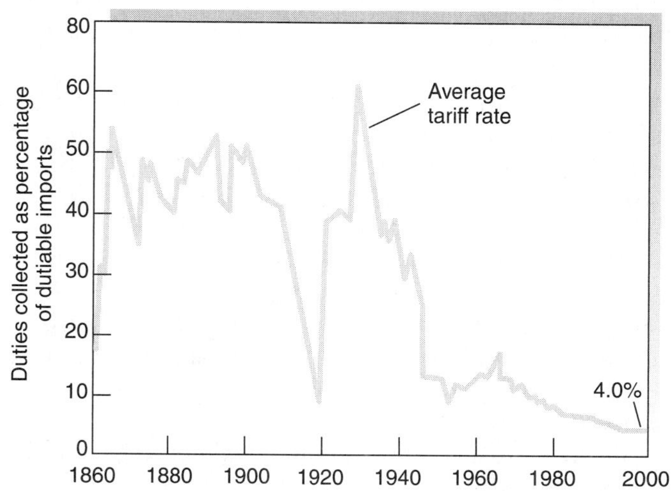

EXHIBIT 26-8 Impact of a Tariff

Here we illustrate the impact of a tariff on automobiles. In the absence of the tariff, the world price of automobiles is P_w; U.S. consumers purchase Q_1 units (Q_d1 from domestic producers plus $Q_1 - Q_d1$ from foreign producers). The tariff makes it more costly for Americans to purchase automobiles from foreigners. Imports decline and the domestic price increases. Consumers lose the sum of the areas $S + U + T + V$ in the form of higher prices and a reduction in consumer surplus. Producers gain the area S and the tariff generates T tax revenues for the government. The areas U and V are deadweight losses due to a reduction in allocative efficiency.

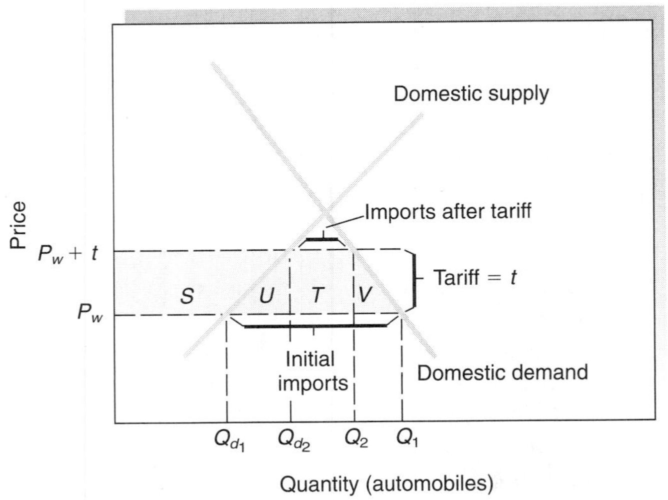

Economics of Quotas

Import quota
A specific limit or maximum quantity (or value) of a good permitted to be imported into a country during a given period.

An **import quota**, like a tariff, is designed to restrict foreign goods and protect domestic industries. A quota places a ceiling on the amount of a product that can be imported during a given period (typically a year). The United States imposes quotas on several products, including brooms, steel, shoes, sugar, dairy products, and peanuts. As in the case of tariffs, the primary purpose of quotas is to protect domestic industries from foreign competition.

Since 1953 the United States has imposed a quota to limit the importation of peanuts to 1.7 million pounds per year, approximately two peanuts per American. Using peanuts as an example, Exhibit 26-9 illustrates the impact of a quota. If there were no trade restraints, the domestic price of peanuts would be equal to the world market price (P_w). Under those circumstances, Americans would purchase Q_1 units. At the price P_w, domestic producers would supply Q_{d1}, and the amount $Q_1 - Q_{d1}$ would be imported from foreign producers.

Now consider what happens when a quota limits imports to $Q_2 - Q_{d2}$, a quantity well below the free-trade level of imports. Since the quota reduces the foreign supply of peanuts to the domestic market, the price of the quota-protected product increases (to P_2). At the higher price, U.S. consumers will reduce their purchases to Q_2, and domestic producers will happily expand their production to Q_{d2}. With regard to the welfare of consumers, the impact of a quota is similar to that of a tariff. Consumers lose the area $S + U + T + V$ in the form of higher prices and the loss of consumer surplus. Similarly, domestic producers gain the area S, while the areas U and V represent deadweight losses in the form of reductions in consumer surplus, gains that buyers would have derived in the absence of the quota.

While the adverse impact of a quota on consumer welfare is similar to that of a tariff, there is a big difference with regard to the area T. Under a tariff,

EXHIBIT 26-9 Impact of a Quota

Here we illustrate the impact of a quota, such as the one the United States imposes on peanuts. The world market price of peanuts is P_w. If there were no trade restraints, the domestic price would also be P_w, and the domestic consumption would be Q_1. Domestic producers would supply Q_{d1} units, while $Q_1 - Q_{d1}$ would be imported. A quota limiting imports to $Q_2 - Q_{d2}$ would push up the domestic price to P_2. At the higher price, the amount supplied by domestic producers increases to Q_{d2}. Consumers lose the sum of the area $S + U + T + V$, while domestic producers gain the area S. In contrast with tariffs, quotas generate no revenue for the government. The area T goes to foreign producers who are granted permission to sell in the U.S. market.

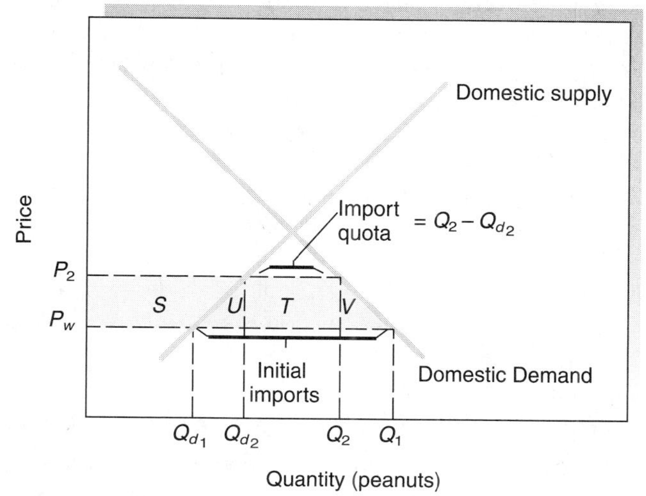

the U.S. government would collect revenues equal to T, representing the tariff rate multiplied by the number of units imported. With a quota, however, these revenues will go to foreign producers, who are granted licenses (quotas) to sell various amounts in the U.S. market. Clearly, this right to sell at a premium price (since the domestic price exceeds the world market price) is extremely valuable. Thus, foreign producers will compete for the permits. They will hire lobbyists, make political contributions, and engage in other rent-seeking activities in an effort to secure the right to sell at a premium price in the U.S. market.

In many ways, quotas are more harmful than tariffs. With a quota, foreign producers are prohibited from selling additional units regardless of how much lower their costs are relative to those of domestic producers. In contrast to a tariff, a quota brings in no revenue for the government. While a tariff transfers revenue from U.S. consumers to the Treasury, quotas transfer these revenues to foreign producers. Obviously, this politically granted privilege creates a strong incentive for foreign producers to engage in wasteful rent-seeking activities. Thus, by rewarding both domestic producers with higher prices and foreign producers with valuable import permits, quotas generate two strong interest groups supportive of their continuation. As a result, removal of a quota is often even more difficult to achieve than a tariff reduction.

In addition to tariffs and quotas, governments sometimes use regulations and political pressure to restrain competition. For example, the United States prohibits foreign airlines from competing in the domestic air travel market. Japanese regulations make it illegal for domestic dealers to handle both foreign and domestically produced autos. This makes it more difficult for foreign manufacturers to establish the network of dealerships needed for effective penetration of the Japanese market. In the 1980s, the United States used political pressure, including the threat of quota restrictions, in order to induce Japanese auto manufacturers to "voluntarily" restrict their imports to the U.S. market. Like tariffs and quotas, regulatory barriers such as these reduce the supply to the domestic market and thereby push prices upward. Overall output is reduced, while producers benefit at the expense of domestic consumers.

Exchange-Rate Controls as a Trade Restriction

Some countries fix the exchange-rate value of their currency above the market rate and impose restrictions on exchange-rate transactions. At the official (artificially high) exchange rate, the country's export goods will be extremely expensive to foreigners. As a result, foreigners will purchase goods elsewhere, and the country's exports will be small. In turn, the low level of exports will make it extremely difficult for domestic residents to obtain the foreign currency required for the purchase of imports. Such exchange-rate controls both reduce the volume of trade and lead to black-market currency exchanges. Indeed, a large black-market premium indicates that the country's exchange-rate policy is substantially limiting the ability of its citizens to trade with foreigners. While exchange rate controls have declined in popularity, they are still an important trade barrier in many less-developed countries.

Protective tariffs are as much applications of force as are blockading squadrons, and their objective is the same—to prevent trade. The difference between the two is that blockading squadrons are a means whereby nations seek to prevent their enemies from trading; protective tariffs are a means whereby nations attempt to prevent their own people from trading.

—Henry George[4]

8 WHY DO NATIONS ADOPT TRADE RESTRICTIONS?

As Henry George notes (see quote), trade restraints are an effort to keep people from trading with foreigners. Why would political officials erect blockades against their own people? Several factors play a role. Trade restrictions reflect the political power of concentrated interests: Even though the populace as a whole is harmed, some people are able to gain. Economic illiteracy may also play a role. We will now take a look at each of these factors.

Partially Valid Arguments for Restrictions

There are three major, at least partially valid, arguments for protecting certain domestic industries from foreign competitors: the national-defense, infant-industry, and anti-dumping arguments.

---

[4] Henry George, *Protection or Free Trade*, 1886, p. 37.

National-Defense Argument

According to the national-defense argument, certain industries—aircraft, petroleum, and weapons, for example—are vital to national defense and therefore should be protected from foreign competitors so that a domestic supply of necessary materials would be available in case of an international conflict. Would we want to be entirely dependent on Arabian or Russian petroleum? Would complete dependence on French aircraft be wise? Many Americans would answer no, even if trade restrictions were required to prevent such dependence by preserving domestic industries.

Although the national-defense argument has some validity, it is often abused. Relatively few industries are truly vital to our national defense. If a resource is important for national defense, often it would make more sense to stockpile the resource during peace-time rather than follow protectionist policies to preserve a domestic industry. Furthermore, it is important to recognize that a strong economy capable of producing large volumes of the goods necessary to sustain a large war effort is itself part of a strong defense. Because the national-defense argument is often used by special interests to justify protection for their industry at the expense of the economy in general, the merits of each specific case must be carefully evaluated.

Infant-Industry Argument

Advocates of the infant-industry argument hold that new domestic industries should be protected from older, established foreign competitors. As the new industry matures, it will be able to stand on its own feet and compete effectively with foreign producers, at which time protection can be removed.

The infant-industry argument has a long and often notorious history. Alexander Hamilton used it to argue for the protection of early U.S. manufacturing. Although it is an argument for only temporary protection, the protection, once granted, is generally difficult to remove. For example, a century ago, this argument was used to gain tariff protection for the newly emerging steel industry in the United States. With time, the steel industry developed and became very powerful, both politically and economically. Despite this maturity, the tariffs remained. To this day, legislation continues to provide the steel industry with various protections that limit competition from abroad.

Anti-Dumping Argument

Dumping involves the sale of goods by a foreign firm at a price below cost or below the price charged in the firm's home-base market. Dumping is illegal and if a domestic industry is harmed, current law provides relief in the form of anti-dumping duties (tariffs imposed against violators). The number of anti-dumping cases has been increasing. In recent years, the United States has levied charges against, for example, Argentine textile producers, Canadian manufacturers of radial tires, and steel producers in Korea and Brazil.

Dumping
The sale of a good by a foreign supplier in another country at a price below that charged by the supplier in its home market.

Dumping raises the concern that foreign producers will temporarily cut prices until the domestic firms are driven from the market and then use their monopoly position to gouge consumers. However, there is reason to question the effectiveness of this strategy. After all, the high prices would soon attract competitors, including other foreign suppliers.

Anti-dumping cases nearly always involve considerable ambiguity. The prices charged in the home market generally vary and the production cost of the firms charged with dumping are not directly observable. This makes it difficult to tell whether a dumping violation has occurred. Furthermore, there is a fine line between dumping and aggressive competitive behavior. Domestic firms facing the latter may well levy charges of the former.

When analyzing the merits of anti-dumping restrictions, it is important to keep two points in mind. First, price cutting is an integral part of the competitive process. When demand is weak and inventories are large, firms will often find it in their interest to offer goods at prices below the average total cost of production. Domestic firms are permitted to engage in this practice. Why should foreign firms be prohibited from doing so? Second, the use of anti-dumping laws to reduce the competitiveness of domestic markets is sure to be contagious. As a few industries are protected from the competition of foreign rivals, others will seek similar treatment. Unless restricted to extreme cases, anti-dumping cases may soon become simply another rather thinly veiled mechanism to stifle competition.

Protectionism is a politician's delight because it delivers visible benefits to the protected parties while imposing the costs as a hidden tax on the public.

—Murray L. Weidenbaum[5]

Special Interests and the Politics of Trade Restrictions

While trade restrictions arise from multiple sources, as Professor Weidenbaum points out, there is no question as to the primary reason for their adoption. ***Trade restrictions provide highly visible, concentrated benefits for a small group of people, while imposing widely dispersed costs that are often difficult to identify on the general citizenry. As we discussed in Chapter 6, politicians have a strong incentive to favor issues of this type, even if they conflict with economic efficiency.***

Trade restrictions nearly always provide sizable benefits to well-organized industrial and labor interests at the expense of consumers and taxpayers. The latter two groups are poorly organized and the costs of the restrictive policies are almost always spread thinly and in ways that are often difficult to identify. As a result, consumers generally ignore protectionist policies, even though, in aggregate, their cost is substantial. In contrast, the beneficiaries of trade restraints often derive sizable personal gain. These gains will motivate them to supply politicians with not only votes, but also campaign funds and other political perks. Thus, politicians can often gain by catering to their views even when the restrictive policies are harmful to the economy.

The sugar program provides a vivid illustration of how the process works. Americans pay about twice the world price for sugar because domestic sugar growers and makers of corn syrup, a sugar substitute, have lobbied the government to impose import quotas that keep low-cost foreign sugar out of the United States. The cost to consumers is estimated at about $3 billion a year. For the fewer than three dozen firms that are the big beneficiaries of the sugar program, the benefits from restricting trade are in the tens or even hundreds of millions of dollars per firm. It is worthwhile for the sugar lobby to spend millions of dollars defending its privileges. For a family of four, though, the average savings from lower-cost sugar would be perhaps $60 a year. It is not worthwhile for consumers to spend time or effort to lobby Congress over such a small amount per family.

---

[5] Personal correspondence with the authors. Professor Weidenbaum is a former chairman of the President's Council of Economic Advisers and long-time director of the Center for the Study of American Business of Washington University.

Hence the U.S. government prevents free trade in sugar even though it is in the best interest of American consumers.

With regard to protectionist policies, this story is repeated over and over again. It explains why trade restrictions are imposed and why it so difficult to remove them. The U.S. tariff code itself is a reflection of these political forces. It is highly complex, lengthy (the schedule fills 3,825 pages), and costly to administer. High tariffs are imposed on some products (for example, apparel, tobacco, and footwear), while low tariffs are imposed on others. Highly restrictive quotas limit the import of a few commodities. Even though this system of targeted trade restrictions squanders resources, it is no accident. It reflects the rent seeking of interest groups and the political side payments, particularly campaign contributions, politicians derive from it. Here, as in the case of other special interest issues, there is often a conflict between sound economics and winning politics. The Applications in Economics box "Tomatoes, Regulations, and Trade Restrictions"on the next page provides additional evidence on this point.

Trade Barriers and Popular Trade Fallacies

Despite the gains derived from trade, fallacies abound. Why is there so much misunderstanding surrounding trade issues? The primary source of confusion is a point we discussed in Chapter 1: the failure to consider the secondary effects. Key elements of international trade are closely linked—you cannot change one element without changing the other. Failure to recognize the secondary effects is undoubtedly the most common source of error in international trade. Two of the most popular trade fallacies involve the effects of imports on employment and the impact of trade with low-wage countries. Let us take a closer look at both.

Trade Fallacy 1: "Trade restrictions that limit imports save jobs for Americans."

Like most other fallacies, this one has just enough truth to give it some credibility. When tariffs, quotas, and other trade barriers limit imports, they may well promote employment in the industries shielded from competition, but this is only half of the story. They will simultaneously destroy jobs in other sectors.

If import restraints reduce the sales of foreigners to us, there will be an automatic secondary effect—foreigners will have fewer dollars with which to buy goods, services, and assets from Americans. As a result, the demand for American exports declines, causing output and employment in export industries to shrink. This will act as an offset to any jobs saved in sectors shielded by the trade barriers.

As Exhibit 26-1 shows, U.S. imports grew rapidly—far more rapidly than GDP—during the 1980s and 1990s. But this did not retard employment. Civilian employment in the United States rose from 99 million in 1980 to 119 million in 1990 and 135 million in 2000. Thus, the unprecedented growth of imports during the last two decades has been accompanied by an unprecedented growth in employment.

Once the link between imports and exports is recognized, this growth of employment is not surprising. As imports grew, so too did exports. There was also an inflow of capital that lowered interest rates, further increasing output and employment. As the trade sector grew, jobs were reshuffled, not destroyed. More Americans were employed producing things we do well (where we had a comparative advantage) and fewer were tied up producing things we do poorly.

APPLICATIONS IN ECONOMICS

Tomatoes, Regulations, and Trade Restrictions

In 1995–1996, Florida tomato growers complained to the Clinton administration and Congress that the import of cheap tomatoes from Mexico was driving them out of business. Blaming the North American Free Trade Agreement (NAFTA) for their plight, they sought to have Congress declare "winter vegetables" a separate industry so they would qualify for greater protection. They also filed an anti-dumping suit with the Commerce Department seeking the imposition of higher tariffs on Mexican tomatoes.

When these strategies failed, the growers asked Congress to pass special package and labeling legislation. While the hard, unripe Florida tomatoes are shipped in solid-tray boxes, the Mexican tomatoes are ripened on the vine, hand-packaged, and shipped in cushioned cartons. At least some consumers believe that this procedure makes the tomatoes tastier. This issue aside, the Florida growers wanted legislation that would require all growers to use the hard-tray cartons. Of course, this would make it difficult for the riper Mexican tomatoes to be shipped without being battered or bruised. Interestingly, the problems of the Florida growers had little to do with NAFTA. The major factor contributing to the increased competitiveness of the Mexican-grown tomatoes was the sharp reduction in the exchange rate of the peso relative to the dollar during 1994–1995.

This case illustrates why it is so difficult to maintain freedom of exchange in international markets. Rather than simply argue for trade restraints, organized interest groups often support regulations that they say will be "safer," or "more convenient," or "facilitate inspection." Of course, such regulations also just happen to give the special-interest groups a competitive edge over their rivals. This is true in all countries. Japan, in particular, has been charged with the use of such diversionary tactics.

Neither is Mexico blameless. For example, the Mexican government attempted to impose cumbersome labeling and inspection procedures in an effort to reduce the competitiveness of American tires in the Mexican market. Mexico continues to prohibit American express delivery firms, such as United Parcel Service, from using large trucks south of the border. Consumers are the losers when restrictions of this type are imposed. Unfortunately, since consumers are disorganized and generally unaware they are being harmed, support of well-organized interest groups is often politically attractive.

As a result, we were able to produce a larger output than would otherwise have been possible.

When trade restraints are lowered (or there is discussion about lowering them), predictably many workers and business officials in import-competitive industries will charge that jobs will be lost to foreign competitors. In contrast, the additional jobs in the export industries do not yet exist. No one will be saying, "I will not be employed next year if the trade restraints are not lowered." Because the jobs (and employees) in the import-competitive industries are highly visible, while the future jobs in the exporting industries are invisible, it is difficult to maintain open markets.

Even though trade does not reduce the availability of jobs, it is nonetheless a mistake to focus on the employment issue. After all, income and high productivity, not jobs, are the sources of prosperity. Consider the following: If import restrictions are a good idea, why don't we use them to restrict trade among the 50 states? After all, think of all the jobs that are lost when, for example, Michigan "imports" oranges from Florida, apples from Washington, wheat from Kansas, and cotton from Georgia. All of these products could be produced in Michigan. However, the residents of Michigan generally find it cheaper to "import" these commodities. Michigan gains by using its resources to produce and "export" automobiles (and other goods it can produce economically) and then using the sales revenue to "import" goods that would be expensive to produce in Michigan.

Most people recognize that free trade among the 50 states is a major source of prosperity for each of the states. Similarly, most recognize that "imports" from other states do not destroy jobs—at least not for long. The implications are identical for trade among nations.

Of course, sudden removal of trade barriers might harm producers and workers in protected industries. It may be costly to transfer quickly the protected resources to other, more productive activities. Gradual removal of the barriers would minimize this shock effect and the accompanying cost of relocation.

Trade Fallacy 2: "Free trade with low-wage countries, such as Mexico and China, will reduce the wages of Americans."

Many Americans believe that if it were not for trade restrictions, American wages would fall to the level of workers in poor countries. How can Americans compete with workers in countries such as Mexico and China who are willing to work for $1 per hour or less? This fallacy stems from a misunderstanding of both the source of high wages and the law of comparative advantage. Workers in the United States are well-educated, possess a high skill level, and work with large amounts of capital equipment. These factors contribute to their high productivity, which is the source of their high wages. Similarly, in countries like Mexico and China, wages are low precisely because productivity is low.

When analyzing the significance of wage and productivity differentials across countries, one must remember that gains from trade emanate from comparative advantage, not absolute advantage (see Exhibits 26-2, 26-3, and 26-4). The United States cannot produce everything cheaper than Mexico or China merely because U.S. workers are more productive and work with more capital than workers in Mexico and China. Neither can the Mexicans and Chinese produce everything cheaper merely because their wage rates are low compared to those of U.S. workers.

Comparative advantage will determine which goods are imported and which are exported. Both high- and low-wage countries will gain when they are able to focus more of their resources on those productive activities that they do well. The comparative advantage of low-wage countries is likely to be in the production of labor-intensive goods, such as toys, textiles, and assembled manufactured products. On the other hand, the comparative advantage of the United States lies in the production of high-tech manufacturing products and other goods produced economically by a well-educated labor force.

Trade reflects relative advantage, not wage levels. We recognize this point with regard to domestic trade. No one argues that trade between doctors and lawn service workers, for example, will cause the wages of doctors to fall. Because of their different skills and costs of providing alternative goods, both high-wage doctors and low-wage lawn care workers can gain from trade. The same is also true for trade between rich and poor nations.

If foreigners, including low-wage foreigners, are willing to sell us a product cheaper than we ourselves can produce it, we can gain by using our scarce resources to produce other things. Perhaps an extreme example will illustrate this point. Suppose a foreign producer (perhaps because workers were willing to work for nothing) was willing to supply us quality automobiles free of charge. Would it make sense to impose tariffs or quotas to keep out the autos? Of course not. Resources that were previously used to produce automobiles could now be freed to produce other goods. The real income and availability of goods would expand. It makes no more sense to erect trade barriers to keep out cheap foreign goods than to keep out free autos.

9 IMPACT OF TRADE OPENNESS—EMPIRICAL EVIDENCE

Economic theory indicates that more open economies should perform better than those that are more closed. Is this really true? In order to address this issue, a measure of openness—the freedom of individuals to engage in voluntary exchange across national boundaries—is needed. One of the authors was recently involved in a study that derived a Trade Openness Index (TOI) for the 1980–98 period.[6] In order to score high on the zero to ten scale of the index, a country must have low tariffs, a freely convertible currency, a large trade sector given its size and location, and avoid capital market controls.

Exhibit 26-10 (column 1) shows the 1980–98 TOI ratings for the 12 highest and 12 lowest rated countries among the 91 for which the required data could be obtained. The TOI ratings reflect the average degree of openness for the entire 1980–98 period. This is important because the gains from increased openness will be realized over a lengthy period. Expanding the openness of trade is a long-term growth strategy, not a short-term quick fix. Credibility is also important. Countries that lower trade barriers and then re-impose them a few years later will derive only limited benefits. In order to isolate the full impact of openness, the key relations must be considered over a lengthy period.

Exhibit 26-10 also presents data for the mean tariff rate and the actual size of the trade sector relative to the expected, given the country's size and location in relationship to the concentration of world demand. When the latter variable is positive, this indicates that the country has a larger trade sector than countries of similar size and location. For example, the 106 percent and 115 percent figures for Hong Kong and Singapore, respectively, indicate that their trade sectors are more than twice as large as what would be expected, given their size and location. On the other hand, the −33 percent figure for Brazil indicates that its trade sector is one-third smaller than expected. Clearly, the more open economies have substantially lower tariff rates and larger trade sectors than those that are more closed. The trade openness ratings reflect these factors, as well as the restrictiveness of exchange rate and capital market controls.

Hong Kong, Singapore, Belgium, Germany, and the United Kingdom head the list of the most open among the 91 economies. The United States ranks ninth tied with Malaysia and Sweden. At the other end of the spectrum, the TOI indicates that Myanmar, Bangladesh, Burundi, Iran, and Sierra Leone were the least open economies during the period.

If trade makes a difference, the countries with persistently high openness ratings should have higher per capita incomes and grow more rapidly than those with persistently low ratings. As Exhibit 26-10 shows, this was indeed the case. The $24,744 GDP per person of the 12 most open economies is almost eight times the comparable figure for the 12 least open economies. The per capita GDP of the 12 most open economies grew at an annual rate of 2.7 percent during 1980–1999, compared to 0.4 percent a year for the 12 least open economies. All 12 of the open economies had positive growth rates and all but one grew at an annual rate of 1.4 percent or more. In contrast, six of the least open economies experienced reductions in per capita GDP and only four of the twelve achieved a growth rate in excess of 1 percent. These striking differences suggest that openness exerts a major impact on growth and prosperity.

A more detailed statistical analysis of the 91 countries showed that there was a strong positive relationship between openness and both per capita GDP and

[6] See James Gwartney, Robert Lawson, and Charles Skipton, "Trade Openness, Income Levels, and Economic Growth," in *Economic Freedom of the World: 2001 Annual Report* (Fraser Institute: Vancouver, B.C., 2001). The analysis of this section borrows freely from that publication.

EXHIBIT 26-10 Trade Openness, Growth, and Income

Country	TOI (80–98)	Effective Average Tariff Rate 1980	Effective Average Tariff Rate 1999	Actual vs. Expected Size of Trade Sector 1998	PPP GDP per Capita 1999	Avg. Annual Growth Rate of Real GDP per Capita 1980–1999
Hong Kong	9.9	1%	1%	106%	$22,090	3.9%
Singapore	9.8	1%	0%	115%	$20,767	4.9%
Belgium	9.1	1%	1%	49%	$25,443	1.7%
Germany	8.5	1%	1%	13%	$23,742	1.4%
UK	8.5	1%	1%	−3%	$22,093	1.9%
Netherlands	8.4	1%	1%	18%	$24,215	1.8%
Luxembourg	8.3	0%	0%	−3%	$42,769	3.9%
Switzerland	8.0	5%	1%	−20%	$27,171	0.9%
USA	7.8	2%	2%	0%	$31,872	1.9%
Malaysia	7.8	15%	3%	286%	$8,209	3.7%
Sweden	7.8	1%	1%	19%	$22,636	1.4%
Ireland	7.7	7%	1%	64%	$25,918	4.4%
Top 12:	**8.5**	**3%**	**1%**	**54%**	**$24,744**	**2.7%**
India	3.5	31%	22%	8%	$2,110	3.7%
Brazil	3.4	20%	17%	−33%	$6,908	0.6%
Argentina	3.3	19%	9%	−37%	$12,554	0.3%
Tanzania	3.2	15%	24%	−1%	$482	3.3%
Madagascar	3.1	17%	20%	−2%	$776	−1.8%
Algeria	2.9		18%	1%	$4,869	−0.5%
Syria	2.5	14%	7%	9%	$3,749	1.1%
Sierra Leone	1.9	27%	32%	−68%	$487	−3.5%
Iran	1.9	34%	18%	−30%	$5,389	−0.2%
Burundi	1.5	36%	18%	−73%	$581	−1.1%
Bangladesh	1.5	27%	19%	−27%	$1,412	2.4%
Myanmar	0.1	28%	72%	−97%	$1,200	−0.1%
Bottom 12:	**2.4**	**24%**	**23%**	**−29%**	**$3,250**	**0.4%**

economic growth. Openness continued to exert a positive and statistically significant impact on both growth and income even after the effects of cross-country differences in the variability of the inflation rate and quality of the legal system were taken into account. Furthermore, the positive impact of openness on economic performance was even stronger when the analysis was undertaken for less developed and small countries separately. These findings provide strong evidence for the economic view that open markets and international trade enhance economic performance.[7]

[7] For additional information on the relationship between international trade and economic growth, see Jeffrey A. Frankel and David Romer. "Does Trade Cause Growth?" *American Economic Review*, June, 1999, pp. 379–399; and Jeffrey D. Sachs and Andrew Warner, "Economic Reform and the Process of Global Integration." *Brookings Papers on Economic Activity*, 1995(1), pp. 1–95.

10 THE CHANGING NATURE OF GLOBAL TRADE

As we previously mentioned, international trade has approximately doubled as a share of the world economy since 1970. The growth of the trade sector has been propelled by technological advancements, lower transport cost, and more liberal trade policies. The growth of trade—some might say the globalization of the economy—has also triggered a reaction. This section will consider the changing nature of the world economy and its implications for the future.

GATT and the WTO

General Agreement on Tariffs and Trade (GATT) An organization formed following the Second World War to set the rules for the conduct of international trade and reduce barriers to trade among nations.

Following World War II, the major industrial nations established the **General Agreement on Tariffs and Trade** (**GATT**). For five decades, GATT played a central role in the multilateral tariff reductions and the relaxation (or elimination) of quotas. The average tariff rates of GATT members fell from approximately 40 percent in 1947 to less than 5 percent in 1998.

When the most recent round of trade negotiations—the Uruguay Round—was completed at year-end 1993, GATT was given a new name: the **World Trade Organization** (**WTO**). This organization of 141 countries is now responsible for the monitoring and enforcement of the trade agreements developed through GATT. The WTO also provides a forum for consideration of trade rules and settlement of trade disputes among members.

World Trade Organization (WTO) The new name given to GATT in 1994; it is currently responsible for monitoring and enforcing the multilateral trade agreements among the 133 member countries.

NAFTA and Other Regional Trade Agreements

North American Free Trade Agreement (NAFTA) A comprehensive trade agreement between the United States, Mexico, and Canada that went into effect in 1994. Tariff barriers will continue to be phased out under the agreement until 2004.

In 1988, the United States and Canada negotiated a trade agreement designed to reduce barriers limiting both trade and the flow of capital between the two countries. A few years later, the United States, Canada, and Mexico finalized the **North American Free Trade Agreement** (**NAFTA**), which took effect in 1994. As the result of NAFTA, tariffs on the shipment of most products among the three countries will be eliminated by 2004. The agreement will also remove limits on financial investments, liberalize trade in services such as banking, and establish uniform legal requirements for the protection of intellectual property.

Reflecting its proximity, Canada has been a major trading partner of the United States for many decades. On the other hand, U.S. trade with Mexico was small prior to the 1990s. Historically, Mexico has been a relatively closed economy. This began to change in the mid-1980s, prior to its NAFTA membership, when Mexico began cutting its tariff rates and unilaterally removing other trade barriers. In addition to its participation in NAFTA, Mexico has also adopted a free trade agreement with the European Union. During the last 15 years Mexico has moved from one of the world's more protectionist to one of its more open economies.

As Exhibit 26-11 shows, U.S. trade with both Mexico and Canada grew rapidly during the 1990s. Measured as a share of GDP, trade with Mexico jumped from 1.1 percent in 1991 to 2.0 percent in 1998. During the same period, trade with Canada rose from 2.9 percent of GDP to 3.8 percent.

This growth of trade, particularly with Mexico, has not been without controversy. Residents along major transportation routes often complain of increased congestion and road damage resulting from the transport of goods by large trucks. Business and labor groups often blame employment contractions and plant closings on competition with Mexican firms. The news media generally gives such stories ample exposure. However, there is no evidence that increased trade with Mexico has adversely affected either output or total employment. While trade with both Mexico and Canada expanded rapidly during the latter

EXHIBIT 26-11 U.S. Trade with Canada and Mexico, 1980–1999

Trade between the United States and Mexico as well as Canada increased with the passage of NAFTA.

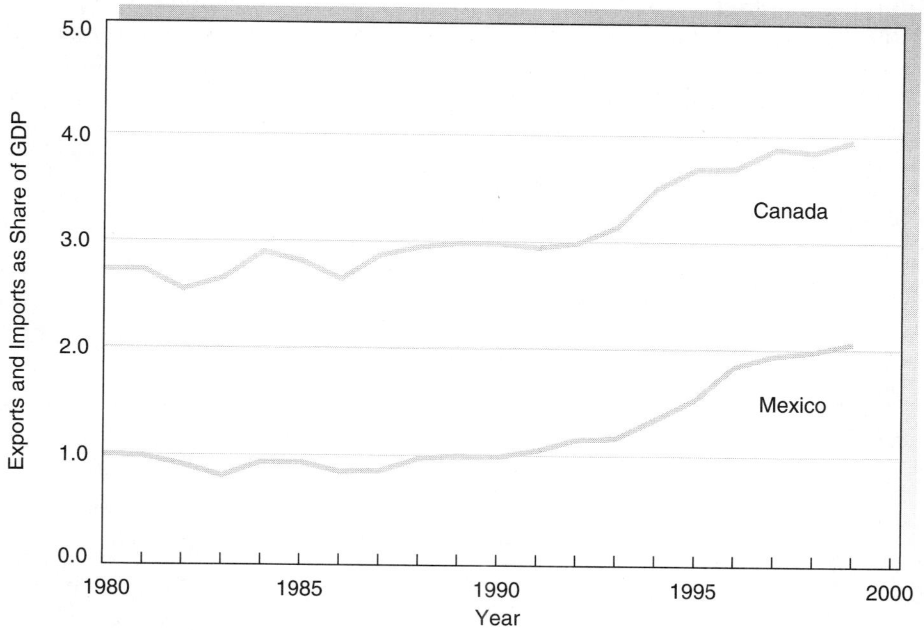

Sources: Statistical Abstract of the United States (various years) and *Economic Report of the President* (2000).

half of the 1990s, the U.S. economy experienced strong growth and unemployment fell to a 30-year low. Clearly the dire predictions about the "jobs going to Mexico" have not been realized.

Historically, Europe has been characterized by trade barriers. During the last several decades, this situation has gradually changed. Most barriers limiting the movement of goods among the 15 members of the European Union have now been removed. With the exception of agricultural and a few other commodities, the external tariff rates of the EU are relatively low. In some cases, the combination of a common market among EU members and low external tariffs has exerted a dramatic impact. As a result, several economies—Ireland, Spain, and Greece, for example—that were relatively closed to trade in the 1970s now rank among the world's more open economies. The 12 members of the European Monetary Union have now taken another dramatic step, the adoption of a common currency. This, too, will reduce the cost of exchange within the union and thereby increase the volume of trade.

The Future

Observing the success of open economies like Hong Kong and Singapore, many less-developed countries have unilaterally reduced their trade restrictions. On average, the tariff rates of less-developed countries are now only about half the level of the early 1980s. Exchange rate controls are becoming increasingly rare and capital market controls are much less restrictive than was true a decade ago. These factors, coupled with the rate reductions of the earlier GATT agreements and increased trade liberalization within regions, have contributed substantially to the worldwide growth of trade.

As demonstrations at recent WTO meetings illustrate, the growth of trade has also generated controversy. Some critics argue that globalization of economic activity is undermining cultural and national identities. Labor and environmental regulations have also been injected into the debate. At the same time, the Internet and other technological changes continue to reduce the costs of transportation and communications, thereby encouraging additional movement of goods, ideas, and people across national boundaries. All of this promises to enliven trade issues in the future.

SUMMARY

- The volume of international trade has grown rapidly in recent decades. Over 20 percent of the world's output is sold outside the country in which it was produced. The size of the trade sector is generally larger in countries with a smaller population.
- Comparative advantage rather than absolute advantage is the source of gains from trade. As long as the relative production costs of goods differ among nations, all nations will be able to gain from trade. Specialization and trade allow trading partners to maximize their joint output and expand their consumption possibilities.
- Exports and imports are closely linked. The exports of a nation are the primary source of purchasing power used to import goods. When a nation restricts imports, it simultaneously limits the ability of foreigners to acquire the purchasing power necessary to buy the nation's exports.
- Relative to the no-trade alternative, international exchange and specialization result in lower prices for products that are imported and higher domestic prices for products that are exported. However, the net effect is an expansion in the aggregate output and consumption possibilities available to a nation.
- Import restrictions, such as tariffs and quotas, reduce foreign supply to the domestic market thereby causing the domestic price to rise. Thus, such restrictions are subsidies to producers (and workers) in protected industries at the expense of (a) consumers and (b) producers (and workers) in export industries. Jobs protected by import restrictions are offset by jobs destroyed in export industries.
- National-defense, infant-industry, and anti-dumping arguments can be used to justify trade restrictions for specific industries under certain conditions. It is clear, though, that the power of special-interest groups and voter ignorance about the harmful effects of trade restrictions are the major explanations for real-world policies.
- Persistently open economies have grown more rapidly and achieved higher per capita income levels than those that are more closed to international trade.

FOREIGN EXCHANGE

READING 27

LEARNING OUTCOMES

The candidate should be able to:

a. define direct and indirect methods of foreign exchange quotations and calculate and interpret the spread on a foreign currency quotation, and convert direct (indirect) foreign exchange quotations into indirect (direct) foreign exchange quotations;

b. explain how spreads on foreign currency quotations can differ as a result of market conditions, bank/dealer positions, and trading volume;

c. calculate and interpret currency cross rates, given two spot exchange quotations involving three currencies;

d. distinguish between the spot and forward markets for foreign exchange;

e. calculate the spread on a forward foreign currency quotation and explain how spreads on forward foreign currency quotations can differ as a result of market conditions, bank/dealer positions, trading volume, and maturity/length of contract;

f. calculate and interpret a forward discount or premium and express it as an annualized rate;

g. explain interest rate parity and illustrate covered interest arbitrage.

INTRODUCTION 1

The international investor is faced with a complex task. The financial markets throughout the world are quite different from one another, and information on them is sometimes difficult to obtain. Trading in different time zones and languages further complicates the task. But the most important aspect of international investment is the use of multiple currencies. An American investing in France must do so in euros; therefore, the performance (and risk) of the investment will depend in part on changes in the euro/U.S. dollar exchange rate. Because of the importance of exchange rates in international investment, this book includes a reading describing foreign exchange transactions.

In this text, we develop the analysis needed for the international investment and portfolio management process. The first three readings lay the foundation of exchange rates, which link the economies of different countries and regions. The next five readings explore the various assets available for international investing. The final five readings develop the techniques and perspective of international investment and portfolio management.

In Chapter 2, we develop the theory of international parity conditions. This theory helps in defining real foreign currency risk, an important factor to be managed in global investing and portfolio management. Chapter 3 then explores the techniques and empirical results in the difficult task of exchange rate forecasting.

Chapter 4 is the first in a series of readings on international assets. In that reading, we develop international asset pricing in general, with attention to foreign currency risk. Then, Chapter 5 places a particular focus on the transaction costs involved in various equity markets and instruments allowing entry into international equity investments. Following this general introduction to international asset pricing, Chapters 6, 7, and 8 focus on the available international assets themselves: equities, bonds, and alternative investments, respectively.

After building cases for and against international diversification in Chapter 9, we move into the foreign currency risk-and-return analysis needed for international portfolio management. We develop the risk-control techniques available with derivatives in Chapter 10 and then apply these techniques to currency risk management in Chapter 11. Then, in Chapter 12, we examine the performance measures to judge the risk–return contributions of international diversification. Finally, we summarize the global investment and portfolio management process in Chapter 13. Throughout the text, we attempt to isolate those elements of the process that have unique international aspects.

Reading 27 begins with foreign exchange quotes and the relationships between different types of quotes, as well as the nature of bid–ask spreads in the foreign exchange market. Then, the implications of no-arbitrage conditions appear in three exchange rate applications. First, the quotes of the domestic currency versus a foreign currency must be aligned when given in the two countries for which the exchange rates are being quoted. Second, the exchange rates quoted between two foreign currencies must be aligned with the exchange rate quotes between the domestic currency and each of the foreign currencies. Finally, the exchange rate quotes for current and future delivery must be aligned with the risk-free interest rates in the two countries for which the quotes are given. Reading 27 presents the basic facts of foreign exchange involving quotation interpretation and arbitrage. Foreign exchange theories are saved for subsequent readings.

FOREIGN EXCHANGE QUOTATIONS 2

Before we can discuss exchange rates, which relate to price levels in two countries, we need to know something about the price level in a single country, and this depends on the supply and demand for money within the country. The domestic money supply is a policy variable set by the domestic central bank. The demand for money comes from the need to buy goods and services, as well as from other motives. The price level in the country is determined by the intersection of the demand and supply curve for money in the economy. Just as the value of money is determined by supply and demand in the domestic economy, its value in relation to foreign currencies is also determined by supply and demand. In Chapters 2 and 3, we explore exchange rate determination in detail. Here, we point out that the demand for domestic currency comes mainly from exports and financial inflows (foreigners' purchases of domestic securities) and that the supply comes from imports and financial outflows (purchases of foreign securities). A higher price for the domestic currency is termed a *strengthening* of the currency and a lower price, a *weakening*.

Basic Principles and the Forex Quotation Convention

For most currencies in worldwide foreign exchange (Forex) markets, all trades take place using one convention. The U.S. dollar is still the major currency so that the interbank market is still mostly dollar. All currencies are still quoted against the U.S. dollar, although there are such regional exceptions as the yen in Asia and the euro in Europe. Over time, exchange rates change, so we will sometimes use assumed values for the current exchange rate. For example, we might assume that the value of the euro is quoted as 0.8 euros per U.S. dollar. In other words, one dollar ($) can be exchanged in the foreign exchange market for 0.8 euros. Conversely, the value of one euro (€) in terms of U.S. dollars is given by the reciprocal of 0.8, which is 1.25 dollars. We will define €/$ as the number of euros per dollar and $/€ as the number of dollars per euro:

$$\text{€}/\$ = 0.80 \quad \text{and}$$
$$\$/\text{€} = 1.25$$

Similarly, the Japanese yen (¥) may be quoted as 120 yen per dollar, so that 100 yen is worth 0.8333 dollars. Quotations for the yen are usually indicated for 100 yen rather than for one yen.

The Forex convention specifies rates for all currencies per dollar (as in ¥/$), except for the pound ($/£) and the euro ($/€). From the quotation of two currencies against the U.S. dollar, one can derive the cross-exchange rate between the two currencies:

$$\$/\text{€} = 1.25 \quad \text{and}$$
$$¥/\$ = 120 \quad \text{implies that}$$
$$¥/\text{€} = 120 \times 1.25 = 150$$

In this example, one euro is worth 150 yen, or 100 yen are worth 0.6667 euros.

Abbreviations are used to refer to the various currencies. These could be commonly used symbols or "official" three-letter codes. For example, the yen is JPY; the pound, GBP; the U.S. dollar, USD; and the euro, EUR.

More on Quotation Conventions

Worldwide, quotations are generally made in terms of the amount of local or domestic currency (DC) required to purchase one unit of foreign currency (FC), and this is called the *direct* exchange rate. For example, the Japanese quote the dollar exchange rate as 120 ¥/$ (120 yen per dollar), a direct rate in Japan. However, the U.S. convention, adapted from the British, is the opposite. In New York and London, traders quote the amount of foreign currency required to purchase one unit of home currency, a rate called an *indirect* rate. In New York, therefore, the yen is also quoted as 120 ¥/$. Because of the central role played by the U.S. dollar, it is important to remember that in countries other than the United States, all exchange rates with the dollar are usually given as direct rates, the domestic currency value of one dollar. However, there are two exceptions that give the indirect rates in countries other than the United States. The British pound played a historical role on the international scene, and it has always been quoted as the dollar price of one pound. When the euro was introduced in 1999, the decision was made to adopt the convention to quote the foreign currency value of one euro. This convention applies for the exchange rate of the euro against any currency, including the dollar. So the exchange rate between the dollar and the euro would appear on trading screens as 1.25 dollars per euro, an indirect quote from the European perspective.

When quotations involve the U.S. dollar, the dollar price of one unit of the second currency is referred to as *American terms,* a direct quote from the U.S. perspective. The amount of the second currency per U.S. dollar is called *European terms,* an indirect quote from the U.S. perspective.

In the foreign exchange market, quotations are generally given with five digits. For example, the ¥/$ could appear as 120.10, the $/€ as 1.2515, and the £/€ as 0.7015.[1]

Because a number is usually quoted without any indication of the role played by each currency, it is important to keep track of which is the domestic currency and what quote convention is being used in order to connect an appreciation or depreciation with an increase or decrease in the exchange rate. For example, the exchange rate between the euro and the U.S. dollar may be quoted in terms of either euros per dollar or dollars per euro. If the domestic country is the United States and the direct quote is given, a depreciation of the quoted euro would mean a decline in its price in dollars. For an indirect quote, an increase in the exchange rate would mean an appreciation of the quoted euro. An appreciation of the foreign currency coincides with a depreciation of the domestic currency.

Domestic Currency	Foreign Currency	Indirect Exchange Rate	Direct Exchange Rate
Appreciates	Depreciates	Increases	Decreases
Depreciates	Appreciates	Decreases	Increases

Bid-Ask (Offer) Quotes and Spreads

The foreign exchange market is a worldwide interbank market. Only the major banks and specialized brokers who act as middlemen for some local markets are admitted to this club, which is linked by telephone. The market is organized like

[1] For exchange rates that are below one, quotes often include five decimal places.

an international over-the-counter market. A customer wanting to buy a specified amount of a currency calls several banks to get the best price. The foreign exchange dealer quotes not one price, but two. The *bid* price is the exchange rate at which the dealer is willing to buy a currency; the *ask* (or *offer*) price is the exchange rate at which the dealer is willing to sell a currency. The midpoint price is the average of the bid and ask price: (ask + bid)/2.

Suppose a dealer provides the following quotes:

Quote in the United States	Bid	Ask
Direct ($/€)	$0.9836	$0.9839
Indirect (€/$)	€1.0164	€1.0167

Paying a $0.9839/euro ask rate is equivalent to a counter-party bidding 1/0.9839 = €1.0164 per dollar.

Two principles apply to cross-rates:

- The DC/FC direct ask exchange rate is the reciprocal of the indirect bid exchange rate.
- The DC/FC direct bid exchange rate is the reciprocal of the indirect ask exchange rate.

For both direct and indirect quotes, the bid–ask spread can be given as a percentage defined as 100 times (ask price − bid price)/ask price.[2] The direct rate bid–ask spread is 100 × (0.9839 − 0.9836)/0.9839 = 0.0305%, or approximately 3 bps. For the indirect rate, the bid–ask spread is 100 × (1.0167 − 1.0164)/1.0167 = 0.0295%.

Spreads differ as a result of market conditions, bank/dealer positions, and trading volume. The size of the bid–ask spread increases with exchange rate uncertainty (volatility) because of bank/dealer risk aversion. In contrast to its relation to market conditions, the size of the bid–ask spread does not depend on bank/dealer positions. Rather, the midpoint of the spread moves in response to dealer positions. For example, a dealer with excess supply of a foreign currency would move the midpoint of his direct quote down rather than adjust the size of his spread. A dealer quoting a large spread relative to other dealers will basically not trade. Neither will the dealer want to quote a smaller spread because that would mean raising his bid price, when he does not want to buy. With excess supply a dealer will make a favorable quote on the ask price or on the bid price, depending on his position. For example, with excess euros, a U.S. dealer will try to sell them and therefore lower his ask price of $0.9839 to, say, $0.9837 and probably also lower his bid to avoid having to buy more euros. Finally, spreads are larger for currencies that have a low trading volume (thinly traded currencies).

Investors need to understand how quotations will be presented. In the following example, we illustrate a likely exchange between a bond portfolio manager and a bank. An example may help to show how a transaction is initiated and completed.

[2] Sometimes the spread is expressed as a percentage of the midpoint price, instead of the ask price. The difference is miniscule. Spreads are often quoted in basis points (bps) where 0.01% equals 1 bp.

Example 27-1

Exchange Rate Quotes and French Bonds

A U.S. portfolio manager wants to buy $10 million worth of French bonds. The manager wants to know how many euros can be obtained to invest using the $10 million. The manager calls several banks to get their €/$ quotation, without indicating whether a sale or a purchase of euros is desired. Bank A gives the following quotation:

€/$ = 0.80000 − 0.80020

In other words, Bank A is willing to buy a dollar for 0.80000 euro or to sell a dollar for 0.80020 euros. These quotes are consistent with the following quotes for the $/€:

$/€ = 1.2497 − 1.2500

To make the quotation faster, only the last digits, called the *points,* are sometimes quoted. The preceding quotation would often be given as follows:

€/$ = 0.80000 − 20

or even

€/$ = 000 − 20

Let's assume that the portfolio manager gets the following quotations from three different banks:

	Bank A	Bank B	Bank C
€/$	0.80000−20	0.79985−05	0.79995−15

Note that the ask prices for all three quotations add 0.00020 to the bid. How many euros will the portfolio manager get to invest?

Solution

The manager will immediately choose Bank A and indicate that she will buy 8 million euros for $10 million. Both parties indicate where each sum should be transferred. The portfolio manager indicates that the euros should be transferred to an account with the Société Générale, the manager's business bank in Paris, whereas Bank A indicates that it will receive the dollars at its account with Citibank in New York. Faxes, telexes, or other electronic messages are exchanged to confirm the oral agreement. The settlement of the transaction takes place simultaneously in Paris and in New York two days later.

3 ARBITRAGE

Arbitrage keeps exchange rates in line with each other and with risk-free interest rates. We will see that triangular arbitrage and interest rate parity are thus reflections of the same principle. Triangular arbitrage and cross-rates involve exchange rates between three currencies and the riskless profit-seeking motive that pushes exchange rates into alignment with each other. Before examining triangular arbitrage, we need to develop the concepts of cross-rate calculations.

Cross-Rate Calculations with Bid-Ask Spreads

Recall that a cross rate is the exchange rate between two countries inferred from each country's exchange rate with a third country. Suppose the dollar per euro exchange rate is 0.9836 and the dollar per pound rate is 1.5231. The euro pound cross-rate can be calculated by multiplying the euro per dollar rate (1/0.9836) by the dollar per pound rate: $(1/0.9836) \times 1.5231 = 1.5485$, or €1.5485 per pound.

In the case of bid and ask (offer) prices, the calculations are only slightly more complex. To calculate a currency cross-rate, we can use the following two equations:

$$(FC_1/FC_2)_{ask} = (FC_1/DC)_{ask} \times (DC/FC_2)_{ask} \quad (27.1)$$

$$(FC_1/FC_2)_{bid} = (FC_1/DC)_{bid} \times (DC/FC_2)_{bid} \quad (27.2)$$

where FC_1, FC_2, and DC are the two foreign currencies and the domestic currency, respectively.

Similarly,

$$(FC_2/FC_1)_{ask} = (DC/FC_1)_{ask} \times (FC_2/DC)_{ask} \quad (27.3)$$

$$(FC_2/FC_1)_{bid} = (DC/FC_1)_{bid} \times (FC_2/DC)_{bid} \quad (27.4)$$

And we must verify that $(FC_2/FC_1)_{ask} = 1/(FC_1/FC_2)_{bid}$ and $(FC_2/FC_1)_{bid} = 1/(FC_1/FC_2)_{ask}$.[3]

Example 27-2

Cross-Rates with the Dollar, Pound, and Euro

Consider the following quotes involving the dollar, the pound, and the euro.

	$ and €		€ and £	
	Bid in Eurozone	**Ask in Eurozone**	**Bid in London**	**Ask in London**
Indirect	$0.9836	$0.9839	€1.5473	€1.5480
Direct	€1.0164	€1.0167	£0.6460	£0.6463

Compute the effective $/£ ask and bid cross-rates, as well as the £/$ ask and bid cross-rates. Assume the euro is the domestic currency.

---

[3] Because of rounding of the quotes to five digits, the cross-rates computed using direct and indirect quotes could yield slightly different results (in the last digit). As mentioned, foreign exchange markets trade and quote using one convention (all exchange rates are the foreign currency value of one dollar, except for the pound and euro), so the cross-rates are best computed using this convention.

Solution

The effective \$/£ ask cross-rate can be calculated from using dollars to buy euros first, and then using the euros to buy pounds:

$\$/£ = \$/€ \times €/£ = 0.9839 \times 1.5480 = 1.5231$ dollars per pound ask rate.

The effective £/\$ bid cross-rate can be calculated by selling dollars for euros first and then selling the euros for pounds.

$£/\$ = €/\$ \times £/€ = 1.0164 \times 0.6460 = 0.6566$ pounds per dollar bid rate.

	\$ and €		€ and £		\$ and £	
	Bid in Eurozone	**Ask in Eurozone**	**Bid in London**	**Ask in London**	**Effective Bid in London**	**Effective Ask in London**
Indirect	\$0.9836	\$0.9839	€1.5473	€1.5480		\$1.5231
Direct	€1.0164	€1.0167	£0.6460	£0.6463	£0.6566	

In the same fashion, we find the \$/£ bid is equal to:

$\$/£ = \$/€ \times €/£ = 0.9836 \times 1.5473 = 1.5219$ dollars per pound bid rate.

And the £/\$ ask rate is equal to:

$£/\$ = €/\$ \times £/€ = 1.0167 \times 0.6463 = 0.6571$ pounds per dollar ask rate, or simply the reciprocal of the dollar per pound bid rate $(1/1.5219 = 0.6571)$.

	\$ and €		€ and £		\$ and £	
	Bid in Eurozone	**Ask in Eurozone**	**Bid in London**	**Ask in London**	**Effective Bid in London**	**Effective Ask in London**
Indirect	\$0.9836	\$0.9839	€1.5473	€1.5480	\$1.5219	\$1.5231
Direct	€1.0164	€1.0167	£0.6460	£0.6463	£0.6566	£0.6571

Other rates can be calculated from dollar or euro quotations and the following example develops familiarity with how to calculate cross-rates from bank quotes. For example, the ¥/€ rate can be calculated using the ¥/\$ and €/\$ rates. This calculation usually implies a larger bid-ask spread on cross-exchange rates.

Example 27-3

Exchange Rate Quotes and Cross-Rates

Following are the quotations given by Bank A:

$$€/\$ = 0.80000 - 0.80020$$
$$¥/\$ = 120.00 - 120.01$$

What should be the ¥/€ bid and ask quotations?

The ¥/€ quotation is obtained as follows:

The ¥/€ bid price is the price at which Bank A is willing to buy euros against yen, that is, the number of yen it is willing to pay to buy one euro. This transaction (buy euros—sell yen) is equivalent to selling yen to buy dollars (at a bid rate of 120.00) and simultaneously reselling those dollars to buy euros (at an ask rate of 0.80020). Mathematically, the transaction is as follows:

$$\text{Bid } ¥/€ = 120.00/0.80020 = 149.96$$

The ¥/€ ask price is the price at which Bank A is willing to sell euros for yen, that is, the number of yen it wants to get for selling one euro. This transaction (sell euros—buy yen) is equivalent to buying yen with dollars (at an ask rate of 120.01) and simultaneously purchasing these dollars with euros (at a bid rate of 0.80000). This may be expressed as follows:

$$\text{Ask } ¥/€ = 120.01/0.80000 = 150.01$$

The resulting quotation by the bank is

$$¥/€ = 149.96 - 150.01$$

To verify that the calculations have been made correctly there are two checks. A *first check* to make sure that you measure the cross-rate in the right direction is to look at the symbols. To get the ¥/€ rate, we divide the ¥/$ rate by the €/$ rate. Observe that the $ symbol disappears:

$$¥/€ = ¥/\$ \,/\, €/\$$$

Similarly, if the euro quotation were given as the number of dollars per euro ($/€), we would have:

$$¥/€ = ¥/\$ \times \$/€$$

A *second check* on the result is to make sure that you maximize the bid–ask spread. To get the bid cross-rate, which is the smaller rate, put the smaller figure (the bid—¥/$) in the numerator and the larger figure (the ask—€/$) in the denominator. To get the ask cross-rate, do the reverse.

Arbitrage aligns exchange rate quotations throughout the world. The quotation for the €/$ rate must be the same, at a given instant, in Frankfurt, Paris, and New York. If quotations were to deviate by more than the spread, a simple phone call would allow a trader to make enormous profits. There are enough professionals in the world watching continuous quote fluctuations to rule out such riskless profit opportunities.

Quotations are directly available online from many financial institutions which have their own computer services. International database services, such as Reuters, provide continuously revised quotations from several banks. Portfolio managers armed with this information on market prices can rapidly arbitrage or hedge their portfolios of foreign assets.

With exchange rates, there are two types of arbitrage opportunities to consider. As with any asset, the law of one price indicates that the exchange rate quotes in two countries should be the same within a transaction cost band. With respect to the exchange rate between two countries, the bid–ask spread in one country should be aligned with the bid–ask spread in the other, or a bilateral arbitrage opportunity would be present. In addition to bid–ask spread alignment, there is also a question of cross-rate alignment. A triangular arbitrage opportunity occurs if the quoted cross-rate between two currencies is higher or lower than the cross-rate implied by the exchange rates of the two currencies against a third currency. We will examine bilateral and triangular arbitrage opportunities in turn.

Bilateral Arbitrage

To detect a bilateral arbitrage opportunity, it is useful to understand the conditions under which no bilateral arbitrage can occur. Suppose that transaction costs are given as 0.015 percent ($t_c = 0.015\%$) of the direct quote midpoint in a foreign country (FC). The direct quote midpoint *in the foreign country* is $S_f = 2$ (i.e., 2 FC units for 1 DC unit). The FC bid–ask spread will be $2 \times (1 \pm 0.00015)$, giving a bid–ask spread of [1.9997, 2.0003]. The equivalent direct bid–ask spread *in the domestic country* must then be given by [1/2.0003, 1/1.9997], or [0.49993, 0.50008]. In examining the possibility of an arbitrage opportunity, we delineate the widest interval within which a bid–ask midpoint in the domestic country would allow no arbitrage profits. Clearly, an arbitrageur would not want to invest 1 DC to buy FC units at the direct bid price in the foreign country, 1.9997 FC, simply to sell those FC units at the direct bid price in the domestic country, 0.49993 DC, to lose money by incurring transaction costs of 0.0003 DC, on every 1 DC unit invested.

A way of expressing this is to develop a formula for the widest interval within which the midpoint of the bid–ask spread in the domestic country must remain in order to allow no arbitrage between the currencies of two countries. With one unit of domestic currency, one could obtain $(1 - t_c) \times S_f = (0.99985 \times 2)$ units of the foreign currency in the foreign country. Then, using the foreign currency in the domestic country, an investor ought to be able to purchase no more than the one unit of domestic currency that the investor started with in the first place. Letting x be the largest no-arbitrage deviation in the domestic midpoint from the reciprocal of the foreign direct midpoint, this implies that $(1 - t_c) \times S_f \times (1 - t_c) \times (1/S_f + x) \leq 1$ unit of domestic currency; for example, $0.99985 \times 2 \times 0.99985 \times (0.5 + x) \leq 1$, or $x = -0.5 + 1 / (0.99985 \times 2 \times 0.99985) = 0.00015$. Given the equivalent direct quote midpoint of $1/S_f = 0.5$, this means that the largest deviation in the no-arbitrage domestic midpoint would be 0.5 ± 0.00015 = [0.49985, 0.50015]. If the midpoint quote is below 0.49985 or above 0.50015, there exists a profitable arbitrage. In general,

$$x = -(1/S_f) + 1/(k^2 \times S_f)$$

where:

S_f is the direct exchange rate quote in the foreign country,

k is 1 minus the transaction cost percentage, t_c, given against the direct quote midpoint (e.g., $k = 0.99985$ if $t_c = 0.015\%$),

and the no-arbitrage range of domestic midpoints is $(1/S_f) \pm x$.

Example 27-4

Bilateral Arbitrage Possibility Detection

Suppose that an arbitrageur in a domestic country faces an indirect exchange rate midpoint of approximately 1.25 FC units for 1 DC unit. The domestic and foreign currency transaction costs are 0.02 percent of the direct quote midpoint in each country. The direct bid–ask spread on the foreign currency in the domestic country is (0.80025 bid, 0.80041 ask). In the foreign country, the direct bid–ask spread is (1.2498 bid, 1.2503 ask). Is there an arbitrage opportunity? What is the widest interval within which the midpoint of the bid–ask spread in the domestic country must remain to allow no arbitrage between the currencies of two countries?

Solution

Multiplying the foreign country direct bid price by the domestic country direct bid price, we get a value $1.2498 \times 0.80025 = 1.00015$ that is greater than one, an indication of an arbitrage opportunity. The transaction cost is $t_c = 0.02\%$, and the direct exchange rate midpoint in the foreign country is $S_f = 1.25$. Hence, $x = -(1/1.25) + 1/(0.9998^2 \times 1.25) = -0.8 + 0.80032 = 0.00032$, and the no-arbitrage range of midpoint exchange rate quotes in the domestic country is [0.79968, 0.80032]. Notice that the midpoint of the domestic bid–ask spread is $0.80033 = (0.80025 + 0.80041)/2$, a midpoint outside the no-arbitrage range.

Triangular Arbitrage

Turning now to triangular arbitrage, we look for a quoted cross-rate between two foreign currencies, FC_1 and FC_2, that is different from the cross-rate implied by the domestic country exchange rate against the two foreign currencies.

Example 27-5

Triangular Arbitrage Profit Without Bid–Ask Spread Considerations

The direct exchange rate is 2 DC units for 1 FC_1 unit, and 3 DC units for 1 FC_2 unit. The quoted cross-rate is 1.48 FC_1 for 1 FC_2 unit. Is there an arbitrage opportunity?

Solution

Ignoring transaction costs, we can find the cross-rates with Equation 27.1:

$$\begin{aligned} FC_1/FC_2 &= (FC_1/DC) \times (DC/FC_2) \\ &= (1/2) \times (3/1) \\ &= 1.5 \end{aligned}$$

The quoted cross-rate is less than the cross-rate implied by the domestic country exchange rate against the two foreign currencies. An arbitrage sequence would be: with 1 DC unit, buy 0.5 FC_1 units; convert to $0.5/1.48 = 0.33784$ FC_2 units; and then convert to $0.33784 \times 3 = 1.0135$ DC units. Notice that this opportunity would not be present if the quoted cross-rate matched the implied cross-rate of 1.5: with 1 DC unit, buy 0.5 FC_1 units; convert to $0.5/1.5 = 1/3$ FC_2 units; and then convert back to $(1/3) \times 3 = 1$ DC unit.

In the realistic case, triangular arbitrage must be examined with bid–ask spreads. There are several steps in calculating the profit from a triangular arbitrage opportunity:

1. Pick the cross-rate currency.
2. Determine whether the cross-rate bid–ask quotes are in line with the direct quotes by determining whether it is cheaper to buy foreign currency directly or indirectly (through the cross-quoted currency).
3. If the actual cross-rate quote is not in line with the quoted cross-rate quote, an arbitrage opportunity exists.

Example 27-6

Triangular Arbitrage Profit with Bid–Ask Spread Considerations

Consider the following quotes involving the dollar, the euro, and the pound. Because these are major currencies, an arbitrage opportunity would not arise. Arbitrage aligns exchange rate quotations throughout the world. As mentioned earlier, the quotation for the €/$ rate, for example, cannot deviate by more than the spread in Frankfurt, Paris, and New York at a given instant. Nevertheless, a hypothetical opportunity will help the reader gain familiarity with the cross-rate concepts already introduced.

Recall the data given in Example 27-2, showing consistent cross-rates.

	$ and €		**€ and £**		**$ and £**	
	Bid in Eurozone	**Ask in Eurozone**	**Bid in London**	**Ask in London**	**Effective Bid in London**	**Effective Ask in London**
Indirect	$0.9836	$0.9839	€1.5473	€1.5480	$1.5219	$1.5231
Direct	€1.0164	€1.0167	£0.6460	£0.6463	£0.6566	£0.6571

Now consider a hypothetical set of rates that might allow an arbitrage opportunity. In gray screens, we show the rates that are out of line with Example 27.2.

	$ and €		€ and £		£ and $	
	Bid in Eurozone	Ask	Bid in London	Ask	Bid in New York	Ask
Indirect	$0.9836	$0.9839	€1.5373	€1.5380	£0.6566	£0.6571
Direct	€1.0164	€1.0167	£0.6502	£0.65049	$1.5219	$1.5231

Is there a hypothetical arbitrage opportunity involving the euro/pound cross-rate? If so, what transactions would permit a U.S. arbitrageur to capture an arbitrage profit? The strategy is to compare two alternatives:

1. Buy pounds directly in New York.
2. Buy pounds indirectly through euros.

Solution
Here the cross-rate quote is €/£.

1. Buy pounds directly in New York for $1.5231.
2. Buy pounds indirectly through euros for 0.9839 × 1.5380 = 1.5132.

Because the indirect rate is cheaper, we conclude that there may be an arbitrage opportunity.

To examine the strategy of buying the pound more cheaply and then selling it in New York, we trace the steps, starting with $1 in New York.

1. With $1, buy 1.0164 euros in Europe; convert these to 0.66086 pounds in London (1.0164 × 0.6502).
2. Sell the 0.66086 pounds in New York for 1.0058 dollars in New York (0.66086 × 1.5219)

We start with $1 and end up with $1.0058, an arbitrage profit of $0.0058. If the cross-rate quote had been in line, it would have been a London indirect ask quote of €1.5480 for one pound. Paying the ask price in Europe ($0.9839) and in London (€1.5480), we would face a $/pound ask price of $1.5231, the same rate as the direct ask rate in New York. Using the "true" London quotes given in Example 27-2, we can verify that the arbitrage constructed above would result in a loss of $0.0007.

Having examined two consequences of arbitrage, alignment of quotes in two countries and alignment of cross-rates, we next examine how the currency exchange quotes for immediate or future delivery are aligned with the risk-free interest rates in the two countries. In order to do this, we need to explain the nature of forward quotes.

4 FORWARD QUOTES

Spot exchange rates are quoted for immediate currency transactions, although in practice the settlement takes place 48 hours later. Spot transactions are used extensively to settle commercial purchases of goods, as well as for investments.

Foreign exchange dealers also quote forward exchange rates in the interbank market. These are rates contracted today but with delivery and settlement in the future, usually 30 or 90 days hence. For example, a bank may quote the one-month €/$ exchange rate as 0.80200–0.80250. This means that the bank is willing to commit itself today to buy dollars for 0.80200 euro or to sell them for 0.80250 euro in one month. In a forward, or futures, contract (described in detail in Chapter 10), a commitment is irrevocably made on the transaction date, but delivery, that is, the exchange of currency, takes place later, on a date set in the contract. The origins of the forward currency market may be traced back to the Middle Ages, when merchants from all over Europe met at major trade fairs and made forward contracts for the next fair.

As with spot rates, bid–ask spreads differ as a result of market conditions, bank/dealer positions, and trading volume. Unique to forward transactions is the feature that liquidity decreases with the increasing maturity of the forward contract. Consequently, bid–ask spreads increase with the increasing maturity of the contract.

Forward exchange rates are often quoted as a *premium,* or *discount,* to the spot exchange rate. With a quote showing the currency price of one dollar, there is a premium on the dollar when the forward exchange rate is higher than the spot rate and a discount otherwise. Clearly, a negative premium is a discount. If the one-month forward exchange rate is €/$ = 0.80200 and the spot rate is €/$ = 0.80000, the dollar quotes with a premium of 0.0020 euro per dollar. In the language of currency traders, the dollar is "strong" relative to the euro, as its forward value is higher than its spot value. Conversely, the euro is traded at a discount, as the forward value of one euro ($/€ = 1/0.80200 = 1.24688) is less than its spot value ($/€ = 1.2500). Consequently, when a trader announces that a currency quotes at a premium, the premium should be added to the spot exchange rate to obtain the value of the forward exchange rate. If a currency quotes at a discount, the discount should be subtracted from the spot exchange rate to obtain the value of the forward rate.

The forward discount, or premium, is often calculated as an annualized percentage deviation from the spot rate as given by the following formula:

Given an exchange rate of x/y, the annualized forward premium on y

$$= \left(\frac{\text{Forward rate} - \text{Spot rate}}{\text{Spot rate}}\right)\left(\frac{12}{\text{No. months forward}}\right)100\%$$

Of course, the annualized forward premium on x can be found by taking the spot rate *minus* the forward rate in this equation.

The percentage premium (discount) is annualized by multiplying by 12 and dividing by the length of the forward contract in months.

Annualized forward premium on the dollar

$$= \left(\frac{0.802 - 0.800}{0.800}\right)\left(\frac{12}{1}\right)100\% = 3.0\%$$

Interbank quotations are often done in the form of an annualized premium (discount) for reasons that will become obvious in the next section. However, forward rates quoted to customers are usually outright (e.g., €/$ = 0.80200 – 0.80250).

Spot and forward dollar exchange rates can be found in newspapers around the world, such as the London-based *Financial Times*. For example, the spot SFr/$ exchange rate could be SFr/$ = 1.3593 × 1.3603. The midpoint is equal to 1.3598. At the same time, the SFr/$ for delivery three months later could be quoted at a midpoint of 1.3471. The dollar quotes at a discount and the Swiss franc at a premium. The dollar's discount is the Swiss franc's premium and the annualized percentage premium of the Swiss franc would then be equal to 3.7 percent per annum; this is obtained by taking the difference between the spot and the forward rate and dividing it by the spot rate:

$$\text{Annualized three-month forward premium} = \left(\frac{0.0127}{1.3598}\right)\left(\frac{12}{3}\right)100\% = 3.7\%$$

Concepts in Action — Strong Currencies

The sign of the premium as reported in newspapers such as the *Financial Times* must be considered carefully. This is because the convention for quotation of the dollar exchange rate differs across currencies. For all currencies except the euro and British pound, a positive premium indicates that the currency on the line is "strong" relative to the dollar because the rates quoted are the currency price of one dollar, e.g., SFr/$. Because the euro and the pound are quoted as the dollar value of one euro or one pound, a premium for these two lines indicates that the currency is "weak" relative to the dollar, while a discount (a negative premium) indicates that the currency is "strong." In the quotations here, positive premiums for the Swiss franc and Japanese yen indicate strength relative to the U.S. dollar but the Canadian dollar's negative discount indicates that it is weak relative to the U.S. dollar. The positive premiums for the euro and the pound indicate that they are both weak relative to the U.S. dollar.

Foreign Exchange Quotations
Dollar Spot Forward Against the Dollar

Aug. 30		Closing Midpoint	Bid/Offer[1]	Three Months Rate	%PA[2]
Euro	(€)	0.9841	839–842	0.9802	1.6
UK	(£)	1.5492	490–494	1.541	2.1
Switzerland	(SFr)	1.4926	922–929	1.4887	1.1
Canada	(C$)	1.5612	610–614	1.566	−1.2
Japan	(¥)	118.185	160–210	117.655	1.8

[1]Bid/offer spreads show only the last three decimal places. UK £ and euro are quoted in U.S. currency.

[2]Means % per annum.

Source: Data from the *Financial Times* and WM/REUTERS.

Interest Rate Parity: The Forward Discount and the Interest Rate Differential

As mentioned earlier, arbitrage aligns exchange rates and risk-free interest rates. Spot exchange rates, forward exchange rates, and interest rates are technically linked for all currencies that are part of the free international market. In the following discussion, we define the exchange rate as the units of foreign currency (FC) for one unit of domestic currency (DC), an indirect rate.

Interest rate parity (IRP) is a relationship linking spot exchange rates, forward exchange rates, and interest rates. For two currencies, DC and FC, the interest rate parity relationship is that the forward discount (premium) equals the discounted interest rate differential between the two currencies. Stated more simply, the product of the forward rate and one plus the domestic risk-free rate equals the product of the spot rate multiplied by one plus the foreign risk-free rate. The relation is driven by arbitrage as illustrated here.

Assume that the following data exist for the FC and DC currencies:

Spot exchange rate	FC/DC = 0.8
One-year forward exchange rate	FC/DC = 0.808
One-year interest rates	
FC	14%
DC	10%

To take advantage of the interest rate differential, a speculator could borrow DC currency units (at 10 percent), convert them immediately into FC units (at the indirect rate of FC/DC = 0.8), and invest the FC currency (at 14 percent). This action is summarized in Exhibit 27-1. (In this exhibit, the U.S. dollar is DC and the euro is FC.) The speculator makes a profit of 4 percent on the borrowing/lending position but runs the risk of a large depreciation of the FC currency.

In Exhibit 27-1, borrowing DC currency means bringing money from the future to the present. Lending DC currency means the reverse. At the end of the period, at time 1, the speculator must convert foreign currency into domestic currency at an unknown rate to honor the claim in DC currency borrowed.

This position may be transformed into a covered (riskless) interest rate arbitrage by simultaneously buying a forward exchange rate contract to repatriate the FC currency into DC currency in one year at a known forward exchange rate of FC/DC = 0.808. In the process shown in Exhibit 27-2, the investor still benefits on the interest rate differential (a gain of 4 percent), but loses on the repa-

EXHIBIT 27-1 Currency Speculation

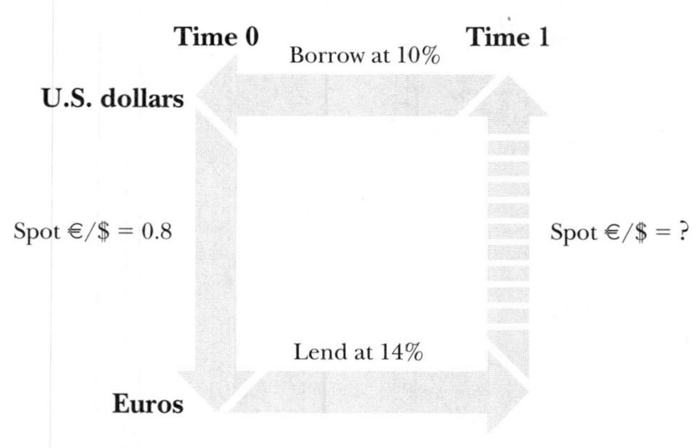

EXHIBIT 27-2 Covered Interest Rate Arbitrage

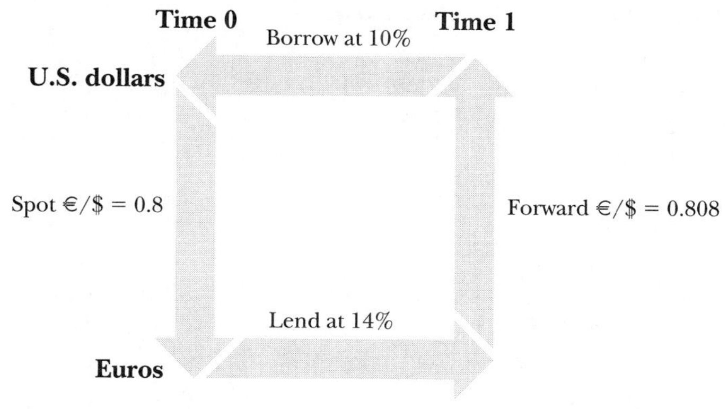

triation of the FC currency into DC currency on the forward contract. In one year, the exchange rate loss will be equal to

$$\frac{0.800 - 0.808}{0.800} = -1\%$$

Per DC currency unit borrowed, the net gain on the position is 3 percent. This gain is certain at time 0, because all interest rates and exchange rates are fixed at that time.

No capital is invested in the position, which is a pure swap with simultaneous borrowing and lending. If such rates were quoted in reality, banks would arbitrage to exploit this riskless profit opportunity. Enormous swaps could occur, because no capital needs to be invested. To prevent this obviously riskless arbitrage, the forward discount must exactly equal the interest rate differential. In other words, the various rates must adjust so that interest rate parity holds. Note that if the forward discount were larger than the interest rate differential, the arbitrage would simply go the other way. Arbitrageurs would borrow FC currency units and swap them for DC currency units.

The exact mathematical relationship is slightly more complicated, because one must buy a forward contract covering both the principal and the accrued interest in order to achieve a perfect arbitrage. In the previous example, for every dollar borrowed, the forward hedge should cover 0.8 FC currency units plus the interest rate of 14 percent, that is, 0.80 (1.14) = 0.912. For two currencies, DC and FC, the interest rate parity relationship is that the forward discount (premium) equals the discounted interest rate differential between the two currencies,

$$(\text{Forward rate} - \text{Spot rate})/\text{Spot rate} = (r_{FC} - r_{DC})/(1 + r_{DC}) \quad \text{or } (F - S)/S = (r_{FC} - r_{DC})/(1 + r_{DC}) \tag{27.5}$$

where:

r_{DC} is the interest rate of currency DC (the domestic currency)
r_{FC} is the interest rate of currency FC (the foreign currency)
the exchange rates are indirect quotes as the number of units of foreign currency FC for one unit of domestic currency DC

Equivalently, we have the relation

$$F(1 + r_{DC}) = S(1 + r_{FC}), \text{ or } F/S = (1 + r_{FC})/(1 + r_{DC}) \tag{27.6}$$

Example 27-7

Interest Rate Parity

If the United States is the domestic country and an indirect quote is provided (rates are quoted as the number of euros per one U.S. dollar), arbitrage ensures that

$$F(1 + r_\$) = S(1 + r_€)$$

where S and F are the spot and forward exchange rates (euro price of one U.S. dollar) and $r_€$ and $r_\$$ are the interest rates in euros and U.S. dollars, respectively. This relation implies that

$$\frac{F - S}{S} = \frac{r_€ - r_\$}{1 + r_\$}$$

If the spot exchange rate is €/$ = 1.05 and the dollar and euro one-year interest rates are 1.76 percent and 3.39 percent, respectively, what is the one-year forward exchange rate?

Solution

Using Equation 27.6, we have

$$F = S(1 + r_€)/(1 + r_\$) = 1.05(1.0339/1.0176) = 1.0668$$

Hence, the one-year forward exchange rate is €1.0668 per dollar.

When the U.S. dollar trades with a forward premium relative to the euro, for example, in a case in which the forward rate is €1.0721 and the spot rate is €1.05, the euro trades with a forward discount relative to the U.S. dollar. Recall that we have defined *strength* by the existence of a premium. The forward premium on the U.S. dollar reflects its strength in this example. Notice that a forward premium is associated with a lower interest rate. A currency with a high risk-free interest rate is considered weak because this rate is needed to compensate for its expected depreciation. A depreciation of the domestic currency coincides with a decrease in the indirect exchange rate. In general, the following table summarizes these relationships:

Domestic Country	Currency Strength	Currency	Indirect Exchange Rate	Direct Exchange Rate	Forward Premium or Discount
Lower risk-free interest rate	Stronger currency	Appreciates	Increases	Decreases	Premium
Higher risk-free interest rate	Weaker currency	Depreciates	Decreases	Increases	Discount

A similar arbitrage relation holds for maturities of less than a year, provided that the right interest rates are used. Annual interest must be converted into rates over the investment period. For a contract with n months maturity, the quoted interest rate must be divided by 12 and multiplied by n.

Example 27-8

Interest Rate Parity with Maturities of Less Than One Year

Consider the following data:

Spot exchange rate $€/\$ = 1.058$

Annual risk-free interest rates for currency investments:

euro	3.39%
U.S. dollar	1.76%

What is the three-month forward exchange rate?

Solution

Three-month interest rates

euro	3.39% (3/12) = 0.8475%
U.S. dollar	1.76% (3/12) = 0.44%

The three-month forward exchange rate is equal to

$$\text{Forward exchange rate} = \text{Spot exchange rate}\,\frac{1 + r_{€}}{1 + r_{\$}}$$
$$= 1.058(1.008475/1.0044) = 1.0623$$

Thus, the three-month forward rate is €1.0623 per dollar.

In working with interest rate parity, one should know which type of rate is being quoted before proceeding any further. The equation for IRP is different for direct exchange rates. With direct exchange rates, the direct spot rate times one plus the domestic risk-free rate (investing domestically the amount of DC units required to purchase one FC unit) equals the forward rate times one plus the foreign risk-free rate (exchanging for one FC unit now, investing in the foreign country, and repatriating later). This means that Equations 27.5 and 27.6 must be rewritten with an interchange of the domestic and foreign currency. With indirect rates, the domestic risk-free rate is in the denominator of both Equations 27.5 and 27.6. The domestic risk-free rate is subtracted from the foreign risk-free rate in the numerator of Equation 27.5 and the foreign risk-free rate appears in the numerator of Equation 27.6. With direct rates, the foreign risk-free rate is in the denominator of both equations. The foreign risk-free rate is subtracted from the domestic risk-free rate in the numerator of Equation 27.7 and the domestic risk-free rate is in the numerator of Equation 27.8.

The forward premium (discount) can be expressed as

$$(\text{Forward rate} - \text{Spot rate})/(\text{Spot rate}) = (r_{DC} - r_{FC})/(1 + r_{FC})$$
$$\text{or } (F - S)/S = (r_{DC} - r_{FC})/(1 + r_{FC}) \qquad \textbf{(27.7)}$$

or, equivalently,

$$\begin{aligned}&(\text{Forward rate/Spot rate})\\&\quad = (1 + \text{Domestic risk-free rate})/(1 + \text{Foreign risk-free rate})\\&\text{or } F/S = (1 + r_{DC})/(1 + r_{FC}).\end{aligned} \tag{27.8}$$

where r_{FC} is the risk-free interest rate of the foreign currency, and r_{DC} is the risk-free interest rate of the domestic currency, and the exchange rates are direct quotes as the number of units of domestic currency DC for one unit of foreign currency FC.

Finally, we note that interest rate parity is sometimes called covered interest rate parity (covered by a forward contract) to distinguish it from uncovered interest rate parity. Uncovered interest rate parity is based on economic theory rather than on arbitrage and involves expected exchange rates rather than forward rates. Uncovered interest rate parity is a theory that links interest rate differentials and the difference between the spot and expected exchange rate. We leave it and other parity theories for Reading 28.

SUMMARY 5

- A direct exchange rate is the domestic price of foreign currency.
- An indirect exchange rate is the amount of foreign currency equivalent to one unit of the domestic currency.
- The spread on a foreign currency transaction is the difference between the rate at which the bank is willing to commit itself today to buy (bid) foreign currency and to sell (ask). When given as a percentage, this spread is given as 100 × (ask − bid)/ask.
- Spreads differ as a result of market conditions and trading volume but not dealer positions. The size of the bid–ask spread increases with exchange rate uncertainty (volatility) because of bank/dealer risk aversion. Spreads are larger for currencies that have a low trading volume (thinly traded currencies).
- To work with currency cross-rates and bid–ask spreads, we can use two principles: the DC/FC direct ask exchange rate is the reciprocal of the FC/DC indirect bid exchange rate, and the DC/FC direct bid exchange rate is the reciprocal of the FC/DC indirect ask exchange rate.
- The largest no-arbitrage deviation in the domestic midpoint from the reciprocal of the direct midpoint of the foreign bid–ask spread that allows no arbitrage between the currencies of two countries is given by

  $$x = -\ (1/S_f) + 1/(k^2 \times S_f)$$

  where S_f is the direct exchange rate quote in the foreign country, and k is 1 minus the transaction cost t_c, which is given as a percentage of the direct quote midpoint (e.g., $k = 0.9997$ if $t_c = 0.03\%$), and the no arbitrage bid–ask spread is $(1/S_f) \pm x$.
- To calculate the profit on a triangular arbitrage opportunity, the basic step is to determine whether the quoted cross-rate is different from the implied cross-rate.
- Spot exchange rates are quoted for immediate currency transactions, but forward change rates are rates contracted today for delivery and settlement in the future.
- As with spot rates, forward contract bid–ask spreads differ as a result of market conditions and trading volume but not bank/dealer positions. Bid–ask spreads increase with increasing maturity of the contract.
- The forward discount (negative) or premium (positive) is defined as the difference between the forward rate and spot rate expressed as a percentage of the spot rate.
- The forward discount, or premium, is often calculated as an annualized percentage deviation from the spot rate as given by the following formula:

  $$\text{Annualized forward premium} = \left(\frac{\text{Forward rate} - \text{Spot rate}}{\text{Spot rate}}\right)\left(\frac{12}{\text{No. months forward}}\right)100\%$$

- For two currencies, A and B, the interest rate parity relationship is that the forward discount (premium) equals the interest rate differential between the two currencies. With the exchange rate quoted as the number of units of B for one unit of A,

$$\frac{\text{Forward rate} - \text{Spot rate}}{\text{Spot rate}} = \frac{r_B - r_A}{1 + r_A}$$

Note that an equivalent relation is

$$\text{forward rate} = \text{spot rate} \times \frac{1 + r_B}{1 + r_A}$$

- Covered interest arbitrage is the process of simultaneously borrowing the domestic currency, transferring it into foreign currency at the spot exchange rate, lending it, and buying a forward exchange rate contract to repatriate the foreign currency into domestic currency at a known forward exchange rate. The net result of such an arbitrage should be nil.

PROBLEMS

1. If the exchange rate value of the British pound goes from US$1.80 to US$1.60, then:
   a. The pound has appreciated, and the British will find U.S. goods cheaper.
   b. The pound has appreciated, and the British will find U.S. goods more expensive.
   c. The pound has depreciated, and the British will find U.S. goods more expensive.
   d. The pound has depreciated, and the British will find U.S. goods cheaper.
2. If the exchange rate between the Australian dollar and the U.S. dollar, A$/$, changes from 1.60 to 1.50, then:
   a. The Australian dollar has appreciated, and the Australians will find U.S. goods cheaper.
   b. The Australian dollar has appreciated, and the Australians will find U.S. goods more expensive.
   c. The Australian dollar has depreciated, and the Australians will find U.S. goods more expensive.
   d. The Australian dollar has depreciated, and the Australians will find U.S. goods cheaper.
3. Over the past six years, the exchange rate between the Swiss franc and the U.S. dollar, SFr/$, has changed from about 1.20 to about 1.60. Would you agree that over this six-year period, the Swiss goods have become cheaper for buyers in the United States?
4. You noticed that the exchange rate between the Thai baht and the dollar has changed considerably. In particular, the baht/$ exchange rate has increased from 25 to 30.
   a. Has the Thai baht appreciated or depreciated with respect to the dollar? By what percentage?
   b. By what percentage has the value of the dollar changed with respect to the Thai baht?
5. A foreign exchange trader with a U.S. bank took a short position of £5,000,000 when the $/£ exchange rate was 1.45. Subsequently, the exchange rate has changed to 1.51. Is this movement in the exchange rate good from the point of view of the position taken by the trader? By how much has the bank's liability changed because of the change in exchange rate?
6. A financial newspaper provided the following midpoint spot exchange rates. Compute all the cross-exchange rates based on these quotes.

$/€	0.9119
SFr/$	1.5971
¥/$	128.17

7. You visit the foreign exchange trading room of a major U.S. bank. A trader asks for quotations of the euro from various correspondents and hears the following quotes:

From Bank A	1.1210–15
From Bank B	12–17

   What do these quotes mean?
8. Do you think the dollar exchange rate of the British pound or the Polish zloty, has a higher percentage bid–ask spread? Why?

9. Here are some quotes of the Japanese yen/U.S. dollar spot exchange rate given simultaneously on the phone by three banks:

Bank A	121.15–121.25
Bank B	121.30–121.35
Bank C	121.15–121.35

Are these quotes reasonable? Is there an arbitrage opportunity?

10. The euro is quoted as $/€ = 1.1610−1.1615, and the Swiss franc is quoted as SFr/$ = 1.4100−1.4120. What is the implicit SFr/€ quotation?

11. A bank is quoting the following exchange rates against the dollar for the Swiss franc and the Australian dollar:

SFr/$ = 1.5960–70

A$/$ = 1.8225–35

An Australian firm asks the bank for a SFr/A$ quote. What cross-rate would the bank quote?

12. A bank is quoting the following exchange rates against the dollar for the Swiss franc and the Australian dollar:

SFr/$ = 1.5960–1.5970

A$/$ = 1.8225–1.8235

A Swiss firm asks the bank for an A$/SFr quote. What cross-rate would the bank quote?

13. Based on the Japanese yen and Canadian dollar direct quotes by a bank, the implicit yen per Canadian dollar cross-rate quotation is ¥/C$ = 82.515−82.575. What would be the implicit Canadian dollar per yen cross-rate, C$/¥, quotation?

14. Paf is a small country that wishes to control international capital flows. The currency of Paf is the pif. Paf put in place an exchange control whereby all current account transactions can be transferred using the normal exchange rate, but financial account transactions must be transferred at a financial pif rate. In other words, foreigners wishing to invest in the assets of Paf must buy them at the financial pif rate, whereas dividends are repatriated at the normal pif rate. The current financial pif rate is 0.8 pifs per dollar or 1.25 dollars per financial pif. The financial rate in dollars/pif quotes at a premium of 25 percent over the normal rate.

- **a.** Assume that the premium of the financial rate stays constant over time. Will a U.S. investor make the same return on investment as will a resident of Paf, once the asset is resold?
- **b.** You hear that the exchange controls may be lifted and that the financial rate may disappear. Would this be good news to an existing foreign investor?
- **c.** Would the lifting of exchange controls and removal of the financial rate be good news to a new foreign investor?

15. You notice the following exchange rates in the newspaper:

$/£ spot: 1.46

$/£ three months forward: 1.42

SFr/$ spot: 1.60

SFr/$ three months forward: 1.65

In the language of currency traders, would the pound be considered "strong" or "weak" relative to the dollar? What about the Swiss franc?

16. The spot dollar to pound exchange rate is $/£ = 1.4570–1.4576. The six-month forward dollar to pound exchange rate is $/£ = 1.4408–1.4434.

a. Is the pound trading at a discount or at a premium relative to the dollar in the forward market?

b. Compute the annualized forward discount or premium on the pound relative to the dollar.

17. The spot Swiss franc to dollar exchange rate is SFr/$ = 1.5960–70. The three-month forward Swiss franc to dollar exchange rate is SFr/$ = 1.5932–62.

a. Is the Swiss franc trading at a discount or at a premium relative to the dollar in the forward market?

b. Compute the annualized forward discount or premium on the Swiss franc relative to the dollar.

FOREIGN EXCHANGE PARITY RELATIONS

READING 28

LEARNING OBJECTIVES

The candidate should be able to:

a. explain how exchange rates are determined in a flexible or floating exchange rate system;

b. explain the role of each component of the balance-of-payments accounts;

c. explain how current account deficits or surpluses and financial account deficits or surpluses affect an economy;

d. describe the factors that cause a nation's currency to appreciate or depreciate;

e. explain how monetary and fiscal policies affect the exchange rate and balance-of-payments components;

f. describe a fixed exchange rate and a pegged exchange rate system;

g. discuss absolute purchasing power parity and relative purchasing power parity.

INTRODUCTION 1

Fluctuations in exchange rates seem to be generated by a large variety of economic and political events. Exchange rate uncertainty adds an important dimension to the economics of capital markets. Reading 28 starts with a review of foreign exchange fundamentals. In the flexible (or floating) exchange rate system of all major currencies, the foreign exchange rate is freely determined by supply and demand. Many international transactions affect foreign exchange demand and supply and these are detailed in the country's balance of payments. After a brief review of the interaction between the two major components of the balance of payments (current account and financial account), we list the major factors that cause a currency to appreciate or depreciate.

Nevertheless, a detailed analysis of exchange rates and their importance in asset management requires a strong conceptual framework. Many domestic and foreign monetary variables interact with exchange rates. Before presenting the basic models of exchange rate determination, it is useful to recall well-known international parity conditions linking domestic and foreign monetary variables: inflation rates, interest rates, and foreign exchange rates. The relations among these are the basis for a simple model of the international monetary environment and are discussed in the second part of this reading. Given the complexity of a multi-currency environment, it is most useful to start by building a simplified model linking the various domestic and foreign monetary variables. The third part of this reading then discusses exchange rate determination theories and their practical implications.

2 FOREIGN EXCHANGE FUNDAMENTALS

Supply and Demand for Foreign Exchange

Just as the value of money is determined by supply and demand in the domestic economy, its value in relation to foreign currencies is also determined by supply and demand. Major currencies, such as the dollar, euro, yen, British pound, or Swiss franc, belong to a *flexible* or *floating exchange rate system.* These currencies are freely exchanged on the foreign exchange market, and their exchange rate depends on supply and demand.

Let's assume that the equilibrium exchange rate between the euro and the U.S. dollar is \$1.25 = 1 euro. So one needs 1.25 dollars to buy one euro. The dollar price of one euro results from the supply and demand for euros. American investors wishing to buy European goods or assets need to sell dollars to buy euros. Conversely, Europeans wishing to buy American goods or assets need to sell euros to buy dollars. If the exchange rate were artificially higher, say \$1.50 = 1 euro, European goods would look more expensive to Americans, as more dollars would be needed to spend the same amount of euros to buy European goods. Americans would decrease their purchase of European goods: The demand for euros from Americans would decrease. Conversely, American goods would look cheaper to Europeans, who would increase their purchase of American goods: The supply of euros from Europeans would increase.

In this two-country example, Exhibit 28-1 illustrates the demand and supply curves for euros. In the marketplace, the current exchange rate of \$1.25 per euro is the price that equilibrates demand and supply. If the exchange rate were set higher, say \$1.50 per euro, there would be excess supply of euros, which would lead to a market disequilibrium.

The illustration presented in Exhibit 28-1 is simple, as we referred only to transactions motivated by trading demand between two countries. In general, there are many types of transactions that affect the demand and supply of one national currency. From an accounting viewpoint, each country keeps track of the payments on all international transactions in its *balance of payments.*

Balance of Payments

The balance of payments tracks all financial flows crossing a country's borders during a given period (a quarter or a year). It is an accounting of all cash flows between residents and nonresidents of a country (called "home country" in the discussion that follows). For example, an export creates a financial inflow for the home country, whereas an import creates an outflow (a negative inflow). A resi-

EXHIBIT 28-1 Foreign Exchange Market Equilibrium

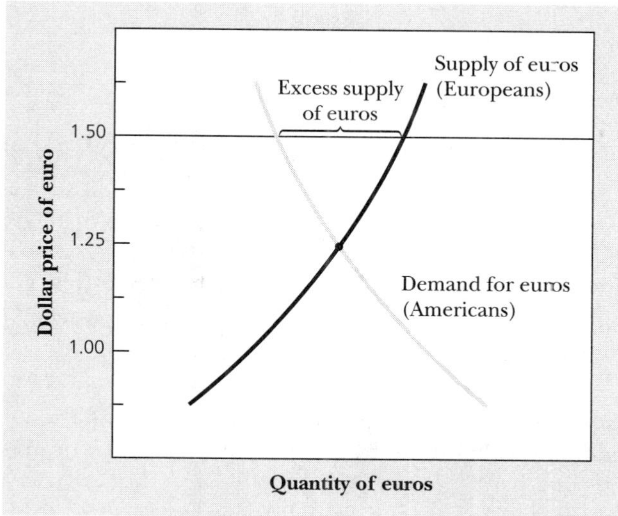

dent's purchase of a foreign security creates a negative financial inflow, whereas a loan made by a foreign bank to a resident bank creates a positive financial inflow. The convention is to treat all inflows (e.g., exports or sale of domestic assets) as a credit to the balance of payments.

For example, assume that a resident imports 100 worth of goods from a foreign country and uses trade credit from the foreign exporter. There will be two accounting entries:

- 100 debit for the goods (imports)
- 100 credit for the loan obtained

International transactions, such as these, are further grouped into two main categories[1]: current account and financial account.

Current Account

The *current account* covers all current transactions that take place in the normal business of residents of a country. It is dominated by the *trade balance,* the balance of all exports and imports. It also includes various other current transactions. To summarize, the current account is made up of

- exports and imports (the trade balance)
- services (such as services in transportation, communication, insurance, and finance)
- income (interest, dividends, and various investment income from cross-border investments)
- current transfers (transfers are gifts and other flows without quid pro quo compensation)

[1] We follow the 1993 IMF (International Monetary Fund) presentation and terminology, which is currently used by the IMF and most countries. A more detailed description of the balance of payments is given later in this reading.

The current account balance represents the net value of all these flows associated with current transactions by residents abroad or by nonresidents in the home country.

Financial Account

The *financial account* covers investments by residents abroad and investments by nonresidents in the home country. It includes

- direct investment made by companies
- portfolio investments in equity, bonds, and other securities of any maturity
- other investments and liabilities (such as deposits or borrowing with foreign banks and vice versa)

The financial account balance represents the net value of all these flows associated with investments and liabilities by residents abroad or by nonresidents in the home country.

The sum of these two accounts, called the *overall balance*,[2] should be zero. If it is not zero, the monetary authority must use reserve assets to fill the gap. If the overall balance is negative, the central bank can use up part of its reserves to restore a zero balance. The *official reserve* account tracks all reserve transactions by the monetary authorities. By accounting definition, the sum of all the balance of payments accounts must be zero.

Current Account Deficits and Financial Account Surpluses

The trade balance, the primary component of the current account, receives major attention in the media of all countries. Monthly trade figures are widely discussed when they are released. The usual undertone is that a current account deficit is "bad." This simple value judgment is based on some economic arguments that are often incorrect. We now address some of the issues.

A Current Account Deficit Is Offset by a Financial Account Surplus

The current account is only one component of a country's balance of payments. A current account deficit should not be confused with an overall balance deficit. A current account deficit has to be offset by a financial account surplus. Of course, official reserves can be used to offset a current account deficit, in a given quarter or year, but this can be only a temporary measure, as the country's reserves will quickly be depleted. To be sustained, a current account deficit must be financed by a financial account surplus. This has been the case for the United States since the mid-nineties. Exhibit 28-2 reports the two major components of the 2001 balance of payments of the United States, Japan, the United Kingdom, and France, as calculated by the IMF.[3]

---

[2] Two other small accounts also exist in the balance of payments terminology. They are the *capital account* (which tracks capital transfers, i.e., capital gifts to other countries such as debt forgiveness) and *net errors and omissions* (to adjust for statistical discrepancies). These accounts are small in magnitude and usually added to the financial account balance for analysis purposes. We follow this convention. A more detailed presentation of the balance of payments is proposed in the third part of this reading.

[3] The capital account and net errors and omissions have been added to the financial account.

EXHIBIT 28-2

Summary 2001 Balance of Payments of the United States, Japan, the United Kingdom, and France
(in billions of U.S. dollars)

Balance	USA	Japan	UK	France
Current account	−417	89	−29	21
Financial account	422	−49	25	−27
Overall balance	5	40	−4	−6

Source: IMF Financial Statistics, September 2002.

The large current account deficit of the United States ($417 billion) is mostly caused by its trade deficit ($424 billion). But foreigners are large investors in the U.S. economy. They are attracted by a stable country with good investment opportunities and a major currency. Investment flows are largely directed at Treasury bonds and other debt securities (around $400 billion), while the balance of direct and equity portfolio investment is almost zero. The overall balance of the United States is close to equilibrium ($5 billion), leading to a small increase in official reserves. If a nation runs a current account deficit, it must also run a financial account surplus and vice versa.

Is a Current Account Deficit a Bad Economic Signal?

A country faces a trade deficit when its imports exceed its exports. As long as foreign investors are willing to finance this difference by net capital flows into the country, the situation poses no economic problem. Actually, U.S. residents consume more than they produce (current account deficit), and the difference is paid by financial inflows from abroad. In terms of the exchange rate, a current account deficit puts depreciation pressures on the home currency (excess demand for foreign currencies to purchase imports), but the financial account surplus puts appreciation pressures on the home currency (excess supply of foreign currencies to buy home securities). If the overall balance is close to zero, the two effects cancel each other.

A current account deficit is sometimes caused by economic growth. When a country grows faster than its trading partners, it tends to need more imports to sustain its output growth. Because other countries do not have the same growth rate, demand for exports does not grow as fast as that for imports. Higher economic growth also yields attractive returns on invested capital and attracts foreign investment. This capital inflow provides natural financing for the current account deficit. Economic growth differentials with other major countries can explain part of the U.S. trade deficit in the nineties. It can also explain part of the Japanese trade surplus in the nineties, as the Japanese economy went into a severe recession that reduced the need for imports. In this case, an excessive current account surplus could be a bad signal, rather than a good one.

Large current account imbalances can have social implications. American unions have repeatedly pointed to the U.S. current account deficit to show that free trade has penalized U.S. labor: U.S. jobs are lost to foreign countries. Periodically, U.S. tariffs have been imposed on some foreign goods for political reasons. Similarly, countries with large current account surpluses can be singled out and become the target of tariffs and other protectionist measures by countries with large current account deficits.

To summarize, a current account deficit is not a bad economic signal as long as nonresidents are willing to offset it by investment flows. But large current account imbalances, positive or negative, can be deemed as "bad" politically.

Is a Large Current Account Deficit Sustainable?

First, we need to judge the size of a deficit relative to some benchmark. This deficit can be compared with total imports or gross domestic product (GDP). For example, the U.S. trade (or current account) deficit was almost 40 percent of total imports in 2001. This is a very large number. It represented around 4 percent of U.S. GDP, a more reasonable number but still large compared with that of most economies. For example, the current account balances of Japan, the United Kingdom, and France represent around 2 percent of their GDP. It is not unusual to see emerging countries sometimes running current account deficits on the order of 5 to 8 percent of their GDP.

Concepts in Action — Balance of Payments Analysis

Let's briefly analyze the 2001 balance of payments of Japan, the United Kingdom, and France using Exhibit 28-2.

Japan: Japan runs a large current account surplus of $89 billion. This is partly offset by a deficit in the financial account balance ($49 billion). Part of this financial account deficit consists of direct investment of Japanese companies to produce abroad (e.g., manufacturing Japanese cars in the United States, or transferring production of electronic equipment to low-cost developing neighbors). Part of it consists in the purchase of U.S. Treasury bonds. But the large current account surplus led to a large increase in official reserves ($40 billion). The case of Japan is unique.

The United Kingdom: The United Kingdom had a current account deficit of $29 billion. This is mostly offset by a financial account surplus of $25 billion. London attracts extensive foreign investments, especially in the banking and financial services industry. Official reserves decreased by a small amount ($4 billion).

France: France had a current account surplus of $21 billion and a financial account deficit of $27 billion. This financial account deficit is mostly explained by extensive foreign direct investments made by French corporations.

A large current account deficit can be sustained as long as nonresidents are willing to finance it continuously. As long as a country offers attractive investment opportunities and a stable "investment climate," it can keep attracting additional financial flows.[4] The situation is no different for a corporation that relies on debt and equity financing to generate more activity. External financing

---

[4] But note that cumulative investment flows will require the payment of dividend and interest income, which will tend to increase the current account deficit.

is a normal recourse for a growing corporation. But as with corporations, external financing of a country also increases the risk of a crisis. As soon as foreign investors reduce their financial flows, or seek to repatriate their invested capital, the financing of the trade deficit will disappear and adjustments will need to take place.

In the early nineties, all developing East Asian countries had a large and sustained current account deficit, offset by large investment flows from America, Japan, and Europe. As illustrated in Exhibit 28-3, Thailand's current account deficit reached $14.7 billion in 1996, some 10 percent of its GDP. This was offset by large capital inflows that induced a positive overall balance. During 1996, the Thai baht had a stable exchange rate around 25 bahts per dollar. But in 1997, foreign investors started to worry that capital was not invested in productive activities, that Thai banks were overextended without proper risk control, and that the local regulatory and legal framework was not progressing quickly enough. This deterioration in the investment climate led to a rapid withdrawal of foreign capital and a negative financial flow balance. The overall balance became a huge deficit in 1997, and the baht was forced to be devalued to a level above 40 bahts per dollar. The financial crisis also affected the local real estate and stock markets, and a severe recession took place. Imports were cut back because of the economic recession and because of their increased price due to the baht depreciation. Exports increased as they became very competitive internationally with the large depreciation of the currency. By 1998, the current account had moved back to a $14 billion surplus, which helped absorb a continuing deficit in the financial account. But the adjustment shock was very painful for the country.

Factors That Cause a Nation's Currency to Appreciate or Depreciate

As discussed previously, a currency appreciates if its price measured in foreign currency units goes up. For example, the euro appreciates if its exchange rate moves from 1.25 dollars per euro to 1.50 dollars per euro. Conversely, the euro depreciates if its exchange rate moves from 1.25 dollars per euro to 1 dollar per euro. In a flexible exchange rate system, the value of a currency is driven by changes in fundamental economic factors. The major factors that move an exchange rate can be associated with the transaction motives on the foreign exchange market, namely, current account transactions and financial account transactions.

EXHIBIT 28-3

Selected Balance of Payments Data for Thailand: 1996–1998
(in billions of U.S. dollars)

Balance	1996	1997	1998
Current account	−14.7	−3.0	14.2
Financial account	16.9	−15.2	−16.9
Overall balance	2.2	−18.2	−2.7

Source: IMF Financial Statistics, September 2002.

Differences in National Inflation Rates

A country's imports and exports depend on the relative prices of foreign-produced and domestically produced goods. A rise in the prices of domestically produced goods (domestic inflation) that is not matched abroad leads to a depreciation of the domestic currency.

For example, suppose that the price of a good-quality golf club is $150 in the United States and £100 in the United Kingdom. Although the clubs are different brands produced locally, they are regarded as equivalent by golfers. The exchange rate is $1.5 = £1. In the coming year, there is no inflation in the United Kingdom, but a 10 percent inflation rate in the United States, so that U.S. clubs now cost $165. If the exchange rate remained at $1.5 = £1, American clubs would not be competitive in the marketplace. Americans would buy more British clubs, and the British would buy fewer American clubs. The current account would deteriorate and the exchange rate would be pushed upward (the pound would appreciate). The pound would need to appreciate against the dollar by 10 percent to restore an equal price between American and British golf clubs.

The currency of a country with high inflation tends to depreciate. The currency of a country with low inflation tends to appreciate. In theory, the movement in the exchange rate between two currencies should exactly offset the difference in inflation rate between the two countries. For example, if there is an annual inflation rate of 5 percent in the United States and 1 percent in the United Kingdom, one would expect the dollar to depreciate by 4 percent against the pound during the course of the year. Conversely, the pound will appreciate by 4 percent against the dollar. This theory is known as "purchasing power parity" and is discussed in detail later in this reading.

Changes in Real Interest Rates

Financial flows are attracted by high expected return. For debt securities, investors search for high real interest rates. The real interest rate is the difference between the interest rate and expected inflation. If exchange rates do indeed adjust to inflation differentials, the country offering the highest real interest rate will provide the highest expected return after an exchange rate adjustment and will attract international loanable funds.

If a country's real interest rate increases, it will lead to an appreciation of its currency. If a country's real interest rate decreases, it will lead to a depreciation of its currency. Of course, if the real interest rate movement of one country is matched by a similar real interest rate movement in another country, their exchange rates should stay unchanged. It is the relative movement in the real interest rate that is of importance for the exchange rate change.

Differences in Economic Performance

Financial flows are attracted by high expected return. For equity securities, investors search for high performance of individual firms and of the economy as a whole. So, good news on the prospect for growth of a nation should attract more international equity capital. The nation's currency should appreciate.

Although growth should boost the financial account of a nation, there is also an opposite effect on the current account. As mentioned, a fast-growing economy has a fast-growing demand for imports. But demand for exports does not grow at the same rate because other countries do not grow as fast. This will put a downward pressure on the current account, which could lead to a depreciation of the nation's currency.

The direction of the cumulative effect is unclear. In the early 1990s, Asian emerging countries grew at a very fast rate with stable currencies. Their imports grew rapidly to sustain the growth in production and to satisfy the consumption needs of their wealthier residents. But this deficit was offset by foreign financial flows. The net result was a stable exchange rate.

It is important to stress that capital flows are motivated by *expected* returns. So, it is the expected future long-run economic growth that affects investment flows. As indicated by its name, the *current* account reflects the influence of current economic growth on imports and exports. Current economic growth affects the current account; future economic growth affects the financial account.

Changes in Investment Climate

Financial flows are attracted by high expected return, but also by low risk. Investors favor countries with a good investment climate and dislike uncertainty. Among desired attributes, one can list

- a stable political system;
- a rigorous but fair legal system, protecting the rights of all investors;
- a tax system that is fair to foreign investors;
- free movements of capital; and
- monetary authorities that favor price stability.

An improvement in a country's investment climate will lead to increased financial inflows and a currency appreciation. Negative news will worsen investment risk perception and tend to lead to capital outflows and a depreciation of the currency.

Government Policies: Monetary and Fiscal

Many of the previously mentioned factors are affected by government policies, such as monetary and fiscal policies. In this section, we sketch the reaction of the exchange rate and components of the balance of payments to an unanticipated change in monetary or fiscal policy. This is a complex issue, and we have to assume that everything else remains the same, including policies of other governments.

Monetary Policy and the Foreign Exchange Rate

Suppose that a country decides to shift to a more expansionary monetary policy. This is a shift that was not anticipated. Most economists would agree that this monetary shock would have, at least, two effects on the domestic economy:

- The real interest rate will temporarily drop.
- There will be an upward pressure on the domestic price level, and inflation will accelerate.

As discussed, both factors would lead to a depreciation of the domestic currency relative to other currencies. Otherwise, both the current account (because of inflation) and the financial account (because of the low real interest rate) would be in deficit.

Whether an expansionary monetary policy creates economic growth in the short and long run is a matter of debate among economists. Many would argue that an unanticipated monetary expansion would induce a short run boost in economic growth, but no long-run stimulation. Because this boost is not likely to be long-lived, it will hardly motivate additional foreign financial flows, but it will put additional pressures on the current account (imports will grow faster than exports).

For all these reasons, an expansionary monetary policy will lead to a depreciation of the home currency, while a restrictive monetary policy will lead to an appreciation of the home currency.[5]

Fiscal Policy and the Foreign Exchange Rate

Suppose that a country decides to use a budget/fiscal policy mix to finance government expenditures. *Everything else equal,* a more restrictive fiscal policy means that a government increases the share of taxes and reduces the share of borrowing to finance government spending. A more expansionary fiscal policy means that a government reduces taxes while increasing the budget deficit.

A more restrictive fiscal policy implies less government borrowing, which should induce a reduction in the domestic real interest rate. In turn, this drop in the domestic real interest rate should lead to a depreciation of the home currency (investment outflows). However, a more restrictive fiscal policy should also slow down economic activity and inflation. These two factors should lead to an appreciation of the home currency (current account improvement).

These influences are conflicting, and it is hard to draw general conclusions on the link between fiscal policy and exchange rates. Many economists believe that the interest rate factor will dominate and that the net result of a more restrictive policy will be a depreciation of the home currency.

A more expansionary fiscal policy has the reverse effect. It will induce a higher domestic real interest rate, which should lead to an appreciation of the currency. However, this expansionary fiscal policy should also induce a rise in output and inflationary pressures, which tend to put depreciation pressure on the home currency. The net result is usually expected to be an appreciation of the home currency. The reaction will be somewhat stronger if the shift in fiscal policy is expected to be permanent rather than temporary.

Exchange Rate Regimes

The previous discussion was conducted assuming that exchange rates were flexible. Historically, exchange rates have operated under three different types of regimes:

- Flexible (or floating) exchange rates
- Fixed exchange rates
- Pegged exchange rates

Flexible (or Floating) Exchange Rates

A *flexible exchange rate regime* is one in which the exchange rate between two currencies fluctuates freely in the foreign exchange market. Today, all major currencies are freely traded, and their pairwise exchange rates fluctuate in the for-

---

[5] A detailed analysis of the dynamics of the exchange rate response to a monetary shock is given in the last part of this reading ("The Asset Market Approach").

eign exchange market in a flexible manner. A central bank can intervene on the foreign exchange market, but it is only one of the many players that contribute to total currency supply and demand, albeit an important one. A government can announce what it believes to be the "normal" exchange rate of its currency, and this announcement will be taken into account by the marketplace.[6] But governments have neither the power nor the will to set official exchange rates (usually called *parities*). In a "pure" floating exchange rate system, governments intervene in the foreign exchange market only to smooth temporary imbalances. If a government has some exchange rate target, it will try to achieve it by adopting the proper macroeconomic policies.

The *advantage* of a flexible exchange rate system is that the exchange rate is a market-determined price that reflects economic fundamentals at each point in time. Governments do not intervene to defend some exchange rate level, so there is no incentive to speculate "against" them. Because exchange rates are flexible, governments are free to adopt independent domestic monetary and fiscal policies.

The *disadvantage* is that flexible exchange rates can be quite volatile. This volatility is unpleasant for agents engaged in trade and investment, but currency risk-hedging strategies are available.

Fixed Exchange Rates

A *fixed exchange rate regime* is one in which the exchange rate between two currencies remains fixed at a present level, known as *official parity*. In a truly fixed system, the exchange rate is expected to remain at its fixed parity forever. It is not sufficient for a country to announce that it will keep a fixed exchange rate with other currencies. To be credible, it must put in place some disciplined system to maintain the official parity at all times.

Historically, the first international exchange rate regime was one of fixed exchange rates, in which all currencies had a value fixed in terms of gold content ("gold standard"). In such a gold standard, the domestic money supply is fully backed by an equivalent of gold reserves. This was a system that worked well in the 1800s and up to the conclusion of World War I, but progressively disappeared thereafter. Today, some countries still attempt to maintain a fixed exchange rate against the dollar or the euro. This is usually done by adopting a *currency board*. In a currency board, a country (say, Argentina) commits to keep a fixed exchange rate (say, 1 peso per dollar) with a major currency (the U.S. dollar), and the supply of home currency is fully backed by an equivalent amount of that major currency.

Suppose there is a deficit in the balance of payments of the home country. It must be financed out of reserves: The amount of dollars held as reserves will be reduced and so will the domestic money supply (100 percent dollar backing). As the country's money supply is reduced, prices of goods must drop and interest rates must rise. In turn, these adjustments make domestic goods more competitive internationally, and the balance of payments equilibrium is restored.

The *advantage* of a fixed exchange rate is that it eliminates exchange rate risk, at least in the short run. It also brings discipline to government policies; this is particularly useful for emerging countries, which are prone to running inflationary policies.

The *disadvantage* of a fixed exchange rate is that it deprives the country of any monetary independence: Its monetary policy is dictated by the "defense" of

---

[6] There is some similarity with a CEO announcing that the corporation's share price is undervalued. The company could decide to use cash reserves to buy back shares.

its parity. It also constrains the country's fiscal policy. A major problem with a fixed exchange rate is its long-term credibility. As soon as a country runs into economic problems, there will be strong speculatory and political pressures to remove the fixed rate system and a push toward a sizable devaluation, with major economic disruption (as happened in Argentina).

Pegged Exchange Rates

A *pegged exchange rate regime* is one characterized as a compromise between a flexible and a fixed exchange rate. A country decides to peg its currency to another major currency (dollar or euro) or to a basket of currencies. A target exchange rate is set (the peg), but this is not a fixed exchange rate to be defended at all costs. First, the exchange rate is allowed to fluctuate within a (small) band around this target exchange rate. Second, periodic changes in the target exchange rate can take place to reflect trends in economic fundamentals (mostly higher inflation in the home country).[7]

Smaller countries, especially emerging countries, frequently use a pegged exchange rate. To defend a target exchange rate against speculation pressures, a country can resort to a variety of measures. Central bank intervention, possibly coordinated with other countries, is the first possibility. The demand and supply for its currency can also be constrained by imposing various restrictions on trade flows (tariffs and quotas) and on capital flows (capital and currency repatriation restrictions, taxes). In the end, aid from international agencies could be requested. But artificially defending a pegged exchange rate could be a costly process for a central bank if devaluation ultimately happens. Speculators will benefit, and this chain of events will also deter foreign investments in the future.

The *advantage* of a pegged exchange rate is that it reduces exchange rate volatility, at least in the short run. This is beneficial to international trade. Setting a fixed exchange rate target also encourages monetary discipline for the home country.

The *disadvantage* of a pegged exchange rate system is that it can induce destabilizing speculation. The more rigid the application of a pegged exchange rate system, the more likely speculation will try to take advantage of the lack of adjustment in the exchange rate.

3 INTERNATIONAL PARITY RELATIONS

We now introduce a simple theoretical framework that is useful to understand the interplay between exchange rates, interest rates, and inflation rates. Traditionally, different nations use different currencies, which allows each nation some independence in setting its national interest rate and monetary policy. Thus, inflation rates and interest rates can differ markedly among countries, which implies that the currencies' exchange rates will not stay constant over time. Consider first how these variables would be linked in a simple and perfect world.

Some Definitions

First, we need to recall some notation introduced in Reading 27 and introduce notation for the inflation rate.

- The *spot exchange rate, S*. The rate of exchange of two currencies tells us the amount of one currency that one unit of another currency can buy. *Spot*

[7] For example, Brazil had a "crawling peg" with the U.S. dollar for many years, whereby the target exchange rate (peg) was automatically adjusted for inflation differential between Brazil and the United States.

means that we refer to the exchange rate for immediate delivery. For example, the U.S. dollar/euro spot exchange rate might be $S = \$1.25$, indicating that one euro is worth 1.25 dollars (one U.S. dollar is worth 0.8 euros).

- The *forward exchange rate, F.* The rate of exchange of two currencies set on one date for delivery at a future specified date, the *forward* rate is quoted today for future delivery. For example, the U.S. dollar/euro forward exchange rate for delivery in one year might be $F = \$1.2061$ per euro.
- The *interest rate, r.* The rate of interest for a given time period is a function of the length of the time period and the denomination of the currency. Interest rates are usually quoted in the marketplace as an annualized rate. With the euro as the domestic currency and the U.S. dollar as the foreign currency, for example, the one-year rate in the domestic country (DC) might be $r_{DC} = 14\%$, and the one-year rate in the foreign country (FC) might be $r_{FC} = 10\%$. In this case, the *interest rate differential* is equal to -4 percent ($r_{FC} - r_{DC} = 10 - 14$).
- The *inflation rate, I.* This is equal to the rate of consumer price increase over the period specified. The *inflation differential* is equal to the difference of inflation rates between two countries. For example, if the inflation in the FC is $I_{FC} = 8.91\%$ and the inflation in the DC is $I_{DC} = 12.87\%$, the inflation differential over the period is approximately -4 percent ($I_{FC} - I_{DC} = 8.91 - 12.87 = -3.96\%$).

The parity relations of international finance are as follows:

1. The *interest rate parity relation,* linking spot exchange rates, forward exchange rates, and interest rates by the no arbitrage condition
2. The *purchasing power parity relation,* linking spot exchange rates and inflation
3. The *international Fisher relation,* linking interest rates and expected inflation
4. The *uncovered interest rate parity relation,* linking spot exchange rates, expected exchange rates, and interest rates
5. The *foreign exchange expectation relation,* linking forward exchange rates and expected spot exchange rates

The last four relations are all theoretical.

Interest Rate Parity

As discussed previously, spot exchange rates, forward exchange rates, and interest rates are linked by the interest rate parity relation:

$$F/S = (1 + r_{FC})/(1 + r_{DC}) \quad \text{or} \quad (F - S)/S = (r_{FC} - r_{DC})/(1 + r_{DC}) \qquad \textbf{(28.1)}$$

where S and F are indirect quotations (the amount of foreign currency that one unit of domestic currency can buy), and r_{DC} and r_{FC} are the domestic and foreign risk-free interest rates, respectively.

Defining $f = (F - S)/S = (r_{FC} - r_{DC})/(1 + r_{DC})$, we have a linear approximation for interest rate parity:[8]

$$f \cong r_{FC} - r_{DC} \qquad \textbf{(28.1')}$$

[8] All parity equations numbered with a prime are expressed in percentage rather than level. This presentation helps to gain an intuitive understanding of the various parity relations.

which states that the percentage difference between the forward and the spot exchange rates is equal to the interest rate differential. This parity relation results from riskless arbitrage and must be true at any point of time (within a transaction cost band).

Example 28-1

The Interest Rate Parity Relation

Suppose that the Eurozone is the domestic country and the United States is the foreign country. The spot exchange rate quote is $S = \$1.25$. Suppose[9] further that the U.S. risk-free interest rate is 10 percent and the Eurozone risk-free interest rate is 14 percent. Calculate the exact forward rate and the approximate forward rate.

Solution

Using Equation 28.1, we have $F/S = (1 + r_{FC})/(1 + r_{DC})$, and $F/1.25 = (1.10)/(1.14)$ gives $F = 1.2061$, \$1.2061 per euro. For a linear approximation with Equation 28.1′, we have $f \cong r_{FC} - r_{DC} = 10\% - 14\% = -4\%$. Then we have $F = (1 + f) \times S = (1 - 0.04) \times 1.25 = 1.20$, \$1.20 per euro.

Purchasing Power Parity: The Exchange Rate and the Inflation Differential

Purchasing power parity (PPP) is a well-known relation in international finance.[10] It states that the spot exchange rate adjusts perfectly to inflation differentials between two countries. There are two versions of PPP: absolute PPP and relative PPP.

Absolute PPP

This version of PPP, inspired by a basic idea known as the law of one price, states that the real price of a good must be the same in all countries. If goods prices rise in one country relative to another, the country's exchange rate must depreciate to maintain a similar real price for the goods in the two countries. This argument is obvious for traded goods with no trade restrictions. Consider the following scenario: Suppose the price of wheat in the Eurozone is 2.68 euros per bushel, and the U.S. price is 2.55 dollars per bushel; the exchange rate is 1.05 euros per dollar. In the next year, suppose the euro price of wheat rises by 3.03 percent, whereas the U.S. dollar price of wheat rises by only 1.4 percent. If the euro depreciation does not offset this hypothetical 1.63 percent inflation differential, Eurozone wheat will be less competitive in the international market and trade flows from the United States to Europe will increase to take advantage of this price differential. If trade could take place instantaneously, at no cost and with no impediments, we would expect the law of one price to hold exactly for all traded goods.

If we take a weighted average of the prices of all goods in the economy, absolute PPP claims that the exchange rate should be equal to the ratio of the

---

[9] Although these rates are unrealistic for the United States and the Eurozone, given today's low inflation policy targets and interest rates, such large rates help illustrate the needed principles and relations.

[10] This theory was originally presented by Cassel (1916). A review of purchasing power parity may be found in Rogoff (1996).

average price levels in the two economies. So absolute PPP is some "average" version of the law of one price. If the weights differ among countries, absolute PPP could be violated even if the law of one price held for each individual good. In practice, determining an average national price level is a daunting task that is never undertaken. Rather than calculating average price levels, expressed in euros in Europe and dollars in the United States, countries calculate movements in price indexes. A price index can be based on a representative sample of produced goods (GDP deflator) or a representative basket of consumed goods (consumer price index). A price index is a pure number, without meaning in itself. Its purpose is to calculate price increases, or inflation rates, from one period to the next.

Relative PPP

Most economists are concerned with relative PPP when they talk about purchasing power parity. Because of domestic inflation, a currency loses some of its purchasing power. For example, a 6 percent annual inflation rate in South Africa implies that one South African rand loses 6 percent of its purchasing power over a year. Relative PPP focuses on the general, across-the-board inflation rates in two countries and claims that the exchange rate movements should exactly offset any inflation differential between the two countries.

The purchasing power parity relation might be written as follows:

$$S_1/S_0 = (1 + I_{FC})/(1 + I_{DC}) \quad \textbf{(28.2)}$$

where

S_0 is the spot exchange rate at the start of the period (the foreign price of one unit of the domestic currency);

S_1 is the spot exchange rate at the end of the period;

I_{FC} is the inflation rate, over the period, in the foreign country (e.g., Canada); and

I_{DC} is the inflation rate, over the period, in the domestic country (e.g., Britain).

Suppose the indirect exchange rate is 2.235 Canadian dollars for one pound and inflation rates are $I_{FC} = 1.3\%$ in Canada and $I_{DC} = 2.1\%$ in Britain. Then the end-of-period spot exchange rate "should" be equal to S_1, such that

$$S_1 = S_0\,(1 + I_{FC})/(1 + I_{DC})$$
$$S_1 = 2.235\,(1 + 0.013)/(1 + 0.021) = 2.2175, \text{ C\\$ per pound}$$

Here, the higher British inflation rate means that the pound depreciates against the Canadian dollar as seen by a decline in the indirect exchange rate. Define s to represent the exchange rate movement:

$$s = (S_1 - S_0)/S_0 = S_1/S_0 - 1$$

The PPP relation is often presented as the linear approximation stating that the exchange rate variation is equal to the inflation rate differential:

$$s = S_1/S_0 - 1 \cong I_{FC} - I_{DC} \quad \textbf{(28.2')}$$

For the preceding example, we would have $I_{FC} - I_{DC} = 1.3 - 2.1 = -0.8$, and expect the indirect exchange rate to decline by 0.8 percent to give $S_1 = (1 - 0.008) \times 2.235 \cong 2.2171$, C\$2.2171 per pound. Compared with the C\$2.2175 per pound calculated with the exact formula, this is close to the exact figure, even though Equation 28.2′ gives us only a first-order approximation of the exact relation (Equation 28.2).

This PPP relation is of major importance in international portfolio management. If it holds, PPP implies that the real return on an asset is identical for investors from any country. For example, consider an Australian asset with an annual rate of return equal to 20 percent in Australian dollars. Assume that the inflation rate is 2.5 percent in Australia and 1.3 percent in Canada and that PPP is verified so that the Australian dollar depreciates against the Canadian dollar by about 1.2 percent. With the linear approximation, the Canadian dollar rate of return on this Australian asset is roughly 18.8 percent (20% − 1.2%). The real rate of return is approximately 17.5 percent for both an Australian investor (20% − 2.5%) and a Canadian investor (18.8% − 1.3%). Because investors should care about real returns, they all agree, whatever their nationality, on the return and risk of a specific asset. Exchange rate movements have no influence, because they only mirror inflation differentials and equalize real return across countries. Of course, PPP is only an economic theory and the relation does not necessarily hold, especially in the short run.

Example 28-2

The Purchasing Power Parity Relation

Suppose that the Eurozone is the domestic country and the United States is the foreign country. The spot exchange rate quote is $S = \$1.25$ per euro. Suppose further that the expected annual U.S. inflation rate is 8.91 percent and the expected Eurozone annual inflation rate is 12.87 percent. Calculate the expected spot rate and the approximate expected spot rate one year away.

Solution

Using Equation 28.2, we have $S_1/S_0 = (1 + I_{FC})/(1 + I_{DC})$ and $S_1/1.25 = (1.0891)/(1.1287)$ gives $S_1 = 1.20614$, or \$1.20614 per euro. For a linear approximation with Equation 28.2′, we have $s \cong I_{FC} - I_{DC} = 8.91\% - 12.87\% = -3.96\%$. This indicates that the indirect exchange rate should decline by approximately 3.96 percent to $(1 - 0.0396) \times 1.25 = 1.2005$, or \$1.2005 per euro.

OPTIONAL SEGMENT

International Fisher Relation: The Interest Rate and Expected Inflation Rate Differentials

Inspired by the *domestic* relation postulated by Irving Fisher (1930), the *international Fisher relation* states that the interest rate differential between two countries should be equal to the expected inflation rate differential over the term of the interest rate. In the *domestic* relation, the nominal interest rate, r, is the sum (or rather, the compounding) of the real interest rate, ρ, and of expected inflation over the term of the interest rate, $E(I)$:

$$(1 + r) = (1 + \rho)\ (1 + E(I)) \quad \textbf{(28.3)}$$

The nominal interest rate is observed in the marketplace and is usually referred to as *the interest rate*, while the real interest rate is calculated from the observed interest rate and the forecasted inflation. For example, consider a nominal FC interest rate of 10 percent and an expected inflation rate of 8.91 percent. The real interest rate is equal to 1 percent, because

$$1 + 0.10 = (1 + 0.01)\ (1 + 0.0891)$$

This relation is often presented with the linear approximation stating that the interest rate is equal to a real interest rate *plus* expected inflation:

$$r \cong \rho + E(I) \qquad \textbf{(28.3')}$$

The economic theory proposed by Fisher is that real interest rates are stable over time. Hence, fluctuations in interest rates are caused by revisions in inflationary expectations, not by movements in real interest rates.[11] The international counterpart of this domestic relation is that the interest rate differential between two countries is linked to the difference in expected inflation:

$$(1 + r_{FC})/(1 + r_{DC}) = ((1 + \rho_{FC})/(1 + \rho_{DC})) \times (1 + E(I_{FC}))/(1 + E(I_{DC}))$$

The international Fisher relation claims that real interest rates are equal across the world; hence, differences in nominal interest rates are caused only by differences in national inflationary expectations. The international Fisher relation can be written as

$$(1 + r_{FC})/(1 + r_{DC}) = (1 + E(I_{FC}))/(1 + E(I_{DC})) \qquad \textbf{(28.4)}$$

or, with the linear approximation,

$$r_{FC} - r_{DC} \cong E(I_{FC}) - E(I_{DC}) \qquad \textbf{(28.4')}$$

Suppose that Thailand is the domestic country and that the expected South Korean inflation rate is 2.3 percent, the expected Thai inflation rate is 0 percent, and the interest rates are 4.74 percent in South Korea and 2.39 percent in Thailand. The real interest rate will then be equal to 2.39 percent in both countries, because

$$(1 + r) = (1 + \rho)\ (1 + E(I))$$

In South Korea,

$$1 + 0.0474 = (1 + 0.0239)\ (1 + 0.023)$$

and in Thailand

$$1 + 0.0239 = (1 + 0.0239)\ (1 + 0)$$

With these equal real rates, the ratio of the nominal interest rates is the same as the ratio of the expected inflation rates:

$$(1 + r_{FC})/(1 + r_{DC}) = 1.0474/1.0239 = 1.023$$

and

$$(1 + E(I_{FC}))/(1 + E(I_{DC})) = 1.023/1 = 1.023$$

[11] Many economists would disagree with this simple approach. They claim that real interest rates vary with liquidity conditions and with the business cycle. Real interest rates would be higher in periods of strong economic growth than in recession periods: High economic growth sustains high real interest rates. See Dornbusch, Fischer, and Startz (2001).

Example 28-3

The International Fisher Relation

Suppose that the Eurozone is the domestic country and the United States is the foreign country. The spot exchange rate quote is $S = \$1.25$ per euro. Suppose further that the expected annual U.S. inflation rate is 8.91 percent and the expected Eurozone annual inflation rate is 12.87 percent. Interest rates are 10 percent in the U.S. and 14 percent in the Eurozone. Demonstrate how interest rates are related to expected inflation rates exactly and by approximation, and calculate the real risk-free interest rate for each country.

Solution

Using Equation 28.4, $(1 + r_{FC})/(1 + r_{DC}) = (1 + E(I_{FC}))/(1 + E(I_{DC}))$, we have

$$(1 + 0.10)/(1 + 0.14) = 0.96491 \text{ and } (1 + 0.0891)/(1 + 0.1287) = 0.96492$$

With Equation 28.4′, $r_{FC} - r_{DC} = E(I_{FC}) - E(I_{DC})$, we have

$$10 - 14 = -4\% \quad \text{and} \quad 8.91 - 12.87 = -3.96\%$$

To calculate the real rate of interest for each country, we take either country and use Equation 28.3. $(1 + r) = (1 + \rho)\ (1 + E(I))$ and solve for ρ. Using the Eurozone, then, we have $\rho = (1 + r)/(1 + E(I)) - 1 = 1.0\%$. The real rates are the same in both countries by the international Fisher assumption.

Again, many economists would not agree that real interest rates should be equalized worldwide, simply because national business cycles are not fully synchronized. Countries with different levels of economic growth could sustain different real interest rates.

Uncovered Interest Rate Parity

Purchasing power parity combined with the international Fisher relation implies that the expected currency depreciation should offset the interest differential between the two countries over the term of the interest rate. To see this, take the expected values of the future exchange rate and the inflation in PPP Equation 28.2. PPP applied to expected values implies

$$E(S_1)/S_0 = (1 + E(I_{FC}))/(1 + E(I_{DC}))$$

Combining with Equation 28.4, we get the theory of uncovered interest rate parity:

$$E(S_1)/S_0 = (1 + r_{FC})/(1 + r_{DC}) \qquad \textbf{(28.5)}$$

or, with the linear approximation,

$$E(s) \cong r_{FC} - r_{DC} \qquad \textbf{(28.5')}$$

Uncovered interest rate parity refers to the idea that the exchange rate exposure is not covered or protected by a forward contract. Although the relation looks similar to covered interest rate parity, the difference is dramatic. Covered interest rate parity must hold by arbitrage. Uncovered interest rate parity is an economic theory whose empirical validity can be questioned.

From the linear approximation to Equation 28.5, the expected movement in the exchange rate should offset the interest rate differential. The basic idea behind the international Fisher relation is that differences in real interest rates among countries would motivate capital flows between countries to take advantage of these real interest rate differentials. These capital flows would lead to an equalization of real interest rates across the world.

Consider for a moment a simple world in which goods and financial markets are perfect. Throughout the world, costless arbitrage can take place instantaneously for physical goods and financial assets. Further assume that all nationals consume the same goods and that there is *no uncertainty*. Hence we know *exactly* what the inflation and the exchange rates will be in the future. In this simple world, arbitrage guarantees that the previous parity relations hold exactly. If the exchange rate does not adjust to the inflation differential as claimed by PPP, one would simply have to buy the goods in the country with the lower real price and ship them for sale in the country with the higher real price to make a certain profit. In a perfect world with costless and instantaneous shipping, such attractive situations cannot exist for long; arbitrage will make the exchange rate movement adjust exactly to inflation in both countries. In the same spirit, if the interest rate differential does not reflect the anticipated and certain exchange rate movement exactly, an arbitrageur would simply borrow in one currency, transfer the amount to the other currency, and lend it at that currency interest rate. By doing so, the arbitrageur would make a certain profit with no capital investment. This riskless profit opportunity would attract huge arbitrage capital, and market rates would adjust to "prevent" such an arbitrage.

In reality, the future exchange rate is uncertain, and arbitrage in the goods market cannot be instantaneous and costless. So, the parity relations developed here are only *theories* claiming that real prices and interest rates should be equalized across the world. The empirical evidence on the validity of these relations is presented in Chapter 3.

Example 28-4

The Uncovered Interest Rate Parity Relation

Suppose that the Eurozone is the domestic country and the United States is the foreign country. The spot exchange rate quote is $S = \$1.25$ per euro, the one-year rate in the domestic country (DC) is $r_{DC} = 14\%$, and the one-year rate in the foreign country (FC) is $r_{FC} = 10\%$. Calculate the exact expected spot rate and the approximate expected spot rate one year forward.

Solution

$E(S_1) = 1.25 \times 1.1/1.14 = 1.2061$, using Equation 28.5. By linear approximation, $s = r_{FC} - r_{DC} = 10\% - 14\% = -4\%$. This means that the spot rate is expected to decline by 4% to $(1 - 0.04) \times 1.25 = \$1.20$ per euro.

Foreign Exchange Expectations: The Forward Premium (Discount) and the Expected Exchange Rate Movement

The *foreign exchange expectation* relation states that the forward exchange rate, quoted at time 0 for delivery at time 1, is equal to the expected value of the spot exchange rate at time 1. This can be written as

$$F = E(S_1) \tag{28.6}$$

This relation would certainly hold if the future values of exchange rates were known with certainty. If one were sure at time 0 that the exchange rate would be worth S_1 at time 1, the current forward rate for delivery at time 1 would have to be S_1; otherwise, a riskless arbitrage opportunity would exist.

Assume, for example, that we know for sure that the spot exchange rate will be 1.2061 \$/€ in a year but, surprisingly, the one-year forward rate is 1.25 \$/€. We could then do the following arbitrage:

- Sell euros forward at 1.25 dollars per euro and hold the contract until maturity.
- At maturity, simultaneously receive delivery of the forward contract and take an offsetting position in the spot exchange rate market.

On the forward contract, the arbitrageur receives 1.25 dollars per euro but pays 1.2061 dollars on the spot market, leading to a profit of 0.0439 dollars per euro. If the expected spot exchange rate is certain, this is a riskless arbitrage that requires no invested capital on the forward commitment. Banks would keep doing this arbitrage until the buying pressure pushed the forward exchange rate to 1.2061 \$/€.

Of course, this parity relation depends strongly on the certainty assumption. Some economists claim, however, that the forward exchange rate should be an unbiased predictor of the future spot exchange rate in the presence of uncertainty thereby leading to Equation 28.6. Others claim the existence of a risk premium appended to this relation.[12]

The foreign exchange expectation relation is often stated relative to the current spot exchange rate. If we subtract S_0 on both sides of Equation 28.6 (remember that the current spot exchange rate is known with certainty) and divide by S_0, we get

$$(F - S_0)/S_0 = E((S_1 - S_0)/S_0) = E(s) \tag{28.7}$$

As mentioned previously, the left-hand side is usually referred to as the forward discount, or premium, and is denoted f. It is the percentage deviation of the forward rate from the current spot rate. This relation states that the forward discount (or premium) is equal to the expected exchange rate movement and can be written as

$$f = E(s) \tag{28.7'}$$

[12] See Chapter 4.

The practical relevance of this foreign exchange expectation relation is obvious. If verified, it means that there is, on the average, no reward for bearing foreign exchange uncertainty. If a risk premium were to be added to the relation, the symmetry of the exchange rate means the risk premium will be paid by some investors (e.g., those selling forward euros for dollars) and received by other investors (e.g., those buying forward euros for dollars). A zero-risk premium means that a forward hedge, that is, the use of forward currency contracts to hedge the exchange risk of a portfolio of foreign assets, will be "costless" in terms of expected returns (except for commissions on the forward contracts).

Example 28-5

The Foreign Exchange Expectation Relation

Suppose that the Eurozone is the domestic country and the United States is the foreign country. The spot exchange rate quote is $S =$ \$1.25. Suppose further that the U.S. risk-free interest rate is 10 percent and the Eurozone risk-free interest rate is 14 percent. Calculate the exact expected spot rate and the approximate expected spot rate one year away.

Solution

Using Equation 28.1, we have $F/S = (1 + r_{FC})/(1 + r_{DC})$ and $F/1.25 = (1.10)/(1.14)$ gives $F = 1.2061$, or \$1.2061 per euro. The expected spot rate is \$1.2061 per euro. Using the linear approximation in Equation 28.1′, $f \cong r_{FC} - r_{DC} = -4\%$. Hence, the exchange rate is expected to depreciate by 4% to $(1 - 0.4) \times 1.25 =$ \$1.20 per euro.

Combining the Relations

The relations link the forward discount to the interest rate differential, the exchange rate movement to the inflation differential, the expected inflation differential to the interest rate differential, and the interest rate differential to the expected currency depreciation, and back to the forward discount:

- *Interest rate differential:* The forward discount (premium) equals the interest rate differential.
- *Inflation differential:* The exchange rate movement should exactly offset any inflation differential.
- *Expected inflation rate differential:* The expected inflation rate differential should be matched by the interest rate differential, assuming (Fisher) real interest rates are equal.
- *The interest rate differential:* The interest rate differential is expected to be offset by the currency depreciation.
- *The expected exchange rate movement:* The forward discount (or premium) is equal to the expected exchange rate movement.

These relations can also be organized in the following manner to show linkages discussed.

Factor	Related to	By
Forward discount	Interest rates	Interest rate parity
Exchange rate movement	Inflation rates	Purchasing power parity
Interest rates	Expected inflation rates	Fisher relation
Expected exchange rate movement	Interest rates	Uncovered interest rate parity (PPP plus Fisher)
Forward discount	Expected exchange rate movement	Foreign exchange expectation

Recall that the *interest rate parity* relation states that the interest rate differential must equal the forward discount (or premium). This is a financial arbitrage condition that does not involve any economic theory. It must hold. Purchasing power parity also relies on some international arbitrage, but in the physical goods markets. Given the heterogeneity in goods and transaction costs, we cannot expect it to hold precisely. All other relations involve expectations on exchange rates and prices; they are based on simple economic theories about agent behavior. The various parity relations are illustrated in Exhibit 28-4, using the linear approximation.

International Parity Relations and Global Asset Management

The multicurrency dimension adds great complexity to global asset management. Interest rates differ among currencies. A foreign investment carries currency risk in addition to market risks. Because of exchange rate fluctuations, an investment could have a positive return when measured in one currency, but a negative one when measured in another currency. International parity relations

EXHIBIT 28-4 International Parity Relations *Linear Approximation*

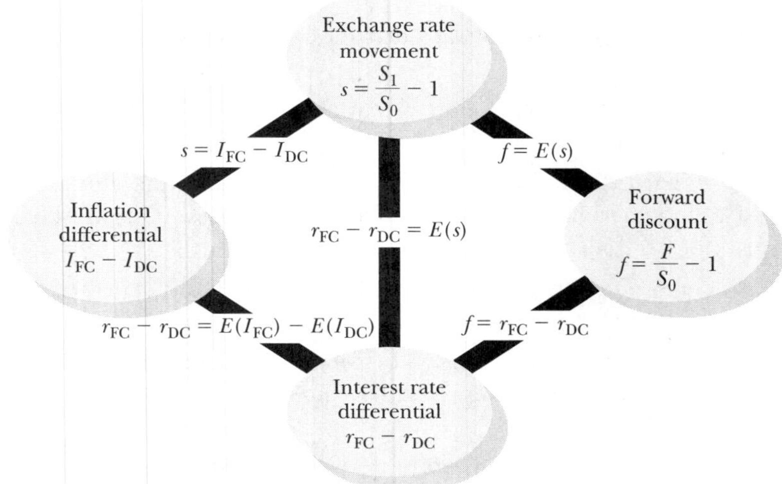

provide the simplest framework to gain a better understanding of global investing in the presence of various exchange rates. From this basic framework, various complexities can be incorporated as done later.

International parity relations provide a useful base for the relationship among exchange rates, inflation, and interest rates. Using this simple framework as a starting point, an international investor can draw several practical implications:

- Interest rate differentials reflect expectations about currency movements. In other words, the expected return on default-free bills should be equal among countries. This is true whether we measure return in a common currency or in real terms.
- Investing in a country with a high interest rate is not a particularly attractive option. The high interest rate is expected to be offset by a matching currency depreciation.
- Investors from different countries expect the same real return on a given asset, once currency is taken into account. For example, consider an investment in a Swiss stock. U.S., French, and Japanese investors will all realize the same real rate of return in their home currency (dollar, euro, and yen).
- Exchange risk reduces to inflation uncertainty if all these relationships hold perfectly. In this instance, an investor concerned with real returns would not be affected by exchange rate uncertainty.
- Currency hedging allows investors to eliminate currency risk without sacrificing expected return, because the forward exchange rate is equal to the expected spot exchange rate.

In this simplified world, currency risk is basically of little real importance; however, deviations from parity relations can introduce complexities. Of primary importance is the observation that currency fluctuations can have real effects if the exchange rate deviates from its PPP value, as illustrated in Example 28-6.

It could also be that real interest rates differ between two countries that are at different stages of the business cycle. Similarly, investors are not risk neutral and could append a risk premium to the foreign exchange expectations relation (see Chapter 4).

We now go one step further and give a brief review of the simple economic models of the exchange rate that could induce deviations from the international parity relations.[13] The empirical validity of these relations is discussed in Chapter 3.

Example 28-6

Are Foreign Risk-Free Investments Risk-Free to a Domestic Investor?

During June 2002, the U.S. dollar depreciated by 7 percent against the euro. One-month bills in euro and in dollar had the same interest rate of 3 percent (annualized), and annual inflation rates were about 2 percent in both regions. Would a European investor holding U.S. Treasury bills have the same return as U.S. investors?

---

[13] These models are detailed in standard international economics textbooks. See, for example, Dornbusch, Fischer, and Startz (2001).

Solution
A U.S. investor has a rate of return of 0.25 percent over the month (3%/12), and a real return of approximately 0.08 percent (1%/12). However, a European investor made a loss of 6.75 percent (7 percent currency loss minus 0.25 percent dollar interest rate) when measured in euro. The real return for European investors is −6.92 percent (−6.75 percent return in euro minus 0.17 percent monthly European inflation rate). The exchange rate movement has a dramatic real impact.

4

EXCHANGE RATE DETERMINATION

In this reading so far, the traditional view indicates that exchange rates should adjust the purchasing power of the two currencies. It is worth looking at this relation again. Other economic variables affecting the exchange rate will then be introduced.

Purchasing Power Parity Revisited

The short-run behavior of exchange rates does not conveniently conform to PPP. The empirical evidence to be introduced in Chapter 3 demonstrates that yearly exchange rates can deviate significantly from the inflation differentials between countries. The real exchange rate is the observed exchange rate adjusted for inflation. Hence, movements in the real exchange rate are equal to movements in the exchange rate minus the actual inflation differential between the two countries. These movements in the real exchange rate are not explained by PPP. However, the theory, supported by extensive empirical evidence, claims that such real exchange rate movements (deviations from PPP) will be corrected in the long run. So, one approach to understanding the path of the exchange rate is to compute its long-run "fundamental" (or "equilibrium") value based on PPP, and to assume that any observed deviation of the current exchange rate from this fundamental value will be progressively corrected. To provide a forecast of the future short-run movement in exchange rates, one must first estimate the *fundamental PPP value* of a currency.

Concepts in Action **Big Mac Currencies (2002)**

Currency forecasters have had it hard in recent years. Most expected the euro to rise after its launch in 1999, yet it fell. When America went into recession last year, the dollar was tipped to decline; it rose. So to help forecasters really get their teeth into exchange rates, *The Economist* has updated its Big Mac index.

Devised 16 years ago as a light-hearted guide to whether currencies are at their "correct" level, the index is based on the theory of purchasing-power parity (PPP). In the long run, countries' exchange rates should move towards rates that would equalize the prices of an identical basket of goods and services. Our basket is a McDonald's Big Mac, produced in 120 countries. The Big Mac PPP is the exchange rate that would leave hamburgers costing the same in America as elsewhere. Comparing these with actual rates signals if a currency is under- or overvalued.

The first column of the table shows the local-currency prices of a Big Mac. The second converts these into dollars. The average American price has fallen slightly over the past year, to $2.49. The cheapest Big Mac is in Argentina (78 cents), after its massive devaluation; the most expensive ($3.81) is in Switzerland. (More countries are listed on our website.) By this measure, the Argentine peso is the most undervalued currency and the Swiss franc the most overvalued.

The third column calculates Big Mac PPPs. Dividing the Japanese price by the American price, for instance, gives a dollar PPP of ¥105, against an actual exchange rate of ¥130. This implies that the yen is 19% undervalued. The euro is only 5% undervalued relative to its Big Mac PPP, far less than many economists claim. The euro area may have a single currency, but the price of a Big Mac varies widely, from €2.15 in Greece to €2.95 in France. However, that range has narrowed from a year ago. And prices vary just as much within America, which is why we use the average price in four cities.

The Australian dollar is the most undervalued rich-world currency, 35% below McParity. No wonder the Australian economy was so strong last year. Sterling, by contrast, is one of the few currencies that is overvalued against the dollar, by 16%; it is 21% too strong against the euro.

Overall, the dollar now looks more overvalued against the average of the other big currencies than at any time in the life of the Big Mac index. Most emerging-market currencies also look cheap against the dollar. Over half the emerging-market currencies are more than 30% undervalued. That implies that any currency close to McParity (e.g., the Argentine peso last year, or the Mexican peso today) will be overvalued against other emerging-market rivals.

Adjustment back toward PPP does not always come through a shift in exchange rates. It can also come about partly through price changes. In 1995 the yen was 100% overvalued. It has since fallen by 35%; but the price of a Japanese burger has also dropped by one-third.

Every time we update our Big Mac index, readers complain that burgernomics does not cut the mustard. The Big Mac is an imperfect basket. Hamburgers cannot be traded across borders; prices may be distorted by taxes, different profit margins or differences in the cost of non-tradable goods and services, such as rents. Yet it seems to pay to follow burgernomics.

In 1999, for instance, the Big Mac index suggested that the euro was already overvalued at its launch, when nearly every economist predicted it would rise. Several studies confirm that, over the long run, purchasing power parity—including the Big Mac PPP—is a fairly good guide to exchange-rate movements.

Still, currencies can deviate from PPP for long periods. In the early 1990s the Big Mac index repeatedly signaled that the dollar was undervalued, yet it continued to slide for several years until it flipped around. Our latest figures suggest that, sooner or later, the mighty dollar will tumble: relish for fans of burgernomics.

The hamburger standard:

	Big Mac Prices In Local Currency	In Dollars	Implied PPP* of the Dollar	Actual Dollar Exchange Rate 23/04/02	Under(−)/over(+) Valuation against the Dollar, %
United States†	$2.49	2.49	—	—	—
Argentina	Peso 2.50	0.78	1.00	3.13	−68
Australia	A$3.00	1.62	1.20	1.86	−35
Brazil	Real 3.60	1.55	1.45	2.34	−38
Britain	£1.99	2.88	1.25‡	1.45‡	+16
Canada	C$3.33	2.12	1.34	1.57	−15
Chile	Peso 1,400	2.16	562	655	−14
China	Yuan 10.50	1.27	4.22	8.28	−49
Czech Rep	Koruna 56.28	1.66	22.6	34.0	−33
Denmark	DKr24.75	2.96	9.94	8.38	+19
Euro area	€2.67	2.37	0.93§	0.89§	−5
Hong Kong	HK$11.20	1.40	4.50	7.80	−42
Hungary	Forint 459	1.69	184	272	−32
Indonesia	Rupiah 16,000	1.71	6,426	9,430	−32
Israel	Shekel 12.00	2.51	4.82	4.79	+1
Japan	¥262	2.01	105	130	−19
Malaysia	M$5.04	1.33	2.02	3.8	−47
Mexico	Peso 21.90	2.37	8.80	9.28	−5
New Zealand	NZ$3.95	1.77	1.59	2.24	−29
Peru	New Sol 8.50	2.48	3.41	3.43	−1
Philippines	Peso 65.00	1.28	26.1	51.0	−49
Poland	Zloty 5.90	1.46	2.37	4.04	−41
Russia	Ruble 39.00	1.25	15.7	31.2	−50
Singapore	S$3.30	1.81	1.33	1.82	−27
South Africa	Rand 9.70	0.87	3.90	10.9	−64
South Korea	Won 3,100	2.36	1,245	1,304	−5
Sweden	SKr26.00	2.52	10.4	10.3	+1
Switzerland	SFr6.30	3.81	2.53	1.66	+53
Taiwan	NT$70.00	2.01	28.1	34.8	−19
Thailand	Baht 55.00	1.27	22.1	43.3	−49
Turkey	Lira 4,000,000	3.06	1,606,426	1,324,500	+21
Venezuela	Bolivar 2,500	2.92	1,004	857	+17

*Purchasing power parity: local price divided by price in the United States

†Average of New York, Chicago, San Francisco, and Atlanta

‡Dollars per pound

§Dollars per euro

Source: "Big Mac Currencies," *The Economist*, April 27, 2002, p. 76. www.economist.com.

Fundamental Value Based on Absolute PPP

Ideally, one would like to compare directly the price of goods in two countries to see if an exchange rate conforms to absolute PPP, or whether it is overvalued or undervalued in real terms. This can only be done for some individual goods that are clearly comparable ("law of one price"), and the estimation for different goods can lead to opposing conclusions.

There is a wide dispersion in the dollar prices of the Big Mac throughout the world. Differences in taxes, rents, and labor costs partly contribute to these differences. But several studies have shown that Big Mac PPP is a useful predictor of future exchange rate movements because deviations tend to be corrected over the long run.[14] This adjustment takes place either by a change in the exchange rate or by a change in the local-currency price of a Big Mac. For example, Cumby (1996) states that, after correcting for currency-specific constants, "a 10 percent undervaluation according to the hamburger standard in one year is associated with a 3.5 percent appreciation over the following year" (p. 13).

In practice, no one would estimate the fundamental value of a currency by applying absolute PPP to a single good, especially a nontraded one, and the preceding discussion is only anecdotal. Some attempts have been made to compare the prices of baskets of goods, but goods consumed in different countries are seldom identical, so a direct comparison of their prices is not realistic. How, for example, can one directly compare the value of a 19th-century Parisian house and that of a Dallas suburban home?

Fundamental Value Based on Relative PPP

Instead, *relative PPP* is most commonly used to explain and forecast currency movements. Remember that relative PPP considers across-the-board movements in prices over time, rather than absolute price levels. Several steps are required to implement this approach:

- Select an inflation index for each country.
- Select a historical period for which to compute long-run PPP.
- Determine the fundamental PPP value of the exchange rate, and hence, the current amount of over- or undervaluation of the currency.

The definition of a proper inflation index is open to question. The estimation of the inflation rate depends on the basket of goods chosen for the index. Different baskets of goods will exhibit different price increases, as the relative prices of the goods change over time. An inflation rate measured from an index of consumed goods (CPI) will be different from an inflation rate measured from an index of produced goods (wholesale price index, WPI), because of differences in imported and exported goods. Differences in price movements between tradable and nontradable goods can also make a difference as illustrated in the case of Japan on the next page.

---

[14] See Cumby (1996) and Annaert and De Ceuster (1997).

Concepts in Action The Case of Japan

The strength of the yen since World War II is a puzzle for many investors. From 1950 to 2002, the yen has appreciated against the dollar from ¥360 per dollar to some ¥120 per dollar. This yen appreciation exceeds the consumer price index (CPI) inflation differential between the two countries. How can such a real appreciation of the yen be sustained?

Several studies, including one by McKinsey et al. (1993), show that Japan has experienced remarkable growth in productivity in many manufacturing industries whose products trade internationally. However, productivity gains for nontradables, such as services and locally consumed agricultural products, have lagged considerably. Locally produced nontradables are a significant share of the Japanese consumption basket (CPI).

The growth in productivity in the tradables sector has allowed wage increases that spread through the economy. Because of the low productivity gains in the nontradables sector, this increase in wages has forced a rapid rise in prices of nontradables. So, the prices of nontradables have risen much faster than the prices of tradables. Calculating the PPP value of the yen based on the CPI results in an apparent real appreciation of the currency. But there is no market pressure to correct such a deviation from PPP, because Japanese traded goods are competitive internationally at that exchange rate.

Because of cultural and regulatory restrictions on imports of competing goods and services (including agricultural products), prices of Japanese nontradables can remain high in the long run. The relative price of nontradables versus tradables has also risen in other countries, but to a much smaller extent.

The historical period selected to compute the fundamental PPP exchange rate value is important. For example, assume that the year is 2002 and you wish to determine the fundamental PPP value of the yen/dollar exchange rate. You can select December 31, 1972, as the base year. Then, the current 2002 fundamental value will be equal to the December 1972 exchange rate, adjusted by the inflation differential over the period 1973–2001. As of the end of 2001, the fundamental PPP value would have been equal to the December 1972 spot exchange rate, $S_{1972} = 302$ ¥/$, multiplied by the ratio of Japanese price indexes at the end of 2001 and at the end of 1972 ($CPI¥_{2001}/CPI¥_{1972}$), and divided by the ratio of U.S. price indexes at the end of 2001 and at the end of 1972 ($CPI\$_{2001}/CPI\$_{1972}$).

This yields a fundamental value of 199 ¥/$ for year-end 2001, compared with an actual spot rate of 131 ¥/$. This is shown in Exhibit 28-5, in which the solid line is the actual spot exchange rate at year-end, and the top dotted line is the PPP value using 1972 as base year. When the dotted line (PPP value) is above the solid line (actual value), the yen is overvalued (or the dollar is undervalued). Conversely, the yen is undervalued when the dotted line is below the solid line. The yen seemed strongly overvalued at the end of 2001. Based on PPP, you can only conclude that the yen should depreciate relative to the dollar.

If a different base year had been selected, however—for example, 1978—the conclusion would have been markedly different. The bottom dotted line in Exhibit 28-5 plots the PPP value using 1978 as base year: 1978 is a year in which

EXHIBIT 28-5 Fundamental Value for the Japanese Yen

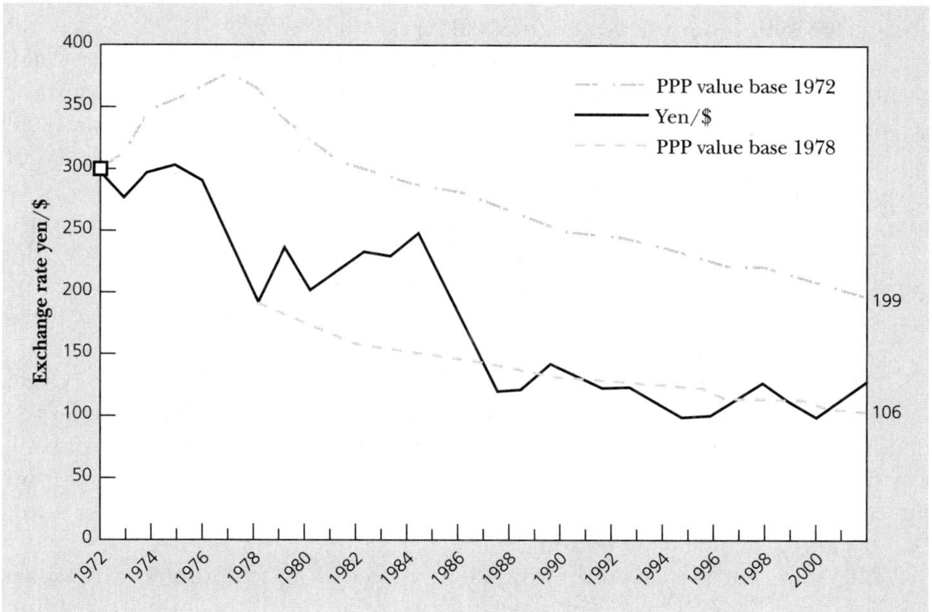

the yen was strong relative to 1972. Hence, calculations using 1978 as a base year lead to a fundamental PPP value equal to only 106 ¥/$ at the end of 2001, a value below the actual spot rate of 131 ¥/$ at the end of 2001. The conclusion would have been that the yen was undervalued in 2001. (Note that the December 31, 2002, exchange rate was ¥120 per dollar, meaning an appreciation of the yen in 2002). Clearly, the choice of base year can make a significant difference. One pragmatic idea implemented by Arnott (1999) is to estimate the fundamental PPP value using a wide range of starting dates. In this smoothing process, the fundamental PPP value is then taken as the average of all the estimates derived with different base years.

To summarize, estimating a currency's fundamental PPP value should help explain future short-term movements in the exchange rate. Such estimation is not an easy task, however, and exchange rates can become grossly misaligned and remain so for several years without a correction. This correction will take place, but it may take several years, and its timing is unclear. Additional models are needed to provide a better understanding of exchange rate movements.

The Balance of Payments Approach

Historically, an analysis of the balance of payments provided the first approach to the economic modeling of the exchange rate. The balance of payments tracks all financial flows crossing a country's borders during a given period (a quarter or a year). For example, an export creates a positive financial inflow for the country, whereas an import creates a financial outflow (a negative financial inflow). A resident's purchase of a foreign security creates a negative financial inflow, whereas a loan made by a foreign bank to a resident bank creates a positive financial inflow. The balance of payments compiles all financial flows. The convention is to treat all financial inflows as a credit to the balance of payments, and all financial outflows as debits.

A balance of payments is not an income statement or a balance sheet, but a cash balance of the country relative to the rest of the world. The balance of all financial flows must be equilibrated, because the foreign exchange market always clears. In other words, the final balance *must* be zero.

This concept can best be confirmed by a simple example. Consider a small country whose only international transactions consist of exports and imports of goods. Its central bank has a large reserve of foreign currencies accumulated over the years. Assume that in the year 2000, this country runs a trade deficit of $1 million (imports greater than exports). Then the central bank will need to use $1 million of reserves to offset this deficit. The net balance will then be zero. Of course, the importers could instead borrow $1 million abroad to finance the payment of the trade balance; this will create a financial inflow that will be recorded in the balance of payments as a positive inflow offsetting the trade deficit. Again, the balance of payments will be equilibrated.

A parallel can be drawn with an individual's cash balance. If expenses exceed receipts at the end of the month, an individual must use his reserves to cover the deficit, borrow money from the outside world, or sell some assets to the outside world. The net balance must be zero. Hence, what is interesting is to analyze and interpret the various components of the balance of payments, because we know that the final balance must be zero.

The tradition is to separate the balance according to the type of transaction involved. There are many types of international transactions, including the following:

- International trade, leading to payment for goods imported and exported
- Payment for services, such as tourism and consulting contracts
- Income received (and paid) on loans and existing investments
- Direct investments made by domestic corporations abroad and by foreign corporations at home
- Portfolio investments, such as purchase of foreign securities by domestic investors and purchase of domestic securities by foreign investors
- All types of short-term and long-term capital flows
- Sale of foreign currency reserves by the central bank

Several readings could be devoted to the accounting details of the balance of payments and to the controversy surrounding the various accounting conventions. The establishment of a balance of payments requires the collection of statistics from many sources, such as customs data, central bank statistics, and bank reports of transactions. Some countries, such as the United States, construct their balance of payments from a sampling of transactions. Most other countries attempt to trace every single international transaction. It is common to see the balance of payments figures revised periodically after a few months or years to reflect corrected data or changes in accounting conventions.

To simplify the presentation of a balance of payments, it is useful to consider four component groups of lines:

- Current account
- Capital account
- Financial account
- Official reserve account

The *current account* includes the balance of goods and services, and income received or paid on existing investments. Exports, or income received from abroad, appear as credits to the balance. It must be stressed that the current account does not include the amounts paid for investments abroad, but only the income received on current holding of foreign assets, usually in the form of dividends or interest payments. Actual investments are reflected in the financial account section. The current account also includes current *transfers*, which are transactions without compensation, such as gifts to relatives living abroad, grants to foreign students, or government aid to developing countries.

An important component of the current account, often mentioned by the news media, is the *trade balance*, which is simply the balance of merchandise exports minus merchandise imports. Many economists believe that the merchandise trade balance is given too much importance and that services should be added to the trade balance. Altogether, the current account gives a more global view of all current (i.e., noninvestment) transactions. Introducing straightforward notation, the current account (*CA*) is the sum of the following:

Trade balance	*TB*
Balance of services	*BS*
Net income received	*NI*
Current transfers	*CT*
Current account	***CA***

The *capital account* (*KA*) section reflects unrequited (or unilateral) transfers corresponding to capital flows entailing no compensation (in the form of goods, services, or assets). These capital transfers are different from current transfers and cover, for example, investment capital given (without future repayment) in favor of poor countries, debt forgiveness, and expropriation losses. It is generally a very small account, whose title is a bit misleading.

The *financial account*[15] (*FA*) includes all short-term and long-term capital transactions. The definition in this textbook excludes transactions made by the central bank, which will be assigned to the official reserve account. The financial account includes direct investment, portfolio investment, and other investment flows (especially short-term capital). Direct investment is the net amount of direct purchases of companies or real estate made by a resident abroad and by foreigners at home. "Direct" means that the purchase did not go through the capital market and involves some form of control in the foreign company, as opposed to portfolio investment. The purchase (sale) of a foreign company by a resident is treated as a debit (credit), because it corresponds to a financial outflow (inflow). The purchase (sale) of a domestic company by a foreign resident is treated as a credit (debit), because it corresponds to a financial inflow (outflow). Portfolio investments correspond to the balance of investments made on financial markets by domestic and foreign investors.[16] "Other investment flows" captures many types of private and official capital flows, including short-term deposits made by foreigners at domestic banks and vice versa. Introducing straightforward notation, the financial account (*FA*) is the sum of these three items:

---

[15] Although the term *current account* is standard in the balance of payments literature, many terms have been used to refer to the sum of all capital flows, defined here as "financial account." Hence, the reader should be careful in applying the concept of "financial account" to published balance of payments data. Here we use the IMF terminology adopted in 1993 and applied since 1995 by most countries (see IMF, 1995).

[16] The balance of payments tracks investment flows. It does not take into account changes in value of foreign investments or liabilities caused by changes in market prices of securities.

Direct investment	*DI*
Portfolio investment	*PI*
Other investment flows	*OI*
Financial account	***FA***

"Net errors and omissions" is very embarrassing for balance-of-payments accountants. At the end of the day, when all statistics are collected from many different sources, the balance of payments must balance, like any cash balance. "Net errors and omissions" includes a few unaffected transactions, but consists mostly of whatever is needed to equilibrate the final balance to zero. Apparently disliking this terminology, the United States in 1976 changed it to "statistical discrepancy." This line is often assigned to the financial account, because transactions in the current account are more reliably tracked than are capital transactions. Aggregating all these items in the *capital and financial account* (*KFA*), we get

Capital account	*KA*
Financial account	*FA*
Net errors and omissions	*NE*
Capital and Financial account	***KFA***

The sum of the current account, the capital account, and the financial account is generally called the *overall balance* (IMF terminology). Denoting *OB*, the overall balance, we have

$$OB = CA + KFA$$

The *official reserve account* reflects net changes in the government's international reserves.[17] These reserves can take the form of foreign currency holdings and loans to foreign governments. Conversely, liabilities that constitute foreign governments' reserves come in the deduction of the domestic reserves. When the U.S. Federal Reserve Bank sells foreign currencies to equilibrate a deficit in the current and financial accounts, it will receive dollars in exchange. This inflow of dollars is treated as a credit to the balance of payments. This means that a *reduction* in the official reserves has a *positive* sign in the balance of payments accounting. This is often a source of confusion, because most of us tend to regard a drop in reserves as "bad" or "negative." However, this convention is quite logical. If a country sells goods or services, it receives a financial inflow in exchange for these goods or services. If its government sells foreign currencies, it also receives a financial inflow. Similarly, if a government is forced to borrow abroad to finance a deficit, the loan will induce a financial inflow and, hence, create a credit to the balance of payments. This credit is treated as an increase in official liabilities and, hence, as a reduction in official reserves.

By definition of a balance of payments, the sum of the current account (*CA*), the capital and the financial account (*KFA*), and the change in official reserves (*OR*) must be equal to zero:

[17] The official reserve account is sometimes included as a subcategory of the financial account.

$$CA + KFA + OR = 0$$

In other words, the change in official reserves simply mirrors the overall balance:

$$OR = -OB$$

The traditional approach to foreign exchange rate determination is to focus on the influence of balance of payments flows. Let's consider a country in which capital flows are restricted, as is often the case with developing nations. A trade deficit would lead to a reduction in the country's reserves and, ultimately, to a depreciation of the home currency. In turn, this depreciation would improve the terms of trade. National exports would become cheaper abroad and more competitive: Exports should increase. Imported goods would become more expensive: Imports should drop. This should lead to an improvement in the trade balance, and the currency should stabilize.

For example, the drop in oil prices in 1985 and 1986 led to a Mexican trade balance deficit; the value of the oil that Mexico exported suddenly dropped, without a corresponding reduction in imports. This deficit forced the Mexican government to borrow abroad to offset the imbalance; it also led to a depreciation of the peso. This devaluation helped restore the terms of trade.

This analysis requires us to estimate the trade flow elasticities in response to a movement in the exchange rate: How will imports and exports react to an exchange rate adjustment? The answers have to be built on often complex models of the economy. For example, oil imports by an emerging country are necessary for the domestic production process, as well as other domestic needs. A devaluation of the home currency is unlikely to strongly affect the demand for oil. Conversely, the demand for some imported goods, such as liquor or luxury items, is going to decrease if such goods become more expensive in home-currency terms.

Furthermore, the model must be dynamic, because the improvement in the trade balance will only be progressive. The immediate technical effect is not a quantity adjustment (more exports and less imports), but a price adjustment. Because imports are more expensive in terms of the home currency, as soon as the devaluation take place, the trade deficit will immediately increase, given the new exchange rate. This is known as the *J-curve effect:* The trade balance will first deteriorate following a devaluation, before improving following the amelioration in the terms of trade. Of course, this scenario is not always rosy: The rise in import prices can feed higher inflation at home, leading to further depreciation of the currency. The monetary authorities will have to adjust their monetary/fiscal policy to control this "imported" inflation.

The analysis becomes even more complex when we consider capital flows, which is necessary to analyze the various components of the balance of payments. We must draw the line between flows that are autonomous—caused by current economic or political conditions—and those that are created to compensate for a potential imbalance.

Concepts in Action The Dollar: A Cliff-Hanger

How Might a Weak Dollar Affect the Global Economy?

Currency forecasters who have long predicted its decline have seen the dollar climb inexorably for years. At last it seems to be turning. Since February the dollar has fallen by 9% against the euro, to a 17-month low of \$0.94. It has also hit a six-month low against the yen, of ¥123. It may well fall further over the coming year.

Two factors weigh against the dollar. First, it is by most yardsticks overvalued. Its trade-weighted level, adjusted for inflation differentials, remains well above its average over the past couple of decades. And second, America's large current-account deficit, at more than 4% of GDP and growing, looks unsustainable. If the dollar stays roughly where it is as the economy rebounds, then the deficit will grow. As a rule, once a country's external deficit approaches 5% of GDP, its currency tends to fall.

To trigger a slide, foreign investors do not have to become net sellers of American assets. The dollar will fall if they merely reduce the pace at which they add to their holdings. It will fall even more if American investors continue or expand this year's buying of foreign assets, notably European equities.

Until recently, net capital inflows more than covered America's current-account deficit. Yet investors are now reassessing their expectations about future relative returns. Recent data appear to confirm that America's recovery is on track. Indeed, The Economist's latest poll of forecasters suggests that the American economy is again expected to outpace Western Europe and Japan this year.

Still, the part of this growth that finds its way into company profits is in greater doubt. America's productivity growth may have risen, but the fruits have so far gone mainly to workers and consumers, rather than to profits. And a growing band of investors guesses that higher potential returns now lie in Europe and Japan—so long as governments carry out reforms and firms continue to restructure.

Currency Complacency?

Most forecasters predict another fall in the dollar, but they generally expect it to be gradual and relatively painless—except, of course, for foreigners with large dollar holdings. For example, UBS Warburg expects the dollar to fall to $1.05 to the euro and to ¥115 by the end of 2003—a drop of around one-sixth from its peak earlier this year. George Magnus, the banker's chief economist, argues that a gradual fall in the dollar would benefit the world economy. It would underpin America's recovery, by helping to bolster exports, profits and investment. A stronger euro and yen would also intensify the pressure for structural reform and corporate restructuring in the euro area and Japan.

By helping to hold down inflation in Europe, a strong euro would also reduce the pressure on the European Central Bank (ECB) to raise interest rates. For Japan, however, a weaker dollar would be bad news, threatening to choke a nascent recovery. With interest rates already close to zero, the exchange rate is one of the few policy tools left for the Bank of Japan. GDP figures for the first quarter, due to be published on June 7th, are widely expected to show strong annualized growth of around 5%. However, Japan's GDP figures are notoriously volatile; many economists reckon that output will stumble again in the second quarter.

The Bank of Japan has intervened four times in the past two weeks in a bid to hold down the yen. Yet intervention rarely has much effect unless it is carried out jointly with other central banks. A new paper by Takatoshi Ito, an economist at the University of Tokyo, finds that joint intervention in the 1990s was 20–50 times more effective than intervention by the Bank of Japan alone. This time round, the Federal Reserve and the ECB are unlikely to join in, as both would be reasonably happy with a weaker dollar.

America's economy would certainly benefit from a moderate fall in the dollar. Some economists fret that this would push up inflation and thus force the Federal Reserve to raise interest rates. Yet the Fed would probably be happy to see some increase in inflation. America's GDP deflator, the broadest measure of inflation, rose by less than 0.5% at an annual rate over the past two quarters, its lowest for almost 50 years. This is getting close to deflation.

While a moderate decline of the dollar might be benign for the world, a sudden plunge would be another story altogether. It would probably trigger a slump in American share prices, and a rise in bond yields, as foreigners pulled out their money. Foreigners own fully two-fifths of American Treasury bonds, a quarter of corporate bonds, and 13% of American equities. Share prices around the world would probably be hit.

A further drop in share prices would erode consumer and business confidence and harm world growth. There is also a question over whether the ECB would react fast enough to a dollar crash by cutting interest rates to offset the deflationary impact on the euro-area economies. Stephen Roach, at Morgan Stanley, estimates that a 20% fall in the dollar over six months could knock up to one percentage point off global growth over the following year.

For now, most economists are sanguine, expecting a moderate fall in the dollar towards its "fair value," rather than a plunge. These are the same forecasters who in 2000 failed to predict a bear market in shares (the S&P 500 is now one-third below its peak) and who last year ruled out a recession. Currencies almost always overshoot, downwards as well as up. From its 1985 peak, the dollar fell by half against the D-mark within two years. A repeat performance is possible.

Source: "The Dollar: A Cliff-Hanger," *The Economist*, June 8, 2002, pp. 59–70. www.economist.com.

The United States has run systematic, large trade deficits from the 1970s through 2002 without a structural depreciation of its currency, because of a financial account surplus. Foreign investors were happy to hold an increasing amount of dollar assets. The 1980s marked an important period for the United States as the dollar developed into the major international reserve currency: The U.S. dollar value swung widely and the U.S. overall balance (OB) moved into a large deficit during the second half of the 1980s. The events from the late 1970s to the early 1990s led to a better understanding of the current situation. The story is told in Exhibit 28-6, which gives the three major components of the U.S. balance of payments, as well as the real effective exchange rate index, as calculated by the IMF. The real effective exchange rate index is the weighted average of the currencies of selected U.S. trading partners, adjusted for relative inflation differentials. It is more representative of the value of the U.S. dollar than any single exchange rate. A real appreciation of the dollar would lead to an increase in the effective exchange rate index. To analyze Exhibit 28-6, remember that a positive official reserve account means a drop in reserves. In 1977 and 1978, the combined deficits of the current and capital accounts led to a drop in official reserves, as well as a depreciation of the dollar. The improvement in the balance of payments (stable reserves, no trade deficit) from 1979 to 1982 led to an appreciation of the dollar. From 1983 to 1985, the United States started to run a huge trade and current account deficit. However, this current deficit was offset by fast-growing foreign

EXHIBIT 28-6 Balance of Payments and the Dollar Exchange Rate

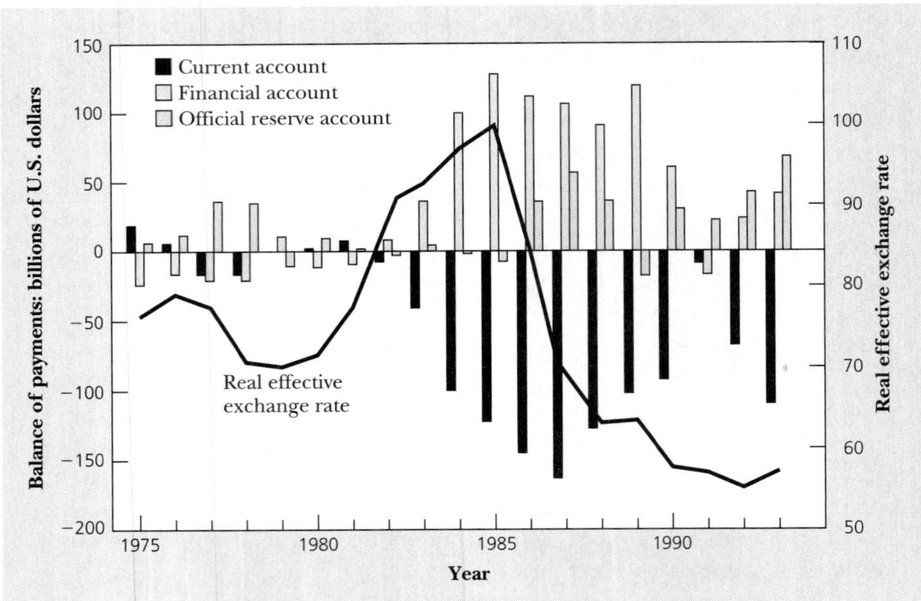

investments, and the reserves did not deteriorate: The dollar kept rising. By 1986, the capital flows became insufficient to cover the current account deficit, the official reserve position deteriorated,[18] and the dollar started to slide. In 1990, the financial account began to deteriorate; it recovered in the mid 1990s. The big surge in capital investment in the 1980s came partly from Japanese investors who engaged in real estate and business acquisitions in the United States. The Japanese were running huge surpluses in their trade and current account balances, which allowed them to invest extensively in the United States and other countries (a Japanese deficit of the financial account). This situation of a huge U.S. trade deficit offset by foreign capital flows still prevailed in the late 1990s.

Although this story sounds reasonable, it is difficult to understand the huge swings in the value of the dollar. The timing of these swings is also difficult to forecast. Small changes in current account flows cannot justify such dramatic turning points and volatility in the exchange rate. In particular, we might ask what drives the behavior of investors and their willingness (or unwillingness) to hold U.S. dollars.

The Asset Market Approach

The General Idea

Many economists reject the view that the short-term behavior of exchange rates is determined in flow markets. Exchange rates are financial prices traded in an efficient asset market. Indeed, an exchange rate is the relative price of two currencies and, therefore, is determined by the willingness to hold each currency.

---

[18] Remember that the IMF changed its accounting convention for official reserves in 1997, and back-calculated all its balance of payments statistics. "Liabilities constituting foreign authorities reserves" were moved from official reserves to the financial flows account. This move has been questioned, because its main implication is to drastically reduce the apparent overall balance deficit of the United States. Here, we use data under the old convention, because it is better suited for our analysis.

Like other asset prices, the exchange rate is determined by expectations about the future, not by current trade flows.[19]

A parallel with other asset prices may illustrate the approach. Consider the stock price of a winery traded on the Paris Bourse. A frost in late spring results in a poor harvest, in terms of both quantity and quality. After harvesting and a year of wine making, the wine is finally sold, and the income is much less than in the previous year. On the day of the final sale, there is no reason for the stock price to be influenced by this low cash flow. First, the unusually low level of income has already been discounted in the winery stock price since the previous spring. Second, the stock price is affected by future, in addition to current, prospects. The stock price is based on expectations of future earnings, and the major cause for a change in stock price is a revision of these expectations.

A similar reasoning applies to exchange rates: Contemporaneous international flows should have little effect on exchange rates to the extent that they are expected. Only news about future economic prospects will affect exchange rates. The mere announcement of some unexpected news is sufficient to trigger an immediate adjustment in market value, even if it will take several months or years to be fully reflected in economic data. Because economic expectations are potentially volatile and influenced by many variables, including those of a political nature, the short-run behavior of exchange rates is volatile.

Several types of news influence exchange rates, but many of them have to do with inflationary expectations and interest rates. The relationship between interest rates and exchange rates is often presented in a confusing fashion in the media. Hence, we will introduce some simple models to help explain this relationship. In particular, we need to distinguish between interest rate movements caused by changes in inflationary expectations and those caused by changes in the real interest rate. We also need to distinguish between short-run and long-run effects.

More on Interest Rates

As mentioned, the interest rate can be separated into an "expected inflation" component and a "real interest rate" component, as in Equation 28.3′:

$$r \cong \rho + E(I)$$

The relation introduced by Irving Fisher is a *long-run* equilibrium relation. It states that an increase in expected inflation causes a proportional increase in money rates. Over the long run, the real interest rate is assumed constant.

But monetary policy affects the real interest rate in the *short run.* To illustrate this point, it is useful to introduce a simple domestic monetary model.

Equilibrium in the money market requires that money supply, M^S, equals money demand, M^D. The money supply is provided by the central bank. Money demand by all agents can be written as the product of the price level, P, and real money demand. Real money demand, M^D/P, can be a function of many variables, but it is generally supposed to be an inverse function of the interest rate.[20] So we can write

$$M^D/P = L(r)$$

[19] A review of this approach can be found in Dornbusch, Fischer, and Startz (2001) or Krugman and Obstfeld (2000).

[20] Demand for real cash balances is also a function of economic activity. To simplify the analysis, we do not explicitly introduce the real sector here, but real output (real GDP) is implicit in L.

This inverse relation between money demand and interest rate is intuitive. Higher interest rates mean that it becomes more costly to hold money balances than to invest in interest-bearing assets. This opportunity cost reduces the demand for money. Equilibrium implies that money supply equals real money demand times the price level:[21]

$$M^S = P \times L(r) \tag{28.8}$$

The interest rate will adjust so that the quantity of money demanded by agents will equal the money supply. For example, assume that the central bank decides to provide more liquidity (unexpected increase in money supply). Agents will have additional cash balances to invest. The supply of loanable funds will increase and the interest rate will drop.

It must be stressed that the money equilibrium Equation 28.8 is commonly used in two very different contexts:

- In the *long run*, monetarists use Equation 28.8 as an equilibrium relation between the money supply and the price level. Everything else equal, an increase in the money supply will cause a proportional increase in the price level. For example, if the money supply doubles, without any change in real output, the price level must also double. In the long run, goods prices adjust to a change in money supply, and real interest rates revert back to their normal equilibrium level.
- In the *short run*, goods prices are inelastic. They react only slowly to monetary shocks and changes in interest rates. An unexpected increase in money supply will not immediately translate into a proportional price increase for physical goods. Goods prices are generally slow to adjust ("sticky prices") and the price level will only increase progressively. This is quite different for financial prices, such as interest rates, which react immediately to new information that affect expectations. So, Equation 28.8 is used, assuming that the price level, P, remains unchanged in the short run. An increase in money supply translates immediately into a drop in the interest rate. This is a drop in the *real* interest rate because expected inflation has clearly not decreased (but rather increased).

This difference between short-run and long-run effects is equally important for the exchange rate.

Exchange Rate Dynamics: Asset Market Approach

The asset market approach is generally used to estimate the impact of some disturbance on the current value of a currency. Typically, a monetary shock (disturbance) such as a central bank intervention on the interest rate will take time to propagate through the economy, but its expected impact will be immediately reflected in current exchange rates. The asset market approach first determines the new equilibrium value of the exchange rate once the influence of the monetary shock has been fully reflected in the economy (long run). Then, knowing that this equilibrium exchange rate is expected to prevail in the long run, one can infer the current exchange rate using uncovered interest parity.

---

21 M^S/P is called the real money supply.

The typical asset market approach to the exchange rate assumes that the parity relations described previously will apply in the long run. The equilibrium value of the exchange rate is driven by PPP, but goods prices are sticky and PPP will not hold in the short run. Because exchange rates are financial prices, however, they will immediately reflect expected changes in this long-run equilibrium value. So, we must clearly differentiate between the long-run and the short-run effects. Thus, the asset market approach studies the dynamics of the exchange rate and proceeds in two steps:

1. Determine the *long run* expected value of the exchange rate based on PPP, $E(S)$. This is its fundamental PPP value expected to prevail in the long run.
2. Infer the *short-run* value of the exchange rate, S_0, assuming that the uncovered interest rate parity relation holds. Using Equation 28.5, we get

$$S_0 = E(S) \times (1 + r_{DC})/(1 + r_{FC}) \quad \text{(28.9)}$$

If the expected long-run exchange rate $E(S)$ were known with certainty, Equation 28.9 could be viewed as an arbitrage condition. S_0 would have to be equal to the expected exchange rate adjusted by the interest rate differential[22]; otherwise arbitrage would occur.

Exchange Rate Dynamics: A Simple Model

A simple model reflects the economic reasoning behind the asset market approach. Assume that the foreign currency is the U.S. dollar and the domestic currency is the euro. $M_\$$ and $M_€$ are the money supplies, and $P_\$$ and $P_€$ are the price levels in both countries. S is the \$/€ spot exchange rate. For the sake of simplicity, assume that there is no inflation in either country and that the money supplies have been constant over time and are expected to remain so in the future. Further, assume that the yield curves are flat in both countries, with $r_\$ = r_€$.

An unexpected increase in money supply takes place in the United States, at time t_0, from $M_\$$ to $M_\$^*$. This is a one-time but permanent money expansion. In other words, the U.S. money supply is now expected to remain at $M_\$^*$ for the foreseeable future. Nothing has changed in Europe: the money supply, interest rate, and price level remain constant at $M_€$, $r_€$, and $P_€$. How should the exchange rate react to this money supply shock?

The time path of the various variables is described on Exhibit 28-7.

- The money supply jumps *permanently* from $M_\$$ to $M_\$^*$ at time t_0 (Exhibit 28-7a).
- The *long-run* equilibrium price level in the United States must increase proportionally to the increase in money supply. In the long run, it will reach a level $P_\$^* = P_\$ \times M_\$^*/M_\$$, as implied by Equation 28.8. Once the price level reaches $P_\$^*$, it will remain at that level because there is no expected monetary expansion beyond the one-time shock. The real money supply will get back to its equilibrium level: $M_\$^*/P_\$^* = M_\$/P_\$$. But goods prices are sticky in

[22] Note Equation 28.9 does not specify the time period necessary for the long-run adjustment. So, the interest rates r_{DC} and r_{FC} are compounded over the whole time period; they are not annualized. For example, assume that it takes two years for the exchange rate to reach its new fundamental value; then the interest rates should be equal to the annualized rates compounded over two years.

EXHIBIT 28-7 Exchange Rate Dynamics

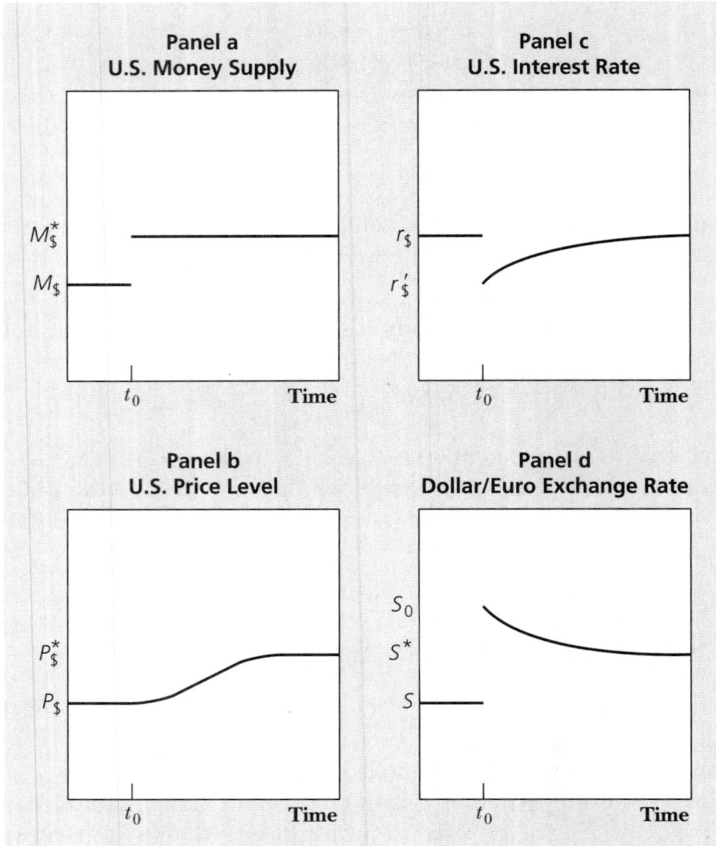

the short run, so it will take time for the price to reach the level $P^*_\$$. The increase in price level will be progressive (Exhibit 28-7b).

- Once the monetary shock is fully absorbed, the U.S. interest rate will revert, in the *long run*, to its normal level of $r_\$$. But, in the *short run*, the price level does not move, so the real money supply increases to $M^*_\$/P_\$$. This increase in money supply will lead to a drop in the U.S. interest rate (say, to a level $r'_\$$), which will progressively get back to its long-run equilibrium value in line with the increase in price level (Exhibit 28-7c).
- The exchange rate started at its PPP value of $S = P_\$/P_€$. In the long run it is expected to rise to its new equilibrium PPP value of $E(S) = S^* = P^*_\$/P_€$. The long-run exchange rate of the euro (number of dollars per euro) will appreciate in proportion to the increase in U.S. money supply, which is also the percentage increase in U.S. price level. Knowing what the exchange rate will be in the long run, we can infer its short-run value using uncovered interest parity. The short-run value (S_0) should be equal to the expected long-run value adjusted by the interest rate differential. Because the U.S. interest rate has dropped, the exchange rate will be higher than its new long-run expected value. The exchange rate will progressively move to its long-run PPP value (Exhibit 28-7d).

Example 28-7

Exchange Rate Dynamics

The United States and Europe have no inflation, a constant money supply, and (annualized) interest rates equal to 3% for all maturities. The exchange rate is equal to one dollar per euro; this is its PPP value, and the price indexes can be assumed to be equal to one in both countries.

Suddenly and unexpectedly, the United States increases its money supply by 2 percent. This is a one-time but permanent shock. Immediately on the announcement, the U.S. interest rate drops from 3 percent to 2 percent for all maturities. It is expected that it will take two years for the shock in money supply to translate fully into a price increase. There is no effect on the real sector, nor any effect on Europe. Assume that the Eurozone is the domestic country. What will be the exchange rate dynamics?

Solution

First, determine the long-run exchange rate. After two years, the U.S. price level will rise by 2 percent to 1.02. The exchange rate expected to prevail at that time, $E(S)$, is the new fundamental PPP value of the exchange rate:

$$S^* = 1 \times \frac{1.02}{1.000} = 1.02 \text{ dollars per euro}$$

After two years, the U.S. interest rate will be back to 3 percent. In the short run (immediately after the announcement), the exchange rate will move to

$$S_0 = E(S) \times (1 + r_{DC})/(1 + r_{FC}) = 1.02 \times \frac{(1 + 3\%)^2}{(1 + 2\%)^2}$$
$$= 1.04 \text{ dollars per euro}$$

Following the money supply shock, the short-run effect on the dollar is a depreciation of 4 percent. This is caused by two phenomena:

- The fundamental PPP value depreciates by 2 percent because of the 2 percent long-run increase in the U.S. price level.
- The drop in the U.S. interest rate leads to an additional 2 percent dollar depreciation (a total of 4 percent).

This second phenomenon is caused by the drop in U.S. interest rates. If the exchange rate S_0 had settled at its long-run value of 1.02 \$/€, an arbitrage could be constructed. Rather than investing dollars at a 2 percent interest rate, it is much more attractive to exchange dollars for euros spot at 1/1.02 euros, to invest those euros at 3 percent and to repatriate the euros into dollars two years from now at the exchange rate of $S^* = 1.02$ \$/€. This would enable a speculator to "pocket" the interest rate differential and put pressure on the spot exchange rate until it reaches $S_0 = 1.04$ \$/€. Of course, such reasoning relies on the assumption that the future exchange rate S^* is known with certainty.

The immediate result of this U.S. monetary shock is a depreciation of the U.S. dollar (appreciation of the euro) beyond its new fundamental PPP value. This phenomenon, caused by the U.S. interest drop, is known as "overshooting": The short-run reaction to a shock is larger than its long-run reaction. Here we see two phenomena at play:

- The dollar depreciates from S to S^* because of the long-run increase in the U.S. price level (*expected inflation*).
- The dollar depreciates even more in the short run (from S to S_0) because of the drop in the U.S. interest rate (drop in the *real interest rate*). As shown in Equation 28.9, the exchange rate S_0 is equal to the long-run expected exchange rate S^*, compounded by the domestic interest rate (euro) and discounted at the foreign interest rate (dollar). A drop in the dollar interest rate implies that S_0 is higher than S^*.

To summarize:

- An increase in expected inflation in the foreign country leads to a depreciation of the foreign currency.
- A drop in the real interest rate in the foreign country leads to a depreciation of the foreign currency.

This simple example illustrates how an exchange rate reacts immediately, and in a volatile fashion, to monetary news. More complex monetary expansion scenarios could be modeled. For example, one could consider an unexpected, but permanent, increase in the *rate of growth* in money supply rather than a quantity shock in its level. Then the long-run interest rate would rise because of the permanent increase in expected inflation, but there would also be short-run effects.

Difficulties

The challenge of the asset market approach is to specify the news that should affect the exchange rate and quantify its *a priori* influence in the short run and the long run. One of the important components of such an approach is modeling the behavior of monetary authorities, because investors will try to guess their reactions. Another important component is risk perception. Investors discount expected events, and a change in risk perception affects the pricing of the exchange rate, as in any forward-looking pricing model. The influence of uncertainty is particularly important for the currencies of weaker economies.

Central banks usually convey their attitude by interest rate announcements. One has to evaluate the content and credibility of interest rate announcements carefully. If the rise in interest rates simply reflects an increase in home inflation, not a rise in the real interest rate, it should not have a positive effect on the currency. Even worse, it could carry some negative information. For example, during currency crises, a rise in interest rates is often interpreted as evidence that the currency is under speculative attack, that the central bank has had serious problems defending the exchange rate, and that its foreign exchange reserves are being exhausted. It prompts other speculators to join the attack and basically sends a negative signal for the home currency.

OPTIONAL SEGMENT ENDS

SUMMARY

5

- In a flexible exchange rate regime, exchange rates are determined by supply and demand.
- In the balance of payments accounts, the current account includes the balance of goods and services, the income received or paid on existing investments, and current transfers. The financial account includes short-term and long-term capital transactions.
- Current account deficits can be balanced by financial account surpluses, and these deficits have a negative effect on the economy only if the country cannot attract financial inflows.
- Factors causing a country's currency to appreciate include lower inflation rates and higher real interest rates, but the effect of differences in economic performance is indeterminate.
- Expansionary monetary policy will generally lead to a depreciation of the home currency.
- Expansionary fiscal policy will generally lead to an appreciation of the home currency.
- A fixed exchange rate system is one in which the exchange rate between two currencies remains fixed at a preset level, known as "official parity."
- A pegged exchange rate system is one in which a target exchange rate (the peg) is set against a major currency, the exchange rate is allowed to fluctuate in a narrow band around the peg, and the peg is adjusted periodically to take account of economic fundamentals.
- Interest rate parity is the relation that the forward discount (premium) equals the interest rate differential between two currencies.
- Absolute purchasing power parity claims that the exchange rate should be equal to the ratio of the average price levels in the two economies.
- Relative purchasing power parity claims that the percentage movement of the exchange rate should be equal to the inflation differential between the two economies.
- Purchasing power parity implies that the ratio of the end-of-period exchange rate to the beginning-of-period exchange rate (in indirect quotes) equals the ratio of one plus the foreign inflation rate to one plus the domestic inflation rate.
- The real interest rate can be approximated for all countries by subtracting the expected inflation rate from the nominal interest rate.
- The international Fisher relation claims that real interest rates are equal across the world and hence, differences in nominal interest rates are caused by differences in national inflationary expectations. Interest rate differences approximately equal expected inflation rate differences if the international Fisher relation holds.
- One plus the real interest rate for any country equals one plus the nominal rate divided by one plus the expected inflation rate for that country.
- Uncovered interest rate parity claims that the expected change in the indirect exchange rate approximately equals the foreign minus the domestic interest rate.
- Uncovered interest rate parity is a theory combining purchasing power parity and the international Fisher relation.

- The forward exchange rate equals the expected exchange rate under the condition of no foreign currency risk premium.
- The forward exchange rate discount or premium equals the expected change in the exchange rate under the condition of no foreign currency risk premium.
- Combining all the parity relations indicates that the expected return on default-free bills should be the same in all countries, and exchange risk reduces to inflation uncertainty because there is no real foreign currency risk.
- Deviations from purchasing power parity should be corrected in the long run.
- The elements in the balance of payments are the current account, the capital account, the financial account, and the official reserves account; without central bank intervention, a current account deficit must be balanced by a financial account surplus. Exchange rate adjustments can be needed to restore balance of payments equilibrium.
- The asset market approach to pricing exchange rate expectations claims that the exchange rate is the relative price of two currencies, determined by investors' expectations about these currencies.
- The long-run exchange rate effect of a sudden and unexpected increase in the money supply is a depreciation of the currency so that purchasing power parity is maintained as the percentage increase in the price level matches the percentage increase in the money supply. Given sticky-goods prices, the short-run exchange rate effect is an immediate drop in the real interest rate and more depreciation of the currency than the depreciation implied by purchasing power parity.

PROBLEMS

1. Consider two countries, A and B, whose currencies are α and β, respectively. The interest rate in A is greater than the interest rate in B. Which of the following is true?

   A. α is expected to appreciate relative to β, and α should trade with a forward discount.

   B. α is expected to appreciate relative to β, and α should trade with a forward premium.

   C. α is expected to depreciate relative to β, and α should trade with a forward discount.

   D. α is expected to depreciate relative to β, and α should trade with a forward premium.

2. The spot $/€ is equal to 1.1795. The annual one-year interest rates on the Eurocurrency market are 4 percent in euros and 5 percent in U.S. dollars. The annualized one-month interest rates are 3 percent in euros and 4 percent in U.S. dollars.

   A. What is the one-year forward exchange rate?

   B. What is the one-month forward exchange rate?

3. You are given the following quotes.

   Spot exchange rates:

$/€	1.1865–1.1870
¥/$	108.10–108.20

   Three-month interest rates (percent per year):

in $	5–5¼
in €	3¼–3½
in ¥	1¼–1½

   What should the quotes be for the

   A. ¥/€ spot exchange rate?

   B. $/€ three-month forward ask exchange rate? *Hint:* Buying euros forward is equivalent to borrowing dollars to buy euros spot and investing the euros.

   C. €/$ three-month forward bid exchange rate?

   D. ¥/$ three-month forward bid and ask exchange rate?

4. Jason Smith is a foreign exchange trader with Citibank. He notices the following quotes.

Spot exchange rate:	SFr1.6627/$
Six-month forward exchange rate:	SFr1.6558/$
Six-month $ interest rate:	3.5% per year
Six-month SFr interest rate:	3.0% per year

   A. Ignoring transaction costs, is the interest rate parity holding?

   B. Is there an arbitrage possibility? If yes, what steps would be needed to make an arbitrage profit? Assuming that Jason Smith is authorized to work with $1,000,000 for this purpose, how much would the arbitrage profit be in dollars?

5. A foreign exchange arbitrageur notices that the Japanese yen to U.S. dollar spot exchange rate is ¥108/$ and the three-month forward exchange rate is ¥107.30/$. The three-month $ interest rate is 5.20 percent per annum and the three-month ¥ interest rate is 1.20 percent per annum.

A. Is the interest rate parity holding?

B. Is there an arbitrage possibility? If yes, what steps would be needed to make an arbitrage profit? Assuming that the arbitrageur is authorized to work with $1,000,000 for this purpose, how much would the arbitrage profit be in dollars?

6. The following chart illustrates the domestic prices of three items (shoes, watches, and electric motors) of similar quality in the United States and Mexico.

Items	United States (dollars)	Mexico (peso)
Shoes	20	80
Watches	40	180
Electric motors	80	600

If one dollar exchanges for five Mexican pesos and transportation costs are zero, Mexico will import

A. shoes and watches, and the United States will import electric motors.

B. shoes, and the United States will import watches and electric motors.

C. all three goods from the United States.

D. electric motors, and the United States will import shoes and watches.

7. A group of countries decides to introduce a common currency. What do you think would happen to the inflation rates of these countries after the introduction of the common currency?

Preparing to Study the CFA Curriculum Materials on Financial Statement Analysis

Before beginning the Reading Assignments, candidates should have a basic mastery of the concepts typically presented in introductory college-level accounting courses. The primary source of Reading Assignments in the CFA Curriculum is *The Analysis and Use of Financial Statements,* Third Edition, by White, Sondhi, and Fried.

These Reading Assignments assume candidates are already knowledgeable in accounting practices and understand the following important subjects:

- the accounting equation and the mechanics of journal entries (debits and credits)
- accounting terms and definitions
- practices for measuring and reporting business and financial activities
- basic principles and rules of financial reporting, as required by U.S. and IASB GAAP
- the relationship between management decisions and financial reporting
- the construction of and interrelationships among the balance sheet, income statement, and statement of cash flows
- basic accounting and business vocabulary related to the use and construction of financial statements and financial reporting.

If you have not taken an introductory accounting course during the past few years, we strongly encourage you to consider additional study of introductory course material. Although examination questions are drawn only from the Reading Assignments, studying the additional introductory material will strengthen candidates' understanding of the required concepts. CFA Institute's book distributor offers a good basic accounting textbook, *Financial Accounting,* Eighth Edition, by Needles and Powers. At a minimum, we recommend that you study the following chapters:

- Chapter 3—Measuring Business Income
- Chapter 5—Financial Reporting and Analysis (pp. 246–258)
- Chapter 8—Inventories
- Chapter 9—Current Liabilities and the Time Value of Money (pp. 412–426)
- Chapter 12—Contributed Capital (pp. 543–553)
- Chapter 13—The Corporate Income Statement and the Statement of Stockholders' Equity (pp. 584–591)

Many accounting textbooks and courses provide similar coverage and will enable you to master the concepts and principles discussed in the Needles and Powers text.

Before you begin your study program, take some time to review the Reading Assignments in the textbook by White, Sondhi, and Fried. If you find the material too difficult, it may be an indication that you would benefit from first studying basic accounting concepts and practices.

FINANCIAL STATEMENT ANALYSIS

The candidate should be able to demonstrate a thorough knowledge of the financial accounting model, principles governing the significant accounting areas affecting valuation, and disclosures in the financial statements. Emphasis is on basic financial statements and how alternative accounting methods affect those statements, financial ratios, and the interrelationships among financial statement items.

Supplemental Materials

Please note that the original publisher of the primary readings in the Financial Statement Analysis Study Sessions, John Wiley & Sons, Inc., continues to make available a supplementary study tool for your use. In Study Session 7 (Readings 29, 31, and 33), Study Session 9 (Readings 39, 40 and 41), and Study Session 10 (Readings 42, 43, and 44), there are examples and assigned problems that illustrate important points through use of actual corporate financial statements, or portions of financial statements. For the full context of the example or problem, candidates may find it helpful to refer to the financial statements, which are provided on the website. The financial statements can be found on the Wiley website at http://he-cda.wiley.com/WileyCDA/HigherEdTitle/productCd-0471375942.html. On the left side of this page, under *Companion Sites,* click on the *Student* link. This will open a new page; on the left side under *Browse by Resource,* click on *Annual Reports.*

STUDY SESSION 7 FINANCIAL STATEMENT: ANALYSIS: BASIC CONCEPTS

READING ASSIGNMENTS

Reading 29 Framework for Financial Statement Analysis
Reading 30 Long-Term Assets
Reading 31 Accounting Income and Assets: The Accrual Concept
Reading 32 The Statement of Cash Flows
Reading 33 Analysis of Cash Flows
Reading 34 Future FASB Changes and the Analytical Challenges of GAAP

LEARNING OUTCOMES

Reading 29: Framework for Financial Statement Analysis

The candidate should be able to:

a. discuss the general principles of the financial reporting system and explain the objectives of financial reporting according to the Financial Accounting Standards Board (FASB) conceptual framework;

b. identify the accounting qualities (e.g., relevance, reliability, predictive value, timeliness) set forth in Statement of Financial Accounting Concepts (SFAC) 2, and discuss how these qualities provide useful information to an analyst;

c. discuss the roles of the International Organization of Securities Commissions (IOSCO) and the International Accounting Standards Board (IASB) in setting and enforcing global accounting standards;

d. describe and distinguish between the principal financial statements: Balance Sheet, Income Statement, Statement of Comprehensive Income, Statement of Cash Flows and Statement of Stockholders' Equity and discuss the additional sources of information accompanying the financial statements, including the financial footnotes, supplementary schedules, Management Discussion and Analysis (MD&A) and Proxy statements;

e. discuss the role of the auditor and the meaning of the audit opinion.

Candidates are responsible for the questions, exercises, and problems following readings. Solutions to the questions, exercises, and problems are found in Appendix A.

Note:
Except where noted as required reading the "Boxes" in Readings 29, 31 and 33 are not part of the Level I reading assignment.

Some of the accounting concepts in the Financial Statement Analysis study sessions (Session 7 through Session 10) may have been superseded by updated rulings and/or pronouncements issued after a reading was published. Candidates are expected to be familiar with the overall analytical framework contained in the study session readings, as well as the implications of alternative accounting methods for financial analysis and valuation, as provided in the assigned readings.

For purposes of the Level I Examination, candidates should assume that U.S. GAAP (generally accepted accounting principles) applies unless otherwise noted.

Reading 30: Long-Term Assets

The candidate should be able to:

a. describe the factors that distinguish long-term assets from other assets, and identify the common types of long-term assets and their carrying values on the balance sheet;

b. determine the cost, and record the purchase, of property, plant, and equipment;

c. explain depreciation accounting (including the reasons for depreciation), calculate depreciation using the straight-line, production (also known as units-of-production), and declining-balance methods, and calculate depreciation after revising the estimated useful life of an asset;

d. describe how to account for the sale, exchange, or disposal of depreciable assets, and determine whether a gain or loss is recorded;

e. identify assets that should be classified as natural resources, and prepare entries to account for such assets, including entries to record depletion;

f. identify the types of intangible assets, and describe how the accounting treatment for goodwill under U.S. GAAP differs from the accounting treatment for other intangible assets.

Reading 31: Accounting Income and Assets: The Accrual Concept

The candidate should be able to:

a. describe the format of the income statement and describe the components of net income;

b. explain the importance of the matching principle for revenue and expense recognition, identify the requirements for revenue recognition to occur, identify and describe the appropriate revenue recognition, given the status of completion of the earning process and the assurance of payment and discuss different revenue recognition methods and their implications for financial analysis;

c. identify the appropriate income statement and balance sheet entries using the percentage-of-completion method and the completed contract method and describe and calculate the effects on cash flows and selected financial ratios that result from using the percentage-of-completion method versus the completed contract method;

d. describe the types and analysis of unusual or infrequent items, extraordinary items, discontinued operations, accounting changes, and prior period adjustments;

e. discuss managerial discretion in areas such as classification of good news/bad news, income smoothing, big bath behavior, and accounting changes, and explain how this discretion can affect the financial statements;

f. describe the format and the components of the balance sheet and describe the format, classification, and use of each component of the statement of stockholders' equity.

Reading 32: The Statement of Cash Flows

The candidate should be able to:

a. identify the types of important information for investment decision making presented in the statement of cash flows;

b. compare and contrast the categories (i.e., cash provided or used by operating activities, investing activities, and financing activities) in a statement of cash flows, and describe how noncash investing and financing transactions are reported;

c. calculate and interpret, using the indirect method, the net cash provided or used by operating activities;

d. prepare and interpret, using the indirect method, the statement of cash flows for investing activities and financing activities.

Reading 33: Analysis of Cash Flows

The candidate should be able to:

a. classify a particular transaction or item as cash flow from 1) operations, 2) investing, or 3) financing;

b. compute and interpret a statement of cash flows, using the direct method and the indirect method;

c. convert an indirect statement of cash flows to a direct basis;

d. explain the two primary factors that may cause discrepancies between balances of operating assets and liabilities reported on the balance sheet and those reported in the cash flow statement;

e. describe and compute free cash flow;

f. distinguish between the U.S. GAAP and IAS GAAP classifications of dividends paid or received and interest paid or received for statement of cash flow purposes.

Reading 34: Future FASB Changes and the Analytical Challenges of GAAP

The candidate should be able to:

a. identify the projects on the FASB agenda that were/are related to international convergence;

b. describe two different guidance rules for revenue recognition discussed by FASB and IASB.

FRAMEWORK FOR FINANCIAL STATEMENT ANALYSIS

READING 29

LEARNING OUTCOMES

The candidate should be able to:

a. discuss the general principles of the financial reporting system and explain the objectives of financial reporting according to the Financial Accounting Standards Board (FASB) conceptual framework;

b. identify the accounting qualities (e.g., relevance, reliability, predictive value, timeliness) set forth in Statement of Financial Accounting Concepts (SFAC) 2, and discuss how these qualities provide useful information to an analyst;

c. discuss the roles of the International Organization of Securities Commissions (IOSCO) and the International Accounting Standards Board (IASB) in setting and enforcing global accounting standards;

d. describe and distinguish between the principal financial statements: Balance Sheet, Income Statement, Statement of Comprehensive Income, Statement of Cash Flows, and Statement of Stockholders' Equity and discuss the additional sources of information accompanying the financial statements, including the financial footnotes, supplementary schedules, Management Discussion and Analysis (MD&A), and Proxy statements;

e. discuss the role of the auditor and the meaning of the audit opinion.

INTRODUCTION 1

Why are financial statements useful? Because they help investors and creditors make better economic decisions. The goal of this book is to enhance financial statement users' understanding of financial reporting in order to facilitate improved decision making. We will examine the impact of the differential application of accounting methods and estimates on financial statements, with particular emphasis on the effect of accounting choices on reported earnings, stockholders' equity, cash flow, and various measures of corporate performance (including, but not limited to, financial ratios). We will also stress the use of cash flow analysis to evaluate the financial health of an enterprise.

Financial statements are, at best, only an approximation of economic reality because of the selective reporting of economic events by the accounting system, compounded by alternative accounting methods and estimates. The tendency to delay accounting recognition of some transactions and valuation changes means that financial statements tend to lag behind reality as well.

This reading provides a framework for the study of financial statement analysis. This framework consists of the users being served, the information system available to them, and the institutional structure within which they interact.

2 NEED FOR FINANCIAL STATEMENT ANALYSIS

The United States has the most complex financial reporting system in the world. Detailed accounting principles are augmented by extensive disclosure requirements. The financial statements of large multinationals add up to dozens of pages, and many of these firms voluntarily publish additional "fact books" for dissemination to financial analysts and other interested users.

Financial reporting in other major developed countries and many emerging markets has also evolved substantially in recent years, with an increasing emphasis on providing information useful to both domestic and foreign creditors and equity investors. International Accounting Standards have become a credible rival to U.S. standards.

In an ideal world, the user of financial statements could focus only on the bottom lines of financial reporting: net income and stockholders' equity. If financial statements were comparable among companies (regardless of country), consistent over time, and always fully reflecting the economic position of the firm, financial statement analysis would be simple, and this text a very short one.

The financial reporting system is not perfect. Economic events and accounting entries do not correspond precisely; they diverge across the dimensions of timing, recognition, and measurement. Financial analysis and investment decisions are further complicated by variations in accounting treatment among countries in each of these dimensions.

Economic events and accounting recognition of those events frequently take place at different times. One example of this phenomenon is the recognition of capital gains and losses only upon sale in most cases. Appreciation of a real estate investment, which took place over a period of many years, for example, receives income statement recognition only in the period management chooses for its disposal.[1]

Similarly, long-lived assets are written down, most of the time, in the fiscal period of management's choice. The period of recognition may be neither the period in which the impairment took place nor the period of sale or disposal.

---

[1] However, in countries (such as the United Kingdom) where periodic asset revaluation is permitted, balance sheet recognition of market value changes may occur much sooner.

Accounting for discontinued operations, in the same manner, results in recognition of a loss in a period different from when the loss occurred or the disposal is consummated.[2]

In addition, many economic events do not receive accounting recognition at all. Most contracts, for example, are not reflected in financial statements when entered into, despite significant effects on financial condition and operating and financial risk. Some contracts, such as leases and hedging activities, are recognized in the financial statements by some companies but disclosed only in footnotes by others. Disclosure requirements for derivatives and hedging activities are in place in many jurisdictions, but recognition and measurement is only recently required[3] in the United States.

Further, generally accepted accounting principles (GAAP) in the United States and elsewhere permit economic events that do receive accounting recognition to be recognized in different ways by different financial statement preparers. Inventory and depreciation of fixed assets are only two of the significant areas where comparability may be lacking.

Financial reports often contain supplementary data that, although not included in the statements themselves, help the financial statement user to interpret the statements or adjust measures of corporate performance (such as financial ratios) to make them more comparable, consistent over time, and more representative of economic reality. When making adjustments to financial statements, we will seek to discern substance from form and exploit the information contained in footnotes and supplementary schedules of data in the annual report and SEC filings. The analytic treatment of "off-balance-sheet" financing activities is a good example of this process. We also illustrate the use of reconciliations to U.S. GAAP in foreign registrants' Form 20-F filings.

Finally, information from outside the financial reporting process can be used to make financial data more useful. Estimating the effects of changing prices on corporate performance, for example, may require the use of price data from outside sources.

FOCUS ON INVESTMENT DECISIONS 3

This book is concerned with the concepts and techniques of financial analysis employed by users of financial statements who are external to the company. Principal emphasis is on the financial statements of companies whose securities are publicly traded. The techniques described are generally applicable to the analysis of financial statements prepared according to U.S. GAAP. However, we will also discuss the pronouncements of the International Accounting Standards Board (IASB) and standard setters in other countries, compare them to U.S. GAAP, and analyze financial statements prepared in accordance with these other reporting standards.

The common characteristic of external users is their general lack of authority to prescribe the information they want from an enterprise. They depend on general-purpose external financial reports provided by management. The

[2] In the United States, Statement of Financial Accounting Standards (SFAS) No. 121, Accounting for the Impairment of Long-Lived Assets and for Long-Lived Assets to Be Disposed of, as amended by SFAS No. 144, Accounting for the Impairment or Disposal of Long-Lived Assets, constrains but does not eliminate management control over the timing of recognition and the measurement of impairments. In most foreign countries there are few, if any, guidelines governing the accounting for impaired assets.

[3] SFAS 133, Accounting for Derivative Instruments and Hedging Activities, became effective in 2000 (Chapter 16).

Financial Accounting Standards Board (FASB) in its Statement of Financial Accounting Concepts (SFAC) 1, Objectives of Financial Reporting by Business Enterprises, aptly describes the objectives of these external users:

> **Information Useful in Investment and Credit Decisions**
>
> Financial reporting should provide information that is useful to present and potential investors and creditors and other users in making rational investment, credit, and similar decisions. The information should be comprehensible to those who have a reasonable understanding of business and economic activities and are willing to study the information with reasonable diligence.[4]

Classes of Users

External users of financial information encompass a wide range of interests but can be classified into three general groups:

1. Credit and equity investors
2. Government (executive and legislative branches), regulatory bodies, and tax authorities
3. The general public and special interest groups, labor unions, and consumer groups

Each of these user groups has a particular objective in financial statement analysis, but, as the FASB stated, the *primary users are equity investors and creditors.* However, the information supplied to investors and creditors is likely to be generally useful to other user groups as well. Hence, financial accounting standards are geared to the purposes and perceptions of investors and creditors. That is the group for whom the analytical techniques in this book are intended.

The underlying objective of financial analysis is the comparative measurement of risk and return to make investment or credit decisions. These decisions require estimates of the future, be it a month, a year, or a decade. General-purpose financial statements, which describe the past, provide one basis for projecting future earnings and cash flows. Many of the techniques used in this analytical process are broadly applicable to all types of decisions, but there are also specialized techniques concerned with specific investment interests or, in other words, risks and returns specific to one class of investors or securities.

The equity investor is primarily interested in the long-term earning power of the company, its ability to grow, and, ultimately, its ability to pay dividends and increase in value. Since the equity investor bears the residual risk in an enterprise, the largest and most volatile risk, the required analysis is the most comprehensive of any user and encompasses techniques employed by all other external users.

Creditors need somewhat different analytical approaches. Short-term creditors, such as banks and trade creditors, place more emphasis on the immediate liquidity of the business because they seek an early payback of their investment. Long-term investors in bonds, such as insurance companies and pension funds, are primarily concerned with the long-term asset position and earning power of the company. They seek assurance of the payment of interest and the capability of retiring or refunding the obligation at maturity. Credit risks are usually smaller than equity risks and may be more easily quantifiable.

More subordinated or junior creditors, especially owners of "high-yield" debt, however, bear risks similar to those of equity investors and may find analytic techniques normally applied to equity investments more relevant than those employed by creditors.

---

[4] SFAC 1, para. 34.

Financial Information and Capital Markets

The usefulness of accounting information in the decision-making processes of investors and creditors has been the subject of much academic research over the last 35 years. That research has examined the interrelationship of accounting information and reporting standards in financial markets in great detail. At times, the research conclusions are highly critical of the accounting standard-setting process and of the utility of financial analysis. This criticism is based on research performed in a capital market setting. These findings do not negate the usefulness of financial analysis of individual securities that may be mispriced or of decisions made outside a capital market setting.[5]

Some researchers argue that financial data are useful to investors only for prediction of a firm's risk characteristics. To a great extent, this line of reasoning is influenced by the finance literature and the prevalent acceptance of the efficient market hypothesis. Others argue that the impact of accounting is not so much in its information content per se, but rather in the "economic consequences" to the firm resulting from contracts (implicit or explicit) that are based on or driven by accounting-determined variables.[6]

By and large, the early conclusions of the academic literature have proven to be somewhat premature. More recent research demonstrates that the interplay between markets and information is richer and more sophisticated than originally thought. In fact, the trend in research is now to incorporate techniques of fundamental analysis in model development and research design.

Various research trends and relevant economic considerations are discussed throughout the book, with varying emphasis from topic to topic. Chapter 5 is devoted entirely to a review of the major strands of empirical research in order to set the stage for discussions of other topics, where appropriate, in subsequent readings. Throughout the text we focus on what the analyst can learn from the research and how its implications are relevant to analysis.

THE FINANCIAL REPORTING SYSTEM 4

An understanding of the conceptual bases of the financial reporting system and of the preparation of financial statements are essential prerequisites to financial analysis. Corporate management issues financial statements and is responsible for their form and content. It is management that selects accounting methods, compiles accounting data, and prepares the financial statements. For smaller companies, auditors may carry out portions of the preparation work.

The accounting process or financial reporting system, which generates financial information for external users, encompasses five principal financial statements:

1. Balance sheet (statement of financial position)
2. Income statement (statement of earnings)
3. Statement of comprehensive income
4. Statement of cash flows
5. Statement of stockholders' equity

---

[5] Examples include acquisitions and credit decisions made by banks or other institutional lenders.

[6] Management compensation contracts and covenants contained in debt agreements are two examples of such contracts.

These five financial statements, augmented by footnotes and supplementary data, are interrelated. Collectively, they are intended to provide relevant, reliable, and timely information essential to making investment, credit, and similar decisions, thus meeting the objectives of financial reporting. An example is the 1999 financial statements of Pfizer,[7] contained in the CD[8] accompanying the text.

General Principles and Measurement Rules

Financial statements provide information about the assets (resources), liabilities (obligations), income and cash flows, and stockholders' equity of the firm. The effects of transactions and other events are recorded in the appropriate financial statement(s). The income statement reports revenues, expenses, and gains and losses. The balance sheet shows assets, liabilities, and stockholders' equity; the statement of stockholders' equity reports capital transactions with owners. The statement of comprehensive income reports changes in certain balance sheet accounts[9] that bypass the income statement. The statement of cash flows includes operating, investing, and financing inflows and outflows. Many transactions are reflected in more than one statement so that the entire set is required to evaluate the firm.

The financial reporting system is based on data generated from *accounting events and selected economic events.* The financial statements recognize events and transactions meeting certain criteria, primarily exchange transactions (the exchange of cash or another asset for a different asset or to create or settle a liability). Other events recognized in the financial reporting system include the passage of time (e.g., accrual of interest), the use of services (e.g., insurance) or assets (e.g., depreciation), estimates such as bad debts or accruals for warranties, and the impact of some contracts (e.g., capital leases). Selected external or economic events, including some market value changes, are also recognized. However, many contractual arrangements and market value changes are disclosed only in the footnotes or in supplementary schedules, if at all.

The emphasis on reporting exchange transactions does not mean that the exchange of cash is necessary for the recognition of revenue and expense events. Under *accrual accounting,* revenues are recognized when goods are delivered or services are performed and expenses are recorded as services are used, rather than when cash is collected or expenditures are incurred for these transactions. Accrual accounting rests on the *matching principle,* which says that performance can be measured only if the related revenues and costs are accounted for in the same period.

Financial statements are prepared using a monetary unit to quantify (measure) the operations of the firm. Transactions are generally measured at their *historical cost,* the amount of cash or other resources exchanged for the asset or liability; changes in value subsequent to acquisition are usually ignored. The advantage of historical cost is that it is objective and verifiable. Its utility declines as specific prices or the general price level changes; as a result, the SEC, FASB, and non-U.S. standard setters have added disclosure and accounting standards for financial instruments.

---

[7] The statement of comprehensive income may be combined with the income statement or balance sheet. Pfizer has chosen to integrate comprehensive income into its balance sheet.

[8] Financial statements for Pfizer and the other companies featured in the text are contained both on the accompanying CD and on the book's website. The icon shown in the margin will appear whenever the financial statements of one of these companies is referenced.

[9] Pfizer shows currency translation adjustments, changes in the market value of marketable securities, and a minimum pension liability. These items are discussed in Chapters 15, 13, and 12, respectively.

Financial reporting also relies on the *going concern assumption*, that the firm will continue in operation indefinitely. The alternative assumes liquidation or sale of the firm, which requires different measures of assets and liabilities. Only by assuming normal future operations is it possible, for example, to depreciate fixed assets over their useful life rather than valuing them at their estimated disposal value.

THE U.S. FINANCIAL REPORTING SYSTEM 5

In the United States, the Securities and Exchange Commission (SEC) through its regulation S-X governs the form and content of the financial statements of companies whose securities are publicly traded. Although the SEC has delegated much of this responsibility to the FASB, it frequently adds its own requirements. The SEC functions as a highly effective enforcement mechanism for standards promulgated in the private sector.

Securities and Exchange Commission

As stated previously, while financial reporting standards are developed primarily in the private sector, the SEC often augments the FASB's work. For example, the SEC-mandated Management Discussion and Analysis (MD&A) provides helpful information regarding past operating results and current financial position. In such areas as segment data, leases, the effects of changing prices, and disclosure of oil and gas reserves, SEC-required disclosures preceded FASB action.

Audited financial statements, related footnotes, and supplementary data are presented in both annual reports sent to stockholders and those filed with the SEC. The SEC filings often contain other valuable information not presented in stockholder reports. Exhibit 29-1 contains a listing of SEC-required filings. Quarterly financial reports and SEC 10-Q filings, both of which contain abbreviated financial statements, may be reviewed by auditors but are rarely audited.

As the SEC reviews the financial statements of public companies, and those wishing to issue securities in the U.S. capital markets, its views on proper financial reporting carry great weight. It promulgates these views through Staff Accounting Bulletins (SAB) and through participation in the FASB's Emerging Issues Task Force (see next section) as well as through the review process and enforcement actions. SABs and EITFs are discussed where appropriate throughout this text.

Financial Accounting Standards Board

The FASB is a nongovernmental body with seven full-time members. The board sets accounting standards for all companies issuing audited financial statements. Because of Rule 203 of the American Institute of Certified Public Accountants (AICPA), all FASB pronouncements are considered authoritative; new FASB statements immediately become part of GAAP. Prior to creation of the FASB in 1973, the Accounting Principles Board (APB), an AICPA committee, set accounting standards. Unless superseded, APB opinions remain part of GAAP.[10]

---

[10] FASB statements and interpretations, Accounting Principles Board (APB) opinions, and AICPA accounting research bulletins constitute the highest level of authority in the hierarchy of accounting principles. These are followed in descending order of authority by FASB technical bulletins, cleared AICPA industry audit guides, and AICPA statements of position at level B. ("Cleared" means that the FASB has not objected to the issuance of the guide or the statement of position.) Positions of the FASB Emerging Issues Task Force and cleared AcSec practice bulletins constitute level C, followed by AICPA accounting interpretations, question-and-answer guides published by the FASB staff, uncleared AICPA statements of position, and uncleared AICPA industry audit and accounting guides. The lowest authoritative level includes FASB concepts statements, APB statements, AICPA issues papers, and IASB statements.

EXHIBIT 29-1

Corporate Filings: Securities and Exchange Commission

10-K Annual Report

Contents (partial listing):
- Business of Company
- Properties
- Legal Proceedings
- Management Discussion and Analysis
- Changes or Disagreements with Auditors
- Financial Statements and Footnotes
- Investee Financial Statements (where applicable)
- Parent Company Financial Statements (where applicable)

Schedules:
- I. Condensed Financial Information
- II. Bad Debt and Other Valuation Accounts
- III. Real Estate and Accumulated Depreciation
- IV. Mortgage Loans on Real Estate
- V. Supplementary Information Concerning Property-Casualty Insurance Operations

Due Date: 3 months following end of fiscal year.

10-Q Quarterly Report

Contents
- Financial Statements
- Management Discussion and Analysis

Due Date: 45 days following end of fiscal quarter. Not required for fourth quarter of fiscal year.

8-K Current Reports

Contents (used to report important events):
- Change in Control
- Acquisitions and Divestitures
- Bankruptcy
- Change in Auditors
- Resignation of Directors

Due Date: 15 days following event.

Source: Adapted from SEC Regulation S-X.

Because the SEC recognizes FASB statements as authoritative (as it recognized APB opinions prior to 1973), there is only one body of GAAP applicable to the United States. There are a few instances (e.g., earnings per share) in which nonpublic companies are exempted from certain GAAP requirements. Generally speaking, however, all audited statements are prepared using the same financial reporting framework.

The FASB is an independent body whose members are required to sever all ties with previous employers. Although historically most board members have been former auditors, others have come from the corporate world, government service, and academia. The analyst community is currently represented on the board by Gary Schieneman; Frank Block, CFA, served from 1979 to 1985, and Anthony Cope, CFA, from 1993 to 2000.

Before issuing a new Statement of Financial Accounting Standards (SFAS), the FASB staff often works with a task force—composed of public accountants, representatives from industry, academics, regulators, and financial statement users—to develop a discussion memorandum. After public comments are received and hearings held, the staff prepares an exposure draft (a proposed standard) for public comment.[11] The FASB also collaborates with other standard-setting authorities. For example, recent standards on earnings per share and segment reporting were developed in conjunction with the IASB and the Canadian Accounting Standards Board.

The Board's due process rules necessitate extensive dissemination of its agenda. SEC rulemaking is also normally preceded by a request for comments on a proposed set of rules. Thus, it is possible to anticipate new accounting and disclosure standards well in advance of their issuance and implementation.

After new standards are issued, and in areas where standards are nonexistent or ambiguous, there may be a need for guidance as to proper accounting. The FASB staff sometimes issues such documents, especially after major new standards (such as the one on hedging). The Emerging Issues Task Force (EITF), with members from auditing firms, preparers, and the SEC (but under FASB purview) tries to achieve consensus on technical issues. Some projects, especially those that are industry specific, are handled by the AICPA's Accounting Standards Committee (AcSec); these Statements of Position (SOPs) must be cleared by the FASB to become effective.

FASB Conceptual Framework

The conceptual basis for U.S. GAAP stems from FASB concepts statements that create a "constitution" or conceptual framework used by the board to set standards. Many critics of the FASB view the conceptual framework as a failure.[12] They state that the definitions are unduly vague and that the board has repeatedly deferred difficult decisions (such as how to measure income). Others believe that the conceptual framework has helped the board set better standards.

For the analyst, the conceptual framework is an important building block in understanding the information provided by financial statements. The conceptual framework delineates the characteristics accounting information must possess to be useful in investment and other economic decisions.

We have already addressed Statement of Financial Accounting Concepts (SFAC) 1, which sets forth the objectives of financial reporting. SFAC 2 is concerned with the Qualitative Characteristics of Accounting Information. These characteristics are shown in Figure 29-1, which is reproduced from the statement. A brief discussion follows.

Qualitative Characteristics of Accounting Information. Analysts' concern with the qualitative characteristics of accounting information derives from the need for information that facilitates comparison of firms using alternative reporting methods and is useful for decision making. Although some of these characteristics are self-evident, others require some explanation. We start with relevance and reliability, key characteristics from the analyst point of view.

---

[11] The FASB sometimes issues an intermediate document, labeled *preliminary views or tentative conclusions,* to obtain comment on difficult issues.

[12] For example, see David Solomons, "The FASB's Conceptual Framework: An Evaluation," *Journal of Accountancy* (June 1986), pp. 114–124.

FIGURE 29-1 A Hierarchy of Accounting Qualities

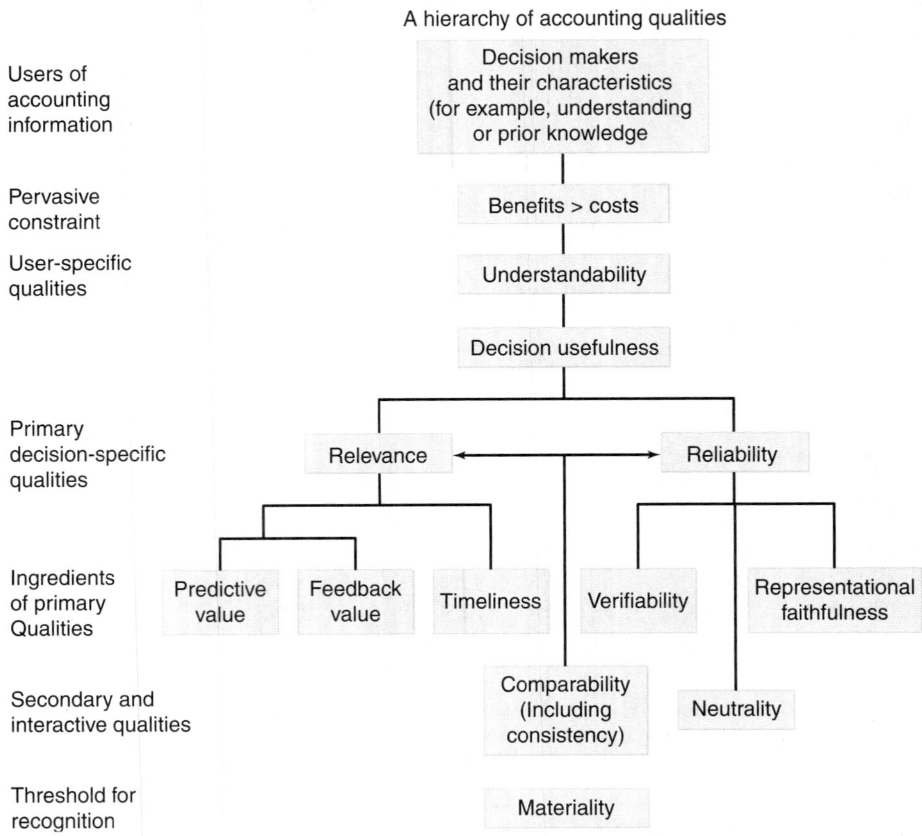

Source: Figure 1 of FASB Concepts Statement No. 2, *Qualitative Characteristics of Accounting Information,* copyright by Financial Accounting Standards Board, Norwalk, CT.

Relevance is defined as "the capacity of information to make a difference in a decision. . . ."[13] In practice, of course, the relevance of information depends on the decision maker. To a technical analyst (chartist), all financial data are irrelevant. For fundamental analysts, the relevance of information varies with the method of analysis (emphasis on income statement, cash flow, balance sheet, etc.).

Timeliness is an important aspect of relevance. Information loses value rapidly in the financial world. Market prices are predicated on estimates of the future; data on the past are helpful in making projections. But as time passes and the future becomes the present, past data become increasingly irrelevant.

Reliability encompasses *verifiability, representational faithfulness,* and *neutrality.* The first two elements (verifiability and representational faithfulness) are concerned with whether financial data have been measured accurately and whether they are what they purport to be. Data without these characteristics cannot be relied on in making investment decisions.

Neutrality is concerned with whether financial statement data are biased. FASB proposals are frequently the object of complaints that companies will be adversely affected by the new standard. The principle of neutrality states that the board should consider only the relevance and reliability of the data, not any possible economic impact.

---

[13] SFAC 2, Glossary.

Unfortunately, relevance and reliability tend to be opposing qualities. For example, the audit process improves the reliability of data, but at the cost of timeliness. For that reason, financial statement users have generally not supported the auditing of quarterly data, believing that the time delay does not compensate for any improved data quality.

Relevance and reliability also clash strongly in a number of accounting areas. Market value data are probably the best example. Information on the current market value of assets such as real estate and agricultural properties may be highly relevant but may be accurate (reliable) only to a limited extent. Yet historical cost, although highly reliable, may have little relevance. It is the old argument as to whether it is better to be "precisely wrong" or "approximately right."

Analysts have generally opted for approximately right. They have supported the disclosure of supplementary data in such areas as natural resources (SFAS 69, Reading 40), off-balance-sheet financing (Reading 44), and segment data (SFAS 131). Auditors and preparers, more concerned with reliability (and legal liability), have often opposed the inclusion of less reliable data in the financial statements.

Consistency and *comparability* are also key characteristics of accounting information from the analyst perspective. Consistency refers to use of the same accounting principles over time. A broader term, comparability, refers to comparisons among companies.

Consistency is affected by new accounting standards and voluntary changes in accounting principles and estimates. Accounting changes hinder the comparison of operating results between periods when the accounting principles used to measure those results differ. As the transition provisions of new accounting standards vary, it is frequently difficult to obtain a consistent time series of earnings properly adjusted for such changes. For voluntary changes (such as depreciation methods and lives), the effect of the change is generally disclosed only for the year of the change.

Comparability is a pervasive problem in financial analysis. Companies are free to choose among different accounting methods and estimates in a variety of areas, making comparisons of different enterprises difficult or impossible. Although the FASB (and to some extent, the IASB) has narrowed these differences somewhat in recent years, new types of transactions (such as securitization of assets) create new sources of noncomparability. Even when accounting differences do not exist, however, comparability may be elusive because of real differences between the firms (e.g., one has foreign operations and the other does not).

Materiality is paradoxically the most elusive accounting quality and arguably the most important. As shown in Figure 29-1, materiality is the threshold for financial statement recognition. FASB statements routinely state that they do not apply to immaterial items.

We define information to be material when it would make a difference in the valuation of the firm. While some use quantitative measures of materiality (e.g., 5% of income), even very small items can affect valuation. For example:

- A firm makes sales (just prior to the end of the quarter) under unusually favorable conditions (to the buyer) to meet sales expectations for the quarter.
- A firm realizes capital gains on long-term investments to achieve projected earnings growth for the period.

In Staff Accounting Bulletin (SAB) 99,[14] the SEC provided additional guidance regarding materiality because of perceived abuses. The SEC stated that financial

[14] August 12, 1999.

statement issuers and auditors must consider qualitative factors as well as quantitative rules of thumb. These qualitative factors include:

1. Obscuring changes in earnings trend
2. Hiding the failure to achieve analyst forecasts
3. Changing a reported loss to income or vice versa
4. Obscuring changes in significant business segments
5. Increasing management compensation
6. Affecting compliance with regulatory requirements, loan covenants, or other contracts
7. Concealing unlawful acts

Materiality is best defined in a firm context. The analyst should always be wary of firms that use "materiality" to hide significant data.

In addition to concept statements 1 and 2, which we have just reviewed, there are four others. SFAC 3, Elements of Financial Statements of Business Enterprises, has been superseded by SFAC 6, Elements of Financial Statements, which is discussed in subsequent sections of this chapter. The topics covered by SFAC 4, Objectives of Financial Reporting by Nonbusiness Organizations, are beyond the scope of this text. SFAC 5, Recognition and Measurement in Financial Statements of Business Enterprises, is referenced in Reading 31. SFAC 7, Using Cash Flow Information and Present Value in Accounting Measurement, is discussed in Box 29-1.

6 INTERNATIONAL ACCOUNTING STANDARDS

Growing international trade, multinational industrial and financial enterprises, and increasingly global capital markets have significantly expanded investment opportunities. Creditors and equity investors need to analyze both domestic and foreign companies. Yet differences in accounting and reporting standards make it difficult to compare domestic companies with those in other countries. Furthermore, as accounting standards are established separately in each country, it is difficult to generalize about those differences.

Financial reporting requirements are a function of tax regulations, corporate law, the comparative significance of capital markets and financial institutions in industrial development, and cultural differences. However, as capital markets and international investments expand, the need for global accounting standards is obvious.

Two questions arise: Who should develop such standards, and who would enforce them?

This section provides a brief discussion of the International Organization of Securities Commissions (IOSCO), the International Accounting Standards Board (IASB), and European financial reporting standards; a review of SEC reporting requirements for foreign registrants follows. These discussions review the significant recent progress toward harmonization of international reporting requirements.

International Organization of Securities Commissions

IOSCO is an organization of securities regulators from more than 65 countries, including the SEC from the United States. IOSCO's Technical Committee investigates regulatory issues related to international securities transactions and is charged with developing solutions to problems in these areas.

BOX 29-1 SFAC 7: USING CASH FLOW INFORMATION AND PRESENT VALUE IN ACCOUNTING MEASUREMENT

SFAC 7 (2000) deals only with measurement. It does not state when assets or liabilities must be measured using these principles. While present values are widely used in financial reporting (e.g., retirement plans), the FASB is expected to extend their use in the future. The statement says:

> The objective of using present value as an accounting measurement is to capture, to the extent possible, the economic difference between sets of future cash flows.*

Capturing the economic difference requires consideration of the following elements of the present value calculation:

1. Estimation of future cash flows
2. Expectations regarding the timing and amounts of those cash flows
3. Time value of money, measured by the risk-free interest rate
4. The effect of uncertainty on the required rate of return
5. Other factors, such as liquidity, that affect the required rate of return

In traditional present value calculations, factors 2 through 5 are rolled up into a single interest rate. SFAC 7, however, requires that each of these factors be considered separately, using the *expected cash flow* approach. We illustrate this method using the following example:†

Cash flow = $10,000 due in 10 years
Probability of collection = 80%
Risk-free rate (10 years) = 5%
Risk premium = $500

The initial step is to compute the expected cash flow:

($10,000 × 80% + $0 × 20%) = $8,000

Second, deduct the risk premium that a risk-averse investor would demand to assume the default risk:

$8,000 − $500 = $7,500

Finally, discount by the risk-free rate:

Present value at 5% of $7,500 due in 10 years = $4,604

Under this approach, the carrying value would be $4,604. This works out to an effective interest rate of 8.065%, which can be broken down into the following components:‡

Risk-free rate	5.000%
Adjustment for expectations	2.370
Adjustment for risk	.695
Total	8.065%

After initial measurement, the asset (or liability) would increase (accrete) at that 8.065 interest rate. Thus, after one year (assuming annual compounding), the carrying amount would be:

$4,604 (1 + .08065) = $4,975

At the end of 10 years, the carrying amount would be $10,000. Depending on the amount actually paid, there would be a gain or loss recognized at that time.

The extent to which SFAC 7 is applied to more assets and liabilities in the future may depend on whether preparers, auditors, and users become convinced that the expected value method provides better information. Auditors are especially concerned that the SFAC 7 method is less auditable than the historical approach of applying a composite discount rate to management's best estimate.

*Para. 20.

†Asset D from Appendix 1 of SFAC 7; see that appendix for comparison with other variations.

‡This example ignores factor 5 (liquidity or other factors).

IOSCO is also involved in standard setting through the Technical Committee's Working Party 1 on Multinational Disclosure and Accounting, which is charged with advocating financial reporting regulation that facilitates cross-border securities offerings and promotes effective and efficient international capital markets.

The Technical Committee's Working Party established a comprehensive core set of international accounting standards that could be recognized by IOSCO members for use in cross-border offerings and global multiple listings. However, each country's regulatory agency must approve these standards. It appears that enforcement would also remain a country-by-country matter.

International Accounting Standards Board

The IASB was established in 1973 to harmonize (conform) the accounting standards of different nations. In 2001, the IASB adopted a new structure, moving away from its "consensus" model[15] to one more like the FASB.

The new IASB structure provides for 19 trustees, headed by Paul Volcker, former chair of the U.S. Federal Reserve Board. The trustees, most of whom are not Americans, perform the functions of a corporate board of directors. The new IASB Board consists of 14 members; its chairman is David Tweedie, former head of the UK Accounting Standards Board. Anthony Cope, CFA, a former analyst and FASB member, is an IASB Board member. The IASB is maintaining its Standing Interpretations Committee (similar to the FASB's EITF), which deals with questions that arise after a new standard is adopted. There is a new Standards Advisory Council, which (like the similar FASB body) provides input from constituents.

As of December 31, 2001, the IASB has issued 41 international accounting standards (IAS) as well as a Framework for the Preparation and Presentation of Financial Statements, similar to the FASB conceptual framework, used to review existing standards and develop future IAS. This framework is also used to promote harmonization of regulations and standard setting by providing a basis for reducing the number of alternative accounting treatments permitted by the IASB.

The IASB has largely "caught up" with the FASB. In October 1993, IOSCO endorsed IAS 7, Cash Flow Statements, and published a list of core standards that would form the basis for a reasonably complete set of global standards. IASB completed work on these "core standards" and the SEC and other IOSCO members are evaluating their suitability for "global GAAP."

As capital markets become more international in scope, the need for global accounting standards and the demand for multiple listings grow. Discussion of financial reporting in Europe will be followed by an examination of the SEC's efforts to facilitate foreign listings.

European Financial Reporting Standards

Financial reporting requirements in Europe differ from those in the United States and other countries because of differences in their economies, relevance of local commercial law to the development of reporting standards, comparative importance of capital markets and banks as a source of financing, and the degree to which tax laws influence financial reporting.

Because of their desire to access other capital markets, a number of European multinational firms have adopted either U.S. standards (Daimler adopted U.S. GAAP even before it merged with Chrysler) or IASB GAAP. Despite occasional talk about "European GAAP," cultural differences and the existence of the IASB model suggest that large European companies will continue to gravitate toward either U.S. or IASB standards, depending on the outcome of the SEC decision concerning the acceptability of IASB standards for U.S. capital markets.

---

[15] The prior IASC had representatives from national accounting federations, stock exchanges, financial institutions, and other groups (including the International Coordinating Committee of Financial Analysts Associations). Because of a supermajority approval requirement a broad consensus was required to adopt a new standard.

SEC REPORTING REQUIREMENTS FOR FOREIGN REGISTRANTS

Foreign issuers that wish to sell securities in the United States must register with the SEC and are subject to substantially the same reporting requirements as their domestic counterparts. Foreign issuers may elect to file the registration and reporting forms used by domestic issuers (see Exhibit 29-1). Alternatively, foreign filers may elect to file the generally less stringent Forms 20-F (similar to 10-K) and 6-K (similar to 8-K). Issuers of American Depositary Receipts (ADRs)[16] may register either Form F-6 or 20-F and are exempt from Form 8-K requirements.

Foreign issuers commonly use Form 20-F filings, thereby exempting them from requirements to file proxies and insider trading reports. Form 20-F annual reports are due six months after the fiscal year-end, quarterly reports are optional, and relatively little business and segment data disclosure is required.

Form 20-F filers must identify both the reporting principles used and the material variations from U.S. GAAP and reconcile reported income and stockholders' equity to U.S. GAAP. These reconciliations provide insights into the differences in reporting requirements across countries and the tasks involved in developing universal financial reporting standards. The data provided in Form 20-F reconciliations are used to illustrate accounting differences throughout the text.

Staff Accounting Bulletin 88 (August 1990) clarified the disclosures and quantitative reconciliations required by Item 17 of Form 20-F. The new guidance requires some additional disclosures regarding pension obligations (SFAS 87) and financial instruments (SFAS 105) in the MD&A. However, SAB 88 does not mandate those disclosures required by U.S. GAAP or the SEC but not required by the foreign issuer's local GAAP.[17]

The SEC no longer requires foreign issuers to reconcile to U.S. GAAP for differences stemming from the use of:

- IAS 7, Cash Flow Statements
- IAS 21, The Effects of Changes in Foreign Exchange Rates
- IAS 22, Business Combinations

These changes reflect two parallel developments. First, some IAS standards are considered equivalent to U.S. GAAP and are deemed acceptable for filings in the United States. Second, U.S. filing requirements for foreign registrants have affected requirements for U.S. entities. FRR 44 (December 13, 1994) eliminated the requirement for domestic issuers to file schedules with data on marketable securities, property, plant, and equipment, accumulated depreciation, and short-term borrowings. Although these amendments "leveled the field" for domestic and foreign filers, they also eliminated a significant amount of information useful in financial analysis.[18]

---

[16] ADRs are depositary shares representing a specified number of shares and are issued against the deposit of a foreign issuer's securities. ADRs must be registered on Form F-6 unless another registration form is more appropriate.

[17] See R. Dieter and J. A. Heyman, "Implications of SEC Staff Accounting Bulletin 88 for Foreign Registrants," *Journal of Accountancy* (August 1991), pp. 121–125.

[18] In 1999, the SEC proposed reinstating disclosure requirements relating to bad debt and other valuation reserves and property, plant, and equipment.

8 PRINCIPAL FINANCIAL STATEMENTS

The preceding sections described the general principles and measurement rules of the basic accounting process applicable to financial reporting in the United States. They also examined the role of international and domestic standard-setting bodies (the SEC and FASB) and the latter's conceptual framework that guides this process, along with the qualitative characteristics of accounting information. This section provides a detailed discussion of the output of this system: the different financial statements, footnotes, and supplementary data.[19]

The Balance Sheet

The balance sheet (statement of financial position) reports major classes and amounts of assets (resources owned or controlled by the firm), liabilities (external claims on those assets), and stockholders' equity (owners' capital contributions and other internally generated sources of capital) and their interrelationships at specific points in time.

Assets reported on the balance sheet are either purchased by the firm or generated through operations; they are, directly or indirectly, financed by the creditors and stockholders of the firm. This fundamental accounting relationship provides the basis for recording all transactions in financial reporting and is expressed as the balance sheet equation:

$$\text{Assets (A)} = \text{Liabilities (L)} + \text{Stockholders' Equity (E)}$$

In the United States, firms issue balance sheets at the end of each quarter and the end of the fiscal year. Annual or semiannual reporting is the norm in most other countries.

Elements of the Balance Sheet

SFAC 6 discusses the elements of financial statements. Although this statement also deals with nonprofit organizations, we restrict our comments to business enterprises.

Assets are defined in SFAC 6 as

> probable future economic benefits obtained or controlled by a particular entity as a result of past transactions or events. (para. 25)

This definition seems to be noncontroversial. Its weakness is its lack of reference to risk. It seems to us that an enterprise that retains the risks of ownership still "owns" the asset. This issue is important, for example, as it relates to the sale of assets (such as accounts receivable, loans, and mortgages; see Reading 44) when the seller retains some risk of loss.

Liabilities are defined, similarly as

> probable future sacrifices of economic benefits arising from present obligations of a particular entity to transfer assets or provide services to other entities in the future as a result of past transactions or events. (para. 35)

Again, the definition reads well Yet it permits the nonrecognition of contractual obligations such as operating leases (see Reading 44). The interpretation of

---

[19] The requirements of IAS standards are very similar; differences are discussed in Readings 31 and 33.

"present obligation" and "result of past transactions or events" is key to accounting for all such contracts; some believe that only payments immediately due as a consequence of completed transactions create liabilities.[20] Others believe that all long-term contracts should be recognized as long-term liabilities. Another important problem area is the derecognition of liabilities that have been prefunded but remain outstanding (see the discussion of defeasance in Reading 43).[21]

As required by the fundamental accounting equation, *stockholders' equity* is therefore

> the residual interest in the net assets of an entity that remains after deducting its liabilities. (para. 49)

In practice, some financial instruments have characteristics of both liabilities and equities, making them difficult to categorize. Convertible debt and redeemable preferreds are two common examples examined in Reading 43. That reading also discusses the FASB Exposure Draft (ED) on recognition and measurement of instruments with equity and liability characteristics.

The Income Statement

The income statement (statement of earnings) reports on the performance of the firm, the result of its operating activities. It explains some but not all of the changes in the assets, liabilities, and equity of the firm between two consecutive balance sheet dates. Use of the accrual concept means that income and the balance sheet are interrelated.

The preparation of the income statement is governed by the matching principle, which states that performance can be measured only if revenues and related costs are accounted for during the same time period. This requires the recognition of expenses incurred to generate revenues in the same period as the related revenues. For example, the cost of a machine is recognized as an expense (it is depreciated) over its useful life (as it is used in production) rather than as an expense in the period it is purchased.[22]

Elements of the Income Statement

Revenues are defined in SFAC 6 as

> inflows . . . of an entity . . . from delivering or producing goods, rendering services, or other activities that constitute the entity's ongoing major or central operations. (para. 78)

Expenses are defined as

> outflows . . . from delivering or producing goods, rendering services, or carrying out other activities that constitute the entity's ongoing major or central operations. (para. 80)

---

[20] The capitalization of all executory contracts was advocated in the AIMR position paper "Financial Reporting in the 1990s and Beyond" (1993).

[21] SFAS 125 (1996), Accounting for Transfers and Servicing of Financial Assets and Extinguishments of Liabilities, prohibits derecognition of liabilities using in-substance defeasance.

[22] Note that no depreciation would be recorded if the products manufactured were not sold in the period the machine was used; the cost of using the machine would be added to work-in-process or finished goods inventories and carried on the balance sheet as an asset until the goods were sold.

These definitions explicitly exclude *gains (and losses)*, defined as

> increases (decreases) in equity (net assets) from peripheral or incidental transactions. . . . (para. 82)

Gains or losses are, therefore, nonoperating events. Examples would include gains and losses from asset sales, lawsuits, and changes in market values (including currency rates).

These definitions are, like the others in SFAC 6, easy to accept as stated. The difficulties come in practice. For example, investment activities may be "central" to a financial institution but "peripheral" to a manufacturing company. Similarly, sales of assets such as automobiles may be "incidental" to a retailer but "central" to a car rental firm. The writedown of inventories due to obsolescence is more difficult to characterize: Is this an operating expense or a loss? To some extent, the distinction between revenue and expense on the one hand and gains and losses on the other is a precursor of the controversies over the characterizations of "recurring versus nonrecurring activities," "operating versus nonoperating activities," and "extraordinary items." From the analyst point of view, disclosure is more important than classification; analysts prefer to make their own distinctions between operating and nonoperating events in many instances. From the point of view of database users, however, the outcome of the debate is important.

Even more important is the decision on when to recognize revenues and expenses. The recognition decision can be a major determinant of reported income, especially for technology and other "new economy" enterprises. This issue is discussed in Reading 31.

Statement of Comprehensive Income

Comprehensive income is defined as:

> the change in equity of a business enterprise during a period from transactions and other events and circumstances from nonowner sources. It includes *all changes in equity during a period except those resulting from investments by owners and distributions to owners.*[23]

Thus, comprehensive income includes both net income and direct-to-equity adjustments such as:

- Cumulative translation adjustments under SFAS 52
- Minimum pension liability under SFAS 87
- Unrealized gains and losses on available-for-sale securities under SFAS 115
- Deferred gains and losses on cash flow hedges under SFAS 133

These adjustments are collectively known as *other comprehensive income.* SFAS 130 (1997) requires that firms with items of other comprehensive income report:

- The closing balance of each such item. Their total is reported as a separate component of equity called *accumulated other comprehensive income.*
- The change (either pretax or after-tax) in each item; the change can be reported either gross (showing both additions and subtractions) or net.

---

[23] SFAC 6 (1985), para. 70, emphasis added.

- Reclassification adjustments to avoid double counting. For example, realized investment gains that include unrealized gains from prior years would be double counted unless those unrealized gains are deducted from other comprehensive income in the year of realization.[24]
- Total comprehensive income in condensed financial statements provided for interim periods.

Alternative displays are permitted. For example, firms can provide a separate statement of comprehensive income or can combine that statement with the income statement. Some data can be reported either on the statement face or in footnotes. IAS 1 (1997), with similar requirements, also permits alternative formats.[25]

Illustration: Pfizer. The shareholders' equity section of Pfizer's balance sheet has a line item: accumulated other comprehensive income. Note 5 shows the Statement of Comprehensive Income, with annual changes and balances for the currency translation adjustment, net unrealized gain on available-for-sale securities, and minimum pension liability.[26] All items are presented net of tax with the tax benefit shown as a single annual total. The individual items will be discussed in the appropriate readings.

Statement of Cash Flows

The statement of cash flows reports cash receipts and payments in the period of their occurrence, classified as to operating, investing, and financing activities. It also provides supplementary disclosures about noncash investing and financing activities. Cash flow data also help explain changes in consecutive balance sheets and supplement the information provided by the income statement.

SFAS 95, Statement of Cash Flows (1987), defines investing cash flows as those resulting from:

- Acquisition or sale of property, plant, and equipment
- Acquisition or sale of a subsidiary or segment
- Purchase or sale of investments in other firms

Similarly, financing cash flows are those resulting from:

- Issuance or retirement of debt and equity securities
- Dividends paid to stockholders

The standard requires gross rather than net reporting of significant investing and financing activities, thereby providing improved disclosure. For example, cash flows for property acquisitions must be shown separately from those related to property sales.

Enterprises with foreign currency transactions or foreign operations must report the effect of exchange rate changes on cash and cash equivalents as a separate component of the reconciliation of cash and cash equivalents for the period.

---

[24] Reclassification adjustments are not required for the minimum pension liability. Such adjustments for the cumulative translation adjustment are limited to translation gains and losses realized upon sale or liquidation of the investment in foreign subsidiaries. Reclassification adjustments in comparative statements provided for earlier periods are encouraged, but not required.

[25] IAS 1 does not use the term comprehensive income; its example is titled "Statement of Recognized Gains and Losses."

[26] These same amounts are shown in Pfizer's statement of shareholders' equity, which follows the balance sheet.

Significant noncash investing and financing activities (such as capitalized leases) must be disclosed separately within the cash flow statement or in a footnote elsewhere in the financial statements. Complex investment and financing transactions sometimes involve combinations of cash, debt, and other resources—these diverse but related components must be reported separately.

Cash from Operations. This key performance measure includes the cash effects of all transactions that do not meet the definition of investing or financing. This measure, moreover, excludes the effect of changes in exchange rates. In effect, it includes the cash flow consequences of the revenue-producing activities of the firm. Cash from operations may be reported either directly, using major categories of gross cash receipts and payments, or indirectly by providing a reconciliation of net income to net cash flow from operating activities. Both methods require separate disclosure of the cash outflows for income taxes and interest within the statement or elsewhere in the financial statements.

Statement of Stockholders' Equity

This statement reports the amounts and sources of changes in equity from capital transactions with owners and may include the following components:

- Preferred shares
- Common shares (at par or stated value)
- Additional paid-in capital
- Retained earnings
- Treasury shares (repurchased equity)
- Employee Stock Ownership Plan (ESOP) adjustments

and as components of other comprehensive income:

- Minimum pension liability
- Unrealized gains and losses on available for sale securities
- Cumulative translation adjustment (foreign operations)
- Unrealized gains and losses on cash flow hedges

Equity events and transactions are generally recognized as they occur, but capital market developments have created significant measurement and classification problems in transactions with owners.

The firm usually records the issuance of preferred and common stock at par (or stated) value and the amounts received in excess of par as additional paid-in capital. Repurchases or retirements of common stock may be reported as Treasury shares, a contra account, which reflects a reduction in common stock outstanding. Retained (reinvested) earnings, which increase with income and decline with dividend declarations, are also reported. Finally, this statement also includes adjustments related to ESOPs.

The minimum pension liability results when the accounting liability for pensions is less than the accumulated benefit obligation. The unrealized gains and losses on available for sale securities and the cumulative foreign currency translation adjustment result from selective recognition of market value changes and exchange rate changes. Unrealized gains and losses on cash flow hedges result from the provisions of SFAS 133.

Footnotes

Information provided in the financial statements is augmented by footnotes and other supplementary disclosures. Footnotes are an integral part of the financial statements and provide data on such subjects as business segments, the financial position of retirement plans, and off-balance-sheet obligations. These data are required by either GAAP (FASB standards) or regulatory authorities (the SEC). The financial statements and footnotes in the annual report and the SEC 10-K filings are audited.

Supplementary schedules, some required by the SEC in 10-K filings (see Exhibit 29-1), provide additional useful information. Some of these supplementary data are unaudited.

Footnotes provide information about the accounting methods, assumptions, and estimates used by management to develop the data reported in the financial statements. They are designed to allow users to improve assessments of the amounts, timing, and uncertainty of the estimates reported in the financial statements. Footnotes provide additional disclosure related to such areas as:

- Fixed assets
- Inventories
- Income taxes
- Pension and other postemployment benefit plans
- Debt (interest rates, maturity schedules, and contractual terms)
- Lawsuits and other loss contingencies
- Marketable securities and other investments
- Hedging and other risk management activities
- Business segments
- Significant customers, sales to related parties, and export sales

Contingencies

Footnotes often contain disclosures relating to contingent[27] losses. Firms are required to accrue a loss (recognize a balance sheet liability) when *both* of the following conditions are met:

1. It is probable that assets have been impaired or a liability has been incurred.
2. The amount of the loss can be reasonably estimated.

If the loss amount lies within a range, the most likely amount should be accrued. When no amount in the range is a better estimate, the firm may report the minimum amount in the range.[28]

SFAS 5 defines *probable* events as those "more likely than not" to occur, suggesting that a probability of more than 50% requires recognition of a loss. However, in practice, firms generally report contingencies as losses only when the probability of loss is significantly higher.

Footnote disclosure of (unrecognized) loss contingencies is required when it is *reasonably possible* (more than remote but less than probable) that a loss has been incurred or when it is probable that a loss has occurred but the amount

[27] The FASB defines a contingency as an "existing condition, situation, or set of circumstances involving uncertainty as to possible gain or loss" (SFAS 5, para. 1).

[28] See FASB Interpretation 14, Reasonable Estimation of the Amount of a Loss.

cannot be reasonably estimated. The standard provides an extensive discussion of loss contingencies.

The recognition and measurement of loss contingencies are problematic because they involve judgment and are subjective at best. External analysis is hampered by the paucity of data, as disclosures are often vague. Footnote disclosures and the SEC-mandated MD&A are the best sources of information.

Significant problem areas include environmental remediation liabilities, litigation, expropriation, self-insurance, debt guarantees, repurchase agreements, take-or-pay contracts, and throughput arrangements. In later readings we provide discussion of analytical techniques applicable to many of these contingencies and examples of losses recognized in the financial statements as well as others disclosed only in footnotes.

Pfizer's Note 18, Litigation, includes substantial disclosures regarding legal and governmental actions affecting the company. As the drug industry is heavily regulated and patents are important assets,[29] most of the note concerns these two areas. Although the note contains considerable uninformative "boilerplate," it does tell us that:

- Pfizer pleaded guilty to price fixing in 1999, and class action suits have been filed against the company.
- In 1999, a jury awarded $143 million in damages against Pfizer in the Trovan case.
- Pfizer is paying claims resulting from settlement of the Shiley lawsuits concerning defective heart valves.
- The company has been designated a "potentially responsible party" for certain waste sites and may be responsible for the cost of environmental remediation.
- A Pfizer subsidiary sold products containing asbestos, and many personal injury claims are pending against the company. The company expects the cost of such claims to be largely covered by insurance.

There is no indication, however, what provision Pfizer has made (if any) for losses from these suits. There are a couple of clues:

1. The Management Discussion and Analysis discloses (under Net Income) that 1998 includes $126 million "other" expense, mainly for legal settlements.
2. Note 8 shows provisions for the cost of antitrust litigation of $2 million and $57 million for 1999 and 1998, respectively.

Footnote and MD&A disclosures of contingencies should be read carefully, as they provide clues about possible future expense provisions and cash outflows.[30] While firms making acquisitions are generally careful to examine environmental and other risks of the acquired company, liability may emerge years later.[31] In extreme cases (asbestos, for example), environmental claims have driven firms into bankruptcy. Lawsuits and claims are, in addition, sometimes indicators of illegal acts or poor management practices.

---

[29] Self-developed patents are not recognized in the financial statements, however. Reading 40 discusses patents and other intangible assets.

[30] See M. E. Barth and M. F. McNichols, "Estimation and Valuation of Environmental Liabilities." *Journal of Accounting Research* (Supplement 1994), pp. 177–209.

[31] In 2000, Aventis (a large French chemicals and pharmaceutical firm) agreed to pay up to $916 million to clean up a defunct copper mine. The mine was owned by Stauffer Chemical, which was acquired by Rhone-Poulenc, which merged with Hoechst to form Aventis in 1999. (*New York Times,* October 22, 2000, p. 32.)

Case 29-1 shows the effect on Bristol Myers, another drug company, of breast implant litigation that took a number of years to be fully reflected in its financial statements.

Risks and Uncertainties

In 1994, the AICPA issued Statement of Position (SOP) 94-6, Disclosure of Certain Significant Risks and Uncertainties.[32] Although most AICPA SOPs are narrow in scope, applying to only one industry or narrow category of transactions, SOP 94-6 has broad application. It requires that audited financial statements report the following information:

1. *Nature of operations.* Description of the firm's major business activities and markets.
2. *Use of estimates.* Statement that financial statements use estimates.
3. *Certain significant estimates.* When it is reasonably possible that an estimate used to prepare financial statements will change in the near term, and such change would have a material impact on those statements, then disclosures must be made regarding the nature of the uncertainty involved. Examples include the effect of technological obsolescence on operating assets, capitalized costs that might not be recoverable from operations, and contingent liabilities for environmental remediation or litigation.
4. *Current vulnerability due to certain concentrations.* Firms must disclose concentrations when it is reasonably possible that there could be a severe impact in the near term. Examples include concentrations in customers, suppliers, or markets.

For companies subject to SEC reporting requirements, the SOP has limited effect,[33] although it was intended to help firms (and their auditors) understand the application of SFAS 5 (Contingencies). The major effect of the SOP is on nonpublic companies, whose disclosures are not governed by the SEC; their disclosures were inadequate to analysts accustomed to reviewing the financial statements of public companies.

Supplementary Schedules

In some cases, additional information about the assets and liabilities of a firm is provided within the financial statement footnotes, or as supplementary data outside the financial statements. Examples include:

- Oil and gas companies provide additional data on their exploration activities, quantities and types of reserves, and the present value of cash flows expected from those reserves (Reading 40).
- Supplemental disclosures of the impact of changing prices.
- Disclosure of sales revenue, operating income, and other data for major business segments and by geographic areas. Firms also provide information about export sales.
- Disclosures related to financial instruments and hedging activities.

---

[32] One of the authors of this text was a member of the task force that prepared the SOP.

[33] SFAS 14 (see Reading 13) requires more detailed segment data. The SOP permits the use of imprecise language such as "approximately."

9 OTHER SOURCES OF FINANCIAL INFORMATION

Stockholder reports often contain useful supplementary financial and statistical data as well as management comments. In some cases, the stockholder report is included ("incorporated by reference") in the SEC filing, or vice versa. The MD&A required by the SEC may appear in either reports to stockholders or SEC filings. A brief discussion of the contents of the MD&A is followed by a discussion of other sources of financial data.

Management Discussion and Analysis

Companies with publicly traded securities have been required since 1968 to provide a discussion of earnings in the MD&A section. The MD&A included in the financial statements of Pfizer is one example. In 1980, the SEC expanded the requirements to a comprehensive, broad-based discussion and analysis of the financial statements to encourage more meaningful disclosure.

The MD&A is required to discuss:

- Results of operations, including discussion of trends in sales and categories of expense
- Capital resources and liquidity, including discussion of cash flow trends
- Outlook based on known trends

In 1989, the SEC issued an interpretive release providing additional guidance on compliance in the following areas:

1. Prospective information and required discussion of significant effects of currently known trends, events, and uncertainties; for example, decline in market share or impact of inventory obsolescence. Firms may voluntarily disclose forward-looking data that anticipate trends or events.
2. Liquidity and capital resources: Firms are expected to use cash flow statements to analyze liquidity; provide a balanced discussion of operating, financing, and investing cash flows; and discuss transactions or events with material current or expected long-term liquidity implications.
3. Discussion of discontinued operations, extraordinary items, and other "unusual or infrequent" events with current or expected material effects on financial condition or results of operations.
4. Extensive disclosures in interim financial statements in keeping with the obligation to periodically update MD&A disclosures.
5. Disclosure of a segment's disproportionate need for cash flows or contribution to revenues or profits. Also, disclosure of any restrictions on a free flow of funds between segments.

On January 22, 2002, the SEC issued a statement reinforcing its views on the importance of MD&A disclosures. The release reminds registrants that disclosure "must be both useful and understandable."

Topics addressed include:

1. Liquidity and capital resources, including the impact of off-balance-sheet arrangements on liquidity and capital resources,
2. Disclosures about contractual obligations and commercial commitments (that is, off-balance-sheet arrangements),

3. Disclosures about trading activities, including non-exchange traded contracts, and
4. The effects of transactions with related parties, including persons (such as former employees) that may fall outside of the technical definition of a related party.

Other Data Sources

Companies that issue securities to the public are required to publish a registration statement, including a prospectus. For large companies, the 10-K and other SEC filings are "incorporated by reference" and little new information is provided. For initial public offerings (IPOs) and smaller companies, however, the prospectus will contain a detailed discussion of the enterprise as well as full financial statements.

Proxy statements, issued in connection with shareholder meetings, contain information about board members and management, executive compensation, stock options, and major stockholders.

Many companies prepare periodic "fact books" containing additional financial and operational data. Corporate press releases also provide new information on a timely basis. Computerized services (e.g., the Dow Jones News Retrieval System) and various on-line services provide databases of corporate releases and other business news. In addition, many companies hold periodic meetings or conference telephone calls to keep the financial community apprised of recent developments regarding the company. In between or in lieu of such meetings, a company officer may be designated to answer questions and provide additional data to analysts following the company.

Industry data and other information about a company also may be obtained from sources outside the company. Trade publications, the general business press, computerized databases, investment research reports, and the publications of competitors are among the sources that may supplement company-originated financial data.

The growth of the Internet has greatly improved access to data relevant to investment decisions. Given the rapid change in Internet offerings, we have not attempted to compile a specific list. Examples include:

- Company home pages that contain financial, product, and other data
- EDGAR, which contains corporate filings with the SEC
- Market data from exchanges and private data providers
- Tax regulations
- Economic data
- Industry data

A comprehensive analysis of a company requires the use of all of these sources of information.

When reviewing corporate reports to stockholders and other publications, it is important to remember that management writes them. Management often views annual reports as public relations or sales materials, intended to impress customers, suppliers, and employees, as well as stockholders. As a result, these reports must be read with at least some degree of skepticism. Only the financial statements (including footnotes and other disclosures labeled "audited") are independently reviewed and attested to by outside auditors.

10 ROLE OF THE AUDITOR

The auditor (independent certified public accountant) is responsible for seeing that the financial statements issued conform with generally accepted accounting principles. Thus, the auditor must agree that management's choice of accounting principles is appropriate and any estimates are reasonable. The auditor also examines the company's accounting and internal control systems, confirms assets and liabilities, and generally tries to ensure that there are no material errors in the financial statements. The auditor will often review interim reports and "unaudited" portions of the annual report. Although hired by the company (often through the audit committee of the board of directors), the auditor is supposed to be independent of management and to serve the stockholders and other users of the financial statements.

Audited financial statements are always accompanied by the auditor's report, often referred to as an "opinion." Because of the boilerplate nature of these reports, there is a tendency to skip over them when reviewing financial statements. Failure to read this report, however, may cause the financial analyst to miss significant information.

Exhibit 29-2 is the independent auditor's report issued by Ernst & Young, LLP after its 1999 audit of Amerada Hess. The first three paragraphs of the report are standard and are required by Statement of Auditing Standards (SAS) 58, Reports on Audited Financial Statements,[34] which addresses the audit report in which auditors express their opinion on the financial statements developed by management. It clarifies the scope of the assurance provided by the auditors and briefly describes the audit work. The report tells us the following:

1. Although the financial statements are prepared by Amerada management and are the responsibility of management, the auditor has performed an independent review of the statements.
2. The audit has been conducted using generally accepted auditing standards (GAAS) that require the auditor to provide "reasonable assurance" that there are no material errors in the financial statements. The auditor does not guarantee that the statements are free from error or no fraud is present. The auditor has performed tests of the company's accounting system designed to ensure that the statements are accurate.
3. Amerada's financial statements are prepared in accordance with GAAP. The auditor is satisfied that the accounting principles chosen and the estimates employed are reasonable.

An auditor's report on GAAP-based financial statements will always include these three claims.

SAS 58 also requires the addition of an explanatory paragraph to the auditor's report when accounting methods have not been used consistently among periods. For Amerada, the final paragraph tells us that the company changed its method of accounting for inventories in 1999 (a change discussed in Reading 39).

Reporting on Uncertainties

In some cases, the SAS requires the addition of an explanatory paragraph (following the "opinion" paragraph) that reports and describes material uncertainties affecting the financial statements, such as:

---

[34] Auditing Standards Board of the American Institute of Certified Public Accountants, 1989.

- Doubt concerning the "going concern" assumption that underlies the preparation of financial statements
- Uncertainty regarding the valuation or realization of assets or liabilities
- Uncertainty due to litigation

EXHIBIT 29-2

Audit Report: Amerada Hess

Report of Ernst & Young LLP, Independent Auditors

The Board of Directors and Stockholders
Amerada Hess Corporation

We have audited the accompanying consolidated balance sheet of Amerada Corporation and consolidated subsidiaries as of December 31, 1999 and 1998 and the related consolidated statements of income, retained earnings, cash flows, changes in common stock and capital in excess of par value and comprehensive income for each of the three years in the period ended December 31, 1999. These financial statements are the responsibility of the Corporation's management. Our responsibility is to express an opinion on these financial statements based on our audits.

We conducted our audits in accordance with auditing standards generally accepted in the United States. Those standards require that we plan and perform the audit to obtain reasonable assurance about whether the financial statements are free of material misstatement. An audit includes examining, on a test basis, evidence supporting the amounts and disclosures in the financial statements. An audit also includes assessing the accounting principles used and significant estimates made by management, as well as evaluating the overall financial statement presentation. We believe that our audits provide a reasonable basis for our opinion.

In our opinion, the financial statements referred to above present fairly, in all material respects, the consolidated financial position of Amerada Hess Corporation and consolidated subsidiaries at December 31, 1999 and 1998 and the consolidated results of their operations and their consolidated cash flows for each of the three years in the period ended December 31, 1999, in conformity with accounting principles generally accepted in the United States.

As discussed in Note 3 to the consolidated financial statements, in 1999 the Corporation adopted the last-in, first-out (LIFO) inventory method for valuing its refining and marketing inventories, and in 1998 the Corporation adopted AICPA Statement of Position 98-1, Accounting for the Costs of Computer Software Developed or Obtained for Internal Use.

/s/ Ernst & Young LLP

New York, NY
February 24, 2000

Source: Amerada Hess, 1999 Annual Report.

For the second and third cases, the opinion references the footnote(s) to the financial statements that further detail those uncertainties. The auditor's report on material uncertainties depends on the probability of material loss due to uncertainty. If the probability of a loss is remote, the auditor issues a standard, unqualified opinion. When a material loss is probable and the amount of the loss cannot be reasonably estimated, an explanatory paragraph is required.

The first category is the most serious. A "going concern" qualification conveys doubt that the firm can continue in business. It may be that the firm requires financing due to losses or a lack of liquidity. This paragraph should be viewed as the equivalent of a flashing red light.[35]

Exhibit 29-3 contains the auditors' report on the financial statements of Read-Rite, a producer of magnetic recording heads for computer disk drives. It indicates that the company was not in compliance with financial covenants of its loan agreements and that "these conditions raise substantial doubt about the Company's ability to continue as a going concern." The paragraph then references the paragraph in Note 1, which discusses the conditions that warranted the going concern qualification and management's plans to remedy them.[36]

The other two categories suggest problems that are significant, but may not threaten the firm's existence. In these cases, the analyst should examine the uncertainty and incorporate any concerns in the investment decision.

Whenever the auditor's report contains any of the three types of disclosures just listed, or the consistency exception, the financial statements should be examined closely. Note that "subject to" and "except for" disclosures no longer appear in auditors' reports; they were replaced in 1989 by the language (SAS 58) discussed previously.

Other Auditor Services

The auditor also performs other services less visible to readers of financial statements. The auditor examines the internal control system of the company and reports any weaknesses to management or the audit committee of the board of directors. The report to the audit committee sometimes also contains information regarding significant audit adjustments, unusual transactions, disagreements with management, or serious audit difficulties. This report is generally not available to outside financial statement users. In 1989, the Auditing Standards Board (ASB) of the American Institute of Certified Public Accountants issued two standards dealing with these reports.

U.S. companies are required to report in their proxy statement the amount paid to the auditor for audit services and (separately) for other services (such as consulting).[37] The intent of this SEC requirement is to alert investors that the auditor's nonaudit fees may be material enough to affect the independence of the audit.

---

[35] Empirical studies [e.g., Carcello et al. (1995) and Rama et al. (1995)] have indicated that approximately 60% of bankrupt firms received a prior going-concern modified audit report and approximately 10% of firms receiving a first-time going-concern qualification entered into bankruptcy within one year of the date of the financial statements. Similarly, Holder-Webb and Wilkins (2000), with respect to SFAS 59, report evidence that resultant going-concern qualifications were useful in "warning" the market of imminent bankruptcies.

[36] In fact, Read-Rite did take steps to reduce its debt and, with the help of improved industry conditions, regained stability. It received a "clean" audit opinion at September 30, 2000. Case 10-1 is concerned with the restructuring of Read-Rite debt.

[37] In July, 2002 U.S. legislation restricted the non-audit services that auditors are permitted to perform for firms that they audit.

EXHIBIT 29-3

Audit Opinion: Read-Rite

Report of Ernst & Young LLP, Independent Auditors

The Board of Directors and Stockholders
Read-Rite Corporation

We have audited the accompanying consolidated balance sheets of Read-Rite Corporation as of September 30, 1999 and 1998, and the related consolidated statements of operations, cash flows and stockholders' equity for each of the three years in the period ended September 30, 1999. Our audits also included the financial statement schedule listed in the index at item 14(a). These financial statements and schedule are the responsibility of the Company's management. Our responsibility is to express an opinion on these financial statements and schedule based on our audits.

We conducted our audits in accordance with generally accepted auditing standards. Those standards require that we plan and perform the audit to obtain reasonable assurance about whether the financial statements are free of material misstatement. An audit includes examining, on a test basis, evidence supporting the amounts and disclosures in the financial statements. An audit also includes assessing the accounting principles used and significant estimates made by management, as well as evaluating the overall financial statement presentation. We believe that our audits provide a reasonable basis for our opinion.

In our opinion, the consolidated financial statements referred to above present fairly, in all material respects, the consolidated financial position of Read-Rite Corporation at September 30, 1999 and 1998, and the consolidated results of its operations and its cash flows for each of the three years in the period ended September 30, 1999, in conformity with generally accepted accounting principles. Also, in our opinion, the related financial statement schedule, when considered in relation to the basic financial statements taken as a whole, presents fairly in all material respects the information set forth therein.

The accompanying financial statements have been prepared assuming that Read-Rite Corporation will continue as a going concern. As more fully described in Note 1, the Company has incurred operating losses and is out of compliance with certain financial covenants of loan agreements with its lenders. These conditions raise substantial doubt about the Company's ability to continue as a going concern. Management's plans in regard to these matters are also described in Note 1. The financial statements do not include any adjustments to reflect the possible future effects on the recoverability and classification of assets or the amounts and classification of liabilities that may result from the outcome of this uncertainty.

/s/ Ernst & Young LLP

San Jose, California
October 22, 1999, except for the
sixth paragraph of Note 1, as to
which the date is December 29, 1999.

Source: Read-Rite Annual Report, September 30, 1999.

Changing Auditors

Changes in auditors have become more frequent in recent years. In many cases, changes are due to an effort to reduce audit costs or to personality issues. Some changes, however, result from disagreements regarding the application of accounting principles. When an auditor is willing to lose a client because of such a disagreement, the financial analyst should exercise extreme caution with respect to the financial statements of the company in question.

Auditing Outside of the United States

The role of the auditor is determined by auditing standards that vary, as do accounting standards, from one jurisdiction to another. Aracruz, while a Brazilian company, follows U.S. GAAP and its audit opinion is based on U.S. auditing standards.

Reviewing the Report of Group Auditors shown in Roche's annual report, we see that:

1. Roche financial statements are prepared in accordance with International Accounting Standards.
2. These statements also comply with Swiss law (Roche is a Swiss company).
3. The audit was conducted in accordance with International Standards on Auditing, issued by the International Federation of Accountants.

Reviewing Note 1 of Roche's financial statements, we see that the company adopted a number of new IAS standards in 2000. The auditor's opinion makes no reference to these changes. This is one example of how standards applied to the audit of non-U.S. companies may differ from those that readers of U.S. GAAP financial statements are used to. Thus it is especially important to read the accounting principles note of the financial statements of non-U.S. companies to determine the accounting and auditing principles followed.

SUMMARY 11

Reading 29 provided an informational background for the study of financial statement analysis. It examined the sources of financial data and the institutional framework in which accounting and disclosure standards are set. In addition, it provided a general guide to the contents of the financial statements and the roles played by statement preparers and auditors. In readings 31 and 33, we build on this informational framework by addressing the financial statements—the raw material of analysis.

LONG-TERM ASSETS

READING 30

LEARNING OUTCOMES

The candidate should be able to:

a. describe the factors that distinguish long-term assets from other assets, and identify the common types of long-term assets and their carrying values on the balance sheet;

b. determine the cost, and record the purchase, of property, plant, and equipment;

c. explain depreciation accounting (including the reasons for depreciation), calculate depreciation using the straight-line, production (also known as units-of-production), and declining-balance methods, and calculate depreciation after revising the estimated useful life of an asset;

d. describe how to account for the sale, exchange, or disposal of depreciable assets, and determine whether a gain or loss is recorded;

e. identify assets that should be classified as natural resources, and prepare entries to account for such assets, including entries to record depletion;

f. identify the types of intangible assets, and describe how the accounting treatment for goodwill under U.S. GAAP differs from the accounting treatment for other intangible assets.

MANAGEMENT ISSUES RELATED TO ACCOUNTING FOR LONG-TERM ASSETS

1

Long-term assets are assets that (1) have a useful life of more than one year, (2) are acquired for use in the operation of a business, and (3) are not intended for resale to customers. For many years, it was common to refer to long-term assets as *fixed assets,* but use of this term is declining because the word *fixed* implies that they last forever. The relative importance of long-term assets to various industries is shown in Figure 30-1. Long-term assets range from 19.8 percent of total assets in the advertising industry to 52.7 percent in interstate trucking.

Study note:
For an asset to be classified as property, plant, and equipment, it must be "put in use." This means that it is available for its intended purpose. An emergency generator is "put in use" when it is available for emergencies, even if it is never used.

Key point:
A computer used in the office would be considered plant and equipment, whereas an identical computer held for sale to customers would be considered inventory.

Stop and think!
Is carrying value ever the same as market value?

On the date of acquisition, the carrying value equals the current market value. After that, it would be a coincidence if it equaled the market value.

Although there is no strict rule for defining the useful life of a long-term asset, the most common criterion is that the asset be capable of repeated use for at least a year. Included in this category is equipment used only in peak or emergency periods, such as generators.

Assets not used in the normal course of business should not be included in this category. Thus, land held for speculative reasons or buildings no longer used in ordinary business operations should not be included in the property, plant, and equipment category. Instead, they should be classified as long-term investments.

Finally, if an item is held for resale to customers, it should be classified as inventory—not plant and equipment—no matter how durable it is. For example, a printing press held for sale by a printing press manufacturer would be considered inventory, whereas the same printing press would be considered plant and equipment if a printing company buys it for use in operations.

Long-term assets differ from current assets in that they support the operating cycle instead of being a part of it. They are also expected to benefit the business for a longer period than do current assets. Current assets are expected to be used up or converted to cash within one year or during the operating cycle, whichever is longer. Long-term assets are expected to last beyond that period. Long-term assets and their related expenses are summarized in Figure 30-2 on page 473.

Generally, long-lived assets are reported at carrying value, as presented in Figure 30-3 on page 473. **Carrying value** is the unexpired part of the cost of an asset, not its market value; it is also called *book value.* If a long-lived asset loses some or all of its revenue-generating potential before the end of its useful life, the asset may be deemed impaired, and its carrying value reduced. **Asset impairment** occurs when the sum of the expected cash flows from the asset is less than the carrying value of the asset.[1] Reducing carrying value to fair value, as meas-

FIGURE 30-1 Long-Term Assets as a Percentage of Total Assets for Selected Industries

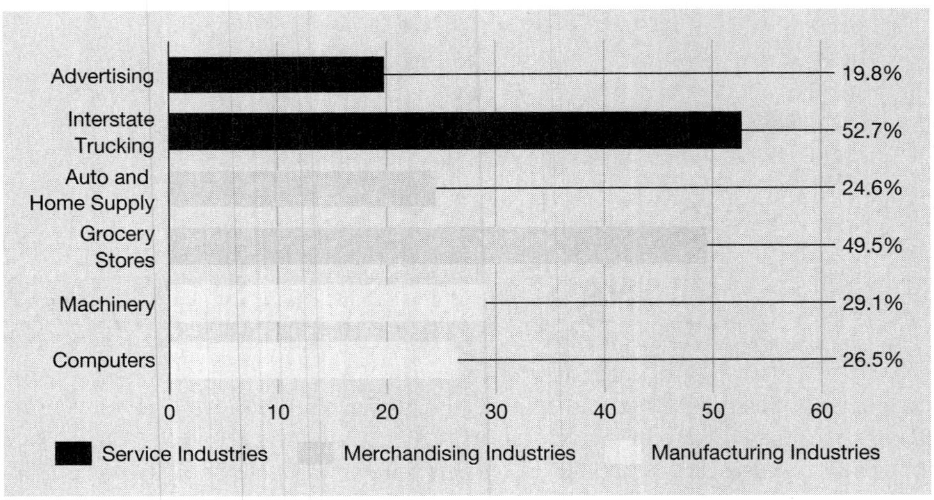

Source: Data from Dun & Bradstreet, *Industry Norms and Key Business Ratios,* 2000–01.

[1] *Statement of Financial Accounting Standards No. 144,* "Accounting for the Impairment or Disposal of Long-Lived Assets" (Norwalk, Conn.: Financial Accounting Standards Board, 2001).

DECISION POINT A USER'S FOCUS

H. J. Heinz Company <www.heinz.com> The effects of management's decisions regarding long-term assets are most apparent in the areas of reported total assets, net income, and cash flows related to investing activities. How does one learn about the significance of those items to a company? An idea of the extent of a company's long-term assets and their importance can be gained from the financial statements. For example, the list of assets in the Financial Highlights from the annual report of H. J. Heinz Company, one of the world's largest food companies. Of the company's $9 billion in total assets, property, plant, and equipment represent about 24 percent, and other noncurrent assets represent about 42 percent.

With 66 percent of Heinz's total assets classified as long-term, management's decisions regarding choice of expected useful life and residual value of the assets can have a material impact on the amount expensed on the income statement. The income statement shows that depreciation and amortization expenses associated with those assets are more than $299 million, or about 63 percent of net income. While depreciation and amortization expenses have no cash effect, the statement of cash flows indicates the amount paid for newly purchased property, plant, and equipment and to what extent a company is reinvesting in its operations. Heinz spent more than $411 million on new long-term assets and expensed almost $300 million as depreciation and amortization expense.[2] In addition to annual expense recognition, long-term assets are reviewed annually to determine if the assets have lost some of their service potential, resulting in asset impairment. Finally, disposals of long-term assets may result in gains or losses on the income statement. Each of these financial-statement issues falls within the scope of accounting for the acquisition, use, and disposal of long-term assets and the related management judgments.

Why are Heinz's long-term assets important to its financial performance as reflected in the balance sheet, the income statement, and the statement of cash flows?

---

[2] H. J. Heinz Company, *Annual Report,* 2001.

Financial Highlights (In thousands)

	2001	2000
Property, Plant, and Equipment:		
Land	**$ 54,774**	$ 45,959
Buildings and leasehold improvements	**878,028**	860,873
Equipment, furniture, and other	**2,947,978**	3,440,915
	3,880,780	4,347,747
Less accumulated depreciation	**1,712,400**	1,988,994
Total property, plant, and equipment, net	**$2,168,380**	$2,358,753
Other Noncurrent Assets:		
Goodwill (net of amortization: 2001—$334,907 and 2000—$312,433)	**$2,077,451**	$1,609,672
Trademarks (net of amortization: 2001—$118,254 and 2000—$104,125)	**567,692**	674,279
Other intangibles (net of amortization: 2001—$157,678 and 2000—$147,343)	**120,749**	127,779
Other noncurrent assets	**984,064**	910,225
Total other noncurrent assets	**$3,749,956**	$3,321,955

ured by the present value of future cash flows, is an application of conservatism. All long-term assets are subject to an asset impairment evaluation. A reduction in carrying value as a result of impairment is recorded as a loss.

www.amazon.com
www.cisco.com
www.lucent.com

Because of a slowdown in the growth of Internet, telecommunications, and technology companies, companies like Amazon.com, Cisco Systems, and Lucent Technologies took write-downs totaling billions of dollars. The carrying value of certain long-term tangible and intangible assets no longer exceeded the cash flows that they would help generate, due to declining revenues or slowing revenue growth. The write-downs caused the companies to report operating losses.[3]

Deciding to Acquire Long-Term Assets

The decision to acquire a long-term asset involves a complex process. Methods of evaluating data to make rational decisions in this area are grouped under a topic called capital budgeting, which is usually covered as a managerial accounting topic. However, an awareness of the general nature of the problem is helpful in understanding the accounting issues related to long-term assets. To illustrate the acquisition decision, let us assume that Irena Markova, M.D., is considering the purchase of a $5,000 computer system for her office. She estimates that if she purchases the computer, she can reduce the hours of a part-time employee sufficiently to save net cash flows of $2,000 per year for four years and that the

[3] David Henry, "The Numbers Game," *BusinessWeek,* May 14, 2001.

FIGURE 30-2 Classification of Long-Term Assets and Corresponding Expenses

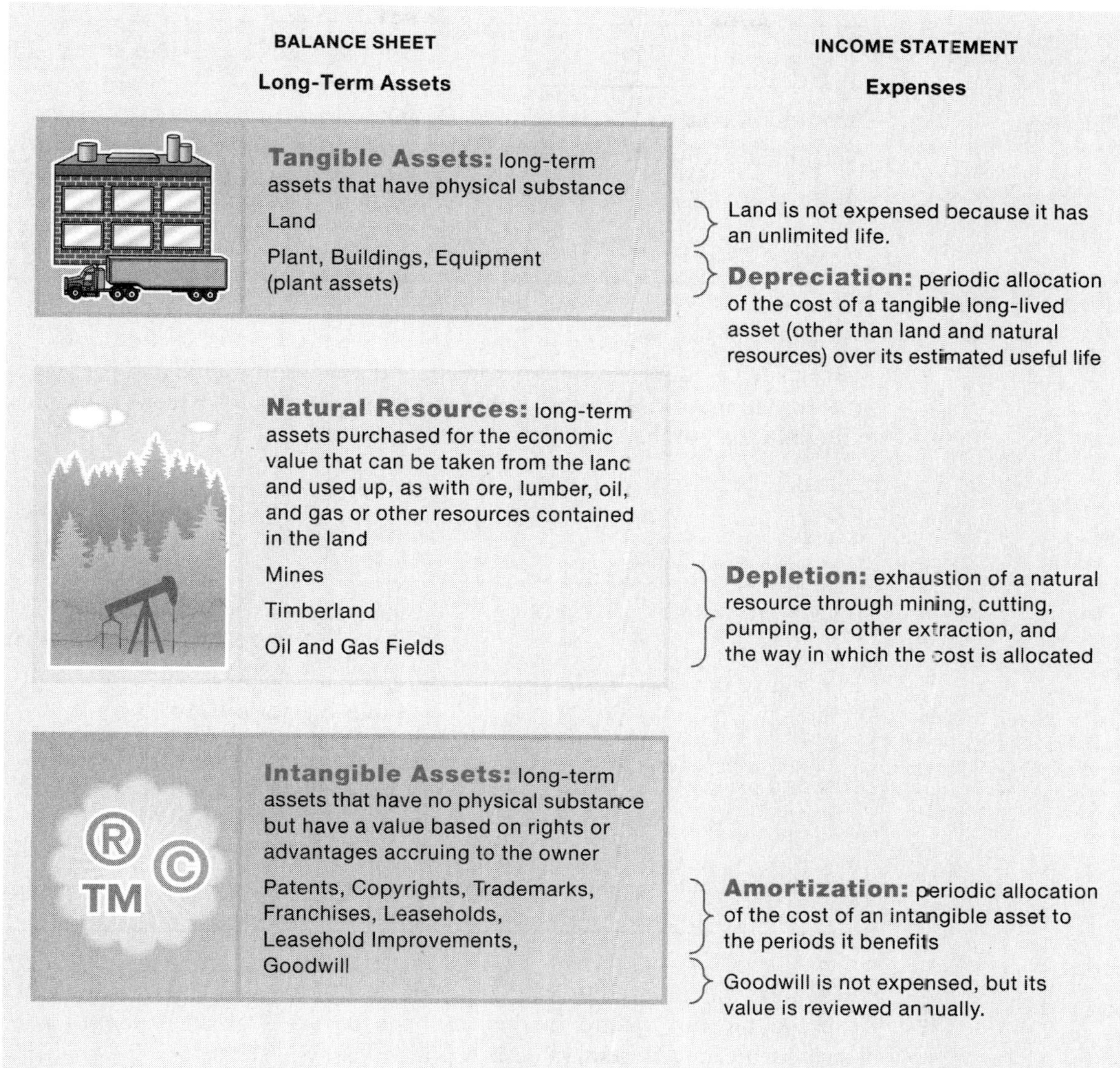

FIGURE 30-3 Carrying Value of Long-Term Assets on the Balance Sheet

Plant Assets	Natural Resources	Intangible Assets
Less Accumulated Depreciation	Less Accumulated Depletion	Less Accumulated Amortization
Carrying Value	Carrying Value	Carrying Value

computer will be worth $1,000 at the end of that period. These data are summarized as follows:

	20x1	20x2	20x3	20x4
Acquisition cost	($5,000)			
Net annual savings in cash flows	$2,000	$2,000	$2,000	$2,000
Disposal price				1,000
Net cash flows	($3,000)	$2,000	$2,000	$3,000

To place the cash flows on a comparable basis, it is helpful to use present value tables, such as Tables 3 and 4 in the appendix on future value and present value tables. Assuming that the appropriate interest rate is 10 percent compounded annually, the purchase may be evaluated as follows:

		Present Value
Acquisition cost	Present value factor = 1.000 1.000 × $5,000	($5,000)
Net annual savings in cash flows	Present value factor = 3.170 (Table 4: 4 periods, 10%) 3.170 × $2,000	6,340
Disposal price	Present value factor = .683 (Table 3: 4 periods, 10%) .683 × $1,000	683
Net present value		$2,023

As long as the net present value is positive, Dr. Markova will earn at least 10 percent on the investment. In this case, the return is greater than 10 percent because the net present value is a positive $2,023. Based on this analysis, Dr. Markova makes the decision to purchase. However, there are other important considerations that have to be taken into account, such as the costs of training and maintenance, and the possibility that because of unforeseen circumstances, the savings may not be as great as expected. In Dr. Markova's case, the decision to purchase is likely to be a good one because the net present value is both positive and large relative to the investment.

www.heinz.com

Information about a company's acquisitions of long-term assets may be found under investing activities in the statement of cash flows. For example, in referring to this section of its 2001 annual report, the management of H.J. Heinz Company makes the following statement:

> Capital expenditures totaled $411.3 million compared to $452.4 million last year. . . . This year's capital expenditures were concentrated in North American Grocery & Foodservice and Europe. Last year's capital expenditures were concentrated across all major segments.[4]

[4] H. J. Heinz Company, *Annual Report*, 2001.

Financing Long-Term Assets

In addition to deciding whether to acquire a long-term asset, management must decide how to finance the asset if it is acquired. Some companies are profitable enough to pay for long-term assets out of cash flows from operations, but when financing is needed, some form of long-term arrangement related to the life of the asset is usually most appropriate. For example, an automobile loan generally spans 4 or 5 years, whereas a mortgage on a house may span as many as 30 years.

For a major long-term acquisition, a company may issue capital stock, long-term notes, or bonds. A good place to study a company's long-term financing is in the financing activities section of the statement of cash flows. For instance, in discussing this section, Ford Motor Company's management states, "Automotive debt at December 31, 2000 totaled $12 billion, which was 39 percent of total capitalization (stockholders' equity and Automotive debt), up from 30 percent of total capitalization a year ago."[5]

www.ford.com

Applying the Matching Rule to Long-Term Assets

Accounting for long-term assets requires the proper application of the matching rule through the resolution of two important issues. The first is how much of the total cost to allocate to expense in the current accounting period. The second is how much to retain on the balance sheet as an asset to benefit future periods. To resolve these issues, four important questions about the acquisition, use, and disposal of each long-term asset must be answered (see Figure 30-4):

FIGURE 30-4 Issues of Accounting for Long-Term Assets

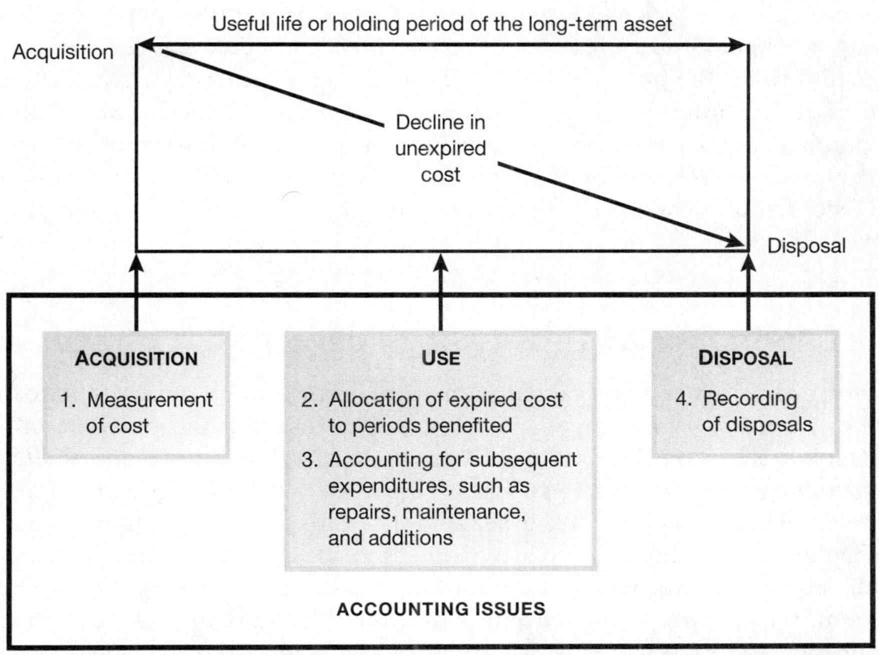

[5] Ford Motor Company, *Annual Report*, 2001.

1. How is the cost of the long-term asset determined?
2. How should the expired portion of the cost of the long-term asset be allocated against revenues over time?
3. How should subsequent expenditures, such as repairs and additions, be treated?
4. How should disposal of the long-term asset be recorded?

Study note: Useful life is measured by the service units a business expects to receive from an asset. It should not be confused with physical life, which is often much longer. If the management of a new business is having difficulty determining an asset's estimated useful life, it may obtain help from trade magazines. Nearly every industry has at least one.

Because of the long life of long-term assets and the complexity of the transactions relating to them, management has many choices and estimates to make. For example, acquisition cost may be complicated by group purchases, trade-ins, or construction costs. In addition, to allocate the cost of the asset to future periods effectively, management must estimate how long the asset will last and what it will be worth at the end of its use. In making such estimates, it is helpful to think of a long-term asset as a bundle of services to be used in the operation of the business over a period of years. A delivery truck may provide 100,000 miles of service over its life. A piece of equipment may have the potential to produce 500,000 parts. A building may provide shelter for 50 years. As each of those assets is purchased, the company is paying in advance for 100,000 miles, the capacity to produce 500,000 parts, or 50 years of service. In essence, each asset is a type of long-term prepaid expense. The accounting problem is to spread the cost of the services over the useful life of the asset. As the services benefit the company over the years, the cost becomes an expense rather than an asset.

2

ACQUISITION COST OF PROPERTY, PLANT, AND EQUIPMENT

Expenditure refers to a payment or an obligation to make future payment for an asset, such as a truck, or a service, such as a repair. Expenditures may be classified as capital expenditures or revenue expenditures. A **capital expenditure** is an expenditure for the purchase or expansion of a long-term asset. Capital expenditures are recorded in the asset accounts because they benefit several future accounting periods. A **revenue expenditure** is an expenditure related to the repair, maintenance, and operation of a long-term asset. Revenue expenditures are recorded in the expense accounts because their benefits are realized in the current period.

Study note: Although dyeing a carpet may make it look almost new, it is not considered a capital expenditure because even though the carpet looks better, its fibers are not stronger, and it probably will not last significantly longer then it would have before the color was changed.

Study note: The cost of mailing lists may be recorded as an asset because the mailing lists will be used over and over and will benefit future accounting periods.

The Importance of Classifying Expenditures Correctly

Careful distinction between capital and revenue expenditures is important to the proper application of the matching rule. For example, if the purchase of an automobile is mistakenly recorded as a revenue expenditure, the total cost of the automobile is recorded as an expense on the income statement. As a result, current net income is reported at a lower amount (understated), and in future periods net income will be reported at a higher amount. If, on the other hand, a revenue expenditure, such as the painting of a building, were charged to an asset account, the expense of the current period would be understated. Current net income would be overstated by the same amount, and the net income of future periods would be understated.

Determining when a payment is an expense and when it is an asset is a matter of judgment in which management takes a leading role. For example, inconsistencies have existed in accounting for the costs of computer programs that run the systems for businesses. Some companies immediately write off the cost as an expense, whereas others treat it as a long-term intangible asset and amortize it year after year. As companies spend billions of dollars a year on this type of software, this is an important variable in the profitability of many companies. Although the AICPA has issued new rules to try to bring more standardization to these accounting issues, considerable latitude does still exist, such as in determining how long the economic life of the software will be.[6]

General Approach to Acquisition Costs

The acquisition cost of property, plant, and equipment includes all expenditures reasonable and necessary to get the asset in place and ready for use. For example, the cost of installing and testing a machine is a legitimate cost of the machine. However, if the machine is damaged during installation, the cost of repairs is an operating expense and not an acquisition cost.

Cost is easiest to determine when a purchase is made for cash. In that case, the cost of the asset is equal to the cash paid for the asset plus expenditures for freight, insurance while in transit, installation, and other necessary related costs. If a debt is incurred in the purchase of the asset, the interest charges are not a cost of the asset, but a cost of borrowing the money to buy the asset. They are therefore an operating expense. An exception to this principle is that interest costs incurred during the construction of an asset are properly included as a cost of the asset.[7]

Key point:
Expenditures necessary to prepare an asset for its intended use are a cost of the asset.

Expenditures like freight, insurance while in transit, and installation are included in the cost of the asset because they are necessary if the asset is to function. Following the matching rule, they are allocated to the useful life of the asset rather than charged as expenses in the current period.

For practical purposes, many companies establish policies defining when an expenditure should be recorded as an expense or an asset. For example, small expenditures for items that would normally be treated as assets may be treated as expenses because the amounts involved are not material in relation to net income. Thus, a wastebasket, which might last for years, would be recorded as a supplies expense rather than as a depreciable asset.

Some of the problems of determining the cost of long-lived plant assets are discussed in the next sections.

Key point:
Many costs may be incurred to prepare land for its intended use and condition. All such costs are a cost of land.

Land

There are often expenditures in addition to the purchase price of land that should be debited to the Land account. Some examples are commissions to real estate agents; lawyers' fees; accrued taxes paid by the purchaser; costs of preparing the land to build on, such as the costs of tearing down old buildings and draining, clearing, and grading the land; and assessments for local improvements, such as putting in streets and sewage systems. The cost of landscaping is usually debited to the Land account because such improvements are relatively permanent. Land is not subject to depreciation because it does not have a limited useful life.

Enrichment note:
The costs of tearing down existing buildings can be major. For example, companies may spend millions of dollars imploding buildings so they can remove them and build new ones.

Let us assume that a company buys land for a new retail operation. It pays a net purchase price of $170,000, pays brokerage fees of $6,000 and legal fees of

[6] *Statement of Position No. 98-1,* "Accounting for the Costs of Computer Software Developed or Planned for Internal Use" (New York: American Institute of Certified Public Accountants, 1996).

[7] *Statement of Financial Accounting Standards No. 34,* "Capitalization of Interest Cost" (Norwalk, Conn.: Financial Accounting Standards Board, 1979), par. 9–11.

$2,000, pays $10,000 to have an old building on the site torn down, receives $4,000 salvage from the old building, and pays $1,000 to have the site graded. The cost of the land is $185,000:

Net purchase price		$170,000
Brokerage fees		6,000
Legal fees		2,000
Tearing down old building	$10,000	
Less salvage	4,000	6,000
Grading		1,000
Total cost		$185,000

Land Improvements

Some improvements to real estate, such as driveways, parking lots, and fences, have a limited life and are thus subject to depreciation. They should be recorded in an account called Land Improvements rather than in the Land account.

Buildings

When an existing building is purchased, its cost includes the purchase price plus all repairs and other expenditures required to put it in usable condition. Buildings are subject to depreciation because they have a limited useful life. When a business constructs its own building, the cost includes all reasonable and necessary expenditures, such as those for materials, labor, part of the overhead and other indirect costs, architects' fees, insurance during construction, interest on construction loans during the period of construction, lawyers' fees, and building permits. If outside contractors are used in the construction, the net contract price plus other expenditures necessary to put the building in usable condition are included in the cost.

Enrichment note:
The electrical wiring and plumbing of a dental chair are included in the cost of the asset since they are a necessary cost of preparing the asset for use.

Equipment

The cost of equipment includes all expenditures connected with purchasing the equipment and preparing it for use. Those expenditures include the invoice price less cash discounts; freight, including insurance; excise taxes and tariffs; buying expenses; installation costs; and test runs to ready the equipment for operation. Equipment is subject to depreciation.

Stop and think!
What incentive does a company have to allocate more of a group purchase price to the land than to the building?

A higher land valuation has the effect of increasing income because a smaller building valuation results in a lower amount to depreciate over its useful life.

Group Purchases

Land and other assets are sometimes purchased for a lump sum. Because land is a nondepreciable asset that has an unlimited life, it must have a separate ledger account, and the lump-sum purchase price must be apportioned between the land and the other assets. For example, assume that a building and the land on which it is situated are purchased for a lump-sum payment of $85,000. The apportionment can be made by determining the price of each if purchased separately and applying the appropriate percentages to the lump-sum price. Assume that appraisals yield estimates of $10,000 for the land and $90,000 for the build-

FOCUS ON BUSINESS ETHICS

Is It an Asset or Expense? The Answer Matters.

Determining whether an expenditure is a long-term asset or an expense is not always as clear-cut as some might imagine. Management has considerable leeway in how to record transactions, but the financial statements must be prepared in accordance with generally accepted accounting principles and the result cannot be deceptive. If management's choices are questioned, the results can sometimes have drastic consequences.

For example, *The Wall Street Journal* reported that the chief financial officer of WorldCom used an unorthodox and unusually aggressive technique to account for one of the long-distance company's biggest expenses. The company recorded charges paid to local telephone networks to complete calls as long-term assets instead of operating expenses. This increased income in the year in question by deferring the costs to a future year, effectively turning a net loss for the year into a net income. In total, the company says that at least $3.8 billion was accounted for in this way. As a result of the report, the company's stock price dropped from a high of $64.50 to less than one dollar. The SEC filed civil fraud charges against WorldCom, saying the company "falsely portrayed itself as a profitable business."[8] Criminal charges may follow and the company will likely face bankruptcy.

This and other notable cases show that accounting is not a passive part of business that can be manipulated at will, but must be taken seriously. The financial statements must reveal the substance of the business's activities.

ing if purchased separately. In that case, 10 percent of the lump-sum price, or $8,500, would be allocated to the land, and 90 percent, or $76,500, would be allocated to the building, as follows:

	Appraisal	Percentage	Apportionment
Land	$ 10,000	10% ($10,000 ÷ $100,000)	$ 8,500 ($85,000 × 10%)
Building	90,000	90% ($90,000 ÷ $100,000)	76,500 ($85,000 × 90%)
Totals	$100,000	100%	$85,000

ACCOUNTING FOR DEPRECIATION 3

The AICPA describes depreciation accounting as follows:

> The cost of a productive facility is one of the costs of the services it renders during its useful economic life. Generally accepted accounting principles require that this cost be spread over the expected useful life of the facility in such a way as to allocate it as equitably as possible to the periods during which services are obtained from the use of the facility. This procedure is known as depreciation accounting, a system of accounting which aims to distribute the cost or other basic value of tangible capital assets, less salvage (if any), over the estimated useful life of the unit . . . in a systematic and rational manner. It is a process of allocation, not of valuation.[9]

[8] Jared Sandberg, Deborah Solomon, and Rebecca Blumenstein, "Inside WorldCom's Unearthing of a Vast Accounting Scandal." *The Wall Street Journal,* June 27, 2002.

[9] *Financial Accounting Standards: Original Pronouncements as of July 1, 1977* (Norwalk, Conn.: Financial Accounting Standards Board, 1977), ARB No. 43, Ch. 9, Sec. C, par. 5.

Parenthetical note:
An older computer may be functioning as well as it did on the day of purchase, but it has become obsolete because much faster, more efficient computers are now available.

This description contains several important points. First, all tangible assets except land have a limited useful life. Because of this, their cost must be distributed as expenses over the years they benefit. Physical deterioration and obsolescence are the major causes of the limited useful life of a depreciable asset. The **physical deterioration** of tangible assets results from use and from exposure to the elements, such as wind and sun. Periodic repairs and a sound maintenance policy may keep buildings and equipment in good operating order and extract the maximum useful life from them, but every machine or building at some point must be discarded. Repairs do not eliminate the need for depreciation. **Obsolescence** is the process of becoming out of date. Because of fast-changing technology and fast-changing demands, machinery and even buildings often become obsolete before they wear out. Accountants do not distinguish between physical deterioration and obsolescence because they are interested in the length of an asset's useful life, not in what limits that useful life.

Second, the term *depreciation*, as used in accounting, does not refer to an asset's physical deterioration or decrease in market value over time. Depreciation means the allocation of the cost of a plant asset to the periods that benefit from the services of that asset. The term is used to describe the gradual conversion of the cost of the asset into an expense.

Key point:
Depreciation is the allocation of the acquisition cost of an asset, and any similarity between undepreciated cost and current market value is pure coincidence.

Third, depreciation is not a process of valuation. Accounting records are kept in accordance with the cost principle; they are not indicators of changing price levels. It is possible that because of an advantageous purchase and specific market conditions, the market value of a building may rise. Nevertheless, depreciation must continue to be recorded because it is the result of an allocation, not a valuation, process. Eventually, the building will wear out or become obsolete regardless of interim fluctuations in market value.

Factors That Affect the Computation of Depreciation

Four factors affect the computation of depreciation: (1) cost, (2) residual value, (3) depreciable cost, and (4) estimated useful life.

Cost

As explained earlier in the reading, cost is the net purchase price plus all reasonable and necessary expenditures to get the asset in place and ready for use.

Residual Value

Key point:
Residual value is the portion of an asset's acquisition cost expected to be recovered at the asset's disposal date.

The **residual value** of an asset is its estimated net scrap, salvage, or trade-in value as of the estimated date of disposal. Other terms often used to describe residual value are *salvage value* and *disposal value.*

Depreciable Cost

Key point:
It is depreciable cost, not acquisition cost, that is allocated over the useful life of a plant asset.

The **depreciable cost** of an asset is its cost less its residual value. For example, a truck that costs $12,000 and has a residual value of $3,000 would have a depreciable cost of $9,000. Depreciable cost must be allocated over the useful life of the asset.

Estimated Useful Life

Estimated useful life is the total number of service units expected from a long-term asset. Service units may be measured in terms of years the asset is expected to be used, units expected to be produced, miles expected to be driven, or simi-

FOCUS ON BUSINESS PRACTICE

The Useful Life of an Aircraft Is How Long?

Most airlines depreciate airplanes over an estimated useful life of 10 to 20 years. But how long will a properly maintained airplane really last? Western Airlines <www.westernairlines.com> paid $3.3 million for a new Boeing 737 in July 1968. More than 78,000 flights and 30 years later, this aircraft was still flying for Vanguard Airlines <www.flyvanguard.com>, a no-frills airline. Among the other airlines that have owned this aircraft during the course of its life are Piedmont, Delta <www.delta.com>, and US Airways <www.usairways.com>. Virtually every part of the plane has been replaced over the years. Boeing believes the plane could theoretically make double the number of flights before it is retired.

The useful lives of many types of assets can be extended indefinitely if the assets are correctly maintained, but proper accounting in accordance with the matching rule requires depreciation over a "reasonable" useful life. Each airline that owned the plane would have accounted for the plane in this way.

lar measures. In computing the estimated useful life of an asset, an accountant should consider all relevant information, including (1) past experience with similar assets, (2) the asset's present condition, (3) the company's repair and maintenance policy, (4) current technological and industry trends, and (5) local conditions, such as weather.

Depreciation is recorded at the end of the accounting period by an adjusting entry that takes the following form:

Depreciation Expense, Asset Name	XXX	
Accumulated Depreciation, Asset Name		XXX
To record depreciation for the period		

A = L + OE
– –

Methods of Computing Depreciation

Many methods are used to allocate the cost of plant assets to accounting periods through depreciation. Each is proper for certain circumstances. The most common methods are (1) the straight-line method, (2) the production method, and (3) an accelerated method known as the declining-balance method.

Straight-Line Method

When the **straight-line method** is used to calculate depreciation, the depreciable cost of the asset is spread evenly over the estimated useful life of the asset. The straight-line method is based on the assumption that depreciation depends only on the passage of time. The depreciation expense for each period is computed by dividing the depreciable cost (cost of the depreciating asset less its estimated residual value) by the number of accounting periods in the asset's estimated useful life. The rate of depreciation is the same in each year. Suppose, for example, that a delivery truck costs $10,000 and has an estimated residual value of $1,000 at the end of its estimated useful life of five years. The annual depreciation would be $1,800 under the straight-line method, calculated as follows:

Clarification note: The straight-line depreciation method should be used when approximately equal asset benefit is obtained each year.

Key point: Residual value and useful life are, at best, educated guesses.

$$\frac{\text{Cost} - \text{Residual Value}}{\text{Estimated Useful Life}} = \frac{\$10{,}000 - \$1{,}000}{5 \text{ years}} = \$1{,}800 \text{ per year}$$

The depreciation for the five years would be as follows:

Depreciation Schedule, Straight-Line Method

	Cost	Yearly Depreciation	Accumulated Depreciation	Carrying Value
Date of purchase	$10,000	—	—	$10,000
End of first year	10,000	$1,800	$1,800	8,200
End of second year	10,000	1,800	3,600	6,400
End of third year	10,000	1,800	5,400	4,600
End of fourth year	10,000	1,800	7,200	2,800
End of fifth year	10,000	1,800	9,000	1,000

There are three important points to note from the depreciation schedule for the straight-line depreciation method. First, the depreciation is the same each year. Second, the accumulated depreciation increases uniformly. Third, the carrying value decreases uniformly until it reaches the estimated residual value.

Production Method

Parenthetical note: The production method is appropriate when a company has widely fluctuating rates of production. For example, carpet mills often close during the first two weeks in July. Charging a full month's depreciation would not achieve the goal of matching cost with revenue. Conversely, the same mills may run double shifts in September. At that time, twice the usual amount of depreciation should be charged.

The **production method** of depreciation is based on the assumption that depreciation is solely the result of use and that the passage of time plays no role in the depreciation process. If we assume that the delivery truck in the previous example has an estimated useful life of 90,000 miles, the depreciation cost per mile would be determined as follows:

$$\frac{\text{Cost} - \text{Residual Value}}{\text{Estimated Units of Useful Life}} = \frac{\$10{,}000 - \$1{,}000}{90{,}000 \text{ miles}} = \$.10 \text{ per mile}$$

If we assume that the use of the truck was 20,000 miles for the first year, 30,000 miles for the second, 10,000 miles for the third, 20,000 miles for the fourth, and 10,000 miles for the fifth, the depreciation schedule for the delivery truck would be as follows:

Depreciation Schedule, Production Method

	Cost	Miles	Yearly Depreciation	Accumulated Depreciation	Carrying Value
Date of purchase	$10,000	—	—	—	$10,000
End of first year	10,000	20,000	$2,000	$2,000	8,000
End of second year	10,000	30,000	3,000	5,000	5,000
End of third year	10,000	10,000	1,000	6,000	4,000
End of fourth year	10,000	20,000	2,000	8,000	2,000
End of fifth year	10,000	10,000	1,000	9,000	1,000

There is a direct relation between the amount of depreciation each year and the units of output or use. Also, the accumulated depreciation increases each year in direct relation to units of output or use. Finally, the carrying value decreases each year in direct relation to units of output or use until it reaches the estimated residual value.

Under the production method, the unit of output or use employed to measure the estimated useful life of each asset should be appropriate for that asset. For example, the number of items produced may be an appropriate measure for one machine, but the number of hours of use may be a better measure for another. The production method should be used only when the output of an asset over its useful life can be estimated with reasonable accuracy.

Declining-Balance Method

An **accelerated method** of depreciation results in relatively large amounts of depreciation in the early years of an asset's life and smaller amounts in later years. Such a method, which is based on the passage of time, assumes that many kinds of plant assets are most efficient when new, and so provide more and better service in the early years of their useful life. It is consistent with the matching rule to allocate more depreciation to earlier years than to later years if the benefits or services received in the earlier years are greater than those received later.

An accelerated method also recognizes that fast-changing technologies cause some equipment to become obsolescent and lose service value rapidly. Thus, it is realistic to allocate more to depreciation in earlier years than in later ones. Another argument in favor of an accelerated method is that repair expense is likely to be greater in later years than in earlier years. Thus, the total of repair and depreciation expense remains fairly constant over a period of years. This result naturally assumes that the services received from the asset are roughly equal from year to year.

The **declining-balance method** is the most common accelerated method of depreciation. Under this method, depreciation is computed by applying a fixed rate to the carrying value (the declining balance) of a tangible long-lived asset, resulting in higher depreciation charges during the early years of the asset's life. Though any fixed rate can be used, the most common rate is a percentage equal to twice the straight-line depreciation percentage. When twice the straight-line rate is used, the method is usually called the **double-declining-balance method**.

In our earlier example, the delivery truck had an estimated useful life of five years. Consequently, under the straight-line method, the depreciation rate for each year was 20 percent (100 percent ÷ 5 years).

Under the double-declining-balance method, the fixed rate is 40 percent (2 × 20 percent). This fixed rate is applied to the *remaining carrying value* at the end of each year. Estimated residual value is not taken into account in figuring depreciation except in a year when calculated depreciation exceeds the amount necessary to bring the carrying value down to the estimated residual value. The depreciation schedule for this method is as follows:

Depreciation Schedule, Double-Declining-Balance Method

	Cost		Yearly Depreciation	Accumulated Depreciation	Carrying Value
Date of purchase	$10,000		—	—	$10,000
End of first year	10,000	(40% × $10,000)	$4,000	$4,000	6,000
End of second year	10,000	(40% × $6,000)	2,400	6,400	3,600
End of third year	10,000	(40% × $3,600)	1,440	7,840	2,160
End of fourth year	10,000	(40% × $2,160)	864	8,704	1,296
End of fifth year	10,000		296*	9,000	1,000

*Depreciation limited to amount necessary to reduce carrying value to residual value: $296 = $1,296 (previous carrying value) − $1,000 (residual value).

Parenthetical note:
Accelerated depreciation is appropriate for assets that provide the greatest benefits in their early years. Under such a method, depreciation charges will be high in years when revenue generation from the asset is high.

Key point:
The double-declining-balance method is the only method presented in which the residual value is not deducted before beginning the depreciation calculation.

Key point:
Under the double-declining-balance method, depreciation in the last year rarely equals the exact amount needed to reduce carrying value to residual value. Depreciation in the last year is limited to the amount necessary to reduce carrying value to residual value.

Parenthetical note:
An asset remains on the books as long as it is in use. Even if the asset is fully depreciated, the company should not remove it from the books until it is taken out of service.

Note that the fixed rate is always applied to the carrying value at the end of the previous year. The depreciation is greatest in the first year and declines each year after that. Finally, the depreciation in the last year is limited to the amount necessary to reduce carrying value to residual value.

Comparison of the Three Methods

Stop and think!
Which depreciation method would best reflect the risk of obsolescence from rapid technological changes?

An accelerated depreciation method is best. Companies facing rapid technological change use it to minimize the risk of obsolescence.

A visual comparison may provide a better understanding of the three depreciation methods described above. Figure 30-5 compares yearly depreciation and carrying value under the three methods. In the left-hand graph, which shows yearly depreciation, straight-line depreciation is uniform at $1,800 per year over the five-year period. However, the double-declining-balance method begins at an amount greater than straight-line ($4,000) and decreases each year to amounts that are less than straight-line (ultimately, $296). The production method does not generate a regular pattern because of the random fluctuation of the depreciation from year to year. The three yearly depreciation patterns are reflected in the graph of carrying value. In that graph, each method starts in the same place (cost of $10,000) and ends at the same place (residual value of $1,000). It is the patterns during the useful life of the asset that differ for each method. For instance, the carrying value under the straight-line method is always greater than that under the double-declining-balance method, except at the beginning and end of useful life.

4 DISPOSAL OF DEPRECIABLE ASSETS

Clarification note:
For financial reporting purposes, the objective is to measure performance accurately. For tax purposes, the objective is to minimize tax liability.

When plant assets are no longer useful because they are worn out or obsolete, they may be discarded, sold, or traded in on the purchase of new plant and equipment. For accounting purposes, a plant asset may be disposed of in one of three ways: It may be (1) discarded, (2) sold for cash, or (3) exchanged for another asset. To illustrate how each of these cases is recorded, assume that MGC Company purchased a machine on January 2, 20×0, for $6,500 and planned to depreciate it on a straight-line basis over an estimated useful life of ten years. The

FIGURE 30-5 Graphic Comparison of Three Methods of Determining Depreciation

FOCUS ON BUSINESS PRACTICE

Accelerated Methods Save Money!

An AICPA study of 600 large companies found that the overwhelming majority used the straight-line method of depreciation for financial reporting purposes, as shown in Figure 30-6. Only about 15 percent used some type of accelerated method, and 6 percent used the production method. These figures tend to be misleading about the importance of accelerated depreciation methods, however, especially when it comes to income taxes. Federal income tax laws allow either the straight-line method or an accelerated method, and for tax purposes, about 75 percent of the 600 companies studied preferred an accelerated method. Companies use different methods of depreciation for good reason. The straight-line method can be advantageous for financial reporting because it can produce the highest net income, and an accelerated method can be beneficial for tax purposes because it can result in lower income taxes.

residual value at the end of ten years was estimated to be $500. On January 2, 20×7, the balances of the relevant accounts appear as follows:

Machinery	
6,500	

Accumulated Depreciation, Machinery	
	4,200

On September 30, 20×7, management disposes of the asset. The next few sections illustrate the accounting treatment to record depreciation for the partial year and the disposal under several assumptions.

Enrichment note:
Plant assets may also be disposed of by involuntary conversion (e.g., fire, theft, mud slide, flood) or condemnation by a governmental authority. For financial reporting purposes, involuntary conversions are treated in the same way as if the assets were discarded or sold.

Discard or Sale of Plant Assets

When a plant asset is discarded or disposed of in some other way, it is first necessary to record depreciation expense for the partial year up to the date of disposal. This step is required because the asset was used until that date and, under

FIGURE 30-6 Depreciation Methods Used by 600 Large Companies for Financial Reporting

Total percentage exceeds 100 because some companies used different methods for different types of depreciable assets.

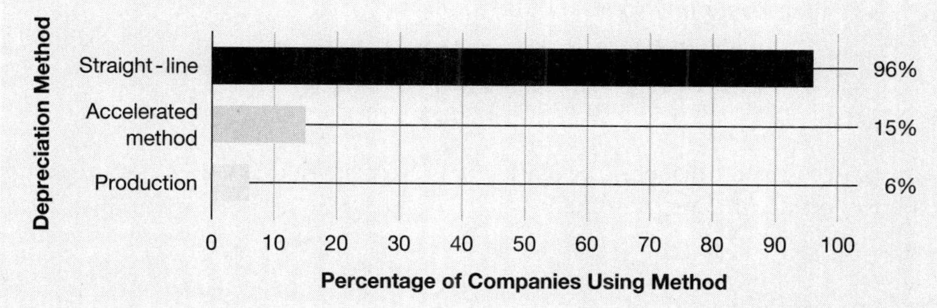

Source: From *Accounting Trends & Techniques.* Copyright © 2000 by the American Institute of Certified Public Accountants, Inc. Reprinted with permission.

the matching rule, the accounting period should receive the proper allocation of depreciation expense.

In this illustration, MGC Company disposes of the machinery on September 30. The entry to record the depreciation for the first nine months of 20×7 (nine-twelfths of a year) is as follows:

A = L + OE
– –

Sept. 30	Depreciation Expense, Machinery	450	
	Accumulated Depreciation, Machinery		450
	To record depreciation up to date of disposal		
	$\frac{\$6,500 - \$500}{10} \times \frac{9}{12} = \$450$		

Key point:
When it disposes of an asset, a company must do two things. First, it must bring the depreciation up to date. Second, it must remove all evidence of ownership of the asset, including the contra account Accumulated Depreciation.

The relevant accounts appear as follows after the entry is posted:

Machinery		Accumulated Depreciation, Machinery	
6,500			4,650

After updating the depreciation, it is then necessary to remove the carrying value of the asset as shown in the following sections.

Discarded Plant Assets

A plant asset rarely lasts exactly as long as its estimated life. If it lasts longer than its estimated life, it is not depreciated past the point at which its carrying value equals its residual value. The purpose of depreciation is to spread the depreciable cost of an asset over the estimated life of the asset. Thus, the total accumulated depreciation should never exceed the total depreciable cost. If an asset remains in use beyond the end of its estimated life, its cost and accumulated depreciation remain in the ledger accounts. Proper records will thus be available for maintaining control over plant assets. If the residual value is zero, the carrying value of a fully depreciated asset is zero until the asset is disposed of. If such an asset is discarded, no gain or loss results.

In the illustration, however, the discarded equipment has a carrying value of $1,850 at the time of its disposal. The carrying value is computed from the T accounts above as machinery of $6,500 less accumulated depreciation of $4,650. A loss equal to the carrying value should be recorded when the machine is discarded, as follows:

A = L + OE
– –
+

Sept. 30	Accumulated Depreciation, Machinery	4,650	
	Loss on Disposal of Machinery	1,850	
	Machinery		6,500
	Discarded machine no longer used in the business		

Gains and losses on disposals of plant assets are classified as other revenues and expenses on the income statement.

Stop and think!
When would the disposal of long-term assets result in no gain or loss?
If cash received for the assets equals their residual value, then no gain or loss occurs.

Plant Assets Sold for Cash

The entry to record a plant asset sold for cash is similar to the one just illustrated, except that the receipt of cash should also be recorded. The following entries show how to record the sale of a machine under three assumptions about the selling price. In the first case, the $1,850 cash received is exactly equal to the $1,850 carrying value of the machine; therefore, no gain or loss occurs.

Sept. 30	Cash	1,850	
	Accumulated Depreciation, Machinery	4,650	
	Machinery		6,500
	Sale of machine for carrying value; no gain or loss		

A = L + OE
+
+
−

In the second case, the $1,000 cash received is less than the carrying value of $1,850, so a loss of $850 is recorded.

Sept. 30	Cash	1,000	
	Accumulated Depreciation, Machinery	4,650	
	Loss on Sale of Machinery	850	
	Machinery		6,500
	Sale of machine at less than carrying value; loss of $850 ($1,850 − $1,000) recorded		

A = L + OE
+ −
+
−

Key point:
For an asset discarded or sold for cash, the gain (loss) on disposal of the asset equals cash received minus carrying value.

In the third case, the $2,000 cash received exceeds the carrying value of $1,850, so a gain of $150 is recorded.

Sept. 30	Cash	2,000	
	Accumulated Depreciation, Machinery	4,650	
	Gain on Sale of Machinery		150
	Machinery		6,500
	Sale of machine at more than the carrying value; gain of $150 ($2,000 − $1,850) recorded		

A = L + OE
+ +
+
−

Exchanges of Plant Assets

Businesses also dispose of plant assets by trading them in on the purchase of other plant assets. Exchanges may involve similar assets, such as an old machine traded in on a newer model, or dissimilar assets, such as a cement mixer traded in on a truck. In either case, the purchase price is reduced by the amount of the trade-in allowance.

Basically, accounting for exchanges of plant assets is similar to accounting for sales of plant assets for cash. If the trade-in allowance received is greater than the carrying value of the asset surrendered, there has been a gain. If the allowance is less, there has been a loss. There are special rules for recognizing these gains and losses, depending on the nature of the assets exchanged:

Exchange	Losses Recognized	Gains Recognized
For financial accounting purposes		
Of dissimilar assets	Yes	Yes
Of similar assets	Yes	No
For income tax purposes		
Of dissimilar assets	Yes	Yes
Of similar assets	No	No

Clarification note:
For assets to be similar, they must be used for similar purposes. A desktop computer, for example, is similar to a laptop computer. Dissimilar assets, such as a truck and a cement mixer, are not used for similar purposes.

Parenthetical note:
Recognizing losses but not gains on similar assets follows the convention of conservatism.

For both financial accounting and income tax purposes, both gains and losses are recognized when a company exchanges dissimilar assets. Assets are dissimilar when they perform different functions or do not meet specific monetary and business criteria for being considered similar assets. For financial accounting purposes, most exchanges are considered exchanges of dissimilar assets. In rare cases, when exchanges meet the specific criteria for exchanges of similar assets, the gains are not recognized. In these cases, you could think of the trade-in as an extension of the life and usefulness of the original machine. Instead of recognizing a gain at the time of the exchange, the company records the new machine at the sum of the carrying value of the older machine plus any cash paid.[10]

Key point:
For exchanges of dissimilar assets, the gain or loss on exchange equals the trade-in allowance minus carrying value of the old asset.

For income tax purposes, similar assets are defined as those performing the same function. Neither gains nor losses on exchanges of these assets are recognized in computing a company's income tax liability. Thus, in practice, accountants face cases in which both gains and losses are recognized (exchanges of dissimilar assets) cases in which losses are recognized and gains are not (exchanges of similar assets for financial reporting purposes), and cases in which neither gains nor losses are recognized (exchanges of similar assets for income tax purposes). Since all these options are used in practice, they are all illustrated in the following sections.

Loss on the Exchange Recognized

A loss is recognized for financial accounting purposes on all exchanges in which a material loss occurs. To illustrate the recognition of a loss, let us assume that the firm in our earlier example exchanges the machine for a newer, more modern machine on the following terms:

Clarification note:
There is no relationship between carrying value and trade-in value. Carrying value is original cost minus accumulated depreciation to date, whereas trade-in value is fair market value on the date of the exchange.

List price of new machine	$12,000
Trade-in allowance for old machine	(1,000)
Cash payment required	$11,000

In this case, the trade-in allowance ($1,000) is less than the carrying value ($1,850) of the old machine. The loss on the exchange is $850 ($1,850 − $1,000). The following journal entry records this transaction under the assumption that the loss is to be recognized:

A = L + OE
+   −
+
−
−

Sept. 30	Machinery (new)	12,000	
	Accumulated Depreciation, Machinery	4,650	
	Loss on Exchange of Machinery	850	
	Machinery (old)		6,500
	Cash		11,000
	Exchange of machines		

Loss on the Exchange Not Recognized

Key point:
For income tax purposes, gains and losses on the exchange of similar assets are not recognized.

In the previous example, in which a loss was recognized, the new asset was recorded at the purchase price of $12,000 and a loss of $850 was recorded. If the transaction involves similar assets and is to be recorded for income tax purposes,

[10] Accounting Principles Board, *Opinion No. 29,* "Accounting for Nonmonetary Transactions" (New York: American Institute of Certified Public Accountants, 1973); Emerging Issues Task Force, *EITF Issue Summary 86-29,* "Nonmonetary Transactions: Magnitude of Boot and the Exceptions to the Use of Fair Value" (Norwalk, Conn.: Financial Accounting Standards Board, 1986).

the loss should not be recognized. In this case, the cost basis of the new asset will reflect the effect of the unrecorded loss. The cost basis is computed by adding the cash payment to the carrying value of the old asset:

Carrying value of old machine	$ 1,850
Cash paid	11,000
Cost basis of new machine	$12,850

Note that no loss is recognized in the entry to record this transaction:

Sept. 30	Machinery (new)	12,850	
	Accumulated Depreciation, Machinery	4,650	
	Machinery (old)		6,500
	Cash		11,000
	Exchange of machines		

A = L + OE
+
+
−
−

Note that the new machinery is reported at the purchase price of $12,000 plus the unrecognized loss of $850. The nonrecognition of the loss on the exchange is, in effect, a postponement of the loss. Since depreciation of the new machine will be computed based on a cost of $12,850 instead of $12,000, the "unrecognized" loss results in more depreciation each year on the new machine than if the loss had been recognized.

Gain on the Exchange Recognized

Gains on exchanges are recognized for accounting purposes when dissimilar assets are involved. To illustrate the recognition of a gain, we continue with our example, assuming the following terms and assuming the machines being exchanged serve different functions:

Key point: For exchanges of assets, the cash payment on the exchange equals list price of the new asset minus trade-in allowance of the old asset.

List price of new machine	$12,000
Trade-in allowance for old machine	(3,000)
Cash payment required	$ 9,000

Here, the trade-in allowance ($3,000) exceeds the carrying value ($1,850) of the old machine by $1,150. Thus, there is a gain on the exchange, assuming that the price of the new machine has not been inflated to allow for an excessive trade-in value. In other words, a gain exists if the trade-in allowance represents the fair market value of the old machine. Assuming that this condition is true, the entry to record the transaction is as follows:

Sept. 30	Machinery (new)	12,000	
	Accumulated Depreciation, Machinery	4,650	
	Gain on Exchange of Machinery		1,150
	Machinery (old)		6,500
	Cash		9,000
	Exchange of machines		

A	= L	+ OE
+		+
+		
−		
−		

Gain on the Exchange Not Recognized

When similar assets are exchanged, gains are not recognized for either accounting or income tax purposes. The cost basis of the new machine must reflect the effect of the unrecorded gain. This cost basis is computed by adding the cash payment to the carrying value of the old asset, as follows:

Carrying value of old machine	$1,850
Cash paid	9,000
Cost basis of new machine	$10,850

The entry to record the transaction is as follows:

A = L + OE
+
+
−
−

Sept. 30	Machinery (new)	10,850	
	Accumulated Depreciation, Machinery	4,650	
	Machinery (old)		6,500
	Cash		9,000
	Exchange of machines		

As with the nonrecognition of losses, the nonrecognition of the gain on an exchange is, in effect, a postponement of the gain. In this illustration, when the new machine is eventually discarded or sold, its cost basis will be $10,850 instead of its original price of $12,000. Since depreciation will be computed on the cost basis of $10,850, the "unrecognized" gain is reflected in lower depreciation each year on the new machine than if the gain had been recognized.

5 ACCOUNTING FOR NATURAL RESOURCES

Clarification note:
Natural resources are not intangible assets. Natural resources are correctly classified as components of property, plant, and equipment.

Natural resources are shown on the balance sheet as long-term assets with such descriptive titles as Timberlands, Oil and Gas Reserves, and Mineral Deposits. The distinguishing characteristic of these assets is that they are converted to inventory by cutting, pumping, mining, or other extraction methods. Natural resources are recorded at acquisition cost, which may include some costs of development. As the resource is extracted and converted to inventory, the asset account must be proportionally reduced. The carrying value of oil reserves on the balance sheet, for example, is reduced by a small amount for each barrel of oil pumped. As a result, the original cost of the oil reserves is gradually reduced, and depletion is recognized in the amount of the decrease.

Depletion

Enrichment note:
When determining the total units available for depletion, management uses only the total units that are economically feasible to extract. This follows the cost-benefit principle—that is, when the cost of extracting a mineral is greater than the expected profit from the sale of the mineral, the company stops extracting it.

The term *depletion* is used to describe not only the exhaustion of a natural resource but also the proportional allocation of the cost of a natural resource to the units extracted. The costs are allocated in a way that closely resembles the production method used to calculate depreciation. When a natural resource is purchased or developed, there must be an estimate of the total units that will be available, such as barrels of oil, tons of coal, or board-feet of lumber. The depletion cost per unit is determined by dividing the cost of the natural resource (less residual value, if any) by the estimated number of units available. The amount of the depletion cost for each accounting period is then computed by multiplying the depletion cost per unit by the number of units extracted and sold. For example, for a mine having an estimated 1,500,000 tons of coal, a cost of $1,800,000, and an estimated residual value of $300,000, the depletion charge per ton of coal is $1:

$$\frac{\$1{,}800{,}000 - \$300{,}000}{1{,}500{,}000 \text{ tons}} = \$1 \text{ per ton}$$

Thus, if 115,000 tons of coal are mined and sold during the first year, the depletion charge for the year is $115,000. This charge is recorded as follows:

Dec. 31	Depletion Expense, Coal Deposits	115,000	
	Accumulated Depletion, Coal Deposits		115,000
	To record depletion of coal mine: $1 per ton for 115,000 tons mined and sold		

A = L + OE
− −

On the balance sheet, data for the mine would be presented as follows:

Coal deposits	$1,800,000	
Less accumulated depletion	115,000	$1,685,000

Key point:
The matching rule dictates that the extracted resource be treated as an asset until it is sold. At that point, the asset cost is converted into an expense.

Sometimes a natural resource is not sold in the year it is extracted. It is important to note that it would then be recorded as a depletion *expense* in the year it is *sold*. The part not sold is considered inventory.

Depreciation of Closely Related Plant Assets

The extraction of natural resources generally requires special on-site buildings and equipment (e.g., conveyors and drilling and pumping devices). If the useful life of those assets is longer than the estimated time it will take to deplete the resource, a special problem arises. Because such long-term assets are often abandoned and have no useful purpose once all the resources have been extracted, they should be depreciated on the same basis as the depletion is computed. For example, if machinery with a useful life of ten years is installed on an oil field that is expected to be depleted in eight years, the machinery should be depreciated over the eight-year period, using the production method. That way, each year's depreciation will be proportional to the year's depletion. If one-sixth of the oil field's total reserves is pumped in one year, then the depreciation should be one-sixth of the machinery's cost minus the residual value. If the useful life of a long-term plant asset is less than the expected life of the depleting resource, the shorter life should be used to compute depreciation. In such cases, or when an asset will not be abandoned once the reserves have been fully depleted, other depreciation methods, such as straight-line or declining-balance, are appropriate.

Parenthetical note:
A company may abandon equipment that is still in good working condition. It may cost the company more to dismantle the equipment and move it to another site than to abandon it.

Development and Exploration Costs in the Oil and Gas Industry

The costs of explorating and developing oil and gas resources can be accounted for under one of two methods. Under **successful efforts accounting**, the cost of successful exploration—for example, producing an oil well—is a cost of the resource. It should be recorded as an asset and depleted over the estimated life of the resource. The cost of an unsuccessful exploration—such as the cost of a dry well—is written off immediately as a loss. Because of these immediate write-offs, successful efforts accounting is considered the more conservative method and is used by most large oil companies.

Exploration-minded independent oil companies, on the other hand, argue that the cost of dry wells is part of the overall cost of the systematic development of an oil field and is thus a part of the cost of producing wells. Under this **full-costing** method, all costs, including the cost of dry wells, are recorded as assets and depleted over the estimated life of the producing resources. This method tends to improve a company's earnings performance in its early years. Either method is permitted by the Financial Accounting Standards Board.[11]

Stop and think!
When would annual depletion not equal depletion expense?

Annual depletion refers to units extracted, but depletion expense includes only units sold. So annual depletion does not equal depletion expense when units extracted do not equal units sold.

[11] *Statement of Financial Accounting Standards No. 25,* "Suspension of Certain Accounting Requirements for Oil and Gas Producing Companies" (Norwalk, Conn.: Financial Accounting Standards Board, 1979).

6 ACCOUNTING FOR INTANGIBLE ASSETS

The purchase of an intangible asset is a special kind of capital expenditure. An intangible asset is long term, but it has no physical substance. Its value comes from the long-term rights or advantages it offers to its owner. The most common examples—goodwill, trademarks, brand names, copyrights, patents, licenses or franchises, leaseholds, leasehold improvements, technology, noncompete covenants, and customer lists—are described in Table 1. Some current assets, such as accounts receivable and certain prepaid expenses, have no physical substance, but they are not classified as intangible assets because they are short term. Intangible assets are both long term and nonphysical.

Figure 30-7 shows the percentage of companies that report the various types of intangible assets. For some companies, intangible assets make up a substantial portion of total assets. As noted in the Decision Point at the beginning of this reading, goodwill, trademarks, and other intangible assets of H.J. Heinz Company amount to over $2.7 billion, or 31 percent of total assets. How these assets are accounted for will have a substantial effect on Heinz's performance.

www.heinz.com

Intangible assets are accounted for at acquisition cost—that is, the amount that was paid for them. Some intangible assets, such as goodwill and trademarks, may be acquired at little or no cost. Even though they may have great value and be needed for profitable operations, they should not appear on the balance sheet unless they have been purchased from another party at a price established in the marketplace.

Key point:
Generally, intangible assets, including goodwill, are recorded only when purchased. An exception is the cost of internally developed computer software after a working prototype has been developed.

The accounting issues connected with intangible assets, other than goodwill are the same as those connected with other long-lived assets. The Accounting Principles Board, in its *Opinion No. 17,* lists them as follows:

1. Determining an initial carrying amount
2. Accounting for that amount after acquisition under normal business conditions—that is, through periodic write-off or amortization—in a manner similar to depreciation
3. Accounting for that amount if the value declines substantially and permanently[12]

In addition to these three problems, an intangible asset, because it has no physical substance, may sometimes be impossible to identify. For these reasons, its value and its useful life may be quite hard to estimate.

Clarification note:
Useful life refers to how long an intangible asset will be contributing income to a firm.

The Accounting Principles Board has decided that a company should record as assets the costs of intangible assets acquired from others. However, the company should record as expenses the costs of developing intangible assets. Also, intangible assets that have a determinable useful life, such as patents, copyrights, and leaseholds, should be written off through periodic amortization over that useful life in much the same way that plant assets are depreciated. Even though some intangible assets, such as brand names and trademarks, have no measurable limit on their lives, they should still be amortized over a reasonable length of time.

To illustrate these procedures, assume that Soda Bottling Company purchases a patent on a unique bottle cap for $18,000. The entry to record the patent would include $18,000 in the asset account Patents. Note that if Soda Bottling Company had developed the bottle cap internally instead of purchasing it from others, the costs of developing the cap, such as salaries of researchers, supplies used in testing, and costs of equipment, would have been expensed as incurred.

---

[12] Adapted from Accounting Principles Board, *Opinion No. 17,* "Intangible Assets" (New York: American Institute of Certified Public Accountants, 1970), par. 2.

Table 30-1 Accounting for Intangible Assets

Type	Description	Accounting Treatment
Goodwill	The excess of the amount paid for the purchase of a business over the fair market value of the net assets.	Debit Goodwill for the acquisition cost, and perform impairment review annually.
Trademark, brand name	A registered symbol or name that can be used only by its owner to identify a product or service.	Debit Trademark or Brand Name for the acquisition cost, and amortize it over a reasonable life, not to exceed 40 years.
Copyright	An exclusive right granted by the federal government to reproduce and sell literary, musical, and other artistic materials and computer programs for a period of the author's life plus 70 years.	Record at acquisition cost, and amortize over the useful life, which is often much shorter than the legal life, but not to exceed 40 years. For example, the cost of paperback rights to a popular novel would typically be amortized over a useful life of two to four years.
Patent	An exclusive right granted by the federal government for a period of 20 years to make a particular product or use a specific process. A design may be granted a patent for 14 years.	The cost of successfully defending a patent in a patent infringement suit is added to the acquisition cost of the patent. Amortize over the useful life, which may be less than the legal life.
License, franchise	A right to an exclusive territory or market, or the right to use a formula, technique, process, or design.	Debit License or Franchise for the acquisition cost, and amortize it over a reasonable life, not to exceed 40 years.
Leasehold	A right to occupy land or buildings under a long-term rental contract. For example, Company A, which owns the right to use but does not want to use a retail location, sells or subleases to Company B the right to use it for ten years in return for one or more rental payments. Company B has purchased a leasehold.	Debit Leasehold for the amount of the rental payment, and amortize it over the remaining life of the lease. Payments to the lessor during the life of the lease should be debited to Lease Expense.
Leasehold improvements	Improvements to leased property that become the property of the lessor (the owner of the property) at the end of the lease.	Debit Leasehold Improvements for the cost of improvements, and amortize the cost of the improvements over the remaining life of the lease.
Technology	Capitalized costs associated with software developed for sale, lease, or internal use.	Record the amount of capitalizable software production costs, and amortize over the estimated economic life of the product.
Noncompete covenant	A contract limiting the rights of others to compete in a specific industry or line of business for a specified period.	Record at the acquisition cost, and amortize over the contract period.
Customer list	A list of customers or subscribers.	Debit Customer Lists for amount paid, and amortize over the expected life.

FIGURE 30-7 Intangible Assets Separately Reported by 600 Large Companies

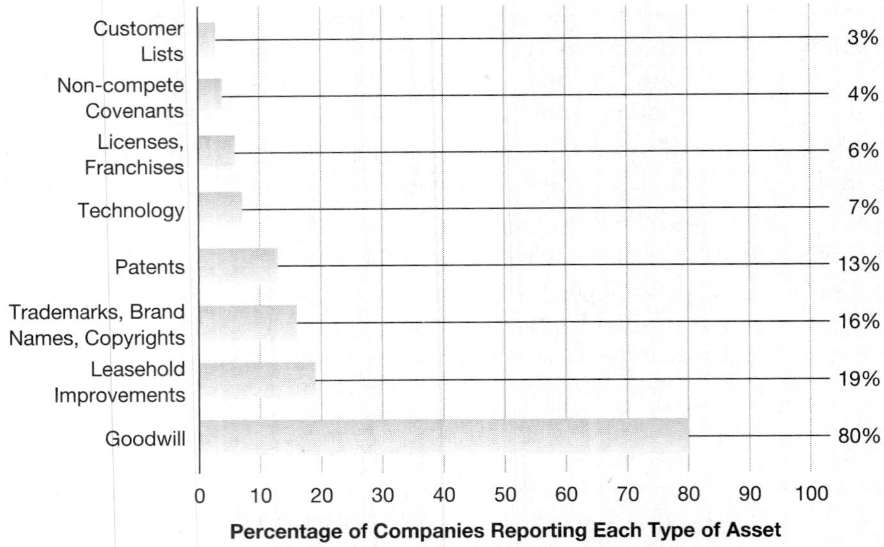

Source: Data from *Accounting Trends and Technology*, 2001.

Assume now that Soda's management determines that although the patent for the bottle cap will last for 20 years, the product using the cap will be sold only for the next six years. The entry to record the annual amortization expense would be for \$3,000 (\$18,000 ÷ 6 years). Note that the Patents account is reduced directly by the amount of the amortization expense. This is in contrast to the treatment of other long-term asset accounts, for which depreciation or depletion is accumulated in separate contra accounts.

If the patent becomes worthless before it is fully amortized, the remaining carrying value is written off as a loss by removing it from the Patents account.

Research and Development Costs

Most successful companies carry out research and development (R&D) activities, often within a separate department. Among these activities are development of new products, testing of existing and proposed products, and pure research. The

FOCUS ON BUSINESS PRACTICE

Take a Closer Look at Subscriber Lists!

One of the most valuable intangible assets some companies have is a list of subscribers. For example, the Newark Morning Ledger Co., a newspaper chain, purchased a chain of Michigan newspapers whose list of 460,000 subscribers was valued at \$68 million. The U.S. Supreme Court upheld the company's right to amortize the value of the subscriber list because the company showed that the list had a limited useful life. The Internal Revenue Service had argued that the list had an indefinite life and therefore could not provide tax deductions through amortization. This ruling will benefit other types of businesses that purchase everything from bank deposits to pharmacy prescription files.[13]

[13] "What's in a Name?" *Time,* May 3, 1993.

costs of these activities are substantial expenditures for many companies. In a recent year, General Motors spent $6.6 billion on research and development, or about 4 percent of its revenues.[14] R&D costs can be even greater in high-tech fields like pharmaceuticals. For example, Abbott Laboratories recently spent $1.4 billion, or almost 10 percent of revenues, on R&D, and Roche Group spent almost $4 billion, or 14 percent of revenues.[15]

www.gm.com
www.abbott.com
www.roche.com

In the past, some companies recorded as assets R&D costs that could be directly traced to the development of specific patents, formulas, or other rights. Other costs, such as those for testing and pure research, were treated as expenses of the accounting period and deducted from income. Since then, the Financial Accounting Standards Board has stated that all R&D costs should be treated as revenue expenditures and charged to expense in the period in which they are incurred.[16] The board argues that it is too hard to trace specific costs to specific profitable developments. Also, the costs of research and development are continuous and necessary for the success of a business and so should be treated as current expenses. To support this conclusion, the board cites studies showing that 30 to 90 percent of all new products fail and that 75 percent of new-product expenses go to unsuccessful products. Thus, their costs do not represent future benefits.

Computer Software Costs

The costs that companies incur in developing computer software for sale or lease or for their own internal use are considered research and development costs until the product has proved technologically feasible. Thus, costs incurred before that point should be charged to expense when incurred. A product is deemed technologically feasible when a detailed working program has been designed. Once that occurs, all software production costs are recorded as assets, such as Technology, and are amortized over the estimated economic life of the product using the straight-line method. If at any time the company cannot expect to realize from a software product the amount of its unamortized costs on the balance sheet, the asset should be written down to the amount expected to be realized.[17]

Leasehold Improvements

As noted in Table 30-1, improvements to leased property that become the property of the lessor (the owner of the property) at the end of the lease are called leasehold improvements. Such improvements are common for both small and large businesses. A study of large companies showed that 19 percent list leasehold improvements separately; the percentage is likely to be much higher for small businesses, since they generally operate in leased premises.[18] The improvement costs are amortized over the remaining term of the lease or the useful life of the improvement, whichever is shorter. Leasehold improvements are often classified as tangible assets in the property, plant, and equipment section of the balance sheet but are included in the intangible asset section because the improvements revert to the lessor at the end of the lease and are therefore more of a right than a tangible asset.

---

[14] General Motors, *Annual Report,* 2000.

[15] Abbott Laboratories, *Annual Report,* 2000; Roche Group, *Annual Report,* 2000.

[16] *Statement of Financial Accounting Standards No. 2,* "Accounting for Research and Development Costs" (Norwalk, Conn.: Financial Accounting Standards Board, 1974), par. 12.

[17] *Statement of Financial Accounting Standards No. 86,* "Accounting for the Costs of Computer Software to be Sold, Leased, or Otherwise Marketed" (Norwalk, Conn.: Financial Accounting Standards Board, 1985).

[18] *Accounting Trends & Techniques,* 2001.

FOCUS ON INTERNATIONAL BUSINESS

Lack of Comparability Is a Real Problem!

Worldwide variability in accounting practice causes problems for those who want to compare the financial statements of companies from different countries. For example, the method of accounting for R&D costs differs, depending on the country in which a company files its financial report. In Germany, Mexico, and the United States, a company must expense its R&D costs, whereas in France, Australia, and Japan, a company may expense R&D or capitalize it (record it as an asset) if it meets certain criteria. Companies complying with the European Directives (European laws affecting financial reporting) have a choice of expensing or capitalizing R&D costs, but companies complying with International Accounting Standards (IAS) must expense research costs and capitalize development costs that meet certain conditions.[19]

Goodwill

Stop and think!
Why would a company spend millions of dollars on goodwill?

The company must be paying for anticipated superior earnings and believes it will more than recoup the goodwill it purchased.

The term *goodwill* means different things to different people. In most cases, goodwill is taken to mean the good reputation of a company. From an accounting standpoint, goodwill exists when a purchaser pays more for a business than the fair market value of the net assets if purchased individually. Because the purchaser has paid more than the fair market value of the physical assets, there must be intangible assets. If the company being purchased does not have patents, copyrights, trademarks, or other identifiable intangible assets of value, the excess payment is assumed to be for goodwill. Goodwill exists because most businesses are worth more as going concerns than as collections of assets. Goodwill reflects all the factors that allow a company to earn a higher-than-market rate of return on its assets, including customer satisfaction, good management, manufacturing efficiency, the advantages of holding a monopoly, good locations, and good employee relations. The payment above and beyond the fair market value of the tangible assets and other specific intangible assets is properly recorded in the Goodwill account.

The FASB has stated that purchased goodwill is an asset to be reported as a separate line item on the balance sheet and is subject to an annual impairment review. The impairment review requires a company to determine the reporting-unit level on which goodwill is to be tested and the specific methodology to calculate the fair value of the reporting unit. If the fair value of goodwill is less than its carrying value on the balance sheet, then goodwill is considered impaired. Impairment results in reducing goodwill to its fair value and reporting the impairment charge on the income statement. A company can perform the fair value measurement for each reporting unit at any time as long as the measurement date is consistent from year to year.[20]

Key point:
Goodwill equals purchase price minus adjusted net asset value.

Goodwill should not be recorded unless it is paid for in connection with the purchase of a whole business. The amount to be recorded as goodwill can be determined by writing the identifiable net assets up to their fair market values at the time of purchase and subtracting the total from the purchase price. For example, assume that the owners of Company A agree to sell the company for \$11,400,000. If the net assets (total assets − total liabilities) are fairly valued at \$10,000,000, then the amount of the goodwill is \$1,400,000 (\$11,400,000 − \$10,000,000). If the fair market value of the net assets is later determined to be more or less than \$10,000,000, an entry is made in the accounting records to

[19] Allan B. Afterman, *International Accounting, Financial Reporting and Analysis* (New York: Warren, Gorham & Lamont, 1995).

[20] *Statement of Financial Accounting Standards No. 144,* "Accounting for the Impairment or Disposal of Long-Lived Assets" (Norwalk, Conn.: Financial Accounting Standards Board, 2001).

FOCUS ON BUSINESS PRACTICE

Wake up, Goodwill Is Growing!

As Figure 30-7 shows, 80 percent of 600 large companies separately report goodwill as an asset. Because much of the growth of these companies has come through purchasing other companies, goodwill as a percentage of total assets has also grown. For some, the amount of goodwill is material:[21]

	Goodwill (in billions)	Percentage of Total Assets
Lucent Technologies <www.lucent.com>	\$9,945	20.4
Sara Lee Corporation <www.saralee.com>	\$2,621	22.6
Tribune Company <www.tribune.com>	\$8,496	57.9

adjust the assets to the fair market value. The goodwill would then represent the difference between the adjusted net assets and the purchase price of \$11,400,000.

SPECIAL PROBLEMS OF DEPRECIATING PLANT ASSETS 7

The illustrations used so far in this reading have been simplified to explain the concepts and methods of depreciation. In actual business practice, there is often a need to (1) calculate depreciation for partial years, (2) revise depreciation rates based on new estimates of useful life or residual value, (3) group like items when calculating depreciation, (4) account for special types of capital expenditures, and (5) use the accelerated cost recovery method for tax purposes. The next sections discuss these five cases.

Depreciation for Partial Years

So far, most illustrations of depreciation methods have assumed that plant assets were purchased at the beginning or end of an accounting period. Usually, however, businesses buy assets when they are needed and sell or discard them when they are no longer useful or needed. The time of year is normally not a factor in the decision. Consequently, it is often necessary to calculate depreciation for partial years.

For example, assume that a piece of equipment is purchased for \$3,600 and that it has an estimated useful life of six years and an estimated residual value of \$600. Assume also that it is purchased on September 5 and that the yearly accounting period ends on December 31. Depreciation must be recorded for four months, September through December, or four-twelfths of the year. This factor is applied to the calculated depreciation for the entire year. The four months' depreciation under the straight-line method is calculated as follows:

$$\frac{\$3{,}600 - \$600}{6 \text{ years}} \times 4/12 = \$167$$

[21] Lucent Technologies, *Annual Report,* 2000; Sara Lee Corporation, *Annual Report,* 2000; Tribune Company, *Annual Report,* 2000.

For the other depreciation methods, most companies compute the first year's depreciation and then multiply by the partial year factor. For example, if the company used the double-declining-balance method on the preceding equipment, the depreciation on the asset would be computed as follows:

$$\$3{,}600 \times 1/3 \times 4/12 = \$400$$

Typically, the depreciation calculation is rounded off to the nearest whole month because a partial month's depreciation is rarely material and the calculation is easier. In this case, depreciation was recorded from the beginning of September even though the purchase was made on September 5.

For all methods, the remainder (eight-twelfths) of the first year's depreciation is recorded in the next annual accounting period together with four-twelfths of the second year's depreciation.

Enrichment note:
A poor estimate can occur when a defective piece of equipment is purchased.

Revision of Depreciation Rates

Clarification note:
A change in an accounting estimate is not considered the correction of an error, but rather a revision based on new information.

Because a depreciation rate is based on an estimate of an asset's useful life, the periodic depreciation charge is seldom precise. It is sometimes very inadequate or excessive. This situation may result from an underestimate or overestimate of the asset's useful life or from a wrong estimate of the residual value. What action should be taken when it is found that after several years of use, a piece of equipment will last less time—or longer—than originally thought? Sometimes, it is necessary to revise the estimate of useful life so that the periodic depreciation expense increases or decreases. Then, to reflect the revised situation, the remaining depreciable cost of the asset is spread over the remaining years of useful life.

With this technique, the annual depreciation expense is increased or decreased to reduce the asset's carrying value to its residual value at the end of its remaining useful life. For example, assume that a delivery truck was purchased for $7,000 and has a residual value of $1,000. At the time of the purchase, the truck was expected to last six years, and it was depreciated on the straight-line basis. However, after two years of intensive use, it is determined that the truck will last only two more years, but that its estimated residual value at the end of the two years will still be $1,000. In other words, at the end of the second year, the truck's estimated useful life is reduced from six years to four years. At that time, the asset account and its related accumulated depreciation account would appear as follows:

Key point:
Allocate the remaining depreciable cost over the estimated remaining life.

Delivery Truck

Cost	7,000		

Accumulated Depreciation, Delivery Truck

		Depreciation, year 1	1,000
		Depreciation, year 2	1,000

The remaining depreciable cost is computed as follows:

Cost	minus	Depreciation Already Taken	minus	Residual Value
$7,000	−	$2,000	−	$1,000 = $4,000

The new annual periodic depreciation charge is computed by dividing the remaining depreciable cost of $4,000 by the remaining useful life of two years. Therefore, the new periodic depreciation charge is $2,000. The annual adjusting entry for depreciation for the next two years would be as follows:

Dec. 31	Depreciation Expense, Delivery Truck	2,000	
	Accumulated Depreciation, Delivery Truck		2,000
	To record depreciation expense for the year		

A = L + OE
− −

This method of revising depreciation is used widely in industry. It is also supported by *Opinion No. 9* and *Opinion No. 20* of the Accounting Principles Board of the AICPA.

Group Depreciation

To say that the estimated useful life of an asset, such as a piece of equipment, is six years means that the average piece of equipment of that type is expected to last six years. In reality, some pieces may last only two or three years, and others may last eight or nine years, or longer. For this reason, and for reasons of convenience, large companies group similar items, such as trucks or pieces of office equipment, to calculate depreciation. This method is called **group depreciation.** Group depreciation is widely used in all fields of industry and business. A survey of large businesses indicated that 65 percent used group depreciation for all or part of their plant assets.[22]

Special Types of Capital Expenditures

Companies make capital expenditures not only for plant assets, natural resources, and intangible assets but also for additions and betterments. An **addition** is an enlargement to the physical layout of a plant asset. As an example, if a new wing is added to a building, the benefits from the expenditure will be received over several years, and the amount paid for it should be debited to the asset account. A **betterment** is an improvement that does not add to the physical layout of a plant asset. Installation of an air-conditioning system is an example of a betterment that will offer benefits over a period of years; therefore, its cost should be charged to an asset account.

Enrichment note:
Other examples of betterments include replacing stairs with an escalator in a department store and paving a gravel parking lot.

Revenue expenditures for plant equipment include the repairs necessary to keep an asset in good working condition. Repairs fall into two categories: ordinary repairs and extraordinary repairs. **Ordinary repairs** are necessary to maintain an asset in good operating condition. Trucks must have periodic tune-ups, their tires and batteries must be regularly replaced, and other routine repairs must be made. Offices and halls must be painted regularly, and broken tiles or woodwork must be replaced. Such repairs are a current expense.

Extraordinary repairs are repairs of a more significant nature—they affect the estimated residual value or estimated useful life of an asset. For example, a boiler for heating a building may be given a complete overhaul, at a cost of several thousand dollars, that will extend its useful life by five years. Typically, extraordinary repairs are recorded by debiting the Accumulated Depreciation account, under the assumption that some of the depreciation previously recorded has now been eliminated. The effect of this reduction in the Accumulated Depreciation account is to increase the carrying value of the asset by the cost of the extraordinary repair. Consequently, the new carrying value of the asset should be depreciated over the new estimated useful life.

Enrichment note:
Putting a new motor in a cement mixer and replacing the roof on a building, thereby extending its life, are other examples of extraordinary repairs.

---

[22] Edward P. McTague, "Accounting for Trade-Ins of Operational Assets," *National Public Accountant* (January 1986), p. 39.

Let us assume that a machine that cost $10,000 has no residual value and an estimated useful life of ten years. After eight years, the accumulated depreciation under the straight-line method is $8,000, and the carrying value is $2,000 ($10,000 − $8,000). At that point, the machine is given a major overhaul costing $1,500. This expenditure extends the machine's useful life three years beyond the original ten years. The entry for the extraordinary repair would be as follows:

A = L + OE
+
−

Jan. 4	Accumulated Depreciation, Machinery	1,500	
	Cash		1,500
	Extraordinary repair to machinery		

The annual periodic depreciation for each of the five years remaining in the machine's useful life would be calculated as follows:

Carrying value before extraordinary repairs	$2,000
Extraordinary repairs	1,500
Total	$3,500

$$\text{Annual periodic depreciation} = \frac{\$3{,}500}{5 \text{ years}} = \$700$$

If the machine remains in use for the five years expected after the major overhaul, the total of the five annual depreciation charges of $700 will exactly equal the new carrying value, including the cost of the extraordinary repair.

Cost Recovery for Federal Income Tax Purposes

The Tax Reform Act of 1986 is arguably the most sweeping revision of federal tax laws since the original enactment of the Internal Revenue Code in 1913. First, it allows a company to expense the first $17,500 (which increases to $25,000 by tax year 2003) of equipment expenditures rather than recording them as an asset. Second, it allows a new method of writing off expenditures recorded as assets, the **Modified Accelerated Cost Recovery System (MACRS)**. MACRS discards the concepts of estimated useful life and residual value. Instead, it requires that a cost recovery allowance be computed (1) on the unadjusted cost of property being recovered, and (2) over a period of years prescribed by the law for all property of similar types. The accelerated method prescribed under MACRS for most property other than real estate is 200 percent declining balance with a half-year convention (only one half-year's depreciation is allowed in the year of purchase, and one half-year's depreciation is taken in the last year). In addition, the period over which the cost may be recovered is specified. Recovery of the cost of property placed in service after December 31, 1986, is calculated as prescribed in the 1986 law.

Congress hoped that MACRS would encourage businesses to invest in new plant and equipment by allowing them to write off such assets rapidly. MACRS accelerates the write-off of these investments in two ways. First, the prescribed recovery periods are often shorter than the estimated useful lives used for calculating depreciation for the financial statements. Second, the accelerated method allowed under the new law enables businesses to recover most of the cost of their investments early in the depreciation process.

Clarification note: MACRS depreciation is used for tax purposes only. It cannot be used for financial reporting.

Tax methods of depreciation are not usually acceptable for financial reporting under generally accepted accounting principles because the recovery periods are shorter than the depreciable assets' estimated useful lives.

REVIEW 8

Review of Learning Objectives

Long-term assets are assets that are used in the operation of a business, are not intended for resale, and have a useful life of more than one year. Long-term assets are either tangible or intangible. In the former category are land, plant assets, and natural resources. In the latter are trademarks, patents, franchises, goodwill, and other rights. The accounting issues associated with long-term assets relate to the decision to acquire the assets, the means of financing the assets, and the methods of accounting for the assets.

It is important to distinguish between capital expenditures, which are recorded as assets, and revenue expenditures, which are recorded as expenses. The error of classifying one as the other will have an important effect on net income. The acquisition cost of property, plant, and equipment includes all expenditures that are reasonable and necessary to get such an asset in place and ready for use. Among these expenditures are purchase price, installation cost, freight charges, and insurance during transit.

Depreciation is the periodic allocation of the cost of a plant asset over its estimated useful life. It is recorded by debiting Depreciation Expense and crediting a related contra-asset account called Accumulated Depreciation. Factors that affect the computation of depreciation are cost, residual value, depreciable cost, and estimated useful life. Depreciation is commonly computed by the straight-line method, the production method, or an accelerated method. The straight-line method is related directly to the passage of time, whereas the production method is related directly to use. An accelerated method, which results in relatively large amounts of depreciation in earlier years and reduced amounts in later years, is based on the assumption that plant assets provide greater economic benefit in their earlier years than in later years. The most common accelerated method is the declining-balance method.

Long-term depreciable assets may be disposed of by being discarded, sold, or exchanged. When long-term assets are disposed of, it is necessary to record the depreciation up to the date of disposal and to remove the carrying value from the accounts by removing the cost from the asset account and the depreciation to date from the accumulated depreciation account. If a long-term asset is sold at a price that differs from its carrying value, the gain or loss should be recorded and reported on the income statement. In recording exchanges of similar plant assets, a gain or loss may arise. Losses, but not gains, should be recognized at the time of the exchange. When a gain is not recognized, the new asset is recorded at the carrying value of the old asset plus any cash paid. For income tax purposes, neither gains nor losses are recognized in the exchange of similar assets. When dissimilar assets are exchanged, gains and losses are recognized under both accounting and income tax rules.

Natural resources are depletable assets that are converted to inventory by cutting, pumping, mining, or other forms of extraction. Natural resources are recorded at cost as long-term assets. They are allocated as expenses through depletion charges as the resources are sold. The depletion charge is based on the ratio of the resource extracted to the total estimated resource. A major issue related to this subject is accounting for oil and gas reserves.

The purchase of an intangible asset should be treated as a capital expenditure and recorded at acquisition cost, which in turn should be amortized over the useful life of the asset. The FASB requires that research and development costs be treated as revenue expenditures and charged as expenses in the periods of expenditure. Software costs are treated as research and development costs and expensed until a feasible working program is developed, after which time the costs may be capitalized and amortized over a reasonable estimated life. Goodwill is the excess of the amount paid for the purchase of a business over the fair market value of the net assets and is usually related to the superior earning potential of the business. It should be recorded only if paid for in connection with the purchase of a business, and it should be reviewed annually for possible impairment.

Supplemental Objective

In actual business practice, many factors affect depreciation calculations. It may be necessary to calculate depreciation for partial years because assets are bought and sold throughout the year, or to revise depreciation rates because of changed conditions. Because it is often difficult to estimate the useful life of a single item, and because it is more convenient, many large businesses group similar items for purposes of depreciation. Companies must also consider certain special capital expenditures when calculating depreciation. For example, expenditures for additions and betterments are capital expenditures. Extraordinary repairs, which increase the residual value or extend the life of an asset, are also treated as capital expenditures, but ordinary repairs are revenue expenditures. For income tax purposes, rapid write-offs of depreciable assets are allowed under the Modified Accelerated Cost Recovery System. Such rapid write-offs are not usually acceptable for financial accounting because the shortened recovery periods violate the matching rule.

REVIEW OF CONCEPTS AND TERMINOLOGY

The following concepts and terms were introduced in this reading:

Accelerated method: A method of depreciation that allocates relatively large amount of the depreciable cost of an asset to earlier years and reduced amounts to later years.

Addition: An enlargement to the physical layout of a plant asset.

Amortization: The periodic allocation of the cost of an intangible asset to the periods it benefits.

Asset impairment: Loss of revenue-generating potential of a long-lived asset before the end of its useful life; the difference between an asset's carrying value and its fair value, as measured by the present value of the expected cash flows.

Betterment: An improvement that does not add to the physical layout of a plant asset.

Brand name: A registered name that can be used only by its owner to identify a product or service.

Capital expenditure: An expenditure for the purchase or expansion of a long-term asset, recorded in an asset account.

Carrying value: The unexpired part of the cost of an asset, not its market value. Also called *book value.*

Copyright: An exclusive right granted by the federal government to reproduce and sell literary, musical, and other artistic materials and computer programs for a period of the author's life plus 70 years.

Customer list: A list of customers or subscribers.

Declining-balance method: An accelerated method of depreciation in which depreciation is computed by applying a fixed rate to the carrying value (the declining balance) of a tangible long-lived asset.

Depletion: The exhaustion of a natural resource through mining, cutting, pumping, or other extraction, and the way in which the cost is allocated.

Depreciable cost: The cost of an asset less its residual value.

Depreciation: The periodic allocation of the cost of a tangible long-lived asset (other than land and natural resources) over its estimated useful life.

Double-declining-balance method: An accelerated method of depreciation in which a fixed rate equal to twice the straight-line percentage is applied to the carrying value (the declining balance) of a tangible long-lived asset.

Estimated useful life: The total number of service units expected from a long-term asset.

Expenditure: A payment or an obligation to make future payment for an asset or a service.

Extraordinary repairs: Repairs that affect the estimated residual value or estimated useful life of an asset thereby increasing its carrying value.

Franchise: The right or license to an exclusive territory or market.

Full-costing: A method of accounting for the costs of exploring and developing oil and gas resources in which all costs are recorded as assets and depleted over the estimated life of the producing resources.

Goodwill: The excess of the cost of a group of assets (usually a business) over the fair market value of the net assets if purchased individually.

Group depreciation: The grouping of similar items to calculate depreciation.

Intangible assets: Long-term assets with no physical substance whose value is based on rights or advantages accruing to the owner.

Leasehold: A right to occupy land or buildings under a long-term rental contract.

Leasehold improvements: Improvements to leased property that become the property of the lessor at the end of the lease.

License: The right to use a formula, technique, process, or design.

Long-term assets: Assets that have a useful life of more than one year, are acquired for use in the operation of a business, and are not intended for resale. Less commonly called *fixed assets.*

Modified Accelerated Cost Recovery System (MACRS): A mandatory system of depreciation for income tax purposes, enacted by Congress in 1986, that requires a cost recovery allowance to be computed (1) on the unadjusted cost of property being recovered, and (2) over a period of years prescribed by the law for all property of similar types.

Natural resources: Long-term assets purchased for the economic value that can be taken from the land and used up.

Noncompete covenant: A contract limiting the rights of others to compete in a specific industry or line of business for a specified period.

Obsolescence: The process of becoming out of date, which is a factor in the limited useful life of tangible assets.

Ordinary repairs: Repairs necessary to maintain an asset in good operating condition, which are recorded as current period expenses.

Patent: An exclusive right granted by the federal government for a period of 20 years to make a particular product or use a specific process or design.

Physical deterioration: Limitations on the useful life of a depreciable asset resulting from use and from exposure to the elements.

Production method: A method of depreciation that assumes depreciation is solely the result of use and that allocates depreciation based on the units of output or use during each period of an asset's useful life.

Residual value: The estimated net scrap, salvage, or trade-in value of a tangible asset at the estimated date of disposal. Also called *salvage value* or *disposal value.*

Revenue expenditure: An expenditure related to repair, maintenance, and operation of a long-term asset, recorded by a debit to an expense account.

Straight-line method: A method of depreciation that assumes depreciation depends only on the passage of time and that allocates an equal amount of depreciation to each accounting period in an asset's useful life.

Successful efforts accounting: A method of accounting for the costs of exploring and developing oil and gas resources in which successful exploration is recorded as an asset and depleted over the estimated life of the resource and all unsuccessful efforts are immediately written off as losses.

Tangible assets: Long-term assets that have physical substance.

Technology: Capitalized costs associated with software developed for sale, lease, or internal use and amortized over the estimated economic life of the software.

Trademark: A registered symbol or brand name that can be used only by its owner to identify a product or service.

READING 31

ACCOUNTING INCOME AND ASSETS: THE ACCRUAL CONCEPT

LEARNING OUTCOMES

The candidate should be able to:

a. describe the format of the income statement and describe the components of net income;

b. explain the importance of the matching principle for revenue and expense recognition, identify the requirements for revenue recognition to occur, identify and describe the appropriate revenue recognition, given the status of completion of the earning process and the assurance of payment, and discuss different revenue recognition methods and their implications for financial analysis;

c. identify the appropriate income statement and balance sheet entries using the percentage-of-completion method and the completed contract method and describe and calculate the effects on cash flows and selected financial ratios that result from using the percentage-of-completion method versus the completed contract method;

d. describe the types and analysis of unusual or infrequent items, extraordinary items, discontinued operations, accounting changes, and prior period adjustments;

e. discuss managerial discretion in areas such as classification of good news/bad news, income smoothing, big bath behavior, and accounting changes, and explain how this discretion can affect the financial statements;

f. describe the format and the components of the balance sheet and describe the format, classification, and use of each component of the statement of stockholders' equity.

1 INTRODUCTION

The primary objective of this book is to help users of financial statements develop the skills needed to analyze financial statement data and use these data when making rational investment, credit, and similar decisions. Such decisions require comparison of the risk and return characteristics of alternative investments. Risk and return projections depend on income and cash flow forecasts and assessments of firm assets and liabilities.

Financial statements are the starting point for analysis as they report data about income, cash flows, and assets and liabilities that users can tailor to their specific needs. To do so, they need to understand the information provided by financial statements and the shortcomings of those data. In addition, financial statement users must be able to rearrange the information provided in a manner consistent with their objectives.

The first question is, How should income and cash flow be defined and measured? Are they simply the amounts provided by financial statements or should reported amounts be adjusted? Reporting methods, measurement techniques, and the presentation of financial information can all be criticized in many cases; good analysis requires skepticism.

Comprehensive financial analysis, therefore, requires a thorough understanding of the financial reporting system and its output. Reading 29 provided a general overview of the accounting process, the reporting system, and their product: the financial statements. We are now ready for the next step. This reading deals with the income statement and balance sheet—products of the accrual system of accounting. Reading 33 considers the statement of cash flows. For exposition purposes, we use Pfizer's financial statements.

2 INCOME, CASH FLOWS, AND ASSETS: DEFINITIONS AND RELATIONSHIPS

As background for the discussion of net income and cash flows in this and in reading 33, we first examine conceptual definitions of "income." We will then explore the relationship between these concepts of income and "accounting income" reported by the current financial reporting system. We use insights from this discussion to delve into the relationship among income, cash flows, and assets as the first stage of the development of our understanding of "return" in our study of comparative risk–return analyses. Later readings will broaden our understanding of the analysis and use of financial statement information in the evaluation of different elements of risk and return.

This section introduces several conceptual definitions of income, measured in terms of cash flows and changes in the market values of assets.

In a world of certainty,[1] the interrelationship among income, cash flow, and assets is captured by the concept of *economic earnings*, defined as net cash flow plus the change in market value of the firm's net assets. The market value of the firm's assets in this certain world is equal to the present value of their future cash flows discounted at the (risk-free) rate r.

We illustrate this concept using a two-period model with the following assumptions:

- The entity has a single asset, an investment with zero liquidation value.
- The entity has no debt; the asset is 100% equity financed.
- The investment generates a return of $100 at the end of each of two years.
- The $100 received at the end of year 1 is distributed to the owners and not reinvested in the firm.
- The (risk-free) rate r equals 5%.

Because the cash received at the end of each period equals $100 and $r = 5\%$, the value of the firm's assets is

Beginning of period 1 = $\$100/(1.05) + \$100/(1.05)^2 = \$185.94$
Beginning of period 2 = $\$100/(1.05) = \$95.24$

and economic earnings equals cash flow plus the change in net asset value:[2]

Period 1: $\$100 + (\$95.24 - \$185.94) = \$9.30$
Period 2: $\$100 + (\$0 - \$95.24) = \$4.76$

Note that economic income in each year is equal to the rate of return times the opening value of the assets:

Period 1: $0.05 \times \$185.94 = \$9.30$
Period 2: $0.05 \times \$95.24 = \$4.76$

Equivalently, the market value at the beginning of the period is equal to a (constant) multiple of earnings equal to $1/r$. In this example, the price/earnings multiple is 20 (1/0.05).

However, future cash flows and interest rates are uncertain in the real world, and the interrelationships are not as neat. Therefore, market prices of assets are also uncertain;[3] available prices may be difficult to relate to the present value of generally unknown, estimated future cash flows discounted at estimated interest rates. These estimates of future cash flows and interest rates and their interrelationships depend on the expectations of different decision makers.

Moreover, the market value of an asset may be measured with different levels of reliability using various (often inconsistent) methods, for example, at its replacement cost or liquidating value. *In this world of uncertainty, income (however measured) is, at best, only a proxy for economic income.* Thus, economists, analysts, and

---

[1] This would include perfect financial markets.

[2] The change in net asset value in this example is often referred to as economic depreciation (see Reading 41).

[3] Some assets are heavily traded on regulated markets (common stock of companies like Pfizer and Sears), others may be thinly traded (stocks of small companies), and still others have limited secondary markets from which verifiable prices can be obtained (most manufacturing equipment).

others have developed a number of analytic and practical definitions of earnings to serve as proxies for economic earnings.

Distributable earnings are defined as the amount of earnings that can be paid out as dividends without changing the value of the firm. This concept is derived from the Hicksian definition of income:

> The amount that a person can consume during a period of time and be as well off at the end of that time as at the beginning.[4]

A related measure, *sustainable income,* refers to the level of income that can be maintained in the future given the firm's stock of capital investment (e.g., fixed assets and inventory).

Another measure, *permanent earnings,*[5] used by analysts for valuation purposes is the amount that can be normally earned given the firm's assets and equals the market value of those assets times the firm's required rate of return. Similar to economic earnings, it is the base to which a multiple is applied to arrive at a "fair price."[6]

All these definitions are attempts to capture the concept of economic earnings. Box 31-1 provides a discussion of the difficulties associated with applying these concepts in practice due to measurement and asset valuation problems.

As a result of these difficulties, the financial reporting concept of income—*accounting income*—is often quite different. The analyst, therefore, needs to relate accounting income to the economic income concepts just discussed.

Accounting income is measured using the accrual concept and provides information about the ability of the enterprise to generate future cash flows. It is not, *a priori,* equivalent to any of the definitions discussed earlier.

3 THE ACCRUAL CONCEPT OF INCOME

Accounting and economic income both define income as the sum of cash flows and changes in net assets. However, in financial reporting, the determination of

- Which cash flows are included in income and when
- Which changes in asset and liability values are included in income
- How and when the selected changes in asset and liability values are measured

are based on accounting rules and principles that make up generally accepted accounting principles (GAAP). With a few exceptions, the accounting process only recognizes value changes arising from actual transactions.

Accounting income represents a *selective* recognition of both current period actual cash flows and changes in asset values. Reported income under the accrual concept provides a measure of current operating performance[7] that is not solely based on actual current period cash flows. Cash inflows and outflows (past, present, and future) are recognized in income in the "appropriate" accounting periods, that is, as goods and services are provided and used rather than as cash is collected and expenditures incurred. *The selected period "best" indicates the firm's present and continuing ability to generate future cash flows.*

---

[4] J. R. Hicks, *Value and Capital,* 2nd ed. (Oxford: Chaundon Press, 1946), p. 176.

[5] Normalized earnings and earnings power are similar concepts.

[6] The price/earnings ratio used by analysts represents this conceptual relationship.

[7] However, see the discussion of nonrecurring items later in this reading.

BOX 31-1 ELABORATION OF CONCEPTUAL INCOME, CASH FLOW, AND ASSET RELATIONSHIPS

The following discussion assumes that all income is paid out as dividends, allowing us to avoid considering reinvestment of income in the firm.

Case A

Assume that a firm purchases an asset at the beginning of each period for $10 and sells it for $12 at the end of each period. Further, assume that this markup of 20% is equivalent to the interest (discount) rate.* Under these conditions, the market value of the firm at the beginning of the period equals the $10 paid for the asset.

The market value of $10 can be derived in a single- or muliperiod context. For a single period, the present value of the end-of-period cash flow is $12/1.20 = $10. If we use a multiperiod model, the firm will earn $2 ($12 sale price less $10 cost of asset). The present value of $2 per period earned for an infinite period equals $2/0.20 = $10.

The economic earnings of the firm equal the cash flow of $2 ($12 − $10), the expected level of earnings in the future; the market value of the firm is a constant $10. Based on this same calculation, the distributable income is also $2, since paying out $2 will not change the value of the firm. Similarly, sustainable income is also $2, as that amount can be distributed without altering the firm's level of operations (buying and selling one asset per period). Finally, since the value of the firm is $10, permanent earnings equal $2 (0.2 × $10). Thus, economic, distributable, sustainable, and permanent earnings are all identical in this simplified case.

However, introducing uncertainty and changing one assumption make the problem much more complex.

Case B

Now assume that the sale price of the asset suddenly increases to $13.20. Accordingly, the purchase price of the asset should also increase as its one-period present value is now $13.20/1.20 = $11.00. Thus, if the firm replaces the asset at the end of that period, economic earnings are the sum of the cash flow of $2.20 ($13.20 − $11.00) and an increase in the market value of the firm of $1.00 (from $10.00 to $11.00), for a total of $3.20.

What are the expected earnings of the firm, given the change in the value of the asset? The answer is clearly not $3.20. It depends on the assumption one makes as to the level of operations the firm maintains.

Maintenance of Physical Level of Assets

If the firm retains the original level of *physical* assets, now valued at $11.00, the expected earnings are $2.20 (20% of $11.00). Note that economic earnings now have two components: operating earnings of $2.20 and a *holding gain* of $1.00. The holding gain results from owning an asset while its market value increases. This "onetime" occurrence cannot be expected to recur. Expected earnings would be the operating earnings as this amount can be expected to continue into the future given the level of physical assets.†

Maintenance of Monetary Level of Assets

If we assume that the asset is divisible and the firm does not replace the entire asset but only maintains its *monetary* level of assets by purchasing $10.00 of the now more expensive asset, economic earnings for the current period will still be $3.20.

Net cash flow will be $3.20 ($13.20 sales proceeds − $10.00 reinvestment). Since the market value of assets remains $10.00, economic earnings are $3.20 as above. Expected earnings, however, differ. If the firm retains the original level of monetary assets of $10.00, expected earnings are $2.00 (20% of $10.00).

What happens to the other definitions of income under this scenario? Distributable income is $3.20, which maintains the initial wealth level of $10.00, equivalent to economic earnings. However, sustainable income, the achievable earnings level of the firm in the future, is only $2.00 (if we assume that $3.20 is distributed).

However, if the firm maintains the same physical level of assets and we consider the Hicksian definition of income in terms of the physical measure of assets, both distributable and sustainable income equal $2.20. Similarly, permanent earnings depend on whether the firm retains its original physical asset base (whose value is now $11.00), or whether it retains its original monetary asset base of $10.00. In the former case, permanent earnings are $2.20; in the latter, they will be $2.00.

Under real-world conditions, income measures become judgmental. The neat mappings from one definition to another no longer hold as they become situation specific.

* Under conditions of certainty, the rate of return earned on the asset (the 20% markup) equals the prevailing interest rate.

† See Box 19-2 for an elaboration of the differing market valuation of permanent and transitory earnings components.

The accrual concept of accounting income assumes that forecasts of future cash flows require more than historical cash flow data:

> Information about enterprise earnings based on accrual accounting generally provides a better indication of an enterprise's present and continuing ability to generate cash flows than information limited to the financial effects of cash receipts and payments.[8]

The accrual basis of accounting thus allocates (recognizes as revenue and expense) many transactions and events producing cash flows to time periods other than those in which the cash flows occur. Accrual accounting principles are, fundamentally, the decision rules that tell preparers of financial statements when to recognize the revenue and expense consequences of cash flows and other events.

The recognition of revenues and expenses in periods other than when cash is actually received or spent has a corollary effect on the balance sheet. *Under accrual accounting, both the recognition and measurement of certain assets and liabilities are results of the application of the accrual concept of income.* The differences between the income recognized and actual cash flows for the period are *accrued* as assets or liabilities.

In case A in Box 31-1, we assume that an item purchased for $10 at the beginning of period 1 is sold for $12 at the end of that period and replaced at the start of the next period at a cost of $10. If we further assume that the sale is made on credit and cash will be collected in the following period, the actual cash outflow in period 1 is $10, the cost of acquiring the asset at the beginning of period 1.

Under accrual accounting, revenue (expected future cash flow) is recognized at the time of sale, and is reported as an increase of $12 in the asset "accounts receivable." Income is measured as the change in assets plus actual cash flows:

Income = $12 Increase in accounts receivable − $10 Cash outflow = $2

Which is a better indicator of the earning power of the firm and its ability to generate future cash flows: the cash outflow of $10 or the income of $2? The accrual accounting concept reports income of $2, providing better forward-looking information than pure cash flow accounting.

The Matching Principle. Revenue and expense recognition are also governed by the *matching principle,* which states that operating performance can be measured only if related revenues and expenses are accounted for during the same time period. It is the matching principle that requires the expense (cost of goods sold) of inventory to be recognized in the same period in which the sale of that inventory is recorded. This facilitates measurement of the periodic income, that is, operating performance generated by selling inventories during the period regardless of when collections or expenditures occur. In the previous example, if we assume that the item also was purchased on credit in period 1 with payment expected in the following period, accrual accounting would still recognize income of $2 in period 1:

Income = $12 Increase in accounts receivable −
$10 Increase in accounts payable = $2

Over the life of the firm, income and cash flows converge. They differ only as to timing of recognition. The recognition of revenues and expenses in "appro-

[8] SFAC 1. Objectives of Financial Reporting by Business Enterprises (November 1978), p. ix.

priate" accounting periods is both the strength and the weakness of the accrual method. It is a strength in that it results in more meaningful measurement of current operating performance (income statement) and is a better indicator of future operating performance and earnings power. If accrual accounting did not exist, financial analysts would have to invent it.[9] The weakness is that the amount and timing of accruals are subject to management discretion and are based on assumptions and estimates that can and do change over time. Analysts need to differentiate between real events and accruals stemming from management choice.

Overall, as the empirical evidence in Box 31-2 indicates, the accrual process does provide information and enhances the predictive ability of cash flows. However, as the evidence also indicates (and as we elaborate on in Reading 33), it does not mean that cash flows are not relevant. They provide information as to the *quality* of accounting earnings and can be used to mitigate the weaknesses of the accrual process.

The determination of accounting earnings is also governed by:

- General principles and measurement rules underlying all accounting transactions and events
- Specific rules to determine revenue, expense, gain, and loss recognition

For example, the *historical cost-based* approach underlying GAAP results in rules that exclude from income *many* unrealized holding gains or losses (increases/decreases in the market value of certain assets and liabilities held by the firm). Recognition of these gains/losses must await the disposal of the assets and the retirement or settlement of the liabilities.

However, some nontransaction-related changes in asset values *can* affect reported income. For example,

- Current assets must be evaluated at each financial statement date and any estimated declines in asset values recognized as losses.
- SFAS 121, Accounting for the Impairment of Long-Lived Assets and for Long-Lived Assets to Be Disposed of, extended this requirement to most classes of fixed assets. The amount and timing of loss recognition remain substantively discretionary because these assets must be evaluated for declines only when certain impairment criteria are present.[10]
- Certain investments in securities are marked to market and changes in market value are reported as a component of income.[11]

Generally, although changes in market values of assets and liabilities may occur over a number of periods, they are recognized in income either in the period of sale or disposal or when certain impairment criteria are met. The result is current period income that may be distorted and may not be indicative of normal earning power. As an initial step, one needs to understand the components that make up the income statement.

---

[9] This occasionally happens. Because of the deficiencies of (cash-based) regulatory accounting in the insurance industry, analysts developed methods of analysis in the 1960s that eventually were adopted as GAAP by the industry. More recently, German analysts developed their own method of adjusting tax-based income statements.

[10] Reading 41 for a discussion of this standard.

[11] Other investments in securities also are reported at fair value with the unrealized gains and losses accumulated in "other comprehensive income"; these changes are moved to income when the investments are sold. See Chapter 13 for a discussion of the accounting for investments in securities.

BOX 31-2 ACCRUAL INCOME VERSUS CASH FLOW: SOME EMPIRICAL EVIDENCE

OPTIONAL SEGMENT

A number of empirical studies have compared the benefits of accrual income with those of cash flows. Some of these studies asked whether one of the measures provided incremental information,* given the other measure. Those studies† offer consistent evidence that, given cash flows from operations (CFO), accruals give incremental information, and given accrual income, CFO provides incremental information.

Bernard and Stober (1989) noted that the variation in cash flow results found by some studies may be caused by using models that do not capture the specific implications of any particular company or situation. That is, in many cases the relative benefits of accruals versus cash flows may be firm-, industry-, and/or situation-specific; they suggest that "further progress in this line of research will require a better understanding of the economic context in which the implications of detailed earnings components are interpreted."‡

Livnat and Zarowin (1990) found that, although aggregate CFO did not provide additional informational content, individual components from both CFO and financing cash flows did add incremental information. This, however, does not mean that cash flow information is superior to accrual information as the relevant comparison would have to be with individual components of accrual income.

Dechow (1994) compared accrual income directly with CFO showing that accrual income more closely measured *firm performance as reflected in stock returns*. Moreover, she found that the "superiority" of accrual income as a predictor of stock returns was more likely to occur when cash flows have significant timing and matching problems. That is, accrual income performed better:

OPTIONAL SEGMENT ENDS

The shorter the interval over which performance is measured

The more volatile the working capital requirements and investment and financing activities

The longer the operating cycle of the firm§

Dechow, Kothari, and Watts (1998) showed (consistent with our conjecture in the chapter) that accrual income is a *better predictor of future (operating) cash flows* than current (operating) cash flows (CFO) themselves. Barth, Cram, and Nelson (2001) extended Dechow et al.'s model and found that disaggregating accrual income into its major components** significantly enhanced the predictive ability of operating cash flows incremental to current cash flow itself and aggregate accrual earnings.

Sloan (1996), on the other hand, found that the CFO component of income was more "persistent" than the accrual component; that is, CFO levels achieved were more likely to carry into the future, whereas accruals were (relative to CFO) more transitory and likely to be reversed. Sloan noted that this finding supported financial analysts who compare CFO with reported net income to test the "quality of earnings." Interestingly, Sloan also found that the market seemed to ignore this distinction, lending credence to investing strategies that attempted to find mispriced securities by exploiting the differences between CFO and net income.

---

* In Chapter 5, we provide a more detailed look at and critique of the nature of the "information content" line of empirical research.

† See, for example, Judy Rayburn (1986), Wilson (1986), and Bowen, Burgstahler, and Dailey (1987).

‡ Victor Bernard and Thomas Stober, "The Nature and Amount of Information in Cash Flows and Accruals," *Accounting Review* (October 1989), p. 648 Dechow (1994), Dechow et al. (1998), and Barth et al. (2001) also examined some of these factors.

§ Similarly, Dechow et al. and Barth et al., using predictive ability of future CFO as the object of interest, also found their results to vary with the length of the operating cash cycle.

** The components they examined (in addition to cash from operations) were changes in accounts receivable, inventory, accounts payable, depreciation, amortization, and other accruals.

Income Statement

Format and Classification

U.S. GAAP do not specify the format of the income statement. Actual formats vary across companies, especially in the reporting of the gain or loss on sale of assets, equity in earnings of affiliates, and other nonoperating income and expense. In some cases, income statement detail appears in financial statement footnotes. Consequently, the sample format presented below should be viewed in a generic sense rather than as a strict rendition of how an income statement is laid out:

Sample Income Statement Format

	Revenues from the sales of goods and services:
+	Other income and revenues
−	Operating expenses
−	Financing costs
+/−	Unusual or infrequent items
=	Pretax earnings from continuing operations
−	Income tax expense
=	Net income from continuing operations*
+/−	Income from discontinued operations (net of tax)*
+/−	Extraordinary items (net of tax)*
+/−	Cumulative effect of accounting changes (net of tax)*
=	Net income*

*Per share amounts are reported for each of these items.

IAS Presentation Requirements

IAS 1 (revised 1997) governs the presentation of financial statements prepared in accordance with IAS GAAP. The requirements are broadly similar to those under U.S. GAAP in that financial statement preparers are permitted considerable flexibility as to format as long as all required information is disclosed either on the face of the financial statements or in the financial statement notes. IAS 1 specifically allows for presentation of the income statement in either of two formats:

1. Classification of expenses by function (the format shown above).
2. Classification of expenses based on their nature. Under this alternative, the company reports expenditures using categories such as raw materials, employees, and changes in inventories.

Components of Net Income

The format typically found in actual statements may not be the most useful for analytical purposes. It is important for the analyst to be cognizant of the various categories or groupings into which the income statement components *can* be combined. These groupings do not necessarily coincide with the classifications presented in actual financial statements (or our sample income statement above). In our discussion of the income statement components, we shall follow the suggested groupings presented below. These groupings provide information about different aspects of a firm's operations:

Suggested Format

	Revenues from the sales of goods and services
−	Operating expenses
=	Operating income from continuing operations
+	Other income and revenues
=	Recurring income before interest and taxes from continuing operations
−	Financing costs
=	Recurring (pretax) income from continuing operations
+/−	Unusual or infrequent items
=	Pretax earnings from continuing operations
−	Income tax expense
=	Net income from continuing operations
+/−	Income from discontinued operations (net of tax)
+/−	Extraordinary items (net of tax)
+/−	Cumulative effect of accounting changes (net of tax)
=	Net income

The income statement reports revenues generated by the sales of goods and services from a firm's continuing operations. The costs and expenses incurred to generate these revenues follow. The costs of manufacturing or purchasing the goods sold are normally listed first since they are directly related to the period's revenues. Indirect costs of selling and administrative activities and expense categories such as research and development are reported next. The excess of revenues over these costs and expenses (excluding interest expense) measures the firm's *operating income from continuing operations*, which is independent of its capital structure.

In addition to its core business, a firm may have income (loss) from other activities, such as interest or dividends from investments, equity in (share of) the income of its unconsolidated affiliates, and gains or losses on sales or disposal of assets. *Recurring earnings before interest and taxes from continuing operations* usually include these items and are also independent of the firm's capital structure. Deducting financing costs (interest expense) results in *recurring (pretax) income from continuing operations.*

Unusual or infrequent items, such as pretax gains and losses from the sale or impairment of assets or investments,[12] are often shown as separate line items yielding *pretax income from continuing operations.* Income tax expense is usually the final deduction before arriving at *net income from continuing operations.*

The income statement effects of discontinued operations (discussed later in this reading) are segregated and reported net of income tax to emphasize the fact that these operations will not contribute to future revenues and income. The

[12] The appropriate income statement classification of such items and their analytic significance are discussed later in this reading.

[13] Actual cash flows are not affected by accounting changes unless the firm also changes the method used for income tax reporting (e.g., LIFO, discussed in reading 39). However, changes in accounting methods may affect the classification of cash flows, as discussed in reading 33.

net of tax effect of "extraordinary items" is also reported separately because they are incidental to the firm's operating activities, unusual in nature, and not expected to be a normal, recurring component of income and cash flows.

Finally, the income statement separately reports the cumulative effect of accounting changes adopted during the period since they are unrelated to the period's income or operating activities and rarely have any cash flow consequences.[13] Footnotes provide detailed information on both mandatory and voluntary changes in accounting methods, which must be analyzed to evaluate the impact on present and future reported earnings.

A more detailed description and discussion of an income statement and related footnotes, using Pfizer, Inc. as an example, are provided in Box 31-3.

Changes in Income Statement Presentation. Companies sometimes change their income statement presentation in order to obscure unfavorable trends. IBM provides an instructive example. Through 1999, the company listed revenues and various expenses in its income statement separately, showing gross profit, operating income, and net income. Using the 1999 format, the analyst could compute the following trends in operating income[14] and net income.

	Years Ended December 31		
	1997	**1998**	**1999**
Percentage change in operating income	5.84%	0.73%	30.15%
Percentage change in net income	12.23%	3.87%	21.87%

In 2000, IBM changed its income statement format to exclude the line item, "operating income," from its income statement. The company continued to report all other line items included in income statements in prior years. This permits us to extend the table through 2000:

	Years Ended December 31			
	1997	**1998**	**1999**	**2000**
Percentage change in operating income	5.84%	0.73%	30.15%	−2.46%
Percentage change in net income	12.23%	3.87%	21.87%	4.94%

Why did IBM change the income statement format? We assume that the company did not wish to highlight the decline in operating income. The lesson is that analysts should use their own formats, allowing them to see trends that management may wish to conceal. Using the same format for all companies within an industry also facilitates comparisons.

Recurring versus Nonrecurring Items

Reported net income is only loosely related to the concept of *comprehensive income* discussed in Reading 29. It contains income from operations as well as all realized (but only some unrealized) changes in the market value of assets and liabilities.

---

[14] See Case 17-1 for a comprehensive analysis of IBM's income statement.

BOX 31-3 PFIZER, INC. INCOME STATEMENT COMPONENTS

OPTIONAL SEGMENT

Pfizer's 1997–1999 income statements illustrate the format used by a manufacturing company. Comments on the individual line items are provided in this box. In addition, we provide below an index listing the readings containing detailed discussions of selected components of the income statement:

Income Statement Component	Reading
Net sales–revenue recognition	2
Alliance revenues	2
Costs and operating expenses, which include:	
Cost of sales (Note 1-C)	6
Employee benefits	12
Amortization of goodwill and other intangibles (Note 8)	14
Depreciation expense (Note 1-D)	8
Research and development	7
Other income (Note 8), which includes:	
Interest Income	2
Interest expense (net of capitalized interest)	7, 10
Asset impairments	8, 14
Restructuring charges	2
Gain (loss) on foreign currency transactions	15
Legal settlements	2
Other "nonrecurring" items	2
Minority interests	13
Income taxes	9
Discontinued operations	2
Earnings per share	4

Net sales include proceeds from human and animal pharmaceutical product sales. Pfizer also reports alliance revenues (generally, a percentage of partners' sales) from co-promoted products developed by other companies. Reported revenue may not be comparable across firms because it depends on management's choice of revenue recognition methods and significant estimates and assumptions.

OPTIONAL SEGMENT ENDS

Costs and operating (selling, informational, and administrative) expenses include the majority of the costs of producing the medical products that constitute Pfizer's operations. Cost of sales includes the cost of raw materials, supplies, and manufacturing outlays. Pfizer's 1999 cost of sales also includes a $310 million write-off of excess inventories of a suspended drug (Note 1-C) and a $6.6 million benefit of a change to the first-in, first-out (FIFO) inventory costing method (Note 6).

Depreciation expense reflects the allocation of past expenditures for property, plant, and equipment. Goodwill amortization (reported in the other deductions—net component) represents a systematic allocation of the excess purchase price (over fair value) of net assets acquired. Pfizer's expenditures for *research and development* are expensed in the period incurred as required by U.S. GAAP.

*Selling, general, and administrative expenses** *(SG&A)* include operating expenses not reported as components of costs of goods sold. The division between costs of goods sold and SG&A depends on the company's accounting choices, and the breakdown may not be comparable among firms. SG&A expenses are not always directly related to sales levels as they contain fixed components. In Note 1-H, Pfizer separately reports its accounting policies and annual expense for advertising and promotional activities.

In *other deductions* (see Note 8) Pfizer reports interest income, interest expense (net of capitalized interest), and costs of legal settlements. The company also incurred a loss on foreign currency transactions.

Note 8 also shows that, in 1998, the company recorded $177 million of restructuring charges and $213 million in asset impairments for workforce reductions and plant and product lines rationalizations. These restructuring plans were substantially completed in 1999. In 1998, Pfizer recorded large expenses for co-promotion payments to Searle and for a contribution to the Pfizer Foundation.

Interest expense reflects financing charges net of capitalized interest. The recognition of minority interest in consolidated subsidiaries and a *provision for income taxes* completes the computation of income from continuing operations.

Note 2, Discontinued Operations, reports a 1999 payment of $20 million to settle antitrust charges concerning a business group divested in 1996. *Earnings per share* are reported separately for income from continuing operations, loss from discontinued operations, and net income. Note 15, earnings per common share, discloses and reconciles the number of shares used to compute both basic and diluted per-share amounts. The note also reports the effect of dilutive securities.

*Unlike most companies, Pfizer uses the term *selling, informational, and administrative (SI&A) expenses*.

From an analyst's perspective, however, it may not be the most informative measure of the income and cash-generating ability of the firm. Generally, income from a firm's recurring operating activities is considered the best indicator of future income. The predictive ability of reported income is enhanced if it excludes the impact of transitory or random components, which are not directly related to operating activities and are generally more volatile. The economic concepts of income discussed earlier (and elaborated on in Box 31-1) tell us that transitory gains or losses should not be regarded as components of permanent or sustainable income. The concept of recurring income is similar to permanent or sustainable income in the sense that it is persistent; that is, its level or rate of growth is relatively predictable, and cash flows will eventually follow at the predicted levels and growth rates.

If we use the terminology above, *recurring income (pretax or post tax[15]) from continuing operations* should be the primary focus of analysis.

Segregation of the results of normal, recurring operations from the effects of nonrecurring items facilitates the forecasting of future earnings and cash flows. Financial reporting defines nonrecurring by the *type of transaction or event.* However, depending on the firm, the nature of the event, and to some extent management discretion, similar transactions may be included in operating income or reported below the line. Operational definitions of "operating," "nonrecurring," and "extraordinary" are elusive and both accounting standards setters and analysts have struggled with this issue for decades.

More recently, companies have increasingly provided early indications of their results for a period by announcing earnings in advance of scheduled annual or quarterly release dates. The nature of these early announcements has further blurred the distinctions between "operating," "nonrecurring," and "extraordinary" components of income. We elaborate on this issue elsewhere in this reading.

For purposes of analysis, however, the important issue is whether each item classified by management as nonrecurring income or loss in a given year is a good predictor of future income or loss. For example, for some firms, a material gain or loss from the sale of fixed assets will be rare; the transaction reported has no predictive value. Other firms retire fixed assets each year and regularly report gains or losses (e.g., consider a car rental company that retires part of its fleet of cars annually). In the latter case, the analytic issue is whether this year's income or loss from the sale of retired property is higher or lower than the "normal" amount.

Ultimately, the analyst must evaluate the significance of nonrecurring items, regardless of whether they are reported in the extraordinary, unusual, or some other category, in the prediction of earnings power. The goal of analysis of the income statement is to derive an effective measure of future earnings and cash flows. Therefore, analysts often exclude components of reported income (regardless of their accounting labels) that may reduce its predictive ability.

Fairfield et al. (1996) examined whether the classification scheme used in financial statements can improve predictive ability. Their results indicated that the forecasting of one-year-ahead profitability, that is, return on equity (ROE), was improved by disaggregating previous year's ROE into the separate components discussed earlier. They found that extraordinary items and discontinued

---

[15] Recurring income on a post-tax basis can be arrived at by either (1) adding back to net income from continuing operations the after-tax consequences of unusual or infrequent items, that is,

Net income from recurring operations = Net income from continuing operations + / − [unusual or infrequent items × (1 − tax rate)]

or (2) adjusting recurring income from continuing operations directly for taxes:

Net income from recurring operations = Recurring income from continuing operations × (1 − tax rate)

operations were not useful in predicting bottom-line ROE or ROE from continuing operations *although unusual and infrequent items were.* This latter result implies that unusual or infrequent items often contain a recurring element.

The predictive ability objective does not mean that financial analysis of the income (or other financial) statements is simply the extrapolation of previous trends. Rather, all financial statement information should be viewed as part of a database that provides limited information about future prospects and opportunities facing the firm. For example, an increase in the sale of semiconductors also provides useful information about the demand for equipment used for their manufacture.

Nonrecurring items can also provide such information, but in a different fashion. The implication of the sale of an operating asset, for example, depends on the utilization of the cash generated by the sale, and how its productive capacity will be replaced.

We return to nonrecurring items later in this reading. First, however, we look at the revenue and expense recognition rules used to report a firm's recurring operations.

Accounting Income: Revenue and Expense Recognition

When accrual accounting is used to prepare financial statements, two revenue and expense recognition issues must be addressed:

1. *Timing.* When should revenue and expense be recognized?
2. *Measurement.* How much revenue and expense should be recognized?

The responses to these questions determine the amount and timing of periodic revenue and expense. In practice, there is considerable scope for management discretion with respect to both revenue and expense recognition. At this point, however, the focus of our discussion is revenue recognition and how the application of the *matching principle* relates expense recognition to revenue recognition.[16] Other issues of expense recognition are discussed, on an issue-by-issue basis, in the readings that follow.

Statement of Financial Accounting Concepts (SFAC) 5, Recognition and Measurement in Financial Statements of Business Enterprises, specifies *two conditions that must be met for revenue recognition to take place.* These conditions are:

1. Completion of the earnings process
2. Assurance of payment

To satisfy the first condition, the firm must have provided all or virtually all the goods or services for which it is to be paid, and it must be possible to measure the total expected cost of providing the goods or services; that is, the seller must have no remaining significant contingent obligation. If the seller is obligated to provide future services, for example, warranty protection for equipment or upgrades and enhancements for software, but cannot estimate the cost of doing so, this condition is not satisfied.

---

[16] Direct costs, such as cost of goods sold, are recognized as related revenue as recognized under accrual accounting. Note that the cost of goods sold often includes depreciation expense or capitalized overhead. However, other expenses cannot be directly related to revenues and must be recognized using different principles. Some, called period costs (e.g., advertising costs), are expensed as incurred. Other costs are recognized as time passes, for example, interest costs. Finally, some costs may be based on other criteria, for example, taxes on income.

Revenue recognition also requires a second condition: the quantification of cash or assets expected to be received for the goods or services provided. Reliable measurement encompasses the realizability (collectibility) of the proceeds of sale. If the seller cannot reasonably estimate the probability of nonpayment, realization is not reasonably assured, and the second condition is not satisfied.

The general rule for revenue recognition includes this concept of realizability: Revenue, measured as the amount expected to be collected, can be recognized when goods or services have been provided and their cost can be reliably determined.

The amount of revenue recognized at any given point in time is measured as

$$\frac{\text{Goods and services provided to date}}{\text{Total goods and services to be provided}} \times \text{Total expected revenue}$$

This equation measures the amount of revenue recognized *cumulatively* to date. Revenue reported for the current period is the *cumulative total less revenue recognized in prior periods.*

The most common case is revenue recognition at the time of sale. Goods or services have been provided, and the sale is for cash or to customers whose ability to pay is reasonably assured.[17]

In some cases, payment is received prior to the delivery of goods or services. Examples include:

- Magazine publishers receive subscription payments in advance; the receipts represent an obligation to provide periodic delivery of the publication. Revenues are recognized in proportion to issues delivered.
- Credit card fees are recognized as advances from customers; revenue is recorded as the right to use the cards expires over time.
- Revenue from leased equipment is recognized as time passes or based on usage (copier rental is sometimes based on a per-copy charge).

These examples show that revenue recognition can be measured by cash expenditures, the passage of time, or the provision of service (measured in physical units) to the customer.

Departures from the Sales Basis of Revenue Recognition

Revenue may be recognized *prior* to sale or delivery when the earnings process is substantially complete and the proceeds of sale can be reasonably measured. For example, revenue is recognized at the completion of production in the case of commodities (such as oil or agricultural products) with highly organized and liquid markets or, in the case of long-term construction contracts, as production takes place.

Alternatively, revenues may not be recognized even at the time of sale if there is significant uncertainty regarding the seller's ability to collect the sales price or to estimate remaining costs. Either the installment method or the more extreme cost recovery method, both discussed shortly, must be used in such cases.

---

[17] In some cases, the buyer has a right to return unsold goods. If the risks or benefits (or both) of ownership are retained by the "seller," the transaction is, in economic substance, a consignment rather than a completed sale. SFAS 48, Revenue Recognition When Right of Return Exists, governs such sales. See also SFAS 49, Accounting for Product Financing Arrangements.

Percentage-of-Completion and Completed Contract Methods

The *percentage-of-completion* method recognizes revenues and costs in proportion to and as work is completed; production activity is considered the critical event in signaling the completion of the earnings process rather than delivery or cash collections. This method is used for long-term projects when there is a contract, and reliable estimates of production completed, revenues, and costs are possible.

The percentage-of-completion method measures progress toward completion using *either*:

- Engineering estimates (or physical milestones such as miles of road completed), or
- Ratios of costs incurred to expected total costs.

This method may overstate revenue and gross profit if expenditures made are recognized before they contribute to completed work, for example, when the costs of raw materials and advance payments to subcontractors are included in the determination of work completed.

When estimates of revenue or costs change, a catch-up effect is included in the earnings of the period in which the change in estimate is made. Earnings of prior periods are not restated because it is a change in accounting estimate. When a loss is expected on the contract, it must be recognized in the period the amount of the loss can be estimated.

The *completed contract method* recognizes revenues and expenses only at the end of the contract. It must be used when any one of the conditions required for the use of the percentage-of-completion method is not met, generally when no contract exists or estimates of the selling price or collectibility are not reliable. It must be used for short-term contracts.[18]

Comparison of Percentage-of-Completion and Completed Contract Methods

Exhibit 31-1 compares the percentage-of-completion and completed contract revenue recognition methods. Part A compares the revenues, expenses, and income reported under each method for each year. Computations for the percentage-of-completion method use the ratio of costs (assumed to provide a reliable measure of actual work performed) incurred each period to expected total costs. In 2001, 16.67% of estimated costs are incurred, so that revenue recognized for that year equals 16.67% of the contract price. As a result, if we use the matching principle, the same percentage (16.67%) of expected total expenses and total income is recognized for 2001. This pattern is repeated as long as actual results closely mirror expectations.

Under the completed contract method, revenues, expenses, and income are recognized only at the end of the contract period; no revenue, expense, or income is reported during the first two years.

As a result, the two different revenue recognition methods produce different patterns of reported revenue, expense, and income, although total revenue, expense, and income over the life of the contract are identical under both methods.

The percentage-of-completion method provides both a better measure of operating activity and a more informative disclosure of the status of incomplete

---

[18] SFAS 56 (1982) emphasizes that the percentage-of-completion and the completed contract method are not "intended to be free-choice alternatives under either Accounting Research Bulletin No. 45 (ARB 45) or AICPA SOP 81-1." ARB 45 states that the percentage-of-completion method is preferable when estimates of costs and degree of completion are reliable. SOP 81-1 reiterates this position.

EXHIBIT 31-1 Comparison of Percentage-of-Completion and Completed Contract Revenue Recognition Methods

In 2001, Justin Corp. entered into a construction project with a total contract price of $6 million and expected costs to complete of $4.8 million resulting in expected profits of $1.2 million.

Actual production costs and cash flow information over the duration of the contract are provided as follows (in $thousands):

	2001	2002	2003
Costs incurred: Current year	$ 800	$2,800	$1,200
Cumulative	800	3,600	4,800
Estimated *remaining* costs to complete (as of December 31)	4,000	1,200	0
Amounts billed and cash received			
Current year	$1,300	$2,500	$2,200
Cumulative	1,300	3,800	6,000

A. Income Statement (in $ thousands)

	Percentage-of-Completion				Completed Contract			
	2001	2002	2003	Total	2001	2002	2003	Total
Revenue*	$1,000	$3,500	$1,500	$6,000	$0	$0	$6,000	$6,000
Expense	(800)	(2,800)	(1,200)	(4,800)	(0)	(0)	(4,800)	(4,800)
Income	$ 200	$ 700	$ 300	$1,200	$0	$0	$1,200	$1,200

$$*2001: \frac{\$800}{\$4,800} \times \$6,000 = \$1,000$$

$$2002: \frac{(\$800 + \$2,800)}{\$4,800} \times \$6,000 = \$4,500 - \$1,000 = \$3,500$$

$$2003: \frac{(\$800 + \$2,800 + \$1,200)}{\$4,800} \times \$6,000 = \$6,000 - \$4,500 = \$1,500$$

B. Balance Sheet (in $ thousands)

	Percentage-of-Completion			Completed Contract		
	2001	2002	2003	2001	2002	2003
Assets						
Cash	$500	$200	$1,200	$500	$200	$1,200
Construction in progress	0	700	0	0	0	0
Total assets	$500	$900	$1,200	$500	$200	$1,200
Liabilities and equity						
Advance billings	$300	$ 0	$ 0	$500	$200	$ 0
Retained earnings	200	900	1,200	0	0	1,200
Total liabilities and equity	$500	$900	$1,200	$500	$200	$1,200

(continued)

EXHIBIT 31-1 (continued)

Explanation:

Cash: Identical for both methods and equivalent to cumulative cash received less costs incurred.

Retained earnings: Cumulative earnings since inception of project.

Construction in progress and advance billings: *Net* amount of following table where advance billings represent cumulative cash received and construction in progress is based on cumulative costs incurred plus profit recognized:

	Percentage-of-Completion			Completed Contract		
	2001	2002	2003	2001	2002	2003
Costs incurred	$ 800	$3,600	$4,800	$ 800	$3,600	$4,800
Profit recognized	200	900	1,200	0	0	1,200
Construction in progress	**$1,000**	**$4,500**	**$6,000**	**$800**	**$3,600**	**$6,000**
Advance billings	**(1,300)**	**(3,800)**	**(6,000)**	**(1,300)**	**(3,800)**	**(6,000)**
Net asset (liability)	**$ (300)**	**$ 700**	**$ 0**	**$ (500)**	**$ (200)**	**$ 0**

C. Change in Estimated Costs to Complete

On December 31, 2002, Justin Corp. determines that the total cost of the project will be $5,400, making remaining costs to complete $1,800, an increase of $600 from the original estimate. This changes *both* revenue and income for 2002 under the percentage-of-completion method. The adjustment is made on a cumulative basis; revenue and expense reported for previous years are *not* restated.

Cumulative revenue recognized is

$$\frac{\$3{,}600 \text{ (cumulative costs incurred} \times \$6{,}000)}{\$5{,}400 \text{ (revised total costs)}}$$

$= \$4{,}000$, of which $1,000 was recognized as revenue in 2001.

Therefore, $3,000 ($4,000 − $1,000) is recognized as revenue for 2002.
Cumulative expense recognized is $3,600, the total incurred. Expense recognized for 2002 remains unchanged at $1,800. As a result, income recognized in 2002 is $3,000 − $2,800 = $200.

The revised income statements for percentage of completion are presented below in panel I. (For completed contract, the revision would all be reflected in year 2003.)

Panel II shows what percentage of completion income would have been had Justin known the actual costs at the beginning of the project.

Percentage-of-Completion

	I. Revised				II. Foreknowledge of Actual Costs			
	2001	2002	2003	Total	2001	2002	2003	Total
Revenue	$1,000	$3,000	$2,000	$6,000	$889	$3,111	$2,000	$6,000
Expense	(800)	(2,800)	(1,800)	(5,400)	(800)	(2,800)	(1,800)	(5,400)
Income	$ 200	$ 200	$ 200	$ 600	$ 89	$ 311	$ 200	$ 600

contracts. For a firm with constant revenues the two methods produce identical results.[19] However, since the business world is rarely in a steady state of equilibrium, *the percentage-of-completion method reports income earlier and is a better indicator of trends in earning power.* Although better disclosure of contracts in progress under the completed contract method would help analysts forecast future operating results and cash flows, the percentage-of-completion method is more informative.

The choice of method also affects the reported assets and liabilities on the balance sheet. Part B shows the balance sheet effects of the two methods.

Under the completed contract method, expenditures prior to completion are reported as inventory (*construction-in-progress*) and cash receipts as advances from customers.

Using the percentage-of-completion method,

- Costs incurred are also accumulated in an asset account titled *construction-in-progress.* However, *gross profit (income) for the period is also accumulated in the construction-in-progress account.* (Periodic gross profit is not recognized under the completed contract method.)
- Amounts billed to customers are recorded as a liability (*advance billings*) and an asset (accounts receivable). When cash is received, the receivable is reduced. The difference between cash received and billings is treated as accounts receivable.[20]

For financial reporting purposes, construction-in-progress and advance billings are netted. For example, at the end of 2001 (percentage of completion method), Justin's balance sheet will show (a liability of) $300 as "amounts billed in excess of contract costs." At the end of 2002 (percentage of completion method), Justin will report (an asset of) $700 as "contract costs in excess of amounts billed." For a company with many contracts in process, it is typical to find both net asset and net liability amounts on the balance sheet. The gross amounts will be reported in footnotes.

At the end of the contract period, under both methods, the construction-in-progress and advance billings accounts are eliminated. Thus, at contract completion under both methods, the only remaining balance sheet amounts are cash and retained earnings. Both amounts equal $1,200, which is the profit on the contract.

Example 31-1

Chicago Bridge & Iron is a global engineering and construction firm. Its 10-K report for the year ended December 31, 1999 lists, among significant accounting policies:

> REVENUE RECOGNITION: Revenues are recognized using the percentage of completion method. Contract revenues are accrued based generally on the percentage that costs-to-date bear to total estimated costs.

---

[19] This statement assumes that, with a large number of contracts, income recognized from contracts completed in each period would be equal to the income recognized from the partial completion of contracts in process.

[20] In our example, amounts billed and cash received were identical, leaving a zero receivables balance.

Footnote 3 contains the following table:

Contracts in Progress	**1999**	**1998**
Revenues recognized on contracts in progress	$808,312	$871,100
Billings on contracts in progress	(813,140)	(896,506)
Shown on balance sheet as:		
Contracts in progress with earned revenues exceeding related progress billings (asset)	$48,486	$ 51,953
Contracts in progress with progress billings exceeding related earned revenues (liability)	(53,314)	(77,359)
	$ (4,828)	$(25,406)

As can be seen from the above table, the netting process reduces very large activities to relatively small net amounts on the balance sheet. As Chicago Bridge had total assets of $337 million at December 31, 1999, reporting revenues and billings gross would have greatly increased total assets and liabilities.

Returning to part B of the Justin example, the only difference in the balance sheet effects of the two methods is that, under the percentage-of-completion method, there is an additional accrual of gross profit in construction-in-progress. When there is an excess of advance billings over costs (e.g., 2001), reported total assets are identical under both methods. When construction-in-progress exceeds billings (e.g., 2002), total assets will be higher under the percentage-of-completion method. For all years, liabilities are lower and retained earnings (equity) higher under the percentage-of-completion method, reflecting the higher level of construction-in-progress.

Generalizing these effects for a company with a continuing flow of profitable contracts, under the percentage-of-completion method:

- Total assets are higher, reflecting the accrual of gross profit during the contract period.
- Liabilities are lower as the higher level of construction-in-progress provides a larger offset.
- Stockholders' equity is higher due to the earlier accrual of gross profit.
- The ratio of liabilities to equity is lower, reflecting lower liabilities and higher equity.

Part C shows the impact of a change in estimate: The estimated cost to complete is increased at the end of the second year (2002). This increase is recognized in 2002, and that year's income reflects the income on work completed during the period offset by the impact of the change in estimate. Note that the cumulative income correctly reflects the degree of completion using the revised cost estimate.[21]

---

[21] The firm has completed two-thirds ($3,600 of costs incurred to date out of total expected costs of $5,400) of the work on the project and at the end of the year will have recognized $400 or two-thirds of expected income of $600 ($200 in 2001 and $200 in 2002).

Similarly, if the firm estimated the remaining cost to complete the project at $2,750 at the end of 2002 (rather than the original $1,200), the expected loss of $350 (on the entire contract) would be recognized in that year. The previously recognized earnings would be offset and the full contract loss would be recognized in 2002, the year in which it can be estimated, even though some of that loss will be incurred in 2003.

Installment Method of Revenue Recognition

Revenues should not be recognized at the time of sale or delivery when there is no reasonable basis to estimate collectibility of the sales proceeds. The installment method recognizes gross profit in proportion to cash collections, resulting in delayed recognition of revenues and expenses as compared with full recognition at the time of sale. This method is sometimes used to report income from sales of noncurrent assets and real estate transactions.

Cost Recovery Method

Revenue recognition on sale or delivery is also precluded when the costs to provide goods or services cannot be reasonably determined, for example, in the development of raw land. This occurs when completion of the sale is dependent on expenditures to be made in the future (e.g., road construction) and it is impossible to estimate the amount of those expenditures (which may depend on zoning or environmental factors).

In many cases, there is also substantial uncertainty about revenue realization since only small down payments may be required with nonrecourse financing provided by the seller. With both future costs and collection uncertain, the cost recovery method requires that all cash receipts be first accounted for as a recovery of costs. Only after all costs are recovered can profit be recognized under this method.[22]

The installment and cost recovery methods may be used to recognize franchise revenues[23] when revenue is collectible over an extended period and there is no reasonable basis to estimate that collectibility. These methods may also be used, under specific circumstances, in real estate sales and retail land sales.[24]

Issues in Revenue and Expense Recognition

While the theoretical basis for revenue and expense recognition appears to be straightforward, the application of these principles has been inconsistent in practice, especially in those areas where GAAP itself lacks definitive standards. Companies have strong incentives to accelerate the recognition of revenues and delay the recording of expense. The significant growth in (1) technology and (2) the use of revenue and gross margin to value companies without earnings have increased the incentives to use accounting methods that increase reported revenues. The result has been new guidelines (a series of consensuses from the Emerging Issues Task Force (EITF) and the U.S. Securities and Exchange Commission). SEC Staff Accounting Bulletin 101, Revenue Recognition in Financial Statements, and Frequently Asked Questions and Answers related to SAB 101[25] forced many companies (including many "old economy" firms) to change their reported revenue and expense.

The accounting issues can be categorized as follows:

1. Revenue recognition
2. Expense recognition
3. Classification

---

[22] When a company markets, sells, or leases software originally developed for internal use, SOP 98-1, Accounting for the Costs of Computer Software Developed for Internal Use, requires the application of the cost recovery method until all unamortized costs have been recovered.

[23] See SFAS 45, Accounting for Franchise Fee Revenue, para. 6 (FASB, 1981).

[24] See SFAS 66, Accounting for Sales of Real Estate (FASB, 1982).

[25] http://www.sec.gov/info/accountants/sab101faq.htm.

We discuss each of these in turn. The end-of-reading problems illustrate the financial statement effects of some of these accounting methods. While some of these issues relate primarily to technology companies, virtually any company's income statement may be affected.

Revenue Recognition

Some accounting issues affect the amount and/or timing of revenue recognition. Examples include:

- Sales incentives (such as discounts or the granting of stock options to customers) to achieve revenue goals. Such incentives may become especially important when a company nears the end of a reporting period and wishes to meet its preannounced revenue goals. In extreme cases, companies may provide rights of return or other privileges that violate the realization principle (and may not be recorded or disclosed to auditors).
- Barter arrangements under which a firm provides goods or services to another in exchange for that firm's goods or services. Barter revenues may be recorded at "list prices" rather than the lower prices that would pertain to arm's-length transactions.
- Recording license fees or membership fees when an agreement is signed, rather than over the term of the agreement.
- Recording revenues based on estimated usage, even when bills have not been sent out.[26]
- Companies that act as agents (e.g., advertising agencies or sales intermediaries) record the gross amount billed as revenue rather than their commission income.
- Recognition of all revenue from a contract even when the customer has not yet agreed that the project is fully installed and operational.
- Reporting shipping and handling costs charged to customers as revenues.

These and other practices vary among companies, making comparisons of revenue levels and growth difficult. When analysts use revenues to value company shares, the incentive to use accounting methods that maximize reported revenues is very high.

When companies are forced to change their revenue recognition policies, the consequences for shareholders can be dire. Consider the example of MicroStrategy [MSTR], a provider of business software, which was required to restate its operating results for 1997 through 1999. Exhibit 31-2 contains an extract from MSTR's 10-K report, showing the effect of the restatement and explaining the accounting changes. Note the significant changes in revenues (1998 and 1999), net income (all three years), accounts receivable, deferred revenues, and stockholders' equity.

MicroStrategy shares, which reached a price of $333 on March 10, 2000 (ten days prior to announcement of the restatement) fell to less than $17 in late May. One year later the share price was below $4.

[26] Many utility companies report "unbilled revenues" as sales.

EXHIBIT 31-2 Microstrategy: Restatement for Change in Revenue Recognition Policies

Notes to Consolidated Financial Statements

(3) Restatement of Financial Statements

Subsequent to the filing of a registration statement on Form S-3 with the SEC which included the Company's audited financial statements for the years ended December 31, 1999, 1998 and 1997 the Company became aware that the timing and amount of reported earned revenues from license transactions in 1999, 1998 and 1997 required revision.

These revisions primarily addressed the recognition of revenue for certain software arrangements which should be accounted for under the subscription method or the percentage of completion method, which spread the recognition of revenue over the entire contract period. For example, when fees are received in a transaction in which the Company is licensing software and also performing significant development, customization or consulting services, the fees should be recognized using the percentage of completion method and, therefore, product license and product support and other services revenue are recognized as work progresses. Revenue from arrangements where the Company provides hosting services is generally recognized over the hosting term, which is generally two to three years. The effect of these revisions is to defer the time in which revenue is recognized for large, complex contracts that combine both products and services. These revisions also resulted in a substantial increase in the amount of deferred revenue reflected on the Company's balance sheet at the end of 1999 and 1998. Additionally, these revisions include the effects of changes in the reporting periods when revenue from certain contracts are recognized. In the course of reviewing its revenue recognition on various transactions, the Company became aware that, in certain instances, the Company had recorded revenue on certain contracts in one reporting period where customer signature and delivery had been completed, but where the contract may not have been fully executed by the Company in that reporting period. The Company subsequently reviewed license agreements executed near the end of the years 1999, 1998 and 1997 and determined that revisions were necessary to ensure that all agreements for which the Company was recognizing revenue in a reporting period were executed by both parties no later than the end of the reporting period in which the revenue is recognized. The total effect of all revisions to revenue was to reduce revenues by $54.0 million, $10.9 million and $1.0 million for the years ended December 31, 1999, 1998 and 1997, respectively.

The Company also made certain revisions to our balance sheet as of December 31, 1999.

Accordingly, such financial statements have been restated as follows:

	1999		1998		1997	
Statements of Operations Data	**Reported**	**Restated**	**Reported**	**Restated**	**Reported**	**Restated**
Revenues:						
Product licenses	$143,193	$85,797	$72,721	$61,635	$36,601	$35,478
Product support and other services	62,136	65,461	33,709	33,854	16,956	17,073
Income (loss) from operations	18,319	(34,533)	9	(2,549)	372	(634)
Provision for income taxes	7,735	1,246	3,442	—	—	—
Net income (loss)	12,620	(33,743)	6,178	(2,255)	121	(885)
Balance sheet data						
Accounts receivable, net	61,149	37,586	33,054	25,377	16,085	15,121
Deferred revenue and advance payments (current and noncurrent)	16,782	71,283	11,478	13,048	9,387	9,429
Retained earnings (deficit)	17,849	(37,953)	5,229	(4,210)	(634)	(1,640)

Source: MicroStrategy 10-K, December 31, 1999.

Expense Recognition

The following accounting issues affect the amount and/or timing of expense recognition:

- Deferral of marketing expenses and sales commissions
- Accrual or deferral of the cost of periodic major maintenance projects
- Bad debt expense
- Warranty expense

Deferral of Marketing Expenses and Sales Commissions. When marketing costs or sales commissions are deferred, reported income increases. While deferred expenses must be recognized sooner or later, the deferral of expenses by growth companies may exceed the recognition of previously deferred costs for extended time periods.

Example 31-2

Sears defers direct marketing expenses associated with catalog and other sales activities. Note 1 states that such capitalized costs rose from $131 million at January 2, 1999 to $180 million at January 1, 2000. If all costs had been expensed, Sears' pretax income would have been $49 million ($180 − $131) lower.

Expensing Periodic Major Maintenance Projects. Some fixed assets require periodic major overhauls. Firms can either accrue the costs in advance (and charge the actual expenditure against the accrued liability) or defer recognizing the expense until it is actually incurred. The latter method delays expense recognition, increasing reported earnings.[27] A third alternative is to capitalize the actual expenditure and amortize it against earnings in subsequent years (as will be discussed in Reading 7).

Example 31-3

Airborne Freight [ABF] stated in its 2000 annual report:

> Effective January 1, 2000, the Company changed its method of accounting for major engine overhaul costs on DC-9 aircraft from the accrual method to the direct expense method where costs are expensed as incurred. Previously, these costs were accrued in advance of the next scheduled overhaul based upon engine usage and estimates of overhaul costs.

The change resulted in a cumulative effect (for prior periods) of $14.2 million and increased earnings for 2000 by $3.7 million. Adding the two components together, the change accounted for 63% of Airborne's total earnings for the year of $28.5 million.

---

[27] For example, a company anticipating a $3 million overhaul in three years would, under the accrual method, recognize an expense (and accrued liability of) $1 million in each of the three years in advance of the overhaul. At the time of the overhaul, the $3 million expenditure would reduce the liability. Recognizing the expense only when incurred would result in a $3 million expense in the year of the overhaul and no expense (or liability) in the years leading up to the overhaul.

Bad Debt Expense. Credit losses affect reported income only indirectly and not at the time they actually occur. The timing of the expense recognition for bad debts and the actual receivable write-off do not coincide. Each year a company makes a provision for bad debt expense reflecting its estimate of the proportion of its credit customers who will default. In making this estimate, the company sets up a reserve for bad debts (allowance for doubtful accounts). When an actual write-off occurs (i.e., it becomes certain that the customer will not pay), the charge is made to the reserve, not earnings.

The procedure is illustrated in the example below. The example also indicates that the estimation process for bad debts can be used to smooth earnings and/or delay the reporting of bad news. Analysts should watch the level of the reserve relative to receivables (considering economic conditions within the industry) as well as the provision against earnings.

Example 31-4: Lucent

The Lucent [LU] 1999 financial statements show the following data ($millions):

	September 30	
	1998	1999
Sales	$31,806	$38,303
Receivables (net of allowance)	7,405	10,438
Allowance for doubtful accounts	416	362
Add back the allowance to get gross receivables	$ 7,821	$10,800
Allowance as % of gross receivables	5.32%	3.35%

There are two red flags here. One is the decline in the allowance relative to gross receivables. The second is the 38% increase in gross receivables, compared with a 1999 sales increase of only 20%.

Lucent's 1999 10-K reveals the following additional data relating to the changes in its bad debt reserve:

	Years Ended September 30	
	1998	1999
Allowance for doubtful accounts (beginning balance)	363	416
Bad debt expense	132	68
Write-offs	(20)	(159)
Other changes	(59)	37
Allowance for doubtful accounts (ending balance)	416	362

[28] Lucent's entries in 1998 were

Bad debt expense $132	and	Allowance for doubtful accounts	$20
Allowance for doubtful accounts $132		Accounts receivable	$20

As the above table indicates, the timing of the expense for bad debt and the actual write-off do not coincide. In 1998 Lucent recorded bad debt expense of $132 million, increasing the allowance for doubtful accounts. The actual accounts receivable written off as uncollectible was only $20 million. That amount was not expensed but charged against the reserve.[28] In 1999, the situation reversed, as the amount expensed ($68 million) was considerably less than the amount actually written off ($159 million).

Lucent reduced its provision for bad debts in 1999 although actual credit losses rose substantially from the 1998 level. Had Lucent made a provision sufficient to bring the allowance relative to gross receivables up to the fiscal 1998 level ($10,800 × .0532 = $575 million), *its pretax income would have been ($575 –* $362) *$213 million (4%) lower.*

It should be noted that in the years 2000 and 2001, Lucent wrote off approximately $1 billion of receivables, evidence that the 1999 year-end provision (of $362 million) was insufficient.

In September 1999, a Lucent subsidiary sold $625 million of accounts receivable to a nonconsolidated entity and the company itself transferred $700 million of accounts receivable as collateral to that entity. Thus, Lucent removed $1,325 million of receivables (but not the related allowance for doubtful accounts).[29] Without these transactions, on September 30, 1999, Lucent's receivables balance would have been $12,125 million (instead of the reported $10,800 million). The actual increase in receivables was 55%, much higher than the 20% increase in sales. The company would have needed an allowance for doubtful accounts balance of $645 million to reflect an allowance comparable to that reported in 1998 and its pretax income would have been ($645 – $362) $283 million (5.4%) lower. *During December 1999, Lucent repurchased $408 million of the $625 million receivables sold in September 1999.*

Warranty Expenses. Many firms provide warranties—guarantees to fix or replace defective products. Expense recognition is similar to that of bad debts. GAAP requires that firms estimate the cost of providing warranties, and deduct that expense from income at the time of sale. A corresponding reserve (liability) is set up on the balance sheet.[30] Such estimates are inherently difficult, especially for new products. The analyst should watch the trend in warranty reserves, as they can be used to smooth reported income.

Example 31-5: AT Cross

AT Cross [ATX] produces pens with a lifetime warranty. In 2000, the company's fourth successive loss year, it reduced its warranty reserve "reflecting lower cost trends among the several factors that impact the company's cost to service the warranty." The data follow ($thousands):

---

[29] See Reading 44 for our discussion of the financial statement impact of sales of receivables.

[30] The reserve is reduced when an actual warranty cost is incurred.

	Years Ended December 31 1998	1999	2000
Sales	$152,783	$126,994	$130,548
Warranty expense	881	720	(761)
% sales	0.6%	0.6%	−0.6%
Warranty reserve			
Opening balance	$ 5,821	$ 5,821	$ 5,821
Expense	881	720	(761)
Costs paid	(881)	(720)	(367)
Closing balance	$ 5,821	$ 5,821	$ 4,693

The accounting change increased operating profit margins by 1.2%. If Cross had recorded sufficient warranty expense to maintain its existing reserve (as in 1998 and 1999), the expense would have been $367,000; if it had accrued expense equal to .6% of sales, the expense would have been $783,000. Either amount would have increased the operating loss further.

Capitalizing current period expenditures can also reduce reported expenses. Reading 40 discusses the capitalization of interest, research and development, and software development expense.

Classification Issues

Many analysts use gross margin (revenues less cost of goods sold) and gross margin percentage (gross margin as a % of sales) to evaluate companies, especially those that have negative earnings. Some reporting methods boost gross margins without affecting operating income:

- Including costs such as discounts and marketing costs as operating expense rather than cost of goods sold
- Recording shipping and handling costs (included in revenue) as operating expense rather than cost of goods sold

Classification issues and changes in classification may not be explicitly disclosed in financial statements. However, differences in classification for the same firm over time and among competing firms may distort analyses and comparisons of gross margin levels, percentages, and growth rates.

The analyst should question companies regarding their revenue and expense recognition practices, and the classification of revenues and expense. Intercompany comparisons may require adjustment for reporting differences.

Software Revenue Recognition

Transactions in the software industry range from the sale or license of a single software product to complex contractual arrangements that involve delivery, significant subsequent production, modification, or customization of the software.

The latter complex arrangements generally must be accounted for in accordance with Accounting Research Bulletin (ARB) 45, Long-Term Construction-Type Contracts, and SOP 81-1, Accounting for the Performance of Construction-Type Contracts and Certain Production-Type Contracts.

SOP 97-2, Software Revenue Recognition, and SOP 98-9, Modification of SOP 97-2, Software Revenue Recognition, With Respect to Certain Transactions, apply to software transactions that do not require significant subsequent production, modification, or customization of the software. SOP 97-2 stipulates four criteria that must *all* be satisfied to recognize revenue for single- or multiple-element software transactions:

1. Persuasive evidence of an arrangement
2. Delivery
3. A fixed or determinable fee
4. Assurance of collectibility

SOP 97-2 requires that revenue be allocated among the components of a multiple-element arrangement based on fair values of the individual elements. In the absence of fair value data, all revenue must be deferred until completion of the project. However, vendor-specific objective evidence (VSOE)[31] of the fair value of the elements can be used to recognize revenue for individual elements.

SOP 98-9 amends SOP 97-2 to require the use of the "residual method" of revenue recognition when:

- VSOE of the fair values of all the undelivered elements is available,
- VSOE of one or more delivered elements is not available, and
- All other revenue recognition criteria of SOP 97-2 are met.

The residual method requires that the total fair value of the undelivered elements be deferred; only the excess of the total sales price over the amount deferred is recognized as revenue. SOP 97-2 applies to the subsequent revenue recognition for the undelivered elements.

Illustration. Assume that a software company agrees to sell a product for \$950, including one year of customer support. The company separately sells customer support for \$150 a year (providing VSOE for the price of customer support). If the company does not have VSOE for the software, customer support (\$150) revenue would be deferred and recognized over the one-year term. Under SOP 98-9, the remaining \$800 would be recognized when the software product is delivered (assuming all other requirements of SOP 97-2 are met).

However, absent VSOE for the customer support price, the entire \$950 would be deferred and recognized over the one-year term. The deferral method would apply even if there were VSOE regarding the software product price. In other words, to recognize the revenue related to one or more elements of a multi-element sale, there must be VSOE to support the revenue allocated to the undelivered elements.

[31] VSOE means the price charged when the element is sold separately or the price established by the vendor for that element.

Example 31-6

Microsoft provides an instructive example of revenue recognition issues in the software industry.[32] Starting in 1996, Microsoft deferred increasing amounts of revenue (designated as unearned revenue), recognizing the deferred revenue in future time periods. The company adopted SOP 97-2 in the fourth quarter of fiscal 1999. Concurrently, Microsoft extended the life cycle of its principal product from two to three years. Maintenance and subscription revenue, based on the average sales prices of each element, are recognized ratably (straight-line basis) over the product's life cycle.

Exhibit 31-3 shows that the company has reported declining revenue growth rates since 1996. The growth rate of cash collections also steadily declined, from 53% in fiscal 1996 to less than 11% in fiscal 2000. However, Microsoft changes accounting methods and estimates as the products mature and as the undelivered components of the products are developed or delivered. Although Microsoft discloses the various components of unearned or deferred revenues, the disclosures do not enable the user to forecast the rate and amount of unearned revenues that will be recognized over the products' life cycles.

EXHIBIT 31-3 Microsoft Corporation

Years Ended June 30 (amounts in $millions)

	1995	1996	1997	1998	1999	2000
Revenues	$5,937	$8,671	$11,936	$15,262	$19,747	$22,956
Unearned revenue*	69	983	1,601	3,268	5,877	6,177
Recognition of prior period unearned revenue*	(54)	(477)	(743)	(1,798)	(4,526)	(5,600)
Change in accounts receivable		(58)	(341)	(480)	(785)	(1,005)
Cash collections	$5,952	$9,119	$12,453	$16,252	$20,313	$22,528
Cash collections growth rate (%)		53.21%	36.56%	30.51%	24.99%	10.90%
Unearned revenue (year-end balance sheet)	$ 54	$ 560	$ 1,418	$ 2,888	$ 4,239	$ 4,816
Prior period revenue as % of reported revenue		5.50%	6.22%	11.78%	22.92%	24.39%
Reported revenue growth rate (%)		46.05%	37.65%	27.87%	29.39%	16.25%

*From statement of cash flows.

Source: Microsoft *Annual Reports, 1996–2000.*

[32] See the footnote on revenue recognition under Accounting Policies in Microsoft's *Annual Report* for the year ended June 30, 2000.

Other Issues

The software industry is not the only one that has particular revenue recognition issues. We have examined it at length given its richness and current relevance. Four examples of other industries and situations follow:

1. In the broadcast industry, television stations buy the rights to show a film for a given period of time. Should the revenue be recognized by the film's owner:
   - When the agreement is signed?
   - When the film is physically transferred to the television station?
   - Over time as the film is shown?
2. Mortgage issuers charge a fee, *origination points,* that is, in effect, interest paid in advance. Points are not refundable even if the mortgage is repaid before its due date. Should the fee be recognized as income:
   - Over time?
   - At the time of origination?
3. An exercise club charges a refundable annual membership fee, payable quarterly. Should revenue be recognized:
   - When the membership is sold?
   - When payments are received?
   - Over one year?

   Should the answer change if payment is made when the contract is signed? What if it is nonrefundable?
4. A company offers price incentives or preferential access to goods to induce customers to purchase future period requirements in advance.[33] The result is an increase in current period revenues. Should all sales be recognized in the current period?

These are but a few examples of complex revenue recognition issues. Case 31-1 contains a comprehensive analysis of revenue and expense recognition issues. Other examples are provided in the problems at the end of this reading. It should be clear, however, that the analyst must have a thorough understanding of the nature of the business and its relationship to revenue recognition. *When valuation is based on revenue or gross margin, pay careful attention to accounting methods that affect these measures, even when net income is unaffected.*

Summary of Revenue Recognition Methods

The preceding sections discuss the conceptual bases and financial statement effects of different revenue recognition methods. The analyst must be aware of the assumptions underlying these methods both for interfirm comparisons and because questionable revenue is a poor predictor of future cash flows.

Furthermore, revenue recognition abuses may also indicate more serious problems. Richard H. Walker, the SEC head of enforcement, stated that:

> . . . the most common type of accounting fraud has been improper recording of revenue. This can occur when a company books revenue for sales that never took place, accelerates or defers revenue to another quarter, or books sales before they

---

[33] In 2002, Bristol-Myers [BMY] reported that it had offered sales incentives to wholesalers in 2000 and 2001 that resulted in approximately $1.5 billion of wholesaler inventory buildup. The required inventory workdown significantly reduced earnings in 2002 and 2003.

are confirmed. . . . Investors have lost billions of dollars in the last few years when companies dropped in market value after restating earnings. . . .[34]

Although the United States has a rich (and growing) body of revenue and expense recognition rules, IAS standards and those of most foreign countries provide little or no guidance. For example, Sir David Tweedie, chairman of the UK Accounting Standards Board, acknowledged the deficiency in UK standards: "It seems ridiculous, we have no rules."[35]

Revenue and expense recognition rules will change as global standard setters respond to the need for improved guidelines. Whichever reporting method is used, the analyst needs to monitor the income statement and its relationship to the cash flow statement. As discussed in the next reading, the statement of cash flows can warn the financial statement user when overly aggressive revenue recognition methods are being used.

NONRECURRING ITEMS 4

Nonrecurring items affect the analysis of the income- and cash-generating ability of most firms. As companies have increased their effort to explain earnings variations, they have made greater use of the "unusual" and "nonrecurring" labels, especially for items that reduce reported income. Many new economy firms have taken this practice to new depths. These firms often announce *pro forma earnings* amounts that exclude goodwill amortization, stock compensation expense, and other selected accruals. We have previously noted that, when estimating a firm's earning power, analysts should exclude items that are unusual or nonrecurring in nature. However, this does not mean that everything management labels nonrecurring should be ignored. In this section, we discuss the extent to which such items provide useful information and how they should be treated in financial analysis.

Types of Nonrecurring Items

The income statement contains four categories of nonrecurring income:

1. Unusual or infrequent items
2. Extraordinary items
3. Discontinued operations
4. Accounting changes

Unusual or infrequent items are reported "above the line" as part of "income from continuing operations" and are presented on a pretax basis. The other three categories are "below the line," excluded from "income from continuing operations," and presented net of tax.[36] We first describe these classifications and then discuss their analytical implications.

---

[34] Interview with Neil Roland of Bloomberg, February 27, 2001.

[35] Quoted in *The Financial Times* (London), December 1, 2000, p. 24. In January 2001, Tweedie became chairman of the reconstituted IASB.

[36] The fact that some nonrecurring items are presented pretax (and included in income from continuing operations) but others are reported after tax (excluded from income from continuing operations) hampers analysis. Attention to detail and a little thought, however, can conquer the inconsistent presentation of nonrecurring items.

Unusual or Infrequent Items

Transactions or events that are *either unusual in nature or infrequent in occurrence but not both* may be disclosed separately (as a single-line item) as a component of income from continuing operations. These items must be reported pretax in the income statement; the tax impact (or the net-of-tax amount) may be disclosed separately. Common examples are:

- Gains or losses from disposal of a portion of a business segment
- Gains or losses from sales of assets or investments in affiliates or subsidiaries
- Provisions for environmental remediation
- Impairments, write-offs, writedowns, and restructuring costs
- Expenses related to the integration of acquired companies

Texaco has reported several "special items" every year for the last several years. The 1999 Management Discussion and Analysis (MD&A) reported write-downs of assets in both domestic and international business segments and gains (losses) on major assets sales in each year, 1997 through 1999. These amounts were recorded as components of depreciation, depletion, and amortization expense. Texaco has also reported:

- Reorganizations, restructurings, and employee separation costs
- Inventory valuation adjustments
- Settlements of royalty valuation issues
- Environmental liabilities

The company provides extensive disclosures for the reorganizations, restructurings, and employee separation programs including the amount and location (in the income statement) of the expenses recorded each year, changes in provisions, cash payments made during the year, amounts transferred to long-term obligations, and the remaining obligations at the end of each year. Note that many of these charges should be considered normal operating charges for a company of the size and complexity of Texaco. While it may be helpful for near-term earnings projections for Texaco to disclose these items, we cannot assume that similar items will not appear in future years. In 2000, for example, Texaco again reported asset impairment and employee separation costs. Thus, while such disclosures are useful adjuncts to the income statement, the analyst should carefully consider case-by-case whether valuation should be based on earnings that exclude "nonrecurring" items.

The Texaco example shows us that nonrecurring items are not always disclosed as separate line items in the income statement. They may be included in the catchall "other income" classification or may be buried in COGS or SG&A. Both footnote disclosures and the MD&A should be scrutinized for events and transactions that may have had a material impact on earnings, but that management has either chosen to treat as normal, recurring items or classified as nonrecurring transactions or events.

Extraordinary Items

APB 30 (1973) created the U.S. GAAP income statement format discussed earlier. It defines *extraordinary items* as transactions and events that are *unusual in nature and infrequent in occurrence and are material in amount.* Extraordinary items must be reported separately, net of income tax. Firms are also required to report per-share amounts for these items and encouraged to provide additional footnote disclosures. Extraordinary items are intended to be rare; based on APB 30, such events as losses due to a foreign government's expropriation of assets qualify as an extraordinary item, whereas gains or losses on the sale of noncurrent assets do not.

In the early 1970s, high interest rates and an economic recession led firms with depressed profits to refinance low coupon debt, whose market value was below the face amount, with high coupon debt, reporting an accounting gain.[37] SFAS 4 (1975) broadened the classification of extraordinary items by requiring that *gains or losses on qualifying early retirement of debt*[38] be classified as extraordinary.

In April 2002, SFAS 145 rescinded SFAS 4. As a result, gains or losses on the early retirement of debt are extraordinary items only when the requirements of APB 30 are met.

In recent years, firms have refinanced high coupon debt, whose market value exceeded face amount after sharp declines in interest rates, and these debt retirements have resulted in reported extraordinary losses. Of the sample of 600 companies in the 2000 *Accounting Trends and Techniques,* 61 companies reported 62 extraordinary items and 56 (10 at a gain and 45 at a loss) of these represented the early retirement of debt. The other items included casualty losses and gains from asset disposals.

Discontinued Operations

The discontinuation or sale of a component of a business may indicate that it:

- Has inadequate or uncertain markets or prospects
- Has an unsatisfactory contribution to earnings and cash flows
- Is no longer considered by management to be a strategic fit
- Can be sold at a significant profit

Operating income from discontinued operations and any gains or losses (net of taxes) from their sale are segregated in the income statement, since these activities will not contribute to future income and cash flows. As in the case of extraordinary items, this segregation makes the reported information more useful for analysis.

A component of business is defined by SFAS 144 (2001) as any business component with separately identifiable operations, assets, and cash flows that has been disposed of or is held for sale. Subsidiaries and investees also qualify as separate components.

To qualify for treatment as discontinued operations, the assets, results of operations, and investing and financing activities of a component must be separable from those of the firm. SFAS 144 states that the separation must be possible physically and operationally, and for financial reporting purposes.

Once management develops or adopts a formal plan for the sale or disposal of a component (the *measurement date*), the operating results of the component are segregated within the income statement. The income statement will report the income or loss from operations of the discontinued component only on a net-of-tax basis. A condensed income statement for the component is usually shown in a footnote. Prior-period income statements are restated as well.

---

[37] See Reading 43 for a comparison of the accounting and economic consequences of refinancing.

[38] Gains and losses on early retirement of debt were considered extraordinary, except for those related to sinking fund requirements (SFAS 4, 1975).

In the period in which a component of an entity is classified as held for sale or has been disposed of, the results of operations of the component and any gain or loss recognized[39] must be reported as discontinued operations in the income statement for current and prior periods.

Pfizer (see Note 2 to 1999 annual report) sold four businesses in 1998, treating them as discontinued operations. The significant effects include:

- The 1997 balance sheet shows a single line item—net assets of discontinued operations.
- The revenues and expenses of the discontinued operations have been removed from the income statement. The operating earnings from these businesses are combined with the net gain on disposal as earnings from discontinued operations, reported separately on the income statement. Note 2 contains a summarized income statement for these operations.
- The operating cash flow from discontinued businesses is *not* shown separately.[40]

Accounting Changes

Accounting changes fall into two general categories: those undertaken voluntarily by the firm and those mandated by new accounting standards. Generally, accounting changes do not have direct cash flow consequences.

The change from one acceptable accounting method to another acceptable method is reported in the period of change. Any cumulative impact on *prior period* earnings is reported net of tax after extraordinary items and discontinued operations on the income statement.[41] Firms are required to provide footnote disclosure of the impact of the change on current period operations (and on each prior period, if restated) and their justification for the change. However, accounting changes also affect future operating results. That impact is rarely disclosed but can sometimes be estimated. Accounting changes are dealt with frequently in the remaining readings of the text.

APB 20 (1971) identifies four exceptions to the general treatment of accounting changes. These are:

1. Change from LIFO to another inventory method (see Reading 39)
2. Change to or from the full cost method (see Reading 40)
3. Change to or from the percentage-of-completion method
4. Change in accounting methods prior to an initial public offering

These exceptions require retroactive restatement of all years presented.

---

[39] A component classified as held for sale must be reported at the lower of its carrying amount or fair value less cost to sell. A loss must be recognized for any initial or subsequent writedown to fair value less cost to sell. Subsequent gain recognition is limited to the cumulative loss recognized. Only a previously unrecognized gain or loss must be recognized on date of sale or disposal.

[40] Separate disclosure of the cash flows from discontinued operations is optional under U.S. GAAP. However, IAS 35 (1998) requires (para. 6) separate disclosure of "the net cash flows attributable to the operating, investing, and financing cash flows of the discontinuing operation."

[41] In most cases, prior period results are not restated. The cumulative impact is computed under the assumption that the new method had been used in all past periods and is therefore the difference between reported income and what income would have been if the new method had been applied.

In some cases, prior period results are restated; the portion of the cumulative impact applicable to periods preceding those for which an income statement is presented is shown as an adjustment to retained earnings.

Example 31-7

In 1999, Lucent changed its method for calculating the market-related value of pension plan assets (see Chapter 12 for a detailed discussion). The cumulative (net-of-tax) effect of the accounting change was $1,308 million (net of income taxes of $842 million) or $0.42 per diluted share, shown as a separate line item in the income statement. Note 10, Employee Benefit Plans, also reports that the accounting change increased reported 1999 income by $260 million (net of taxes of $167) or $0.08 per diluted share. Lucent reported 1999 net income of $1.52 per diluted share of which nearly one-third ($0.50 per diluted share) came from this accounting change.

Prior Period Adjustments

A change from an incorrect to an acceptable accounting method is treated as an error, and its impact is reported as a *prior period adjustment.* On occasion, newly available information clarifies transactions that were accounted for in prior periods. In some cases, the appropriate adjustment is not reported as a component of current period income, but recorded directly to retained earnings. SFAS 16, Prior Period Adjustments, restricts this treatment to accounting errors. In most cases, however, these adjustments are included in reported income of the period in which the new information becomes available.

IAS Standards for Nonrecurring Items

IAS 8 (revised 1993) governs the treatment of nonrecurring items under IAS GAAP. While these standards are similar to U.S. GAAP, there are several significant differences:

- The IAS definition of extraordinary differs slightly from the U.S. definition, allowing for the possibility of different treatments of the same item.
- IAS 8 does not require the separate presentation of earnings from continuing operations, earnings from discontinued operations, and income before extraordinary items.
- For accounting changes, IAS 8 permits *either* the cumulative change method *or* the restatement of prior periods.[42]
- Errors can be corrected by *either* restating prior periods *or* including the item in current period results.

IAS 35 (1998), which provides standards for discontinued operations, also differs slightly from U.S. GAAP. The most important differences are:

- IAS GAAP requires the estimated losses from a discontinued unit to be reported as incurred, rather than accrued as under U.S. GAAP.
- Impairment losses associated with discontinued operations may be reported as part of the loss from continued operations under IAS GAAP, even if recognized prior to the announcement date.

---

[42] IAS standards do not require the restatement of prior period results in deference to the prohibition against restatement in the GAAP of many countries.

- Under IAS 35, the "discontinuation" date may differ from that under SFAS 144.

Example 31-8

In 1999, Roche announced plans to spin off its flavors and fragrances division, Givaudan (see Note 7 to Roche annual report). Yet the results of Givaudan are included in the Roche income statement for 1999 and its assets and liabilities remain on Roche's December 31, 1999 balance sheet. Givaudan's operating results and cash flows were included in those of Roche through the spinoff date (June 8, 2000).

Analysis of Nonrecurring Items

The preceding discussion of unusual items, extraordinary items, and discontinued operations illustrates the difficulty presented by nonrecurring items. Accounting standard setters cannot draw "bright lines" that are adequate to separate clearly unusual items. In practice, gains tend to be buried in continuing operations, whereas losses are often shown separately; disclosure is not always sufficient. In some cases, the MD&A provides more information about unusual items than the financial statements themselves.

When estimating a firm's "earning power," analysts normally exclude items that are unusual or nonrecurring in nature. Yet such events seem to recur, more so in some companies than others. Some companies seem to be "accident prone," although each "accident" is different. Nonrecurring items are not all alike. Although the sale of assets, divisions, or segments may not be part of continuing operations, such sales may recur, albeit sporadically. Recurring and nonrecurring are not two distinct categories but rather a continuum. The objective, therefore, is to place each item in its appropriate place on the spectrum. *When determining the earnings amount used for firm valuation, the analyst must classify income and expenses between operating and nonrecurring using the preceding discussion rather than relying on the classification provided by the company.*

Income Statement Impact of Nonrecurring Items

The current period income statement effect of nonrecurring items is generally clearly stated. However, such items also have implications for previously reported income and future earnings.

Some nonrecurring items are, in effect, a correction of prior period income. A common example is asset writedowns, frequently included in "restructuring" provisions. Such writedowns suggest that prior period depreciation or amortization changes were insufficient and reported income for these periods was overstated. The recognition of liabilities for environmental remediation is another indication that prior year earnings were overstated.

Asset impairment and "restructuring" charges result in increases in future reported income. To the extent that assets are written down, future depreciation and amortization expense will be lower than would otherwise have been the case. The accrual of future lease rental expense and employee severance costs also affects future earnings, which will no longer be saddled with these costs. The restructuring charges recorded by Texaco contain asset writedowns that reflect on both past and future reported earnings.

These implications for previous and future earnings must be carefully considered. *If nonrecurring charges are really prior year expenses taken too late or future expenses charged off early, then the practice of ignoring nonrecurring charges and focusing on recurring operating income results in an overestimation of the firm's earnings trend.*

Some commentators have criticized the ever-increasing spate of restructurings and special charges (e.g., Texaco reports several in each of the years 1997 to 2000) as being motivated by the desire to paint a better earnings picture:

> How can repeated write-offs be nonrecurring or extraordinary? *How can investors believe that reported earnings are real and won't be canceled by subsequent write-offs?* . . .
>
> Here's how this kind of charge can boost earnings. Say Company XYZ reports rising profits of $1 million in year 1 and $1.2 million in year 2; in year 3, XYZ takes a restructuring charge of $5 million for the cost of closing a few businesses. The charge turned year 3's net into a loss of $3.5 million—but XYZ says profit would have been $1.5 million before the charge. The next year, year 4, the upward trend resumes as XYZ reports profits of $1.8 million. But the results are helped because $2 million of the company's year 4 expenses—say, for severance payments and plant closings—can be counted against the charge already taken in year 3. . . .
>
> *The most obvious way restructuring charges make companies' earnings look better is if the companies can convince investors that operating earnings—before the charges—provide a more meaningful indication of trends.* . . .
>
> Wall Street analysts often use some version of operating earnings—not counting charges—to track a company's earnings trend. Thus, many analysts and research services that follow AT&T show a tidy growth track for the company: $3.13 a share for 1994, $3.45 for 1995, and $3.95 for 1996. But that doesn't include AT&T's 1995 charges of $5.4 billion, or $3.35 a share. . . . [43]

We believe that the need to assess "nonrecurring" charges has increased since these words were written. Moreover, the increased use of pro forma earnings for valuation purposes (discussed in Box 31-4) has made these issues even more pressing.

Cash Flow and Valuation Impact

Nonrecurring items with cash flow consequences do affect the wealth of the firm. However, they should still be segregated because their valuation implications differ from those for recurring income. As outlined in Box 31-1 and discussed in greater detail in Reading 19, (true) nonrecurring components of income have only a onetime dollar-for-dollar effect on valuation, whereas the multiple for changes in recurring income (the price-earnings multiple) is greater.

The analyst must distinguish among items that:

- Have no cash flow implications (e.g., asset writedowns)
- Affect current period cash flow only (e.g., employee severance costs)
- Have future cash flow effects (e.g., lease payments for closed facilities)

Careful attention must be paid to footnote disclosures to ascertain the cash flow effects of "restructuring" provisions in particular. In some cases, the cash drain from such provisions extends years into the future.

---

[43] Quotations are excerpted from "Are Companies Using Restructuring Costs to Fudge the Figures?: A Repeated Strategic Move Makes Future Earnings Seem Unrealistically Rosy," *Wall Street Journal* (January 30, 1996), emphasis added.

BOX 31-4 PRO FORMA EARNINGS

An increasing number of companies are reporting pro forma earnings in press releases announcing their earnings before filing quarterly reports with the SEC. Companies use varying definitions of "pro forma earnings" and some companies report more than one category of such earnings. Unlike GAAP-based earnings, pro forma earnings *exclude one or more of the following* expenses and gains or losses:

- Goodwill amortization
- Other intangible-asset amortization
- Stock-compensation expense
- Writedowns of impaired assets
- Restructuring charges
- Severance pay and early or involuntary termination benefits
- Interest expense
- Marketing expenses
- Results of Internet operations (and other wholly or majority-owned subsidiaries, and equity-method investees)
- Gain or loss on sale of stock in subsidiaries, investees, or other affiliates

Companies have advanced several reasons to justify reporting pro forma earnings:

- Users of financial statements and analysts prefer "cash earnings" that exclude amortization of goodwill and other noncash charges.
- Management's breakdown of earnings and cash flows enhances the transparency of financial statements and is more informative.
- Restructuring charges, impairments, and other one-time or nonrecurring charges are not relevant as they are not expected to contribute to future earnings and cash flows.
- The results of operations of Internet operations and other subsidiaries or affiliates may not be relevant if the company plans to spin off the operations at some unspecified or uncertain future date.

The SEC has expressed concern about but has no authority to specify what companies say in press releases. Unfortunately, some analysts have acceded to management demands to forecast pro forma earnings rather than GAAP-based earnings.

In 2001, Financial Executives International (FEI) proposed guidelines for press releases intended to reflect best practices and reduce abusive practices.

Example 31-9

In a January 30, 2001 press release, Amazon.com announced its fourth quarter 2000 results, with the following headline:

Fourth-Quarter 2000 Pro Forma Operating Loss Improves from 26 Percent to 6 Percent of Net Sales

The release reported a pro forma operating loss for the fourth quarter of 2000 of $60 million, or 6% of net sales. The reported pro forma net loss was $90 million. Later in the press release the company reported that its fourth-quarter GAAP loss from operations was $322 million and the GAAP-based net loss was $545 million, including charges of $339 million for impairment of goodwill and equity investments. Stock-based compensation charges and equity in losses of equity-method investees were among the other items excluded from the pro forma operating loss.

When a company has truly nonrecurring gains or losses, or has made a large acquisition or divestiture, data that remove the effects of these distortions may be very informative. However, in most cases, the reporting of pro forma operating results is an effort to persuade analysts to ignore certain expenses or categories of expense and thereby improve the valuation of the firm's securities. Thus it is important to cast a skeptical eye on such reports; the analyst should use reported GAAP data (after appropriate adjustments by the analyst) for valuation decisions.

The 1995 pretax business restructuring charges of $2,467 million and asset impairment and other charges of $188 million reported by Lucent are a good example of the continuing income and cash flow consequences of such announcements. Its 1999 annual report shows deductions from business restructuring reserves, noncash charges, and cash payments continuing through fiscal 1999. In 1999, Lucent reversed $141 million of the business restructuring charges due to favorable experience in employee separation and lower costs of other restructuring projects announced in 1995.

Implications for Continuing Operations

Nonrecurring events, even those without cash flow effects, may also provide useful information about the firm. A plant closing and the write-off of its book value are one example. The actual cash outflows occurred in the past and are only now being expensed. The value implication of the gain or loss reported on the income statement may be nonexistent. The plant closing itself may, however, help forecast the firm's future sales, earnings, and cash flows. Similarly, Lucent's 1995 restructuring charge included employee severance costs. Future reported earnings should be higher than previously expected because its employment costs are reduced. The reduced number of employees also will affect benefit accruals (see Chapter 12).

Management Discretion and Earnings Manipulation

When estimating earnings trends, the analyst must also be wary of the discretionary nature of the income statement. Items requiring separate disclosure on the income statement may be discretionary with respect to the:

- Timing of the occurrence (e.g., the disposal of an asset or the discontinuation of a segment)
- Classification of the item (ordinary, unusual, or extraordinary)

In addition, changes in accounting methods can alter reported income statement trends. In many cases, there is no disclosure (except in the aggregate) of the effects of the accounting change on income reported in individual prior periods, making adjustment difficult.

The discretionary nature of income recognition permits an examination of the degree of management manipulation of earnings under one or more of the following guises:

- Classification of good news/bad news
- Income smoothing
- Big-bath behavior
- Accounting changes

Classification of Good News/Bad News. Management prefers to report good news "above the line" as part of continuing operations and bad news "below the line" as extraordinary or discontinued operations. For example, management determines whether the component of the firm sold meets the definition of a discontinued operation and hence is given below-the-line treatment as income from discontinued operations. As SFAS 131 notes, the

> management approach (to segmentation) is based on the way the management organizes the segments within the enterprise for making operating decisions and assessing performance.[44]

This discretion permits management to report unusual items most favorably.[45]

Income Smoothing. Some firms reduce earnings in good years (defer gains or recognize losses) and inflate earnings in bad years (recognize gains or defer losses) in order to report stable earnings. Empirical evidence indicates that managements can and do engage in such behavior by engaging in two types of smoothing. *Intertemporal smoothing* refers to either:

- Timing expenditures such as research and development, repairs and maintenance, and asset disposals, or
- Choosing accounting methods (e.g., capitalization or expensing) that allocate the expenditure over time.

Classificatory smoothing is smoothing by choosing to classify an item as either income from continuing operations, or extraordinary income. The implicit assumption is that analysts focus on ordinary income and ignore nonrecurring/extraordinary items. Thus, by shifting items above or below the line, management can report a desired trend.

Asset sales are an example of a nonrecurring item that has been used as both an intertemporal and classificatory smoothing instrument. Bartov (1993) showed that such sales have been *timed* to smooth income. Furthermore, as there is discretion in how a segment is defined, the sale of a portion of a business can be classified as part of continuing operations or as a discontinued operation. Fried et al. (1996) showed that the *classification* choices made by their sample of firms were consistent with smoothing.

Ronen and Sadan (1981) have argued that smoothing is not necessarily bad. Rather, by engaging in smoothing, management may be aiding the predictive ability of reported earnings by conveying information about the future prospects of the firm. Moses (1987) made similar arguments. Possible incentives for earnings manipulation are varied [see the discussion in Bartov (1993) and the survey paper by Healy and Wahlen (1999)] and not necessarily limited to the desire to show stable earnings and/or aid predictive ability. A number of authors [e.g., Healy (1985), Holthausen et al. (1995), and Gaver et al. (1995)] examined executive bonus plans and showed that depending on the structure of such plans, management may be motivated to engage in discretionary accruals, manipulating earnings in an upward or downward direction. Jones (1991) showed that firms that would benefit from import relief (e.g., tariff increases and quota reductions) decrease income through earnings manipulation in order to influence the U.S. International Trade Commission. Bartov, on the other hand, demonstrated that firms attempt to manipulate earnings in an upward direction in order to escape possible restrictions imposed by their bond covenant agreements.

---

[44] SFAS 131, para. 4.

[45] Rapacciolli and Schiff (1991) show that in their sample of about 500 disposals, approximately 60% of the cases were accorded the more favorable treatment, with 61% of gains reported above the line and 57% of losses reported below the line.

More recently, research has focused on earnings management geared to meet (or just beat) analysts' expectations. Burgstahler and Eames (1998) found that managers manage earnings upward to avoid missing analyst expectations.[46] In this spirit, Bradshaw, Moberg, and Sloan (2000) broaden the definition of earnings management to include "management of the 'perception' of earnings" and argue that managers have taken earnings management a step further by encouraging analysts to focus on (management defined) pro forma earnings (discussed in Box 31-4) rather than GAAP earnings.

Big-Bath Accounting. In contrast to income smoothing, the big-bath hypothesis suggests that management will report additional losses in bad years in the hope that, by taking all available losses at one time, they will "clear the decks" once and for all. The implicit assumption is that future reported profits will increase.

This hypothesis is more widely accepted in the financial press than in the academic literature. Francis, Hanna, and Vincent (1996) and Elliott and Shaw (1988) found that analyst forecasts following large write-offs are not consistent with the big-bath theory. Rather than increasing following a write-off, indicating a clearing of the deck, forecast earnings tended to decrease. Fried et al. (1989) reported that a firm taking an asset writedown in one year is likely to take another one soon after. This is inconsistent with big-bath behavior, which argues that firms would overestimate rather than underestimate the size and amounts of write-offs.[47]

Accounting Changes. Regardless of whether accounting changes are voluntary or mandatory, they typically have no direct cash flow consequences for a U.S. company.[48] Thus, such changes can be viewed as a form of earnings manipulation. Empirical research has studied accounting changes extensively, focusing on both managerial motivations and stock market reaction. We shall refer to many of these studies in later readings.

Elliott and Philbrick (1990) examined the effects of accounting changes on earnings predictability. Not surprisingly, they found that analysts had difficulty forecasting earnings for the year of the change. That difficulty was more pronounced for mandatory changes, for which there was no prior information regarding the change. Moreover, they found that when analysts had no prior information about the change, the effect of the accounting change tended to be in the *opposite* direction of forecast revisions made by analysts in the latter part of the fiscal year (fourth quarter). For example, accounting changes that *increased* income were associated with *downward* forecast revisions; that is, when income was lower than originally expected (causing downward forecast revisions), accounting changes were adopted that raised reported income. This behavior, the authors concluded, was consistent with management's use of accounting changes to manipulate or smooth earnings.

Quality of Earnings

The term "quality of earnings" is used in two different senses. We use it to mean the use of accounting methods and assumptions that tend not to overstate reported revenues and earnings. The discussion of revenue and expense recognition earlier in this reading should already have provided a sense of how accounting methods and assumptions can affect reported operating results.

---

46 Similar evidence was found by Kaznick (1999) with respect to meeting management's own earnings forecasts.

47 See the discussion of impairment in Reading 8 for more details of these results.

48 The FIFO to LIFO change is the major exception in the United States (see Reading 39).

However, some use the term to indicate consistency of reported earnings (lack of volatility). The two meanings are somewhat contradictory. Firms that report "consistent" earnings growth often do so by managing earnings in ways that the external analyst cannot see. Earnings management may include the use of aggressive accounting assumptions when required to meet analyst expectations. Companies that stretch the financial reporting system to meet unattainable expectations may also cross the line into financial fraud. Companies that use conservative methods are unlikely to commit fraud, as they can change accounting methods and assumptions first.

We return to the subject of quality of earnings in Chapter 17, as the discussion is more useful after all of the intervening readings have been covered.

5 THE BALANCE SHEET

The balance sheet (statement of financial position) reports the categories and amounts of assets (firm resources), liabilities (claims on those resources), and stockholders' equity at specific points in time. In the United States, balance sheets are generally issued at the end of each quarter and the end of the fiscal year; outside of the United States, annual or semiannual reporting is the general rule.

Format and Classification

The definitions of assets, liabilities, and stockholders' equity are discussed in Reading 1. We now discuss the format and classification prevalent in most companies. IAS standards are similar to those used by firms in the United States. Box 31-5 on page 548 lists and discusses Pfizer's balance sheet components.

Assets and liabilities are classified according to liquidity, that is, their expected use in operations or conversion to cash in the case of assets and time to maturity for liabilities. Assets expected to be converted to cash or used within one year (or one operating cycle, if longer than one year) are classified as current assets. Current liabilities include obligations the firm expects to settle within one year (or one operating cycle, if longer).

Assets expected to provide benefits and services over periods exceeding one year and liabilities to be repaid after one year are classified as long-term assets and liabilities. Tangible assets and liabilities are generally reported before intangibles and other assets and liabilities whose measurement is less certain.

This classification scheme can be used to develop ratios employed in financial analysis. The current–noncurrent distinction can be used to measure liquidity, for example. In recent years, however, that distinction has become somewhat arbitrary as differences between short-term and long-term investments and debt are sometimes difficult to discern.

The most liquid assets, cash and cash equivalents, precede marketable equity securities, receivables, inventories, and prepaid expenses in the current asset section of the balance sheet. Long-lived assets, including property, plant, and equipment, investments in affiliated companies, and intangible assets such as brand names, patents, copyrights, and goodwill, are reported as noncurrent assets.

Short-term bank and other debt, the current portion of long-term debt and capitalized leases, accounts payable to suppliers, accrued liabilities (amounts owed to employees and others), interest, and taxes payable are classified as current liabilities. Long-term debt, capitalized lease obligations, pension obligations, and other "liabilities" (such as deferred income taxes and minority interest in the net assets of consolidated affiliates) are commonly observed noncurrent liabilities.

Stockholders' equity (the residual interest in the firm) lists components in order of their priority in liquidation with any preference (preferred) stock listed before common stock, Treasury stock, and reinvested earnings. This section may also include the additional components shown in Box 31-5.

Measurement of Assets and Liabilities

Most components of the balance sheet are reported at historical cost, that is, the exchange price at their acquisition date. As noted earlier in this reading, in the discussion of the accrual concept of income, the nature (and amount) of a recognized asset is a function of the firm's revenue recognition method.

In some cases (e.g., accounts receivable), valuation allowances (reserve for uncollectible receivables) adjust the originally recorded amount to an approximation of net realizable value. The reserve for uncollectibles is an estimate of bad debts, reported as a deduction from the gross receivables balance; this is called a *contra* account. (Accumulated depreciation is also a contra account since it reduces the carrying value of long-lived assets to reflect their use.)

Changes in some other assets or liabilities are accumulated in *adjunct* accounts, such as the premium on bonds payable that records the excess of the bond's issue price over its face value. These contra and adjunct accounts allow firms to report both the original, historical cost (e.g., gross plant assets) and the net carrying amount (plant assets net of accumulated depreciation). They also reflect management's estimate of realizable values of the underlying assets, for example, receivables net of the allowance for uncollectibles. However, these are accounting estimates of net realizable values and not market values.[49]

Lower of cost or market and impairment rules[50] may, however, require writedowns to fair or market values when they are below cost. In most cases, however, market values are not reflected in the balance sheet prior to realization, and recoveries (reversal of previous writedowns) to the original acquisition cost are not allowed under U.S. GAAP.[51] The exception to this rule is the accounting for investments in securities (see Chapter 13).[52]

Finally, the assets and liabilities of foreign affiliates or those denominated in other currencies are reported at amounts translated from other currencies at the exchange rate prevailing on the financial statement date or a combination of this current rate and specific historical rates for certain components.[53]

The balance sheet does not report all assets and liabilities of the firm, but reflects only those meeting specific recognition criteria.[54] Some assets and liabilities meet these criteria, but are not reported because they cannot be reliably measured (see the discussion of contingencies in Reading 29).

---

[49] The level and trend of the allowance for uncollectible receivables may, however, help assess the market value of receivables, as well as the firm's credit policies and revenue recognition method.

[50] See Reading 41.

[51] Under IASB standards, however, writedowns of fixed and intangible assets can be written back up to the original carrying amount if conditions change (see Reading 41).

[52] Companies also record acquired assets and liabilities at fair market value when the purchase method is used. See Chapter 14 for a comparison of the purchase and pooling methods.

[53] See Chapter 15 for a detailed discussion.

[54] SFAC 5, Recognition and Measurement in Financial Statements of Business Enterprises (FASB 1984), requires financial statement recognition when four basic criteria are met:

Definition. The item qualifies as an element (e.g., asset or liability) of financial statements.

Measurability. It can be reliably measured.

Relevance. The information provided by the item can make a difference in user decisions.

Reliability. The information is representationally faithful, verifiable and neutral.

Recognition is subject to cost/benefit and materiality constraints.

BOX 31-5 PFIZER, INC. BALANCE SHEET COMPONENTS

Although every firm's financial statements are unique, we can use Pfizer's 1997–1999 balance sheets* to review the components of the balance sheet. These components are discussed in greater detail in various readings as listed below:

Assets	Reading
Cash and cash equivalents	3
Investments and loans	13
Accounts receivable	2, 4
Inventories	4, 6
Deferred income taxes	9
Prepaid expenses	2
Deferred taxes	9
Current assets	4
Net assets of discontinued operations	2
Fixed assets	7
(Accumulated depreciation)	8
Capital leases	11
Investments in affiliates	13, 15
Prepaid pension costs	12
Intangible assets†	7, 14
Liabilities	
Accounts payable	4
Income tax liability	9
Advance billings	2
Current liabilities	4, 10
Debt—short- and long-term	10
Capital leases	11
Pensions and other postretirement benefits	12
Deferred income tax	9
Minority interest	13
Stockholders' equity	2
Cumulative translation adjustment	15
Minimum pension liability	12
Unrealized gains and losses	13
Treasury stock	2

In the discussion that follows, all "Note" references are to the financial statement footnotes of Pfizer.

Assets

SFAS 95 defines *cash and cash equivalents* as risk-free assets with original maturities of 90 days or less. Examples include bank accounts, U.S. Treasury Bills, and similar assets. The net change in cash and cash equivalents for the period is reported in the statement of cash flows. Other investments (Note 4-A), which do not meet the criteria for reporting as cash equivalents, are shown separately (broken out into short-term and long-term components).

Accounts receivable may contain both trade receivables (which may include loans to customers) and notes receivable (e.g., from asset sales or loans to management). The distinction is important. Trade receivables are a result of credit sales of products and services and they are important indicators of liquidity and the soundness of revenue recognition methods. The maturity and collectibility of notes receivable may have important implications for the future cash flow and the liquidity of the firm. As Pfizer shows loans separately, its accounts receivable may be trade-only.

The accounting method used for *inventories* (Notes 1-C and 6) can significantly affect the measurement of this important operating asset as well as the level and trend of reported income. As noted in Box 31-3, Pfizer wrote off $310 million of excess inventories of a suspended drug and it switched to the first-in, first-out inventory costing method in 1999, recording a pretax benefit of $6.6 million.

Deferred income taxes represent deferred tax debits. Note 9 provides details regarding the firm's income tax position. Prepaid expenses and taxes (some companies use the "other current assets" caption) may include prepaid expenses such as tax and insurance prepayments, items that will be reported as expenses in future income statements.

Total current assets include all of Pfizer's assets that are expected to generate cash (or reduce cash outflows) within one year or one operating cycle. However, most of these assets revolve; new receivables and inventories arise as old ones are used in the manufacturing process and turned into cash. Thus, current assets alone are not a forecast of future cash flow.

As required by U.S. GAAP, Pfizer shows the assets of discontinued operations net of liabilities.

Property, plant, and equipment (PPE) is the largest asset category for many industrial and manufacturing companies. The stated amount is a function of accounting policies regarding the capitalization, depreciation, and impairment. Note 7 contains a breakdown of Pfizer's fixed assets and Note 11 tells us that a small amount of operating properties have been leased. Assets under operating leases are not included in the PPE totals; Note 11 provides data on Pfizer's operating leases.

We assume that Pfizer has included prepaid pension cost (Note 10) in its "other assets, deferred taxes, and deferred charges" category. Pensions are discussed in Chapter 12. Pfizer reports *goodwill and other acquired intangibles* reflecting the excess of the purchase price over the fair value of identifiable net assets acquired in purchase method business acquisitions.

"Other assets, deferred taxes, and deferred charges" may contain long-term deferred tax debits, investments in securities, and intangible assets such as goodwill. Unlike some firms, Pfizer does not provide complete footnote disclosure of the components of this category, although Note 9 does report the location of all deferred tax accruals.

Liabilities

Total current liabilities include *accounts payable* (trade payables represent amounts owed to the suppliers of operating assets such as inventories), *payroll and benefit-related liabilities* (obligations to employees for services received), debt maturing within one year (amounts expected to be repaid during the next year; see Notes 4-B and C), and the relatively significant (15% of current liabilities) other current liabilities.

Note 10 provides necessary detail for *postretirement and benefit-related liabilities. Long-term debt* (Notes 4-C and 11 for operating leases) reflects amounts to be paid after one year. Note 9 lists the sources of *deferred income taxes—net*, and the poorly explained *other noncurrent liabilities* rounds out the long-term liabilities.

Stockholders' Equity

Pfizer has authorized but never issued *preferred stock*. When issued, preferred stock would represent a claim senior to that represented by the outstanding *common stock*. The *additional paid-in capital* and common stock in total represent the total amount received by the firm from issuance or other sales of stock. Pfizer reports adjustments to additional paid-in capital due to employee stock option and benefit trust transactions. Pfizer, as most companies, separately reports Treasury stock, representing expenditures incurred to repurchase common stock. Pfizer also reports shares held by its employee benefit trusts (Note 14).

Retained earnings report the accumulated earnings that were not paid as dividends to stockholders. For most companies, the distinction between these three components of capital is unimportant. In rare cases, however, a low level of (or absence of) retained earnings may affect the firm's ability to declare dividends or the tax treatment of those dividends. The *employee benefit trusts* reflects transactions with or commitments to those plans.

Accumulated other comprehensive income (loss) includes (Note 5):

- Foreign currency translation adjustment,
- Minimum pension liability, and
- Unrealized holding gains (or losses) on investments carried at market value.

---

* Pfizer reports three consecutive balance sheets, facilitating analysis. Most companies report only two years.

† Not shown in these years.

Some intangible assets have extremely uncertain or hard-to-measure benefits, for example, customer lists or brand names, and they are recognized only when acquired in a purchase method acquisition. Others, such as research and development, are never recognized as assets under U.S. GAAP. Similarly, liabilities may exist as a result of legal action, but because they are not reliably measurable, only footnote disclosure may be required (see, e.g., Note 18 on litigation in Pfizer's 1999 financial statements).

Thus, a balance sheet does not report the market value of a firm's assets, liabilities, or equity, although the information provided can be useful when estimating the market value of the firm or its securities.

Uses of the Balance Sheet

The reported balance sheet is one starting point for the analysis of a firm. It provides information about a firm's resources (assets) and obligations (liabilities), including liquidity and solvency. For creditors, the balance sheet provides information about the nature of assets that the firm uses as debt collateral.

The balance sheet also reports on a firm's earnings-generating ability in two ways. First, assets are defined as economic resources that are expected to provide future benefits. Consistent with the long-run going concern perspective of the firm, these future benefits are not only cash flows but also the ability to generate earnings.

Receivables are forecasts of cash collections. Fixed assets and inventory, on the other hand, are assets that generate future sales. Increases and decreases in such assets assist forecasts of the firm's sales and profitability.

Second, proper evaluation of a firm's profitability must consider the amount of resources, that is, the level of investment, required for a specified level of sales or profitability. The balance sheet provides such data and (together with the income statement) can be used to measure the efficiency of a firm's operations and its return on investment.

The balance sheet can also generate forecasts about a firm's future cash flow needs. The asset levels needed to generate certain operating levels as well as the age of the firm's assets are useful inputs in assessing when a firm may have to replace its assets.

Finally, the reported balance sheet is the starting point for the preparation of an adjusted balance sheet and book value using current cost data. In Reading 17, we show how to prepare a current cost balance sheet, using adjustments discussed in many chapters along the way.

Limitations of the Balance Sheet. The usefulness of the balance sheet is limited by the following three factors:

1. *Selective reporting.* Important assets and liabilities may be omitted from the balance sheet because GAAP does not require their inclusion. One example is operating leases and other off-balance-sheet financing techniques (see Reading 44). Some included assets may have no economic value (see the discussion of goodwill in Chapter 14).
2. *Measurement.* Some assets and liabilities are carried at historical cost, others at market value. Historical costs may bear little relationship to their real market value. Inventories (Reading 39) and long-lived assets (Reading 40) are good examples.
3. *Delayed recognition.* GAAP permits companies to delay recognition of value changes. An important example is employee benefit plans, discussed in Chapter 12.

Fortunately, footnote and supplementary data are often used by analysts to adjust reported balance sheets and thereby improve their usefulness. Starting with Reading 39, we discuss the adjustments that can be made to prepare a current cost balance sheet that provides a better measure of a firm's resources and obligations. In Chapter 17, as already stated, we show how to prepare a current cost balance sheet.

6 STATEMENT OF STOCKHOLDERS' EQUITY

This statement reports components of stockholders' equity or the investment of the owners in the firm, the earnings reinvested in the business, and various accounting adjustments that reflect selected market value changes in certain investments in securities, any minimum pension liability, certain unrealized gains and losses on cash flow hedges, and the effect of exchange rate changes on certain foreign subsidiaries. U.S. and IAS GAAP have similar requirements for the presentation of stockholders' equity.

Format, Classification, and Use

Companies generally report components of stockholders' equity in order of preference upon liquidation. For each class of shares, firms report the number of shares authorized, issued, and outstanding at each balance sheet date.

Preferred (preference) stock has priority for liquidation and dividends. Common characteristics and related disclosure requirements include but are not limited to:

- Cumulative rights to dividends that may be:
  - Fixed.
  - Floating rate.
  - Tied to amounts declared for common stock.
- Callable by issuer; call price must be disclosed.
- Convertible into common stock at option of holder; specified prices must be disclosed.
- Mandatory conversion into common shares at a specified date or under certain conditions; terms must be disclosed.

These features must be evaluated to determine the treatment of different classes of preferred stock in the analysis of leverage, capital structure, and earnings per share.

Redeemable preferred stock is redeemable at the option of the holder or according to a fixed time schedule. Such issues must be excluded from stockholders' equity, and reported after liabilities but before the equity section of the balance sheet.[55] The liquidation preference or redemption price should be used in the computation of book value per share, leverage, and capital ratios.

Common stock represents the owners' residual interest in the firm after all other claims have been met. Firms may issue one or more classes of common stock. The balance sheet or related footnotes generally disclose the various rights (such as voting rights and dividends) of the different classes of common stock. The par (or stated) value of common stock is normally reported separately from any additional paid-in capital. The latter represents the cumulative difference between the par value of common and the amount received when issued.

Firms often purchase their own common stock on the open market when management thinks it is undervalued, for reissue, or to prevent hostile takeovers. Treasury stock is usually reported as a contra account within stockholders' equity.[56] Although such repurchases were largely a U.S. phenomenon, they have become increasingly common in other countries.

The statement of stockholders' equity also reconciles the beginning and ending balance of retained earnings reinvested in the firm. This reconciliation reports the net income for the period, preferred and common dividends declared during the year, and any adjustments for stock splits, stock dividends, and acquisitions or quasi-reorganizations.

---

[55] Rule 5-02(28) of Regulation S-X requires the exclusion of mandatorily redeemable preferred stock from the equity section of the financial statements. Preferred stocks that are not redeemable or are redeemable only at the option of the issuer and common stock should be included in the equity section. Staff Accounting Bulletin 64 details the accounting treatment of redeemable preferred.

[56] Some companies report the difference between the purchase price of Treasury stock and the price at subsequent reissuance of that Treasury stock as a component of additional paid-in capital. Other firms reflect this difference as an adjustment to retained earnings.

The statement must also report changes in comprehensive income (see Reading 29 for presentation and discussion). There may be changes in the:

- Minimum liability recognized for underfunded pension plans (see Chapter 12)
- Market values of noncurrent investments (see Chapter 13)
- Unrealized gains and losses on cash flow hedges (see Chapter 16)
- Cumulative effect of exchange rate changes (Chapter 15)
- Unearned shares issued to employee stock ownership plans (ESOPs)

However, these items are sometimes different under IAS standards than under U.S. GAAP.

The valuation allowance for changes in the carrying amount of investment securities and the cumulative translation adjustment are examples of reserves permitted by U.S. or IAS GAAP. For many foreign companies, the statement of stockholders' equity includes reserve accounts that are required or discretionary under financial reporting standards or tax rules. Some foreign firms appropriate some percentage of earnings to preserve liquidity by limiting earnings available for dividends. The use of conservative accounting rules can achieve the same goal.

Some foreign countries permit firms to account for selected transactions as direct charges to the additional paid-in capital account. These include debt and equity issue and repurchase costs (including premiums and discounts on debt) and organization costs. Finally, some countries allow the revaluation of assets with the resulting gain or loss reported in a revaluation reserve. UK GAAP (SSAP 6) requires a statement or a separate footnote on changes in reserves.

The growth of international capital markets has increased the transparency of reserves reported by foreign multinationals. Examples are provided and analyzed in various readings in the text.

Example 31-10

Pfizer's 1999 Consolidated Balance Sheet and Statement of Shareholders' Equity report the:

1. Number of preferred shares authorized (none are outstanding).
2. Par value and number of common shares authorized and issued as of year-end.[57]
3. Additional paid-in capital.
4. Retained earnings and changes due to net income and common dividends declared.
5. Accumulated other comprehensive income (expense) and changes in each of its after-tax components.
6. Deduction for shares held by employee benefit trusts, and the annual changes (see Note 14 for discussion).
7. Deduction for Treasury stock repurchased (see Note 12 for details).

---

[57] Note that the 1999 stock split increased par value by $138 million and reduced APIC by an equal amount.

When a company has preferred shares outstanding, careful attention should be paid to their terms. When shares are convertible into common, the analyst should consider treating them as common shares when conversion is highly likely. When computing book value per common share, preferred shares should be stated at their redemption value when higher than the par or stated *amount.*

Example 31-11

Hecla Mining reported the following in its annual report for the year ended December 31, 2000:

Shareholders' Equity

December 31 Amounts in $thousands	**2000**	**1999**
Preferred stock, $0.25 par value, authorized 5,000,000 shares; issued and outstanding—2,300,000 shares, liquidation preference $119,025	575	575
Common stock, $0.25 par value, authorized 100,000,000 shares; issued 2000—66,859,752 shares, issued 1999—66,844,575 shares	16,715	16,711
Capital surplus	400,236	400,205
Accumulated deficit	(366,523)	(278,533)
Accumulated other comprehensive loss	(4,858)	(4,871)
Less stock held by grantor trust; 2000—139,467 common shares, 1999—132,290 common shares	(514)	(500)
Less treasury stock, at cost; 2000—62,114 common shares, 1999—62,111 common shares	(886)	(886)
Total shareholders' equity	44,745	132,701

Note 11: Shareholders' Equity
Preferred Stock

Hecla has 2.3 million shares of Series B Cumulative Convertible Preferred Stock (the Preferred Shares) outstanding. Holders of the Preferred Shares are entitled to receive cumulative cash dividends at the annual rate of $3.50 per share payable quarterly, when and if declared by the Board of Directors. As of January 31, 2001, Hecla has failed to pay the equivalent of two quarterly dividends of $4.0 million.

The Preferred Shares are convertible, in whole or in part, at the option of the holders thereof, into shares of common stock at an initial conversion price of $15.55 per share of common stock. The Preferred Shares were not redeemable by Hecla prior to July 1, 1996. After such date, the shares are redeemable at the option of Hecla at any time, in whole or in part, initially at $52.45 per share and thereafter at prices declining ratably on each July 1 to $50.00 per share on or after July 1, 2003.

While the preferred shares are shown at their carrying amount (575,000) they should be valued at their liquidating preference of $119 million [(2.3 million shares × $50 per share) + $4 million of unpaid dividends].[58] Correctly valuing the preferred shows that Hecla's common stockholders' equity was negative. As the market price of Hecla's common shares was $.50 at December 31, 2000, clearly the conversion feature had insignificant value at that date.

---

[58] One can also argue for a liquidating value of $121.4 million [(2.3 million shares × $51.05 per share) + $4 million of unpaid dividends], where $51.05 is the redemption price at December 31, 2000.

SUMMARY

7

This introduces the balance sheet, the income statement, and the accrual concept that links them together. Financial statements are interrelated and good financial analysis requires the use of all available information. Our introduction, therefore, is incomplete.

The next reading discusses the use of the cash flow statement and cash flow data in the assessment of the firm. It begins with the cash flow statement and the information it contains, and then develops the relationship between cash flow and income. Reading 33 concludes our introduction to a firm's financial statements—the raw material of analysis.

PROBLEMS

1. [Revenue recognition criteria] Describe the conditions under which revenue would be recognized:
   a. At the time of production, but prior to sale
   b. At the time of sale, but prior to cash collection
   c. Only when cash collection has occurred
2. [Contract accounting; CFA© adapted] On December 31, 1999, LAS1 Construction entered into a major long-term construction with the following terms:

   Total contract price $3,000,000

   Total expected cost $2,400,000

   Construction is expected to take three years. Production costs and cash flows are shown in the following table:

   Projected Production Costs and Cash Flows

Year	Costs Incurred	Cash Received
2000	$ 900,000	$1,000,000
2001	800,000	1,000,000
2002	700,000	1,000,000
Totals	$2,400,000	$3,000,000

   a. Show the revenue and pretax income for each year under *both* the percentage-of-completion and completed contract methods.
   b. Show the balance sheet accounts at December 31, 2000 resulting from the contract under the
      (i) Percentage-of-completion method
      (ii) Completed contract method
   c. Assume that total projected costs increase by $100,000 and the change in estimate is made at December 31, 2001. Compute the revenue and pretax income for 2001 under the revised assumption.
3. [Balance sheet effects of revenue recognition methods] Lucent's balance sheet shows the following accounts:
   - Contracts in process (current assets)
   - Advance billings (current liabilities)

   a. Describe the nature of the two accounts listed above.
   b. State the other accounts on the company's balance sheet to which these accounts are similar.
   c. Determine the accounting method that Lucent uses to account for its long-term construction projects.
4. [Provision for bad debts] Nucor [NUE], a large U.S. steel producer, reported the following (amounts in $millions):

	Years Ended December 31			
	1997	1998	1999	2000
Allowance for Doubtful Accounts				
Opening balance	$ 14.6	$ 18.0	$ 16.3	$ 21.1
Charged to earnings	4.2	(1.4)	5.3	
Write-offs (net of recoveries)	(0.8)	(0.3)	(0.5)	
Closing balance	$ 18.0	$ 16.3	$ 21.1	$ 27.6
Other Financial Data				
Accounts receivable (net)	$ 386.4	$ 299.2	$ 393.8	$ 350.2
Sales	4,184.5	4,151.2	4,009.3	4,586.1
Pretax income	460.2	415.3	379.2	478.3

a. Compute the following ratios (in %):

(i) Ending balance of reserves to gross receivables for all years

(ii) Accounts written off to revenues for 1997 to 1999

b. Assuming that Nucor had expensed accounts written off rather than accruing a reserve for bad debts, compute pretax income for 1997 through 2000.

c. Assuming that Nucor had maintained its bad debt reserve at the 1997 ratio of gross receivables, compute the effect on pretax income for 1998 through 2000.

d. Discuss two reasons that might explain the level of reserve accrual by Nucor for 1998 through 2000.

Nucor did not disclose the charge to earnings and writeoffs in 2000. Nucor's CFO told one of the authors that: "the amounts are clearly immaterial, bad debt writeoffs for the last six years averaged .02% of sales, and in no year were more than .03% of sales."

e. Evaluate the CFO's statement that the amounts are immaterial, stating one argument that supports his statement and one argument against it.

f. Explain why a chief financial officer would prefer not to disclose the charge to earnings and writeoffs.

g. Explain why a financial analyst would want those disclosures.

THE STATEMENT OF CASH FLOWS

READING 32

LEARNING OUTCOMES

The candidate should be able to:

a. identify the types of important information for investment decision making presented in the statement of cash flows;

b. compare and contrast the categories (i.e., cash provided or used by operating activities, investing activities, and financing activities) in a statement of cash flows, and describe how noncash investing and financing transactions are reported;

c. calculate and interpret, using the indirect method, the net cash provided or used by operating activities;

d. prepare and interpret, using the indirect method, the statement of cash flows for investing activities and financing activities.

OVERVIEW OF THE STATEMENT OF CASH FLOWS 1

The **statement of cash flows** shows how a company's operating, investing, and financing activities have affected cash during an accounting period. It explains the net increase (or decrease) in cash during the period. For purposes of preparing this statement, **cash** is defined as including both cash and cash equivalents. The FASB defines **cash equivalents** as short-term, highly liquid investments, including money market accounts, commercial paper, and U.S. Treasury bills. A company maintains cash equivalents to earn interest on cash that would otherwise remain unused temporarily. Suppose, for example, that a company has $1,000,000 that it will not need for 30 days. To earn a return on this amount, the company may place the cash in an account that earns interest (such as a money market account), it may lend the cash to another corporation by purchasing that corporation's short-term notes (commercial paper), or it may purchase a short-term obligation of the U.S. government (Treasury bills). In this context, short-term refers to original

DECISION POINT: A USER'S FOCUS

Marriott International, Inc. <www.marriott.com> Marriott International, Inc., is a world leader in lodging and contract hotel services. The balance sheet, income statement, and statement of stockholders' equity presented in Marriott's annual report give an excellent picture of the company's philosophy and performance.

Although these three financial statements are essential to the evaluation of any company, they do not tell the entire story. A fourth statement, the statement of cash flows, contains some additional information, as shown in the Financial Highlights on page 549.[1] This statement shows how much cash the company's operations generated during the past three years and how much cash investing and financing activities used or provided.

Marriott feels that maintaining adequate cash flows is important to the future of the company. In fact, Marriott's emphasis on cash flows is reflected in its compensation plan for top executives. A review of the plan indicates that cash flows, at the firm or business group level, are the financial measure given the greatest weight in determining compensation. Why would Marriott emphasize cash flows to such an extent?

Strong cash flows are essential to management's key goal of liquidity. If cash flows exceed the amount needed for operations and expansion, the company will not have to borrow additional funds. The excess cash flows will be available to reduce the company's debt and improve its financial position by lowering its debt to equity ratio. Another reason for the emphasis on cash flows may be the belief that strong cash flows from operations generate shareholder value and increase the market value of the company's stock.

The statement of cash flows demonstrates management's commitments in ways that are not readily apparent in the other financial statements. For example, it can show whether management's focus is on the short term or the long term. This statement, which is required by the FASB, satisfies the board's long-held position that a primary objective of financial statements is to provide investors and creditors with information about a company's cash flows.[2]

What does Marriott's statement of cash flows reveal about the company's success in providing top-notch lodging and hotel services?

---

[1] Marriott International, Inc., *Annual Report*, 2000.

[2] *Statement of Financial Accounting Standards No. 95*, "Statement of Cash Flows" (Norwalk, Conn.: Financial Accounting Standards Board, 1987); *Statement of Financial Accounting Concepts No. 1*, "Objectives of Financial Reporting for Business Enterprises" (Norwalk, Conn.: Financial Accounting Standards Board, 1978), par. 37–39.

Financial Highlights: Consolidated Statement of Cash Flows

Marriott International, Inc., and Subsidiaries (In millions)

	2000	1999	1998
OPERATING ACTIVITIES			
Net income	**$ 479**	$400	$390
Adjustments to reconcile to cash provided by operations:			
Depreciation and amortization	**195**	162	140
Income taxes	**133**	87	76
Timeshare activity, net	**(195)**	(102)	28
Other	**48**	19	(22)
Working capital changes:			
Accounts receivable	**(53)**	(126)	(104)
Inventories	**(4)**	(17)	15
Other current assets	**28**	(38)	(16)
Accounts payable and accruals	**219**	326	98
Cash provided by operations	**850**	711	605
INVESTING ACTIVITIES			
Capital expenditures	**(1,095)**	(929)	(937)
Acquisitions	**—**	(61)	(48)
Dispositions	**742**	436	332
Loan advances	**(389)**	(144)	(48)
Loan collections and sales	**93**	54	169
Other	**(377)**	(143)	(192)
Cash used in investing activities	**(1,026)**	(787)	(724)
FINANCING ACTIVITIES			
Commercial paper, net	**46**	355	426
Issuance of long-term debt	**338**	366	868
Repayment of long-term debt	**(26)**	(63)	(473)
Redemption of convertible subordinated debt	**—**	(120)	—
Issuance of Class A common stock	**58**	43	15
Dividends paid	**(55)**	(52)	(37)
Purchase of treasury stock	**(340)**	(354)	(398)
Advances to Old Marriott	**—**	—	(100)
Cash provided by financing activities	**21**	175	301
(DECREASE) INCREASE IN CASH AND EQUIVALENTS	**(155)**	99	182
CASH AND EQUIVALENTS, beginning of year	**489**	390	208
CASH AND EQUIVALENTS, end of year	**$ 334**	$489	$390

maturities of 90 days or less. Since cash and cash equivalents are considered the same, transfers between the Cash account and cash equivalents are not treated as cash receipts or cash payments. In effect, cash equivalents are combined with the Cash account on the statement of cash flows.

Key point:
Money market accounts, commercial paper (short-term notes), and U.S. Treasury bills are considered cash equivalents because they are highly liquid, temporary (90 days or less) holding places for cash not currently needed to operate the business. They can be quickly converted into cash if the need arises.

Cash equivalents should not be confused with short-term investments or marketable securities, which are not combined with the Cash account on the statement of cash flows. Purchases of marketable securities are treated as cash outflows and sales of marketable securities as cash inflows on the statement of cash flows. In this reading, we assume that cash includes cash and cash equivalents.

Purposes of the Statement of Cash Flows

The primary purpose of the statement of cash flows is to provide information about a company's cash receipts and cash payments during an accounting period. A secondary purpose of the statement is to provide information about a company's operating, investing, and financing activities during the accounting period. Some information about those activities may be inferred from other financial statements, but it is on the statement of cash flows that all the transactions affecting cash are summarized.

Stop and Think!
Which statement is more useful—the income statement or the statement of cash flows?

The statements are equally useful. The income statement relates most directly to the goal of profitability, whereas the statement of cash flows is more closely tied to the goal of liquidity.

Internal and External Uses of the Statement of Cash Flows

The statement of cash flows is useful internally to management and externally to investors and creditors. Management uses the statement to assess liquidity, to determine dividend policy, and to evaluate the effects of major policy decisions involving investments and financing. In other words, management may use the statement to determine if short-term financing is needed to pay current liabilities, to decide whether to raise or lower dividends, and to plan for investing and financing needs.

Investors and creditors find the statement useful in assessing the company's ability to manage cash flows, to generate positive future cash flows, to pay its liabilities, to pay dividends and interest, and to anticipate its need for additional financing. Also, they may use the statement to explain the differences between net income on the income statement and the net cash flows generated from operations. In addition, the statement shows both the cash and the noncash effects of investing and financing activities during the accounting period.

Key point:
Management uses the statement of cash flows to make various investing and financing decisions. Investors and creditors, on the other hand, use the statement primarily to assess cash flow prospects.

Classification of Cash Flows

The statement of cash flows classifies cash receipts and cash payments into the categories of operating, investing, and financing activities. The components of these activities are illustrated in Figure 32-1 and summarized below.

Key point:
Operating activities arise from the day-to-day sale of goods and services, investing activities involve long-term assets and investments, and financing activities deal with stockholders' equity accounts and debt (borrowing).

1. **Operating activities** include the cash effects of transactions and other events that enter into the determination of net income. Included in this category as cash inflows are cash receipts from customers for goods and services, interest and dividends received on loans and investments, and sales of trading securities. Included as cash outflows are cash payments for wages, inventory, expenses, interest, taxes, and purchases of trading securities. In effect, the income statement is changed from an accrual to a cash basis.
2. **Investing activities** include the acquisition and sale of long-term assets and marketable securities, other than trading securities or cash equivalents, and the making and collecting of loans. Cash inflows include the cash received

FIGURE 32-1 Classification of Cash Inflows and Cash Outflows

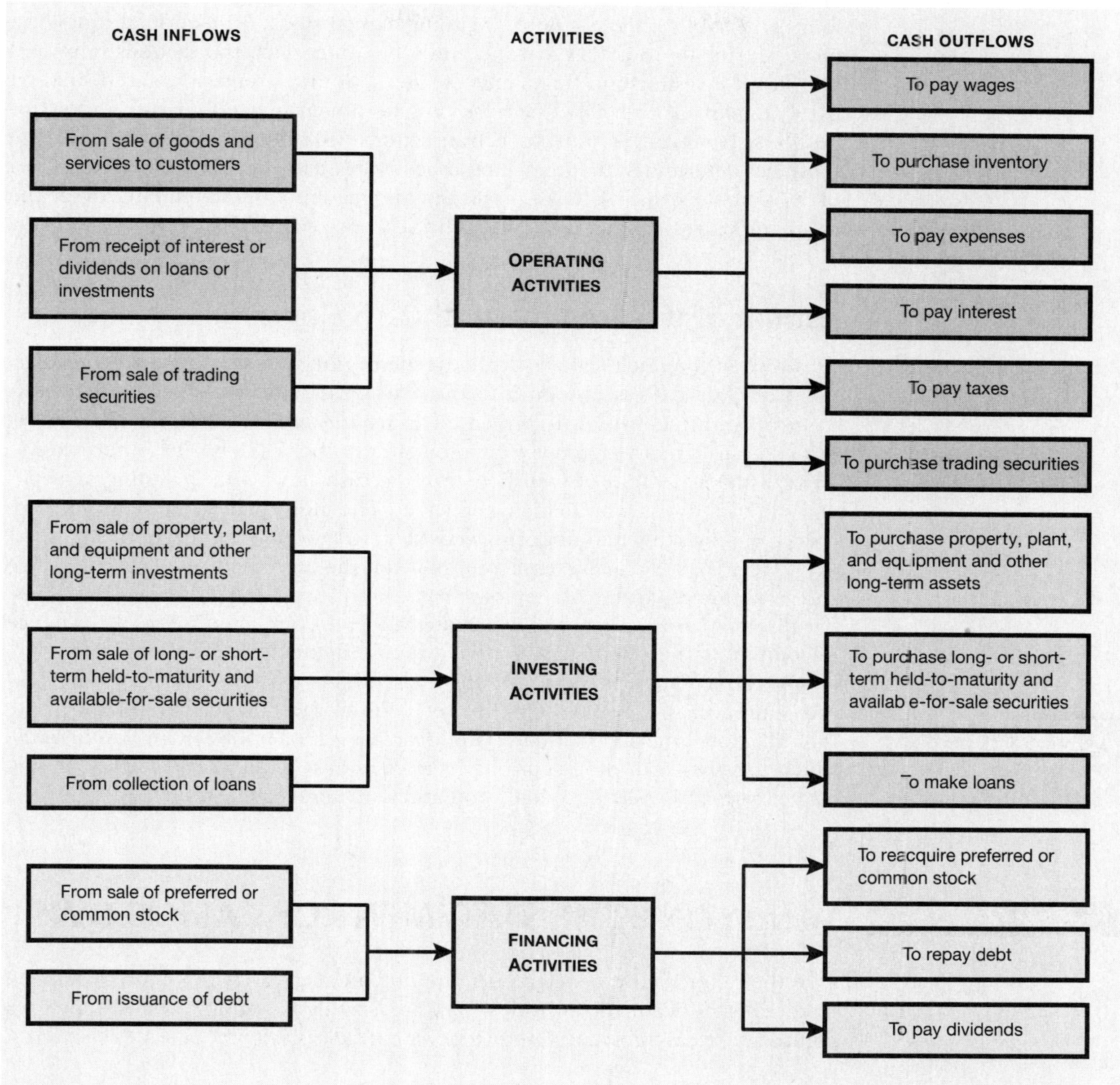

from selling long-term assets and marketable securities and from collecting loans. Cash outflows include the cash expended for purchases of long-term assets and marketable securities and the cash lent to borrowers.

3. **Financing activities** include obtaining resources from stockholders and providing them with a return on their investments, and obtaining resources from creditors and repaying the amounts borrowed or otherwise settling the obligations. Cash inflows include the proceeds from issues of stocks and from short-term and long-term borrowing. Cash outflows include the repayments of loans (excluding interest) and payments to owners, including cash dividends. Treasury stock transactions are also considered financing activities. Repayments of accounts payable or accrued liabilities are not considered repayments of loans under financing activities; they are classified as cash outflows under operating activities.

Companies occasionally engage in significant **noncash investing and financing transactions** involving only long-term assets, long-term liabilities, or stockholders' equity. For instance, a company might exchange a long-term asset for a long-term liability, settle a debt by issuing capital stock, or take out a long-term mortgage for the purchase of land and a building. Such transactions represent significant investing and financing activities, but they would not be reflected on the statement of cash flows because they do not involve either cash inflows or outflows. However, because such transactions will affect future cash flows, the FASB has determined that they should be disclosed in a separate schedule as part of the statement of cash flows. In this way, the reader of the statement can see the company's investing and financing activities more clearly.

Format of the Statement of Cash Flows

As shown in the Financial Highlights at the beginning of this reading, the statement of cash flows is divided into three sections. The first section, cash flows from operating activities, is presented using the indirect method. This is the most common method and is explained later in the reading. The other two sections of the statement of cash flows are the cash flows from investing activities and the cash flows from financing activities. The individual cash inflows and outflows from investing and financing activities are shown separately in their respective categories. Normally, cash outflows for the purchase of plant assets are shown separately from cash inflows from the disposal of plant assets. However, because the inflows are not usually material, some companies follow the practice of combining these two lines in order to show the net amount of outflow.

A reconciliation of the beginning and ending balances of cash appears near the bottom of the statement. Again referring to the Financial Highlights, note that Marriott International had a net decrease in cash of $155 million in 2000, which together with the beginning balance of $489 million results in $334 million of cash and cash equivalents on hand at the end of the year.

www.marriott.com

2 ANALYZING THE STATEMENT OF CASH FLOWS

Like the other financial statements, the statement of cash flows can be analyzed to reveal significant relationships. Two areas analysts examine when studying a company are cash-generating efficiency and free cash flow.

FOCUS ON INTERNATIONAL BUSINESS

How Universal Is the Statement of Cash Flows?

Despite the importance of the statement of cash flows in assessing the liquidity of companies in the United States, considerable variation in its use and format has existed in other countries. For example, the principal directives related to financial reporting for the European Union do not address the statement of cash flows. In many countries, the statement shows the change in working capital instead of the change in cash and cash equivalents. However, international accounting standards require the statement of cash flows, and international financial markets expect it to be presented. As a result, most multinational companies include the statement in their financial reports. Most European countries will adopt the statement of cash flows by 2006, when the European Union will require the use of international accounting standards.

Cash-Generating Efficiency

Cash-generating efficiency is the ability of a company to generate cash from its current or continuing operations. Three ratios are helpful in measuring cash-generating efficiency: cash flow yield, cash flows to sales, and cash flows to assets. We compute these ratios for Marriott International in 2000 using data from the Financial Highlights at the beginning of this reading and those presented below.[3] All dollar amounts are stated in millions.

www.marriott.com

Financial Highlights for Marriott International (In millions of dollars)

	2000	1999	1998
Net Sales	$10,017	$8,739	$7,968
Total Assets	8,237	7,324	6,233

Cash flow yield is the ratio of net cash flows from operating activities to net income, computed as follows:

$$\text{Cash Flow Yield} = \frac{\text{Net Cash Flows from Operating Activities}}{\text{New Income}}$$

$$= \frac{\$850}{\$479}$$

$$= 1.8 \text{ times}$$

Enrichment note: The cash flow yield enables users to assess whether sufficient cash flows underlie earnings. Serious questions would be raised if cash flow yield was less than 1.0. For example, receivables and inventories might be growing too fast, perhaps signaling a slowdown in sales growth or a problem in managing receivables collection or inventory levels.

Marriott International has a good cash flow yield of 1.8 times; that is, the corporation's operating activities are generating about 80 percent more cash flow than net income. If special items, such as discontinued operations, appear on the income statement and are material, income from continuing operations should be used as the denominator.

Cash flows to sales is the ratio of net cash flows from operating activities to sales, computed as follows:

Key point: The change in cash shown in the comparative balance sheets provides a check figure for the statement of cash flows.

$$\text{Cash Flows to Sales} = \frac{\text{Net Cash Flows from Operating Activities}}{\text{Net Sales}}$$

$$= \frac{\$850}{\$10{,}017}$$

$$= 8.5\%$$

Marriott generates cash flows to sales of 8.5 percent. The company generated a positive but relatively small percentage of net cash from sales.

Cash flows to assets is the ratio of net cash flows from operating activities to average total assets, computed as follows:

$$\text{Cash Flows to Assets} = \frac{\text{Net Cash Flows from Operating Activities}}{\text{Average Total Assets}}$$

$$= \frac{\$850}{(\$8{,}237 + \$7{,}324) \div 2}$$

$$= 10.9\%$$

[3] Marriott International, Inc., *Annual Report,* 2000.

Stop and think!
If cash flow yield is less than 1.0, would cash flows to sales and cash flows to assets be greater or less than profit margin and return on assets, respectively?

Cash flows to sales and cash flows to assets would be less than profit margin and return on assets, respectively, because a cash flow yield of 1.0 means that cash flows from operations are less than net income. Both are numerators in ratios that have the same denominators.

www.marriott.com

The cash flows to assets ratio is higher than the cash flows to sales ratio because Marriott International has a good asset turnover ratio (sales ÷ average total assets) of approximately 1.3 times (10.9% ÷ 8.5%). Cash flows to sales and cash flows to assets are closely related to the profitability measures of profit margin and return on assets. They exceed those measures by the amount of the cash flow yield ratio because cash flow yield is the ratio of net cash flows from operating activities to net income.

Although Marriott's cash flow yield and cash flows to assets are relatively good, its efficiency at generating cash flows from operating activities, as measured by cash flows to sales, could be improved.

Free Cash Flow

In 2000, Marriott had a net cash outflow of $1,026 million for investing activities, which could indicate that the company was expanding. However, that figure mixes capital expenditures for plant assets, which reflect management's expansion of operations, with the acquisition of hotel chains and loan advances and collections. Cash flows from financing activities provided $21 million, but that figure combines financing activities associated with long-term debt and stocks with dividends paid to stockholders. While something can be learned by looking at those broad categories, many analysts find it more informative to go beyond them to focus on a computation called free cash flow.

Key point:
Free cash flow should be interpreted in light of the company's overall need for cash. For instance, the purchase of treasury stock will reduce the amount of cash that is free for operating uses.

Free cash flow is the amount of cash that remains after deducting the funds a company must commit to continue operating at its planned level. The commitments must cover current or continuing operations, interest, income taxes, dividends, and net capital expenditures. Cash requirements for current or continuing operations, interest, and income taxes must be paid or the company's creditors and the government can take legal action. Although the payment of dividends is not strictly required, dividends normally represent a commitment to stockholders. If these payments are reduced or eliminated, stockholders will be unhappy and the price of the company's stock will fall. Net capital expenditures represent management's plans for the future.

FOCUS ON BUSINESS PRACTICE

What Do You Mean, "Free Cash Flow"?

Because the statement of cash flows has been around for less than 20 years, no generally accepted analyses have yet been developed. For example, the term *free cash flow* is commonly used in the business press, but there is no agreement on its definition. An article in *Forbes* defines *free cash flow* as "cash available after paying out capital expenditures and dividends, *but before taxes and interest*"[4] [emphasis added]. An article in *The Wall Street Journal* defines it as "operating income less maintenance-level capital expenditures."[5] The definition with which we are most in agreement is the one used in *Business Week:* free cash flow is net cash flows from operating activities less net capital expenditures and dividends. This "measures truly discretionary funds—company money that an owner could pocket without harming the business."[6]

---

[4] Gary Slutsker, "Look at the Birdie and Say: 'Cash Flow,'" *Forbes,* October 25, 1993.

[5] Jonathan Clements, "Yacktman Fund Is Bloodied but Unbowed," *The Wall Street Journal,* November 8, 1993.

[6] Jeffrey Laderman, "Earnings, Schmearnings—Look at the Cash," *BusinessWeek,* July 24, 1989.

FOCUS ON BUSINESS PRACTICE

Cash Flows Tell All

In early 2001, the telecommunications industry began one of the biggest market crashes in history. Could it have been predicted? The telecommunications industry depends on heavy capital expenditures in equipment, such as cable lines and computers. When the cash flows from sales of 41 telecommunications companies are compared with their capital expenditures (a negative component of free cash flow) over the six years preceding the crash, an interesting pattern emerges. In the first three years, both cash flows from sales and capital expenditures were about 20 percent of sales. In other words, free cash flows were neutral, with operations generating enough cash flows to cover capital expenditures. In the next three years, these measures diverged. Cash flows to sales stayed at about 20 percent of sales, but the companies increased capital expenditure dramatically, to 35 percent of sales. Thus, free cash flows turned very negative, and almost half of capital expenditures had to be financed by debt instead of operations, making these companies more vulnerable to the downturn in the economy that occurred in 2001.[7]

If free cash flow is positive, it means that the company has met all its planned cash commitments and has cash available to reduce debt or to expand. A negative free cash flow means that the company will have to sell investments, borrow money, or issue stock in the short term to continue at its planned level. If free cash flow remains negative for several years, a company may not be able to raise cash by issuing stock or bonds.

Since cash commitments for current or continuing operations, interest, and income taxes are incorporated in cash flows from current operations, free cash flow for Marriott is computed as follows (in millions):

$$\begin{aligned}\text{Free Cash Flow} &= \begin{array}{l}\text{Net Cash Flows from Operating Activities} - \text{Dividends} - \\ \text{Purchases of Plant Assets} + \text{Sales of Plant Assets}\end{array} \\ &= \$850 - \$55 - \$1{,}095 + \$742 \\ &= \$442\end{aligned}$$

Purchases and sales of plant assets appear in the investing activities section of the statement of cash flows. Marriott reported both capital expenditures and dispositions of property and equipment. Dividends are found in the financing activities section. Marriott had positive free cash flow of $442 million due primarily to its strong operating cash flow of $850 million and $742 million cash received on disposal of property and equipment. The cash provided by financing activities was the lowest in three years, only $21 million, and was possible because of increasing cash provided by operations. The company repaid long-term debt of $26 million while issuing new debt of $338 million. Marriott also issued common stock in the amount of $58 million and purchased treasury stock for $340 million. The result is that financing activities were a positive $21 million.

Cash flows can vary from year to year, so it is best to look at trends in cash flow measures over several years when analyzing a company's cash flows. Marriott's cash flow yield has shown little variation over the past three years. Management summed this up in the company's annual report:

> ***Cash from Operations***
>
> The company's operating cash flow is stable, and typically does not fluctuate widely within an economic cycle.[8]

---

[7] "Deadweight on the Markets," *BusinessWeek,* February 19, 2001.

[8] Marriott International, Inc., *Annual Report,* 2000.

3 PREPARING THE STATEMENT OF CASH FLOWS: OPERATING ACTIVITIES

To demonstrate the preparation of the statement of cash flows, we will work through an example step by step. The data for this example are presented in Exhibits 32-1 and 32-2, which show Ryan Corporation's balance sheets for December 31, 20x4 and 20x3, and its 20x4 income statement. Exhibit 32-1 shows the balance sheet accounts that we use for analysis and whether the change in each account is an increase or a decrease. Exhibit 32-2 contains data about transactions that affected non-current accounts. The company's accountants would identify those transactions from the records.

The first step in preparing the statement of cash flows is to determine cash flows from operating activities. The income statement indicates a business's success or failure in earning an income from its operating activities. However, because the income statement is prepared on an accrual basis, it does not reflect the inflow and outflow of cash from those activities. Revenues are recorded even though the cash for them may not have been received, and expenses are recorded even though the cash for them may not have been expended. Thus, to arrive at cash flows from operations, the figures on the income statement must be converted from an accrual basis to a cash basis.

Key point:
The direct and indirect methods relate only to the operating activities section of the statement of cash flows. They are both acceptable for financial reporting purposes.

There are two methods of converting the income statement from an accrual basis to a cash basis: the direct method and the indirect method. Under the **direct method**, each item on the income statement is adjusted from the accrual basis to the cash basis. The result is a statement that begins with cash receipts from sales and interest and deducts cash payments for purchases, operating expenses, interest payments, and income taxes to arrive at net cash flows from operating activities. The **indirect method**, on the other hand, does not require the individual adjustment of each item on the income statement; it lists only those adjustments necessary to convert net income to cash flows from operations.

Key point:
The indirect method begins with net income and adjusts up or down to produce net cash flows from operating activities.

The direct and indirect methods always produce the same net figure. The direct method is more easily understood by the average reader because it results in a more straightforward presentation of operating cash flows than does the indirect method. However, the indirect method is the overwhelming choice of most companies and accountants. A survey of large companies shows that 99 percent use this method.[9] The indirect method is superior to the direct method from the analysts' perspective because its format begins with net income and derives cash flows from operations. The analyst can readily identify the factors that cause cash flows from operations. Further, from the company's standpoint, the indirect method is easier and less expensive to prepare. For these reasons, we use the indirect method in this book.

As illustrated in Figure 32-2, the indirect method focuses on items from the income statement that must be adjusted to reconcile net income to net cash flows from operating activities. The items that require adjustment are those that affect net income but not net cash flows from operating activities. They include depreciation and amortization, gains and losses, and changes in the balances of current asset and current liability accounts. The reconciliation of Ryan Corporation's net income to net cash flows from operating activities is shown in Exhibit 32-3 on page 571. Each adjustment is discussed in the following sections.

---

[9] American Institute of Certified Public Accountants, *Accounting Trends & Techniques* (New York: AICPA, 2001).

EXHIBIT 32-1 Comparative Balance Sheets with Changes in Accounts Indicated

Ryan Corporation
Comparative Balance Sheets
December 31, 20x4 and 20x3

	20x4	20x3	Change	Increase or Decrease
		Assets		
Current assets				
Cash	$ 46,000	$ 15,000	$ 31,000	Increase
Accounts receivable (net)	47,000	55,000	(8,000)	Decrease
Inventory	144,000	110,000	34,000	Increase
Prepaid expenses	1,000	5,000	(4,000)	Decrease
Total current assets	$238,000	$185,000	$ 53,000	
Investments available for sale	$115,000	$127,000	($ 12,000)	Decrease
Plant assets				
Plant assets	$715,000	$505,000	$210,000	Increase
Accumulated depreciation	(103,000)	(68,000)	(35,000)	Increase
Total plant assets	$612,000	$437,000	$175,000	
Total assets	$965,000	$749,000	$216,000	
		Liabilities		
Current liabilities				
Accounts payable	$ 50,000	$ 43,000	$ 7,000	Increase
Accrued liabilities	12,000	9,000	3,000	Increase
Income taxes payable	3,000	5,000	(2,000)	Decrease
Total current liabilities	$ 65,000	$ 57,000	$ 8,000	
Long-term liabilities				
Bonds payable	295,000	245,000	50,000	Increase
Total liabilities	$360,000	$302,000	$ 58,000	
		Stockholders' Equity		
Common stock, $5 par value	$276,000	$200,000	$ 76,000	Increase
Paid-in capital in excess of par value, common	214,000	115,000	99,000	Increase
Retained earnings	140,000	132,000	8,000	Increase
Treasury stock	(25,000)	0	(25,000)	Increase
Total stockholders' equity	$605,000	$447,000	$158,000	
Total liabilities and stockholders' equity	$965,000	$749,000	$216,000	

EXHIBIT 32-2 Income Statement and Other Information on Noncurrent Accounts

Ryan Corporation
Income Statement
For the Year Ended December 31, 20x4

Net sales		$698,000
Cost of goods sold		520,000
Gross margin		$178,000
Operating expenses (including depreciation expense of $37,000)		147,000
Operating income		$ 31,000
Other income (expenses)		
Interest expense	($23,000)	
Interest income	6,000	
Gain on sale of investments	12,000	
Loss on sale of plant assets	(3,000)	(8,000)
Income before income taxes		$ 23,000
Income taxes		7,000
Net income		$ 16,000

Other transactions affecting noncurrent accounts during 20x4:

1. Purchased investments in the amount of $78,000.
2. Sold investments that cost $90,000 for $102,000.
3. Purchased plant assets in the amount of $120,000.
4. Sold plant assets that cost $10,000 with accumulated depreciation of $2,000 for $5,000.
5. Issued $100,000 of bonds at face value in a noncash exchange for plant assets.
6. Repaid $50,000 of bonds at face value at maturity.
7. Issued 15,200 shares of $5 par value common stock for $175,000.
8. Purchased treasury stock in the amount of $25,000.
9. Paid cash dividends in the amount of $8,000.

FIGURE 32-2 Indirect Method of Determining Net Cash Flows from Operating Activities

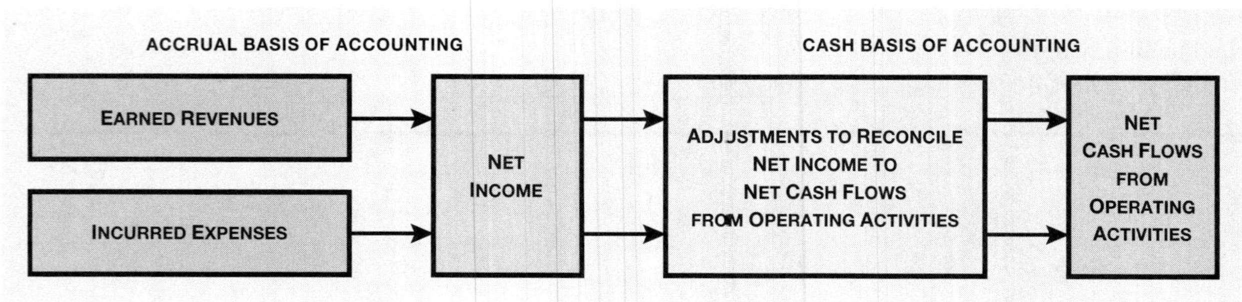

EXHIBIT 32-3 Schedule of Cash Flows from Operating Activities: Indirect Method

Ryan Corporation
Schedule of Cash Flows from Operating Activities
For the Year Ended December 31, 20x4

Cash flows from operating activities		
Net income		$16,000
Adjustments to reconcile net income to net cash flows from operating activities		
Depreciation	$37,000	
Gain on sale of investments	(12,000)	
Loss on sale of plant assets	3,000	
Changes in current assets and current liabilities		
Decrease in accounts receivable	8,000	
Increase in inventory	(34,000)	
Decrease in prepaid expenses	4,000	
Increase in accounts payable	7,000	
Increase in accrued liabilities	3,000	
Decrease in income taxes payable	(2,000)	14,000
Net cash flows from operating activities		$30,000

Stop and Think!
If a company has positive earnings, can cash flows from operating activities ever be negative?

If a company has large gains, large increases in current assets, or decreases in current liabilities, the results could overwhelm the earnings and create negative cash flows from operating activities.

Depreciation

Cash payments for plant assets, intangibles, and natural resources occur when the assets are purchased and are reflected as investing activities on the statement of cash flows at that time. When depreciation expense, amortization expense, and depletion expense appear on the income statement, they simply indicate allocations of the costs of the original purchases to the current accounting period; they do not affect net cash flows in the current period. The amount of such expenses can usually be found by referring to the income statement or a note to the financial statements. For Ryan Corporation, the income statement reveals depreciation expense of $37,000, which would have been recorded as follows:

Key Point:
Operating expenses on the income statement include depreciation expense, which does not require a cash outlay.

Depreciation Expense	37,000	
Accumulated Depreciation		37,000
To record annual depreciation on plant assets		

A = L + OE
− −

The recording of depreciation involved no outlay of cash even though depreciation expense appears on the income statement. Thus, to derive cash flows from operations, an adjustment for depreciation is needed to increase net income by the amount of depreciation recorded.

Gains and Losses

Gains and losses that appear on the income statement also do not affect cash flows from operating activities and need to be removed from this section of the statement of cash flows. The cash receipts generated by the disposal of the assets that resulted in the gains or losses are shown in the investing section of the statement of cash flows. Thus, gains and losses are removed from net income (preventing double

Study Note:
Gains and losses by themselves do not represent cash flows; they are merely bookkeeping adjustments. For example, when a long-term asset is sold, it is the *proceeds* (cash received), not the gain or loss, that constitute cash flow.

counting) to reconcile net income to cash flows from operating activities. For example, on its income statement, Ryan Corporation showed a $12,000 gain on the sale of investments, and this is subtracted from net income to reconcile net income to net cash flows from operating activities. The reason for this is that the $12,000 is already included (added) in the investing activities section as part of the $102,000 cash from the sale of the investment. Because the gain is included in the calculation of net income, the $12,000 gain needs to be subtracted to prevent double counting. Also, Ryan Corporation showed a $3,000 loss on the sale of plant assets. Following the same logic, the $3,000 loss is already reflected in the $5,000 sale of plant assets in the investing activities section. Thus, the $3,000 is added to net income to reconcile net income to net cash flows from operating activities.

Changes in Current Assets

Decreases in current assets other than cash have positive effects on cash flows, and increases in current assets have negative effects on cash flows. A decrease in a current asset frees up invested cash, thereby increasing cash flow. An increase in a current asset consumes cash, thereby decreasing cash flow. For example, refer to the balance sheets and income statement for Ryan Corporation in Exhibits 32-1 and 32-2. Note that net sales in 20x4 were $698,000 and that Accounts Receivable decreased by $8,000. Thus, cash received from sales was $706,000, calculated as follows:

$$\$706,000 = \$698,000 + \$8,000$$

Collections were $8,000 more than sales recorded for the year. This relationship may be illustrated as follows:

Accounts Receivable

		Debit	Credit	
	Beg. Bal.	55,000	706,000 →	Cash Receipts from Customers
Sales to Customers →		698,000		
	End. Bal.	**47,000**		

Thus, to reconcile net income to net cash flows from operating activities, the $8,000 decrease in Accounts Receivable is added to net income.

Inventory may be analyzed in the same way. For example, Exhibit 32-1 shows that Inventory increased by $34,000 from 20x3 to 20x4. This means that Ryan Corporation expended $34,000 more in cash for purchases than was included in cost of goods sold on the income statement. As a result of this expenditure, net income is higher than the net cash flows from operating activities, so $34,000 must be deducted from net income. Using the same logic, the decrease of $4,000 in Prepaid Expenses is added to net income to reconcile net income to net cash flows from operations.

Changes in Current Liabilities

Changes in current liabilities have the opposite effects on cash flows from those of changes in current assets. Increases in current liabilities are added to net income, and decreases in current liabilities are deducted from net income to reconcile net income to net cash flows from operating activities. An increase in a current liability represents a postponement of a cash payment, which frees up cash and increases cash flow in the current period. A decrease in current liabilities consumes cash, thereby decreasing cash flow. For example, Exhibit 32-1 shows that Ryan Corporation had a $7,000 increase in accounts payable from 20x3 to 20x4. This means that Ryan Corporation paid $7,000 less to creditors than the amount of purchases indicates in cost of goods sold on the income statement. This relationship may be visualized as follows:

Accounts Payable

	Debit	Credit	
Cash Payments to Suppliers →	547,000	Beg. Bal. 43,000	
		554,000*	← Purchases
		End. Bal. 50,000	

* Purchases = Cost of Goods Sold ($520,000) + Increase in Inventory ($34,000).

As a result, $7,000 is added to net income to reconcile net income to net cash flows from operating activities. By the same logic, the increase of $3,000 in accrued liabilities is added to net income, and the decrease of $2,000 in income taxes payable is deducted from net income.

Schedule of Cash Flows from Operating Activities

In summary, Exhibit 32-3 shows that by using the indirect method, net income of $16,000 has been adjusted by reconciling items totaling $14,000 to arrive at net cash flows from operating activities of $30,000. This means that although net income was $16,000, Ryan actually had net cash flows of $30,000 available from operating activities to use for purchasing assets, reducing debts, or paying dividends.

The effects of items on the income statement that do not affect cash flows may be summarized as follows:

	Add to or Deduct from Net Income
Depreciation expense	Add
Amortization expense	Add
Depletion expense	Add
Losses	Add
Gains	Deduct

The adjustments for increases and decreases in current assets and current liabilities may be summarized as follows:

	Add to Net Income	Deduct from Net Income
Current assets		
Accounts receivable (net)	Decrease	Increase
Inventory	Decrease	Increase
Prepaid expenses	Decrease	Increase
Current liabilities		
Accounts payable	Increase	Decrease
Accrued liabilities	Increase	Decrease
Income taxes payable	Increase	Decrease

FOCUS ON BUSINESS PRACTICE

What's Your "Burn Rate"?

Why would a company have a total market value less than the amount of cash it has on hand? The answer is "burn rate." Burn rate is the pace at which companies use cash in their operations. A major contributor to the market crash of the stocks of dot-com companies was the difficulty these firms had in generating enough revenue to produce positive cash flows from operations. For example, when investors thought Webvan Group, Inc., the Internet grocer, would be the delivery service model of the future, the company was valued as high as $11.4 billion. However, as Webvan's burn rate reached $55 million a month, its market value dropped to a mere $132 million, even though the company had $212 million in cash.[10] The company was never able to generate sufficient revenues and soon declared bankruptcy.

4 PREPARING THE STATEMENT OF CASH FLOWS: INVESTING ACTIVITIES

To determine cash flows from investing activities, each account involving cash receipts and cash payments from investing activities is examined individually. The objective is to explain the change in each account balance from one year to the next.

Investing activities center on the long-term assets shown on the balance sheet, but they also include transactions affecting short-term investments from the current assets section of the balance sheet and investment gains and losses from the income statement. The balance sheets in Exhibit 32-1 show that Ryan Corporation had long-term assets of investments and plant assets, but no short-term investments. The income statement in Exhibit 32-2 shows that Ryan had investment-related items in the form of a gain on the sale of investments and a loss on the sale of plant assets.

Key point:
Investing activities involve long-term assets and short- or long-term investments. Both inflows and outflows of cash are shown in the investing activities section of the statement of cash flows.

The schedule at the bottom of Exhibit 32-2 lists the following five items pertaining to investing activities in 20x4:

1. Purchased investments in the amount of $78,000.
2. Sold investments that cost $90,000 for $102,000.
3. Purchased plant assets in the amount of $120,000.
4. Sold plant assets that cost $10,000 with accumulated depreciation of $2,000 for $5,000.
5. Issued $100,000 of bonds at face value in a noncash exchange for plant assets.

The following sections analyze the accounts related to investing activities to determine their effects on Ryan Corporation's cash flows.

Investments

The objective here is to explain Ryan Corporation's $12,000 decrease in investments, all of which are classified as available-for-sale securities. This is accomplished by analyzing the increases and decreases in the Investments account to determine the effects on the Cash account. Purchases increase investments, and sales decrease investments.

---

[10] Pallavi Gogoi, "Cash-Rich, So?" *BusinessWeek,* March 19, 2001.

Item **1** in Ryan's list of investing activities shows purchases of $78,000 during 20x4. This transaction is recorded as follows:

Investments	78,000	
Cash		78,000
Purchase of investments		

A = L + OE
+
−

The entry shows that the effect of this transaction is a $78,000 decrease in cash flows.

Item **2** in the list shows that Ryan sold investments that cost $90,000 for $102,000, resulting in a gain of $12,000. This transaction is recorded in the following way:

Cash	102,000	
Investments		90,000
Gain on Sale of Investments		12,000
Sale of investments for a gain		

A = L + OE
+ +
−

The effect of this transaction is a $102,000 increase in cash flows. Note that the gain on sale of investments is included in the $102,000. This is why we excluded it in computing cash flows from operations. If it had been included in that section, it would have been counted twice.

Key point: The $102,000 price obtained, not the $12,000 gain, constitutes the cash flow here.

The $12,000 decrease in the Investments account (unrelated to the $12,000 gain above) during 20x4 has now been explained, as seen in the following T account:

Investments

Beg. Bal.	127,000	Sales	90,000
Purchases	78,000		
End. Bal.	**115,000**		

The cash flow effects from these transactions are shown in the investing activities section on the statement of cash flows as follows:

Purchase of investments	($ 78,000)
Sale of investments	102,000

Notice that purchases and sales are listed separately as cash outflows and inflows to give readers of the statement a complete view of investing activity. Some companies prefer to combine them into a single net amount.

If Ryan Corporation had short-term investments or marketable securities, the analysis of cash flows would be the same.

Stop and think!
Which adjustments to net income in the operating activities section of the statement of cash flows are directly related to cash flows reported in other sections?

Gains and losses from operating activities are directly related to the cash flows from the sale of assets reported in the investing activities section.

Plant Assets

In the case of plant assets, it is necessary to explain the changes in both the Plant Assets account and the related Accumulated Depreciation account. According to Exhibit 32-1, Ryan Corporation's plant assets increased by $210,000, and accumulated depreciation increased by $35,000. Purchases increase plant assets, and sales decrease plant assets. Accumulated depreciation is increased by the amount of depreciation expense and decreased by the removal of the accumulated depreciation associated with plant assets that are sold. Three items listed in Exhibit 32-2 affect plant assets. Item 3 in the list indicates that Ryan Corporation purchased plant assets totaling $120,000 during 20x4, as shown by the following entry:

A = L + OE
+
−

Plant Assets	120,000	
Cash		120,000
Purchase of plant assets		

This transaction results in a cash outflow of $120,000.

Item **4** states that Ryan Corporation sold for $5,000 plant assets that cost $10,000 and had accumulated depreciation of $2,000, which resulted in a loss of $3,000. The entry to record this transaction is as follows:

A = L + OE
+ −
+
−

Cash	5,000	
Accumulated Depreciation	2,000	
Loss on Sale of Plant Assets	3,000	
Plant Assets		10,000
Sale of plant assets at a loss		

Key point:
Even though Ryan had a loss on the sale, it realized a positive cash flow of $5,000, which will be reported in the investing activities section of the statement of cash flows. When the indirect approach is used, the loss is eliminated with an "add-back" to net income.

Note that in this transaction the positive cash flow is equal to the amount of cash received, or $5,000. The loss on the sale of plant assets is included here, and excluded from the operating activities section (see page 561), by adjusting net income for the amount of the loss. The amount of a loss or gain on the sale of an asset is determined by the amount of cash received and does not represent a cash outflow or inflow.

The disclosure of these two transactions in the investing activities section of the statement of cash flows is as follows:

Purchase of plant assets	($120,000)
Sale of plant assets	5,000

Cash outflows and cash inflows are listed separately here, though companies sometimes combine them into a single net amount, as they do the purchase and sale of investments.

Item **5** on the list of Ryan's investing activities is a noncash exchange that affects two long-term accounts, Plant Assets and Bonds Payable. It is recorded as follows:

A = L + OE
+ +

Plant Assets	100,000	
Bonds Payable		100,000
Issued bonds at face value for plant assets		

Although this transaction does not involve an inflow or outflow of cash, it is a significant transaction involving both an investing activity (the purchase of plant assets) and a financing activity (the issue of bonds payable). Because one purpose of the statement of cash flows is to show important investing and financing activities, the transaction is listed in a separate schedule, either at the bottom of the statement of cash flows or accompanying the statement, as follows:

Schedule of Noncash Investing and Financing Transactions

Issue of bonds payable for plant assets	$100,000

Through our analysis of the preceding transactions and the depreciation expense for plant assets, we have now accounted for all the changes in the Plant Assets accounts as shown in the following T accounts:

Plant Assets

Beg. Bal.	**505,000**	Sale	10,000
Cash Purchase	120,000		
Noncash Purchase	100,000		
End. Bal.	**715,000**		

Accumulated Depreciation

Sale	2,000	**Beg. Bal.**	**68,000**
		Dep. Exp.	37,000
		End. Bal.	**103,000**

Had the balance sheet included specific plant asset accounts (e.g., Buildings and Equipment and related accumulated depreciation accounts) or other long-term asset accounts (e.g., Intangibles), the analysis would have been the same.

PREPARING THE STATEMENT OF CASH FLOWS: FINANCING ACTIVITIES

5

Key point:
Financing activities involve stockholders' equity accounts and short- and long-term borrowings. Because dividends paid involve retained earnings, they are appropriately included in this category.

The procedure for determining cash flows from financing activities is like the analysis of investing activities, including treatment of related gains or losses, but the accounts analyzed are short-term borrowings, long-term liabilities, and stockholders' equity accounts. Cash dividends from the statement of stockholders' equity must also be considered. Since Ryan Corporation does not have short-term borrowings, we deal only with long-term liabilities and stockholders' equity accounts.

These items from Exhibit 32-2 pertain to Ryan's financing activities in 20x4:

5. Issued $100,000 of bonds at face value in a noncash exchange for plant assets.
6. Repaid $50,000 of bonds at face value at maturity.
7. Issued 15,200 shares of $5 par value common stock for $175,000.
8. Purchased treasury stock for $25,000.
9. Paid cash dividends in the amount of $8,000.

Bonds Payable

Exhibit 32-1 shows that Bonds Payable increased by $50,000 in 20x4. This account is affected by items **5** and **6**. Item **5** was analyzed in connection with plant assets. As noted above, it is reported on the schedule of noncash investing and financing transactions, but it must be remembered here in preparing the T account for Bonds Payable. Item **6** results in a cash outflow, which is recorded as follows:

Bonds Payable	50,000	
Cash		50,000
Repayment of bonds at face value at maturity		

A = L + OE
− −

This cash outflow is shown in the financing activities section of the statement of cash flows as follows:

Repayment of bonds	($50,000)

The following T account explains the change in Bonds Payable:

Bonds Payable

Repayment	50,000	**Beg. Bal.**	**245,000**
		Noncash Issue	100,000
		End. Bal.	**295,000**

If Ryan Corporation had any notes payable, the analysis would be the same.

Common Stock

Like the Plant Asset account and its related accounts, related stockholders' equity accounts should be analyzed together. For example, Paid-in Capital in Excess of Par Value, Common should be examined with Common Stock. In 20x4, Ryan Corporation's Common Stock account increased by $76,000, and Paid-in Capital in Excess of Par Value, Common increased by $99,000. Those increases are explained by item **7** in the list in Exhibit 32-2, which states that Ryan issued 15,200 shares of common stock for $175,000. The entry to record the cash inflow is as follows:

A = L + OE
+ +
+

Cash	175,000	
Common Stock		76,000
Paid-in Capital in Excess of Par Value, Common		99,000
Issued 15,200 shares of $5 par value common stock		

Study note:
The purchase of treasury stock would also qualify as a financing activity, but would appear as a cash outflow.

This cash inflow is shown in the financing activities section of the statement of cash flows as follows:

Issue of common stock	$175,000

The following analysis of this transaction is all that is needed to explain the changes in the two accounts during 20x4:

Common Stock

	Beg. Bal.	200,000
	Issue	76,000
	End. Bal.	**276,000**

Paid-in Capital in Excess of Par Value, Common

	Beg. Bal.	115,000
	Issue	99,000
	End. Bal.	**214,000**

Retained Earnings

At this point, we have dealt with several items that affect retained earnings. For instance, we used Ryan's net income in the analysis of cash flows from operating activities. The only other item affecting Ryan's retained earnings is the payment of $8,000 in cash dividends (item **9** in Exhibit 32-2), which is recorded as follows:

A = L + OE
− −

Retained Earnings	8,000	
Cash		8,000
Cash dividends for 20x4		

Ryan Corporation would have declared the dividend before paying it and therefore would have debited the Cash Dividends Declared account instead of Retained

Earnings, but after paying the dividend and closing the Cash Dividends Declared account to Retained Earnings, the effect is as shown. Cash dividends are displayed in the financing activities section of the statement of cash flows as follows:

Dividends paid	($8,000)

Key point:
It is dividends paid, not dividends declared, that appear on the statement of cash flows.

The following T account shows the change in the Retained Earnings account:

Retained Earnings

Dividends	8,000	Beg. Bal.	132,000
		Net Income	16,000
		End. Bal.	**140,000**

Treasury Stock

As noted in the reading on contributed capital, many companies buy back their own stock on the open market. These buybacks use cash, as this entry shows:

Treasury Stock	25,000	
Cash		25,000

A	=	L	+	OE
−				−

This use of cash is classified in the statement of cash flows as a financing activity as follows:

Purchase of treasury stock	($25,000)

The T account for this transaction is as follows:

Treasury Stock

Purchase	25,000		

Stop and think!
In computing free cash flow, what is an argument for treating purchases of treasury stock like dividend payments?

Both purchases of treasury stock and dividend payments represent payments to stockholders. Each diverts cash from productive use in the business (as assets), and thus each reduces free cash flow.

At this point in the analysis, we have analyzed all income statement items, explained all balance sheet changes, and taken all additional information into account. The resulting information may now be assembled into a statement of cash flows for Ryan Corporation, which is presented in Exhibit 32-4.

EXHIBIT 32-4 Statement of Cash Flows: Indirect Method

Ryan Corporation
Statement of Cash Flows
For the Year Ended December 31, 20x4

Cash flows from operating activities		
Net income		$ 16,000
Adjustments to reconcile net income to net cash flows from operating activities		
Depreciation	$ 37,000	
Gain on sale of investments	(12,000)	
Loss on sale of plant assets	3,000	
Changes in current assets and current liabilities		
Decrease in accounts receivable	8,000	
Increase in inventory	(34,000)	
Decrease in prepaid expenses	4,000	
Increase in accounts payable	7,000	
Increase in accrued liabilities	3,000	
Decrease in income taxes payable	(2,000)	14,000
Net cash flows from operating activities		$ 30,000
Cash flows from investing activities		
Purchase of investments	($ 78,000)	
Sale of investments	102,000	
Purchase of plant assets	(120,000)	
Sale of plant assets	5,000	
Net cash flows from investing activities		(91,000)
Cash flows from financing activities		
Repayment of bonds	($ 50,000)	
Issue of common stock	175,000	
Dividends paid	(8,000)	
Purchase of treasury stock	(25,000)	
Net cash flows from financing activities		92,000
Net increase (decrease) in cash		$ 31,000
Cash at beginning of year		15,000
Cash at end of year		$ 46,000

Schedule of Noncash Investing and Financing Transactions

Issue of bonds payable for plant assets	$100,000

REVIEW

6

Review of Learning Objectives

The statement of cash flows explains the changes in cash and cash equivalents from one accounting period to the next by showing cash inflows and outflows from the operating, investing, and financing activities of a company for an accounting period. For the statement of cash flows, *cash* is defined as including both cash and cash equivalents. The primary purpose of the statement is to provide information about a firm's cash receipts and cash payments during an accounting period. A secondary purpose is to provide information about a firm's operating, investing, and financing activities. The statement is useful to management and to investors and creditors in assessing the liquidity of a business, including its ability to generate future cash flows and to pay debts and dividends.

Cash flows may be classified as stemming from (1) operating activities, which include the cash effects of transactions and other events that enter into the determination of net income; (2) investing activities, which include the acquisition and sale of marketable securities and property, plant, and equipment, and the making and collecting of loans, excluding interest; or (3) financing activities, which include obtaining resources from stockholders and creditors and providing the former with a return on their investments and the latter with repayment. Noncash investing and financing transactions are also important because they affect future cash flows; these exchanges of long-term assets or liabilities are of interest to investors and creditors when evaluating the financing and investing activities of a business.

In analyzing a firm's statement of cash flows, analysts tend to focus on cash-generating efficiency and free cash flow. Cash-generating efficiency is a firm's ability to generate cash from its current or continuing operations. Three ratios used in measuring cash generating efficiency are cash flow yield, cash flows to sales, and cash flows to assets. Free cash flow is the cash that remains after deducting the funds a firm must commit to continue operating at its planned level. Such commitments must cover current or continuing operations, interest, income taxes, dividends, and net capital expenditures.

Under the indirect method, net income is adjusted for all noncash effects and for items that need to be converted from an accrual to a cash basis to arrive at a cash flow basis, as follows:

Cash flows from operating activities		
Net income		xxx
Adjustments to reconcile net income to net cash flows from operating activities (list of individual items)	xxx	xxx
Net cash flows from operating activities		xxx

Cash flows from investing activities are determined by identifying the cash flow effects of the transactions that affect each account relevant to investing activities. Such accounts include all long-term assets and short-term marketable securities.

The procedure for determining cash flows from financing activities is almost identical to that for investing activities. The difference is that the accounts involved are short-term borrowings, long-term liabilities, and stockholders' equity. The effects of gains and losses reported on the income statement must also be considered. After the changes in the balance sheet accounts from one accounting period to the next have been explained, all the cash flow effects should have been identified.

Review of Concepts and Terminology

The following concepts and terms were introduced in this reading:

Cash: For purposes of the statement of cash flows, both cash and cash equivalents.

Cash equivalents: Short-term (90 days or less), highly liquid investments, including money market accounts, commercial paper, and U.S. Treasury bills.

Cash flows to assets: The ratio of net cash flows from operating activities to average total assets.

Cash flows to sales: The ratio of net cash flows from operating activities to sales.

Cash flow yield: The ratio of net cash flows from operating activities to net income.

Cash-generating efficiency: The ability of a company to generate cash from its current or continuing operations.

Direct method: The procedure for converting the income statement from an accrual basis to a cash basis by separately adjusting each item on the income statement.

Financing activities: Business activities that involve obtaining resources from stock-holders and creditors and providing the former with a return on their investments and the latter with repayment.

Free cash flow: The amount of cash that remains after deducting the funds a company must commit to continue operating at its planned level; net cash flows from operating activities minus dividends paid minus net capital expenditures.

Indirect method: The procedure for converting the income statement from an accrual basis to a cash basis by adjusting net income for items that do not affect cash flows, including depreciation, amortization, depletion, gains, losses, and changes in current assets and current liabilities.

Investing activities: Business activities that involve the acquisition and sale of long-term assets and marketable securities, other than trading securities or cash equivalents, and the making and collecting of loans.

Noncash investing and financing transactions: Significant investing and financing transactions involving only long-term assets, long-term liabilities, or stockholders' equity that do not affect current cash inflows or outflows.

Operating activities: Business activities that involve the cash effects of transactions and other events that enter into the determination of net income.

Statement of cash flows: A financial statement that shows how a company's operating, investing, and financing activities have affected cash during an accounting period.

ANALYSIS OF CASH FLOWS

READING 33

LEARNING OUTCOMES

The candidate should be able to:

a. classify a particular transaction or item as cash flow from 1) operations, 2) investing, or 3) financing;

b. compute and interpret a statement of cash flows, using the direct method and the indirect method;

c. convert an indirect statement of cash flows to a direct basis;

d. explain the two primary factors that may cause discrepancies between balances of operating assets and liabilities reported on the balance sheet and those reported in the cash flow statement;

e. describe and compute free cash flow;

f. distinguish between the U.S. GAAP and IAS GAAP classifications of dividends paid or received and interest paid or received for statement of cash flow purposes.

STATEMENT OF CASH FLOWS 1

Cash flow data supplement the information provided by the income statement as both link consecutive balance sheets. The statement of cash flows reports all the cash inflows and outflows (classified among operating, investing, and financing activities) of the firm for a specified period. It also includes disclosures about that period's noncash investing and financing activities.

The classification of cash flows among operating, financing, and investing activities is essential to the analysis of cash flow data. Net cash flow (the change in cash and cash equivalents during the period) has little informational content by itself; it is the classification and individual components that are informative.

Cash flow from operating activities (cash from operations or CFO) measures the amount of cash generated or used by the firm as a result of its production and sales of goods and services. Although deficits or negative cash flows from operations are expected in some circumstances (e.g., rapid growth), for most firms positive operating cash flows are essential for long-run survival. Internally generated funds can be used to pay dividends or repurchase equity, repay loans, replace existing capacity, or invest in acquisitions and growth.

Investing cash flow (*CFI*) reports the amount of cash used to acquire assets such as plant and equipment as well as investments and entire businesses. These outlays are necessary to maintain a firm's current operating capacity and to provide capacity for future growth. CFI also includes cash received from the sale or disposal of assets or segments of the business.

Financing cash flow (*CFF*) contains the cash flow consequences of the firm's capital structure (debt and equity) decisions, including proceeds from the issuance of equity, returns to shareholders in the form of dividends and repurchase of equity, and the incurrence and repayment of debt.

Firms with significant foreign operations separately report a fourth category, *the effect of exchange rate changes on cash,* which accumulates the effects of changes in exchange rates on the translation of foreign currencies. This segregation is essential to accurately report the cash flow consequences of operating, investing, and financing decisions, unaffected by the impact of changes in exchange rates.

Direct and Indirect Method Cash Flow Statements

SFAS 95, Statement of Cash Flows (1987), and IAS 7 (1992) govern the preparation of cash flow statements under U.S. and IAS GAAP, respectively. Both standards permit firms to report cash from operations either *directly* by reporting major categories of gross cash receipts and payments, or *indirectly* by reconciling accrual-based net income to CFO.[1] Both investing and financing cash flows are usually computed identically under the two methods. However, there are reporting options under IAS 7 that can create noncomparability between cash flow statements prepared under the two standards.[2]

Exhibit 33-1 contrasts the direct and indirect cash flow statements of the WSF Company. These statements are generated from the company's balance sheet (Exhibit 33-2) and income statement (Exhibit 33-3).

Under the indirect method, CFO is computed by adjusting net income[3] for all:

1. Noncash revenues and expenses (for example, depreciation expense)
2. Nonoperating items included in net income (for example, gains from property sales)
3. Noncash changes in operating assets and liabilities (operating changes in receivables, payables, etc.)

Enterprises using the direct method must also provide this reconciliation. Firms using either method must disclose the cash outflows for income taxes and interest within the statement or elsewhere in the financial statements (e.g., in the footnotes).[4]

---

[1] Para. 19 of IAS 7 encourages use of the direct method.

[2] See table in "Cash Flow Statements: An International Perspective," later in this reading.

[3] Income from continuing operations may be used when the cash flows from discontinued operations are shown separately. IAS 35 (1998) requires separate disclosure of cash flows from discontinued operations; SFAS 95 does not.

[4] Required by para. 29 of SFAS 95. The AICPA's 2000 *Accounting Trends and Techniques* reports that 33 of the 600 firms surveyed did not disclose interest payments and 22 firms did not disclose income tax payments.

EXHIBIT 33-1 The WSF Company Statement of Cash Flows for Year Ended December 31, 2001

A. Direct Method

Cash collections		$ 2,675,000
Less: Cash inputs	$(1,750,000)	
Cash expenses (rent, operating)	(430,000)	
Cash interest	(125,000)	(2,305,000)
Cash flow from operations		**$370,000**
Capital expenditures	(500,000)	
Investment in affiliate	(710,000)	
Cash flow from investing		**(1,210,000)**
Short-term borrowing	500,000	
Dividends paid	(35,000)	
Cash flow from financing		**465,000**
Net cash flow		**$ (375,000)**
Cash balance, as of December 31		
2001	$ 3,625,000	
2000	4,000,000	
Net change		**$ (375,000)**

B. Indirect Method

Net income		78,870
Add: Noncash expenses		
Depreciation expense		175,000
Changes in operating accounts		$ 253,870
(Increase) in receivables	(224,500)	
Decrease in inventories	425,000	
(Decrease) in accounts payable	(475,000)	
Increase in accrued liabilities	50,000	
Increase in interest payable	125,000	
Increase in taxes payable	40,630	
Increase in advances from customers	175,000	116,130
Cash flows from operations		**$ 370,000**

Note: Cash flow from investing and financing identical to that shown on direct method. The firm would also provide a separate footnote on cash payments for interest and taxes. The WSF Company paid $125,000 in interest, but it made no tax payments during the year ended December 31, 2001.

Cash flow statements prepared using the indirect method have a significant drawback. Because the *indirect format reports the net cash flow from operations, it does not facilitate the comparison and analysis of operating cash inflows and outflows by function with the revenue and expense activities that generated them, as is possible from direct method cash flow statements.* In the absence of acquisitions, divestitures, and significant foreign operations, the indirect method simply recasts the income statement and the balance sheet, providing little new information on or insight into

EXHIBIT 33-2 The WSF Company
Balance Sheets at December 31, 2000 and 2001

	2000	2001
Assets		
Cash	$4,000,000	$3,625,000
Accounts receivable	0	224,500
Inventory	850,000	425,000
Current assets	$4,850,000	$4,274,500
Investment in affiliates	0	710,000
Buildings	3,500,000	4,000,000
Less: Accumulated depreciation	0	(175,000)
Long-term assets	$3,500,000	$4,535,000
Total assets	$8,350,000	$8,350,000
Liabilities		
Short-term debt	$ 0	$500,000
Advances from customers	0	175,000
Accounts payable	850,000	375,000
Accrued liabilities	0	50,000
Interest payable	0	125,000
Taxes payable	0	40,630
Dividends payable	0	35,000
Current liabilities	$ 850,000	$1,300,630
Bonds payable	2,500,000	2,500,000
Total liabilities	$3,350,000	$3,800,630
Common stock	1,000,000	1,000,000
Additional paid-in capital	4,000,000	4,000,000
Retained earnings	0	8,870
Stockholders' equity	$5,000,000	$5,008,870
Total liabilities and equities	$8,350,000	$8,809,500

the specific components of a firm's cash-generating ability. As a majority of firms prepare the SoCF using the indirect method,[5] it is often necessary to convert an indirect statement into a direct one.

Preparation of a Statement of Cash Flows

The cash flow statement combines cash flows for events that are reported on the balance sheet (e.g., purchases of inventories) and the income statement (e.g., the cost of goods sold). The process is complicated by timing differences

[5] Of the 600 firms surveyed by the AICPA in the 2000 *Accounting Trends and Techniques*, only 7 report using the direct method.

EXHIBIT 33-3 The WSF Company
Income Statement for Year Ended December 31, 2001

Net sales		$ 2,724,500
Less: Cost of goods sold		(1,700,000)
Gross margin		$ 1,024,500
Less: Operating expense	$360,000	
Depreciation expense	175,000	
Rent expense	120,000	
Interest expense	250,000	(905,000)
Income before taxes		119,500
Tax expense		(40,630)
Net income		$ 78,870

Statement of Retained Earnings

Beginning balance, January 1, 2001	$ 0
Net income	78,870
Dividends declared	(70,000)
Ending balance, December 31, 2001	$ 8,870

between when cash flows occur and when they are recognized as revenues, expenses, assets, or liabilities. The next section discusses methods used to prepare direct and indirect method cash flow statements.

Transactional Analysis

Transactional analysis[6] is a technique that can be used to create a cash flow statement for firms that do not prepare such statements in accordance with SFAS 95 and IAS 7.[7] It can also be used to convert indirect method cash flow from operations to the direct method.

One objective of transactional analysis is to understand the relationship between the accruals of revenues, expenses, assets, and liabilities and their cash flow consequences. Another goal is to facilitate analysis by classifying gross cash flows between operating, financing, and investing activities.

The method reconciles line-item changes in the balance sheet with their related income statement components to derive the cash flow consequences of the reported transactions and events. These changes are grouped according to whether they are operating,

[6] See Ashwinpaul C. Sondhi, George H. Sorter, and Gerald I. White, "Transactional Analysis," *Financial Analysts Journal* (September/October 1987), pp. 57–64. "Cash Flow Redefined: FAS 95 and Security Analysis," *Financial Analysts Journal* (November/December 1988), pp. 19–20 by the same authors links the transactional analysis method of preparing cash flow statements to those required by SFAS 95.

[7] The number of non-U.S. companies preparing statements of cash flows is on the increase. Firms using IAS 7 are not required to reconcile their cash flow statements to U.S. GAAP. Despite the increased use of IAS GAAP by non-U.S. firms, many foreign firms do not report any cash flow statement or report changes in funds (see "Cash Flow Statements: An International Perspective," near the end of this reading).

investing, or financing in nature. The classification and cash flow description for a typical firm follow:

Changes in Balance Sheet Accounts	Income Statement Items	Cash Flow Description
Cash Flow from Operating Activities (CFO)		
Accounts receivable	Net sales	Cash received from customers
Advances from customers	Net sales	Cash received from customers
Inventories and accounts payable	COGS	Cash paid for inputs
Prepaid expenses	SG&A expense	Cash operating expenses
Rent payable	Rent expense	Cash operating expenses
Accrued expenses	SG&A expense	Cash operating expenses
Interest payable	Interest expense	Interest paid
Income tax payable and deferred income taxes	Income tax expense	Income tax paid
Cash Flow from Investing Activities (CFI)		
Property, plant, and equipment	Depreciation expense	Capital expenditures
Intangible assets	Amortization expense	Capital expenditures
Investment in affiliates	Equity in income of affiliates	Cash paid for and received from investments in affiliates
Short and long-term investments and gains (losses) on certain investments	Realized gains or losses on investments	Cash paid for and received from investments
Assets and liabilities resulting from acquisitions and divestitures		Cash paid for acquisitions or received from divestitures
Cash Flow from Financing Activities (CFF)		
Dividends payable		Dividends paid
Notes payable		Increase or decrease in debt
Short-term debt		Increase or decrease in debt
Long-term debt		Increase or decrease in debt
Bonds payable		Increase or decrease in debt
Common stock and APIC		Increase or decrease in equity
Retained earnings		Dividends paid

The relationship between balance sheet changes and cash flows can be summarized as follows:

- Increases (decreases) in assets represent net cash outflows (inflows). If an asset increases, the firm must have paid cash in exchange.

- Increases (decreases) in liabilities represent net cash inflows (outflows). When a liability increases, the firm must have received cash in exchange.

While these points are simple (they ignore payments or receipts other than cash), they are useful in practice.

Two examples clarify the application of these points to transactional analysis:

1. When accounts receivable increase, the period's credit sales (revenues) must have exceeded cash collections. Thus, the increase in receivables must be deducted from the accrued sales revenue to derive the cash collected from customers during the period.
2. When interest payable increases, the firm has not paid all the interest expense accrued during the period. Hence, the increase in interest payable must be deducted from the interest expense to compute the amount of interest paid during the period.

Preparation of a Direct Method Statement of Cash Flows

Exhibit 33-4 illustrates the use of transactional analysis to prepare a direct method statement of cash flows for the WSF Company. We use the data from Exhibits 33-2 and 33-3 to explain the method without the complications present in most actual financial statements. A brief discussion of the most critical problems in the preparation of cash flow statements is provided later.

Cash Flows from Operations

Cash Collections. The principal component of CFO is the cash collections for the period. To derive this amount, we start with WSF net sales of $2,724,500 in 2001. The increase of $224,500 in the balance of accounts receivable means that cash has not yet been collected for all the sales recognized. In addition, the firm received cash advances ($175,000) for which revenue has not yet been recognized.

We modify net sales by deducting the increase in accounts receivable and adding the increase in advances, to arrive at cash collections. This is the amount of cash actually received during the period as a result of sales activities, regardless of when the related revenues are recognized.

Cash Outflows. The next stage involves the computation of operating cash outflows incurred to generate the cash collections. The first component is the cash outflow for inputs into the manufacturing or retailing process. The decrease in inventory balances[8] (cash outflow occurred in the prior period) is subtracted from, and the decrease in accounts payable (cash outflow in the current period for goods received in a prior period) is added to the cost of goods sold to determine the cash inputs or outflow for the manufacturing process.

The remaining income statement accounts and their related balance sheet accounts are similarly modified to their cash analogs to determine the cash outflows for operating expenses, interest, and taxes. In each case, the goal is to link the income statement account with related balance sheet accounts. By related, we mean the balance sheet account that contains cash flows that either have

---

[8] The cash outflow for inputs is not affected by the inventory valuation method used by the firm, facilitating comparison across firms.

EXHIBIT 33-4 The WSF Company
Transactional Analysis ($000)

	Income Statement	Balance Sheet 12/31/00	Balance Sheet 12/31/01	Change	Cash Effect	Cash	
Cash Collections							
Net sales	2,724.5				Increase	2,724.5	
Accounts receivable		—	224.5	224.5	(Decrease)	(224.5)	
Advances		—	175.0	175.0	Increase	175.0	**2,675.0**
Cash Inputs							
COGS	(1,700.0)				(Decrease)	(1,700.0)	
Inventory		850.0	425.0	(425.0)	Increase	425.0	
Accounts payable		850.0	375.0	(475.0)	(Decrease)	(475.0)	**(1,750.0)**
Cash Expenses							
Operating expense	(360.0)				(Decrease)	(360.0)	
Rent expense	(120.0)				(Decrease)	(120.0)	
Accrued liabilities		—	50.0	50.0	Increase	50.0	**(430.0)**
Cash Taxes Paid							
Tax expense	(40.63)				(Decrease)	(40.63)	
Taxes payable		0	40.63	40.63	Increase	40.63	—
Cash Interest paid							
Interest expense	(250.0)				(Decrease)	(250.0)	
Interest payable		0	125	125	Increase	125.0	**(125.0)**
Operating Cash Flow							**370.0**
Capital Expenditures							
Depreciation	(175.0)				(Decrease)	(175.0)	
Buildings—Net		3,500	3,825	325.0	(Decrease)	(325.0)	**(500.0)**
Cash Invested in Affiliates							
Investment in affiliates		—	710.0	710.0	(Decrease)		**(710.0)**
Investing Cash Flow							**(1,210.0)**
Cash from Borrowing							
Short-term debt		—	500.0	500.0	Increase	500.0	
Bonds payable		2,500	2,500	—		—	**500.0**
Equity Financing							
Common stock		1,000	1,000	—			
Additional paid-in capital		4,000	4,000	—			
Net income	78.87						
Dividends							
Dividends declared					(Decrease)	(70.0)	
Dividends payable		—	35.0		Increase	35.0	**(35.0)**
Financing Cash Flow							**465.0**
Change in cash							**(375.0)**

been recognized in that income statement account (accruals and payables) or will be recognized in the future (prepayments).

In many cases, disclosures are inadequate to do this precisely. Educated guesses and approximations may be necessary. For example, we assume that accounts payable reported by WSF relate only to the purchase of inventory for operating purposes although they may also be related to other operating expenses.

A careful reading of footnote data is necessary to obtain additional information on aggregated balance sheet accounts, permitting finer breakdowns of assets and liabilities. For example, in addition to trade accounts receivable, the amounts reported on the balance sheet may include notes and loans receivable, which represent investment cash flows.

Additionally, balance sheet and income statement accounts may require reallocation of some components. For example, when depreciation expense is not reported separately in the income statement, we must reduce COGS by the amount of depreciation expense to accurately reflect cash inputs and create a "depreciation expense" account to correctly estimate cash invested in property. The depreciation expense may be disclosed separately in footnotes, or in the indirect cash flow statement.

Cash flows that are considered nonrecurring[9] or peripheral to the basic activities of the firm are combined in the miscellaneous category, which also includes the cash impact of transactions for which the financial statements and the footnotes do not provide information enabling more precise classification.

Investing Cash Flow

Capital expenditures for long-term assets such as plant and machinery are usually the primary component of investing cash flow. As depreciation changes (net) property, plant, and equipment, the calculation of capital expenditures requires the amount of depreciation, depletion, and amortization expense in addition to the changes in all related long-term asset accounts.[10]

Capital expenditures may be calculated net or gross of proceeds on the sales of these assets. The cash flows from such sales are considered investment cash flows, regardless of whether they are netted in capital expenditures. Trends in gross capital expenditures contain useful insights into management plans.

Other components of cash flows from investing activities include cash flows from investments in joint ventures and affiliates and long-term investments in securities.[11] The cash flow consequences of acquisitions and divestitures must also be reported in this category. Footnote disclosures (when available) should be used to segregate operating assets and liabilities obtained (relinquished) in acquisitions (divestitures). This analysis, as discussed later, may be necessary to calculate CFO.

---

[9] However, the transaction should be analyzed to determine whether it is best classified as operating, investing, or financing.

[10] The deduction for depreciation expense is not taken because depreciation represents a cash flow; rather, it is needed to calculate the cash capital expenditures.

[11] The nature of the relationship between parent and subsidiary or joint venture affiliate should be periodically reviewed to ensure proper classification; in some cases, affiliates may be more accurately considered part of operations. However, contractual arrangements may constrain the parent's control over or access to cash flows from affiliates. (See Reading 13 for a detailed discussion of these issues.)

Financing Cash Flow

Components of financing cash flow include inflows from additional borrowing and equity financing, and outflows for repayment of debt, dividend payments, and equity repurchases. Debt financing for the period is the sum of the changes in short- and long-term debt accounts.

The calculation of equity financing cash flows requires analysis of the change in stock-holders' equity, separating:

- Net income.
- Dividends declared.
- Shares issued or repurchased.
- Changes in valuation accounts included in equity (each of these may require reallocation to appropriate operating or investing cash flow categories[12]).

Once this is done, every change in the balance sheet has been included (net income is included by incorporating each of its components) except cash. The net cash flow must, by definition, be equal to the change in cash. This identity provides a check on computations.[13]

The last step is to summarize the cash flows from operations, financing, and investing activities. The result is a direct method statement of cash flows, as shown in Exhibit 33-1A.

Indirect Method

Exhibit 33-1B presents the indirect method statement of cash flows for the WSF Company. The reporting of investing and financing activities is identical to the direct method. *The reporting of cash flow from operations, however, is quite different.* Under the indirect method, the starting point is the period's net income. Two types of adjustments are then made to net income to arrive at the CFO:

1. All "noncash" expense (revenue) components of the income statement are added (subtracted).
2. Changes in operating accounts are added/subtracted as follows:
    - Increases (decreases) in the balances of operating asset accounts are subtracted (added).
    - Increases (decreases) in the balances of operating liability accounts are added (subtracted).

The second type of adjustment represents the same balance sheet changes that were used to derive individual components of cash from operations under the direct method. As these adjustments are provided by the reconciliation in the indirect cash flow method, they can be used to derive a direct method cash flow statement from an indirect one.

In Box 33-1, we demonstrate this process using Pfizer's indirect method statement of cash flows. As the discussion in the box indicates, careful analysis of footnote information is required to make the necessary adjustments.

---

[12] For example, the change in the unrealized gains (losses) on investments account must be reflected as a component of investment cash flows (see Chapter 13).

[13] As an additional check, make sure that the income statement components used in the transactional analysis add up to net income.

BOX 33-1 PFIZER: DERIVATION OF DIRECT METHOD CFO ($ IN MILLIONS)

1999 Income Statement

Net sales	$14,133
Alliance revenue	2,071
Total revenues	$16,204
Costs and expenses:	
Cost of sales	(2,528)
Selling, informational, and administrative expenses	(6,351)
Research and development expenses	(2,776)
Other deductions—net	(101)
Income from continuing operations before provision for taxes on income and minority interests	$ 4,448
Provision for taxes on income	(1,244)
Minority interests	(5)
Income from continuing operations	$ 3,199

Indirect CFO from SoCF

Income from continuing operations	$ 3,199
Adjustments:	
Depreciation and amortization	542
Trovan inventory write-off	310
Deferred taxes and other	286
Changes in assets and liabilities:	
Accounts receivable	(978)
Inventories	(240)
Prepaid and other assets	68
Accounts payable and accrued liabilities	61
Income taxes payable	(179)
Other deferred items	7
Net cash provided by operating activities	$ 3,076

Two important requirements of SFAS 95 must, however, be explained before proceeding to Box 33-1:

1. *Changes in operating accounts shown on Pfizer's statement of cash flows do not equal the balance sheet changes.* For example, in the 1999 cash flow statement, accounts receivable are reported to *increase by $978*; the balance sheet shows an *increase of $950*. What accounts for this and similar discrepancies in other operating assets and liabilities?

Derivation of Direct Method CFO

Cash collections from customers		
Net sales (excluding alliance revenues)	$14,133	
Change in accounts receivable	(978)	**$13,155**
Cash from alliance revenues		**2,071**
Cash payments for inputs		
COGS	(2,528)	
Depreciation and amortization	542	
Trovan inventory write-off	310	
Change in inventories	(240)	
Change in accounts payable	61	**(1,855)**
Cash payments for SI&A		
Selling, informational, and administrative expenses	(6,351)	
Prepaid and other assets	68	**(6,283)**
Cash for research and development		**(2,776)**
Cash taxes paid		**(1,293)**
Cash interest paid		**(238)**
Miscellaneous cash flows (including minority interest)		**295**
Cash flow from operations		**$ 3,076**

Discussion

The direct method CFO is derived from the income statement and indirect method CFO.* Unlike many other companies, Pfizer does not provide details for most balance sheet categories. A number of assumptions were used to develop the direct method cash flow statement.

Cash collections are derived by deducting the $978 million increase in accounts receivable [see the reported indirect method statement of cash flows (SoCF)] from reported net sales of $14,133 million.

Pfizer reported cost of sales of $2,528 million; depreciation and amortization expense of $542 and the $310 million inventory write-off are added back as they reflect non-cash portions of COGS.† We also adjust for the changes in inventory and accounts payable. This latter adjustment requires the simplifying assumption that the accounts payable are related primarily to inventories.

To derive cash expenses, we add the $68 million of prepaid expenses to the reported selling, informational, and administrative expenses of $6,351 million. Research and development expenses are taken directly from the income statement. Pfizer discloses cash tax payments of $1,293 million and cash interest payments of $238 million.

The miscellaneous amount of $295 million is a "plug" amount used to arrive at the reported CFO of $3,076 million.

*Note that the CFI and CFF portions of the SoCF are identical under the direct and indirect methods. Thus we need only adjust the CFO portion.

† Many companies disclose depreciation as a separate item on the income statement. For those companies, depreciation on the SoCF equals the depreciation expense shown on the income statement. For companies that do not disclose depreciation separately, an assumption has to be made as to whether the depreciation is (primarily) included in COGS or SG&A. The rule of thumb is to assume COGS for manufacturing firms and SG&A for other firms.

2. Pfizer's statement of cash flows contains the *effect of exchange rate changes on cash* (in addition to the three cash flow categories: operating, investing, and financing). The 1999 amount is $26 million. What does it represent?

We address both issues later in this reading.

Reported versus Operating Changes in Assets and Liabilities

The discrepancies between the changes in accounts reported on the balance sheet and those reported in the cash flow statement are primarily due to two[14] factors:

- Acquisitions and divestitures
- Foreign subsidiaries

Acquisitions and Divestitures

Changes in reported balances of operating asset and liability accounts may include the effects of both operating activities and acquisitions or divestitures. For example, the inventory account may have increased as a result of:

1. Purchase of inventory from a supplier (an operating activity)
2. Acquisition of (merger with) another firm that has inventory as a component of its balance sheet (an investing activity)

SFAS 95 requires that CFO include only operating transactions and events. Thus, for firms that acquire the operating assets and liabilities of another company, the changes reported in the statement of cash flows as adjustments to income to arrive at CFO will not match the increase or decrease reported on the balance sheet.

The difference between the changes reported in the two statements provides useful information to the analyst. If the difference for any balance sheet account represents the amount of that component acquired through a merger, *the analyst can reconstruct the assets and liabilities obtained by the firm through an acquisition.*[15] This information is generally not provided anywhere else.

Although the reporting requirements accomplish the necessary segregation in the period of the acquisition (or divestiture), cash flows for subsequent periods may be distorted. For example, cash paid for the accounts receivable of an acquired firm is reported as an investment cash outflow. However, collection of the acquired receivable in a subsequent period will be reported as a component of operating cash flows. The result is overstated cash flows from operations, as the cost of acquiring the accounts receivable was never reflected in cash outflows for operations.[16] *Acquisitions, divestitures, and continuing corporate reorganizations can therefore distort trends in both cash flows from operations and investing cash flows.* These issues are examined in greater detail in Chapter 14.

---

[14] As previously discussed, balance sheet accounts may include both operating and nonoperating (investing or financing) items. The cash flow statement must allocate balance sheet changes to the appropriate activity.

[15] This can be done if we assume that the confounding effect of exchange rate changes (discussed next) is not significant. Thus, ignoring that issue for the moment, one would estimate that Pfizer's accounts receivable increased by $978 million and the balance sheet change reflects a divestiture of $28 million ($978 − $950).

[16] Similarly, cash received for accounts receivable of a divested business is reflected as an investment cash inflow, whereas the cash outflow required to generate the receivable (purchase of inventory, selling costs) was previously reported as a component of CFO. However, the CFI characterization is correct since the divested business will no longer contribute to cash flows from continuing operations. Prior period receivables (and CFO) would also exclude balances related to the divested business.

Translation of Foreign Subsidiaries

The second difference between the changes reported on the cash flow statement and those reported on the balance sheet relates to foreign operations. The assets and liabilities of foreign subsidiaries must be translated into the reporting currency (i.e., U.S. dollars) upon preparation of consolidated financial statements. This process generates a U.S. dollar balance for each asset and liability account that includes both operating changes (representing real cash flow effects) and exchange rate effects that have no current cash flow consequences.

For example, assume a firm has a foreign subsidiary that has an opening and closing accounts receivable balance of £10,000. Assume further that at the beginning of year 1, the pound is worth \$1.00, but at the end of the year a pound is worth \$1.10. Upon consolidation, the parent's balance sheet will include

Opening accounts receivable from foreign subsidiary (£10,000 × opening exchange rate of £1 = \$1)	\$10,000
Closing accounts receivable from foreign subsidiary (£10,000 × closing exchange rate of £1 = \$1.1)	11,000
Increase	\$ 1,000

This \$1,000 increase is included in accounts receivable shown on the balance sheet. However, it will not appear as a component of cash collections for the period because it is not a change resulting from operations. Thus, CFO does not include the effects of the translation process.

Translation gains and losses resulting from exchange rate changes are excluded from cash flows from operating, investing, and financing activities.[17] The effect of these excluded gains and losses is reported as the effect of exchange rate changes on cash (see the next section). The \$28 million discrepancy between the balance sheet increase in receivables (\$950 million) and that reported in Pfizer's cash flow statement (\$978 million) most likely reflects the impact of changes in exchange rates as the \$U.S. appreciated during 1999, reducing the \$U.S. equivalent of foreign currency receivables.

Effect of Exchange Rate Changes on Cash

An explanation of the *effect of exchange rate changes on cash* follows directly from our previous discussion. Suppose the foreign subsidiary in our previous example had a cash balance of £4,000 at the beginning and end of the year. Upon consolidation, the parent's reported cash balance includes \$4,000 at the beginning of the year and \$4,400 (£4,000 × 1.10) at the end of the year. This increase of \$400 needs to be reported as it does not appear as an operating, investing, or financing activity.

In Pfizer's case, the \$26 million reported as "effect of exchange rate on cash" reflects the effect of exchange rate changes on the firm's foreign currency cash holdings.

---

[17] These issues are discussed in greater detail in Chapter 15.

Example: Pfizer

We examine each component of Pfizer's cash flow statement, in turn, to demonstrate the use and analysis of cash flow statements.

Cash from Operations. Pfizer reports cash flows using the *indirect method.* As a result, the company provides a reconciliation of the difference between income from continuing operations[18] and CFO. The reconciling adjustments fall into three categories:

1. Noncash expenses
2. Nonoperating cash flows
3. Changes in operating assets and liabilities

Noncash expenses consist mostly of the amortization of past investment outflows. Although the matching principle requires amortization when computing net income, it is not a current-period cash flow. Pfizer adds back depreciation and amortization expense. The company also adjusts the income from continuing operations for the noncash effect of the Trovan inventory write-off.[19]

Nonoperating cash flows relate to investment and financing activities. For example, gains and losses from the sales of investments result from investment activities (discussed below) and must be excluded from the CFO. Similarly, extraordinary losses relate to the early extinguishment of debt, a financing activity, and must also be excluded from the computation of the cash flows from operations.

Finally, cash from operations reports changes in balance sheet accounts that are operating in nature. Such accounts include inventories, accounts receivable and payable (excluding amounts relating to investing and financing activities), and accruals for such operating items as interest,[20] income taxes, and employee benefits.

The reconciliation uses only the changes due to operating activities and, as discussed in the preceding section, excludes two other sources of changes in operating assets and liabilities: acquisitions/divestitures and the impact of changes in exchange rates.

Investing Cash Flow. Pfizer's net investment in property, plant, and equipment (PPE) grew steadily each year from $831 million (purchases of $878 million less disposal proceeds of $47 million) in 1997 to $1,490 million in 1999. Pfizer received cash inflows from the sale of businesses, most significantly proceeds of $3,059 million from the sale of the medical technology segment (see Note 2 for details). The company also reports significant transactions in short-term financial instruments, purchases of long-term investments, and other investing activities.

---

[18] Net cash used in (provided by) discontinued operations is separately reported for each year from 1997 to 1999. This distinction is important for the analysis of current CFO and future forecasts of CFO because the discontinued operations will no longer contribute to cash flows.

[19] Other examples of noncash expenses include the cumulative effect of adopting new accounting standards when those standards have no cash flow consequences.

[20] In a subsequent section of this reading, we argue that cash flows for interest represent financing rather than operating activities.

The separate disclosure of cash outflows for acquisitions is an important feature of the cash flow statement. These amounts reflect the assets purchased less liabilities assumed in acquisitions accounted for using the purchase method. *The cash outflows for the acquisitions of operating assets and liabilities of the acquired firm are excluded from CFO but included in CFI.*

Pfizer's transactions in short-term investments require some discussion. These investments are not considered "cash equivalents" because they do not meet the SFAS 95 definition (risk-free with maturities of less than three months). Nonetheless, from a practical point of view, they may be little different. If their risk is low and liquidity high, they should be treated analytically as cash equivalents as they represent additional short-term liquidity. Note that changes in the level of these investments may be reported net, one of the exceptions to the "gross" reporting requirements of SFAS 95. Under that standard, changes in balance sheet assets and liabilities that turn over frequently (another example is credit card receivables) may be reported net. Investments that are long-term, less liquid, and riskier (e.g., stocks or long-term bonds) must be treated differently (such investments are discussed in Reading 13).

Financing Cash Flow. This category contains cash flows between the firm and suppliers of its debt and equity capital. Pfizer reports a net increase in short-term debt and repayment of long-term debt. CFF also includes dividends paid to shareholders, purchases of common stock, cash effects of stock option transactions, and cash received from the sale of common stock.

Effect of Exchange Rate Changes on Cash. Pfizer has foreign subsidiaries and cash balances denominated in foreign currencies. Changes in exchange rates create translation gains and losses that are not cash flows, but must be reported for the cash flow statement to balance. The $26 million reported by Pfizer captures, in a single number, the effect of exchange rate changes on the firm's foreign cash holdings.

Change in Cash and Cash Equivalents. The net reconciling number is the period's change in the balance of cash and equivalents, equal to the sum of the three major cash flow components (CFO, CFI, and CFF) and any exchange rate effects. This number is necessarily equal to the difference between cash at the beginning of the year and the amount at the end of the year. However, although this number is easy to measure, it has no analytic value. Firms can influence the net change by accelerating or delaying payments, or by making use of short-term financing facilities.

2 ANALYSIS OF CASH FLOW INFORMATION

The cash flow statement is intended to help predict the firm's ability to sustain (and increase) cash from current operations. In doing so, the statement provides more objective information about:

- A firm's ability to generate cash flows from operations
- Trends in cash flow components and cash consequences of investing and financing decisions
- Management decisions regarding such critical areas as financial policy (leverage), dividend policy, and investment for growth

Neither the statement of cash flows nor the income statement alone contains sufficient information for decision making. (See Box 2-2 for some empirical evidence in this respect.) Income statement and balance sheet data must be combined with cash flows for insights into the firm's ability to turn its assets into cash inflows, repay its liabilities, and generate positive returns to shareholders. All three financial statements are needed to value the firm appropriately.

Free Cash Flows and Valuation

An important but elusive concept often used in cash flow analysis is *free cash flow* (FCF). It is intended to measure the cash available to the firm for discretionary uses after making all required cash outlays. The concept is widely used by analysts and in the finance literature as the basis for many valuation models (see Chapter 19). The basic elements required to calculate FCF are available from the cash flow statement. In practice, however, the definition of FCF varies widely, depending on how one defines required and discretionary uses.

The basic definition used by many analysts is cash from operations less the amount of capital expenditures required to maintain the firm's *present* productive capacity.[21] Discretionary uses include growth-oriented capital expenditures and acquisitions, debt reduction, and payments to stockholders (dividends and stock repurchase). The larger the firm's FCF, the healthier it is, because it has more cash available for growth, debt payment, and dividends.

The argument for this definition is similar to Hicks's argument regarding the computation of net income, discussed in the previous reading. If historical cost depreciation provided a good measure of the use of productive capacity, then FCF would equal CFO less depreciation expense. However (as discussed in Reading 41), historical cost depreciation is arbitrary and measures the cost to replace operating capacity only by coincidence.

The obvious alternative to depreciation is the amount of capital expenditures made to maintain current capacity, excluding capital expenditures for growth. In practice, however, it is difficult to separate capital expenditures into expansion and replacement components. Lacking better information, all capital expenditures are subtracted from CFO to obtain FCF.

Subtracting all capital expenditures from CFO to arrive at FCF brings the definition of FCF closer to the one used in finance valuation models. In these models, required outflows are defined as operating cash flows less capital expenditures to replace current operating capacity *as well as capital expenditures necessary to finance the firm's growth opportunities.* Growth opportunities are defined as those in which the firm can make "above-normal" returns. It is difficult to determine *a priori* the amount of capital expenditures required to maintain growth and the discretionary portion of these expenditures; pragmatically, FCF is generally measured as CFO less capital expenditures.

Valuation models do, however, differ as to whether FCF is measured as *FCF available to the firm* [*i.e., all providers of capital (debt and equity)*] or as *FCF available to equity shareholders.* In the former case, required payments *do not* include outlays for interest and debt. In the latter case, they do. Thus, for FCF to the firm, one cannot use reported CFO (less capital expenditures) because CFO includes outlays for interest expense. We return to this issue later in this reading. In Chapter 19, we elaborate on the differing definitions of FCF and their implications for valuation models.

---

[21] IAS 7 recommends this disclosure.

Relationship of Income and Cash Flows

When periodic financial statements are prepared, estimates of the revenues earned and expenses incurred during the reporting interval are required. As discussed in the previous reading, these estimates require management judgment and are subject to modification as more information about the operating cycle becomes available. Accrual accounting can therefore be affected by management's choice of accounting policies and estimates. Furthermore, accrual accounting *by itself* fails to provide adequate information about the liquidity of the firm and long-term solvency. Some of these problems can be alleviated by the use of the cash flow statement in conjunction with the income statement.

Cash flow is relatively (but not completely) free of the drawbacks of the accrual concept. It is less likely to be affected by variations in accounting principles and estimates, making it more useful than reported income in assessing liquidity and solvency.

Figure 33-1 compares the level and trend of net income, cash from operations, and two measures of free cash flow for three different companies: Kmart, Westvaco, and Intel. Reported income and CFO were taken directly from the firms' financial statements. Two measures of free cash flow are used:

FCF1 equals CFO minus (net) capital expenditures.

FCF2 equals CFO minus CFI and thus includes expenditures (receipts) for acquisitions (divestitures) and other investments.

Note that CFO exceeds income for all three companies because CFO is not reduced by the cost of productive capacity.[22] Depreciation is usually the largest component of the adjustment from income to CFO. When the cost of productive capacity is included, as in FCF1, the relationship is company specific and varies from year to year.

Intel is a "growth" company; its income[23] and CFO (except 1998) show steady growth from 1997 to 2000. FCF1 is below income in each period (except 1999), reflecting capital expenditures for expansion as well as for replacement. FCF1 is positive in each year, a healthy sign given rapid growth. FCF2 is also positive each year. FCF patterns have to be monitored carefully for growth companies to ensure that they are not growing too fast, which can cause liquidity problems.

While the 1998 and 1999 increases in free cash flow (due to declines in Intel's CFI) are surprising for a growth company, the decrease may simply mean that Intel avoided overexpansion during those years. The 2000 declines in FCF1 and FCF2 are the result of increased capital expenditures and acquisitions.

Kmart reported increases in both income and cash flow from 1997 to 1998, lower CFO in 1999 and 2000, and a decline in income in 1999 and a loss in 2000. CFO remained positive despite a loss in 2000. Both FCF1 and FCF2 deteriorated over the four-year period as capital expenditures and CFI increased. Investments in operating assets, new businesses, and the acquisition of leases of other companies explain the difference between the income and cash flow measures.

Westvaco is an example of a cyclical company. Income declined from 1997–1999 with significant improvement in 2000. Debt and interest costs increased every year. After peaking in 1997, capital expenditures declined every year. Net operating assets declined as well until 2000. The result was high and

---

[22] This point is elaborated on further in the section entitled "Cash Flow Classification Issues."

[23] Although Intel reported increasing income, one source of that increase was gains on investments in new technology companies, which proved to be ephemeral. Net income was also increased by substantial interest income. Since management has considerable discretion over the amount and timing of realized gains on investments, and the measurement of unrealized gains, the analyst needs to be wary of income growth stemming from nonoperating sources.

FIGURE 33-1 Comparison of Patterns of Income, CFO, and Free Cash Flows

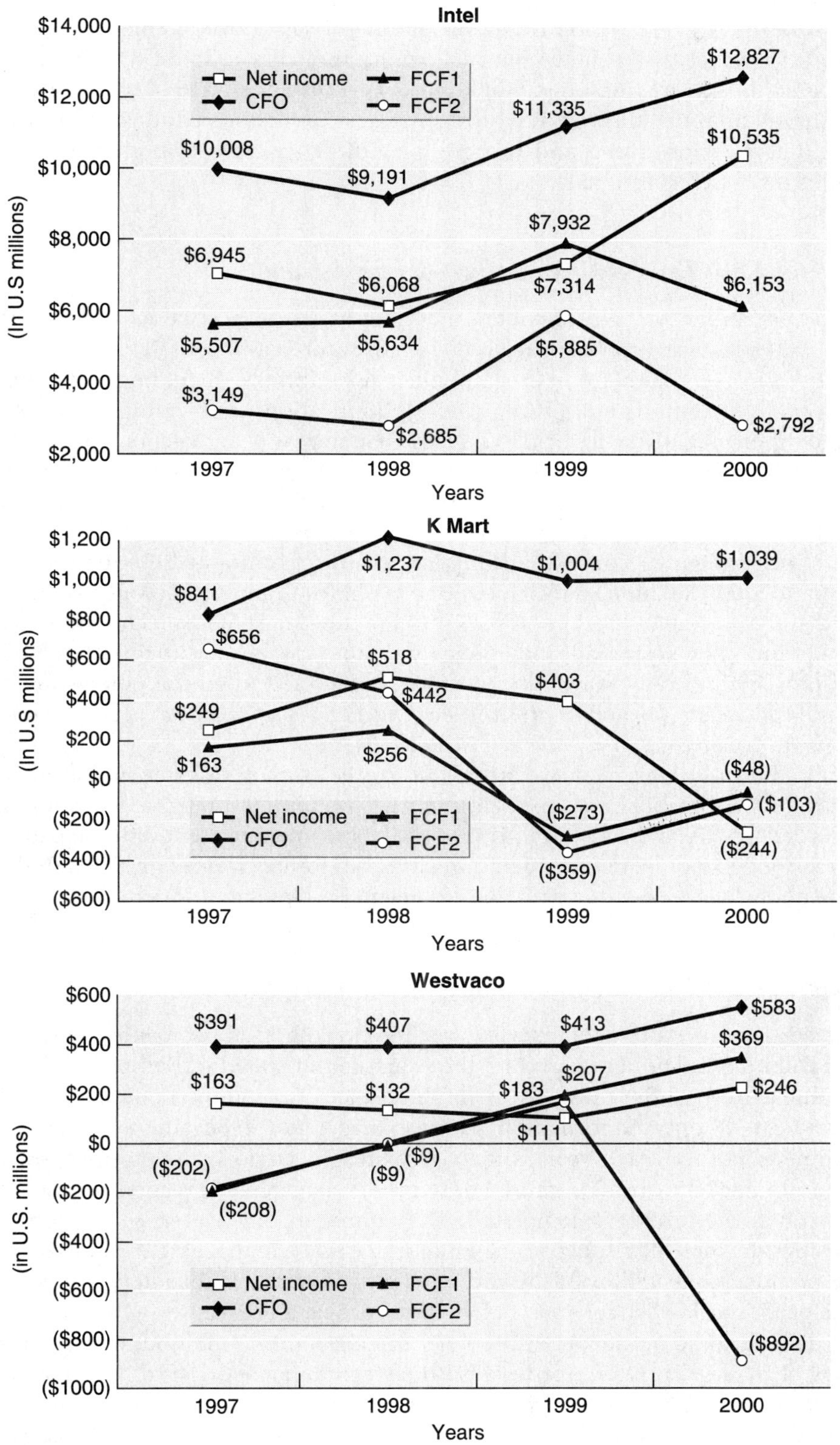

increasing (relative to income) CFO every year from 1997 to 2000. FCF1 was positive in 1999 and 2000 but FCF2 was positive only in 1999. The 2000 decline in FCF2 reflects significant global acquisitions as the company expanded its packaging business.

The previous discussion illustrates the use of cash flow statements together with information from the income statement, the balance sheet, and footnotes to assess the cash-generating ability of a firm. This assessment should consider the firm's liquidity, the viability of income as a predictor of future cash flows, and the effect of timing and recognition differences. We elaborate on these points in the next sections.

Income, Cash Flow, and the Going-Concern Assumption

As noted earlier, income statement amounts based on accrual accounting are generally presumed to be good predictors of future cash flows. That predictive ability is subject to a number of implicit assumptions, including the going-concern assumption. For example, the classification of inventories as assets rather than expenses implicitly assumes that they will be sold in the normal course of business. Similarly, the accrual of revenue from credit sales and the valuation of receivables assume that the firm will continue to operate normally; failing firms may find that customers are unwilling to pay.

When the going concern assumption is subject to doubt, revenue recognition and asset valuation can no longer be taken for granted. The value of inventory and receivables declines sharply when they must be quickly liquidated. Long-term assets (especially intangibles and other assets with little or no value in a nonoperating framework) also must be reexamined when the going-concern assumption is questioned. In this respect, *the statement of cash flows serves as a check on the assumptions inherent in the income statement.*

To find out why income can fail as a predictor of cash-generating ability (uncollected receivables or unsold inventories) requires a comparison of amounts recorded as sales and cost of goods sold on the income statement with the pattern of cash collections from customers and cash paid for inventories on the cash flow statement. A direct method cash flow statement is helpful in this regard.

Income, Cash Flow, and the Choice of Accounting Policies

Consider the income statements for the three hypothetical companies presented in Exhibit 33-5. They are based on the example illustrated in Exhibit 2-1. Their income patterns differ only because of the choice of accounting policy. The policies selected convey information about management expectations. In case A, income is positive each year as management expects to complete the project within budget. In case B, a more conservative management recognizes income only when the project is completed. The annual income statement reports no activities during the first two years. Finally, in case C, management assumes that the eventual collectibility of the revenues is uncertain and thus does not recognize profit until collections are sufficient to recover all costs.

The periodic net income differs because accounting methods and assumptions of managers differ, not because their economic activities differ. *The cash flow statement allows the analyst to distinguish between the actual events that have occurred and the accounting assumptions that have been used to report these events.* This is not to say that the assumptions made by management are wrong. These assumptions may provide useful information. The user of financial statements needs to understand the interrelationship between these events and financial reporting choices.

Exhibit 33-5 Derivation of Cash from Operations Under Alternative Accounting Methods

	Year			
Indirect Method	**1**	**2**	**3**	**Total**
Company A: Percentage of Completion				
Revenue	$1,000	$3,500	$1,500	$6,000
Expense	(800)	(2,800)	(1,200)	(4,800)
Net income	$ 200	$ 700	$ 300	$1,200
Add (deduct): Increase (decrease in advances)	300	(300)	—	—
Add (deduct): Decreases (increases) in construction in progress	—	(700)	700	—
Cash from operations	$ 500	$ (300)	$1,000	$1,200
Company B: Completed Contract				
Revenue	$ —	$ —	$6,000	$6,000
Expense	—	—	(4,800)	(4,800)
Net income	$ —	$ —	$1,200	$1,200
Add (deduct): Increase (decrease in advances)	500	(300)	(200)	—
Cash from operations	$ 500	$ (300)	$1,000	$1,200
Company C: Cost Recovery				
Revenue	$ 800	$2,800	$2,400	$6,000
Expense	(800)	(2,800)	(1,200)	(4,800)
Net income	$ —	$ —	$1,200	$1,200
Add (deduct): Increase (decrease in advances)	500	(300)	(200)	—
Cash from operations	$ 500	$ (300)	$1,000	$1,200
Direct Method: Identical for All Three Companies				
Cash collections	$1,300	$2,500	$2,200	$6,000
Cash disbursements	(800)	(2,800)	(1,200)	(4,800)
Cash from operations	$ 500	$ (300)	$1,000	$1,200

The cash flow statement shows that the cash collected, cash disbursed, and the cash flow from operations is identical for all three companies because the economic activities of these companies are identical. The three companies differ only with respect to reported income, which is a function of different accounting assumptions and policies.

Income, Cash Flow, and Liquidity

Companies can grow too fast, resulting in liquidity problems. Although Intel, discussed above, does not suffer from liquidity problems, its cash flow pattern can be a prelude to such problems. Another fast-growing company, The Discovery

Zone, an operator of children's indoor entertainment facilities, provides such an example. The company filed for bankruptcy reorganization under Chapter 11 in 1995. At that time, its CEO stated:

> A successful Chapter 11 reorganization will address the problems caused by the company's *rapid expansion* and put Discovery Zone on stronger financial footing.

Rapid growth is often accompanied by increases in capital expenditures and negative free cash flows. Moreover, growth companies may also report weak operating cash flows because they must finance growth in current operating assets. As firms usually pay for inventories before they are sold and collect sales proceeds subsequent to sale, there may be a long time lag between payments to suppliers and receipts from customers.

The cash flow statement provides information about the firm's liquidity and its ability to finance its growth from internally generated funds. It can highlight potential liquidity problems, such as an increasing need for operating capital or lagging cash collections.

However, reliance on the cash flow statement is insufficient for a complete assessment of the underlying strength of the company. Trends in sales and earnings must be evaluated from income statement data to determine whether there is a strong growth pattern that indicates a sustainable ability to generate cash flows in the future.

Analysis of Cash Flow Trends

The data contained in the statement of cash flows can be used to:

1. Review individual cash flow items for analytic significance.
2. Examine the trend of different cash flow components over time and their relationship to related income statement items.
3. Consider the interrelationship between cash flow components over time.

We examine each of these uses continuing with Pfizer as an example. A summary of Pfizer's cash flow statements for 1997–1999 is presented below:

Pfizer Statement of Cash Flows

	1997–1999 (in $millions)		
	1997	**1998**	**1999**
Cash from operations (CFO)	$1,580	$3,282	$3,076
Investing cash flow (CFI)	(963)	(335)	(2,768)
Financing cash flow (CFF)	(981)	(2,277)	(1,127)
Cash provided by (used in) discontinued operations	118	4	(20)
Effect of exchange rate changes	(27)	1	26
Change in cash and equivalents	$ (273)	$ 675	$ (813)

The CFI portion of Pfizer's cash flow statement shows a significant increase in investment[24] in property, plant, and equipment from $831 million in 1997 to $1,490 million in 1999. Pfizer's segment data (Note 19) tell us that more than 90% of the investment has been made in the pharmaceutical segment. The company derives most of its revenues and profits from that segment. Pfizer's merger with the Warner-Lambert Company indicates a continuing emphasis on pharmaceuticals. Revenues are nearly unchanged and profits have been erratic in the only other segment of operations, animal health.

The CFF component reports significant and increasing payments to stockholders; net repurchases of stock and dividend payments were $1,467, $2,888, and $3,586 million in 1997, 1998, and 1999 respectively. Pfizer's free cash flow (CFO—capital expenditures) was not sufficient to meet the demands of its capital structure choices in 1997 and 1999. The company borrowed (short-term debt) $2,083 million in 1999 and Note 4B tells us that weighted-average interest rate on those borrowings during that year was 4.3%. Note that the company reports significant investments in securities during these three years while it increased both Treasury stock and short-term debt. These actions raise the following questions:

- Why is the company borrowing and investing short-term?
- What do the share repurchases say about the company's investment opportunities?

For an example of the second type of analysis, we look at cash from operations. Because CFO is subject to random and cyclical influences, it should be analyzed over long periods (three to five years). In general, CFO should be positive and increase over time because it provides the resources to service debt, invest in growth, and reward shareholders.

Pfizer's CFO grew by $1,496 million or 95% from 1997–1999. Given the company's sales growth (47%) and increasing profitability (44%), higher CFO is a healthy sign. Significant growth often results in negative CFO for brief periods, as the required increase in working capital more than offsets growth in income. This is not the case for Pfizer, which reports improved CFO despite an increase in operating assets.[25]

In other cases, however, weak CFO may reflect operating problems such as unrealistic revenue recognition accounting policies or the inability to collect receivables. A comparison of revenue and expense trends with the pattern of cash collections from customers and cash payments should reveal the causes of lower CFO and suggest whether the trend is likely to reverse.

Direct method statements allow analysts to make such comparisons because they provide information better suited to trend analysis. Direct method statements reveal, for example, whether CFO is increasing because cash collections are increasing or payments to suppliers are decreasing. The discussion of Pfizer uses the 1999 data derived in Box 33-1, and 1997 and 1998 data derived using the same method.

---

[24] The capital expenditures are calculated net of disposals. In 1997, for example, there were purchases of $878 million less disposal proceeds of $47 million.

[25] The ratio analysis of Pfizer in Chapter 4 provides further insight into this issue.

First, we compute a "cash gross margin" percentage and compare it to one based on income:

Pfizer: Cash and Income-based Gross Margins

	1997 to 1999 (in $millions)		
	1997	**1998**	**1999**
Cash Flow Statement			
Cash collections	$10,262	$11,912	$13,155
Cash inputs	(2,189)	(1,905)	(1,855)
Cash gross margin	$8,073	$10,007	$11,300
Percent	78.7%	84.0%	85.9%
Income Statement			
Sales	$10,739	$12,677	$14,133
COGS	(1,776)	(2,094)	(2,528)
Gross margin	$ 8,963	$10,583	$11,605
Percent	83.5%	83.5%	82.1%
Other Ratios			
Cash collections/sales	95.6%	94.0%	93.1%
Cash inputs/COGS	123.3%	91.0%	73.4%

Pfizer's cash gross margin increased by $3,227 million (40%) over the 1997–1999 period, more than twice the $1,496 million improvement in CFO. Pfizer has reported increases in both cash expenses and research and development expenditures. Cash gross margin improved in both 1998 and 1999. The income statement–based gross margin held steady at 83.5% in 1997 and 1998, falling to 82.1% in 1999.[26] Future pricing pressures combined with required increases in expenditures may limit growth in Pfizer's CFO.

The cash collections/sales ratio has declined marginally as receivables have increased 74% while sales rose only 32% during this period. *The major improvement over time derives from cash inputs.* The cash for inputs/COGS ratio declined, as inputs declined despite rising COGS. Inventories have generally increased, with 1999 inventories declining partly because of the Trovan inventory write-off. The cash for inputs/COGS ratio would be 84% if we exclude the write-off from COGS.

The third type of analysis of cash flow components looks at the relationship among those components over time. An example is provided by Pfizer's free cash flows defined here as CFO less capital expenditures.

---

[26] Excluding the Trovan inventory write-off, this gross margin would have risen to 84.3%.

Pfizer Free Cash Flows

1997 to 1999 (in $millions)

	1997	1998	1999
Cash from operations	$1,580	$3,282	$3,076
Capital expenditures	(831)	(1,119)	(1,490)
Free cash flow	$ 749	$2,163	$1,586
CFF	(981)	(2,277)	(1,127)

Pfizer's FCF increased significantly (by $837 million or nearly 112%) over the 1997–1999 period. This increase reflects the improvement in CFO despite higher capital expenditures. As noted in a preceding section, Pfizer did not generate sufficient free cash flow to fund its dividend and share repurchase programs. In 1999, the stockholder payments (share repurchases and dividend payments) were offset by a significant increase in short-term borrowing.

Trend analysis of cyclical companies requires more than the evaluation of data for individual years; aggregated data should be evaluated as well. In Box 33-2, we provide an analysis of A. M. Castle (a cyclical company) over the five-year period 1996 through 2000.

Cash Flow Classification Issues

Although the classification of cash flows into the three main categories is important, we must recognize that classification guidelines can be arbitrary. The resulting data may require selective adjustment before they are used to make investment decisions. The classification guidelines of SFAS 95 often create problems for users of the cash flow statement in the following areas:

- Cash flows involving property, plant, and equipment
- Differences due to some accounting methods
- Interest and dividends received
- Interest paid
- Noncash transactions

Some of these issues have been touched on earlier in this reading. We discuss each in greater detail now.

Classification of Cash Flows for Property, Plant, and Equipment

Consider the components of cash flow from operations in the following simple example:

Net income	$30,000
Noncash expense: depreciation	5,000
	$35,000
Change in operating accounts: decrease in inventory	15,000
= Cash from operations	$50,000

BOX 33-2 A. M. CASTLE

Analysis of Cash Flows, 1996–2000 (in $thousands)

	1996	1997	1998	1999	2000	Total
Cash collections	$675,236	$742,275	$802,283	$710,024	$736,235	$3,666,053
Cash inputs	(479,343)	(555,006)	(617,401)	(431,424)	(537,847)	(2,621,021)
Cash expenses	(142,596)	(164,214)	(188,791)	(190,856)	(197,972)	(884,429)
Cash joint ventures and minority interest					(2,547)	(2,547)
Cash taxes	(15,268)	(13,729)	(10,134)	(3,302)	(5,402)	(47,835)
Cash interest	(2,997)	(4,209)	(7,987)	(11,353)	(10,992)	(37,538)
Miscellaneous	(117)	48	(1,498)	508	(81)	(1,140)
CFO	$ 34,915	$ 5,165	$(23,528)	$ 73,597	$(18,606)	$ 71,543
Capital expenditures	$(22,544)	$(16,182)	$(30,236)	$(17,770)	$(13,231)	$ (99,963)
Proceeds from sales of PPE	2,521	2,470	9,640	7,399	8,264	30,294
Investments and acquisitions	(17,984)	(29,265)	(26,171)	(3,129)	(4,050)	(80,599)
CFI	**(38,007)**	**$ (42,977)**	**$ (46,767)**	**$ (13,500)**	**$ (9,017)**	**$ (150,268)**
CFF	**4,230**	**38,782**	**70,474**	**(60,473)**	**27,124**	**80,137**
Change in cash	**$ 1,138**	**$ 970**	**$ 179**	**$ (376)**	**$ (499)**	**$ 1,412**
Beginning balance	667	1,805	2,775	2,954	2,578	10,779
Ending balance	$ 1,805	$ 2,775	$ 2,954	$ 2,578	$ 2,954	$ 13,066
Cash inputs/cash collections	70.99%	74.77%	76.96%	60.76%	73.05%	
CFO/cash collections	5.17%	0.70%	−2.93%	10.37%	−2.53%	
COGS/net sales*	71.58%	71.57%	70.52%	68.29%	70.23%	
Operating expense/net sales*	20.84%	21.81%	23.35%	26.73%	26.26%	

*These ratios are based on income statement data not shown.

Discussion

A direct method cash flow statement for A. M. Castle (Castle) for the five years from 1996 to 2000 is presented. These statements were derived from the reported indirect method statements using the methodology depicted in Box 33-1.

Castle is a metal wholesaler. Its revenues and earnings are heavily influenced by the business cycle. Because of the cyclicality, we start by reviewing cash flows over the entire five-year period.

Aggregate cash from operations was approximately $71.5 million, although CFO was negative for two of the five years. Net capital expenditures were nearly $70 million (capital expenditures of $100 million less proceeds from sales of $30 million). The company also reported investment and acquisition outflows of $80.5 million during the same period. Even if we assume that the capital expenditures reflect replacement of productive capacity, free cash flow of $1.5 million would have been inadequate for expansion. Sales have risen from $672 million in 1996 to $745 million in 2000, peaking at $793 million in 1998.

Castle has paid its stockholders nearly $50 million in dividends over the five-year period and borrowed nearly $130 million to finance its investments and acquisitions. Total balance sheet debt has grown from $43 million in 1996 to $164.5 million in 2000 with the debt-to-equity ratio rising from about 36% in 1996 to 127% in 2000.

During this five-year period, cash for inputs (production costs) ranged from 61% in 1999 to as much as 77% in 1998 while the COGS as a percentage of net sales remained comparatively stable (68% to 71.6%). The difference is due to swings in inventory levels and prices.

The cash flow statement adds both depreciation expense (a noncash expense) and the decrease in inventory (change in an operating asset) to net income to arrive at cash from operations for the current period. Their differing classifications suggest that the reason for these addbacks is not identical. Both adjustments reflect prior-period cash outflows that are recognized in income in the current period. Depreciation allocates the cost of fixed assets to the period in which they are used. Similarly, the cost of goods sold allocates the cost of inventory to the period in which the inventory is actually sold.

The difference between the two adjustments is the classification of the initial cash outlays. In one sense, both initial outlays were for investments. In one case, the firm invested in fixed assets; in the other, it invested in inventories. The latter, however, is classified as an operating cash outflow,[27] deducted from CFO in the period of the initial outlay and added back to income when expensed to avoid double counting.

The original investment in fixed assets was reported as an investment cash outflow, and its allocation (depreciation expense) is added back to income and never classified as an operating flow, but always as an investment flow.[28]

The implications of this classification issue follow:

1. Cash from operations does not include a charge for use of the firm's operating capacity. Cash required to replace the productive capacity or physical plant used during operations is not included in CFO.
2. Firms reporting positive CFO may not thrive unless the CFO (generated and retained) is sufficient to replace the productive capacity used to generate the operating cash flow.
3. Identical firms with equal capital intensity will report different CFOs when one firm leases plant assets and the other owns its assets. The firm that leases reports lower CFO because lease rentals are operating expenditures (operating cash flows), whereas the other firm's expenditures are reported as investment cash flows.
4. Cash payments for operating assets and obligations to pay operating liabilities may also be excluded from CFO. For example, the cash paid for an acquired firm's inventories is included in investing cash flow. However, the proceeds from the sale of such "purchased" inventory in subsequent periods are included in CFO, distorting reported CFO because its purchase cost is never reported in CFO. Similarly, cash paid to settle acquired operating liabilities would be reported in CFO in subsequent periods.
5. An additional problem is that "investment" is not precisely defined. Two examples follow:
   - Hertz classifies its investment in rental cars as inventory, and purchases are included in CFO. In this case, CFO is understated relative to a firm that classifies its operating assets as property.
   - Media companies consider programming purchases as long-term fixed assets. Although amortization impacts reported earnings, purchase costs are never reported in CFO. Yet financial markets seem to value such firms based on multiples of CFO per share rather than earnings per share!

---

[27] An exception occurs, as previously discussed, when inventory is acquired as part of an acquisition.

[28] As discussed later in this reading, this applies to all expenditures that are capitalized and amortized rather than expensed.

Free cash flow, which deducts capital expenditures (however defined) from CFO, is generally free from the classification issue. However, the classification decision can have a significant impact on reported CFO.

Effect of Differences in Accounting Methods

We previously demonstrated that CFO is not affected by the timing differences generated by revenue and expense recognition methods. In that sense, CFO is less affected by differing accounting policies. However, *CFO is affected by reporting methods that alter the classification of cash flows among operating, investing, and financing categories.* If one accounting method results in the classification of a cash flow as investing and an alternative results in its classification as operating, then the reported CFOs will differ. Moreover, unlike revenue and expense differences in accounting policies that reverse over time, *the differences in CFO classification caused by reporting methods are permanent.*[29]

The capitalization of expenditures such as internal-use computer software leads to the classification of cash outflows as investing cash flows. However, they are reported as operating cash flows when expensed immediately.[30] Reading 40 contains an extensive discussion of this issue. Lease classification (discussed in Reading 44) also affects cash flow components for both lessors and lessees. We shall demonstrate other examples throughout the book.

Example

On July 1, 2000, Amazon.com, Inc. adopted the consensus of Emerging Issues Task Force Issue 00-2, Accounting for Web Site Development Costs. For the year ended December 31, 2000, the company capitalized costs of $3.0 million, reported as a component of fixed assets, and amortized over a period of two years. The company also capitalized the cost of internal-use software including the costs of operating the company's website. *None of these capitalized costs will ever be reported as components of CFO.*

Interest and Dividends Received

Interest income and dividends received from investments in other firms are classified under SFAS 95 as operating cash flows. *As a result, the return on capital is separated from the return of capital.*[31] Combining these two returns to report cash flow to and from investees facilitates analysis. More important, the reclassification of

---

[29] The effects on the calculation of free cash flows must also be considered. If the classification difference is just between CFO and CFI, then Free Cash Flow = CFO − CFI will not be affected. However, if the classification difference results in a shift between CFO and CFF (as in the case of leasing), FCF is affected as well.

[30] This effect depends on the cash flow classification of the capitalized amount. Overhead capitalized in inventory, for example, will not change reported CFO because changes in inventory are also included in CFO. Overhead capitalized in fixed assets, however, will result in reclassification of the outflow from operating to investing cash flow.

[31] Only the nominal (cash) return (dividend or interest received) is reported as an operating cash flow: the real (total) return (which includes capital gain or loss) is split between operating and investing cash flow.

after-tax dividend and interest from operating to investing cash flows has the advantage of reporting operating cash flows that reflect only the operating activities of the firm's core business.[32]

Interest Paid

Interest payments are classified as operating cash outflows under SFAS 95. Such payments are the result of capital structure and leverage decisions and they reflect financing rather than operating risk. The reported CFOs of two firms with different capital structures are not comparable because returns to creditors (interest) are included in CFO, whereas returns to stockholders (dividends) are reported as financing cash flows. For analytical purposes, therefore, interest payments (after tax to reflect the cash flow benefits of tax deductibility) should be reclassified as financing cash flows. The resulting operating cash flow is independent of the firm's capitalization, facilitating the comparison of firms with different capital structures.

The treatment of interest payments in cash flow statements has an important valuation impact. The telecommunications company Sprint has issued two tracking stocks. One is the wireless unit, Sprint PCS, and the other is Sprint FON, comprised of the local, long-distance, and data businesses. Sprint allocated $14 billion of debt to Sprint PCS and $4 billion to Sprint FON. Sprint PCS pays nearly 8% interest (2% more than the actual cost) on its debt. In its 10-Q filings, Sprint says that the difference between actual interest cost and the amount charged to Sprint PCS is reported as a deduction from Sprint FON's interest expense.

The August 6, 2001 issue of *Barron's* suggests a reason: Sprint PCS (as a start-up, without earnings) is valued on pretax cash flow before interest by the financial markets whereas Sprint FON is valued on after-tax earnings.

Noncash Transactions

Some investing and financing activities do not require direct outlays of cash. For example, a building may be acquired by assuming a mortgage. Under current disclosure rules, such transactions do not appear as cash from financing or investing activities but are given separate footnote disclosure as "significant noncash financing and investment activities."

For analytical purposes, however, this transaction is identical to the issuance of a bond to a third party, using the proceeds to acquire the building. *The "noncash" transaction reflects both a financing and investing activity and should be included in each category.* Knowledge of the firm's cash requirements for investing activities is as important as the method of financing. The latter provides information about future cash flow needs for interest and the repayment of principal.

The classification issues discussed in this section should provide the reader with an awareness that the cash flow statement is based on assumptions, definitions, and (somewhat arbitrary) accounting rules. Knowledge of these assumptions and rules allows the analyst to make informed adjustments that may be better suited for analytical purposes.

---

[32] However, some investments and joint ventures are operating in nature. Such investments may assist in current and future operations, require significant financing commitments, and provide some control over the cash flows generated by the investee. See Chapter 13 for more discussion of these issues.

3 CASH FLOW STATEMENTS: AN INTERNATIONAL PERSPECTIVE

As discussed earlier in this reading, the requirements of IAS 7 are quite similar to those of SFAS 95. The following table highlights the most significant differences:

Issue	US GAAP (SFAS 95)	IAS GAAP (IAS 7)
Bank overdrafts	Shown as liability; changes are shown in cash flow statement	May be shown as part of cash equivalents, in countries where it is customary to use overdrafts as part of cash management programs; changes *not* shown in cash flow statement
Interest and dividends received	Cash from operations (CFO)	May be shown as *either* CFO *or* cash from investing (CFI)
Interest paid	Cash from operations (CFO)	May be shown as *either* CFO *or* cash from financing (CFF)
Dividends paid	Cash from financing (CFF)	May be shown as *either* CFO *or* cash from financing (CFF)
Reconciliation from net income to CFO	Always required	Not required when direct method used

The cash flow classification differences are especially significant for companies using IAS GAAP that choose the alternative that differs from U.S. GAAP. For example, the cash flow statement in the 2000 annual report of Roche includes interest and dividends received in cash flows from investing activities and interest paid in financing activities. Financial statement users must watch for such differences and adjust for them to make cash flow measures comparable.

The International Organization of Securities Commissions (IOSCO) has endorsed IAS 7 in financial statements used in cross-border offerings; the U.S. SEC does not require reconciliation when foreign issuers prepare cash flow statements using IAS 7.

Although income statements and balance sheets are required as part of the periodic financial statements virtually around the world, there is no cash flow statement requirement in many countries. For example, Germany and The Netherlands have no requirement; in Japan, it is only required of listed companies as part of an unaudited schedule. Takeda includes a cash flow statement in its English language reports (as explained in Note 1) although Japanese GAAP do not require it. Holmen's cash flow statement uses a quite different format. When no cash flow statement is provided, the analyst should use the transactional analysis method (Exhibit 33-4) to generate a direct method cash flow statement.

When cash flow statements are required, their format varies greatly across countries. Australian GAAP require the use of the direct method. In the United Kingdom, interest and dividends paid (returns to providers of capital) are grouped in a separate category, not included as part of either CFO or CFF.

Although we believe this format is superior to the SFAS 95 format, reported cash flows are not comparable without adjustment.[33]

Cash flow analysis is an important tool for international comparisons because of significant accounting differences across countries. As noted, cash flows (CFO and FCF) are generally less susceptible than income to variations resulting from differences in accounting methods. However, differences in accounting methods do affect cash flow classifications. Thus, international comparisons may require the adjustment of reported cash flows.[34]

[33] A few countries still present a statement of changes in funds (working capital). The focus on working capital ignores changes in operating accounts. Such statements do not add informational value to net income. Problem 3-13 requires adjustment of a statement of source and application of funds to a cash flow statement.

[34] See, for example, Kenneth S. Hackel and Joshua Livnat, "International Investments Based on Free Cash Flow: A Practical Approach," *Journal of Financial Statement Analysis* (Fall 1995), pp. 5–14, where such an approach is applied to a sample of firms. See also Chapter 10 of *Cash Flow and Security Analysis,* 2nd ed. (Irwin, 1995) by the same authors.

4 SUMMARY

This reading completes our discussion of the basic framework for financial statement analysis. We have discussed financial statements that are the raw data of financial analysis and introduced users of financial statements to the interrelationship among them.

In the next reading, we examine financial statement ratios, which are used as shorthand indicators of firm performance. Although some ratios use data from only one financial statement (debt/equity ratio), others use data from several statements (return on equity). Sound investment decisions, based on the comparative assessment of alternative investments, require the use and analysis of all three financial statements as well as footnote and supplementary disclosures.

In the following reading, we review trends in empirical research to gain insight into the information content of financial data. Starting in Reading 39, we examine areas of financial reporting more specifically, seeking to apply the general principles articulated in these first three readings.

PROBLEMS

1. [Cash flows; CFA © adapted] Cash flow data of Palomba Pizza Stores for the year ended December 31, 2000 follow:

Cash payment of dividends	$(35,000)
Acquisition of Naples' Pizza	(14,000)
Cash payments for interest	(10,000)
Cash payments for salaries	(45,000)
Sale of equipment	38,000
Retirement of common stock	(25,000)
Purchase of equipment	(30,000)
Cash payments to suppliers	(85,000)
Cash collections from customers	250,000
Cash at December 31, 1999	50,000

a. Prepare a statement of cash flows for Palomba for 2000. Classify cash flows as required by SFAS 95.

b. Discuss, from an analyst's viewpoint, the purpose of classifying cash flows into the three categories used in part a.

c. Discuss whether any of the cash flows should be classified differently.

d. Discuss the significance of the change in cash during 2000 as an indicator of Palomba's performance.

e. Calculate Palomba's *free cash flow*.

f. In your calculation of free cash flow, justify your treatment of cash payments for interest and cash paid for acquisitions.

2. [Revenue and expense recognition: cash flow analysis] The Stengel Company showed the following pattern of sales, bad debt expense, and net receivables for 1997 through 2001 (in $ millions):

	1997	1998	1999	2000	2001
Sales	$140	$150	$165	$175	$195
Bad debt expense	7	7	8	10	10
Net receivables*	40	50	60	75	95
Net receivables* at 1996 = 30					

*At year-end.

a. Calculate the cash collected from customers each year from 1997 to 2001.

b. For each year presented, calculate the following ratios:

(i) Bad debt expense/sales

(ii) Net receivables/sales

(iii) Cash collections/sales

c. Based on the patterns of sales, net receivables, and cash collections in part A and ratios calculated in part B, discuss the adequacy of the provision for bad debts.

3. [Cash flow: transactional analysis; CFA© adapted] The following financial statements are from the *2001 Annual Report* of the Niagara Company:

Income Statement for Year Ended December 31, 2001

Sales	$1,000
Cost of goods sold	(650)
Depreciation expense	(100)
Sales and general expense	(100)
Interest expense	(50)
Income tax expense	(40)
Net income	$ 60

Balance Sheets at December 31, 2000 and 2001

	2000	2001
Assets		
Cash	$ 50	$ 60
Accounts receivable	500	520
Inventory	750	770
Current assets	$1,300	$1,350
Fixed assets (net)	500	550
Total assets	$1,800	$1,900
Liabilities and Equity		
Notes payable to banks	$ 100	$ 75
Accounts payable	590	615
Interest payable	10	20
Current liabilities	$ 700	$ 710
Long-term debt	300	350
Deferred income tax	300	310
Capital stock	400	400
Retained earnings	100	130
Total liabilities and equity	$1,800	$1,900

Use the direct method to prepare a statement of cash flows for the year ended December 31, 2001.

4. [Preparation of cash flow statement—direct and indirect methods; CFA © adapted] The balance sheet and income statement for the Green Company are presented in Exhibit 33P-1.

a. Based on the financial statements provided, prepare a statement of cash flows for 2001 using the

(i) Indirect method

(ii) Direct method

b. Calculate the company's free cash flow.

EXHIBIT 33P-1 The Green Company
Balance Sheet and Income Statement

Balance Sheet As of December 31	2000	2001
Assets		
Cash	$ 1,000	$ 1,100
Accounts receivable	1,500	1,650
Inventory	2,000	2,200
Total current assets	$ 4,500	$ 4,950
Fixed assets—at cost*	11,000	12,150
Accumulated depreciation	4,500	5,100
Net fixed assets	6,500	7,050
Total assets	$11,000	$12,000
Liabilities and Equity		
Accrued liabilities	$ 800	$ 880
Accounts payable	1,200	1,320
Notes payable	5,500	6,050
Total current liabilities	7,500	8,250
Long-term debt	2,000	1,602
Common stock	1,000	1,000
Retained earnings	500	1,148
Total liabilities and equity	$11,000	$12,000

Income Statement for the Year Ending December 31, 2001	
Sales	$10,000
Cost of goods sold	6,000
Depreciation	600
Selling, general, and administrative expenses	1,000
Interest expense	600
Taxable income	$ 1,800
Taxes	720
Net income	$ 1,080

*No fixed assets were sold during 1996.

FUTURE FASB CHANGES AND THE ANALYTICAL CHALLENGES OF GAAP

READING 34

Patricia A. McConnell
Senior Managing Director
Bear, Stearns & Co., Inc.
New York City

LEARNING OUTCOMES

The candidate should be able to:

a. identify the projects on the FASB agenda that were/are related to international convergence;

b. describe the two different guidance rules for revenue recognition discussed by FASB and IASB.

INTRODUCTION 1

The Financial Accounting Standards Board (FASB) is trying to bring U.S. GAAP in harmony with International Accounting Standards. Toward that end, the FASB has several projects that it is tackling, notably accounting for stock compensation, business combinations, and revenue recognition. The resulting new rules will clearly affect not only how companies report their financial conditions but also how analysts value companies.

The agenda of the Financial Accounting Standards Board (FASB) in the United States is being driven by the convergence to International Accounting Standards (IAS) globally, which is being driven by events that are taking place in Europe. The European Commission has issued a regulation that will require publicly traded European companies to adopt the IAS as set by the International Accounting Standards Board (IASB) by 2005. Although companies that reconcile their statements to U.S. GAAP for American Depositary Receipts will need to adopt the new standards soon, an exception exists for European public companies that currently apply U.S. GAAP in their primary financial statements. These companies will have until 2007 to adopt the IAS.

Consequently, in an effort to facilitate the listing of European companies in the United States, the IASB and the FASB are working furiously on a program to eliminate as many differences as possible between IAS and U.S. GAAP. Because U.S. SEC regulation requires non-U.S. issuers to reconcile to U.S. GAAP, the critical issue that the IASB and the FASB are working to address is the minimization of reconciliation adjustment that European companies will need to make.

The minimization of reconciliation adjustment is just one example of the FASB's increasingly globalized agenda. Once the European Commission adopted IAS, numerous countries around the world jumped on the bandwagon. By 2005, more than 90 countries will require or permit their publicly traded companies to use IAS. In short, the world is moving rapidly toward a set of high-quality global standards. This trend has had an influence on the FASB's agenda and the U.S. accounting changes on the horizon.

The projects currently on the FASB agenda are all related to international convergence:

- accounting for stock compensation,
- changes in the methodology used for purchase accounting,
- revenue recognition changes,
- accounting conventions for convertible debt and other exotic instruments with both equity and liability characteristics (under a project called "Instruments"),
- financial performance reporting in regards to revising the form and the content of the income statement,
- fair-value measurement, and
- elimination of many small differences between IAS GAAP and U.S. GAAP. (Many of these differences exist for no particular reason other than the preference of a board member when the standards were originally issued.)

This reading will concentrate on three of these projects: accounting for stock compensation, business combinations, and revenue recognition.

2 STOCK-BASED COMPENSATION

It is well known that the FASB has an active project on accounting for stock-based compensation, namely employee stock options. Less well known is that this project is being done in tandem with the IASB so that the two standards will ultimately be virtually identical. Note that they are working in *tandem*, not simultaneously, because the IASB started a little bit before the FASB. In the early 1990s, the FASB got burned when it tried to enforce expensing of employee stock options. Thus, the FASB was not willing to take on this project until the IASB was serious and committed to take action. So, the FASB is a little bit behind.

The IASB will issue its final standard in the first quarter of 2004. The FASB will issue its exposure draft in the first quarter of 2004 but expects to finalize the standard before the end of the year. Both organizations intend for the standards to take effect beginning 15 December 2004. This new accounting rule will require that employee stock options be valued using an option-pricing model. The value as calculated at the grant date of the options will be amortized to compensation expense in the income statement over the vesting period of the option, which will bring the accounting for employee stock options in line with all other forms of compensation, including other forms of stock compensation, such as restricted stock. As a result, all forms of compensation will be on a level playing field from an accounting standpoint.

Neither the IASB nor the FASB intends to mandate a particular option-pricing model, but they are leaning toward what is called a binomial option-pricing model. This type of model is based on a decision tree and is sometimes referred to as a lattice model.

The reason they favor the binomial model is because they believe that if it is applied honestly, it is a more rigorous model and produces a better valuation of the option than other alternatives. But in all likelihood, the binomial model will be eliminated by the time they issue the final standards. Some field testing of the model has highlighted a lack of transparency in the application of the model. The model can be applied in too many ways, which reduces the comparability from one company to the next.

With a Black–Scholes valuation model, if one knows the assumptions and is familiar with the model, one can get a pretty good feel for how the value would have been affected by changes in the assumptions. Conversely, because a binomial model is a decision-tree model, one cannot get a good sense for sensitivity to the various assumptions because the probabilities assigned to the outcomes will not be known. So, the boards' bias toward the binomial model will likely be removed from the final standards.

Regardless of the methodology ultimately used, the valuation at the grant date will be amortized to compensation expense over the vesting period. No subsequent adjustments are necessary for changes in the value of the option. Once the value of the option is calculated at the grant date, it will remain fixed in spite of what happens to the company's stock price after the grant date.

Finally, deferred-tax accounting will apply. This change means that the expense going into the income statement will be treated as if it were deducted on the company's tax return. In other words, an after-tax effect on net income will occur.

This change will result in lower reported GAAP earnings and EPS. Fortunately, companies have been required to disclose what their earnings and EPS would have been under an expensing methodology for employee stock options in the footnotes to their financial statements since 1995. Consequently, investors should be able to estimate the magnitude of the accounting change's impact on U.S. companies.

Investors should keep in mind, however, that the impact in 2005 will likely not be as great as indicated by these past disclosures. At Bear, Stearns & Co., we have been looking at the footnotes for all the companies in the S&P 500 Index since 1995 and have found that the estimated aggregate operating income of the S&P 500 would have been 12 percent lower in 2001, 8 percent lower in 2002, and 5 percent lower in 1999 if it had been adjusted for employee stock option compensation. We do not believe that impact is representative of what will happen in 2005.

In 2002, the number of options (not the dollar amount) granted to employees declined by a third for the companies in the S&P 500. We believe a couple of conclusions can be drawn from this fact. First, employee stock options really are a form of compensation. Earnings were down in 2002, and accordingly, compensation was down in 2002, including the part of compensation paid in the form of stock options. Second, companies in the aggregate believed the FASB was serious about expensing options this time. They realized that it was necessary to start cutting back on the number of options granted beginning in 2002 to avoid having a big expense in the future when the FASB mandates the accounting change.

The analytic impact on the balance sheet is interesting. If not for tax effects, the balance sheet would see no effect. The charge to the income statement for the stock option compensation expense would be offset by an increase in equity, which would show up as an increase to additional paid-in capital for the value of the options. Because the charge on the income statement has an impact on taxes, a deferred-tax asset shows up on the balance sheet. Assets will increase and equity will increase by the amount of the employee stock option compensation expense.

My view is that this transaction should be treated as having a cash flow impact. Analytically, I view this transaction as an operating cash outflow. That is, the payment of compensation to the employees is offset by a financing cash inflow, a sale of options in exchange for services. So, it should have an analytical impact on operating cash flow. But reported operating cash flow will not change because, from a GAAP accounting standpoint, it is a noncash transaction and nothing happens to the company's bank account.

3 BUSINESS COMBINATIONS: PURCHASE METHOD PROCEDURES

OPTIONAL SEGMENT

The next project on the FASB's agenda involves proposed changes to business combination accounting and how purchase accounting is actually applied. A couple of years ago, the FASB issued two new standards: Statement of Financial Accounting Standards (SFAS) No. 141, *Business Combinations*,[1] and No. 142, *Goodwill and Other Intangible Assets*.[2] SFAS No. 141 eliminated the pooling-of-interest method for business combinations, which left purchase accounting as the sole method of accounting for business combinations. SFAS No. 142 addresses how a company accounts for the goodwill created in a purchased business combination.

When the FASB was developing SFAS No. 141, it realized the purchase accounting methodology had a lot of flaws. Accordingly, the FASB and the IASB initiated a joint project to adjust some of the perceived flaws. Both boards will issue their exposure drafts in the first quarter of 2004 to become effective for business combinations entered into after 15 December 2004. In my view, the nature of some of these proposed changes may accelerate some business combinations in 2004. Just as occurred before SFAS No. 141 went into effect, a flurry of business combinations may precede the new standard.

The project covers a multitude of flaws in purchase accounting, such as the accounting for in-process R&D, the costs of restructuring the acquired company, the treatment of merger and acquisition costs at the date of the acquisition, how the purchase price is measured when the consideration paid is the company's own common stock, and the treatment of contingent purchase price (i.e., "earn-out agreements"). In addition, it is expected to change the way step acquisitions

---

[1] See www.fasb.org/st/summary/stsum141.shtml.

[2] See www.fasb.org/st/summary/stsum142.shtml.

are recorded—that is, acquisitions in which control is obtained in a series of transactions rather than in one transaction. Also expected to change is the accounting for the sale of a minority interest in a company that is already controlled. Finally, it is expected to change the way minority interest is displayed in the balance sheet and income statement.

In the interest of time, I will discuss only in-process R&D, the cost of restructuring an acquired company, and the measurement date of the purchase price when payment is made with stock.

In-Process R&D

Probably the most significant of the proposed FASB changes is the change in accounting for in-process R&D. Currently, when a company acquires another company, the acquirer is required to allocate the fair value of the consideration. That is, the purchase price must be allocated to the fair value of both the tangible and the identifiable intangible assets acquired. Goodwill is the difference between the fair value of the purchase price and the fair value of the acquired assets.

One of the identifiable intangible assets acquired is in-process R&D. Companies are required to value this identifiable intangible in-process R&D and allocate part of the purchase price to that fair value. But unlike all the other identifiable intangible assets acquired, in-process R&D is expensed at the date of acquisition, which results in a large one-time charge. Historically, the financial markets have tended to ignore this charge for in-process R&D. Under the new rule, the value assigned to the in-process R&D will no longer be expensed. It will be capitalized and recorded as an intangible asset in the consolidated financial statements from the date of acquisition. After the date of acquisition, no additional research expenditures to develop the research will be capitalized. Rather, post-acquisition research will continue to be expensed.

When the product or process that results from the R&D is launched, the amortization of acquired in-process R&D would generally begin. Presumably, the amortization period would match the expected life of the product. If, subsequent to the business combination, it becomes apparent that the acquired in-process R&D is not going to result in a marketable product or process, the in-process R&D intangible asset would be deemed impaired and would be written off and expensed.

The implications for financial analysis will be fairly significant because the change will affect the income statement, the balance sheet, and thus the ratios used for financial analysis. We expect the amortization will be treated as a production cost. In the future, with in-process R&D being capitalized, the amortization will be embedded as a cost in the income statement. Thus, analysts will likely pay more attention to the figure than they do now. It will be factored into the ongoing earnings of the company.

This difference is one of the reasons why I think companies will accelerate their transactions before the rule goes into effect. Company managers are presently fairly certain about how the financial markets will regard one-time charges for in-process R&D at the date of acquisition. They are less certain, and perhaps less comfortable, with how the financial markets will likely view the amortization of in-process R&D when products are launched.

To illustrate the significance of this change, Table 34-1 shows four recent business combinations involving Medimmune, Amgen, Pfizer, and Johnson & Johnson. For example, 72 percent of what Medimmune paid for Aviron was considered in-process R&D. With Amgen, only 17 percent of the purchase price was assigned to in-process R&D. In the Pfizer–Pharmacia acquisition, only 9 percent was allocated to in-process R&D, and in the case of Johnson & Johnson, only 32 percent was allocated to in-process R&D. To estimate what the impact would have been had the new rule been in effect, we asked our pharmaceutical analysts

Table 34-1 Example Potential Income Statement Effects on Amortization of In-Process R&D

($ millions, except per share)

Item	Medimmune–Aviron	Amgen–Immunex	Pfizer–Pharmacia	Johnson & Johnson–Scios
Acquisition closing date	10/Jan/02	15/Jul/02	16/Apr/03	29/Apr/03
Total acquisition price	$1,635	$17,772	$55,962	$2,300
Amount recorded as in-process R&D	$1,179	$ 2,992	$ 5,130	$ 730
In-process R&D as a percentage of acquisition price	72%	17%	9%	32%
Percentage of in-process R&D costs with future benefits[a]	75%	50%	50%	50%
Amortizable in-process R&D	$ 884	$ 1,496	$ 2,565	$ 365
Amortizable life (years)[a]	7	7	7	7
Annual amortization expense	$ 126	$ 214	$ 366	$ 52
After-tax amortization expense[b]	$ 82	$ 139	$ 238	$ 34
Diluted shares outstanding[c]	258	1,347	7,453	3,016
Potential annual impact of in-process R&D amortization on diluted EPS	$ 0.32	$ 0.10	$ 0.03	$ 0.01

Notes: This table constitutes Bear, Stearns & Co. estimates for illustration purposes only. The FASB's proposed standard would not apply retroactively.

[a] Estimated average remaining patent/product life after drugs are launched based on BSC Pharmaceutical Equity Research.

[b] Assumes marginal tax rate of 35 percent.

[c] Based on company filings.

Sources: Data based on company reports and Bear, Stearns & Co. estimates.

how much of the acquired research would likely find its way into successful products or processes. They estimate that only about 50 percent of research generally leads to successful products. In the case of Medimmune, they assigned a higher rate, 75 percent, because the product actually passed the appropriate U.S. Food and Drug Administration requirements one quarter after the acquisition. Our estimate of the amount of R&D that would end up being amortizable in the future for Medimmune is $884 million, and the expected life of the product generated by the research is approximately seven years. Thus, the annual amortization expense would be $126 million. When this number is adjusted for taxes and divided by the diluted shares outstanding, the result is that Medimmune would have had an additional charge to earnings of about 32 cents per share if the new rule had been in effect. For Johnson & Johnson, the charge would have been only about 1 cent. Obviously, companies have an incentive to complete acquisitions before the new accounting rule takes effect.

Costs of Restructuring an Acquired Company

The costs of restructuring an acquired company have been an especially challenging issue in recent years, particularly because of the perception that restructuring reserves are used to manage future earnings. Currently, the accounting for the restructuring reserves of a target company is different from the accounting treatment for the restructuring reserves of the acquiring company. Generally, when a company does a restructuring, it takes a charge to earnings and records a liability for the estimated costs of restructuring. These costs include such items as severance, lease termination, and facility shutdowns. For a target company, the same costs are treated as liabilities recorded as part of the purchase accounting adjustments. So, there is no charge to earnings, and this treatment generally increases the amount of goodwill recorded in the acquisition. Currently, the costs of restructuring the target do not flow through the combined company's income statement under GAAP. In this project, the FASB is proposing that the costs of restructuring the target be treated the same way as the costs of restructuring the acquiring company. That is, the costs would be charged to earnings when the liabilities are recorded. The new standard will bring the treatment of the two into line.

This change will obviously affect income statements, balance sheets, and financial ratios. Because the restructuring reserves will be expensed, goodwill recorded in the acquisition will be lower by that amount. Net income will be reduced in the period of acquisition by the amount of the restructuring costs for the target. Ultimately, equity of the combined company will be reduced as a result of the expensing.

Measurement Date

The measurement date of the purchase price of a company is generally not a problem when the purchase price is paid in cash. But given the elimination of pooling-of-interest transactions, valuating purchase prices for stock transactions has become more of a problem. Under current GAAP, when the consideration paid is the stock of the acquiring corporation, the value is determined on the announcement date of the transaction.

The FASB is proposing in this new project that the stock be valued instead at the closing date of the transaction. The rationale behind this change is that if the market has changed the value of the consideration paid, the new value is a better indication of the value of the entity being acquired than the value on the announcement date.

For accounting, this change means that the amount of goodwill recorded will be either higher or lower than it would have been under the old rule, depending on whether the acquiring company's stock price increased or decreased after the announcement of the transaction. The change in the amount of goodwill recorded is likely to affect any future goodwill impairment charges.

To illustrate this impact, consider the example of AOL Time Warner, as shown in Table 34-2. This deal was a stock-for-stock transaction. At the date the transaction was announced, AOL's share price was $67.75. At the closing date of the transaction, it was only $47.23. The resulting difference in the transaction value was $44.7 billion. In other words, if the new rule had been in effect at the

Table 34-2 AOL Acquisition of Time Warner

Item	Current GAAP (announcement date)	Proposed GAAP (closing date)
AOL's share price	\$ 67.75[a]	\$ 47.23[b]
Shares issued to Time Warner's shareholders	1,973	1,973
Acquisition price of common stock acquired	\$133,671	\$ 93,185
Preferred stock	2,270	2,270
Stock options	10,409	6,547[c]
Transaction costs	300	0
Total accounting transaction value	\$146,650	\$102,001
Difference in recorded acquisition values	**\$44.7 billion**	
Estimated goodwill recorded	\$ 94,705	\$ 50,057

[a] Based on AOL's average market price a few days before and after the announcement of the merger.

[b] AOL's closing date share price on 11 January 2001.

[c] Reflects fair market value of \$33.37 per share for options assumed to purchase 196.182 million shares of AOL common stock. Adjusted based on the following assumptions—expected volatility, 46.3 percent; expected lives, five years; risk-free interest rate, 6.37 percent; expected dividend yield, zero; and share price, \$47.23.

Sources: Based on data from company reports and Bear, Stearns & Co. estimates.

date of the transaction, AOL Time Warner would have recorded \$44.7 billion less goodwill. The difference is significant. When SFAS No. 142 came in effect, AOL Time Warner had to test its goodwill for impairment. If AOL had been operating under the new standard, its goodwill impairment charge would have been significantly less. It wrote off goodwill in excess of \$50 billion, and a good chunk of that write-off was needed because of the measurement date of the stock price. If the new rule had been in effect and AOL Time Warner had been able to reflect the market's assessment of the value of the transaction, the impact of a goodwill impairment charge would have been much lower.

OPTIONAL SEGMENT ENDS

4 REVENUE RECOGNITION

Revenue recognition is a forward-looking project, and the FASB will not be able to issue a document on it in the immediate future. Nevertheless, a change is coming, and analysts should be aware of it because it may produce monumental changes in the reporting of revenue and cost of sales. The project is a joint effort between the FASB and the IASB. That these two standard setters have the same standard on revenue recognition is critically important because revenue is the largest number on a company's income statement and is a crucial valuation metric. Ideally, public companies around the world should recognize and measure revenue according to the same principles.

The objectives of the project are to eliminate inconsistencies between authoritative literature and practice. Eliminating inconsistencies not only means inconsistencies between the FASB standards and the IASB standards or GAAP in other jurisdictions but it also means inconsistencies within U.S. GAAP with regard to revenue recognition.

The inconsistencies in U.S. GAAP result from a number of factors. First, the GAAP guidance for revenue recognition in most cases developed long before the FASB was formed in 1972 and long before a conceptual framework of accounting even existed. In many cases, the policies for revenue recognition really are generally accepted accounting principles in the sense that they were what most people were following; thus, they were presumed to be generally acceptable. Compounding the problem of revenue recognition is that the FASB's conceptual framework includes two different guidance rules for revenue recognition. Concept Statement 6 defines revenue in terms of changes in the company's assets and liabilities. Essentially, Concept Statement 6 says that income is the increase in the company's net assets (assets − liabilities) and income. In other words, income is any increase in the net assets that results from transactions other than with shareholders. Any transaction, other than selling stock, that increases the net assets would result in a revenue gain. Any transaction that decreases net assets, other than buying back stock or paying dividends, is an expense or a loss. This simple concept is tied to the fundamental accounting equation:

Assets − Liabilities = Equity

Concept Statement 5, however, includes revenue recognition criteria that have nothing to do with changes in assets and liabilities. Concept Statement 5 includes the more familiar revenue recognition criteria that the earnings process must be complete and collectibility of the revenue must be reasonably assured. Most people probably remember this standard about when revenue should be recognized from their accounting courses.

These two concepts are in conflict. Consider the example of a health club that sells three-year memberships. After 60 days, the membership fee is not refundable to the client. So, the health club gets the cash and has no responsibility to return that cash once the 60-day period elapses. The company built the health club, purchased equipment, and hired trainers. The question is: When does it recognize revenue? Under the more familiar guidance, which says revenue recognition is complete when the earnings process is complete, the company would have to amortize that revenue over the membership period. But under the Concept Statement 5 definition, the company has an increase in the net assets by the amount of cash that it does not have to give back. Should it recognize revenue once the right to refund goes away? These two concepts conflict. Accounting standards have been derived from both of them, and few standards can satisfy both concepts simultaneously.

The FASB and the IASB have tentatively decided that the approach they take should be consistent with the asset − liability approach. That is, if there is an increase in the net assets from a transaction with customers, the company has revenue. This criterion will not be overridden by any test based on realization or completion of an earnings process. But it may result in the need to record some sort of performance liability at the date of the transaction. So, revenues will arise from changes in assets and liabilities that result from some combination of performance and liability extinguishment.

If the standard setters continue in this direction, one implication of the new approach is that new assets and liabilities will appear on the balance sheet. The situation is similar to accounting for a lease that is capitalized under SFAS No. 13, *Accounting for Leases.*[3] The company acquires an asset and records a lease obligation—no change in the net assets and no revenue or expense. If the

---

[3] See www.fasb.org/st/summary/stsum13.shtml.

recorded assets were greater than the recorded liability, there would be revenue at the date the executory contract was signed.

This change is likely to have a significant impact on the world of accounting. It could potentially result in revenue recognition earlier than has been customary. Correspondingly, it would result in cost of goods sold or expenses being recorded earlier. If the assets are a performance liability, the offsetting entry for that performance liability would be an expense affecting cost of goods sold.

How will the performance liability be measured? Standard setters generally agree that the best way to measure the performance liability at the initiation of the executory contract is fair value (i.e., what it would cost the company to engage someone else to perform that obligation for them). This number would be recorded as the performance liability.

5 CONCLUSION

This revenue recognition project is in its early stages, but the investment community needs to keep an eye on it. The investment community should get involved in helping the two boards formulate the outcome of the project. Once the standard setters get their minds set too firmly, dissuading them will be difficult. At this early stage, the likely problems with this new mechanism cannot be specified, but I know from long experience that every accounting rule change has both a bright side and a dark side. Investors need to make sure that the dark side of this accounting rule change is not darker than the bright side is bright.

The near future holds a great many changes. Remember, the goal is to harmonize U.S. GAAP and IAS by 2007. This goal will not be achieved completely, but the standard setters will do their best to reconcile as many of the differences as possible by that time. Many of the necessary changes could radically alter financial reporting.

QUESTION AND ANSWER SESSION 6

Patricia A. McConnell

Question: What will happen with the stock options issued between 2003 and 2005?

McConnell: The FASB recently did a bait and switch on corporate America. The FASB decided in its exposure draft that it will require this new methodology to be applied using what it refers to as the "modified prospective method." Under the modified prospective method, companies will expense in 2005 the amortized value of all options granted since 1995. This change means that their 2005 income statements will report the exact same number that would have been disclosed in their stock option footnote.

As an example, assume that a company had a policy of always granting options with a fair value of $300 million every year and has had this policy since 1995. Its options vest over three years. So, in 1995, the expense pretax that it takes to its income will be $300 million, but that is not fully from the value of the grant in 2005. What that $300 million would actually represent is one-third of the 2005 grant, one-third of the 2004 grant, and one-third of the 2003 grant. In other words, it would have been the same number as in the company's footnote.

The bait and switch is as follows: Currently, more than 350 companies have voluntarily adopted the fair-value method of accounting for employee stock options. Those companies can apply what is called the prospective method. In fact, nearly all of those 350 companies use the prospective method. Under the prospective method, companies can only expense the value of options granted in the year of adoption and thereafter. If the same company from my example had voluntarily adopted to expense the stock options beginning in 2003, its stock option expense in 2003 would have been $100 million, which is one-third of the value of the options granted in 2003. In 2004, its expense would have been $200 million—one-third of 2003 and one-third of 2004. When it got to 2005, it would expense $300 million.

The FASB has said that when 2005 comes along, even if you're already on the fair-value method, you have to go to the modified prospective method. So, if the company in my example had an amortization or vesting period longer than three years, it would have had a sudden jump in its expense in 2005. For that reason, there will be a slowdown in the number of companies voluntarily adopting the fair-value method.

Question: Given that some companies do not announce the date of options granted until year-end, will they be required to make announcements throughout the year as options are granted?

McConnell: The expense will be adjusted every time a company makes a grant.

My research has indicated that companies tend to issue options in the first quarter of the year because they tend to be used as a portion of bonuses.

Question: Do you believe companies may try to time options with a lull in the market?

McConnell: Companies really don't try to find a lull. But companies have not had to account for options, so the practice may change. A lot of managerial behavior may change once managers have to account for employee stock options. My experience tells me that if a company does not have to account for a cost, it does not typically manage that cost. Once it has to account for that cost, it manages the cost carefully. I expect a lot of behavioral changes as the standards change.

Question: When is the taxable event for the recipient of stock options?

McConnell: Generally speaking, the taxable event for the recipient is when the option is exercised because that creates taxable ordinary income from the difference between the market price of the stock and option's exercise price. Currently, the company has a tax deduction for an equal amount at the date of exercise. This is why companies will be doing deferred-tax accounting on the fair-value expense—there will be a timing difference between when they take the charge to the income statement and when they take the deduction on the tax return.

Question: With regard to options accounting, aren't we double counting when options are expensed against diluted net earnings?

McConnell: There is a lot of disagreement on that point. My personal opinion is that we are not double counting. There are really two different transactions that are being measured. The first transaction involves the company's decision on how much it will pay its employees. That is compensation expense, which is deducted in arriving at net income.

The second decision relates to how the company will finance the payment of that compensation to its employees. It could be paid from operating cash flows or through borrowings. If the money is to be borrowed, the company has many alternatives, including issuing debentures, selling stock, selling options to a firm like Bear Stearns, or selling options to its employees. Companies often choose to sell options to the employees because of the significant tax benefits for both the employee and the corporation.

It is that second decision, the financing decision, that is being measured in the denominator of the EPS calculation. The dilution does not occur because employees have been paid in options or because employees have been compensated. Rather, the dilution stems from management's decision to finance the payment of the compensation by issuing options. Under our current accounting model, the only way to measure that financing cost is by including the options in the denominator of the fully diluted EPS calculation using the Treasury stock method.

This discussion further illustrates my point about how the investment community really needs to be aware of forthcoming changes. Remember the FASB agenda item I mentioned earlier that pertains to liabilities and equity? One of the potential implications of that project is that the FASB will change the current definition of a liability. Presently, a liability is a current obligation that will be settled in the future by the transfer of cash or other assets. So, an employee stock option does not meet the definition of a liability because it is satisfied not by the transfer of cash or other assets but by the transfer of equity instruments—shares of stock. They are recorded in equity, and GAAP says companies do not recognize gains or losses in their own equity securities.

The FASB is thinking of changing the definition of a liability so that an option on a company's stock would be a liability. In this case, options would fall under SFAS No. 133, *Accounting for Derivative Instruments and Hedging Activities*, as derivative securities.[4] That standard will require companies to mark to market the change in value of the option going to earnings each period. If that

---

[4] See www.fasb.org/st/summary/stsum133.shtml.

were to happen, then I would agree that including options in the denominator of the EPS calculation would be double counting.

Fortunately, this change is still a way down the road, and there is still a significant chance that the change ultimately will not be adopted.

Question: With the new rules, will companies grant fewer or more options?

McConnell: As I said earlier, I think management behavior is going to change. Additionally, I mentioned that when companies do not have to account for an expense, they often do not manage the expense. I think that is what was going on with options. Perhaps this isn't a problem in every company, but I think it happens with many companies.

I think the first thing they will do is look more closely at their compensation policies. There is a good chance they will pull back on the number of options that they grant. In fact, we have already seen some of that. Last year, one-third less options were granted than in previous years. I also think they will begin to substitute other kinds of compensation, such as restricted stock.

Restricted stock has some advantages from the employee standpoint. On the one hand, as long as the company's stock does not decline all the way to zero, employees will at least have something. On the other hand, option-holding employees may have nothing after a stock price decline.

There are some advantages to the company as well, particularly if it expects its stock price to rise significantly. It can give the same amount of compensation with restricted stock as with options but see less dilution in EPS. For example, assume that a company's stock price is $100 and the fair value of an option with a strike price of $100 is $40. If company management wanted to pay the employee $200, it could give the employee two shares of stock or five options to get to the $200. If the stock price went up significantly, then the company would see EPS diluted by five shares for options, but the dilution from restricted stock would remain two shares. So, there would be less dilution with restricted shares. Of course, the trade-off is that the dilution with restricted stock would be immediate rather than delayed as it would be with options.

Question: Who decides how much and where is the gaming room of capitalizing R&D?

McConnell: The financial statements are the primary responsibility of management. Management decides how much. The auditors are then supposed to assess whether that value is reasonable. In the past, it has been a real problem that many auditors have not taken finance courses, much less courses in valuation. That is changing, but auditors are unfortunately still not very good at valuation. After the auditors, the third backstop is the SEC. Of course, the SEC comes into play after the fact and determines with hindsight that research was not properly reported.

Before SFAS No. 142 and No. 141, when goodwill had to be amortized, companies appeared to be stuffing as much value as they could into this in-process R&D. Companies would then write this intangible off at the date of acquisition. In doing so, companies could reduce the amount of goodwill recorded and, by extension, the goodwill amortization charge. So, there was a bias toward overvaluing in-process R&D.

Now, we are in a situation where goodwill is not being amortized, which has certainly reduced the overvaluation bias. Who cares whether it gets written off immediately as in-process R&D or whether it ends up being goodwill? So, I think we now have a balance where there really isn't any incentive or disincentive for management to overvalue or undervalue in-process R&D, except to justify to the marketplace why management is doing the acquisition in the first place.

When we go to a situation where a company has to capitalize in-process R&D, then I think we will see a bias to undervaluing R&D acquired in an acquisition. Rather than having to amortize it, companies will then be able to let it simply fall down into goodwill. Ultimately, these are all very soft numbers and there is obviously room for management to maneuver. Part of the problem with setting an accounting standard is that there is always a relevant-versus-reliability trade-off. Is it more relevant to see the value that a company paid for the asset and all the other assets it acquired on the balance sheet? Or, do you want to err toward reliability and just let all the value go to goodwill?

Question: When companies do the annual 142 impairment (i.e., when they go back in and write down the purchased R&D), do you think investors will overlook those write-downs?

McConnell: In-process R&D will be an intangible asset on the balance sheet and subject to an annual impairment test under SFAS No. 142 just like goodwill and all the other identifiable intangible assets. From time to time, it will get written off if it isn't going to produce anything of value. I guess whether the market decides to ignore those charges or whether it factors them in will depend on the sign and the persistency of those charges. If a company is consistently acquiring its R&D rather than doing R&D in-house, then those charges, in a sense, become a replacement for the company's annual R&D cost.

OPTIONAL SEGMENT ENDS

STUDY SESSION 8
FINANCIAL STATEMENT ANALYSIS: FINANCIAL RATIOS AND EARNINGS PER SHARE

READING ASSIGNMENTS

Reading 35 Analysis of Financial Statements
Reading 36 Dilutive Securities and Earnings per Share
Reading 37 Seek and Ye Shall Find
Reading 38 Searching for Shenanigans

LEARNING OUTCOMES

Reading 35: Analysis of Financial Statements

The candidate should be able to:

a. interpret common-size balance sheets and common-size income statements, and discuss the circumstances under which the use of common-size financial statements is appropriate;

b. calculate, interpret, and discuss the uses of measures of a company's internal liquidity, operating performance (i.e., operating efficiency (activity) and operating profitability), risk profile, and growth potential;

c. calculate and interpret the various components of the company's return on equity using the original and extended DuPont systems and calculate and interpret a company's financial ratios relative to its industry, to the aggregate economy, and to the company's own performance over time;

Reading 36: Dilutive Securities and Earnings per Share

The candidate should be able to:

a. differentiate between simple and complex capital structures for purposes of calculating earnings per share (EPS), describe the components of EPS, and calculate a company's EPS in a simple capital structure;

Note:
Candidates should be aware that certain ratios may be defined slightly differently in the readings assigned in the Financial Statement Analysis (FSA) study sessions. Authors may also use different names for the same ratio or category of ratios. Such differences are part of the nature of financial analysis. **For Level I examination purposes, when a ratio is defined and calculated differently, candidates should use the definition given in Reading 35, Analysis of Financial Statements**

Candidates should also note in Reading 35 that the operating performance ratios are divided into two categories: operating efficiency and operating profitability. In other FSA readings, operating efficiency ratios are called "activity ratios." Efficiency (activity) ratios typically include those ratios identified as "turnover" ratios.

Note:
Candidates are responsible for the questions, exercises, and problems listed following the readings. Solutions to the questions, exercises and problems appear in Appendix A.

b. calculate a company's weighted average number of shares outstanding;

c. describe stock dividends and stock splits, and determine the effect of each on a company's weighted average number of shares outstanding;

d. distinguish between dilutive and antidilutive securities and calculate a company's basic and diluted EPS in a complex capital structure, and describe and determine the effects of convertible securities, options, and warrants on a company's EPS;

e. compare and contrast the requirements for EPS reporting in simple versus complex capital structures.

Reading 37: Seek and Ye Shall Find

The candidate should be able to:

a. explain the two basic strategies underlying all accounting "shenanigans," and describe seven categories of techniques that may be used by management to distort a company's reported financial performance and financial condition;

b. identify conservative and aggressive accounting policies;

c. describe why "shenanigans" exist, and explain where they are most likely to occur;

d. list the documents that an analyst should use to identify "shenanigans," and explain what information to look for in such documents.

Reading 38: Searching for Shenanigans

The candidate should be able to:

a. explain the two basic strategies underlying all accounting "shenanigans," and describe seven categories of techniques that may be used by management to distort a company's reported financial performance and financial condition;

b. identify conservative and aggressive accounting policies;

c. describe why "shenanigans" exist, and explain where they are most likely to occur;

d. list the documents that an analyst should use to identify "shenanigans," and explain what information to look for in such documents.

ANALYSIS OF FINANCIAL STATEMENTS

READING 35

LEARNING OUTCOMES

The candidate should be able to:

a. interpret common-size balance sheets and common-size income statements, and discuss the circumstances under which the use of common-size financial statements is appropriate;

b. calculate, interpret, and discuss the uses of measures of a company's internal liquidity, operating performance (i.e., operating efficiency (activity) and operating profitability), risk profile, and growth potential;

c. calculate and interpret the various components of the company's return on equity using the original and extended DuPont systems and calculate and interpret a company's financial ratios relative to its industry, to the aggregate economy, and to the company's own performance over time;

INTRODUCTION 1

You have probably already flipped through the pages of this reading and recognized that it is a fairly long reading with several financial statements and numerous financial ratios. A logical question is, What is the purpose of this extensive discussion of how to analyze financial statements? To answer this very reasonable question, we need to recall the process of investing. Early on, the point was made that our ultimate goal is to construct a portfolio of investments that will provide rates of return that are consistent with the risk involved with the portfolio. In turn, to determine the expected rates of return on alternative assets, it is necessary to *estimate the future value* of the asset since a major component of the rate of return is the change in value for the asset over time. Therefore, the crux of investments is valuation! While we will consider alternative valuation models in the next reading, you are already aware from prior coursework that the value of any earning asset is the present value of the expected cash flows generated by the asset. Therefore, to estimate the value of an asset, you must derive an estimate of (1) the discount rate for the asset (your required rate of return) and (2) its expected cash flows. The point is, the main source of information that will help you make these two estimates is the financial statements. To derive an estimate of your required rate of return, you need to understand the business and financial risk of the firm, which is specifically considered in this reading. To estimate future cash flows, you must understand the composition of cash flows and what will contribute to the shortrun and long-run growth of this series. An analysis of the composition and growth of cash flow is a topic of this reading. Put another way, a primary purpose of this reading is to help you understand how to estimate the variables in alternative valuation models.

Financial statements are also the main source of information when deciding whether to lend money to a firm (invest in its bonds) or to buy warrants or options on a firm's stock. In this reading, we first introduce a corporation's major financial statements and discuss why and how financial ratios are useful. In subsequent sections, we provide example computations of ratios that reflect internal liquidity, operating performance, risk analysis, and growth analysis. In the final section, we address four major areas in investments where financial ratios have been effectively employed.

Our example company in this reading is Walgreen Co., the largest retail drugstore chain in the United States. It operates 3,165 drugstores in 43 states and Puerto Rico. General merchandise accounts for 26 percent and pharmacy generates over 55 percent of total sales. The firm leads its industry (retail drugstores) in sales, profit, and store growth. The firm's goal is to be America's most convenient and technologically advanced health care retailer. It takes great pride in its steady sales and earnings growth that has been reflected in outstanding stock performance—for example, dividends have been increased in each of the past 25 years and, since 1980, the stock has been split two-for-one seven times.

2 MAJOR FINANCIAL STATEMENTS

OPTIONAL SEGMENT

Financial statements are intended to provide information on the resources available to management, how these resources were financed, and what the firm accomplished with them. Corporate shareholder annual and quarterly reports include three required financial statements: the balance sheet, the income statement, and the statement of cash flows. In addition, reports that must be filed with the Securities and Exchange Commission (SEC) (for example, the 10-K and 10-Q reports) carry detailed information about the firm, such as information on loan agreements and data on product line and subsidiary performance. Information from the basic financial statements can be used to calculate financial ratios and to analyze the operations of the firm to determine what factors influence a firm's earnings, cash flows, and risk characteristics.

Generally Accepted Accounting Principles

Among the input used to construct the financial statements are **generally accepted accounting principles** (**GAAP**), which are formulated by the Financial Accounting Standards Board (FASB). The FASB recognizes that it would be improper for all companies to use identical and restrictive accounting principles. Some flexibility and choice are needed because industries and firms within industries differ in their operating environments. Therefore, the FASB allows companies some flexibility to choose among appropriate GAAP. This flexibility allows the firm's managers to choose accounting standards that best reflect company practice. On the negative side, this flexibility can allow firms to appear healthier than they really are.[1] Given this possibility, the financial analyst must rigorously analyze the available financial information to separate those firms that *appear* attractive from those that actually are in good financial shape.

Fortunately, the FASB requires that financial statements include footnotes that inform analysts regarding which accounting principles were used by the firm. Because accounting principles frequently differ among firms, the footnote information assists the financial analyst in adjusting the financial statements of companies so the analyst can better compare "apples with apples."

Balance Sheet

The **balance sheet** shows what resources (assets) the firm controls and how it has financed these assets. Specifically, it indicates the current and fixed assets available to the firm *at a point in time* (the end of the fiscal year or the end of a quarter). In most cases, the firm owns these assets, but some firms lease assets on long-term bases. How the firm has financed the acquisition of these assets is indicated by its mixture of current liabilities (accounts payable or short-term borrowing), long-term liabilities (fixed-income debt), and owners' equity (preferred stock, common stock, and retained earnings).

The balance sheet for Walgreens in Exhibit 35-1 represents the *stock* of assets and its financing mix as of the end of Walgreens' fiscal year, August 31, 1999, 2000, and 2001.

Income Statement

The **income statement** contains information on the profitability of the firm during some *period of time* (a quarter or a year). In contrast to the balance sheet, which indicates the firm's financial position at a fixed point in time, the income statement indicates the *flow* of sales, expenses, and earnings during a period of time. The income statement for Walgreens for the years 1999, 2000, and 2001 appears in Exhibit 35-2. We concentrate on earnings from operations after tax as the relevant net earnings figure. In the case of Walgreens, this is typically the same as net income; the firm generally has no nonrecurring or unusual income or expense items.

Statement of Cash Flows

Based upon our earlier discussion on valuation, you know that cash flows are a critical input. In response to a growing interest in this data, accountants now require firms to provide such information. The **statement of cash flows**

---

[1] The recent Enron fiasco clearly makes this point. For a general discussion on this topic, see Nanette Byrnes and David Henry, "Confused About Earnings?" *Business Week* (26 November 2001): 77–84; David Henry, "The Numbers Game," *Business Week* (14 May 2001): 100–110; and Nanetta Byrnes, Mike McNamee, Diane Brady, Louis Lavelle, and Christopher Palmeri, "Accounting in Crises," *Business Week* (28 January 2002): 44–48.

EXHIBIT 35-1 Walgreen Co. and Subsidiaries Consolidated Balance Sheet ($ Millions): Years Ended August 31, 1999, 2000, and 2001

	2001	2000	1999
Assets			
Current Assets			
Cash and cash equivalents	$ 17	$ 13	$ 142
Trade accounts receivable—net of allowances	798	615	487
Inventories	3,482	2,831	2,463
Other current assets	96	92	131
Total Current Assets	4,394	3,550	3,222
Property, plant, and equipment	5,503	4,420	3,473
Less accumulated depreciation	1,158	992	879
Property—Net	4,345	3,428	2,594
Other noncurrent assets	95	125	91
Total Assets	$8,834	$7,104	$5,907
Liabilities and Shareholders' Equity			
Current Liabilities			
Short-term debt	$ 441	$ 0	$ 0
Current portion of long-term debt	0	0	0
Trade accounts payable	1,547	1,364	1,130
Accrued expenses and other liabilities	938	848	730
Income taxes payable	87	92	63
Other accrued liabilities	0	0	0
Total Current Liabilities	3,012	2,304	1,923
Long-term Debt	0	0	0
Other Noncurrent Liabilities	478	464	424
Deferred Income Taxes	137	102	75
Preferred Stock, $.0625 par value, authorized 32,000,000 shares; none issued			
Common Shareholders' Equity			
Common stock, $.078125 par value, authorized 3.2 billion shares; issued and outstanding 1,010,818,890 in 2000 and 1,004,022,258 in 1999	80	79	78
Paid-in capital	597	367	259
Retained earnings	4,531	3,788	3,147
Total Common Shareholders' Equity	5,207	4,234	3,484
Total Liabilities and Common Shareholders' Equity Co.	$8,834	$7,104	$5,907

Reprinted with permission from Walgreen Co., Deerfield, IL.

EXHIBIT 35-2 Walgreen Co. and Subsidiaries Consolidated Statement of Income ($ Millions, Except Per-Share Data): Years Ended August 31, 1999, 2000, and 2001

	2001	2000	1999
Net sales	$24,623	$21,207	$17,839
Cost of goods sold	18,049	15,466	12,979
Gross profit	6,574	5,741	4,860
Selling, general and administrative expenses	5,176	4,517	3,845
Operating profit (EBIT)	1,398	1,224	1,015
Interest income	(5)	(6)	(12)
Interest expense	3	0	0
Other Income	(22)	(34)	0
Gain on sale of long-term care pharmacies	0	0	0
Operating income before income taxes	1,422	1,263	1,027
Provision for income taxes	537	486	403
Operating income after taxes[b]	886	777	624
Cumulative effect of accounting change	0	0	0
Reported net income	886	777	624
Reported net income available for Common	886	777	624
Per Share Data[a]			
Operating income after taxes[b]	$ 0.86	$ 0.76	$ 0.62
Reported net income	$ 0.86	$ 0.76	$ 0.62
Dividends declared	$ 0.14	$ 0.14	$ 0.13
Average number of common shares outstanding (millions)[a]	1,029	1,020	1,014

[a] Adjusted for stock splits.

[b] Does not include gain on sale of pharmacies and effect of accounting changes.

Reprinted with permission from Walgreen Co., Deerfield, IL.

integrates the information on the balance sheet and income statement. For a given period, it shows the effects on the firm's cash flow of income flows (based on the most recent year's income statement) and changes in various items on the balance sheet (based on the two most recent annual balance sheets). The result is a set of cash flow values that you can use to estimate the value of a firm and to evaluate the risk and return of the firm's bonds and stock.

The statement of cash flows has three sections: cash flows from operating activities, cash flows from investing activities, and cash flows from financing activities. The sum total of the cash flows from the three sections is the net change in the cash position of the firm. This bottom-line number should equal the difference in the cash balance between the ending and beginning balance sheets. The statements of cash flow for Walgreens for 1999, 2000, and 2001 appear in Exhibit 35-3.

Cash Flow from Operating Activities

This section lists the sources and uses of cash that arise from the normal operations of a firm. In general, the net cash flow from operations is computed as the net income reported on the income statement, including changes in net

EXHIBIT 35-3 Walgreen Co. and Subsidiaries Consolidated Statement of Cash Flows ($ Millions): Years Ended August 31, 1999, 2000, and 2001

	2001	2000	1999
Cash Flows from Operating Activities:			
Net Income	$ 886	$ 777	$ 624
Adjustments to Reconcile Net Income to Net Cash Provided by Operating Activities:			
Cumulative effect of accounting changes	0	0	0
Depreciation and amortization	269	230	210
Deferred income taxes and other items	47	21	(9)
Gain on sale of long-term care pharmacies	0	0	0
Income tax savings from employee stock plans	67	39	27
Other	2	14	12
Changes in Operating Assets and Liabilities (Used in) Provided from Continuing Operations:			
(Increase) decrease in trade accounts receivable	(177)	(135)	(106)
(Increase) decrease in inventories	(652)	(368)	(436)
(Increase) decrease in other current assets	0	0	0
Increase (decrease) in trade accounts payable	183	234	223
Increase (decrease) in other current liabilities	0	0	0
Accrued expenses and other liabilities	82	101	104
Income taxes	(5)	29	9
Other	17	32	(6)
Net Cash Provided by Operating Activities	$ 719	$ 972	$ 652
Cash Flows from Investing Activities:			
Additions to property, plant, and equipment	$(1,237)	$(1119)	$(696)
Net borrowing against corporate-owned life insurance	59	11	9
Net proceeds from marketable securities	0	48	0
Disposition of property and equipment	44	23	42
Net Cash Used in Investing Activities	$(1,135)	$(1037)	$(646)
Cash Flows from Financing Activities:			
Proceeds from short-term borrowings	$ 441	$ —	$ —
Cash dividends	(141)	(135)	(129)
Proceeds from employee stock plans	126	79	105
Other	(7)	(8)	15
Net Cash Used in Financing Activities	419	$ (63)	$ (9)
Net increase (decrease) in cash and cash equivalents	4	(129)	(3)
Cash and cash equivalents—beginning of year	13	142	144
Cash and cash equivalents—end of year	$ 17	$ 13	$ 142

working capital items (i.e., receivables, inventories, and so on) plus adjustments for noncash revenues and expenses (such as depreciation) or:

$$\text{Cash Flow from Operating Activities} = \text{Net Income} + \text{Noncash Revenue and Expenses} + \text{Changes in Net Working Capital Items}$$

Consistent with the preceding discussion, the cash account is not included in the calculations of cash flow from operations. Notably, Walgreens has been able to generate consistently large cash flows from operations even after accounting for consistent increases in receivables and inventory.

Cash Flows from Investing Activities

A firm makes investments in both its own noncurrent and fixed assets and the equity of other firms (which may be subsidiaries or joint ventures of the parent firm; they are listed in the "investment" account of the balance sheet). Increases and decreases in these noncurrent accounts are considered investment activities. The cash flow from investing activities is the change in gross plant and equipment plus the change in the investment account. The changes are positive if they represent a source of funds (e.g., sale of some plant and/or equipment); otherwise, they are negative. The dollar changes in these accounts are computed using the firm's two most recent balance sheets. Most firms (including Walgreens) experience negative cash flows from investments due to significant capital expenditures.

Cash Flows from Financing Activities

Cash flow from financing activities is computed as financing sources minus financing uses. Cash inflows are created by actions increasing notes payable and long-term liability and equity accounts, such as bond and stock issues. Financing uses (cash outflows) include decreases in such accounts (that is, the paydown of liability and debt accounts or the repurchase of common shares). Dividend payments to equityholders are a significant financing cash outflow.

The sum total of the cash flows from operating, investing, and financing activities is the net increase or decrease in the firm's cash. The statement of cash flows provides some of the cash flow detail that is lacking in the balance sheet and income statement.

Alternative Measures of Cash Flow

There are several cash flow measures an analyst can use to determine the underlying health of the corporation.

Cash Flow from Operations

This includes the traditional measure of cash flow, which is equal to net income plus depreciation expense and deferred taxes; but, as we have just seen, it is also necessary to adjust for changes in operating (current) assets and liabilities that either use or provide cash. For example, an increase in accounts receivable implies that either the firm is using cash to support this increase or the firm did not collect all the sales reported. In contrast, an increase in a current liability account, such as accounts payable, means that the firm acquired some assets but has not paid for them, which is a source (increase) of cash flow (that is, the firm's suppliers are implicitly providing financing to the firm). These changes in operating assets or liabilities can add to or subtract from the cash flow estimated from the traditional measure of cash flow: net income plus noncash expenses.

The following table compares the cash flow from operations figures (Exhibit 35-3) to the traditional cash flow figures for Walgreens from 1999 to 2001:

	Traditional Cash Flow Equals Net Income + Depreciation + Change in Deferred Taxes	Cash Flow from Operations from Statement of Cash Flows
2001	1,045	719
2000	1,034	972
1999	820	652

In all three years, the cash flow from operations was less than the traditional cash flow estimate because of the several adjustments needed to arrive at cash flow from operations. Therefore, using this more exact measure of cash flow, the Walgreens ratios would not have been as strong. This is fairly typical because the effect of working-capital changes is often a large negative cash flow due to necessary increases in receivables or inventory to support sales growth (especially for high-growth companies like Walgreens).

Free Cash Flow

Free cash flow modifies cash flow from operations to recognize that some investing and financing activities are critical to the firm. It is assumed that these "necessary" expenditures must be made before a firm can use its cash flow for other purposes such as reducing debt outstanding or repurchasing common stock. Two additional items are considered: (1) capital expenditures (an investing expenditure) and (2) the disposition of property and equipment (a divestment source of cash). These two items are used to modify cash flow from operations for Walgreens as follows (some analysts only subtract capital expenditures, and those who are conservative also subtract dividends):

	Cash Flow from Operations	−	Capital Expenditures	+	Disposition of Property and Equipment	=	Free Cash Flow
2001	719	−	1,237	+	44	=	(474)
2000	972	−	1,119	+	23	=	(124)
1999	652	−	696	+	42	=	(2)

For firms involved in leveraged buyouts, this free cash flow number is critical because the new owners typically want to use the firm's free cash flow as funds available for retiring outstanding debt. As noted, it is not unusual for a firm's free cash flow to be a negative value. The free cash flow for Walgreens has been negative for these three years even though the firm has large cash flow from operations because the firm has committed to very heavy capital expenditures for new stores. Notably, this free cash flow value or a variation of it will be used in the subsequent cash flow valuations models.[2]

Purpose of Financial Statement Analysis

Financial statement analysis seeks to evaluate management performance in several important areas, including profitability, efficiency, and risk. Although we will necessarily analyze historical data, the ultimate goal of this analysis is to provide insights that will help you to *project* future management performance, including pro forma balance sheets, income statements, cash flows, and risk. It is the firm's *expected future* performance that determines whether you should lend money to a firm or invest in it.

OPTIONAL SEGMENT ENDS

ANALYSIS OF FINANCIAL RATIOS 3

Analysts use financial ratios because numbers in isolation typically convey little meaning. Knowing that a firm earned a net income of $100,000 is less informative than also knowing the sales figure that generated this income ($1 million or $10 million) and the assets or capital committed to the enterprise. Thus, ratios are intended to provide meaningful *relationships* between individual values in the financial statements.

Because the major financial statements include numerous individual items, it is possible to produce a vast number of potential ratios, many of which will have little value. Therefore, you want to limit your examination to the most relevant ratios and categorize them into groups that will provide information on important economic characteristics of the firm. It is also important to recognize the need for relative analysis.

Importance of Relative Financial Ratios

Just as a single number from a financial statement is of little use, an individual financial ratio has little value except in relation to comparable ratios for other entities. That is, *only relative financial ratios are relevant.* The important comparisons examine a firm's performance relative to

- The aggregate economy
- Its industry or industries
- Its major competitors within the industry
- Its past performance (time-series analysis)

The comparison to the aggregate economy is important because almost all firms are influenced by the economy's expansions and contractions (recessions) in the business cycle. For example, it is unreasonable to expect an increase in the profit margin for a firm during a recession; a stable margin might be encouraging under such conditions. In contrast, no change or a small increase in a firm's

---

[2] As will be shown in Reading 55 that deals with valuation, small modifications of this free cash flow, entitled free cash flow to equity (FCFE), free cash flow to the firm (FCFF), and NOPLAT are used in alternative valuation models and also in the well-regarded economic value added (EVA) model.

profit margin during a major business expansion may be a sign of weakness. Comparing a firm's financial ratios relative to a similar set of ratios for the economy will also help you to understand how a firm reacts to the business cycle and will help you *estimate* the future performance of the firm during subsequent business cycles.

Probably the most significant comparison relates a firm's performance to that of its industry. Different industries affect the firms within them differently, but this company-industry relationship is always significant. The industry effect is strongest for industries with homogeneous products, such as steel, rubber, glass, and wood products, because all firms within these industries experience coincidental shifts in demand. In addition, these firms employ fairly similar technology and production processes. For example, even the best-managed steel firm experiences a decline in sales and profit margins during a recession. In such a case, the relevant question is not whether sales and margins declined but how bad was the decline and how did the firm perform relative to other steel firms? As part of this, you should examine an industry's performance relative to aggregate economic activity to understand how the industry responds to the business cycle.

When comparing a firm's financial ratios to industry ratios, you may not feel comfortable using the average (mean) industry value when there is wide variation among individual firm ratios within the industry. Alternatively, you may believe that the firm being analyzed is not typical—that is, it has a unique component. Under these conditions, a **cross-sectional analysis** may be appropriate, in which you compare the firm to a subset of firms within the industry that are comparable in size or characteristics. As an example, if you were interested in Kroger, you would want to compare its performance to that of other national food chains rather than some regional chains or specialty food chains.

Another practical problem with comparing a firm's ratios to an industry average is that many large firms are multiproduct and multi-industry in nature. Inappropriate comparisons can arise when a multi-industry firm is evaluated against the ratios from a single industry. Two approaches can help mitigate this problem. First, you can use a cross-sectional analysis by comparing the firm against a rival that operates in many of the same industries. Second, you can construct composite industry average ratios for the firm. To do this, the firm's annual report or 10-K filing is used to identify each industry in which the firm operates and the proportion of total firm sales derived from each industry. Following this, composite industry average ratios are constructed by computing weighted average ratios based on the proportion of firm sales derived from each industry.

Finally, you should examine a firm's relative performance over time to determine whether it is progressing or declining. This **time-series analysis** is helpful when estimating future performance. For example, some analysts calculate the average of a ratio for a 5- or 10-year period without considering the trend. This can result in misleading conclusions. For example, an average rate of return of 10 percent can be based on rates of return that have increased from 5 percent to 15 percent over time, or it can be based on a series that begins at 15 percent and declines to 5 percent. Obviously, the difference in the trend for these series would have a major impact on your estimate for the future. Ideally, you want to examine a firm's time series of *relative* financial ratios compared to its industry and the economy.

4 COMPUTATION OF FINANCIAL RATIOS

We divide the financial ratios into five major categories that will help us understand the important economic characteristics of a firm. In this section, we focus on describing the various ratios and computing them using Walgreens data. Comparative analysis of Walgreens ratios with the economy and industry will be discussed in a later section. The five categories are as follows:

1. Common size statement
2. Internal liquidity (solvency)
3. Operating performance
   a. Operating efficiency
   b. Operating profitability
4. Risk analysis
   a. Business risk
   b. Financial risk
   c. Liquidity risk
5. Growth analysis

Common-Size Statements

Common-size statements "normalize" balance sheet and income statement items to allow easier comparison of different-size firms. A common-size balance sheet expresses all balance sheet accounts as a *percentage of total assets.* A common-size income statement expresses all income statement items as a *percentage of sales.* Exhibit 35-4 is the common-size balance sheet for Walgreens, and Exhibit 35-5 contains the common-size income statement. Common-size ratios are useful to quickly compare two different-size firms and to examine trends over time within a single firm. Common-size statements also give an analyst insight into the structure of a firm's financial statements—that is, the proportion of assets that are liquid, the proportion of liabilities that are short-term obligations, or the percentage of sales consumed by production costs. For example, for Walgreens, the common-size balance sheet shows a small decline in the percent of current assets and a steady increase in the proportion of net property. Alternatively, the common-size income statement in Exhibit 35-5 shows Walgreens' cost of goods sold was relatively stable during the five years with a small increase overall in proportion to sales. As a result of this stability combined with a consistent small decline in the ratio for selling, general, and administrative (SG+A) expenses, the firm has experienced an overall increase in its operating profit margin before and after taxes. The ability of Walgreens to experience strong growth in sales (over 14 percent a year) *and* an overall increase in its profit margin is very impressive.

EVALUATING INTERNAL LIQUIDITY 5

Internal liquidity (solvency) ratios indicate the ability of the firm to meet future short-term financial obligations. They compare near-term financial obligations, such as accounts payable or notes payable, to current assets or cash flows that will be available to meet these obligations.

Internal Liquidity Ratios

Current Ratio

Clearly the best-known liquidity measure is the *current ratio,* which examines the relationship between current assets and current liabilities as follows:

$$\text{Current Ratio} = \frac{\text{Current Assets}}{\text{Current Liabilities}}$$

EXHIBIT 35-4 Walgreen Co. and Subsidiaries Common-Size Balance Sheet[a]: Years Ended August 31, 1997, 1998, 1999, 2000, and 2001

	2001	2000	1999	1998	1997
Assets					
Current Assets					
Cash and cash equivalents	0.19%	0.18%	2.40%	2.95%	1.74%
Trade accounts receivable—net of allowances	9.04	8.65	8.24	7.61	8.94
Inventories	39.42	39.85	41.69	41.35	41.19
Other Current assets	1.09	1.30	2.21	1.60	3.42
Total Current Assets	49.74	49.98	54.54	53.52	55.29
Property, plant, and equipment	62.30	62.22	58.79	60.39	59.47
Less accumulated depreciation	13.11	13.96	14.88	16.66	17.78
Property—Net	49.19	48.26	43.91	43.73	41.69
Other noncurrent assets	1.07	1.77	1.54	2.76	3.02
Total Assets	100.00%	100.00%	100.00%	100.00%	100.00%
Liabilities and Shareholders' Equity					
Current Liabilities					
Short-term debt	4.99%	0.00%	0.00%	0.00%	0.00%
Current portion of long-term debt	0.00	0.00	0.00	0.00	0.00
Trade accounts payable	17.51	19.20	19.14	18.50	19.32
Accrued expenses and other liabilities	10.62	11.93	12.36	12.62	13.17
Income taxes payable	0.98	1.30	1.07	1.12	1.71
Total Current Liabilities	34.09	32.43	32.57	32.24	34.20
Long-term Debt	0.00	0.00	0.00	0.00	0.00
Other Noncurrent Liabilities	5.41	6.54	7.17	7.82	6.70
Deferred Income Taxes	1.55	1.43	1.27	1.82	2.69
Preferred Stock, $.0625 par value, authorized 32,000,000 shares; none issued					
Common Shareholders' Equity					
Common stock, $.078125 par value, authorized 3.2 billion shares; issued and outstanding 1,010,818,890 in 2000 and 1,004,022,258 in 1999	0.91	1.11	1.33	1.59	1.83
Paid-in capital	6.76	5.17	4.38	2.41	0.71
Retained Earnings	51.32	53.32	53.28	54.13	53.86
Total Common Shareholders' Equity	58.95	59.60	58.99	58.12	56.41
Total Liabilities and Common Shareholders' Equity	100.00%	100.00%	100.00%	100.00%	100.00%

[a] Percentages may not add to 100% due to rounding.

EXHIBIT 35-5 Walgreen Co. and Subsidiaries Common-Size Income Statement[a]: Years Ended August 31, 1997, 1998, 1999, 2000, and 2001

	2001	%	2000	%	1999	%	1998	%	1997	%
Net sales	$24,623	100.00%	$21,207	100.00%	$17,839	100.00%	$15,307	100.00%	$13,363	100.00%
Cost of goods sold	18,049	73.30	15,466	72.93	12,979	72.75	11,139	72.78	9,682	72.45
Gross profit	6,574	26.70	5,741	27.07	4,860	27.25	4,167	27.22	3,681	27.55
Selling, general and administrative expenses	5,176	21.02	4,517	21.30	3,845	21.55	3,332	21.77	2,973	22.25
Operating profit	1,398	5.68	1,224	5.77	1,015	5.69	835	5.46	708	5.30
Interest income	(5)	(0.02)	(6)	(0.03)	(12)	(0.07)	(6)	(0.04)	(6)	(0.04)
Interest expense	3	0.01	0	0.00	0	0.00	1	0.01	2	0.01
Other income	(22)	(0.09)	(34)	(0.16)						
Gain on sale of long-term care pharmacies							(37)	(0.24)		
Operating income before income taxes	1,423	5.78	1,263	5.96	1,027	5.76	877	5.73	712	5.33
Provision for income taxes	537	2.18	486	2.29	403	2.26	340	2.22	276	2.07
Operating income after taxes	886	3.60	777	3.66	624	3.50	537	3.51	436	3.26
Extraordinary loss (income)	0	–	0	–	0	–	0	–	0	–
Cumulative effect of accounting change	0	–	0	–	0	–	(26)	(0.17)	0	–
Reported net income	886	3.60	777	3.66	624	3.50	511	3.34	436	3.26
Operating income after taxes available for common	886	3.60	777	3.66	624	3.50	537	3.51	436	3.26
Reported net income available for common	886	3.60	777	3.66	624	3.50	511	3.34	436	3.26

[a] Percentages may not add to 100% due to rounding.

For Walgreens, the current ratios were (all ratios are computed using dollars in 1,000s):

$$2001: \frac{4394}{3012} = 1.46$$

$$2000: \frac{3550}{2304} = 1.54$$

$$1999: \frac{3222}{1924} = 1.67$$

These current ratios experienced a small decline during the three years and are consistent with the "typical" current ratio. As always, it is important to compare these values with similar figures for the firm's industry and the aggregate market. If the ratios differ from the industry results, it is necessary to determine what might explain it. This comparative analysis is considered in a subsequent section.

Quick Ratio

Some observers believe you should not consider total current assets when gauging the ability of the firm to meet current obligations because inventories and some other assets included in current assets might not be very liquid. As an alternative, they prefer the *quick ratio*, which relates current liabilities to only relatively liquid current assets (cash items and accounts receivable) as follows:

$$\text{Quick Ratio} = \frac{\text{Cash} + \text{Marketable Securities} + \text{Receivables}}{\text{Current Liabilities}}$$

Walgreens' quick ratios were:

$$2001: \frac{815}{3012} = 0.27$$

$$2000: \frac{627}{2304} = 0.27$$

$$1999: \frac{628}{1924} = 0.33$$

These quick ratios for Walgreens were small, but were fairly constant over the three years. As before, you should compare these values relative to other firms in the industry and to the aggregate economy. When possible, you should question management regarding the reason for these relatively low liquidity ratios (e.g., small receivables due to heavy cash sales?).

Cash Ratio

The most conservative liquidity ratio is the *cash ratio*, which relates the firm's cash and short-term marketable securities to its current liabilities as follows:

$$\text{Cash Ratio} = \frac{\text{Cash} + \text{Marketable Securities}}{\text{Current Liabilities}}$$

Walgreens' cash ratios were:

$$2001: \frac{17}{3012} = 0.01$$

$$2000: \frac{13}{2304} = 0.01$$

$$1999: \frac{142}{1924} = 0.07$$

The cash ratios during these three years have been quite low and they would be cause for concern except that such cash ratios are typical for a fast-growing retailer with larger inventories being financed by accounts payable to its suppliers. In addition, the firm has strong lines of credit available on short notice at various banks. Still, as an investor, you would want to confirm how the firm can justify such a low ratio and how it is able to accomplish this.

Receivables Turnover

In addition to examining total liquid assets relative to near-term liabilities, it is useful to analyze the quality (liquidity) of the accounts receivable. One way to do this is to calculate how often the firm's receivables turn over, which implies an average collection period. The faster these accounts are paid, the sooner the firm gets the funds that can be used to pay off its own current liabilities. Receivables turnover is computed as follows:

$$\text{Receivables Turnover} = \frac{\text{Net Annual Sales}}{\text{Average Receivables}}$$

Analysts typically derive the average receivables figure from the beginning receivables figure plus the ending value divided by two. Walgreens' receivables turnover ratios were:

$$2001: \frac{24{,}623}{(798 + 615)\ /\ 2} = 34.9 \text{ Times}$$

$$2000: \frac{21{,}207}{(615 + 487)\ /\ 2} = 38.5 \text{ Times}$$

It is not possible to compute a turnover value for 1999 because the tables used do not include a beginning receivables figure for 1999 (that is, we lack the ending receivables figure for 1998).

Given these annual receivables turnover figures, an average collection period is as follows:

$$\text{Average Receivable Collection Period} = \frac{365}{\text{Average Receivables Turnover}}$$

$$2001: \frac{365}{34.9} = 10.5 \text{ Days}$$

$$2000: \frac{365}{38.5} = 9.4 \text{ Days}$$

These results indicate that Walgreens currently collects its accounts receivable in about 10 days on average, and this collection period has increased slightly over the recent five years. To determine whether these receivable collection numbers are good or bad, it is essential that they be related to the firm's credit policy and to comparable collection figures for other firms in the industry. The point is, the receivable collection period value varies dramatically for different firms (e.g., from 10 to over 60) and it is mainly due to the product and the industry. Such an analysis would indicate similar rapid collection periods for other drugstore chains since this is basically a cash business for the majority of sales. Still, a significant change has occurred for drugstores because about 90 percent of pharmacy sales are to a third party (i.e., these pharmacy sales are reimbursed by a managed-care company), which, in turn, generates a receivable.

The receivables turnover is one of the ratios where *you do not want to deviate too much from the norm.* For example, in an industry where the "normal" collection period is 40 days, a collection period of 80 days would indicate slow-paying customers, which increases the capital tied up in receivables and the possibility of bad debts. Therefore, you would want the firm to be somewhat below the norm (for example, 35 days versus 40 days). At the same time, a figure *substantially below* the norm, such as 20 days, might indicate overly stringent credit terms relative to your competition, which could be detrimental to sales.

Inventory Turnover

Another current asset that should be examined in terms of its liquidity is inventory based upon the firm's inventory turnover and the implied processing time. Inventory turnover can be calculated relative to sales or cost of goods sold. The preferred turnover ratio is relative to cost of goods sold (CGS) because CGS does not include the profit implied in sales.

$$\text{Inventory Turnover} = \frac{\text{CGS}}{\text{Average Inventory}}$$

For Walgreens, the inventory turnover ratios are as follows:

$$2001: \frac{18{,}049}{(3{,}482 + 2{,}831)\ /\ 2} = 5.7 \text{ Times}$$

$$2000: \frac{15{,}466}{(2{,}831 + 2{,}463)\ /\ 2} = 5.8 \text{ Times}$$

Given the turnover values, you can compute the average inventory processing time as follows:

$$\text{Average Inventory Processing Period} = \frac{365}{\text{Average Annual Turnover}}$$

$$2001: \frac{365}{5.7} = 64 \text{ Days}$$

$$2000: \frac{365}{5.8} = 63 \text{ Days}$$

Although this seems like a low turnover figure, it is encouraging that the inventory processing period is very stable and has declined slightly compared to the longer run period. Still, it is essential to examine this figure relative to an industry norm and/or the firm's prime competition. Notably, it will also be affected by the products carried by the chain—for instance, if a drugstore chain adds high-profit-margin items, such as cosmetics and liquor, these products may have a lower turnover.

As with receivables, you do not want an extremely low inventory turnover value and long processing time because this implies that capital is being tied up in inventory and could signal obsolete inventory (especially for firms in the technology sector). Alternatively, an abnormally high inventory turnover and a very short processing time relative to competitors could mean inadequate inventory that could lead to outages, backorders, and slow delivery to customers, which would eventually have an adverse effect on sales.

Cash Conversion Cycle

A very useful measure of overall internal liquidity is the cash conversion cycle, which combines information from the receivables turnover, the inventory turnover, and the accounts payable turnover. The point is, cash is tied up in assets for a certain number of days. Specifically, cash is committed to receivables for the collection period and is also tied up for a number of days in inventory—the inventory processing period. At the same time, the firm receives an offset to this capital commitment from its own suppliers, who provide interest-free loans to the firm by carrying the firm's payables. Specifically, the payables payment period is equal to 365/the payables turnover ratio. In turn, the payables turnover ratio is equal to:

$$\text{Payables Turnover Ratio} = \frac{\text{Cost of Goods Sold}}{\text{Average Trade Payables}}$$

For Walgreens, the payables turnover ratio is:

$$2001: \frac{18{,}049}{(1{,}547 + 1{,}364)\ /\ 2} = 12.4 \text{ Times}$$

$$2000: \frac{15{,}466}{(1{,}364 + 1{,}130)\ /\ 2} = 12.4 \text{ Times}$$

$$\text{Payables Payment Period} = \frac{365}{\text{Payables Turnover}}$$

$$2001: \frac{365}{12.4} = 29 \text{ Days}$$

$$2000: \frac{365}{12.4} = 29 \text{ Days}$$

Therefore, the cash conversion cycle for Walgreens equals:

Year	Receivables Days	+	Inventory Processing Days	−	Payables Payment Period	=	Cash Conversion Cycle
2001	10	+	64	−	29	=	45 days
2000	9	+	63	−	29	=	43 days

Walgreens has experienced a small decline in its receivables days, it has been stable regarding its inventory processing days, and it is paying its bills at the same speed. Overall, the result has been a small decrease in its cash conversion cycle. Although the overall cash conversion cycle appears to be quite good (about 46 days), as always, you should examine the firm's long-term trend and compare it to other drugstore chains.

EVALUATING OPERATING PERFORMANCE 6

The ratios that indicate how well the management is operating the business can be divided into two subcategories: (1) **operating efficiency ratios** and (2) **operating profitability ratios**. Efficiency ratios examine how the management uses its assets and capital, measured in terms of the dollars of sales generated by various asset or capital categories. Profitability ratios analyze the profits as a percentage of sales and as a percentage of assets and capital employed.

Operating Efficiency Ratios

Total Asset Turnover

The total asset turnover ratio indicates the effectiveness of the firm's use of its total asset base (net assets equals gross assets minus depreciation on fixed assets). It is computed as follows:

$$\text{Total Asset Turnover} = \frac{\text{Net Sales}}{\text{Average Total Net Assets}}$$

Walgreens' total asset turnover values were:

$$2001: \frac{24{,}623}{(8{,}834 + 7{,}104)\ /\ 2} = 3.09 \text{ Times}$$

$$2000: \frac{21{,}207}{(7{,}104 + 5{,}907)\ /\ 2} = 3.3 \text{ Times}$$

It is essential that you compare this ratio to that of other firms in an industry because this particular ratio varies substantially between industries. For example, total asset turnover ratios range from about 1 (or less) for large, capital-intensive industries (steel, autos, and other heavy manufacturing companies) to over 10 for some retailing or service operations. This ratio can also be affected by the use of leased facilities.

Again, you should consider a *range* of turnover values consistent with the industry. It is poor management to have an exceedingly high asset turnover relative to your industry because this might imply too few assets for the potential business (sales), or it could be due to the use of outdated, fully depreciated assets. It is equally poor management to have a low relative asset turnover because this implies tying up capital in an excess of assets relative to the needs of the firm.

Beyond analyzing the firm's total assets, it is insightful to examine the utilization of some specific assets, such as receivables, inventories, and fixed assets. This is especially important to do if the firm has experienced a major decline or increase in total asset turnover because you want to know the cause of the change—that is, which of the component turnovers (receivables, inventory, fixed asset) contributed to the change. Because we have already examined the receivables and inventory turnover as part of our liquidity analysis, we will examine the fixed asset ratio.

Net Fixed Asset Turnover

The net fixed asset turnover ratio reflects the firm's utilization of fixed assets. It is computed as follows:

$$\text{Fixed Asset Turnover} = \frac{\text{Net Sales}}{\text{Average Net Fixed Assets}}$$

Walgreens' fixed asset turnover ratios were

$$2001: \frac{24{,}623}{(4{,}345 + 3{,}428)\ /\ 2} = 6.3 \text{ Times}$$

$$2000: \frac{21{,}207}{(3{,}428 + 2{,}594)\ /\ 2} = 7.0 \text{ Times}$$

These turnover ratios, which indicate a decline for Walgreens during the last few years, must be compared with those of firms in the same industry and should consider the impact of leased assets.[3] Also remember that an abnormally low turnover implies capital tied up in excessive fixed assets, while an abnormally high asset turnover ratio can indicate a lack of productive capacity to meet sales demand or it might imply the use of old, fully depreciated equipment that may be obsolete.[4]

Equity Turnover

In addition to specific asset turnover ratios, it is useful to examine the turnover for alternative capital components. An important one, equity turnover, is computed as follows:

$$\text{Equity Turnover} = \frac{\text{Net Sales}}{\text{Average Equity}}$$

Equity includes preferred and common stock, paid-in capital, and total retained earnings.[5] The difference between this ratio and total asset turnover is that it excludes current liabilities and long-term debt. Therefore, when examining this series, it is important to consider the firm's capital structure ratios because a firm can increase its equity turnover ratio by increasing its proportion of debt capital (that is, by having a higher debt/equity ratio).

Walgreens' equity turnover ratios were:

$$2001: \frac{24{,}623}{(5{,}207 + 4{,}234)\ /\ 2} = 5.2 \text{ Times}$$

$$2000: \frac{21{,}207}{(4{,}234 + 3{,}484)\ /\ 2} = 5.5 \text{ Times}$$

Walgreens has experienced a small decline in this ratio during the past several years. In our later analysis of sustainable growth, we examine the variables that affect the equity turnover ratio to understand what caused any changes.

Following an analysis of the firm's record of operating efficiency based upon its ability to generate sales from its assets and capital, the next step is to examine its profitability in relation to its sales and capital.

Operating Profitability Ratios

The ratios in this category indicate two facets of profitability: (1) the rate of profit on sales (profit margin) and (2) the percentage return on capital employed.

---

[3] The impact of leased assets is especially significant for retail firms that lease most of their stores and for airlines that lease their planes. We will consider this off-balance-sheet financing in the subsequent section on financial risk.

[4] There will be a longer-term analysis of the firm's total asset turnover ratio in the subsequent DuPont analysis section.

[5] Some investors prefer to consider only *owner's* equity, which would not include preferred stock.

Gross Profit Margin

Gross profit equals net sales minus the cost of goods sold. The gross profit margin is computed as:

$$\text{Gross Profit Margin} = \frac{\text{Gross Profit}}{\text{Net Sales}}$$

The gross profit margins for Walgreens were:

$$2001: \frac{6{,}574}{24{,}623} = 26.7\%$$

$$2000: \frac{5{,}741}{21{,}207} = 27.1\%$$

$$1999: \frac{4{,}860}{17{,}839} = 27.2\%$$

This ratio indicates the basic cost structure of the firm. An analysis of this ratio over time relative to a comparable industry figure shows the firm's relative cost-price position. Walgreens has experienced stability in this margin during the last several years. As always, it is important to compare these margins and any changes with the industry and strong competitors. Notably, this margin can be impacted by a change in the firm's product mix toward higher or lower profit margin items. In the case of Walgreens, the shift has been slightly negative because of the high rate of growth in the pharmacy business, which has a lower gross profit margin than other product sales.

Operating Profit Margin

Operating profit is gross profit minus sales, general, and administrative (SG&A) expenses. The operating profit margin is computed as:

$$\text{Operating Profit Margin} = \frac{\text{Operating Profit}}{\text{Net Sales}}$$

For Walgreens, the operating profit margins were:

$$2001: \frac{1{,}398}{24{,}623} = 5.7\%$$

$$2000: \frac{1{,}224}{21{,}207} = 5.8\%$$

$$1999: \frac{1{,}015}{17{,}839} = 5.7\%$$

The variability of the operating profit margin over time is a prime indicator of the business risk for a firm. As noted earlier for Walgreens, this margin has experienced an overall steady increase during the last several years. Because there has been a small decline in the gross profit margin, it is clearly the firm's ability to control its SG&A expense as it has experienced strong sales growth that has resulted in the higher operating profit margin.

There are two additional deductions from operating profit (also referred to as EBIT—earnings before interest rate and taxes)—interest expense and net foreign exchange loss. This indicates operating income before income taxes.

In some instances, investors add back to operating income depreciation expense and compute a profit margin that consists of earnings before interest, taxes, depreciation, and amortization (EBITDA). This alternative operating profit margin reflects all controllable expenses and is used as a proxy for pre-tax cash flow.[6]

Net Profit Margin

This margin relates net income to sales. In the case of Walgreens, this is the same as operating income after taxes because the firm does not have any significant nonoperating adjustments. The net income used is earnings after taxes but before dividends on preferred and common stock. For most firms, this margin is equal to:

$$\text{Net Profit Margin} = \frac{\text{Net Income}}{\text{Net Sales}}$$

As noted, Walgreens' net profit margin is based on income after taxes as follows:

$$2001{:}\ \frac{886}{24{,}623} = 3.6\%$$
$$2000{:}\ \frac{777}{21{,}207} = 3.7\%$$
$$1999{:}\ \frac{624}{17{,}839} = 3.5\%$$

This ratio should be computed based on sales and earnings from *continuing* operations because our analysis seeks to derive insights about *future* expectations. Therefore, results for continuing operations are relevant rather than the profit or loss that considers earnings from discontinued operations, the gain or loss from the sale of these operations, or any truly nonrecurring income or expenses. Consistent with prior profit margins for Walgreens, this one also shows a small long-run increase.

Common-Size Income Statement

Beyond these ratios, an additional technique for analyzing operating profitability is a common-size income statement, which lists all expense and income items as a percentage of sales. Analyzing this statement for several years (five at least) will provide useful insights regarding the trends in cost figures and profit margins. Earlier, we discussed the common-size statement for Walgreens (Exhibit 35-5). Beyond the analysis of earnings related to sales, the ultimate measure of the success of management is the profits earned on the assets or the capital committed to the enterprise. Several ratios help us evaluate this important relationship.

---

[6] While this measure of "cash flow" has grown in popularity, there are a growing number of concerned observers who point out that this measure does *not* consider the necessary cash outflows for working capital items (which are considered in "cash flow from operations") or capital expenditures (which are considered in "free cash flow"). For a brief discussion, see Herb Greenberg, "Alphabet Dupe: Why EBITDA Falls Short," *Fortune* 10 July 2000): 240–241.

Return on Total Capital

The return on total capital (ROTC) ratio relates the firm's earnings to all the capital involved in the enterprise (debt, preferred stock, and common stock). Therefore, the earnings figure used is the net income from continuing operations (before any dividends) *plus* the interest paid on debt.

$$\text{Return on Total Capital} = \frac{\text{Net Income} + \text{Gross Interest Expense}}{\text{Average Total Capital}}$$

Walgreens incurred interest expense for long- and short-term debt. The gross interest expense value used in this ratio differs from the "net" interest expense item in the income statement, which is measured as gross interest expense minus interest income.

Walgreens' rate of return on total capital was:

$$2001: \frac{886 + 3}{(8{,}834 + 7{,}104) / 2} = 11.2\%$$

$$2000: \frac{777 + 0.4}{(7{,}104 + 5{,}907) / 2} = 11.9\%$$

This ratio indicates the firm's return on all the capital it employed. It should be compared with the ratio for other firms in the industry and the economy. If this rate of return does not match the perceived risk of the firm, one might question if the entity should continue to exist because the capital involved in the enterprise could be used more productively elsewhere in the economy. For Walgreens, the results are stable and indicate a small increase over the last several years.

ROTC Including Leases

An alternative computation of ROTC is appropriate for a firm such as Walgreens that employs operating leases for its stores. This treatment would be similar for most retail firms and for airlines that lease most of their aircraft. In such instances, it is appropriate to capitalize the lease payments and put the resulting value on the balance sheet as a fixed asset and as a long-term liability.[7]

An estimate of the discounted value of the future lease payments can be done one of two ways: (1) a multiple of the forthcoming minimum lease payments or (2) the discounted value of the future minimum lease payments provided in the annual report at the firm's cost of long-term debt. The traditional multiple technique multiplies the minimum lease payment in year $t + 1$ by 8. In the case of Walgreens, the future minimum lease payments in the annual report for the year 2001 are as follows:

Years relating to year end	2002	2003	2004	2005	2006	later
Minimum payments (in $millions)	783	826	817	805	785	9,010

Given these data, the estimate using the first technique (referred to as "the 8 times rule") would produce an estimate of *$6.26 billion* (8 × $783 million). To

[7] In a subsequent section where we discuss measures for financial risk, we will include the capitalized value as part of the firm's debt and include an imputed interest expense in ratios that include interest expense—for example, fixed charge coverage ratios.

derive an estimate using the second technique, we need to estimate the firm's cost of long-term debt and consider how to handle the lump sum "later" payments. Our debt rate estimate is 8 percent, which is consistent with the prevailing rate on AA-A rated corporate bonds. Regarding the "later" lump sum payment, it is necessary to derive a reasonable estimate regarding how many years to assume for this amortization. A liberal assumption is that the later payment is amortized over 15 years based upon a typical building lease of 20 years (this assumption would imply \$9,010/15 = \$601 million per year). This assumption implies that the firm will have a lease payment of \$601 million each year for the 15 years beginning in 2007. An alternative estimate of the amortization period is derived by dividing the lump sum payment by the payment in the latest year (2006), which implies a time estimate (9,010 ÷ 785 = 11.5 years). If we round this up to 12 years, it implies an annual payment of \$751 million per year for 12 years (\$9,010/12 = \$751).

If we discount all the minimum annual flows and the amortized flows over 15 years at 8 percent, we derive an estimate of the lease debt of *\$6.71 billion.* A similar computation using the 12-year amortization indicates an estimate of lease debt of *\$7.06 billion.* Therefore, we have the following three estimates:[8]

Eight times the $t + 1$ lease payment	\$6.26 billion
Discounting the lease payments assuming a 15-year amortization	\$6.71 billion
Discounting the lease payments assuming a 12-year amortization	\$7.06 billion

We will use the \$6.71 billion discounted value estimate, which assumes a 15-year amortization period since this provides an estimate that is more theoretically correct than the "8 times rule" but not as aggressive as assuming a 12-year amortization period—that is, it provides an estimate between the two alternatives.

If we add this amount to both fixed assets and long-term debt, we will have a better measure of the assets utilized by the firm and a better estimate of the complete financing of the assets. Notably, the value that we calculated using future minimum lease payments is an appropriate value to be included on the August 31, 2001, financial statement. To properly calculate several of the subsequent financial risk ratios, we need comparable estimates for each of the year ends of 1998, 1999, and 2000, which entails estimating the present value of minimum lease payments at the end of each of these years as shown in the annual reports.

Implied Interest for Leased Assets

When computing the return on total capital (ROTC) that considers these leased assets, it is also necessary to add the implied interest expense for the leases. Again, there are two estimating techniques: (1) a rule of thumb and (2) an interest rate applied to the discounted value of minimum lease payments. The interest expense component of a lease is estimated by some analysts using the rule-of-thumb technique, which contends interest is equal to one-third of the lease

[8] Notably, the "8 times" estimate almost always provides the lowest estimate of debt value, which means that this "rule of thumb" will tend to underestimate the financial leverage for these firms and the resulting implied interest expense. Therefore, the authors prefer one of the specific discounted value estimates but feel that this relatively small underestimate is minor compared to not capitalizing these lease obligations.

payment during the year in question. In the current example, if we wanted an estimate for the implied interest for the year 2001, we would use one-third of the lease payment in 2001, which was $730 million. Thus, the implied interest would be estimated at $243 million ($730/3).

An alternative to this "rule of thumb" would be to derive a specific estimate based on an estimate of the firm's cost of debt capital (8 percent) and the estimate of the present value (PV) of the lease obligation as follows:

Estimating Technique	PV of Lease Obligation (billion $)	Interest Expense @ 8 percent (million $)
8 times estimate of rent	6.26	501
P.V. with 15-year amortization	6.71	537
P.V. with 12-year amortization	7.06	565

Notably, all of these estimates of the implied interest expense that used the capitalized lease value are substantially higher than the "one-third of lease payment" rule-of-thumb estimate of $243 million. Again, the rule of thumb underestimates the financial leverage related to these lease obligations. For our calculations, we will apply the 8 percent debt cost to the present value of the lease payments assuming the 15-year amortization of the lump sum. Because the lease obligations are for future periods, it is necessary to use lagged values of the obligations—that is, the estimate for 2001 is 8 percent of the obligation estimated at the end of fiscal 2000. These values are as follows:

	Estimate of PV of Lease Obligation (Billion $)[a]	Estimate of Interest Expense of Lease (Million $)[b]
2002	$6.71	$537
2001	5.76	461
2000	4.48	358
1999	3.65	292

[a] These are the capitalized lease payments on the books for year $t - 1$—for example, to get the 2002 value, we discount the minimum payments reported in the 2001 annual report.

[b] Equal to 8 percent of the PV of lease obligation.

Adding these values to the prior ratios results in the following lease-adjusted return on total capital values:

$$2001: \frac{886 + 3 + 461}{(15{,}094 + 12{,}494) / 2} = \frac{1{,}350}{13{,}454} = 10.03\%$$

$$2000: \frac{777 + 0.4 + 358}{(12{,}494 + 10{,}137) / 2} = \frac{1{,}135.4}{11{,}315.5} = 10.03\%$$

As shown, the ROTCs that include the leased assets and lease debt are lower (about 10 percent versus 12 percent), but they are still quite reasonable.

Implied Depreciation on Leased Assets

Beyond the implied interest expense, another factor is the implied depreciation expense that would be taken if these were not leased assets. One alternative is to simply use the typical term of the lease or weighted average term. In the case of Walgreens, this is reasonably clear since almost all leases are for 20 years on buildings. A second alternative, if it is not clear, would be the depreciation expense as a percent of beginning of year net fixed assets. In the case of Walgreens, for 2000, this would be: depreciation—$230 million; net fixed assets at end of 1999—$2,594, which implies a percent of .089 (230/2,594), which is clearly higher than the 5 percent on buildings. Obviously, Walgreens has many assets being depreciated over shorter lives. For these calculations, we prefer to assume the 20-year life as follows:

	Estimate of PV of Lease Obligation (Billion $)	Estimate of Implied Depreciation Expense of Lease (Million $)[a]
2001	5.76	288
2000	4.48	224
1999	3.65	183

[a] This assumes straight-line depreciation over a 20-year life.

These implied depreciation charges should be included in ratios that include depreciation expenses.

Return on Owner's Equity

The return on owner's equity (ROE) ratio is extremely important to the owner of the enterprise (the common stockholder) because it indicates the rate of return that management has earned on the capital provided by the owner after accounting for payments to all other capital suppliers. If you consider all equity (including preferred stock), this return would equal:

$$\text{Return on Total Equity} = \frac{\text{Net Income}}{\text{Average Total Equity}}$$

If an investor is concerned only with owner's equity (the common shareholder's equity), the ratio would be calculated

$$\text{Return on Owner's Equity} = \frac{\text{Net Income} - \text{Preferred Dividend}}{\text{Average Common Equity}}$$

Walgreens generated return on owner's equity of:

$$2001: \frac{886 - 0}{(5{,}207 + 4{,}234)\ /\ 2} = 18.8\%$$

$$2000: \frac{777 - 0}{(4{,}234 + 3{,}484)\ /\ 2} = 20.1\%$$

This ratio reflects the rate of return on the equity capital provided by the owners. It should correspond to the firm's overall business risk, but also the financial risk assumed by the common stockholder because of the prior claims of bondholders and store lessors.

The DuPont System

The importance of ROE as an indicator of performance makes it desirable to divide the ratio into several components that provide insights into the causes of a firm's ROE or any changes in it. This breakdown of ROE into component ratios is generally referred to as the **DuPont system**. To begin, the return on equity (ROE) ratio can be broken down into two ratios that we have discussed—net profit margin and equity turnover.

$$\text{ROE} = \frac{\text{Net Income}}{\text{Common Equity}} = \frac{\text{Net Income}}{\text{Net Sales}} \times \frac{\text{Net Sales}}{\text{Common Equity}}$$

This breakdown is an identity because we have both multiplied and divided by net sales. To maintain the identity, the common equity value used is the year-end figure rather than the average of the beginning and ending value. This identity reveals that ROE equals the net profit margin times the equity turnover, which implies that a firm can improve its return on equity by *either* using its equity more efficiently (increasing its equity turnover) or by becoming more profitable (increasing its net profit margin).

As noted previously, a firm's equity turnover is affected by its capital structure. Specifically, a firm can increase its equity turnover by employing a higher proportion of debt capital. We can see this effect by considering the following relationship:

$$\frac{\text{Net Sales}}{\text{Equity}} = \frac{\text{Net Sales}}{\text{Total Assets}} \times \frac{\text{Total Assets}}{\text{Equity}}$$

Similar to the prior breakdown, this is an identity because we have both multiplied and divided the equity turnover ratio by total assets. This equation indicates that the equity turnover ratio equals the firm's *total asset turnover* (a measure of efficiency) times the ratio of *total assets to equity*, a measure of financial leverage. Specifically, this latter ratio of total assets to equity indicates the proportion of total assets financed with debt. *All assets have to be financed by either equity or some form of debt* (either current liabilities or long-term debt). Therefore, the higher the ratio of assets to equity, the higher the proportion of debt to equity. A total asset/equity ratio of 2, for example, indicates that for every two dollars of assets there is a dollar of equity, which means the firm financed one-half of its assets with equity. This implies that it financed the other half with debt. A total asset/equity ratio of 3 indicates that only one third of total assets was financed with equity, so two-thirds must have been financed with debt. This breakdown of the equity turnover ratio implies that a firm can increase its equity turnover either by increasing its total asset turnover (becoming more efficient) or by increasing its financial leverage ratio (financing assets with a higher proportion of debt capital). This financial leverage ratio is also referred to as the *financial leverage multiplier* whereby the first two ratios (profit margin and total asset turnover) equal return on total assets (ROTA) and ROTA times the financial leverage multiplier equals ROE.

Combining these two breakdowns, we see that a firm's ROE is composed of three ratios as follows:

$$\begin{aligned}\frac{\text{Net Income}}{\text{Common Equity}} &= \frac{\text{Net Income}}{\text{Net Sales}} \times \frac{\text{Net Sales}}{\text{Total Assets}} \times \frac{\text{Total Assets}}{\text{Common Equity}} \\ &= \text{Profit Margin} \times \text{Total Asset Turnover} \times \\ &\quad\ \text{Financial Leverage}\end{aligned}$$

As an example of this important set of relationships, the figures in Exhibit 35-6 indicate what has happened to the ROE for Walgreens and the components of

EXHIBIT 35-6 Components of Return on Total Equity for Walgreen Co.[a]

Year	1 Sales/Total Assets	2 Net Profit Margin (%)	3[b] Return on Total Assets	4 Total Assets/Equity	5[c] Return on Equity (%)
1982	3.31	2.75	9.09	2.06	18.73
1983	3.29	2.96	9.72	2.04	19.84
1984	3.26	3.11	10.16	2.03	20.60
1985	3.29	2.98	9.79	2.00	19.58
1986	3.06	2.82	8.62	2.16	18.64
1987	3.14	2.42	7.60	2.19	16.63
1988	3.23	2.64	8.54	2.12	18.12
1989	3.20	2.87	9.18	2.04	18.74
1990	3.16	2.89	9.12	2.02	18.42
1991	3.21	2.90	9.31	1.94	18.04
1992	3.15	2.95	9.30	1.92	17.90
1993	3.27	2.67	8.74	1.84	16.07
1994	3.17	3.05	9.69	1.85	17.91
1995	3.20	3.09	9.86	1.81	17.85
1996	3.24	3.16	10.23	1.78	18.19
1997	3.18	3.26	10.37	1.77	18.35
1998	3.12	3.34	10.42	1.72	17.93
1999	3.02	3.50	10.57	1.70	17.91
2000	2.99	3.66	10.94	1.68	18.35
2001	2.79	3.60	10.04	1.70	17.07

[a] Ratios use year-end data for total assets and common equity rather than averages of the year.

[b] Column 3 is equal to Column 1 times Column 2.

[c] Column 5 is equal to Column 3 times Column 4.

its ROE during the 20-year period from 1982 to 2001. As noted, these ratio values employ year-end balance sheet figures (assets and equity) rather than the average of beginning and ending data so they will differ from our individual ratio computations.

The DuPont results in Exhibit 35-6 indicate several significant trends:

1. The total asset turnover ratio experienced an overall decline with a total range of 2.79 to 3.31. Notably, the ratio declined to its lowest level in 2001.
2. The profit margin series experienced a stable increase from 2.75 to its peak value of 3.66 in 2000.
3. The product of the total asset turnover and the net profit margin is equal to return on total assets (ROTA), which experienced an overall increase from 9.09 percent to a peak of 10.94 percent in 2000.
4. The financial leverage multiplier (total assets/equity) experienced a steady decline from 2.06 to 1.68. Notably, most of this debt is trade credit, which is noninterest bearing. The fact is, the firm has almost no interest-bearing debt, except for the long-term leases on drugstores that were discussed and

analyzed in the prior subsection and will be considered in the financial risk section.

5. Finally, as a result of the increasing ROTA and the declining financial leverage, the firm's ROE has experienced a small decline, beginning at 18.73 and ending at 17.07.

An Extended DuPont System[9]

Beyond the original DuPont system, some analysts have suggested using an extended DuPont system, which provides additional insights into the effect of financial leverage on the firm and also pinpoints the effect of income taxes on the firm's ROE. Because both financial leverage and tax rates have changed dramatically over the past decade, these additional insights are important.

In the prior presentation, we started with the ROE and divided it into components. In contrast, we now begin with the operating profit margin (EBIT divided by sales) and introduce additional ratios to derive an ROE value. Combining the operating profit margin and the total asset turnover ratio yields the following:

$$\frac{\text{EBIT}}{\text{Net Sales}} \times \frac{\text{Net Sales}}{\text{Total Assets}} = \frac{\text{EBIT}}{\text{Total Assets}}$$

This ratio is the operating profit return on total assets. To consider the negative effects of financial leverage, we examine the effect of interest expense as a percentage of total assets:

$$\frac{\text{EBIT}}{\text{Total Assets}} - \frac{\text{Interest Expense}}{\text{Total Assets}} = \frac{\text{Net Before Tax (NBT)}}{\text{Total Assets}}$$

We consider the positive effect of financial leverage with the financial leverage multiplier as follows:

$$\frac{\text{Net Before Tax (NBT)}}{\text{Total Assets}} \times \frac{\text{Total Assets}}{\text{Common Equity}} = \frac{\text{Net Before Tax (NBT)}}{\text{Common Equity}}$$

This indicates the pretax return on equity. To arrive at ROE, we must consider the tax-rate effect. We do this by multiplying the pre-tax ROE by a tax-retention rate as follows:

$$\frac{\text{Net Before Tax}}{\text{Common Equity}} \times \left(100\% - \frac{\text{Income Taxes}}{\text{Net Before Tax}}\right) = \frac{\text{Net Income}}{\text{Common Equity}}$$

In summary, we have the following five components:

1. $\frac{\text{EBIT}}{\text{Sales}} = \text{Operating Profit Margin}$
2. $\frac{\text{Sales}}{\text{Total Assets}} = \text{Total Asset Turnover}$
3. $\frac{\text{Interest Expense}}{\text{Total Assets}} = \text{Interest Expense Rate}$

[9] The original DuPont system was the three-component breakdown discussed in the prior section. Because this extended analysis also involves the components of ROE, some still refer to it as the DuPont system. In our presentation, we refer to it as the extended DuPont system to differentiate it from the original three-component analysis.

$$4.\ \frac{\text{Total Assets}}{\text{Common Equity}} = \text{Financial Leverage Multiplier}$$

$$5.\ \left(100\% - \frac{\text{Income Taxes}}{\text{Net Before Tax}}\right) = \text{Tax Retention Rate}$$

To demonstrate the use of this extended DuPont system, Exhibit 35-7 contains the calculations using the five components for the years 1982 through 2001. The first column indicates that the firm's operating profit margin peaked in 1985, subsequently declined to a low point in 1990, increased to a new peak of 5.77 percent in 2000 prior to a decline in 2001. We know from the prior discussion that the firm's total asset turnover (column 2) experienced an overall decline to a low point in 2001. The resulting operating return on assets increased prior to

EXHIBIT 35-7 Extended DuPont System Analysis for Walgreens: 1982–2000[a]

	1	2	3	4	5	6	7	8	9
Year	EBIT/ Sales (Percent)	Sales/ Total Assets (Times)	EBIT/ Total Assets (Percent)[b]	Interest Expense/ Total Assets (Percent)	Net Before Tax/Total Assets Equity (Percent)[c]	Total Assets/ Common Equity (Times)	Net Before Tax/ Common Equity (Percent)[d]	Tax Retention Rate	Return on Equity (Percent)[e]
1982	4.32	3.31	14.30	(0.85)	15.15	2.06	31.20	0.60	18.75
1983	5.16	3.29	17.00	0.25	16.75	2.04	34.20	0.56	19.30
1984	5.57	3.26	18.20	(0.24)	18.44	2.03	37.40	0.55	20.65
1985	5.63	3.29	18.50	0.43	18.07	2.00	36.10	0.54	19.57
1986	5.37	3.06	16.40	0.74	15.66	2.16	33.90	0.55	18.63
1987	4.92	3.14	15.50	1.22	14.28	2.19	31.30	0.53	16.69
1988	4.59	3.23	14.80	1.01	13.79	2.12	29.30	0.62	18.10
1989	4.71	3.20	15.10	0.57	14.53	2.04	29.70	0.63	18.79
1990	4.70	3.16	14.90	0.17	14.73	2.02	29.80	0.62	18.52
1991	4.77	3.21	15.30	0.44	14.86	1.94	28.80	0.63	18.00
1992	4.80	3.15	15.10	0.23	14.87	1.92	28.60	0.62	17.87
1993	4.90	3.31	16.20	0.26	15.94	1.82	29.00	0.61	17.80
1994	4.93	3.21	15.90	(0.10)	16.00	1.83	29.20	0.62	17.96
1995	5.00	3.20	15.99	0.04	15.95	1.81	28.90	0.61	17.70
1996	5.13	3.24	16.62	0.06	16.56	1.78	29.50	0.61	18.07
1997	5.30	3.18	16.85	0.05	16.80	1.77	29.74	0.61	18.14
1998	5.46	3.12	17.04	0.02	17.02	1.72	29.28	0.61	17.93
1999	5.69	3.02	17.19	0.00	17.19	1.70	29.22	0.61	17.83
2000	5.77	2.99	17.25	0.00	17.25	1.68	28.98	0.61	17.78
2001	5.08	2.79	15.84	0.00	16.11	1.70	27.33	0.62	17.07

[a] The percents in this table may not be the same as in Exhibit 35-6 due to rounding.

[b] Column 3 is equal to Column 1 times Column 2.

[c] Column 5 is equal to Column 3 minus Column 4.

[d] Column 7 is equal to Column 5 times Column 6.

[e] Column 9 is equal to Column 7 times Column 8.

a decline in 2001. As discussed, because of virtually no interest-bearing debt (except off-balance sheet leases), Column 4 shows zero negative impact on leverage.

Column 5 reflects the firm's operating performance before the positive impact of financing (the leverage multiplier) and the impact of taxes. These results show strong performance by the firm overall. Column 6 reflects the steady decline in non-lease financial leverage. As a result of the reduced leverage multiplier, the before-tax ROE in Column 7 has declined since 1982. Column 8 shows the strong positive effect of lower tax rates, which caused a higher tax-retention rate that increased from the mid-50 percent range to the recent 62 percent rate.

In summary, this breakdown helps you to understand *what* happened to a firm's ROE and *why* it happened. The intent is to determine what happened to the firm's internal operating results, what has been the effect of its financial leverage policy, and what was the effect of external government tax policy. Although the two breakdowns should provide the same ending value, they typically differ by small amounts because of the rounding of components.

7 RISK ANALYSIS

Risk analysis examines the uncertainty of income flows for the total firm and for the individual sources of capital (that is, debt, preferred stock, and common stock). This involves examining the major factors that cause a firm's income flows to vary. More volatile income flows mean greater risk (uncertainty) facing the investor.

The total risk of the firm has two internal components: business risk and financial risk. The next section discusses the concept of business risk: how you measure it, what causes it, and how you measure its individual causes. The following section discusses financial risk and the several ratios used to measure it. After we examine the firm's internal risk factors, we discuss an important external risk factor, external liquidity risk—that is, the ability to buy or sell the firm's stock in the secondary equity market.

Business Risk[10]

Recall that **business risk** is the uncertainty of income caused by the firm's industry. In turn, this uncertainty is due to the firm's variability of sales caused by its products, customers, and the way it produces its products. Specifically, a firm's operating earnings vary over time because its sales and production costs vary. As an example, the earnings for a steel firm will probably vary more than those of a grocery chain because (1) over the business cycle, steel sales are more volatile than grocery sales; and (2) the steel firm's large fixed production costs (operating leverage) make its earnings vary more than its sales.

Business risk is generally measured by the variability of the firm's operating income over time. In turn, the earnings variability is measured by the standard deviation of the historical operating earnings series. You will recall from Chapter 1 that the standard deviation is influenced by the size of the numbers, so investors standardize this measure of volatility by dividing it by the mean value for the series (i.e., the average operating earnings). The resulting ratio of the

---

[10] For a further discussion on this general topic, see Eugene Brigham and Louis C. Gapenski, *Financial Management: Theory and Practice*, 9th ed. (Fort Worth, Tex.: Dryden, 2000), Chapters 6 and 10.

standard deviation of operating earnings divided by the average operating earnings is the coefficient of variation (CV) of operating earnings:

$$\begin{aligned}\text{Business Risk} &= f\,(\text{Coefficient of Variation of Operating Earnings})\\ &= \frac{\text{Standard Deviation of Operating Earnings (OE)}}{\text{Mean Operating Earnings}}\\ &= \frac{\sqrt{\sum_{i=1}^{n}(OE_i - \overline{OE})^2/n}}{\sum_{i=1}^{n} OE_i/n}\end{aligned}$$

The CV of operating earnings allows comparisons between standardized measures of business risk for firms of different sizes. To compute the CV of operating earnings, you need a minimum of 5 years up to about 10 years. Less than 5 years is not very meaningful, and data more than 10 years old are typically out of date. We cannot compute the CV of operating earnings of Walgreens because we have data for only 3 years.

Besides measuring overall business risk, it is very insightful to examine the two factors that contribute to the variability of operating earnings: sales variability and operating leverage.

Sales Variability

Sales variability is the prime determinant of earnings variability. In turn, the variability of sales is mainly caused by a firm's industry and is largely outside the control of management. For example, sales for a firm in a cyclical industry, such as automobiles or steel, will be quite volatile over the business cycle compared to sales of a firm in a noncyclical industry, such as retail food or hospital supplies. Like operating earnings, the variability of a firm's sales is typically measured by the CV of sales during the most recent 5 to 10 years. The CV of sales equals the standard deviation of sales divided by the mean sales for the period.[11]

$$\begin{aligned}\text{Sales Volatility} &= f\,(\text{Coefficient of Variation of Sales})\\ &= \frac{\sqrt{\sum_{i=1}^{n}(S_i - \bar{S})^2/n}}{\sum_{i=1}^{n} S_i/n}\end{aligned}$$

Operating Leverage

The variability of a firm's operating earnings also depends on its mixture of production costs. Total production costs of a firm with no *fixed* production costs would vary directly with sales, and operating profits would be a constant proportion of sales. In such an example, the firm's operating profit margin would be constant and its operating profits would have the same relative volatility as its

[11] Besides normalizing the standard deviation for size by computing the CV, it is also important to recognize that the standard deviation is measured relative to the mean value for the series—that is, it computes deviations from "expected value." The problem arises for firms that experience significant growth that will create very large deviations from the mean for the series even if it is *constant* growth. The way to avoid this bias is to measure deviations from the growth path of the series.

sales. Realistically, firms always have some fixed production costs such as buildings, machinery, or relatively permanent personnel. Fixed production costs cause operating profits to vary more than sales over the business cycle. Specifically, during slow periods, operating profits will decline by a larger percentage than sales, while during an economic expansion, operating profits will increase by a larger percentage than sales.

The employment of fixed production costs is referred to as **operating leverage.** Clearly, greater operating leverage (caused by a higher proportion of fixed production costs) makes the operating earnings series more volatile relative to the sales series.[12] This basic relationship between operating profit and sales leads us to measure operating leverage as the percentage change in operating earnings relative to the percentage change in sales during a specified period as follows:

$$\text{Operating Leverage} = \frac{\sum_{i=1}^{n} \left| \frac{\% \Delta OE}{\% \Delta S} \right|}{n}$$

We take the absolute value of the percentage changes because the two series can move in opposite directions. The direction of the change is not important, but the relative size of the change is relevant. By implication, the more volatile the operating earnings as compared to the volatility of sales, the greater the firm's operating leverage.

Financial Risk

Financial risk, you will recall, is the additional uncertainty of returns to equity holders due to a firm's use of fixed obligation debt securities. This financial uncertainty is in addition to the firm's business risk. When a firm sells bonds to raise capital, the interest payments on this capital precede the computation of common stock earnings, and these interest payments are fixed contractual obligations. As with operating leverage, during an economic expansion, the net earnings available for common stock after the fixed interest payments will experience a larger percentage increase than operating earnings. In contrast, during a business decline, the earnings available to stockholders will decline by a larger percentage than operating earnings because of these fixed financial costs. Also, as a firm increases its relative debt financing with fixed contractual obligations, it increases its financial risk and the possibility of default and bankruptcy.

A very important point to remember is that *the acceptable level of financial risk for a firm depends on its business risk.* If the firm has low business risk (i.e., stable operating earnings), investors are willing to accept higher financial risk. For example, retail food companies typically have rather stable operating earnings over time and, therefore, relatively *low* business risk. As a result, investors and bond-rating firms will allow a firm in this industry to have *higher* financial risk.[13]

---

[12] See C. F. Lee, Joseph Finnerty, and Edgar Norton, *Foundations of Financial Management* (St. Paul, Minn. West Publishing, 1997).

[13] Support for this specific relationship is a set of tables published by Standard & Poor's Credit Rating division that suggests specific required financial risk ratios needed to be considered for a specific bond rating, and the required ratios differ based upon the perceived business risk of the firm. See *Corporate Ratings Criteria* (New York: Standard & Poor's, 55 Water Street, New York, NY 10041, 2002), p. 57.

In our analysis of financial risk, we employ three sets of financial ratios to measure financial risk; and *all three* sets should be considered. First, there are balance sheet ratios that indicate the proportion of capital derived from debt securities compared to equity capital. Second are ratios that compare the earnings available to pay fixed financial charges to the required interest payments. Third are ratios that compare the cash flows available to the financial charges or compare cash flows to the book value of the outstanding debt.

Proportion of Debt (Balance Sheet) Ratios

The proportion of debt ratios indicate what proportion of the firm's capital is derived from debt compared to other sources of capital, such as preferred stock, common stock, and retained earnings. A higher proportion of debt capital compared to equity capital makes earnings more volatile because of larger fixed financial charges and increases the probability that a firm will be unable to meet the required interest payments and will default on the debt. Therefore, higher proportion of debt ratios indicate greater financial risk. In this subsection, we describe the major proportion of debt ratios used to measure this risk.

Debt-Equity Ratio

The debt-equity ratio is:

$$\text{Debt-Equity Ratio} = \frac{\text{Total Long-Term Debt}}{\text{Total Equity}}$$

The debt figure includes all long-term fixed obligations, including lease obligations and subordinated convertible bonds. The equity typically is the book value of equity and includes preferred stock, common stock, and retained earnings. Some analysts prefer to exclude preferred stock and consider only common equity. Total equity is preferable if you are examining an industry in which some of the firms being analyzed have preferred stock.

Notably, debt ratios can be computed *with and without deferred taxes.* Most balance sheets include an accumulated deferred tax figure, which comes just below long-term debt and other liabilities on the balance sheet. There is some controversy regarding whether you should treat these deferred taxes as a liability or as part of permanent capital. Some argue that if the deferred tax has accumulated because of the difference in accelerated and straight-line depreciation, this liability may never be paid. That is, as long as the firm continues to grow and add new assets, this total deferred tax account continues to grow and is never paid off. Alternatively, if the deferred tax account results from differences in the recognition of income on long-term contracts, such as government contracts, there will be a reversal, and this liability must eventually be paid. To resolve this question, you must determine the reason for the deferred tax account and examine its long-term trend.[14] Walgreens' deferred tax account is because of a depreciation difference and has grown over time.

A second factor that must be considered when computing debt ratios is the existence of operating leases, as mentioned previously. Given a firm like Walgreens with extensive leased facilities, it is necessary to estimate the present value of the lease payments as long-term debt.

---

[14] For a further discussion of this, see Gerald I. White, Ashwinpaul C. Sondhi, and Dov Fried, *The Analysis and Use of Financial Statements,* 2d ed. (New York: Wiley, 1997), 1017–1018.

To show the effect of these two significant items on the financial risk of Walgreens, we will be conservative and define the ratios to include both of these factors, but they will be broken out so that you can identify the effect of each of the components of total debt. Thus, the debt-equity ratio is:

$$\text{Debt-Equity Ratio} = \frac{\text{Total Long-Term Debt}}{\text{Total Equity}}$$
$$= \frac{\text{Noncurrent Liabilities} + \text{Deferred Taxes} + \text{PV of Lease Obligations}}{\text{Total Equity}}$$

Therefore, for Walgreens, the debt-equity ratios were:

$$2001: \frac{478 + 137 + 6{,}710}{5{,}207} = \frac{7{,}325}{5{,}207} = 140.68\%$$
$$2000: \frac{464 + 102 + 5{,}760}{4{,}234} = \frac{6{,}326}{4{,}234} = 149.41\%$$
$$1999: \frac{424 + 75 + 4{,}480}{3{,}484} = \frac{4{,}979}{3{,}484} = 142.91\%$$

These ratios demonstrate the significant impact of including the present value of the lease payments as part of long-term debt—for example, the debt-equity percent for 2001 went from less than 14 percent when only long-term debt on the balance sheet was considered to over 140 percent.

Long-Term Debt/Total Capital Ratio

The debt–total capital ratio indicates the proportion of long-term capital derived from long-term debt capital. It is computed as:

$$\text{Long-Term Debt/Total Long-Term Capital Ratio} = \frac{\text{Total Long-Term Debt}}{\text{Total Long-Term Capital}}$$

The total long-term debt values are the same as before. The total long-term capital would include all long-term debt, any preferred stock, and total equity. The debt–total capital ratios for Walgreens were:

Including Deferred Taxes and Lease Obligations as Long-Term Debt

$$2001: \frac{7{,}325}{7{,}325 + 5{,}207} = \frac{7{,}325}{12{,}532} = 58.45\%$$
$$2000: \frac{6{,}326}{6{,}326 + 4{,}234} = \frac{6{,}326}{10{,}560} = 59.90\%$$
$$1999: \frac{4{,}979}{4{,}979 + 3{,}484} = \frac{4{,}979}{8{,}463} = 58.83\%$$

Again, this ratio, which includes the present value of lease obligations, shows that a significant percent of long-term capital for Walgreens is derived from debt obligations. This is very different from the impression without the lease obligations included.

Total Debt Ratios

In many cases, it is useful to compare *total* debt to *total* capital computed as:

$$\text{Total Debt Ratios} = \frac{\text{Current Liabilities} + \text{Total Long-Term Debt}}{\text{Total Debt} + \text{Total Equity}}$$

This ratio is especially revealing for a firm that derives substantial capital from short-term borrowing. The total debt/total capital ratios for Walgreens were:

Including Deferred Taxes and Lease Obligations as Long-Term Debt

$$2001: \frac{3{,}012 + 7{,}325}{10{,}337 + 5{,}207} = \frac{10{,}337}{15{,}544} = 66.50\%$$

$$2000: \frac{2{,}304 + 6{,}326}{8{,}630 + 4{,}234} = \frac{8{,}630}{12{,}864} = 67.09\%$$

$$1999: \frac{1{,}924 + 4{,}979}{6{,}903 + 3{,}484} = \frac{6{,}903}{10{,}387} = 66.46\%$$

This ratio indicates that currently almost 67 percent of Walgreens assets are financed with debt. These ratios should be compared with those of other companies in the industry (after capitalizing leases) to evaluate their consistency with the business risk of this industry. Such a comparison with industry peers also would indicate how much higher this total debt ratio can go (i.e., the firm's unused debt capacity).

While this ratio indicates a relatively high proportion of total debt, some observers would consider it too conservative because it includes accounts payable and accrued expenses, which are *non-interest-bearing debt*. In the case of Walgreens, if this non-interest-bearing debt, along with deferred taxes, is excluded from debt and from total capital, the total debt ratio declines as follows:

$$\text{Total Interest-Bearing Debt/Total Funded Capital} = \frac{\text{Total Interest-Bearing Debt}}{\text{Total Capital} - \text{Non-Interest Liabilities}}$$

$$2001: \frac{919 + 6{,}710}{15{,}544 - 2{,}708} = \frac{7{,}629}{12{,}836} = 59.43\%$$

$$2000: \frac{464 + 5{,}760}{12{,}864 - 2{,}405} = \frac{6{,}224}{10{,}459} = 59.51\%$$

$$1999: \frac{424 + 4{,}480}{10{,}381 - 1{,}999} = \frac{4{,}904}{8{,}382} = 58.51\%$$

While these ratios are lower, the percents are still quite high, which confirms the importance of considering the impact of lease obligations on the financial risk of firms like Walgreens that employ this form of financing.

Earnings Flow Ratios

In addition to ratios that indicate the proportion of debt on the balance sheet, investors are giving greater attention to ratios that relate the *flow* of earnings that is available to meet the required interest and lease payments. A higher ratio of available earnings relative to fixed financial charges indicates lower financial risk.

Interest Coverage

The standard interest coverage ratio is computed as follows:

$$\text{Interest Coverage} = \frac{\text{Income Before Interest and Taxes (EBIT)}}{\text{Debt Interest Charges}}$$
$$= \frac{\text{Net Income} + \text{Income Taxes} + \text{Interest Expense}}{\text{Interest Expense}}$$

This ratio indicates how many times the fixed interest charges are earned, based on the earnings available to pay these expenses.[15] Alternatively, one minus the reciprocal of the coverage ratio indicates how far earnings could decline before it would be impossible to pay the interest charges from current earnings. For example, a coverage ratio of 5 means that earnings could decline by 80 percent (1 minus 1/5), and the firm could still pay its fixed financial charges. Again, it is necessary to consider the impact of the lease obligations on this ratio because if you only consider the firm's public interest-bearing debt, the interest cost is about one-half million dollars and the coverage ratio exceeds 3,000 times. In contrast, if we recognize the lease obligations as debt and use the estimated interest expenses derived earlier, the coverage ratio would be computed as follows:

$$\text{Interest Coverage} = \frac{\text{Earnings Before Interest and Taxes} + \text{Estimated Lease Interest Expense}}{\text{Gross Interest Expense} + \text{Estimated Lease Interest Expense}}$$

Hence, the coverage ratios for Walgreens were:

$$2001: \frac{886 + 537 + (3 + 461)}{3 + 461} = \frac{1{,}887}{464} = 4.07 \text{ times}$$
$$2000: \frac{777 + 486 + 358}{358} = \frac{1{,}621}{358} = 4.53 \text{ times}$$
$$1999: \frac{624 + 403 + 292}{292} = \frac{1{,}319}{292} = 4.52 \text{ times}$$

These interest coverage ratios show a substantially different picture than the coverage ratios that do not consider the impact of the lease obligations. Still, these coverage ratios show reasonable financial risk for a firm with very low business risk.

The trend of Walgreens' coverage ratios has been consistent with the overall trend in the proportion of debt ratios. The proportion of debt ratios and the earnings flow ratios do not always give consistent results because the proportion of debt ratios is not sensitive to changes in earnings or to changes in the interest rates on the debt. For example, if interest rates increase or if the firm replaces old debt with new debt that has a higher interest rate, no change would occur in the proportion of debt ratios, but the interest coverage ratio would decline. Also, the interest coverage ratio is sensitive to an increase or decrease in earnings. Therefore, the indications regarding the financial risk of the firm using balance sheet ratios and coverage ratios can differ. Given a difference between the two sets of financial risk ratios, the authors have a strong preference for the coverage ratios that reflect the ability of the firm to meet its financial obligations.

---

[15] The net income figure used in the analysis is the operating income after taxes because, once again, it is important to exclude earnings and cash flows that are considered nonrecurring. The idea is to consider only those earnings that should be available in the future (that is, those from ongoing operations).

Cash Flow Ratios

As an alternative to these earnings coverage ratios, analysts employ several cash flow ratios that relate the cash flow available from operations to either interest expense, total fixed charges, or the face value of outstanding debt. The first set of cash-flow-to-interest-expense ratios or cash-flow-to-total-fixed-charge ratios is an extension of the earnings coverage ratios. The second set of cash flow ratios is unique because it relates to the *flow* of earnings plus noncash expenses to the *stock* of outstanding debt. These cash-flow-to-outstanding-debt ratios have been significant variables in numerous studies concerned with predicting bankruptcies and bond ratings.

Cash Flow Coverage Ratios

These ratios are an alternative to the earnings coverage ratio. The motivation is that a firm's earnings and its cash flow typically will differ substantially (these differences have been noted and will be considered further in a subsequent section). To have ratios that can be compared to similar values for other firms in the industry, the measure of cash flow used is the "cash flow from operating activities" figure contained in the cash flow statement. As such, it includes depreciation expense, deferred taxes, and the impact of all working capital changes. Again, it is appropriate to specify the ratio in terms of total interest charges including estimated leases interest expense as follows:

$$\text{Cash Flow Coverage of Fixed Financial Costs} = \frac{\text{Net Cash Flow Provided by Operating Activities} + \text{Interest Expense} + \text{Estimated Lease Interest Expense}}{\text{Interest Expense} + \text{Estimated Lease Interest Expense}}$$

Notably, the "change in deferred tax" component can be either a negative or positive value (positive cash flow is when deferred taxes increased; negative cash flow is when deferred taxes declined). The depreciation expense item can be found in the cash flow statement. The "change in deferred tax" item can be derived from changes in the balance sheet, or the change is reported in the cash flow statement. If the two approaches do not give the same number, we use the values given in the cash flow statement since we are specifically interested in the cash flow effect. The estimated lease interest expense was derived earlier, based on footnote data. The cash flow coverage ratios for Walgreens were:

$$2001: \frac{719 + 3 + 461}{3 + 461} = \frac{1{,}183}{464} = 2.55 \text{ times}$$

$$2000: \frac{972 + 358}{358} = \frac{1{,}330}{358} = 3.72 \text{ times}$$

$$1999: \frac{652 + 292}{292} = \frac{944}{292} = 3.23 \text{ times}$$

These coverage ratios are clearly not overpowering but are respectable for a firm with low business risk and should be compared to other firms in the industry after adjusting for leases.

Cash Flow/Long-Term Debt Ratio

Beyond relating cash flow to the required financing expense, several studies have used a ratio that relates cash flow to a firm's outstanding long-term debt as a predictor of bankruptcy and have found that this ratio was an excellent explanatory variable. The cash flow figure used in most of these studies was the traditional measure of cash flow (net income plus noncash expenses) that prevailed at the time the studies were done. In the current analysis, as shown earlier, we use the "cash flow from operating activities," which goes beyond the traditional measure and also considers the effect of working capital changes. This is a more conservative measure of cash flow because working capital changes typically have a negative impact on cash flow for a growing firm like Walgreens. Therefore, this ratio would be computed as:

$$\text{Cash Flow/Long-Term Debt} = \frac{\text{Cash Flow Provided by Operating Activities}}{\text{Book Value of Long-Term Debt} + \text{Present Value of Lease Obligations}}$$

Again, we computed these ratios assuming that deferred taxes and lease obligations were included as long-term debt as follows:

$$2001: \frac{719}{615 + 6{,}710} = \frac{719}{7{,}325} = 9.82\%$$

$$2000: \frac{972}{566 + 5{,}760} = \frac{972}{6{,}326} = 15.37\%$$

$$1999: \frac{652}{499 + 4{,}480} = \frac{652}{4{,}979} = 13.09\%$$

Cash Flow/Total Debt Ratio

Investors also should consider the relationship of cash flow to *total* interest-bearing debt to check that a firm has not had a significant increase in its short-term borrowing. For Walgreens, these ratios were:

$$\text{Cash Flow/Total Interest-Bearing Debt} = \frac{\text{Cash Flow Provided by Operating Activities}}{\text{Total Long-Term Debt} + \text{Current Interest-Bearing Liabilities}}$$

$$2001: \frac{719}{7{,}325 + 441} = \frac{719}{7{,}766} = 9.26\%$$

$$2000: \frac{972}{6{,}326 + 0} = \frac{972}{6{,}326} = 15.37\%$$

$$1999: \frac{652}{4{,}979 + 0} = \frac{652}{4{,}979} = 13.09\%$$

When you compare these ratios to those with only long-term debt (that includes deferred taxes), they reflect the firm's proportion of short-term debt due to short-term borrowing. In this analysis we exclude accounts payable and accrued expenses because they are non-interest-bearing. In the case of Walgreens, this eliminates almost all current liabilities. As before, it is important to compare these flow ratios with similar ratios for other companies in the industry and with the overall economy to gauge the firm's relative performance.

Alternative Measures of Cash Flow[16]

As noted, many past studies that included a cash flow variable used the traditional measure of cash flow. The requirement that companies must prepare and report the statement of cash flows to stockholders has raised interest in other exact measures of cash flow. The first alternative is the *cash flow from operations,*

---

[16] A list of studies in which ratios or cash flow variables are used to predict bankruptcies or bond ratings is included in the reference section.

which is taken directly from the statement of cash flows and is the one we have used. A second alternative measure is *free cash flow,* which is a modification of the cash flow from operations—that is, capital expenditures are also deducted. Some analysts are very conservative and also subtract dividends. The following table summarizes the values derived earlier in the reading.

				Free Cash Flow	
Year	**Traditional Cash Flow**	**Cash Flow from Operations**	**Net Capital Expenditures***	**Before Dividends**	**After Dividends**
2001	1,045	719	1,193	(474)	(615)
2000	1,034	972	1,096	(124)	(259)
1999	820	652	654	(2)	(131)

* Net Capital Expenditures = Property and Equipment Additions minus Dispositions

As shown, Walgreens has strong and growing cash flow from operations after considering working capital requirements, but the firm experiences small or negative free cash flow because of substantial capital expenditures related to growth.

External Liquidity Risk

External Liquidity Defined

In Reading 52, we discuss *external market liquidity* as the ability to buy or sell an asset quickly with little price change from a prior transaction assuming no new information. AT&T and IBM are examples of liquid common stocks because you can sell them quickly with little price change from the prior trade. You might be able to sell an illiquid stock quickly, but the price would be significantly different from the prior price. Alternatively, the broker might be able to get a specified price but could take several days doing so.

Determinants of Market Liquidity

As an investor, you should know the liquidity characteristics of the securities you currently own or may buy because liquidity can be important if you want to change the composition of your portfolio. Although the major determinants of market liquidity are reflected in market trading data, several internal corporate variables are good proxies for these market variables. The most important determinant of external market liquidity is the number of shares or dollar value of shares traded (the dollar value adjusts for different price levels). More trading activity indicates a greater probability that you can find someone to take the other side of a desired transaction.

A measure that is usually available is **trading turnover** (the percentage of outstanding shares traded during a period of time), which indicates relative trading activity. During calendar year 2001, about 705 million Walgreens shares were traded, which indicates turnover of approximately 70 percent (705 million/1,020 million).[17] This compares with the average turnover of the NYSE of about 68 percent.

[17] An excellent source of information on shares traded during the calendar year for stocks on the NYSE, the AMEX, and the Nasdaq National Market System is the "Year-End Review" section of *The Wall Street Journal,* which is published on the first business day of the new year—for example, data for calendar 2001 were in the review published January 2, 2002.

Another measure of market liquidity is the bid-ask spread (a smaller spread indicates greater liquidity). In addition, there are certain internal corporate variables that correlate highly with these market trading variables:

1. Total market value of outstanding securities (number of common shares outstanding times the market price per share)
2. Number of security owners

Numerous studies have shown that the main determinant of the bid-ask spread (besides price) is the dollar value of trading.[18] In turn, the value of trading correlates highly with the market value of the outstanding securities and the number of security holders. This relationship holds because, with more shares outstanding, there will be more stockholders to buy or sell at any time for a variety of purposes. Numerous buyers and sellers provide liquidity.

You can estimate the market value of Walgreens' outstanding stock as the average number of shares outstanding during the year (adjusted for stock splits) times the average market price for the year (equal to the high price plus the low price divided by two) as follows:[19]

2001: 1,029 × [(45 + 28)/2] = \$37.56 Billion
2000: 1,017 × [(46 + 23)/2] = \$35.09 Billion
1999: 1,010 × [(33 + 23)/2] = \$28.28 Billion

These market values would place Walgreens in the large-capitalization category, which usually begins at about \$6 billion. Walgreens stockholders number 88,000, including more than 650 institutions that own approximately 56 percent of the outstanding stock. These large values for market value, the number of stockholders and institutional holders, along with the high trading turnover indicate a highly liquid market in the common stock of Walgreens. That is, Walgreens has extremely low external liquidity risk.

8 ANALYSIS OF GROWTH POTENTIAL

Importance of Growth Potential

The analysis of **sustainable growth potential** examines ratios that indicate how fast a firm should grow. Analysis of a firm's growth potential is important for both lenders and owners. Owners know that the value of the firm depends on its future growth in earnings, cash flow, and dividends. In Reading 55, we discuss various valuation models that determine the value of the firm based on your required rate of return for the stock and the expected growth rate of the firm's alternative cash flows.

Creditors also are interested in a firm's growth potential because the firm's future success is the major determinant of its ability to pay obligations, and the firm's future success is influenced by its growth. Some financial ratios used in credit analysis measure the book value of a firm's assets relative to its financial obligations, assuming the firm can sell these assets to pay off the loan

[18] Studies on this topic are discussed in Reading 52.

[19] These values are for Walgreens' fiscal year. Stock prices are rounded to the nearest whole dollar.

in case of default. Selling assets in a forced liquidation will typically yield only about 10 to 15 cents on the dollar. Currently, it is widely recognized that the more relevant analysis is the ability of the firm to pay off its obligations as an ongoing enterprise, and its growth potential indicates its future status as an ongoing enterprise. This analysis is also relevant if you are interested in changes of bond ratings.

Determinants of Growth

The growth of business, like the growth of any economic entity, including the aggregate economy, depends on

1. the amount of resources retained and reinvested in the entity, and
2. the rate of return earned on the resources retained and reinvested.

The greater the proportion of earnings that a firm reinvests, the greater its potential for growth. Alternatively, for a given level of reinvestment, a firm will grow faster if it earns a higher rate of return on the resources reinvested. Therefore, the growth of equity earnings is a function of two variables: (1) the percentage of net earnings retained and reinvested into the business (the firm's retention rate) and (2) the rate of return earned on the firm's equity capital (the firm's ROE) because when earnings are retained they become part of the firm's equity (i.e., its retained earnings). This can be summarized as follows:

$$\begin{aligned} g &= \text{Percentage of Earnings Retained} \times \text{Return on Equity} \\ &= \text{RR} \times \text{ROE} \end{aligned}$$

where:

$$\begin{aligned} g &= \text{potential (i.e., sustainable) growth rate} \\ \text{RR} &= \text{the retention rate of earnings} \\ \text{ROE} &= \text{the firm's return on equity} \end{aligned}$$

The retention rate is a decision by the board of directors based on the investment opportunities available to the firm. Theory suggests that the firm should retain earnings and reinvest them as long as the expected rate of return on the investment exceeds the firm's cost of capital.

As discussed earlier in this reading, using the DuPont system, the firm's ROE is a function of three components:

- Net profit margin
- Total asset turnover
- Financial leverage (total assets/equity)

Therefore, a firm can increase its ROE by increasing its profit margin, by becoming more efficient (increasing its total asset turnover), or by increasing its financial leverage and financial risk. As discussed, you should examine and estimate each of these components when estimating the ROE for a firm.

An analysis of the sustainable growth potential for Walgreens begins with the retention rate (RR):

$$\text{Retention Rate} = 1 - \frac{\text{Dividends Declared}}{\text{Operating Income After Taxes}}$$

Walgreens' RR figures were:

$$2001: 1 - \frac{0.14}{0.86} = 0.84$$

$$2000: 1 - \frac{0.14}{0.76} = 0.82$$

$$1999: 1 - \frac{0.13}{0.62} = 0.79$$

The historical results shown in Exhibit 35-8 indicate that the retention rate for Walgreens has been relatively stable during the 20-year period at an average rate in excess of 70 percent.

Exhibit 35-6 contains the three components of ROE for the period 1982–2001. Exhibit 35-8 contains the two factors that determine a firm's growth potential and the implied growth rate during the past 20 years. Overall, Walgreens experienced a slight decline in its growth potential during the early 1990s, but since 1995 the firm increased its potential growth rate to over 15 percent prior to a small decline in 2001.

EXHIBIT 35-8 Walgreen Co. Components of Growth and the Implied Sustainable Growth Rate

Year	1 Retention Rate	2 Return on Equity[a]	3[b] Sustainable Growth Rate
1982	0.72	18.73	13.49
1983	0.74	19.84	14.68
1984	0.74	20.60	15.24
1985	0.71	19.58	13.90
1986	0.70	18.64	13.05
1987	0.68	16.63	11.31
1988	0.71	18.12	12.87
1989	0.73	18.74	13.68
1990	0.72	18.42	13.26
1991	0.71	18.04	12.81
1992	0.71	17.90	12.71
1993	0.67	16.07	10.77
1994	0.70	17.91	12.54
1995	0.69	17.89	12.34
1996	0.71	18.19	12.91
1997	0.73	18.35	13.40
1998	0.75	17.92	13.44
1999	0.79	17.91	14.13
2000	0.82	18.35	15.09
2001	0.84	17.07	14.29

[a] From Exhibit 35-6.

[b] Column 3 is equal to Column 1 times Column 2.

Exhibit 35-8 reinforces the importance of the firm's ROE. Walgreens' retention rate was quite stable throughout the period with an increase during the last six years. Even with this, it has been the firm's ROE that has mainly determined its sustainable growth rate. This analysis indicates that the important consideration is *the long-run outlook for the components of sustainable growth.* As an investor, you need to *project* changes in each of the components of ROE and employ these projections to estimate an ROE to use in the growth model along with an estimate of the firm's long-run retention rate. We will come back to these concepts on numerous occasions when valuing the market, alternative industries, and individual firms. This detailed analysis of ROE is extremely important for growth companies where the ROEs are notably above average for the economy and vulnerable to competition.

COMPARATIVE ANALYSIS OF RATIOS 9

We have discussed the importance of comparative analysis, but so far we have concentrated on the selection and computation of specific ratios. Exhibit 35-9 contains most of the ratios discussed for Walgreens, the retail drug store industry (as derived from the S&P *Analysts Handbook*), and the S&P Industrials Index. The three-year comparison should provide some insights, although you typically would want to examine data for a 5-to 10-year period. It is necessary to do the comparison for the period 1998 to 2000 because industry and market data from Standard and Poors were not available for 2001 until late 2002.

Internal Liquidity

The three basic ratios (current ratio, quick ratio, and cash ratio) provided mixed results regarding liquidity for Walgreens relative to the industry and market. The current ratio is above the industry and market. The firm's receivables turnover has declined due to a high percentage of the pharmacy sales being paid by a third party. Still, its collection period is substantially less than the S&P Industrials and the retail drug store industry (9 days versus 12 and 78 in 2000). Because the collection period has been fairly steady, the difference is because of the firm's basic credit policy.

Overall, the comparisons indicate reasonably strong internal liquidity. An additional positive factor related to liquidity is the firm's ability to sell high-grade commercial paper and the existence of several major bank credit lines.

Operating Performance

This segment of the analysis considers efficiency ratios (turnovers) and profitability ratios. Given the nature of the analysis, the major comparison is relative to the industry. Walgreens turnover ratios were consistently substantially above those of the retail drug store (RDS) industry.

The comparison of profitability from sales was mixed. Operating profit margins were consistently below the industry, but net margins beat the industry performance. The lower operating profit margin is due to the higher growth rate of new stores for Walgreens relative to the competition. The fact is, new stores require 18 to 24 months to reach the firm's "normal" profit rate.

The profit performance related to invested capital was historically strong. The return on total capital (including capitalized leases) for Walgreens was above both the S&P Industrials and the RDS industry in all three years. Walgreens likewise consistently attained higher ROEs than its industry and the market.

EXHIBIT 35-9 Summary of Financial Ratios for Walgreens, S&P Retail Drugstores, S&P Industrial Index, 1998–2000

	2000			1999		
	Walgreens[a]	Drugstores	S&P Industrials	Walgreens	Drugstores	S&P Industrials
Internal Liquidity						
Current ratio	1.54	1.26	1.02	1.67	1.18	1.07
Quick ratio	0.27	0.26	0.72	0.33	0.24	0.75
Cash ratio	0.01	0.04	0.18	0.07	0.05	0.18
Receivables turnover	38.52	29.86	4.70	41.50	28.35	4.59
Average collection period	9.46	12.22	77.66	8.80	12.87	79.56
Working capital/sales	0.06	0.04	0.01	0.07	0.03	0.03
Operation Performance						
Total asset turnover	3.26	2.92	0.84	3.30	2.22	0.88
Inventory turnover (sales)[b]	8.01	6.59	12.09	7.95	6.17	11.17
Working capital turnover	17.01	27.95	30.50	13.74	30.21	33.33
Net fixed asset turnover	7.04	7.98	3.10	7.53	7.58	2.81
Equity turnover	5.49	5.27	2.72	5.63	5.52	3.06
Profitability						
Gross profit margin	27.07	—	—	27.25	—	—
Operating profit margin	5.77	6.18	15.42	5.69	6.82	15.92
Net profit margin	3.66	3.00	6.32	3.50	2.70	6.27
Return on total capital	10.03	7.75	7.10	8.86	7.10	7.17
Return on owner's equity	20.13	16.05	17.14	19.71	14.90	19.19
Financial Risk						
Debt/equity ratio	149.41	7.96	100.87	135.73	46.44	116.98
Long-term debt/long-term capital	59.90	7.38	50.22	57.58	34.11	76.07
Total debt/total capital[c]	67.09	48.38	67.39	65.63	58.70	68.39
Interest coverage	4.53	28.57	6.26	6.82	9.79	6.05
Cash flow/long-term debt	15.37	295.56	38.99	17.34	58.55	51.70
Cash flow/total debt[c]	15.36	25.11	12.77	12.33	14.88	14.57
Growth Analysis[d]						
Retention rate	0.82	0.64	0.69	0.79	0.75	0.65
Return on equity	18.35	17.22	16.22	17.91	14.08	17.46
Total asset turnover	2.99	2.92	0.84	3.02	2.09	0.84
Total assets/equity	1.67	1.94	3.07	1.70	2.49	3.32
Net profit margin	3.66	3.00	6.32	3.50	2.70	6.27
Sustainable growth rate	15.09	11.02	11.19	14.13	10.57	11.4

[a] Ratios for Walgreens are consistent with calculations in this reading.
[b] Computed using sales since cost of sales not available for industry and S&P Industrials.
[c] Total debt equal to total assets minus (common stock plus retained earnings).
[d] Calculated using year-end data.

EXHIBIT 35-9 (continued)

	1998		
	Walgreens	Drugstores	S&P Industrials
Internal Liquidity			
Current ratio	1.66	1.28	1.37
Quick ratio	0.33	0.26	0.93
Cash ratio	0.09	0.05	0.20
Receivables turnover	40.86	31.89	4.43
Average collection period	8.93	11.44	82.41
Working capital/sales	0.07	0.05	0.12
Operation Performance			
Total asset turnover	3.36	2.24	0.91
Inventory turnover (sales)[b]	8.14	5.62	10.31
Working capital turnover	14.68	19.06	8.33
Net fixed asset turnover	7.85	7.57	2.58
Equity turnover	5.86	5.34	3.15
Profitability			
Gross profit margin	27.22	—	—
Operating profit margin	5.46	7.00	16.70
Net profit margin	3.34	2.58	5.14
Return on total capital	8.62	7.11	6.40
Return on owner's equity	19.56	13.77	16.21
Financial Risk			
Debt/equity ratio	140.51	49.25	129.09
Long-term debt/long-term capital	58.42	35.77	76.07
Total debt/total capital[c]	66.21	58.52	62.29
Interest coverage	6.77	8.06	5.10
Cash flow/long-term debt	16.91	46.45	44.16
Cash flow/total debt[c]	12.31	12.41	13.61
Growth Analysis[d]			
Retention rate	0.75	0.71	0.55
Return on equity	17.93	13.12	16.26
Total asset turnover	3.12	2.04	0.85
Total assets/equity	1.72	2.49	3.70
Net profit margin	3.34	2.58	5.14
Sustainable growth rate	13.45	9.32	8.94

[a] Ratios for Walgreens are consistent with calculations in this reading.

[b] Computed using sales since cost of sales not available for industry and S&P Industrials.

[c] Total debt equal to total assets minus (common stock plus retained earnings).

[d] Calculated using year-end data.

Risk Analysis

Walgreens' financial risk ratios, measured in terms of proportion of debt, were consistently much higher than its industry and the market when both deferred taxes and capitalized leases were included as long-term debt for Walgreens, because it was not possible to do a comparable adjustment for the S&P Industrials or the RDS industry. The lack of such an adjustment would have a significant impact on the industry results. Similarly, the financial risk flow ratios for Walgreens were always below the market and its industry. These comparisons indicate that Walgreens has a reasonable amount of financial risk, but it is not a major concern because the firm has very low business risk based upon a high stable growth rate in sales and operating profit. While there are no specific comparative ratios available for both business and external liquidity risk, it is note-worthy that in both cases the prior analysis concluded that Walgreens had very low business and liquidity risk.

Growth Analysis

Walgreens has generally maintained a sustainable growth rate above its industry and the aggregate market based upon both a higher ROE and a consistently higher retention rate.

In sum, Walgreens has adequate liquidity; a good operating record, including a consistent growth record that implies low business risk; "reasonable" financial risk, even when you consider the leases on stores; and above-average growth performance. Your success as an investor depends on how well you use these historical numbers to derive meaningful *estimates* of future performance for use in a valuation model. Everybody is generally aware of the valuation models, so it is the individual who can provide the best *estimates* of relevant valuation variables who will experience superior risk-adjusted performance.

10 ANALYSIS OF NON-U.S. FINANCIAL STATEMENTS

As noted previously, your portfolio should encompass other economies and markets, numerous global industries, and many foreign firms in these global industries. You should recognize, however, that non-U.S. financial statements will differ widely from those in this reading and be different from what you will see in a typical accounting course because accounting conventions differ substantially among countries.

11 THE QUALITY OF FINANCIAL STATEMENTS

Analysts sometimes speak of the quality of a firm's earnings, or the quality of a firm's balance sheet. In general, **quality financial statements** are a good reflection of reality; accounting tricks and one-time charges are not used to make the firm appear stronger than it really is. Some factors that lead to lower-quality financial statements were mentioned previously when we discussed ratio analysis. Other quality influences are discussed in the following sections.[20]

---

[20] For additional discussion, see K. G. Palepu, Victor L. Bernard, and P. M. Healy, *Business Analysis and Valuation* (Cincinnati, Ohio: South-Western Publishing Co., 1996), Chapter 3.

Balance Sheet

A high-quality balance sheet typically has a conservative use of debt and leverage. Therefore, the potential of experiencing financial distress resulting from the need to service debt is quite low. Little use of debt also implies the firm has unused borrowing capacity; should an attractive investment opportunity arise, the firm can draw on that unused capacity to invest wisely for the shareholders' benefit.

A quality balance sheet contains assets with a market value greater than their book value. The capacity of management and the existence of intangible assets, such as goodwill, trademarks, or patents, will make the market value of the firm's assets exceed their book values. In general, as a result of inflation and historical cost accounting, we might expect the market value of assets to exceed their book values. Some situations in which the opposite may occur include the use of outdated, technologically inferior assets; unwanted or out-of-fashion inventory; and the presence of nonperforming assets on the firm's books (an example would be a bank that has not written off nonperforming loans).

The presence of off-balance-sheet liabilities also harms the quality of a balance sheet. Such liabilities may include joint ventures and loan commitments or guarantees to subsidiaries.[21]

Income Statement

High-quality earnings are *repeatable* earnings. For example, they arise from sales to customers who are expected to do repeat business with the firm and from costs that are not artificially low as a result of unusual or temporary price reductions. One-time and nonrecurring items, such as accounting changes, mergers, and asset sales, should be ignored when examining earnings. Unexpected exchange rate fluctuations that raise revenues or reduce costs should also be viewed as nonrecurring.

High-quality earnings result from the use of conservative accounting principles that do not result in overstated revenues and understated costs. The closer the earnings are to cash, the higher the quality of the income statement. Suppose a firm sells furniture "on time" by allowing customers to make monthly payments. A higher-quality income statement will recognize revenue using the "installment" principle; that is, as the cash is collected each month, in turn, annual sales will reflect only the cash collected from sales during the year. A lower-quality income statement will recognize 100 percent of the revenue from a sale at the time of sale, even though payments may stretch well into the next year.[22]

Footnotes

A word to the wise—READ THE FOOTNOTES! The purpose of the footnotes (that have come to include three or more pages in most annual reports) is to provide information on how the firm handles balance sheet and income items. While the footnotes may not reveal everything you should know (e.g., Enron), if you do not read them you cannot hope to be informed.

---

[21] For detailed analysis of these items, see Clyde P. Stickney, *Financial Reporting and Statement Analysis*, 3d ed. (Fort Worth, Tex.: Dryden, 1996), Chapter 6.

[22] For detailed analysis of income items, see Stickney, *Financial Reporting and Statement Analysis*, 3d ed., Chapter 5.

12

THE VALUE OF FINANCIAL STATEMENT ANALYSIS

Financial statements, by their nature, are backward-looking. They report the firm's assets, liabilities, and equity as of a certain (past) date; they report a firm's revenues, expenses, or cash flows over some (past) time period. An efficient capital market will have already incorporated this past information into security prices; so it may seem, at first glance, that the analysis of a firm's financial statements and ratios is a waste of the analyst's time.

The fact is, the opposite is true. Analysis of financial statements allows the analyst to gain knowledge of a firm's operating and financial strategy and structure. This, in turn, assists the analyst in determining the effect of *future* events on the firm's cash flows. Likely future scenarios can be analyzed and a knowledge of the firm's operating and financial leverage can help the analyst gauge the risk and expected cash flows of the firm. Combining knowledge of the firm's strategy, operating and financial leverage, and possible macro- and microeconomic scenarios is necessary to determine an appropriate market price for the firm's stock. Combining what is known about the firm, based on the analysis of historical data, with potential future scenarios allows analysts to evaluate the risks facing the firm and then to develop an expected return forecast based on these risks. The final outcome of the process, as future readings will detail, is a determination of the firm's current value based on expected cash flows and an appropriate discount rate that is compared to the firm's security price. The point is, the detailed analysis of the historical results will help you estimate the required discount rate and the expected cash flows and, thus, derive a superior valuation of the firm.

13

SPECIFIC USES OF FINANCIAL RATIOS

We have discussed the role of financial ratios in measuring firm performance and risk. Financial ratios have been used in four major areas in investments: (1) stock valuation, (2) the identification of internal corporate variables that affect a stock's systematic risk (beta), (3) assigning credit quality ratings on bonds, and (4) predicting insolvency (bankruptcy) of firms. In this section, we discuss how ratios have been used in each of these four areas and the specific ratios found to be most useful.

Stock Valuation Models

As will be discussed in Reading 55, most valuation models attempt to derive a value based upon one of several cash flow models or relative valuation ratios for a stock. As we will discuss, all the valuation models are influenced by the expected growth rate of earnings, cash flows, or dividends and the required rate of return on the stock. Clearly, financial ratios can help in estimating these critical inputs. The estimate of the growth rate for earnings, cash flow, or dividends employs the ratios discussed in the potential growth rate section—the retention rate and the return on investments (either equity or total assets).

When estimating the required rate of return on an investment (i.e., either the cost of equity, *k,* or the weighted average cost of capital, WACC), you will recall from Chapter 1 that these estimates depend on the risk premium for the security, which is a function of business risk, financial risk, and liquidity risk. Business risk typically is measured in terms of earnings variability; financial risk is identified by either the debt proportion ratios or the earnings or cash flow ratios;

insights regarding a stock's liquidity risk can be derived from the external liquidity measures discussed.

The typical empirical valuation model has examined a cross section of companies and has used a multivariate statistical model that relates one of the relative valuation ratios (i.e., P/E; P/sales; P/book value) for the sample firms to some of the following corporate variables (the averages generally consider the past 5 or 10 years):

Financial Ratios

1. Average debt/equity
2. Average interest coverage
3. Average dividend payout
4. Average return on equity
5. Average retention rate
6. Average market price to book value
7. Average market price to cash flow
8. Average market price to sales

Variability Measures

1. Coefficient of variation of operating earnings
2. Coefficient of variation of sales
3. Coefficient of variation of net income
4. Systematic risk (beta)

Nonratio Variables

1. Average growth rate of sales and earnings
2. Average growth rate of cash flow

Estimating Systematic Risk

As we discuss in Reading 79, the capital asset pricing model (CAPM) asserts that the relevant risk variable for an asset should be its systematic risk, which is its beta coefficient related to the market portfolio of all risky assets. In efficient markets, a relationship should exist between internal corporate risk variables and market-determined risk variables, such as beta. Numerous studies have tested the relationship between a stock's systematic risk (beta) and the firm's internal corporate variables intended to reflect business risk and financial risk. Some of the significant variables (usually five-year averages) included were:

Financial Ratios

1. Dividend payouts
2. Total debt/total assets
3. Cash flow/total debt
4. Fixed charge (interest) coverage
5. Working capital/total assets
6. Current ratio

Variability Measures

1. Variance of operating earnings
2. Coefficient of variation of operating earnings
3. Coefficient of variation of operating profit margins
4. Operating earnings beta (company earnings related to aggregate earnings)

Nonratio Variables

1. Asset size of firm
2. Market value of stock outstanding

Estimating the Credit Ratings on Bonds

As will be discussed in the initial bond reading, three financial service firms assign credit ratings to bonds on the basis of the issuing company's ability to meet all its obligations related to the bond. An AAA or Aaa rating indicates high quality and almost no chance of default, whereas a C rating indicates the bond is already in default. Studies have used financial ratios to predict the credit rating to be assigned to a bond. The major financial variables considered in these studies (again, typically five-year averages) were as follows:

Financial Ratios

1. Long-term debt/total assets
2. Total debt/total capital
3. Net income plus depreciation (cash flow)/long-term senior debt
4. Cash flow/total debt
5. Earnings before interest and taxes (EBIT)/interest expense (fixed charge coverage)
6. Cash flow from operations plus interest/interest expense
7. Market value of stock/par value of bonds
8. Net operating profit/sales
9. Net income/owners' equity (ROE)
10. Net income plus interest/total assets
11. Working capital/sales
12. Sales/owners' equity (equity turnover)

Variability Measures

1. Coefficient of variation (CV) of sales
2. Coefficient of variation of operating earnings
3. Coefficient of variation of net earnings
4. Coefficient of variation of return on assets

Nonratio Variables

1. Subordination of the bond issue
2. Size of the firm (total assets)
3. Issue size
4. Par value of all publicly traded bonds of the firm

Predicting Insolvency (Bankruptcy)

Analysts have always been interested in using financial ratios to identify which firms might default on a loan or declare bankruptcy. Several studies have attempted to identify a set of ratios for this purpose. The typical study examines a sample of firms that have declared bankruptcy against a matched sample of firms in the same industry and of comparable size that have not failed. The analysis involves examining a number of financial ratios or cash flow variables expected to reflect declining liquidity for several years (usually five years) prior to the declaration of bankruptcy. The goal is to determine which ratios or set of ratios provides the best predictions of bankruptcy—that is, correctly predicts that the firm will be in the bankrupt or non-bankrupt group. The models have typically been able to properly classify more than 80 percent of the firms one year prior to failure, and some achieve high classification results three to five years before failure. The financial ratios typically included in successful models were:[23]

Financial Ratios

1. Cash flow/total debt
2. Cash flow/long-term debt
3. Sales/total assets*
4. Net income/total assets
5. EBIT/total assets*
6. Total debt/total assets
7. Market value of stock/book value of debt*
8. Working capital/total assets*
9. Retained earnings/total assets*
10. Current ratio
11. Cash/current liabilities
12. Working capital/sales

Limitations of Financial Ratios

We must reinforce the earlier point that you should always consider *relative* financial ratios. In addition, you should be aware of other questions and limitations of financial ratios:

1. Are alternative firms' accounting treatments comparable? As you know from prior accounting courses, there are several generally accepted methods of treating various accounting items, and the alternatives can cause a difference in results for the same event. Therefore, you should check on the accounting treatment of significant items and adjust the values for major differences. This becomes a critical consideration when dealing with non-U.S. firms.
2. How homogeneous is the firm? Many companies have several divisions that operate in different industries. This may make it difficult to derive comparable industry ratios.

---

[23] In addition to the several studies that have used financial ratios to predict bond ratings and failures, other studies have used cash flow variables or a combination of financial ratios and cash flow variables for these predictions, and the results have been quite successful. The five ratios designated by an asterisk (*) are the ratios used in the well-known Altman Z-score model advocated by Edward I. Altman, "Financial Ratios, Discriminant Analysis and the Prediction of Corporate Bankruptcy," *Journal of Finance* 23, no. 4 (September 1968): 589–609.

3. Are the implied results consistent? It is important to develop a total profile of the firm and not depend on only one set of ratios (for example, internal liquidity ratios). As an example, a firm may be having short-term liquidity problems but be very profitable, and the profitability will eventually alleviate the short-run liquidity problems.
4. Is the ratio within a reasonable range for the industry? As noted on several occasions, you typically want to consider a *range* of appropriate values for the ratio because a value that is either too high or too low for the industry can be a cause for concern.

SUMMARY

- The overall purpose of financial statement analysis is to help you make decisions on investing in a firm's bonds or stocks. Financial ratios should be examined relative to the economy, the firm's industry, the firm's main competitors, and the firm's past relative ratios.
- The specific ratios can be divided into four categories, depending on the purpose of the analysis: internal liquidity, operating performance, risk analysis, and growth analysis.
- When analyzing the financial statements for non-U.S. firms, you must consider differences in format and in accounting principles that cause different values for specific ratios in alternative countries.
- An important consideration for domestic or international financial statements is to READ THE FOOTNOTES to ensure that you understand how the GAAP was applied and the accounting philosophy of the firm.
- Four major uses of financial ratios are (1) stock valuations, (2) the identification of variables affecting a stock's systematic risk (beta), (3) assigning credit quality ratings on bonds, and (4) predicting insolvency (bankruptcy).
- A final caveat: You can envision a large number of potential financial ratios through which to examine almost every possible relationship. The trick is not to come up with more ratios but to attempt to limit the number of ratios so you can examine them in a meaningful way. This entails an analysis of the ratios over time relative to the economy, the industry, or the past. Any additional effort should be spent on deriving better comparisons for a limited number of ratios that provide insights into the questions of interest to you (for example, the firm's future operating performance or its business and financial risk).

QUESTIONS

1. Why do analysts use financial ratios rather than the absolute numbers? Give an example.
2. How might a jewelry store and a grocery store differ in terms of asset turnover and profit margin? Would you expect their return on total assets to differ assuming equal business risk? Discuss.
3. Why is the analysis of growth potential important to the common stockholder? Why is it important to the debt investor?

THE INTERNET

Investments Online

Many publicly traded companies have websites which, among other pieces of information, contain financial information. Sometimes complete copies of the firm's annual report and SEC filings are on their home page. Since the focus of this reading has been Walgreen's financial statements, here are some relevant sites:

http://www.walgreens.com Walgreen's home page, with financial information available through links from this page. At least three of Walgreen's competitors have websites featuring financial information. These include:

http://www.cvs.com The home page for CVS Pharmacy.

http://www.rlteald.com The Rite Aid Corporation's home page.

http://www.longs.com The website for Longs Drug Stores.

http://www.duanereade.com Duane Reade's home page.

Commercially oriented and government-sponsored databases are also available through the Web:

http://www.sec.gov The Web home page for the Securities and Exchange Commission allows entrance into the SEC's EDGAR (electronic data gathering, analysis, and retrieval) database. Most firm's SEC filings are accessible through EDGAR, including filings for executive compensation, 10-K, and 10-Q forms.

http://www.hoovers.com Hoovers Online is a commercial source of company-specific information, including financial statements and stock performance. Some data are available for free, including a company profile, news, stock price and chart of recent stock price performance. It contains links to a number of sources, including the firm's annual report, SEC filings, and earnings per share estimates by First Call.

http://www.dnb.com Dun & Bradstreet is a well-known gatherer of financial information. Corporations use its business credit reporting services. D&B publishes industry average financial ratios that are useful in equity and fixed income analysis.

PROBLEMS

1. Three companies have the following results during the recent period.

	K	L	M
Net profit margin	.04	.06	.10
Total asset turnover	2.20	2.00	1.40
Total assets/equity	2.40	2.20	1.50

a. Derive for each its return on equity based on the three DuPont components.

b. Given the following earnings and dividends, compute the estimated sustainable growth rate for each firm.

	K	L	M
Earnings/share	2.75	3.00	4.50
Dividends/share	1.25	1.00	1.00

2. Given the following balance sheet, fill in the ratio values for 2003 and discuss how these results compare with both the industry average and Eddies' past performance.

Eddies Enterprises Consolidated Balance Sheet: Years Ended December 31, 2002 and 2003

Assets (Dollars in Thousands)

	2003	2002
Cash	$ 100	$ 90
Receivables	220	170
Inventories	330	230
Total current assets	650	490
Property, plant, and equipment	1,850	1,650
Depreciation	350	225
Net properties	1,500	1,425
Intangibles	150	150
Total assets	2,300	2,065

Liabilities and Shareholders' Equity

	2003	2002
Accounts payable	$ 85	$ 105
Short-term bank notes	125	110
Current portion of long-term debt	75	—
Accruals	65	85
Total current liabilities	350	300
Long-term debt	625	540
Deferred taxes	100	80
Preferred stock (10%, $100 par)	150	150
Common stock ($2 par, 100,000 issued)	200	200
Additional paid-in capital	325	325
Retained earnings	550	470
Common shareholders' equity	1,075	995
Total liabilities and shareholders' equity	2,300	2,065

Eddies Enterprises Consolidated Statement of Income: Years Ended December 31, 2002 and 2003

(Dollars in Thousands)		
	2003	**2002**
Net sales	$3,500	$2,990
Cost of goods sold	2,135	1,823
Selling, general, and administrative expenses	1,107	974
Operating profit	258	193
Net interest expense	62	54
Income from operations	195	139
Income taxes	66	47
Net income	129	91
Preferred dividends	15	15
Net income available for common shares	114	76
Dividends declared	40	30

	Eddies (2003)	**Eddies' Average**	**Industry Average**
Current ratio	________	2.00	2.20
Quick ratio	________	1.00	1.10
Receivable turnover	________	18.00	18.00
Average collection period	________	20.00	21.00
Total asset turnover	________	1.50	1.40
Inventory turnover	________	11.00	12.50
Fixed-asset turnover	________	2.50	2.40
Equity turnover	________	3.20	3.00
Gross profit margin	________	.40	.35
Operating profit margin	________	8.00	7.50
Return on capital	________	.107	.120
Return on equity	________	.118	.126
Return on common equity	________	.128	.135
Debt/equity ratio	________	.60	.50
Debt/total capital ratio	________	.40	.37
Interest coverage	________	4.00	4.50
Fixed charge coverage	________	3.00	4.00
Cash flow/long-term debt	________	.40	.45
Cash flow/total debt	________	.25	.30
Retention rate	________	.35	.40

3. *CFA Examination Level I (adapted)*

[Question 3 is composed of two parts, for a total of 20 minutes.]

The DuPont formula defines the net return on shareholders' equity as a function of the following components:

- Operating margin
- Asset turnover
- Interest burden
- Financial leverage
- Income tax rate

Using *only* the data in the following table:

a. Calculate *each* of the *five* components listed for 1999 *and* 2003, and calculate the return on equity (ROE) for 1999 *and* 2003, using all of the *five* components. Show calculations. [15 minutes]

b. Briefly discuss the impact of the changes in asset turnover *and* financial leverage on the change in ROE from 1999 to 2003. [5 minutes]

	1999	2003
Income Statement Data		
Revenues	$542	$979
Operating income	38	76
Depreciation and amortization	3	9
Interest expense	3	0
Pretax income	32	67
Income taxes	13	37
Net income after tax	19	30
Balance Sheet Data		
Fixed assets	$ 41	$ 70
Total assets	245	291
Working capital	123	157
Total debt	16	0
Total shareholders' equity	159	220

DILUTIVE SECURITIES AND EARNINGS PER SHARE

READING 36

LEARNING OUTCOMES

The candidate should be able to:

a. differentiate between simple and complex capital structures for purposes of calculating earnings per share (EPS), describe the components of EPS, and calculate a company's EPS in a simple capital structure;

b. calculate a company's weighted average number of shares outstanding;

c. describe stock dividends and stock splits, and determine the effect of each on a company's weighted average number of shares outstanding;

d. distinguish between dilutive and antidilutive securities and calculate a company's basic and diluted EPS in a complex capital structure, and describe and determine the effects of convertible securities, options, and warrants on a company's EPS;

e. compare and contrast the requirements for EPS reporting in simple versus complex capital structures.

COMPUTING EARNINGS PER SHARE 1

Earnings per share data are frequently reported in the financial press and are widely used by stockholders and potential investors in evaluating the profitability of a company. **Earnings per share (EPS)** indicates the income earned by each share of common stock. Thus, **earnings per share is reported only for common stock.** For example, if Oscar Co. has net income of $300,000 and a weighted average of 100,000 shares of common stock outstanding for the year, earnings per share is $3 ($300,000 ÷ 100,000).

Because of the importance of earnings per share information, most companies are required to report this information on the face of the income statement.[1] The exception is nonpublic companies: because of cost-benefit considerations they do not have to report this information.[2] Generally, earnings per share information is reported below net income in the income statement. For Oscar Co. the presentation would be as given in Illustration 36-1.

ILLUSTRATION 36-1 Income Statement Presentation of EPS

Net income	$300,000
Earnings per share	$3.00

International Insight
In many nations (e.g., Switzerland, Sweden, Spain, and Mexico) there is no legal requirement to disclose earnings per share.

When the income statement contains intermediate components of income, earnings per share should be disclosed for each component. Illustration 36-2 shows the income statement presentation of EPS components.

ILLUSTRATION 36-2 Income Statement Presentation of EPS Components

Earnings per share:	
Income from continuing operations	$4.00
Loss from discontinued operations, net of tax	0.60
Income before extraordinary item and cumulative effect of change in accounting principle	3.40
Extraordinary gain, net of tax	1.00
Cumulative effect of change in accounting principle, net of tax	0.50
Net income	$4.90

These disclosures enable the user of the financial statements to recognize the effects of income from continuing operations on EPS, as distinguished from income or loss from irregular items.[3]

[1] "Earnings per Share," *Statement of Financial Accounting Standards No. 128* (Norwalk, Conn.: FASB, 1997). For an article on the usefulness of EPS reported data and the application of the qualitative characteristics of accounting information to EPS data, see Lola W. Dudley, "A Critical Look at EPS," *Journal of Accountancy* (August 1985), pp. 102–11.

[2] A nonpublic enterprise is an enterprise (1) whose debt or equity securities are not traded in a public market on a foreign or domestic stock exchange or in the over-the-counter market (including securities quoted locally or regionally) or (2) that is not required to file financial statements with the SEC. An enterprise is no longer considered a nonpublic enterprise when its financial statements are issued in preparation for the sale of any class of securities in a public market.

[3] Per share amounts for discontinued operations, an extraordinary item, or the cumulative effect of an accounting change in a period should be presented either on the face of the income statement or in the notes to the financial statements.

EARNINGS PER SHARE—SIMPLE CAPITAL STRUCTURE

2

A corporation's capital structure is considered **simple** if it consists only of common stock or includes no **potential common stock** that upon conversion or exercise could dilute earnings per common share. (A capital structure is considered **complex** if it includes securities that could have a dilutive effect on earnings per common share.) The computation of earnings per share for a simple capital structure involves two items (other than net income)—preferred stock dividends and weighted average number of shares outstanding.

Preferred Stock Dividends

As indicated earlier, earnings per share relates to earnings per common share. When a company has both common and preferred stock outstanding, **the current-year preferred stock dividend is subtracted from net income to arrive at income available to common stockholders**. The formula for computing earnings per share is given in Illustration 36-3.

ILLUSTRATION 36-3 Formula for Computing Earnings per Share

$$\text{Earnings per Share} = \frac{\text{Net Income} - \text{Preferred Dividends}}{\text{Weighted Average Number of Shares Outstanding}}$$

In reporting earnings per share information, dividends on preferred stock should be subtracted from each of the intermediate components of income (income from continuing operations and income before extraordinary items) and finally from net income to arrive at income available to common stockholders. If dividends on preferred stock are declared and a net loss occurs, **the preferred dividend is added to the loss** in order to compute the loss per share. If the preferred stock is cumulative and the dividend is not declared in the current year, **an amount equal to the dividend that should have been declared for the current year only** should be subtracted from net income or added to the net loss. Dividends in arrears for previous years should have been included in the previous years' computations.

Weighted Average Number of Shares Outstanding

In all computations of earnings per share, the **weighted average number of shares outstanding** during the period constitutes the basis for the per share amounts reported. Shares issued or purchased during the period affect the amount outstanding and must be **weighted by the fraction of the period they are outstanding**. The rationale for this approach is to find the equivalent number of **whole shares** outstanding for the year.

To illustrate, assume that Stallone Inc. has the following changes in its common stock shares outstanding for the period (Illustration 36-4).

ILLUSTRATION 36-4 Shares Outstanding, Ending Balance Stallone Inc.

Date	Share Changes	Shares Outstanding
January 1	Beginning balance	90,000
April 1	Issued 30,000 shares for cash	30,000
		120,000
July 1	Purchased 39,000 shares	39,000
		81,000
November 1	Issued 60,000 shares for cash	60,000
December 31	Ending balance	141,000

To compute the weighted average number of shares outstanding, the following computation is made (Illustration 36-5).

ILLUSTRATION 36-5 Weighted Average Number of Shares Outstanding

Dates Outstanding	(A) Shares Outstanding	(B) Fraction of Year	(C) Weighted Shares (A × B)
Jan. 1–Apr. 1	90,000	3/12	22,500
Apr. 1–July 1	120,000	3/12	30,000
July 1–Nov. 1	81,000	4/12	27,000
Nov. 1–Dec. 31	141,000	2/12	23,500
Weighted average number of shares outstanding			103,000

International Insight
Where EPS disclosure is prevalent, it is usually based on the weighted average of shares outstanding.

As illustrated, 90,000 shares were outstanding for 3 months, which translates to 22,500 whole shares for the entire year. Because additional shares were issued on April 1, the shares outstanding change, and these shares must be weighted for the time outstanding. When 39,000 shares were purchased on July 1, the shares outstanding were reduced, and again a new computation must be made to determine the proper weighted shares outstanding.

Stock Dividends and Stock Splits

When **stock dividends** or **stock splits** occur, computation of the weighted average number of shares requires restatement of the shares outstanding before the stock dividend or split. For example, assume that a corporation had 100,000 shares outstanding on January 1 and issued a 25 percent stock dividend on June 30. For purposes of computing a weighted average for the current year, the additional 25,000 shares outstanding as a result of the stock dividend are assumed to have been **outstanding since the beginning of the year**. Thus the weighted average for the year would be 125,000 shares.

The issuance of a stock dividend or stock split is restated, but the issuance or repurchase of stock for cash is not. Why? The reason is that stock splits and stock dividends do not increase or decrease the net assets of the enterprise; only additional shares of stock are issued, and therefore the weighted average shares must be restated. By restating, valid comparisons of earnings per share can be made between periods before and after the stock split or stock dividend. Conversely, the issuance or purchase of stock for cash changes the amount of net assets. As a result, the company either earns more or less in the future as a result of this change in net assets. Stated another way, **a stock dividend or split does not change the shareholders' total investment**—it only increases (unless it is a reverse stock split) the number of common shares representing this investment.

To illustrate how a stock dividend affects the computation of the weighted average number of shares outstanding, assume that Rambo Company has the following changes in its common stock shares during the year (Illustration 36-6).

ILLUSTRATION 36-6 Shares Outstanding, Ending Balance Rambo Company

Date	Share Changes	Shares Outstanding
January 1	Beginning balance	100,000
March 1	Issued 20,000 shares for cash	20,000
		120,000
June 1	60,000 additional shares (50% stock dividend)	60,000
		180,000
November 1	Issued 30,000 shares for cash	30,000
December 31	Ending balance	210,000

The computation of the weighted average number of shares outstanding would be as follows (Illustration 36-7).

ILLUSTRATION 36-7 Weighted Average Number of Shares Outstanding—Stock Issue and Stock Dividend

Dates Outstanding	(A) Shares Outstanding	(B) Restatement	(C) Fraction of Year	(D) Weighted Shares (A × B × C)
Jan. 1–Mar. 1	100,000	1.50	2/12	25,000
Mar. 1–June 1	120,000	1.50	3/12	45,000
June 1–Nov. 1	180,000		5/12	75,000
Nov. 1–Dec. 31	210,000		2/12	35,000
Weighted average number of shares outstanding				180,000

The shares outstanding prior to the stock dividend must be restated. The shares outstanding from January 1 to June 1 are adjusted for the stock dividend, so that these shares are stated on the same basis as shares issued subsequent to the stock dividend. Shares issued after the stock dividend do not have to be restated because they are on the new basis. The stock dividend simply restates existing shares. **The same type of treatment applies to a stock split.**

If a stock dividend or stock split occurs after the end of the year, but before the financial statements are issued, the weighted average number of shares outstanding for the year (and for any other years presented in comparative form) must be restated. For example, assume that Hendricks Company computes its weighted average number of shares to be 100,000 for the year ended December 31, 2004. On January 15, 2005, before the financial statements are issued, the company splits its stock 3 for 1. In this case, the weighted average number of shares used in computing earnings per share for 2004 would be 300,000 shares. If earnings per share information for 2003 is provided as comparative information, it also must be adjusted for the stock split.

Comprehensive Illustration

Sylvester Corporation has income before extraordinary item of $580,000 and an extraordinary gain, net of tax, of $240,000. In addition, it has declared preferred dividends of $1 per share on 100,000 shares of preferred stock outstanding. Sylvester Corporation also has the following changes in its common stock shares outstanding during 2004 (Illustration 36-8).

ILLUSTRATION 36-8 Shares Outstanding, Ending Balance Sylvester Corp.

Dates	Share Changes	Shares Outstanding
January 1	Beginning balance	180,000
May 1	Purchased 30,000 treasury shares	30,000
		150,000
July 1	300,000 additional shares (3-for-1 stock split)	300,000
		450,000
December 31	Issued 50,000 shares for cash	50,000
December 31	Ending balance	500,000

To compute the earnings per share information, the weighted average number of shares outstanding is determined in Illustration 36-9.

ILLUSTRATION 36-9 Weighted Average Number of Shares Outstanding

Dates Outstanding	(A) Shares Outstanding	(B) Restatement	(C) Fraction of Year	(D) Weighted Shares (A × B × C)
Jan. 1–May 1	180,000	3	4/12	180,000
May 1–Dec. 31	150,000	3	8/12	300,000
Weighted average number of shares outstanding				480,000

In computing the weighted average number of shares, the shares sold on December 31, 2004, are ignored because they have not been outstanding during the year. The weighted average number of shares is then divided into income before extraordinary item and net income to determine earnings per share (Illustration 36-10). Sylvester Corporation's preferred dividends of $100,000 are subtracted from income before extraordinary item ($580,000) to arrive at income before extraordinary item available to common stockholders of $480,000 ($580,000 − $100,000).

Deducting the preferred dividends from the income before extraordinary item has the effect of also reducing net income without affecting the amount of the extraordinary item. The final amount is referred to as **income available to common stockholders**.

ILLUSTRATION 36-10 Computation of Income Available to Common Stockholders

	(A) Income Information	(B) Weighted Shares	(C) Earnings per Share (A ÷ B)
Income before extraordinary item available to common stockholders	$480,000*	480,000	$1.00
Extraordinary gain (net of tax)	240,000	480,000	0.50
Income available to common stockholders	$720,000	480,000	$1.50

* $580,000 − $100,000

Disclosure of the per share amount for the extraordinary item (net of tax) must be reported either on the face of the income statement or in the notes to the financial statements. Income and per share information reported on the face of the income statement is given in Illustration 36-11.

ILLUSTRATION 36-11 Earnings per Share, with Extraordinary Item

Income before extraordinary item	$580,000
Extraordinary gain, net of tax	240,000
Net income	$820,000
Earnings per share:	
Income before extraordinary item	$1.00
Extraordinary item, net of tax	0.50
Net income	$1.50

3 EARNINGS PER SHARE—COMPLEX CAPITAL STRUCTURE

One problem with a **basic EPS** computation is that it fails to recognize the potentially dilutive impact on outstanding stock when a corporation has dilutive securities in its capital structure. **Dilutive securities** are securities that can be converted to common stock and that upon conversion or exercise reduce—dilute—earnings per share. Dilutive securities present a serious problem because conversion or exercise often has an adverse effect on earnings per share. This adverse effect can be significant and, more important, unexpected, unless financial statements call attention to the potential dilutive effect in some manner.[4]

A complex capital structure exists when a corporation has convertible securities, options, warrants or other rights that upon conversion or exercise could dilute earnings per share. Therefore when a company has a complex capital structure, both a basic and diluted earnings per share are generally reported.

The computation of **diluted EPS** is similar to the computation of basic EPS. The difference is that diluted EPS includes the effect of all dilutive potential common shares that were outstanding during the period. The formula in Illustration 36-12 shows the relationship between basic EPS and diluted EPS.

International Insight
The provisions in U.S. GAAP are substantially the same as those in International Accounting Standard No. 33, *Earnings per Share*, issued by the IASB.

Note that companies with complex capital structures will not report diluted EPS if the securities in their capital structure are antidilutive. **Antidilutive securities** are securities that upon conversion or exercise increase earnings per share (or reduce the loss per share). The purpose of the dual presentation is to inform financial statement users of situations that will likely occur and to provide "worst case" dilutive situations. If the securities are antidilutive, the likelihood of conversion or exercise is considered remote. Thus, companies that have only antidilutive securities are not permitted to increase earnings per share and are required to report only the basic EPS number.

ILLUSTRATION 36-12 Relation between Basic and Diluted EPS

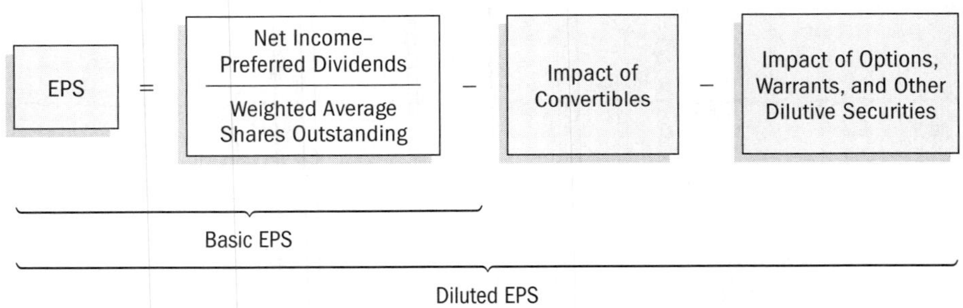

The computation of basic EPS was illustrated in the prior section. The discussion in the following sections addresses the effects of convertible and other dilutive securities on EPS calculations.

Diluted EPS—Convertible Securities

At conversion, convertible securities are exchanged for common stock. The method used to measure the dilutive effects of potential conversion on EPS is called the **if-converted method**. The if-converted method for a convertible bond assumes the following: (1) the conversion of the convertible securities at the beginning of the period (or at the time of issuance of the security, if issued during the period), and (2) the elimination of related interest, net of tax. Thus the **denominator**—the weighted average number of shares outstanding—is increased by the additional shares assumed issued. The **numerator**—net income—is increased by the amount of interest expense, net of tax associated with those convertible securities.

[4] Issuance of these types of securities is typical in mergers and compensation plans.

WHAT DO THE NUMBERS MEAN?

The Source of My Dilution

What is the source of dilutive securities, which give rise to complex capital structures? Merger activity is a major source.

Typical mergers in the 1990s were combinations of information, entertainment, or financial (banking) companies. For example, **Bell Atlantic Corp.** and **Nynex Corp.** combined in a $22.7 billion deal, **Time** acquired **Warner Communications** for $10.1 billion, and **Walt Disney Co.** purchased **Capital Cities/ABC, Inc.** Even larger were the mergers of **Nations Bank** and **BankAmerica** ($62 billion), and **Bell Atlantic** and **GTE** ($71 billion) in 1998.

One consequence of heavy merger activity is an increase in the use of securities such as convertible bonds, convertible preferred stocks, stock warrants, and contingent shares to structure these deals. Although not common stock in form, these securities enable their holders to obtain common stock upon exercise or conversion.

Although merger and acquisition activity has declined in the recent bear market, the presence of dilutive securities on corporate balance sheets is still very prevalent. As discussed in the prior section, the use of stock option plans, which also are dilutive in nature, is increasing. In addition, companies that have difficulty selling common stock at a reasonable price often use some form of convertible preferred or bond to help finance their operations.

Source: Farrell Kramer, "Mergers Have Been in Fashion in 1996, With Seven Big Ones," *St. Louis Post-Dispatch* (December 16, 1996), p. A7; and Geoffrey Colvin, "The Year of the Mega Merger," *Fortune* (January 11, 1999), p. 62.

Comprehensive Illustration—If-Converted Method

As an example, Marshy Field Corporation has net income for the year of $210,000 and a weighted average number of common shares outstanding during the period of 100,000 shares. The basic earnings per share is, therefore, $2.10 ($210,000 ÷ 100,000). The company has two convertible debenture bond issues outstanding. One is a 6 percent issue sold at 100 (total $1,000,000) in a prior year and convertible into 20,000 common shares. The other is a 10 percent issue sold at 100 (total $1,000,000) on April 1 of the current year and convertible into 32,000 common shares. The tax rate is 40 percent.

As shown in Illustration 36-13, to determine the numerator, we add back the interest on the if-converted securities, less the related tax effect. Because the if-converted method assumes conversion as of the beginning of the year, no interest on the convertibles is assumed to be paid during the year. The interest on the 6 percent convertibles is $60,000 for the year ($1,000,000 × 6%). The increased tax expense is $24,000 ($60,000 × .40), and the interest added back net of taxes is **$36,000** [$60,000 − $24,000 or simply $60,000 × (1 − .40)].

Because 10 percent convertibles are issued subsequent to the beginning of the year, the shares assumed to have been issued on that date, April 1, are weighted as outstanding from April 1 to the end of the year. In addition, the interest adjustment to the numerator for these bonds would reflect the interest for only 9 months. Thus the interest added back on the 10 percent convertible would be **$45,000** [$1,000,000 × 10% × 9/12 year × (1 − .40)]. The computation of earnings (the numerator) for diluted earnings per share is shown in Illustration 36-13.

The computation for shares adjusted for dilutive securities (the denominator) for diluted earnings per share is shown in Illustration 36-14.

Marshy Field would then report earnings per share based on a dual presentation on the face of the income statement; basic and diluted earnings per share are reported.[5] The presentation is shown in Illustration 36-15.

[5] Conversion of bonds is dilutive because EPS with conversion ($2.02) is less than basic EPS ($2.10).

ILLUSTRATION 36-13 Computation of Adjusted Net Income

Net income for the year	$210,000
Add: Adjustment for interest (net of tax)	
6% debentures ($60,000 × [1 − .40])	36,000
10% debentures ($100,000 × 9/12 × [1 − .40])	45,000
Adjusted net income	$291,000

ILLUSTRATION 36-14 Computation of Weighted Average Number of Shares

Weighted average number of shares outstanding	100,000
Add: Shares assumed to be issued:	
6% debentures (as of beginning of year)	20,000
10% debentures (as of date of issue, April 1; 9/12 × 32,000)	24,000
Weighted average number of shares adjusted for dilutive securities	144,000

ILLUSTRATION 36-15 Earnings per Share Disclosure

Net income for the year	$210,000
Earnings per Share (Note X)	
Basic earnings per share ($210,000 ÷ 100,000)	$2.10
Diluted earnings per share ($291,000 ÷ 144,000)	$2.02

Other Factors

The example above assumed that Marshy Field's bonds were sold at the face amount. If the bonds are sold at a premium or discount, interest expense must be adjusted each period to account for this occurrence. Therefore, the amount of interest expense added back, net of tax, to net income is the interest expense reported on the income statement, not the interest paid in cash during the period.

In addition, the conversion rate on a dilutive security may change over the period during which the dilutive security is outstanding. In this situation, for the diluted EPS computation, the **most advantageous conversion rate available to the holder is used**. For example, assume that a convertible bond was issued January 1, 2003, with a conversion rate of 10 common shares for each bond starting January 1, 2005. Beginning January 1, 2008, the conversion rate is 12 common shares for each bond, and beginning January 1, 2012, it is 15 common shares for each bond. In computing diluted EPS in 2003, the conversion rate of 15 shares to one bond is used.

Finally, if the 6 percent convertible debentures were instead 6 percent convertible preferred stock, the convertible preferred would be considered potential common shares and included in shares outstanding in diluted EPS calculations. Preferred dividends are not subtracted from net income in computing the numerator. Why not? Because it is assumed that the convertible preferreds are converted and are outstanding as common stock for purposes of computing EPS. Net income is used as the numerator—**no tax effect** is computed because preferred dividends generally are not deductible for tax purposes.

Diluted EPS—Options and Warrants

Stock options and warrants outstanding (whether or not presently exercisable) are included in diluted earnings per share unless they are antidilutive. Options and warrants and their equivalents are included in earnings per share computations through the **treasury stock method**.

The treasury stock method assumes that the options or warrants are exercised at the beginning of the year (or date of issue if later) and that the proceeds from the exercise of options and warrants are used to purchase common stock for the treasury. If the exercise price is lower than the market price of the stock, then the proceeds from exercise are not sufficient to buy back all the shares. The incremental shares remaining are added to the weighted average number of shares outstanding for purposes of computing diluted earnings per share.

For example, if the exercise price of a warrant is $5 and the fair market value of the stock is $15, the treasury stock method would increase the shares outstanding. Exercise of the warrant would result in one additional share outstanding, but the $5 received for the one share issued is not sufficient to purchase one share in the market at $15. Three warrants would have to be exercised (and three additional shares issued) to produce enough money ($15) to acquire one share in the market. Thus, a net increase of two shares outstanding would result.

To see this computation using larger numbers, assume 1,500 options outstanding at an exercise price of $30 for a common share and a common stock market price per share of $50. Through application of the treasury stock method there would be 600 **incremental shares** outstanding, computed in Illustration 36-16.[6]

ILLUSTRATION 36-16 Computation of Incremental Shares

Proceeds from exercise of 1,500 options (1,500 × $30)	$45,000
Shares issued upon exercise of options	1,500
Treasury shares purchasable with proceeds ($45,000 ÷ $50)	900
Incremental shares outstanding (potential common shares)	600

Thus, if the exercise price of the option or warrant is **lower than** the market price of the stock, dilution occurs. If the exercise price of the option or warrant is **higher than** the market price of the stock, common shares are reduced. In this case, the options or warrants are **antidilutive** because their assumed exercise leads to an increase in earnings per share.

[6] The incremental number of shares may be more simply computed:

$$\frac{\text{Market price} - \text{Option price}}{\text{Market price}} \times \text{Number of options} = \text{Number of shares}$$

$$\frac{\$50 - \$30}{\$50} \times 1{,}500 \text{ options} = 600 \text{ shares}$$

For both options and warrants, exercise is not assumed unless the average market price of the stock is above the exercise price during the period being reported.[7] As a practical matter, a simple average of the weekly or monthly prices is adequate, so long as the prices do not fluctuate significantly.

Comprehensive Illustration—Treasury Stock Method

To illustrate application of the treasury stock method, assume that Kubitz Industries, Inc. has net income for the period of $220,000. The average number of shares outstanding for the period was 100,000 shares. Hence, basic EPS—ignoring all dilutive securities—is $2.20. The average number of shares under outstanding options (although not exercisable at this time), at an option price of $20 per share, is 5,000 shares. The average market price of the common stock during the year was $28. The computation is shown in Illustration 36-17.

ILLUSTRATION 36-17 Computation of Earnings per Share—Treasury Stock Method

	Basic Earnings per Share	Diluted Earnings per Share
Average number of shares under option outstanding:		5,000
Option price per share		× $20
Proceeds upon exercise of options		$100,000
Average market price of common stock		$28
Treasury shares that could be repurchased with proceeds ($100,000 ÷ $28)		3,571
Excess of shares under option over the treasury shares that could be repurchased (5,000 − 3,571)—potential common incremental shares		1,429
Average number of common shares outstanding	100,000	100,000
Total average number of common shares outstanding and potential common shares	100,000 (A)	101,429 (C)
Net income for the year	$220,000 (B)	$220,000 (D)
Earnings per share	$2.20 (B ÷ A)	$2.17 (D ÷ C)

Contingent Issue Agreement

In business combinations, the acquirer may promise to issue additional shares—referred to as **contingent shares**—if certain conditions are met. If these shares are issuable upon the **mere passage of time or upon the attainment of a certain**

[7] Options and warrants have essentially the same assumptions and computational problems, although the warrants may allow or require the tendering of some other security, such as debt, in lieu of cash upon exercise. In such situations the accounting becomes quite complex. *SFAS No. 128* explains the proper disposition in this situation.

earnings or market price level, and this level is met at the end of the year, the contingent shares should be considered as outstanding for the computation of diluted earnings per share.[8]

For example, assume that Walz Corporation purchased Cardella Company and agreed to give Cardella's stockholders 20,000 additional shares in 2007 if Cardella's net income in 2006 is $90,000. In 2005 Cardella Company's net income is $100,000. Because the 2006 stipulated earnings of $90,000 are already being attained, diluted earnings per share of Walz for 2005 would include the 20,000 contingent shares in the shares outstanding computation.

Antidilution Revisited

In computing diluted EPS, the aggregate of all dilutive securities must be considered. But first we must determine which potentially dilutive securities are in fact individually dilutive and which are antidilutive. **Any security that is antidilutive should be excluded** and cannot be used to offset dilutive securities.

Recall that antidilutive securities are securities whose inclusion in earnings per share computations would increase earnings per share (or reduce net loss per share). Convertible debt is antidilutive if the addition to income of the interest (net of tax) causes a greater percentage increase in income (numerator) than conversion of the bonds causes a percentage increase in common and potentially dilutive shares (denominator). In other words, convertible debt is antidilutive if conversion of the security causes common stock earnings to increase by a greater amount per additional common share than earnings per share was before the conversion.

To illustrate, assume that Kohl Corporation has a 6 percent, $1,000,000 debt issue that is convertible into 10,000 common shares. Net income for the year is $210,000, the weighted average number of common shares outstanding is 100,000 shares, and the tax rate is 40 percent. In this case, assumed conversion of the debt into common stock at the beginning of the year requires the following adjustments of net income and the weighted average number of shares outstanding (Illustration 36-18).

ILLUSTRATION 36-18 Test for Antidilution

Net income for the year	$210,000	Average number of shares outstanding	100,000
Add: Adjustment for interest (net of tax) on 6% debentures $60,000 × (1 − .40)	36,000	Add: Shares issued upon assumed conversion of debt	10,000
Adjusted net income	$246,000	Average number of common and potential common shares	110,000

Basic EPS = $210,000 ÷ 100,000 = $2.10

Diluted EPS = $246,000 ÷ 110,000 = $2.24 = **Antidilutive**

[8] In addition to contingent issuances of stock, other types of situations that might lead to dilution are the issuance of participating securities and two-class common shares. The reporting of these types of securities in EPS computations is beyond the scope of this textbook.

WHAT DO THE NUMBERS MEAN?

Pro Forma EPS Confusion

Many companies are reporting pro forma EPS numbers along with U.S. GAAP-based EPS numbers in the financial information provided to investors. Pro forma earnings generally exceed GAAP earnings because the pro forma numbers exclude such items as restructuring charges, impairments of assets, R&D expenditures, and stock compensation expense. Here are some examples.

Company	U.S. GAAP EPS	Pro Forma EPS
Adaptec, Inc.	$(0.62)	$ 0.05
Corning Inc.	(0.24)	0.09
General Motors Corp.	(0.41)	0.85
Honeywell International Inc.	(0.38)	0.44
International Paper Co.	(0.57)	0.14
QUALCOMM Inc.	(0.06)	0.20
Broadcom Corp.	(6.36)	(0.13)
Lucent Technologies Inc.	(2.16)	(0.27)

Source: Company press releases.

The SEC has expressed concern that pro forma earnings may be misleading. For example, **Trump Hotels & Casino Resorts Inc.** (DJT) was cited for abuses related to its 1999 third-quarter pro forma EPS release. The SEC noted that the firm misrepresented its operating results by excluding a material, one-time $81.4 million charge in its pro forma EPS statement and including an undisclosed nonrecurring gain of $17.2 million. The gain enabled DJT to post a profit in the quarter. The SEC emphasized that DJT's pro forma EPS statement deviated from conservative U.S. GAAP reporting. Therefore, it was "fraudulent" because it created a "false and misleading impression" that DJT had actually (1) recorded a profit in the third quarter of 1999 and (2) exceeded consensus earnings expectations by enhancing its operating fundamentals.

The Sarbanes-Oxley Act of 2002 requires the SEC to develop regulations on pro forma reporting. As a consequence, the SEC now requires companies that provide pro forma financial information to make sure that the information is not misleading. In addition, a reconciliation between pro forma and GAAP information is required.

Sources: SEC Accounting and Enforcement Release No. 1499 (January 16, 2002); "SEC Proposes Rules to Implement Sarbanes-Oxley Act Reforms," SEC Press Release 2002-155 (October 30, 2002).

As a shortcut, the convertible debt also can be identified as antidilutive by comparing the EPS resulting from conversion, $3.60 ($36,000 additional earnings ÷ 10,000 additional shares), with EPS before inclusion of the convertible debt, $2.10.

With options or warrants, whenever the exercise price is higher than the market price, the security is antidilutive. **Antidilutive securities should be ignored in all calculations and should not be considered in computing diluted earnings per share.** This approach is reasonable because the profession's intent was to inform the investor of the **possible dilution** that might occur in reported earnings per share. The intent was not to highlight securities that, if converted or exercised, would result in an increase in earnings per share. The appendix to this reading provides an extended example of how antidilution is considered in a complex situation with multiple securities.

EPS Presentation and Disclosure

If a company's capital structure is complex, the EPS presentation would be as given in Illustration 36-19.

ILLUSTRATION 36-19 EPS Presentation—Complex Capital Structure

Earnings per common share	
Basic earnings per share	$3.30
Diluted earnings per share	$2.70

When the earnings of a period include irregular items, per share amounts (where applicable) should be shown for income from continuing operations, income before extraordinary items, income before accounting change, and net income. Companies that report a discontinued operation, an extraordinary item, or the cumulative effect of an accounting change should present per share amounts for those line items either on the face of the income statement or in the notes to the financial statements. A presentation reporting extraordinary items only is presented in Illustration 36-20.

ILLUSTRATION 36-20 EPS Presentation, with Extraordinary Item

Basic earnings per share	
Income before extraordinary item	$3.80
Extraordinary item	0.80
Net income	$3.00
Diluted earnings per share	
Income before extraordinary item	$3.35
Extraordinary item	0.65
Net income	$2.70

Earnings per share amounts must be shown for all periods presented. Also, all prior period earnings per share amounts presented should be restated for stock dividends and stock splits. If diluted EPS data are reported for at least one period, they should be reported for all periods presented, even if they are the same as basic EPS. When results of operations of a prior period have been restated as a result of a prior period adjustment, the earnings per share data shown for the prior periods should also be restated. The effect of the restatement should be disclosed in the year of the restatement.

Complex capital structures and dual presentation of earnings per share require the following additional disclosures in note form.

1. Description of pertinent rights and privileges of the various securities outstanding.
2. A reconciliation of the numerators and denominators of the basic and diluted per share computations, including individual income and share amount effects of all securities that affect EPS.
3. The effect given preferred dividends in determining income available to common stockholders in computing basic EPS.

4. Securities that could potentially dilute basic EPS in the future that were not included in the computation because they would be antidilutive.
5. Effect of conversions subsequent to year-end, but before statements have been issued.

Illustration 36-21 presents the reconciliation and the related disclosure that is needed to meet disclosure requirements for EPS.

ILLUSTRATION 36-21 Reconciliation for Basic and Diluted EPS

	For the Year Ended 2005		
	Income (Numerator)	**Shares (Denominator)**	**Per Share Amount**
Income before extraordinary item and accounting change	$7,500,000		
Less: Preferred stock dividends	(45,000)		
Basic EPS			
Income available to common stockholders	7,455,000	3,991,666	$1.87
Warrants		30,768	
Convertible preferred stock	45,000	308,333	
4% convertible bonds (net of tax)	60,000	50,000	
Diluted EPS			
Income available to common stockholders + assumed conversions	$7,560,000	$4,380,767	$1.73

Stock options to purchase 1,000,000 shares of common stock at $85 per share were outstanding during the second half of 2005 but were not included in the computation of diluted EPS because the options' exercise price was greater than the average market price of the common shares. The options were still outstanding at the end of year 2005 and expire on June 30, 2015.[9]

[9] Note that *Statement No. 123* has specific disclosure requirements as well regarding stock option plans and earnings per share disclosures.

SUMMARY

4

As you can see, computation of earnings per share is a complex issue. It is a controversial area because many securities, although technically not common stock, have many of its basic characteristics. Some companies have issued these types of securities rather than common stock in order to avoid an adverse dilutive effect on earnings per share.

Illustrations 36-22 and 36-23 show the elementary points of calculating earnings per share in a simple capital structure and in a complex capital structure.

ILLUSTRATION 36-22 Calculating EPS, Simple Capital Structure

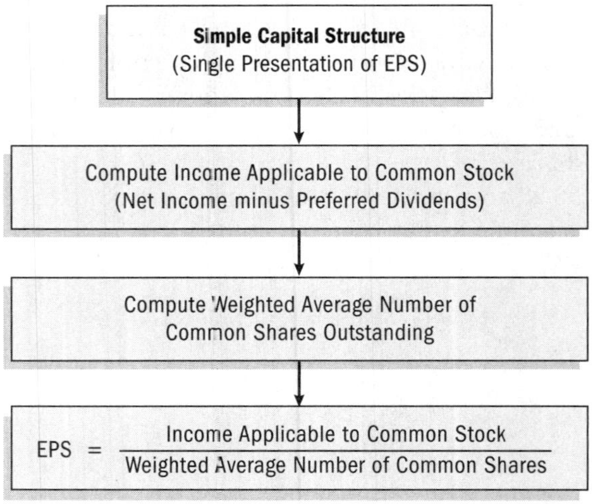

ILLUSTRATION 36-23 Calculating EPS, Complex Capital Structure

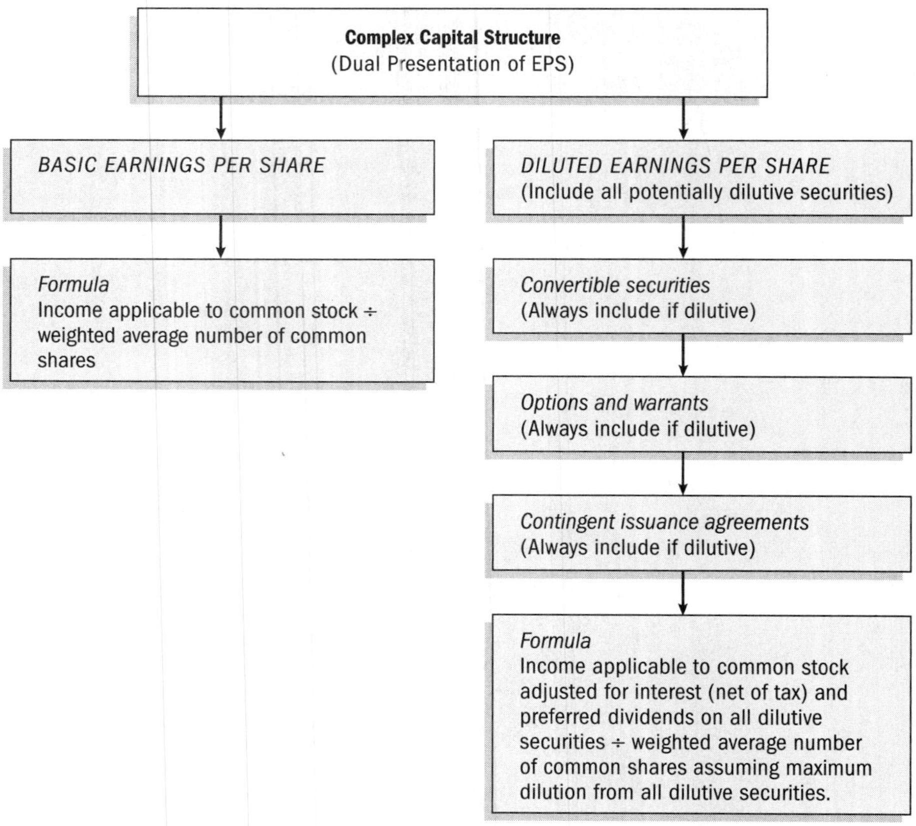

APPENDIX 36B

Comprehensive Earnings per Share Illustration

The purpose of this appendix is to illustrate the method of computing dilution when many securities are involved. The following section of the balance sheet of Webster Corporation is presented for analysis (Illustration 36B-1). Assumptions related to the capital structure follow the balance sheet.

ILLUSTRATION 36B-1 Balance Sheet for Comprehensive Illustration

Webster Corporation
Balance Sheet (Partial)
At December 31, 2004

Long-term debt	
Notes payable, 14%	$ 1,000,000
8% convertible bonds payable	2,500,000
10% convertible bonds payable	2,500,000
Total long-term debt	$6,000,000
Stockholders' equity	
10% cumulative, convertible preferred stock, par value $100; 100,000 shares authorized, 25,000 shares issued and outstanding	$ 2,500,000
Common stock, par value $1, 5,000,000 shares authorized, 500,000 shares issued and outstanding	500,000
Additional paid-in capital	2,000,000
Retained earnings	9,000,000
Total stockholders' equity	$14,000,000

Notes and Assumptions
December 31, 2004

1. Options were granted in July 2002 to purchase 50,000 shares of common stock at $20 per share. The average market price of Webster's common stock during 2004 was $30 per share. No options were exercised during 2004.
2. Both the 8 percent and 10 percent convertible bonds were issued in 2003 at face value. Each convertible bond is convertible into 40 shares of common stock. (Each bond has a face value of $1,000.)
3. The 10 percent cumulative, convertible preferred stock was issued at the beginning of 2004 at par. Each share of preferred is convertible into four shares of common stock.
4. The average income tax rate is 40 percent.

5. The 500,000 shares of common stock were outstanding during the entire year.
6. Preferred dividends were not declared in 2004.
7. Net income was $1,750,000 in 2004.
8. No bonds or preferred stock were converted during 2004.

The computation of basic earnings per share for 2004 starts with the amount based upon the weighted average of common shares outstanding, as shown in Illustration 36B-2.

ILLUSTRATION 36B-2 Computation of Earnings per Share—Simple Capital Structure

Net income	$1,750,000
Less: 10% cumulative, convertible preferred stock dividend requirements	250,000
Income applicable to common stockholders	$1,500,000
Weighted average number of common shares outstanding	500,000
Earnings per common share	$3.00

Note the following points concerning the calculation above.

1. When preferred stock is cumulative, the preferred dividend is subtracted to arrive at income applicable to common stock whether the dividend is declared or not.
2. The earnings per share of $3 must be computed as a starting point, because it is the per share amount that is subject to reduction due to the existence of convertible securities and options.

DILUTED EARNINGS PER SHARE

The steps for computing diluted earnings per share are:

1. Determine, for each dilutive security, the per share effect assuming exercise/conversion.
2. Rank the results from step 1 from smallest to largest earnings effect per share. That is, rank the results from most dilutive to least dilutive.
3. Beginning with the earnings per share based upon the weighted average of common shares outstanding ($3), recalculate earnings per share by adding the smallest per share effects from step 2. If the results from this recalculation are less than $3, proceed to the next smallest per share effect and recalculate earnings per share. Continue this process so long as each recalculated earnings per share is smaller than the previous amount. The process will end either because there are no more securities to test or a particular security maintains or increases earnings per share (is antidilutive).

We'll now apply the three steps to Webster Corporation. (Note that net income and income available to common stockholders are not the same if preferred dividends are declared or cumulative.) Webster Corporation has four securities (options, 8 percent and 10 percent convertible bonds, and the convertible preferred stock) that could reduce EPS.

The first step in the computation of diluted earnings per share is to determine a per share effect for each potentially dilutive security. Illustrations 36B-3 through 36B-6 illustrate these computations.

ILLUSTRATION 36B-3 Per Share Effect of Options (Treasury Stock Method), Diluted Earnings per Share

Number of shares under option	50,000
Option price per share	× $20
Proceeds upon assumed exercise of options	$1,000,000
Average 2004 market price of common	$30
Treasury shares that could be acquired with proceeds ($1,000,000 ÷ $30)	33,333
Excess of shares under option over treasury shares that could be repurchased (50,000 − 33,333)	16,667
Per share effect:	

$$\frac{\text{Incremental Numerator Effect}}{\text{Incremental Denominator Effect}} = \frac{\text{None}}{16{,}667 \text{ shares}} = \$0$$

ILLUSTRATION 36B-4 Per Share Effect of 8% Bonds (If-Converted Method), Diluted Earnings per Share

Interest expense for year (8% × $2,500,000)	$200,000
Income tax reduction due to interest (40% × $200,000)	80,000
Interest expense avoided (net of tax)	$120,000
Number of common shares issued assuming conversion of bonds (2,500 bonds × 40 shares)	100,000
Per share effect:	

$$\frac{\text{Incremental Numerator Effect}}{\text{Incremental Denominator Effect}} = \frac{\$120{,}000}{100{,}000 \text{ shares}} = \$1.20$$

ILLUSTRATION 36B-5 Per Share Effect of 10% Bonds (If-Converted Method), Diluted Earnings per Share

Interest expense for year (10% × $2,500,000)	$250,000
Income tax reduction due to interest (40% × $250,000)	100,000
Interest expense avoided (net of tax)	$150,000
Number of common shares issued assuming conversion of bonds (2,500 bonds × 40 shares)	100,000
Per share effect:	

$$\frac{\text{Incremental Numerator Effect}}{\text{Incremental Denominator Effect}} = \frac{\$150{,}000}{100{,}000 \text{ shares}} = \$1.50$$

ILLUSTRATION 36B-6 Per Share Effect of 10% Convertible Preferred (If-Converted Method), Diluted Earnings per Share

Dividend requirement on cumulative preferred (25,000 shares × $10)	$250,000
Income tax effect (dividends not a tax deduction)	none
Dividend requirement avoided	$250,000
Number of common shares issued assuming conversion of preferred (4 × 25,000 shares)	100,000
Per share effect:	

$$\frac{\text{Incremental Numerator Effect}}{\text{Incremental Denominator Effect}} = \frac{\$250{,}000}{100{,}000 \text{ shares}} = \$2.50$$

Illustration 36B-7 shows the ranking of all four potentially dilutive securities.

ILLUSTRATION 36B-7 Ranking of per Share Effects (Smallest to Largest), Diluted Earnings per Share

	Effect per Share
1. Options	$ 0
2. 8% convertible bonds	1.20
3. 10% convertible bonds	1.50
4. 10% convertible preferred	2.50

The next step is to determine earnings per share giving effect to the ranking in Illustration 36B-7. Starting with the earnings per share of $3 computed previously, add the incremental effects of the options to the original calculation, as in illustration 36B-8.

ILLUSTRATION 36B-8 Recomputation of EPS Using Incremental Effect of Options

Options	
Income applicable to common stockholders	$1,500,000
Add: Incremental numerator effect of options	none
Total	$1,500,000
Weighted average number of common shares outstanding	500,000
Add: Incremental denominator effect of options (Illustration 36B-3)	16,667
Total	516,667
Recomputed earnings per share ($1,500,000 ÷ 516,667 shares)	$2.90

Since the recomputed earnings per share is reduced (from $3 to $2.90), the effect of the options is dilutive. Again, this effect could have been anticipated because the average market price ($30) exceeded the option price ($20).

Recomputed earnings per share, assuming the 8 percent bonds are converted, is given in Illustration 36B-9.

ILLUSTRATION 36B-9 Recomputation of EPS Using Incremental Effect of 8% Convertible Bonds

8% Convertible Bonds	
Numerator from previous calculation	$1,500,000
Add: Interest expense avoided (net of tax)	120,000
Total	$1,620,000
Denominator from previous calculation (shares)	516,667
Add: Number of common shares assumed issued upon conversion of bonds	100,000
Total	616,667
Recomputed earnings per share ($1,620,000 ÷ 616,667 shares)	$2.63

Since the recomputed earnings per share is reduced (from $2.90 to $2.63), the effect of the 8 percent bonds is dilutive.

Next, earnings per share is recomputed assuming the conversion of the 10 percent bonds. This is shown in Illustration 36B-10.

ILLUSTRATION 36B-10 Recomputation of EPS Using Incremental Effect of 10% Convertible Bonds

10% Convertible Bonds	
Numerator from previous calculation	$1,620,000
Add: Interest expense avoided (net of tax)	150,000
Total	$1,770,000
Denominator from previous calculation (shares)	616,667
Add: Number of common shares assumed issued upon conversion of bonds	100,000
Total	716,667
Recomputed earnings per share ($1,770,000 ÷ 716,667 shares)	$2.47

Since the recomputed earnings per share is reduced (from $2.63 to $2.47), the effect of the 10 percent convertible bonds is dilutive.

The final step is the recomputation that includes the 10 percent preferred stock. This is shown in Illustration 36B-11.

ILLUSTRATION 36B-11 Recomputation of EPS Using Incremental Effect of 10% Convertible Preferred

10% Convertible Preferred	
Numerator from previous calculation	$1,770,000
Add: Dividend requirement avoided	250,000
Total	$2,020,000
Denominator from previous calculation (shares)	716,667
Add: Number of common shares assumed issued upon conversion of preferred	100,000
Total	816,667
Recomputed earnings per share ($2,020,000 ÷ 816,667 shares)	$2.47

Since the recomputed earnings per share is not reduced, the effect of the 10 percent convertible preferred is not dilutive. Diluted earnings per share is $2.47, and the per share effects of the preferred are not used in the computation.

Finally, the disclosure of earnings per share on the income statement for Webster Corporation is shown in Illustration 36B-12.

ILLUSTRATION 36B-12 Income Statement Presentation, EPS

Net income	$1,750,000
Basic earnings per common share (Note X)	$3.00
Diluted earnings per common share	$2.47

A company uses **income from continuing operations (adjusted for preferred dividends) to determine whether potential common stock is dilutive or antidilutive**. (Some refer to this measure as the **control number**.) To illustrate, assume that Barton Company provides the following information (Illustration 36B-13).

ILLUSTRATION 36B-13 Barton Company Data

Income from continuing operations	$2,400,000
Loss from discontinued operations	3,600,000
Net loss	$1,200,000
Weighted average shares of common stock outstanding	1,000,000
Potential common stock	200,000

The computation of basic and dilutive earnings per share is given in Illustration 36B-14.

ILLUSTRATION 36B-14 Basic and Diluted EPS

Basic earnings per share	
Income from continuing operations	$2.40
Loss from discontinued operations	3.60
Net loss	$1.20
Diluted earnings per share	
Income from continuing operations	$2.00
Loss from discontinued operations	3.00
Net loss	$1.00

As shown in Illustration 36B-14, basic earnings per share from continuing operations is higher than the diluted earnings per share from continuing operations. The reason: The diluted earnings per share from continuing operations includes an additional 200,000 shares of potential common stock in its denominator.[1]

Income from continuing operations is used as the control number because many companies will show income from continuing operations (or a similar line item above net income if it appears on the income statement), but report a final net loss due to a loss on discontinued operations. If the final net loss is used as the control number, basic and diluted earnings per share would be the same because the potential common shares are antidilutive.[2]

[1] A company that does not report a discontinued operation but reports an extraordinary item or the cumulative effect of a change in accounting principle should use that line item (for example, income before extraordinary items) as the control number.

[2] If a loss from continuing operations is reported, basic and diluted earnings per share will be the same because potential common stock will be antidilutive, even if the company reports final net income. The FASB believes that comparability of EPS information will be improved by using income from continuing operations as the control number.

SUMMARY OF LEARNING OBJECTIVE FOR APPENDIX 36B

Compute earnings per share in a complex situation. For diluted EPS, make the following computations: (1) Determine, for each potentially dilutive security, the per share effect assuming exercise/conversion. (2) Rank the results from most dilutive to least dilutive. (3) Recalculate EPS starting with the most dilutive, and continue adding securities until EPS increases (is antidilutive).

QUESTIONS

1. Define the following terms.
   (a) Basic earnings per share.
   (b) Potentially dilutive security.
2. Discuss why options and warrants may be considered potentially dilutive common shares for the computation of diluted earnings per share.
3. Explain how convertible securities are determined to be potentially dilutive common shares and how those convertible securities that are not considered to be potentially dilutive common shares enter into the determination of earnings per share data.

EXERCISES

1. **(EPS: Simple Capital Structure)** On January 1, 2005, Wilke Corp. had 480,000 shares of common stock outstanding. During 2005, it had the following transactions that affected the common stock account.

February 1	Issued 120,000 shares
March 1	Issued a 10% stock dividend
May 1	Acquired 100,000 shares of treasury stock
June 1	Issued a 3-for-1 stock split
October 1	Reissued 60,000 shares of treasury stock

Instructions

(a) Determine the weighted average number of shares outstanding as of December 31, 2005.

(b) Assume that Wilke Corp. earned net income of $3,456,000 during 2005. In addition, it had 100,000 shares of 9%, $100 par nonconvertible, noncumulative preferred stock outstanding for the entire year. Because of liquidity considerations, however, the company did not declare and pay a preferred dividend in 2005. Compute earnings per share for 2005, using the weighted-average number of shares determined in part (a).

(c) Assume the same facts as in part (b), except that the preferred stock was cumulative. Compute earnings per share for 2005.

(d) Assume the same facts as in part (b), except that net income included an extraordinary gain of $864,000 and a loss from discontinued operations of $432,000. Both items are net of applicable income taxes. Compute earnings per share for 2005.

2. (EPS with Complex Capital Structure) Diane Leto, controller at Dewey Yaeger Pharmaceutical Industries, a public company, is currently preparing the calculation for basic and diluted earnings per share and the related disclosure for Yaeger's external financial statements. Following is selected financial information for the fiscal year ended June 30, 2005.

Dewey Yaeger Pharmaceutical Industries
Selected Statement of
Financial Position Information
June 30, 2005

Long-term debt	
Notes payable, 10%	$ 1,000,000
7% convertible bonds payable	5,000,000
10% bonds payable	6,000,000
Total long-term debt	$12,000,000
Shareholders' equity	
Preferred stock, 8.5% cumulative, $50 par value, 100,000 shares authorized, 25,000 shares issued and outstanding	$ 1,250,000
Common stock, $1 par, 10,000,000 shares authorized, 1,000,000 shares issued and outstanding	1,000,000
Additional paid-in capital	4,000,000
Retained earnings	6,000,000
Total shareholders' equity	$12,250,000

The following transactions have also occurred at Yaeger.

1. Options were granted in 2003 to purchase 100,000 shares at $15 per share. Although no options were exercised during 2005, the average price per common share during fiscal year 2005 was $20 per share.
2. Each bond was issued at face value. The 7% convertible debenture will convert into common stock at 50 shares per $1,000 bond. It is exercisable after 5 years and was issued in 2004.
3. The 8.5% preferred stock was issued in 2003.
4. There are no preferred dividends in arrears; however, preferred dividends were not declared in fiscal year 2005.
5. The 1,000,000 shares of common stock were outstanding for the entire 2005 fiscal year.
6. Net income for fiscal year 2005 was $1,500,000, and the average income tax rate is 40%.

Instructions

For the fiscal year ended June 30, 2005, calculate the following for Dewey Yaeger Pharmaceutical Industries.

(a) Basic earnings per share.

(b) Diluted earnings per share.

SEEK AND YE SHALL FIND

READING 37

LEARNING OUTCOMES

The candidate should be able to:

a. explain the two basic strategies underlying all accounting "shenanigans," and describe seven categories of techniques that may be used by management to distort a company's reported financial performance and financial condition;

b. identify conservative and aggressive accounting policies;

c. describe why "shenanigans" exist, and explain where they are most likely to occur;

d. list the documents that an analyst should use to identify "shenanigans," and explain what information to look for in such documents.

INTRODUCTION 1

Financial shenanigans range from benign tricks to outright fraud. They occur at companies of all sizes, from small, unknown firms to the most prominent global ones. This reading provides some important building blocks for identifying companies that are using accounting tricks. It also provides an important case study showing the very different fates of two companies that employed improper accounting: One company never recovered, and the other bounced back from a "bump in the road" to achieve great success.

To strive, to seek, to find, and not to yield.

Alfred, Lord Tennyson, British poet

Reading 37 answers the following seven questions about shenanigans:

- What are financial shenanigans in general?
- What specific techniques are used?
- What are the basic strategies underlying the shenanigans?

- How do the shenanigans relate to one another?
- Should investors be more concerned about certain shenanigans?
- Why do shenanigans exist and where are they most likely to occur?
- What is the profile of a "big" story?

2 WHAT ARE FINANCIAL SHENANIGANS, IN GENERAL?

Financial shenanigans are actions that intentionally distort a company's reported financial performance and financial condition. They range from benign (changes in accounting estimates) to egregious (fraudulent recognition of bogus revenue).

3 WHAT SPECIFIC TECHNIQUES ARE USED?

The CFRA has identified thirty techniques (grouped into seven categories) that companies use to trick investors and other stakeholders.

SEVEN FINANCIAL SHENANIGANS

Shenanigan No. 1: Recording Revenue Too Soon or of Questionable Quality

- Recording revenue when future services remain to be provided
- Recording revenue before shipment or before the customer's unconditional acceptance
- Recording revenue even though the customer is not obligated to pay
- Selling to an affiliated party
- Giving the customer something of value as a quid pro quo
- Grossing up revenue

Shenanigan No. 2: Recording Bogus Revenue

- Recording sales that lack economic substance
- Recording cash received in lending transactions as revenue
- Recording investment income as revenue
- Recording as revenue supplier rebates tied to future required purchases
- Releasing revenue that was improperly held back before a merger

Shenanigan No. 3: Boosting Income with One-Time Gains

- Boosting profits by selling undervalued assets
- Including investment income or gains as part of revenue
- Reporting investment income or gains as a reduction in operating expenses
- Creating income by reclassification of balance sheet accounts

Shenanigan No. 4: Shifting Current Expenses to a Later or Earlier Period

- Capitalizing normal operating costs, particularly if recently changed from expensing
- Changing accounting policies and shifting current expenses to an earlier period
- Amortizing costs too slowly
- Failing to write down or write off impaired assets
- Reducing asset reserves

Shenanigan No. 5: Failing to Record or Improperly Reducing Liabilities

- Failing to record expenses and related liabilities when future obligations remain
- Reducing liabilities by changing accounting assumptions
- Releasing questionable reserves into income
- Creating sham rebates
- Recording revenue when cash is received, even though future obligations remain

Shenanigan No. 6: Shifting Current Revenue to a Later Period

- Creating reserves and releasing them into income in a later period
- Improperly holding back revenue just before an acquisition closes

Shenanigan No. 7: Shifting Future Expenses to the Current Period as a Special Charge

- Improperly inflating amount included in a special charge
- Improperly writing off in-process R&D costs from an acquisition
- Accelerating discretionary expenses into current period

WHAT ARE THE BASIC STRATEGIES UNDERLYING THE SHENANIGANS? 4

The following are two basic strategies underlying all accounting tricks:

- To *inflate* current-period earnings by *inflating* current-period revenue and gains or by *deflating* current-period expenses
- To *deflate* current-period earnings (and, consequently, inflate future periods' results) by *deflating* current-period revenue or by *inflating* current-period expenses

The first strategy, inflating profits, is intuitive and needs no further clarification. In contrast, the strategy of intentionally making the company look worse than it really is may be confusing. The larger objective of this strategy is to shift earnings to a later period when they will really be needed—in other words, to *inflate tomorrow's profits.* Table 37-1 summarizes the relationship between these strategies and the seven shenanigan tactics.

Table 37-1 Accounting Strategies and the 7 Shenanigans

	Strategies			
Accounts	**Inflate Current Period**	**Tactic**	**Deflate Current Period**	**Tactic**
Revenue (or gains)	Recording revenue too soon	No. 1	Shifting current revenue to a later period	No. 6
	Recording bogus revenue	No. 2		
	Boosting income with one-time gains	No. 3		
	Failing to record or improperly reducing liabilities	No. 5		
Expenses (or losses)	Boosting income with one-time gains	No. 3	Shifting future expenses to the current period as a special charge	No. 7
	Shifting current expenses to a later or earlier period	No. 4		
	Failing to record or improperly reducing liabilities	No. 5		

5 HOW DO THE SHENANIGANS RELATE TO ONE ANOTHER?

Although all financial shenanigans fit into seven finite categories, there are important connections and intersections among certain of these categories.

For example, Shenanigans No. 1 and Shenanigan No. 5 can be thought of as close cousins. A company that receives an advance payment from a customer for future services and improperly recording revenue immediately has employed both Shenanigan No. 1 (recording revenue too soon) and Shenanigan No. 5 (failing to record or improperly reducing liabilities).

Shenanigan No. 2 is related to Shenanigan No. 6. A company that improperly holds back recording all of today's revenue (No. 6) will invariably record that revenue in a later period (No. 2).

There is also an important connection between Shenanigan No. 5 and Shenanigan No. 7. Consider the following example: A company takes a big restructuring charge (Shenanigan No. 7, shifting future expenses to the current period as a special charge) and in the next quarter releases the reserves with the charge credited (Shenanigan No. 5, failing to record or improperly reducing liabilities).

SHOULD INVESTORS BE MORE CONCERNED ABOUT CERTAIN SHENANIGANS? 6

Certain shenanigans can be fairly benign, whereas others may be more harmful for investors. In general, shenanigans that inflate revenue should be considered more serious than those that affect expenses. If a company's revenue growth appears solid and its accounting is proper, the company's prospects typically remain strong.

The Continuum—From Benign to Outright Fraud

Not all financial shenanigans are illegal acts or violations of generally accepted accounting principles (GAAP). They include a broad array of activities that intentionally misreport the financial performance or financial condition of a company. Shenanigans range from the fairly benign (amortizing costs too slowly, a technique under Shenanigan No. 4) to outright fraud (recording bogus revenue, Shenanigan No. 37-2). Table 37-2 shows the continuum and gives some examples.

Table 37-2. The Shenanigan Continuum

More Benign ←——→ Most Egregious

1	2	3	4
Change in accounting estimates	Releasing reserves	Capitalizing operating costs	Including bricks in inventory boxes to trick the auditors who weigh the boxes

Not Great News for Investors

Not surprisingly, the share price invariably performs poorly after a company begins using financial shenanigans. Moreover, when companies use particularly egregious shenanigans, the stock price decline will generally be steeper and more permanent. There are two obvious reasons for this:

- Generally, companies that use such accounting chicanery are attempting to cover some major operational deterioration in the business. The truth concerning the operating problem will soon become known by investors.
- Such chicanery leads investors to lose faith in management's integrity, causing the stock to remain out of favor for a long time.

WHY DO SHENANIGANS EXIST AND WHERE ARE THEY MOST LIKELY TO OCCUR? 7

While most people agree that gimmicks can distort financial statements, there are many theories about the reasons why these gimmicks exist. Based on my research, there are three general reasons for shenanigans: (1) It pays to do it, (2) it's easy to do, and (3) it's unlikely that you'll get caught.

It Pays to Do It

Some managers will resort to accounting gimmicks if they are personally enriched by doing so. Thus, when bonuses encourage managers to post higher sales and profits and no questions are asked about how those gains were achieved, an incentive for using shenanigans can be created. Unfortunately, misguided incentive plans are not uncommon today in corporations. In explaining why companies use financial shenanigans to manage earnings, Baruch College's Professor Abraham Briloff remarked, "Because it's their report card." Executives like their bonuses and the other perquisites that are tied to reported earnings.

Be Alert for Misguided Management Incentives.

Like most of us, managers are affected in their behavior by rewards and punishments. Since many companies offer bonuses and stock options based on financial statement measures, executives and managers are motivated to report more favorable financial results. Similarly, if underperforming divisions in companies are threatened with layoffs or lower compensation for their managers, those managers will often search for ways to report stronger results. Because of this pressure to report higher sales and higher profits, managers may be creative in their interpretation of GAAP.

A compensation structure that heavily emphasizes the bottom line creates an environment that sometimes encourages accounting chicanery. Professor Paul Healy of MIT undertook a study to show empirically that management benefited by choosing accounting procedures that produced higher earnings. Healy found a connection between bonus schemes and the accounting choices that executives made. Specifically, he found that executives whose bonuses were already at the maximum level tended to choose accounting options that minimized reported profits, whereas those who had no ceiling chose profit-boosting options. Thus, if no additional bonus is paid once profits reach a certain level, it is not in the executive's interest to have reported profits exceed that amount. In such a case, the manager would be better off deferring any profits above the maximum bonus level to some future period when they might be needed to sustain the manager's own income.

It's Easy to Do It

Managers select accounting methods (e.g., for inventory valuation or amortization of intangible assets) from a variety of acceptable choices. Thus, depending on the methods selected and the numerous estimates that must be made, a company's reported profit can vary considerably and yet still be in compliance with GAAP.

Honest managers grapple with the many choices and judgments required with the goal of finding accounting policies that portray the company's financial performance fairly. Unscrupulous managers, unfortunately, use the flexibility in GAAP to distort the financial reports.

Indeed, it is surprisingly easy for managers to use accounting gimmicks to manipulate financial statements. This is true for various reasons, including the following: (1) There is substantial flexibility in interpreting GAAP, (2) GAAP can be applied in ways that boost a company's reported profits, and (3) changes in GAAP by the Financial Accounting Standards Board (FASB) often occur long after a deficiency in financial reporting becomes evident.

Unlike tax legislation and the related U.S. Treasury Department regulations, financial accounting standards are fairly broad, and consequently management has considerable flexibility in interpreting them. Thus, decisions on whether to capitalize a cost or categorize it as an expense, or on selecting amortization periods for fixed assets, depend on management judgment.

Furthermore, management can structure transactions or decide when and how to implement new accounting rules to maximize its reporting goals. For example, the use of stock compensation plans (which produce no change in income) as a substitute for other forms of compensation has become increasingly popular at many corporations. Similarly, companies can structure lease agreements to keep the debt off their books (e.g., using an operating lease approach).

Question Overly Liberal Accounting Rules.

Because management has substantial control over the numbers that are reported, consider whether the accounting policies selected are overly aggressive. Consider various accounting policies of a company, such as inventory method, amortization period, and revenue recognition policy. Further, consider any changes in accounting policies and the reasons cited for them.

Beyond the realm of ethics, judgment plays an especially important role in the banking and insurance industries. Bankers use judgment in determining whether and when to write off loans that may not be repaid. If they are slow to recognize problem loans and fail to write them off, the bank will continue accruing interest on shaky loans. The result is an overstatement of assets, interest income, and profits on the bank's financial statements.

Watch for Poor Internal Controls.

In addition to taking advantage of the flexibility of GAAP, management may have little difficulty distorting financial reports if the company has weak internal controls. Such controls relate to the organizational structure and to corporate procedures for safeguarding assets against losses and ensuring the reliability of financial records for external reporting purposes. Strong controls (i.e., checks and balances) tend to reduce the temptation for management to engage in shenanigans. If safeguards and controls are lacking, however, unethical employees may engage in shenanigans with impunity. While independent auditors scrutinize the adequacy of these controls, it may be difficult for readers of financial statements to ascertain whether the controls contain weaknesses.

It's Unlikely That You'll Get Caught

Just as some people cheat on their tax returns because they think they won't get caught by the IRS, companies may use accounting tricks because they believe that they won't get caught by auditors or regulators. Unfortunately, for the reasons outlined in this reading, they are usually right. And, even when they are caught, the penalty is often too little, too late.

Note that Quarterly Financial Statements Are Unaudited.

Investors and bankers who rely on quarterly financial statements and press releases on financial performance may believe that those reports have the blessing of an independent CPA. Unfortunately, that's not usually true. Only the annual financial statements of publicly held companies must be audited; quarterly statements need not be. Moreover, most companies are privately held and are rarely audited by an outside CPA. When companies use accounting tricks on unaudited financial statements, there is little risk that they will be caught. As a result, investors must be especially careful when reading quarterly financial statements.

What Types of Companies Are Most Likely to Use Shenanigans?

While it is relatively easy for managers to use shenanigans and there is only a moderate chance of their getting caught, most companies *do not* intentionally distort their financial reports. Unfortunately, since you never know in advance which companies *do* publish misleading information, it is prudent to be a bit suspicious of all companies and to search for early warning signs of problems. Such signs often include (1) a weak control environment (i.e., lack of independent members on the board of directors or lack of a competent/independent external auditor), (2) management facing extreme competitive pressure, and (3) management known or suspected of having questionable character. Be particularly alert for these factors in the following types of companies: fast-growth companies whose real growth is beginning to slow, basket-case companies that are struggling to survive, newly public companies, and private companies.

The growth of all fast-growth companies will eventually slow considerably. At that point, managers may be tempted to use accounting gimmicks. Investors and lenders should be alert for shenanigans in all such companies. At the other extreme, managers of very weak companies might be tempted to use accounting tricks to deceive the outside world into thinking that their companies' problems are minor. Investors and lenders should be particularly alert when a company may not be in compliance with bank lending covenants on such financial measures as minimum net worth and working capital. Many newly public companies whose shares are first issued through an initial public offering, or IPO, have never been audited before and may lack strong internal controls. Shenanigans may be prevalent. Finally, private companies, particularly those that are closely held and have not been audited, are more likely to use shenanigans.

8 WHAT IS THE PROFILE OF A "BIG" STORY?

As indicated earlier, some accounting tricks are considered fairly benign and others are lethal. Knowing the difference between the two is essential. The story of two companies, AOL and Medaphis, provides an example of this.

AOL: An Interesting Story

Back in 1994, AOL was far different from the media giant AOL Time Warner of today. In fact, there were real doubts that AOL would survive against its larger and more formidable competitors of that era, CompuServe and Prodigy.

AOL needed sizable capital infusions from investors, but it had one glaring problem: It was spending considerably more than it was receiving from subscribers. That fact would have been clear to investors had AOL used more conventional accounting.

Specifically, in 1994 AOL decided to exclude current marketing costs in calculating its profit—an unusual and aggressive policy. Instead of immediately expensing these costs, AOL shifted them to the balance sheet (as an asset) and charged them off in future periods. Table 37-3 shows the resulting effect on AOL's revenue, income, and profits.

Table 37-3 AOL Revenue ($ in millions)

	1996	1995	1994	1993
Revenue	1,093.9	394.3	115.7	52.0
Operating income	65.2	(21.4)	4.2	1.7
Net income	29.8	(35.8)	2.2	1.4
Total assets	958.8	405.4	155.2	39.3
Deferred subscriber acquisition costs	314.2	77.2	26.0	—

By the following year, profits were becoming more elusive and AOL's accounting became even more aggressive. The company began amortizing marketing costs over eighteen months, rather than twelve. The shine started coming off AOL in 1996, and the share price sagged. With rapid growth of the number of subscribers, AOL's infrastructure proved to be inadequate to meet customers' needs. The result, not surprisingly, was massive subscriber defections. In fact, during the March 1996 quarter, net additions to AOL's subscriber base were virtually zero. The company again started tinkering with its accounting for marketing costs, pushing out the amortization period from eighteen to twenty-four months.

Those who had been bullish on AOL apparently had seen enough, and they dumped the stock, cutting the share price from a (pre-split) high in May 1996 of $75 to only $25 in September (see Figure 37-1). The very survival of the company was now being debated. On top of the soft subscriber growth, investors worried about the impact on future earnings of amortizing the $385 million of marketing costs that AOL had shifted to future periods.

In October 1996, management announced a bold plan to turn the company around. The plan included a scheme to write off the $385 million of marketing costs as a one-time, nonrecurring (and to be ignored) restructuring charge.

Over the subsequent months and years, AOL's business strengthened, making it the dominant Internet data provider. Investors have been richly rewarded,

FIGURE 37-1 AOL Share Price, 1994–1998

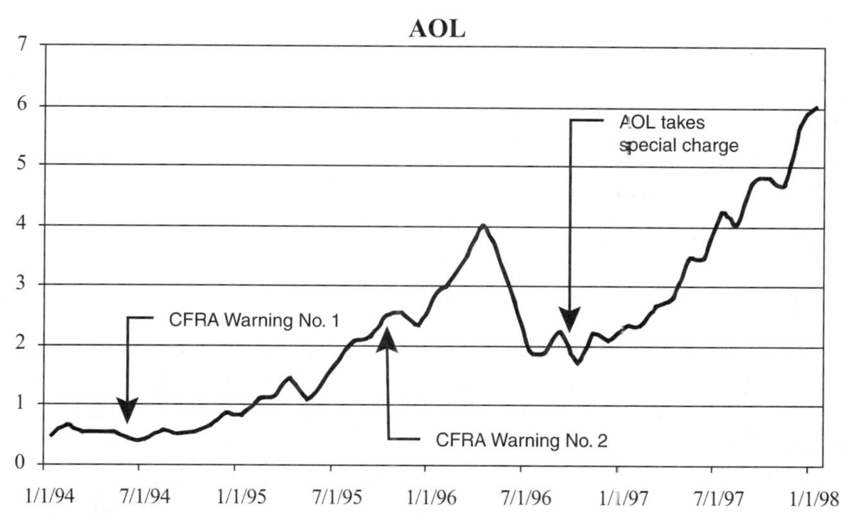

as the share price has appreciated almost twentyfold off its 1996 low. AOL used its richly valued stock to acquire Netscape and its nemesis CompuServe. Finally, in 2000, AOL swallowed media giant Time Warner.

Justice Is Not Always Swift in Coming . . . and May Arrive Too Late.

For years, AOL inflated earnings by aggressively deferring the marketing expenses related to sending out millions of computer disks to potential customers. That enabled AOL to look more profitable than it really was, helping it issue securities to raise cash and to make the acquisitions that fed its growth.

Although AOL's accounting transgressions failed to derail its aggressive plans, the regulators finally caught up with it. On May 15, 2000, AOL submitted to an SEC settlement (without admitting or denying any wrongdoing), paid a $3.5 million fine, and restated its former income to losses. The company was home free.

Warning Signs and Lessons from AOL. CFRA issued three separate warnings (June 1994, October 1995, and June 1996), focusing on AOL's aggressive and unusual accounting for marketing costs (see Table 37-4). Instead of charging those costs against income immediately, AOL pushed them to future periods, thereby inflating current-period income. Finally, in 1996, AOL changed to the more conservative approach of expensing such costs. In so doing, it also wrote off the previously deferred costs as a "special charge." As a result, future-period operating income received a boost from the exclusion of the already written off amortization costs.

Table 37-4 Warning Signs: AOL

Problem Indicated	Evidence	Shenanigan
Aggressive accounting: Capitalized normal operating costs	AOL capitalized marketing costs as "deferred subscriber acquisition costs."	No. 4
Aggressive accounting: Amortized costs too slowly	Stretched out amortization from twelve to twenty-four months.	No. 4
Aggressive accounting: Shifted future expenses to the current period as a special charge	AOL changed the accounting for marketing costs and wrote off the $385 million of deferred subscriber acquisition costs as a one-time nonrecurring charge.	No. 7

Medaphis: A Big Story

In April 1995, a CFRA analyst (electronically) searched through financial reports for any mention of "unbilled revenue"—a tip-off that aggressive revenue recognition was going on. That's when Medaphis Corporation (MEDA), a medical information company, first came to our attention. Based on its 1994 filing, the company would book 100 percent of a contract as revenue, although it had collected only 15 percent of that amount from the customer. CFRA calculated that of the $17.2 million of profit reported, only $3.1 million (or 18 percent) was appropriate.

After the release of our April 1995 report to investors, the share price declined markedly as a result of the accounting concerns (see Figure 37-2). Almost immediately thereafter, eight brokerage firms published harsh rebuttals to CFRA's warnings, helping the share price recover. By year-end, the share price had increased by another 25 percent. On March 20, 1996, it reached an all-time high of $53.25, giving the company a market value of $3.5 billion.

Medaphis had reported impressive growth during the period 1993 to 1995. Revenue for 1995 hit $467.7 million, up almost 50 percent from the prior year. Operating profits raced ahead 65 percent, hitting $75.2 million during 1995 (see Table 37-5). However, in June 1996, one year after our first warning, we noticed a more troubling sign. Specifically, MEDA had recorded as part of its revenue $12.5 million that represented its share of the earnings from an investment partnership. Investment income is certainly nice to have, but it should not be included as part of revenue. After the CFRA analyst restated the reported revenue and operating income by excluding the investment gains, the results were shocking—MEDA's operating profits were off 37 percent.

FIGURE 37-2 Medaphis Stock Price, 1994–1997

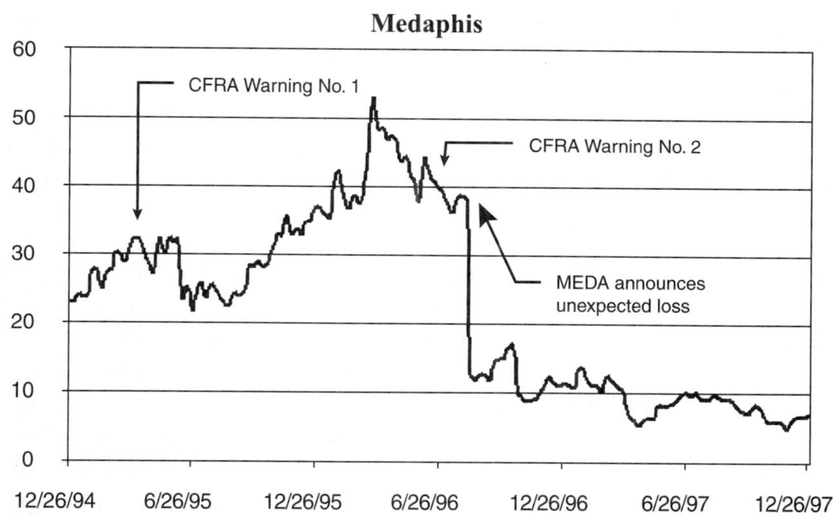

Table 37-5 Medaphis Operating Profits, 1994–1996

	Quarterly ($ in millions)		
	March 1996	March 1995	
Revenue	136.6	110.1	+24.1%
Operating income	24.0	18.2	+31.9%

	Annual ($ in millions)		
	December 1995	December 1994	
Revenues	467.7	319.1	+46.6%
Operating income	75.2	45.6	+64.9%

Two months after CFRA's second warning to investors was issued, MEDA shocked the markets by announcing a big unexpected loss. The company said that it was having problems with a major European contract and was reporting a loss on that contract, which involved designing and installing a computerized accounting system. The stock price (which had peaked in March at $53.25) melted down, falling 60 percent to $14.25 on volume of more than 42 million shares, well over half the 71 million shares outstanding.

Over the coming months, the news got worse. On October 22, when Medaphis reported a far larger loss than it had forecast in August, the stock fell 38 percent from its already depressed level. Medaphis also announced that it would restate earnings for the fourth quarter and full year of 1995. The restatements were necessary because of improperly recorded revenues booked in connection with a major license agreement executed in December 1995 and other unspecified transactions. These agreements had side letters relieving the customer of obligations under the agreement. The restatement reduced reported fourth-quarter 1995 operating results from a net income of approximately $4 million to a loss of $1.1 million *for the quarter* (a shocking 120 percent reversal). In a similar vein, the previously reported loss of $3.4 million for full year 1995 more than doubled to a restated loss of approximately $8.5 million. By March 1997, the stock had reached a low of $3 and MEDA's auditors were questioning whether the company could continue as a going concern. The company's accountants said that they did not expect the company to generate enough cash to pay off its debt.

Warning Signs and Lessons from Medaphis. While Medaphis's revenue and earnings growth *was* impressive, most of it was coming from the company's rapid acquisition program, not from organic growth. Since 1988, the company had made approximately fifty acquisitions, with the pace accelerating in more recent periods. In the March 1996 quarter alone, MEDA had announced six new acquisitions. In addition, CFRA found a number of other concerns related to operational deterioration and very aggressive accounting practices. (Reports were published in April 1995 and June 1996.) Evidence of the operational problems included an enormous operating cash flow deficit, bulging *unbilled* receivables, and deteriorating operating margins. Telltale signs of aggressive accounting included shifting certain operating costs to future periods by capitalizing software costs and including in revenue certain investment gains from a joint venture (see Table 37-6).

Particularly troubling was the ploy related to inflating revenue. During the quarter ended March 1996, MEDA and a German telecommunications company signed an agreement to provide systems integration and workflow engineering systems and services over a multiyear period.

Comparison of AOL and MEDA—Why Did AOL Recover and MEDA Not?

The MEDA vignette illustrates a most egregious accounting transgression: recording bogus revenue. By including in revenue the proceeds from an investment, the company hid from its investors a substantial revenue slowdown (revenue grew 12 percent rather than the reported 24 percent) and deteriorating operating margins. Once the truth was revealed in August 1996, investors fled. In contrast, despite AOL's aggressive accounting practice of pushing expenses to a later period, its revenue was solid and was reported accurately. After a rocky period in 1996, AOL's share price recovered its loss and went on to greater heights. MEDA had a very different fate: Its share price continued falling, only bottoming out at a level 90 percent off its high. Today MEDA is part of Atlanta-based Per Se Technologies.

Table 37-6 Warning Signs: Medaphis

Problem Indicated	Evidence	Shenanigan
Aggressive accounting: Recorded revenue too soon	▸ MEDA used percentage-of-completion accounting, thereby recording revenue before the product was shipped. ▸ There was a big increase in unbilled revenue.	No. 1
Aggressive accounting: Recorded investment income as revenue	▸ MEDA included in March 1996 revenue $12.5 million of net earnings from a joint venture.	No. 2
Aggressive accounting: Capitalized normal operating costs	▸ During 1995, MEDA capitalized $33.5 million (52 percent of pretax earnings), up an astonishing 423 percent from 1994.	No. 4
Aggressive accounting: Amortized costs too slowly	▸ MEDA lengthened the amortization period from five to seven years in 1995.	No. 4
Operational problems	▸ MEDA's cash flow from operations was deteriorating. ▸ MEDA's margins were deteriorating. ▸ MEDA had made acquisitions of troubled companies.	—
Aggressive Accounting: Shifted future expenses to the current period as a special charge	▸ MEDA recorded a $25 million restructuring charge and created reserves.	No. 7

SEARCHING FOR SHENANIGANS

READING 38

LEARNING OUTCOMES

The candidate should be able to:

a. explain the two basic strategies underlying all accounting "shenanigans," and describe seven categories of techniques that may be used by management to distort a company's reported financial performance and financial condition;

b. identify conservative and aggressive accounting policies;

c. describe why "shenanigans" exist, and explain where they are most likely to occur;

d. list the documents that an analyst should use to identify "shenanigans," and explain what information to look for in such documents.

Detection is, or ought to be, an exact science, and should be treated in the same cold and unemotional way.

When you have eliminated the impossible, whatever remains, however improbable, must be the truth.

SIR ARTHUR CONAN DOYLE
Author and creator of Sherlock Holmes

INTRODUCTION 1

Sherlock Holmes and other good detectives search for clues, examine all the evidence, and deduce what actually happened. Similarly, successful investors, lenders, and analysts read financial reports and other information, searching for clues and deducing how the company actually performed in the past and how it is likely to perform in the future. This reading describes the process of evaluating financial evidence.

An essential skill for analysts is the ability to detect early signs that companies are using financial shenanigans to camouflage problems. This reading discusses the sources of information analysts use (see Table 38-1), including database searches that enable them to systematically hone in on the problems.

Table 38-1 Sources of Information

- Press releases
- SEC filings
- Company interview
- Commercial databases (screening)

2 LIVING A DREAM—AND A NIGHTMARE

Imagine living the American dream during the Internet era. You and your college buddy form a software company. For the first few years you work around the clock, but you take virtually no cash compensation. Instead, you reward yourself and your valued employees with stock and stock options. You begin meeting with investment bankers to plan your much anticipated initial public offering (IPO). Then it happens—the bankers successfully peddle your shares to the public. You now have your first millions. But that's only the beginning. The share price of your (now public) company begins to levitate, appreciating more than 1,000 percent. You are one of the wealthiest people in America and you are not even old enough to run for the presidency. The media treat you like royalty.

That was the real-life dream of MicroStrategy's (MSTR) founder, Michael Saylor. Founded in 1989, MSTR went public in 1998. At that time, Saylor's stock was worth over $200 million. That was only the beginning of an incredible odyssey. In the last four months of 1999, the share price began to rise dramatically, from $20 to over $100 (see Figure 38-1). Over the next ten weeks, the stock reached the stratospheric price of $333. Michael Saylor's net worth reached an almost inconceivable $14 billion; he was the richest person in the nation's capital.

Then the dream turned into a nightmare of epic proportions. In March 2000, MSTR disclosed to investors that its financial reports contained accounting irregularities. The financial reports for the years 1997 to 1999 had to be restated,

FIGURE 38-1 Microstrategy Stock Prices, 1999–2000+

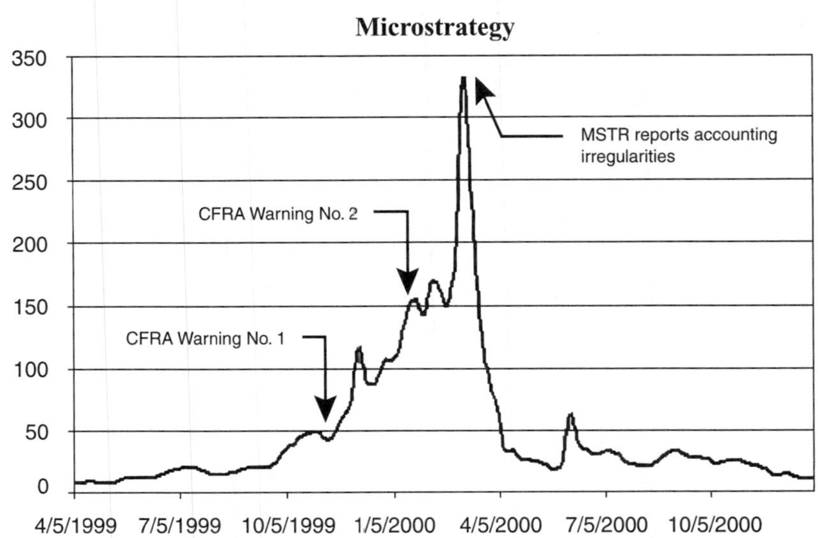

resulting in massive losses rather than the previously reported profits. Shocked investors started dumping the stock, dropping the share price $140 the day the news broke. That was only the beginning. The once $333 stock didn't bottom out until it reached $1.75 in March 2001.

What Led to the Collapse?

In early March 2000, only weeks after the auditors at PricewaterhouseCoopers (PWC) had blessed MSTR's 1999 financial reports, contained in the prospectus for a proposed stock offering, *Forbes* magazine questioned the company's accounting.

PWC conducted an internal investigation and concluded that the company's audited financial reports were false and misleading. The auditor's swift about-face, an extremely rare event, sent the share price into a free fall.

The Punishment

In addition to watching their net worth dwindle by billions, senior management had to disgorge $10 million of improper gains from stock sales and pay a fine of $1 million. That was a pittance compared to the fines paid by the auditors to settle the litigation: those fines totaled $55 million.

Warning Signs in Press Releases. On October 5, 1999, MSTR announced in a press release that it had signed a deal with NCR Corporation. The following month, the CFRA warned investors about an unusual revenue-generating transaction that was first disclosed in that press release. In the release, MSTR described a $52.5 million licensing agreement and a partnership with NCR Corporation. Under the agreement, MSTR invested in an NCR partnership and NCR returned the favor and purchased MSTR's products. We refer to that practice as a "boomerang." As the press release put it,

> Under the terms of the partnership, NCR signed a $27.5 million OEM {Original Equipment Manufacturer} agreement for MicroStrategy's entire suite of Intelligent E-Business products. . . . The agreement also includes several ongoing royalty streams associated with the reselling of MicroStrategy's products and personal information services. In addition, MicroStrategy has chosen to purchase an NCR Teradata Warehouse worth $11 million to power the Strategy.com network.
>
> As part of the OEM agreement, NCR will become a master affiliate of Strategy.com. As a master affiliate, NCR will join the network, sell Strategy.com affiliations, and sell MicroStrategy products and services. As part of the agreement, MicroStrategy will provide NCR's future OLAP technology. MicroStrategy has agreed to purchase NCR's TeraCube business and all related intellectual property in exchange for $14 million in MicroStrategy stock.

Initially, Wall Street seemed concerned about CFRA's warnings, and the share price fell 10 percent. However, investment bankers and analysts at Merrill Lynch, who were helping MSTR float a secondary stock offering, issued a stern rebuttal of CFRA's warning. This seemed to alleviate investors' concerns, as the stock price strengthened and began to rise rapidly.

It's Déjà Vu All Over Again

By the time CFRA issued its second warning in late January 2000, the share price was approaching $100, double the price at the time of our November warning. Again, we found an unusual disclosure about revenue recorded from a new joint venture partner in a press release issued by the company. The facts are quite similar to those in the NCR ploy, with a press release issued a week after the quarter closed. The other player this time was Exchange Application, Inc., and the press release (excerpts from which are shown below) was dated January 6, 2000. However, MSTR, curiously, recorded the revenue in December 1999.

> Under the terms of the agreement, Exchange Applications will pay MicroStrategy an initial $30 million fee, payable through a combination of cash and Exchange Applications stock, of which approximately one-third will be recognized by MicroStrategy as revenue during the fourth quarter of 1999. In addition, MicroStrategy can earn up to an additional $35 million for future eCRM applications over the next two to three years.
>
> As part of the agreement, Exchange Applications will become a master affiliate of Strategy.com. As a master affiliate, Exchange Applications will join the network, sell Strategy.com affiliations, and sell MicroStrategy products and services.

Press Releases Were the Key

The MSTR story underscores the fact that important information may be contained in corporate press releases. The auditors at PricewaterhouseCoopers missed the problem and certified that the financial reports could be relied upon. Yet investors who read MSTR's press releases in October 1999 and January 2000 would have seen the warning signs.

3 THE "PRO FORMA" GAME

As the MSTR example illustrates, disclosures contained in press releases can provide useful information for investors. One problem, however, is the occasional attempt to obfuscate the truth by using a new metric called *pro forma* earnings. This measure removes from net income items that management believes are not related to the company's normal recurring business. Traditionally, pro forma numbers were provided to give investors an idea of what the earnings of a completely new business or the business that would result from a merger would look like.

Recently, some companies have issued press releases that contained misleading earnings, using the pro forma metric. They have whimsically excluded expenses that really are related to the company's normal recurring business. For example, some companies have excluded such costs as stock-based compensation and amortization expense in computing pro forma earnings.

This subjective approach to accounting and financial reporting can turn losses into profits. That's just what happened at Computer Associates International (CA), whose accounting was challenged in an April 2001 story in *The New York Times.* By changing the terms of its software sales and how it accounts for them, CA reported 42 cents of pro forma earnings per share in the final quarter of last year, versus a 59-cent loss under GAAP. Company officials say that the new presentation is actually more conservative and that the purpose of the change was not enhancing growth.

Similarly, giant telecom carrier Qwest Communications International Inc. reported $2 billion in quarterly earnings before interest, taxes, depreciation, and amortization, or EBITDA (one version of pro forma), in a January 2001 press release. Shareholders had to wait weeks to find out, in a footnote to the annual results, that according to GAAP rules, Qwest had actually lost $116 million.

SEC Not Amused by Pro Forma Chicanery

The SEC has taken note of these schemes. In a March 2001 speech, the agency's chief accountant, Lynn Turner, attacked company disclosures that appeared to "turn straw into gold." He described how the fixation on corporate profits has led companies to move from reporting EPS (earnings per share) to creating the turbocharged pro forma EBS—Everything but the Bad Stuff.

Mr. Buffett Says It Best

Investment guru Warren Buffett (chairman of Berkshire Hathaway) has poked fun at the managements that create pro forma metrics by comparing this practice to someone who first shoots an arrow and then, after seeing where it is headed, draws the bull's-eye on the target. Similarly, management first decides what it would like to highlight and then comes up with a descriptor. *It's pretty difficult to lose that game.*

Table 38-2 shows the enormous difference between the actual GAAP-based earnings and the inflated pro forma earnings recently reported by various technology companies. JDS Uniphase (JDSU), for example, actually lost $1.13 per share, yet in its pro forma disclosure, JDSU reported profits of $0.14 per share. That's some difference!

GATHERING FINANCIAL DATA 4

The main source of financial information on public companies is found in documents filed with the SEC. The financial shenanigans can be detected in SEC filings. These filings fall into two broad categories: regular and irregular. All companies regularly file annual (Form 10-K and the proxy) and quarterly (Form 10-Q) reports. In addition, companies are required to file when specific events occur, such as when insiders sell stock (Form 144), when additional stock or debt is offered to the public (Registration S-1 or S-4), and when other special events occur (Form 8-K).

Table 38-2 Comparison of Pro Forma and GAAP Results of Selected Companies (March 2001 Quarter)

Company	Pro Forma	GAAP	Difference
JDS Uniphase	$0.14	−$1.13	1.27
Checkfree	−0.04	−1.17	1.13
Terayon	−0.43	−1.01	0.58
Amazon.com	−0.22	−0.66	0.44
PMC-Sierra	0.02	−0.38	0.40
Corning	0.29	0.14	0.15
Qualcomm	0.29	0.18	0.11
Cisco Systems	0.18	0.12	0.06

A SUMMARY OF CORPORATE FILINGS

I. Regular Filings

A. Annual

Form 10-K[1]	All publicly held companies report detailed financial results to the SEC on an annual basis using Form 10-K. This report, audited by an independent accountant, is due 90 days after the close of the fiscal year.
Annual report	Publicly held companies generally report their financial results to their shareholders once a year in an annual report. This report, a condensed version of Form 10-K, contains the basic financial statements, the accompanying footnotes, a report by an independent CPA, and a letter from the company president.
Proxy	A proxy statement is mailed to stockholders in connection with the annual stockholders' meeting. This document explains proposals to be voted on by shareholders, including such routine items as the reappointment of the company's accounting firm. More important, it contains information about management compensation, management stock options, special deals for management and directors, related-party transactions, and changes of auditors.

B. Quarterly

Form 10-Q	Publicly held companies must file quarterly reports within 45 days after the close of each quarter using Form 10-Q. This report, which is far less detailed than Form 10-K, is *not* audited by a CPA. It contains a balance sheet, a statement of operations and cash flow, footnotes, and management discussion and analysis.
Form 8-K	Using Form 8-K, a company must inform the SEC of special events, including changes in control of the company, the acquisitions, dispositions, auditor changes, the resignation of directors, and bankruptcy. These reports are due within 15 days after the occurrence of the event, except in the case of auditor changes, which must be reported within 5 days.
Form 144	Insiders must register whenever they buy or sell stock.
Registration	Whenever a publicly held company plans to issue securities, it must first file a registration statement, including a prospectus and exhibits, with the SEC (using Form S-1 or Form S-18 for initial public offerings). The prospectus describes the company's background, financial performance, and future plans. It is a detailed business plan; it provides many valuable clues that can be used for predicting a company's future performance.

[1] Publicly held companies must file a Form 10-K, an annual shareholders' report, and a proxy. They have some flexibility concerning what to disclose in each one, so readers should view these three filings as an integrated document. A typical Form 10-K contains the following sections: Audited Balance Sheet, Statement of Operations, Cash Flow Statement, Footnotes to the Financial Statements, Management Discussion and Analysis, Auditor's Report, and Liquidity Position and Capital Expenditures.

Finding Data on Non-U.S. Companies Creates Challenges

Foreign companies that are not traded on U.S. stock exchanges have less stringent reporting requirements. Such companies rarely file quarterly results, and the annual report (Form 20-F) is due 180 days (rather than the 90 days for U.S. companies) after year-end. However, foreign companies typically report their results on their websites at least semiannually.

BEGINNING THE SEARCH FOR FINANCIAL SHENANIGANS

5

With these documents in hand, you are ready to begin the search. So, where should you start? Interestingly, you should *not* begin with the balance sheet, statement of operations, or statement of cash flows. Instead, your search should begin with the accompanying information, such as the auditor's report, proxy statements, footnotes to the financial statements, the letter from the president, management discussion and analysis (MD&A), and Form 8-K filings. Table 38-3 lists what you should look for in this material.

The Auditor's Report

Since the auditor has spent weeks reviewing the financial records and searching for accounting tricks, first read the auditor's opinion and see what he or she has to say. Generally, this letter contains a "clean" opinion. However, if the auditor has a strong reservation about the company's financial condition or the fairness of its financial statements, he or she will generally "qualify" the report.

Table 38-3 Using the Documents to Find Shenanigans

Where to Look	What to Look For
Auditor's report	Absence of opinion or qualified report
	Reputation of auditor
Proxy statement	Litigation
	Executive compensation
	Related-party transactions
Footnotes	Accounting policies/changes in those policies
	Related-party transactions
	Contingencies or commitments
President's letter	Forthrightness
MD&A	Specific concise disclosure
	Consistency with footnote disclosure
Form 8-K	Disagreements over accounting policies
Registration statement	Past performance
	Quality of management and directors

Watch for Qualified Opinions

Investors should be cautious about investing in any company that receives a qualified opinion—especially if it is a "going concern" qualification. That was the opinion that auditors Ernst & Young gave on Carolco Pictures' 1991 financial statements. Ernst & Young indicated "substantial doubts" about the movie company's ability to continue as a going concern after it posted a loss of $265 million. A going concern qualification warns investors and others that the company is experiencing major financial difficulties.

Be Wary When No Audit Committee Exists

Another warning sign for investors is the absence of an audit committee composed of outside members of the board of directors. This committee serves as a buffer between management and the independent auditor. While companies that are listed on the New York Stock Exchange are required to have audit committees, there is no such requirement for the majority of publicly traded companies. Investors should be concerned if (1) no audit committee exists, and/or (2) members of the audit committee appear not to be independent of management.

Proxy Statements

Although proxy statements are separate from the annual report, investors should consider them an integral part of the financial report. Astute investors read the proxy statement to search for important information that is not included in the financial reports, such as special compensation "perks" for officers and directors, and also lawsuits and other contingent obligations facing the company. One such investor, Hugo Quackenbush, senior vice president of Charles Schwab & Co., describes proxy statements as follows:

> They are like a soap opera in black and white. Management has to disclose all the stuff they don't want to and investors can get more of the texture and flavor of a company reading the proxy statement than the glossy annual report.

Footnotes to the Financial Statements

Appended to the financial statements are footnotes. They provide the reader with a wealth of information for assessing the financial condition of a company and the quality of its reported earnings. Specifically, the footnotes detail such matters as accounting policies selected, pending or imminent litigation, long-term purchase commitments, changes in accounting principles or estimates, industry-specific notes (e.g., unbilled receivables for a government contractor), and segment information showing which operations are healthy and which are not.

Many analysts agree that the information in the footnotes is actually more important than what is shown on the financial statements. Columnist Kenneth Fisher, for example, wrote in *Forbes:*

> The back of the report, the footnotes is where they hide the bad stuff they didn't want to disclose but had to . . . they bury the bodies where the fewest folks find them—in the fine print.

Table 38-4 gives criteria for evaluating a company's accounting policies, whether they are conservative or aggressive.

Table 38-4 Evaluating Accounting Policies

Accounting Policies	Conservative	Aggressive
Revenue recognition	After sale, when risk has passed to buyer	At sale, although risk remains
Depreciation choice	Accelerated over shorter period	Straight-line over longer period
Inventory method	LIFO (assuming prices are rising)	FIFO (assuming prices are rising)
Amortization of goodwill	Over a shorter period	Over 40 years
Estimate of warranty	High estimate	Low estimate
Estimate of bad debts	High estimate	Low estimate
Treatment of advertising	Expense	Capitalize
Loss contingencies	Accrue loss	Footnote only

Favor Companies with Conservative Accounting Policies

Footnotes can provide signs of "creative" accounting or gimmicks. Some footnotes should lead you to question not only the validity of the financial statements, but also the integrity of management. Companies that fail to use conservative accounting methods may be demonstrating a lack of integrity in their financial reporting process. Indeed, many analysts place a premium on companies that use conservative accounting policies. In searching for excellent companies, for example, the widely respected analyst and shenanigan buster Thornton O'glove offers the following advice:

> Look for companies that use very conservative accounting principles. In my experience, if a company does not cut corners in its accounting, there's a good chance it doesn't cut corners in its operations. You know you've got your money with a high quality management.

Be Alert for an Aggressive or Inappropriate Inventory Valuation

The selection of an inventory valuation method, which can substantially affect a company's reported profits, often indicates the degree of conservatism of a company's accounting policies. The most popular methods are last-in, first-out (LIFO) and first-in, first-out (FIFO). LIFO charges the latest inventory costs as an expense first; conversely, FIFO charges the earliest costs first.

During inflationary periods (i.e., when inventory costs are rising), the difference between LIFO and FIFO can affect profits substantially. Under these circumstances, LIFO generally produces lower reported profits for a company than does FIFO (this also results in lower taxes and therefore in higher cash flows). FIFO undervalues the rising costs of inventory and produces a higher level of reported profits. Thus FIFO is often considered a more aggressive inventory valuation technique.

Consider Pending or Imminent Litigation

In addition to searching the footnotes for nonconservative accounting principles, note any pending or imminent litigation. (The litigation footnote is usually less informative than a company's response to item 3 on Form 10-K.) Such litigation may have serious consequences for a company's future operations.

Question Long-Term Purchase Commitments

As well as letting investors know about litigation, footnotes also can alert them to long-term purchase commitments. Buried in the footnotes of Columbia Gas Systems' first-quarter 1991 10-Q was notification that the company had a long-term commitment to purchase natural gas at inflated prices. Investors who noted this footnote and understood its significance should have been nervous. The company had signed a long-term contract in early 1991 (during Operation Desert Storm in Kuwait), when gas prices were at their highest. Since Columbia's customers were not locked into buying this high-priced gas, investors should have concluded that the company would be unable to sell it at a profit. Sure enough, Columbia was unable to sell the gas, and in April 1991 it filed for bankruptcy. In subsequent lawsuits, investors and lenders alleged that Columbia had misled them by failing to disclose a substantial contingent liability.

Watch for Changes in Accounting Principles

As indicated earlier, management has substantial flexibility in choosing accounting principles, and that choice generally affects a company's profits. Investors and lenders should thus take note whenever a company changes accounting principles for no apparent reason. Such changes can also sometimes signal bookkeeping games to boost weak financial statements.

Slowing down a company's depreciation schedule or changing its depreciation method can dress up earnings quite nicely. In 1988, according to stock analyst David Healy, General Motors was able to post record earnings directly because of its decision to liberalize its accounting policies. Healy calculated that about $1.8 billion of GM's $4.9 billion in profits came from such tricks: $790 million from changing its depreciation period for plant assets from 35 to 45 years, $480 million from changing its accounting for pensions, $217 million from changing its inventory valuation policies, and $270 million from changing its assumptions about the residual value of cars leased out by the company.

The Letter from the President

After reading the footnotes, you should turn to the front of the annual report, where you will be greeted with a picture of and some words from the president. Sometimes the president announces some recent event that will significantly hurt the company's future performance. But don't count on it. The tone of this letter is almost invariably upbeat—regardless of the real conditions. In a recent study intended to identify the words used most frequently to disguise the fact that a company is in serious trouble, Professor Martin Kellman found that no word is more ominous than *challenging*. His interpretation of "challenging": "Your company has lost money, is losing money, and will continue to lose money." His recommendation: "If the C-word appears in any form three or more times in the front pages of any annual report—sell immediately!"

> The first four months of 2001 were extremely challenging as we went from year-over-year bookings in excess of 70% in November, to 30% negative growth within a span of months.—John Chambers, CEO of Cisco Corporation, May 2001

Read the Letter from the President with a Grain of Salt

Many professional analysts agree that the letter from the president is used to bias the reader into thinking that the company is doing better than it really is. Thornton O'glove describes the president's letter this way:

> It is designed to serve as a veil for the striptease—namely, to offer a hint of what is underneath, to indicate shape and form but not to permit too much insight.

O'glove also suggests reading the president's letter for the previous three or four years to determine how earlier predictions turned out. Like O'glove, Raymond DeVoe (an analyst with Legg Mason Wood Walker, Inc.) has made a hobby of perusing annual reports and their letters from the president. DeVoe has developed a way of translating what the president is really saying. Here are a few of his "translations" of presidential declarations:

> ANNUAL REPORT: "Your company is now poised for significant earnings growth."
> (TRANSLATION: "We lost so much last year and wrote off everything possible, so earnings couldn't get much worse.")
> ANNUAL REPORT: "These results were somewhat below the projections that management had announced publicly during the quarter."
> (TRANSLATION: "We lied.")
> ANNUAL REPORT: "The quarter's earnings contained a substantial contribution from a settlement arising from the involuntary termination of operating equipment."
> (TRANSLATION: "If the plane hadn't crashed, we would have been in the red. Fortunately, only one was killed, and the insurance company paid off a helluva lot.")

While most letters from presidents are short on informative disclosure and long on fluff, Warren Buffett's letter stands out for its candor. Buffett often uses his letter to discuss mistakes that he has made and to reflect on important issues of the time. Of particular interest in his 1992 letter was his criticism of the financial shenanigans used in the insurance industry to prop up earnings. He stated:

> Loss-reserve data for the [insurance] industry indicate that there is reason to be skeptical of the outcome, and it may turn out that 1991's ratio should have been worse than was reported. In the long run, of course, trouble awaits managements that paper-over operating problems with accounting maneuvers. Eventually, managements of this kind achieve the same result as the seriously-ill patient who tells his doctor: "I can't afford the operation, but would you accept a small payment to touch up the X-rays?"

Focus on Management and Its Estimates

Reading the president's letter is a good way of assessing the integrity of management. Things to look for:

- Does management cast a rosy glow on unfavorable developments?
- Has there been a significant turnover of high-ranking managers from year to year? (That could be a tipoff to corporate turmoil.)

Management Discussion and Analysis

If the information in the president's letter lacks substance, try reading the section in the annual report and Form 10-K entitled "Management Discussion and Analysis." This section requires management to discuss specific issues on the financial statements and to assess the company's current financial situation, its liquidity, and its planned capital expenditures for the next year. This section is also a good place to learn about management's candor. If the company is clearly having financial difficulties, the MD&A section should level with the readers and not try to avoid or sugar-coat the problem.

Form 8-K

After you have reviewed the company's annual report (and Form 10-K), scan the SEC website, http://www.sec.gov, to learn whether there have been any recent Form 8-K filings for the company. Besides telling investors about major acquisitions or divestitures by the company, Form 8-K highlights any changes in auditors. Changes could offer clues to financial shenanigans, especially in those cases in which the auditors may have been fired because they found some problem that they were unwilling to suppress.

A company that fires its auditor because of a disagreement over financial principles and then shops around for a new auditor that is more agreeable to its interpretation of GAAP has engaged in what is known as "opinion shopping." To prevent this practice, the SEC requires a company that changes auditors to file a Form 8-K, notifying the commission of the termination and giving the details of any accounting disagreements. Unfortunately, few disagreements are ever actually disclosed in these filings.

Form 144: Insider Stock Transactions

Management and directors must notify the SEC of their intention to purchase or sell company stock. Substantial insider sales might indicate impending problems at the company.

Company Interview

After you have thoroughly read and analyzed the company's SEC filings, consider interviewing a senior financial executive at the company. Typically, the chief financial officer (CFO) would be the first choice. Others who may be helpful are the head of investor relations, the corporate comptroller, and the treasurer. Since these companies are publicly held, their officers expect telephone calls from investors concerning issues raised in SEC filings.

During the course of the interview, you have a wonderful opportunity to not only gather specific factual information, but also assess the "tone" of senior management through the way they address your concerns.

Fair Disclosure (FD) Guidelines

Private discussions with analysts and investors have become somewhat less open since the SEC issued new guidelines called Regulation FD. These guidelines were issued because certain professional investors and brokerage firm analysts were being given information before other investors or information that was not available to other investors.

While Regulation FD may cause companies to not answer all your questions, it should help individual investors in two ways: Big investors will no longer be able to obtain information before the rest of us, and companies will probably send out more frequent and more complete press releases to ensure compliance with full and fair disclosure.

Commercial Database

Financial analysts use commercial databases to screen for companies exhibiting certain warning signs. CFRA's analysts use Compustat (a division of Standard & Poor's) and Lexis/Nexis (a division of Reed Elsevier).

STUDY SESSION 9
FINANCIAL STATEMENT ANALYSIS: ASSETS

READING ASSIGNMENTS

Reading 39 Analysis of Inventories
Reading 40 Analysis of Long-Lived Assets: Part I—The Capitalization Decision
Reading 41 Analysis of Long-Lived Assets: Part II—Analysis of Depreciation and Impairment

LEARNING OUTCOMES

Reading 39: Analysis of Inventories

The candidate should be able to:

a. compute ending inventory balances and cost of goods sold using the LIFO, FIFO, and average cost methods to account for product inventory and explain the relationship among and the usefulness of inventory and cost-of-goods-sold data provided by the LIFO, FIFO, and average cost methods when prices are 1) stable or 2) changing;

b. adjust the financial statements of companies using different inventory accounting methods to compare and describe the effect of the different methods on cost of goods sold and inventory balances discuss how a company's choice of inventory accounting method affects other financial items such as income, cash flow, and working capital, and compute and describe the effects of the choice of inventory method on profitability, liquidity, activity, and solvency ratios;

c. discuss the reasons that a LIFO reserve might decline during a given period, and discuss the implications of such a decline for financial analysis;

d. discuss how inventories are reported in the financial statements and how cost, market, and net realizable value are generally determined.

Note:
See the discussion in Study Session 8 about different names and definitions for financial ratios in the readings assigned in the Financial Statement Analysis study sessions.

Note:
Except where noted as required reading the "Boxes" in Readings 39, 40 and 41 are not part of the Level I reading assignment.

Reading 40: Analysis of Long-Lived Assets: Part I—The Capitalization Decision

The candidate should be able to:

a. compute and describe the effects of capitalizing versus expensing on net income, shareholders' equity, cash flow from operations, and financial ratios, explain the effects on financial statements and the interest coverage ratios (times interest earned) of capitalizing interest costs, and explain the circumstances in which intangible assets, including software development costs and research and development costs, are capitalized;

b. calculate and describe both the initial and long-term effects of asset revaluations on financial ratios.

Reading 41: Analysis of Long-Lived Assets: Part II—Analysis of Depreciation and Impairment

The candidate should be able to:

a. identify the different depreciation methods, discuss how the choice of a depreciation method affects a company's financial statements, ratios, and taxes, explain the role of depreciable lives and salvage values in the computation of depreciation expenses, and compute and describe how changing depreciation methods or changing the estimated useful life or salvage value of an asset affects financial statements and ratios;

b. discuss the use of fixed asset disclosures to compare companies' average age of depreciable assets, and calculate, using such disclosures, the average age and average depreciable life of fixed assets;

c. define impairment of long-lived assets and explain what effect such impairment has on a company's financial statements and ratios;

d. list the requirements of SFAS 143, Accounting for Asset Retirement Obligations (AROs), and explain the likely financial statement and ratio effects for most firms.

ANALYSIS OF INVENTORIES

READING

39

LEARNING OUTCOMES

The candidate should be able to:

a. compute ending inventory balances and cost of goods sold using the LIFO, FIFO, and average cost methods to account for product inventory and explain the relationship among and the usefulness of inventory and cost-of-goods-sold data provided by the LIFO, FIFO, and average cost methods when prices are 1) stable or 2) changing;

b. adjust the financial statements of companies using different inventory accounting methods to compare and describe the effect of the different methods on cost of goods sold and inventory balances, discuss how a company's choice of inventory accounting method affects other financial items such as income, cash flow, and working capital, and compute and describe the effects of the choice of inventory method on profitability, liquidity, activity, and solvency ratios;

c. discuss the reasons that a LIFO reserve might decline during a given period, and discuss the implications of such a decline for financial analysis;

d. discuss how inventories are reported in the financial statements and how cost, market and net realizable value are generally determined.

INTRODUCTION 1

During 1999, the spot price of crude oil[1] rose from less than $10 per barrel to more than $25 per barrel, an increase of more than 150%. Crude oil continued to rise in early 2000, nearing $32 per barrel in March. Simultaneously, the price of gasoline sold at the pump increased dramatically in most countries. Consumers

[1] Measured by the Brent Crude "near contract generic future" as reported on Bloomberg.

and politicians criticized oil companies for immediately raising the price of gasoline sold at the retail level. They argued that the gasoline being sold had been refined from oil purchased at a price of $10 per barrel and, hence, raising the price of this "old" gasoline resulted in windfall profits.

The oil companies countered that since the market price of oil had risen, replacing the old oil now cost more and thus raising the price of gasoline was justified by current market conditions.

The accounting choice of last-in, first-out (LIFO) versus first-in, first-out (FIFO) for inventory and cost of goods sold (COGS) mirrors this debate as to the more appropriate measure of income. The choice affects the firm's income statement, balance sheet, and related ratios. Perhaps more important, in contrast to most financial reporting choices, the choice of inventory method has real cash flow effects as it affects income taxes paid by the firm.

2 INVENTORY AND COST OF GOODS SOLD: BASIC RELATIONSHIPS

The inventory account is affected by two events: the purchase (or manufacture) of goods (P) and their subsequent sale (COGS). The relationship between these events and the balance of beginning inventory (BI) and ending inventory (EI) can be expressed as

(1) $EI = BI + P - \text{COGS}$ or
(2) $BI + P = \text{COGS} + EI$

For any period, prior to the preparation of financial statements for the period, the left side of the second equation is known: the beginning inventory plus purchases (cost of goods acquired for sale during the period). Preparation of the income statement and balance sheet for the period requires the allocation of these costs ($BI + P$) between COGS and ending inventory. This process is illustrated under two scenarios:

Beginning inventory: 200 units @ $10/unit = $2,000

		Scenario 1: Stable Prices		Scenario 2: Rising Prices	
Quarter	**Purchases Units**	**Unit Cost**	**Purchases Dollars**	**Unit Cost**	**Purchases Dollars**
1	100	$10	$1,000	$11	$1,100
2	150	10	1,500	12	1,800
3	150	10	1,500	13	1,950
4	100	10	1,000	14	1,400
Total	500		$5,000		$6,250
			$BI + P =$ $7,000		$BI + P =$ $8,250

Units sold: 100 units per quarter for a total of 400 units
Ending inventory: 300 units

Scenario 1: Stable Prices

Beginning inventory plus purchases equals \$7,000. Since unit costs are constant at \$10 per unit and 400 units were sold, the COGS equals \$4,000 (400 × \$10) and the cost of the 300 units in ending inventory equals \$3,000 (300 × \$10).

$$BI + P = \text{COGS} + EI$$
$$\$2{,}000 + \$5{,}000 = \$4{,}000 + \$3{,}000$$

However, perfectly stable prices are the exception rather than the norm. In addition to general inflationary pressures, costs and prices for specific goods are constantly changing. Accounting for inventory and COGS in such an environment, as a result, becomes more complex.

Scenario 2: Rising Prices

Beginning inventory plus purchases equals \$8,250. Unlike the case of stable prices, the allocation between COGS and the cost of ending inventory requires an assumption as to the flow of costs. Essentially, three alternative assumptions are possible: *FIFO, LIFO, and weighted-average cost.*

FIFO accounting assumes that the costs of items *first purchased* are deemed to be the costs of items *first sold* and these costs enter COGS; ending inventory is made up of the cost of the most recent items purchased.

At the opposite extreme is LIFO accounting where items *last purchased* are assumed to be the ones *first sold* and the ending inventory is made up of the earliest costs incurred.

Finally, as its name implies, weighted-average cost accounting uses the (same) average cost for both the items sold and those remaining in closing inventory.

In our example, *the assumptions of rising prices and an increase in the inventory balance generate three alternative allocations of the cost of goods available for sale* ($BI + P$), on the income statement and balance sheet (the calculations are shown in Exhibit 39-1):

Method	*BI*	+	*P*	=	COGS	+	*EI*
FIFO	\$2,000	+	\$6,250	=	\$4,300	+	\$3,950
Weighted-average	2,000	+	6,250	=	4,714	+	3,536
LIFO	2,000	+	6,250	=	5,150	+	3,100

COMPARISON OF INFORMATION PROVIDED BY ALTERNATIVE METHODS

3

This section compares the information provided by the three alternative accounting methods.

Balance Sheet Information: Inventory Account

The ending inventory consists of 300 units. At current replacement cost (i.e., the fourth-quarter unit cost of \$14), the inventory would have a carrying value of \$4,200. The FIFO inventory of \$3,950 comes closest to this amount because FIFO allocates the earliest costs to COGS, leaving the most recent costs in ending inventory.

EXHIBIT 39-1 Allocation of Costs Under Different Inventory Methods, Scenario 2

A. FIFO

The 400 units sold (COGS) are assumed to carry the earliest costs incurred and the 300 units left in inventory carry the latest costs:

COGS		Ending Inventory	
200 @ \$10 =	\$2,000	100 @ \$14 =	\$1,400
100 @ \$11 =	\$1,100	150 @ \$13 =	\$1,950
100 @ \$12 =	\$1,200	50 @ \$12 =	\$ 600
400	\$4,300	300	\$3,950

B. LIFO

The 400 units sold (COGS) are assumed to carry the latest costs incurred and the 300 units left in inventory carry the earliest costs:

COGS		Ending Inventory	
100 @ \$14 =	\$1,400	200 @ \$10 =	\$2,000
150 @ \$13 =	\$1,950	100 @ \$11 =	\$1,100
150 @ \$12 =	\$1,800		
400	\$5,150	300	\$3,100

C. Weighted-Average

The total costs for the 700 units = \$8,250. On a per-unit basis, this results in a weighted-average unit cost of:

$$\frac{\$8{,}250}{700} = \$11.786$$

$$\text{COGS} = 400 \times \$11.786 = \$4{,}714$$

$$\text{Ending inventory} = 300 \times \$11.786 = \$3{,}536$$

Conversely, the LIFO balance of \$3,100 is furthest from the current cost as LIFO accounting allocates the earliest (outdated) costs to ending inventory. In fact, the cost of ending inventory for many companies using LIFO may be decades old[2] and virtually useless as an indicator of the current or replacement cost of inventories on hand.

From a balance sheet perspective, therefore, inventories based on FIFO are preferable to those presented under LIFO, as carrying values most closely reflect current cost. In other words, FIFO provides a measure of inventory that is closer to its current (economic) value.

[2] For example, Caterpillar has stated that the LIFO method "was first adopted for the major portion of inventories in 1950."

The carrying amount of inventory can also be affected by changes in market value as discussed below.

Inventory Valuation: Lower of Cost or Market

GAAP requires the use of the lower-of-cost-or-market valuation basis (LCM) for inventories, with market value defined as replacement cost.[3] The LCM valuation basis follows the principle of conservatism (on both the balance sheet and income statement) since it recognizes losses or declines in market value as they occur, whereas increases are reported only when inventory is sold. LCM can be used with LIFO for financial statement purposes. However, for tax purposes LIFO cannot be combined with LCM. Firms using LIFO cannot recognize (and obtain tax benefits from) writedowns and declines in market value for tax purposes.[4]

Income Statement Information: Cost of Goods Sold

Consider a situation where an item purchased for $6 is sold for $10 at a time when it costs $7 to replace it. Prior to replacement of the item, reported income is $4 ($10 − $6). However, if income is defined as the amount available for distribution to shareholders without impairing the firm's operations, then it can be argued that income is only $3, as $7 (not the original cost of $6) are needed to replace the item in inventory and continue operations. The $1 difference between the original cost of the item and the cost of replacement is referred to as a holding gain or inventory profit,[5] and it is debatable whether this amount should be considered income.[6]

In our hypothetical case, *only if the item were not replaced* would there be $10 to distribute to shareholders, indicating income of $4. Under a going-concern assumption, however, firms that sell their inventory need to replenish it constantly for sales in the future. Thus, income should be measured after providing for the replacement of inventory. In addition, the increase in inventory costs suggests that income of $3 is a better indicator of expected future income than $4.

In our example, the replacement cost of the items sold (using the unit cost for each quarter) is $5,000[7] [(100 × $11) + (100 × $12) + (100 × $13) + (100 × $14)]. As U.S. GAAP uses a historical cost framework, however, replacement cost accounting is not permitted. LIFO allocates the most recent purchase prices

---

[3] However, replacement cost cannot exceed the net realizable value or be below the net realizable value less the normal profit margin.

[4] Otherwise, the firm could have the best of both worlds and obtain tax savings whether costs were rising or declining.

[5] If we use terminology, economic income equals $4. As the holding gain is $1, sustainable (future) income is $3. Jennings, Simko, and Thompson (1996) confirm that LIFO-based cost of goods sold is a more useful indicator of the firm's future resource outflows than ("as-if") non-LIFO cost of goods sold as LIFO-based income statements explained more of the variation in equity valuations than non-LIFO income statements. However, in contrast to our earlier argument, they did not find ("as-if") non-LIFO balance sheets to be more informative than LIFO-based balance sheets.

[6] The situation is analogous to having purchased a home before a rapid increase in real estate prices and not being able to benefit from your good fortune because any replacement home would cost as much as the home you live in now.

[7] If the computation were done on an annual basis, the replacement cost would be $5,600 (400 × $14) using the most recent purchase price to measure replacement cost.

to COGS. The reported LIFO COGS of $5,150 is, therefore, closest to the replacement cost, with the FIFO COGS of $4,300 furthest from this cost. *During periods of changing prices and stable or growing inventories, LIFO is the most informative accounting method for income statement purposes, in that it provides a better measure of current income and future profitability*. This leaves us in something of a quandary, since FIFO provides the best measure for the balance sheet.[8]

The preceding discussion implied the use of a single method for all inventories of the firm. In practice, firms often use more than one inventory method. They may use different methods for their foreign operations since LIFO is rarely used outside the United States, or they may use different methods for particular business segments. This factor serves to disguise further the impact of reported inventory on the income statement and balance sheet.

Additionally, the LIFO measurements are based on assumptions and estimates that are complex in a multiproduct environment and are affected by management choice.

Finally, the use of FIFO, LIFO, or weighted-average for the allocation of cost of goods available for sale is preceded by the measurement of costs included in inventory. In a manufacturing environment, as Box 39-1 illustrates, such measurement is also affected by management choice.

From an analyst's perspective the use of different methods is not so grim. Information is often available to permit restatement of financial statements from one method to the other. Such restatement is illustrated later in this reading. Our discussion now, however, turns to the financial statement effects of the choice between LIFO and FIFO.

4 LIFO VERSUS FIFO: INCOME, CASH FLOW, AND WORKING CAPITAL EFFECTS

The above example illustrates that, in periods of rising prices and stable or increasing inventory quantities, the use of LIFO results in higher COGS expense and lower reported income. In the absence of income taxes, there would be no difference in cash flow. Cash flow would equal payments made for inventory purchases and be independent of the accounting method used.

When LIFO is a permitted method for income taxes, however, lower income translates into lower taxes and thus higher operating cash flows. In the United States, unlike other accounting policy choices that allow differing methods of accounting for financial statements and tax purposes, *IRS regulations require that the same method of inventory accounting used for tax purposes also be used for financial reporting*. From an economic perspective, given rising prices, LIFO is the better choice, as taxes will be lower and cash flows will be higher despite the lower reported income.[9]

---

[8] The weighted-average method falls someplace in between the FIFO and LIFO methods both in terms of the balance sheet and income statement. It is seen by some as a compromise method. Alternatively, we can argue that it is the worst of the three choices: Unlike LIFO and FIFO, which provide good information on one financial statement, the weighted-average method does not do so for either statement. Practically speaking, however, the weighted-average method tends to be closer to FIFO than LIFO, especially with respect to inventory costs on the balance sheet.

[9] The question of why, given the foregoing, all firms do not use LIFO will be considered later in the reading.

BOX 39-1 INVENTORY COSTING IN A MANUFACTURING ENVIRONMENT

Accounting for inventories in a manufacturing environment adds another dimension to the problem of inventory costing. Unlike merchandising operations, which carry only finished goods inventory, manufacturing operations carry three types of inventory: (1) raw material, (2) work in process, and (3) finished goods.

Inventories include raw material costs as well as labor and overhead costs required to transform the raw materials into finished goods. Determining the amount of overhead (indirect) costs poses the most problems. Included in (factory) overhead are items such as: supervisors' salaries, depreciation/rent of factory plant and equipment, utilities, repairs and maintenance, and quality control costs.

Such costs are *joint costs* and, in a multiproduct environment, are difficult to allocate among products. As the inventory carrying amount of any one product line depends on the allocation procedure, that amount can be somewhat arbitrary and capable of manipulation. For example, a manufacturer can increase reported income by choosing an allocation method that charges more of the joint costs to slower moving items. These costs then remain in inventory longer, and products with higher turnover rates appear more profitable.

A second aspect of this problem is the fixed nature (in the short run) of items such as depreciation, rent, or supervisors' salaries. Allocating such costs to products involves an averaging process that is affected by changing levels of production. A simple example in a single-product environment will illustrate this effect.

Assume a company has factory rent of $12,000 and it sells 10,000 units. If it produces 10,000 units, the full $12,000 of factor rent will be expensed through COGS (at a rate of $1.20/unit). If production increases to 12,000 units, then factory rent is allocated to inventory at $1.00/unit. But if only 10,000 units are sold, then only $10,000 is expensed as part of COGS and $2,000 of unallocated (but incurred) rent remains in inventory. Income increases by changing production levels rather than increasing sales.

OPTIONAL SEGMENT

The income effect of changing production rates can be the result of either intentional management decision (manipulation) or the unintended result of sales levels that differ from expectation. In either case it is imperative for the analyst to recognize:

- The accounting policies used by different firms in the same industry
- The effects of fluctuations in production on COGS and reported income

Finally, which costs are charged to inventory (and expensed when sold) and which costs are expensed as incurred vary among firms. Schiff (1987) notes that, although it is commonly suggested in accounting textbooks that fixed overhead costs must be allocated to inventory, in practice, many companies* have (historically) charged certain overhead costs (e.g., depreciation, pension costs, and property taxes) directly to expense. For such companies, variations in production and inventory levels will not affect the amount expensed. However, for firms that allocate such costs to inventory, when inventory levels increase, the amount expensed will be less than the amount actually incurred, with the difference remaining in inventory. On the balance sheet, those firms that capitalize more indirect costs in inventory will have higher carrying values of inventory, working capital, and equity balances. Unfortunately, not all companies disclose their practices in this respect. This can make comparisons between companies difficult.†

* The steel industry is one example noted by Schiff.

† The matter is further complicated by the increased emphasis in recent years in improvements in manufacturing processes. As a result, many firms have adjusted their method of inventory costing. [Bartley and Chen (1992) also report tax-related motivations for firms to switch from expensing to capitalization of certain items.]

OPTIONAL SEGMENT ENDS

It was noted that working capital is used as a broad liquidity measure because it includes cash and near-cash assets. Inventory accounting can distort the working capital measure and lead to erroneous and contradictory conclusions. LIFO accounting results in higher cash flows, but it reports lower working capital because the inventory balances retain earlier (lower) costs and the cash saved is only a percentage (the marginal tax rate) of the difference in inventory values.

In periods of rising prices and stable or increasing inventory quantities, the impact of LIFO and FIFO on the financial statements can be summarized as

	LIFO	FIFO
COGS	Higher	Lower
Income before taxes	Lower	Higher
Income taxes	Lower	Higher
Net Income	Lower	Higher
Cash flow	**Higher**	**Lower**
Inventory balance	Lower	Higher
Working capital	Lower	Higher

Cash flow has been highlighted because it is the only amount with direct economic impact. The others are accounting constructs and their economic significance is indirect and informational.

Continuing with the previous numeric example and assuming that 400 units are sold for $10,000 (average price of $25) with a tax rate of 40%, we can illustrate the above differences as follows. The resulting income statements are

	FIFO	LIFO	LIFO Higher/(Lower) by
Sales	$10,000	$10,000	$ 0
COGS	(4,300)	(5,150)	850
Income before tax	$ 5,700	$ 4,850	$(850)
Income tax @ 40%	(2,280)	(1,940)	(340)
Net income	$ 3,420	$ 2,910	$(510)

If we assume that sales are for cash and payments for purchases and taxes are made immediately, then cash flows are

	FIFO	LIFO	LIFO Higher/(Lower) by
Sales inflows	$10,000	$10,000	$ 0
Purchases	(6,250)	(6,250)	0
Inflows before tax	$ 3,750	$ 3,750	$ 0
Income tax paid	(2,280)	(1,940)	(340)
Operating cash flow	$ 1,470	$ 1,810	$340

Therefore, changes in balance sheet accounts are

Assets

	FIFO	LIFO	LIFO Higher/(Lower) by
Operating cash*	$1,470	$1,810	$340
Inventory†	1,950	1,100	(850)
Working capital	$3,420	$2,910	$(510)

Liabilities and Stockholders' Equity

Retained earnings‡	$3,420	$2,910	$(510)

* Net cash flow for period.
† Purchases less COGS.
‡ Net income for period.

The difference in net income of $510 and the difference in cash flows of $340 are related to the difference in COGS (equivalently the difference in inventory balances) of $850 as follows:

$$\begin{aligned} \text{Income Difference} &= (\text{1-Tax Rate}) \times \text{COGS Difference} \\ \$510 &= 0.6 \times \$850 \\ \text{Cash Flow Difference} &= \text{Tax Rate} \times \text{COGS Difference} \\ \$340 &= 0.4 \times \$850 \end{aligned}$$

However, these differences are in *opposite directions*, with higher income for the FIFO firm and higher operating cash flows for the LIFO firm. The difference in working capital is the net of the difference in inventory balance and cash flow:

$$\$510 = \$850 - \$340$$

This results in misleading liquidity measures for the LIFO firm as its working capital is understated.[10] The increase in cash is more than offset by the understatement of inventory.

Our illustration shows that the choice of inventory method can greatly affect reported operating results. Moreover, depending on whether the focus is the balance sheet or income statement, differing methods may be preferred. Thus, the analyst needs to be able to adjust between LIFO and FIFO in order to:

- Eliminate differences between firms due to accounting methods so that any remaining differences reflect economic and operating variations.
- Obtain the measure(s) most relevant for their analytical purpose.

The next sections describe how such adjustments can be made.

[10] Johnson and Dhaliwal (1988) studied firms that abandoned LIFO in favor of FIFO. Their evidence suggests one possible motivation for the abandonment decision was to increase their reported working capital. Compared to firms that retained LIFO, the abandonment firms had tighter working capital constraints under their debt covenants.

5 ADJUSTMENT FROM LIFO TO FIFO

Adjustment of Inventory Balances

LIFO inventory balances generally contain older costs with little or no relationship to current costs. Because of this deficiency, firms are required to disclose the *LIFO reserve.* The LIFO reserve (usually shown in the financial statement footnotes, but sometimes on the face of the balance sheet) is the difference between the inventory balance shown on the balance sheet and the (approximately current or replacement cost) amount that would have been reported had the firm used FIFO.

To adjust inventory balances of firms using LIFO to current or FIFO cost, we must add the LIFO reserve to the LIFO inventory amount. We can express this as

$$\text{LIFO Reserve} = \text{Inventory}_F - \text{Inventory}_L$$

or

$$\text{Inventory}_F = \text{Inventory}_L + \text{LIFO Reserve}$$

(where the subscripts F and L represent the accounting methods FIFO and LIFO, respectively).

Example:

Sunoco

Exhibit 39-2 contains details of inventory and portions of financial statement footnotes from the 1996–1999 annual reports of Sunoco, a large U.S. oil refiner. Sunoco uses the LIFO method to account for virtually all crude oil and refined product inventories.

Exhibit 39-3A shows the adjustment of inventory from LIFO to FIFO, adding the LIFO reserve to the LIFO inventory. Sunoco's LIFO reserve is large, indicating that the balance sheet carrying amount significantly understates inventories. This understatement is typical of firms whose products have risen in price and that have used LIFO for many years. In the case of Sunoco, the LIFO cost of inventories is only 30% of the FIFO cost in 1999. As the price of oil is volatile, the difference between Inventory_F and Inventory_L is highly variable over the period shown in Exhibit 39-3.

Adjustment of Cost of Goods Sold

COGS can be derived using the opening and closing inventory balances and purchases for the period:

$$\text{COGS} = BI + P - EI$$

Thus, to arrive at FIFO cost of goods sold (COGS_F), these amounts must be restated from LIFO to FIFO. The adjustment of inventory balances was illustrated earlier. Purchases (which are not a function of the accounting method used) need not be adjusted and can be derived directly from the (opening and closing) inventory balances and COGS reported in the financial statements:

$$P = \text{COGS}_L + EI_L - BI_L$$

EXHIBIT 39-2 Sunoco

Inventory Disclosures

Inventories of crude oil and refined products are valued at the lower of cost or market. The cost of such inventories is determined principally using LIFO.

	Inventories* at December 31 (in $millions)			
	1996	1997	1998	1999
Crude oil	$157	$150	$184	$158
Refined products	252	214	219	163
Inventories valued at LIFO	**$409**	**$364**	**$403**	**$321**

The current replacement cost of all inventories valued at LIFO exceeded their carrying cost by $780, $492, $205, and $763 million at December 31, 1996 through 1999, respectively.

	1996	1997	1998	1999
Cost of goods sold (in $millions)	$8,718	$7,610	$5,646	$7,365

* The above data only include inventories intended for resale. Sunoco also carries materials and supplies on its balance sheet as inventories.

Source: Sunoco, 1996–1999 annual reports.

EXHIBIT 39-3 Sunoco

Adjustment from LIFO to FIFO, 1996–1999

A. Adjusting LIFO Inventory to FIFO (Current Cost)

	1996	1997	1998	1999
Inventories carried at LIFO	$ 409	$364	$403	$ 321
LIFO reserve	780	492	205	763
Inventories adjusted to FIFO	$1,189	$856	$608	$1,084

B. Adjusting LIFO COGS to FIFO COGS

Cost of goods sold at LIFO ($COGS_L$)	$7,610	$5,646	$7,365
Less: LIFO effect*	(288)	(287)	558
Equals: cost of goods sold at FIFO ($COGS_F$)	$7,898	$5,933	$6,807

*Change in LIFO reserve from previous year-end.

Source: Data from Sunoco, 1996–1999 annual reports.

Example:

Sunoco

Sunoco's purchases for 1999 can be calculated (in $millions) as

$$P = \$7{,}365 \text{ million} + \$321 \text{ million} - \$403 \text{ million}$$
$$= \$7{,}283 \text{ million}$$

Using 1999 purchases, just calculated, and the FIFO inventory amounts derived in Exhibit 3A yields the 1999 COGS on a FIFO basis for Sunoco:

$$COGS_F = BI_F + P - EI_F$$
$$= \$608 \text{ million} + \$7{,}283 \text{ million} - \$1{,}084 \text{ million}$$
$$= \$6{,}807 \text{ million}$$

Thus COGS on a FIFO basis is lower than on a LIFO basis by $558 million ($7,365 million − $6,807 million). The astute reader will note that this amount equals the increase in the LIFO reserve during the year (from $205 to $763 million). This is no coincidence and the adjustment from LIFO to FIFO COGS can be made directly from the LIFO reserve accounts without going through the intermediate steps of calculating purchases and adjusting inventories. The direct adjustment (shown in Exhibit 39-3B) is[11]

$$COGS_F = COGS_L - \text{Change in LIFO Reserve}$$

or

$$COGS_F = COGS_L - (\text{LIFO Reserve}_E - \text{LIFO Reserve}_B)$$
$$\$6{,}807 \text{ million} = \$7{,}365 \text{ million} - (\$763 \text{ million} - \$205 \text{ million})$$

where the subscripts E and B refer to ending (inventory) and beginning (inventory), respectively. The change in LIFO reserve during the year, sometimes called the *LIFO effect* for the year, is thus the difference between the COGS computed under the two methods.

Before leaving this discussion, consider two questions. First, why does conversion to FIFO in 1996 to 1998 increase COGS (see Exhibit 39-3B) when we normally expect $COGS_F$ to be lower than $COGS_L$? Second, why did the LIFO reserve decrease in those years?

The answer to both questions is the same: Oil prices decreased. This decline reduced the difference between inventory cost on a LIFO basis and cost on a FIFO basis. The LIFO reserve, which represents this difference, is thus reduced. In both years, use of the LIFO method reduced COGS by almost $290 million, increasing pretax earnings by an equal amount. The lesson here should be clear: *When prices are declining, LIFO produces lower COGS and, therefore, higher earnings.*

---

[11] For those with a more mathematical bent, this result can be proven as follows:

Purchases ($P = COGS + EI - BI$) are identical for both accounting methods.
Thus $COGS_F + EI_F - BI_F = COGS_L + EI_L - BI_L$.
Rearranging terms yields $COGS_F = COGS_L - [(EI_F - EI_L) - (BI_F - BI_L)]$.
or $COGS_F = COGS_L - [(\text{LIFO Reserve}_E - \text{LIFO Reserve}_B)]$.

In 1999, when prices (and the LIFO reserve) increased, the expected effect was obtained. $COGS_L$ was higher and pretax income was reduced by the amount of increase in the LIFO reserve. In industries such as oil and gas, based on volatile commodity prices, fluctuations in the LIFO reserve due to price changes are common.

ADJUSTMENT OF INCOME TO CURRENT COST INCOME

6

This section discusses the adjustment of FIFO (and weighted-average) COGS to reflect current costs.[12] There are two reasons for making this adjustment. One is to estimate the impact of price changes on a firm's COGS and earnings; we wish to separate price effects from operating effects. The second reason is to compare the firm with other firms in the same industry using LIFO accounting.

Note that *only the adjustment of COGS to LIFO COGS is relevant.* Adjustments of inventory balances to LIFO serve no purpose, as LIFO inventory costs are outdated and almost meaningless.

Unlike the adjustment from LIFO to FIFO discussed in the previous section, information needed to adjust COGS to LIFO is not generally provided in the financial statements of firms using FIFO (or average cost). An approximate adjustment, however, is often possible.[13]

This adjustment requires multiplying the opening inventory by the (specific) inflation rate and adding the result to $COGS_F$ to arrive at $COGS_L$. More formally,

$$COGS_L = COGS_F + (BI_F \times r)$$

where r is the *specific inflation rate appropriate for the products in which the firm deals.*[14]

---

[12] Although we use the terms LIFO and current cost COGS interchangeably, our objective is to estimate current cost COGS. Generally, as long as the firm does not deplete any of its opening inventory, these two are equivalent. When opening inventory quantities are reduced (known as a LIFO liquidation), LIFO COGS and income are both distorted, as old costs flow into the income statement and COGS no longer reflects the current cost of inventory sold. When a LIFO liquidation occurs, LIFO COGS does not equal current cost COGS; in a subsequent section of the reading we illustrate how to adjust for this distortion.

[13] A more complex adjustment taking into consideration the firm's inventory turnover is possible. Falkenstein and Weil (1977) discuss the use of turnover, but note (p. 51 of their article) that estimates from the more basic procedure (used here) have always approximated the estimates from the more complex methods.

[14] The appropriateness of the approximation can be illustrated by the following proof. Assume that a firm carries a *quantity* Q of inventory and this quantity is equal to three months of inventory. The inventory level Q is replenished every three months. Assume further that the inflation rate over the year is equal to r. Finally, let P be the unit cost at which the opening inventory Q_o was purchased at the end of the previous year. Thus, the unit cost of the inventory at the end of the current year will equal $P(1 + r)$. The following illustrates the actual flow of goods purchased throughout the year:

Beginning inventory = Q_0 = Sales during 1st Quarter
End of 1st Quarter Purchase = Q_1 = Sales during 2nd Quarter
End of 2nd Quarter Purchase = Q_2 = Sales during 3rd Quarter
End of 3rd Quarter Purchase = Q_3 = Sales during 4th Quarter
End of 4th Quarter Purchase = Q_4 = Ending Inventory

Under FIFO, the cost of Q_0, Q_1, Q_2, and Q_3 will appear in COGS. Under LIFO, the cost of Q_1, Q_2, Q_3, and Q_4 will appear in COGS. Thus, the difference between the two methods lies in the difference between the cost of the beginning (Q_0) and ending (Q_4) inventory. Hence, the difference between LIFO and FIFO equals

$$Q_4P(1 + r) - Q_0P = Q_0Pr$$

since the inventory quantity purchased each period is the same.

To the extent that a firm's inventory purchases are steady throughout the period, the above adjustment will approximate the actual FIFO-to-LIFO (current cost) adjustment.

Weighted-average COGS (with subscript w) can be similarly adjusted to current cost (LIFO); the adjustment to opening inventory can be appoximated[15] by one-half the (specific) inflation rate:

$$COGS_L = COGS_W + (BI_W \times r/2)$$

Obtaining r. The inflation rate needed for the adjustment is not a general producer or consumer price index, but rather should be the specific price index appropriate to the firm in question. (For a multi-industry firm, the calculation should be done on a segmented basis.) Many industry indices are readily available, published by government or private sources. For companies whose inputs are commodities (oil, coffee, steel scrap), the spot price for the commodity may be used.

Alternatively, the specific price level change, r, for a given FIFO (or weighted average) firm can be estimated from data of a competing (LIFO) firm (in the same industry) by making use of the following relationship:[16]

$$r = \frac{\Delta \text{LIFO reserve}}{BI_F}$$

This procedure provides a reasonable approximation of r as long as the LIFO firm has not had a *significant* reduction of its inventory from year to year. The example that follows illustrates the adjustment procedure to LIFO.

Example:

Caltex Australia

Exhibit 39-4 part A contains relevant income statement and balance sheet information for Caltex Australia, a major oil producer and refiner in Australia. LIFO is not permitted under Australian GAAP and Caltex Australia uses the weighted-average cost method to account for inventory. Our objective is to demonstrate the adjustment of COGS and earnings to a current cost basis using the methodology described previously.

One advantage of using Caltex Australia as our example is that the company discloses (Exhibit 39-4, part B) the estimated effects of inventory holding gains on its earnings. Thus, we can double-check our estimates

---

15 When weighted-average cost is used, the inventory turnover rate affects the adjustment.

16 This can be proven since

$$COGS_F = COGS_L - \Delta \text{LIFO reserve}$$

and

$$COGS_L = COGS_F + (r \times BI_F)$$

Therefore

$$(r \times BI_F) = \Delta \text{ LIFO reserve}$$

and

$$r = \frac{\Delta \text{ LIFO reserve}}{BI_F}$$

EXHIBIT 39-4 Caltex Australia

Selected Income, Balance Sheet and Replacement Cost Disclosures (in $AUS millions)

A. Income Statement and Balance Sheet Data

	1998	1999
Net revenue	$2,891	$3,153
Operating costs and expenses	(2,693)	(2,936)
Operating profit (before interest, income tax, and abnormal items)	$ 198	$ 217
Ending inventory	234.8	429.0

Caltex Australia uses the weighted-average method to account for its inventory.

B. Replacement Cost of Sales Basis of Accounting

- To assist in understanding the company's operating performance, the directors have provided additional disclosure of the company's results for the year on a replacement-cost-of-sales basis, which excludes net inventory gains and losses adjusted for foreign exchange.
- Operating profit before interest, income tax, and abnormal items on a replacement-cost-of-sales basis was $75.0 million, a reduction of $221.8 million over 1998.

	1995	1996	1997	1998	1999	Total
Historical cost operating profit before interest, income tax, and abnormal items	$263.7	$272.6	$200.6	$216.7	$198.2	$1,151.8
Add/(deduct) inventory losses/(gains)*	(15.5)	(27.9)	53.4	98.6	(141.7)	(33.1)
Replacement cost operating profit before interest, income tax, and abnormal items	$248.2	$244.7	$254.0	$296.8	$ 75.0	$1,118.7

* Historical cost results includes gross inventory gains or losses from the movement in crude prices, net of the related exchange impact. In 1999, historical cost result includes $141.7 million net inventory gain (1998: $98.6 million net inventory loss) from the increase in crude oil prices, made up of **$144.9** million in inventory gains (1998: $124.7 million in inventory losses) net of an unfavorable exchange impact of $3.2 million (1998: $26.1 million gain).

Source: Caltex Australia, *Annual Review 1999.*

with those provided by management. The company states that it provides this information because:

> As a general rule using the historic cost basis of accounting, rising crude prices will result in increased operating profit for Caltex, falling crude oil prices will result in decreased operating profit. This movement in operating profit, often referred to as an inventory gain or loss, can create large variations in Caltex's results as calculated by the historic cost method. *Consequently, in order to provide a better insight into the operating performance of the company, Caltex's Financial reporting now includes earnings on a replacement cost of sales basis.* Replacement cost of sales earnings exclude inventory gains and losses and are calculated by restating cost of sale using the replacement cost of goods sold rather than the historic cost. (Caltex Australia's *1999 Annual Review*, emphasis added.)

The price of crude oil increased dramatically in 1999. In Australia, the price increased from \$10.60/barrel at the beginning of the year to \$23.85/barrel at year-end.[17] This implies a specific price index (r) of 125% for oil products.[18] The adjustment to Caltex Australia's weighted average COGS (the LIFO effect) is

$$(BI_W \times r / 2) = (\$AUS\ 235 \text{ million} \times 1.25/2) = \$AUS\ 147 \text{ million}$$

where the \$AUS 235 million is the inventory balance at the beginning of 1999.

This \$AUS 147 million is the holding gain included in income reported under the weighted-average method. Removing the holding gain from income (adding it to COGS) results in a better measure of reported income (\$AUS in millions):

Operating income (reported)	\$AUS 217
Adjustment for holding gain	(147)
Operating income (approximate current cost)	\$AUS 70

Note that this approximation almost equals the estimated (\$AUS 144.9 million) inventory holding gain provided by the firm itself in the footnote to part B of Exhibit 39-4.

An alternative approach to arrive at the specific price index appropriate for the oil refining industry would be to examine the financial statements of a competing firm in that industry using LIFO. The LIFO reserve information presented earlier in Exhibit 39-3 for Sunoco Company can be used to approximate the effect of inflation on Caltex Australia.

The 1999 increase in Sunoco's LIFO reserve of \$558 million (\$205 to \$763 million) represents the increase in current costs during 1999. The specific inflation rate r was, therefore,

$$\$558 \text{ million}/\$608 \text{ million} = 92\%$$

where \$608 million is Sunoco's Inventory_F on December 31, 1998.

[17] *Source:* U.S. Energy Information Administration, Department of Energy.

[18] This estimate of r reflects the price increase in U.S. dollars. To more accurately measure the effect on Caltex Australia, the analysis should be done with oil prices expressed in Australian dollars, thereby taking into account exchange rate effects as well. However, as the method demonstrated is only an approximation and the exchange rate effect is relatively small, for ease of exposition we have ignored this technicality. (Exhibit 39-4 indicates that the exchange rate effect was only \$3.2 million of the total \$142 million effect.)

This estimated r of 92% is considerably smaller than the estimated r of 125% derived from the spot price of oil. However, from Exhibit 39-3, we see that Sunoco's *physical* inventory must have been reduced by approximately 20%. $Inventory_L$ decreased from \$403 million to \$321 million. As noted, the estimate of r is biased when inventory is reduced dramatically and the greater the change in the relevant price index, the greater the distortion.

We can eliminate the distortion by estimating r based on only 80% of the opening inventory:

Estimating *r* from Sunoco Data After Adjusting for Reduction in Inventory

	1999 Opening Inventory	80% of 1999 Opening Inventory	1999 Closing Inventory
$Inventory_L$	\$403	**\$321**	**\$321**
LIFO reserve	205	**164**	**763**
$Inventory_F$	\$608	**\$485**	**\$1,084**

Using the second and third columns, the change in the LIFO Reserve equals \$599 (\$763 − \$164) and BI_F = \$485. By using the price change (LIFO effect) only for those inventories that Sunoco retained the whole year, our estimate of r becomes 123.5% (\$599/\$485). This estimate is virtually identical to the 125% estimate using the alternative methodology and, as we showed earlier, is consistent with Caltex Australia's estimate of 1999 inventory holding gains.

Before proceeding to the next section it is worthwhile to explore further Caltex Australia's estimates of its inventory holding gains/losses for the years 1997–1999.

First, compare the pattern of Caltex Australia's adjustments to replacement cost with the pattern of Sunoco's COGS on a FIFO and LIFO basis (Exhibit 39-3). For both companies, the effect of declining prices in 1997 and 1998 was that replacement cost income exceeded operating income ($COGS_L < COGS_F$); in 1999, when prices rose, the situation reversed.

The data in Exhibit 39-4 speak for themselves. Historical cost profit experienced a sharp decline in 1997–1998 relative to 1995–1996 and then recovered slightly in 1999. When holding gains and losses are excluded, however, a different picture emerges: replacement cost profit rose steadily from 1995–1998 (20% increase) and experienced a dramatic 75% decrease in 1999 as prices rose. *Reported operating earnings over this time period were significantly affected by inventory holding gains or losses virtually every year.*

If we recall our discussion of the meaning of income, it seems clear that replacement cost profit is a better measure of earnings. Holding gains and losses are not predictable. Moreover, holding gains must be reinvested in inventory for the firm to remain in business; they are not available for distribution.

Although Caltex Australia, given wide swings in the price of oil, may be an extreme case, it illustrates the necessity of analyzing the inventory accounting of a firm to understand the impact of changing prices on its earnings and net worth.

7 FINANCIAL RATIOS: LIFO VERSUS FIFO

Exhibit 39-5, based on Dopuch and Pincus (1988), compares selected financial characteristics of FIFO and LIFO firms.[19] The comparison is made first on the basis of amounts reported in financial statements (part A) and again after adjusting to the alternative accounting method (part B).

Using reported financial data, part A shows that, based on median values, LIFO firms have higher turnover ratios, less inventory as a percentage of sales or total assets, and lower variation in inventory levels and pretax income.[20] However, for the most part, these differences are not real operating differences but rather are differences due to the accounting choice. In part B the FIFO firms are adjusted to LIFO and the LIFO firms are adjusted to FIFO. The appropriate comparison can now be made with all firms using the same accounting method; that is, the numbers in part B should be compared with those directly above them in part A.

Once the data are adjusted for accounting methods, the differences tend to disappear. For example, the inventory turnover ratio as reported is 4.97 for LIFO

EXHIBIT 39-5 Analysis of FIFO/LIFO Firms Based on Median Data, 1963–1981

A. Data as Reported

	LIFO	FIFO
COGS/average Inventory	4.97	3.88
Inventory/sales	0.16	0.20
Inventory/assets	0.21	0.29
C.V. inventory*	0.42	0.63
C.V. pretax income	0.74	0.79

B. FIFO Firms Adjusted to LIFO and LIFO Firms to FIFO

	FIFO to LIFO	LIFO to FIFO
COGS/average inventory	4.72	4.03
Inventory/sales	0.17	0.22
Inventory/assets	0.25	0.24
C.V. inventory	0.52	0.67
C.V. pretax income	0.81	0.77

* C.V. is the coefficient of variation (standard deviation divided by the mean).

Source: Nicholas Dopuch and Morton Pincus, "Evidence of the Choice of Inventory Accounting Methods: LIFO Versus FIFO," *Journal of Accounting Research* (Spring 1988), pp. 28–59, Tables 4 and 5, p. 44 (adapted).

[19] Although the data used in their sample (1963–1981) may be outdated, (the direction and degree of) distortion resulting from inventory accounting differences remains relevant.

[20] The variation in inventory and pretax income is measured by the coefficient of variation—(standard deviation divided by the mean).

firms and 3.88 for FIFO firms—a difference of 28%. After we adjust to the same method, the turnover ratios are:

- With all firms on FIFO, 4.03 for LIFO-reporting firms and 3.88 for FIFO-reporting firms—a difference of only 4%
- With all firms on a LIFO basis, 4.97 versus 4.72, respectively—a difference of only 5%

Similar patterns exist for the other variables.

With Exhibit 39-5 as a prologue, we now focus on how the FIFO/LIFO choice distorts measures of financial performance.

The FIFO/LIFO choice impacts reported profitability, liquidity, activity, and leverage ratios. For some ratios, LIFO provides a better measure, whereas for others, FIFO does. The LIFO-to-FIFO and FIFO-to-LIFO adjustment procedures discussed earlier, however, allow the analyst to make the appropriate adjustments to arrive at the "correct" ratio regardless of the firm's choice of accounting method. *The general guideline is to use LIFO numbers for ratio components that are income related and FIFO-based data for components that are balance sheet related.*

Profitability: Gross Profit Margin

The argument that LIFO better measures current income can be made with reference to gross profit margins. When input prices increase, firms pass along the added costs to customers. Moreover, they try to mark up not only those items purchased at the higher price but also all goods previously purchased. (This policy is economically defensible using the argument made earlier that the real cost of an item sold is its replacement cost.)

Thus, if the pricing policy of the firm in our opening example is to mark up cost by 100% (implying gross profit margin of 50% of sales), the $10,000 of sales in our example would have been arrived at as follows:

Sales: 100 units per quarter for a total of 400 units

Sales Price: Assume 100% markup over current costs

	Unit		Sales	
Quarter	**Cost**	**Price**	**Units**	**Dollars**
1	$11	$22	100	$ 2,200
2	12	24	100	2,400
3	13	26	100	2,600
4	14	28	100	2,800
Total			400	$10,000

Gross profit margin under FIFO and LIFO would be

Method	Sales	–	COGS	=	Gross Profit	Percent Margin
FIFO	$10,000	–	$4,300	=	$5,700	$5,700/$10,000 = 57.0%
LIFO	$10,000	–	$5,150	=	$4,850	$4,850/$10,000 = 48.5%

The 48.5% gross profit margin reported when LIFO is used is clearly closer to the profit margin intended by the firm's pricing policy. FIFO accounting, in times of rising (falling) prices, will tend to overstate (understate) reported profit margins.

The gross profit margin, by measuring the profitability of current sales, also provides an indication of the future profitability of a firm. Clearly, FIFO net income (which includes holding gains resulting from rising prices) inflates expectations regarding future profitability as future holding gains may be smaller (or negative) if future price increases are lower (or prices fall). *LIFO gives a more accurate forecast of the firm's prospects by removing the impact of price changes.*

Liquidity: Working Capital

LIFO misstates working-capital-based ratios because, as discussed, the inventory component of working capital reports outdated costs. As the purpose of the current ratio is to compare a firm's cash or near-cash assets and liabilities, use of the current value of inventory (FIFO) results in the better measure.

For Sunoco, working capital and current ratios for 1996 to 1999 based on reported data are:

Sunoco
Current Position Based on Reported LIFO Inventory

	Years Ended December 31 (in $millions)			
	1996	**1997**	**1998**	**1999**
Current assets	$1,535	$1,248	$1,180	$1,456
Current liabilities	(1,817)	(1,464)	(1,384)	(1,766)
Working capital	**$ (282)**	**$ (216)**	**$ (204)**	**$ (310)**
Current ratio	**0.84**	**0.85**	**0.85**	**0.82**

Adjusting LIFO inventory (and hence current assets) to current cost (FIFO) by adding the LIFO reserves (see Exhibits 39-2 and 39-3) changes Sunoco's current position to:

Sunoco
Adjusted Current Position Based on Current Cost (FIFO) Inventory

	Years Ended December 31 (in $millions)			
	1996	**1997**	**1998**	**1999**
Current assets	$1,535	$1,248	$1,180	$1,456
LIFO reserve	780	492	205	763
Adjusted current assets	$2,315	$1,740	$1,385	$2,219
Current liabilities	(1,817)	(1,464)	(1,384)	(1,766)
Adjusted working capital	**$ 498**	**$ 276**	**$ 1**	**$ 453**
Adjusted current ratio	**1.27**	**1.19**	**1.00**	**1.26**

The adjustments convert negative working capital to a positive measure for each year. Similarly, adjusted current ratios are (approximately 20–50%) higher than the unadjusted measures. The adjusted current ratio is also more volatile than the original ratio, reflecting the volatility of the current cost of oil-based inventories.

Activity: Inventory Turnover

Inventory turnover, defined as COGS/average inventory, is often meaningless for LIFO firms due to the mismatching of costs. The numerator represents current costs, whereas the denominator reports outdated historical costs. Thus, the turnover ratio under LIFO will, when prices increase, trend higher irrespective of the trend of physical turnover.

This point is illustrated in Exhibit 39-6. We assume an actual physical turnover of four times per year; that is, the average inventory is sufficient for one quarter. Further, it is assumed that unit costs increase 10% per quarter.

The FIFO inventory ratio is unaffected by the change in price, and at 3.77 is a rough approximation of the actual physical turnover of 4. The LIFO-based ratios of 5.11 and 7.47 are, however, far from the actual measure of 4, and the discrepancy grows over time. *Thus, to arrive at a reasonable approximation of the inventory turnover ratio for a LIFO firm, we must first convert stated inventory to FIFO.*

The preferred measure of inventory turnover (labeled "current cost" in Exhibit 39-6), however, is based solely on current cost. It combines the two methods, using LIFO COGS in the numerator and the FIFO inventory balance in the

EXHIBIT 39-6 Illustration of Turnover Ratio Under LIFO and FIFO

Year	Quarter	Purchases = Sales	Cost per Unit	Total	For Entire Year		
Opening inventory		100	$10.00	$1,000			
1	1	100	$11.00	$1,100	FIFO	COGS	$4,641
1	2	100	$12.10	$1,210		Avg. inv.	$1,232
1	3	100	$13.31	$1,331	LIFO	COGS	$5,105
1	4	100	$14.64	$1,464		Avg. inv.	$1,000
2	1	100	$16.11	$1,611	FIFO	COGS	$6,795
2	2	100	$17.72	$1,772		Avg. inv.	$1,804
2	3	100	$19.49	$1,949	LIFO	COGS	$7,474
2	4	100	$21.44	$2,144		Avg. inv.	$1,000

	Turnover Ratios: Year 1	Turnover Ratios: Year 2
FIFO	3.77	3.77
LIFO	5.11	7.47
Current cost	4.14	4.14

denominator. This approach provides the best matching of costs, as current costs are used in both the numerator and denominator. The current cost ratio (4.14) comes closest to the actual measure (based on physical units) of 4.

Using data for Sunoco (Exhibit 39-3), the computed inventory turnover ratios for 1998 and 1999 are (in $millions)

	1998		1999	
Method	**Turnover**	**#Days**	**Turnover**	**#Days**
LIFO (reported)	$\frac{\$5,646}{(\$364 + \$403)/2} = \mathbf{14.72}$	**25**	$\frac{\$7,365}{(\$403 + \$321)/2} = \mathbf{20.34}$	**18**
FIFO (adjusted)	$\frac{\$5,933}{(\$856 + \$608)/2} = \mathbf{8.10}$	**45**	$\frac{\$6,807}{(\$608 + \$1,084)/2} = \mathbf{8.04}$	**45**
Current cost	$\frac{\$5,646}{(\$856 + \$608)/2} = \mathbf{7.71}$	**47**	$\frac{\$7,365}{(\$608 + \$1,084)/2} = \mathbf{8.70}$	**42**

Comparing the 1998 and 1999 inventory turnover ratios for Sunoco, we see the importance of making current cost adjustments. Based on reported data, it appears that Sunoco turns its inventory very rapidly and increased its efficiency (turnover ratio) by almost 50% in 1999. After adjustment to current cost, however, a different picture emerges as the adjusted ratios imply a six-week rather than a three-week supply of inventory on hand and a much smaller year-to-year improvement in turnover.

Note also the small differences between the FIFO turnover ratios and the more refined current cost ratios. The ratio levels are similar although the current cost ratio shows higher turnover in 1999 whereas the FIFO ratio does not. The similarity is empirically true in most situations and for all practical purposes these two ratio calculations are equivalent as long as prices are not rising too rapidly (as was the case for 1999 oil prices).

Our example illustrates the usefulness of the LIFO-to-current cost adjustment for the analysis of a given company's turnover ratio. The same methodology can be used to compare two companies in the same industry when one uses FIFO and the other LIFO. The first step would be to adjust the LIFO turnover ratio to current cost. *Having made the ratios comparable (by eliminating the effect of different accounting methods), the analyst can then look for other explanations for any difference in the current cost turnover ratio.*

Inventory Theory and Turnover Ratios

Computing the inventory turnover ratio implies that there is some standard against which to measure or that there is an optimal ratio. As for all turnover ratios, one's first instinct is to believe that higher is better, that more rapid inventory turnover indicates a more efficient use of capital. In practice, however, that assumption may be overly simplistic.

The management science literature has devoted much study to the design of optimal inventory ordering policies. The traditional literature in the United States has focused on the economic order quantity (EOQ). More recently, in line with developments in Japanese management practices, focus has turned to just-in-time inventory policies. It is worthwhile to note the implications of these theories for the interpretation of the turnover ratio.

Economic Order Quantity

The construction and use of ratios for cross-sectional and time-series comparisons implicitly assume that the relationship between the numerator and denominator is linear. Applying this assumption to the inventory turnover ratio implies that, as demand increases, the quantity of inventory held should increase proportionately. The EOQ model, however, argues that the optimal level of inventory is proportionate to the *square root* of demand.

Thus, for example, if demand (COGS) increases by four times, one would expect average inventory to double (2 = the square root of 4). As a result, the turnover ratio would also double. Generally, under the EOQ model, turnover ratios should rise as sales increase and smaller firms should have lower turnover ratios. A high turnover ratio for a small firm might not be a sign of efficiency but, on the contrary, an indication that the firm was not managing its inventories in the most economic fashion.

Just in Time

Japanese management practices strive for the ideal that firms should not hold any inventory but rather should receive and ship orders "just in time" (JIT) as needed. Carried to its ultimate conclusion, this would argue for a turnover ratio approaching infinity with zero inventory held. Hence, we would expect the turnover ratios of Japanese firms to be considerably higher than those of American firms. To the extent that U.S. firms adopt these practices, they can be expected to have higher turnover ratios in the future.

One interesting byproduct of the trend toward JIT inventory is that it renders the LIFO/FIFO choice less meaningful. If a firm has no inventories (or relatively small quantities), then there is no significant difference between FIFO and LIFO.[21]

The FIFO/LIFO Choice and Inventory Holding Policy

Another important consideration is that the LIFO/FIFO choice may be related to a firm's actual inventory holding policy. Biddle (1980) found that LIFO firms tend to maintain higher inventory balances (in units) than comparably sized FIFO firms.[22] This finding is consistent with the following three factors:

1. Firms with higher inventory balances have larger potential tax savings from the use of LIFO. Thus, the higher inventory levels that result from the firm's production and operating environment may explain why the firm chose LIFO in the first place.
2. These higher balances may result from the LIFO choice, as LIFO firms attempt to get the most advantage from it by increasing their inventory levels.

---

[21] However, suppliers may hold inventory and if a firm owns or controls its suppliers, it may indirectly bear the residual risk usually borne by the suppliers. To properly include the effect of captive suppliers, turnover ratios and other inventory measures should be based on consolidated financial statements, where consolidation reflects economic rather than legal or regulatory control. Admittedly, such consolidation is not always feasible given the paucity of disclosure regarding such relationships.

[22] Barlev et al. (1984) examined Canadian and Israeli firms that were not permitted to use LIFO but used an alternative method of tax adjustment for inflation. They found that inventory balances were higher for firms with large tax benefits from the inflation adjustment.

3. To avoid LIFO liquidations and consequent higher income taxes, LIFO firms must buy (produce) at least as many items as they sell each year. For LIFO firms it is costly to reduce inventory levels, even when lower expected levels of demand might dictate lower levels.

Solvency: Debt-to-Equity Ratio

We have argued that, to compute liquidity ratios, understated LIFO inventory balances should be restated to current cost by adding the LIFO reserve. For the same reason, the firm's stockholders' equity should be increased by the same amount.[23] The rationale for this adjustment is that the reported equity of the firm is understated because the firm owns inventory whose current value exceeds its carrying value.[24]

For analytical purposes, the inventory choice should be treated like other accounting choices. The fact that the Internal Revenue Service does not permit any difference between financial reporting and tax accounting methods should not tie the hands of the analyst. The valuation of a LIFO firm should not be penalized because it takes advantage of the tax savings inherent in LIFO.

8 DECLINES IN LIFO RESERVE

LIFO reserves can decline for either of the following reasons:

- Liquidation of inventories
- Price declines

In either case, COGS will be smaller (and income larger) relative to what it would have been had the reserve not declined. *The response of the analyst should not be the same in both cases, however.* For LIFO liquidations, the analyst should exclude the effects of the LIFO liquidation to arrive at a better measure of the firm's operating performance. In the second case, no adjustment is required, as price decreases are a normal part of the firm's operating results (just as much as price increases).

LIFO Liquidations

The discussion of LIFO in this reading thus far has assumed that inventory quantities are stable or increasing. When more goods are sold than are purchased (or manufactured), goods held in opening inventory are included in COGS. For

---

[23] Lasman and Weil (1978) suggest that the LIFO reserve should not be adjusted for taxes unless a liquidation of LIFO layers is assumed. Further, as liquidations are reported in reverse LIFO order (latest layers are liquidated first), the largest gains reside in the earliest layers. Thus, there is a low probability that the tax effect of "minor" liquidations will be significant and (if we assume that the firm remains in business) extensive liquidations are unlikely, also arguing against tax adjustment. Note that firms have strong incentives to avoid liquidations that would result in significant tax payments. See, however, the discussion regarding the Dhaliwal, Trezevant and Wilkins (2000) paper.

[24] Using FIFO values for equity does not contradict our statement that the optimal choice for income presentation is LIFO. Recalling the example in footnote 6, the fact that your house doubled in value from $100,000 to $200,000 at a time when all houses doubled in value means that you do not benefit from selling the house as you will need the larger amount to buy a replacement house. The value of (your equity in) your house is, nevertheless, $200,000.

LIFO companies, this results in the liquidation of LIFO layers established in prior years, and such *LIFO liquidations* can materially distort reported operating results.

The carrying cost of the old (in an accounting sense) inventories (which becomes the cost of goods sold associated with the inventory reduction) may be abnormally low and the gross profit margin abnormally high. Thus, LIFO cost no longer approximates current cost. For companies whose base inventory is very old, the distortion from these "paper profits" can be quite large;[25] for analysis, that distortion needs to be removed.

The higher income resulting from LIFO liquidations translates into increased income taxes and lower operating cash flows as taxes that were postponed through the use of LIFO must now be paid. To postpone taxes indefinitely, purchases (production) must always be greater than or equal to sales.[26]

LIFO liquidations may result from inventory reductions because of strikes, recession, or declining demand for a particular product line.[27] The paradoxical result is that companies may report surprisingly high profits during economic downturns, as production cuts result in the liquidation of low-cost LIFO inventories. Given the trend toward lower inventory levels in recent years as companies move toward just-in-time or other means of reducing their investment in inventories, LIFO liquidations have become common. Such liquidations are usually disclosed in the inventory footnote of the financial statements. *As profits from LIFO liquidations are nonoperating in nature, they should be excluded from earnings for purposes of analysis.*

Example:

Oilgear

Exhibit 39-7 presents data from the inventory footnote for Oilgear, a manufacturer and distributor of systems and value-engineered components for a broad range of industrial machinery and industrial processes. The company uses the LIFO method of inventory for more than two-thirds of its inventory and reported inventory declines and LIFO liquidations in each of the years 1995–1999.[28] The motivation for the inventory declines (reported in the company's Management Discussion and Analysis) was to "align inventory levels with current (lower) customer demand."

LIFO liquidations added to Oilgear's reported earnings in each of the years 1995 to 1999. As the effect of LIFO liquidations is completely

[25] Schiff (1983) showed that in the recession of 1980–1981, LIFO layers that were liquidated dated back as far as World War II.

[26] See Biddle (1980) for a discussion of the impact of LIFO/FIFO on inventory purchases and holding policy.

[27] A LIFO liquidation may not be a one-time, random occurrence but a signal that a company is entering an extended period of decline. Stober (1986) found that over 60% of his sample of firms had liquidations in more than one year and 33% experienced liquidations in three or more years. Similarly, Davis et al. (1984) found that liquidations were industry related, indicating a systematic effect, and Fried et al. (1989) found that writedowns and/or restructurings were often preceded by LIFO liquidations.

[28] Exhibit 39-7, from the *1999 Annual Report*, provides information only about 1997–1999 liquidations. Information as to prior-year liquidations was obtained from prior-year annual reports.

nonoperating in nature, operating results (COGS) should be adjusted to exclude it. Adjustments for each year follow (data in $000):

	1995	1996	1997	1998	1999
Sales	$82,157	$89,621	$90,904	$96,455	$90,709
COGS	(55,858)	(60,184)	(62,507)	(70,634)	(65,521)
Gross margin (reported)	**$26,299**	**$29,437**	**$28,397**	**$25,821**	**$25,188**
LIFO liquidation	800	1,350	750	740	850
Adjusted gross margin	**$25,499**	**$28,087**	**$27,647**	**$25,081**	**$24,338**
Liquidation effect:					
Gross margin increases	**3%**	**5%**	**3%**	**3%**	**3%**
Pretax income (reported)	**$ 3,070**	**$ 3,620**	**$ 3,363**	**$ 1,284**	**$ 1,864**
LIFO liquidation	800	1,350	750	740	850
Adjusted pretax income	**$ 2,270**	**$ 2,270**	**$ 2,613**	**$ 544**	**$ 1,014**
Liquidation effect:					
Pretax income increases	**35%**	**59%**	**29%**	**136%**	**84%**

Removing the LIFO liquidation effectively adjusts reported LIFO COGS to a current cost basis. Although the effects on gross margin are relatively small (3% to 5%), the effects on income are significant. As a result of the liquidation, Oilgear's reported (pretax) income was 29% to 136% higher than without the liquidation!

EXHIBIT 39-7 Oilgear

LIFO Liquidations

From Notes to Financial Statements

INVENTORIES

Inventories at December 31, 1999 and 1998 consist of the following:

	1998	1999
Raw materials	$ 2,601.718	$ 2,447,402
Work in process	21,773,524	17,634,558
Finished goods	6,281,776	4,777,960
Total	$30,657,018	$24,859,920
LIFO reserve	(1,996,000)	(1,627,000)
Total (net of LIFO reserve)	$28,661,018	$23,232,920

During 1999, 1998, and 1997, LIFO inventory layers were reduced. These reductions resulted in charging lower inventory costs prevailing in previous years to cost of sales, thus reducing cost of sales by approximately $850,000, $740,000, and $750,000 below the amount that would have resulted from liquidating inventory recorded at December 31, 1999, 1998, and 1997 prices, respectively.

EXHIBIT 39-7 (continued)

From Income Statement (in $millions)

	1997	1998	1999
Sales	$90,904	$96,455	$90,709
COGS	(62,507)	(70,634)	(65,521)
Gross margin	28,397	25,821	25,188
Pretax income	3,363	1,284	1,864

Source: Oilgear, *1999 Annual Report.*

Declining Prices

Our discussion thus far has assumed rising price levels. In the analysis of Sunoco, we saw that the LIFO reserve declines when prices fall. In some industries (notably those that are technology related), input prices decline steadily over time; in others (mainly commodity-based industries such as metals and petroleum), prices may fluctuate cyclically.

Declines in LIFO reserves occur whenever inventory costs fall as the lower-cost current purchases enter reported LIFO COGS, decreasing the cost difference between LIFO and FIFO ending inventories. Such declines are not considered LIFO liquidations, and disclosure of their impact is not required.

The theoretical arguments as to which accounting method provides better information still hold. LIFO provides more recent (or current) cost on the income statement and outdated costs on the balance sheet. The direction of the LIFO versus FIFO differences, however, reverses when prices decline. LIFO closing inventories are overstated, and FIFO COGS tends to be higher. Thus, although the pragmatic incentives to use LIFO for tax purposes are lost in an environment of declining prices[29] (LIFO results in higher taxes and lower cash flow), the nature of the information provided does not change. *The LIFO amounts on the balance sheet are not current and require adjustment, whereas the income statement amounts are current and do not need adjustment.*

Example:

Wyman-Gordon

Exhibit 39-8 presents data from the inventory footnote for Wyman-Gordon,[30] a producer of components for the aerospace industry. Wyman-Gordon used the LIFO method for many years and had a large LIFO reserve on its balance sheet. Weak industry conditions led to inventory declines, resulting in significant LIFO liquidations; declining prices also reduced the LIFO reserve. The exhibit indicates that in 1992 and 1993

[29] In addition, companies whose inventories are subject to obsolescence often take advantage of the ability (not available, for tax purposes, under LIFO) to write down inventory to market value.

[30] Wyman-Gordon is no longer a public company.

the LIFO reserve declined $22.838 and $7.917 million, respectively. Wyman-Gordon separated the effects of liquidations and price declines:

	(in $thousands)	
	1992	**1993**
Effect of LIFO liquidation	$(18,388)	$(5,469)
Effect of lower prices	(4,450)	(2,448)
Total LIFO effect	$(22,838)	$(7,917)

When analyzing Wyman-Gordon, the LIFO liquidation effect and the declining price effect should be treated differently. If the analyst's objective is to obtain a more accurate estimate of current cost income, then (*just*) the LIFO liquidation effect should be removed; the effects of declining prices on current purchases and sales, which are operating in nature, should not be removed. However, *for purposes of comparison with firms using FIFO* (i.e., calculating COGS on a FIFO basis), adjustment should be made for the total LIFO effect (liquidations *and* declining prices).

EXHIBIT 39-8 Wyman-Gordon

Inventories and Declines in LIFO Reserve

	in ($thousands)		
	1991	**1992**	**1993**
Inventory		$ 53,688	$42,388
LIFO reserve	64,203	41,365	33,448
Change in LIFO reserve (LIFO effect)		$(22,838)	$(7,917)

If all inventories valued at LIFO cost had been valued at FIFO cost or market, which approximates current replacement cost, inventories would have been $41,365,000 and $33,448,000 higher than reported at December 31, 1992 and 1993, respectively.

Inventory quantities were reduced in 1991, 1992, and 1993, resulting in the liquidation of LIFO inventories carried at lower costs prevailing in prior years as compared with the cost of current purchases. The effect of lower quantities decreased 1991 loss from operations by $1,529,000, increased 1992 income from operations by $18,388,000, and decreased 1993 loss from operations by $5,469,000, whereas the effect of deflation had no impact on 1991 loss from operations, increased 1992 income from operations by $4,450,000, and decreased 1993 loss from operations by $2,448,000.

Source: Wyman-Gordon, *1993 Annual Report.*

INITIAL ADOPTION OF LIFO AND CHANGES TO AND FROM LIFO

9

Changes in the inventory accounting method require examination for two reasons:

1. Reporting methods for these changes are not symmetric; changing from FIFO to LIFO is not accorded the same treatment as a LIFO to FIFO switch.
2. The implications and motivation behind the accounting change are equally important; the change itself may convey information about the company's operations.

Initial Adoption of LIFO

In the United States the change to LIFO is made only on a prospective basis: GAAP do not require either retroactive restatement or the disclosure of any cumulative effect of the adoption of LIFO. Records necessary for restatement or *pro forma* disclosures often do not exist. Opening inventory in the year of adoption is the base-period inventory for subsequent LIFO computations.

When LIFO is adopted, required footnote disclosures include the impact of the adoption on the period's income before extraordinary items, net income, and related earnings per share amounts. A brief explanation of the reasons for the change in method must be provided and the absence of any cumulative effect disclosures or retroactive adjustment must be noted.

Exhibit 39-9 provides an example of the required disclosures. Effective January 1, 1999, Amerada Hess adopted the LIFO method for its crude oil and refined petroleum products. As Amerada Hess reported earnings per share of $4.88 for that year, the LIFO adoption reduced reported earnings by 18% from the $5.96 that would have been reported without the change. On the other hand, the change to LIFO resulted in a substantial tax saving as calculated below:

From inventory note: LIFO adjustment (effect)	$149,309,000
From accounting change note: effect on net income	97,051,000
Tax savings	$ 52,258,000

Amerada Hess was the last major U.S. oil refiner to adopt LIFO. In its footnote the company states that it switched to LIFO because the "LIFO method more closely matches current costs and revenues and will improve comparability with other oil companies." That may be so but the $52.3 million tax savings may also have had something to do with the company's decision. Note that the company chose to adopt LIFO in 1999, a year in which oil prices rose significantly, justifying the cost of changing accounting methods.

Indeed, adoptions of LIFO are often made to take advantage of the tax benefits inherent in the LIFO method and the propensity to switch is often a function of inflationary conditions. For example, in the early 1970s, over 400 firms switched to LIFO, reflecting double-digit inflation. Interestingly, the stock market has not always regarded such switches favorably despite their (positive) cash flow implications. The empirical section of the reading examines the reasons for this market reaction more closely.

Change from LIFO Method

Unlike changes to LIFO, changes from LIFO to other methods require retroactive restatement of reported earnings to the new method for prior years. The cumulative effect of adopting the new inventory accounting method is credited

EXHIBIT 39-9 Amerada Hess

Initial Adoption of LIFO

Accounting Changes

Effective January 1, 1999, the Corporation adopted the last-in, first-out (LIFO) inventory method for valuing its refining and marketing inventories. The corporation believes that the LIFO method more closely matches current costs and revenues and will improve comparability with other oil companies. The change to LIFO decreased net income by $97,051,000 for the year ended December 31, 1999 ($1.08 per share basic and diluted). There is no cumulative effect adjustment as of the beginning of the year for this type of accounting change.

Inventories

Inventories at December 31 are as follows:

	Thousands of Dollars	
	1998	1999
Crude oil and other charge stocks	$ 35,818	$ 67,539
Refined and other finished products	386,917	393,064
	$422,735	$460,603
Less: LIFO adjustment		(149,309)
		$311,294
Materials and supplies	59,447	61,419
Total	$482,182	$372,713

Source: Amerada Hess, *Annual Report 1999.*

to retained earnings at the beginning of the earliest restated year to avoid a misstatement of current period income.

SEC regulations require a preferability letter from the firm's independent auditor stating its concurrence with and the rationale for the change. Additionally, a change from LIFO requires Internal Revenue Service approval.[31] The IRS considers changes from LIFO as a loss of tax deferral privileges, and the previous LIFO reserve becomes immediately taxable. Thus, a change from LIFO may bring significant adverse tax and cash flow consequences and requires evaluation of the impact on operations as well as management incentives for the switch. These motivations are also discussed in the following section.

[31] Firms switching from LIFO to another method also agree not to switch back to LIFO for at least 10 years, except under "extraordinary circumstances."

LIFO: A HISTORICAL AND EMPIRICAL PERSPECTIVE

Overview of FIFO/LIFO Choice

Out of 600 (generally very large) firms sampled in *Accounting Trends and Techniques*,[32] about half use LIFO for at least part of their inventories. Few firms use LIFO for all inventories. Use by industry classification varies widely. LIFO is used by all rubber and plastic product firms (in this sample) and virtually all firms in the food and drug store, petroleum refining, furniture, and textile industries. None of the firms in the computer and data services, computer software, semiconductors, or telecommunications sectors do so.

Given the powerful incentives to use LIFO (tax savings and cash flow), two interrelated[33] questions arise:

1. Why do some firms continue to use FIFO?
2. Are firms that use LIFO perceived as being "better off" by the market despite lower reported earnings?

Many empirical studies have examined these issues; in this section we summarize their findings. Before doing so, we note that empirical research related to inventories is not confined to the FIFO/LIFO choice. Box 39-2 shows how analysts can use trends in inventory balances as an aid in forecasting future sales and profitability.

The large number of studies devoted to the FIFO/LIFO choice is due to its richness as the choice has opposite effects on reported income and cash flow. Moreover, the ability to adjust from one method to the other permits "as-if" comparisons in research design. The main empirical findings are relevant to the analyst as they provide evidence that the implications of the FIFO/LIFO choice (or any other accounting choice) are often complex and go beyond the simple trade-off of lower taxes (higher cash flow) versus higher reported income articulated in research designs. We provide a synopsis of the findings in the next section, using the work of Cushing and LeClere (1992) to motivate the discussion.

Summary of FIFO/LIFO Choice

Cushing and LeClere (1992) asked 32 LIFO firms and 70 FIFO firms to rank their reasons for their choice of inventory method. For LIFO firms, the overwhelming primary reason was the favorable tax effect. This result is consistent with research findings that firms using LIFO are primarily motivated by its favorable tax effects and these firms stand to gain the most from using LIFO.

The market, however, does not always regard a switch to LIFO favorably. By switching to LIFO, the firm may be providing (unfavorable) information about its sensitivity to changing prices (or other firm characteristics). Thus, reaction to

[32] American Institute of Certified Public Accountants, 2000 edition.

[33] These questions are interrelated because if the market reacts (for whatever reason) negatively to a switch to LIFO, it may explain why some firms choose to remain on FIFO.

BOX 39-2 USING INVENTORY BALANCES TO AID IN FORECASTING*

OPTIONAL SEGMENT

Changes in inventory balances can provide ambiguous signals about a firm's future sales and earnings prospects. An unanticipated (from the analyst's perspective) increase in the inventory balance may signal either:†

1. An unexpected decrease in recent demand, causing an unplanned increase in inventory that signals lower future demand, or‡
2. A (planned) increase in inventory levels by management anticipating higher future demand.

These two arguments are, of course, mutually exclusive. Which condition prevails cannot be determined from changes in the inventory account itself. Rather, the change itself acts as a signal for the analyst to investigate (using other sources of information) which condition is most likely for the company in question.§

The previous dichotomy relates only to changes in finished goods inventory. In a manufacturing environment, changes in work-in-process inventory (and to some degree changes in raw materials inventory) may indicate that management is increasing production to meet an increase in actual or anticipated orders.

Consistent with the above, Bernard and Noel (1991) examined whether changes in inventory could be used to forecast future sales and earnings. They found that the implications of inventory changes are not homogeneous for all firms, but differ between retailers and manufacturers.

For retailers, inventory increases signal higher sales but lower earnings and profit margins. This may seem paradoxical but the explanation is straightforward; a drop in demand results in increased inventory. To eliminate "excess" inventory, retailers reduce prices to stimulate sales ("dumping" inventory). Therefore, sales increase but with lower earnings. These effects generally are short-lived as the effect on sales dissipates over time.

OPTIONAL SEGMENT ENDS

For manufacturers, increases in finished goods inventory again indicate lower future demand; higher sales and owers earnings in the short run follow these increases as manufacturers dump unwanted inventory. However, unlike retailers, in the long run (once the initial increase is worked down) the drop in demand persists and future sales and earnings decrease. For raw materials and work in process, on the other hand, increases in inventory levels are consistent with higher future demand and higher future sales.

The foregoing discussion provides a different analytical application of information contained in financial reports. The lessons of the reading, however, must not be forgotten. Any changes in inventory balances must take into consideration the inventory method used. Thus, for a LIFO company, analysis of changes should be based on current cost inventory amounts. In addition, an effort should be made to ensure that the change in inventory balances is driven by quantity changes, not increased prices for the same inventory quantity.

* See Bernard and Noel (1991) for a more elaborate discussion of the issues discussed here.

† Unplanned inventory changes may also have a direct impact on future unit production costs. When excess inventory must be reduced, production levels decline and unit costs increase as fixed overhead is spread over fewer units. Conversely, inventory building reduces unit costs by spreading overhead over increased production.

‡ Throughout this section, a distinction between demand and sales must be kept in mind. Lower current demand can be associated with higher future sales if a company, in response to lower demand, cuts prices, thus stimulating sales.

§ The analyst must also be sure that the change is not (1) a result of a change in accounting method, (2) due to acquisitions of other companies, or (3) management's acquisition of more inventory in an attempt to beat an anticipated price increase.

a change in accounting method may reflect this other information rather than the tax advantage alone.

Reasons for choosing FIFO are complex. Based on the responses in Cushing and LeClere, no single reason emerges as most important for FIFO firms. Over half suggested economic reasons as their motivation. Twenty of the 70 firms (approximately 30%) indicated that LIFO did not provide them with any tax benefits (e.g., declining prices). Others claimed that the accounting and administrative costs to maintain LIFO records and/or ensure that there are no LIFO liquidations kept them from using LIFO. However, just as many firms stated that they chose FIFO because it was a "better accounting method" as it better reflected the physical flow of goods. Close to 40% indicated, as one of their two primary reasons, their concern about the lower earnings resulting from LIFO.[34]

Consistent with the tax effects argument, Dopuch and Pincus (1988) found that FIFO firms were less likely (relative to LIFO firms) to have significant tax savings from LIFO. With respect to the income-enhancing arguments, Hunt (1985) did find some evidence that supported the bonus plan hypothesis.

Many of the inventory studies found the choice of inventory method closely related to industry and size factors, with larger firms opting for LIFO. The industry factor is a consequence of similar production, operating, and *inflation conditions* faced by firms in the same industry. The size factor has been explained in two ways. As noted, adoption of LIFO increases inventory management and control costs, which mitigate the benefit received from tax savings. For large firms, these costs are more readily absorbed and small relative to the potential tax benefits. Alternatively, the size effect reflects the fact that, for political reasons, larger firms tend to choose accounting methods that lower reported earnings.

Exhibit 39-10, based on Cushing and LeClere (1992), summarizes their findings; the variables and the rationale behind them are indicated in the table. Seven of the eight variables that explain the FIFO/LIFO choice are significant in the predicted direction. The estimated tax savings are significantly greater for

EXHIBIT 39-10 Variables Hypothesized to Affect FIFO-LIFO Choice

1. *Estimated tax savings* from use of LIFO expected to be larger for LIFO companies.
2. *Inventory materiality:* The larger a firm's inventory balance, the greater the incentive to use LIFO as the potential tax savings is larger.
3. *Tax loss carryforward:* The larger a firm's tax loss carryforward, the less incentive it has to use LIFO.
4. *Inventory variability:* The more variable a firm's inventory balance, the more likely it is to face inventory liquidations. This would tend to favor choosing FIFO over LIFO.
5. *Inventory obsolescence:* If a firm's inventory tends to become obsolete because of new product innovation, then the replacement of old products by new ones raises a difficult LIFO accounting question for which there is no authoritative answer. Such companies may prefer FIFO.
6. *Size as proxy for bookkeeping costs:* The larger the accounting costs required to use LIFO, the less likely a firm would choose LIFO. Larger firms would be able to absorb these costs more readily.
7. *Leverage:* Under the debt covenant hypothesis, firms with higher leverage would prefer FIFO as it would improve their debt/equity ratios.
8. *Current ratio:* Under the debt covenant hypothesis, firms with low current ratios would prefer FIFO, which improves their current ratio.

Source: Barry E. Cushing and Marc J. LeClere, "Evidence on the Determinants of Inventory Accounting Policy Choice," *Accounting Review* (April 1992), pp. 355–366, Table 4, p. 363.

[34] These percentages are considerably higher than those reported by Granof and Short (1984) in an earlier survey.

LIFO firms. Consistent with this, FIFO firms have higher average loss carryforwards. Inventory variability is higher for FIFO firms, increasing the chances of LIFO liquidations. FIFO firms tend to be smaller, more highly leveraged, and less liquid. Similarly, the likelihood of inventory obsolescence is also a significant factor. Only the materiality measure is not statistically significant.

These variables indicate possible motivations to stay on FIFO. For a given firm, the analyst should try to determine which of these motivations apply and, thus, whether the firm is justified in staying on FIFO or management is inefficient (or self-serving) by foregoing tax savings from the use of LIFO. Management that remains on FIFO for motives that are either selfish or based on the belief that the market can be fooled should not inspire confidence.

OPTIONAL SEGMENT ENDS

11 INTERNATIONAL ACCOUNTING AND REPORTING PRACTICES

FIFO and the weighted-average method are the most commonly used methods worldwide. Historically, the use of LIFO was essentially limited to companies in the United States, and the significant tax benefits this method can provide suggest that the method will continue to enjoy widespread acceptance. These benefits have resulted in gradual adoption of LIFO as a permitted alternative in countries such as Germany, Italy, and Japan.[35] In some countries, LIFO is allowed for financial reporting but not income taxes, which may account for its lack of popularity in these countries. In practice, LIFO is rarely used in these countries, perhaps because of the low inflation rates of recent years. Non-U.S. reporting standards do not require disclosure of LIFO reserves, reducing the analyst's ability to make the adjustments discussed in this reading.

In the United Kingdom, Statement of Standard Accounting Practice (SSAP) 9 holds that LIFO may not result in a true and fair valuation and, in addition, the method is not allowed for tax purposes.

Average cost is the most widely used method in Germany, although LIFO has been allowed for tax purposes since 1990, and it may change reporting habits.

IASB Standard 2

In 1993, the IASB issued revised International Accounting Standard (IAS) 2, designating FIFO and weighted-average costs as the benchmark treatments and LIFO as the allowed alternative. Firms using LIFO are required to provide FIFO/weighted-average or current cost disclosures, facilitating the adjustments discussed in this reading.

Inventories are reported at the lower of cost or market value; cost depends on the method used. Market is generally defined as the net realizable value with specific limitations in the United States;[36] any writedown is determined on an item-by-item basis. Revised IAS 2 limits itself to net realizable value (NRV), and it does not specify whether the cost versus NRV comparison should be made on an item-by-item basis or by groups of similar items. This standard is similar to those of most other countries.

---

[35] Financial reporting and tax reporting are identical in these countries.

[36] Generally, these limitations ensure that inventories are written down to approximate current cost.

SUMMARY AND CONCLUDING COMMENTS 12

The choice of accounting method for inventories is one of the basic decisions made by nearly all companies engaged in the manufacturing and distribution of goods. Ideally, the method chosen should result in the best measure of income and financial condition. However, no single method accomplishes these objectives in most cases and, in an environment of changing prices, assumptions as to the flow of costs affect reported income, balance sheet amounts, and associated ratios.

For companies operating in the United States, under conditions of rising prices, the cash flow advantage of LIFO usually dictates the choice of that method. When LIFO is not chosen, therefore, the first question should be: Why not? As the empirical work indicates, managers offer a number of reasons for not using LIFO, only some of which appear valid. Thus, companies that should use LIFO but do not may appear unattractive to investors.

In many cases, the analytical techniques presented in this reading enable the analyst to approximate the effect of LIFO on a company using FIFO or average cost. Such analysis can provide estimates of both the cash savings foregone (relevant to the discussion in the previous paragraph) and the holding gains included in reported income. Similarly, the reading demonstrates how the analyst can adjust from LIFO to FIFO where appropriate. The reading also explores the effects of liquidations and the incentives for the FIFO/LIFO choice, and concludes with a review of inventory accounting standards applied internationally.

PROBLEMS

1. [Allocation of purchase costs under different inventory methods; CFA © adapted] Assume the following:

Quarter	Units Purchased	Per Unit Cost	Dollar Purchases	Unit Sales
I	200	$22	$ 4,400	200
II	300	24	7,200	200
III	300	26	7,800	200
IV	200	28	5,600	200
Year	1,000		$25,000	800

Inventory at beginning of Quarter I: 400 units at $20 per unit = $8,000
Inventory at end of Quarter IV: 600 units

A. Calculate reported inventory at the end of the year under *each* of the following inventory methods:

(i) FIFO
(ii) LIFO
(iii) Average cost

B. Calculate the cost of goods sold for the year under each method listed in part A.

C. Discuss the effect of the differences among the three methods on:

(i) Reported income for the year
(ii) Stockholders' equity at the end of the year

2. [Effect of inventory methods on financial statements; CFA © adapted] Compare the effect of the use of the LIFO inventory method with use of the FIFO method on each of the following, assuming rising prices and stable inventory quantities:

(i) Gross profit margin
(ii) Net income
(iii) Cash from operations
(iv) Inventories
(v) Inventory turnover ratio
(vi) Working capital
(vii) Total assets
(viii) Debt-to-equity ratio

3. [Inventory methods; basic relationships] The M&J Company begins operations on January 1, 20X0 with the following balance sheet:

Cash	$10,000	Common stock	$10,000

During the year, the company maintains its inventory accounts using the FIFO method. Before a provision for income tax, the balance sheet at December 31, 20X0, is:

Cash	$ 5,000	Common stock	$10,000
Inventory	10,000	Pretax income	5,000
	$15,000		$15,000

M&J has 20X0 sales of $25,000. The company sells half of the *units* purchased during the year. Operating expenses (excluding COGS) are $12,000.

Prior to issuing financial statements, the company considers its choice of inventory method. Assume a tax rate of 40% and a dividend payout ratio of 50%.

A. Using the information provided, complete the following table:

	FIFO	Weighted Average	LIFO
Sales	$25,000	$25,000	$25,000
COGS			
Other expenses	12,000	12,000	12,000
Pretax income			
Income tax expense			
Net income			
Dividends paid			
Retained earnings			
Cash from operations			
Closing cash balance			
Closing inventory			
Inventory purchases			

B. Prepare a balance sheet for M&J at December 31, 20X0, assuming use of the:

(i) LIFO inventory method

(ii) Weighted-average method

(iii) FIFO inventory method

C. Discuss the advantages and disadvantages of each of the three possible choices of inventory method.

4. [LIFO versus FIFO; effect on ratios; adjusting ratios; CFA © adapted] The Zeta Corp. uses LIFO inventory accounting. The footnotes to the 20X4 financial statements contain the following data as of December 31:

	20X3	20X4
Raw materials	$392,675	$369,725
Finished products	401,325	377,075
Inventory on FIFO basis	$794,000	$746,800
LIFO reserve	(46,000)	(50,000)
Inventory on LIFO basis	$748,000	$696,800

You are also provided with the following data:

- The company has a marginal tax rate of 35%.
- COGS for 20X4 is $3,800,000.
- Net income for 20X4 is $340,000.
- Return on equity for 20X4 is 4.6%.

A. Calculate 20X4 net income for Zeta, assuming that it uses the FIFO inventory method.

B. Calculate the company's inventory turnover ratio on both a FIFO and LIFO basis.

C. Calculate Zeta's return on equity on a FIFO basis. (Remember to adjust both the numerator and denominator.)

D. Discuss the usefulness of the adjustments made in parts A, B, and C to a financial analyst.

E. Describe alternative measures of inventory turnover and return on equity that would be more useful to assess Zeta's operating performance.

5. [Decline in LIFO reserve] The following footnote appeared in the annual report of A. T. Cross [ATX], a pen manufacturer:

Note B—Inventories

Domestic writing instrument inventories, approximating $13,404,000 and $5,695,000 at December 30, 2000 and January 1, 2000, respectively, are priced at the lower of LIFO cost or market. The remaining inventories are priced at the lower of FIFO cost or market. If the FIFO method of inventory valuation had been used for those inventories priced using the LIFO method, inventories would have been approximately $9,614,000 and $11,227,000 higher than reported at December 30, 2000 and January 1, 2000, respectively. The Company believes the LIFO method of inventory valuation ordinarily results in a more appropriate matching of its revenues to their related costs, since current costs are included in cost of goods sold, and distortions in reported income due to the effect of changing prices are reduced.

A. Cross did not report any LIFO liquidation for 2000. Explain how its LIFO reserve could decline.

B. State two reasons why Cross might choose to continue to use the LIFO method despite the decline in the LIFO reserve.

6. [Effect of LIFO liquidations on gross margins] The following data were obtained from annual reports of Stride-Rite [SRR], a shoe manufacturer and retailer:

Years Ended December 31 (in $thousands)

	1997	1998	1999
Sales	$515,728	$539,413	$572,696
COGS	(328,172)	(348,587)	(362,108)
Gross profit	$187,556	$190,826	$210,588
LIFO liquidation (net of tax)	$ 3,379	$ 1,733	0

A. Compute the gross margin percentage for each year, 1997–1999.

B. Stride-Rite disclosed the effect of LIFO liquidations net of income tax. Assuming a tax rate of 35%, recompute Stride-Rite's gross margin for the years 1997–1999 after removing the effect of LIFO liquidations.

C. Explain why the trend in gross margins shown in part B is a better indicator of Stride-Rite's performance than the reported gross margins.

ANALYSIS OF LONG-LIVED ASSETS: PART I — THE CAPITALIZATION DECISION

READING 40

LEARNING OUTCOMES

The candidate should be able to:

a. compute and describe the effects of capitalizing versus expensing on net income, shareholders' equity, cash flow from operations, and financia ratios, explain the effects on financial statements and the interest coverage ratio (times interest earned) of capitalizing interest costs, and explain the circumstances in which intangible assets, including software development costs and research and development costs, are capitalized;

b. calculate and describe both the initial and long-term effects of asset revaluations on financial ratios.

INTRODUCTION 1

The long-lived operating assets of a firm, unlike inventory, are not held for resale but are used in the firm's manufacturing, sales, and administrative operations. Such assets include tangible fixed assets (plant, machinery, and office facilities) as well as intangible assets such as computer software, patents, and trademarks.

This reading examines financial reporting and analysis issues when these assets are originally acquired, with emphasis on:

- Which costs are included in the carrying amount of fixed assets
- The financial statement effects of capitalization versus expensing
- The capitalization of interest
- The circumstances under which research and development, computer software, and other intangible costs can be capitalized

- Analytical adjustments required to compare companies with different capitalization policies
- The analysis of fixed asset disclosures

Reading 41 discusses the accounting for and analysis of the use, impairment, and disposal of these long-lived assets.

2 ACQUIRING THE ASSET: THE CAPITALIZATION DECISION

The costs of acquiring resources that provide services over more than one operating cycle are capitalized and carried as assets on the balance sheet. All costs incurred until the asset is ready for use must be capitalized, including the invoice price, applicable sales tax, freight and insurance costs incurred delivering the equipment, and any installation costs.[1]

However, considerable debate surrounds the application of these principles and significant differences remain (across countries and firms) with respect to three major issues:

1. Should some components of acquisition cost be included in the capitalized cost (e.g., interest during construction)?
2. Do some types of costs merit capitalization (e.g., software development and research and development costs)?
3. What accounting method should be used to determine the amount of costs capitalized (e.g., oil and gas properties)?

These choices affect the balance sheet, income and cash flow statements, and ratios both in the year the choice is made and over the life of the asset. Management discretion can result in smoothing or manipulation of reported income, cash flows, and other measures of financial performance. Moreover, unlike some accounting choices whose effects reverse over time, some effects of the decision to capitalize or expense may never reverse.

This reading is devoted to the controversial issue of capitalization versus expensing of expenditures for long-lived assets. We start with an overview of the conceptual issues and a review of the implications of capitalization for financial statement analysis. The remaining sections then examine the specific components and categories of cost where capitalization practices vary.

---

[1] In June 2001, the Accounting Standards Executive Committee (AcSEC) of the AICPA issued an exposure draft of a proposed Statement of Position: Accounting for Certain Costs and Activities Related to Property, Plant, and Equipment. The SOP would require that:

- Costs incurred prior to asset acquisition must be expensed, with the exception of option payments and other costs directly related to specific PPE assets.
- All repair and maintenance costs during the life of PPE assets must be expensed.
- Overhead costs (including general and administrative and other support costs) must be expensed.

CAPITALIZATION VERSUS EXPENSING: CONCEPTUAL ISSUES

The Financial Accounting Standards Board (FASB), in its Statement of Financial Accounting Concepts (SFAC) 6,[2] defines accounting assets as probable future economic benefits. Analytically, the concept of long-lived assets can also serve as:

1. An index of initial investment outlays, used as a base for measuring profitability (return on assets)
2. A measure of the firm's wealth, used for valuation and to measure solvency
3. Inputs in the firm's production function, used to measure capital intensity, leverage, and operating efficiency

Different analytical objectives require distinct definitions of what constitutes an asset. Although returns on research and development should be evaluated in the same way as returns on a purchased factory, measurement problems may preclude recognition of such expenditures as assets for assessment of shareholder wealth or collateral for bondholders.

For this reason, traditional, historical cost-based accounting rules cannot satisfy all contexts; analysts must evaluate asset definitions used for financial reporting and make necessary adjustments. The appropriate adjustment may require the capitalization of previously expensed costs, or the reverse. In some cases, particularly for intangible assets, there is no one "correct" choice that serves all analytical needs.

Financial Statement Effects of Capitalization

Box 40-1 (Figures 40-1 to 40-5) uses a simple illustration to demonstrate the financial statement effects of the capitalize-versus-expense choice on growing firms. That choice will have significant effects on reported cash flows, as well as on the balance sheet and income statement.

Income Variability

Firms that capitalize costs and depreciate them (systematically allocate them to income) over time show smoother patterns of reported income (Figure 40-2). Firms that expense costs as incurred have greater variance in reported income, as the variance in spending is transmitted directly to income. That variance declines as the firm matures and is lower for larger firms (or those with other sources of income).

Profitability

In the early years, expensing lowers profitability, both in absolute terms (as the cost of new assets exceeds depreciation of previously capitalized expenditures) and relative to assets, sales, etc. *Profitability remains lower for expensing firms as long*

[2] See Chapter 1 for a discussion of SFAC 6.

BOX 40-1 COMPARISON OF FINANCIAL STATEMENT EFFECTS: CAPITALIZATION VERSUS EXPENSING

For our illustration we consider two hypothetical firms, each with an asset base of $1,000 on which it earns $150, which begin to grow. Growth requires the acquisition of an "asset," which has a three-year life. Each asset costs $100 and generates cash flows of $50 per year. The pattern of growth* (the number of assets acquired each year and the replacement of old assets) is illustrated in Figure 40-1.

Growth is assumed to continue for 15 years after which maturity is reached, and all subsequent acquisitions are for replacement only. We further assume that the asset cost may be capitalized or expensed at the discretion of management under the provisions of generally accepted accounting principles (GAAP). One firm capitalizes the acquisition cost; the other expenses it. The firms are otherwise operationally identical. Their reported income, cash flow from operations, and related ratios, however, will differ markedly.

Figure 40-2 compares the pattern of reported income. The "expensing" firm exhibits a fluctuating pattern of income growth through maturity. The "capitalizing" firm, on the other hand, exhibits a smooth pattern of income growth. For firms that are initially larger,† the fluctuations are not as great throughout the growth and maturity cycle because of the larger base.

Figure 40-3 compares the return on assets (ROA) ratio for the two firms. The choice of accounting method affects both the numerator and denominator of the ROA. The expensing firm, having fewer recorded assets, will have a smaller denominator, increasing its reported ROA. The numerator (earnings) is volatile, so that sometimes ROA increases but at other times decreases. At the early stage of growth, the expensing firm's ROA gyrates about that of the capitalizing firm but will initially tend to be lower. As the expensing firm grows larger, the fluctuations persist, but its ROA is higher because the effect of lower reported assets on the denominator dominates.

Figure 40-4 compares reported cash from operations for the capitalizing and expensing firms. The capitalizing firm always shows higher cash from operations; the difference increases and does not reverse over the life of the asset (see Figure 40-5).

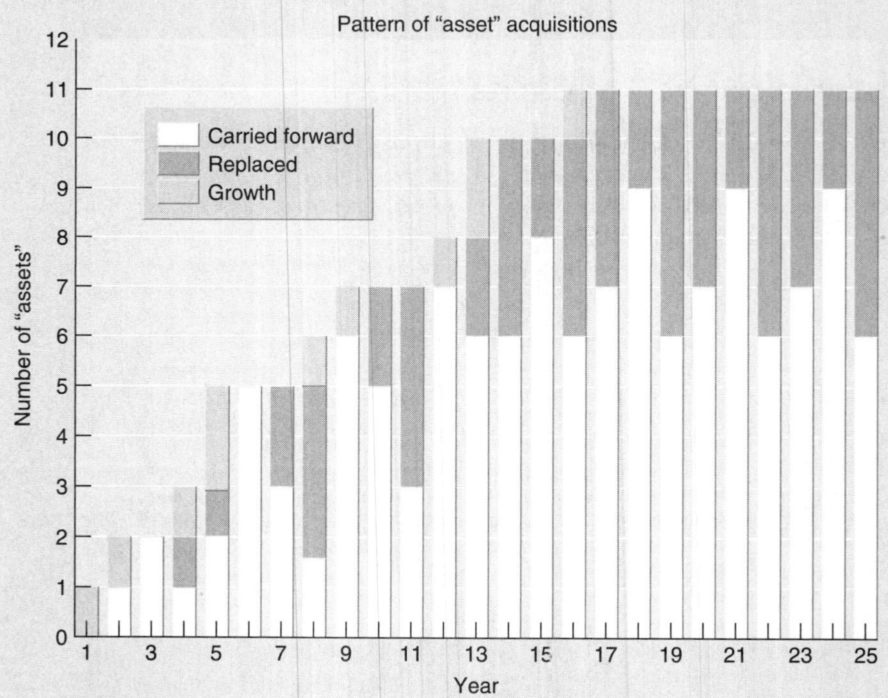

FIGURE 40-1

* A variable growth rate is used in the illustration because it is more descriptive of reality (it has greater external validity). Any growth rate, other than a perfectly constant one, will create a similar pattern of differences between a capitalizing and expensing firm. At maturity or steady state, a constant growth rate generates identical (and constant) total expense for both firms. (ROA and cash flow from operations would still differ.)

† The term "larger" does not necessarily relate only to absolute size. It can also denote that the firm engages in other activities that offset the variability of the costs that are expensed.

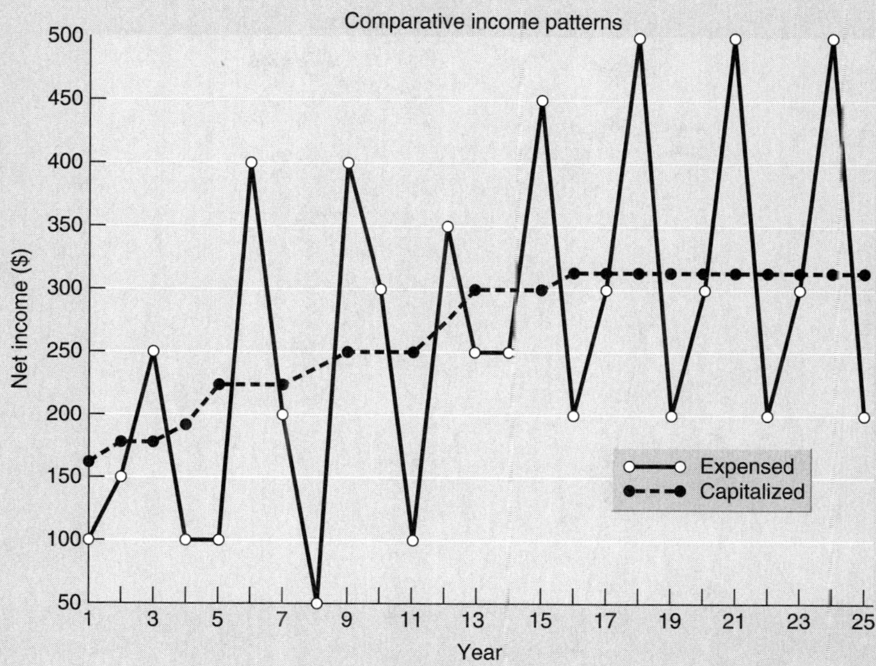

FIGURE 40-2

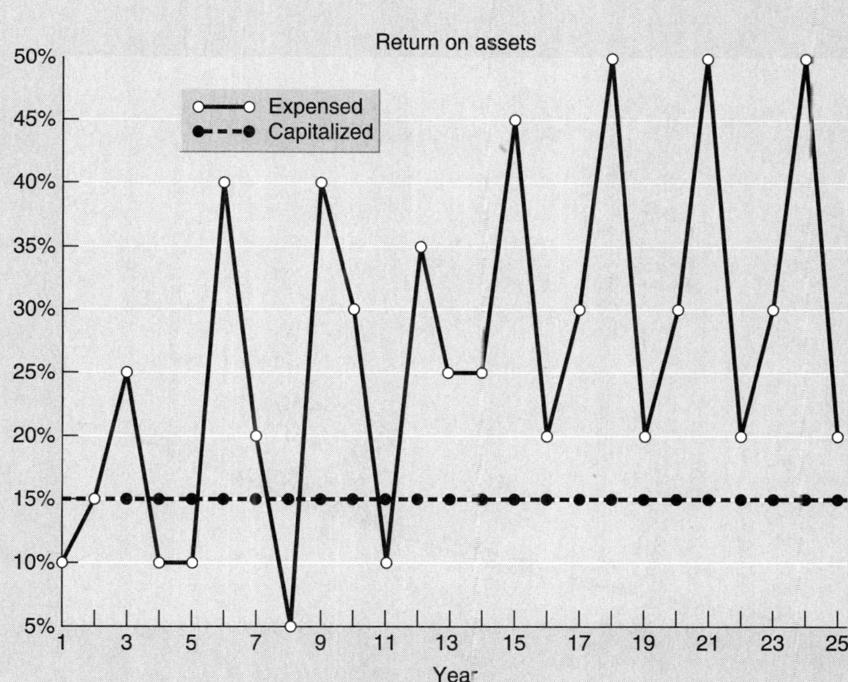

FIGURE 40-3

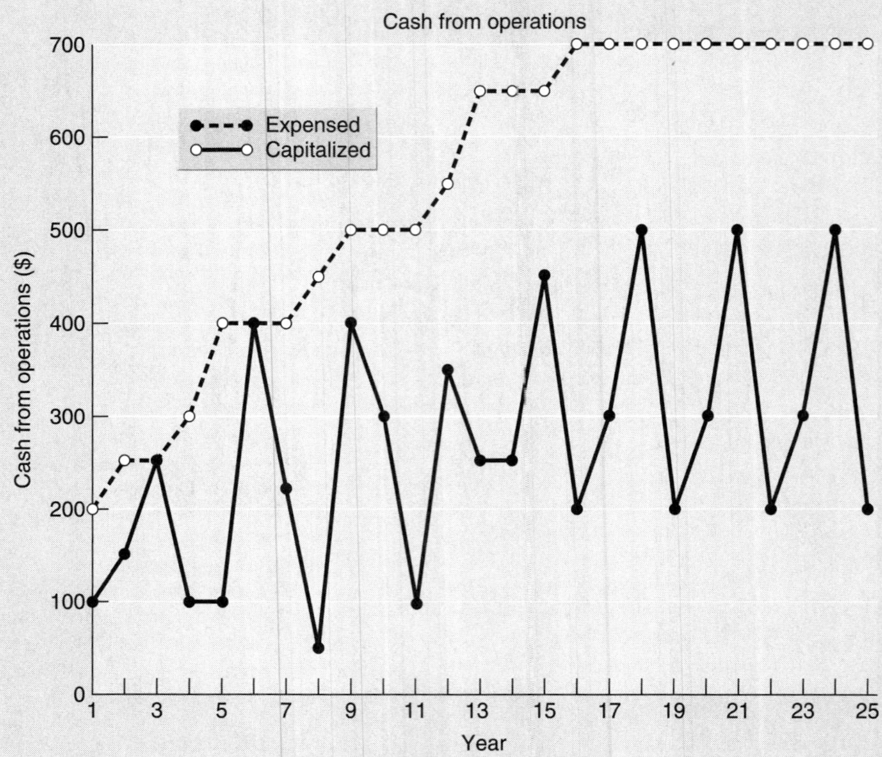

FIGURE 40-4

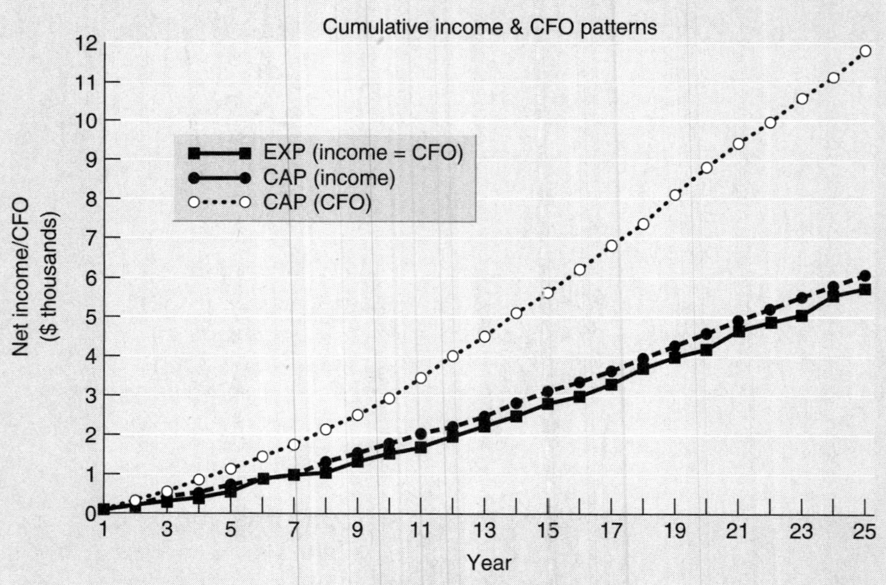

FIGURE 40-5

as the level of expenditures is increasing (positive growth). However, because they report lower assets (and equity), their ROA/ROE measures can be higher than those of firms that capitalize costs (Figure 40-3). In general, whether ROA and ROE will be higher depends on the relationship between profitability and growth.[3]

Cash Flow from Operations

Reported *net cash flow,* unlike net income, is immune to accounting alternatives.[4] However, the capitalization decision has a significant impact on the components of cash flow, with a trade-off between *cash from operations (CFO) and cash from investment (CFI).* As discussed in Reading 33, cash expenditures for capitalized assets are included in investing cash flow and *never* flow through CFO. Firms that expense these outlays, however, include these expenditures in CFO. Thus, CFO will always be higher for the capitalizing firm (Figure 40-4),[5] and the cumulative difference (rather than reversing) increases over time (Figure 40-5). *Thus, the capitalization of long-lived assets results in a permanent shift of expenditures from CFO to CFI.*

Leverage Ratios

Expensing firms report lower assets and equity balances.[6] As a result, debt-to-equity and debt-to-assets solvency ratios will appear worse for expensing firms as compared with firms that capitalize the same costs.

Given management discretion as to capitalization, a great deal of care must be exercised when assessing financial performance. The remainder of this reading considers particular areas where this problem occurs. Some issues are pervasive and cut across all industries; others are industry specific.

CAPITALIZATION VERSUS EXPENSING: GENERAL ISSUES 4

Capitalization of Interest Costs

Companies often construct long-lived assets, such as new operating facilities, for their own use and capitalize costs incurred during construction until the assets are ready to be placed in service. How should the firm measure the cost of these self-constructed assets? Should the interest cost on funds used for

---

[3] Sarath, Lev, and Sougiannis (2000) show that for a firm whose relevant expenditures are growing at a rate g, ROE on an expensing basis will be higher if that ROE $> g/(1 + g/2)$. For growth rates (in the relevant range) below 30%, that relationship is equivalent to comparing ROE and g. As long as they are close, there is little difference between ROE on an expense basis and ROE on a capitalized basis. The greater the difference between ROE and g, the greater the difference between ROE on an expense basis and ROE on a capitalized basis. (A similar relationship holds for pretax ROA.)

For (after-tax) ROA, ROA will be higher for the expensing firm if its ROA $> (1 - \text{tax rate})\ g/(1 + g/2)$.

[4] Ignoring any income tax effects.

[5] This affects the cash from operations/capital expenditures ratio that measures the degree to which the firm's internally generated funds finance the replacement and expansion of productive capacity.

[6] These effects are not directly shown in Box 40-1. However, they can be deduced from the discussion of the return-on-investment (ROA/ROE) measures.

construction be capitalized or expensed? Should interest capitalization require specific borrowing to finance construction? Should the firm capitalize a return on equity when there is no debt or the firm has borrowed less than the total construction cost? The answers to these questions vary from country to country.

In the United States, SFAS 34 (1979) requires the capitalization of interest costs incurred during the construction period. When a specific borrowing is associated with the construction, the interest cost incurred on that borrowing is capitalized. If no specific borrowing is identifiable, the weighted-average interest rate on outstanding debt (up to the amount invested in the project) is capitalized. When the firm has no interest expense, no borrowing costs may be capitalized. Capitalization of the cost of equity is not permitted under any circumstances. SFAS 34 requires the disclosure of the amount of interest capitalized.

The argument for interest capitalization is that the cost of a self-constructed asset should equal the cost of one purchased after completion. In the latter case, the purchase price would presumably include the cost of capital of the seller. Capitalization of interest for self-constructed assets, it is argued, replicates this process. This argument should apply even when the firm has no debt; in that case, return on equity capital used for construction should be capitalized.

On the other hand, there are strong arguments against the capitalization of interest in general and SFAS 34 in particular. On a conceptual level, interest, as a financing cost, is different from the other costs of acquiring and getting the asset ready for service. It results from a financing decision rather than an operating decision.

Under SFAS 34, interest is capitalized only if the firm is leveraged. It seems illogical that two identical assets should be carried at different costs, depending on the firm's financing decisions. Further, the capitalization of interest creates differences between reported earnings and cash flow. Given these arguments, we believe that expensing of all interest is the preferable treatment.

For purposes of analysis, therefore, the income statement capitalization of interest should be reversed, resulting in the following effects:

1. *Capitalized interest should be added back to interest expense.* The adjusted interest expense provides a better representation of the level and trend of a firm's financing costs.
2. *Adding capitalized interest back to interest expense reduces net income.* Unfortunately, although the amount of interest capitalized in the current year must be disclosed, disclosure of the amortization of previously capitalized interest (included in the fixed asset account) is not required and is rarely provided.[7] This amortization must be deducted from depreciation expense to accurately determine the net effect of interest capitalization on net income. *However, if the amount of interest capitalization in previous years is not large and asset lives are long, the amortization (over the asset life) is likely to be immaterial and can be ignored.* If interest capitalization has been large, the analyst must estimate the amortization.[8]

---

[7] See Problem 40-1, based on Chevron, which does disclose the amortization of previously capitalized interest.

[8] The amortization of capitalized interest is included in depreciation expense. Thus, one can use the historical ratio of interest capitalized to total capital expenditures to estimate the portion of depreciation applicable to capitalized interest expense.

3. *The capitalization of interest also distorts the classification of cash flows. Interest capitalized as part of the cost of fixed assets will never be reported as CFO, but as an investment outflow. To restore comparability with firms that do not capitalize interest, the amount of interest capitalized should be added back to cash for investment and subtracted from CFO.* The cash flows for capitalized interest are then included with other interest payments.[9]
4. *The interest coverage ratio should be calculated with interest expense adjusted to add back capitalized interest.* Otherwise, it is overstated.[10]

These adjustments tend to be small relative to cash flows but may be significant for interest expense and net income. The following example illustrates how adding back capitalized interest affects profitability and the interest coverage ratio.

Example:

Westvaco

Note F in Westvaco's fiscal 1999 financial statements reports capitalized interest, which can be used to adjust the interest coverage ratio:[11]

Westvaco, Years Ended October 31 (in $thousands)

	1997	1998	1999	% Change 1997–1999
As reported:				
EBIT	$339,872	$314,575	$271,514	(20%)
Interest expense	93,272	110,162	123,538	32%
Pretax income	$246,600	$204,413	$147,976	(40%)
Interest coverage	3.64X	2.86X	2.20X	(39%)
Interest capitalized	$ 25,962	$ 20,752	$ 8,890	(66%)
After adjustment:				
EBIT (unchanged)	$339,872	$314,575	$271,514	(20%)
Interest expense	119,234	130,914	132,428	11%
Pretax income	$220,638	$183,661	$139,086	(37%)
Interest coverage	2.85X	2.40X	2.05X	(28%)

---

[9] These interest payments would be deducted from cash from operations, as required by SFAS 95. Alternatively, as we argue in Reading 33, interest payments should be considered financing cash flows and thus excluded from both CFO and cash for investment regardless of capitalization.

[10] The SFAS 95 requirement for the disclosure of interest paid makes it possible to make this adjustment and compute interest coverage accurately on a cash flow basis. On an accrual basis, the numerator, EBIT (and hence the coverage ratio), will be underestimated if the amortization of previous years' capitalized interest is not removed. However, as noted, this effect is relatively insignificant.

[11] Due to lack of disclosure, no adjustment has been made for the amortization of previously capitalized interest.

Based on Westvaco's reported data, the interest coverage ratio fell 39% due to declining earnings before interest and taxes (EBIT) and rising interest expense. While adding back capitalized interest does not radically change the data, it does show that:

- Adjusted interest coverage, based on interest incurred before capitalization, is, as expected, below the (reported) ratio based on interest expense after capitalization.
- Interest expense over the period rose only 11% rather than 32% as reported.
- Interest coverage fell 28% based on interest incurred, a smaller decline than the 39% decline based on reported data.
- While pretax income is lower each year, the two-year decline in pretax income was slightly lower after adjustment.

Capitalization of interest provides additional information. Despite rising interest costs, capitalized interest declined 66%, apparently due to a lower level of qualifying assets. *A significant change in capitalized interest may signal a shift in the amount or nature of capital spending, and should be investigated by the analyst.*

Interest Capitalization Outside the United States

IAS 23, Borrowing Costs (revised 1993), makes expensing all borrowing costs the benchmark treatment. Alternatively, borrowing costs that are directly attributable to the acquisition, construction, or production of qualifying assets may be capitalized. Interest capitalization is also permitted in many jurisdictions worldwide. When comparing firms that capitalize interest with those do not, adjustment is required to achieve a base for proper valuation.

Intangible Assets

Growth of the computer, Internet, telecommunications, and service industries has led to significantly increased investment in and use of intangible assets. Licenses, computer software, patents, leasehold rights, brand names, and copyrights are among the more familiar examples of assets without tangible, physical substance. As a result of their increased use, the financial reporting and analysis of such intangible assets have gained importance; for some firms they are important on- or off-balance-sheet revenue-producing assets that account for a substantial portion of the value of a firm.

Intangible assets are identifiable, nonmonetary resources controlled by firms.[12] When acquired in an arm's-length transaction, recognition and measurement rules are similar to those for tangible assets. However, practice is diverse with respect to the recognition and measurement of such assets when they are internally developed. In addition, practices differ with respect to the revaluation, amortization, and impairment of intangible assets, regardless of their origin.

[12] Goodwill is an intangible asset although it is not identifiable. See Chapter 14 for a discussion of acquisition goodwill.

The decision whether to capitalize or expense the cost of asset acquisition is especially difficult when applied to intangible resources. The variations in legal protection available for intellectual property and other intangible assets in many countries also make the assessment of value more difficult than for tangible assets. We begin, therefore, with a review of the recognition and measurement issues associated with intangible assets.

Recognition and Measurement Issues

The cost of acquiring intangible assets from unrelated entities is capitalized at acquisition, measured by the amount paid to acquire them. Given an arm's-length transaction, the acquisition price is assumed to equal the market value of the assets acquired.

Intangible assets may also be received through government grants or generated internally by the firm. Few, if any, costs may be incurred in obtaining assets through government grants. Financial statement recognition of such assets would be informative, but in the absence of secondary markets it is difficult to defend any measurement basis other than cost. When active secondary markets do exist (such as for broadcast properties and cellular licenses), then market price can be a reliable measure of the value of these assets.

Internally generated intangible assets are the most troublesome category because:

- The costs incurred in developing these assets may not be easily separable.
- It is difficult to measure the amount and duration of benefits from such expenditures as advertising when they are made, or even later.
- There may be little relationship between the costs incurred and the value of the asset created.

For many internally generated intangible assets, discounted cash flow analysis may be the only way to measure their fair value. However, such measurement is subject to accurate forecasting of the amount and timing of cash flows and the choice of discount rates.

To illustrate these issues, we turn to a discussion of capitalization issues for specific intangible assets.

Research and Development

Companies invest in research and development (R&D) because they expect the investment to produce profitable future products. However, absent a resultant commercial product, these expenditures may have no value to the firm. Further, the value of the resulting product may be unrelated to the amount spent on R&D. Due to such valuation uncertainties, R&D is generally unacceptable to creditors as security for loans.

SFAS 2, Accounting for Research and Development Costs. SFAS 2 (1974) requires that virtually all R&D costs be expensed[13] in the period incurred and the amount disclosed. In effect, assets with uncertain future economic benefits are barred from the balance sheet. The impact of SFAS 2 on the financial

[13] The main exception is contract R&D performed for unrelated entities. In this case, R&D is carried as an asset (similar to inventory) until completion of the contract.

statements of firms with significant R&D is substantial, and there is some evidence of a decrease in R&D expenditures when SFAS 2 was adopted. Accounting aside, R&D expenditures are clearly investments in the economic sense, albeit risky ones. Further, empirical evidence[14] suggests that benefits from R&D expenditures last, on average, seven to nine years (depending on the industry), supporting the argument that R&D is an economic asset. Pfizer, for example, spent nearly $2.8 billion (17.1% of revenue) on R&D in 1999.

Accounting for Research and Development Costs Outside the United States. IAS 9 (1993) requires the expensing of research costs but requires capitalization of development costs[15] when all of the following criteria are met:

1. The product (process) is clearly defined.
2. Costs can be clearly identified.
3. Technical feasibility has been established.
4. The firm intends to produce the product (use the process).
5. The market has been clearly defined.
6. The firm has sufficient resources to complete the project.

Capitalized costs must be reviewed periodically to ensure that these conditions are still operable and that capitalized costs do not exceed net realizable value.[16] The standard also requires disclosure of the accounting methods followed, amortization methods and lives, and a reconciliation of the carrying amount.

Example:

Nokia

Nokia, an international telecommunications manufacturer, follows IASB GAAP and capitalized R&D costs in its 1998 and 1999 financial statements.

As expensing research and development costs is the dominant accounting method worldwide, financial statements of companies such as Nokia that capitalize R&D must be restated (by expensing all such expenditures) to make them comparable with similar companies that expense these costs. Alternatively (or for other analytical purposes), it may be desirable to restate another firm's financial statements by capitalizing previously expensed R&D costs. Box 2 describes the procedures required to make the adjustments in both directions. Next we illustrate the capitalization-to-expense adjustment, using Nokia as an example. Later (see Microsoft example) we adjust from expense to capitalization.

---

[14] Research in this area can be found in both the accounting and economics literature. Lev and Sougiannis (1996) provide a brief review of the literature in this area. See also the discussion of valuation in Box 40-3.

[15] IAS 9 defines development costs as expenditures incurred to translate research output into the production of materials, devices, products, processes, systems, and services.

[16] See Reading 41 for a discussion of impairment.

Nokia: Capitalized R&D Costs

	Years Ended December 31 (millions of euros)		
	1997	**1998**	**1999**
Opening balance	€426	€469	€650
Additions	156	182	271
Disposals	(113)	(1)	(110)
Closing balance	€469	€650	€811
Accumulated depreciation (year-end)*	(242)	(361)	(398)
Closing balance (net)	€227	€289	€413
Depreciation expense		119	110

*Note that the 1998 depreciation expense equals the change in accumulated depreciation; in 1999 accumulated depreciation has been reduced by the amount allocated to the disposal of R&D. We can deduce that reduction to equal €73 (361 + 110 − 398).

We can use these disclosures to compute the effect of capitalization compared to expense.

Adjustment to Pretax Income: Subtract the difference between R&D expenditure (additions) and depreciation/writedowns from reported income. This adjustment essentially amounts to subtracting the change in net (unamortized) closing balance from reported income:

(Millions of Euros)	**1998**	**1999**
Pretax income (reported)	€2,456	€3,845
Less: change in net (unamortized) closing balance	62	124
Pretax income (adjusted)	€2,394	€3,721
% reduction	2.5%	3.2%

We can also adjust reported cash flows:

Adjustment to Cash Flows: Subtract R&D expenditure (additions) from CFO and add back to CFI:

(Millions of Euros)	**1998**	**1999**
Cash from operations	€1,687	€3,102
Cash flow from investing	(780)	(1,341)
Additions (R&D expenditures)	182	271
After adjustment		
Cash from operations	1,505	2,831
% reduction	10.8%	8.7%
Cash flow from investing	€(598)	€(1,070)

BOX 40-2 ADJUSTING FINANCING STATEMENTS FOR CAPITALIZATION VERSUS EXPENSING

OPTIONAL SEGMENT

The capitalization-versus-expense decision has pervasive effects on firms' financial statements and ratios. In this box, we illustrate the adjustments from one method to the other. For convenience we use research and development (R&D) as the expenditure that can either be capitalized or expensed.

Adjusting from Capitalization to Expense

Income Statement:	
Pretax Income:	Deduct difference between R&D additions (expenditures) and amount amortized (or written off). This adjustment is equivalent to the *change in the net (unamortized) R&D asset.*
Net Income:	Deduct (1 − tax rate) × (change in the net (unamortized) R&D asset).
Balance Sheet:	
Assets:	Deduct net (unamortized) R&D asset from assets.
Liabilities:	Deduct (tax rate) × (decrease in assets) from deferred tax liability.*
Equity:	Deduct (1 − tax rate) × (decrease in assets) from equity.
Cash Flow Statement:	Deduct R&D expenditures from CFO and add same amount to CFI.

Adjusting from Expense to Capitalization

To capitalize expenditures, we need an assumption as to the period of amortization. This illustration assumes amortization over three years beginning in the year of the expenditure (year t).

Income Statement:	
Pretax Income:†	In year t, increase pretax income by $R\&D_t - 1/3(R\&D_t + R\&D_{t-1} + R\&D_{t-2})$.
Net Income:	Add (1 − tax rate) × (pretax income adjustment).
Balance Sheet:‡	
Assets:	Increase by $[2/3\ R\&D_t + 1/3\ R\&D_{t-1}]$.
Liabilities:	Add (tax rate) × (increase in assets) to deferred tax liability.§
Equity:	Increase by (1 − tax rate) × (increase in assets).
Cash Flow Statement:	Add $R\&D_t$ to CFO and deduct same amount from CFI.

* Assumes that R&D was expensed for tax purposes, creating a deferred tax liability (see Reading 42).

† General case, for amortization over n years: Increase pretax income by $[R\&D_t - 1/n\ (R\&D_t + R\&D_{t-1} + \ldots\ R\&D_{t-(n-1)})]$.

‡ Increase assets by $[(n-1)/n\ R\&D_t + (n-2)/n\ R\&D_{t-1} + \ldots\ 1/n\ R\&D_{t-(n-2)}]$.

§ Assumes that R&D is expensed for tax purposes, so that capitalization results in a deferred tax liability (see Reading 42).

OPTIONAL SEGMENT ENDS

Finally, to make Nokia comparable to companies that expense all R&D, we must reduce equity[17] by the closing balance of unamortized R&D expense, net of tax effect:

(Millions of Euros)	1998	1999
Shareholders' equity (as reported)	€5,109	€7,378
Closing R&D balance (net of depreciation)	289	413
Less tax @ 28% (rate in Finland)	(81)	(116)
Net reduction in equity	€208	€297
Shareholders' equity (adjusted)	4,901	7,081
% reduction	4.1%	4.0%

These adjustments vary from 2% to 10% depending on the item being adjusted. Nokia is a very large company (1999 sales were nearly €20 billion). Depending on the size of the firm and the variability in expenditures, the effect on other firms may be more significant.[18]

One additional benefit of this analysis is that it highlights the actual expenditures on R&D activities. Changes in amount or trend (note the large 1999 increase for Nokia) should be examined for implications regarding the company's future sales and earnings.

Research and Development Affiliates. Although SFAS 2 does not permit the capitalization of R&D costs, companies have found ways to defer the recognition of such costs. One method is the R&D partnership. Another involves the issuance of "callable common" shares to the public.

Patents and Copyrights

All costs incurred in developing patents and copyrights are expensed in conformity with the treatment of R&D costs.[19] Only the legal fees incurred in registering internally developed patents and copyrights can be capitalized. However, the full acquisition cost is capitalized when such assets are purchased from other entities.

Patents have a legal life of 17 years under U.S. patent law; copyrights have a legal life of 50 years beyond the creator's life. However, these periods should be viewed as upper limits. Successful patented products invite competition and the development of comparable or improved products that can diminish the value of the patent or make it obsolete. In addition, there is often a gap between the time that a patent is registered and the time the product comes to market.

---

[17] To adjust assets, we would deduct the closing balance of unamortized R&D expense.

[18] Nokia's 20-F report, in the required reconciliation between IASB and U.S. GAAP, shows somewhat different amounts for the income statement and balance sheet adjustments. These differences reflect the fact that, even under U.S. GAAP, Nokia could have capitalized a portion of these expenditures (computer software). The adjustments shown here eliminate the entire capitalized amount, facilitating comparison with firms that expense all R&D.

[19] However, publishers and motion picture producers capitalize all costs of creating their inventory.

In the pharmaceutical industry, for example, even after a patent is registered, the product cannot be marketed in most countries until it obtains regulatory approval, which can take a number of years. The analysis of companies that are heavily dependent on patented or proprietary products must consider the remaining legal life of patents on existing products and the number of patents in the pipeline.

Franchises and Licenses

Companies may sell the right to use their name, products, processes, or management expertise to others for some negotiated time period or market. The franchisee or licensee capitalizes the cost of purchasing these rights.

Brands and Trademarks

The cost of acquiring brands and trademarks in arm's-length transactions is capitalized. However, as in the case of other intangibles, U.S. GAAP prohibit recognition of the value of *internally created* brands or trademarks. IAS 38 also prohibits recognition of internally generated brands, mastheads, publishing titles, customer lists, and similar items. Some national accounting standards do permit recognition of such assets.

Advertising Costs

Successful advertising campaigns can contribute to generating a customer base and establishing brand or firm loyalty for many years. However, as with R&D, these benefits are uncertain and difficult to measure, and hence advertising costs are expensed as incurred. Even though there may be economic benefits, no asset is recorded because of measurement problems.

In December 1994, the Accounting Standards Executive Committee (AcSEC) of the AICPA issued Practice Bulletin 13,[20] Direct-Response Advertising and Probable Future Benefits, requiring capitalization of the costs of direct-response advertising that result in probable future benefits.[21] These costs are amortized over the estimated life of the future benefits. Capitalization is not allowed when the advertising produces leads that require additional marketing efforts to convert into sales.[22]

Goodwill

The difference between the cost of an acquired firm and the fair market value of its net assets is accounted for as an intangible asset, goodwill. It represents the amount paid for the acquired firm's ability to earn excess profits, or value that cannot be assigned to tangible assets like property. The United States and most

---

[20] This bulletin provides an interpretation of AICPA SOP 93-7, Reporting on Advertising Costs.

[21] An example would be advertising that results in a telephone response with an order.

[22] America On Line (AOL) capitalized marketing costs prior to 1996 as "deferred subscriber acquisition costs." After pressure from the SEC and analysts, AOL took a $385 million write-off in 1997 to eliminate these assets from its financial statements. In March 2000, AOL paid a $3.5 million fine to the SEC to settle charges that it had inflated profits in the years prior to 1997.

other GAAP limit the recognition of goodwill to cases where it is acquired in purchase method transactions.

Asset Revaluation

The balance sheet is more informative when assets and liabilities are stated at market value rather than historical cost. Although the recognition of changes in fixed asset value is not permitted under U.S. GAAP, IASB standards do permit such revaluations.

IAS 16 (revised 1998), Property, Plant, and Equipment, allows firms to report fixed assets at fair value less accumulated depreciation.[23] Revaluations must be made with sufficient regularity to keep them current. All items in an asset class must be revalued if any are. Revaluation decreases that place the asset value below historical cost must be included in reported earnings. Revaluations are credited directly to equity except when they reverse writedowns that were included in reported income. IAS 16 has extensive disclosure provisions regarding revaluations and requires a full reconciliation of fixed assets. Footnote 12 to the Roche 2000 financial statements is a typical reconciliation.

IAS 41 (2000), Agriculture, requires that agricultural produce (e.g. cotton, milk, and logs) and biological assets (plants and animals) be measured at fair value for financial reporting. This standard becomes effective in 2003.

Revaluation is permitted under some non-U.S. GAAP as well.[24] Unfortunately, revaluation is applied inconsistently as standards in most countries do not specify either the method(s) to be used for revaluations or the intervals at which they must be made. The resulting balance sheet accounts are not comparable and, in some cases, may be misleading.

Example:

Holmen

Footnote 10 to Holmen's 1999 financial statements reports total revaluation surplus of SKr 4,372, almost all of which reflects the revaluation of forest land. No other data are provided although this item exceeds 27% of equity.

The revaluation of forest land has the following effects on Holmen compared with firms that do not revalue:

- Lower asset turnover due to the higher asset value for land
- Lower return on assets (ROA) due to higher assets
- Higher reported book value per share
- Lower return on equity (ROE) due to higher equity
- Lower debt ratios due to higher equity

[23] Although historical cost is the benchmark treatment, revaluation is an allowed alternative.

[24] Australian GAAP, for example, permits revaluations. Barth and Clinch (1998) examined a sample of revaluations in Australia and found that both tangible and intangible revaluations tended to be value relevant.

As forestland is not depreciated, there is no effect on reported income. For assets that are depreciated, revaluation has the following additional effects:

- Lower earnings due to higher depreciation expense
- Lower interest coverage due to reduced EBIT

The earnings reduction further reduces ROA and ROE and dilutes the positive impact of the revaluation on book value per share.

5 CAPITALIZATION VERSUS EXPENSING: INDUSTRY ISSUES

Regulated Utilities

Even prior to the issuance of SFAS 34, almost all U.S. regulated utilities capitalized interest on construction work in progress. In addition, utilities capitalize many cash outflows that unregulated companies cannot. The reason is that accounting rules have direct economic impact for utilities. Rates charged to customers are largely a function of accounting-generated numbers.[25]

Regulators allow utilities to earn profits equal to a specified allowable rate of return on assets (rate base). Adding expenses to this allowable profit yields the rates they can charge their customers. Revenues are derived as follows:

$$\text{Revenues} = \text{Expenses} + (\text{Rate of Return} \times \text{Rate Base})$$

Using interest for a self-constructed asset as an example, expensing increases revenue immediately as the interest expense is recovered in the year incurred. Capitalizing results in recovery of the expense over time as depreciation of the additional fixed asset. However, the total allowable profit is increased due to the fact that the asset base has been increased. Hence, although revenues are deferred, the total amount collected over the life of the asset is greater. As the average life of utility fixed assets (mainly generating plants) is quite long, the incentive to capitalize costs in fixed assets (increasing the rate base) is powerful.

Fairness to customers is often one argument for capitalization; as current customers do not (yet) benefit from investments in capacity growth, they should not bear the cost. Thus, the cost of financing new capacity is capitalized and spread over time, matching the costs with the benefits (service to ratepayers). This logic is also appealing to regulators who prefer (for political reasons) to defer rate increases to future time periods. Logic and fairness aside, utilities have a direct economic incentive to capitalize.[26]

---

[25] For this reason, virtually all regulators that set prices also mandate the accounting principles followed by the companies that they regulate. This has given rise to so-called RAP (regulatory accounting principles), which may differ materially from GAAP.

[26] This discussion assumes that the capitalized interest will, in fact, be recovered from future revenues. In practice, "regulatory lag" often results in actual rates of return below the "allowable" rate of return. In addition, by capitalizing interest, the recovery of that interest is delayed to a later period and thus current period cash flow is reduced. For these reasons, some utilities have successfully petitioned regulators to allow some portion of the interest on construction work in progress (CWIP) to be recovered currently (expensed) rather than capitalized.

Regulatory accounting results in the creation of *regulatory assets* and *regulatory liabilities.* Regulatory assets are expenditures that regulators will permit the utility to recover in future periods, even though these expenditures do not qualify as assets for unregulated companies under GAAP. Examples include:

- Capitalization (as part of fixed assets) of return on equity as well as interest. These are called the allowance for funds used during construction (AFUDC).
- Capitalization (as part of fixed assets) of employee costs and other overhead.
- Demand-side management costs (expenditures to reduce demand).
- Costs to buy out coal or gas purchase contracts.

Under SFAS 71, such expenditures can be recorded as regulatory assets (regulatory liabilities) as long as recovery (settlement) is expected. If an adverse regulatory ruling is made, such assets must be written off.

When deregulation occurs, the company must reassess the carrying value of its assets and liabilities under these new circumstances. In the United States, deregulation of the telephone industry resulted in significant write-offs by companies in that industry as they:

- Wrote down fixed assets to reflect shorter economic lives
- Wrote off regulatory assets that were no longer recoverable

The use of shorter asset lives as a result of the accounting change increases depreciation expense, somewhat offset by the elimination of depreciation on older assets that were fully written off as part of the change. The change also sharply reduces reported stockholders' equity, increasing the reported debt-to-equity ratio.

The deregulation of the electric utility industry in the United States is in its early stages. Such deregulation is likely to result in similar write-offs of regulatory assets and the use of shorter lives for fixed assets.[27]

OPTIONAL SEGMENT ENDS

Computer Software Development Costs

The growing importance of computer software led the FASB to issue SFAS 86 (1985), which applies to software intended for sale or lease to others. SFAS 86 requires that all costs incurred to establish the technological and/or economic feasibility of software be viewed as R&D costs and expensed as incurred. Once economic feasibility has been established, subsequent costs can be capitalized as part of product inventory and amortized based on product revenues or on a straight-line basis.

Although this provision allows software firms to increase reported assets and income, some software firms[28] (most notably, Microsoft[29]) have not taken

---

[27] Deregulation also eliminates the incentives for investments in generating plants by eliminating the guaranteed recovery of the investment and a return on investment. Shortages of generating capacity started to appear in 1999.

[28] In 1996, the Software Publishers Association (SPA) petitioned the FASB to abolish SFAS 86 and make expensing the required method of accounting. The SPA argued that the uncertainty surrounding eventual product sales made capitalization both inappropriate and not beneficial to investors. As noted in Box 40-3, Aboody and Lev (1998) found, on the contrary, that software capitalization was indeed value relevant to investors. Aboody and Lev suggested (using recent trends in software development costs) that perhaps the SPA was motivated by the fact that software development expenditures had declined to a low level and that expensing would now show higher income than capitalization. By eliminating the previous years' capitalization overhang with a onetime accounting charge, software developers could (under the SPA's proposal) get the best of both worlds, using capitalization when costs were growing and expensing when costs declined.

[29] Microsoft's fiscal 2000 annual report states that it adopted SOP 98-1 (discussed shortly) in 2000 but provides no disclosure of the effects. On page 22 it states that SFAS 86 "does not materially affect the Company."

advantage of the provisions of SFAS 86. Disparate accounting for software hinders the comparison of computer software firms, requiring restatement to the same accounting method. SFAS 86 disclosures are sufficient to evaluate (and eliminate) the impact of capitalization. For some firms, the effect may be significant, as illustrated by the following example.

Example:

Lucent

The following data were obtained from Lucent's annual report for fiscal 1999:

Capitalized Software

(in $millions)	1998	1999
Opening balance	$293	$298
Closing balance	298	470
Amortization	234	249

where the balances were obtained from Lucent's balance sheet and the amortization amount from the statement of cash flows. By adding the year-to-year increase in the balance to the amortization, we can deduce the amount invested during the year (which is included in capital expenditures under investing activities):

(in $millions)	1998	1999
New investment	$239	$421

If Lucent expensed this amount each year (as does Microsoft), its income would have been reduced by:

	(in $millions)	1998	1999
Income adjustment	Investment less amortization	$ 5	$ 172
	Tax offset (35%)	(2)	(60)
	Net adjustment	$ 3	$ 112
Net Income	Reported	$1,035	$3,458
	Adjusted	1,032	3,346
	% reduction	−0.3%	−3.2%

Note that the 1999 effect is much greater than the 1998 effect, reflecting the substantial increase in expenditures. Capitalization and amortization smoothes the effect of spending changes on reported income. It also obscures the large increase, which may suggest that Lucent hopes to expand its software sales.

Perhaps more important, however, is that amounts capitalized are included in cash for investing activities rather than cash from operations. By subtracting the new investment amount, we can adjust cash from operations:

Cash from Operations

(in $millions)	1998	1999
Reported	$1,860	$(276)
Adjusted	1,621	(697)
% reduction	−12.8%	−152.5%

While reported CFO turned negative in 1999, the effect is even greater when software expenditures are reclassified from investing to operating activities.

SOP 98-1 governs accounting for the cost of developing computer software for internal use (rather than sale or lease).[30] This standard requires the capitalization and subsequent amortization of the cost of developing internal-use software once technical feasibility has been established. EITF Issue 00-2[31] extends SOP 98-1 to website development costs, allowing capitalization of costs to develop or add applications for websites. IBM, for example, capitalized $81 million of website development costs in 2000.

Example:

Lucent

The 10-Q report filed by Lucent for the first quarter of fiscal 2000 (ending December 31, 1999) states:

> Effective October 1, 1999, Lucent adopted Statement of Position 98-1, "Accounting for the Costs of Computer Software Developed or Obtained for Internal Use" ("SOP 98-1"). As a result, certain costs of computer software developed or obtained for internal use have been capitalized and will be amortized over a three-year period. The impact of adopting SOP 98-1 was a reduction of costs and operating expenses of $80 million during the three months ended December 31, 1999.

[30] Issued by the Accounting Standards Executive Committee of the American Institute of Certified Public Accountants. For full discussion of SOP 98-1, see Daniel Noll, "Accounting for Internal Use Software," *Journal of Accountancy* (September 1998), pp. 95–98.

[31] Accounting for Web Site Development Costs, issued by the Emerging Issues Task Force based on discussions in January and March 2000. EITF 00-2 was effective for costs incurred after June 30, 2000.

The impact of the new standard increased pretax income by $80 million, equal to nearly 5% of pretax income excluding "one-time items." If not for the accounting change, that adjusted pretax income would have declined by more than 28% instead of the reported decline of 25%. The effect of the accounting change was not reported in the January 20, 2000 press release announcing Lucent's first quarter earnings, providing an illustration of the importance of reviewing SEC filings.

Case 40-1 uses International Business Machines to explore the financial statement effects and information content of capitalization of software costs in greater detail.

OPTIONAL SEGMENT

Accounting for Oil and Gas Exploration

Oil and gas exploration results in drilling both productive wells and dry holes.[32] As failure is an integral part of successful exploration, the cost of dry holes can be considered part of the cost of drilling productive ones. As in the case of R&D, the value of an oil discovery is frequently unrelated to the cost of drilling.

The FASB, in SFAS 19 (1977), required all firms to use the successful efforts (SE) accounting method that expenses all dry hole costs. Like the FASB's R&D reporting standard, this rule was conservative and eliminated assets with uncertain future benefits from the balance sheet. The Securities and Exchange Commission (SEC), fearing that the adoption of this rule would result in the curtailment of oil exploration (especially by smaller companies), forced the FASB to suspend SFAS 19 (SFAS 25, 1979). The SEC (ASR 253, 1978) permits public companies to use either SE or full cost (FC) methods of accounting. The latter permits the capitalization of dry hole costs.

Under current accounting practice, therefore, firms have the option of capitalizing the cost of dry holes (FC method) or expensing them as they occur (SE method). The choice between these two methods has a significant impact on the financial statements of oil and gas exploration companies and on many ratios as well. Exhibit 40-1 illustrates the difference between the SE and FC methods of accounting for oil and gas exploration costs. The balance sheet carrying amount of reserves, $4,000, is higher under the FC method because of the inclusion of the cost of dry holes ($3,000). The SE firm carries its reserves at only $1,000.[33]

The reported profitability (both levels and trends over time) of production is also affected. The SE firm reports a net loss of $250 in year 1 but net income of $2,750 per year for years 2 through 4, for a total net income of $8,000. The FC firm shows constant net income of $2,000 per year, again for a total of $8,000 over the four years. The effect of the FC method is to defer (capitalize) exploration costs and, therefore, accelerate the recognition of profit.

CFO may also differ. As previously discussed, although the income difference reverses over time, the difference in CFO does not. The cumulative CFO over the life of the well is higher for the FC firm by the cost of the capitalized dry holes ($12,000 − $9,000 = $3,000).

---

[32] Dry holes are wells drilled that do not find commercial quantities of oil or gas.

[33] Using a sample of oil and gas companies, Harris and Ohlson (1987) found that the market distinguished between SE and FC companies in a rational fashion. Book values of full cost companies were given less weight than those of SE companies. Additionally, they found that FC book values had less explanatory power than those of SE companies. This finding is consistent with a survey that indicated analysts prefer SE.

The differences between the methods cause SE firms to report:

- Lower carrying costs of oil and gas reserves than FC firms
- Lower stockholders' equity due to lower asset values
- Lower earnings than FC firms when exploration efforts are rising
- Lower cash from operations than FC firms

EXHIBIT 40-1 Comparison of Successful Efforts and Full Cost Impact on Net Income and Cash from Operations

Assumptions:

1. $1,000 cost of drilling well (dry or productive).
2. Four wells are drilled: One is productive, the other three are dry.
3. The productive well has a four-year life, with revenues (net of cost of production) of $3,000 per year.

Successful Efforts Method

The $3,000 cost of dry holes is expensed immediately. Only the $1,000 cost of the productive well is capitalized and amortized over its four-year life.

Year	1	2	3	4	Total
Net revenues	$ 3,000	$3,000	$3,000	$3,000	$12,000
Dry hole expense	(3,000)	0	0	0	(3,000)
Amortization	(250)	(250)	(250)	(250)	(1,000)
Net income	$ (250)	$2,750	$2,750	$2,750	$ 8,000
Cash Flows					
Operations*	$ 0	$3,000	$3,000	$3,000	$ 9,000
Investment	(1,000)	0	0	0	(1,000)
Total	$(1,000)	$3,000	$3,000	$3,000	$ 8,000

* Net revenues less dry hole expense.

Full Cost Method

The entire $4,000 drilling cost ($3,000 for dry holes and $1,000 for the productive well) is capitalized and amortized over the four-year life of the productive well.

Year	1	2	3	4	Total
Net revenues	$ 3,000	$3,000	$3,000	$3,000	$12,000
Amortization	(1,000)	(1,000)	(1,000)	(1,000)	(4,000)
Net income	$ 2,000	$2,000	$2,000	$2,000	$ 8,000
Cash Flows					
Operations*	$ 3,000	$3,000	$3,000	$3,000	$12,000
Investment	(4,000)	0	0	0	(4,000)
Total	$(1,000)	$3,000	$3,000	$3,000	$ 8,000

* Net revenues.

In practice, however, oil and gas firms using the SE method adjust their reported cash flow statements for this difference. They add exploration costs expensed back to net income (assuming use of the indirect method) and include those costs in capital expenditures. For example, Texaco's 1999 annual report states:

> We present cash flows from operating activities using the indirect method. We exclude exploratory expenses from cash flows of operating activities and apply them to cash flows of investing activities. On this basis, we reflect all capital and exploratory expenditures as investing activities.

However, Repsol, the large Spanish oil company, does not appear to make this adjustment. As a result, its reported cash flow components are not comparable with those of companies that make the adjustment.

6 ANALYTICAL ADJUSTMENTS FOR CAPITALIZATION AND EXPENSING

Need for Analytical Adjustments

Because the choices between capitalization and expensing discussed in this chapter affect reported corporate performance, analysts must sometimes adjust reported data to facilitate analysis and comparisons.

Software companies, as noted earlier, are allowed to capitalize software costs, and most do so. A notable exception is Microsoft. Comparisons with other (software) companies can be facilitated and insight as to Microsoft's motivations can be gained by comparing Microsoft's reported income with income had it capitalized R&D. In our analysis, we assume a three-year amortization period.

(in $millions)

	1996	1997	1998	1999	2000
Net income as reported			$4,490	$7,785	$9,421
Adjustment					
R&D as reported	$1,432	$1,925	2,601	2,970	3,775
Amortization of R&D*			(1,986)	(2,499)	(3,115)
Pretax adjustment			$ 615	$ 471	$ 660
After-tax @ 35% tax rate			400	306	429
Adjusted income			4,890	8,091	9,850
% increase in income			8.9%	3.9%	4.6%

* For example, for 2000: ($2,601 + $2,970 − $3,775)/3 = $3,115.

Note that, as Microsoft's R&D is increasing, expensing R&D reduces reported income by 4% to 9%. Although one cannot be sure, it is possible that Microsoft opted not to capitalize costs in order to lessen pressure from antitrust authorities by reporting lower income.

In Microsoft's case, the adjustments to R&D do not significantly affect ROE and ROA.[34] However, that is a function of Microsoft's profitability and pattern of R&D expenditures. For other industries, the effects on ROE and ROA can be considerable.

The pharmaceutical industry, for example, reports ROE that is among the highest of all U.S. industries. Some suggest that this reflects a higher return for the risks inherent in R&D. Others contend that the industry simply earns excess profits, and drug prices have periodically become a political issue. To some extent, however, high drug-industry returns reflect the accounting method used for R&D. Expensing these costs understates equity, the denominator of the ROE ratio. Capitalizing R&D costs (treating them as an investment) would give a more accurate measure of ROE.

Figure 40-6 illustrates this point. Sougiannis (1994) and Lev and Sougiannis (1996) examined the effect on return on equity (ROE) of recalculating the financial results of Merck as if the company capitalized R&D expense and amortized the capitalized amounts over seven years.[35] Using the implied amortization schedule for Merck,[36] Figure 6 shows the effects of their conversion process graphically for the period 1982 to 1991. Adjusted ROE is significantly lower for all years, although the trend is unchanged.[37]

From the analyst's perspective, the problem is that accounting does not (and probably cannot) accurately measure the value of expenditures on research and development.[38] Thus the analyst must perform two tasks:

1. Adjust financial data to reflect differences in capitalization policy among firms.
2. Evaluate the flow of new products resulting from R&D expenditures.

The Merck example shows the effects of restating by capitalizing an expense. At times, it may be more appropriate to restate capitalized expenditures to expenses. Westvaco (capitalized interest) and Nokia (capitalized development costs) are examples of such restatements. The second task, far more difficult, is beyond the scope of financial statement analysis.

Similar adjustments are required for firms that differ in the extent to which they buy operating assets or lease them. Airlines, for example, may buy or lease airplanes. Similarly, retail store chains may own or lease stores. This choice has financial statement effects similar to those stemming from capitalizing or expensing. Reported ROA may be misleading; adjustments are required for comparability. Reading 11 discusses leasing and other off-balance-sheet financing techniques in detail.

---

[34] In 2000, average equity was \$34,903 million, yielding ROE of 27.0%. Capitalizing R&D would increase equity for

$$1999\left[.65x\left(\left(\frac{2}{3}\right)2{,}970+\left(\frac{1}{3}\right)2{,}601\right)\right]=1{,}851 \text{ and for } 2000\left[.65x\left(\left(\frac{2}{3}\right)3{,}775+\left(\frac{1}{3}\right)2{,}970\right)\right]=2{,}280$$

Average equity would increase by [.5 × (\$1,851 + \$2,280) = \$2,065] to \$36,968 and adjusted ROE would be (\$9,850/\$36,968=) 26.6%. The reason for the small adjustment is related to the discussion in footnote 3. Note the growth rate in Microsoft's R&D expenditures for 2000 is 27.1%. As that growth rate is almost identical to the ROE of 27.0%, the differences in reported and adjusted ROE (ROA) will be negligible.

[35] Their analysis suggests that R&D has (on average) a seven-year duration for the pharmaceutical industry.

[36] The amortization schedule is neither straight-line nor declining balance. Rather, it amortizes capitalized R&D in proportion to the benefits received. As there is a lag between the time of the expenditure and benefits received, amortization increases over the first three years and declines thereafter.

[37] In this case, Merck's profitability as measured by ROE was in the 40% range whereas growth in R&D expenditures was considerably smaller at 15%.

[38] It is precisely this difficulty that prompted the FASB to require the expensing of R&D expenditures.

FIGURE 40-6 Recalculation of Profitability Ratios Assuming Capitalization of R&D Expenditures

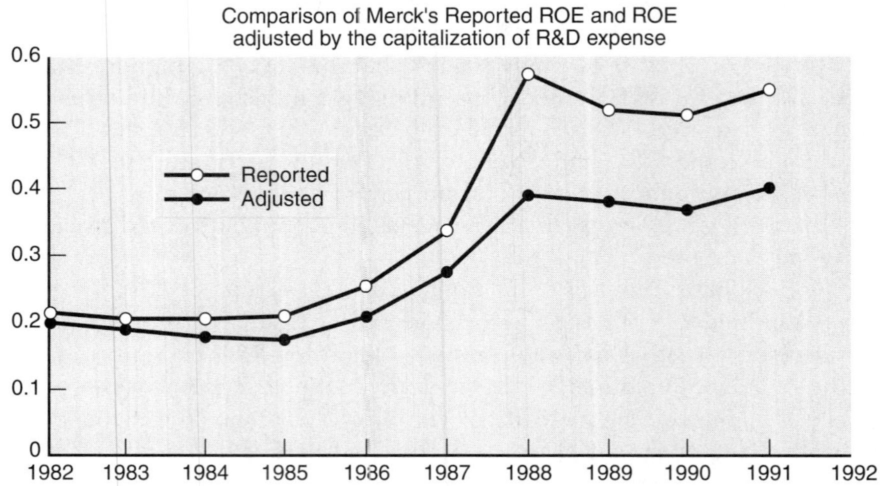

Source: "The Capitalization, Amortization, and Value-Relevance of R&D," *Journal of Accounting and Economics*, Baruch Lev and Theodore Sougiannis, Table 6 (Feb. 1996), pp. 107–138.

Valuation Implications

Expenditures for R&D and advertising are generally expensed because it is difficult, if not impossible, to reliably estimate their future benefits. That does not mean that these expenditures do not affect firm valuation. An outflow that is truly an expense reduces stockholder wealth; an outflow that generates future cash flows may actually increase it.

Chapter 19 discusses two types of valuation models: earnings based and asset based. Box 40-3 discusses how the capitalization decision affects these valuation models and presents empirical evidence that the market recognizes the asset characteristics of outflows in categories such as R&D, advertising, and oil and gas wells. These results suggest that the analyst cannot apply either capitalization or expensing mechanically, but must try to forecast the future benefits of these expenditures.

Other Economic Consequences

Although differences in accounting methods are cosmetic, they can have real consequences, as suggested by positive theory.[39]

First, a firm's borrowing ability may be limited by unfavorable profitability or leverage ratios resulting from, for example, expensing R&D expenditures. Second, because of these unfavorable ratios, a firm may curtail these expenditures, effectively scaling back operations. Finally, whether or not managers actually reduce R&D, the fact that the market perceives such a possibility can cause negative market reaction.

Mandated accounting changes is one area where such effects can be examined, as they provide a laboratory environment permitting before-and-after comparisons. Box 40-4 reviews empirical evidence regarding mandated accounting changes for R&D and oil and gas accounting.

[40] See Chapter 5.

BOX 40-3 CAPITALIZATION AND VALUATION

Consider the following simplified valuation model:

$$\text{Value} = p \times \text{Net Inflows}$$

The model can be used to represent a (constant) discounted earnings model, where net inflows represent revenue and expense flows and the coefficient *p* is simply the price/earnings (P/E) ratio. Disaggregating the net inflows into inflows and outflows yields

$$\text{Value} = p \times \text{Inflows} - p \times \text{Expense Outflows} + b \times \text{Asset Outflows}$$

where asset outflows represent expenditures for such categories as R&D. If these outflows are actually expenses, then $b = -p$.

From a valuation perspective, the difference between asset and expense outflows should be whether the associated outflow has expected future benefits. The level and sign of the coefficient *b* measure whether the outflow should be considered an expense. An expense benefits only the period of occurrence, and the outlay reduces value by $-p$ times the outflow.* An asset outflow benefits future periods and, therefore, the coefficient *b* should be positive.†

Bublitz and Ettredge (1989) compared the market valuation of unexpected changes in advertising, R&D, and other expenses. Advertising was included because, like R&D, it is expected to provide benefits for more than one period, albeit for a shorter term than R&D. They expected the coefficient for R&D to be larger (more positive) than the coefficient for advertising, and both larger than the coefficient for other expenses. The results were mixed, but on balance they were consistent with a market assessment of advertising as short-lived and R&D as long-lived.‡

Their valuation model used a discounted earnings-based perspective. Shevlin (1991) used an asset-based valuation model for R&D partnerships. In such a model, the value of the firm is defined as

$$\text{Value} = \text{Assets} - \text{Liabilities}$$

Shevlin[§] found that when R&D expenditures were considered assets, they contributed to firm value. Moreover, the market weighting given these expenditures was larger than for other assets, indicating that the expected benefit from these expenditures exceeds their book value.

Lev and Sougiannis (1996) and Sougiannis (1994) estimated stock prices and returns as functions of *both* earnings and book values. They also found that the capitalized components of R&D have value relevance** and are associated with current-period stock returns. More important, Lev and Sougiannis found a significant association between capitalized R&D and *subsequent* stock returns. This implied either a (systematic) mispricing by the market of R&D-intensive companies or compensation for (extra-market) risk associated with R&D.

Aboody and Lev (1998) compared companies that capitalized software development costs with those that chose not to. They found software capitalization (as well as the subsequent amortization) to be value relevant. Amounts capitalized were strongly associated with (contemporaneous) market prices and returns and were also positively associated with subsequent earnings changes. Moreover, consistent with the reasoning underlying SFAS 86,

> the coefficient of capitalized software . . . is larger than the coefficient of the development costs expensed by "expensers" . . . which in turn is larger than the coefficient of the development costs expensed by "capitalizers". . . . *This order of coefficient sizes is consistent with the reasoning of SFAS No. 86 that capitalized software reflects the costs of projects close to fruition and should be strongly associated with near-term earnings, whereas the development costs of "expensers" reflect the costs of both feasible and prefeasibility projects, which should not be as strongly associated with near-term earnings. The development costs expensed by "capitalizers" reflect both prefeasibility costs and costs of failed projects, consistent with little or no association with subsequent earnings.*[††]

Lev, in a series of publications,[‡‡] attempts to arrive at capitalization values in an indirect manner. Rather than capitalizing intangible expenditures, he capitalizes *intangible-driven earnings*. More specifically, Lev argues that a firm's earnings are a function of its physical, financial, and intangible assets; i.e.,

$$\text{Earnings} = f(\text{Physical Assets, Financial Assets, Intangible Assets})$$

Using a combination of past and forecasted earnings as well as "normal" returns on (known) physical and financial assets, he imputes *intangible-driven earnings* (i.e., earnings above those normally generated by a firm's physical and financial assets). Forecasted values of these intangible-driven earnings are then discounted to arrive at a capitalized value of intangible assets.

Such assets, known alternatively as "knowledge," "intellectual," or "intangible" capital, are not confined to technology companies. Lev shows that in addition to industries such as aerospace, telecommunications, computer hardware/software, and pharmaceuticals, the home products and food and beverage industries are also rich in intangible capital. This intangible capital he attributes to strong brand recognition.

Gu and Lev (2001) also test the valuation relevance of intangibles-driven earnings. They argue that their findings indicate that intangibles-driven earnings provide more relevant information to investors than conventional earnings and cash flows.

* The current benefits are reflected in the inflows.

† The asset outflows representing future benefits can be thought of as a growth component. In Chapter 19, we show that for a firm with growth, its value can be expressed as

$$\text{Value} = \frac{E}{r} + \left[\frac{1}{r}\left(\frac{r* - r}{r - ar*}\right)\right]\text{aE}$$

where *E* is earnings, *r* the appropriate discount rate, r^* the amount the firm earns on its nvestment, and *aE* the amount the firm reinvests. In our example, $p = 1/r$ and *b* is the coefficient of the asset investment *aE*. That is, *b* is equal to the term in brackets. On the margin, it may be zero (if $r^* = r$) as the firm undertakes zero or break-even net present value investments.

‡ Their R&D results are consistent with those of Hirschey and Weygandt (1985), who found that the market valuation of R&D implies it is an asset outflow. Hirschey and Weygandt also found that advertising had characteristics similar to a long-lived asset.

§ Shevlin applied option-pricing models to the valuation of R&D partnerships.

** Sougiannis, for example, shows that (on average) a one-dollar increase in R&D expenditures produces a five-dollar increase in market value.

†† David Aboody and Baruch Lev, "The Value Relevance of Intangibles: The Case of Software Capitalization, *Journal of Accounting Research* (Supplement 1998), p. 178, emphasis added.

‡‡ See, for example, Lev (2001), Gu and Lev (2001), and articles published in *Fortune* ("Accounting Gets Radical," by Thomas A. Stewart, April 16, 2001) and *CFO* ("Knowledge Capital Scorecard: Treasures Revealed," by Andrew Osterland, April 2001) for a general description of the methodology and results. The exact methodology is proprietary.

The research confirms that, even if an accounting change has no direct economic impact, the effects of the change on reported income can have real indirect consequences, such as the curtailment of expenditures and negative market reaction. Indirect effects may also result from debt covenant constraints or the influence of management compensation contracts. Accounting choices may also be motivated by firm characteristics.

Additional Analysis of Fixed Asset Data

Changes in the balance sheet cost of fixed assets result from four types of events:

1. Capital spending (acquisition of fixed assets)
2. Sale, impairment, or retirement (no longer in use) of fixed assets
3. Increases (decreases) in fixed assets due to acquisitions (disposals)
4. Changes due to the effects of foreign currency translation

The effects of acquisitions and foreign currency translation are considered in Chapters 14 and 15, respectively. The following sections discuss capital expenditures and the sale/retirement of assets.

Capital Expenditures

The capital expenditure decision provides information to the investor as to a firm's future profitability and growth prospects. Management often announces major capital expenditure plans separately. McConnell and Muscarella (1986) and Kerstein and Kim (1995) provide evidence that there is positive (negative) market reaction to unexpected increases (decreases) in capital expenditures. Similarly, Lev and Thiagarajan (1993) show that firms with higher (lower)

BOX 40-4 MANDATED ACCOUNTING CHANGES: ECONOMIC CONSEQUENCES AND MARKET REACTION

The capitalization-versus-expense issue has proved a fruitful area of empirical research. The issues examined provide interesting parallels between R&D (SFAS 2) and oil and gas accounting (SFAS 19). In both cases, mandated accounting changes favored expensing over capitalization (albeit in the case of SFAS 19, the standard was suspended).

Economic Consequences

Proponents of capitalization argued that the accounting change would lead to a reduction of risk-taking activities such as expenditures for R&D and exploration activities, as the cost of risk taking would increase. These fears were generally expressed for smaller companies* who feared that markets (at least private lenders) would focus on the effects on reported income (both amounts and variability). The change would thus impair their ability to raise capital.

As SFAS 19 was never implemented, the validity of these claims could not be verified. However, for SFAS 2, a number of studies attempted to verify whether the new standard curtailed R&D.

Horwitz and Kolodny (1980) reported that a majority of firms (58% to 67%) believed that small firms reduced planned R&D expenditures as a consequence of SFAS 2. Using a sample of small high-technology firms, they found evidence that the actual levels of R&D expenditures dropped following the introduction of SFAS 2.

In contrast, Dukes et al. (1980) found no evidence of curtailment of R&D subsequent to the adoption of SFAS 2. Their sample, however, consisted of larger companies, and in a subsequent study Elliott et al. (1984) confirmed the finding that small companies that had previously capitalized R&D curtailed R&D expenditures after the issuance of SFAS 2. However, they noted that the downward trend in R&D expenditures for these companies had already begun years prior to the issuance of SFAS 2. Comparing the operating performance of the "capitalizers" with a control sample of firms that had always expensed R&D, they found that the operating performance of the capitalizers was worse. They conjectured that financial difficulties, rather than the accounting change, may have caused the curtailment of R&D. In fact, it could be argued that the original decision to capitalize R&D by these firms may have been motivated by an effort to improve reported financial performance in the face of financial stress.

Selto and Clouse (1985) argued that firms would be likely to anticipate the effects of an accounting change such as SFAS 2 and adapt to it. Thus, if divisional managers would be motivated to reduce R&D expenditures because of the effect on their compensation (through earnings-based compensation plans), firms would adjust their compensation plans accordingly or, alternatively, take steps to centralize the R&D decision-making process. They found that although not all firms made such changes, those that did were the ones most likely to be affected by the provisions of SFAS 2. Thus, to the extent accounting changes have economic consequences, they may be manifested internally rather than externally.

Market Reaction

Vigeland (1981) found no market reaction to the mandated accounting change for R&D expenditures. There is little controversy with respect to this mandated accounting change. This is not true with respect to the mandated change(s) affecting accounting for oil and gas exploration. This issue spawned a cottage industry of research with studies examining the reaction to the announcement of (the exposure draft of) SFAS 19 and Accounting Series Release (ASR) 253, issued by the SEC, that suspended SFAS 19.

The research examined whether firms using the full cost method (FC) had negative (positive) returns when SFAS 19 (ASR 253) was announced. Generally negative reaction was found around the time of the announcement of the SFAS 19 exposure draft. Not everyone, however, agreed with its significance† and the results were found to be sensitive to the time period examined and (at the time of the exposure draft announcement) "confounding" news affecting the oil industry. Thus, even though negative market reaction was found, its cause was not clear.

With respect to the ASR 253 announcement, Collins et al. (1982) compared the market reaction at the time the SFAS 19 exposure draft was announced with the reaction experienced when ASR 253 was announced. They found that there was a significant negative correlation for the FC firms; that is, negative reaction to the first announcement was followed by positive reaction to the subsequent (suspension) announcement.

These studies tested market reaction without considering any factors that might cause differential market reactions across firms due to differential impacts on income and equity. Such factors might include firm size, the relative importance of exploration, firm leverage, and the existence of debt covenants and accounting-based management compensation schemes. Collins et al. (1981) and Lys (1984) tested for such factors with some success, finding, for example, that the degree of market reaction was related to (1) the size of the reduction in owner's equity that would result from SFAS 19, (2) the existence of debt covenants, and (3) management compensation schemes based on reported income.

---

* The standards primarily affected smaller firms, as for both R&D and exploration costs, larger firms generally used the expensing method. See Box 40-1 for further discussion of the differential impact of the capitalize-versus-expense decision on larger and small firms.

† Collins and Dent (1979) and Lev (1979) claimed that the results were statistically significant, whereas Dyckman and Smith (1979) argued that the market reaction was not statistically different from that experienced by firms using successful efforts (SE).

changes in capital expenditures than their industry average experience positive (negative) market reaction. Thus, it is important to monitor (changes in) the level of a firm's capital expenditures.

In doing so, note that capital expenditures tend to be seasonal, with the majority of such expenditures being carried out in the fourth quarter. Different theories exist as to whether this phenomenon is tied to a firm's budgetary cycle [Callen et al. (1996)] or the timing is tax related [Kinney and Trezevant (1993)].

Sale, Impairment, or Retirement of Assets

The sale or retirement of fixed assets removes these assets from the balance sheet. For most firms, sale or retirement also generates gains or losses, included in reported income.

In the case of Westvaco, gains on asset sales are included in other income (see financial statement Note B). In 1999, such gains accounted for 12% of pretax income. Some companies report gains or losses on a separate line in the income statement, whereas others include them elsewhere.[40] The analyst should examine such gains or losses for several reasons.

First, gains and losses resulting from asset sales are considered nonrecurring and the inclusion of such gains in reported income lowers the quality of earnings. However, if such gains or losses occur in most years, it is difficult to consider them "nonrecurring." As asset sales are to a great extent subject to management discretion, their timing and variation from year to year must be closely monitored as they can be used to distort operating trends. Bartov (1993) reported that firms use gains or losses from asset sales to smooth reported income.[41] Additionally, highly leveraged firms sell more long-lived assets than less leveraged firms in an effort to improve their reported debt-to-equity ratios.

A second reason for looking at asset sales is more fundamental. Sale of a significant portion of fixed assets is an indicator of change—in product line or production location. The examination of trends in capital spending and fixed asset sales can help the analyst ask perceptive questions regarding changes in future operations.

Finally, a pattern of gains suggests that the company's depreciation method is conservative, understating reported income and the net carrying amounts of fixed assets. A pattern of losses suggests that depreciation expense is understated (income is overstated) and fixed assets are overvalued on the balance sheet. In extreme cases, such losses are recognized as "impairments." Issues relating to depreciation and impairments are discussed in Reading 41.

OPTIONAL SEGMENT ENDS

[40] Undisclosed gains and losses can sometimes be deduced from the statement of cash flows. Gains and losses from asset sales are non-operating in nature, and must be subtracted from cash from operations. The proceeds from asset sales must be reported in cash from investment.

[41] Whether this constitutes "good" or "bad" behavior depends on whether one views income smoothing (see Reading 31) as "variance reducing" (providing information to investors as to a firm's expected performance) or manipulative behavior that hides a firm's actual performance.

SUMMARY 7

This reading considers the financial statement effects of the capitalize-versus-expense decision for long-lived assets. This decision is significant not only for firms with large investments in buildings and machinery, but also for those who have large expenditures on research, development, and computer software. The reading reviews the analytical techniques that can be used to restore comparability despite the use of differing accounting methods for similar transactions.

Once the capitalized amount is determined, the firm must choose an appropriate pattern of depreciation or amortization. Analysts must also contend with financial reporting for impairments and disposal of these assets. We discuss these issues in the next reading.

PROBLEMS

1. [Capitalization of interest] The following data were obtained from the annual reports of Chevron, a multinational oil company (all data in $millions):

	1995	1996	1997	1998	1999
Interest expense	$ 401	$ 364	$ 312	$ 405	$ 472
Pretax income	1,789	4,740	5,502	1,834	3,648
Net income	930	2,607	3,256	1,339	2,070
Capitalized interest	141	108	82	39	59
Amortization of capitalized interest	47	24	28	35	9

a. Using reported interest expense, compute the earnings coverage ratio (times interest earned) for each year, 1995 to 1999.

b. Assuming that Chevron had always expensed interest as incurred:

(i) Recompute the earnings coverage ratio for each year.

(ii) Compare the two ratios (based on reported versus restated data).

(iii) Recompute income (assume a 35% tax rate each year).

(iv) Discuss the effect on net income of restatement to expense all interest.

c. Discuss the effect of restatement on the five-year trend of Chevron's:

(i) Interest expense

(ii) Interest coverage ratio

(iii) Pretax and net income

d. State which calculation of the interest coverage ratio is better for financial analysis and justify your choice.

2. [Capitalization versus expensing] American Woodmark [AMWD] is a manufacturer of kitchen cabinets and similar items. Its fiscal year 2000 annual report contains the following footnote under Significant Accounting Policies:

> *Promotional Displays:* The Company's investment in promotional displays is carried at cost less applicable amortization. Amortization is provided by the straightline method on an individual display basis over the estimated period of benefit (approximately 30 months).

Financial data at April 30 (in $thousands)

	1999	2000
Promotional displays	$ 8,451	$ 10,099
Total assets	140,609	166,656
Shareholders' equity	78,337	92,612
Sales	327,013	387,301
Net income	17,509	14,467

a. Explain why American Woodmark may have chosen to capitalize the cost of promotional displays rather than expense them.

b. Calculate the effect of that accounting choice on the following reported amounts for fiscal year 2000:

(i) Net income

(ii) Shareholders' equity

(iii) Return on assets

(Assume a 35% tax rate.)

3. [Capitalization of research and development] Pfizer's 1999 annual report contains a financial summary (p. 62) with 11 years of data including research and development expense.

a. Compute R&D expense as a % of sales for the five years ending in 1999. Discuss what this trend tells you about the importance of R&D to Pfizer's business. Describe the effect of that trend on Pfizer's reported earnings.

b. Pfizer expenses all R&D. Assuming Pfizer had capitalized and amortized R&D costs, compute the following adjusted amounts for 1997–1999:

(i) Net

(ii) Return on equity

Your calculations should assume a tax rate of 35% and three-year amortization starting in the year of the R&D expenditure.

c. Compare the adjusted results in part b with those reported by Pfizer.

d. Discuss how the change in accounting method would affect the trend of Pfizer's:

(i) Asset turnover

(ii) Cash from operations

ANALYSIS OF LONG-LIVED ASSETS: PART II — ANALYSIS OF DEPRECIATION AND IMPAIRMENT

READING 41

LEARNING OUTCOMES

The candidate should be able to:

a. identify the different depreciation methods, and discuss how the choice of depreciation method affects a company's financial statements, ratios, and taxes, explain the role of depreciable lives and salvage values in the computation of depreciation expenses, and compute and describe how changing depreciation methods or changing the estimated useful life or salvage value of an asset affects financial statements and ratios;

b. discuss the use of fixed asset disclosures to compare companies' average age of depreciable assets, and calculate, using such disclosures, the average age and average depreciable life of fixed assets;

c. define impairment of long-lived assets and explain what effect such impairment has on a company's financial statements and ratios;

d. list the requirements of SFAS 143, Accounting for Asset Retirement Obligations (AROs), and explain the likely financial statement and ratio effects for most firms.

INTRODUCTION 1

This reading continues the analysis of long-lived assets begun in the previous reading where we examined financial reporting and analysis issues arising at acquisition. We now consider the reporting and analysis of long-lived assets:

1. Over their useful lives, with emphasis on

- Depreciation methods
- Depreciable lives and salvage values
- Impact of choices on financial statements

2. When they are disposed of, or written off when impaired, or at the end of their useful lives, with particu ar attention to the effects of impairment write-downs on financial statements and ratios

Amortization, depletion, and depreciation are all terms used for the systematic allocation of the capitalized cost of an asset to income over its useful life. Depreciation, the most frequently used of these terms, is often used generically in discussions of the concept. Strictly speaking, *depreciation* represents the allocation of the cost of tangible fixed assets, *amortization* refers to the cost of intangible assets, and *depletion* applies to natural resource assets.

2 THE DEPRECIATION CONCEPT

For accountants, depreciation is an allocation process, not a valuation process. It is important, therefore, for analysts to differentiate between accounting depreciation and economic depreciation. Although the accounting process may be purely allocative, the concept of depreciation also has economic meaning.

In Reading 31, income was defined as the amount that can be distributed during the period without impairing the productive capacity of the firm. The cash flows generated by an asset over its life, therefore, cannot be considered income until a provision is made for its replacement. These cash flows must be reduced by the amount required to replace the asset to determine the earnings generated by that asset.

This is the underlying principle of economic depreciation; profits are overstated if no allowance is made for the replacement of the asset. The periodic depreciation expense, therefore, segregates a portion of cash flows for reinvestment, preserving that sum from distribution as dividends and taxes.[1]

Continuing this conceptual argument, suppose an asset costs $240 and is expected to generate net cash flows of $100 per year over its three-year life. Over the life of the asset, income equals $60 ($300 – $240) as $240 is required to replace the asset (if we assume that the asset is worthless at the end of the three-year period and price levels do not change). As financial statements report income annually, it is necessary to determine how much income (how much depreciation) to report each year. This requires the allocation of a portion of the multiperiod return to each period.

The next section describes the depreciation methods used in financial reporting, followed by a discussion of the impact of depreciation methods on financial statements. A separate analysis of accelerated depreciation methods used for income taxes is followed by a discussion of the interaction of inflation and depreciation methods. Analysis of financial statement depreciation disclosures, changes in depreciation methods, and a comprehensive examination of fixed asset disclosures round out the discussion.

Depreciation Methods

Annuity or Sinking Fund Depreciation

From an economic perspective, the income reported each year should reflect the rate of return earned by the asset. For example, the asset just described gen-

[1] This does not mean that cash equal to depreciation expense is set aside for reinvestment but, rather, that the definition of income requires a subtraction for asset replacement.

EXHIBIT 41-1 Sinking Fund Depreciation

Year	(1) Opening Balance Asset	(2) Cash Flow	(3) Depreciation Expense	(4) = (2) − (3) Net Income	(5) = (4)/(1) Rate of Return
1	$240	$100	$ 71	$29	12%
2	169	100	80	20	12
3	89	100	89	11	12
Totals		$300	$240	$60	

erates a return of 12% over its three-year life.[2] To report a 12% return for each year requires the pattern of depreciation shown in Exhibit 41-1.

This pattern, with the amount of depreciation increasing every year, is known as *annuity or sinking fund depreciation.* U.S. GAAP, however, do not permit this form of depreciation. In Canada, increasing charge methods are used for income-producing properties in the real estate industry and by a few utilities, but they are not generally acceptable depreciation methods.

Straight-line and accelerated depreciation (discussed shortly) can also produce a constant rate of return when cash flows generated by the asset decline over time. Exhibit 41-2 illustrates this case; the rate of return is constant and reflects the true return earned by the asset.

Instead of depreciation patterns that generate a constant rate of return, accountants generally use depreciation patterns that result in constant or declining expense. These patterns are sometimes justified by the matching principle. Generally, however, they are arbitrary, their sole purpose being a systematic allocation of the asset cost over time.

Straight-Line Depreciation

Given the same asset and the pattern of constant cash flows shown in Exhibit 41-1, accountants (using the matching principle) argue that since the revenues (cash flows of $100) generated by the asset are the same each year, the income shown each year should also be the same. The result of this line of reasoning is the

EXHIBIT 41-2 Straight-Line Depreciation with Declining Cash Flows

Year	(1) Opening Balance Asset	(2) Cash Flow	(3) Depreciation Expense	(4) = (2) − (3) Net Income	(5) = (4)/(1) Rate of Return
1	$240	$109	$ 80	$29	12%
2	160	99	80	19	12
3	80	90	80	10	12
Totals		$298	$240	$58	

[2] The present value of a three-year annuity of $100 per year discounted at 12% is (approximately) equal to $240.

EXHIBIT 41-3 Straight-Line Depreciation with Constant Cash Flows

Year	(1) Opening Balance Asset	(2) Cash Flow	(3) Depreciation Expense	(4) = (2) − (3) Net Income	(5) = (4)/(1) Rate of Return
1	$240	$100	$ 80	$20	8.3%
2	160	100	80	20	12.5
3	80	100	80	20	25.0
Totals		$300	$240	$60	

straight-line method, the pattern of depreciation expense exhibited in Exhibit 41-3. *Straight-line depreciation is the dominant method in the United States and most countries worldwide.* Westvaco, for example, states in the summary of significant accounting policies in its fiscal 1999 annual report:

> The cost of plant and equipment is depreciated, generally by the straight-line method, over the estimated useful lives of the respective assets. . . .

Note that the use of this method results in an *increasing* rate of return rather than the actual rate of return earned over the life of the asset.

Accelerated Depreciation Methods

The matching principle can also justify accelerated depreciation patterns, with higher depreciation charges in early years and smaller amounts in later years. There are two arguments:

1. Benefits (revenues) from an asset may be higher in early years, declining in later years as efficiency falls (the asset wears out). The matching process suggests that depreciation should decline with benefits.
2. Even if revenues are constant over time, an asset requires maintenance and repairs over time, costs that tend to increase as the asset ages. Accelerated depreciation methods compensate for the rising trend of maintenance and repair costs so that total asset costs are level over the asset's life.

However, both the efficiency and maintenance of an asset are difficult to forecast, and, in any case, accelerated depreciation methods are (like straight-line) arbitrary procedures designed to yield the desired pattern of higher depreciation amounts in earlier years. Accelerated methods have historically been used for tax reporting, where they are justified by the desire to promote capital investment, rather than accounting theory.

The two most common accelerated methods are the *sum-of-years' digits* (SYD) method and the family of *declining-balance* methods. A comparison of these methods (using the double-declining-balance method) with straight-line (SL) depreciation is presented in Exhibit 41-4. In the example used, the concept of *salvage value,* the estimated amount for which the asset can be sold at the end of its useful life, is introduced into the calculations.

While U.S. firms rarely use accelerated methods, they are more widely used outside of the United States. Takeda, for example, states in its summary of significant accounting policies (Note 2 in fiscal 1999 annual report) that:

> Depreciation is primarily computed by the declining balance method. . . .

EXHIBIT 41-4 Comparison of Straight-Line and Accelerated Depreciation Methods

Original Cost = $18,000

Salvage Value = $3,000

Depreciable Life $n = 5$

A. Straight-Line Depreciation

$$\text{Depreciation in Year } i = \frac{1}{n} \times (\text{Original Cost} - \text{Salvage Value})$$

Depreciation expense is constant each year; at the end of the five-year period, the net book value of the asset equals its salvage value of $3,000.

Year	Rate	(Original Cost— Salvage Value)	Depreciation Expense	Accumulated Depreciation	Net Book Value
0					$18,000
1	1/5	$15,000	$ 3,000	$ 3,000	15,000
2	1/5	15,000	3,000	6,000	12,000
3	1/5	15,000	3,000	9,000	9,000
4	1/5	15,000	3,000	12,000	6,000
5	1/5	15,000	3,000	15,000	3,000
Total			$15,000		

B and C. Accelerated Depreciation Methods
B. Sum-of-Years' Digits (SYD) Method

$$\text{Depreciation in Year } i = \frac{(n - i + 1)}{\text{SYD}} \times (\text{Original Cost} - \text{Salvage Value})$$

where $\text{SYD} = 1 + 2 + 3 + \ldots + n$ the summation over the depreciable life of n years or simply $\text{SYD} = n(n + 1)/2$. For our example, $n = 5$.

$$\text{SYD} = 1 + 2 + 3 + 4 + 5 = 15$$

or, alternatively,

$$\text{SYD} = \frac{(5)(5 + 1)}{2} = 15$$

The rate of depreciation thus varies from year to year (as i varies) in reverse counting order of the years; that is, the pattern is 5/15, 4/15, 3/15, 2/15, and 1/15 and is depicted as follows:

Year	Rate	(Original Cost— Salvage Value)	Depreciation Expense	Accumulated Depreciation	Net Book Value
0					$18,000
1	5/15	$15,000	$ 5,000	$5,000	13,000
2	4/15	15,000	4,000	9,000	9,000
3	3/15	15,000	3,000	12,000	6,000
4	2/15	15,000	2,000	14,000	4,000
5	1/15	15,000	1,000	15,000	3,000
Total			$15,000		

EXHIBIT 41-4 (continued)

C. Double-Declining-Balance

$$\text{Depreciation in Year } i = \frac{2}{n} \times (\text{Original Cost} - \text{Accumulated Depreciation})$$

or

$$\frac{2}{n} \times (\text{Net Book Value})$$

The rate of $(2/n)$ is what gives the double-declining-balance (DDB) method its name. The depreciation rate is double* the straight-line rate. The declining pattern occurs because the fixed rate is applied to an ever-decreasing asset balance (net book value),† and in our example it is calculated as follows:

Year	Rate	Net Book Value	Depreciation Expense	Accumulated Depreciation	Net Book Value
0					$18,000
1	2/5	$18,000	$ 7,200	$ 7,200	10,800
2	2/5	10,800	4,320	11,520	6,480
3	2/5	6,480	2,592	14,112	3,888
4	NA	NA	888	15,000	3,000
5	NA	NA	0	15,000	3,000
Total			$15,000		

Note that in year 4 the DDB procedure is discontinued. This is because depreciation can be taken only until the salvage value is reached. Following DDB in year 4 and beyond would have reduced net book value below salvage. When the DDB method is applied to longer-lived assets, a switch to the straight-line method often occurs in later years, when the latter method results in higher depreciation expense.

NA = not applicable.

* The DDB method is actually only one case of the family of declining-balance methods. The same principle can be applied to other multiples of the straight-line rate (e.g., 150% declining balance). Higher multiples result in more accelerated patterns of depreciation expense.

† Note that salvage value is not used to calculate depreciation under declining-balance methods but acts as a floor for net book value.

Units-of-Production and Service Hours Method

These methods depreciate assets in proportion to their actual use rather than as a function of the passage of time. Thus, more depreciation is recognized in years of higher production. Measurement requires an initial estimate of the total number of units of output or service hours expected over the life of the machine. The methods differ in whether asset usage is measured by output or hours used.

Assume that the asset described in Exhibit 41-4 is expected to produce 60,000 units of output over its life and have a service life of 150,000 hours. The actual hours of service and output, and the resultant depreciation schedules, are presented in Exhibit 41-5.

EXHIBIT 41-5 Service Hours and Units-of-Production Methods

Original Cost = $18,000
Salvage Value = $3,000

	Service Hours Method Expected Service Hours = 150,000 Cost/Service Hour = $0.10*			Units-of-Production Method Expected Output = 60,000 Cost/Unit of Output = $0.25†		
Year	**Hours Worked**	**Depreciation**	**Net Book Value**	**Units of Output**	**Depreciation**	**Net Book Value**
0			$18,000			$18,000
1	40,000	$ 4,000	14,000	15,000	$ 3,750	14,250
2	35,000	3,500	10,500	16,000	4,000	10,250
3	45,000	4,500	6,000	20,000	5,000	5,250
4	20,000	2,000	4,000	10,000	2,250‡	3,000
5	40,000	1,000‡	3,000	12,500	0‡	3,000
Total		$15,000			$15,000	

* ($18,000 − $3,000)/150,000.
† ($18,000 − $3,000)/60,000.
‡ Note that in both cases, the asset is never depreciated below the salvage value even when actual use exceeds estimated use.

These methods make depreciation expense a variable rather than a fixed cost, decreasing the volatility of reported earnings as compared to straight-line or accelerated methods. Some companies use a mix of depreciation methods.

International Paper, for example, reports on its depreciation methods as follows:

> **Plants, Properties and Equipment**
>
> Plants, properties and equipment are stated at cost, less accumulated depreciation. For financial reporting purposes, we use the units-of-production method of depreciation for our major pulp and paper mills and certain wood products facilities and the straight-line method for other plants and equipment.[3]

A significant drawback of these two methods occurs when the firm's productive capacity becomes obsolete as it loses business to more efficient competitors. The units-of-production and service hours methods decrease depreciation expense during periods of low production. The result is to overstate reported income and asset values at the same time as the asset's economic value declines. This danger is particularly acute for mature industries facing increased competition from new entrants or imports. Competition frequently increases the rate of economic depreciation of fixed assets. However, the corporate response is often to relieve the pressure on earnings by decreasing depreciation expense by changing to a method such as units-of-production. Alternatively, firms may get the same effect by lengthening lives.

[3] *Source:* International Paper, 10-K report, year ended December 31, 1999.

Sooner or later, however, the firm will recognize the impairment (see the discussion later in this reading) of its productive capacity. Once impairment exists, companies report "restructuring" or similar charges to correct the overvaluation of fixed assets. Analysts often exclude such "nonrecurring" charges when evaluating corporate earnings. But to the extent that these charges represent an adjustment for past underdepreciation of assets, they correct a systematic overstatement of past earnings. As past earnings are used to forecast the future, this issue should not be ignored.

The following footnote from the 1992 financial statements of Brown & Sharpe, a machine tool manufacturer, illustrates this phenomenon:

> In 1992, the Company extended the estimated useful lives of machinery and equipment at its Swiss subsidiary, based upon the current low rate of utilization. The effect of this change was to reduce 1992 depreciation expense and net loss by $921,000 or $.19 per share.

Total depreciation expense for Brown & Sharpe fell from $8 million in 1992 to $6.8 million in 1993; the change in accounting estimate was apparently the major factor in that decline. In 1994, however, Brown & Sharpe reported restructuring charges that included: "costs . . . for . . . property, plant, and equipment . . . writeoffs . . . due to a plant closing in Switzerland."

Although the corporate temptation to change accounting methods when business is weak is understandable, that change can mislead investors. Furthermore, on occasion, a company recognizes the impairment of fixed assets gradually, by accelerating depreciation on a group of assets in danger of becoming obsolete. From an analytical point of view, it is preferable to recognize the impairment immediately. Because accounting depreciation is a systematic allocation of cost, its acceleration when the asset is impaired (and its use has declined or it has been temporarily idled) fails to match costs and revenues and misstates the earning power of the company.

Group and Composite Depreciation Methods

Depreciation methods described in the preceding sections apply to single assets; they may be impractical when firms use large numbers of similar assets in their operations. Group (composite) depreciation methods allocate the costs of similar (dissimilar) assets using depreciation rates based on a weighted average of the service lives of the assets.

Gains or losses on the disposal of assets depreciated using group or composite methods are either:

- Recognized in reported income, or
- Reported instead as a component of accumulated depreciation[4]

Example. Texaco uses group methods for most assets (see the Description of Significant Accounting Policies). Gains and losses are recognized only when a complete unit is disposed of.

---

[4] At the time of the sale, the proceeds are added to cash, the original asset cost is removed from gross PPE, and the accumulated depreciation for the asset is removed from that account. The difference between the cash proceeds and the net book value of the assets sold is then credited-debited to the accumulated depreciation account; no gain or loss is recorded.

Depletion

Financial reporting requirements for natural resources are similar to those for tangible assets. The carrying costs of natural resources include the costs of acquiring the land or mines and the costs of exploration and development of the resources. These costs may be capitalized or expensed as a function of the firm's accounting policies (such as successful efforts or full cost for oil and gas exploration).

The carrying costs of natural resources (excluding costs of machinery and equipment used in extraction or production) are allocated to accounting periods using the units-of-production method. This method requires an initial estimate of the units (of oil, coal, gold, or timber) in the resource base to compute a unit cost, which is then applied to the actual units produced, extracted, or harvested.

Amortization

Amortization of intangible assets may be based on useful lives as defined by law (e.g., patents) or regulation, or such assets may be depreciated over the period during which the firm expects to receive benefits from them (computer software). Companies use either straight-line or units-of-production methods. Goodwill and indefinite-term franchises and licenses may be amortized over periods not exceeding 40 years.[5] Note that SFAS 142 (2001) eliminated the amortization of goodwill and certain intangible assets.

Example. In Reading 40 we examined Lucent's capitalization of software development costs; now we discuss amortization. The accounting policies footnote is vague about amortization periods.

Lucent's financial statements show the following (in $millions):

Years Ended September 30

	1997	1998	1999
Capitalized software costs (net)	293	298	470
Amortization	380	234	249

Amortization of capitalized software declined sharply in fiscal 1998. Amortization rose only slightly in fiscal 1999 despite the large increase in capitalized cost. There is no discussion of amortization in Lucent's Management Discussion and Analysis.

Depreciation Method Disclosures

As we have shown, the choice of the depreciation method can greatly affect the pattern of reported income. Disclosure of the depreciation method used is required and can usually be found in the footnote listing accounting policies. Most (more than 90%) American firms use straight-line depreciation, but accelerated methods are more widely used in other countries. The use of accelerated methods in the United States has declined in recent years as firms have changed to straight-line depreciation.

[5] See Chapter 14 for an extensive discussion of goodwill.

Depreciation Lives and Salvage Values

Even when the same depreciation method is used, comparability for a firm over time and among companies at a given point in time may be lacking. The *useful life* (the period over which the asset is depreciated) can vary from firm to firm, and excessively long lives understate reported depreciation expense. Although companies are required to disclose depreciation lives, in practice such disclosures are often vague, providing ranges rather than precise data. In such cases, the analyst must use available data to compute approximate depreciation lives (see the analysis of fixed asset disclosures later in the reading).

Example:

Westvaco

Westvaco's summary of significant accounting policies states that:

> The cost of plant and equipment is depreciated . . . over the estimated useful lives . . . which range from 20 to 40 years for buildings and 5 to 30 years for machinery and equipment.

Although usually a less significant factor, *salvage values* also affect comparisons; they (like asset lives) are also management estimates. High estimates reduce the depreciation base (cost less salvage value) and, therefore, reduce depreciation expense. (Note that salvage values are not employed in declining-balance depreciation methods.) In practice, companies rarely disclose data regarding salvage values, except when estimates are changed.[6]

Impact of Depreciation Methods on Financial Statements

The choice of depreciation method impacts both the income statement and balance sheet; for capital-intensive companies, the impact can be significant. As depreciation is an allocation of past cash flows, the method chosen for financial reporting purposes has no impact on the statement of cash flows.[7]

Accelerated depreciation methods, with higher depreciation expense in the early years of asset life, tend to depress both net income and stockholders' equity when compared with the straight-line method. As the percentage effect on net income is usually greater than the effect on net assets, return ratios tend to be lower when accelerated depreciation methods are used. Consequently, these methods are considered more conservative.

Toward the end of an asset's life, however, the effect on net income reverses. In Exhibit 41-4, depreciation expense in years 4 and 5 is lower using accelerated methods than under the straight-line method. This is true for individual assets. However, for companies with stable or rising capital expenditures, the early-year

[6] Changes in accounting estimates receive less disclosure than changes in method. APB 20 (para. 33) requires disclosure of the effect of a change that affects future periods, such as changes in depreciable lives.

[7] This assumes that the method chosen for tax purposes is independent of the method chosen for financial statement purposes.

impact of new assets acquired dominates, and depreciation expense on a total firm basis is higher under an accelerated method. When capital expenditures decline, however, accelerated depreciation decreases depreciation expense as the later-year effect on older assets dominates.

Depreciable lives and salvage values impact both depreciation expense and stated asset values. Shorter lives and lower salvage values are considered conservative in that they lead to higher depreciation expense. These factors interact with the depreciation method to determine the expense; for example, use of the straight-line method with short depreciation lives may result in depreciation expense similar to that obtained from the use of an accelerated method with longer lives. Conservative depreciation practices also increase asset turnover ratios by decreasing the denominator of that ratio. Fixed-asset turnover ratios should be computed using gross fixed-asset investment in the denominator, although that is not done in practice.

Accelerated Depreciation and Taxes

Notwithstanding the theoretical arguments and the financial statement effects discussed, the primary reason for accelerated depreciation methods is their beneficial effect on the firm's tax burden. At the onset of an asset's life, the total amount of depreciable cost available is fixed. Depreciation acts as a tax shield by reducing the amount of taxes paid in any given year. Given a positive interest rate, firms are better off using accelerated depreciation methods to obtain the benefit of increased cash flows (from reduced taxes) in the earlier years.

Governments have long used the tax code to encourage investment, and this was the intent of the U.S. government when it first allowed accelerated depreciation methods for tax purposes in 1954. Many foreign governments also permit the use of accelerated depreciation methods. Since 1954, the U.S. government has frequently changed tax depreciation regulations to increase or decrease investment incentives in certain types of fixed assets or simply to raise revenues. The present system is known as MACRS—modified accelerated cost recovery system—which consists of specified depreciation patterns and depreciable lives (generally shorter than actual useful service lives) for different property classes.

MACRS uses the double-declining-balance and 150% declining-balance methods, which few companies use for financial reporting purposes. Thus, in the United States the depreciation method and lives used for financial statements almost always differ from those used for tax purposes. The implications of these differences are discussed in Reading 42, which also illustrates the use of tax disclosures to obtain insights into the depreciation practices used for financial reporting.

Impact of Inflation on Depreciation

Historical cost-based depreciation expense may be used to define income as long as the total expense over the asset's life is enough to replace the asset after it has been fully utilized. If, however, the replacement cost of the asset increases, then depreciation expense based on the original cost will be insufficient.

Returning to the example in Exhibit 41-1, assume that after three years the firm requires $300 to replace the asset. Now the total economic income earned by the firm is $0, as total cash flows equal the cost to replace. If we use the historical cost basis, however, total depreciation is limited to the original $240 cost, and reported income is overstated. In addition, because firms are only allowed to use historical cost basis depreciation for tax reporting, the resultant taxes are too high. Income taxes become, in effect, a tax on capital rather than a tax on income. Box 41-1 illustrates the resulting disincentives for investment in the context of a simple capital budgeting model.

BOX 41-1 DISINCENTIVES FOR INVESTMENT ARISING FROM HISTORICAL COST DEPRECIATION

OPTIONAL SEGMENT

We begin by assuming that the inflation rate p is equal to zero. A project is profitable if the net present value (NPV) of the cash flows of the investment:

$$\mathbf{NPV}_{(p=0)} = -I + (1 - t)\sum \frac{C_i}{(1 + r)^i} + t\sum \frac{d_i I}{(1 + r)^i}$$

is greater than zero (i.e., NPV > 0), where C_i is the pretax (real) cash flow in period i, t is the marginal tax rate, d_i is the rate of depreciation in period i, I is the cost of the original investment, and r is the appropriate real discount rate.* The summation on the right reflects the depreciation tax shelter, and the NPV can be disaggregated into

NPV = −investment + present value (after-tax cash flows)
+ present value (depreciation tax shelter)

If we introduce an annual inflation rate of $p > 0$, then the expected (nominal) cash flows in any period will increase. In addition, the discount rate will change to reflect inflation. The depreciation deduction based on historical costs will not change. The expression for net present value now becomes

$$\mathbf{NPV}_{(p>0)} = -I + (1 - t)\sum \frac{(1 + p)^i C_i}{(1 + p)^i (1 + r)^i} + t\sum \frac{d_i I}{(1 + p)^i (1 + r)^i}$$

As the $(1 + p)^i$ terms in the first summation cancel, inflation (when it is expected) will not affect the after-tax cash flows. However, the depreciation tax shelter will now be worth less as

$$t\sum \frac{d_i I}{(1 + r)^i} > t\sum \frac{d_i I}{(1 + p)^i (1 + r)^i}$$

The decline in the depreciation tax shelter will reduce the profitability of the project:

$$\mathbf{NPV}_{(p>0)} < \mathbf{NPV}_{(p=0)}$$

and *ceteris paribus*, there is less likelihood that the project will be undertaken.

OPTIONAL SEGMENT ENDS

* Generally, the depreciation tax shelter would be discounted at a rate lower than the cash flows themselves as the tax deduction is "riskless." We do not make the distinction here for the sake of simplification. Alternatively, one can view this problem in the context of certainty, and r is the risk-free rate.

Accelerated depreciation methods partially compensate for this inflation effect by shortening the (tax) recovery period. Depreciating the asset over a shorter life serves a similar purpose. A number of studies have examined whether accelerated methods compensate for inflation and/or reflect economic depreciation (variously defined).

Kim and Moore (1988), for example, report that, for the Canadian trucking industry, tax depreciation exceeded economic depreciation, resulting in a tax subsidy. Most (1984), focusing on reported income, found that in the United States the useful life (used for financial reporting) is generally longer than the economic life of the asset, understating reported depreciation and overstating reported income. Skinner (1982), on the other hand, reported the opposite phenomenon in the United Kingdom.

Beaver and Dukes (1973) examined firm price/earnings ratios and found that market prices, on average

> assign a more accelerated form of depreciation than is implied by reported earnings.[8]

They did not attempt to discern the reasons for this result but recognized that it was consistent with either a constant rate of return depreciation model (with declining cash flows) or depreciation based on current costs rather than a historical cost system.

Generalizing these results to other time periods, particularly for studies that examined whether depreciation practices (whether for tax or book purposes) compensated for the actual economic or physical depreciation of assets, requires a great deal of caution, given changing economic environments. These comparisons are a function of the provisions of the tax code, the inflation rate, and varying degrees of technological obsolescence across industries during the comparison period. During the 1980s, the depreciation provisions of the U.S. tax code were changed three times, inflation declined to approximately 4% from double-digit rates, and technological change was rapid in many industries. International differences are an additional difficulty.

The benchmark issue emerging from these studies is: How does one determine the "correct" useful life and economic depreciation rate? This is an important question for analytical purposes. Estimates of economic lives on an aggregate industry basis can be derived from Department of Commerce data.

In 1982, the FASB issued SFAS 33 (Changing Prices), which required very large firms[9] to disclose supplementary, unaudited data on the effects of changing prices. Among the required disclosures were:

- The current cost of fixed assets
- Depreciation expense on a current cost basis

These disclosures were intended to help financial statement users adjust for the shortcomings of historical cost depreciation discussed earlier. However, studies that examined the informational content of the replacement cost data found that, although historical cost earnings had informational content above and beyond that of current cost data provided by SFAS 33, the reverse did not hold.[10] Inflation-adjusted data did not appear to have any marginal information content above that provided by historical cost data. The reasons offered for this surprising result were that the data were:

- Too difficult to comprehend, and the market had not yet learned how to use them
- Not new, as the market knew how to adjust historical costs for inflation without SFAS 33 disclosures[11]

---

[8] William H. Beaver and Roland E. Dukes, "Interperiod Tax Allocation and δ-Depreciation Methods: Some Empirical Results," *Accounting Review* (July 1973), pp. 549–559.

[9] SFAS 33 applied to firms with inventories and gross (before deducting depreciation) property exceeding $125 million (in the aggregate) or with total assets exceeding $1 billion.

[10] Some studies [e.g., Beaver et al. (1980, 1982)] found little information content, focusing on ASR 190 disclosures. Others [Beaver and Landsman (1983)] examined the SFAS 33 data with similar results. Although the consensus was that these data did not have information content, the conclusions were by no means unanimous [see, e.g., Easman et al. (1979) and Murdoch (1986)].

[11] One example is the work of Angela Falkenstein and Roman L. Weil, "Replacement Cost Accounting: What Will Income Statements Based on the SEC Disclosures Show?—Part I," *Financial Analysts Journal* (January–February 1977), pp. 46–57 and "Replacement Cost Accounting: What Will Income Statements Based on the SEC Disclosures Show?—Part II," *Financial Analysts Journal* (March—April 1977), pp. 48–57.

- Irrelevant, either from a conceptual point of view or in the manner in which they were prepared and reported

Whatever the reason, in practice the data were difficult to prepare and use. Facing intense complaints regarding the cost of the disclosures and empirical research that seemed to belie the usefulness of the data, the FASB subsequently made the disclosures voluntary.

Changes in Depreciation Method

Companies may change the reported depreciation of fixed assets in different ways:

- Change in method applicable only to newly acquired assets
- Change in method applicable to all assets
- Changes in asset lives or salvage value

Change in Method Applicable Only to Newly Acquired Assets. A company can change its depreciation method only for newly acquired assets and continue to depreciate previously acquired similar assets using the same method(s) as in the past. The impact of the new method will be gradual, increasing as fixed assets acquired after the change grow in relative importance.

DuPont, for example, changed from the sum-of-the-years' digits method (for nonpetroleum properties) to the straight-line method for properties placed in service in 1995, with the following footnote disclosure:

> Property, plant and equipment (PP&E) is carried at cost and, except for petroleum PP&E, PP&E placed in service prior to 1995 is depreciated under the sum-of-the-years' digits method and other substantially similar methods. PP&E placed in service after 1994 is depreciated using the straight-line method. This change in accounting was made to reflect management's belief that the productivity of such PP&E will not appreciably diminish in the early years of its useful life, and it will not be subject to significant additional maintenance in the later years of its useful life. In these circumstances, straight-line depreciation is preferable in that it provides a better matching of costs with revenues. Additionally, the change to the straight-line method conforms to predominant industry practice. The effect of this change on net income will be dependent on the level of future capital spending; it did not have a material effect in 1995.[12]

This is a common method of changing accounting principles, as it does not require the restatement of past earnings.

The company made the uninformative statement that "the change is not expected to have a material effect on 1995 results." Nonetheless, *the change increased subsequent reported income* as depreciation charges for new PPE were lower (depreciation charges on old PPE continued to be computed using the SYD method).

Exhibit 41-6 contains an extract from DuPont's segment disclosures for the years 1994 to 1996. As petroleum assets are depreciated by the units of production method, we must remove the capital spending and depreciation for that segment:

---

[12] *Source:* DuPont 10-K report, 1995.

EXHIBIT 41-6 DuPont Segment Disclosures ($millions)

	Chemicals	Fibers	Polymers	Petroleum	Life Sciences	Diversified Businesses	Consolidated
1996:							
Depreciation, etc.	$330	$609	$350	$1,128	$70	$232	$2,719
Capital expenditures	338	611	446	1,616	93	213	3,317
1995:							
Depreciation, etc.	352	626	362	1,111	78	294	2,823
Capital expenditures	417	593	399	1,714	73	198	3,394
1994:							
Depreciation, etc.	405	686	386	1,266	79	284	3,106
Capital expenditures	258	640	356	1,635	47	215	3,151

Source: DuPont 10-K report, December 31, 1996.

	1994	1995	1996
Capital spending	$3,151	$3,394	$3,317
Petroleum segment	(1,635)	(1,714)	(1,616)
All nonpetroleum	$1,516	$1,680	$1,701
% change		10.8%	1.3%
Total depreciation	$3,106	$2,823	$2,719
Petroleum segment	(1,266)	(1,111)	(1,128)
All nonpetroleum	$1,840	$1,712	$1,591
% change		−7.0%	−7.1%

Although nonpetroleum capital spending rose in both 1995 and 1996, depreciation expense fell 7% in both years. The decline is clearly due to the combined effect of straight-line (lower than SYD) depreciation expense relating to new assets and declining SYD depreciation on old assets.

Change in Method Applicable to All Assets. Instead of being implemented prospectively, the new method can be applied retroactively so that all fixed assets are depreciated using the new method. In this case, the effect is greater and can be significant in the year of the switch as well as in future years. For a sample of 38 companies that switched to straight-line depreciation, Healy et al. (1987) estimated that the median increase in income was 8% to 10% in the 10-year period following the change. In addition to the effect on current and future depreciation expense (and net income), there is a cumulative effect, given the retroactive nature of the change: the cumulative difference between originally reported depreciation and the restated depreciation for all past periods. When the new method is applied retroactively, companies must also disclose the pro forma impact of the new method on prior periods.

A change in depreciation method for all assets is considered a change in accounting principle under APB 20, Accounting Changes. *The cumulative effect of the change must be reported separately and net of taxes.*

Changes in Asset Lives or Salvage Value. *Changes in asset lives and salvage values are changes in accounting estimates and are not considered changes in accounting principle.* Their impact is only prospective, and no retroactive or cumulative effects are recognized. Estimate changes attract much less notice than do changes in depreciation methods (see footnote 6). They are not, for example, referred to in the auditor's opinion. Thus, it is important to read financial statement footnotes carefully to be sure that no changes in accounting estimates have been made.

Example: AMR

Exhibit 41-7 contains extracts from the *1999 Annual Report* of AMR, the parent of American Airlines, which changed the estimated useful lives *and* the salvage values used to compute depreciation on its flight equipment, effective January 1, 1999. Given the asset intensity of airlines, this change had a significant impact on reported earnings, as shown in the following table:

AMR (in $millions)

	Years Ended December 31		
	1997	**1998**	**1999**
As Reported (with Depreciation Changes)			
Depreciation expense	$1,040	$1,040	$1,092
% Change from previous year		0.0%	5.0%
Operating income	$1,595	$1,988	$1,156
% Change from previous year		24.6%	−41.9%
After Adjustment for Depreciation Change			
Depreciation expense	$1,040	$1,040	$1,250
% Change from previous year		0.0%	20.2%
Operating income	$1,595	$1,988	$ 998
% Change from previous year		24.6%	−49.8%

Despite the accounting change, depreciation expense rose 5% in 1991 due to new equipment. If not for the change, depreciation expense would have been more than 20% higher. Without the accounting change, the 1999 decline in operating income would have been steeper, 50% instead of 42%. This may have been the motivation for the change. *When analyzing firms that change depreciation methods or assumptions, it is important to remember that the effect of such changes persists, as depreciation on both old and new fixed assets is stretched out, increasing reported income.*

EXHIBIT 41-7 AMR Corporation
Change in Depreciation Lives of Flight Equipment

A. Extract from Depreciation Footnote

Effective January 1, 1999, in order to more accurately reflect the expected useful life of its aircraft, the Company changed its estimate of the depreciable lives of certain aircraft types from 20 to 25 years and increased the residual value from five to 10 percent. It also established a 30-year life for its new Boeing 777 aircraft, first delivered in the first quarter of 1999. As a result of this change, depreciation and amortization expense was reduced by approximately $158 million and net earnings were increased by approximately $99 million, or $0.63 per common share diluted, for the year ended December 31, 1999.

B. Extract from Income Statement

	Years Ended December 31 (in $millions)		
	1999	**1998**	**1997**
Revenues	$17,730	$17,516	$16,957
Expenses:			
Depreciation and amortization	1,092	1,040	1,040
Total operating expenses	16,574	15,528	15,362
Operating Income	1,156	1,988	1,595

C. Extract from Management Discussion and Analysis

Depreciation and amortization expense increased $52 million, or 5.0 percent, due primarily to the addition of new aircraft, partially offset by the change in depreciable lives and residual values for certain types of aircraft in 1999 (see Note 1 to the consolidated financial statements).

Source: AMR Corp. 10-K Report, December 31, 1999.

Increases in asset lives have been common in recent years. The effect of such increases is, of course, to increase reported earnings. Such changes are often made by more than one firm in an industry, as firms compete to show higher reported earnings and ROE. For example, in the airline industry, Delta Airlines changed both the estimated lives and the salvage values used to compute depreciation on flight equipment in 1993. Both Southwest Airlines and UAL (United Airlines) extended aircraft depreciable lives in 1999.

Box 41-2 examines the motivation for and reaction to depreciation changes. Whenever a change in depreciation method or lives is reported, the effect of the change on current year reported earnings should be removed to evaluate operating performance on a comparable basis. The change should also be factored into estimates of future reported income.

BOX 41-2 CHANGES IN DEPRECIATION METHODS: MOTIVATION AND REACTION

OPTIONAL SEGMENT

When the Internal Revenue Code of 1954 permitted the use of accelerated depreciation for tax purposes, many firms also adopted these methods for financial statement purposes. Subsequently, many of these firms "switched back" to straight-line depreciation for financial reporting purposes. The effect of the switch-back was to increase the firm's reported net income, (tangible) assets, and retained earnings.

Unlike the FIFO-LIFO switch discussed in Reading 39, the depreciation switch-back was a "pure accounting" change without any direct cash flow consequences as accelerated depreciation was retained for tax purposes. The phenomenon was originally studied by Archibald (1972) and Kaplan and Roll (1972) as a test of whether the efficient market hypothesis (EMH) or the functional fixation hypothesis prevailed with respect to financial statements; that is, was the market "fooled" by the numbers, or did it see through the accounting change, realizing that it had no economic consequence? As detailed in Chapter 5, the results of these studies (using weekly and monthly data) were consistent with the EMH, finding no market reaction to the switch.

With the advent of positive accounting research, the assumption of no economic consequences to a "pure accounting" change was reexamined. Management compensation contracts as well as debt covenants based on accounting numbers are affected by accounting changes. Holthausen (1981) examined the accounting switch-backs in this framework. He argued that an accounting change that increases reported income, given earnings-based management contracts, should result in negative market reaction, as there would be a wealth transfer from the owners of the firm to the managers. Conversely, the presence of debt covenants should result in a positive market reaction, as the increase in reported earnings and assets would generally increase the slack associated with any leverage constraints. Empirical results did not confirm these hypotheses.

OPTIONAL SEGMENT ENDS

As noted in Chapter 5, studies of market reaction to voluntary accounting changes have generally not found results consistent with the positive accounting framework, as (it is argued that) by the time the change is made, it has been generally anticipated that the firm (or its managers) will make the change to improve reported performance. Thus, although the motivation for the change (compensation, debt covenants) is as specified, the market has already taken it into account.

Evidence consistent with the compensation motivation for depreciation switch-backs is reported by Dhaliwal et al. (1982), who found that management-controlled firms are more likely to adopt straight-line depreciation methods. Furthermore, Healy et al. (1987) found that when firms changed reporting methods to straight-line depreciation,

> the CEO's bonus and salary awards are based on reported earnings both before and after the accounting changes. We find no evidence that subsequent to either the inventory change or the depreciation change, reported earnings are transformed to earnings under the original accounting method for computing compensation awards.*

Generally, however, they note that the percentage of the CEO's compensation attributable to the accounting change is small relative to their overall compensation package. On average, these results do not find a debt covenant or (significant) management compensation motivation for the change in depreciation method. For a given company, however, an analyst would be wise to check these factors whenever an income-increasing accounting change is implemented.

* Paul H. Healy, Sok-Hyon Kang, and Krishna Palepu, "The Effect of Accounting Procedure Changes on CEO's Cash Salary and Bonus Compensation," *Journal of Accounting and Economics* (1987), pp. 7–34.

3 ANALYSIS OF FIXED ASSET DISCLOSURES

In practice, firms use varying accounting methods, lives, and residual value assumptions for fixed assets, hampering comparisons between firms. To improve comparability, the analyst must use financial statement disclosures to gain insight into a company's depreciation accounting. Unfortunately, in 1994 the SEC deleted the requirement for firms to disclose details of their property accounts.[13]

[13] Financial Reporting Release (FRR) 44 (December 13, 1994) amended Rule 5-04 of Regulation S-X to eliminate Schedule V, Property, Plant and Equipment, and Schedule VI, Accumulated Depreciation, Depletion and Amortization of Property, Plant and Equipment. See FRR 44 for a listing of other schedules eliminated.

However, the Commission has proposed restoring the requirement following complaints from financial analysts regarding the loss of these useful data. As a result, for American firms, only a broad analysis is possible except when detailed data are made available by the company. However, IAS 16 and many foreign GAAP require detailed disclosures about fixed assets, permitting detailed analysis as shown later in this reading.

Estimating Relative Age and Useful Lives

Fixed-asset data can be used to estimate the relative age of companies' property, plant, and equipment. The relative age as a percentage of depreciable ("useful") life is calculated as

Relative Age (%) = Accumulated Depreciation/Ending Gross Investment

As long as straight-line depreciation is used,[14] this is an accurate estimate of asset age as a percentage of depreciable life. Neither changes in asset mix (additions with longer or shorter lives than existing assets) nor the timing of purchases affect the calculation. The relative age is a useful measure of whether the firm's fixed-asset base is old or new. Newer assets are likely to be more efficient; when relative age is high, the firm has not been adding to (or modernizing) its capital stock and may find it difficult to compete with firms that have more modern facilities. Remember, however, that this calculation is affected by the firm's accounting methods in the following areas:

- Depreciation lives[15]
- Salvage values

Another useful calculation is the average depreciable life of fixed assets:

Average Depreciable Life = Ending Gross Investment/Depreciation Expense

This calculation is only a rough approximation as it can be affected by changes in asset mix. During periods of rapid growth in fixed assets, the time (within the year) when assets are placed into service can also affect the ratio. Over longer time periods, however, this ratio is a useful measure of a firm's depreciation policy and can be used for comparisons with competitors.

Estimating the Age of Assets

We can also calculate the approximate age (in years) of a firm's fixed assets by comparing accumulated depreciation with depreciation expense:[16]

Average Age = Accumulated Depreciation/Depreciation Expense

---

[14] The use of accelerated depreciation methods invalidates this analysis. However, since more than 90% of companies use straight-line depreciation, the method has general application.

[15] As noted earlier, depreciable lives and economic lives for reporting purposes are not equivalent. See the earlier reference to Most (1984).

[16] Average age can also be computed as relative age multiplied by average depreciable life.

As in the case of depreciable life, average age calculations may be distorted by changes in asset mix and by acquisitions. Nonetheless, these data are useful for comparison purposes and can suggest a useful line of questioning when meeting with management.

Average age data, either as a percentage of gross cost or in absolute terms, are useful for two reasons. First, older assets tend to be less efficient; inefficient or obsolete fixed assets may make the firm uncompetitive. Second, knowing past patterns of capital replacement helps the analyst estimate when major capital expenditures will be required. The financing implications of capital expenditure requirements may be significant. Furthermore, when forecasting capital expenditures, the data should be compared with benchmark data on the useful (economic) life of fixed assets for that industry.

Example:

Forest Products Industry Comparison

Exhibit 41-8 contains average age and average depreciable life statistics for four Scandinavian companies in the forest products industry for 1999. Statistics for buildings and for machinery and equipment are shown separately, as required by Swedish GAAP.[17]

The statistics show significant differences among these four companies:

- SCA's fixed assets appear youngest and Assidoman's appear oldest.
- Holmen appears to use the shortest depreciable lives, followed by SCA.

EXHIBIT 41-8 Analysis of Fixed Assets for Scandinavian Forest Products Industry

1999	Assidoman	Holmen	SCA	Stora Enso
Buildings				
Average age %	41.6	49.1	29.4	35.1
Average depreciable life years	27.3	21.0	24.4	27.6
Average age years	11.3	10.3	7.2	9.7
Machinery and Equipment				
Average age %	55.7	50.0	42.7	48.3
Average depreciable life years	16.3	13.4	15.2	17.4
Average age years	9.1	6.7	6.5	8.4

Source: Data from 1999 annual reports.

[17] IAS 16 requirements are similar.

These statistics are, however, only the starting point for analysis. They assume that all four firms have comparable assets when in fact they may have differing mixes of assets with different depreciable lives. Differences in product mix (requiring different fixed-asset mixes) and acquisitions and divestitures also affect the comparison. These statistics should be used to ask questions of management rather than to make decisions.

Several of these firms had major acquisitions or divestitures over the 1997–1999 period, making three-year comparisons meaningless. However data for SCA follow:

SCA: Analysis of Fixed Asset Disclosures by Property Class (SEK millions)

	1997	1998	1999
Buildings et al.			
Gross investment	12,566	13,986	12,513
Accumulated depreciation	(3,299)	(3,909)	(3,680)
Net investment	9,267	10,077	8,833
Depreciation expense	519	515	513
Average age %	26.3%	27.9%	29.4%
Average depreciable life years	24.2	27.2	24.4
Average age years	6.4	7.6	7.2
Machinery and Equipment			
Gross investment	42,404	47,256	47,487
Accumulated depreciation	(17,488)	(20,729)	(20,289)
Net investment	24,916	26,527	27,198
Depreciation expense	3,117	2,912	3,117
Average age %	41.2%	43.9%	42.7%
Average depreciable life years	13.6	16.2	15.2
Average age years	5.6	7.1	6.5

Even within one company, the fixed asset statistics can show significant change over short periods. The apparent increase in average depreciable life in 1998 and the 1999 decline may be due to significant asset acquisitions and dispositions in those years (note the changes in gross investment and accumulated depreciation). As in the case of comparisons with other companies, these statistics are a means rather than an end.

IMPAIRMENT OF LONG-LIVED ASSETS 4

Fixed assets used in continuing operations are carried at acquisition cost less accumulated depreciation. The carrying amount of fixed assets may also be affected by changes in market conditions and technology. These changes may increase or decrease the fair value of fixed assets. Unlike some foreign countries (and the IASB), U.S. GAAP do not allow firms to recognize increases in value.

This section is concerned with the recognition, measurement, and disclosure problems associated with decreases in fair value, often called impairment, of long-lived assets. Impairment means that some or all of the carrying cost cannot be recovered from expected levels of operations. Due to unfavorable economic conditions, technological developments, or declines in market demand, firms may temporarily idle, continue to operate at a significantly reduced level, sell, or abandon impaired assets. These economic conditions may also call for fewer employees or those with different skills.

Financial Reporting of Impaired Assets

Impairments are sometimes reported as part of "restructuring" provisions. Such provisions (see Reading 31 for further discussion) contain elements that fall into two general categories. Some elements, including impairment writedowns, write off past cash flows.[18] Others reflect a major restructuring of the firm and may result in current and expected future cash outflows for such items as employee severance and lease payments. Restructuring provisions must, therefore, be separated into impairment (noncash writedowns of past cash outflows) and those with cash flow implications.

In October 2001, the FASB issued SFAS 144, Accounting for the Impairment or Disposal of Long-Lived Assets. The new standard superseded SFAS 121 (Accounting for Impairment) and APB 30,[19] and also nullified most of the guidance (EITF 94-3) on obligations associated with disposal activities.

SFAS 144 broadened the application of "discontinued operation" accounting[20] and changed the treatment of assets intended for disposal. SFAS 121 (1995) had distinguished between assets held for sale and those remaining in use.

Impairment of Assets Held for Sale

The new standard requires that long-lived assets held for sale:

- Be written down to fair value less cost to sell when lower than the carrying amount. In most cases estimated fair value would be the present value of expected cash flows, discounted at the credit-adjusted risk-free rate.[21] Costs to sell exclude costs associated with the ongoing operations of assets held for sale.
- Cease to be depreciated after reclassification as held for sale.

Subsequent increases in fair value less cost to sell would be recognized as gains only to the extent of previously recognized writedowns.

Impairment of Assets Remaining in Use

The standard requires the recognition of impairment when there is evidence that the carrying amount of an asset or a group of assets still in use can no longer be recovered. One or more of the following indicators may signal lack of recoverability:

---

[18] However, they may signal departure from a business segment or the need for significant capital expenditures for investments in new and improved technologies.

[19] APB 30 deals with disposal of a segment and the classification of items as extraordinary.

[20] See Reading 31 for discussion of discontinued operations accounting.

[21] See discussion of SFAC 7 in Box 29-1.

- A significant decrease in the market value, physical change, or use of the assets
- Adverse changes in the legal or business climate
- Significant cost overruns
- Current period operating or cash flow losses combined with a history of operating or cash flow losses and a forecast of a significant decline in the long-term profitability of the asset

SFAS 144 provides a two-step process. First is the recoverability test: Impairment must be recognized when the carrying value of the assets exceeds the *undiscounted* expected future cash flows from their use and disposal. The second stage is loss measurement: the excess of the carrying amount over the fair value of the assets. When fair value cannot be determined, the *discounted* present value of future cash flows (discounted at the firm's incremental borrowing rate) must be used.[22]

For assets to be held and used, the new standard permits either a probability-weighted or a best-estimate approach when applying the undiscounted cash flows recoverability test. Estimates of future cash flows used in these tests would be based on the remaining useful life of the primary asset of the group, which may be recognized identifiable intangible assets that are being amortized. The standard includes guidance on the present value methods described in SFAC 7.

The recoverability test and loss measurement are based on assets grouped at the lowest level for which cash flows can be identified independently of cash flows of other asset groups. The impairment loss is reported pretax as a component of income from continuing operations.

The standard prohibits restoration of previous impairments. It requires disclosure of the amount of the loss, segments affected, events and circumstances surrounding the impairment, and how fair value was determined.

SFAS 144 does not require firms to disclose cash flows and discount rates used to measure impairment. Firms do not have to disclose impaired assets (even though one or more impairment indicators are present) as long as their gross *undiscounted* cash flows exceed their carrying amount (even when the discounted cash flows are below the carrying amount). Thus, there is no disclosure of early-warning signals.

SFAS 144 was effective in fiscal years beginning after December 15, 2001. The new standard applied prospectively to new disposal activities. Retroactive application was prohibited except for restatement for comparative purposes.

Analysts must develop supplementary techniques to counter inadequate disclosure requirements and the absence of early-warning signals. Significant declines in market value, abnormal technological changes, and overcapacity are good indicators of possible asset impairments. Research indicates that managers are slow to report impairments.

The telecommunications industry provides a good example; the three indicators mentioned earlier in the preceding paragraph were present during 2001. A June 25, 2001 article in the *Wall Street Journal* asked whether companies had delayed impairment announcements because asset writedowns would violate bond covenants based on minimum levels of fixed assets relative to debt. Impairment recognition would have reduced access to capital markets and risked technical insolvency.

[22] When the recoverability test is applied to assets acquired in purchase method business combinations, the standard requires the elimination of goodwill before recording writedowns of related impaired tangible and identifiable intangible assets. When only some of the acquired assets are subject to the recoverability test, goodwill must be allocated to the affected assets on a pro-rata basis using the relative fair values of all assets acquired. SFAS 142 (2001) made significant changes in accounting for the impairment of goodwill. See the discussion in Chapter 14.

The need to evaluate recoverability periodically may result in the review of depreciation methods, lives, and salvage values. Changes in depreciation may precede or accompany a firm's reporting of asset impairment.

Example:

Texaco

Note 6 of Texaco's 1999 financial statements provides an example of impairment recognition and disclosure. Texaco, a multinational oil company, reported asset impairments (included in unusual items) in 1997, 1998, and 1999. While the impairment amounts are small compared to Texaco's net income, the disclosures illustrate the poor quality of disclosures in this area. Texaco's disclosures are very broad and uninformative. The statement that "fair value was determined by discounting expected future cash flows" provides no detail regarding the assumptions used.

Financial Statement Impact of Impairments

Impairment writedowns of long-lived assets have pervasive and significant effects on financial statements and financial ratios.

The principal balance sheet impacts of the writedowns are reductions in the:

- Carrying value of plant, equipment, and other production assets
- Deferred tax liabilities
- Stockholders' equity

The lower level of fixed assets is a direct consequence of the impairment writedown. As a result, the firm's fixed-asset and total-asset turnover increases, affecting any comparison with firms that have not recognized impairments.

The reduction in deferred tax liabilities reflects the fact that the impairment loss is not recognized for tax purposes until the property is disposed of. However, because virtually all firms depreciate fixed assets more quickly for tax purposes than for financial reporting, the impairment has the effect of reducing the difference between the tax basis and reporting basis of these assets. Thus, previously established deferred tax liabilities are reduced (see Reading 42 for further discussion of deferred taxes).

The reduction in equity is the net effect of the impairment provision. This reduction increases the firm's debt-to-equity ratio and decreases reported book value per share. The price-to-book value ratio is increased.

Future financial statements are also affected by the writedown. Depreciation expense declines as a direct result of the reduction in the carrying value of fixed assets; reported earnings are higher than if no impairment were recognized. With higher earnings and lower assets and equity, return ratios (ROA and ROE) also increase.

The ratios used to evaluate fixed assets and depreciation policy earlier in this reading are also distorted by the impairment writedown. For example, the apparent average age of fixed assets increases, and fixed assets appear older than they really are.

Effect of SFAS 121 on Analysis of Impairment

The lack of reporting guidelines for impairments prior to SFAS 121 resulted in widely divergent timing, measurement, and reporting practices. Fried, Schiff, and Sondhi (FSS) (1989) and two Financial Executives Institute surveys[23] found that a majority of companies used net realizable values (NRV) to measure impairments. However, NRV meant different things to different firms, and the definition used was rarely disclosed.[24] The use of undiscounted cash flows under SFAS 121 reduces the probability of recognition of impairments and overstates asset values because of the failure to recognize the time value of money.

It is difficult to forecast impairment writedowns because managements have so much discretion as to timing. Substandard profitability, especially when persistent, is probably the surest sign of impaired assets. LIFO liquidations and changes in depreciation methods, estimated useful lives, and salvage values provide useful but very imprecise signals. Segment data can help the analyst spot underperforming operations.

The cash flow and tax implications of write-offs are also unclear in some cases. Generally, impairments recognized for financial reporting are not deductible for tax purposes until the affected assets are disposed of. Recognition of the impairment, therefore, leads to a deferred tax asset (a probable future tax benefit), not a current refund. Beneficial cash flow impacts may occur only in the future, when tax deductions are realized. Close attention to the income tax footnote should be helpful, but a complete understanding may require posing questions to management.

Timely recognition of impairments may correct understated past depreciation or permit recognition of the effect of changes in markets or technology on operating assets. Higher frequency of impairment announcements and the absence of reporting guidelines resulted in diverse accounting practices that were not comparable across companies and inconsistently applied within firms over time. The FASB recognized this problem when it placed asset impairment on its agenda. SFAS 144, and SEC efforts to improve disclosures regarding "restructuring" provisions have improved disclosure.

Empirical Findings

OPTIONAL SEGMENT

The frequency and dollar amount of writedowns have increased considerably in the last 25 years.[25] Elliott and Hanna (1996) report that fewer than 200 (5%) firms in the Compustat database reported write-offs in 1975, almost 800 (14%) did so in 1985, and over 1,200 (21%) in 1993. Moreover, in a phenomenon dubbed by Bleakley (1995) as a "recurring nonrecurring item," firms that report write-offs in one year tend to report write-offs again in subsequent years.[26]

The analysis of write-offs has been confounded by the existence of conflicting beliefs as to the nature and motivations behind such actions. Some view

---

[23] Financial Executives Institute, Committee on Corporate Reporting, "Survey on Unusual Charges," 1986 and 1991.

[24] The problem is compounded by SFAC 5, in which NRV is defined as a short-term, gross, undiscounted cash flow.

[25] The majority of write-offs (55%–60%) are taken in the fourth quarter. Given the detailed review (both by management and auditors) during preparation of the annual report, it is likely that the fourth quarter will always contain the largest number of write-offs.

[26] Elliott and Hanna found that 27% of the companies that take a write-off report a subsequent one the next year and approximately 60% do so within three years. Fried et al. (1990) also document multiple write-offs. Their probabilities, however, are higher (45% within one year and approximately 70% within three years).

managers as manipulating earnings[27] by recognizing impairments only when it is to their benefit rather than as they occur. Others view impairment announcements as information provided by managers as to declines in asset values due to poor performance, technological shifts, and/or changes in the firm's objectives.

Articles in the financial and popular press as well as in academic journals often talk about the "big bath"—a tendency to take large write-offs during adverse times—and about "house cleaning"—large write-offs assumed to accompany changes in senior management. Consequently, write-off announcements often are viewed as a signal of improvement in future reported performance. However, debate lingers as to whether the subsequent improvement (should it materialize) is evidence that the upturn is real or merely a consequence of earnings management.

A number of studies have examined the write-off phenomenon. These studies document a number of recurring characteristics of write-offs.

1. *Poor financial as well as stock market performance usually precede write-offs.*

   Francis, Hanna, and Vincent (1996), Rees, Gill, and Gore (1996), and Elliott and Shaw (1988) all report poor stock market performance of write-off firms from three to five years prior to the write-off. Consistent with the foregoing, within their respective industries, firms with write-offs had lower operating performance as measured by ROA (Rees et al.), earnings, and ROE (Elliott and Shaw). These results hold for the year of the write-off[28] as well as the three-year period preceding the write-off.[29] Francis et al. showed similar results (with respect to ROA) but only for firms classifying their write-offs as restructurings.

2. *Overall, negative returns occur around the time of the write-off and for up to 18 months following the write-off. These results, however, depend on the nature of the write-off.*

   Elliott and Shaw reported that the negative return experienced around the time of the write-off was directly related to the size of the write-off; the larger the write-off, the more negative the reaction. On the other hand, Francis et al., as well as Lindhal and Ricks (1990), indicate that although, in general, market reaction to write-offs was negative, the results depend on whether the event is

   a. A *writedown* comprising purely accounting decisions to reduce the carrying value of assets with no (apparent) change in operations; or

   b. A *restructuring* that consists of decisions to modify operations (e.g., asset sales, employee layoffs, plant closings)

   For the latter type of event, they report positive market reaction. Francis et al. argue that restructurings are associated with positive returns because they indicate decisions taken to modify and improve future operations and corporate strategy.[30]

---

[27] Earnings management can operate in both directions. Zucca and Campbell (1992) argue that firms may engage in big-bath behavior, taking write-offs when earnings are severely depressed, as well as smoothing behavior by taking write-offs when earnings are "too high."

[28] These conditions hold even without taking the write-off into consideration.

[29] FSS (1989), using a control group of firms matched by industry and size, found similar results. Strong and Meyer (1987), however, reported that although the write-off firms were not the best performers in their industry, they were not the worst either, but tended to cluster in the middle quintiles.

[30] Bartov, Lindhal, and Ricks (1996) similarly partitioned their write-off sample into a *writedown category* and an *operating decision category*. Although they found negative returns for both categories, the stock performance of the writedown category was much worse than that of the operating decision category.

3. *Problems leading to write-offs are rarely short-lived and generally persist after the write-off.*

   This persistence is especially true for firms taking multiple write-offs. Rees et al. show that such firms had market-adjusted returns that were significantly negative for up to two years after the initial write-off. Furthermore, (industry-adjusted) ROA for these firms did not recover after the write-off. These results are consistent with Elliott and Hanna, who found that bond ratings were lower and default probability higher for firms with sequential write-offs.

Taken together, the evidence seems to indicate that firms write down assets during periods of poor performance. However, the assumption of big-bath behavior may not be well founded. The writedown may also be a response to the (negative) change in the firm's economic situation. The prevalence of multiple write-offs and their increasing size is inconsistent with big-bath behavior, usually associated with a once-and-for-all write-off.[31] Similarly, the persistent negative financial performance and market returns following writedowns are consistent not with an expected reversal following a big-bath but rather with a permanent deterioration in the firm's prospects. Furthermore, positive returns following write-offs are generally confined to those situations where the firm has made explicit operating decisions (restructurings) to modify operations.

Given the significance and frequency of impairments, it is unfortunate that indicators of initial write-offs other than poor financial condition are hard to find.[32] Better disclosure in financial statements (or the Management Discussion and Analysis) of problems with particular segments would make it easier to predict write-offs. However, the evidence indicates that care must be taken to distinguish whether the write-off is purely an accounting decision or is coupled with corrective operating decisions.

OPTIONAL SEGMENT ENDS

LIABILITIES FOR ASSET RETIREMENT OBLIGATIONS 5

Governments often require that owners of operating assets remedy the environmental damage caused by operating those assets or restore land to its preexisting condition. Common examples include:

- Restoration of strip mines after mining is completed
- Dismantlement of an offshore oil platform after the end of its useful life
- Removal of toxic wastes caused by production
- Decontamination of site when a nuclear power plant is decommissioned

Prior to SFAS 143, current period costs of these activities were often expensed except for capital expenditures that were capitalized.[33] As no standards have

---

[31] In effect, if anything, firms seem to warehouse bad news and report it through multiple write-offs.

[32] FSS (1989) do report that LIFO liquidations are leading indicators of writedowns.

[33] SFAS 19 required the accrual of an asset retirement obligation in some cases. Under SFAS 19, ARO was recognized over the life of the asset and measured using a cost-accumulation approach; it was not discounted, and was often recorded as a contra asset with no recognition of a separate liability. In addition, many electricity producers accrued for the decontamination of nuclear facilities.

existed for the accrual of future expenditures, practice has been inconsistent with respect to:

- Whether (or when) accrual takes place
- Whether accruals increase the carrying amount of the related asset (and whether they must be depreciated)
- Whether accruals are included in depreciation expense
- Measurement of the liability (whether or not discounted, and at what rate)
- Disclosure

Because of inconsistent accounting practice, the FASB issued SFAS 143, Accounting for Asset Retirement Obligations (AROs), in June 2001.

Provisions of SFAS 143

The requirements of SFAS 143 become effective for fiscal years starting after June 15, 2002 (calendar 2003 for most companies). However some companies will apply the standard earlier.

This standard changes accounting standards for ARO in the following ways:

- It applies to all entities[34] and to all legal obligations (including contractual obligations[35]) connected with the retirement of tangible fixed assets.
- Affected firms must recognize the fair value of an ARO liability in the period in which it is incurred (normally at acquisition).
- Absent a market value, fair value is the present value of the expected cash flows required to extinguish the liability.[36]
- As the liability is carried at its present value, the firm must recognize accretion expense in its income statement each period.
- An amount equal to the initial liability must be added to the carrying value of the asset, and depreciated over its useful life.
- Changes in the estimated liability are accounted for prospectively; prior period amounts are not restated.
- Required disclosures include:
  - Description of the ARO and associated asset
  - Reconciliation of the ARO liability, showing the effect of:
    - New liabilities incurred
    - Liabilities extinguished
    - Accretion expense
    - Revisions of the estimated AROs
  - Fair value of any restricted assets (such as funds) set aside for ARO obligations.

Further detail regarding SFAS 143 is contained in Box 41-3.

---

[34] Paragraph 17 of SFAS 143 governs its application to leased assets.

[35] The standard also applies to legally enforceable contracts arising from promises made. One example would be a company's publicly stated promise to restore a site it is not required to restore by existing laws.

[36] See Box 41-3 for details.

BOX 41-3 SFAS 143 (2001): ACCOUNTING FOR ASSET RETIREMENT OBLIGATIONS

Explanation of Accounting Method

Initial Recognition and Measurement

SFAS 143 requires the recognition of the fair value of the ARO liability in the period it is incurred if a reasonable estimate of fair value can be made. The fair value of the liability is defined as the amount at which the liability can be settled in a current transaction between willing parties. Quoted market prices are presumed to be the best evidence of fair value. In their absence, firms must estimate fair value using the best available information on prices of similar liabilities and present value (or other valuation) methods.

For present value techniques, SFAS 143 applies the provisions of SFAC 7 (see Box 29-1) to the measurement of ARO liabilities:

A. Estimate the expected (gross) cash flows required to extinguish the obligation, assuming an outside contractor is hired. Given uncertainty regarding future costs, the firm uses the expected value. Other assumptions (such as inflation rates) may be required.

B. The present value of the expected cash flows is computed using an interest rate based on the risk-free rate, but increased to reflect the credit risk of the firm (credit-adjusted risk-free rate).

C. The resulting measure of the ARO is recognized on the balance sheet, with periodic accretion (using the interest method) so that the liability equals the expected gross cash flows at the expected payment date. Use of the interest method means that accretion increases each year.

D. An equal amount is added to the carrying basis of the related asset and depreciated over that asset's useful life, using the same method used to depreciate the cost of the asset.

Subsequent Recognition and Measurement

OPTIONAL SEGMENT

E. If the timing or the amount of estimated gross cash flows change after the initial recognition, the ARO (and the related asset) is increased or decreased accordingly. Any increase is discounted using interest rates at the date of change; any decrease is discounted at the original interest rate. Accretion and depreciation charges change prospectively; there is no restatement of prior periods.

F. When the liability is extinguished (the cash flows occur), any difference between the amount paid and the carrying amount of the ARO liability is recognized as a gain or loss in the income statement.

Transition Method

The provisions of SFAS 143 were effective in fiscal years beginning after June 15, 2001, with earlier application encouraged. The new standard required use of the cumulative change method to recognize existing AROs. Such recognition was accomplished as follows:

1. Estimate gross obligation based on information available at the (current) transition date.
2. Discount to present value using current interest rates.
3. Replace any previous accrual with the following:
   - **a.** Asset equal to ARO at date of asset acquisition
   - **b.** Accumulated depreciation to transition date, assuming SFAS 143 implemented at asset acquisition date
   - **c.** ARO liability at transition date
4. Record the difference between any previous accruals and those listed in the previous paragraph as the *cumulative effect* of implementing the new standard, shown in the income statement on a separate line.
5. Provide pro forma disclosure of the ARO liability for each year presented in the financial statement.

OPTIONAL SEGMENT ENDS

Effects of SFAS 143

Implementation of the new standard will result in the following financial statement effects for most firms:[37]

- Increase in the carrying value of fixed assets.
- Increase in liabilities due to recognition of the ARO.

[37] For firms that have already recognized ARO liabilities (based on expected gross cash outflows), it is possible that the ARO liability will decrease under SFAS 143 because that standard measures the ARO at its present value.

- Lower net income due to recognition of additional depreciation (higher fixed assets) and accretion expense (on the ARO). Due to the nature of the accretion process, this expense will increase every year.

The following ratio effects will also occur:

- Lower asset turnover (higher asset levels)
- Lower debt-to-equity ratio as equity is depressed by lower net income[38]
- Lower return on assets (lower income, higher assets)
- Lower interest coverage (lower income due to higher depreciation, higher interest expense)

Bond covenants that rely on these ratios will also be affected, unless rewritten to ignore the accounting change. Disclosures will be improved in almost all cases. Cash flows will be unaffected.

IAS 16 (1998) requires firms that recognize the liability for remediation costs to include such cost in the carrying amount of fixed assets and depreciate it. The liability recognition is governed by IAS 37 (1998), which (similar to SFAS 143) requires that companies recognize the present value of asset retirement obligations.

Example:

Texaco

In the Management Discussion and Analysis section of its 1999 annual report, Texaco reports (p. 29):

Restoration and Abandonment Costs and Liabilities

> Expenditures in 1999 for restoration and abandonment of our oil and gas producing properties amounted to $26 million. At year-end 1999, accruals to cover the cost of restoration and abandonment were $911 million.

Further, in its accounting policy section (p. 30), Texaco states that:

> We include estimated future restoration and abandonment costs in determining amortization and depreciation rates of productive properties.

These minimal disclosures are representative of practice prior to SFAS 143. The December 31, 1999 total accrual equals 7.6% of stockholders' equity. Note that the accrual is undiscounted and may be offset by expected recoveries from state funds. While it appears that accruals are made through depreciation charges, Texaco does not write up fixed assets. The accounting effect of the proposed accounting standard cannot be estimated due to the complexity of the transition requirements.

---

[38] The debt-to-equity ratio is also affected by whether AROs are considered debt or operating liabilities.

SUMMARY

6

The capitalization decision is only the start of the accounting cycle for long-lived assets. Depreciation expense depends on the choice of accounting method and asset life and salvage value assumptions. Thus, the same asset can produce different amounts of depreciation expense, limiting the comparability of reported income. Economic depreciation may be entirely different from accounting depreciation.

Economic changes often result in asset lives that differ from those anticipated by accounting conventions. In such cases, asset impairment may require accounting recognition. Although SFAS 144 provides standards for impairment writedowns in the United States, management retains considerable discretion over their timing and amounts. The accrual (if any) for future environmental costs related to long-lived assets is another area where practice is highly inconsistent.

PROBLEMS

1. [Depreciation methods; CFA© adapted] An analyst gathered the following information about a fixed asset purchased by a company:
   - Purchase price: $12,000,000
   - Estimated useful life: 5 years
   - Estimated salvage value: $2,000,000

   Compute the depreciation expense for this asset over its useful life using *each* of the following methods:
   - **a.** Straight-line
   - **b.** Sum-of-years' digits (SYD)
   - **c.** Double-declining balance
2. [Effect of depreciation methods; CFA© adapted] Compare the straight-line method of depreciation with accelerated methods with respect to their impact on:
   - **a.** Trend of depreciation expense
   - **b.** Trend of net income
   - **c.** Reported return on equity
   - **d.** Reported return on assets
   - **e.** Reported cash from operations
   - **f.** Asset turnover
3. [Depreciation methods and cash flows, courtesy of Professor Stephen Ryan] The Capital Company considers investing in either of two assets. Cash flows of these assets are:

Year	Asset A	Asset B
1	$36	$26
2	23	24
3	11	22

   - **a.** At an interest rate of 10%, how much should Capital be willing to pay for each asset?
   - **b.** Assuming that the amount calculated in part a is paid for each asset, calculate the depreciation schedule for each asset that results in a constant rate of return.
   - **c.** What type of historical cost depreciation is equal to present value depreciation for Asset A? Asset B?
4. [Change in depreciation method; effect and motivation] Pope and Talbot [POP] changed the method of depreciation for its U.S. pulp production assets from straight-line to units-of-production in 1998 in order to bring the accounting methods of the Company's pulp mills into conformity with its Canadian operations. The company stated:

> The Company believes this method, common within the industry, more appropriately matches production costs with pulp sales revenues. The impact to the 1998 loss from continuing operations was a reduction of depreciation expense before tax of $.8 million. The cumulative effect of this accounting change on years prior to 1998 was income of $.7 million, net of tax, or $.06 per share.

The company's 1998 net income was $342,000.

a. Compute POP's net income before the cumulative effect of the accounting change.

b. Compute POP's net income before the change in depreciation method. (Assume a 35% tax rate.)

c. Present another reason, other than conformity, that might explain why the firm made the accounting change in 1998.

5. [Change in depreciation lives] On March 6, 2000, Pepsi Bottling Group [PBG] issued a press release containing the following:

> In recognition of its long-standing success in preventive maintenance programs, The Pepsi Bottling Group, Inc. (NYSE: PBG) today announced a change in the depreciation lives of certain categories of assets. This change will result in a reduction of about $58 million in depreciation expense, an increase in earnings per share of $0.22 and an increase in return on invested capital of 0.6% in the year 2000.

Exhibit P-2 contains extracts from the first-quarter 10-Q issued by PBG.

a. Compute each of the following ratios for the first quarter of 1999 and 2000, using reported data:

(i) Gross profit margin

(ii) Operating margin

b. Compute each of the following ratios for the first quarter of 1999 and 2000, after adjusting reported data for the depreciation change:

(i) Gross profit margin

(ii) Operating margin

c. Compute how much of the apparent improvement of each of these two ratios was due to the depreciation change.

d. Discuss the effect of the depreciation change on PBG's:

(i) Fixed-asset turnover ratio

(ii) Trend of reported earnings, 1999–2004

(iii) Quality of earnings

(iv) Cash from operations

The March 6 press release also contained the following statement:

> "We maintain that cash profits remain the best method of tracking our performance. However, since some investors look at us and other bottlers in terms of reported earnings, we thought it was important to reflect our depreciation expenses and reported profit more accurately," said John Cahill, Executive Vice President and Chief Financial Officer for PBG. "Even with these changes, the new policies still present our financial results conservatively."

e. Evaluate the benefits to PBG of making the depreciation change.

EXHIBIT P-2 Pepsi Bottling Group

The Pepsi Bottling Group, Inc.
Condensed Consolidated Statements of Operations
(in millions, unaudited)

	12 Weeks Ended	
	March 20, 1999	March 18, 2000
Net revenues	$1,452	$1,545
Cost of sales	(835)	(845)
Gross profit	$ 617	$ 700
Selling, delivery and administrative expenses	(575)	(625)
Operating income	$ 42	$ 75

Note 6. Comparability of Results

Asset Lives

At the beginning of fiscal year 2000, we changed the estimated useful lives of certain categories of assets to reflect the success of our preventive maintenance programs in extending the useful lives of these assets. The changes, which are detailed in the table below, lowered total depreciation cost for the quarter by $14 million ($8 million after tax and minority interest, or $0.05 per share) reducing cost of sales by $8 million and selling, delivery and administrative expenses by $6 million.

Estimated Useful Lives

	1999	2000
Manufacturing equipment	10	15
Heavy fleet	8	10
Fountain dispensing equipment	5	7
Small speciality coolers and marketing equipment	5 to 7	3

Source: Pepsi Bottling Group, 10-Q Report, March 18, 2000.

6. [Analysis of fixed assets] Roche's summary of significant accounting policies states:

> Property, plant and equipment are initially recorded at cost of purchase or construction and are depreciated on a straight-line basis, except for land, which is not depreciated. Estimated useful lives of major classes of depreciable assets are as follows:

Buildings and land improvements	40 years
Machinery and equipment	5–15 years
Office equipment	3 years
Motor vehicles	5 years

The following data were obtained from Roche's annual reports (the 1999 data are located in Note 12 of its 2000 annual report):

Property, plant, and equipment (CHF millions)

	1997	1998	1999
Buildings and land improvements:			
Gross investment	$ 7,576	$ 7,947	$ 8,578
Accumulated depreciation	(2,580)	(2,695)	(2,944)
Net investment	$ 4,996	$ 5,252	$ 5,634
Depreciation expense	233	195	210
Machinery and equipment:			
Gross investment	$10,529	$11,350	$13,174
Accumulated depreciation	(5,755)	(6,079)	(7,015)
Net investment	$ 4,774	$ 5,271	$ 6,159
Depreciation expense	692	948	1,036

a. Using the above data, compute each of the following ratios for all three years:

(i) Average depreciable life (years)

(ii) Average age (years)

(iii) Average age (%)

b. Compare the result of part a (i) with the accounting policy statement above.

c. Discuss the three-year trend of the three ratios in part a for both fixed-asset classes.

d. State the questions you would ask management after reviewing parts a through c above.

STUDY SESSION 10 FINANCIAL STATEMENT ANALYSIS: LIABILITIES

READING ASSIGNMENTS

Reading 42 Analysis of Income Taxes
Reading 43 Analysis of Financing Liabilities
Reading 44 Leases and Off-Balance-Sheet Debt

Note:
See the discussion in Study Session 8 about different names and definitions for financial ratios in the readings in the Financial Statement Analysis study sessions.

Note:
Except where noted as required reading the "Boxes" in Readings 42, 43 and 44 are not part of the Level I reading assignment.

LEARNING OUTCOMES

Reading 42: Analysis of Income Taxes

The candidate should be able to:

a. list and explain the key terms used in income tax accounting, explain why and how deferred tax liabilities and assets are created, and describe the liability method of accounting for deferred taxes;

b. discuss the implications of a valuation allowance (i.e., when it is required, what impact it has on the financial statements, and how it might affect an analyst's view of a company);

c. explain the factors that determine whether a company's deferred tax liabilities should be treated as a liability or as equity for purposes of financial analysis;

d. distinguish between temporary and permanent items in pretax financial income and taxable income;

e. compute income tax expense, income taxes payable, deferred tax assets, and deferred tax liabilities;

f. calculate the adjustment to the financial statements related to a change in the tax rate.

Reading 43: Analysis of Financing Liabilities

The candidate should be able to:

a. compute the effects of debt issuance and amortization of bond discounts and premiums on the financial statements and ratios, discuss the effect on reported cash flows of issuing zero-coupon debt; determine the appropriate classification for debt with equity features and calculate the effect of issuance of such instruments on the debt to total capital ratio;

b. discuss the effect of changing interest rates on the market value of debt and on financial statements and ratios;

Reading 44: Leases and Off-Balance-Sheet Debt

The candidate should be able to:

a. classify a lease as capital or operating and discuss the factors that determine whether a company would tend to favor leasing over outright asset purchases and more specifically, factors that would favor capital or operating leases;

b. calculate the effects of capital and operating leases on the financial statements and ratios of the lessees;

c. explain and differentiate the accounting treatment for a sale and leaseback of assets under U.S. and IASB GAAP;

d. describe the types and economic consequences of off-balance-sheet financing and determine how take-or-pay contracts, throughput arrangements, and the sale of receivables affect selected financial ratios;

e. distinguish between a sales-type lease and a direct-financing lease and describe the effects on the financial statements and ratios of sales-type and operating leases.

ANALYSIS OF INCOME TAXES

READING 42

LEARNING OUTCOMES

The candidate should be able to:

a. list and explain the key terms used in income tax accounting, explain why and how deferred tax liabilities and assets are created, and describe the liability method of accounting for deferred taxes;

b. discuss the implications of a valuation allowance (i.e., when it is required, what impact it has on the financial statements, and how it might affect an analyst's view of a company);

c. explain the factors that determine whether a company's deferred tax liabilities should be treated as a liability or as equity for purposes of f nancial analysis;

d. distinguish between temporary and permanent items in pretax financial income and taxable income;

e. compute income tax expense, income taxes payable, deferred tax assets, and deferred tax liabilities;

f. calculate the adjustment to the financial statements related to a change in the tax rate.

Note:
Deferred taxes are applicable globally with respect to consolidated financial statements and, therefore, are the focus of the Learning Outcomes for this reading.

INTRODUCTION 1

Differences in the objectives of financial and tax reporting make income taxes a troublesome issue in financial reporting. The objective of financial reporting is to provide users with information needed to evaluate a firm's financial position, performance, and cash flows. The accrual basis of financial reporting allows management to select revenue and expense recognition methods that best reflect performance and smooth or otherwise manage (maximize or minimize) reported net income. As discussed throughout the text, management incentives to manage reported income result from management compensation contracts, bond

The Analysis and Use of Financial Statements, Third Edition, by Gerald I. White, Ashwinpaul C. Sondhi, and Dov Fried,

covenants, political considerations, and the (presumed) effect of those factors on financial markets.

Tax reporting, in contrast, is the product of political and social objectives. Current-period *taxable income* is measured using the modified cash basis; revenue and expense recognition methods used in tax reporting often differ from those used for financial reporting as the firm has strong incentives to select methods allowing it to minimize taxable income and, therefore, taxes paid, maximizing cash from operations.[1]

Thus, differences between *taxes payable* for the period and reported *income tax expense* result from:

- The difference between accrual and modified cash bases of accounting
- Differences in reporting methods and estimates

These differences create *deferred tax liabilities* (credits) and prepaid taxes or *deferred tax assets* (debits) that are difficult to interpret. There are disagreements as to (1) whether they are true assets or liabilities and (2) their usefulness as indicators of future cash flows. When these deferrals become very large, their interpretation can have a significant effect on the financial analysis of a firm or group of firms.

Note: Terminology related to income tax accounting can be confusing because two terms that seem similar can have very different meanings. A glossary of terms used in this reading is therefore provided in Box 42-1. Each term in the glossary is shown in italics when first used in the reading.

2 BASIC INCOME TAX ACCOUNTING ISSUES

Basic accounting issues are discussed in Box 42-2. There we provide a discussion and an illustration of how temporary differences between tax and financial reporting affect the balance sheet and the income statement. The box also contains a review of the impact of tax law and rate changes on deferred tax assets and liabilities. This permits us to focus on analytical issues in the reading.

3 THE LIABILITY METHOD: SFAS 109 AND IAS 12

The central accounting issue is whether the tax effects of transactions for which GAAP-based and tax-based accounting rules differ should be recognized in the period(s) in which they affect taxable income (in which case no deferred taxes

[1] In countries such as Japan, Germany, and Switzerland, statutory financial reporting is required to conform to tax reporting. In these countries, the problems discussed in this reading do not occur for statutory (usually, parent company only) statements. However, consolidated financial statements, for example, those prepared under IAS GAAP, do not conform to tax reporting and deferred tax issues must be dealt with. See the discussion of financial reporting practices outside the United States later in this reading.

BOX 42-1 GLOSSARY: INCOME TAX ACCOUNTING

Amounts in Tax Return:

Taxable income	Income subject to tax.
Taxes payable	Tax return liability resulting from current period taxable income.
(current tax expense)	SFAS 109 calls this "current tax expense or benefit"
Income tax paid	Actual cash outflow for income taxes, including payments (refunds) for other years.
Tax loss carryforward	Tax return loss that can be used to reduce taxable income in future years.

Amounts in Financial Statements:

Pretax income	Income before income tax expense.
Income tax expense	Expense based on current period pre-tax income; includes taxes payable and deferred income tax expense.
Deferred income tax expense	Accrued income tax expense expected to be paid (or recovered) in future years; difference between taxes payable and income tax expense. Under SFAS 109, the amount depends on changes in deferred tax assets and liabilities.
Deferred tax asset (debit)	Balance sheet amounts; expected to be recovered from future operations.
Deferred tax liability (credit)	Balance sheet amounts; expected to result in future cash outflows.
Valuation allowance	Reserve against deferred tax assets (debits) based on likelihood that those assets will not be realized.
Timing difference	The difference between tax return and financial statement treatment (timing or amount) of a transaction.
Temporary difference	Difference between tax and financial statement reporting, which will affect taxable income when those differences reverse; similar to but broader than timing differences (see footnote 3 on page 849).

Note: SFAS 109 contains a more technical glossary of terms used in that standard.

would be recognized) or in the period(s) in which they are recognized in the financial statements (giving rise to deferred taxes). These alternatives produce different measures of operating and financial performance, affecting the evaluation of a firm's operating performance and earning power. Cash flows for taxes are not affected by financial reporting choices except when conformity between tax and financial reporting is required.

Both U.S. and IAS standards are based on the liability method, which is consistent with the second alternative.[2] This method measures the balance sheet deferred tax assets and liabilities first, under the assumption that temporary differences will reverse. Income tax expense reflects both the effect of any current period pretax income and future changes in the tax rate used to measure the tax effect of tax expense resulting from those reversals.

[2] The deferral method (also consistent with the second alternative) measures income tax expense first. Changes in deferred tax assets and liabilities result *only* from current year deferred tax expense. These assets and liabilities are based on tax rates when they originated; the effect of tax rate changes is recognized only when timing differences actually reverse.

BOX 42-2 BASIC INCOME TAX ACCOUNTING ISSUES

We use a simple example to illustrate the issues faced when tax accounting differs from accounting for financial statements. We begin this example assuming that depreciation is the only item of expense. Part A of Exhibit 42-B1 depicts income tax reporting where the company depreciates a $6,000 asset over two years, giving rise to *taxes payable* of $800, $800, and $2,000 over the three-year period.

For financial reporting (Part B of Exhibit 42-B1), the firm depreciates the asset over three years. *Pretax income* exceeds taxable income in the first two years; taxable income is higher in year 3.* What *tax expense* should the company report in its financial statements?

Part B1 of Exhibit 42-B1 displays one approach (not permitted under U.S. GAAP) where the tax expense equals taxes payable. Pretax income is the same for all three years, but tax expense differs as the tax deferred in earlier years is paid in year 3. As a result, tax expense, as a percentage of pretax income, does not reflect the prevailing statutory tax rate, 40%. The reported tax rate is 26.7% for the first two years and 66.7% for year 3.

Timing Differences: Deferred Tax Liabilities

Part B2 of Exhibit 42-B1 illustrates the U.S. GAAP treatment, SFAS 109, which requires the recognition of deferred tax liabilities when future taxable income is expected to exceed pretax income. IAS 12 has the same requirement. In our example, pretax income exceeds taxable income in years 1 and 2, but year 3 taxable income is expected to exceed pretax income by $2,000. At the end of years 1 and 2, a deferred tax liability of $400 (timing difference of $1,000 × 40% tax rate) is recognized to reflect the tax on the $1,000 *timing difference* that will be paid in year 3. This liability is reported each year as a portion of that year's tax expense. Thus, income tax expense is $1,200 in both years 1 and 2: tax payable or current tax expense ($800) plus *deferred income tax expense* ($400). The matching principle is satisfied as the relationship between revenues and expenses (40% tax rate) is maintained. At the end of year 2, the cumulative timing difference is $2,000 and the aggregate deferred tax liability is $800.

No tax depreciation remains to be recorded in year 3, but book depreciation expense equals $2,000. At the end of year 3, the machine has been fully depreciated for both tax and financial reporting purposes. The effect of the year 1 and 2 timing differences must be reversed; year 3 income tax expense equals $1,200 or taxes payable ($2,000) *less* the reversal of the deferred tax liability of $800 accumulated over the first two years.

Timing Differences: Deferred Tax Assets

Differences between financial accounting and tax accounting can also give rise to *deferred tax assets* (debits) when future pretax income is expected to exceed taxable income. Part B3 of Exhibit 42-B1 introduces another timing difference, warranty expense, which gives rise to a deferred tax asset in years 1 and 2. As warranty payments are tax-deductible when paid rather than when accrued, larger amounts are charged to warranty expense earlier for financial statement purposes; tax deductions occur in later periods when the repairs or replacement services are provided.

As shown in part B3,† the firm recognizes a warranty expense of $500 in each of years 1 and 2, but receives no tax deduction because no expenditures are incurred in those years. The higher taxable income results in a prepayment of taxes; tax expense in the financial statements reflects lower pretax income. The difference of $500 in each of the first two years generates a deferred tax debit of $200 ($500 × 0.40) each year and decreases tax expense by that amount each year. At the end of year 2, there is a deferred tax asset of $400.

In year 3, tax-deductible expenditures of $1,500 are incurred for repairs, reducing taxable income and tax payments. These expenditures exceed the $500 of financial statement warranty expense of year 3 by $1,000; equal to the total additional expense accrued in the first two years. The temporary difference reverses, deferred income tax expense is reduced by $400 ($1,000 × 0.40), and the deferred tax debit generated during the first two years is eliminated.

* Of the $3,000 pretax income reported in years 1 and 2, $1,000 (the excess tax depreciation) is not subject to taxes in those years. The $2,000 (2 × $1,000) deferred in the first two years is subject to taxation in the third as taxable income ($5,000) exceeds pretax income ($3,000) by $2,000.

† In part B3, we ignore depreciation expense to illustrate the accounting treatment of timing differences that generate deferred tax assets.

‡ In these examples, income tax expense could also have been computed by applying the income tax rate of 40% directly to pretax income in each year. However, in more complex situations, discussed later, this approach would produce a different result.

Comprehensive Example: Deferred Tax Liabilities and Deferred Tax Assets

Exhibit 42-B1 separately illustrates the treatment of timing differences that gave rise to a deferred tax liability and a deferred tax asset. In practice, firms report both deferred tax assets and liabilities, resulting from multiple timing differences. Exhibit 42-B2 shows the accounting when a firm has both types of timing differences.

Taxes payable equal the tax rate multiplied by taxable income and reflect the effects of tax depreciation and allowable warranty deductions on the tax return. Income tax expense is based on pretax income, which reflects financial statement depreciation and estimated warranty expense for products sold. Over the three-year period, total revenues are $15,000, total depreciation expense is $6,000, and total warranty expense is $1,500 for both financial and tax reporting. The timing of expense recognition differs, but the total amount is the same.[§]

EXHIBIT 42-B1 Alternative Approaches to Reported Income Tax Expense

Assumptions:

- The firm purchases a machine costing $6,000 with a three-year estimated service life and no salvage value.
- For financial reporting purposes, the firm uses straight-line depreciation over the three-year life.
- For income tax reporting, the machine is depreciated over two years using the straight-line depreciation method.
- Products manufactured using the machine generate annual revenues of $5,000 for three years.
- The statutory tax rate is 40% in all three years.

Part A. Income Tax Reporting: Straight-line Depreciation over Two Years

	Year 1	Year 2	Year 3	Total
Revenues	$5,000	$5,000	$5,000	$15,000
Depreciation expense	(3,000)	(3,000)	0	(6,000)
Taxable income	$2,000	$2,000	$5,000	$ 9,000
Taxes payable @ 40%	(800)	(800)	(2,000)	(3,600)
Net income	$1,200	$1,200	$3,000	$ 5,400

Part B. Financial Statements: Straight-line Depreciation over Three Years

B1: Flow-Through Method—Not Permitted by GAAP

- No recognition of deferred taxes.
- Tax expense defined as taxes payable.

	Year 1	Year 2	Year 3	Total
Revenues	$5,000	$5,000	$5,000	$15,000
Depreciation expense	(2,000)	(2,000)	(2,000)	(6,000)
Pretax income	$3,000	$3,000	$3,000	$ 9,000
Tax expense = taxes payable	(800)	(800)	(2,000)	(3,600)
Net income	$2,200	$2,200	$1,000	$ 5,400

§ Warranty expense and actual repair costs are assumed to be identical for illustration only; it is difficult to predict the frequency and level of repair costs perfectly. Bad debt expenses and litigation losses are other examples of timing differences where predictions are uncertain.

EXHIBIT 42-B1 (continued)

B2: SFAS 109 and IAS 12—Deferred Tax Liabilities

- Recognition of deferred taxes.
- Tax expense differs from taxes payable.

	Year 1	Year 2	Year 3	Total
Revenues	$5,000	$5,000	$5,000	$15,000
Depreciation expense	(2,000)	(2,000)	(2,000)	(6,000)
Pretax income	$3,000	$3,000	$3,000	$ 9,000
Tax expense @ 40%	(1,200)	(1,200)	(1,200)	(3,600)
Net income	$1,800	$1,800	$1,800	$ 5,400
Taxes payable (from part A)	800	800	2,000	3,600
Deferred tax expense	400	400	(800)	0
Balance sheet deferred tax liability	400	800	0	N. A.

Journal Entries

Years 1 and 2: Origination of the deferred tax liability

	Debit	Credit
Tax expense	$1,200	
Deferred tax liability		$ 400
Taxes payable		800

Year 3: Reversal of the deferred tax liability

	Debit	Credit
Tax expense	$1,200	
Deferred tax liability	800	
Taxes payable		$2,000

B3: SFAS 109 and IAS 12—Deferred Tax Assets

Assumption: Warranty expenses estimated at 10% of revenues each year; all repairs provided in year 3

Income Tax Reporting	Year 1	Year 2	Year 3	Total
Revenues	$5,000	$5,000	$5,000	$15,000
Warranty expense	0	0	(1,500)	(1,500)
Taxable income	$5,000	$5,000	$3,500	$13,500
Tax payable @ 40%	(2,000)	(2,000)	(1,400)	(5,400)
Net income	$3,000	$3,000	$2,100	$ 8,100

EXHIBIT 42-B1 (continued)

Financial Statements

Revenues	$5,000	$5,000	$5,000	$15,000
Warranty expense	(500)	(500)	(500)	(1,500)
Pretax income	$4,500	$4,500	$4,500	$13,500
Tax expense @ 40%	(1,800)	(1,800)	(1,800)	(5,400)
Net income	$2,700	$2,700	$2,700	$ 8,100
Prepaid (deferred) tax	200	200	(400)	0
Balance sheet deferred tax asset	200	400	(400)	N. A.

Journal Entries

Years 1 and 2: Origination of deferred tax assets

Tax expense	$1,800	
Deferred tax asset	200	
Taxes payable		$2,000

Year 3: Reversal of deferred tax asset

Tax expense	$1,800	
Deferred tax asset		$ 400
Taxes payable		1,400

Do the deferred tax liabilities at the end of years 1 and 2 actually represent a liability for tax payments due in year 3? Similarly, does the deferred tax asset qualify as an asset? In this simple case, they do, as the forecast reversals occurred as expected and the firm did not engage in any other transactions with timing differences. In the real world, the answer is not so clear; these are important issues from an analytical perspective and the reading provides a comprehensive discussion of those issues.

Effect of Tax Rate and Tax Law Changes

The balance sheet orientation of SFAS 109 requires adjustments to deferred tax assets and liabilities to reflect the impact of a change in tax rates or tax laws. Using the example in Exhibit 42-B2, Exhibit 42-B3 depicts the impact of a tax rate decrease from 40% to 35% at the beginning of year 2. In panel A, we assume that the future tax decrease *was enacted before* the year 1 financial statements were prepared. Panel B illustrates the accounting under the assumption that the year 2 tax decrease *was enacted after* year 1 financial statements were prepared.

Panel A: Future Tax Rate Change Enacted in Current Year.

Taxes payable for year 1 are based on the current tax rate of 40%, and the deferred tax assets and liabilities are based on the tax rate expected to be in effect when the differences reverse, 35%.

Note that year 1 tax expense as a percentage of pretax income (the effective tax rate) is 39% ($975/$2,500): a weighted average of the current tax rate of 40% and the 35% rate that will be in effect when the timing differences that gave rise to the deferred taxes reverse. There is no attempt to match income tax expense directly with pretax income, and one cannot calculate tax expense directly by multiplying pretax income by the current tax rate. For years 2 and 3, the calculations are similar to those in Exhibit 42-B2 except that the new tax rate of 35% (rather than 40%) is used for all calculations.

EXHIBIT 42-B2 Financial Reporting Under SFAS 109

Income Tax Reporting	Year 1	Year 2	Year 3	Total
Revenues	$5,000	$5,000	$5,000	$15,000
Depreciation expense	(3,000)	(3,000)	0	(6,000)
Warranty expense	0	0	(1,500)	(1,500)
Taxable income	$2,000	$2,000	$3,500	$ 7,500
Tax payable @ 40%	(800)	(800)	(1,400)	(3,000)
Net Income	$1,200	$1,200	$2,100	$ 4,500
Financial Statements				
Revenues	$5,000	$5,000	$5,000	$15,000
Depreciation expense	(2,000)	(2,000)	(2,000)	(6,000)
Warranty expense	(500)	(500)	(500)	(1,500)
Pretax income	$2,500	$2,500	$2,500	$ 7,500
Tax expense @ 40%	(1,000)	(1,000)	(1,000)	(3,000)
Net Income	$1,500	$1,500	$1,500	$ 4,500
Deferred tax expense	400	400	(800)	0
Balance sheet deferred tax liability	400	800	0	N. A.
Prepaid tax	200	200	(400)	0
Balance sheet deferred tax asset	200	400	0	N. A.

Journal Entries

Years 1 and 2: Origination of deferred tax liabilities and deferred tax assets

	Debit	Credit
Tax expense	$1,000	
Deferred tax asset	200	
Deferred tax liability		$ 400
Taxes payable		800

Year 3: Reversal of deferred tax liabilities and deferred tax assets

	Debit	Credit
Tax expense	$1,000	
Deferred tax liability	800	
Deferred tax asset		$ 400
Taxes payable		1,400

EXHIBIT 42-B3 Impact of Tax Rate Change: The Liability Method

Assumptions

Identical to Exhibit 42-B2

- A firm purchases a machine costing $6,000 with a three-year estimated service life and no salvage value.
- For financial reporting purposes, the firm uses straight-line depreciation with a three-year life.
- For income tax reporting, the machine is depreciated straight-line over two years.
- The machine is used to manufacture a product that will generate annual revenue of $5,000 for three years.
- Warranty expenses are estimated at 10% of revenues each year; all repairs are provided in year 3.

A. Year 2 Tax Rate Change Enacted in Year 1

Year 1: Tax Rate = 40%

Year 2 Tax Rate Will Be 35%

	Debit	Credit
Income tax expense	975	
Deferred tax asset	175	
Deferred tax liability		350
Taxes payable		800

Selected T-Accounts

Deferred Tax Asset (Dr)	Deferred Tax Asset (Cr)	Deferred Tax Liability (Dr)	Deferred Tax Liability (Cr)
$175			$350
$175			$350

Year 2: Tax Rate = 35%

	Debit	Credit
Income tax expense	875	
Deferred tax asset	175	
Deferred tax liability		350
Taxes payable		700

Deferred Tax Asset (Dr)	Deferred Tax Asset (Cr)	Deferred Tax Liability (Dr)	Deferred Tax Liability (Cr)
$175			$350
175			350
$350			$700

Year 3: Tax Rate = 35%

	Debit	Credit
Income tax expense	875	
Deferred tax liability	700	
Deferred tax asset		350
Taxes payable		1,225

Deferred Tax Asset (Dr)	Deferred Tax Asset (Cr)	Deferred Tax Liability (Dr)	Deferred Tax Liability (Cr)
$350			$700
		700	
	350		
$ 0			$ 0

Calculations

	Temporary Differences: Depreciation (Liability)	Temporary Differences: Warranty (Asset)	Taxes Payable	Income Tax Expense
Year 1	35% × $1,000	35% × $(500)	40% × $2,000	$350 − $175 + $ 800
Year 2	35% × 1,000	35% × (500)	35% × 2,000	350 − 175 + 700
Year 3	35% × (2,000)	35% × 1,000	35% × 3,500	− 700 + 350 + 1,225

EXHIBIT 42-B3 (continued)

B. Year 2 Tax Rate Change Enacted in Year 2

Year 1: Tax Rate = 40%

Selected T-Accounts

Journal entry	Dr	Cr	Deferred Tax Asset (Dr)	Deferred Tax Asset (Cr)	Deferred Tax Liability (Dr)	Deferred Tax Liability (Cr)
Income tax expense	1,000					
Deferred tax asset	200					
Deferred tax liability		400	$200			$400
Taxes payable		800	$200			$400

Year 2: Tax Rate Reduced to 35%

(i) *Adjustment of Prior-Year Deferrals*

Journal entry	Dr	Cr	Deferred Tax Asset (Dr)	Deferred Tax Asset (Cr)	Deferred Tax Liability (Dr)	Deferred Tax Liability (Cr)
Deferred tax liability	50		$200			$400
Deferred tax asset		25		25	50	
Income tax expense		25	$175			$350

(ii) *Current Year Operations*

Journal entry	Dr	Cr	Deferred Tax Asset (Dr)	Deferred Tax Asset (Cr)	Deferred Tax Liability (Dr)	Deferred Tax Liability (Cr)
Income tax expense	875		$175			$350
Deferred tax asset	175		175			
Deferred tax liability		350				350
Taxes payable		700	$350			$700

Year 3: Tax Rate = 35%

Journal entry	Dr	Cr	Deferred Tax Asset (Dr)	Deferred Tax Asset (Cr)	Deferred Tax Liability (Dr)	Deferred Tax Liability (Cr)
Income tax expense	875		$350			$700
Deferred tax liability	700				700	
Deferred tax asset		350		350		
Taxes payable		1,225	$ 0			$ 0

Calculations

	Temporary Differences			
	Depreciation (Liability)	Warranty (Asset)	Taxes Payable	Income Tax Expense
Year 1	40% × $1,000	40% × $(500)	40% × $2,000	$400 − $200 + $ 800
Year 2	(5%) × 1,000	(5%) × (500)		−50 + 25
	35% × 1,000	35% × (500)	35% × 2,000	350 − 175 + 700
Year 3	35% × (2,000)	35% × 1,000	35% × 3,500	−700 + 350 + 1,225

Panel B: Future Tax Rate Change Enacted after Year 1 Statements Have Been Prepared.

Calculations for year 1 tax expense, taxes payable, and deferred taxes are based on the year 1 tax rate of 40% and are identical to those in Exhibit 42-B2. A deferred tax asset of $200 and a deferred tax liability of $400 are created.

In year 2, when the rate decrease is effective, two steps are necessary to calculate the current year's tax expense:

1. Exhibit 42-B3 illustrates the restatement of end of year 1 deferred tax asset and liability balances to the new (lower) tax rate of 35% (assumed to be in effect when the deferred taxes will be paid). Year 2 tax expense is reduced (income is increased) since the lower rate reduces the expected tax payment when the depreciation difference reverses, partially offset by a lower expected tax benefit when the warranty expense difference reverses. The adjustment results in a deferred tax asset of $175 and liability of $350.**
2. The taxes payable and deferred taxes arising from current year operations are calculated using the new rate of 35%.

Tax expense for year 2 is calculated as follows:

Adjustment of Year 1 Balances to New Rate:	
Deferred tax asset of $200 restated to $175	$ 25
Deferred tax liability of $400 restated to $350	(50)
Year 2 Taxes Payable and New Temporary Differences:	
Taxes payable = $2,000 taxable income × 35%	700
Deferred tax asset = $500 temporary difference × 35%	(175)
Deferred tax liability = $1,000 temporary difference × 35%	350
Income tax expense	$850

Note that, as in panel A, the income tax expense of $850 is affected by changes in the deferred tax liability and asset accounts and there is no attempt to directly match the relationship of tax expense to pretax income.

** These balances are now identical to those shown in panel A of the exhibit when the tax law change was known prior to the issuance of the year 1 financial statements. The only difference between the two panels is the timing of the restatement at the lower rate.

Accounting for taxes in the United States is based on SFAS 109 (1992), whose two objectives are to recognize:

1. Taxes payable or refundable for the current year
2. The deferred tax liabilities and assets (adjusted for recoverability) measured as the future tax consequences of events that have been recognized in financial statements or tax returns

SFAS 109 recognizes the deferred tax consequences of *temporary differences.*[3] Deferred tax assets (adjusted for recoverability) and liabilities are calculated directly and reported on the balance sheet; *deferred income tax expense* used to determine reported income is a consequence of the resulting balance sheet amounts.

IAS 12 (2000) is also based on the liability method, with minor differences. Those differences are explained in the "Financial Reporting Outside the United States" section of this reading.

[3] This concept extends beyond chronological (timing) differences (e.g., earlier recognition of revenues and expenses on either the financial statements or tax returns), and also includes certain other events that result in differences between the tax bases of assets and liabilities and their carrying amounts in financial statements. Such differences arise when

1. The tax basis of an asset is reduced by tax credits.
2. Investment tax credits are deferred and amortized.
3. The tax basis of a foreign subsidiary's assets is increased as a result of indexing.
4. The carrying amounts and tax bases of assets differ in purchase method acquisitions.

Deferred Tax Liabilities

SFAS 109 emphasizes tax liabilities, focusing on the balance sheet. *The standard mandates the recognition of deferred tax liabilities for all temporary differences expected to generate net taxable amounts in future years.*

The FASB argued that deferred tax consequences of temporary differences that will result in net taxable amounts in future years meet the SFAC 6 definition of liabilities.[4] The board contended that deferred taxes are legal obligations imposed by tax laws and temporary differences will affect taxable income in future years as they reverse.

Treatment of Operating Losses

Operating losses are due to an excess of tax deductions over taxable revenues. Tax losses can be carried back to prior years to obtain refunds of taxes paid; the impact of the carryback on income tax expense is recognized in the loss period because it can be measured and is recoverable.

Tax losses may also be carried forward to future periods if insufficient taxes were paid during the carryback period or the firm would lose valuable tax credits if losses were carried back to that period. Because the realization of *tax loss carryforwards* depends on future taxable income, the expected benefits are recognized as deferred tax assets. Under SFAS 109, such assets are recognized in full but a *valuation allowance* may be required if recoverability is unlikely.

Deferred Tax Assets and the Valuation Allowance

SFAS 109 is permissive regarding the recognition of deferred tax assets whenever deductible temporary differences generate an operating loss or tax credit carryforward. However, management (and its auditors) must defend recognition of all deferred tax assets. A valuation allowance reducing the deferred tax asset is required if an analysis of the sources of future taxable income suggests that it is more likely than not that some portion or all of the deferred tax asset will not be realized.[5]

Example

Bethlehem Steel [BS] reported a net deferred tax asset at December 31, 2000 of about $985 million ($1,325 million less a valuation allowance of $340 million). This asset equaled 88% of stockholders' equity on that date. The company provided a valuation allowance equal to 50% of the deferred tax asset related to operating loss carryforwards and some temporary differences. BS stated,

---

[4] A common temporary difference is a firm's use of longer depreciation lives for financial reporting than for tax return reporting, creating a difference between the carrying amount of the asset and its tax basis. Use of the asset in operations results in taxable income in the year(s) no depreciation can be recorded on the tax return. The board acknowledged that other events may offset the net taxable amounts that would be generated when temporary differences reverse, but because those events have not yet occurred, and they are not assumed in the financial statements, their tax consequences should not be recognized. See SFAS 109 (paras. 75–79) for more discussion of this issue.

[5] Sources of future taxable income include existing taxable temporary differences, future taxable income net of reversing temporary differences, taxable income recognized during qualifying carryback periods, and applicable tax-planning strategies.

> Based on our current outlook for 2001 and beyond, we believe that our net deferred tax asset will be realized by future operating results, asset sales, and tax planning opportunities.[6]

In the quarter ended June 30, 2001, however, BS recognized a 100% valuation allowance for its deferred tax assets, increasing income tax expense and net loss for the quarter by $1,009 million ($7.77 per diluted share) and for the first half of 2001 by $984 million ($7.58 per diluted share). Mainly due to the increased valuation allowance, Bethlehem's equity at June 30, 2001 became negative. The company stated that it now expected a financial accounting and tax loss in 2001 and that the outlook for the balance of 2001 was worse than earlier anticipated. Given its record of cumulative financial accounting losses, excluding unusual items, SFAS 109 required the increased valuation allowance. This is an excellent example of how management discretion with respect to the amount and timing of recognition of the valuation allowance affords management significant opportunity to manage earnings.

Tax-planning strategies can be used to reduce required valuation allowances, but they must be disclosed. SFAS 109 provides examples of positive and negative evidence that must be weighed to determine the need for a valuation allowance and to measure the amount of the allowance.[7] *Changes in the valuation allowance are included in income from continuing operations except when they are generated by unrecognized changes in the carrying amount of assets or liabilities.*[8]

Bethlehem reported that it expected to realize the deferred tax assets from future operating results and tax planning opportunities. The company included choices of depreciation methods and lives, sales of assets, and the timing of contributions to the pension trust fund as examples of tax-planning opportunities.

When there are significant deferred tax assets, the analyst should review the company's financial performance and its accounting choices to assess the likelihood of realization of those assets.

Financial Statement Presentation and Disclosure Requirements

Large multinational companies operate in dozens of tax jurisdictions and their financial reports must summarize their tax position for all consolidated entities. Such firms often generate deferred tax assets and liabilities in different tax jurisdictions. *SFAS 109 permits offsets of deferred tax effects only within each tax-paying component and tax jurisdiction of the firm.*

---

[6] *Source:* Note D to 2000 financial statements.

[7] Existing contracts or backlogs expected to be profitable, appreciated assets, earnings over the past few years, and the nature (nonrecurring) of the loss would suggest that a valuation allowance is not needed. Examples of negative evidence include cumulative losses in recent years and the past inability to use loss or tax credit carryforwards.

[8] The most common example is the deferred tax assets that arise when the market value of "available-for-sale" securities is less than cost; the unrealized loss is included in equity, under SFAS 115, net of the related deferred income tax assets.

Example

Texaco reported (Note 8) a valuation allowance of $800 million at December 31, 1999, mostly related to foreign tax loss carryforwards and related book versus tax asset differences stemming from operations in Denmark. The company notes that the valuation allowance was required because these loss carryforwards are based on individual (oil and gas) fields and cannot be netted against taxable income from other fields.

Deferred tax assets and liabilities must be separated into current and noncurrent components based on the types of the assets and liabilities generating the deferral. However, deferred tax assets due to carryforwards are classified by reference to expected reversal dates. SFAS 109 specifically requires:

1. Separate disclosure of all deferred tax assets and liabilities, any valuation allowance, and the net change in that allowance for each reporting period.
2. Disclosure of any unrecognized deferred tax liability for the undistributed earnings of domestic or foreign subsidiaries and joint ventures. These disclosures should facilitate the comparison of the operating results of firms that have different policies with respect to deferred tax recognition or the remission of income from such affiliates.
3. Disclosure of the current-year tax effect of each type of temporary difference.
4. Disclosure of the components of income tax expense.
5. Reconciliation of reported income tax expense with the amount based on the statutory income tax rate (the reconciliation can use either amounts or percentages of pre-tax income).
6. Disclosure of tax loss carryforwards and credits.

These six requirements determine income tax disclosures in financial statements, the raw material for the analysis provided later in this reading.

4 DEFERRED TAXES: ANALYTICAL ISSUES

Estimates of the firm's future cash flows and earning power and the analysis of financial leverage must consider changes in deferred tax assets and liabilities, deferred tax expense, and any changes in the valuation allowance. *The key analytic issue is whether the deferred tax assets and liabilities will reverse in the future. If they will not, then it is highly debatable whether deferred taxes are assets or liabilities (that is, have cash flow consequences); it may be more appropriate to consider them as decreases or increases to equity.*

To resolve that issue, we need to understand the factors that determine the level of and trends in reported deferred taxes, to decide whether they are assets (or liabilities) and to evaluate their expected cash consequences.

Factors Influencing the Level and Trend of Deferred Taxes

In general, temporary differences originated by individual transactions will reverse and offset future taxable income and tax payments. However, *these reversals may be offset by other transactions, for example, newly originating temporary differ-*

ences. The cash consequences of deferred tax debits and credits depend on the following factors:

- Future tax rates and tax laws
- Changes in accounting methods
- The firm's growth rate (real or nominal)
- Nonrecurring items and equity adjustments

We discuss these factors next.

Effects of Changes in Tax Laws and Accounting Methods

Management incentives for choosing revenue and expense recognition methods on the tax return and financial statements differ, as mentioned previously. Choices (and subsequent changes) of tax and/or accounting methods determine taxes payable, income tax expense, and both the amounts and rate of change of reported deferred tax balances.

Under the liability method,[9] when a new tax law is enacted its effects must be recognized immediately. Thus, lower tax rates will reduce deferred tax liabilities and assets, and the adjustment is included in current-period income tax expense. Assuming a net deferred tax liability, equity will increase. The larger the net deferred tax liability, the greater the impact of the tax cut, as previous-year deferrals are adjusted to the lower rate. For analytical purposes, one need not wait for the actual tax change to be enacted; estimates can be made when legislation is proposed.

Changes in GAAP can also significantly impact deferred taxes. For example, in 1992, many companies adopted SFAS 106, Accounting for Postretirement Benefits Other Than Pensions. That standard required accrual accounting for postretirement costs (mainly medical benefits for current employees after retirement) rather than cash-basis accounting. As cash-basis accounting was used for income tax purposes, there was no temporary difference associated with these benefits prior to the adoption of SFAS 106.

Example

Upon adoption of SFAS 106 in 1992, DuPont recognized a postretirement benefit liability of $5.9 billion and deferred tax asset of $2.1 billion. Was this $2.1 billion an asset? Would it reduce future taxes? The answers depend on the $5.9 billion liability associated with it. Eight years later, at December 31, 2000, DuPont's postretirement benefit liability was $5.76 billion. Benefits paid exceeded cost recognized in both 1999 and 2000, reducing the liability. Assuming this trend continues, DuPont will realize the deferred tax asset, but over a very long time period. A fair-value balance sheet should recognize the discounted present value of the deferred tax asset rather than its gross amount.

Thus, *realization of a deferred tax asset or liability depends on the realization of the temporary difference that created it.*

---

9 See the illustration in Exhibit 42-B3 of Box 42-2.

Effect of the Growth Rate of the Firm

For most firms, the deferred tax liability grows over time; temporary differences do not reverse on balance.[10] For growing firms, increased or higher-cost investments in fixed assets result in ever-increasing deferred tax liabilities due to the use of accelerated depreciation methods for tax reporting.

Exhibit 42-1 illustrates this effect by focusing on the deferred tax consequences of depreciation differences. Assume that a firm purchases one machine each year for $6,000 and uses the straight-line depreciation method over two

EXHIBIT 42-1 Impact of Growth on Deferred Tax Liability

Assumptions

A firm purchases one machine during each year of operation. All other assumptions are identical to those used in Exhibit 42-B1. Most important, temporary differences are originated and reversed as in Exhibit 42-B1 and at the same tax rate, which is assumed to remain constant over time.

	Deferred Tax Liability	
Year 1	$ 400	Machine 1 (origination)
Year 2	400	Beginning balance
	400	Machine 1 (origination)
	400	Machine 2 (origination)
Year 3	$1,200	Beginning balance
	(800)	Machine 1 (reversal)
	400	Machine 2 (origination)
	400	Machine 3 (origination)
Year 4	$1,200	Beginning balance
	(800)	Machine 2 (reversal)
	400	Machine 3 (origination)
	400	Machine 4 (origination)
Year 5	$1,200	Beginning balance

Note: The balance stabilizes at $1,200 in this example at the end of year 3, with the originations exactly offset by the reversals. This result assumes constant levels of asset acquisitions, price levels, tax rates, and regulations. Increases in either price levels or acquisitions would result in rising balances of deferred tax liabilities.

[10] This statement may not apply to deferred tax assets. Deferred tax assets (more precisely, prepaid taxes) stem from both recurring transactions (such as deferred revenues, warranty expenses, management compensation, employee benefits, and bad-debt reserves), and from more irregular events (such as restructuring costs, impairments, environmental remediation obligations, and provisions for litigation losses) that are accrued on the financial statements prior to their deduction on the tax return.

Management often has substantial discretion over the amount and timing of the origination of these debit balances as it controls the recognition of these expenses. However, the amount and timing of their reversal may not be as discretionary or predictable as the temporary differences (such as depreciation differences) that generate deferred tax liabilities.

years on its tax return and over three years in its financial statements. If we assume a 40% tax rate and zero residual value on both the tax return and the financial statements, the depreciation differences will produce a deferred tax expense (a deferred tax liability) of $400 in each year during the first two years of each machine's operation, with a reversal of $800 in its third year to eliminate the deferred tax liability generated over the first two years.

The acquisition of a second machine in year 2 generates another difference of $400; the deferred tax liability increases to $1,200 at the end of year 2. In year 3, the firm acquires and uses the third machine, originating its first-year temporary difference, and the asset acquired in year 2 originates its second-year difference. However, these originating differences are offset by the reversal of the accumulated temporary differences on the machine acquired in year 1 as it is depreciated in the financial statements, but no depreciation remains to be recorded for the asset on the tax return.

The deferred tax liability remains $1,200 and *stabilizes at that level* if asset acquisitions, depreciation methods, and tax rates and tax laws remain unchanged. Increased asset purchases above present levels (either in physical quantity or due to higher prices) would result in a growing deferred tax liability as originations exceeded reversals. Thus, as a result of growth, either in real or nominal terms, the net deferred tax liability will increase over time; *in effect, it will never be paid.*

If the firm reduces its acquisition of fixed assets and reversals exceed originations, the related deferred tax liability will decline. The cash consequences of this scenario, however, are uncertain. If the decrease in asset acquisitions results from declining product demand, then lower asset acquisitions may be accompanied by poor profitability. Without taxable income, the deferred taxes will never be paid. Alternatively, the firm may originate other temporary differences that offset depreciation reversals; in the aggregate, deferred tax liabilities may not decline.

The cash consequences of reversing temporary differences, therefore, depend on both future profitability and other activities of the firm that affect future taxable income.

Effects of Nonrecurring Items and Equity Adjustments

The following may also affect income tax expense, taxes paid, and deferred tax assets and liabilities:

- Nonrecurring items
- Extraordinary items
- Accounting changes
- Equity adjustments

Nonrecurring items (such as restructuring charges) may have future as well as current-period tax consequences, and complicate the analysis of the firm's tax position. Texaco, for example, reported restructuring changes in 1999, as detailed throughout its MD&A. These charges generated deferred tax assets.

Extraordinary items, such as a loss from the early retirement of debt, are reported after tax; the tax effect is often shown separately in the tax footnote. Transition effects of accounting changes often generate deferred tax effects, especially when the new method is not a permitted method of tax reporting. The large deferred tax asset resulting from the adoption of SFAS 106 (as discussed using DuPont) is a typical example.

Finally, equity adjustments that bypass the income statement may have current and deferred tax consequences. Common examples include:

- Unrealized gains or losses on marketable securities
- Currency translation adjustments

The items discussed previously may obscure the cash and deferred tax effects of continuing operations. Although firms generally disclose their associated tax effect, discerning their cash and deferred tax impact may require careful reading of the tax footnote supplemented by discussions with management.

Liability or Equity?

How should analysts treat deferred tax liabilities in the analysis of a firm's solvency?

As indicated previously, changes in a firm's operations or tax laws may result in deferred taxes that are never paid (or recovered). Moreover, a firm's growth may continually generate deferred tax liabilities. Even if temporary differences do reverse, future losses may forestall tax payments. These factors suggest that, in many cases, deferred taxes are unlikely to be paid.

Even if deferred taxes are eventually paid, the present value of those payments is considerably lower than the stated amounts. Thus, the deferred tax liability should be discounted at an appropriate interest rate.[11]

These arguments suggest that the components of the deferred tax liability should be analyzed to evaluate the likelihood of reversal or continued growth. Only those components that are likely to reverse should be considered a liability.[12] In addition, the liability should be discounted to its present value based on an estimate of the year(s) of reversal. If the temporary differences giving rise to deferred tax liabilities are not expected to reverse, those amounts should not be considered liabilities.

SFAS 109 requires disclosure of the components of the deferred tax liability at each year-end. These components should be examined over time to see which tend to reverse and which do not. For example, the effect of using accelerated depreciation methods for tax reporting tends not to reverse.[13] If reversal is expected, as capital expenditures decline, the liability should be discounted to present value. Similar analysis can be applied to other major differences, keeping in mind any expected tax law changes.

To the extent that deferred taxes are not a liability, then they are stockholders' equity. Had they not been recorded, prior-period tax expense would have been lower

---

[11] Discounting of deferred taxes is not allowed under either U.S. or IAS GAAP and is rare elsewhere. It is currently allowed in the Netherlands; however, few firms discount. The UK accounting standard FRS 19, Deferred Tax, permits but does not require discounting of deferred tax liabilities (only for the time value of money) that are not expected to settle for some time.

[12] Prior to the issuance of FRS 19, Deferred Tax, the United Kingdom allowed partial allocation and deferred taxes were recognized only when reversal was expected within the foreseeable future.

[13] However, the recognition of fixed asset impairment (see the discussion in Reading 41) may instantaneously offset many years of accelerated depreciation. Such writedowns do not affect tax reporting unless the affected assets are sold. As a result, previously established deferred tax liabilities relating to these assets reverse. If the carrying value of the impaired assets is reduced below their tax basis, deferred tax assets must be established. But this reversal has no effect on taxable income or, therefore, taxes payable. This is another case where the reversal of temporary differences may not generate income tax cash outflows.

and both net income and equity higher. This adjustment reduces the debt-to-equity ratio, in some cases considerably.[14]

In some cases, however, deferred taxes are neither liability nor equity. For example, if tax depreciation is a better measure of economic depreciation than financial statement depreciation, adding the deferred tax liability to equity overstates the value of the firm. However, if the deferred tax liability is unlikely to result in a cash outflow, it is not a liability either. Ultimately, the financial analyst must decide on the appropriate treatment of deferred taxes on a case-by-case basis.

In practice, the analytical treatment of deferred tax liabilities varies. Some creditors, notably banks, do not consider them to be liabilities (but neither do they include them as part of equity). In calculating solvency and other ratios, many analysts ignore deferred taxes altogether.

Standard and Poor's, a major U.S. rating agency, includes noncurrent deferred taxes in permanent capital for its computation of pretax return on permanent capital. However, it does not consider deferred tax liabilities as debt.[15].

Box 42-3 discusses evidence provided by market research regarding the relevance of deferred taxes to securities valuation. The evidence indicates that the market incorporates the growth rate of an entity, the probability of reversal of deferred taxes, and the time value of money in its assessment of deferred taxes as liability or equity.

Analysis of Deferred Tax Assets and the Valuation Allowance

Deferred tax assets may be indicators of future cash flow, reported income, or both. Therefore, as with liabilities, one should examine the source of those assets and evaluate the likelihood and timing of reversal. Any valuation allowance should also be reviewed. To the extent that deferred tax assets have been offset by a valuation allowance, realization of those assets will increase reported income (and stockholders' equity) as well as generate cash flow. If no valuation allowance has been provided, then realization will have no effect on reported income or equity, although cash flow will still benefit.

Conversely, when deferred tax assets are no longer realizable, if no valuation allowance had been provided, then the establishment of such an allowance reduces reported income and equity (see the Bethlehem Steel example earlier in the reading).

Given management discretion, the valuation allowance has become another factor used to evaluate the quality of earnings. Some firms are conservative, offsetting most or all deferred tax assets with valuation allowances. Other firms are more optimistic and assume that no valuation allowance is necessary.

The important point is that changes in the valuation allowance often affect reported earnings and can be used to manage them.

---

[14] Some creditors treat deferred tax liabilities as debt. In this case, there is a double effect; debt is decreased and equity increased by the same amount, with an even greater decrease in the debt-to-equity ratio.

[15] See Standard and Poor's "Formulas for Key Ratios," *Corporate Ratings Criteria* (New York: McGraw-Hill, 2000), p. 55.

BOX 42-3 VALUATION OF DEFERRED TAXES

OPTIONAL SEGMENT

Surprisingly, not many empirical studies have examined whether the market as a whole treats deferred taxes as debt. However, the results of those few studies that examined this issue are consistent with our view that the extent to which deferred tax liabilities should be treated as debt is a function of the probability that the deferrals will be reversed and the debt (if considered) should be discounted to its present value.

Amir, Kirschenheiter, and Willard (1997) found that, overall, deferred taxes are value relevant in explaining the cross-sectional variation in market values of equity. However, the degree of value relevance was related to the probability of future reversal. For example, the valuation coefficient on deferred tax liabilities arising from depreciation was close to zero, reflecting investors' expectations that firms would continue to invest in depreciable assets, increasing the likelihood that tax deferrals would not reverse in the future. On the other hand, deferred tax components related to restructurings had the highest valuation coefficients, consistent with an expectation that they would reverse in the short run (as written-down plants are sold at a loss and/or severance payments are made to employees).

Givoly and Hayn (1992) examined these issues in the context of the Tax Reform Act (TRA) of 1986. The TRA cut the statutory tax rate for U.S. corporations from 46% to 34%. This rate reduction reduced both the current tax obligation and the amount that would have to be repaid if and when future reversals of temporary differences occurred.

The TRA was debated for over two years in Congress. Givoly and Hayn examined the effects on stock prices of events that increased (decreased) the chance of the measure passing. After controlling for the effects on current tax payments, they argued that if the market treated the deferred tax liability as debt, then:

1. The larger the deferred tax liability, the more positive the impact of the TRA on the firm's market price.
2. If temporary differences will not be reversed, or future tax losses will result in nonpayment of the tax at reversal, the effects of the TRA should be minimal regardless of the liability amount. Thus, they argued that the larger the growth rate in the deferred tax account and the greater the probability of tax losses; the less likely there would be a positive impact on stock prices.

OPTIONAL SEGMENT ENDS

If the market ignored the deferred tax liability, none of these factors would have any impact. Overall, their results confirmed that the market incorporated the deferred tax liability into valuation.

When chances of the TRA adoption increased (decreased), then:

1. The larger the deferred tax liability, the more positive (negative) the market reaction.
2. A high liability growth rate and increased probability of losses decreased (increased) the abnormal return.

Givoly and Hayn also found that the market incorporated a discount factor in valuing the deferred tax liability. The deferred tax accounts of high-risk* firms tended to affect market valuation less than low-risk firms. This result is consistent with a higher discount rate being applied to the higher-risk firms.

Sansing (1998), and Guenther and Sansing (2000), however, using a theoretical model, demonstrate analytically that deferred taxes should have value-relevance† *irrespective of the probability of eventual reversal*. However, the valuation coefficient on deferred taxes (which in their model is a function of the tax depreciation rate and the (market) rate of interest) is *considerably less than one*. Thus, they argue that the findings of Amir et al. and Givoly and Hayn should not be interpreted as reflecting the effects of the expected timing of the reversal of deferred taxes.

The above studies took a balance sheet perspective and found that deferred taxes are incorporated in valuation. Beaver and Dukes (1972), with an income statement perspective, had also found that market prices reflect the deferral method. They found that market reaction was more closely associated with income that incorporated deferred income taxes than with current tax expense.‡ Rayburn (1986), however, found that the association between deferred tax accruals and security returns was dependent on the expectations model assumed.

---

* Based on the firm's market beta.

† Their reasoning is that, according to their model, the market (resale) value of the asset includes the tax basis of the asset. Deferred taxes reflect this factor, although not on a dollar-for-dollar basis.

‡ The authors found this result surprising as they expected the measure closer to cash flow (earnings without deferral) to be more closely associated with security prices. In a subsequent paper (Beaver and Dukes, 1973) the authors offered a different explanation. They demonstrated (see the discussion in Reading 41) that the market generally imputes accelerated depreciation rather than straight-line depreciation. As deferred taxes increase total expense for firms using straight-line depreciation, they argued that the observed results may be due to deferred taxes masking as a form of accelerated depreciation.

Example

Apple Computer had recorded a significant valuation allowance against its deferred tax assets due to losses in the mid-1990s. With its return to profitability, it realized its loss carryforwards, reducing both deferred tax assets and the valuation allowance. The result was to lower the effective tax rate, as seen below:

	Years Ended September 30			Percent Change	
Amounts in $millions	**1998**	**1999**	**2000**	**1999**	**2000**
As reported:					
Pretax income	$329	$ 676	$1,092	105%	62%
Income tax expense	(20)	(75)	(306)		
Net income	$309	$ 601	$ 786	94%	31%
Tax rate	6.1%	11.1%	28.0%		
Change in valuation allowance	$(97)	$(153)	$ (27)		
Excluding valuation allowance:					
Pretax income	$329	$ 676	$1,092	105%	62%
Income tax expense	(117)	(228)	(333)		
Net income	$212	$ 448	$ 759	111%	69%
Tax rate	35.6%	33.7%	30.5%		

Apple's pretax income increased by 105% in 1999 and 62% in 2000. The growth rate of net income was lower due to the diminishing effect of the valuation allowance. However, net income was inflated by the valuation allowance reductions. To eliminate these distortions, analysis should be based on net income excluding changes in the valuation allowance.

Effective Tax Rates

Valuation models that forecast future income or cash flows use the firm's effective tax rate as one input. Moreover, trends in effective tax rates over time for a firm and the relative effective tax rates for comparable firms within an industry can help assess operating performance and the income available for stockholders. Several alternative measures can be used to assess the firm's effective tax rate. The *reported* effective tax rate is measured as:

$$\frac{\text{Income tax expense}}{\text{Pretax income}}$$

However, both reported tax expense and pretax income are affected by management choices of revenue and expense recognition methods. Although pretax income is a key indicator of financial performance and is an appropriate denominator, other numerators generate tax rates that provide additional information.[16]

The first alternative tax rate uses taxes payable (current tax expense) for the period, based on the revenue and the expense recognition methods used on the tax return:

$$\frac{\text{Taxes payable}}{\text{Pretax income}}$$

This ratio may also be used with cash taxes paid instead of taxes payable. The resulting ratio focuses more on cash flows:

$$\frac{\text{Income tax paid}}{\text{Pretax income}}$$

The amount of cash taxes paid can be easily obtained as both SFAS 95 (Statement of Cash Flows) and IAS 7 (Cash Flow Statements) require separate disclosure of this amount. Due to interim tax payments and refunds, cash taxes paid may be quite different from taxes payable.

Exhibit 42-2 calculates these differing measures of the effective tax rate for Pfizer.

Pfizer's reported effective tax rate (income tax expense/pretax income) rose from 27.0% in 1997 to 28% in 1999; the three-year average rate is 26.9%. All these rates are below the U.S. statutory rate for the period.[17]

EXHIBIT 42-2 Pfizer

Effective Tax Rates

	1997	1998	1999	Total
Taxes payable	$ 815	$ 918	$1,265	$2,998
Deferred tax expense	(40)	(276)	(21)	(337)
Income tax expense	$ 775	$ 642	$1,244	$2,661
Income taxes paid	809	1,073	1,293	3,175
Pretax income	2,867	2,594	4,448	9,909
Statutory tax rate	35.0%	35.0%	35.0%	35.0%
Income tax expense/pretax income	27.0%	24.7%	28.0%	26.9%
Taxes payable/pretax income	28.4%	35.4%	28.4%	30.3%
Taxes paid/pretax income	28.2%	41.4%	29.1%	32.0%

Source: Data from Pfizer annual reports.

[16] Some empirical evidence (see Zimmerman, 1983) indicates that effective tax rates calculated using income tax paid and/or current tax expense tend to be higher for large firms. This is cited as evidence of the political cost hypothesis as large firms, being more politically sensitive, are required to make (relatively) larger wealth transfers than smaller firms. As the research results are largely due to the oil and gas industry, it is difficult to tell whether political costs result from size or industrial classification. Wang (1991) notes that because smaller firms are more likely to have operating losses than larger firms, their effective tax rate is more likely to be zero. Ignoring these losses may bias Zimmerman's research results.

[17] The average statutory rate for a multiyear period should be a weighted average, with pretax income providing the weights.

Two questions are suggested by these data:

1. Why is Pfizer's effective tax rate below the statutory rate?
2. What is Pfizer's effective tax rate likely to be in the future?

We seek answers to these questions shortly.

The second effective tax rate (taxes payable/pretax income) calculated in Exhibit 42-2 was 35.4% in 1998 and 28.4% in both 1997 and 1999. The average rate is 30.3% over the three-year period, above the first effective rate and below the statutory rate. Again, we will try to understand the factors causing these differences and the likelihood that they will persist in the future.

The third measure of the effective tax rate, which compares income tax paid with pretax income, is also variable over the three-year period. The average rate of 32.0% is close to the average rate for taxes payable. This congruence should be expected as the timing of taxes paid is affected by technical payment requirements and by errors in management's forecast of tax liability in each jurisdiction. Over time, these factors should cancel out.

We return to the analysis of Pfizer's income tax position shortly. To provide additional background for that analysis, we must first discuss the effect of temporary versus permanent differences on effective tax rates and other specialized issues that highlight differences between tax and financial reporting.

ACCOUNTING FOR TAXES: SPECIALIZED ISSUES 5

Temporary versus Permanent Differences

The different objectives of financial and tax reporting generate temporary differences between pretax financial income and taxable income. In addition, *permanent differences* result from revenues and expenses that are reportable either on tax returns or in financial statements but not both. In the United States, for example, interest income on tax-exempt bonds, premiums paid on officers' life insurance, and amortization of goodwill (in some cases) are included in financial statements but are never reported on the tax return. Similarly, certain dividends are not fully taxed, and tax or statutory depletion may exceed cost-based depletion reported in the financial statements.

Tax credits are another type of permanent difference. Such credits directly reduce taxes payable and are different from tax deductions that reduce taxable income. The Puerto Rico operations credit reported by Pfizer is one example. It partially exempts Pfizer from income, property, and municipal taxes.

No deferred tax consequences are recognized for permanent differences; however, they result in a difference between the effective tax rate and the statutory tax rate that should be considered in the analysis of effective tax rates.

Indefinite Reversals

The amount and timing of the reversal of some temporary differences are subject to management influence or control. Some differences may never reverse. The accounting for these differences is especially troublesome. The uncertainty as to the amount and timing of their cash consequences affects the estimation of cash flows and firm valuation.

The undistributed earnings of unconsolidated subsidiaries and joint ventures are the most common example of this problem. The U.S. tax code requires 80% ownership to consolidate for tax purposes, excluding joint ventures and many subsidiaries that are consolidated for accounting purposes. In addition, foreign subsidiaries are not consolidated in the U.S. tax return.[18]

As a result, the income of these affiliates is taxable on the parent's (U.S.) tax return only when dividends are received or the affiliate is sold, not when earnings are recognized. There is a difference between (tax return) taxable income and (financial reporting) pretax income. If the affiliate earnings are permanently reinvested, then affiliate earnings may never be taxable on the parent company's tax return.

SFAS 109 requires the recognition of deferred tax liabilities for temporary differences due to the undistributed earnings of essentially permanent domestic subsidiaries and joint ventures for fiscal years beginning on or after December 15, 1992.[19] SFAS 109 does not, however, require deferred tax provisions in the following cases:

- Undistributed earnings of a foreign subsidiary or joint venture that are considered to be permanently reinvested.
- Undistributed earnings of a domestic subsidiary or joint venture for fiscal years prior to December 15, 1992.

In its income tax note (Note 9), Pfizer reports that the firm has not recorded a U.S. tax provision of $1.9 billion on $8.2 billion of undistributed earnings of foreign affiliates at December 31, 1999. If the indefinite reversal assumption had not been applicable, the firm would have reported $1.9 billion of additional deferred tax liabilities, reducing equity by 21%. Earnings would also have been reduced in the years during which those provisions were not made.

Accounting for Acquisitions

SFAS 109 requires separate recognition of the deferred tax effects of any differences between the financial statement carrying amounts and tax bases of assets and liabilities recognized in purchase method acquisitions.

In some cases, a valuation allowance must be recorded for deferred tax assets due to the acquired firm's temporary differences or its operating loss or tax credit carryforwards. The tax benefits of subsequent reversals of the valuation allowance must be used, first, to reduce all related goodwill, second, to eliminate all other related noncurrent intangible assets, and third, to reduce reported income tax expense.

6 ANALYSIS OF INCOME TAX DISCLOSURES: PFIZER

Accounting for income taxes is complex; a large company may have many permanent and temporary differences between financial statement income and taxable income. A large multinational pays taxes in a number of jurisdictions, further complicating the process. From an analyst's perspective, unraveling these layers can seem daunting indeed.

---

[18] In some cases, even wholly owned U.S. subsidiaries may not be consolidated for tax purposes. Insurance subsidiaries, which are governed by special tax regulations, are one example.

[19] But if the parent has the statutory ability to realize those earnings tax free, no deferred tax provision is required (para. 33, SFAS 109).

Some analysts respond to this complexity by ignoring the issues. They analyze corporate performance on a pretax basis and simply accept that variations in the reported tax rate occur. We agree that analysis on a pretax basis is sound, but also believe that a firm's income tax accounting is too important to ignore.

The goals of income tax analysis are to:

1. Understand why the firm's effective tax rate differs (or does not differ) from the statutory rate in its home country.
2. Forecast changes in the effective tax rate, improving forecasts of earnings.
3. Review the historical differences between income tax expense and income taxes paid.
4. Forecast the future relationship between income tax expense and income tax payments.
5. Examine deferred tax liabilities and assets, including any valuation allowance, for
    - Possible effects on future earnings and cash flows
    - Their relevance to firm valuation
    - Their relevance in assessing a firm's capital structure

We pursue these five goals, using Pfizer as an example, and illustrate the insights regarding a firm that can be derived from its income tax disclosures.

Analysis of the Effective Tax Rate

The first step is an examination of the firm's tax rate, the trend in that rate, and the rate relative to similar companies. Variations are generally the consequence of:

- Different statutory tax rates in different jurisdictions; analysis can offer important clues as to the sources of income.
- Tax holidays that some countries offer; earnings from such operations usually cannot be remitted without payment of tax. Be alert to possible changes in the operations in such countries or the need to remit the accumulated earnings.
- Permanent differences between financial and taxable income: tax-exempt income, tax credits, and nondeductible expenses.
- The effect of tax rate and other tax law changes which, under SFAS 109, are included in income tax expense (a separate disclosure of this effect is required).
- Deferred taxes provided on the reinvested earnings of foreign affiliates and unconsolidated domestic affiliates.

As noted earlier, Pfizer's effective tax rate averaged 26.9% over the 1997 to 1999 period. Pfizer's tax footnote provides the required reconciliation between its statutory rate and effective rate for each year.[20] Because of the significance of some of these differences and variation in pretax income over the period, the rate-based disclosures are difficult to analyze. For that reason, Exhibit 42-3 converts them to dollar-based disclosures.

[20] The reconciliation can be done in either percentages (relative to the statutory tax rate) or monetary amounts (relative to "statutory" income tax expense equal to pretax income multiplied by the statutory rate).

EXHIBIT 42-3 Pfizer

Reconciliation of Effective and Statutory Tax Rates

				1997 to 1999	
	1997	**1998**	**1999**	**Total**	**Rate**
Pretax income	$2,867	$2,594	$4,448	$9,909	
Statutory rate	35.0%	35.0%	35.0%		35.0%
Variations from Statutory Rate (in percent)					
Partially tax-exempt operations in Puerto Rico	−1.8%	−2.2%	−1.5%		
International operations	−5.0%	−5.5%	−4.8%		
Other-net	−1.2%	−2.5%	−0.7%		
Net difference	−8.0%	−10.2%	−7.0%		
Effective tax rate (Income tax expense/pretax income)	27.0%	24.7%	28.0%		
Tax in millions of dollars = Rate × Pretax Income					
At statutory rate	$1,003.5	$ 907.9	$1,556.8	$3,468.1	
Effect of					
Partially tax-exempt operations in Puerto Rico	$ (51.6)	$ (57.1)	$ (66.7)	$ (175.4)	−1.8%
International operations	(143.4)	(142.7)	(213.5)	(499.5)	−5.0%
Other-net	(34.4)	(64.9)	(31.1)	(130.4)	−1.3%
Net effect	$ (229.4)	$(264.6)	$ (311.4)	$ (805.3)	−8.1%
Income tax expense	$ 774.1	$ 643.3	$1,245.4	$2,662.8	26.9%

Source: Adapted from Pfizer, Note 9, 1999 annual report.

Starting with the three-year totals, the lower tax rate on non-U.S. earnings is the largest single factor in Pfizer's low effective tax rate, deducting nearly $500 million or 5 percentage points over the three-year period. Pfizer's international operations accounted for 39% of revenues and 42.5% of income from continuing operations in 1999, as shown in Pfizer's segment data. Thus, Pfizer's low effective tax rate is largely a function of its non-U.S. operations. Forecasting future effective tax rates, therefore, requires explicit forecasts of the earnings of these operations.

Pfizer's effective tax rate also benefits from lower tax rates paid by partially tax-exempt operations in Puerto Rico. This factor reduced the composite three-year tax rate by nearly two percentage points, adding $175 million to net income. Pfizer provides additional data regarding these operations, permitting a determination of the remaining benefits. Unexplained "other" benefits averaging 1.5 percentage points per year (but with considerable variability) further reduce the effective tax rate. Discussion with management should result in a better understanding of the source and likelihood of continuation of these benefits.

The Belgian tax assessment[21] and the limited term of the Puerto Rican tax exemption suggest that significant contributors to Pfizer's lower effective tax rate may not be available in the future.

Now that we understand the reasons for Pfizer's low effective tax rate in the past, we turn to the future. A forecast of future income tax expense should start with estimated pretax income and apply the statutory rate of 35%. The analyst should then adjust for:

- Effects of the lower tax rate on foreign income
- Effects of the lower tax rate on U.S. possession operations
- "Other" effects

These adjustments may require input from Pfizer management or trade publications. Some firms provide periodic forecasts of their tax rate because of the difficulty of making such forecasts externally.

Analysis of Deferred Income Tax Expense

We now examine the effects of temporary differences on income tax expense. Companies are required to provide details of these differences, although formats vary. Pfizer's disclosure is typical, showing a breakdown in dollars for each year.

Temporary differences are generally the result of the use of different accounting policies or estimates for tax purposes than for financial reporting differences. Some of these differences are systematic; others are transaction specific. Frequent examples include:

- *Depreciation.* Different methods and/or lives result in different measures of depreciation expense.
- *Impairment.* Financial reporting writedowns do not generate tax deductions unless assets are sold.
- *Restructuring costs.* Usually tax-deductible when paid rather than when accrued.
- *Inventories.* Companies using last-in, first-out (LIFO) accounting for tax purposes in the United States must also use LIFO for reporting purposes; but when other methods are used, differences may occur.
- *Postemployment benefits.* The accruals required by SFAS 87 (pensions), SFAS 106 (other retiree benefits), and SFAS 112 (other post-employment benefits) are discussed in Chapter 12. Tax treatment of these costs is generally cash based, generating deferred tax effects.
- *Deferred compensation.* Tax-deductible only when payments are made.

On a cumulative basis, Pfizer generated negative deferred tax expense (taxes payable > income tax expense) over the 1997 to 1999 period.[22] Depreciation generated positive deferred tax expense over this period, reflected in a rising level of deferred tax liabilities for property, plant, and equipment (PP&E). Pfizer used accelerated depreciation methods for most property on its tax return and the straight-line method on its financial statements.

---

[21] However, Pfizer may have benefited from the allocation and transfers of property to selected foreign operations. In 1994, Belgian tax authorities assessed additional taxes ($432 million) and interest ($97 million), claiming jurisdiction on certain income related to property transferred from non-Belgian subsidiaries to Pfizer's operations in Ireland.

[22] See Note 9 in Pfizer's financial statements and data in Exhibit 42-2.

Pfizer also reports deferred tax debits from PP&E, likely due to its asset impairments in both 1997 and 1998. Pfizer reports that, in 1999, it had substantially completed the restructuring announced in 1998; the deferred tax debits due to restructuring and PP&E declined in 1999 after increasing in 1998. *When a restructuring charge is taken, the tax effects generally occur as expenditures are made, with significant effects on deferred tax expense both in the year of the charge and the year(s) of payment.*

Pfizer's Note 9 also shows numerous other sources of deferred tax assets and liabilities, some of them poorly explained. Significant year-to-changes in deferred tax balances reflect differences between the tax and financial reporting treatment of transactions, and should be examined for their implications for cash flow and quality of earnings. The most significant deferred tax assets relate to inventories and employee benefits. There is a significant deferred tax liability for "unremitted earnings." These items are discussed in the next section as part of the analysis of deferred tax assets and liabilities.

Because Pfizer's deferred tax expense was negative over the 1997 to 1999 period, taxes payable (and income tax paid) exceeded income tax expense. Given increasing deferred tax debits for inventories, employee benefits, foreign tax credit, and other carryforwards, deferred tax expense may remain negative in the future.

Using Deferred Taxes to Estimate Taxable Income

Deferred tax expense reflects the difference between taxable income reported to tax authorities and pretax income reported to shareholders. This relationship can be used to estimate components of taxable income. The difference between taxable income and pretax income equals

$$\frac{\text{Deferred tax expense}}{\text{Statutory tax rate}}$$

For example, Pfizer's 1999 financial statement depreciation expense was $499 million (depreciation and amortization expense of $542 reported in the statement of cash flows less amortization of $43 million for goodwill and other intangibles in Note 8). The deferred tax liability related to depreciation was $514 million in 1999, an increase of $81 million over the amount reported in 1998 (Note 9). Using that amount and the statutory tax rate of 35%, we estimate that the additional depreciation expense under tax reporting was $231 million ($81 million divided by 0.35) and tax basis depreciation was $730 million ($499 + $231).

These calculations should be viewed as estimates. They are most reliable when they relate to a single tax jurisdiction as the appropriate tax rate and the difference between tax and financial reporting rules are clear. Although this method can, in theory, be used to calculate taxable income for the entire firm, such calculations for large multinationals are less reliable.

Similar calculations can be made for the cumulative financial reporting-tax differences using deferred tax asset and liability data. The calculation for Pfizer's fixed assets is shown in the next section of this reading.

Deferred tax disclosures can also be used, in some cases, to estimate the taxes paid associated with components of income and expense.

Analysis of Deferred Tax Assets and Liabilities

Our final step is an examination of the balance sheet consequences of Pfizer's income tax accounting. As required by SFAS 109, Note 9 contains a table of significant deferred tax assets and liabilities, as well as the valuation allowance, at each balance sheet date.

The most significant deferred tax asset relates to accrued employee benefits. Financial reporting rules for pension and postretirement benefits often result in large deferred tax assets. The second-largest deferred tax asset is associated with inventories, probably due to the 1999 Trovan write-off. Other contributors include prepaid/deferred items, restructuring charges, and various carryforwards. Pfizer reports a valuation allowance of $27 million at December 31, 1999 ($30 million at December 31, 1998). Note 9 says that tax credit carryforwards are the source of that allowance.

Pfizer's largest single source of deferred tax liabilities, as for most firms, is depreciation. If we assume a 35% tax rate for all depreciation-related deferred tax credits, the reporting difference can be estimated as $1.47 billion ($514/0.35) or 55% of accumulated depreciation of $2.7 billion. This is due to Pfizer's use of accelerated depreciation for tax purposes compared with straight-line for financial reporting.

Another source of large deferred tax credits is unremitted earnings of subsidiaries and joint venture affiliates that are included in financial statement income; the tax return only reflects dividends received.

Pfizer's net balance sheet debit (asset) for income tax is:

Deferred tax debits	$2,109
Less: valuation allowance	(27)
Less: deferred tax credits	(1,456)
Net debits	$ 626

Where do these debits and credits appear on Pfizer's balance sheet? The answer is: *in several places.* As required by SFAS 109, Note 9 discloses their location (in $millions):

Assets		Liabilities	
Prepaid expenses and taxes	$744		
Other assets, deferred taxes, and deferred charges	183	Deferred taxes on income	$301
Totals	$927		$301
		Net debit	$626

Is this $626 million a real asset? Or, to rephrase the question, What are the likely future cash flow effects of Pfizer's deferred tax assets and liabilities?

We begin with the largest deferred tax liability associated with accumulated depreciation. Capital expenditures have been rising (79% since 1997); unless there are decreases in capital spending, it seems unlikely that the deferred tax liability from depreciation will decline over the next few years. The trend in capital spending must, however, be monitored. Based on data available in the annual report, deferred tax credits due to unremitted earnings and other sources seem unlikely to reverse.

Pfizer's largest deferred tax asset, related to accrued employee benefits, might start to reverse at some point if employee levels stabilize or decrease. As retiree benefit payments increase, they may exceed the accrual for additional benefits earned (as in the case of DuPont, discussed earlier). Trends in these amounts can be monitored using the techniques in Chapter 12. The deferred tax debit from restructuring charges will reduce tax payments as severance payments are made and impaired PP&E is sold.

In total, therefore, it appears unlikely that Pfizer's deferred tax accruals will generate any significant cash flows over the next few years. In addition, given the unlikelihood of near-term reversal, the deferred tax credit should be discounted for the time value of money. The combination of these factors suggests that neither an asset nor a liability should be recognized for valuation purposes.

Other Issues in Income Tax Analysis

The following issues, although not relevant to an analysis of Pfizer, occur frequently enough to warrant brief mention:

- Watch for companies that report substantial income for financial reporting purposes but little or no taxes payable (implying little or no taxable income). Such differences often reflect aggressive revenue and expense recognition methods used for financial reporting, and low quality of earnings. In such cases, caution is indicated as the methods used for financial reporting purposes may be based on optimistic assumptions.[23]
- Look for current or pending reversals of past temporary differences. For example, a decline in capital spending may result in a greater proportion of depreciation coming from old assets that have already been heavily depreciated for tax purposes. Thus, financial reporting depreciation may exceed tax depreciation, generating a tax liability.
- Remember that deferred tax assets and liabilities may point to near-term cash consequences. Restructuring provisions often generate little cash or tax effect in the year they occur, but substantial effects in following years.
- Tax law changes may also result in the reversal of past temporary differences. In the United States, tax law changes in recent years have curtailed the use of the completed contract and installment methods for tax purposes, generating substantial tax liabilities for affected companies.

7 FINANCIAL REPORTING OUTSIDE THE UNITED STATES

OPTIONAL SEGMENT

As already noted, many foreign jurisdictions require conformity between financial reporting and tax reporting in separate (parent company) financial statements. In such cases, the issues discussed in this reading do not occur. That statement is no longer true, however, once consolidated statements include subsidiaries that are not consolidated for tax purposes. Given the worldwide tendency toward consolidated reporting, even firms in tax-conformity countries must grapple with the question of deferred tax accounting.

IASB Standards

IAS 12 (revised 2000) requires use of the liability method but *permits* companies to use "indefinite reversal" criteria to avoid recognizing deferred taxes on the reinvested earnings of subsidiaries, associates, and joint ventures, when both of the following conditions are met:

1. The parent, investor, or venturer can control the manner and timing of the reversal of the temporary difference.
2. It is probable that the temporary difference will not reverse in the foreseeable future.

---

[23] Empirical evidence also suggests that firms cannot costlessly increase financial reporting income and at the same time keep taxable income very low. Mills (1998) shows that IRS audit adjustments increase as book—tax differences increase; that is, "The more book income (or tax expense) exceeds taxable income (or tax payable), the greater the proposed IRS audit adjustments."

As a result, there are significant differences in the recognition of deferred tax liabilities among firms using IAS and U.S. GAAP; the latter group must record deferred taxes for the reinvested earnings of domestic affiliates. In addition, deferred taxes are based on enacted laws and rates whereas IAS 12 uses substantially enacted rates (tax rate changes that have been announced by the government but not yet enacted).

Other National Standards

Virtually all countries require the recognition of deferred taxes on temporary differences. Germany and the United Kingdom use the liability method, whereas France and Japan allow either the deferral (see footnote 2) or liability method. Most countries limit the recognition of deferred tax liabilities and few address the issue of deferred tax assets. In Switzerland, deferred taxes not expected to reverse need not be recognized and the recognition of certain deferred tax assets is discretionary.

German GAAP permits the recognition of deferred tax assets for the elimination of intercompany profits. In general, deferred taxes are computed under the liability method, but the amounts recognized are limited to the excess of consolidated deferred tax liabilities over consolidated deferred tax assets.

The accounting differences among U.S., IAS, and foreign GAAP affect reported net income and stockholders' equity (lower when deferred tax assets are unrecognized or offset by a valuation allowance). Another difficulty when comparing firms using different GAAP is the paucity of disclosure requirements in many cases. Both SFAS 109 and IAS 12 have substantial disclosure requirements; similar information is rarely available in the financial statements of most foreign countries.

Form 20-F reconciliations of reported net income and stockholders' equity show the adjustments due to differences in deferred tax accounting. These differences can be used to restore comparability between U.S. firms and foreign firms that file Form 20-F. In some cases, these adjustments can be used to approximate adjustments for firms not providing Form 20-F reconciliations, when they are similar to firms that do provide them.

Exhibit 42-4 contains disclosures provided by Cadbury Schweppes in its 2000 Form 20-F. Applying UK GAAP, the company calculated deferred tax liabilities of £105 million (1999: £93) using the partial allocation method.[24] Had it used comprehensive allocation (U.S. GAAP), it would have recorded an additional deferred tax liability of £58 million in 2000 (1999: £62 million); most of the difference is attributed to the accelerated depreciation method. No deferred tax is recorded for the effect of accelerated depreciation because it is not expected to reverse.

Although we have recommended this approach in the section "Liability or Equity" and agree that partial allocation is a logical alternative to the comprehensive allocation method, it presents two analytical problems. First, it makes Cadbury's financial statements not comparable to its U.S. competitors, Coca-Cola and PepsiCo, who use comprehensive allocation. Comparability can be restored either by adjusting Cadbury's income statement provision, its deferred taxes (and equity), or by converting its competitors' financial statements to the partial allocation method.

The second problem with partial allocation is management discretion that can be used to manage earnings. This discretion is comparable to that available in the application of valuation allowances under SFAS 109 and IAS 12.

---

[24] The partial allocation method in UK GAAP limits the recognition of net deferred tax assets to amounts expected to be recovered without the assumption of future taxable income. The standard is permissive regarding deferred tax consequences of pension and postretirement benefits; firms may use either comprehensive or partial allocation with disclosure of the method selected.

In December 2000, the UK Accounting Standards Board issued FRS 19, Deferred Tax, requiring comprehensive allocation. Cadbury will most likely adopt this standard in 2002 and the resulting financial statements will be more comparable to its U.S. competitors. The UK—U.S. GAAP reconciliation in the form 20-F as it relates to deferred taxes is reproduced in Panel B of Exhibit 42-4. On December 31, 2000, the U.S. GAAP—based deferred tax liability is £163 million (1999: £152 million). This information can be used to make Cadbury's financial statements comparable to those of its U.S. competitors.

EXHIBIT 42-4 Cadbury Schweppes

Panel A—Deferred Taxes: Partial Allocation

The analysis of the deferred tax liabilities/(assets) included in the financial statements at the end of the year is as follows:

in £millions	1999	2000
Accelerated capital allowances	£ 2	£ 3
Other timing differences	91	102
Deferred taxation liability	£93	£105

The deferred taxation liability is included in provisions for liabilities and charges. Gross deferred tax assets at year-end are £15 million (1999: £18 million). The potential liability for deferred taxation not provided comprised:

in £millions	1999	2000
UK accelerated capital allowances	£48	£77
UK property values	5	5
Other timing differences	9	(30)
	£62	£52

To the extent that dividends from overseas undertakings are expected to result in additional taxes, appropriate amounts have been provided. No taxes have been provided for other unremitted earnings since these amounts are considered permanently reinvested by subsidiary undertakings and in the case of associated undertakings the taxes would not be material. Distributable earnings retained by overseas subsidiary undertakings and the principal associated undertakings totaled approximately £846 million at 31 December 2000. The remittance of these amounts would incur tax at varying rates depending on available foreign tax credits.

Tax losses carried forward as at 31 December 2000 for offset against future earnings of overseas companies were approximately £103 million (1999: £103 million). The utilization of losses is dependent upon the level of future earnings and other limiting factors within the countries concerned. Tax losses totaling £22 million have expiration periods in 2001 and 2002, tax losses of £25 million expire in 2003 to 2012 and tax losses totaling £56 million have no expiry date.

EXHIBIT 42-4 (continued)

Panel B—US GAAP

The US GAAP analysis of deferred tax liability is as follows:

in £millions	1999	2000
Liabilities		
Fixed asset timing differences	£ 84	£ 84
Other timing differences	71	79
	£155	£163
Assets		
Operating loss carryforwards	(37)	(37)
Less: Valuation allowance	37	37
Net deferred tax liability	£155	£163

Source: Cadbury *20-F*, December 31, 2000

OPTIONAL SEGMENT ENDS

8 SUMMARY

In this reading, we have seen how income tax expense and deferred tax assets and liabilities are affected by the accounting method used and by management choices and assumptions. As all business enterprises are subject to income tax, no financial analysis is complete until the issues raised in this reading have been examined. Analysts must examine, in particular, the effective tax rate, the cash flow effects of deferred tax accruals, and the relevance of such accruals for valuation.

PROBLEMS

1. [Deferred tax classification; CFA© adapted] Explain in which of the following categories deferred taxes can be found. Provide an example for each category in your answer.
   - **A.** Current liabilities
   - **B.** Long-term liabilities
   - **C.** Stockholders' equity
   - **D.** Current assets
   - **E.** Long-term assets
2. [Deferred taxes; CFA© adapted] State which of the following statements are correct under SFAS 109. Explain why.
   - **A.** The deferred tax liability account must be adjusted for the effect of enacted changes in tax laws or rates in the period of enactment.
   - **B.** The deferred tax asset account must be adjusted for the effect of enacted changes in tax laws or rates in the period of enactment.
   - **C.** The tax consequences of an event must not be recognized until that event is recognized in the financial statements.
   - **D.** Both deferred tax liabilities and deferred tax assets must be accounted for based on the tax laws and rates in effect at their origin.
   - **E.** Changes in deferred tax assets and liabilities are classified as extraordinary items in the income statement.
3. [Permanent versus temporary differences; CFA© adapted]
   - **A.** Define *permanent differences* and describe two events or transactions that generate such differences.
   - **B.** Describe the impact of permanent differences on a firm's effective tax rate.
4. [Treatment of deferred tax liability; CFA© adapted]
   - **A.** When computing a firm's debt-to-equity ratio, describe the conditions for treating the deferred tax liability:
     - **(i)** As equity
     - **(ii)** As debt
   - **B.** Provide arguments for excluding deferred tax liabilities from both the numerator and the denominator of the debt-to-equity ratio.
   - **C.** Describe the arguments for including a portion of the deferred taxes as equity and a portion as debt.
5. [Depreciation methods and deferred taxes] The Incurious George Company acquires assets K, L, and M at the beginning of year 1. Each asset has the same cost, a five-year life, and an expected salvage value of $3,000. For financial reporting, the firm uses the straight-line, sum-of-the-years' digits, and double-declining-balance depreciation methods for assets K, L, and M, respectively. It uses the double-declining-balance method for all assets on its tax return; its tax rate is 34%. Depreciation expense of $12,000 was reported for asset L for financial reporting purposes in year 2. Using this information:
   - **A.** Calculate the tax return depreciation expense for each asset in year 2.
   - **B.** Calculate the financial statement depreciation expense for assets K and M in year 2.

C. Calculate the deferred tax credit (liability) or debit (asset) for each asset at the end of:

(i) Year 2

(ii) Year 5

6. [Analysis of deferred tax; CFA© adapted] On December 29, 2000, Mother Prewitt's Handmade Cookies Corp. acquires a numerically controlled chocolate chip-milling machine. Due to differences in tax and financial accounting, depreciation for tax purposes is $150,000 more than depreciation in the financial statements, adding $52,500 to deferred taxes. At the same time, Mother Prewitt's sells $200,000 worth of cookies on an installment contract, recognizing the $100,000 profit immediately. For tax purposes, however, $80,000 of the profit will be recognized in 2001, requiring $27,200 of deferred taxes.

A. Compare the expected cash consequences of the two deferred tax items just described.

B. Explain your treatment of deferred taxes when calculating Mother Prewitt's solvency and leverage ratios.

C. In 2001, Mother Prewitt's tax rate will be 40%. Discuss the adjustments to *each* of the two deferred tax items in 2001 because of the change in the tax rate, assuming the use of SFAS 109.

ANALYSIS OF FINANCING LIABILITIES

READING 43

LEARNING OUTCOMES

The candidate should be able to:

a. compute the effects of debt issuance and amortization of bond discounts and premiums on the financial statements and ratios, discuss the effect on reported cash flows of issuing zero-coupon debt and determine the appropriate classification for debt with equity features and calculate the effect of issuance of such instruments on the debt to total capital ratio;

b. discuss the effect of changing interest rates on the market value of debt and on financial statements and ratios.

INTRODUCTION 1

The assessment of a firm's liabilities is crucial to the analysis of its long-run viability and growth. A firm can incur obligations in myriad ways; some are a consequence of the firm's operating activities, whereas others result from its financing decisions. The former are characterized by exchanges of goods and services for the later payment of cash (or vice versa), whereas debt arising from financing decisions generally involves current receipts of cash in exchange for later payments of cash. Both forms of debt are generally reported "on balance sheet," and our focus in this reading is on their measurement, interpretation, and analysis.

More complex arrangements, often based on contracts rather than immediate cash exchanges, involve promises to purchase (or use) products, services, or distribution systems in return for specified future payments of cash or equivalent resources. Such contractual arrangements are usually not recorded on the firm's balance sheet but may receive footnote disclosure. A thorough analysis of the firm's financial structure requires recognition of these liabilities as well. Such "off-balance-sheet" debt must first be identified, then measured, interpreted, and analyzed.

The analysis of a firm's short-term liquidity and long-term solvency position requires evaluation of both on- and off-balance-sheet debt. Debt-to-equity and interest coverage ratios based on reported financial data, for example, are affected by the form of transactions (rather than their substance), which determines whether they are recognized and how they are accounted for. This analysis must also consider incentives for management decisions regarding the proportion of on- versus off-balance-sheet debt.

An additional focus of analysis is debt covenants, used by creditors to protect themselves. These restrictions limit the firm's operations, its distributions to shareholders, and the amount of additional debt or leverage the firm can assume. Firms may alter their operating and financing activities and change accounting policies in an effort to operate within the confines of these covenants.

This reading is the first of a series of readings that deal with these issues. It primarily examines liabilities resulting from financing activities, the nature of various debt instruments, the impact of market rate (and credit) changes on reported and economic liabilities, and the nature and effect of covenants imposed by creditors. Liabilities arising from contractual obligations such as leases (a combined financing and investment activity) and other off-balance-sheet debt, debt guarantees, and obligations of the firm's affiliates are the subject of Reading 44.

2 BALANCE SHEET DEBT

The liability amount reported on the balance sheet does not equal the total cash outflow required to satisfy the debt. Only the principal portion, that is, the present value of the future cash flow, is recorded. For example, if a firm borrows $100 at an interest rate of 10%, the actual amount payable at year-end is $110. The balance sheet liability equals the present value of the future payment or $100.

Current Liabilities

Current liabilities are defined as those due within one year or one operating cycle; they result from both operating and financing activities. Analysis must distinguish among different types of current operating and financing liabilities:

Consequences of Operating Activities

1. *Operating and trade liabilities*, the most frequent type, are the result of credit granted to the company by its suppliers and employees.
2. *Advances from customers* arise when customers pay in advance for services to be rendered by the company. The firm is obligated to render the service and/or deliver a product to the customer in the near future.

Consequences of Financing Activities

3. *Short-term debt* represents amounts borrowed from banks or the credit markets that are expected to be repaid within one year or less.
4. *Current portion of long-term debt* identifies the portion of long-term debt that is payable within the next year; it is excluded from the long-term liability section of the balance sheet.

Operating and trade debt is reported at the expected (undiscounted) cash flow and is an important exception to the rule that liabilities are recorded at present value. A purchase of goods for $100 on credit, to be paid for within the normal operating cycle of the firm, is recorded at $100 even though its present value is lower. This treatment is justified by the short period between the incurrence of the debt and its payment, rendering the adjustment to present value immaterial.

When analyzing a firm's liquidity, advances from customers should be distinguished from other payables. Payables require a future outlay of cash. Advances from customers, on the other hand, are satisfied by delivery of goods or services,[1] requiring a cash outlay lower[2] than the advances recorded; otherwise, the firm would be selling below cost. Increases in advances should be viewed favorably as *advances are a prediction of future revenues rather than of cash outflows.*

Short-term debt and the current portion of long-term debt are the result of prior financing cash inflows. They indicate the firm's need for either cash or a means of refinancing the debt. The inability to repay short-term credit is a sign of financial distress.

It is important to monitor the relative levels of debt from operating as compared to financing activities. The former arise from the normal course of business activities and represent the required operating capital for a given level of production and sales: *A shift from operating to financing liabilities may signal the beginning of a liquidity crisis, as reduced access to trade credit results in increased reliance on borrowings.*

Example:

Warnaco

The following data for Warnaco Group, a major clothing manufacturer, illustrates this point:

Warnaco Group
Amounts in $000

	1/1/00	12/30/00	Change
Accounts payable	$ 599,768	$ 413,786	$(185,982)
Total debt	1,332,755	1,493,483	160,728

Over one year Warnaco's trade credit fell 31%, requiring borrowing that increased the company's already-large debt burden. The company filed for bankruptcy on June 11, 2001.

---

[1] The firm will have a cash obligation only if the goods and services are not delivered. Thus, the primary liability does not require cash.

[2] This is especially true in industries with high fixed/low variable cost structures (e.g., airlines). The marginal cost for any individual customer is low relative to the selling cost.

Long-Term Debt

Firms obtain long-term debt financing from public issuance; from private placements with insurance companies, pension plans, and other institutional investors; or from long-term bank credit agreements. Creditors may receive a claim on specific assets pledged as security for the debt (e.g., mortgages), or they may have only general claims on the assets of the firm. Some debt, known as *project financing*, is repaid solely from the operations of a particular activity (e.g., a coal mine or office building). Some creditor claims are *subordinated*, in that they rank below those of *senior* creditors, whose claims have priority.

Long-term liabilities are interest-bearing in nature, but the structure of interest and principal payments varies widely. The different payment terms are, however, conceptually identical. As the subtleties of the financing equation(s) can be overwhelming and obscure the sight of the forest for the trees, *we suggest that the reader keep two basic principles in mind:*

1. Debt equals the present value of the remaining future stream of (interest and principal) payments. The book value reported in the financial statements uses the discount rate (market interest rate) in effect when the debt was incurred. Market value measurements use the current market interest rate.
2. Interest expense is the amount paid by the debtor to the creditor in excess of the amount borrowed. Even when the *total* amount of interest paid over time is known, its allocation to individual time periods (both cash outflows and accrual of expense in periodic income statements) may vary with the form of the debt.

These points seem simplistic but reference to them from time to time may help focus the discussions that follow.

Although bonds are only part of the debt universe, they are used for convenience to illustrate the accounting and analysis issues.

A bond is a "contract" or written agreement that obligates the borrower (bond issuer) to make certain payments to the lender (bondholder) over the life of the bond. A typical bond promises two types of payments: periodic interest payments (usually semiannual in the United States but annual in other countries) and a lump-sum payment when the bond matures.

The *face value* of the bond is the lump-sum payment due at maturity. The *coupon rate* is the stated cash interest rate (but not necessarily the actual rate of return).

Periodic Payment = "Coupon Rate" × Face Value

The coupon rate is in quotation marks because it is stated on an annual basis, whereas payments are made semiannually. The coupon rate (CR) used for the payment calculation is therefore equal to one-half the stated coupon rate.

The example in Exhibit 43-1 is based on a three-year bond[3] with the following terms:

Face Value (FV):	$100,000
Coupon:	10%
Interest Payment:	Semiannual

[3] Bonds issued for periods of 10 years or less are usually called *notes*. There is no analytical distinction, and we call all debt issues *bonds* for convenience.

EXHIBIT 43-1 Comparison of Bond Issued at Par, Premium, and Discount

Face Value (FV) of bond = $100,000
Coupon (CR) = 5% (semiannual payment; 10% annual rate)
Maturity = 3 years
Semiannual payments of $5,000 (0.5 × 10% × $100,000)

A. Bond Issued at Par: Market Rate = 10% (MR = 5%)

Period Ending	(1) Liability Opening	(2) (1) × MR Interest Expense	(3) FV × CR Coupon Payment	(4) (2) − (3) Change in Liability	(5) (1) + (4) Liability Closing	(6) FV Face Value of Bond
01/01/01	Proceeds (see below)				$100,000	$100,000
06/30/01	$100,000	$ 5,000	$ 5,000	$0	100,000	100,000
12/31/01	100,000	5,000	5,000	0	100,000	100,000
06/30/02	100,000	5,000	5,000	0	100,000	100,000
12/31/02	100,000	5,000	5,000	0	100,000	100,000
06/30/03	100,000	5,000	5,000	0	100,000	100,000
12/31/03	100,000	5,000	5,000	0	100,000	100,000
Totals		$30,000	$30,000			

Calculation of Proceeds

Present value of annuity of $5,000 for 6 periods, discounted at 5%: $5,000 × 5.0756 =	$ 25,378
Present value of $100,000 in 6 periods, discounted at 5%: $100,000 × 0.74622 =	74,622
Total	$100,000

B. Bond Issued at Premium: Market Rate = 8% (MR = 4%)

Period Ending	(1) Liability Opening	(2) (1) × MR Interest Expense	(3) FV × CR Coupon Payment	(4) (2) − (3) Change in Liability	(5) (1) + (4) Liability Closing	(6) FV Face Value of Bond	(7) (5) − (6) Closing Premium
01/01/01	Proceeds (see below)				$105,242	$100,000	$5,242
06/30/01	$105,242	$ 4,210	$ 5,000	$ (790)	104,452	100,000	4,452
12/31/01	104,452	4,178	5,000	(822)	103,630	100,000	3,630
06/30/02	103,630	4,145	5,000	(855)	102,775	100,000	2,775
12/31/02	102,775	4,111	5,000	(889)	101,886	100,000	1,886
06/30/03	101,886	4,075	5,000	(925)	100,961	100,000	961
12/31/03	100,961	4,039	5,000	(961)	100,000	100,000	0
Totals		$24,758	$30,000	$(5,242)			

EXHIBIT 43-1 (continued)

Calculation of Proceeds

Present value of annuity of \$5,000 for 6 periods, discounted at 4%:	
\$5,000 × 5.2421 =	\$ 26,211
Present value of \$100,000 in 6 periods, discounted at 4%:	
\$100,000 × 0.79031 =	79,031
Total	\$105,242

C. Bond Issued at Discount: Market Rate = 12% (MR = 6%)

Period Ending	(1) Liability Opening	(2) (1) × MR Interest Expense	(3) FV × CR Coupon Payment	(4) (2) − (3) Change in Liability	(5) (1) + (4) Liability Closing	(6) FV Face Value of Bond	(7) (5) − (6) Discount
01/01/01	Proceeds (see below)				\$95,083	\$100,000	\$(4,917)
06/30/01	\$95,083	\$ 5,705	\$ 5,000	\$ 705	95,788	100,000	(4,212)
12/31/01	95,788	5,747	5,000	747	96,535	100,000	(3,465)
06/30/02	96,535	5,792	5,000	792	97,327	100,000	(2,673)
12/31/02	97,327	5,840	5,000	840	98,167	100,000	(1,833)
06/30/03	98,167	5,890	5,000	890	99,057	100,000	(943)
12/31/03	99,057	5,943	5,000	943	100,000	100,000	0
Totals		\$34,917	\$30,000	\$4,917			

Calculation of Proceeds

Present value of annuity of \$5,000 for 6 periods, discounted at 6%:	
\$5,000 × 4.9173 =	\$24,587
Present value of \$100,000 in 6 periods, discounted at 6%:	
\$100,000 × 0.70496 =	70,496
Total	\$95,083

The purchaser of the bond expects six payments of interest (each payment is \$5,000) and a final principal payment of \$100,000 for a total of \$130,000. Note that this stream of payments does not uniquely determine the principal amount borrowed by the bond issuer. *The amount borrowed (the proceeds received on issuance) depends on the market rate of interest for bonds of a similar maturity and risk as well as the payment stream.*

The market rate may be less than, equal to, or greater than the coupon rate. *It is the current market interest rate that allocates payments between interest and principal.*

Exhibit 43-1, parts A through C, shows how the economics of the bond and the accounting treatment of the payments are affected by the relationship between the market and coupon rates. The following points should be noted:

1. The initial liability is the amount paid to the issuer by the creditor (present value of the stream of payments discounted at the market rate), not necessarily the face value of the debt.

2. The *effective interest rate* on the bond is the market (not the coupon) rate at the time of issuance, and interest expense is that market rate times the bond liability.
3. The coupon rate and face value determine the actual cash flows (stream of payments from the issuer).
4. Total interest expense is equal to the payments by the issuer to the creditor in excess of the amount received. (Thus, total interest expense = $130,000 – initial liability.)
5. The balance sheet liability over time is a function of (a) the initial liability and the relationship of (b) periodic interest expense to (c) the actual cash payments.
6. The balance sheet liability at any point in time is equal to the present value of the remaining payments, discounted at the market rate in effect at the time of the issuance of the bonds.

Exhibit 43-1A: Market Rate = Coupon Rate. When the market rate equals the coupon rate of 10% (compounded semiannually), the bond is issued at par; that is, the proceeds equal the face value.[4] The creditor is willing to pay $100,000, the present value of the stream of payments and the face value of the bond. In this case, the initial liability equals the face value.

Since the debt has been issued at a market rate of 10% (equal to the coupon rate), periodic interest expense (Exhibit 43-1A, column 2) equals the periodic cash payments (column 3). The liability remains $100,000 (column 5) throughout the life of the bond.

Exhibit 43-1B: Market Rate < Coupon Rate. When the market rate is less than the coupon rate, the creditor is willing to pay (and the bond issuer will demand) a premium above the face value of $100,000.[5] If we assume a market rate of 8%, the proceeds and initial liability (Exhibit 43-1B) equal $105,242 (face value of $100,000 plus premium of $5,242).

After six months, the bondholder earns interest of $4,210 (4% × $105,242) but receives a payment of $5,000 (coupon rate times face value). This $5,000 payment includes interest expense of $4,210 and a $790 principal payment, reducing the liability to $104,452. For the second period, interest expense is $4,178 (4% × $104,452), lower than the first period expense since the liability has been reduced. After the second payment of $5,000, the liability is further reduced. This process is continued until the bond matures. At that time, as shown in Exhibit 43-1B, the liability is reduced to $100,000, the face value of the bond, which is repaid at maturity.

The process by which a bond premium (or discount) is amortized over the life of the bond is known as the *effective interest method.* This process, which results in a constant rate of interest over the life of the obligation, is widely used in financial reporting.

---

[4] We ignore, for simplicity, the underwriting costs and expenses associated with the bond issuance. These costs are generally capitalized and amortized over the life of the bond issue.

[5] Assuming a market interest rate of 8%, the bond issuer could find an investor willing to lend $100,000 in exchange for a semiannual annuity stream of $4,000 (4% × $100,000) in addition to the lump-sum payment at maturity. For the borrower to obligate itself to pay the higher annuity of $5,000 requires additional proceeds above the face value.

Exhibit 43-1C: Market Rate > Coupon Rate. When the market rate exceeds the coupon rate, the bond buyer is unwilling to pay the full face value of the bond.[6] At a market rate of 12%, the bond would be issued at a discount of $4,917, and the proceeds and initial liability equal $95,083.

Interest expense for the first six months is $5,705 (6% × $95,083), but cash interest paid is only $5,000; the shortfall of $705 is added to the balance sheet liability. As a result, a higher liability is used to calculate interest expense for the second period, increasing interest expense, increasing the shortfall, and further increasing the liability. This cycle is repeated for all remaining periods until the bond matures. At that point, the initial principal of $95,083 plus the accumulated (unpaid) interest of $4,917 equals $100,000, the face value payment that retires the debt. The zero-coupon bond, discussed shortly, is the extreme case; all interest is unpaid until the bond matures.

Financial Statement Effects

Interest expense reported in the income statement (column 2 of Exhibit 43-1) is the effective interest on the loan based on the market rate in effect at issuance times the balance sheet liability at the beginning of the period. The actual cash payments (column 3) may not equal interest expense, but do equal the reduction in cash from operations (CFO). The balance sheet liability is shown in column 5. The initial cash received and the final face value payment of $100,000 are both treated as cash from financing (CFF). The financial statement effects on an annual basis (if we assume a December fiscal year-end) are summarized in Exhibit 43-2. Note that for bonds issued at a premium (discount), the interest expense decreases (increases) over time. This is a direct function of the declining (rising) balance sheet liability; for each period, interest expense is the product of the beginning liability and the effective interest rate. At any point in time, the balance sheet liability equals the present value of the remaining payments discounted at the effective interest rate at the issuance date.[7,8]

The reported cash flows for each period over the life of the bond (Exhibit 43-2) are identical across all three scenarios; the $100,000 face value payment is treated as cash from financing, and the periodic cash payments of $5,000 are reported as reductions in CFO.[9] For bonds issued at a premium or discount, however, these cash flows *incorrectly* describe the economics of the bond transaction.

The misclassification of cash flows results from reporting the coupon payments rather than interest expense as CFO. For bonds sold at a premium, part of the coupon payment is a reduction of principal and should be treated as a financing cash (out)flow. CFO is understated and financing cash flow is over-

---

[6] The bondholder can purchase a 12% bond and receive periodic payments of $6,000. The periodic payments from this bond are only $5,000. Thus, an investor would only purchase this bond at a *discount*.

[7] To illustrate this property, compute the balance sheet liability of $96,535 at December 31, 2001, for the bond issued at a discount. The present value of the remaining four periodic payments and lump-sum payment equals:

Present value of annuity of $5,000 for 4 periods discounted at 6%: $5,000 × 3.46511 =	$17,326
Present value of $100,000 for 4 periods discounted at 6%: $100,000 × 0.79209 =	79,209
	$96,535

[8] The *market* value of the debt, however, is equal to the present value of all remaining payments discounted at the *current market* interest rate.

[9] Under the indirect method, net income is adjusted by the change in bond discount/premium (the periodic amortization of the bond/discount premium) to derive CFO. Thus for the first year, the cash flow statement will show an addback of $1,612 in the premium case and a deduction of $1,452 in the discount case.

EXHIBIT 43-2 Comparison of Financial Statement Effects of Bonds Issued at Par, Premium, and Discount

Bond Face Value = \$100,000
Maturity = 3 years
Coupon Rate = 10% (semiannual payments)

Premium Case: Market Rate = 8%
Discount Case: Market Rate = 12%

	Interest Expense Bond Issued at			Balance Sheet Liability Bond Issued at			Cash Flow from	
Year	Par	Premium	Discount	Par	Premium	Discount	Operations (for all cases)	Financing (for all cases)
2001	\$10,000	\$ 8,388	\$11,452	\$100,000	\$103,630	\$ 96,535	\$10,000	
2002*	10,000	8,256	11,632	100,000	101,886	98,167	10,000	
2003*	10,000	8,114	11,833	100,000	100,000	100,000	10,000	\$100,000
Totals	\$30,000	\$24,758	\$34,917				\$30,000	\$100,000

*Interest expense and cash flow total of June 30 and December 31 amounts for each year. All data from Exhibit 43-1.

stated by an equal amount. Similarly, when bonds are issued at a discount, part of the discount amortization represents additional interest expense. Consequently, CFO is overstated and financing cash flow is understated by that amount.

In summary, the cash flow classification of the debt payments depends on the coupon rates, not the effective interest rate. When these differ, CFO is misstated.

Exhibit 43-3 presents two cash flow reclassifications. The first correctly allocates cash outflows based on interest expense. After reallocation, the cash flows reflect the economics of the debt rather than the coupon payments alone.

The second reclassification, however, goes much further. We argue that all debt-related cash flows should be separated from operating cash flows. The "functional" reclassification in Exhibit 43-3 makes that separation so CFO is unaffected by borrowing. All debt-related cash flows are included in financing cash flow regardless of the coupon or effective interest rates.

Most debt is issued at or close to par (face value), making the distortion from bond premium or discount immaterial. However, when the discount is large, for example, with zero-coupon bonds, the difference between coupon and effective interest rates leads to the significant distortion of reported cash flows.

Zero-Coupon Debt

A zero-coupon bond has no periodic payments (coupon = 0).[10] For that reason, it must be issued at a deep discount to face value. The lump-sum payment at maturity includes all unpaid interest (equal to the face value minus the proceeds) from the time of issuance.

[10] The following discussion also applies to bonds sold at deep discounts, that is, with coupons that are far below market interest rates, and to bonds issued with attached warrants that generate debt discount (discussed later in the reading).

EXHIBIT 43-3 Reclassification of Cash Flows for Bonds in Exhibits 43-1 and 43-2

		SFAS 95		Reclassification Based on Interest Expense				Functional Reclassification For All Bonds	
	Actual Cash	Cash Flow for All Bonds		Premium Bond		Discount Bond			
Year	Flow	Operations	Financing	Operations	Financing	Operations	Financing	Operations	Financing
2001	$ 10,000	$10,000	0	$ 8,388	$ 1,612	$11,452	$ (1,452)	0	$ 10,000
2002	10,000	10,000	0	8,256	1,744	11,632	(1,632)	0	10,000
2003	110,000	10,000	100,000	8,114	101,886	11,833	98,167	0	110,000
Totals	$130,000	$30,000	$100,000	$24,758	$105,242	$34,917	$95,083	0	$130,000

SFAS 95 requires that cash flows be allocated between operations and financing based on the coupon interest rate.

The first reclassification allocates cash outflows based on interest expense. In 2001, for the premium case, $8,388 is shown as operating cash flow and the balance of $1,612 ($10,000 − $8,388) as financing. The interest expense reported for the discount issue, $11,452, is shown as operating cash flow and the excess over interest paid $1,452 ($11,452 − $10,000) is reported as a financing cash inflow. The 2003 financing cash flow for the discount issue, therefore, equals the outflow of $100,000 to repay the debt less $1,833 (interest expense in excess of interest paid).

The second reclassification is based on the authors' view that financing cash flow should include both principal and interest paid. Regardless of whether debt is issued at par, premium, or discount, financing cash flow reflects all payments made in the year of the actual payments.

The proceeds at issuance equal the present value of the face amount, discounted at the market interest rate. Thus, at a market rate of 10%, a $100,000 face value zero-coupon bond payable in three years will be issued at $74,622.

Exhibit 43-4 shows the income statement, cash flow, and balance sheet effects for this bond. Note that the repayment of $100,000 includes $25,378 of interest that is *never* reported as CFO; the full $100,000 payment is treated as cash from financing. The contrast with the bond issued at par (Exhibit 43-1A) is striking.

The interest on a zero-coupon bond never reduces operating cash flow. This surprising result has important analytic consequences. *One is that reported CFO is systematically overstated when a zero-coupon (or deep discount) bond is issued.* Furthermore, solvency ratios, such as cash-basis interest coverage, are improved relative to the issuance of par bonds. Finally, the cash eventually required to repay the obligation may become a significant burden.[11]

EQK Realty Investors (EQK), a real estate investment trust, illustrates this phenomenon. The company issued zero-coupon mortgage notes in 1985 and 1988. Adjustment of reported cash flow for the effect of interest on these zero-coupon bonds results in a quite different CFO trend.

[11] In fact, interest expense increases cash flow by generating income tax deductions. (Zero-coupon bond interest expense is tax-deductible even though it is not paid.) This result can have real-world consequences. When valuing a company for leveraged buyout (LBO) purposes, the use of zero-coupon or low-coupon debt (issued at a discount) can result in the following anomaly: The higher the interest rate, the higher the cash flow, mistakenly resulting in a higher price for the company. An investment banker commented to one of the authors that this factor contributed to overbidding in the late 1980s. Of course, when the zero-coupon bond comes due, the cash must be found to repay the (much higher) face amount.

EXHIBIT 43-4 Zero-Coupon Bond Analysis

Bond: Face Value (FV) = $100,000 Coupon 0%
Maturity = 3 years
Market Rate = 10% (MR = 5%)

	(1) Liability Opening	(2) (1) × MR Interest Expense	(3) FV × CR Coupon Payment	(4) (2) − (3) Change in Liability	(5) (1) + (4) Liability Closing	(6) FV Face Value of Bond	(7) (5) − (6) Discount
01/01/01	Proceeds (see below)				$ 74,622	$100,000	$(25,378)
06/30/01	$74,622	$ 3,731	$0	$ 3,731	78,353	100,000	(21,647)
12/31/01	78,353	3,917	0	3,917	82,270	100,000	(17,730)
06/30/02	82,270	4,114	0	4,114	86,384	100,000	(13,616)
12/31/02	86,384	4,319	0	4,319	90,703	100,000	(9,297)
06/30/03	90,703	4,535	0	4,535	95,238	100,000	(4,762)
12/31/03	95,238	4,762	0	4,762	100,000	100,000	(0)
Totals		$25,378	$0	$25,378			

Calculation of Proceeds

Present value of $100,000 in 6 periods, discounted at 5%: $100,000 × 0.74622 = $74,622

Cash flow from operations: Zero in all periods

Cash flow from financing: $74,622 inflow at 1/1/01; $100,000 outflow at 12/31/03

Exhibit 43-5 presents excerpts from EQK's 1992 Balance Sheet, Cash Flow Statement, and Financial Statement Notes. The zero-coupon notes were retired in December 1992, using cash and a new (conventional) mortgage bond.

Given the opening (January 1, 1992) balance of $89,410 on the zero-coupon bond and the issuance of a mortgage bond having a face value of $75,716 ($75,324 + $392 debt discount), the cash required to retire the bond should have been $13,694 ($89,410 − $75,716). Why then did EQK report a cash payment of $23,038, an excess of $9,344, as cash from financing?

The answer can be found in the cash flows from operating activities section of the statement of cash flows. "Amortization of discount on zero-coupon mortgage notes" of $9,344 appears as an addback to net income, thereby *removing it from CFO;* $9,344 is the amount of interest that accrued on the zero-coupon bond from January 1992 through its retirement in December 1992. This interest, paid in 1992, was treated as a financing rather than an operating cash outflow. The impact of this misclassification on CFO is significant. Reclassifying the interest expense as CFO turns a positive cash flow of over $8 million into a negative $1.276 million:

Reported CFO	$8,068
Reclassify 1992 interest portion	(9,344)
Adjusted CFO	($1,276)

EXHIBIT 43-5 EQK Realty
Zero Coupon Financing, Financial Statement Excerpts

Balance Sheet

Year Ended December 31	1991	1992
Liabilities		
Mortgage note payable, net of debt discount of $392	—	$75,324
Zero-coupon mortgage notes, net of unamortized discount of $9,574	$89,410	—

Statement of Cash Flows

Year Ended December 31	1992
Cash flows from operating activities	
Net loss	$ (8,850)
Adjustments to reconcile net loss to net cash provided by operating activities	
Amortization of discount on zero-coupon mortgage notes	9,344
Other adjustments	7,574
Net cash provided by operating activities	$ 8,068
Cash flows from financing activities	
Prepayment of zero-coupon note	$(23,038)
Other adjustments	1,572
Net cash provided by (used in) financing activities	$(21,466)

Note 2: Debt Restructuring

In December 1992, the Company refinanced $75,689,000 representing the balance of its zero-coupon mortgage note that remained after reducing this indebtedness with the proceeds from the sale of properties. . . . The new financing, which is collateralized by first mortgage liens . . . matures in December 1995.

Source: EQK Realty Investors, *1992 Annual Report.*

Similar reclassification can be extended to previous years, when the company accrued (but did not pay) interest cost (amortization of discount) on these notes. Reported CFO obscured the fact that at some point the accrued interest must be repaid. As the maturity of the debt approached, the company faced a liquidity crisis.[12]

The following table presents reported and adjusted CFO for the period 1989 to 1994. The treatment of the interest on the zero-coupon bond causes significant distortions both prior to and following the 1992 refinancing.[13]

[12] In 1991 EQK's auditors issued a "going concern qualification" due to the impending maturity of the zero-coupon bond.

[13] The adjustment ignores small amounts of amortization of other discount notes.

EQK Realty Investors Adjustment of Operating Cash Flow (CFO), Years Ending December 31, 1989 to 1994 (in $thousands)

	1989	1990	1991	1992	1993	1994
Reported CFO	$10,458	$9,795	$ 5,728	$ 8,068	$4,087	$2,184
Less: zero-coupon interest	7,486	8,318	9,229	9,344	0	0
Adjusted CFO	$ 2,972	$1,477	$(3,501)	$(1,276)	$4,087	$2,184

After adjustment, the 1989 to 1991 deterioration in CFO is even more striking as 1991 CFO is negative.[14] The 1992 recovery is less impressive as adjusted CFO remains negative. In 1993, CFO rises despite the burden of full-coupon debt; the unadjusted data obscure this improvement. The adjusted CFO data provide better information regarding the operating cash flow trend.

Variable-Rate Debt

Some debt issues do not have a fixed coupon payment; the periodic interest payment varies with the level of interest rates. Such debt instruments are generally designed to trade at their face value. To achieve this objective, the interest rate "floats" above the rate on a specified-maturity U.S. Treasury obligation or some other benchmark rate such as the prime rate or LIBOR (London InterBank Offered Rate). The "spread" above the benchmark depends on the credit rating of the issuer.

Fixed- versus Variable-Rate Debt and Interest Rate Swaps

Borrowers can issue fixed-rate or variable-rate debt directly; alternatively, they can enter into interest rate swap agreements that convert a fixed-rate obligation to a floating-rate obligation or vice versa.

Whether a firm prefers to incur fixed-rate or variable-rate debt depends on a number of factors. Variable-rate debt exposes the firm's interest expense, cash flows, and related ratios to higher volatility due to interest rate changes.[15] On the other hand, when the firm's operating cash flows are correlated with movements in interest rates, variable-rate debt minimizes risk. The common notion that fixed rates minimize risk by reducing the volatility of a firm's income and cash flows is, thus, only a half-truth.[16]

Financial intermediaries (banks, finance companies) generally issue a high proportion of variable-rate debt, as their assets tend to be variable-rate in nature. Thus, they match the variability of their assets and liabilities.

---

[14] Note the increasing trend of interest expense on the zero-coupon debt, similar to the trend in Exhibit 43-4.

[15] The impact of interest rate changes can, of course, be either positive or negative.

[16] The investor point of view, however, is different. Variable-rate debt has low price risk; interest rate changes should have minimal impact on its market price. Significant market fluctuation should result only from perceived changes in credit quality. However, the variability of income is higher than for fixed-rate debt.

However, a nonfinancial firm may also view variable-rate debt as hedging variable operating cash flows. For example, the 1996 financial statements of AMR (American Airlines) state:

> Because American's operating results tend to be better in economic cycles with relatively high interest rates and its capital instruments tend to be financed with long-term fixed-rate instruments, interest rate swaps in which American pays the floating rate and receives the fixed rate are used to reduce the impact of economic cycles on American's net income.[17]

Alternatively, a firm may prefer to issue variable-rate debt because management believes that interest rates will fall or short-term rates (the usual basis for variable debt) will remain below long-term rates charged on fixed-rate loans. The analysis of a firm's debt should include a consideration of whether management's choice of financing alternatives is based on the inherent economics of the business or management speculation on future interest rate changes.

Debtors use interest rate swaps to manage the fixed- and variable-rate mix of total borrowings. Box 43-1 presents the mechanics of interest rate swaps.

Example:

Nash-Finch

Nash-Finch [NAFC] is a food wholesaler with annual sales exceeding $4 billion. The company's debt at December 31, 1998 and 1999 was $300 million and $315 million, respectively. For both years, the variable-rate debt was approximately 42% of the total debt ($128 million in 1998 and $132 million in 1999).

The company engaged in interest rate swaps, converting variable-rate to fixed-rate debt. The company disclosed the following information regarding interest rate swaps outstanding at the 1998 and 1999 year-ends (amounts in $thousands):

	Years Ended December 31	
	1998	**1999**
Receive variable/pay fixed	$90,000	$30,000
Average receive rate	5.5%	5.3%
Average pay rate	6.5%	6.5%

Note that Nash remains liable for the original principal and interest payments on the fixed-rate debt (see Box 43-1). *At the inception of the swap, no accounting recognition is required although Nash has altered its debt obligation.* Presumably at that time, the swap was "fair," that is, the net present value of the swap payments was zero. The transaction is an *off-balance-sheet contract.*

[17] AMR Corporation, 1996 Financial Statements, Note 6.

BOX 43-1 INTEREST RATE SWAPS

Firms use interest rate swaps* to exchange variable- (floating-) rate debt for obligations with fixed interest rates or, alternatively, to exchange fixed-rate debt for obligations with variable rates.

Swaps are contractual obligations that supplement existing debt agreements. Each firm remains liable for its original debt, makes all payments on that debt, and carries that debt on its books. The firm with variable-rate debt agrees to pay, at specified intervals, amounts equal to a fixed rate times the *notional principal amount*. In return, the counterparty pays variable amounts equal to the variable interest rate (pegged to a specified rate or index) times that same notional principal amount.

Because firms wish to minimize credit risk, they do not engage in swaps with other industrial firms, even when a swap would meet the objectives of both parties. The counterparty is normally a bank or other financial institution with a high credit rating. Money center banks, as a result, have large portfolios of swaps.†

Given that some firms prefer variable-rate debt and others fixed-rate debt, why do they not arrange their preferred form of financing directly with their creditors? Why incur the additional costs and/or risks of swaps? Frictions in the credit markets and/or the institutional setting of the firm may result in differential borrowing costs that make it cheaper to borrow in the non-preferred mode and swap into the preferred mode of borrowing rather than borrowing directly in the preferred mode. For example, some "household name" American firms can borrow at very low rates in certain foreign markets. A second factor leading to swaps is that preferences change over time. This is especially true of firms that use swaps to "match" assets and liabilities (see Chapter 16 for a discussion of hedging activities).

Illustration

The Triple A and Triple B companies each want to borrow $100 million. Assume that the Triple A company prefers variable-rate debt, whereas the Triple B company prefers fixed-rate debt. The companies' respective borrowing rates and preferences are:

Company	Fixed-Rate	Variable-Rate	Preferred Mode
Triple A	8%	Prime	Variable
Triple B	10%	Prime + 1%	Fixed

The Triple-A company is considered to be more creditworthy than the Triple B company and, hence, is offered more favorable borrowing terms. Note that the rate differential on fixed-rate debt (2%) is greater than the differential (1%) on floating-rate debt. This discrepancy makes it profitable for firms to enter into swaps.

Based on these rates, we demonstrate that the combined borrowing cost for the two firms is 1% lower when each company *borrows in its nonpreferred mode*. This 1% difference is independent of changes in the prime rate.

Company	Borrow Preferred Mode	Borrow Nonpreferred Mode
Triple A	Prime	8%
Triple B	10%	Prime + 1%
Total cost	Prime + 10%	Prime + 9%

The two firms are both better off borrowing in their nonpreferred mode, "swapping" the debt and splitting the 1% savings. The swap agreement requires the following payments:

- The Triple A company pays the Triple B company the prime rate (times the notional amount of $100 million).
- The Triple B company pays the Triple A company 8.5% (times the notional amount of $100 million).

The cost of the original borrowing and the swap for each company is

	Original Loan	+ To Swap Counter-party	− From Swap Counter-party	= Net Cost
Triple A	8%	Prime	(8.5%)	Prime − 0.5%
Triple B	Prime + 1%	8.5%	(Prime)	9.5%

Each company has obtained debt in its preferred mode at a rate one-half percent below the rate available on its preferred mode of borrowing.

* For a further elaboration of these issues, see James Bicksler and Andrew Chen, "An Economic Analysis of Interest Rate Swaps," *Journal of Finance*, July 1986 and John Hull, *Introduction to Futures and Options Markets* (Englewood Cliffs, NJ: Prentice-Hall, 1995), Chapter 6.

† See Chapter 16 for further discussion of derivatives held by financial institutions.

Economic Effects of the Swap

Assume that the swap illustrated has a five-year term, the prime rate is 6% at inception, payments are made semiannually, and adjustments for changes in the prime rate are also semiannual. The first semiannual assessment results in a net payment of \$1.25 million [0.5 × (8.5% − 6%) × \$100 million] from Triple B to Triple A. If, for the second semiannual period, the prime rate increases to 7%, then the second scheduled payment will be \$0.75 million [0.5 × (8.5% − 7%) × \$100 million]. *Although Triple B has borrowed at a variable rate, increases in that rate are passed on to Triple A as Triple B's payments decline. Thus, Triple B's economic cost is the fixed rate of 9.5%. Conversely, Triple A is exposed to rising interest rates although it has incurred only fixed-rate debt. The swap has changed the economic position of both firms.*

Economic Effects of Termination

Now assume that Triple A, expecting increases in interest rates, wishes to terminate the swap agreement after the first payment. How much should Triple A pay to do so? The required payment should equal the fair value of the swap agreement, calculated as follows.[‡]

Triple B is liable for 9 semiannual payments of \$4.25 million (0.5 × 8.5% × \$100 million). If Triple B enters into another swap agreement, it would be based on current interest rates. If the fixed rate has increased by 0.5% (while the prime rate has increased by 1%), Triple B would have to make 9 payments of \$4.5 million (0.5 × 9% × \$100 million), an increase of \$250 thousand. The present value of the increase discounted at the *new* rate of 9% is equal to approximately \$1.8 million. Thus, to terminate the swap, Triple A must pay Triple B that amount.

[‡] In our simplified example, we assume that the swap is terminated at the same time when the floating rate is reset. Were this not the case, then a similar calculation would have to be made for the variable-rate bond to compensate for the fact that if Triple B entered into a new swap agreement, while it is true that it would pay a higher fixed rate, it would receive immediately floating-rate payments based on the higher floating rate and not have to wait for the next adjustment date. This calculation, however, is usually not very material; it is for only one payment and the discounting period is less than six months (from the termination date to the interest rate adjustment date).

The effect of the swap was to reduce the sensitivity of Nash to changes in interest rates:

Effect of Swap on Debt Structure (amounts in \$thousands)

	1998		1999	
	Before Swap	**After Swap**	**Before Swap**	**After Swap**
Fixed	\$172,125	\$262,125	\$183,609	\$213,609
Variable	127,665	37,665	131,990	101,990
Total	\$299,790	\$299,790	\$315,599	\$315,599
% Variable	42.6%	12.6%	41.8%	32.3%

The swap has also affected Nash's interest expense as the required payments (fixed) exceeded the amounts received (based on variable rates):

	Years Ended December 31	
	1998	**1999**
Swap	\$90,000	\$30,000
Interest received	4,950	1,590
Interest paid	(5,850)	(1,950)
Net payment	\$ (900)	\$ (360)
Interest expense:		
Reported	\$29,034	\$31,213
Ex-swap	28,134	30,853
Increase due to swap	3.2%	1.2%

What conclusions can we draw from these data?

1. Nash entered into the swaps to reduce its vulnerability to higher interest rates. It did not replace swaps expiring in 1999, thus increasing its exposure. Yet total debt (and variable debt) increased from 1998 to 1999.
2. The swaps increased Nash's interest expense as the fixed-rate payments exceeded the variable rate payments. The net payments can be viewed as the cost of insurance against the effect of higher interest rates.
3. While the fair value of the swaps at inception (net present value) can be assumed to be zero, the fair value will fluctuate over the swap term. If the changes are favorable, Nash-Finch will have an unrealized gain; if unfavorable there will be an unrealized loss.[18]
4. Nash also assumed *counterparty risk*, the risk that the other party will default. When Nash must make net payments (as in 1998 and 1999) there is no risk. If variable rates rose sharply, resulting in payments to Nash, then default risk would be present.[19] *When a company enters into swaps that are material to its financial position, the analyst should ensure that the counterparties are sufficiently strong so that the likelihood of default is insignificant.*[20]

These conclusions result in questions that the analyst may want to pursue by discussing them with management. Especially in the first case, the answer might yield useful insights regarding management's strategy regarding interest rate risk.

Debt Denominated in a Foreign Currency

Companies sometimes issue debt for which all interest and principal payments are made in a foreign currency. There are three motivations for such issuance:

1. More favorable terms in foreign markets than domestic ones.[21]
2. Assets denominated in the foreign currency and debt denominated in that currency can hedge[22] against exchange rate movements.
3. Need for foreign currency for a particular investment or other transaction.

The carrying value of foreign currency debt is adjusted for changes in exchange rates.

For example, Note 24 of the 2000 financial statements of Roche reports debt in Japanese yen and U.S. dollars as well as Roche's parent currency of

---

[18] See Chapter 16 for discussion of when and how gains and losses from derivatives must be recognized in the financial statements.

[19] When the fair value of the swap changes so that Nash-Finch has an unrealized gain, realization of that gain depends on the creditworthiness of the counterparty.

[20] If we assume that the counterparty is a highly rated financial institution, it would not provide collateral to protect Nash against default.

[21] For example, in July 1998, Pepsico issued one-year notes in Japan (to retail investors) and swapped the fixed-rate obligation for floating rate U.S. dollar payments. The company stated that its net borrowing cost was *comfortably below one-month LIBOR*.

[22] If the parent currency strengthens relative to the foreign currency, then the carrying amount of assets denominated in foreign currencies decreases. This decrease is offset by the decrease (in the parent currency) of the debt to be repaid.

Swiss francs. Note that the carrying amounts for the yen and U.S. dollar bonds[23] rose in 2000 due to appreciation of those currencies against the Swiss franc.[24]

This adjustment for exchange rate changes is distinct from any adjustment to current market value. Market value adjustments are based on changes in interest rates.[25] The market value of this debt in local currencies may have increased if interest rates declined since the debt was issued; this change is *not* reflected on the balance sheet. *Thus, the balance sheet liability has been adjusted for exchange rate changes but not interest rate changes.*

Project Debt

Some debt is issued to finance a single project, such as a factory, pipeline, or real estate. In these cases, the debt terms are tailored to the expected cash flows generated by the project. Project debt may be *nonrecourse,* meaning that the lender will be paid only from project cash flows and cannot demand payment from the debtor if the project is unsuccessful. Mortgages on real estate are the major example of nonrecourse debt. Even though such debt is shown on the debtor's balance sheet, the debt is a claim only against the project cash flows and assets. Some project debt is incurred by joint ventures, discussed in Reading 44.

Example:

Forest City Enterprises

Forest City [FCE], a U.S. developer of commercial and residential real estate, finances most of its projects with nonrecourse mortgage debt. The company's capital structure at January 31, 2000 was (in $millions):

Mortgage debt, nonrecourse	$2,382.4	74.5%
Recourse debt	429.9	13.4%
Shareholders' equity	386.5	12.1%
Total capital	$3,198.8	100.0%

The large proportion of nonrecourse debt protects the company from adversity. The effects of one poorly performing project cannot jeopardize others, as the company cannot lose more than its total investment in that project.

[23] The rise in the carrying amount of the zero coupon U.S. dollar obligations is due to accretion of discount as well as the appreciation of the U.S. dollar.

[24] See the financial review (p. 51 of the Roche annual report) for foreign currency data.

[25] In theory, exchange rates are also affected by interest rates. However, that influence is based on the *difference* in interest rate levels between the two countries, *not the level* of interest rates.

OPTIONAL SEGMENT ENDS

Debt with Equity Features

Convertible Bonds and Warrants

To reduce borrowing costs, many companies issue debt convertible into their common shares or issue a combination of bonds and warrants to purchase common shares. Although conceptually these two types of "equity-linked" debt are identical, their accounting consequences may differ.[26]

Convertible Bonds. Under APB 14 (1969), the conversion feature of a bond is completely ignored when the bond is issued. Thus, the entire proceeds of the bond are recorded as a liability, and interest expense is recorded as if the bond were nonconvertible. However, the conversion feature lowers interest expense. When the bondholder converts the convertible bond into common stock, the entire proceeds are reclassified from debt to equity. As discussed in Box 43-2, however, the FASB issued an exposure draft that would change the accounting for convertible debt.

From an analytic perspective, however, recognition should be given to the equity feature prior to the conversion. When the stock price is (significantly) greater than the conversion price, it is likely that the debt will not have to be repaid, and the convertible bond should be treated as equity rather than debt when calculating solvency ratios such as debt-to-equity. When the stock price is significantly below the conversion price, the bond should be treated as debt. At levels close to the conversion price, the instrument has both debt and equity features, and its treatment becomes a more difficult issue.

One possibility is to separate the debt and equity values of the convertible bond, using option pricing models. This analysis is complex, however, and beyond the scope of this book. IAS 32 (2000) requires issuers to split compound instruments into their component parts. The FASB ED would require such separation. Alternatively, the analyst can examine the sensitivity of key ratios to bond classification, first treating the bond as debt and then as equity to see whether the differences are significant. If they are, then the question of whether the debt will be ultimately converted becomes a key issue, which may depend on the purpose of the analysis.[27]

Example:

Holmen

Note 18 of Holmen's annual report shows that in 1998, the company issued debt of SKr 361 million, convertible into class B common shares in 2004 at a price of SKr 148.10. As the market price of Holmen's class B

[26] A convertible bond can be disaggregated into a bond plus an option to convert the bond into common shares. An important difference between a convertible and a debt-plus-warrant issue is that, in the former case, the bond must be surrendered to exercise the option, whereas in the latter case, the bond and warrant are not linked. Thus, the issuer can use the proceeds of exercised warrants for purposes other than the retirement of the associated debt. Another difference is their impact on earnings-per-share calculations. The interest expense on the convertible issue is eliminated when diluted earnings per share are computed, whereas the interest on the debt component of the bond-plus-option alternative will never affect earnings-per-share calculations (however, there is an adjustment for the exercise of dilutive warrants).

[27] For example, in takeover analysis, the intended purchase price will determine whether convertible bonds will be converted to common or remain outstanding debt.

BOX 43-2 FASB EXPOSURE DRAFT: ACCOUNTING FOR FINANCIAL INSTRUMENTS WITH CHARACTERISTICS OF LIABILITIES, EQUITY, OR BOTH

OPTIONAL SEGMENT

On October 27, 2000, the Board issued an exposure draft (ED) that would change the accounting for:

- Convertible debt
- Redeemable preferred shares

In general, the ED would classify as equity all financial instruments components that establish an ownership relationship with the issuer. A component establishes an ownership relationship if it

1. Is an outstanding equity share not subject to redemption, or
2. Is an obligation that can or must be settled by the issuance of equity shares, and all changes in the monetary value of the obligation are attributable to, equal to, and in the same direction as the change in the fair value of the issuer's equity shares.

The new standard would require that proceeds of issuance of securities with both liability and equity components be allocated between the value of the liability component and that of the equity component. The most important example is the issuance of convertible debt, which would be accounted for as if the company sold a combination of debt and warrants.

When a company issued convertible debt, it would be required to allocate the proceeds (net of underwriting fees and other direct costs of issuance) between the debt (liability) component and the warrant (equity) component using their relative fair values. If the warrant could not be valued, the issuer would estimate the fair value of the debt component, and allocate the remaining proceeds to the equity component.*

Further, if the debt is repurchased or converted, the issuer must recognize gain or loss† equal to the difference between the fair value of the debt component and the carrying amount of the liability.

There would also be a gain or loss on the equity component at the date of repurchase or conversion. This gain or loss would be excluded from income but would affect stockholders' equity.

OPTIONAL SEGMENT ENDS

The accounting change would have the following effects:

1. The difference between the fair value of the debt component and its face value would be amortized over the life of the debt, using the effective interest method. This would result in higher interest expense and lower income than under current accounting.
2. Only the debt component would be shown as a liability; the equity component would be recorded in stockholders' equity. As a result, the debt-to-equity ratio would be lower than under the current accounting method.
3. At redemption or conversion, the company would recognize a gain or loss on the liability component. In general, companies would recognize a loss when interest rates were lower at the time of repurchase or conversion than when the debt was issued. In the case of conversion, the fair value of the liability component would be added to equity, rather than the carrying amount under current accounting.
4. At redemption or conversion, stockholders' equity would reflect the change in value of the equity component. When the underlying shares have risen in value, equity would rise, reducing the debt-to-equity ratio. Under current accounting, the market value at redemption or conversion date has no effect on the balance sheet.

The ED would also change the classification of redeemable preferred shares (and similar instruments such as Trust Preferreds) by requiring that they be recorded as debt in the issuer's balance sheet. Similarly, the "dividends" paid on such shares would be included in interest expense.

The effect of this change would be to increase the reported debt-equity ratio and reduce the interest coverage ratio of affected firms.

A final standard was expected to be issued prior to the end of 2002. It is likely that affected companies would be required to restate their financial statements for the accounting change.

* This method is styled the "with-and-without method" in the ED.

† Under SFAS 145 (2002), gains and losses from the extinguishment of debt are treated as extraordinary items only when they meet the APB 30 criteria for classification as an extraordinary item (see Reading 31).

shares was SKr 307 at December 31, 1999, these bonds should be considered equity. The reclassification decreases the debt/total capital ratio:

Holmen Capital Structure
December 31, 1999

	Reported	Reclassification	Adjusted
SKr millions			
Financial liabilities	6,845	(361)	6,484
Equity	15,883	361	16,244
Total capital	22,728		22,728
Financial liabilities	30.1%		28.5%
Equity	69.9%		71.5%

Exchangeable Bonds. Some bond issues are convertible into shares of another firm rather than those of the issuing firm. The analysis of such issues is more complex than the analysis of convertible debt. Exercise of the conversion privilege results in:

- Extinguishment of the debt
- Elimination of the investment in the underlying shares
- Recognition of gain or loss from the "sale" (via debt conversion) of the underlying shares

The motivation for such debt issues may include:

1. The desire to obtain cash while retaining the underlying shares for strategic reasons.
2. Minimizing the market effect of sales; the underlying shares are sold over time as bonds are exchanged.
3. Financial benefits: The interest rate on the exchangeable bonds will be lower (because of the exchange feature) than on straight debt, and the exercise price will contain a premium over the current market price.
4. Delayed recognition of a large unrealized gain; recognition is postponed until the exchange privilege is exercised. This delays the income tax recognition of the gain and may permit management some control over the timing of the gain (it can call the bonds, forcing exchange, when it wishes to report the gain).
5. Hedging the investment. SFAS 133 changed the accounting for such hedges.

Example:

Times Mirror

In March 1996, Times Mirror [TMC] sold 1.3 million shares of Premium Equity Participating Securities (PEPS) redeemable for shares of Netscape. TMC had purchased Netscape shares less than one year earlier, before

Netscape's initial public offering, at a price of $2.25 per share. TMC's Netscape shares were restricted from public sale. The PEPS were sold at a price of $39.25 with a 4.25% coupon and a March 15, 2001 maturity. At that date, each PEPS was redeemable for the cash equivalent of:

- One Netscape share if that share's price was below $39.25
- .87 Netscape share if its price was $45.15 or higher
- $39.25 cash if Netscape's share price was between $45.15 and $39.25

The advantages to TMC of offering PEPS were that TMC:

1. Received the fair market value of its Netscape shares, at a low interest rate of 4.25%, despite the fact that the shares could not be legally sold.
2. Hedged its investment; if Netscape shares declined, the PEPS holders would receive smaller payments at maturity.
3. Maintained part of the upside potential given the reduced conversion rate if Netscape shares exceeded $45.15 in price at maturity.
4. Postponed capital gains tax until the actual sale of Netscape shares was effected through conversion of the PEPS.
5. Enabled TMC to control the timing of its realization of the large gain on the Netscape investment.

The last two advantages are illustrated by events in 1998 and 1999:

- In 1998, TMC sold part of its Netscape holding, redeemed a corresponding portion of the PEPS, and realized a pretax gain of $16 million.[28]
- In 1999, TMC sold shares of AOL (which had acquired Netscape) and redeemed additional PEPS, reporting a pretax gain of nearly $17 million.

Bonds with Warrants. When warrants and bonds are issued together, the accounting treatment differs from that of convertible bonds. The proceeds must be allocated between the two financial instruments.[29] The fair value of the bond portion is the recorded liability. As a result, the bond is issued at a discount, and interest expense includes amortization of that discount. The fair value of the warrants is included in equity and has no income statement impact. When warrants are exercised, the additional cash increases equity capital.

Roche has made extensive use of bonds with equity features (see Note 24 and pages 99–101 of the Roche annual report).

Comparison of Convertible Bonds and Bonds with Warrants. As bonds with warrants are accounted for as if they were issued at a discount, the reported liability is lower (but increases as the discount is amortized) as compared to that of

[28] This gain was previously reflected in equity as TMC carried its investment in Netscape at market value.

[29] As discussed in Box 43-2, the FASB has proposed extending this accounting treatment to convertible bonds as well.

a convertible bond. However, reported interest expense is higher.[30] As discussed earlier in this reading, reported cash flow from operations is the same, equal to the coupon interest.

These differences are summarized in the list below, which also includes a comparison with a conventional bond. Note that issuing debt with equity features:

- Lowers interest expense
- Increases operating cash flows
- Results in a balance sheet liability equal to or below that of a conventional bond

In all respects, such debt appears less costly.

Interest Expense	Balance Sheet Liability	Operating Cash Flow
Conventional bond	Conventional bond	Conventional bond
greater than	*equal to*	*less than*
Bond with warrants	Convertible bond	Convertible bond
greater than	*greater than*	*equal to*
Convertible bond	Bond with warrants	Bond with warrants

However, the financial statement effects are misleading as the cost of the equity feature is ignored. When convertible debt is issued, there is a systematic understatement of interest expense.[31]

Commodity Bonds

The interest and principal payments on bond issues are sometimes tied to the price of a commodity, such as gold, silver, or oil. Firms producing the commodity, as part of a hedge strategy, may issue such bonds. A higher commodity price increases the payments to bondholders but is offset by higher operating profitability. These bonds, therefore, convert interest from a fixed to a variable cost. Such bonds were issued during time periods when commodity prices were rising, making the bonds attractive to purchasers. A recent variation on this theme is the issuance of bonds whose payoff depends on losses due to insurance losses resulting from natural catastrophes.

Perpetual Debt

Some debt issues have no stated maturity. When debt does not have a maturity date, it may be considered preferred equity rather than a liability for analytic purposes. An exception would be cases where debt covenants are likely to force repayment or refinancing of the debt.

---

[30] Because of the accounting difference, American companies rarely issue debt/warrant combinations. However, such issues are common outside of the United States.

[31] Moreover, the impact of equity-linked bonds on earnings per share must always be taken into consideration.

Example:

SAS

In 1986, SAS (Scandinavian Airlines) issued a perpetual 200 million Swiss franc–denominated subordinated loan, with the interest rate fixed for 10 years and reset every 10 years. While there is no set maturity date, SAS has the exclusive right to terminate the loan once every five years.

In 1994, SAS repurchased SFR 55.35 million at a price of 72. This repurchase shows that perpetual notes are not the same as equity, as changes in market conditions may lead the issuer to refinance them. However, given management control over the refinancing decision, treatment as preferred equity is appropriate absent evidence of refinancing intent.

When long-term interest rates were at low levels, some firms issued debt with a maturity of 100 years. Although such issues are technically debt, their long maturity suggests that, for all practical purposes, they represent permanent capital and should be treated as equity when computing the debt-to-equity ratio. For example, Walt Disney issued 100-year bonds in 1993.[32]

Preferred Stock

Many companies issue more than one class of shares. Preferred (or preference) shares have priority over common shares with respect to dividends and entitlement to the proceeds of sale or liquidation. In exchange for this privileged position, preferred shareholders usually give up their right to participate fully in the success of the company.

Preferred shares generally have a fixed dividend payment and a fixed preference on liquidation. Dividend payments are almost always *cumulative;* if not paid when due, they remain a liability (but one that is not recorded). Dividend arrears must be paid before any dividend can be paid to common shareholders. When calculating the net worth of a company with preferred shares outstanding, the analyst should:

1. Subtract the liquidating value of the preferred, not the par or stated value, which may be lower.
2. Subtract any cumulative dividends that are in arrears.

Some preferred shares have a variable interest rate. "Auction rate" preferred shares have interest rates that change frequently, making them attractive to buyers seeking "money-market"-type investments.[33] From an analytical perspective, these preferred shares function as short-term liabilities and should be treated as such. They are often called when market conditions change, making them a less permanent source of funds.

---

[32] These bonds have a fixed interest rate of 7.55%, protecting Disney against future interest rate increases. As the bonds are not callable until 2023, the buyers were protected against lower interest rates for 30 years.

[33] For U.S. corporate buyers, preferred dividends are 70% tax-free when ownership is below 20%, making these issues more attractive on an after-tax basis than many other short-term investments. The exclusion is 80% for ownership of 20% but below 80%.

Preferred shares are almost always callable by the issuer. Many issues are, however, redeemable by the preferred shareholder, often over a period of years.[34] Because of these "sinking fund" provisions, redeemable preferreds should be treated as debt for analysis; they should be included as debt in solvency ratios, and dividend payments should be treated as interest. The FASB has issued an exposure draft (see Box 43-2) that would require redeemable preferred shares to be reported as debt, and the "dividends" on such shares included in interest expense, as required by IAS 32 (2000).

Consistent with this view, the SEC requires that redeemable preferred shares be excluded from stockholders' equity. However, at the same time, the SEC does not require their classification as debt. The argument against debt classification is that, ultimately, *firms cannot be forced to pay the dividends or redeem the preferred shares. Unlike creditors, preferred shareholders do not have the power to force the firm into bankruptcy for noncompliance* with the terms of the agreement.[35] Often, when dividends are in arrears, they do gain representation on the board of directors.

The ambiguity as to whether these shares are debt or equity was shown in two studies by Kimmel and Warfield (1993, 1995). They found that only 60% of redeemable preferred shares are actually redeemed; the other 40% are eventually converted to common shares, arguing against treating these hybrids as debt. Furthermore, as a firm's systematic risk (its beta) is related to a firm's debt-to-equity ratio, they tested whether the relationship had a better "fit" with the redeemables treated as debt or equity. They found that they *did not fit into either category unless the redeemables had voting rights and were convertible.* Only when these attributes were present did the securities exhibit equitylike qualities. Thus, on average, one cannot generalize as to the nature of these hybrid securities.

The line between debt and equity has become increasingly blurred in recent years. Companies prefer to issue securities that minimize the after-tax cost of financing yet provide maximum flexibility.[36] Some issues are designated preferreds but are really debt; others are called debt but are functionally equity. Although help from accounting standards setters is on the way, analysts must evaluate such instruments on a case-by-case basis and decide whether to treat them as debt or equity.

Effects of Changes in Interest Rates

Debt reported on the balance sheet is equal to the present value of future cash payments discounted at the *market rate on the date of issuance*. Increases (decreases) in the *current market rate* decrease (increase) the *market value* of the debt. A company that issues fixed-rate debt prior to an increase (decrease) in market rates experiences an economic gain (loss) as a result of the rate change. This economic gain or loss is not reflected in either the income statement or balance sheet.

For some analytical purposes, however, the market value of a company's debt may be more relevant than its book value. It better reflects the firm's economic position and is as important as the current market values of a firm's assets. Analysis of a firm's absolute and relative level of debt and borrowing capacity should be

[34] These provisions provide preferred shareholders with a guaranteed future value for the shares.

[35] In many states, a firm cannot pay dividends or redeem shares if such payments will jeopardize the company's survival.

[36] Trust Preferred Securities (TPS) are an example of such securities. For tax purposes, they are treated as debt. While they cannot be classified as equity, they are not reported as debt but rather as preferred shares or minority interest. Similarly, "dividend" payments are reported as preferred dividends or minority interest. Frischmann, Kimmel, and Warfield (1999) refer to TPSs as the "Holy Grail" of financial instruments and report that, since their introduction in 1993, they have become the primary mode of new issues of preferred shares.

based on current market conditions. Consider two firms reporting the same book value of debt. One firm issued the debt when interest rates were low; the other at higher current interest rates. Debt-to-equity ratios based on book values may be the same. However, the firm that issued the bonds at the lower interest rate has higher borrowing capacity as the economic value of its debt is lower.[37] Ratios calculated using the market value of debt would reflect the stronger solvency position.

Furthermore, in valuation models that deduct the value of debt from the value of the firm (or of its assets), that debt should be measured at market value rather than book value.[38] Firms that issued debt at lower rates are relatively better off when interest rates increase, and this advantage should increase the equity value of the firm.

In the United States, SFAS 107, Disclosures about Fair Value of Financial Instruments, requires that firms report the fair value of outstanding debt. IAS 32 (1998) has similar requirements. Box 43-3 restates the debt of Westvaco from book to market value. This exercise is useful for several reasons.

First, financial statement disclosures are based on year-end (or quarter) prices. When interest rates have changed significantly since the last report date, the analyst may need to recalculate the market value of the firm's debt. Second, most non-U.S. firms, and firms in the United States that are not subject to FASB disclosure requirements, do not provide market value disclosures; analysts must know how to estimate the market value of debt for such firms. Finally, market valuation requires assumptions and (especially for firms with complex financial instruments) often there are competing valuation methods. In some cases, analysts may want to perform their own market value calculations. To do so, they must disaggregate management's aggregate fair value disclosure; this requires an understanding of how market values are estimated.

Example:

Westvaco

The book value of Westvaco's long-term debt was $1,477 million at October 31, 1999; its market value was $1,494 million, or 1% higher. The October 31, 1998 book value was $1,557 million; its market value was $1,636 million, or 5% higher. Thus, during the 1999 fiscal year, market value relative to book value declined 4%. This decline reflected the rise in interest rates (see Box 43-3), which reduced the fair value. The decline reflects the structure of Westvaco's debt, which is mostly fixed-rate debt with long maturities.

OPTIONAL SEGMENT

The Westvaco example above is not unique. The market value of the long-term debt of Mead [MEA] was 6.6% higher than book value at December 31, 1998 (Mead was on a calendar year). One year later, the market value was 2.9% below the book value; during calendar 1999, therefore, market value relative to book value declined by 9.5% as interest rates rose. Mead, which merged with Westvaco early in 2002, had a similar debt structure, mostly fixed rate debt with long maturities.

---

[37] Theoretically, it could refinance its current debt at the same interest rate as the other firm, lowering the book value of debt.

[38] Similarly, in discounted cash flow valuation analysis, the calculation of a firm's (weighted-average) cost of capital is based on market rather than book values of debt (and equity).

BOX 43-3 ESTIMATING THE MARKET VALUE OF DEBT

In many cases, the replacement of book value with market value is simple. For publicly traded debt, market values are readily available.* If the debt is not publicly traded, its present value can be calculated by applying the current market rate to the original debt terms. The maturity, coupon rate, and other terms of long-term debt are generally disclosed for each debt security issued.

The appropriate current market rate can be obtained from:

1. Other publicly traded debt of the company having approximately the same maturity; estimate the rate used by the market to discount that debt.
2. Publicly traded debt of equivalent companies in the same industry; estimate the rate used to discount that debt.
3. Estimating the risk premium over the rate on government debt of the same maturity. The risk premium depends on the bond-rating "risk" class of the company's bonds.

Calculating the Market Value of Debt

Footnote J in Westvaco's financial statements shows notes payable and long-term obligations at October 31, 1999. The company reports the fair value as required by SFAS 107.† The book and fair values for the three years ended October 31, 2000 are (in $thousands):

October 31	1998	1999	2000
Book value	$1,557,477	$1,477,162	$2,716,772
Fair value	1,636,093	1,494,290	2,627,696
Difference	$ 78,616	$ 17,128	$ (89,076)

Source: Westvaco *Annual Reports, 1999 and 2000.*

The maturities, coupon rates, and carrying amounts for most obligations are listed in footnote J. Some obligations are publicly traded while others are not.

As Westvaco discloses the fair (market) value of its debt, we forgo the laborious task of calculating the estimated market value for each issue. The following comments are intended as a guide for use when such calculations are required.

Most of Westvaco's debt at October 31, 1999 consists of fixed-rate long-term debentures, some of which have sinking funds. Because the rate is fixed and the duration is long, the fair value of these bonds fluctuates with interest rates.

Example:

In 1990 Westvaco, which was A rated, issued $100 million of 9 75% bonds due June 15, 2020. At the issue date, the yield‡ was 130 basis points (1.3%) above the yield on the U.S. Treasury 8.75% bonds due in May, 2020. The price and yield to maturity of the U.S. Treasury 8.75% issue at October 31, 1998–2001 was reported by Bloomberg as follows:

October 31	1998	1999	2000	2001
Price	142-11*	124-30	131-4	145-11
Yield-to-maturity	5.40%	6.53%	6.02%	4.98%

* US government securities with maturities longer than one year are quoted as a % of face value in 32nds. Thus 142-11 means 142 11/32% of face value or $1,423.44 per $1,000 bond.

Source: Price and yield data from Bloomberg.

Estimation of the fair value of the Westvaco 9¾% bonds requires an estimate of the spread over the U.S. Treasury bond. That spread is a function of the rating of the corporate issuer (Westvaco) and the spread between bonds of different ratings classes.§ Bond quality spreads are variable over time, tending to compress when the economy is strong (and concerns about credit quality are low) and to widen when economic conditions weaken.

Westvaco was A rated by Standard & Poor's at October 31, 1997 and A rated at October 31, 1998. Standard & Poor's data show little change in quality spreads in 1998 and 1999. Thus, our calculations assume that the Westvaco bonds had a yield to maturity of 130 basis points for both years.

Extending this analysis to 2000 and 2001, we find two changes:

1. Westvaco's S&P rating was reduced from A− to BBB+ in May 2000 and further reduced to BBB in June 2001. These rating reductions reflected Westvaco's higher leverage.
2. Quality spreads started to widen in 2000 and 2001 as concerns grew about the economic outlook and the possible effect of recession on corporate credit quality. The September 11, 2001 terrorist attacks accelerated this trend.

* Sources include rating service publications (such as Standard & Poor's *Bond Guide*), newspapers, and electronic quotation services.

† The book value does not match the total of current and noncurrent obligations in footnote J. The company has apparently excluded some long-term obligations that it considers not to be financial instruments.

‡ Throughout this box, yield means yield-to-maturity.

§ See Chapter 18 for discussion of bond ratings.

Thus our estimated yield spread for the Westvaco bonds is 180 basis points at October 31, 2000 and 220 basis points at October 31, 2001.

The following table shows the results of these assumptions and the calculated fair value of the Westvaco bonds. These fair value estimates differ from the actual market value reported in Bloomberg by less than 2% each year.

October 31	1998	1999	2000	2001
Yield on U.S. 8.75% bond	5.40%	6.53%	6.02%	4.98%
Assumed spread	1.30%	1.30%	1.80%	2.20%
Assumed yield on Westvaco 9.75% bond	6.70%	7.83%	7.82%	7.18%
Calculated value of Westvaco bond	$1,344.85	$1,194.43	$1,191.50	$1,260.88
Bloomberg value of Westvaco bond	1,369.80	1,217.40	1,169.30	1,245.60
Difference	−1.8%	−1.9%	1.9%	1.2%

Source: Price and yield data from Bloomberg.

Complexities in Market Value Estimation

Because of the conventional nature of Westvaco's debt, the calculation of its market value is straightforward. Westvaco's debt is virtually all fixed rate and dollar denominated. Simple debt structures, however, are becoming the exception rather than the rule for large companies, given globalization and the increased sophistication of financial markets.

Some complexities make the calculation of market values almost impossible as the requisite information is lacking. A few of the complexities summarized below have been discussed earlier, others will be addressed in later sections of the text, and some remain beyond the scope of our book.

Convertible Bonds

Market prices are readily available for most convertible debt issues. However, these prices incorporate both the debt and equity features of the security. Only the debt component of the market value should be included as part of debt.

Variable-Rate Debt

Variable-rate debt usually requires no market value adjustment. Because of the continuous adjustment of the interest rate on the debt, market value approximates book value.**

Debt Denominated in a Foreign Currency

For debt denominated in a foreign currency, the present value calculations should be based on current interest rates for the currency in which the debt is denominated.

Hedges and Derivatives

Firms can protect themselves against changes in interest rates and/or currency exchange rates using instruments such as options or forward contracts (including swap agreements). We defer a discussion of the accounting treatment and economic impact of these instruments on the value of a firm's debt, for the most part, to Chapter 16. In this reading we confine ourselves to a discussion of *interest rate swaps*.

As previously discussed, *the original debt instrument with its original parameters remains in effect and is reported in the firm's financial statements; if publicly traded, market prices are available*. However, the estimated market value of the underlying debt instrument must reflect any interest rate swap.

When fixed-rate debt has been converted to floating-rate debt with an interest rate swap covering its full term, no adjustment to market value is required. If a swap does not cover the full term of fixed-rate debt, changes in interest rates after the end of the swap term will affect market values. Thus, it is important to discern the terms of any swaps by careful reading of footnotes.

When a swap converts floating-rate debt to fixed-rate debt, however, the market value is exposed to changes in interest rates. Even though the market value of the original obligation does not change, the fair value of the effective (because of the swap) obligation does and should be calculated.

** This is not precisely accurate. The variable-rate adjustment may lag the interest rate change. Nevertheless, given the short period until adjustment, the effect of any lag on present value is usually immaterial. Because of this, SFAS 107 states that, for variable-rate debt, the book value can be used to approximate the market or fair value.

These factors (confirmed by empirical results discussed in Box 43-4) suggest the conditions to be considered before deciding whether the restatement of debt to market value is a useful exercise. All of the following factors should be considered.

Debt: Market or Book Value?

Given the effort and assumptions required to estimate market values when they are not provided, we now turn to a discussion of the factors that determine whether the adjustment from book value to market value is a useful exercise. Empirical results with respect to these factors are discussed in Box 43-4.

Debt Maturities. The effect of interest rate changes on the market value of debt increases with the maturity of the debt. If a firm's debt is mostly short-term, changes in interest rates will not appreciably affect its market value.[39]

Interest Rates on Debt. For adjustable-rate debt, whose interest rate varies with the market rate of interest, book value approximates market value and no adjustment is required. On the other hand, the market value of fixed-rate debt issues does change with interest rates. This is especially true of zero-coupon and other discount debt, due to their longer duration relative to debt of the same maturity issued at par.

When a firm has swapped its fixed debt for floating-rate debt, there should be no adjustment, as the value of that debt is no longer exposed to interest rate changes. Conversely, when a firm swaps variable rates for fixed rates, the market value of that portion of its debt will vary with interest rates and adjustment is required.

Changes in Market Interest Rates. The adjustment to market value depends on changes in the market rate of interest. As long as there is no long-term trend, fluctuations in market value tend to offset, leaving the difference between book and market values small. However, when rates rise or fall greatly over several years, the differences between book and market value can be significant.

Embedded Interest Rate. Westvaco issued debt at various times and its (weighted) average outstanding coupon rate (*embedded rate*) was approximately 8.39%,[40] within the range of interest rates over the late 1990s. The adjustment from book value does not depend on the change in interest rates itself, but rate changes relative to the imbedded rate. As interest rates were below the embedded rate for both 1998 and 1999, the fair value exceeds book value.

Unless there are limits on the firm's ability to refinance (noncallable debt or deterioration in credit quality), the embedded rate should decline (with some lag) as interest rates fall. The reverse is not true; firms with long-term fixed-rate debt can enjoy low interest costs for many years even though interest rates in general have risen.

---

[39] Thus, even if its long-term debt is adjusted by 10%, total debt will only be affected by 10% times the percentage of long-term debt. The lower the percentage of long-term debt, the smaller the overall adjustment.

[40] Calculated as interest incurred (from Westvaco footnote F) divided by the average debt level. For 1999, the calculation is

$$\frac{\$132{,}428}{(\$1{,}552{,}377 + \$1{,}605{,}415)/2} = 8.39\%$$

BOX 43-4 MARKET OR BOOK VALUES: EMPIRICAL EVIDENCE

Bowman (1980) examined the relationship between firms' market betas and the debt-to-equity ratio. Finance theory predicts (see Chapter 18) that the higher a firm's debt-to-equity ratio (using market values), the higher the firm's beta.

Letting the superscripts M and B refer to the market and book value, respectively, Bowman examined which of the following four measures of the debt-to-equity ratio, D^M/E^M, D^M/E^B, D^B/E^M, and D^B/E^M, were more closely associated with the firm's beta.

Bowman obtained the best results when he used the market value of equity in the denominator. Whether debt was measured on a market basis or book basis made little difference as the ratios D^B/E^M and D^M/E^M yielded similar results. The pure book value ratio D^B/E^B did not perform as well; the measure of the market value of the debt-to-book value of equity (D^M/E^B) performed the poorest.

These results can be partly attributable to the fact that for close to 60% of the debt in Bowman's sample, book value and market value were equivalent. Furthermore, the correlation between the market value of debt and the book value of debt was close to 100%. As the study ranked debtors by relative rather than absolute levels of debt, changes in the market rates of interest shifted debt valuations without changing ranks.

Mulford (1986) replicated Bowman's study by using a later time period. Bowman's analysis was based on 1973 data, predating the dramatic rise in market interest rates of the late 1970s. Mulford, referring to Bowman's study, noted:

> His failure to find evidence of superior performance for a debt-to-equity ratio based on market values of debt may have been due to small differences between the book and market values of debt which accompanied the general level of interest rates at that time.*

To remedy this deficiency, Mulford focused on 1980, when market rates of interest were historically high. In addition, to alleviate potential measurement problems arising from the conversion of book to market values, he examined the performance of portfolios of firms in addition to individual firms. Mulford's results were more in line with theory, but only on a portfolio basis. No matter which variation was used to measure the relationship between beta and debt-to-equity, the market-based debt-to-equity ratio was always the most closely associated with beta on a portfolio basis. On an individual basis, D^M/E^M did not always perform as well, but the differences between it and the best performing ratio were minimal.

These results suggest, not surprisingly, that the market value of debt is not superior to book value when the difference between the stated and market rates of interest is small; the additional cost of obtaining market values is not worthwhile.† Adjustment is necessary only when the gap between the historic and market rates of interest is large. Even then, potential measurement problems‡ in estimating market values may offset any benefits from the adjustment process.

* Charles W. Mulford, "The Importance of a Market Value Measurement of Debt in Leverage Ratios: Replications and Extensions," *Journal of Accounting Research*, Autumn 1984, pp. 897–906.

† Given the high correlation between market and book values of debt, this is especially true for analyses that focus on relative rather than absolute debt burdens.

‡ The issue of a measurement problem also calls into question the results of both Bowman and Mulford from a different perspective. They adjusted only on-balance-sheet debt, ignoring any "off-balance-sheet" debt. As Reading 44 will make clear, the latter can be significant.

Debt of Firms in Distress

When the credit quality of a firm changes significantly (in either direction), the market price of debt will follow, independent of interest rate trends. When credit quality and the market value of debt decline, there appears to be a gain to the firm, yet it is difficult to argue that shareholders are better off. This apparent paradox reflects simultaneous changes in the value of assets as credit quality changes. It is reasonable to assume that some assets of such troubled companies are impaired (see the discussion in Reading 41). Case 10-1 discusses the convertible debt of Read-Rite, a troubled debtor, the exchange of that debt for a new debt issue, and the ultimate conversion of that new issue into equity.

Accounting for Restructured and Impaired Debt

When a debtor is in financial difficulty, creditors may agree to accept assets in payment of the debt or to "restructure" the obligation by modifying its terms (e.g., reducing the interest rate or deferring principal payments). When debt is extinguished, both the debtor and creditor will recognize gain or loss measured as the difference between the fair value of the assets (cash or other assets) used to repay the debt and its carrying amount. This accounting treatment raises neither accounting nor analysis issues.

When the obligation is restructured, however, different accounting rules apply to creditors and debtors. Creditors adhere to SFAS 114 (1993), as amended by SFAS 118 (1994), whereas debtors use SFAS 15 (1977) to account for these transactions.

Under SFAS 114, the creditor must recognize a loss equal to the difference between the carrying value of the loan and the present value of the restructured payment stream *discounted at the original discount rate* (effective interest rate). Thus, if a 12% coupon loan with a face value of \$100,000 and three years remaining to maturity is restructured by reducing the interest rate to 8%, the creditor recognizes a loss of \$9,610 as the new carrying value of the loan is \$90,390.[41] The loan impairment may also be measured using the observable market price of the loan or the fair value of collateral when the loan is collateral dependent.[42]

The FASB was reluctant, however, to allow debtors to record gains resulting from financial distress. SFAS 15 provides that the debtor's carrying amount of the debt be compared with the *undiscounted gross cash flows* (principal and interest) due after restructuring. As long as the gross cash flows exceed the carrying amount, the debtor recognizes no gain. In our example, the future payments are (\$100,000 + 3 × \$8,000) = \$124,000. No gain is recognized.[43]

However, the present value of the cash flows has been reduced; in economic terms, the debtor has gained at the expense of the creditor. The accounting mandated by SFAS 15 recognizes this transfer only over the life of the loan as payments are made; the debtor will show lower interest expense as the loan is amortized at the implicit interest rate of the loan. In our example, interest expense is now calculated at an interest rate of 8% rather than 12%.

A similar approach is mandated by the FASB for loans considered to be "impaired." Creditors are required to recognize the probable loss, but recognition of gains by debtors is not allowed. Under SFAS 114, creditors are required to carry impaired loans at the present value of cash flows expected after modification of the loan terms, *discounted at the original effective interest rate.* For the debtor, however, no gain recognition is permitted.

For purposes of analysis, however, both impaired and restructured debt should be restated to fair market value using a *current market interest rate* to discount the cash flows required by the (actual or expected) restructured obligation. However, as noted earlier, debtor "gains" should be viewed warily; gains resulting from an inability to repay loans are almost certainly offset by asset impairment.

---

[41] If we assume annual payments, the present value of a three-year annuity of \$8,000 discounted at 12% + present value of \$100,000 in three years discounted at 12% equals \$90,390.

[42] SFAS 118 amended SFAS 114 to allow creditors to continue income-recognition methods for impaired loans that had been used prior to the adoption of SFAS 114. For example, cost-recovery or cash-basis methods report investments in impaired loans at less than the present value of expected future cash flows. In these cases, no additional impairment needs to be recognized under SFAS 118. SFAS 114 was also amended to require additional disclosures regarding the investment in certain impaired loans and the recognition of interest income on those loans.

[43] If the payments do not exceed the carrying value, then the gain is limited to the difference between those amounts; the debt is discounted at an implicit interest rate of zero.

Retirement of Debt Prior to Maturity

Firms generally choose the initial debt maturity of their obligations based on such considerations as cost and investment horizon (when projects funded with debt are expected to generate cash flows). Subsequently, conditions may change and a firm may wish to refinance or retire debt prior to the original maturity. Examples include:

- Declining interest rates permit the reduction of interest cost.
- Increasing cash from operations permits debt retirement earlier than expected.
- Sale of assets or additional equity generates funds and the firm decides to reduce financial leverage.

In such cases, the firm can reduce bank debt, commercial paper, and other short-term debt quickly and at small expense. For longer-maturity debt, the firm may exercise call provisions, tender offers, or in-substance defeasance. We examine the economic and accounting effects of these choices shortly.

Accounting for Debt Retirement

When firms retire debt prior to maturity, the gain or loss (difference between the book value of the liability and the amount paid at retirement) is treated as a component of continuing operations.[44]

Using the par bond example in Exhibit 43-1A (see p. 901), assume that on December 31, 2001, the market interest rate for the firm is 12%. As a result, the market price of the bonds should be $96,535.[45] If the firm paid $96,535 to retire the bond, the resulting gain on the bond retirement is $3,465 since the book value is $100,000.[46] While this gain must be included in income from continuing operations, there are two reasons why an analyst should consider treating it as a nonoperating item:

- In reality, the firm is no better off as a result of the refinancing. To finance the retirement of the bond, it must issue new debt[47] bearing at least the same effective interest rate (and must incur transaction costs). Effectively, over the remaining life of the original bond, the net borrowing cost would be identical; the company has simply replaced 10% coupon debt with 12% coupon debt. In economic terms, the gain took place as interest rates rose, not when the refinancing took place. Because of the use of historical cost as a measure of the bond liability, however, only refinancing results in a recognized gain.[48]

---

[44] SFAS 145 (2002) rescinded both SFAS 4 (1975), which mandated extraordinary item treatment for these gains and losses, and SFAS 64 (1982), which provided an exemption from extraordinary item reporting for gains and losses on normal sinking fund repurchases. Under SFAS 145, gains and losses on retirement of debt are reported as extraordinary items only if they meet APB 30 criteria (see page 54 of text).

[45] This can be seen from Exhibit 43-1C as the carrying amount of the discount bond is the present value at the (original) 12% interest rate.

[46] We have ignored unamortized debt issuance costs. When bonds are retired, the firm must write off these costs that were capitalized when the bonds were issued. This write-off becomes a component of the gain or loss on retirement.

[47] Even if it did not issue new debt to retire the bond but rather used internal funds, the firm would experience an opportunity cost equal to the forgone interest revenue.

[48] If the gain or loss is recognized at all, it should be in the period in which interest rates change, not in the year in which the refinancing takes place. In our example, the year is the same, but that coincidence is rare in practice.

- The decision to refinance is a function of the change in market interest rates. The analyst should evaluate the transaction to determine whether the gain or loss should be considered as part of normal operations or treated analytically as an extraordinary item.

In the early 1970s, interest rates rose sharply at the same time the U.S. economy entered recession. Firms found their outstanding low-coupon bonds selling at deep discounts. Many of these firms had poor operating profitability, but were able to increase reported income by retiring bonds. The issuance of SFAS 4 in 1975 was partially a response to this income manipulation activity.

In the late 1990s, lower interest rates resulted in the refinancing of higher coupon debt, resulting in a recognized loss. That loss should be viewed, however, as a signal of lower future interest expense, as high-coupon debt is replaced by lower-coupon debt (also see the following discussion of callable bonds).

Example:

DaimlerChrysler

In 1990, predecessor Chrysler had issued $1.1 billion of 12% debt, due in 2020. The high interest rate was due to the higher level of interest rates and Chrysler's poor debt rating. As a result of lower interest rates and improved financial condition, the bonds sold at a large premium in the late 1990s. Late in 1996, Chrysler repurchased half of the issue, recording an extraordinary pretax loss of $309 million. In 1998, DaimlerChrysler repurchased an additional $300 million of the bonds, recording an extraordinary pretax loss of $230 million (€203 million). The company replaced this high-cost debt with lower coupon debt, reducing interest expense significantly. The combined effect of the extraordinary loss from debt retirement (decreasing equity) and reduced future interest expense (increasing earnings) is a higher reported future return on equity.

Our discussion of discretionary debt retirements indicates that the amounts and timing of the accounting gain and the economic gain from debt retirement are quite different. This especially applies to callable bonds, whose retirement may give rise to economic profit but may generate a loss for accounting purposes.

Callable Bonds

When a bond is callable, the issuer has the option to buy back (call) the bond from bondholders at predetermined dates and prices. This differs from the case in which the issuer retires the old bond at a market price equal to the present value of the future payment stream. The call price is usually set at a premium over the face value of the bond, but is independent of the present value of the payment stream at the time the call is made. However, the actual exercise does depend on the relationship of the call price to that present value.

Exhibit 43-6 contains an analysis of a callable bond. The decline in interest rates constitutes an economic loss at the time of the rate change, as the market value of the bond rises. In the absence of the call provision, a decision to refinance would not impact Cole, which would incur new debt equal to $106,624 to

EXHIBIT 43-6 Analysis of Callable Bond

On January 1, 2001, Cole issues the following bond:

Face value:	$100,000
Coupon:	10% (annual payments assumed for simplicity
Maturity:	5 years
Call provision:	Callable at any time after one year at 102

If the market interest rate applicable to Cole is 10%, then the bonds will be issued at par.

Reported Liability = $100,000
Annual Interest Expense = $10,000 (10% × $100,000)

Assume that, on December 31, 2001, the market rate applicable to Cole has declined to 8%. The rate change has no accounting impact on the company. However, the present value of the cash flows associated with the debt rises to $106,624 (discounted at 8%). Absent the call provision, the expected market price of the bonds is 106.624.

By calling the bonds at a price of 102, Cole realizes an economic gain of $4,624 [(106.624 − 102) × ($100,000)].

However, the call results in an accounting loss of $2,000 [(100 − 102) × ($100,000)].

refinance the debt at market rates. However, the call provision permits the firm to retire the bonds for only $102,000; the economic gain is the difference.[49]

Economically, it is beneficial to refinance the debt, but the income statement reports a loss. One can only speculate as to how many firms have not refinanced under such conditions because of the financial statement impact. This is yet another reason why analysts should ignore gains and losses from the retirement of debt.

Defeasance

In some cases, the firm wishes to retire debt but is unable to do so because the debt is non-callable. *In-substance defeasance* involves setting aside riskless securities sufficient to pay all remaining installments of principal and interest. The cash flow characteristics of the securities used must match those of the debt being defeased and must be placed in a trust fund restricted for that purpose.

Although the original debt remained outstanding, U.S. GAAP permitted debtor firms to derecognize the defeased obligations through December 31, 1996.[50] However, SFAS 125 (1996)[51] disallows in-substance defeasance and debt may be extinguished only on repayment or when the debtor is legally released from being the primary obligor. IAS 32 (2000) disallowed defeasance for firms following IAS GAAP.

---

[49] When bonds are issued, the call provisions are often an important ingredient in the market reception. As call provisions benefit only the issuer, bond buyers will bargain against them. Option-adjusted bond analysis is now routine. See, for example, Frank J. Fabozzi, *Fixed Income Analysis for the Chartered Financial Analyst Program*, New Hope, Pennsylvania; Frank J. Fabozzi Associates, 2000 (pp. 347ff). Many shorter-term issues are noncallable.

[50] See SFAS 76 (1983) and FASB Technical Bulletin 84-4 for accounting and disclosure requirements related to defeasance.

[51] See SFAS 125, Accounting for the Transfers and Servicing of Financial Assets and Extinguishments of Liabilities.

BOND COVENANTS 3

Creditors use debt covenants in lending agreements to protect their interests by restricting activities of the debtor that could jeopardize the creditor's position. Auditors and management must certify that the firm has not violated the covenants. If any covenant is violated, the firm is in *technical default* of its lending agreement, and the creditor can demand repayment of the debt after the stated grace period. Generally, however, as we shall see, the terms are renegotiated but at a cost to the debtor as the lender demands concessions. The analysis of a firm's debt position must therefore take into consideration the nature of these covenants and the risk that the firm may violate them.

Information on debt covenants is important both to evaluate the firm's credit risk as well as to understand the implications of such restrictions for the firm's dividend and growth (investment) prospects. In addition, to the extent these covenants are accounting-based, they may affect the choice of accounting policies.

Nature of Covenants

Smith and Warner (1979) characterize debt covenants as placing limits on one or more of the following activities:

1. Payment of dividends (includes share repurchases)
2. Production and investment (includes mergers and acquisitions, sale and leaseback, or outright disposal of certain assets)
3. Issuance of new debt (or incurrence of other liabilities)
4. Payoff patterns (includes sinking fund requirements and the priorities of claims on assets)

In addition to direct restrictions on activities, covenants may require maintenance of certain levels of such accounting-based financial variables as stockholders' equity (or retained earnings), working capital, interest coverage, and debt-to-equity ratios. These levels are often related to the four types of activities listed above by restricting a certain activity if the accounting variable violates the specified target level. In some cases, the violation itself may signal a breach of the covenant even without any subsequent firm activity.

Bond covenants may also require that interest rates depend on certain financial ratios.

Example:

Luby's

Based in Texas, Luby's [LUB] operates cafeterias. It entered into a credit agreement with a group of banks early in 1996. That agreement was subsequently amended four times:

1. January 24, 1997
2. July 3, 1997
3. October 27, 2000
4. June 29, 2001

The second and third amendments are of particular interest. The second amendment increased the credit line from $100 million to $125 million but added the following provision with respect to the spread over the LIBOR rate ("applicable margin"):

Applicable margin means the following per-annum percentages, applicable in the following situations:

Applicability **If the leverage is:**	**LIBOR Basis for Advances of One, Two, Three, or Six Months**	**LIBOR Basis for Advances of Seven to Fourteen Days**
not less than 2 to 1	0.225	0.325
less than 2 to 1	0.200	0.300
Difference	0.025	0.025

This provision gives the lender an additional margin over LIBOR of 2.5 basis points (.025%) if the leverage ratio (debt-to-equity ratio as defined in the original credit agreement) exceeds 2.0. This additional margin was presumably intended to compensate the lender for the additional risk.

The third amendment, adopted when Luby's earnings had fallen sharply, changed the *applicable margin* as follows:

Applicability If the Leverage Is:	**LIBOR Basis for Advances of One, Two, Three, or Six Months**	**LIBOR Basis for Advances of Seven to Fourteen Days**
greater than or equal to 2.75 to 1	0.500	2.500
greater than or equal to 2.50 to 1 but less than 2.75 to 1	0.375	2.125
greater than or equal to 2.25 to 1 but less than 2.50 to 1	0.000	1.750
less than 2.25 to 1	0.000	1.250

This amendment increased the lending spread to reflect the higher leverage ratio, and provided a sliding scale under which the spread increases and decreases with the leverage ratio (a measure of risk).

Additionally, as detailed in Exhibit 43-7, the third amendment introduced a covenant based on the fixed-charge coverage ratio as well as imposing restrictions on net worth (stockholders' equity) and the leverage ratio. Note the extent to which the ratios as well as their components are defined by the agreement.

These provisions had several effects:

1. To restrict the ability of Luby's to incur additional debt that would dilute the interest of the creditors.

2. To require Luby's to maintain stockholders' equity, limiting its ability to pay dividends (it eliminated its dividend in October 2000) or buy back stock, either of which would reduce cash and the equity cushion.
3. To reward creditors for the level of risk by increasing the interest rate margin as the leverage ratio increases.

Luby's provides an example of bond covenants. Additional discussion regarding the nature of accounting-based debt covenants can be found in Box 43-5.

EXHIBIT 43-7 Excerpts from Luby's Bond Covenants

Fixed Charge Coverage Provision

"Earnings Available for Fixed Charges" means, for any period, calculated for the Borrower and its Subsidiaries on a consolidated basis in accordance with GAAP, the sum of (a) EBITDA, plus (b) all lease and rental expense pursuant to Operating Leases, minus (c) cash taxes paid, minus (d) Capital Expenditures.

"Fixed Charges" means, for any period, calculated for the Borrower and its Subsidiaries on a consolidated basis in accordance with GAAP, the sum of (a) all interest, premium payments, fees, charges and related expenses (including, but not limited to, interest expense pursuant to Capitalized Lease Obligations) in connection with borrowed money or in connection with the deferred purchase price of assets, in each case to the extent treated as interest in accordance with GAAP, (b) all dividends and distributions paid in respect of Capital Stock and (c) all lease and rental expenses pursuant to Operating Leases.

"Fixed Charges Coverage Ratio" means, for any date of determination, the ratio of (a) Earnings Available for Fixed Charges for the period of four consecutive fiscal quarters ending on such date to (b) Fixed Charges for the period of four consecutive fiscal quarters ending on such date.

The Borrower covenants and agrees that it will not allow the Fixed Charges Coverage Ratio to be less than 1.20 to 1 at the fiscal quarter ending November 30, 2000 or at the end of any fiscal quarter thereafter.

Net Worth Provision

The Borrower covenants and agrees that it will not allow its Net Worth at any time to be less than the sum of (i) $190,000,000 plus (ii) 50% of Consolidated Net Income (excluding Consolidated Net Income for any fiscal quarter in which Consolidated Net Income was a negative number) earned on or after September 1, 2000, plus (iii) 75% of the Net Cash Proceeds of any equity issues of the Borrower's Capital Stock in an underwritten public offering pursuant to an effective registration statement under the Securities Act of 1933, as amended, after September 1, 2000.

Leverage Ratio Provision

The Borrower covenants and agrees that it will not allow the Leverage Ratio to be greater than (a) 3.00 to 1 at the fiscal quarters ending November 30, 2000, February 28, 2001 and May 31, 2001, (b) 2.60 to 1 at the fiscal quarter ending August 31, 2001 and (c) 2.50 to 1 at the fiscal quarter ending November 30, 2001 and each fiscal quarter thereafter.

Source: Third Amendment to Credit Agreement, dated October 27, 2000, Exhibit 4(j) to Luby's Form 10-K for year ended August 31, 2000.

BOX 43-5 ACCOUNTING-BASED DEBT COVENANTS

Exhibit 43-8 contains a summary of the nature of accounting-based debt covenant restrictions, adapted from Duke and Hunt (1990). *Restricted retained earnings* as a constraint on dividend payments, one of the most common forms used, is outlined in Exhibit 43-9. The Luby's covenants discussed in the text are examples of these restrictions.

Information regarding these covenants was obtained by Smith and Warner (1979) and Duke and Hunt (1990) from the American Bar Foundation's *Commentaries on Debentures*, which summarizes typical covenants found in lending agreements. A cursory examination of these restrictions makes it clear that creditors seek to limit the firm's level of risk (investment and debt restrictions) and preserve the assets of the firm to ensure that debts are repaid (payment restrictions). Thus, covenants attempt to limit shareholders' ability to transfer assets to themselves (dividend restrictions), new shareholders (merger and acquisition restrictions), or new creditors (debt restrictions).

The best source of information on specific covenants (and other terms of the bond issue) for publicly issued bonds is the bond indenture, the legal document created when the bond is issued and filed with the registration statement filed with the SEC. The trustee (normally a bank) will have a copy of the indenture and is responsible for the enforcement of its terms. The bond prospectus should contain a good summary of these terms. Bank credit agreements entered into by public companies are filed with SEC annual (10-K) or quarterly (10-Q) reports.

For all debt issues, summarized data can be found in:

- Services such as Moody's Industrial Manual
- Annual reports
- SEC filings by debtors

Press and Weintrop (1990 and 1991) contend that information obtained from annual reports and Moody's is not comprehensive, especially with respect to covenants relating to privately placed debt, and that in these cases, it is necessary to access the original SEC filings.

Calculation of Accounting-Based Constraints

Each type of constraint is defined in the covenants. In addition, the covenants specify:

- Whether GAAP definitions are to be used or GAAP is to be modified. Leftwich (1983) noted that such modifications are most often associated with private rather than public debt indentures.
- Whether GAAP in effect at the time of the debt issuance are maintained throughout the life of the bond ("frozen" GAAP), or calculations in subsequent years are to be based on GAAP in effect at the date of the calculation ("rolling" GAAP). This is important when important new accounting standards are adopted.

Mohrman (1996) examined a sample of 174 lending agreements that contained covenants based on financial statement information. She found that over half (90) the covenants were based on *fixed* GAAP specified in the agreements. That is, the covenants were not affected by voluntary or FASB-mandated accounting changes, nor were they originally designed to mimic GAAP in effect at the time the contract was signed. Additionally, she found that contracts that contained more accounting-based covenants were more likely to specify fixed GAAP provisions and the use of such provisions in contracts was increasing over time.

EXHIBIT 43-8 Common Accounting-Based Debt Covenant Restrictions

Attribute:	Retained earnings
Measured as:	Restricted retained earnings
Limits:	Payments of dividends or stock repurchase below minimum level of restricted retained earnings
Attribute:	Net assets
Measured as:	Net tangible assets or net assets
Limits:	Investments, dividend payments, and new debt issues if net assets fall below a certain level
Attribute:	Working capital
Measured as:	Minimum working capital or current ratio
Limits:	Mergers and acquisitions, dividend payments, and new debt issues if the working capital or the current ratio fall below a certain level
Attribute:	Debt-to-equity
Measured as:	Debt divided by net tangible assets or debt divided by net assets
Limits:	Issuance of additional debt

Source: Joanne C. Duke and Herbert G. Hunt III, "An Empirical Examination of Debt Covenant Restrictions and Accounting-Related Debt Proxies," *Journal of Accounting and Economics,* Jan. 1990, adapted from Table 1, p. 52.

EXHIBIT 43-9 Unrestricted Retained Earnings: Inventory of Payable Funds

The most frequent accounting-based restriction specified is the dividend constraint. Dividends cannot be paid out of restricted retained earnings. Only unrestricted retained earnings, often referred to as the inventory of payable funds (IPF), are available for dividends. The general formulation of IPF is defined (see Smith and Warner, 1979) as the sum of:

1. A specified percentage k of earnings E from the date of the debt issuance to the present period, plus
2. Proceeds from the sale of common shares CS from the date of the debt issuance to the present period, plus
3. A prespecified constant F, less
4. The sum of dividends DV and stock repurchases from the date of the debt issuance to the present period

Algebraically, this is equal to

$$\text{IPF}_t = k \sum_{i=0}^{t} E_i + \sum_{i=0}^{t} CS_i + F - \sum_{i=0}^{t} DV_i$$

where period 0 represents the date of the debt issuance and period t refers to the current date. The prespecified constant F is usually set at approximately one year's earnings.* This builds some slack into the system in the event the firm has a loss.

*See Smith and Warner (1979), Note 36.

Costs and Effects of Covenant Violations

Although creditors have a right to demand immediate payment when an accounting-based debt covenant is violated, they do not usually do so. This does not mean that violating such covenants is costless. Waivers of such violations often come with strings attached. Creditors may renegotiate the terms of the debt to demand:

- Accelerated principal payments
- An increased interest rate
- Liens on assets (such as accounts receivable)
- New covenants increasing restrictions on the firm's investing, borrowing, and dividend-paying ability

Chen and Wei (1993) examined a sample of 128 companies that disclosed violations of their accounting-based debt covenants. For 71 of these firms, the creditors did not waive the violation but demanded accelerated payments or higher interest rates. Beneish and Press (1993) found the median interest rate increase to be 80 basis points; they estimated that the overall cost of such renegotiations averaged from 1 to 2% of the market value of the firm's equity or 4 to 7% of the balance on the loan.

When waivers were granted, not surprisingly, they were more often granted for secured debt and for smaller-size loans. Similarly, waivers were more likely to be granted to "healthier" firms considered less likely to become bankrupt. When waivers were granted, they were often (24 of the 57 companies) given only for limited time periods.

Successful renegotiation of the debt terms or receipt of a waiver may not be the last word. Chen and Wei found that by the following year creditors demanded payment of the debt for 39 companies (30% of the sample), forcing 13 companies into bankruptcy.

Beneish and Press found that accounting-based covenants were often relaxed as a result of renegotiation. However, they were supplanted with more direct covenants restricting capital expenditures, mergers, assets sales, stock repurchases, and future borrowings.

These results indicate the importance of monitoring debt covenants to ensure that the firm is not close to violating them. Such violations can expose the firm to direct out-of-pocket costs in the form of higher borrowing costs and/or limit the scope of a firm's investing and financing choices.*

* Given these costs, one can understand why DeFond and Jiambalvo (1994) reported that managements engage in (accounting) manipulations in an effort to satisfy the covenants.

SUMMARY

4

In this reading, we have examined the different forms that debt financing can take. The choice of debt issue can have significant effects on the pattern of reported income, cash flows, and financial position. In addition, different debt instruments respond differently to changes in interest rates. The reader should now have an understanding of the following issues:

1. The effects of zero-coupon or low-coupon debt, variable rate debt, and foreign currency debt on the firm's financial statements.
2. The economic and financial statement effects of interest rate swaps.
3. The implications for financial analysis of variable-rate debt versus fixed-rate debt.
4. The economic and accounting effects of debt with equity features.
5. The analyst's need to classify between debt and equity based on the essence of the financial instrument rather than its form.
6. The effect of changes in interest rates on the market value of debt and when the market value should be used instead of carrying value.
7. The accounting effects of debt retirement and analytical adjustments required.
8. The importance of debt covenants to the analysis of the firm.

Debt can also take forms that do not require recognition on the balance sheet. Such off-balance-sheet debt is the subject of the next reading.

PROBLEMS

1. [Zero-coupon debt; CFA© adapted] Compare the effect of issuing zero-coupon debt with that of issuing full-coupon debt with the same effective interest rate on a company's:
   A. Cash flow from operations over the life of the debt
   B. Cash flow from financing in the year of issuance, the year of maturity, and over the life of the debt.
   C. Cash flow from investing over the life of the debt
   D. Trend of net income over the life of the debt
2. [Zero-coupon bonds] The Null Company issued a zero-coupon bond on January 1, 2000, due December 31, 2004. The face value of the bond was \$100,000. The bond was issued at an effective rate of 12% (compounded annually).
   A. Calculate the cash proceeds of the bond issue.
   B. Complete the following table on a *pretax* basis, assuming that all interest is paid in the year it is due:

	2000	2001	2002	2003	2004
Earnings before interest and taxes	\$50,000	\$50,000	\$50,000	\$50,000	\$50,000
Cash flow from operations before interest and taxes	60,000	60,000	60,000	60,000	60,000
Cash flow from operations					
Times interest earned					
Times interest earned (cash basis)					

   C. Assume that Null had raised the same cash proceeds with a conventional bond issued at par, paying interest annually and the principal at maturity. Complete the following table, under the assumptions in part B:

	2000	2001	2002	2003	2004
Earnings before interest and taxes	\$50,000	\$50,000	\$50,000	\$50,000	\$50,000
Cash flow from operations before interest and taxes	60,000	60,000	60,000	60,000	60,000
Cash flow from operations					
Times interest earned					
Times interest earned (cash basis)					

   D. Using the results of parts B and C, discuss the impact on reported cash flow from operations and interest coverage of Null's choice of bond.
   E. Explain how consideration of income taxes would change your answers to parts B through D.

3. [Understanding bond relationships; coupon versus effective interest] The Walk & Field Co. has outstanding bonds originally issued at a discount. During 2000, the unamortized bond discount decreased from $8,652 to $7,290. Annual interest paid was $7,200. The market rate of interest was 12% when the bond was issued.

Using the data provided, calculate:

A. Interest expense for 2000

B. The face value of the bond

C. The coupon rate of the bond

(*Note:* You do not need present value calculations or tables to solve this problem.)

4. [Convertible debt] Note 5 of Takeda's annual report states that the company had convertible bonds outstanding at March 31, 1998 but none outstanding at March 31, 1999. From the statement of stockholders' equity and cash flow statement we can deduce that most of the bonds (more than 22 billion yen) were converted into approximately 11 million shares, implying a conversion price of approximately 2,000 yen per share. The market price of Takeda shares exceeded 3,000 yen during all of calendar 1998.

Years Ended March 31 *As reported in millions yen*	**1998**	**1999**
Bank loans	9,509	9,361
Current debt	24,077	2,119
Long-term debt	10,896	9,858
Total debt	44,482	21,338
Equity	829,381	907,373
Total capital	873,863	928,711

A. Describe the advantages to Takeda of having issued these convertible notes rather than nonconvertible notes. State one disadvantage.

B. Compute Takeda's debt-to-total capital ratio at March 31, 1998 and March 31, 1999. State the factor that accounted for most of the change in that ratio.

C. State the appropriate classification for the convertible notes at March 31, 1998 (debt or equity) and justify your choice.

5. [Debt refinancing] On July 14, 2000, the *Wall Street Journal* reported on the earnings report by Fannie Mae [FNM], the largest mortgage lender in the United States. Fannie Mae has substantial outstanding debt and uses hedging techniques to manage its exposure to changing interest rates. Excerpts from that article follow:

> *Fannie Mae Posts 15% Earnings Gain for the Quarter*
> By Patrick Barta
>
> Fannie Mae overcame a cooling housing market to report double-digit earnings growth for the second quarter. . . .
>
> However, some pointed out that the company's results included a one-time after-tax gain of $32.7 million from the retirement of debt that helped compensate for a one-time trading loss. Typically, such gains are omitted when a company calculates its earnings-per-share results.

"In our mind, [the gain] should be excluded," says Charles L. Hill, First Call's director of research.

Fannie Mae says the company has long included retirement of debt in its earnings-per-share calculations, because it considers retirement of debt to be part of its continuing operations. The company notes that it reported gains and losses from debt retirement in its earnings-per-share calculations in 27 of the last 40 quarters. "It's something we do on a regular basis," says Mary Lou Christy, vice-president of investor relations.

At the heart of the debate was a one-time loss of about $60 million, attributed to a hedging strategy that lost money after interest rates for Fannie Mae debt rose unexpectedly.

The company was able to offset much of the loss by repurchasing debt at favorable rates, which produced the $32.7 million gain.[53]

A. Present one reason why the gain from debt retirement should be considered part of Fannie Mae's operating earnings and one reason why it should not.

B. Present one reason why the loss from the hedging strategy should be considered part of Fannie Mae's operating earnings and one reason why it should not.

C. Recommend the proper treatment for both items, from an analyst viewpoint, and justify your recommendation.

---

[53] *Wall Street Journal,* July 14, 2000, p. A2.

LEASES AND OFF-BALANCE-SHEET DEBT

READING 44

LEARNING OUTCOMES

The candidate should be able to:

a. classify a lease as capital or operating and discuss the factors that determine whether a company would tend to favor leasing over outright asset purchases and more specifically, factors that would favor capital or operating leases;

b. calculate the effects of capital and operating leases on the financial statements and ratios of the lessees;

c. explain and differentiate the accounting treatment for a sale and leaseback of assets under U.S. and IASB GAAP;

d. describe the types of off-balance-sheet financing; determine how take-or-pay contracts, throughput arrangements, and the sale of receivables affect selected financial ratios;

f. distinguish between a sales-type lease and a direct-financing lease and describe the effects on the financial statements and ratios of sales-type and operating leases.

INTRODUCTION 1

Rapid changes in manufacturing and information technology and expanding international trade and capital markets have resulted in the growth of multinational corporations that must cope with increasingly mobile capital, labor, and product markets. Volatile commodity and other factor price levels, fluctuating interest and foreign currency exchange rates, and continuous tax and regulatory changes have accompanied these changes. In addition, general inflation and industry-specific price changes have raised many asset prices and have increased the risks of operations and investments.

This economic climate has required increasing amounts of capital as firms acquire operating capacity (both for expansion and replacement purposes) at ever-higher prices. Because of the volatility of prices and cash flows, the risks of owning operating assets have also increased. These trends have driven firms to seek methods of:

1. Acquiring the rights to assets through methods other than traditional direct purchases (financed by debt)
2. Controlling the risks of operation through derivative and hedging transactions

Executory contracts are the primary alternative form of transactions used by firms to acquire operating capacity, supplies of raw materials, and other inputs. Such contracts or arrangements are the subject of this reading.

The increased use of these financing techniques and hedging transactions has been encouraged by drawbacks in the historical cost-based financial reporting system, in which recognition and measurement depend primarily on actual transactions. As contracts are considered legal promises, and neither cash nor goods may be exchanged at the inception of these contracts, accounting recognition is not required in many cases. The emphasis on accounting assets and liabilities rather than the recognition of economic resources and obligations further encourages firms to keep resources and obligations off the balance sheet.

Firms may engage in these transactions to avoid reporting high debt levels and leverage ratios and to reduce the probability of technical default under restrictive covenants in debt indentures. Off-balance-sheet transactions may also keep assets and potential gains out of the financial statements but under the control of management, which can orchestrate the timing of gain recognition to offset periods of poor operating performance.

Footnote disclosures constitute the best source of information about off-balance-sheet activities. Additional information may be available from disclosures in 10-K filings and from other company publications. In some cases, the economic meaning behind the disclosures requires explanation from management. Thus, a complete analysis of the firm must include a review of all financial statement disclosures to obtain data on off-balance-sheet activities. In many cases, straightforward adjustments can be used to reflect off-balance-sheet assets and liabilities on the balance sheet. Such adjustments result in a balance sheet that presents a more complete portrait of the firm's resources and obligations and financial ratios that are more comparable to those of competitors whose use of off-balance-sheet techniques is different.

The reading begins with a discussion of leases, the most common form of executory contract entered into by firms. The methods used to analyze and adjust for leases serve as a model for the analysis of other off-balance-sheet activities that comprise the second part of the reading.

LEASES 2

Accounting policy makers have grappled with leases for years to develop reporting requirements that emphasize the economic substance rather than the legal form of the leasing transaction. We begin our discussion of leases with a review of incentives for leases. A discussion of reporting requirements and the analysis of leases complete this section of the reading.

Incentives for Leasing

Firms generally acquire rights to use property, plant, and equipment by outright purchase, partially or fully funded by internal resources or externally borrowed funds. In a purchase transaction, the buyer acquires (and the seller surrenders) ownership, which includes all the benefits and risks embodied in the asset. Alternatively, firms may also acquire the use of property, including some or all of the benefits and risks of ownership, for specific periods of time and stipulated rental payments through contractual arrangements called *leases.*

Short-term, or *operating,* leases allow the lessee to use leased property for only a portion of its economic life. The lessee accounts for such leases as contracts, reporting (as rental expense) only the required rental payments as they are made. Because the lessor retains substantially all the risks of ownership of leased property, the leased assets remain on its balance sheet and are depreciated over their estimated economic lives; rental payments are recognized as revenues over time according to the terms of the lease.

However, longer-term leases may effectively transfer all (or substantially all) the risks and rewards of the leased property to the lessee. Such leases are the economic equivalent of sales with financing arrangements designed to effect the purchase (by the lessee) and sale (by the lessor) of the leased property. *Such leases, referred to as finance or capital leases, are treated for accounting purposes as sales.* The asset and associated debt are carried on the books of the lessee, and the lessor records a gain on "sale" at the inception of the lease. The lessee depreciates the asset over its life, and treats lease payments as payments of principal and interest.[1] The lessor records a financing profit over the lease term. The financial reporting differences between accounting for a lease as an operating or capital lease are far-reaching and affect the balance sheet, income statement, cash flow statement, and associated ratios.

One motivation for leasing rather than borrowing and buying an asset is to avoid recognition of the debt and asset on the lessee's financial statements.[2] Lease capitalization eliminates this advantage. Whether a lease is reported as operating or capitalized depends, as we shall see, on the terms of the lease and their relationship to criteria specified by SFAS 13 and IAS 17.

---

[1] The lease payments made by the lessee to the lessor are recorded by the latter as receipts of principal and interest.

[2] Firms may believe that investors, lenders, and rating services do not adjust for leases. However, debt covenants sometimes explicitly include operating leases. Ratings services also incorporate leases when setting debt ratings (see, for example, Moody's Investors Service, *Off-Balance-Sheet Leases: Capitalization and Ratings Implications,* October 1999).

Notwithstanding these financial reporting requirements, leases may be structured to qualify as operating leases to achieve desired financial reporting effects and capital structure benefits. Operating leases allow lessees to avoid recognition of the asset and report higher profitability ratios and indicators of operating efficiency. Reported leverage is also lower because the related liability for contractual payments is not recognized.

Extensive use of operating leases needs careful evaluation and the analyst must adjust financial statements (to reflect unrecognized assets and liabilities) and the leverage, coverage, and profitability ratios for the effects of operating leases.

Box 44-1 reviews the finance literature on the competing incentives of the lease-versus-purchase decision. The impact of the financial reporting alternatives (operating vs. capitalization) on this decision is also discussed.

Lease Classification: Lessees

The preceding discussion suggests that lessees prefer to structure and report leases as operating leases. Their counterparts, lessors, however, prefer to structure leases as capital leases. This allows earlier recognition of revenue and income by reporting transactions that are in substance installment sales or financing arrangements as completed sales. The resulting higher profitability and turnover ratios are powerful incentives for lessors. The final section of the reading is devoted to a discussion of lease accounting from the perspective of the lessor. The discussion that follows retains the lessee perspective.

Lease classifications are not intended to be alternative reporting methods. However, management actively negotiates the provisions of lease agreements and the preferred accounting treatment is an important element of these contractual negotiations.

SFAS 13 (1976) and IAS 17 (revised 1997) attempt to promulgate "objective" and "reliable" criteria to facilitate the evaluation of the economic substance of lease agreements. One goal was to discourage off-balance-sheet financing by lessees and front-end loading of income by lessors. The criteria are designed to ensure that either the lessee or lessor recognize the leased assets on their books.

Capital Leases

A lease that, in economic substance, transfers to the lessee substantially all the risks and rewards inherent in the leased property is a financing or capital lease and should be capitalized. Under U.S. GAAP, the lessee must classify a lease meeting any one of the following SFAS 13 criteria at the inception of the lease as a capital lease:

1. The lease transfers ownership of the property to the lessee at the end of the lease term.
2. The lease contains a bargain purchase option.
3. The lease term is equal to 75% or more of the estimated economic life of the leased property (not applicable to land or when the lease term begins within the final 25% of the economic life of the asset).
4. The present value[3] of the minimum lease payments[4] (MLPs) equals or exceeds 90% of the fair value of leased property to the lessor.

---

[3] The discount rate used to compute the present values should be the lessee's incremental borrowing rate or the implicit interest rate of the lessor, whichever is *lower.* The use of the lower rate generates the higher of two present values, increasing the probability that this criterion will be met and the lease capitalized. Under IAS 17, there is a similar (but less precise) requirement.

[4] MLPs include residual values when they are guaranteed by lessees since the guarantee results in a contractually fixed residual value and effectively transfers the risk of changes in residual values to the lessee.

BOX 44-1 INCENTIVES FOR LEASING AND THEIR EFFECT ON THE CAPITAL VERSUS OPERATING LEASE CHOICE

Management may have a number of reasons to prefer leasing compared to outright asset purchases. The choice may be a function of strategic investment and capital structure objectives, the comparative costs* of leasing versus equity or debt financing, the availability of tax benefits, and perceived financial reporting advantages. Some of these factors influence whether the lease will be treated as an operating or capital lease; others are unrelated to reporting methods.

Tax Incentives

The tax benefits of owning assets are exploited best by transferring them to the party in the higher marginal tax bracket. Firms with low effective tax rates more readily engage in leasing than firms in high tax brackets as the tax benefits can be passed on to the lessor. El-Gazzar et al. (1986) found that, consistent with this hypothesis, firms with lower effective tax rates had a higher proportion of lease debt to total assets than did firms with higher effective tax rates. Moreover, lessees with high effective tax rates tended to capitalize their leases for financial statement purposes. El-Gazzar et al. argue that tax effects also influence the choice of accounting method as the lessee attempts to influence the tax interpretation (by the IRS) of lease contracts. That is, it is more difficult to argue for capital lease treatment for tax purposes if the lease is treated as an operating lease for book purposes.

Nontax Incentives

Smith and Wakeman (1985) analyzed nontax incentives related to the lease-versus-purchase decision. Their list of eight nontax factors that make leasing more likely than purchase is presented here. Some of these factors are not directly related to the lessee's choice, but are motivated by the manufacturer or lessor and/or the type of asset involved. We have sorted these conditions by their potential impact on the operating-versus-capitalization accounting choice.

Nontax Incentives for Leasing versus Purchase: Incentives Classified by Potential Impact on Operating versus Capital Lease Choice

Favors Operating Lease per SFAS 13

1. Period of use is short relative to the overall life of the asset.
2. Lessor has comparative advantage in reselling the asset.

Favors Structuring Lease as Operating Lease

3. Corporate bond covenants contain specific covenants relating to financial policies that the firm must follow.
4. Management compensation contracts contain provisions expressing compensation as a function of returns on invested capital.

Not Relevant to Operating versus Capital Lease Decision

5. Lessee ownership is closely held so that risk reduction is important.
6. Lessor (manufacturer) has market power and can thus generate higher profits by leasing the asset (and controlling the terms of the lease) rather than selling it.
7. Asset is not specialized to the firm.
8. Asset's value is not sensitive to use or abuse (owner takes better care of asset than lessee).

Short periods of use and the resale factor favor the use of operating leases, and under GAAP, these conditions would lead to lease agreements consistent with operating leases. The bond covenant and management compensation incentives also favor the negotiated structuring of the agreement as an operating lease.

Consistent with the foregoing, both Abdel-Khalik (1981) and Nakayama et al. (1981) note that the expected covenant violations resulting from SFAS 13 influenced firms to lobby against its adoption. Furthermore, Abdel-Khalik notes that firms renegotiated the terms of their leases during SFAS 13's transition period to make them eligible for treatment as operating leases. Imhoff and Thomas (1988) found that subsequent to SFAS 13, there was a general decline in leases as a form of financing.† Taken together, these results confirm that debt covenant and compensation factors affect both the choice of leasing as a form of financing as well as the choice of accounting treatment of the lease.

Based on Smith and Wakeman (1985).

* Related to these costs are the risks related to residual values and obsolescence.

† Further evidence is provided by El-Gazzar et al., who note that in the pre-SFAS 13 period, firms that had high debt-to-equity ratios and/or had incentive-based contracts based on income after interest expense were more likely to have leases classified as operating leases.

The ownership and bargain purchase criteria imply a transfer of all the risks and benefits of the leased property to the lessee; in economic substance, such leases are financing arrangements. Lease terms extending to at least 75% of the economic life of the leased asset are also considered to achieve such a transfer; there is an implicit assumption that most of the value of an asset accrues to the user within that period. Finally, a lease must be capitalized when the present value of the minimum lease payments is equal to or exceeds 90% of the fair value of the leased property at the inception of the lease. In effect, the lessee has contractually agreed to payments ensuring that the lessor will recover its investment along with a reasonable return. The transaction is, therefore, an installment purchase for the lessee financed by the lessor, and capitalization reflects this economic interpretation of the leasing transaction.[5]

The provisions of IAS 17 are less precise. That standard defines a finance lease (the IAS term for a capital lease) as one:

> that transfers substantially all of the risks and rewards incident to ownership of an asset. Title may or may not eventually be transferred.[6]

As IAS 17 lacks the quantitative criteria of SFAS 13, it is easier for a lease to be classified as an operating lease under IAS standards than under U.S. GAAP.

Operating Leases

Under U.S. GAAP, leases not meeting any of the four SFAS 13 criteria listed above are not capitalized and no asset or obligation is reported in the financial statements of the lessee since no purchase is deemed to have occurred. Such leases are classified as operating leases, and payments are reported as rental expense. SFAS 13 mandates the use of the straight-line method of recognizing periodic rental payments unless another, systematic basis provides a better representation of the use of leased property. As a result, for leases with rising rental payments, lease expense and cash flow will not be identical.

Financial Reporting by Lessees: Capital versus Operating Leases

Financial reporting by lessees will be illustrated using a noncancellable lease beginning December 31, 2000, with annual MLPs of $10,000 made at the end of each year for four years. Ten percent is assumed to be the appropriate discount rate.

Operating Lease. If the lease does not meet any criteria requiring capitalization:

- No entry is made at the inception of the lease.
- Over the life of the lease, only the annual rental expense of $10,000 will be charged to income and CFO.

Capital Lease. If the lease meets any one of the four criteria of a capital lease:

- At the inception of the lease, an asset (leasehold asset) and liability (leasehold liability) equal to the present value of the lease payments, $31,700, is recognized.

---

[5] Leases are classified at the inception of the lease; the classification is not changed when the lessee or lessor is acquired unless the provisions of the lease agreement are changed. See FASB Interpretation 21 (1978).

[6] IAS 17, para. 3. An operating lease is defined as a "lease other than a finance lease."

Over the life of the lease:

1. The annual rental expense of $10,000 will be allocated between interest and principal payments on the $31,700 leasehold liability according to the following amortization schedule:

Allocation of Payment of $10,000

Year	Opening Liability	Interest*	Principal	Closing Liability†
2000				$31,700
2001	$31,700	$3,170	$6,830	24,870
2002	24,870	2,487	7,513	17,357
2003	17,357	1,735	8,265	9,092
2004	9,092	909	9,092	0

* 10% of the opening liability.

† Equals the opening liability less the periodic amortization of the lease obligation. Also equals the present value of the remaining MLPs discounted at the interest rate in effect at the inception of the lease.

2. The cost of the leasehold asset of $31,700 is charged to operations (annual depreciation is $7,925) using the straight-line method over the term of the lease.[7]

Comparative Analysis of Capitalized and Operating Leases

Balance Sheet Effects. No assets or liabilities are recognized if the lease is treated as an operating lease. When leases are capitalized, there is a major impact on a firm's balance sheet at inception and throughout the life of the lease. At the inception of the lease, an asset and a liability equal to the present value of the lease payments are recognized.

Balance Sheet Effects of Lease Capitalization

	2000	2001	2002	2003	2004
Assets					
Leased assets	$31,700	$31,700	$31,700	$31,700	$31,700
Accumulated depreciation	0	7,925	15,850	23,775	31,700
Leased assets, net	$31,700	$23,775	$15,850	$ 7,925	$ 0
Liabilities					
Current portion of lease obligation	6,830	7,513	8,265	9,092	0
Long-term debt: lease obligation	24,870	17,357	9,092	0	0
	$31,700	$24,870	$17,357	$ 9,092	$ 0

The gross and net (of accumulated depreciation) amounts are reported at each balance sheet date. The current and noncurrent components of the lease obligation are reported as liabilities under capitalization. The current component

[7] Generally, depreciation methods used for similar purchased property are applied to leased assets over their estimated economic lives when one of the transfer of ownership criteria (1 or 2) is met and over the lease term when one of the other capitalization criteria (3 or 4) is satisfied.

is the principal portion of the lease payment to be made in the following year. Note that, at the inception of the lease, the leased asset and liability are equal at $31,700. Since the asset and liability are amortized using different methods, this equality is not again observed until the end of the lease term when both asset and liability are equal to zero.

Effect on Financial Ratios. Lease capitalization increases asset balances, resulting in lower asset turnover and return on asset ratios, as compared with the operating lease method, which does not record leased assets.

The most important effect of lease capitalization, however, is its impact on leverage ratios. As lease obligations are not recognized for operating leases, leverage ratios are understated. Lease capitalization adds both current and noncurrent liabilities to debt, resulting in a corresponding decrease in working capital and increases in the debt-to-equity and other leverage ratios.

Income Statement Effects. The income statement effects of lease reporting are also significant and impact operating income as well as net income. The operating lease method charges the periodic rental payments to expense as accrued, whereas capitalization recognizes depreciation and interest expense over the lease term.

Income Effects of Lease Classification

	Operating Lease	Capital Lease		
	Operating = Total Expense	Operating Expense	Nonoperating Expense	
Year	Rent	Depreciation	Interest	Total Expense
2001	$10,000	$ 7,925	$3,170	$11,095
2002	10,000	7,925	2,487	10,412
2003	10,000	7,925	1,735	9,660
2004	10,000	7,925	909	8,834
Totals	$40,000	$31,700	$8,300	$40,000

Operating Income. Capitalization results in higher operating income (earnings before interest and taxes, or EBIT) since the annual straight-line depreciation expense of $7,925 is lower than the annual rental expense of $10,000 reported under the operating lease method. For an individual lease, this difference is never reversed and remains constant over the lease term given use of the straight-line depreciation method. Accelerated depreciation methods would generate smaller differences in early years, with an increasing difference as depreciation declines, increasing both the level and trend of EBIT.

Total Expense and Net Income. Under capitalization, lease expense includes interest expense and depreciation of the leased asset. Initially, total expense for a capital lease exceeds rental expense reported for an operating lease, but declines over the lease term as interest expense falls.[8] In later years, total lease expense will be less than rental expense reported for an operating lease.

[8] If the company uses accelerated depreciation, then the difference in earlier years will be greater but the subsequent decline will also be rapid.

Note that total expense (interest plus depreciation) for a capital lease must equal total rental expense for an operating lease over the life of the lease.[9] Consequently, although total net income over the lease term is not affected by capitalization, the timing of income recognition is changed; lower net income is reported in the early years, followed by higher income in later years. This relationship holds for individual leases, but the effect on a firm depends on any additional leases entered into in subsequent periods. When asset prices (and lease rentals) are rising, the impact of old leases nearing expiration may be swamped by the impact of new leases. If a firm enters into new leases at the same or increasing rate over time, reported net income will remain lower under capitalization.

Effect on Financial Ratios. In general, firms with operating leases report higher profitability, interest coverage (as interest expense is lower), return on equity, and return on assets ratios. The higher ROE ratios are due to the higher profitability (numerator effect), whereas the higher ROA is due primarily to the lower assets (denominator effect).

Cash Flow Effects of Lease Classification. Lease classification provides another example where accounting methods affect the classification of cash flows.[10] Under the operating lease method, all cash flows are operating and there is an operating cash outflow of $10,000 per year. However, lease capitalization results in both operating and financing cash flows as the rental payments of $10,000 are allocated between interest expense (treated as CFO) and amortization of the lease obligation (reported as cash from financing).

Cash Flow Effects of Lease Classification

	Operating Lease	Capital Lease	
Year	Operations	Operations	Financing
2001	$10,000	$3,170	$6,830
2002	10,000	2,487	7,513
2003	10,000	1,735	8,265
2004	10,000	909	9,091

In 2001, for example, CFO differs between the two methods by $6,830, the amortization of the lease obligation. Because interest expense declines over the lease term and an increasing proportion of the annual payment is allocated to the lease obligation, the difference in CFO increases over the lease term. Thus, lease capitalization systematically decreases the operating cash outflow while increasing the financing cash outflow.

Therefore, although the capital lease method adversely affects some financial statement ratios, it allows firms to report higher operating cash flows compared to those reported using the operating lease method.

Before proceeding, it is important to point out that *at the inception of the lease (year 2000), no cash flows are reported.* This is true even though a capital lease implies

[9] This equality does not hold when the residual value is not zero.

[10] We discuss only the classification of cash flows. After-tax cash flows are not affected by lease classification as *generally* firms that use the capital lease method for financial reporting purposes use the operating lease method for tax purposes. Tax payments and actual cash flows are therefore identical. Under the capital lease method, the lease expense under financial reporting exceeds the lease expense reported for tax purposes, resulting in a deferred tax asset.

the purchase of an asset (cash outflow for investment) financed by the issuance of new debt (cash inflow from financing). Disclosure of the event is reported as part of the "significant noncash financing and investing activities." Analysts attempting to estimate a firm's cash flow requirements for operating capacity should, however, include the present value of such leases as a cash requirement. *Moreover, free cash flow calculations for valuation purposes should incorporate the present value of leases as a cash outflow for investment at the inception of the lease.*

Analysis of Lease Disclosures

A noncancellable lease, whether reported as a capital or operating lease, in effect, constitutes debt and the right to use an asset. If the lease is reported as a capital lease, this information is on-balance-sheet. If it is reported as an operating lease, then the debt and asset are off-balance-sheet and the analyst must adjust accordingly.

This is especially true in industries such as airlines and retailers where some firms own operating assets (i.e., airplanes or stores), other firms lease them and report the leases as capital leases, and still other lessees account for them as operating leases. Given the same conditions, the firms using operating leases may report the "best" results as they will show minimal debt and their higher profits will appear to be generated by a relatively smaller investment in assets.

However, the disclosure requirements of firms with leases, capital or operating, are sufficiently detailed to provide the information required for adjustments.

Lease Disclosure Requirements

SFAS 13 requires the disclosure of gross amounts of capitalized lease assets as of each balance sheet date, by major classes or grouped by their nature or function; they may be combined with owned assets.

Lessees must also disclose future MLPs for each of the five succeeding fiscal years and the aggregate thereafter as well as the net present value of the capitalized leases.

Lessees reporting operating leases must also disclose future MLPs for each of the five succeeding fiscal years and in the aggregate thereafter (see Exhibit 44-1 for an example). The present value of the MLPs is not required but is occasionally provided. The rental expense under operating leases (classified as to minimum, contingent, and sublease rentals) for each period for which an income statement is presented must be disclosed as of the balance sheet date.

For both operating and capital leases, lessees must also disclose aggregate minimum rentals receivable under noncancellable subleases. Information regarding renewal terms, purchase options, contingent rentals, any escalation clauses, and restrictions on dividends, additional debt, and leasing is also required. However, rather than being informative, such disclosure is usually vague and general in nature.

IAS 17 disclosure requirements are far less extensive:

- MLPs due within one year
- MLPs due in more than one but less than five years
- MLPs due after five years

This abbreviated disclosure (for an example, see Note 12 of the Roche 2000 annual report) makes the analysis that follows less precise, but does permit approximations.

EXHIBIT 44-1 AMR
Excerpts from Balance Sheet and Lease Footnote, December 31, 1999 (in $millions)

Assets		
Equipment and property (net of accumulated depreciation of 7,403)		$14,338
Equipment and property under capital leases (net of accumulated amortization of 1,347)		1,949
Total assets		24,374
Liabilities		
Long-term debt		
Current maturity	$ 302	
Noncurrent	4,078	4,380
Capital lease obligations		
Current	$ 236	
Noncurrent	1,611	1,847
Total long-term debt and capital lease obligations		$ 6,227
Shareholders' equity		6,858

Leases

AMR's subsidiaries lease various types of equipment and property, including aircraft and airport and off-airport facilities. The future minimum lease payments required under capital leases, together with the present value of net minimum lease payments, and future minimum lease payments required under operating leases that have initial or remaining noncancellable lease terms in excess of one year as of December 31, 1999, were (in millions):

Years Ending December 31	Capital Leases	Operating Leases
2000	$ 347	$ 1,015
2001	329	1,006
2002	280	952
2003	198	965
2004	249	954
2005 and subsequent	1,081	12,169
	$2,484	$17,061
Less amount representing interest	(637)	
Present value of net minimum lease payments	$1,847	

At December 31, 1999, the Company had 205 jet aircraft and 71 turboprop aircraft under operating leases, and 79 jet aircraft and 61 turboprop aircraft under capital leases.

Source: AMR, *1999 Annual Report.*

Financial Reporting by Lessees: An Example

Exhibit 44-1 contains balance sheet information and the lease footnote of AMR Corp. [AMR], the parent of American Airlines. From the balance sheet alone, it would seem that AMR primarily purchases rather than leases its equipment. The carrying value of purchased equipment is over seven times that of leased equipment.

The footnote paints an entirely different picture. AMR has substantial leases that are mostly structured as operating leases. As required by GAAP, capital lease obligations and operating leases are shown separately. Future MLPs for the next five years, and the aggregate thereafter, are disclosed for both capital and operating leases. For capital leases, interest has been deducted to report their present value of $1,847 million ($236 million is reported as current and $1,611 million as long-term debt).

Note that the (aggregate) operating lease payments of $17,061 million are almost seven times the capital lease payments ($2,484 million). Moreover, the data suggest that the operating leases are of longer term than the capital leases!

Aggregate MLPs of the capital leases for the next five years are about 56% of total future MLPs, or $1,403 million. Total MLPs for the remaining years are $1,081 million, or 44% of the total MLPs of $2,484 million over the lease terms. The average lease term of the capitalized leases can be estimated by computing the number of payments included in the "later years" amount of $1,081 million; that is, ($1,081 million/$249 million) if we assume that annual payments remain at the 2004 level. This suggests a lease term of approximately 9 (initial five plus the estimated remaining four) years.

For operating leases, the proportion of payments after the first five years is ($12,169/ $17,061) 71% of total payments. This suggests a longer term than for the capital leases. Dividing the remaining payments of $12,169 by the 2004 payment of $954 yields 13, suggesting a lease term of 18 years (5 plus 13) or *twice as long as the term of the capital leases.*

The note indicates that 205 jet aircraft and 71 turboprops are under operating leases. *Neither these assets nor the debt associated with them appear on the balance sheet.*

Investors and analysts can use the lease disclosures to adjust the balance sheet appropriately. The present value of the operating leases can be estimated by discounting the future minimum lease payments. This estimate requires assumptions about the pattern of MLPs after the first five years and the discount rate. The estimation procedure (described below) is "robust," with the calculated present value relatively invariant to the assumptions.

Assumed Pattern of MLPs. Footnote disclosures reflect the payments to be made over each of the next five years and the total payments thereafter. The present value computation requires an estimate of the number of payments implicit in the latter lump sum. Either the rate of decline suggested by the cash outflows for the next five years or a constant amount over the remaining term may be used to derive the present value of the operating lease payments.

Discount Rate. The discount rate should reflect the risk class of the leased assets as well as the company being analyzed. The interest rate implicit in the reported capital leases is a good approximation of that rate.[11]

Box 44-2 uses AMR to illustrate the estimation method(s). The procedure yields a rate of between 6.0% and 6.5% depending on the assumptions made; we use 6.4%. The two assumptions regarding pattern of cash flows over the lease term generate present value estimates of $10.1 and $9.9 billion, a difference of only 2%.

---

[11] Because the implicit rate is an average rate based on terms at inception, it may be significantly different from either the reported or marginal long-term borrowing rate the company faces in the capital markets. The analyst may use a long-term borrowing rate estimated from the debt footnote or based on current market conditions.

BOX 44-2 ESTIMATION OF THE PRESENT VALUE OF OPERATING LEASES

A. The Implicit Discount Rate of a Firm's Capital Leases

Two approaches may be employed to estimate the average discount rate used to capitalize a firm's capital leases. The first uses only the next period's MLP; the second incorporates all future MLPs in the estimation procedure.

1. Using Next Period's MLP

The 2000 MLP for AMR's capital leases is $347 million. That payment includes interest and principal. The principal portion is shown in AMR's current liabilities section as $236 million. The difference, $111 million, represents the interest component of the MLP. As the present value of AMR's capital leases equals $1,847, the interest rate on the capitalized leases can be estimated as ($111/$1,847) 6.01%.

This calculation assumes that the principal payment of $236 million will be made at the end of the year. If it is made early in the year, then the interest expense is based on the principal outstanding after payment of the current portion. The results can be biased if the current portion is a significant portion of the overall liability. An alternative estimate of the implicit interest rate may be derived using the average liability balance; that is, $111/[0.5 × ($1,847 + $1,611)] = 6.42%.

2. Using All Future MLPs

The interest rate can also be estimated by solving for the implicit interest rate (internal rate of return) that equates the MLPs and their present value. This calculation requires an assumption about the pattern of MLPs after the first five years as the MLPs for the first five years (2000 to 2004) are given. From 2004 and on, two assumptions are possible:

1. Constant rate, or
2. Declining rate

Constant Rate

Under the simpler constant rate assumption, it is assumed that the payment level ($249 million) in the fifth year (2004) continues into the future, implying the following payment stream:

Year	2000	2001	2002	2003	2004	2005
MLP	$347	$329	$280	$198	$249	$249
Year	2006	2007	2008	2009[r]	Total	
MLP	$249	$249	$249	$85	$2,484	

[r] Residual.

The internal rate of return that equates this stream to the present value of $1,847 is 6.55%.

Declining Rate

Alternatively, and more realistically, one would expect the payments to decline over time. The rate of decline implicit in the MLPs reported indiv dually for the first five years may be used to estimate the payment pattern after the initial five years. In AMR's case, payments decrease initially and then jump in 2004. On average, the payments are approximately 94% of the previous year.* Using this rate we obtain the following pattern of payments:

Year	2000	2001	2002	2003	2004	2005
MLP	$347	$329	$280	$198	$249	$234
Year	2006	2007	2008	2009	2010[r]	Total
MLP	$220	$207	$194	$183	$43	$2,484

[r] Residual.

The internal rate of return that equates this stream to the present value of $1,847 is 6.40%; a rate close to the 6.55% based on the constant rate assumption. Generally, the differences are not significant and unless the rate of decline is very steep, the constant rate assumption simplifies the computation. *The first procedure yields an estimate of 6.0 to 6.4%; the second yields estimates of 6.40 to 6.55%. Based on these estimates, we use 6.4% for our analysis of AMR's operating leases.*

B. Finding the Present Value of the Operating Leases

For operating leases the MLPs for the first five years (2000 to 2004) are given. Again we can make two assumptions as to the pattern of payments for 2005 and on.

Under the constant rate assumption, it is assumed that MLPs from the year 2005 and on equal the 2004 payment of $954. Alternatively, based on the payment pattern of the operating lease MLPs over the first five years, one would expect the payments to decline at a rate of 1.5% a year. The assumed patterns and the resultant present values using the discount rate of 6.4% are presented below.

Constant Rate

Year	2000	2001	2002	2003	2004
MLP	$1,015	$1,006	$952	$965	$954
Year	2005–2016	2017[r]	Total	Present Value	
MLP	$954	$721	$17,061	$10,060	

[r] Residual.

Declining Rate

Year	2000	2001	2002	2003	2004	2005
MLP	$1,015	$1,006	$952	$965	$954	$940

Year	2006	...	2018	2019[r]	Total	Present Value
MLP	$926	...	$772	$221	$17,061	$9,911

[r] Residual.

Note that the two present value estimates of $10.1 and $9.9 billion are within 2% of each other.

C. Executory Costs

Reported MLPs at times include such executory costs as maintenance, taxes, and insurance on the leased assets. These costs are not financing costs and should be excluded from the calculation of the lease present value. However, because footnote disclosures generally do not reduce MLPs by executory costs, the present value calculation described previously is biased.

OPTIONAL SEGMENT ENDS

In most cases that bias is small and can be ignored. However, the estimation method can be modified to adjust for this bias. When the firm discloses the total of the executory costs, we can assume that the pattern of the executory costs follows that of the MLPs. If we define p as the proportion of total executory costs to total MLPs,

$$p = \frac{\text{Total executory costs}}{\text{Total MLPs}}$$

then the procedures described above can be applied[†] to a pattern of *adjusted MLPs*, where the

Adjusted MLP (for any year) = $(1 - p) \times$ unadjusted MLP (for that year)

* We have used the arithmetic mean. The geometric mean is 92%.

[†] Alternatively, one can use the unadjusted MLPs and make the following two adjustments:

1. In calculating the implicit interest rate of the capital leases, gross up the present value of the capital leases by *dividing* by $(1 - p)$.
2. Using the interest rate calculated in step 1, find the present value of the unadjusted MLPs. *Multiply* that present value by $(1 - p)$.

Impact of Operating Lease Adjustments

Liabilities. The impact of the adjustment is highly significant. AMR's reported long-term debt and capital leases total $6.2 billion. Adding approximately $10 billion for off-balance-sheet operating leases increases debt by more than 160% to approximately $16.2 billion. *AMR has more debt off the balance sheet than on the balance sheet.* With equity of $6.9 billion, the debt-to-equity ratio of 0.9 mushrooms to 2.3.

AMR: Effects of Operating Lease Adjustments (in $billions)

	Reported	+	Operating Leases	=	Adjusted
Debt	$ 6.2		$10.0		$16.2
Equity	6.9				6.9
Debt/equity ratio	0.9X				2.3X
Assets	$24.4		$10.0		$34.4

Assets. Exhibit 44-1 reports total assets of $24.4 billion. Capitalization of the operating leases increases total assets by $10 billion. AMR is operating 41% more assets than reported on its balance sheet. *Efficiency measures such as turnover or ROA use total assets in the denominator and are highly overstated; adjusted ratios more accurately portray AMR's asset efficiency.*

Income and Cash Flow Effects. Adjustments for operating leases also affect the income and cash flow statements (as well as related ratios). These effects can be illustrated using the 2000 MLP of $1,015 million as an example. Under the operating lease method, both rent expense and the CFO outflow equal $1,015 million. Capitalization results in allocation of that $1,015 million between interest expense and principal payments; in addition, the leased asset must be depreciated. These changes reduce reported income but increase CFO.

AMR: Effects of Operating Lease Adjustment, 2000 (in $millions)

	As Reported	Adjusted
Income Statement		
Rent expense	$1,015	
Interest expense		$ 640*
Amortization expense		555†
Total expense	$1,015	$1,195
Cash Flow Statement		
If interest payments are treated as CFO (per SFAS 95)		
CFO outflow	$1,015	$ 640
CFF outflow	0	$ 375
If interest payments are treated as CFF (per Reading 33)		
CFO outflow	$1,015	0
CFF outflow	0	$1,015

* Interest expense = interest rate × PV of leases = 0.064 × $10 billion = $640 million.

† Amortization expense = PV of leases divided by lease term = $10 billion/18 = $555 million.

Other Lease-Related Issues

While lease classification affects how leases are reported in financial statements, it is not the only issue that affects financial analysis. The following may also be significant for some companies:

1. *Lease impairment.* Because of changes in market conditions, leased assets can become uneconomic to the firm. In such cases, the firm may recognize an impairment charge similar to the impairment charges for fixed assets. For example, OMI [OMM], an operator of oil tankers, recorded a loss of $6.3 million in June 1999 when it "determined that its current lease obligations for vessels exceeded its undiscounted forecasted future net cash flows."
2. *Sale and leaseback of assets.* Such sales can be a cost-effective source of funds, especially for firms with low credit ratings. Because the assets sold secure the obligation, lenders charge a lower interest rate than for unsecured borrowings. Both SFAS 13 and IAS 17 require the lessee to defer any gain on the asset sale, and recognize it over the lease term, when the lease is a capital (finance) lease. Amortization over the lease term is also required for sale/leasebacks classified as operating leases under SFAS 13. However, under IAS 17, gains on sale/leasebacks classified as operating leases are recognized immediately.[12]

[12] The accounting for sale/leasebacks can be quite complex, with numerous variations and exceptions under both U.S. and IAS GAAP. See Box 44-4 for further discussion.

3. *Lease guarantees.* Firms may guarantee leases for affiliates (see discussion of Texaco later in the reading). Companies may also remain obligated for leases when operating units are sold. For example, Kmart [KM] sold its Builders Square subsidiary in 1997 to Hechinger, another chain of home improvement stores. When Hechinger filed for bankruptcy in June 1999, Kmart recognized a pretax charge of $350 million for its guarantees of long-term leases with a net present value of $711 million.
4. *Straight-line recognition.* Both SFAS 13 and IAS 17 require both lessors and lessees to recognize operating lease payments over the life of the lease on a straight-line basis (equal amounts in each year). However, the lease payments may take a different form, resulting in either prepaid rent or rent receivable.

   For example, in the first quarter of 2001, Cisco [CSCO] paid Catellus [CDX] $68 million in connection with a California ground lease. Catellus reported that this sum would be amortized over the 34-year lease term.
5. *Synthetic leases.* Such leases use a special purpose entity to finance an asset purchase. The asset is then leased to the user. While the user receives the tax benefits of ownership, the transaction is accounted for as an operating lease, keeping it off-balance-sheet.

   For example, AOL Time Warner [AOL] used a synthetic lease to finance the construction of its New York headquarters, keeping a reported one billion dollars of debt off its balance sheet.

3 OFF-BALANCE-SHEET FINANCING ACTIVITIES

Leases are but one example of contractual arrangements that give rise to off-balance-sheet debt. In this section, we discuss other such arrangements and show how financial statements should be adjusted to reflect the underlying economic consequences. Like leases, some of these off-balance-sheet activities are commonplace and can be found in many firms and industries. Others tend to be industry specific or are the product of specific market conditions.

Take-or-Pay and Throughput Arrangements

Firms use take-or-pay contracts to ensure the long-term availability of raw materials and other inputs necessary for operations.[13] These agreements are common in the energy, chemical, paper, and metal industries. Under these arrangements, the purchasing firm commits to buy a minimum quantity of an input over a specified time period. Input prices may be fixed by contract or may be related to market prices. Energy companies use throughput arrangements with pipelines or processors (such as refiners) to ensure future distribution or processing requirements.

These contracts are often used as collateral for bank or other financing by unrelated suppliers or by investors in joint ventures. The contract serves as an indirect guarantee of the related debt. However, neither the assets nor the debt

---

[13] Inventories can also be financed through product financing arrangements under which inventories are sold and later repurchased. SFAS 49 (1981) requires that such arrangements that do not effectively transfer the risk of ownership to the buyer must be accounted for as debt financing rather than sale of inventory. In such cases, the cost of holding inventories (storage and insurance) and interest cost on the imputed debt must be recognized as incurred. Prior to SFAS 49, companies sometimes used these arrangements to defer these costs and accelerate the recognition of profit. Product financing arrangements may still be accounted for as sales outside of the United States.

incurred to obtain (or guarantee availability of) operating capacity are reflected on the balance sheet of the purchaser. SFAS 47 (1981) requires that, when a long-term commitment is used to obtain financing, the purchaser must disclose the nature of the commitment and the minimum required payments in its financial statement footnotes.

As take-or-pay contracts and throughput agreements effectively keep some operating assets and liabilities off the balance sheet, the analyst should add the present value of minimum future commitments to both property and debt.

Exhibit 44-2 contains the commitments and contingencies footnote from the 1999 annual report of Alcoa [AA], disclosing a take-or-pay obligation of Alcoa of Australia, a consolidated subsidiary. Note that the disclosure is similar to that required for (capital and operating) leases. We can apply the method used earlier to compute the present value of the debt. The calculation is shown in panel B of the exhibit.

The take-or-pay contracts reported by Alcoa represent $1,780 million of off-balance-sheet assets and debt. The impact of this adjustment on the leverage ratio is as follows:

Alcoa Balance Sheet, at December 31, 1999 (in $millions)

	Reported	Adjusted	Increase
Total debt	$3,067	$4,847	58%
Stockholders' equity	6,318	6,318	None
Debt-to-equity ratio	0.49X	0.77X	58%

Sale of Receivables

Receivables are sometimes financed by their sale (or securitization) to unrelated parties. That is, the firm sells the receivables to a buyer (normally a financial institution or investor group). Depending on the interest (if any) paid by customers and the effective interest rate on the sale transaction, the seller may recognize a gain or loss on the receivables sold. The seller uses the proceeds from the sale for operations or to reduce existing or planned debt. The firm continues to service the original receivables; customer payments are transferred to the new owner of the receivables. Some arrangements are revolving in nature as collected receivables are periodically replaced by new ones.

Such transactions are recorded as sales under SFAS 140, Accounting for Transfers and Servicing of Financial Assets and Extinguishments of Liabilities (2000), as long as there has been a *legal* transfer of ownership from the seller to the buyer.[14] To effect such transactions, firms often set up distinct (nonconsolidated) trusts or subsidiaries (often referred to as a *qualifying special-purpose entity, QSPE*) that the firm's creditors cannot access in the event of bankruptcy.[15] By selling the receivables through such entities, the firm has adhered to the strict legal definition of ownership transfer. Exhibit 44-3 provides examples of such arrangements from the financial statements of Lucent Technologies [LU]. Note that in

[14] SFAS 140 states that the transferor (seller) accounts for the transfer as a sale when it surrenders effective control over those assets (see SFAS 140 for details).

[15] LTV, a steel company, filed for bankruptcy late in 2000. LTV argued that the transfer of receivables (and a similar transfer of inventories) to a QSPE was a "disguised finance transaction" and that it still had an interest in the transferred assets. However, the bankruptcy court ruled against the company in March 2001.

EXHIBIT 44-2 Alcoa
Analysis of Take-or-Pay Contracts

A: Footnote: Contingent Liabilities

Alcoa of Australia (AofA) is party to a number of natural gas and electricity contracts that expire between 2001 and 2022. Under these take-or-pay contracts, AofA is obligated to pay for a minimum amount of natural gas or electricity even if these commodities are not required for operations. Commitments related to these contracts total \$190 in 2000, \$182 in 2001, \$179 in 2002, \$176 in 2003, \$176 in 2004, and \$2,222 thereafter.

Source: Alcoa, *1999 Annual Report.*

B. Analysis: Take-or-pay Contracts, 2000 to 2004 and Beyond (in \$millions)

Year	Take-or-Pay Obligation
2000	\$ 190
2001	182
2002	179
2003	176
2004	176
Thereafter	2,222

Using the technique for capitalizing operating leases discussed earlier in the chapter, the above payment stream can be discounted to its present value. Estimated payments continue after 2004 (using, for simplifying purposes, the constant rate assumption) for

$$\frac{\$2{,}222 \text{ million}}{\$176 \text{ million}} = 12.63 \text{ years}$$

Given this payment stream, the present value can be arrived at using an estimated cost of debt (based on capitalized lease disclosures or other long-term debt). For Alcoa, we estimate an interest rate of 7%. When applied to the minimum payments shown above, the resulting present value equals \$1,780 million for take-or-pay obligations. Thus approximately \$1.8 billion should be added as an adjustment to Alcoa's consolidated property and total debt.

2000, Lucent's receivables and loans were sold through a "bankruptcy-remote subsidiary," as required by GAAP for sale recognition.

By reporting such transactions as sales, the company decreases accounts receivable and increases cash from operations in the period of sale. However, most such receivable sales and/or securitizations provide that the seller retains the effective credit risk by either:

- Retaining a portion of the receivables and receiving payment only after the securitized amount has been repaid. If the retained percentage exceeds the historic loss ratio, the seller has retained the effective risk.
- Providing other collateral, or agreeing to replace delinquent receivables with current receivables.

EXHIBIT 44-3 Lucent Technologies Receivable Securitization Activities (years ended September 30)

1999

- Subsidiary of Lucent sold approximately $625 million of accounts receivable to a nonconsolidated qualified special-purpose entity (QSPE).
- The QSPE resold the receivables to an unaffiliated financial institution.
- Lucent transferred $700 million of other receivables to the QSPE as collateral.

2000

- Lucent and a third-party financial institution arranged for the creation of a nonconsolidated Special Purpose Trust.
- Trust purchases, from a wholly owned (bankruptcy-remote) subsidiary of Lucent, customer finance loans, and receivables on a limited-recourse basis.
- Balance of receivables sold but uncollected was $1,329 million.

Source: Information from Lucent Technologies, *2000 Annual Report.*

As shown in Exhibit 44-3, Lucent provided the second form of implicit guarantee. *When the seller retains the entire expected loss experience, these transactions are effectively collateralized borrowings with the receivables serving as collateral.* Sales of receivables are another form of off-balance-sheet financing and should be adjusted as follows:

1. *Balance Sheet.* Both accounts receivable and current liabilities should be increased by the amount of receivables sold that have not yet been collected.
2. *Cash Flow Statement.* CFO must be adjusted; the change in the uncollected amount should be classified as cash from financing rather than CFO.

These two adjustments usually capture the analytical effects of receivable sales. However, as sales/securitizations of receivables transactions can be quite complex, other aspects of the financial statements may also be affected. Moreover, to the extent amounts received from receivable sales are not equal to the "face value" of receivables sold, the (cash flow) adjustment is only an approximation, albeit a reasonably accurate one.

Box 44-3 illustrates the effects of sales/securitizations on the income statement. Treating the transaction as a sale results in earlier income recognition as compared to treating it as a collateralized borrowing.

Example:

Lucent Technologies

Exhibit 44-4 continues with our Lucent example. Panel A summarizes data from the financial statements. As indicated in Exhibit 44-3, Lucent engaged in receivables securitization and reported balances of $625 and $1,329 million of outstanding uncollected receivables in 1999 and 2000, respectively. In both years, the receivables were sold through an entity established specifically for this purpose.

BOX 44-3 INCOME STATEMENT EFFECTS OF RECEIVABLE SALES AND SECURITIZATIONS

Our illustration assumes that the company is selling (credit) receivables that it carries on its books at $1,000,000. Depending on the interest rate structure of the credit receivables and the risk, the buyer may pay more or less than $1,000,000.

Buyer Pays Less: $900,000

Transaction qualifies as a sale: The seller will *immediately* recognize a $100,000 loss on the sale.*

Transaction does not qualify as a sale and is treated as a financing: The $100,000 is treated as a "discount" on the loan payable taken by the seller.† The income statement is not affected at the time of the sale. Over time (as the receivables are collected) the discount is amortized as additional interest expense.‡

Buyer Pays More: $1,100,000

Transaction qualifies as a sale: The mirror image of the previous transaction occurs (i.e., the seller will *immediately* recognize a $100,000 gain on the sale).

Transaction does not qualify as a sale and is treated as a financing: The $100,000 is treated as a "premium" on the loan payable taken by the seller.§ The income statement is not affected at the time of the sale. Over time (as the receivables are collected) the premium is amortized and interest expense is reduced.**

Analytical procedures: From an analytical perspective, the two approaches result in different timing of income or loss recognition. Thus, if a company recognized a securitization as a sale and the analyst felt that it would be more appropriate to view the transaction as a financing event, then the financial statement adjustments would be as follows:

- Remove gain/loss from current period income.
- Add the securitized receivables to the balance sheet amount.
- Classify the securitization proceeds as debt.

---

* The entry would be

Cash	$900,000	
Loss on sale	100,000	
Accounts receivable		$1,000,000

† The entry would be

Cash	$900,000	
Loan payable (net of discount)		$900,000

‡ For example, when $200,000 of the receivables are collected, the entry for the "passthrough" would be

Amortization of discount	$ 20,000	
Loan payable	180,000	
Cash		200,000

Note, if the transaction were treated as a sale, there would be no entry at the time of collection.

§ The entry would be

Cash	$1,100,000	
Loan payable (includes premium)		$1,100,000

** For example, when $200,000 of the receivables are collected, the entry would be

Loan payable	220,000	
Amortization of premium		20,000
Cash		200,000

Note, if the transaction were treated as a sale, there would be no entry at the time of collection.

Balance Sheet. Lucent recorded the securitizations as sales as they were structured to satisfy the (legalistic) requirements of SFAS 125 and 140. Lucent, however, transferred other (not sold) receivables to the subsidiary as collateral for the receivables sold and therefore ultimately bears the credit risk.

The sale proceeds should therefore not be viewed as a reduction of accounts receivable, but rather as an increase in (short-term) borrowing. As panel B of Exhibit 44-4 indicates, Lucent's 1999 (2000) accounts receivable, current assets, and current liabilities should be increased by $625 ($1,329) million.[16]

---

16 The manner in which Lucent set up its QSPE in 1999 results in another, more subtle "off-balance-sheet activity." (See subsequent section entitled "Joint Ventures, Finance Subsidiaries, and Investment in Affiliates.") By transferring $700 million of its receivables to the subsidiary as collateral, Lucent effectively removed this amount from its receivables balances (where they belong) and buried it within the investment in subsidiary accounts. Total assets are not affected but the composition of those assets is. To keep the exposition for sale of receivables straightforward, we have ignored this factor in our presentation.

EXHIBIT 44-4 Lucent Technologies
Analysis of Receivables Securitization

	A. Reported Data				B. Adjusted Data	
	1998	1999	2000		1999	2000
From Footnotes						
Balance of uncollected receivables	$ 0	$ 625	$ 1,329			
From Balance Sheet				*Adjustment:*	*Add $625*	*Add $1,329*
Accounts receivable	7,821	9,097	10,059		9,722	11,388
Current assets		19,240	21,490		19,865	22,819
Current liabilities		9,150	10,877		9,775	12,206
From Cash Flow Statement				*Adjustment:*	*Deduct $625*	*Deduct $704*
CFO	1,452	(962)	304		(1,587)	(400)
From Income Statement						
Sales	24,367	30,617	33,813			
Selected Trends and Ratios						
% Change in sales from 1998		26%	39%		26%	39%
% Change in A/R from 1998		16%	26%		24%	46%
# of days A/R outstanding	117	101	103		105	114
Current ratio	1.45	2.10	1.98		2.03	1.87
CFO/Current liabilities	0.13	(0.11)	0.03		(0.16)	(0.03)

Source: Data from Lucent Technologies, *1998–2000 Annual Reports.*

Cash Flow Classification. Accounting for these transactions as sales distorts the amount and timing of CFO as the firm received cash earlier than if the receivables had been collected in the normal course of business. An adjustment is required to reclassify *the change in the uncollected receivables sold*[17] from CFO to cash from financing.

Since 1999 was the first year Lucent engaged in sales securitization, the full $625 million should be deducted from CFO (and classified as CFF). For 2000, the adjustment should be the change in sold but uncollected receivables; that is, ($1,329 − $625 =) $704 million. These adjustments are made in Exhibit 44-4, panel B.

Effects of Adjustments. The effects of these adjustments are also demonstrated in Exhibit 44-4. Relative to 1998, sales in 1999 and 2000 increased 26% and 39%, respectively. *Reported* accounts receivable, however, increased only 16% and 26% over that same period; an apparent

[17] In Reading 33, it was shown that the change in accounts receivable is an adjustment to net income when deriving CFO. Because the uncollected balance of the receivables sold must be added to the reported balance of accounts receivable, calculation of the adjusted CFO requires exclusion of any change in the balance of uncollected receivables sold.

improvement in receivables management. This improvement is reflected in the receivable turnover with days receivables outstanding improving by 14 days from 117 to 103 days over the 1998–2000 period.

However, after adjustment for receivables sold, the improvement disappears. Restoring the $625 million of receivables sold in 1999 results in an (adjusted) increase of 24% in receivables relative to 1998, similar to the 26% sales increase over the same period. For 2000, we find that, after adjustment, receivables increased 46%, greater than the 39% increase in sales. After adjustment, the number of days of outstanding receivables, which declined on a reported basis, rose to 114 in 2000, similar to the 1998 level.[18]

Moving to Lucent's liquidity ratios, we note that both the adjusted current ratio and the CFO/current liabilities ratio are below the reported amounts. For these ratios, there is an adjustment to both the numerator and denominator. For the current ratio, the same amount is added to both; the numerator adjustment improves the ratio whereas the denominator adjustment reduces the ratio. It is only because the (reported) ratio is greater than 1 that the net effect is a lower ratio. Were the ratio less than 1 to begin with, the effect of the adjustment would be to improve the ratio. Both adjustments to the CFO/current liabilities ratio, on the other hand, reduce the ratio as CFO is decreased and current liabilities are increased.

Turning to CFO, we find that the receivables sales masked the deterioration of the company's operating cash flow: 1998 CFO was $1,452 million; 1999 reported CFO plunged to ($962) million, recovering to $304 million in 2000.

After adjustment for receivables sold, CFO was considerably below the amounts reported. For 1999, adjusted CFO was ($1,587) million, an outflow two-thirds greater than the reported amount of ($962) million. Although 2000 CFO improved, on an adjusted basis it remained negative at ($400) million.

The cash flow trend may have been the motivation for Lucent beginning a program of receivable securitization in 1999; as CFO deteriorated, the company needed another source of cash.

Other Securitizations

While the securitization of accounts receivable remains a major source of financing, other forms of securitization have emerged. A few examples follow:

1. PolyGram, the Dutch film producer, issued bonds in 1998 backed by expected revenues from films.
2. Marne et Champagne issued bonds in 2000 backed by its champagne inventories.
3. Toys "R" Us [TOY] issued bonds in 2000 secured by license-fee income from its Japanese affiliate.
4. Yasuda Fire & Marine Insurance [8755] used auto and mortgage loans and leasing credits to back bonds issued in 2000.

---

[18] As discussed in Reading 31 (using Lucent as an example), sales of receivables should be added back when assessing the provision for bad debts.

Such issues are a growing form of off-balance-sheet financing, used worldwide, with significant implications for current and future period cash flows. The financial analyst must be alert to such transactions and make the appropriate analytical adjustments.[19]

Joint Ventures, Finance Subsidiaries, and Investment in Affiliates

Firms may acquire manufacturing and distribution capacity through investments in affiliated firms, including suppliers and end users. Joint ventures with other firms may offer economies of scale and provide opportunities to share operating, technological, and financial risks. To obtain financing, the venture may enter into take-or-pay or throughput contracts with minimum payments designed to meet the venture's debt service requirements. Direct or indirect guarantees of the joint venture debt may also be present. Generally, firms account for their investments in joint ventures and affiliates (where they have 20 to 50% ownership) using the equity method whereby the balance sheet reports the firm's *net investment* in the affiliate. The net investment reflects the parent's proportionate share of the assets minus the liabilities of the subsidiary (*i.e., the parent's financial statements do not report its share of the debt of these affiliates*).

For example, Micron [MU] stated in its August 31, 2000 10-K report that it participated in two joint ventures (in Singapore and Japan). Micron entered into take-or-pay contracts requiring it to purchase all of the output of the joint ventures and to provide technology, systems support, and other services. These joint ventures are not consolidated although they are clearly part of Micron operationally. They supplied more than one-third of all memory produced by Micron in fiscal 2001 and Micron reported all transactions with the venture as part of cost of goods sold.

Similarly, many firms have long used legally separate finance subsidiaries to borrow funds to finance parent-company receivables. Such debt is often lower-cost than general-purpose borrowings because of the well-defined collateral. Finance subsidiaries enable the parent to generate sales by granting credit to dealers and customers for purchases of its goods and services. Until 1987, most firms used the equity method to account for finance subsidiaries.[20] The FASB eliminated the nonconsolidation option (SFAS 94) and firms must now consolidate the assets and liabilities of controlled financial subsidiaries. As a result, some parent firms reduced their ownership of finance subsidiaries below 50% to gain the benefit of "debt suppression" afforded by the equity method.

From an overall economic entity (parent firm plus share in the affiliate) perspective, however, affiliate debt should be considered explicitly because it is clearly required to maintain the parent's operations. Additionally, the parent firm generally supports affiliate borrowings through extensive income maintenance agreements and direct or indirect guarantees of debt.

---

[19] Bond ratings services recognize the effect of securitizations on a company's debt structure. For example, Moody's March 2000 analysis of Federal-Mogul [FMO] included $450 million of securitized receivables in its calculation of Federal Mogul's total debt.

[20] Livnat and Sondhi (1986) showed that the exclusion of finance subsidiary debt allowed firms to report higher coverage and lower leverage ratios, stabilized reported debt ratios over time, and reduced the probability of a technical violation of bond covenants. Heian and Thies (1989) identified 182 companies (in 35 industry groups) reporting unconsolidated finance subsidiaries in 1985. Supplementary disclosures provided by 140 of these companies indicated a total of $205 billion in subsidiary debt that had not been reported on the parent's balance sheet. The authors also computed debt-to-capital ratios on the basis of pro forma consolidation and compared them to the pre-consolidation ratios; the average increase in the ratio for the sample was 34%, but nearly 90% for the firms with the 21 largest finance units.

EXHIBIT 44-5 Georgia-Pacific Joint Venture Financing

Note 13: Related Party Transactions

The Corporation is a 50% partner in a joint venture (GA-MET) with Metropolitan Life Insurance Company (Metropolitan). GA-MET owns and operates the Corporation's main office building in Atlanta, Georgia. The Corporation accounts for its investment in GA-MET under the equity method.

At January 1, 2000, GA-MET had an outstanding mortgage loan payable to Metropolitan in the amount of $144 million. The note bears interest at 9½%, requires monthly payments of principal and interest through 2011, and is secured by the land and building owned by the joint venture. In the event of foreclosure, each partner has severally guaranteed payment of one-half of any shortfall of collateral value to the outstanding secured indebtedness. Based on the present market conditions and building occupancy, the likelihood of any obligation to the Corporation with respect to this guarantee is considered remote.

Source: Georgia-Pacific, *1999 Annual Report.*

The information required for these adjustments to debt and related interest coverage and leverage ratios can be obtained from the footnotes, which may disclose the assets, liabilities, and results of operations of finance subsidiaries in a summarized format.[21]

Exhibit 44-5 contains an excerpt from the footnote on commitments and contingencies in the *1999 Annual Report* issued by Georgia Pacific [GP]. It discloses a joint venture with Metropolitan Life [MET]. GP is clearly liable for one-half of this off-balance-sheet debt, and $72 million should be added to GP's (property and) debt. In the GP example, the parent explicitly guaranteed the debt of the affiliate. Even in the absence of such guarantees, the proportionate share of the affiliate's debt should be added to the reported debt of the investor and the financial statements should be adjusted accordingly. These adjustments will be illustrated shortly in the analysis of Texaco and Exhibits 44-6 and 44-7. Case 11-1 carries this analysis further and examines Texaco and its 50%-owned affiliate, Caltex, to explore the use of off-balance-sheet activities in a more complex setting.

4 ANALYSIS OF OBS ACTIVITIES: TEXACO

Texaco is a major worldwide refiner, marketer, and distributor of oil products. Exhibit 44-6 contains excerpts from footnotes to Texaco's 1999 financial statements relating to its unconsolidated subsidiaries, leases, and commitments and contingencies. *A complete assessment of a company's off-balance-sheet activities requires a review of all financial statement disclosures.*

Exhibit 44-7 illustrates the adjustments for off-balance-sheet financing activities discussed in this reading. Panel A presents Texaco's reported and adjusted debt, total liabilities, and equity. Panel B shows each adjustment to the reported amounts, based on the information provided in Exhibit 44-6. The result is a more comprehensive measure of the firm's leverage.

---

[21] When the subsidiary or joint venture issues publicly traded debt, then full financial statements are available and can be used for more accurate adjustments.

EXHIBIT 44-6 Texaco Off-Balance-Sheet Activities

Excerpts from 1999 Notes to Financial Statements
Note 5: Investments and Advances

We account for our investments in affiliates, including corporate joint ventures and partnerships owned 50% or less, on the equity method. . . . The following table provides summarized financial information on a 100% basis for the Caltex Group, Equilon, Motiva, Star and all other affiliates that we account for on the equity method, as well as Texaco's total share of the information.

As of December 31, 1999
(Millions of dollars)

	Equilon	Motiva	Caltex Group	Other Affiliates	Texaco's Total Share
Current assets	$ 4,209	$ 1,271	$ 2,705	$ 801	$ 3,796
Noncurrent assets	7,208	5,307	7,604	2,230	9,321
Current liabilities	(5,636)	(1,278)	(3,395)	(736)	(4,916)
Noncurrent liabilities	(735)	(2,095)	(2,639)	(792)	(2,638)
Net equity	$ 5,046	$ 3,205	$ 4,275	$1,503	$ 5,563

Note 10: Lease Commitments and Rental Expense

We have leasing arrangements involving service stations, tanker charters, crude oil production and processing equipment and other facilities. We reflect amounts due under capital leases in our balance sheet as obligations, while we reflect our interest in the related assets as properties, plant and equipment. The remaining lease commitments are operating leases, and we record payments on such leases as rental expense.

As of December 31, 1999, we had estimated minimum commitments for payment of rentals (net of noncancelable sublease rentals) under leases which, at inception, had a noncancellable term of more than one year, as follows:

(millions of dollars)

	Operating Leases	Capital Leases
2000	$ 134	$ 9
2001	93	9
2002	416	8
2003	50	7
2004	54	7
After 2004	315	14
Total lease commitments	$1,062	$54
Less interest		(8)
Present value of total capital lease obligations		$46

EXHIBIT 44-6 (continued)

Note 15: Other Financial Information, Commitments and Contingencies

Preferred Shares of Subsidiaries

Minority holders own $602 million of preferred shares of our subsidiary companies, which is reflected as minority interest in subsidiary companies in the Consolidated Balance Sheet.

The above preferred stock issues currently require annual dividend payments of approximately $34 million. We are required to redeem $75 million of this preferred stock in 2003, $65 million (plus accreted dividends of $59 million) in 2005, $112 million in 2024 and $350 million in 2043. We have the ability to extend the required redemption dates for the $112 million and $350 million of preferred stock beyond 2024 and 2043.

Financial Guarantees

We have guaranteed the payment of certain debt, lease commitments and other obligations of third parties and affiliate companies. These guarantees totaled $716 million and $797 million at December 31, 1999 and 1998. The year-end 1999 and 1998 amounts include $336 million and $387 million of operating lease commitments of Equilon, our affiliate.

Throughput Agreements

Texaco Inc. and certain of its subsidiary companies previously entered into certain long-term agreements wherein we committed to ship through affiliated pipeline companies and an offshore oil port sufficient volume of crude oil or petroleum products to enable these affiliated companies to meet a specified portion of their individual debt obligations, or, in lieu thereof, to advance sufficient funds to enable these affiliated companies to meet these obligations. In 1998, we assigned the shipping obligations to Equilon, our affiliate, but Texaco remains responsible for deficiency payments on virtually all of these agreements. Additionally, Texaco has entered into long-term purchase commitments with third parties for take or pay gas transportation. At December 31, 1999 and 1998, our maximum exposure to loss was estimated to be $445 million and $500 million.

However, based on our right of counterclaim against Equilon and unaffiliated third parties in the event of non-performance, our net exposure was estimated to be $173 million and $195 million at December 31, 1999 and 1998.

No significant losses are anticipated as a result of these obligations.

Litigation

Texaco and approximately 50 other oil companies are defendants in 17 purported class actions. The actions are pending in Texas, New Mexico, Oklahoma, Louisiana, Utah, Mississippi, and Alabama. . . . Plaintiffs seek to recover royalty underpayments and interest. In some cases plaintiffs also seek to recover severance taxes and treble and punitive damages. Texaco and 24 other defendants have executed a settlement agreement with most of the plaintiffs that will resolve many of these disputes. The federal court in Texas gave final approval to the settlement in April 1999 and the matter is now pending before the U.S. Fifth Circuit Court of Appeal.

Texaco has reached an agreement with the federal government to resolve similar claims. The claims of various state governments remain unresolved.

It is impossible for us to ascertain the ultimate legal and financial liability with respect to contingencies and commitments. However, we do not anticipate that the aggregate amount of such liability in excess of accrued liabilities will be materially important in relation to our consolidated financial position or results of operations.

Source: Texaco, *1999 Annual Report.*

EXHIBIT 44-7 Texaco
Adjusted Long-Term Debt, Liabilities, and Solvency Analysis (amounts in $millions)

A. Reported and Adjusted Debt, Liabilities, and Capitalization Ratios

	Reported	Adjustments (Panel B below)	Adjusted	% increase
Debt	$ 7,647	$4,613	$12,260	60%
Total liabilities	16,930	8,927	25,857	53%
Shareholders' equity	12,042		12,042	
Capitalization Ratios				
Debt to equity	0.64		1.02	60%
Total liabilities to equity	1.41		2.15	53%

B. Adjustments for Off-Balance-Sheet Data

	Debt	Liabilities
Share of affiliate debt	$2,638	$7,554
Capitalization of operating leases	864	864
Redeemable preferred shares	602	—
Guarantees	336	336
Throughput agreements	173	173
Total Adjustments to Debt and Liabilities	**$4,613**	**$8,927**

Adjustments to 1999 Debt

Share of Affiliate Debt. Texaco has entered into a number of joint ventures with other major oil companies. The three primary ones are:

Joint Venture	Partners	Texaco's Share
Equilon	Shell Oil	44.0%
Motiva	Shell Oil, Saudi Refining	32.5%
Caltex	Chevron	50.0%

As Texaco is not the majority owner of any of these ventures, their financial results are not consolidated with Texaco's financial statements and (Texaco's portion of) the debt and liabilities of these joint ventures remains off-balance-sheet. Texaco, however, reports its proportionate share of its joint ventures' assets and liabilities in the final column of Note 5. The adjustment to debt equals Texaco's share in the noncurrent[22] liabilities of its joint ventures;

[22] Current liabilities may include financing obligations, but they are excluded in calculating the debt adjustment as no disclosures were provided. This "undercounting" may be partially offset by the "overcount" implied in including all noncurrent liabilities as certain noncurrent liabilities (e.g., deferred taxes) may not constitute debt.

Texaco's liabilities are increased by its share of total (current plus noncurrent) liabilities of its joint ventures.

Capitalization of Operating Leases. Note 10 (in Exhibit 44-6) provides information on Texaco's operating and capital leases. The interest rate implicit in the 1999 capital leases is 4.5%, relatively low even considering the low interest rate levels prevalent in the late 1990s. Texaco's long-term debt footnote (not shown) indicated a cost of debt of about 5.5% for new 10-year debt issued in 1999. We used a discount rate of 5% (and a straight-line assumption for payments after 2004), resulting in a present value adjustment of $864 million.

Redeemable Preferred Shares. Redeemable preferred shares should be treated as debt. Note 15 (in Exhibit 44-6) states that Texaco includes $602 million of such preferred shares as part of minority interest. As minority interest is included in total liabilities, no adjustment is required there. However, debt must be increased by $602 million.

Financial Guarantees. As a portion of the $716 million of guarantees relates to affiliate debt, including it would result in double counting as we have already adjusted for Texaco's share of affiliate debt. Thus, we adjust only for $336 million of guarantees of Equilon's operating leases, as that amount is off-balance-sheet for Equilon as well. Note that Texaco's guarantee includes a guarantee of lease residual values.

Throughput Agreements. We have used the net exposure of $173 million, although a conservative approach would use the gross exposure of $445 million.

Litigation. We note only that potential liabilities related to litigation exist. However, a numeric adjustment is not possible based on the information provided.

The effect of these adjustments is summarized in Exhibit 44-7, panel A. Adjusted debt is 60% higher than reported debt in 1999 and total liabilities increase by 53%. The adjusted debt-to-equity and liabilities-to-equity ratios are significantly higher than the reported ratios.

OPTIONAL SEGMENT ENDS

5 FINANCIAL REPORTING BY LESSORS

Many manufacturers and dealers offer customers leases to market their products. Such *sales-type leases* include both a manufacturing or merchandising profit (the difference between the fair value at the inception of the lease and the cost or carrying value of the leased property) and interest income due to the financing nature of the transaction. Financial institutions and leasing intermediaries offer direct financing leases that generate interest income only. Either class of lessors may create operating leases.

The remainder of the reading discusses the accounting by lessors for sales-type and direct financing leases. Leveraged leases are beyond the scope of this text and sales with leasebacks are discussed in Box 44-4.

Lessor financial reporting is illustrated using the lessee example of the beginning of the chapter with the additional assumptions that the leased equipment cost $20,000 to manufacture and the expected residual value (not guaranteed by the lessee) is $2,500 after four years.

Lease Classification: Lessors

Lease capitalization by lessors is required when the lease meets *any one* of the four criteria specified for capitalization by lessees and *both* of the following revenue-recognition criteria:

BOX 44-4 FINANCIAL REPORTING FOR SALES WITH LEASEBACKS

Sale leaseback transactions are sales of property by the owner who then leases it back from the buyer-lessor. Financial reporting for these transactions is governed by SFAS 28, Accounting for Sales with Leasebacks (1979), as amended by SFAS 66, Accounting for Sales of Real Estate (1982).

The amount and timing of profit (or loss) recognized on a sale leaseback transaction are determined by the proportion of the rights to use the leased property retained by the owner-lessee after the sale. If all or substantially all the use rights are retained by the owner-lessee, it is a financing transaction, and no profit or loss on the transaction should be recognized.

The extent of continuing use is determined by the proportion of the present value of reasonable rentals relative to the fair value of assets sold and leased back. This proportion is used to assign sale leaseback transactions to the following financial reporting categories.

Minor Leasebacks. Present value of reasonable rentals is less than 10% of the fair value of the leased property; the buyer-lessor obtains substantially all the rights to use the leased property. Any gain (or loss) on the transaction is recognized in full at the inception of the lease.

More than Minor but Less than "Substantially All" Leasebacks. Present value of reasonable rentals exceeds 10% but is less than 90% of the fair value of the asset sold; depending on specific criteria, some or all of the gain or loss must be deferred and amortized over the lease term.

Substantially All Leasebacks. Present value of MLPs equals or exceeds 90% of the fair value of property sold; the total gain (loss) must be deferred and amortized over the lease term. The leaseback is a financing transaction, and the gain (loss) is recognized as the leased property is used.

OPTIONAL SEGMENT

Example

OM [OMM], an oil tanker operator, sold a vessel in May 1997 for $39.9 million and leased it back for five years. The $15.7 million gain was deferred and recognized as an adjustment to lease expense over the five-year lease term. Had the gain been recognized immediately, 1997 pretax income would have been more than twice the reported level.

IAS Standards for Sales with Leasebacks

IAS 17, the accounting standard for these transactions, is significantly different from U.S. GAAP as it requires that:

- When a sale/leaseback results in a finance lease, any profit on the sale must be deferred and recognized over the lease term.
- When a sale/leaseback results in an operating lease, and the sales price equals the asset's fair value, the seller recognizes any gain or loss.
- When a sale/leaseback results in an operating lease, and the sales price is below fair value, the seller recognizes any gain or loss. The exception is that any loss is deferred and amortized when the lease provides for payments that are below market.
- When a sale/leaseback results in an operating lease, and the sales price exceeds fair value, the seller defers any gain and amortizes it over the lease term.

OPTIONAL SEGMENT ENDS

1. Collectibility of the MLPs is reasonably predictable.
2. There are no significant uncertainties regarding the amount of unreimbursable costs yet to be incurred by the lessor under the provisions of the lease agreement.

Leases not meeting these criteria must be reported as operating leases since either the risks and benefits of leased assets have not been transferred, or the earnings process is not complete.

Sales-Type Leases

Exhibit 44-8 presents financial reporting by a lessor for a sales-type lease using the lessee example. Part A illustrates the accounting recognition at inception and the determination of gross and net investment in the lease; part B provides the lessor's amortization schedule for the sales-type lease.

The lessor recognizes sales revenue of $31,700, the present value of the MLPs. The cost of goods sold is the carrying amount of the leased property. The present value of the unguaranteed residual value of the leased property constitutes continuing investment by the lessor and is not included in costs charged against income; that is, it is deducted from cost to manufacture.

EXHIBIT 44-8 Lessor Financial Reporting

A. Sales-Type Lease

Lessor's Gross Investment in Leased Equipment		
MLPs: $10,000 × 4		$40,000
Unguaranteed residual value		2,500
		$42,500
Lessor's Net Investment in Leased Equipment		
Present value at 10% of an annuity of 4 payments of $10,000		$31,700
Present value at 10% of $2,500, 4 periods hence		1,707
		$33,407
Unearned Income		
Gross investment in lease		$42,500
Less: Net investment		33,407
		$ 9,093
Accounting Recognition at Lease Inception		
Sales revenue*	$ 31,700	
Cost of goods sold†	(18,293)	
Gross profit on sale		$13,407
Gross investment in lease	$ 42,500	
Unearned income	(9,093)	
Net investment in lease		$33,407

* Present value of lease payments, excluding residual value.

† Cost to manufacture (assumed to be $20,000) less PV of residual value.

B. Lessor Amortization Schedule: Sales-Type Lease

Year	Annual Payment Received (A)	Interest Income (B)	Reduction in Investment (C) = (A) − (B)	Net Investment (D)
2000				$33,407
2001	$10,000	$3,340	$ 6,660	26,747
2002	10,000	2,675	7,325	19,422
2003	10,000	1,942	8,058	11,364
2004	10,000	1,136	8,864	2,500
Totals	$40,000	$9,093	$30,907	

The lessor's gross investment in the lease is $42,500, the sum of the MLPs and the unguaranteed residual value. Net investment in the lease is $33,407, determined by discounting the MLPs and the unguaranteed residual value at the interest rate implicit in the lease (10%), as shown in part A.

The difference between the gross and net investment represents unearned income, the interest component of the transaction. Unearned income is system-

EXHIBIT 44-8 (continued)

C. Balance Sheet Effects

	Capital (Sales-Type) Lease			Operating Lease		
	Net Investment in Leases					
Year	Current	Long-Term	Total	Assets Under Lease	Accumulated Depreciation	Net
2000	$6,660	$26,747	$33,407	$20,000	$ 0	$20,000
2001	7,325	19,422	26,747	20,000	4,375	15,625
2002	8,058	11,364	19,422	20,000	8,750	11,250
2003	8,864	2,500	11,364	20,000	13,125	6,875
2004	2,500	0	2,500	20,000	17,500	2,500

D. Income Statement Effects

	Capital (Sales-Type) Lease		Operating Lease		
Year		Income	Rental Revenue	Depreciation	Income
2000	Gain on Sale	$13,407			
2001	Interest	3,340	$10,000	$ 4,375	$ 5,625
2002	Interest	2,675	10,000	4,375	5,625
2003	Interest	1,942	10,000	4,375	5,625
2004	Interest	1,136	10,000	4,375	5,625
Totals		$22,500	$40,000	$17,500	$22,500

E. Cash Flow Statement Effects

	Capital (Sales-Type) Lease			Operating Lease
Year	CFO	Cash from Investment	Total	CFO
2000	$13,407	$(13,407)	$ 0	$ 0
2001	3,340	6,660	10,000	10,000
2002	2,675	7,325	10,000	10,000
2003	1,942	8,058	10,000	10,000
2004	1,136	8,864	10,000	10,000
Totals	$22,500	$ 17,500	$40,000	$40,000

atically amortized to income over the lease term, using the interest method that reports a constant rate of return of 10% on the net investment in the lease. The lessor reports its net investment in the lease on the balance sheet (see the next section). Contingent rentals, if any, are reported as they are earned. SFAS 13 requires an annual review of the estimated residual value. Nontemporary declines must be recognized; however, increases in value or subsequent reversals of declines cannot be reported.

Balance Sheet Effects (Exhibit 44-8C). The lessor reports the current and non-current components of its net investment in sales-type leases. Lessors using the operating lease method do not report any investment in leases, but they continue to report the assets on the balance sheet as long-term assets, net of accumulated depreciation. These amounts assume straight-line depreciation over four years of the original cost of the asset less estimated residual value ($20,000 − $2,500). Note that the operating lease method reports lower net assets each year and, ignoring income effects, tends to increase return on assets relative to the sales-type lease method.

Income Statement Effects (Exhibit 44-8D). For the sales-type lease, the lessor records profit at inception of $13,407. The annual rental of $10,000 is allocated to interest income and return of principal. Reported interest income reflects a constant 10% return on the declining net investment in the lease. The balance of the rental payment is applied to amortize (reduce principal) the net investment systematically over the lease term.

The operating lease method reports constant income over the lease term as straight-line depreciation is charged against the constant annual rental. The use of accelerated depreciation would result in a pattern of increasing income over the lease term as depreciation declines.

The sales-type lease reports substantially higher income in the first year of the lease due to recognition of manufacturing profit at the inception of the lease. However, reported income declines thereafter due to declining interest income over the remainder of the lease term, relative to constant or increasing income under the operating lease method. In our example, reported net income is higher under the operating lease method after the initial year. *Over the lease term, the total net income is the same under both methods.*

Cash Flow Effects (Exhibit 44-8E). At the inception of the lease, no cash changes hands. The operating lease method reports no cash flow effects on the statement of cash flows. In contrast, the sales-type lease method reports 2000 operating cash flow of $13,407, equal to the sales profit at the inception of the lease. This cash inflow is offset by a net cash outflow for investment equal to $13,407 (the investment of $33,407 less the $20,000 prior carrying amount of the leased property). Net cash flow remains zero.

In subsequent years, under the operating lease method, CFO is equal to the rental payment of $10,000/year. Under the sale-type lease method, the $10,000 payment is allocated between CFO and cash from investment; CFO is equal to interest income and cash from investment is equal to the reduction in the net investment. Thus, after inception, the operating lease method reports higher CFO and, since interest income declines over the lease term, this difference in CFO increases. Simultaneously, a correspondingly larger reduction in net investment is reported in investment cash flow.

Note that total cash flow (operating plus investing) is unaffected by the method of lease accounting. The actual cash flow in each year is $10,000, the lease payment received. Only under the operating lease method does CFO equal the cash flows associated with the lease. Capitalization of the lease by the lessor reclassifies reported cash flows between operating and investing activities.

The use of sales-type lease accounting allows firms to recognize income earlier than the operating lease method. Lease capitalization also allows firms to report higher CFO at the inception of the lease. This aggressive recognition of income and cash flows ("front-end loading") improves financial ratios; it accurately reflects the firm's operations only if the risks and benefits of leased property have been fully transferred to the lessee and the lessor has no further performance obligation.

Footnote Disclosures. Footnote disclosure for lessors under U.S. GAAP is similar to that of lessees. The sales-type lease method requires the disclosure of gross MLPs receivable, unearned income, and the current and noncurrent components of the net investment in leases. Lessors must also provide information on lease terms, future MLPs receivable over the next five years, and the aggregate thereafter. Disclosure for operating leases is limited to MLPs receivable over the next five years and the aggregate thereafter.

Direct Financing Leases

In a direct financing lease, the lessor's original cost or carrying value (prior to the lease) of the asset approximates the market value of the leased asset (the present value of the MLPs). Such leases are pure financing transactions and financial reporting for direct financing leases reflects this fact. *No sale is recognized at the inception of the lease, and there is no manufacturing or dealer profit. Only financing income is reported.*

Unearned income is the difference between the gross investment in the lease and the cost or carrying amount of the leased property. It is amortized to report a constant periodic return (effective interest method) on the net investment in the lease (gross investment plus initial direct costs less unearned income). Thus, in our example, the lessor would report (interest) income and cash flows similar to those reported for the sales-type lease over the period 2001–2004. There are no income or cash flow consequences at the inception of the lease in 2000.

Disclosure requirements for financing leases are similar to those for sales-type leases. Lessors must disclose MLPs receivable over the next five fiscal years and the aggregate thereafter. Any allowance for uncollectibles, executory costs, unguaranteed residual value, and unearned income must also be reported.

The income reported on financing leases depends on assumptions made, particularly those regarding uncollectible payments and residual values. When uncollectibles are underestimated, or residual values overestimated, income is overstated. For example, the *New York Times* reported[23] that automobile lessors would lose more than $10 billion in 2000 because they overestimated the residual values of cars and trucks that they had leased to customers.

Financial Reporting by Lessors: An Example

Exhibit 44-9 contains IBM Credit Corp.'s footnote on its activities as lessor. The company finances customer purchases of information-handling equipment through direct financing leases; shorter-term leases of such equipment are treated as operating leases.

IBM discloses aggregate MLPs receivable and reports the periodic payments in each of the next five years and in the aggregate thereafter as a percentage of this total. The terms of both the direct financing leases and operating leases range from two to three years.[24] However, the operating leases generally have shorter terms: 57% of the operating leases are due within one year, higher than the 50% of direct financing leases due within 12 months of the financial statement date.

---

[23] December 15, 2000, p. F1.

[24] In its 1994 annual report, IBM Credit reported financing lease terms ranging three to five years and operating leases that spanned two to four years. The shortening of lease terms is consistent with the rapid technological changes in the computer industry.

EXHIBIT 44-9 IBM Credit Corp. Net Investment in Capital Leases

The Company's capital lease portfolio includes direct financing and leveraged leases. The Company originates financing for customers in a variety of industries and throughout the United States. The Company has a diversified portfolio of capital equipment financing for end users.

Direct financing leases consist principally of IBM advanced information processing products with terms generally from two to three years. The components of the net investment in direct financing leases at December 31, 1999 and 1998 are as follows:

(dollars in thousands)

	1999	1998
Gross lease payments receivable	$5,335,352	$5,278,060
Estimated unguaranteed residual values	442,288	397,529
Deferred initial direct costs	18,339	30,634
Unearned income	(604,035)	(571,168)
Allowance for receivable losses	(47,220)	(65,644)
Total	$5,144,724	$5,069,411

The scheduled maturities of minimum lease payments outstanding at December 31, 1999, expressed as a percentage of the total, are due approximately as follows:

Within 12 months	50%
13 to 24 months	33
25 to 36 months	13
37 to 48 months	3
After 48 months	1
	100%

Included in the net investment in capital leases is $17.7 million of seller interest at December 31, 1998, relating to the securitization of such leases. These securitizations were terminated and settled in 1999.

Refer to the note on page 31, Allowance for Receivable Losses, for a reconciliation of the direct financing leases and leveraged leases allowances for receivable losses.

Additional disclosures are required for the capitalized direct financing leases: current and noncurrent components, allowance for uncollectibles, estimated unguaranteed residual values, and unearned interest. IBM Credit provides most applicable disclosures. No contingent rentals are reported; they may not be significant. However, the current and noncurrent components have not been reported separately. Computation of the implicit interest rate requires additional assumptions.

The footnote disclosure includes the securitization of direct financing lease receivables and reference to a reconciliation of the allowance for losses.

EXHIBIT 44-9 (continued)

Equipment on Operating Leases:

Operating leases consist principally of IBM advanced information processing products with terms generally from two to three years. The components of equipment on operating leases at December 31, 1999 and 1998 are as follows:

(dollars in thousands)

	1999	1998
Cost	$ 7,166,892	$ 7,046,757
Accumulated depreciation	(3,780,206)	(3,427,172)
Total	$ 3,386,686	$ 3,619,585

Minimum future rentals were approximately $3,094.2 million at December 31, 1999. The scheduled maturities of the minimum future rentals at December 31, 1999, expressed as a percentage of the total, are due approximately as follows:

Within 12 months	57%
13 to 24 months	30
25 to 36 months	10
37 to 48 months	2
After 48 months	1
	100%

Source: IBM Credit Corp., *1999 Annual Report.*

Going beyond the financial effects of IBM's lessor activities, the footnote data indicate that the company is experiencing minimal lease growth. Direct financing leases increased by 1% (using MLPs) during 1999 while operating leases grew at a rate less than 2%. These patterns may represent stable volume and prices, or higher volume offset by lower lease prices, or a shift from leases to sales (reflecting changes in relative prices or customer preferences). This is another example of how attention to footnote detail can suggest worthwhile questions about changes in operations to ask management.

IAS Standards for Lessors

IAS 17 provides accounting standards for lessors that are broadly similar to those of U.S. GAAP. The most significant differences are:

- Lease classification as a finance lease depends on broad principles (see discussion for lessees earlier in the reading) rather than the SFAS 13 rules.
- Disclosure requirements are the same as for lessees, with MLPs disclosed for amounts due
  1. Within one year
  2. One to five years
  3. In more than five years

6 SUMMARY

Financial liabilities can take many forms, from simple, full-coupon debt to leasing and other more esoteric forms of off-balance-sheet activities. This reading and the previous one illustrated the far-reaching effects of such transactions on a firm's income, cash flow, and capital structure. The principal points made in this reading are:

1. Operating leases are the most common form of off-balance-sheet financing. Such leases should be capitalized and adjustments made to reported financial data.
2. In addition to leases, there are other means of acquiring the use of assets without reflecting them on the balance sheet, such as
   - Joint ventures
   - Take-or-pay and throughput agreements
   - Sales of receivables

   The reading illustrates techniques that can be used to adjust financial statements for these activities as well.

The discussion and analysis of OBS activities is not yet complete.

PROBLEMS

1. [Lease classification and financial statement effects; CFA© adapted] On January 1, 2001, a company entered into a capital lease, recording a balance sheet obligation of $10,000, using an interest rate of 12%. The lease payment for 2001 was $1,300. Compute each of the following:

A. Interest expense for 2001

B. The lease obligation at the end of 2001

C. The effect of the lease payments on each of the three components of cash flow for 2001

D. Each of items (A) through (C) if the lease had been recorded as an operating lease

2. [Analysis of lessee] The Tolrem Company has decided to lease an airplane on January 1, 2002. The firm and its lessor have not yet decided the terms of the lease. Assume that the terms can be adjusted to permit Tolrem to either capitalize the lease or record it as an operating lease.

A. State the effect (higher, lower, or equal) of the choice of capitalizing the lease on the following for 2002 (the initial year of the lease):

(i) Cash flow from operations
(ii) Financing cash flow
(iii) Investing cash flow
(iv) Net cash flow
(v) Debt-to-equity ratio
(vi) Interest coverage ratio
(vii) Operating income
(viii) Net income
(ix) Deferred tax asset or liability
(x) Taxes paid
(xi) Pre- and posttax return on assets
(xii) Pre- and posttax return on equity

B. Recall that the difference between net income under the two methods changes direction at some point during the lease term. State which answers to part A will change in the year after the switch occurs and describe the change.

C. Assume that Tolrem enters into new aircraft leases at a constant annual rate. Describe the effect of the choice of accounting method on the items in part A.

3. [Sale of receivables; ratio and cash flow effects] Foster Wheeler [FWC] entered into arrangements to sell receivables in 1998 and 1999. The accounts receivable footnote in the firm's *1999 Annual Report* noted that

> As of December 31, 1999 and December 25, 1998, $50 million and $38.4 million, respectively, in receivables were sold under the agreement and are therefore not reflected in the accounts receivable–trade balance in the Consolidated Balance Sheet.

Selected reported financial data for the company follow:

Years Ended December (in $millions)

	1997	1998	1999
Sales	$4,060	$4,537	$3,867
Trade accounts receivable	664	720	739
Current assets		1,673	1,615
Current liabilities		1,492	1,472
Total short- and long-term debt		963	961
Stockholders' equity		572	376
Cash flow from operations	(113)	(59)	(6)

A. Compute the impact of the sale of receivables on FWC's receivable turnover ratio and cash cycle for 1998 and 1999.

B. Compute the reported and adjusted (for the sale of receivables) current and debt-to-equity ratios for 1998 and 1999.

C. Discuss the impact of the sale on (the trend of) the firm's cash flow from operations over the period 1997 to 1999.

4. [Off-balance-sheet obligations; CFA© adapted] Extracts from The Bowie Company's December 31, 2001, balance sheet and income statement are presented in the following schedule, along with its interest coverage ratio:

Debt	$12 million
Equity	20
Interest expense	1
Times interest earned	5.0X

The Bowie Corporation's financial statement footnotes include the following:

(i) At the beginning of 2001, Bowie entered into an operating lease with future payments of $40 million ($5 million/year) with a discounted present value of $20 million.

(ii) Bowie has guaranteed a $5 million, 10% bond issue, due in 2007, issued by Crockett, a nonconsolidated 30%-owned affiliate.

(iii) Bowie has committed itself (starting in 2002) to purchase a total of $12 million of phosphorous from PEPE, Inc., its major supplier, over the next five years. The estimated present value of these payments is $7 million.

A. Adjust Bowie's debt and equity and recompute the debt-to-equity ratio, using the information in footnotes (i) to (iii).

B. Adjust the times-interest-earned ratio for 2001 for these commitments.

C. Discuss the reasons (both financial and operating) why Bowie may have entered into these arrangements.

D. Describe the additional information required to fully evaluate the impact of these commitments on Bowie's current financial condition and future operating trends.

5. [Analysis of lessor] Carignane Corp., a manufacturer/lessor, enters into a sales-type lease agreement with Mourvedre, Inc., as lessee. The lessor capitalizes the lease rather than reporting it as an operating lease.

Describe the effect (lower, higher, or none) of this choice on the following accounts and ratios of Carignane (the lessor) in the first and ninth years of a 10-year lease:

A. Total assets

B. Revenues

C. Expenses

D. Asset turnover ratio

E. Interest income

F. Cost of goods sold

G. Net income

H. Retained earnings

I. Income taxes paid

J. Posttax return on assets

K. Cash flow from operations

L. Investment cash flow

SOLUTIONS TO END-OF-READING PROBLEMS

APPENDIX

A

SOLUTIONS TO PROBLEMS IN READING 27

1. Since the value of the British pound in U.S. dollars has gone down, it has depreciated with respect to the U.S. dollar. Therefore, the British will have to spend more British pounds to purchase U.S. goods. Accordingly, the correct answer is (c).
2. Since the number of Australian dollars needed to purchase one U.S. dollar has decreased from 1.60 to 1.50, the Australian dollar has appreciated with respect to the U.S. dollar. Therefore, the Australians will have to spend fewer Australian dollars to purchase U.S. goods. Accordingly, the correct answer is (a).
3. The value of the dollar in Swiss francs has gone up from about 1.20 to about 1.60. Therefore, the dollar has appreciated relative to the Swiss franc, and the dollars needed by Americans to purchase Swiss goods have decreased. Thus, the statement is correct.
4. **a.** One baht was worth 1/25 or 0.04 dollars earlier. It is worth 1/30 or 0.0333 dollars now. Thus, the baht has depreciated with respect to the dollar. Percentage change in the dollar value of baht = $((0.0333 - 0.04)/0.04)100\% = -16.7\%$.

   b. One dollar was worth 25 bahts earlier and is worth 30 bahts now. Percentage change in the value of dollar $= ((30 - 25)/25)100\% = 20.0\%$.
5. The increase in $/£ exchange rate implies that the pound has appreciated with respect to the dollar. This is unfavorable to the trader since the trader has a short position in pounds.

   Bank's liability in dollars initially was 5,000,0000 × 1.45 = $7,250,000
   Bank's liability in dollars now is 5,000,0000 × 1.51 = $7,550,000

   Thus, the bank's liability has increased by $300,000.
6. Three cross-exchange rates need to be computed: SFr/€, ¥/€, SFr/¥.

   SFr/€ = SFr/$ × $/€ = SFr 1.5971/$ × $ 0.9119/€ = 1.4564
   ¥/€ = ¥/$ × $/€ = ¥ 128.17/$ × $ 0.9119/€ = 116.88
   SFr/¥ = SFr/$ × $/¥ = (SFr/$)/(¥/$) =
   (SFr 1.5971/$)/(¥ 128.17/$) = 0.0125
7. These quotations mean that Bank A is willing to buy a euro for 1.1210 dollars (bid rate) or to sell one for 1.1215 dollars (ask rate). Bank B's $/€ bid rate is 1.1212; its ask rate is 1.1217. That is, Bank B is willing to buy a euro for 1.1212 dollars or to sell one for 1.1217 dollars.
8. The percentage spread is considerably higher for the Polish zloty than for the British pound. The market for the Polish zloty is much less liquid than the market for the British pound. There is a lot more competition between market makers for the British pound than for the Polish zloty. Consequently, the percentage spread is considerably higher for the Polish zloty than for the British pound.

9. These quotes are unreasonable because they deviate from Bank A to Bank B by more than the spread; for example, Bank A's ask rate (121.25) is smaller than Bank B's bid rate (121.30). There is, therefore, an arbitrage opportunity. One can buy Bank A's dollars for 121.25 yen per dollar, sell these dollars to Bank B for 121.30 yen per dollar, and thereby make a profit of 0.05 yen per dollar traded. This is a riskless, instantaneous operation that requires no initial investment.

10. The SFr/€ quotation is obtained as follows. In obtaining this quotation, we keep in mind that SFr/€ = SFr/\$ × \$/€, and that the price for each transaction (bid or ask) is the one that is more advantageous to the trader.

The SFr/€ bid price is the number of Swiss francs that a trader is willing to pay for one euro. This transaction (buy euro—sell Swiss francs) is equivalent to selling Swiss francs to buy dollars (at a bid rate of 1.4100) and then selling those dollars to buy euros (at a bid rate of 1.1610). Mathematically, the transaction is as follows:

$$(\text{bid SFr}/\$) \times (\text{bid }\$/€) = 1.4100 \times 1.1610 = 1.6370$$

The SFr/€ ask price is the number of Swiss francs that a trader is asking for one euro. This transaction (sell euros—buy Swiss francs) is equivalent to buying Swiss francs with dollars (at an ask rate of 1.4120) and simultaneously purchasing these dollars against euros (at an ask rate of 1.1615). Mathematically, this can be expressed as follows:

$$(\text{ask SFr}/\$) \times (\text{ask }\$/€) = 1.4120 \times 1.1615 = 1.6400$$

So the resulting quotation by the trader is

$$\text{SFr}/€ = 1.6370 - 1.6400$$

11. The SFr/A\$ quotation is obtained as follows. In obtaining this quotation, we keep in mind that SFr/A\$ = SFr/\$/A\$/\$, and that the price (bid or ask) for each transaction is the one that is more advantageous to the bank.

The SFr/A\$ bid price is the number of SFr the bank is willing to pay to buy one A\$. This transaction (buy A\$—sell SFr) is equivalent to selling SFr to buy dollars (at a bid rate of 1.5960) and then selling those dollars to buy A\$ (at an ask rate of 1.8235). Mathematically, the transaction is as follows:

$$\text{bid SFr/A}\$ = (\text{bid SFr}/\$)/(\text{ask A}\$/\$) = 1.5960/1.8235 = 0.8752$$

The SFr/A\$ ask price is the number of SFr that the bank is asking for one A\$. This transaction (sell A\$—buy SFr) is equivalent to buying SFr with dollars (at an ask rate of 1.5970) and simultaneously purchasing these dollars against A\$ (at a bid rate of 1.8225). This may be expressed as follows:

$$\text{ask SFr/A}\$ = (\text{ask SFr}/\$)/(\text{bid A}\$/\$) = 1.5970/1.8225 = 0.8763$$

The resulting quotation by the bank is

$$\text{SFr/A}\$ = 0.8752 - 0.8763$$

12. The A$/SFr quotation is obtained as follows. In obtaining this quotation, we keep in mind that A$/SFr = A$/$ / SFr/$, and that the price (bid or ask) for each transaction is the one that is more advantageous to the bank.

The A$/SFr bid price is the number of A$ the bank is willing to pay to buy one SFr. This transaction (buy SFr—sell A$) is equivalent to selling A$ to buy dollars (at a bid rate of 1.8225) and then selling those dollars to buy SFr (at an ask rate of 1.5970). Mathematically, the transaction is as follows:

bid A$/SFr = (bid A$/$)/(ask SFr/$) = 1.8225/1.5970 = 1.1412

The A$/SFr ask price is the number of A$ that the bank is asking for one SFr. This transaction (sell SFr—buy A$) is equivalent to buying A$ with dollars (at an ask rate of 1.8235) and simultaneously purchasing these dollars against SFr (at a bid rate of 1.5960). This may be expressed as follows:

ask A$/SFr = (ask A$/$)/(bid SFr/$) = 1.8235/1.5960 = 1.1425

The resulting quotation by the bank is

A$/SFr = 1.1412 – 1.1425

13. The bid C$/¥ rate would be the inverse of the ask ¥/C$ rate, and the ask C$/¥ rate would be the inverse of the bid ¥/C$ rate. Therefore,

bid C$/¥ = 1/ask (¥/C$) = 1/82.5750 = 0.01211
ask C$/¥ = 1/bid (¥/C$) = 1/82.5150 = 0.01212

Thus, the quote is C$/¥ = 0.01211–0.01212.

14. a. The American investor has paid a 25 percent premium over the price paid by a domestic investor. Yet, he receives the same dividends as the domestic investor. Therefore, his investment bears a smaller yield than it would for a domestic investor.

b. Lifting of the exchange controls would be bad news to an existing foreign investor in Paf, since her asset could only be repatriated at the normal pif rate (1.00), while she had bought it at the financial rate (1.25)

c. Lifting of the exchange controls would be good news to foreign investors planning to invest in Paf in the future, because they would no longer have to pay the 25 percent premium when buying assets in Paf.

15. The value of the £ in $ is worth less three months forward than it is now. Thus, the £ is trading at a forward discount relative to the $. Therefore, the £ is "weak" relative to the $. Because a $ is worth SFr1.60 now but worth SFr1.65 three months forward, the $ is "strong" relative to the SFr. That is, the SFr is "weak" relative to the $.

16. The midpoint of the spot dollar to pound exchange rate is $/£ = 1.4573. The midpoint of the six-month forward dollar to pound exchange rate is $/£ = 1.4421.

a. Based on the midpoints, the dollar value of a pound is 1.4573 now and only 1.4421 six months forward. Thus, the pound is worth less six months forward than now. That is, the pound is trading at a discount relative to the dollar in the forward market.

b. The difference between midpoints of the forward and spot rates = 0.0152.

Annualized discount

$$= \left(\frac{\text{Difference between forward and spot rates}}{\text{Spot rate}}\right)\left(\frac{12}{\text{No. months forward}}\right)100\%$$

$$= \left(\frac{0.0152}{1.4573}\right)\left(\frac{12}{6}\right)100\% = 2.09\%$$

17. The midpoint of the spot Swiss franc to dollar exchange rate is SFr/$ = 1.5965. The midpoint of the three-month forward Swiss franc to dollar exchange rate is SFr/$ = 1.5947.

a. Based on the midpoints, a dollar is worth SFr1.5965 now and only 1.5947 three months forward. So, the dollar is trading at a discount relative to the SFr in the forward market. That is, the SFr is trading at a premium relative to the dollar in the forward market.

b. The difference between midpoints of the forward and spot rates = 0.0018.

Annualized premium

$$= \left(\frac{\text{Difference between forward and spot rates}}{\text{Spot rate}}\right)\left(\frac{12}{\text{No. months forward}}\right)100\%$$

$$= \left(\frac{0.0018}{1.5965}\right)\left(\frac{12}{3}\right)100\% = 0.45\%$$

SOLUTIONS TO PROBLEMS IN READING 28

1. Because the interest rate in A is greater than the interest rate in B, α is expected to depreciate relative to β and should trade with a forward discount. Accordingly, the correct answer is (c).
2. Because the exchange rate is given in $/€ terms, the appropriate expression for the interest rate parity relation is

$$\frac{F}{S} = \frac{1 + r_{\$}}{1 + r_{€}}$$

($r_{\$}$ is a part of the numerator and $r_{€}$ is a part of the denominator).

a. The one-year $/€ forward rate is given by

$$\$/€ = 1.1795\,\frac{1.05}{1.04} = 1.1908$$

b. The one-month $/€ forward rate is given by

$$\$/€ = 1.1795\,\frac{1 + (0.04/12)}{1 + (0.03/12)} = 1.1805$$

Of course, these are central rates, and bid–ask rates could also be determined on the basis of bid–ask rates for the spot exchange and interest rates.

3. **a.** bid ¥/€ = (bid ¥/$) × (bid $/€) = 108.10 × 1.1865 = 128.2607.
ask ¥/€ = (ask ¥/$) × (ask $/€) = 108.20 × 1.1870 = 128.4334.

b. Because the exchange rate is in $/€ terms, the appropriate expression for the interest rate parity relation is $F/S = (1 + r_{\$})/(1 + r_{€})$.

$$\$/\text{ 3-month ask} = (\text{spot ask } \$/€)\,\frac{1 + (\text{ask } r_{\$})}{1 + (\text{bid } r_{€})} = 1.1870\,\frac{1 + (0.0525/4)}{1 + (0.0325/4)}$$

$$= 1.1929$$

Thus, the $/€ 3-month forward ask exchange rate is: 1.1929.

c. bid €/$ = 1/ask $/€ = 1/1.1929 = 0.8383.

Thus, the 3-month forward bid exchange rate is €/$ = 0.8383.

d. Because the exchange rate is in ¥/$ terms, the appropriate expression for the interest rate parity relation is $F/S = 1 + r_{¥}/1 + r_{\$}$.

$$¥/\$\text{ 3-month bid} = (\text{spot bid } ¥/\$)\,\frac{1 + (\text{bid } r_{¥})}{1 + (\text{ask } r_{\$})} =$$

$$108.10\,\frac{1 + (0.0125/4)}{1 + (0.0525/4)} = 107.03$$

$$¥/\$\text{ 3-month ask} = (\text{spot ask } ¥/\$)\,\frac{1 + (\text{ask } r_{¥})}{1 + (\text{bid } r_{\$})} =$$

$$108.20\,\frac{1 + (0.0150/4)}{1 + (0.0500/4)} = 107.26$$

Thus, the ¥/$ 3-month forward exchange rate is: 107.03–107.26. *Note:* The interest rates one uses in all such computations are those that result in a lower forward bid (so, bid interest rates in the numerator and ask rates in the denominator) and a higher forward ask (so, ask interest rates in the numerator and bid rates in the denominator).

4. a. For six months, $r_{SFr} = 1.50$ percent and $r_{\$} = 1.75$ percent. Because the exchange rate is in SFr/$ terms, the appropriate expression for the interest rate parity relation is

$$\frac{F}{S} = \frac{1 + r_{SFr}}{1 + r_{\$}}, \text{ or } \frac{F}{S}(1 + r_{\$}) = (1 + r_{SFr})$$

The left side of this expression is

$$\frac{F}{S}(1 + r_{\$}) = \frac{1.6558}{1.6627}(1 + 0.0175) = 1.0133$$

The right side of the expression is: $1 + r_{SFr} = 1.0150$. Because the left and right sides are not equal, IRP is not holding.

b. Because IRP is not holding, there is an arbitrage possibility: Because $1.0133 < 1.0150$, we can say that the SFr interest rate quote is more than what it should be as per the quotes for the other three variables. Equivalently, we can also say that the $ interest rate quote is less than what it should be as per the quotes for the other three variables. Therefore, the arbitrage strategy should be based on borrowing in the $ market and lending in the SFr market. The steps would be as follows:

- Borrow $1,000,000 for six months at 3.5 percent per year. Need to pay back $1,000,000 × (1 + 0.0175) = $1,017,500 six months later.
- Convert $1,000,000 to SFr at the spot rate to get SFr1,662,700.
- Lend SFr1,662,700 for six months at 3 percent per year. Will get back SFr1,662,700 × (1 + 0.0150) = SFr1,687,641 six months later.
- Sell SFr1,687,641 six months forward. The transaction will be contracted as of the current date but delivery and settlement will only take place six months later. So, six months later, exchange SFr1,687,641 for SFr1,687,641/SFr1.6558/$ = $1,019,230.

The arbitrage profit six months later is 1,019,230 − 1,017,500 = $1,730.

5. a. For three months, $r_{\$} = 1.30$ percent and $r_{¥} = 0.30$ percent. Because the exchange rate is in ¥/$ terms, the appropriate expression for the interest rate parity relation

$$\frac{F}{S} = \frac{1 + r_{¥}}{1 + r_{\$}}, \text{ or } \frac{F}{S}(1 + r_{\$}) = (1 + r_{¥})$$

The left side of this expression is

$$\frac{F}{S}(1 + r_{\$}) = \frac{107.30}{108.00}(1 + 0.0130) = 1.0064$$

The right side of this expression is: $1 + r_{¥} = 1.0030$. Because the left and right sides are not equal, IRP is not holding.

b. Because IRP is not holding, there is an arbitrage possibility. Because $1.0064 > 1.0030$, we can say that the \$ interest rate quote is more than what it should be as per the quotes for the other three variables. Equivalently, we can also say that the ¥ interest rate quote is less than what it should be as per the quotes for the other three variables. Therefore, the arbitrage strategy should be based on lending in the \$ market and borrowing in the ¥ market. The steps would be as follows:

- Borrow the yen equivalent of \$1,000,000. Because the spot rate is ¥108/\$, borrow \$1,000,000 × ¥108/\$ = ¥108,000,000. Need to pay back ¥108,000,000 × (1 + 0.0030) = ¥108,324,000 three months later.
- Exchange ¥108,000,000 for \$1,000,000 at the spot exchange rate.
- Lend \$1,000,000 for three months at 5.20 percent per year. Will get back \$1,000,000 × (1 + 0.0130) = \$1,013,000 three months later.
- Buy ¥108,324,000 three months forward. The transaction will be contracted as of the current date, but delivery and settlement will only take place three months later. So, three months later, get ¥108,324,000 for ¥108,324,000/¥107.30/\$ = \$1,009,543.

The arbitrage profit three months later is 1,013,000 − 1,009,543 = \$3,457.

6. At the given exchange rate of 5 pesos/\$, the cost in Mexico in dollar terms is \$16 for shoes, \$36 for watches, and \$120 for electric motors. Thus, compared with the United States, shoes and watches are cheaper in Mexico, and electric motors are more expensive in Mexico. Therefore, Mexico will import electric motors from the United States, and the United States will import shoes and watches from Mexico. Accordingly, the correct answer is (d).

7. Consider two countries, A and B. Based on relative PPP,

$$\frac{S_1}{S_0} = \frac{1 + I_A}{1 + I_B}$$

where S_1 and S_0 are the expected and the current exchange rates between the currencies of A and B, and I_A and I_B are the inflation rates in A and B. If A and B belong to the group of countries that introduces the same currency, then one could think of both S_1 and S_0 being one. Then, I_A and I_B should both be equal for relative PPP to hold. Thus, introduction of a common currency by a group of countries would result in the convergence of the inflation rates among these countries. A similar argument could be applied to inflation among the various states of the United States.

SOLUTIONS TO PROBLEMS IN READING 31

1. {S} **a.** When the product is a commodity with a known price and liquid market.

b. When collection is assured because the risk of nonpayment can be estimated.

c. When collection is uncertain because the risk of nonpayment cannot be estimated.

2. {S} a. (All data in $ millions)

Under the completed contract method, neither revenue nor pretax income would be reported until the project is completed. When the project has been completed, at the end of 2002, LASI Construction would report revenues of $3.0 and pretax income of $0.6 (revenues of $3.0 minus costs of $2.4).

Under the percentage-of-completion method, revenues and pretax income must be reported each year as follows:

Year	Cumulative % Completion	Cumulative Revenue	Current Period Revenue	Current Period Expense	Pretax Income
2000	0.9/2.4 = 37.5%	$1.125	$1.125	$0.900	$0.225
2001	1.7/2.4 = 70.8%	2.125	1.000	0.800	0.200
2002	2.4/2.4 = 100.0%	3.000	0.875	0.700	0.175
Total			$3.000	$2.400	$0.600

b. Computation of construction in progress and advance billings (in $ millions)

	Percentage-of-Completion	Completed Contract
Costs incurred	$ 0.900	$ 0.900
Profit recognized	0.225	0.000
Construction in progress	$ 1.125	$ 0.900
Advance billings	(1.000)	(1.000)
Net asset (liability)	$ 0.125	$(0.100)

Balance Sheet on December 31, 2000 (in $ millions)

	Percentage-of-Completion	Completed Contract
Assets		
Cash	$0.100	$0.100
Construction in progress (net)	0.125	0.000
Total assets	$0.225	$0.100
Liabilities and equity		
Advance billings (net)	$0.000	$0.100
Retained earnings	0.225	0.000
Total liabilities and equity	$0.225	$0.100

c. The effect on 2001 revenue and pretax income of a change in estimated costs to complete is as follows:

There is no change in 2001 revenues and pretax income (both are $0.000) under the completed contract method because no revenue or income can be recognized prior to completion.

Under the percentage-of-completion method, both revenue and pretax income change and are computed as follows:

Year	Cumulative % Completion	Cumulative Revenue	Current Period Revenue	Current Period Expense	Pretax Income
2001	1.7/**2.5** = **68.0%**	**$2.040**	**$0.915**	$0.800	**$0.115**

Note: All changes are in bold. The change in estimated costs to complete raises the total expected costs to complete to $2.500 from the previous estimate of $2.400. Costs incurred at the end of Year 2001 are $1.700 ($0.900 in 2000 and $0.800 in 2001) because we have assumed that the incremental costs ($0.100) will be incurred in Year 2002. Cumulative revenue of $2.040 must be recognized at the end of 2001; since we recognized $1.125 in revenue in 2000, the difference ($2.040 − $1.125) or $0.915 must be recognized in 2001. The effect of the change is recognized in Year 2001 and Year 2000 results are not changed.

3. {S}

Account	Part a	Part b
Contracts in process	This account reflects the costs actually incurred and the proportionate share of profits on those contracts for which the amount of revenue recognized exceeds payments received from customers.	The account is similar to accounts receivable that also reflects the excess of revenue recognized over cash payments received.
Advance billings	This account reflects those contracts for which payments received exceed revenue recognized.	The account is similar to advances from customers.

c. The company most likely uses the percentage-of-completion method. Under that method, the ***contracts in process*** account includes estimated earnings on uncompleted contracts, making it larger than under the completed contract method. As a result, it is more likely that some or all contracts will have an excess of contracts in process over advance billings, as illustrated in Exhibit 31-1B on pages 521–522.

4. {M} Required calculations are shown in the table below.

($millions)	**1997**	**1998**	**1999**	**2000**
Allowance for doubtful accounts				
Opening balance	$ 14.6	$ 18.0	$ 16.3	$ 21.1
Charged to earnings	4.2	(1.4)	5.3	
Writeoffs (net of recoveries)	(0.8)	(0.3)	(0.5)	
Closing balance	$ 18.0	$ 16.3	$ 21.1	$ 27.6
Accounts receivable (net)	386.4	299.2	393.8	350.2
Sales	4,184.5	4,151.2	4,009.3	4,586.1
Pretax income	460.2	415.3	379.2	478.3
Gross receivables*	404.4	315.5	414.9	377.8
a. (i) Closing balance of reserves to gross receivables (%)	**4.45%**	**5.17%**	**5.09%**	**7.31**
(ii) Writeoffs (net of recoveries) to revenues (%)	**0.02%**	**0.01%**	**0.01%**	
b. Adjusted pretax income^	**$ 463.6**	**$ 416.4**	**$ 384.0**	**$ 478.3**
c. Adjusted pretax income^^	**460.2**	**417.6**	**379.6**	**478.3**

* Net receivables plus amounts charged to earnings.

^ Reported pretax income plus amounts charged to earnings minus writeoffs (net of recoveries). (No adjustment made for 2000)

^^ See calculations below.

The following calculation is based on the assumption that Nucor maintained its closing balance of bad debt reserves at the 1997 ratio of 4.45% of gross receivables. Annual amounts charged to earnings are determined after calculation of required closing balance of bad debt reserve at 4.45% of gross receivables.

($millions)	**1997**	**1998**	**1999**	**2000**
Allowance for doubtful accounts				
Opening balance	$ 14.6	$ 18.0	$ 14.0	$ 18.5
Charged to earnings (plug)	4.2	(3.7)	4.9	
Writeoffs (net of recoveries)	(0.8)	(0.3)	(0.5)	
Closing balance at 4.45% of gross receivables	$ 18.0	$ 14.0	$ 18.5	$ 16.8
Difference between plug and actual charge	0.0	(2.3)	(0.4)	0.0
Adjusted pretax income	460.2	417.6	379.6	478.3

d. One factor should be the actual loss experience (writeoffs). Yet the accrual varied despite continuing low losses. A second factor should be the reserve level relative to receivables. This percentage may reflect economic conditions and should rise when the risk of customer financial distress increases. Nucor's reserve as a percent of gross receivables rose significantly from 1997 to 2000.

e. The actual writeoffs (through 1999) were immaterial, supporting the CFO's statement. However, as the table above shows, Nucor's accruals do not seem to reflect either the actual loss experience or maintaining a reserve that is a fixed percentage of gross receivables.

f. A CFO would prefer not to disclose the actual charge as it preserves management's ability to make accounting decisions without the risk of misinterpretation by analysts. For managements that use this reserve to manage earnings (see chapter discussion) nondisclosure hides such activity from investors and analysts.

g. From the analyst perspective, disclosure permits the analyst to see the effect of management decisions regarding the appropriate reserve level. It also allows the analyst to see the actual loss experience. Finally, disclosure permits the analyst to decide whether management is using the reserve to manage reported earnings.

SOLUTIONS TO PROBLEMS IN READING 33

1. {S} a. Palomba Pizza Stores
Statement of Cash Flows
Year Ended December 31, 2000

Cash Flows from Operating Activities:		
Cash Collections from Customers	$250,000	
Cash Payments to Suppliers	(85,000)	
Cash Payments for Salaries	(45,000)	
Cash Payments for Interest	(10,000)	
Net Cash from Operating Activities		$110,000
Cash Flows from Investing Activities:		
Sales of Equipment	38,000	
Purchase of Equipment	(30,000)	
Purchase of Land	(14,000)	
Net Cash for Investing Activities		(6,000)
Cash Flows from Financing Activities:		
Retirement of Common Stock	(25,000)	
Payment of Dividends	(35,000)	
Net Cash for Financing Activities		(60,000)
Net Increase in Cash		$ 44,000
Cash at Beginning of Year		50,000
Cash at End of Year		$ 94,000

b. Cash Flow from Operations (CFO) measures the cash generating ability of operations, in addition to profitability. If used as a measure of performance, CFO is less subject to distortion than net income. Analysts use the CFO as a check on the quality of reported earnings, although it is not a substitute for net income. Companies with high net income and low CFO may be using overly aggressive income recognition techniques. The ability of a firm to generate cash from operations on a consistent basis is one indication of the financial health of the firm. Analysts search for trends in CFO to indicate future cash conditions and potential liquidity or solvency problems.

Cash Flow from Investing Activities (CFI) reports how the firm is investing its excess cash. The analyst must consider the ability of the firm to continue to grow and CFI is a good indication of the attitude of management in this area. This component of total cash flow includes the capital expenditures made by management to maintain and expand productive capacity. Decreasing CFI may be a forecast of slower future growth.

Cash Flow from Financing (CFF) indicates the sources of financing for the firm. For firms that require external sources of financing (either borrowing or equity financing) it communicates management's preferences regarding financial leverage. Debt financing indicates future cash requirements for principal and interest payments. Equity financing will cause future earnings per share dilution.

For firms whose operating cash flow exceeds investment needs, CFF indicates whether that excess is used to repay debt, pay (or increase) cash dividends, or repurchase outstanding shares.

c. Cash payments for interest should be classified as CFF for purposes of analysis. This classification separates the effect of financial leverage decisions from operating results. It also facilitates the comparison of Palomba with other firms whose financial leverage differs.

d. The change in cash has no analytic significance. The change in cash (and hence, the cash balance at the end of the year) is a product of management decisions regarding financing. For example, the firm can show a large cash balance by drawing on bank lines just prior to year end.

e. and f. There are a number of definitions of free cash flows. In the text, free cash flow is defined as cash from operations less the amount of capital expenditures required to maintain the firm's current productive capacity. This definition requires the exclusion of costs of growth and acquisitions. However, few firms provide separate disclosures of expenditures incurred to maintain productive capacity. Capital costs of acquisitions may be obtained from proxy statements and other disclosures of acquisitions (See Chapter 14).

In the finance literature, free cash flows available to equity holders are often measured as cash from operations less capital expenditures. Interest paid is a deduction when computing cash from operations as it is paid to creditors. Palomba's free cash flow available to equity holders is calculated as follows:

Net cash flow from operating activities less net cash for investing activities:

$110,000 − $6,000 = **$104,000**

The investment activities disclosed in the problem do not indicate any acquisitions.

Another definition of free cash flows, which focuses on free cash flow available to all providers of capital, would exclude payments for interest ($10,000 in this case) and debt. Thus, Palomba's free cash flow available to all providers of capital would be $114,000.

2. {M} a.

	1996	1997	1998	1999	2000	2001
Sales	$ —	$140	$150	$165	$175	$195
Bad debt expense	—	7	7	8	10	10
Net receivables	30	40	50	60	75	95
Cash collections[1]	**$ —**	**$123**	**$133**	**$147**	**$150**	**$165**

[1] Sales − bad debt expense − increase in net receivables

b.

	1997	1998	1999	2000	2001
Bad debt expense/sales	5.0%	4.7%	4.9%	5.7%	5.1%
Net receivables/sales	28.6	33.3	36.4	42.8	48.7
Cash collections/sales	87.9	88.7	89.1	85.7	84.6

c. The bad debt provision does not seem to be adequate. From 1997–2001 sales increased by approximately 40%, while net receivables more than doubled, indicating that collections have been lagging. The ratios calculated in part b also indicate the problem. While bad debt expense has remained fairly constant at 5% of sales over the 5-year period, net receivables as a percentage of sales have increased from 29% to 49%; cash collections relative to sales have declined. Other possible explanations for these data are that stated payment terms have lengthened or that Stengel has allowed customers to delay payment for competitive reasons.

3. {S} Niagara Company
Statement of Cash Flows 2001

Cash collections	$ 980	[Sales − Δ Accounts Receivable]
Cash inputs	(670)	[COGS + Δ Inventory
Cash expenses	(75)	[Selling & General Expense − Δ Accounts Payable[1]]
Cash interest paid	(40)	[Interest Expense − Δ Interest Payable]
Income taxes paid	(30)	[Income Tax Expense − Δ Deferred Tax]
Cash from Operations	$ 165	
Purchase of fixed assets	(150)	
Cash used for Investing	(150)	[Depreciation Expense + Δ Fixed Assets (net)]
Increase in LT debt	50	
Decrease in notes payable	(25)	
Dividends paid	(30)	[Net Income − Δ Retained earnings]
Cash Used for Financing	(5)	
Net Change in Cash	$ 10	
Cash Balance 12/31/00	50	
Cash Balance 12/31/01	$ 60	

[1] Can also be used to calculate cash inputs, decreasing that outflow to $645 while increasing cash expenses to $100.

4. {L} a. (i) **Statement of Cash Flows—Indirect Method**

Cash from operations:		
Net income		$1,080
Add noncash expense: depreciation		600
Add/Subtract changes in working capital:		
Accounts receivable	(150)	
Inventory	(200)	
Accruals	80	
Accounts payable	120	(150)
		$1,530
Cash from investing:		
Capital expenditures		**1,150**
Cash from financing:		
Short-term borrowing		550
Long-term repayment		(398)
Dividends		(432)
		$ (280)
Net change in cash		**$ 100**

Worksheet for (Indirect Method) Cash Flow Statement

	Income Statement	Balance Sheet 12/31/00	12/31/01	Change	Cash Effect
Net income	$1,080				$ 1,080
Depreciation	600				600
Accounts receivable		$1,500	$1,650	$150	(150)
Inventory		2,000	2,200	200	(200)
Accruals		800	880	80	80
Accounts payable		1,200	1,320	120	120
Depreciation	(600)				(600)
Net fixed assets		6,500	7,050	550	(550)
Capital expenditures					***$(1,150)***
Note payable		5,500	6,050	550	550
Short-term borrowing					***$ 550***
Long-term debt		2,000	1,602	(398)	(398)
Long-term debt repayment					***$ (398)***
Net income	(1,080)				(1,080)
Retained earnings		500	1,148	648	648
Dividends paid					***$ (432)***
	0				$ 100

The worksheet to create the cash flow statement is presented above. Each balance sheet change (other than cash) is accounted for and matched with its corresponding activity. As a last check, the net income and the add-backs of non-cash items are balanced and "closed" to their respective accounts (PP&E and retained earnings), providing the amounts of capital expenditures and dividends.

a. (ii) Statement of Cash Flows—Direct Method

Cash from Operations:	
Cash collections	$9,850
Cash payments for merchandise	(6,080)
Cash paid for SG&A	(920)
Cash paid for interest	(600)
Cash paid for taxes	(720)
	$1,530
Cash for Investing Activities:	
Capital expenditures	**(1,150)**
Cash for Financing Activities:	
Short-term borrowing	550
Long-term debt repayment	(398)
Dividends	(432)
	$ (280)
Net Change in Cash	**$ 100**

b. The worksheet to create the cash flow statement is presented below. Each balance sheet change (other than cash) is accounted for and matched with its corresponding activity. Furthermore the operating account changes are matched to their corresponding income statement item. As a last check, the net income is balanced and "closed" to retained earnings providing the amount of dividends.

Note that there is no difference between the indirect and direct methods in the cash flow statement and in the worksheet for cash for investing and financing activities.

Worksheet for (Direct Method) Cash Flow Statement

	Income Statement	Balance Sheet 12/31/00	Balance Sheet 12/31/01	Change	Cash Effect
Sales	$10,000				$10,000
Accounts receivable		$1,500	$1,650	$ 150	(150)
Cash Collections					*$ 9,850*
COGS	(6,000)				(6,000)
Inventory		2,000	2,200	200	(200)
Accounts payable		1,200	1,320	120	120
Cash Paid for Merchandise					*$ (6,080)*
SG&A expense	(1,000)				(1,000)
Accruals		800	880	80	80
Cash Paid for SG&A					*$ (920)*
Interest expense	(600)				(600)
Cash Paid for Interest					*$ (600)*
Taxes	(720)				(720)
Cash Paid for Taxes					*$ (720)*
Depreciation	(600)				(600)
Net fixed assets		6,500	7,050	550	(550)
Capital Expenditures					*$ (1,150)*
Note payable		5,500	6,050	550	550
Short-term Borrowing					*$ 550*
Long-term debt		2,000	1,602	(398)	(398)
Long-term Debt Repaid					*$ (398)*
Net income	(1,080)				(1,080)
Retained earnings		500	1,148	648	648
Dividends					*$ (432)*
	$ 0				$ 100

SOLUTIONS TO PROBLEMS IN READING 35

Answers to Questions

1. Analysts employ financial ratios simply because numbers in isolation are typically of little value. For example, a net income of $100,000 has little meaning unless analysts know the sales figure that generated the income and the assets or capital employed in generating these sales or this income. Therefore, ratios are used to provide meaningful relationships between individual values in the financial statements. Ratios also allow analysts to compare firms of different sizes.

2. In general, jewelry stores have very high profit margins but low asset turnover. It could take them months to sell a 1-carat diamond ring, but once it is sold, the profit could be tremendous. On the other hand, grocery stores usually have very low profit margins but very high asset turnover. Assuming both business risk and financial risk of the firms are equal, the ROE's should likewise be equal.

3. Growth analysis is important to common stockholders because the future value of the firm is heavily dependent on future growth in earnings and dividends. The present value of a firm with perpetual dividends payment is:

$$V = \frac{\text{Dividend Next Period}}{\text{Required Rate of Return} - \text{Growth Rate}}$$

Therefore, an estimation of expected growth of earnings and dividends on the basis of the variables that influence growth is obviously crucial. Growth analysis is also important to debt-investors because the major determinant of the firm's ability to pay an obligation is the firm's future success which, in turn, is influenced by its growth.

The rate of growth of any economic unit depends on the amount of resources retained and reinvested in the entity and the rate of return earned on the resources retained. The more reinvested, the greater the potential for growth. In general:

$$\text{Growth} = \text{Retention Rate} \times \text{Return on Equity}$$

Answers to Problems

1. a. ROE = Total asset turnover × Total assets/equity × Net profit margin

Company K: $\text{ROE} = 2.2 \times 2.4 \times .04 = .21$

Company L: $\text{ROE} = 2.0 \times 2.2 \times .06 = .26$

Company M: $\text{ROE} = 1.4 \times 1.5 \times .10 = .21$

1. b. $\text{Growth Rate} = \text{Retention Rate} \times \text{ROE}$

$= (1 - \text{Payout Rate}) \times \text{ROE}$

Company K: $\text{Growth Rate} = (1 - 1.25/2.75) \times .21$

$= .55 \times .21 = .1155$

Company L: $\text{Growth Rate} = (1 - 1.00/3.00) \times .26$

$= .67 \times .26 = .1742$

Company M: $\text{Growth Rate} = (1 - 1.00/4.50) \times .21$

$= .78 \times .21 = .1638$

2. Current ratio = 650/350 = 1.857

Quick ratio = 320/350 = 0.914

Receivables turnover = 3500/195 = 17.95x

Average collection period = 365/17.95 = 20.33 days

Total asset turnover = 3500/2182.5 = 1.60x

Inventory turnover = 2135/280 = 7.625x

Fixed asset turnover = 3500/1462.5 = 2.39x

Equity turnover = 3500/1035 = 3.382x

Gross profit margin = (3500 − 2135)/3500 = .39

Operating profit margin = 258/3500 = .074

Return on capital (129 + 62)/2182.5 = .088

Return on equity = 129/1185 = .109

Return on common equity = 114/1035 = .110

Debt/equity ratio = 625/1225 = .51

Debt/total capital ratio = 625/1850 = .338

Interest coverage = 258/62 = 4.16x

Fixed charge coverage = 258/[62 + (15/.66)] = 3.045x

Cash flow/long-term debt = (129 + 125 + 20)/625 = .438

Cash flow/total debt = (129 + 125 + 20)/975 = .281

Retention rate = 1 − (40/114) = .65

Eddie's current performance appears in line with its historical performance and the industry average except in the areas of profitability (measured by return on capital and return on equity) and leverage (debt/equity and debt/total capital ratios).

3. CFA Examination I (1990)

	1999	2003
3. a. Operating Margin = (Operating Income − Depreciation)/Sales	= (38 − 3)/542 = 6.46%	= (76 − 9)/979 = 6.84%
Asset Turnover = Sales/Total Assets	= 542/245 = 2.21x	= 979/291 = 3.36x
Interest Burden = Interest Expense/Total Assets	= 3/245 = 1.22%	= 0/291 = 0%
Financial Leverage = Total Assets/Common Shareholders Equity	= 245/159 = 1.54x	= 291/220 = 1.32x
Tax Rate = Income Taxes/Pre-tax Income	= 13/32 = 40.63%	= 37/67 = 55.22%

The recommended formula is:

Return on (ROE) = [(Op. Margin × Asset Turnover) − Int. Burden] × Equity Financial Leverage × (100% − Income Tax Rate)

1999 = [(6.46% × 2.21x) − 1.22%] × 1.54 × (100% − 40.63%)
= 13.05 × 1.54 × .5937 = 11.93%

2003 = [(6.84% × 3.36x) − 0%] × 1.32 × (100% − 55.22%)
= 22.98 × 1.32 × .4478 = 13.58%

Two alternative approaches are also correct.

ROE = [(Op. Margin − (Int. Burden/Asset Turnover)] × Financial Leverage × Asset Turnover × (100% − Income Tax Rate)

ROE = [(Financial Leverage × Asset Turnover × Operating Margin) − (Financial Leverage × Interest Burden)] × (100% − Income Tax Rate)

3. b. Asset turnover measures the ability of a company to minimize the level of assets (current and fixed) to support its level of sales. The asset turnover increased substantially over the period thus contributing to an increase in the ROE.

Financial leverage measures the amount of financing outside of equity including short- and long-term debt. Financial leverage declined over the period thus adversely affecting the ROE. Since asset turnover rose substantially more than financial leverage declined, the net effect was an increase in ROE.

SOLUTIONS TO PROBLEMS IN READING 36

1. a. Basic earnings per share is the amount of earnings for the period available to each share of common stock outstanding during the reporting period.

   b. A potentially dilutive security is a security which can be exchanged for or converted into common stock and therefore upon conversion or exercise could dilute (or decrease) earnings per share. Included in this category are convertible securities, options, warrants, and other rights.

2. The concept that a security may be the equivalent of common stock has evolved to meet the reporting needs of investors in corporations that have issued certain types of convertible securities, options, and warrants. A potentially dilutive security is a security which is not, in form, common stock but which enables its holder to obtain common stock upon exercise or conversion. The holders of these securities can expect to participate in the appreciation of the value of the common stock resulting principally from the earnings and earnings potential of the issuing corporation. This participation is essentially the same as that of a common stockholder except that the security may carry a specified dividend yielding a return different from that received by a common stockholder. The attractiveness to investors of this type of security is often based principally upon this potential right to share in increases in the earnings potential of the issuing corporation rather than upon its fixed return or upon other senior security characteristics. In addition, the call characteristic of the stock options and warrants gives the investor potential control over a far greater number of shares per dollar of investment than if the investor owned the shares outright.

3. Convertible securities are considered to be potentially dilutive securities whenever their conversion causes a greater percentage increase in the EPS numerator than in the EPS denominator. If this situation does not result, conversion is not assumed and only basic EPS is reported.

Answers to Exercises

1. a.

Event	Dates Outstanding	Shares Outstanding	Restatement	Fraction of Year	Weighted Shares
Beginning balance	Jan. 1–Feb. 1	480,000	1.1 × 3.0	1/12	132,000
Issued shares	Feb. 1–Mar. 1	600,000	1.1 × 3.0	1/12	165,000
Stock dividend	Mar. 1–May 1	660,000	3.0	2/12	330,000
Reacquired shares	May 1–June 1	560,000	3.0	1/12	140,000
Stock split	June 1–Oct. 1	1,680,000		4/12	560,000
Reissued shares	Oct. 1–Dec. 31	1,740,000		3/12	435,000
Weighted average number of shares outstanding					1,762,000

b. Earnings Per Share $= \dfrac{\$3{,}456{,}000 \text{ (Net Income)}}{1{,}762{,}000 \text{ (Weighted Average Shares)}} = \$1.96$

c. Earnings Per Share $= \dfrac{\$3{,}456{,}000 - \$900{,}000}{1{,}762{,}000} = \$1.45$

d.

Income from continuing operations[a]	$1.72
Loss from discontinued operations[b]	(.25)
Income before extraordinary item	1.47
Extraordinary gain[c]	.49
Net income	$1.96
[a]Net income	$3,456,000
Deduct extraordinary gain	(864,000)
Add loss from discontinued operations	432,000
Income from continuing operations	$3,024,000

[a] $\dfrac{\$3{,}024{,}000}{1{,}762{,}000} = \$1.72$

[b] $\dfrac{\$(432{,}000)}{1{,}762{,}000} = \$(.25)$

[c] $\dfrac{\$864{,}000}{1{,}762{,}000} = \$.49$

2. The computation of Dewey Yaeger Pharmaceutical Industries' basic earnings per share and the diluted earnings per share for the fiscal year ended June 30, 2005, are shown below.

a. Basic earnings per share $= \dfrac{\text{Net income} - \text{Preferred dividends}}{\text{Average common shares outstanding}}$

$= \dfrac{\$1{,}500{,}000 - \$106{,}250^{1}}{1{,}000{,}000}$

$= \dfrac{\$1{,}393{,}750}{1{,}000{,}000}$

$= \$1.3937$ or $\$1.39$ per share

[1] Preferred dividend = .085 × $1,250,000
= $106,250

b. Diluted earnings per share $= \dfrac{\text{Net income} - \text{Preferred dividends} + \text{Interest (net of tax)}}{\text{Average common shares} + \text{Potentially dilutive common shares}}$

$= \dfrac{\$1{,}500{,}000 - \$106{,}250 + \$210{,}000^{2}}{1{,}000{,}000 + 250{,}000^{3} + 25{,}000^{4}}$

$= \dfrac{\$1{,}603{,}750}{1{,}275{,}000}$

$= \$1.2578$ or $\$1.26$ per share

[2] Use "if converted" method for 7% bonds

Adjustment for interest expense (net of tax) ($5,000,000 × .07 × .6)	$210,000

[3] Shares assumed to be issued if converted

$5,000,000 ÷ $1,000/bond × 50 shares	250,000

[4] Use treasury stock method to determine incremental shares outstanding

Proceeds from exercise of options (100,000 × $15)	$1,500,000
Shares issued upon exercise of options	100,000
Shares purchasable with proceeds (Proceeds ÷ Average market price) ($1,500,000 ÷ $20)	75,000
Incremental shares outstanding	25,000

SOLUTIONS TO PROBLEMS IN READING 39

1. {S} a. Start with the basic inventory relationship

BI + P = COGS + EI

Opening inventory	400 units @ $20	$ 8,000
Purchases	1,000	25,000
Total	1,400 units	$33,000

(i) Under FIFO, ending inventory consists of 600 units:

100 purchased in second quarter at $24	$ 2,400
300 purchased in third quarter at $26	7,800
200 purchased in fourth quarter at $28	5,600
600 units total	$15,800

(ii) Under LIFO, ending inventory consists of 600 units:

400 inventory at January 1 at $20	$ 8,000
200 purchased in first quarter at $22	4,400
600 units total	$12,400

(iii) Under average cost, ending inventory consists of 600 units with an average cost of $33,000/1,400 = $23.5714 per unit or $14,142.84 total.

b. COGS for the year equals the $33,000 total of opening inventory plus purchases, less closing inventory under the method chosen:

(i) FIFO: $33,000 less $15,800 = $17,200

(ii) LIFO: $33,000 less $12,400 = $20,600

(iii) Average cost: $33,000 less $14,142.84 = $18,857.16

c. (i) Reported income is highest under FIFO (lowest COGS) and lowest under LIFO (highest COGS). Average cost is in between FIFO and LIFO.

(ii) Stockholders' equity is highest under FIFO (highest inventory and retained earnings) and lowest under LIFO (lowest inventory and retained earnings), with average cost in between.

2. {S} Using FIFO instead of LIFO when prices are rising and inventory quantities are stable has the following effects:

a. Gross profit margins are higher under FIFO than under LIFO because revenues at higher current prices are matched with cost-of-goods-sold measured using older (lower) prices.

b. Net income is lower under LIFO than under FIFO because cost-of-goods-sold is higher.

c. Cash from operations is higher under LIFO than under FIFO because income tax paid is lower.

d. Inventory balances are lower under LIFO than under FIFO because cost-of-goods-sold is higher and lower prices remain in inventory.

e. Inventory turnover is lower under FIFO than under LIFO because cost-of-goods-sold is lower and inventory balances higher. Both factors decrease the inventory turnover ratio.

f. Working capital is lower under LIFO than under FIFO because inventory balances are lower, despite partial offset from higher cash balances (because of lower tax payments).

g. Total assets are higher under FIFO because FIFO inventory balances are higher.

h. The debt-to-equity ratio is lower under FIFO than under LIFO because equity is higher, reflecting higher retained earnings.

3. {L} a. The first step is to obtain FIFO cost-of-goods-sold:

Pretax income = sales − COGS − other expenses

$5,000 = $25,000 − COGS − $12,000

Solving: COGS = $8,000

Purchases are equal to COGS + Closing Inventory = $8,000 + $10,000 = $18,000.

The key to this problem is to distinguish between the flow of units and the flow of costs. Purchases are independent of the accounting method used.

Since half the units were sold, half remain in inventory. Under LIFO, therefore, the cost allocations to inventory and COGS are the reverse of those allocated under FIFO. That is, under LIFO, COGS = $10,000 and Closing Inventory = $8,000.

Under the weighted average method, as total purchases equal $18,000, the allocation between COGS and closing inventory will be equal: COGS = Closing Inventory = $9,000.

Recalling that pretax CFO depends on purchases, not COGS, we can now fill in the rest of the table.

	FIFO	Weighted Average	LIFO
Sales	$25,000	$25,000	$25,000
Cost of goods sold	8,000	9,000	10,000
Other expenses	12,000	12,000	12,000
Pretax income	5,000	4,000	3,000
Tax expense	2,000	1,600	1,200
Net income	3,000	2,400	1,800
Retained earnings	3,000	2,400	1,800
Cash from operations[1]	(7,000)	(6,600)	(6,200)
Cash balance[2]	3,000	3,400	3,800
Closing inventory	10,000	9,000	8,000
Purchases	18,000	18,000	18,000

[1] Cash from operations = Sales − Other expenses − Purchases − Tax expense.

[2] Cash balance = $10,000 + Cash from operations

b. M & J Company
Balance Sheet, December 31, 20X0

	FIFO	Weighted Average	LIFO
Cash	$ 3,000	$ 3,400	$ 3,800
Inventory	10,000	9,000	8,000
Total assets	$13,000	$12,400	$11,800
Common stock	$10,000	$10,000	$10,000
Retained earnings	3,000	2,400	1,800
Total equities	$13,000	$12,400	$11,800

c. The advantages of LIFO are that it results in the highest cash flow (by reducing income taxes) and it best measures net income by matching the cost of sales with most recent costs to replace inventory sold. The disadvantage of LIFO is that inventory on the balance sheet is understated.

The advantage of FIFO is that inventory is measured at most recent costs. Its disadvantages are the reduced cash flow and overstatement of reported income.

Average cost has the disadvantage of misreporting both the balance sheet inventory and net income. Income taxes are higher than under the LIFO method (but lower than under FIFO). The "advantage" of average cost is that it is "less wrong" than LIFO on the balance sheet and "less wrong" than FIFO on the income statement.

4. {M} a. The LIFO Reserve increased by $4,000. If the company used FIFO, its pretax income would be $4,000 higher. After-tax income would be higher by .65 × $4,000 = $2,600.

b. Inventory turnover is COGS/average inventory:

LIFO $3,800,000/[.5 ($748,000 + $696,800)] = 5.26X
FIFO $3,796,000/[.5 ($794,000 + $746,800)] = 4.93X

c. Since the firm's ROE is 4.6% and net income is $340,000, then average equity = $340,000/.046 = $7,391,304

If the company used FIFO, equity would be higher by the LIFO reserve amount adjusted for taxes. The average LIFO reserve is $48,000. Therefore, average equity should be higher by $31,200 (.65 × $48,000) after tax.

FIFO average equity = $7,391,304 + $31,200 = $7,422,504
ROE_{FIFO} = $342,600/$7,422,504 = 4.62%

The adjustment of ROE is insignificant in this case because the increase in the numerator (income) and denominator (equity) are proportionate.

d. There are two reasons to make adjustments for accounting methods:

1. To more accurately measure the firm's operations

2. To facilitate comparisons of different firms on the same basis

For inventory turnover, the adjustment results in a more accurate measure of performance. However, the main purpose of the LIFO to FIFO adjustment is to enable the analyst to compare Zeta to other firms that use FIFO.

e. The current cost method (inventory and equity at FIFO, COGS and net income at LIFO) should be used for both inventory turnover and ROE. For inventory turnover, this method better approximates the actual (physical) turnover. The argument for ROE is that FIFO equity better reflects the Company's current value, while LIFO income reflects the current operating profit earned on that equity. For Zeta, these adjustments offset. In some cases, however, the current cost method ratios are quite different.

5. {S} a. The cost of inventory may have declined due to deflation.

b. (1) They might believe that the price decrease is temporary and in the future prices will increase again.

(2) Since the LIFO reserve is large, a switch to FIFO would require a large tax expense (equal to tax rate times the LIFO reserve) immediately. Thus, even if they felt that prices would continue to decrease in the future, they are still better off paying the higher taxes slowly over time (as the LIFO reserve declines) rather than paying the full amount immediately.

6. {S}

	1997	1998	1999
a. Sales	$515,728	$539,413	$572,696
Gross margin	187,556	190,826	210,588
Gross margin %	**36.4%**	**35.4%**	**36.8%**
b. LIFO liquidation	$ 3,379	$ 1,733	none
Pretax liquidation*	**5,198**	**2,666**	
Adjusted			
Gross margin	$182,358	$188,160	$210,588
Gross margin %	**35.4%**	**34.9%**	**36.8%**

* Equals LIFO liquidation (net of tax)/.65

c. The adjusted gross margin percentage is more indicative of the longer-term trend of the company. By removing the effects of the LIFO liquidation(s), COGS and subsequently gross margin are more reflective of current cost income. Removing the effect of the liquidation shows that gross margins improved significantly from 1997–1998 to 1999.

SOLUTIONS TO PROBLEMS IN READING 40

1. **{M}** Exhibit 40-1 contains the calculations required.

Exhibit 40-1. Chevron
Adjustments for Capitalization of Interest
Amounts in $ millions

Year	1995	1996	1997	1998	1999	part c 1999/95
As reported						
Interest expense	$ 401	$ 364	$ 312	$ 405	$ 472	**1.18**
Pretax income	1,789	4,740	5,502	1,834	3,648	**2.04**
Net income	930	2,607	3,256	1,339	2,070	**2.23**
Capitalized interest	141	108	82	39	59	
Amortization of capitalized interest	47	24	28	35	9	
a. Calculations						
EBIT	$2,190	$5,104	$5,814	$2,239	$4,120	
Times interest earned	**5.46**	**14.02**	**18.63**	**5.53**	**8.73**	**1.60**
b. Adjusted						
Net capitalized interest	$ 94	$ 84	$ 54	$ 4	$50	
After 35% income tax	61	55	35	3	33	
Interest expense	542	472	394	444	531	**0.98**
EBIT	2,237	5,128	5,842	2,274	4,129	
(i) Times interest earned	**4.13**	**10.86**	**14.83**	**5.12**	**7.78**	**1.88**
(ii) % reduction from reported ratio	**−24.4%**	**−22.5%**	**−20.4%**	**−7.4%**	**−10.9%**	
Pretax income	$1,695	$4,656	$5,448	$1,830	$3,598	**2.12**
(iii) Net income	**869**	**2,552**	**3,221**	**1,336**	**2,038**	**2.34**
% reduction from reported	−6.6%	−2.1%	−1.1%	−0.2%	−1.6%	

b. (iv) Expensing all interest reduces net income for each year. However, the effect diminishes over time.

c. (i) Because the amount of interest capitalized declined over time, restatement reduces the rate of increase in interest expense.

(ii) While the interest coverage ratio is lower after restatement, its trend improves due to the lower growth rate of interest expense.

(iii) Both pretax and net income are lower after restatement but their growth rate improves due to the lower growth rate of interest expense.

d. The restated data are more useful for financial analysis because they are based on actual interest expense. They provide better comparability with firms that do not capitalize interest.

2. {S} a. The capitalization of the investment in displays delays their impact on income as compared with expensing. In addition, cash from operations is permanently increased as the expenditures are classified as cash flows for investment. Finally, if these expenditures are volatile, capitalization and amortization smoothes the impact on reported income.

b. (i) In 2000, the capitalized amount increased by $1,648,000. Had promotional displays been expensed, net income would be $1,071,200 (after 35% tax) lower. Expensing would have reduced net income by 7.4% ($1,071.2/$14,467).

(ii) Shareholders' equity would be reduced by 65% of $10,099,000 equal to $6,564,350 or 7.1%.

(iii) Reported return on (average) assets equals
$14,467/[($166,656 + $140,609)/2] = 9.42%
Adjusted return on (average) assets equals
$14,467 − $1,071)/[($166,656 − $10,099) + ($140,609 − $8,451)/2] = 9.28% as assets must be reduced by the investment in promotional displays.

3. {M} Exhibit 40-2 on page 981 contains the calculations required by parts a and b.

a. R&D is clearly very important to Pfizer's business. Its R&D expenditures are very high relative to sales and the percentage has been growing even though sales growth is rapid. These expenditures, at least in the short run, reduce Pfizer's reported earnings given the long time lag between discovery and profitable sales of prescription drugs.

c. Capitalization and amortization of R & D increases net income each year, the expected result given rising expenditures. There is little impact on ROE as higher equity offsets higher net income. (This latter result is not surprising given the findings of Sarath et al., discussed in footnote 3 on page 775.)

d. (i) Asset turnover will decline under capitalization due to the higher level of assets; sales are unchanged.

(ii) Cash from operations will rise under capitalization as R&D expenditures will be classified as investing cash flows and will never be reported as a component of cash flows from operations.

EXHIBIT 40-2 Pfizer

Amounts in $millions	**1995**	**1996**	**1997**	**1998**	**1999**
	Years ended December 31				
Net sales	$8,684	$9,864	$10,739	$12,677	$14,133
R & D expense	1,340	1,567	1,805	2,279	2,776
a. % sales	**15.4%**	**15.9%**	**16.8%**	**18.0%**	**19.6%**
b. Adjustments					
3 year amortization:					
1/3 current year			$ 602	$ 760	$ 925
1/3 prior year			522	602	760
1/3 2nd prior year			447	522	602
Total amortization			$1,571	$1,884	$2,287
Expense less amortization			(234)	(395)	(489)
Adjusted pretax income			$3,101	$2,989	$4,937
Adjusted tax expense			(857)	(780)	(1,415)
(i) Adjusted net income			**$2,244**	**$2,209**	**$3,522**
Reported net income			2,092	1,952	3,204
R & D asset (net)	$1,239	$1,491	$1,726	$ 2,121	$ 2,610
R & D asset after-tax	805	969	1,122	1,379	1,697
Shareholders' equity	5,506	6,954	7,933	8,810	8,887
Adjusted equity	$6,311	$7,923	$9,055	$10,189	$10,584
Adjusted average equity	5,637	7,117	8,489	9,622	10,386
(ii) Adjusted ROE			**26.4%**	**23.0%**	**33.9%**
Reported ROE			28.1%	23.3%	36.2%

SOLUTIONS TO PROBLEMS IN READING 41

1. {M} a. Straight-line depreciation

b. Sum-of-years' digits

Depreciable base	$10,000,000	$10,000,000
Sum-of-years'-digits		15

Year	Straight line Method	Sum-of-years' Digits
1	$ 2,000,000	$ 3,333,333
2	2,000,000	2,666,667
3	2,000,000	2,000,000
4	2,000,000	1,333,333
5	2,000,000	666,667
Total	$10,000,000	$10,000,000

c. Double declining balance

Depreciable base $12,000,000 Rate = 40%

Year	Double-declining balance Depreciation	Balance
1	$ 4,800,000	$ 7,200,000
2	2,880,000	4,320,000
3	1,728,000	2,592,000
4	592,000	2,000,000
5		2,000,000
Total	$10,000,000	

2. {S} a. Straight-line methods report constant depreciation expense throughout the life of the asset. Accelerated methods result in higher depreciation expense initially, but a declining trend thereafter. The effect on total depreciation expense depends on the growth rate of capital spending (whether the effect of higher depreciation expense on new assets offsets the impact of declining depreciation expense on old ones). Using the same economic life, accelerated methods will report higher depreciation expense than the straight-line method during the early years and lower expense thereafter.

b. The effect on net income is the reverse of the above. Net income is lower initially. Its reversal will depend on the level and growth of capital expenditures in the future.

c. Accelerated depreciation methods report lower net income (higher depreciation expense), lower assets, and lower equity (higher accumulated depreciation) than the straight-line method. The numerator effect may dominate, producing lower return ratios. For a growing firm with increasing capital expenditures, the early years' depreciation expense difference will persist, resulting in lower return ratios.

d. Accelerated depreciation methods report lower income in the first year but higher income in later years as depreciation expense declines. Reported assets are lower throughout. Companies with rapidly growing capital expenditures are likely to report lower ROA as the income effect dominates. As they mature, however, slowing capital expenditures and the growing effect of the reduced denominator (assets) is likely to result in higher ROA than under the straight-line method.

e. For financial reporting purposes, the choice of method has no effect on reported cash flows, as depreciation is a noncash expense. However, for tax purposes, the use of accelerated methods rather than the straight-line method reduces taxes paid, increasing cash from operations.

f. As depreciation expense has no effect on revenues, accelerated depreciation methods increase reported asset turnover, as the denominator is lower.

3. {S} a. The present value of the cash flows, discounted at 10%, is $60 for each asset.

b. Asset A:

Year	Net Asset	Cash Flow	Depreciation Expense	Income	ROA
1	$60	$36	$30	$6	10%
2	30	23	20	3	10%
3	10	11	10	1	10%

Asset B:

Year	Net Asset	Cash Flow	Depreciation Expense	Income	ROA
1	$60	$26	$20	$6	10%
2	40	24	20	4	10%
3	20	22	20	2	10%

c. The pattern for Asset A is the sum-of-the-years' digits method. The pattern for Asset B is the straight-line method.

4. {S} a.

Reported net income	$ 342,000
Cumulative effect of change	(700,000)
Net income before cumulative effect	**$(358,000)**

b.

1998 effect of change	$ 800,000
Less: 35% income tax	(280,000)
1998 effect net	$ 520,000
Net income before cumulative effect	$(358,000)
1998 effect net	(520,000)
Net income before accounting change	**$(878,000)**

c. Pope and Talbot had an operating loss of $(878,000) in 1998. The accounting change enabled POP to report net income of $342,000.

5. {M} a.–c.

As shown in the following table, the accounting change improved the 2000 gross margin ratio by 0.5% and the operating ratio by 0.9%.

	As Reported 1999	2000	Accounting Change	Adjusted 2000
Net revenues	$1,452	$1,545		$1,545
Cost of sales	(835)	(845)	$ 8	(853)
Gross profit	$ 617	$ 700	$ 8	$ 692
S, D, & A expense	(575)	(625)	6	(631)
Operating income	$ 42	$ 75	$14	$ 61
% of Sales				
Net revenues	100.0%	100.0%		100.0%
Cost of sales	−57.5%	−54.7%	0.5%	−55.2%
Gross margin	**42.5%**	**45.3%**	**0.5%**	**44.8%**
S, D, & A expense	−39.6%	−40.5%	0.4%	−40.8%
Operating margin	**2.9%**	**4.9%**	**0.9%**	**3.9%**

d. **(i)** Fixed asset turnover is reduced as lower depreciation expense increases the net carrying amount of fixed assets.

(ii) The accounting change improves the reported income trend as 2000 and following years benefit from the reduced depreciation expense.

(iii) PBG's quality of earnings is reduced as the accounting change increases reported earnings.

(iv) Cash from operations is unchanged as depreciation is a noncash expense.

e. If the company believes that its performance is best measured using cash flow data, the accounting change has no benefit whatsoever. However reported income is increased, reducing the reported price-earnings ratio.

6. {M} a. Calculations below use the following definitions:

(i) Average depreciable life (years) = Gross investment/depreciation expense

(ii) Average age (years) = Accumulated depreciation/depreciation expense

(iii) Average age (%) = Accumulated depreciation/gross investment

	1997	1998	1999
Buildings and land improvements			
(i) Average depreciable life (years)	32.5	40.8	40.8
(ii) Average age (years)	11.1	13.8	14.0
(iii) Average age (%)	34.1%	33.9%	34.3%
Machinery and equipment			
(i) Average depreciable life (years)	15.2	12.0	12.7
(ii) Average age (years)	8.3	6.4	6.8
(iii) Average age (%)	54.7%	53.6%	53.2%

b. The average depreciable life for buildings and land improvements is just over 40 years for 1998 and 1999, very close to the 40 year stated life. The 1997 ratio is much lower. The high depreciation for that year suggests that there was some special factor accounting for the discrepancy.

The average for machinery and equipment varies over the three-year period but is consistent with the 15-year maximum stated life. The ratio suggests that most assets in this category are depreciated over 15 years despite the stated policy of 5–15 years.

c. The average age (years) of buildings and land improvements has been increasing but is still low (and stable) compared with the average depreciable life (average age (%)). For machinery and equipment the average age fell in 1998 and was stable in 1999. These ratios suggest that Roche's physical facilities are modern, although it would be useful to compare the ratios with those of Roche competitors.

d. Questions worth asking include:

- Why was 1997 depreciation on buildings and land improvements abnormally high?
- Was 1997 depreciation on machinery and equipment abnormally low and, if so, why?
- What types of machinery and equipment are depreciated over 15 years versus shorter time periods?
- What is the breakdown of future capital expenditures between land and land improvements and machinery and equipment?
- Will future capital expenditures change the average depreciable life due to changes in the asset mix?

SOLUTIONS TO PROBLEMS IN READING 42

1. {S} Deferred taxes can be found in all of the categories listed. Examples are:

a. Current liabilities may include deferred tax liabilities arising from an installment sale with cash payments expected within one year.

b. Deferred income tax credits resulting from the use of accelerated depreciation for tax purposes and straight line for financial reporting are reported in long-term liabilities.

c. The stockholders' equity account may include the deferred tax offset to the valuation allowance for available-for-sale securities or the cumulative translation adjustment account.

d. The deferred tax asset (debit) due to accrued compensation with cash payment expected within one year is a component of current assets.

e. Long-term assets would include deferred tax assets (debits) recognized, (for example for, postretirement benefits or restructuring charges), but not expected to be funded within one year.

2. {S} a. Correct: Under SFAS 109, changes in tax laws must be reflected in the deferred tax liability in the period of enactment.

b. Correct: Answer to (i) also applies to deferred tax assets.

c. Correct: The tax consequences of events that have not been reflected in the financial statements (such as future earnings or losses) are not recognized.

d. Incorrect: See answers to (i) and (ii) above. This statement is true for the deferral method (see footnote 2 on text page 839).

e. Incorrect: Changes in deferred tax assets and liabilities are included in income tax expense except for those charged directly to stockholders' equity.

3. {S} a. Permanent differences are items of income or expense that affect *either tax return income or financial income, but not both.* Examples include:

- Tax-exempt interest income (not reported on the tax return,
- Interest expense on amounts borrowed to purchase tax-exempt securities (not deductible on the tax return).
- Tax or other nondeductible government penalties (not reported on the tax return),
- Statutory mineral depletion in excess of cost basis depletion (not reported in the financial statements),
- Premiums on key-person life insurance policies (not deductible on the tax return),
- Proceeds from key-person life insurance policies (not reported on the tax return).

b. Permanent differences, depending on their nature, either increase or decrease the firm's effective tax rate relative to the statutory rate. For example, tax-exempt interest income (the first example listed) reduces the effective tax rate as there is no tax expense associated with this income.

4. {S} a.(i) If the deferred tax liability is not expected to reverse, there is no expectation of a cash outflow and the liability should be considered as equity.

(ii) If the deferred tax liability is the result of a temporary difference that is expected to reverse, with consequent tax payment, it should be treated as a liability.

b. Because both the amounts and timing of tax payments resulting from the reversals of temporary differences are uncertain, deferred taxes should be excluded from both liabilities and equity.

c. The portion of the deferred tax liability that represents (the present value of) expected payments should be treated as debt. Accounting-based timing differences that are not expected to reverse should be treated as equity.

5. {M} We begin by determining the cost of each asset using the information about asset L. Year 2 depreciation under the sum-of-the-years' digits method with a five-year life is 4/15ths. Therefore, the depreciable base (cost − salvage value) must be \$12,000/(4/15) = \$45,000 and the cost must be \$48,000 because salvage value is \$3,000. We can now prepare a depreciation schedule for each method:

Depreciation Expense

Year	Asset K Straight-line[1]	Asset L SYD[2]	Asset M DDB[3]
1	\$ 9,000	\$15,000	\$19,200
2	9,000	12,000	11,520
3	9,000	9,000	6,912
4	9,000	6,000	4,147
5	9,000	3,000	3,221
Total	\$45,000	\$45,000	\$45,000

[1] Base = \$45,000 (cost − salvage value); expense = \$45,000/5 = \$9,000.

[2] Base = \$45,000; expense = 5/15ths, 4/15ths, 3/15ths, etc.

[3] Base = \$48,000 (salvage value ignored); rate = 40%

Year 1 expense = .40 × \$48,000 = \$19,200, leaving \$28,800

Year 2 expense = .40 × \$28,800 = \$11,520, leaving \$17,280

Year 3 expense = .40 × \$17,280 = \$6,912, leaving \$10,368

Year 4 expense = .40 × \$10,368 = \$4,147, leaving \$6,221

Year 5 expense = \$3,221 leaving \$3,000

a. The double declining balance method is used on the tax return for all three assets; year 2 depreciation expense under that method is **\$11,520.**

b. Financial statement depreciation expense in year two (from the table above) is:

Asset K (straight line)	**\$ 9,000**
Asset M (double declining balance)	**11,520**

c. (i) At the end of year two, accumulated depreciation equals (from the table above):

Asset K (straight line)	$18,000
Asset L (SYD)	27,000
Asset M (DDB)	30,720
Tax return (DDB)	30,720

Therefore, the deferred tax liability is:

Asset K: .34 ($30,720 − $18,000) = **$4,324.80**

Asset L: .34 ($30,720 − $27,000) = **1,264.80**

Asset M: No deferred tax as the same method is used for financial and tax reporting.

(ii) At the end of year five, accumulated depreciation is the same under all methods and there is no deferred tax asset or liability.

6. {S} a. b. Assuming that Mother Prewitt continues to buy machines in the future, the depreciation timing difference will never reverse and there is no expected cash consequence. In this case, the deferred tax can be treated as equity.

If the installment sale is not expected to recur, the tax on that sale will be paid in 2001 and will require cash. For that reason, the $27,200 of deferred taxes should be considered a liability when calculating liquidity, solvency, and leverage ratios.

If, on the other hand, installment sales are expected to recur, such sales are no different from the depreciation case. The cash consequences of deferred tax items depend on the probability of their reversal, not on their nature.

c. Under SFAS 109 (liability method), enacted changes in tax rates are recognized, and the deferred tax liabilities must be restated to amounts based on the 40% tax rate. The incremental liability is recorded as a component of income tax expense regardless of when (or if) paid.

SOLUTIONS TO PROBLEMS IN READING 43

1. {S} a. When full-coupon debt is issued, interest paid reduces cash from operations (CFO). When zero-coupon debt is issued, however, no cash interest is paid. CFO is unaffected, and is therefore higher than when full-coupon debt is issued. In addition, when imputed interest on zero-coupon debt is tax deductible, CFO is further increased by the tax benefit.

b. When full-coupon debt is issued, the proceeds are included in cash from financing (CFF). When that debt matures, the amount paid reduces CFF. Assuming the debt is issued and redeemed at par, the net effect on CFF is zero over the life of the debt.

Zero-coupon debt is issued at a discount; CFF is below the full-coupon case. However at maturity the full face amount is paid (same as full-coupon case). The net amount of CFF (outflow) is therefore greater than when full-coupon debt is issued.

c. No effect.

d. Interest on the zero-coupon bond rises each year as the carrying amount rises, increasing the base on which each year's interest expense is computed. All other things being equal, net income declines each year.

2. {M} a. Proceeds equal $\$100{,}000/(1.12)^5 = \$56{,}742$

b.	**2000**	**2001**	**2002**	**2003**	**2004**
EBIT	$50,000	$50,000	$50,000	$50,000	$50,000
CFO before interest & taxes	60,000	60,000	60,000	60,000	60,000
Interest expense	6,809	7,626	8,541	9,566	10,714
CFO	60,000	60,000	60,000	60,000	60,000
Times interest earned	7.34	6.56	5.85	5.23	4.67
Times interest earned (cash basis)	[Infinite, since no interest is paid. In 2004, when the bond is retired, the payment will be reported as a financing cash outflow.]				

c. For a full-coupon bond, annual interest expense paid in cash would be $\$56{,}742 \times .12 = \$6{,}809$

	2000	**2001**	**2002**	**2003**	**2004**
EBIT	$50,000	$50,000	$50,000	$50,000	$50,000
CFO before interest & taxes	60,000	60,000	60,000	60,000	60,000
Interest expense	6,809	6,809	6,809	6,809	6,809
CFO	53,191	53,191	53,191	53,191	53,191
Times interest earned	7.34	7.34	7.34	7.34	7.34
Times interest earned (cash basis)	8.81	8.81	8.81	8.81	8.81

d. Cash flow from operations is higher when zero-coupon bonds are issued because interest is never reported as an operating cash outflow. [Note the infinite cash-basis coverage ratio.] Interest coverage, however, is lower after the first year, and declines as interest expense increases over time, reflecting the steadily increasing principal amount. Full-coupon bonds (if sold at par) result in a constant cash outflow from operations and constant interest expense. Given the Null Company's "steady state," the interest coverage ratio is constant on both accrual and cash flow bases.

e. Given the tax deductibility of accrued but unpaid interest on zero-coupon bonds, cash flow from operations will be higher for both cases. The reported cash flow differences will remain unchanged. For the zero-coupon case, cash flow from operations is even more misleading as the firm must generate sufficient cash from operations to repay the debt at maturity. The obligation must be repaid, regardless of its cash flow classification.

3. {S} a. Interest expense = Interest paid + change in bond discount
\$8,562 = \$7,200 + \$1,362

b. = Market rate × [face value − discount]
= .12 × [face value − \$8,652]

Therefore, face value = (\$8,562/.12) + \$8,652 = **\$80,000**

c. Coupon rate = interest paid/face value = \$7,200/\$80,000 = **9%**

4. {S} a. The advantage is that, when Takeda's share price rose, the debt was converted into equity, strengthening the balance sheet. As convertible notes are issued with a conversion price that exceeds the then market price, the company effectively sold common shares at a premium. In addition, because of the conversion feature, the interest rate would have been below the rate required by nonconvertible notes.

The disadvantage is that the debt was converted into common shares at a time when Takeda could have sold new shares at a much higher price, obtaining the same capital at a lower cost.

b. Reported data (Yen millions)

	1998	1999
Total debt	44,482	21,338
Equity	829,381	907,373
Total capital	873,863	928,711
Debt/total capital	5.1%	2.3%

The more than 50% debt decrease was the largest factor reducing the debt/total capital ratio.

c. As the market price of Takeda shares was well above the conversion price in 1998, the convertible debt should be classified as equity. After that adjustment (subtracting 22,000 from debt and adding the same amount to equity) Takeda's debt was virtually unchanged from 1998 to 1999 and the decline in the debt/total capital ratio was small:

Adjusted data (Yen millions)

	1998
Total debt	22,482
Equity	851,381
Total capital	873,863
Debt/total capital	2.6%

This analysis underscores the discussion in the reading; the analyst must classify convertible debt based on market considerations. Proper classification results in a more appropriate leverage measure.

5. {S} a. An argument for inclusion is that, for Fannie Mae, the issuance and retirement of debt are recurring operating activities whose consequences should be included in operating earnings.

An argument for exclusion is that gains or losses from debt repurchase reflect economic changes during the entire period the debt was outstanding and should not be included in operating earnings for the period in which management chose to realize the gain.

b. An argument for including the hedging loss is that hedging activities are part of Fannie Mae's normal operating activities.

An argument for exclusion is that the hedging loss was unusually large and inclusion distorts the trend of operating earnings.

c. We believe that gains and losses from debt retirement should be excluded from operating earnings for most firms. These gains and losses result from management decisions and because (as discussed in the reading) refinancing may not yield any economic gain or loss despite the accounting gain or loss. Hedging results should be included in operating earnings as hedging gains and losses should offset other economic effects that are also included.

However, Fannie Mae may be an exception. As stated in part a, the company routinely issues and retires debt, suggesting that gains and losses should be included in operating earnings. Before doing so, the analyst should try to determine whether the gains or losses for the particular quarter are unusual or reflect interest rate changes over multiple periods, suggesting that the gains or losses should (analytically) be spread over several quarters.

SOLUTIONS TO PROBLEMS IN READING 44

1. **{S} a.** Interest expense = 12% × $10,000 (beginning balance of lease obligation) = $1,200.

   b. The lease obligation will be reduced by $100 ($1,300 − $1,200) leaving an obligation of $9,900.

   c. Cash from Operations will be reduced by the interest payment of $1,200. Cash from investing activities will not be affected. (However, the firm will report the capital lease as a "noncash investment and financing activity." Cash from financing will be reduced by the amount of the principal payment of $100.

   d. Under an operating lease there is no lease obligation on the balance sheet. The only effect on income is Rent Expense of $1,300. Similarly, CFO is reduced by $1,300. (CFI and CFF are not affected).

2. **{M} a.** The following states the effects of Tolrem using the capital lease method as compared with the operating lease method.

   (i) Cash from operations is higher as only the interest portion of lease expense is deducted from operating cash flows; total lease expense is deducted for operating leases.

   (ii) Financing cash flow is lower for capital lease, as part of lease rental is treated as amortization of liability and classified as financing cash outflow.

   (iii) Investing cash flow is not affected by the lease treatment. However, the firm will report capital leases in the statement of cash flows (or a footnote) as noncash investment activities.

   (iv) Net cash flow reflects the actual rental payment and is unaffected by the financial reporting treatment of the lease.

   (v) Debt/equity ratio is higher for capital lease, as it records the present value of minimum lease payments as debt *and* reduces net income (and therefore equity) in first year.

   (vi) Interest coverage ratio is usually (not always) lower for capital lease method, which reports interest expense but also higher EBIT, see (vii). For coverage ratios well above 1.0, the ratio will decline. If the increase in interest expense exceeds the increase in EBIT, the ratio will decline even for firms with very low coverage ratios.

3. {M} a. All amounts in $ millions

	1997	1998	1999
Receivables reported	$664.0	$ 720.0	$ 739.0
Receivables sold	—	38.4	50.0
Adjusted receivables	$664.0	$ 758.4	$ 789.0
Average receivables			
as reported		692.0	729.5
adjusted		711.2	773.7
Sales		$4,537.0	$3,867.0
Receivable turnover			
Reported		6.56	5.30
Adjusted		6.38	5.00
# of days receivable			
Reported		56 days	69 days
Adjusted		57 days	73 days
Cash cycle effect		**1 day**	**4 days**

The sale of receivables allowed the company to show an improved receivable turnover and cash cycle; the improvement was more significant for 1999 as the amount of receivables sold increased and sales declined.

b. The effect on the current ratio is minimal as the same amount is added to both numerator and denominator of the ratio and that ratio is close to 1. The debt-to-equity ratio adjustment is more significant in 1999 due to the increase in receivables sold and the lower equity amount.

	1998	1999
Current assets	$1,673.0	$1,615.0
Current liabilities	1,492.0	1,472.0
Current ratio	**1.121**	**1.097**
Adjusted (add receivables sold)		
Current assets	$1,711.4	$1,665.0
Current liabilities	1,530.4	1,522.0
Current ratio adjusted	**1.118**	**1.094**
Debt reported	$ 963.0	$ 961.0
Debt adjusted	1,001.4	1,011.0
Equity	572.0	376.0
Debt-to-equity reported	**1.68**	**2.56**
Debt-to-equity adjusted	**1.75**	**2.69**

c. As the calculation below indicates, both the level and trend in CFO are overstated as a result of the sale of receivables.

	1997	1998	1999
CFO as reported	$(113.0)	$(59.0)	$ (6.0)
Change in receivables sold	—	38.4	11.6
CFO adjusted	$(113.0)	$(97.4)	$(17.6)

4. {M} a. Debt should be increased by:

$20 million	(present value of operating lease)
5	(guarantee)
7	(present value of take-or-pay agreement)
$32 million	

There is no effect on equity as each obligation is offset by a correspon-ding asset:

Leased assets for operating lease
Receivable for Crockett's obligation to repay debt
Supply agreement

The recomputed debt-to-equity ratio is:
($12 + $32)/$20 = **2.2X** as compared to .6X before adjustment

b. Additional interest expense is:

Lease (effective interest rate is about 18%)

	.18 × $20 = $3.6 million
Bond guarantee	.10 × 5 = 0.5
Total	$4.1 million

Before adjustment, the interest expense is $1.0 million and the times interest earned ratio is 5.0, implying EBIT of $5.0 million.

After adjustment, the ratio is:
($5.0 + $4.1)/($1.0 + $4.1) = **1.78X**

No adjustment has been made for the take-or-pay contract, as it does not affect 1993 interest expense. Adjustments in future years will be based on the implicit interest rate of 21%.

c. Reasons for entering into off-balance-sheet obligations:

1. Avoidance of or mitigation of the risk of violating debt covenant restrictions.
2. Leased assets revert to lessor after eight years, limiting risk of obsolescence.
3. Guarantee of Crockett's debt may lower interest costs, increasing profitability of investment.
4. Contract with PEPE secures source of supply and possibly advantageous pricing.

d. Additional information needed for full evaluation:

1. (Lease) Useful life of leased assets; conditions under which lease can be canceled; nature of leased assets.
2. (Guarantee) Financial condition of Crockett; bond covenants.
3. (Take-or-pay) Alternate sources of supply; quantity to be purchased relative to total needs; price provisions of contract.

5. {M}

	1st Year	9th Year
a. Assets	Higher	Higher
b. Revenues	Higher	Lower
c. Expenses	Higher	Lower
d. Asset turnover ratio	Higher	Lower
e. Interest income	Higher	Higher
f. Cost of goods sold	Higher	No effect
g. Net income	Higher	Lower
h. Retained earnings	Higher	Higher
i. Taxes paid	No effect	No effect
j. Post-tax ROA	Higher	Lower
k. Cash from operations	Higher	Lower
l. Investment cash flow	Lower	Higher

Assets are higher because inventory is replaced with (higher) receivables because of the recognition of manufacturing profit. Assets remain higher throughout the lease term.

Revenues are higher in Year 1 as the sales-type lease recognizes a sale whereas the operating lease method does not. In later years, interest revenue from the sales-type lease should be lower than lease revenue for the operating lease. This effect is more pronounced over time; in year 9, interest income is low given the small remaining receivable. The revenue effect increases the asset turnover ratio in the first year. But the revenue effect reduces turnover in the ninth year.

Expenses are higher in year 1 due to the recognition of cost of goods sold. In later years, there is no expense for the sales-type lease; the operating lease method reports depreciation expense in every year, however.

Initial period income and income-related ratios are higher for the sales-type lease because the sale (and income) is recognized at the inception of the lease. In later years, however, income is higher for the operating lease.

Income taxes paid are the same since the lease cannot be considered a completed sale for tax purposes.

Cash from operations is higher for the first year due to recognition of the sale (the investment in the lease is classified as an investing cash outflow). In later years the operating lease method shows higher cash from operations as rental income exceeds the interest income recorded for the sales-type lease (income taxes paid are the same).

GLOSSARY

Abnormal rate of return The amount by which a security's return differs from its expected rate of return based on the market's rate of return and the security's relationship with the market.

Absolute advantage A situation in which a nation, as the result of its previous experience and/or natural endowments, can produce more of a good (with the same amount of resources) than another nation.

Absolute dispersion The amount of variability present without comparison to any reference point or benchmark.

Absolute frequency The number of observations in a given interval (for grouped data).

Accelerated method A method of depreciation that allocates relatively large amounts of the depreciable cost of an asset to earlier years and reduced amounts to later years.

Accounting beta method A method of estimating a project's beta by running a regression of the company's return on assets against the average return on assets for a large sample of firms.

Accounting estimates Estimates of items such as the useful lives of assets, warranty costs, and the amount of uncollectible receivables.

Accounting profits The sales revenues minus the expenses of a firm over a designated time period, usually one year. Accounting profits typically make allowances for changes in the firm's inventories and depreciation of its assets. No allowance is made, however, for the opportunity cost of the equity capital of the firm's owners, or other implicit costs.

Accounting risk The risk associated with accounting standards that vary from country to country or with any uncertainty about how certain transactions should be recorded.

Accrued interest (1) Interest earned but not yet due and payable. This is equal to the next coupon to be paid on a bond multiplied by the time elapsed since the last payment date and divided by the total coupon period. Exact conventions differ across bond markets. (2) Interest earned but not yet paid.

Accumulation phase Phase in the investment life cycle during which individuals in the early-to-middle years of their working career attempt to accumulate assets to satisfy short-term needs and longer-term goals.

Active factor risk The contribution to active risk squared resulting from the portfolio's different-than-benchmark exposures relative to factors specified in the risk model.

Active return The return on a portfolio minus the return on the portfolio's benchmark.

Active risk The standard deviation of active returns.

Active risk squared The variance of active returns; active risk raised to the second power.

Active specific risk or asset selection risk The contribution to active risk squared resulting from the portfolio's active weights on individual assets as those weights interact with assets' residual risk.

Activist strategy Deliberate changes in monetary and fiscal policy in order to inject demand stimulus during a recession and apply restraint during an inflationary boom and thereby, it is hoped, minimize economic instability.

Actuarial rate of return The discount rate used to find the present value of a defined benefit pension plan's future obligations and thus determine the size of the firm's annual contribution to the plan.

Actuarial yield The total yield on a bond, obtained by setting the bond's current market value equal to the discounted cash flows promised by the bond. Also called yield to maturity.

Adaptive-expectations hypothesis The hypothesis that economic decision makers base their future expectations on actual outcomes observed during recent periods. For example, according to this view, the rate of inflation actually experienced during the past two or three years would be the major determinant of the rate of inflation expected for the next year.

Addition An enlargement to the physical layout of a plant asset.

Addition rule for probabilities A principle stating that the probability that A or B occurs (both occur) equals the probability that A occurs, plus the probability that B occurs, minus the probability that both A and B occur.

Add-on interest A procedure for determining the interest on a bond or loan in which the interest is added onto the face value of a contract.

Adjusted beta Historical beta adjusted to reflect the tendency of beta to be mean reverting.

Adjusted R^2 A measure of goodness-of-fit of a regression that is adjusted for degrees of freedom and hence does not automatically increase when another independent variable is added to a regression.

Administrative lag The time period after the need for a policy change is recognized but before the policy is actually implemented.

After-tax Cost of Debt, $k_d(1 - T)$ The relevant cost of new debt, taking into account the tax deductibility of interest; used to calculate the WACC.

Agency problem A potential conflict of interest between the agent (manager) and (1) the outside stockholders or (2) the creditors (debtholders).

Agency trade A trade in which a broker acts as an agent only, not taking a position on the opposite side of the trade.

Aggregate demand curve A downward-sloping curve indicating an inverse relationship between the price level and the quantity of domestically produced goods and services that households, business firms, governments, and foreigners (net exports) are willing to purchase during a period.

Aggregate supply curve A curve indicating the relationship between the nation's price level and quantity of goods supplied by its producers. In the short run, it is probably an upward-sloping curve, but in the long run most economists believe the aggregate supply curve is vertical (or nearly so).

AIMR The Association for Investment Management and Research (AIMR®) awards the CFA® certification and sets professional standards that must be applied by its members worldwide.

Allocative efficiency The allocation of resources to the production of goods and services most desired by consumers, at the lowest possible cost.

Alternative hypothesis The hypothesis accepted when the null hypothesis is rejected.

American Depositary Receipt (ADR) (1) A certificate of ownership issued by a U.S. bank to promote local trading in a foreign stock. The U.S. bank holds the foreign shares and issues ADRs against them. (2) Certificates of ownership issued by a U.S. bank that represent indirect ownership of a certain number of shares of a specific foreign firm. Shares are held on deposit in a bank in the firm's home country.

American option (1) An option contract that can be exercised at any time until its expiration date. (2) An option that can be exercised on any day through the expiration day. Also referred to as American-style exercise.

American terms With reference to U.S. dollar exchange rate quotations, the U.S. dollar price of a unit of another currency.

Amortization The periodic allocation of the cost of an intangible asset to the periods it benefits.

Amortizing and accreting swaps A swap in which the notional principal changes according to a formula related to changes in the underlying.

Analysis effect The difference in performance of a bond portfolio from that of a chosen index due to acquisition of temporarily mispriced issues that then move to their correct prices.

Analysis of variance (ANOVA) The analysis of the total variability of a dataset (such as observations on the dependent variable in a regression) into components representing different sources of variation; with reference to regression, ANOVA provides the inputs for an F-test of the significance of the regression as a whole.

Annual percentage rate The cost of borrowing expressed as a yearly rate.

Annuity A finite set of level sequential cash flows.

Annuity due An annuity having a first cash flow that is paid immediately.

Anomalies Security price relationships that appear to contradict a well-regarded hypothesis; in this case, the efficient market hypothesis.

Anticipated change A change that is foreseen by decision makers in time for them to adjust.

Anticipated inflation An increase in the general level of prices that was expected by most decision makers.

Appreciation An increase in the value of the domestic currency relative to foreign currencies. An appreciation increases the purchasing power of the domestic currency for foreign goods.

A priori probability A probability based on logical analysis rather than on observation or personal judgment.

Arbitrage (1) The simultaneous purchase of an undervalued asset or portfolio and sale of an overvalued but equivalent asset or portfolio, in order to obtain a riskless profit on the price differential. Taking advantage of a market inefficiency in a risk-free manner. (2) A trading strategy designed to generate a guaranteed profit from a transaction that requires no capital commitment or risk bearing on the part of the trader. A simple example of an arbitrage trade would be the simultaneous purchase and sale of the same security in different markets at different prices. (3) The condition in a financial market in which equivalent assets or combinations of assets sell for two different prices, creating an opportunity to profit at no risk with no commitment of money. In a well-functioning financial market, few arbitrage opportunities are possible. Equivalent to the law of one price. (4) A risk-free operation that earns an expected positive net profit but requires no net investment of money.

Arbitrage approach A common approach used to value derivative securities, based on an arbitrage strategy involving the underlying securities.

Arbitrage opportunity An opportunity to conduct an arbitrage; an opportunity to earn an expected positive net profit without risk and with no net investment of money.

Arbitrage portfolio The portfolio that exploits an arbitrage opportunity.

Arbitrage pricing theory (APT) A theory that posits that the expected return to a financial asset can be described by its relationship with several common risk factors. The APT can be contrasted with the single-factor CAPM.

Arithmetic mean (AM) (1) A measure of mean annual rates of return equal to the sum of annual holding period rates of return divided by the number of years. (2) The sum of the observations divided by the number of observations.

Arrears swap A type of interest rate swap in which the floating payment is set at the end of the period and the interest is paid at that same time.

Asian call option A European-style option with a value at maturity equal to the difference between the stock price at maturity and the average stock price during the life of the option, or $0, whichever is greater.

Ask price The price at which a market maker is willing to sell a security (also called offer price).

Asset allocation (1) Dividing of investment funds among several asset classes to achieve diversification. (2) The process of deciding how to distribute an investor's wealth among different asset classes for investment purposes.

Asset class Securities that have similar characteristics, attributes, and risk/return relationships.

Asset impairment Loss of revenue-generating potential of a long-lived asset before the end of its useful life; the difference between an asset's carrying value and its fair value, as measured by the present value of the expected cash flows.

Assets under management (AUM) The total market value of the assets managed by an investment firm.

Asymmetric Information The situation in which managers have different (better) information about firms' prospects than do investors.

At-the-money option An option for which the strike (or exercise) price is close to (at) the current market price of the underlying asset.

Attribution analysis An assessment technique designed to establish whether a manager's performance relative to a benchmark resulted from market timing or security selection skills.

Autocorrelation The correlation of a time series with its own past values.

Autocorrelation test A test of the efficient market hypothesis that compares security price changes over time to check for predictable correlation patterns.

Automatic stabilizers Built-in features that tend automatically to promote a budget deficit during a recession and a budget surplus during an inflationary boom, even without a change in policy.

Automation A production technique that reduces the amount of labor required to produce a good or service. It is beneficial to adopt the new labor-saving technology only if it reduces the cost of production.

Autonomous expenditures Expenditures that do not vary with the level of income. They are determined by factors (such as business expectations and economic policy) that are outside the basic income-expenditure model.

Autoregressive (AR) model A time series regressed on its own past values, in which the independent variable is a lagged value of the dependent variable.

Average fixed cost Total fixed cost divided by the number of units produced. It always declines as output increases.

Average product The total product (output) divided by the number of units of the variable input required to produce that output level.

Average tax rate (ATR) (1) Tax liability divided by taxable income. It is the percentage of income paid in taxes. (2) A person's total tax payment divided by his or her total income.

Average total cost Total cost divided by the number of units produced. It is sometimes called per-unit cost.

Average variable cost The total variable cost divided by the number of units produced.

Back office Settlement and related processes.

Back simulation *See* Historical simulation method.

Backtest A method of testing a quantitative model in which computers are used to examine the composition and returns of portfolios based on historical data to determine if the selected strategy would have worked in the past.

Back-to-back Transactions in which a loan is made in one currency against a loan in another currency.

Backwardated A situation in a futures market where the current contract price is less than the current spot price for the underlying asset.

Backwardation A condition in the futures markets in which the benefits of holding an asset exceed the costs, leaving the futures price less than the spot price.

Balanced budget A situation in which current government revenue from taxes, fees, and other sources is just equal to current government expenditures.

Balanced fund A mutual fund with, generally, a three-part investment objective: (1) to conserve the investor's principal, (2) to pay current income, and (3) to increase both principal and income. The fund aims to achieve this by owning a mixture of bonds, preferred stocks, and common stocks.

Balance of merchandise trade The difference between the value of merchandise exports and the value of merchandise imports for a nation. The balance of merchandise trade is only one component of a nation's total balance of payments. Also called simply balance of trade or net exports.

Balance of payments (1) A summary of all economic transactions between a country and all other countries for a specific time period, usually a year. The balance-of-payments account reflects all payments and liabilities to foreigners (debits) and all payments and obligations received from foreigners (credits). (2) A record of all financial flows crossing the borders of a country during a given time period (a quarter or a year).

Balance of trade *See* Trade balance.

Balance on current account The import-export balance of goods and services, plus net investment income earned abroad, plus net private and government transfers. If the value of the nation's export-type items exceeds (is less than) the value of the nation's import-type items plus net unilateral transfers to foreigners, a current-account surplus (deficit) is present.

Balance on goods and services The exports of goods (merchandise) and services of a nation minus its imports of goods and services.

Balance sheet A financial statement that shows what assets the firm controls at a fixed point in time and how it has financed these assets.

Bank discount basis A quoting convention that annualizes, on a 360-day year, the discount as a percentage of face value.

Bank reserves Vault cash plus deposits of the bank with Federal Reserve banks.

Barriers to entry Obstacles that limit the freedom of potential rivals to enter and compete in an industry or market.

Base case An analysis in which all of the input variables are set at their most likely values.

Basic earnings per share Total earnings divided by the weighted average number of shares actually outstanding during the period.

Basis (1) The difference between the futures (or forward) price of an asset and its spot (or cash) price. The basis can be expressed as a value or as a percentage of the spot price. (2) The difference between the spot price of the underlying asset and the futures contract price at any point in time (e.g., the initial basis at the time of contract origination, the cover basis at the time of contract termination).

Basis of an asset For tax purposes, the cost of an asset.

Basis point One hundredth of 1 percent (0.01%).

Basis point value (BPV) Also called present value of a basis point or price value of a basis point (PVBP), the change in the bond price for a 1 basis point change in yield.

Basis risk (1) The risk that arises from fluctuation in the basis. (2) The residual exposure to the price volatility of an underlying asset that results from a cross hedge transaction.

Basis swap (1) An interest rate swap involving two floating rates. (2) A swap in which both parties pay a floating rate.

Bayes' formula A method for updating probabilities based on new information.

Bearer bond An unregistered bond for which ownership is determined by possession. The holder receives interest payments by clipping coupons attached to the security and sending them to the issuer for payment.

Bearer security A negotiable security. All cash flows paid on the security are remitted to its bearer. No register of ownership is kept by the issuing company.

Bear spread An option strategy that involves selling a put with a lower exercise price and buying a put with a higher exercise price. It can also be executed with calls.

Behavioral finance Involves the analysis of various psychological traits of individuals and how these traits affect how they act as investors, analysts, and portfolio managers.

Benchmark (1) A standard measurement used to evaluate the performance of a portfolio. The benchmark may be some passive index or the aggregate performance on a universe of comparable portfolios (*see* Composite). (2) A comparison portfolio; a point of reference or comparison.

Benchmark bond A bond representative of current market conditions and used for performance comparison.

Benchmark error Situation where an inappropriate or incorrect benchmark is used to compare and assess portfolio returns and management.

Benchmark portfolio A comparison standard of risk and assets included in the policy statement and similar to the investor's risk preference and investment needs, which can be used to evaluate the investment performance of the portfolio manager.

Benchmark value of the multiple In using the method of comparables, the value of a price multiple for the comparison asset; when we have comparison assets (a group), the mean or median value of the multiple for the group of assets.

Bernoulli random variable A random variable having the outcomes 0 and 1.

Bernoulli trial An experiment that can produce one of two outcomes.

Best-case scenario An analysis in which all of the input variables are set at their best reasonably forecasted values.

Beta (β) (1) A statistical measure of market risk on a portfolio; traditionally used to estimate the elasticity of a stock portfolio's return relative to the market index. (2) A standardized measure of systematic risk based upon an asset's covariance with the market portfolio. (3) A measure of the relationship between the return on a stock portfolio and the return on the market portfolio, which is a portfolio containing all risky assets in the market. (4) A measure of an asset's sensitivity to movements in the market.

Betterment An improvement that does not add to the physical layout of the plant.

Bid-ask spread The difference between the quoted ask and the bid prices.

Bid price The price at which a market maker is willing to buy a security.

Bilateral arbitrage With reference to currencies, an arbitrage involving two currencies only.

Bill-and-hold basis Sales on a bill-and-hold basis involve selling products but not delivering those products until a later date.

Binomial model A model for pricing options in which the underlying price can move to only one of two possible new prices.

Binomial option pricing model A valuation equation that assumes the price of the underlying asset changes through a series of discrete upward or downward movements.

Binomial random variable The number of successes in n Bernoulli trials for which the probability of success is constant for all trials and the trials are independent.

Binomial tree (1) A diagram representing price movements of the underlying in a binomial model. (2) The graphical representation of a model of asset price dynamics in which, at each period, the asset moves up with probability p or down with probability $(1 - p)$.

Bird-in-the-hand theory MM's name for the theory that a firm's value will be maximized by setting a high dividend payout ratio.

Black market A market that operates outside the legal system, either by selling illegal goods or by selling goods at illegal prices or terms.

Black-Scholes or Black-Scholes-Merton formula A standard option pricing formula derived by F. Black and M. Scholes and also by R. Merton.

Block Orders to buy or sell that are too large for the liquidity ordinarily available in dealer networks or stock exchanges.

Bond A long-term debt security with contractual obligations regarding interest payments and redemption.

Bond-equivalent basis A basis for stating an annual yield that annualizes a semiannual yield by doubling it.

Bond-equivalent yield The yield to maturity on a basis that ignores compounding.

Bond option An option in which the underlying is a bond; primarily traded in over-the-counter markets.

Bond price volatility The percentage changes in bond prices over time.

Bond swap An active bond portfolio management strategy that exchanges one position for another to take advantage of some difference between them.

Book value of equity (or book value) (1) Shareholders' equity (total assets minus total liabilities) minus the value of preferred stock; common shareholders' equity. (2) The accounting value of a firm.

Book value per share Book value of equity divided by the number of common shares outstanding.

Bottom-up investing With respect to investment approaches, a focus on selecting individual securities with whatever allocation of money to asset classes, countries, or industry securities results.

Bourse A French term often used to refer to a stock market.

Box spread An option strategy that combines a bull spread and a bear spread having two different exercise prices, which produces a risk-free payoff of the difference in the exercise prices.

Brand name A registered name that can be used only by its owner to identify a product or service.

Brady bonds Bonds issued by emerging countries under a debt-reduction plan named after Mr. Brady, former U.S. Secretary of the Treasury.

Break-even exchange rate The future exchange rate such that the return in two bond markets would be even for a given maturity. Also called implied forward exchange rate.

Breakeven point The volume of sales at which total costs equal total revenues, causing operating profits (or EBIT) to equal zero.

Break Point (BP) The dollar value of new capital that can be raised before an increase in the firm's weighted average cost of capital occurs.

Bretton Woods The site of a 1944 conference that led to the establishment of a semifixed exchange rate system.

Breusch–Pagan test A test for conditional heteroskedasticity in the error term of a regression.

Broker (1) An agent who executes orders to buy or sell securities on behalf of a client in exchange for a commission. (2) *See* Futures commission merchants.

Budget constraint The constraint that separates the bundles of goods that the consumer can purchase from those that cannot be purchased, given a limited income and the prices of the products.

Budget deficit A situation in which total government spending exceeds total government revenue during a specific time period, usually one year.

Budget surplus A situation in which total government spending is less than total government revenue during a time period, usually a year.

Bull floating-rate note A floating-rate note whose coupon increases if interest rates drop; an inverse floater.

Bull spread An option strategy that involves buying a call with a lower exercise price and selling a call with a higher exercise price. It can also be executed with puts.

Business cycle Fluctuations in the general level of economic activity as measured by such variables as the rate of unemployment and changes in real GDP.

Business risk The variability of operating income arising from the characteristics of the firm's industry. Two sources of business risk are sales variability and operating leverage.

Butterfly spread An option strategy that combines two bull or bear spreads and has three exercise prices.

Buy-and-hold strategy A passive portfolio management strategy in which bonds are bought and held to maturity.

Call An option that gives the holder the right to buy an underlying asset from another party at a fixed price over a specific period of time.

Call auction *See* Fixing.

Call market A market in which trading for individual stocks only takes place at specified times. All the bids and asks available at the time are combined and the market administrators specify a single price that will possibly clear the market at that time.

Call option (1) A contract giving the right to buy an asset at a specific price on or before a specified date. (2) Option to buy an asset within a certain period at a specified price called the exercise price.

Call premium Amount above par issuer must pay to bondholder for retiring the bond before its stated maturity.

Call provisions Specifies when and how a firm can issue a call for bonds outstanding prior to their maturity.

Cannibalization Occurs when the introduction of a new product causes sales of existing projects to decline.

Cap (1) A contract on an interest rate, whereby at periodic payment dates, the writer of the cap pays the difference between the market interest rate and a specified cap rate if, and only if, this difference is positive. This is equivalent to a stream of call options on the interest rate. (2) A combination of interest rate call options designed to hedge a borrower against rate increases on a floating-rate loan.

Cap agreement A contract that on each settlement date pays the holder the greater of the difference between the reference rate and the cap rate or zero; it is equivalent to a series of call options on the reference rate.

Capital Man-made resources (such as tools, equipment, and structures) that are used to produce other goods and services. Resources that enhance our ability to produce output in the future.

Capital account (1) The record of transactions with foreigners that involve either (a) the exchange of ownership rights to real or financial assets or (b) the extension of loans. (2) A component of the balance of payments that reflects unrequited (or unilateral) transfers corresponding to capital flows entailing no compensation (in the form of goods, services, or assets). Examples include investment capital given (without future repayment) in favor of poor countries, debt forgiveness, and expropriation losses.

Capital allocation line (CAL) A graph line that describes the combinations of expected return and standard deviation of return available to an investor from combining the optimal portfolio of risky assets with the risk-free asset.

Capital appreciation A return objective in which the investor seeks to increase the portfolio value, primarily through capital gains, over time to meet a future need rather than dividend yield.

Capital asset pricing model (CAPM) (1) An equilibrium theory that relates the expected return of an asset to its market risk (*see* Beta). (2) A theory concerned with deriving the expected or required rates of return on risky assets based on the assets' systematic risk levels. (3) An equation describing the expected return on any asset (or portfolio) as a linear function of its beta.

Capital budgeting The process of planning expenditures on assets whose cash flows are expected to extend beyond one year.

Capital component One of the types of capital used by firms to make money.

Capital expenditure An expenditure for the purchase or expansion of a long-term asset, recorded in an asset account.

Capitalism An economic system based on private ownership of productive resources and allocation of goods according to the signals provided by market prices.

Capital market instruments Fixed-income or equity investments that trade in the secondary market.

Capital market line (CML) (1) The line from the intercept point that represents the risk-free rate tangent to the original efficient frontier; it becomes the new efficient frontier since investments on this line dominate all the portfolios on the original Markowitz efficient frontier. (2) A form of the capital allocation line in which investors share identical expectations about the mean returns, variance of returns, and correlations of risky assets.

Capital preservation A return objective in which the investor seeks to minimize the risk of loss; generally a goal of the risk-averse investor.

Capital rationing A situation in which a constraint is placed on the total size of the firm's capital budget.

Capital structure A company's specific mixture of long-term financing.

Caplet Each component call option in a cap.

Capped swap A swap in which the floating payments have an upper limit.

Carrying value The unexpired part of the cost of an asset, not its market value. Also called *book value.*

Cartel An organization of sellers designed to coordinate supply decisions so that the joint profits of the members will be maximized. A cartel will seek to create a monopoly in the market.

Cash-and-carry arbitrage An arbitrage strategy with a simultaneous spot purchase and forward sale of an asset. The reverse transaction (borrowing the asset, selling it spot, and buying it forward) is known as a reverse cash and carry, or as a carry-and-cash arbitrage. These arbitrages lead to a relation between spot and forward, or futures, prices of the same asset.

Cash flow additivity principle The principle that dollar amounts indexed at the same point in time are additive.

Cash flow at risk (CFAR) A variation of VAR that reflects the risk of a company's cash flow instead of its market value.

Cash price or spot price The price for immediate purchase of the underlying asset.

Cash settlement (1) A procedure for settling futures contracts in which the cash difference between the futures price and the spot price is paid instead of physical delivery. (2) A procedure used in certain derivative transactions that specifies that the long and short parties engage in the equivalent cash value of a delivery transaction.

CD equivalent yield *See* Money market yield.

Central bank An institution that regulates the banking system and controls the supply of money of a country.

Centralized risk management or companywide risk management When a company has a single risk management group that monitors and controls all of the risk-taking activities of the organization. Centralization permits economies of scale and allows a company to use some of its risks to offset other risks. *See also* Enterprise risk management.

Central limit theorem A result in statistics that states that the sample mean computed from large samples of size n from a population with finite variance will follow an approximate normal distribution with a mean equal to the population mean and a variance equal to the population variance divided by n.

Certificates of deposit (CDs) Instruments issued by banks and S&Ls that require minimum deposits for specified terms and that pay higher rates of interest than deposit accounts.

Ceteris paribus A Latin term meaning "other things constant," used when the effect of one change is being described, recognizing that if other things changed, they also could affect the result. Economists often describe the effects of one change, knowing that in the real world, other things might change and also exert an effect.

Chain rule of forecasting A forecasting process in which the next period's value as predicted by the forecasting equation is substituted into the right-hand side of the equation to give a predicted value two periods ahead.

Change in net working capital The increased current assets resulting from a new project, minus the spontaneous increase in accounts payable and accruals.

Characteristic line Regression line that indicates the systematic risk of a risky asset.

Cheapest to deliver A bond in which the amount received for delivering the bond is largest compared with the amount paid in the market for the bond.

Cherry-picking When a bankrupt company is allowed to enforce contracts that are favorable to it while walking away from contracts that are unfavorable to it.

Choice The act of selecting among alternatives.

Civilian labor force The number of persons 16 years of age and over who are either employed or unemployed. In order to be classified as unemployed, one must be looking for a job.

Classical economists Economists from Adam Smith to the time of Keynes who focused their analyses on economic efficiency and production. With regard to business instability, they thought market prices and wages would decline during a recession quickly enough to bring the economy back to full employment within a short period of time.

Clean price The price of a bond obtained as the total price of the bond minus accrued interest. Most bonds are traded on the basis of their clean price.

Clearinghouse (1) An organization that settles and guarantees trades in some financial markets. (2) An entity associated with a futures market that acts as middleman between the contracting parties and guarantees to each party the performance of the other.

Clientele Effect The tendency of a firm to attract a set of investors who like its dividend policy.

Closed-end fund An investment company with a fixed number of shares. New shares cannot be issued and the old shares cannot be redeemed. Shares are traded in the marketplace, and their value may differ from the underlying net asset value of the fund.

Closed-end investment company An investment company that issues only a limited number of shares, which it does not redeem (buy back). Instead, shares of a closed-end fund are traded in securities markets at prices determined by supply and demand.

Closeout netting Netting the market values of all derivative contracts between two parties to determine one overall value owed by one party to another in the event of bankruptcy.

Coefficient of variation (CV) (1) A measure of relative variability that indicates risk per unit of return. It is equal to: standard deviation divided by the mean value. When used in investments, it is equal to: standard deviation of returns divided by the expected rate of return. (2) The ratio of a set of observations' standard deviation to the observations' mean value.

Coincident indicators A set of economic variables whose values reach peaks and troughs at about the same time as the aggregate economy.

Cointegrated Describes two time series that have a long-term financial or economic relationship such that they do not diverge from each other without bound in the long run.

Collar (1) A combination of a cap and a floor. (2) An option strategy involving the purchase of a put and sale of a call in which the holder of an asset gains protection below a certain level, the exercise price of the put, and pays for it by giving up gains above a certain level, the exercise price of the call. Collars also can be used to provide protection against rising interest rates on a floating-rate loan by giving up gains from lower interest rates.

Collar agreement A hedging arrangement where an underlying asset is protected against decreases in value by the simultaneous purchase of a put option and sale of a call option.

Collateral trust bonds A mortgage bond wherein the assets backing the bond are financial assets like stocks and bonds.

Collateralized mortgage obligation (CMO) A debt security based on a pool of mortgage loans that provides a relatively stable stream of payments for a relatively predictable term.

Collective decision making The method of organization that relies on public-sector decision making (voting, political bargaining, lobbying, and so on) to resolve basic issues.

Collusion Agreement among firms to avoid various competitive practices, particularly price reductions. It may involve either formal agreements or merely tacit recognition that competitive practices will be self-defeating in the long run. Tacit collusion is difficult to detect. In the United States, antitrust laws prohibit collusion and conspiracies to restrain trade.

Combination A listing in which the order of the listed items does not matter.

Commercial banks Financial institutions that offer a wide range of services (for example, checking accounts, savings accounts, and extension of loans) to their customers. Commercial banks are owned by stockholders and seek to operate at a profit.

Commercial paper Unsecured short-term corporate debt that is characterized by a single payment at maturity.

Comparative advantage The ability to produce a good at a lower opportunity cost than others can produce it. Relative costs determine comparative advantage.

Commission brokers Employees of a member firm who buy or sell securities for the customers of the firm.

Commodity forward A contract in which the underlying asset is oil, a precious metal, or some other commodity.

Commodity futures Futures contracts in which the underlying is a traditional agricultural, metal, or petroleum product.

Commodity option An option in which the asset underlying the futures is a commodity, such as oil, gold, wheat, or soybeans.

Commodity swap A swap in which the underlying is a commodity such as oil, gold, or an agricultural product.

Common size statements (1) Financial statements in which all elements (accounts) are stated as a percentage of a key figure such as revenue for an income statement or total assets for a balance sheet. (2) The normalization of balance sheet and income statement items to allow for more meaningful comparison of different-size firms. Balance sheet items are divided by total assets; income statement items are divided by total sales.

Common stock An equity investment that represents ownership of a firm, with full participation in its success or failure. The firm's directors must approve dividend payments.

Company fundamental factors Factors related to the company's internal performance, such as factors relating to earnings growth, earnings variability, earnings momentum, and financial leverage.

Company share-related factors Valuation measures and other factors related to share price or the trading characteristics of the shares, such as earnings yield, dividend yield, and book-to-market value.

Compensating wage differentials Wage differences that compensate workers for risk, unpleasant working conditions, and other undesirable nonpecuniary aspects of a job.

Competition as a dynamic process A term that denotes rivalry or competitiveness between or among parties (for example, producers or input suppliers), each of which seeks to deliver a better deal to buyers when quality, price, and product information are all considered. Competition implies a lack of collusion among sellers.

Competitive bid An underwriting alternative wherein an issuing entity (governmental body or a corporation) specifies the type of security to be offered (bonds or stocks) and the general characteristics of the issue, and the issuer solicits bids from competing investment banking firms with the understanding that the issuer will accept the highest bid from the bankers.

Competitive environment The level of intensity of competition among firms in an industry, determined by an examination of five competitive forces.

Competitive price-searcher market A market where the firms have a downward-sloping demand curve, and entry into and exit from the market are relatively easy.

Competitive strategy The search by a firm for a favorable competitive position within an industry, which affects evaluation of the industry's prospects.

Complement With reference to an event S, the event that S does not occur.

Complements Products that are usually consumed jointly (for example, peanut butter and jelly). They are related such that a decrease in the price of one will cause an increase in demand for the other.

Completely diversified portfolio A portfolio in which all unsystematic risk has been eliminated by diversification.

Completeness fund A specialized index used to form the basis of a passive portfolio whose purpose is to provide diversification to a client's total portfolio by excluding those segments in which the client's active managers invest.

Composite A universe of portfolios with similar investment objectives.

Composite measure An investment performance statistic that considers both the return and risk associated with a portfolio (e.g., Sharpe measure, Treynor measure, Jensen measure).

Compounding The process of accumulating interest on interest.

Conditional expected value (1) Expected value of a variable conditional on some available information set. The expected value changes over time with changes in the information set. (2) The expected value of a stated event given that another event has occurred.

Conditional heteroskedasticity Heteroskedasticity in the error variance that is correlated with the values of the independent variable(s) in the regression.

Conditional probability The probability of an event given (conditioned on) another event.

Conditional variance (1) Variance of a variable conditional on some available information set. (2) The variance of one variable, given the outcome of another.

Confidence interval A range that has a given probability that it will contain the population parameter it is intended to estimate.

Consistency A desirable property of estimators; a consistent estimator is one for which the probability of estimates close to the value of the population parameter increases as sample size increases.

Consistent With reference to estimators, describes an estimator for which the probability of estimates close to the value of the population parameter increases as sample size increases.

Consolidation phase Phase in the investment life cycle during which individuals who are typically past the midpoint of their career have earnings that exceed expenses and invest them for future retirement or estate planning needs.

Constant-cost industry An industry for which factor prices and costs of production remain constant as market output is expanded. Thus, the long-run market supply curve is horizontal.

Constant maturity swap or CMT swap A swap in which the floating rate is the rate on a security known as a constant maturity treasury or CMT security.

Constant maturity treasury or CMT A hypothetical U.S. Treasury note with a constant maturity. A CMT exists for various years in the range of 2 to 10.

Constant returns to scale Unit costs that are constant as the scale of the firm is altered. Neither economies nor diseconomies of scale are present.

Construct the portfolio Given the strategy and economic outlook, what specific stocks and/or bonds will be put into the portfolio at the present time that are consistent with the client's policy statement.

Consumer price index (CPI) (1) An indicator of the general level of prices. It attempts to compare the cost of purchasing the market basket bought by a typical consumer during a specific period with the cost of purchasing the same market basket during an earlier period. (2) A price index defined on a basket of goods consumed.

Consumer surplus The difference between the maximum price consumers are willing to pay and the price they actually pay. It is the net gain derived by the buyers of the good.

Consumption function A fundamental relationship between disposable income and consumption, in which, as disposable income increases, current consumption expenditures rise, but by a smaller amount than the increase in income.

Consumption opportunity constraint The constraint that separates consumption bundles that are attainable from those that are unattainable. In a money income economy, this is usually a budget constraint.

Contango (1) A situation in a futures market where the current contract price is greater than the current spot price for the underlying asset. (2) A condition in the futures markets in which the costs of holding an asset exceed the benefits, leaving the futures price more than the spot price.

Contingent claims Derivatives in which the payoffs occur if a specific event occurs; generally referred to as options.

Contingent deferred sales load A mutual fund that imposes a sales charge when the investor sells or redeems shares. Also referred to as rear-end loads or redemption charges.

Continual monitoring This involves constant evaluation of the economic environment, the policy statement, and the portfolio to ensure that it is consistent with the policy statement. Also involves evaluating performance to determine if changes are required in the portfolio, the strategy, or the policy statement.

Continuing earnings *See* Underlying earnings.

Continuously compounded return The natural logarithm of 1 plus the holding period return, or equivalently, the natural logarithm of the ending price over the beginning price.

Continuous market A market where stocks are priced and traded continuously by an auction process or by dealers when the market is open.

Continuous random variable A random variable for which the range of possible outcomes is the real line (all real numbers between $-\infty$ and $+\infty$) or some subset of the real line.

Continuous time Time thought of as advancing in extremely small increments.

Contract for difference (CFD) A contract between an investor and a broker in which the investor receives (or pays) the difference between the price of the underlying share when the contract is closed and the price when the contract was opened.

Convexity A measure of the change in duration with respect to changes in interest rates.

Contestable market A market in which the costs of entry and exit are low, so a firm risks little by entering. Efficient production and zero economic profits should prevail in a contestable market. A market can be contestable even if capital requirements are high.

Contract price The transaction price specified in a forward or futures contract.

Contrarian An investment strategy that attempts to buy (sell) securities on which the majority of other investors are bearish (bullish).

Convenience yield (1) An adjustment made to the theoretical forward or futures contract delivery price to account for the preference that consumers have for holding spot positions in the underlying asset. (2) The nonmonetary return offered by an asset when the asset is in short supply, often associated with assets with seasonal production processes.

Conversion factors (1) The adjustments made to Treasury bond futures contract terms to allow for the delivery of an instrument other than the standardized underlying asset. (2) An adjustment used to facilitate delivery on bond futures contracts in which any of a number of bonds with different characteristics are eligible for delivery.

Conversion parity price The price at which common stock can be obtained by surrendering the convertible instrument at par value.

Conversion premium The excess of the market value of the convertible security over its equity value if immediately converted into common stock. Typically expressed as a percentage of the equity value.

Conversion ratio The number of shares of common stock for which a convertible security may be exchanged.

Conversion value The value of the convertible security if converted into common stock at the stock's current market price

Convertible bonds A bond with the added feature that the bondholder has the option to turn the bond back to the firm in exchange for a specified number of common shares of the firm.

Convexity A measure of the degree to which a bond's price-yield curve departs from a straight line. This characteristic affects estimates of a bond's price volatility for a given change in yields.

Copyright An exclusive right granted by the federal government to reproduce and sell literary, musical, and other artistic materials and computer programs for a period of the author's life plus 70 years.

Core earnings *See* Underlying earnings.

Core-plus bond portfolio management This is a combination approach to bond portfolio management wherein a significant (core) part of the portfolio (e.g., 70–75 percent) of the portfolio is managed passively in a widely recognized sector of the bond market, such as an aggregate bond index or a U.S. Government/corporate sector. The rest of the portfolio would be actively managed in one or several "plus" sectors that are less efficient than the core component—for example, high-yield bonds, foreign bonds, or emerging market debt.

Corporate, or Within-Firm, risk Risk not considering the effects of stockholders' diversification; it is measured by a project's effect on uncertainty about the firm's future earnings.

Corporation A business firm owned by shareholders who possess ownership rights to the firm's profits, but whose liability is limited to the amount of their investment in the firm.

Correlation A number between −1 and +1 that measures the co-movement (linear association) between two random variables.

Correlation analysis The analysis of the strength of the linear relationship between two data series.

Correlation coefficient A standardized measure of the relationship between two variables that ranges from −1.00 to +1.00.

Cost averaging The periodic investment of a fixed amount of money.

Cost of carry (1) The cost associated with holding some asset, including financing, storage, and insurance costs. Any yield received on the asset is treated as a negative carrying cost. (2) The net amount that would be required to store a commodity or security for future delivery, usually calculated as physical storage costs plus financial capital costs less dividends paid to the underlying asset. (3) The costs of holding an asset.

Cost of carry model A model for pricing futures contracts in which the futures price is determined by adding the cost of carry to the spot price.

Cost of new common equity, k_e The cost of external equity; based on the cost of retained earnings, but increased for flotation costs.

Cost of Preferred Stock, k_{ps} The rate of return investors require on the firm's preferred stock. k_{ps} is calculated as the preferred dividend, D_{ps}, divided by the net issuing price, P_n.

Cost of retained earnings, k_s The rate of return required by stockholders on a firm's common stock.

Countercyclical policy A policy that tends to move the economy in an opposite direction from the forces of the business cycle. Such a policy would stimulate demand during the contraction phase of the business cycle and restrain demand during the expansion phase.

Counterparty A participant to a derivative transaction.

Country risk Uncertainty due to the possibility of major political or economic change in the country where an investment is located. Also called political risk.

Coupon Indicates the interest payment on a debt security. It is the coupon rate times the par value that indicates the interest payments on a debt security.

Coupon reinvestment risk The component of interest rate risk due to the uncertainty of the rate at which coupon payments will be reinvested.

Covariance (1) A measure of the degree to which two variables, such as rates of return for investment assets, move together over time relative to their individual mean returns. (2) A measure of the extent to which the returns on two assets move together. (3) A measure of the co-movement (linear association) between two random variables.

Covariance matrix A matrix or square array whose entries are covariances; also known as a variance–covariance matrix.

Covariance stationary Describes a time series when its expected value and variance are constant and finite in all periods and when its covariance with itself for a fixed number of periods in the past or future is constant and finite in all periods.

Covered call (1) A trading strategy in which a call option is sold as a supplement to a long position in an underlying asset or portfolio of assets. (2) An option strategy involving the holding of an asset and sale of a call on the asset.

Covered interest arbitrage (1) A trading strategy involving borrowing money in one country and lending it to another designed to exploit price deviations from the interest rate parity model. (2) A transaction executed in the foreign exchange market in which a currency is purchased (sold) and a forward contract is sold (purchased) to lock in the exchange rate for future delivery of the currency. This transaction should earn the risk-free rate of the investor's home country.

Covered option An option position that is offset by an equal and opposite position in the underlying security.

Credit Funds acquired by borrowing.

Credit analysis An active bond portfolio management strategy designed to identify bonds that are expected to experience changes in rating. This strategy is critical when investing in high-yield bonds.

Credit derivatives A contract in which one party has the right to claim a payment from another party in the event that a specific credit event occurs over the life of the contract.

Credit risk or default risk The risk of loss due to nonpayment by a counterparty.

Credit spread option An option on the yield spread on a bond.

Credit swap A type of swap transaction used as a credit derivative in which one party makes periodic payments to the other and receives the promise of a payoff if a third party defaults.

Credit unions Financial cooperative organizations of individuals with a common affiliation (such as an employer or a labor union). They accept deposits, including checkable deposits, pay interest (or dividends) on them out of earnings, and channel funds primarily into loans to members.

Credit VAR, Default VAR, or Credit at Risk A variation of VAR that reflects credit risk.

Credit-linked notes Fixed-income securities in which the holder of the security has the right to withhold payment of the full amount due at maturity if a credit event occurs.

Critical value *See* Rejection point.

Cross hedge A trading strategy in which the price volatility of a commodity or security position is hedged with a forward or futures contract based on a different underlying asset or different settlement terms.

Crossover price The price at which the yield to maturity equals the yield to call. Above this price, yield to call is the appropriate yield measure; below this price, yield to maturity is the appropriate yield measure.

Crossover rate The discount rate at which the NPV profiles of two projects cross and, thus, at which the projects' NPVs are equal.

Cross-product netting Netting the market values of all contracts, not just derivatives, between parties.

Cross-rate The exchange rate between two currencies, derived from their exchange rates with a third currency.

Cross-sectional analysis An examination of a firm's performance in comparison to other firms in the industry with similar characteristics to the firm being studied.

Cross-sectional data Observations over individual units at a point in time, as opposed to time-series data.

Cross-sectional return studies Studies wherein investigators look for public information regarding individual stocks that predict the cross-sectional distribution of risk-adjusted returns—e.g., is there an inverse relationship between market-value size of a firm and future risk-adjusted rates of return for its stock?

Crowding-out effect A reduction in private spending as a result of higher interest rates generated by budget deficits that are financed by borrowing in the private loanable funds market.

Cumulative distribution function A function giving the probability that a random variable is less than or equal to a specified value.

Cumulative relative frequency For data grouped into intervals, the fraction of total observations that are less than the value of the upper limit of a stated interval.

Currency board An entity that (a) issues a currency with a fixed designated value relative to a widely accepted currency (for example, the U.S. dollar), (b) promises to continue to redeem the issued currency at the fixed rate, and (c) maintains bonds and other liquid assets denominated in the other currency that provide 100 percent backing for all currency issued.

Currency exposure The sensitivity of the asset return, measured in the investor's domestic currency, to a movement in the exchange rate.

Currency forward A forward contract in which the underlying is a foreign currency.

Currency option An option that allows the holder to buy (if a call) or sell (if a put) an underlying currency at a fixed exercise rate, expressed as an exchange rate.

Currency-option bond A bond in which the coupons and/or the principal may be paid in more than one currency, at the option of the bondholder.

Currency overlay In currency risk management, the delegation of the management of currency risk in an international portfolio to a currency specialist.

Currency swap (1) A contract to exchange streams of fixed cash flows denominated in two different currencies. (2) A swap transaction in which the cash flows, which can be either fixed or variable, are denominated in different currencies. (3) A swap in which each party makes interest payments to the other in different currencies.

Current account (1) The record of all transactions with foreign nations that involve the exchange of merchandise goods and services, current income derived from investments, and unilateral gifts. (2) A component of the balance of payments covering all current transactions that take place in the normal business of the residents of a country, such as exports and imports, services, income, and current transfers.

Current credit risk The risk associated with the possibility that a payment currently due will not be made.

Current income A return objective in which the investor seeks to generate income rather than capital gains; generally a goal of an investor who wants to supplement earnings with income to meet living expenses.

Current P/E *See* Trailing P/E.

Current yield A bond's yield as measured by its current income (coupon) as a percentage of its market price.

Customer list A list of customers or subscribers.

Cyclical businesses Businesses with high sensitivity to business- or industry-cycle influences.

Cyclical change An economic trend arising from the ups and downs of the business cycle.

Cyclical company A firm whose earnings rise and fall with general economic activity.

Cyclical stock A stock with a high beta; its gains typically exceed those of a rising market and its losses typically exceed those of a falling market.

Cyclical unemployment Unemployment due to recessionary business conditions and inadequate aggregate demand for labor.

Daily settlement *See* Marking to market.

Data mining The practice of determining a model by extensive searching through a dataset for statistically significant patterns.

Day trader A trader holding a position open somewhat longer than a scalper but closing all positions at the end of the day.

Deadweight loss A loss of gains from trade resulting from the imposition of a tax. It imposes a burden of taxation over and above the burden associated with the transfer of revenues to the government.

Dealer An agent that buys and sells securities as a principal (for its own account) rather than as a broker for clients. A dealer may function, at different times, as a broker or as a dealer. Sometimes called a market maker.

Debentures Bonds that promise payments of interest and principal but pledge no specific assets. Holders have first claim on the issuer's income and unpledged assets. Also known as unsecured bonds.

Decentralized risk management A system that allows individual units within an organization to manage risk. Decentralization results in duplication of effort but has the advantage of having people closer to the risk be more directly involved in its management.

Deciles Quantiles that divide a distribution into 10 equal parts.

Decision rule With respect to hypothesis testing, the rule according to which the null hypothesis will be rejected or not rejected; involves the comparison of the test statistic to rejection point(s).

Declaration date The date on which a firm's directors issue a statement declaring a dividend.

Declining-balance method An accelerated method of depreciation in which depreciation is computed by applying a fixed rate to the carrying value (the declining balance) of a tangible long-lived asset.

Declining trend channel The range defined by security prices as they move progressively lower.

Decreasing-cost industry An industry for which costs of production decline as the industry expands. The market supply is therefore inversely related to price. Such industries are atypical.

Dedication A portfolio management technique in which the portfolio's cash flows are used to retire a set of liabilities over time.

Dedication with reinvestment A dedication strategy in which portfolio cash flows may precede their corresponding liabilities. Such cash flows can be reinvested to earn a return until the date the liability is due to be paid.

Deep in the money Options that are far in-the-money.

Deep out of the money Options that are far out-of-the-money.

Default risk The risk that an issuer will be unable to make interest and principal payments on time.

Default risk premium An extra return that compensates investors for the possibility that the borrower will fail to make a promised payment at the contracted time and in the contracted amount.

Defensive company Firms whose future earnings are likely to withstand an economic downturn.

Defensive competitive strategy Positioning the firm so that its capabilities provide the best means to deflect the effect of the competitive forces in the industry.

Defensive stock A stock whose return is not expected to decline as much as that of the overall market during a bear market.

Defined benefit pension plan A pension plan to which the company contributes a certain amount each year and that pays employees an income after they retire. The benefit size is based on factors such as workers' salary and time of employment.

Defined contribution pension plan A pension plan in which worker benefits are determined by the size of employees' contributions to the plan and the returns earned on the fund's investments.

Degree of confidence The probability that a confidence interval includes the unknown population parameter.

Degrees of freedom (df) The number of independent observations used.

Delivery A process used in a deliverable forward contract in which the long pays the agreed-upon price to the short, which in turn delivers the underlying asset to the long.

Delivery option The feature of a futures contract giving the short the right to make decisions about what, when, and where to deliver.

Delta (Δ) (1) Ratio of change in the option price to a small change in the price of the underlying asset. Also equal to the derivative of the option price with respect to the asset price. (2) The change in the price of the option with respect to a one dollar change in the price of the underlying asset; this is the option's hedge ratio, or the number of units of the underlying asset that can be hedged by a single option contract. (3) The relationship between the option price and the underlying price, which reflects the sensitivity of the price of the option to changes in the price of the underlying.

Delta hedge (1) A dynamic hedging strategy using options with continuous adjustment of the number of options used, as a function of the delta of the option. (2) An option strategy in which a position in an asset is converted to a risk-free position with a position in a specific number of options. The number of options per unit of the underlying changes through time, and the position must be revised to maintain the hedge.

Delta-normal method A measure of VAR equivalent to the analytical method but that refers to the use of delta to estimate the option's price sensitivity.

Demand deposits Non-interest-earning checking deposits that can be either withdrawn or made payable on demand to a third party. Like currency, these deposits are widely used as a means of payment.

Demand for money A curve that indicates the relationship between the interest rate and the quantity of money people want to hold. Because higher interest rates increase the opportunity cost of holding money, the quantity demanded of money will be inversely related to the interest rate.

Dependent With reference to events, the property that the probability of one event occurring depends on (is related to) the occurrence of another event.

Dependent variable The variable whose variation about its mean is to be explained by the regression; the left-hand-side variable in a regression equation.

Depletion The exhaustion of a natural resource through mining, cutting, pumping, or other extraction, and the way in which the cost is allocated.

Depository institutions Businesses that accept checking and savings deposits and use a portion of them to extend loans and make investments. Banks, savings and loan associations, and credit unions are examples.

Depreciable cost The cost of an asset less its residual value.

Depreciation (1) A reduction in the value of the domestic currency relative to foreign currencies. A depreciation reduces the purchasing power of the domestic currency for foreign goods. (2) The periodic allocation of the cost of a tangible long-lived asset (other than land and natural resources) over its estimated useful life.

Depression A prolonged and very severe recession.

Derivatives (1) Securities bearing a contractual relation to some underlying asset or rate. Options, futures, forward, and swap contracts, as well as many forms of bonds, are derivative securities.

(2) A financial instrument that offers a return based on the return of some other underlying asset.

Derivatives dealers The commercial and investment banks that make markets in derivatives. Also referred to as market makers.

Derivative security An instrument whose market value ultimately depends upon, or derives from, the value of a more fundamental investment vehicle called the underlying asset or security.

Derived demand The demand for a resource; it stems from the demand for the final good the resource helps to produce.

Descriptive statistics The study of how data can be summarized effectively.

Devaluation Deliberate downward adjustment of a currency against its fixed parity.

Differentiated products Products distinguished from similar products by such characteristics as quality, design, location, and method of promotion.

Diff swaps A swap in which the payments are based on the difference between interest rates in two countries but payments are made in only a single currency.

Diffuse prior The assumption of equal prior probabilities.

Diffusion index An indicator of the number of stocks rising during a specified period of time relative to the number of stocks declining and not changing price.

Diluted earnings per share Total earnings divided by the number of shares that would be outstanding if holders of securities such as executive stock options and convertible bonds exercised their options to obtain common stock.

Direct exchange rate The amount of local or domestic currency required to purchase one unit of foreign currency.

Discount (1) A bond selling at a price below par value due to capital market conditions. (2) To reduce the value of a future payment in allowance for how far away it is in time; to calculate the present value of some future amount. Also, the amount by which an instrument is priced below its face value.

Discounted cash flow (DCF) techniques Methods for ranking investment proposals that employ time value of money concepts.

Discounted payback period The length of time required for an investment's cash flows, discounted at the cost of capital, to cover its cost.

Discounting The procedure used to calculate the present value of future income, which is inversely related to both the interest rate and the amount of time that passes before the funds are received.

Discount interest A procedure for determining the interest on a loan or bond in which the interest is deducted from the face value in advance.

Discount rate The interest rate the Federal Reserve charges banking institutions for borrowing funds.

Discrete random variable A random variable that can take on at most a countable number of possible values.

Discrete time Time thought of as advancing in distinct finite increments.

Discretionary fiscal policy A change in laws or appropriation levels that alters government revenues and/or expenditures.

Discriminant analysis A multivariate classification technique used to discriminate between groups, such as companies that either will or will not become bankrupt during some time frame.

Dispersion The variability around the central tendency.

Disposable income The income available to individuals after personal taxes. It can be either spent on consumption or saved.

Dividend discount model (DDM) A technique for estimating the value of a stock issue as the present value of all future dividends.

Dividend irrelevance theory The theory that a firm's dividend policy has no effect on either its value or its cost of capital.

Dividend reinvestment plan (DRP) A plan that enables a stockholder to automatically reinvest dividends received back into the stock of the paying firm.

Dollar-weighted return The discount rate that sets the present value of a future set of cash flows equal to the investment's current value; also known as the internal rate of return.

Double-declining-balance method An accelerated method of depreciation in which a fixed rate equal to twice the straight-line percentage is applied to the carrying value (the declining balance) of a tangible long-lived asset.

Downtick A price decline in a transaction price compared to the previous transaction price.

Down transition probability The probability that an asset's value moves down in a model of asset price dynamics.

Dual-currency bond A bond with coupons fixed in one currency and principal repayment fixed in another currency.

Dummy variable A type of qualitative variable that takes on a value of 1 if a particular condition is true and 0 if that condition is false.

Dumping The sale of a good by a foreign supplier in another country at a price below that charged by the supplier in its home market.

DuPont system A method of examining ROE by breaking it down into three component parts: (1) profit margin, (2) total asset turnover, and (3) financial leverage.

Duration (1) A measure of an option-free bond's average maturity. Specifically, the weighted average maturity of all future cash flows paid by a security, in which the weights are the present value of these cash flows as a fraction of the bond's price. More importantly, a measure of a bond's price sensitivity to interest rate movements (*see* Modified duration). (2) A measure of the interest rate sensitivity of a bond's market price taking into consideration its coupon and term to maturity. (3) A measure of the size and timing of the cash flows paid by a bond. It quantifies these factors by summarizing them in the form of a single number. For bonds without option features attached, duration is interpreted as a weighted average maturity of the bond.

Duration strategy A portfolio management strategy employed to reduce the interest rate risk of a bond portfolio by matching the modified duration of the portfolio with its investment horizon. For example, if the investment horizon is 10 years, the portfolio manager would construct a portfolio that has a modified duration of 10 years. This strategy is referred to as immunization of the portfolio.

Dutch Book Theorem A result in probability theory stating that inconsistent probabilities create profit opportunities.

Dynamic hedging A strategy in which a position is hedged by making frequent adjustments to the quantity of the instrument used for hedging in relation to the instrument being hedged.

EAFE index A stock index for Europe, Australia, and the Far East published by Morgan Stanley Capital International.

Early stage With reference to venture capital financing, the stage associated with moving into operation and before commercial manufacturing and sales have occurred. Includes the start-up and first stages.

Earned Income Tax Credit A provision of the tax code that provides a credit or rebate to persons with low earnings (income from work activities). The credit is eventually phased out if the recipient's earnings increase.

Earnings at risk (EAR) A variation of VAR that reflects the risk of a company's earnings instead of its market value.

Earnings momentum A strategy in which portfolios are constructed of stocks of firms with rising earnings.

Earnings multiplier Also known as the price/earnings ratio, it is a measure of the relationship between a company's, or the aggregate stock market's, stock prices and earnings. *See also* Price-earnings (P/E) ratio. (I prefer the slash, but can live with either)

Earnings multiplier model A technique for estimating the value of a stock issue as a multiple of its earnings per share.

Earnings surprise A company announcement of earnings that differ from analysts' prevailing expectations. *See also* Unexpected earnings.

Earnings yield Earnings per share divided by price; the reciprocal of the P/E ratio.

Economic efficiency 1) A market meets the criterion of economic efficiency if all the gains from trade have been realized. With well-defined property rights and competition, market equilibrium is efficient. 2) Economizing behavior. When applied to a community, it implies that (1) an activity should be undertaken if the sum of the benefits to the individuals exceeds the sum of their costs and (2) no activity should be undertaken if the costs borne by the individuals exceed the benefits.

Economic exposure The risk associated with changes in the relative attractiveness of products and services offered for sale, arising out of the competitive effects of changes in exchange rates.

Economic profit The difference between the firm's total revenues and its total costs, including both the explicit and implicit cost components.

Economic risk As used in currency risk management, the risk that arises when the foreign currency value of a foreign investment reacts systematically to an exchange rate movement.

Economic regulation Regulation of product price or industrial structure, usually imposed on a specific industry. By and large, the production processes used by the regulated firms are unaffected by this type of regulation.

Economic theory A set of definitions, postulates, and principles assembled in a manner that makes clear the "cause-and-effect" relationships of economic data.

Economic value added (EVA) Internal management performance measure that compares net operating profit to total cost of capital. Indicates how profitable company projects are as a sign of management performance.

Economies of scale Reductions in the firm's per-unit costs that are associated with the use of large plants to produce a large volume of output.

Economizing behavior Choosing with the objective of gaining a specific benefit at the least possible cost. A corollary of economizing behavior implies that, when choosing among items of equal cost, individuals will choose the option that yields the greatest benefit.

Effective annual rate The amount by which a unit of currency will grow in a year with interest on interest included.

Effective annual yield (EAY) An annualized return that accounts for the effect of interest on interest; EAY is computed by compounding 1 plus the holding period yield forward to one year, then subtracting 1.

Effective duration Direct measure of the interest rate sensitivity of a bond (or any financial instrument) based upon price changes derived from a pricing model.

Efficiency A desirable property of estimators; an efficient estimator is the unbiased estimator with the smallest variance among unbiased estimators of the same parameter.

Efficient capital market A market in which security prices rapidly reflect all information about securities.

Efficient frontier (1) The set of all efficient portfolios for various levels of risk. (2) The set of portfolios that has the maximum rate of return for every given level of risk, or the minimum risk for every potential rate of return. (3) The portion of the minimum-variance frontier beginning with the global minimum-variance portfolio and continuing above it; the graph of the set of portfolios offering the maximum expected return for their level of variance of return.

Efficient portfolio (1) A portfolio that provides the best expected return for a given level of risk. (2) A portfolio offering the highest expected return for a given level of risk as measured by variance or standard deviation of return.

Electronic communications networks Order-driven trading systems in which the book of limit orders plays a central role.

Electronic crossing networks Order-driven trading systems in which market orders are anonymously matched at prespecified times at prices determined in the primary market for the system.

Empirical duration Measures directly the interest rate sensitivity of an asset by examining the percentage price change for an asset in response to a change in yield during a specified period of time.

Empirical probability The probability of an event estimated as a relative frequency of occurrence.

Employment discrimination Unequal treatment of persons on the basis of their race, sex, or religion, restricting their employment and earnings opportunities compared to others of similar productivity. Employment discrimination may stem from the prejudices of employers, customers, fellow employees, or all three.

Ending-wealth value The total amount of money derived from investment in a bond until maturity, including principal, coupon payments, and income from reinvestment of coupon payments.

Endogenous growth theory A theory of economic growth that does not assume that the marginal productivity of capital declines as capital is added.

Enhanced derivatives products companies (EDPC) (or special purpose vehicles [SPVs]) A type of subsidiary engaged in derivatives transactions that is separated from the parent company in order to have a higher credit rating than the parent company.

Entrepreneur A profit-seeking decision maker who decides which projects to undertake and how they should be undertaken. A successful entrepreneur's actions will increase the value of resources and expand the size of the economic pie.

Enterprise risk management A form of centralized risk management that typically encompasses the management of a broad variety of risks, including insurance risk.

Equation of exchange $MV = PY$, where M is the money supply, V is the velocity of money, P is the price level, and Y is the output of goods and services produced.

Equilibrium A state of balance between conflicting forces, such as supply and demand, permitting the simultaneous fulfillment of plans by buyers and sellers.

Equipment trust certificates Mortgage bonds that are secured by specific pieces of transportation equipment like boxcars and planes.

Equitizing cash A strategy used to replicate an index. It is also used to take a given amount of cash and turn it into an equity position while maintaining the liquidity provided by the cash.

Equity collar An option-based hedging strategy that protects a stock position from price declines by purchasing a put option that is paid for by the sale of a call option.

Equity forward A contract calling for the purchase of an individual stock, a stock portfolio, or a stock index at a later date at an agreed-upon price.

Equity mutual fund A corporation that pools the funds of investors, including small investors, and uses them to purchase a bundle of stocks.

Equity options Options on individual stocks; also known as stock options.

Equity swap (1) A swap transaction in which one cash flow is tied to the return to an equity portfolio position, often an index such as the Standard and Poor's 500, while the other is based on a floating-rate index. (2) A swap in which the rate is the return on a stock or stock index.

Equivalent annual annuity (EAA) method A method which calculates the annual payments a project would provide if it were an annuity. When comparing projects of unequal lives, the one with the higher equivalent annual annuity should be chosen.

Error autocorrelation The autocorrelation of the error term.

Error term The portion of the dependent variable that is not explained by the independent variable(s) in the regression.

Escalator clause A contractual agreement that periodically and automatically adjusts money wage rates upward as the price level rises. They are sometimes referred to as cost-of-living adjustments or COLAs.

Estimate The particular value calculated from sample observations using an estimator.

Estimated (or fitted) parameters With reference to regression analysis, the estimated values of the population intercept and population slope coefficient(s) in a regression.

Estimated rate of return The rate of return an investor anticipates earning from a specific investment over a particular future holding period.

Estimated useful life The total number of service units expected from a long-term asset.

Estimation With reference to statistical inference, the subdivision dealing with estimating the value of a population parameter.

Estimator An estimation formula; the formula used to compute the sample mean and other sample statistics are examples of estimators.

Euribor Interbank offer rate for short-term deposits in euros. Euribor is determined by an association of European banks.

Euro The common currency of many European countries.

Eurobond (1) A bond underwritten by a multinational syndicate of banks and placed mainly in countries other than the country of the issuer; sometimes called an international bond. (2) Bonds denominated in a currency not native to the country in which they are issued.

Eurocurrency market Interbank market for short-term borrowing and lending in a currency outside of its home country. For example, borrowing and lending of U.S. dollars outside the United States. Thus, it is an offshore market escaping national regulations. This is the largest money market for several major currencies.

Eurodollar A dollar deposited outside the United States.

Eurodollar market The U.S. dollar segment of the Eurocurrency market.

European Monetary System A formal arrangement linking some, but not all, of the currencies of the EU.

European option (1) An option contract that can only be exercised on its expiration date. (2) An option that can be exercised only at expiration. Also referred to as European-style exercise.

European-style option or European option An option exercisable only at maturity.

European terms With reference to U.S. dollar exchange rate quotations, the price of a U.S. dollar in terms of another currency.

European Union (EU) A formal association of European countries founded by the Treaty of Rome in 1957. Formerly known as the EEC.

European-type option An option that can be exercised only at expiration.

Event Any outcome or specified set of outcomes of a random variable.

Event study Research that examines the reaction of a security's price to a specific company, world event, or news announcement.

Excess burden of taxation Another term for deadweight loss. It reflects losses that occur when beneficial activities are forgone because they are taxed.

Excess kurtosis Degree of peakedness (fatness of tails) in excess of the peakedness of the normal distribution.

Exchange clearinghouse The functional unit attached to a futures exchange that guarantees contract performance, oversees delivery, serves as a bookkeeper, and calculates settlement transactions.

Exchange for physicals (EEP) A permissible delivery procedure used by futures market participants, in which the long and short arrange a delivery procedure other than the normal procedures stipulated by the futures exchange.

Exchange rate The price of one unit of foreign currency in terms of the domestic currency. For example, if it takes $1.50 to purchase an English pound, the dollar-pound exchange rate is 1.50.

Exchange rate risk Uncertainty due to the denomination of an investment in a currency other than that of the investor's own country.

Exchange traded funds (ETFs) A type of mutual fund traded like other shares on a stock market, having special characteristics particularly related to redemption, and generally designed to closely track the performance of a specified stock market index.

Ex-dividend A synonym for "without dividend." The buyer of a security ex-dividend does not receive the next dividend.

Ex-dividend date The date on which the right to the current dividend no longer accompanies a stock; it is usually four working days prior to the holder-of-record date.

Executive stock option An option to buy stock at a stated price within a specified time period that is granted to an executive as part of his or her compensation package.

Exercise (or exercising the option) The process of using an option to buy or sell the underlying.

Exercise price (or strike price or striking price, or strike) (1) The transaction price specified in an option contract. *See* also Strike price. (2) The fixed price at which an option holder can buy or sell the underlying.

Exercise rate or strike rate The fixed rate at which the holder of an interest rate option can buy or sell the underlying.

Exhaustive Covering or containing all possible outcomes.

Exotic option Designed to have payoffs that differ from those of standard contract options. Three such nonstandard contracts are Asian, lookback, and digital options.

Expansionary fiscal policy An increase in government expenditures and/or a reduction in tax rates such that the expected size of the budget deficit expands.

Expansionary monetary policy A shift in monetary policy designed to stimulate aggregate demand. Bond purchases, creation of additional bank reserves, and an increase in the growth rate of the money supply are generally indicative of a shift to a more expansionary monetary policy.

Expansion project A project that is intended to increase sales.

Expected rate of return The return that analysts' calculations suggest a security should provide, based on the market's rate of return during the period and the security's relationship to the market.

Expected return The rate of return that an investor expects to get on an investment.

Expected value The probability-weighted average of the possible outcomes of a random variable.

Expenditure A payment or obligation to make future payment for an asset or a service.

Expenditure multiplier The ratio of the change in equilibrium output to the independent change in investment, consumption, or government spending that brings about the change. Numerically, the multiplier is equal to 1 *divided by* (1 − MPCC) when the price level is constant.

Expiration date The date on which a derivative contract expires.

Expiry The expiration date of a derivative security.

Explicit costs Payments by a firm to purchase the services of productive resources.

Exports Goods and services produced domestically but sold to foreigners.

External debt The portion of the national debt owed to foreign investors.

External efficiency When prices reflect all available information about an asset, which implies that prices adjust quickly to new information regarding supply or demand. Also referred to as informational efficiency.

Externalities (1) The side effects, or spillover effects, of an action that influence the well-being of nonconsenting parties. The nonconsenting parties may be either helped (by external benefits) or harmed (by external costs). (2) The effects of a project on cash flows in other parts of the firm.

Extraordinary repairs Repairs that affect the estimated residual value or estimated useful life of an asset thereby increasing its carrying value.

Face value (1) The amount paid on a bond at redemption and traditionally printed on the bond certificate. This face value excludes the final coupon payment. Sometimes referred to as par value. (2) The promised payment at maturity separate from any coupon payment.

Factor A common or underlying element with which several variables are correlated.

Factor risk premium (or factor price) The expected return in excess of the risk-free rate for a portfolio with a sensitivity of 1 to one factor and a sensitivity of 0 to all other factors.

Factor sensitivity (also factor betas or factor loadings) A measure of the response of return to each unit of increase in a factor, holding all other factors constant.

Fair value (1) The price at which an asset or liability would change hands between a willing buyer and a willing seller when the former is not under any compulsion to buy and the latter is not under any compulsion to sell. (2) The theoretical value of a security based on current market conditions. The fair value is the value such that no arbitrage opportunities exist.

Fallacy of composition Erroneous view that what is true for the individual (or the part) will also be true for the group (or the whole).

Federal funds market A loanable funds market in which banks seeking additional reserves borrow short-term (generally for seven days or less) funds from banks with excess reserves. The interest rate in this market is called the federal funds rate.

Federal Reserve System The central bank of the United States; it carries out banking regulatory policies and is responsible for the conduct of monetary policy.

Fiat money Money that has neither intrinsic value nor the backing of a commodity with intrinsic value; paper currency is an example.

Fiduciary A person who supervises or oversees the investment portfolio of a third party, such as in a trust account, and makes investment decisions in accordance with the owner's wishes.

Fiduciary call A combination of a European call and a risk-free bond that matures on the option expiration day and has a face value equal to the exercise price of the call.

Filter rule A trading rule that recommends security transactions when price changes exceed a previously determined percentage.

Final market goods and services Goods and services purchased by their ultimate user.

Financial account A component of the balance of payments covering investments by residents abroad and investments by nonresidents in the home country. Examples include direct investment made by companies, portfolio investments in equity and bonds, and other investments and liabilities.

Financial futures Futures contracts in which the underlying is a stock, bond, or currency.

Financial leverage The extent to which fixed-income securities (debt and preferred stock) are used in a firm's capital structure.

Financial risk (1) The variability of future income arising from the firm's fixed financing costs, for example, interest payments. The effect of fixed financial costs is to magnify the effect of changes in operating profit on net income or earnings per share. (2) Risk relating to asset prices and other financial variables.

First-differencing A transformation that subtracts the value of the time series in period $t - 1$ from its value in period t.

First-order serial correlation Correlation between adjacent observations in a time series.

Fiscal policy The use of government taxation and expenditure policies for the purpose of achieving macroeconomic goals.

Fixed exchange rate An exchange rate that is set at a determined amount by government policy.

Fixed exchange rate regime A system in which the exchange rate between two currencies remains fixed at a preset level, known as official parity.

Fixed-income forward A forward contract in which the underlying is a bond.

Fixed-income investments Loans with contractually mandated payment schedules from investors to firms or governments.

Fixing A method for determining the market price of a security by finding the price that balances buyers and sellers. A fixing takes place periodically each day at defined times. Sometimes called a call auction.

Flat trend channel The range defined by security prices as they maintain a relatively steady level.

Flexible exchange rates Exchange rates that are determined by the market forces of supply and demand. They are sometimes called floating exchange rates.

Flexible exchange rate system A system in which exchange rates are determined by supply and demand.

Flexible portfolio fund Mutual fund that allows managers to shift assets between stocks, bonds, and cash according to changing market conditions; also known as asset allocation fund.

Floating-rate loan A loan in which the interest rate is reset at least once after the starting date.

Floating-rate note (FRN) (1) Bond issued with variable quarterly or semiannual interest rate payments, generally linked to LIBOR. (2) Short- to intermediate-term bonds with regularly scheduled coupon payments linked to a variable interest rate, most often LIBOR.

Floor (1) A contract on an interest rate, whereby the writer of the floor periodically pays the difference between a specified floor rate and the market interest rate if, and only if, this difference is positive. This is equivalent to a stream of put options on the interest rate. (2) A combination of interest rate put options designed to hedge a lender against lower rates on a floating-rate loan.

Floor agreement A contract that on each settlement date pays the holder the greater of the difference between the floor rate and the reference rate or zero; it is equivalent to a series of put options on the reference rate.

Floor brokers Independent members of an exchange who act as brokers for other members.

Floored swap A swap in which the floating payments have a lower limit.

Floorlet Each component put option in a floor.

Floor traders or locals Market makers that buy and sell by quoting a bid and an ask price. They are the primary providers of liquidity to the market.

Flotation Cost, F The percentage cost of issuing new common stock.

Foreign bond A bond issued by a foreign company on the local market and in the local currency (e.g., Yankee bonds in the United States, Bulldog bonds in the United Kingdom, or Samurai bonds in Japan).

Foreign currency risk premium The expected movement in the (direct) exchange rate minus the interest rate differential (domestic risk-free rate minus foreign risk-free rate).

Foreign exchange The purchase (sale) of a currency against the sale (purchase) of another.

Foreign exchange controls Various forms of government-imposed controls on the purchase (sale) of foreign currencies by residents or on the purchase (sale) of local currency by nonresidents.

Foreign exchange expectation A relation that states that the forward exchange rate, quoted at time 0 for delivery at time 1, is equal to the expected value of the spot exchange rate at time 1. When stated relative to the current spot exchange rate, the relation states that the forward discount (premium) is equal to the expected exchange rate movement.

Foreign exchange market The market in which the currencies of different countries are bought and sold.

Foreign exchange parity A foreign exchange rate of two currencies that is officially fixed by international agreement.

Forex Foreign exchange.

Formative stage With respect to venture capital financing, the seed and early stages.

Forward contract (1) A customized contract to buy (sell) an asset at a specified date and a specified price (forward price). No payment takes place until maturity. (2) An agreement between two counterparties that requires the exchange of a commodity or security at a fixed time in the future at a predetermined price. (3) An agreement between two parties in which one party, the buyer, agrees to buy from the other party, the seller, an underlying asset at a later date for a price established at the start of the contract.

Forward discount or premium Refers to the percentage difference between the forward exchange rate and the spot exchange rate (premium if positive, discount if negative).

Forward P/E *See* Leading P/E.

Forward premium A situation where, from the perspective of the domestic country, the spot exchange rate is larger than the forward exchange rate with a foreign country.

Forward price or forward rate The fixed price or rate at which the transaction scheduled to occur at the expiration of a forward contract will take place. This price is agreed on at the initiation date of the contract.

Forward rate A short-term yield for a future holding period implied by the spot rates of two securities with different maturities.

Forward rate agreement (FRA) (1) An agreement between two parties that will apply to a future notional loan or deposit. (2) A transaction in which two counterparties agree to a single exchange of cash flows based on a fixed and floating rate, respectively. (3) A forward contract calling for one party to make a fixed interest payment and the other to make an interest payment at a rate to be determined at the contract expiration.

Forward swap A forward contract to enter into a swap.

Fourth market Direct trading of securities between owners, usually institutions, without any broker intermediation.

Franchise The right or license to an exclusive territory or market.

Franchise factor A firm's unique competitive advantage that makes it possible for a firm to earn excess returns (rates of return above a firm's cost of capital) on its capital projects. In turn, these excess returns and the franchise factor cause the firm's stock price to have a P/E ratio above its base P/E ratio that is equal to $1/k$.

Franchise value In P/E ratio analysis, the present value of growth opportunities divided by next year's expected earnings.

Free cash flow This cash flow measure equals cash flow from operations minus capital expenditures and debt payments.

Free rider One who receives the benefit of a good without contributing to its costs. Public goods and commodities that generate external benefits offer people the opportunity to become free riders.

Frequency distribution A tabular display of data summarized into a relatively small number of intervals.

Frequency polygon A graph of a frequency distribution obtained by drawing straight lines joining successive points representing the class frequencies.

Frictional unemployment Unemployment due to constant changes in the economy that prevent qualified unemployed workers from being immediately matched up with existing job openings. It results from the scarcity of information and the search activities of both employers and employees for information that will help them make better employment choices.

Fringe benefits Benefits other than normal money wages that are supplied to employees in exchange for their labor services. Higher fringe benefits come at the expense of lower money wages.

Full-costing A method of accounting for the costs of exploring and developing oil and gas resources in which all costs are recorded as assets and depleted over the estimated life of the producing resources.

Full employment The level of employment that results from the efficient use of the labor force after allowance is made for the normal (natural) rate of unemployment due to information cost, dynamic changes, and the structural conditions of the economy. For the United States, full employment is thought to exist when approximately 95 percent of the labor force is employed.

Full price (or dirty price) (1) The total price of a bond, including accrued interest. (2) The price of a security with accrued interest.

Full replication A technique for constructing a passive index portfolio in which all securities in an index are purchased in proportion to their weights in the index.

Fully taxable equivalent yield (FTEY) A yield on a tax-exempt bond that adjusts for its tax benefits to allow comparisons with taxable bonds.

Fundamental beta A beta that is based at least in part on fundamental data for a company.

Fundamental factor models A multifactor model in which the factors are attributes of stocks or companies that are important in explaining cross-sectional differences in stock prices.

Futures commission merchants (FCMs) Individuals or companies that execute futures transactions for other parties off the exchange.

Futures contract (1) A standardized contract to buy (sell) an asset at a specified date and a specified price (futures price). The contract is traded on an organized exchange, and the potential gain/loss is realized each day (marking to market). (2) An agreement that provides for the future exchange of a particular asset at a specified delivery date in exchange for a specified payment at the time of delivery. (3) A variation of a forward contract that has essentially the same basic definition but with some additional features, such as a clearinghouse guarantee against credit losses, a daily settlement of gains and losses, and an organized electronic or floor trading facility.

Futures exchange A legal corporate entity whose shareholders are its members. The members of the exchange have the privilege of executing transactions directly on the exchange.

Future value (FV) The amount to which a payment or series of payments will grow by a stated future date.

Gamma A numerical measure of how sensitive an option's delta is to a change in the underlying.

Game theory Analyzes the strategic choices made by competitors in a conflict situation, such as decisions made by members of an oligopoly.

GDP deflator A price index that reveals the cost during the current period of purchasing the items included in GDP relative to the cost during a base year (currently, 1996). Because the base year is assigned a value of 100, as the GDP deflator takes on values greater than 100, it indicates that prices are higher than during the base year.

General Agreement on Tariffs and Trade (GATT) An organization formed following the Second World War to set the rules for the conduct of international trade and reduce barriers to trade among nations.

Generalized least squares A regression estimation technique that addresses heteroskedasticity of the error term.

Generally accepted accounting principles (GAAP) Accounting principles formulated by the Financial Accounting Standards Board and used to construct financial statements.

General obligation bond (GO) A municipal issue serviced from and guaranteed by the issuer's full taxing authority.

Generic *See* Plain-vanilla.

Geometric mean (GM) (1) The *n*th root of the product of the annual holding period returns for *n* years minus 1. (2) A measure of central tendency computed by taking the nth root of the product of *n* non-negative values.

Gifting phase Phase in the investment life cycle during which individuals use excess assets to financially assist relatives or friends, establish charitable trusts, or construct trusts to minimize estate taxes.

Gilt (or Gilt-edged) A U.K. government bond.

Global Investment Performance Standards™ (GIPS®) A global industry standard for the ethical presentation of investment performance results promulgated by the Association for Investment Management and Research.

Going out of business The sale of a firm's assets and its permanent exit from the market. By going out of business, a firm is able to avoid fixed costs, which would continue during a shutdown.

Gold standard An international monetary system in which the parity of a currency is fixed in terms of its gold content.

Goods and services market A highly aggregated market encompassing the flow of all final-user goods and services. The market counts all items that enter into GDP. Thus, real output in this market is equal to real GDP.

Goodwill The excess of the cost of a group of assets (usually a business) over the fair market value of the assets if purchased individually.

Gray market A forward market for newly issued bonds before the final terms on the bond are set.

Gross domestic product (GDP) (1) The market value of all final goods and services produced within a country during a specific period. (2) Total value of a country's output produced by residents within the country's physical borders.

Gross national product (GNP) (1) The total market value of all final goods and services produced by the citizens of a country. It is equal to GDP minus the net income of foreigners. (2) Total value of a country's output produced by residents both within the country's physical borders and abroad.

Group depreciation The grouping of similar items to calculate depreciation.

Group of Seven (G-7) The seven countries (Canada, France, Germany, Italy, Japan, the United Kingdom, and the United States) that meet periodically to enhance cooperative action on international economic matters. [The Group of Eight (G-8) includes Russia.]

Growth company A company that consistently has the opportunities and ability to invest in projects that provide rates of return that exceed the firm's cost of capital. Because of these investment opportunities, it retains a high proportion of earnings, and its earnings grow faster than those of average firms.

Growth stock A stock issue that generates a higher rate of return than other stocks in the market with similar risk characteristics; usually identified by high P/E or high price-to-book ratios.

Harmonic mean A type of weighted mean computed by averaging the reciprocals of the observations, then taking the reciprocal of that average.

Health and safety regulation Legislation designed to improve the health, safety, and environmental conditions available to workers and/or consumers. The legislation usually mandates production procedures, minimum standards, and/or product characteristics to be met by producers and employers.

Hedge fund A type of investment vehicle often set up as a limited partnership, limited liability corporation, or offshore corporation to be exempt from most governmental regulation.

Hedge ratio (1) The percentage of the position in an asset that is hedged with derivatives. (2) The number of derivative contracts that must be transacted to offset the price volatility of an underlying commodity or security position. (3) The relationship of the quantity of an asset being hedged to the quantity of the derivative used for hedging.

Hedging (1) The process of reducing the uncertainty of the future value of a portfolio by taking positions in various derivatives (e.g., forward and futures contracts). (2) A general strategy usually thought of as reducing, if not eliminating, risk.

Herfindahl index A measure of industry concentration equal to the sum of the squared market shares of the firms in the industry.

Heteroskedasticity The property of having a nonconstant variance; refers to an error term with the property that its variance differs across observations.

Heteroskedasticity-consistent standard errors Standard errors of the estimated parameters of a regression that correct for the presence of heteroskedasticity in the regression's error term.

High-yield bond A bond rated below investment grade. Also referred to as speculative-grade bonds or junk bonds.

Histogram A bar chart of data that have been grouped into a frequency distribution.

Historical method A method of estimating VAR that uses data from the returns of the portfolio over a recent past period and compiles this data in the form of a histogram.

Historical simulation method (or back simulation) (1) Another term for the historical method of estimating VAR. This term is somewhat misleading in that the method involves not a simulation of the past but rather what actually happened in the past, sometimes adjusted to reflect the fact that a different portfolio may have existed in the past than is planned for the future. (2) Simulation involving sampling from a historical data series.

Holder-of-record date If the company lists the stockholder as an owner on this date, then the stockholder receives the dividend.

Holding period return (HPR) (1) The total return from an investment, including all sources of income, for a given period of time. A value of 1.0 indicates no gain or loss. (2) The return that an investor earns during a specified holding period; a synonym for total return.

Holding period yield (HPY) (1) The total return from an investment for a given period of time stated as a percentage. (2) The return that an investor earns during a specified holding period; holding period return with reference to a fixed-income instrument.

Homogenization Creating a contract with standard and generally accepted terms, which makes it more acceptable to a broader group of participants.

Homoskedasticity The property of having a constant variance; refers to an error term that is constant across observations.

Hostile takeover The acquisition of a company over the opposition of its management.

Human capital The value of skills and knowledge possessed by the workforce.

Human resources The abilities, skills, and health of human beings that can contribute to the production of both current and future output. Investment in training and education can increase the supply of human resources.

Hurdle rate The discount rate (cost of capital) which the IRR must exceed if a project is to be accepted.

Hypothesis With reference to statistical inference, a statement about one or more populations.

Hypothesis testing With reference to statistical inference, the subdivision dealing with the testing of hypotheses about one or more populations.

Immunization A bond portfolio management technique of matching modified duration to the investment horizon of the portfolio to eliminate interest rate risk.

Impact lag The time period after a policy change is implemented but before the change begins to exert its primary effects.

Implementation shortfall With respect to execution costs, the difference between the value of the executed portfolio or share position and the value of the same portfolio at the time the trading decision was made.

Implicit costs The opportunity costs associated with a firm's use of resources that it owns. These costs do not involve a direct money payment. Examples include wage income and interest forgone by the owner of a firm who also provides labor services and equity capital to the firm.

Implicit marginal tax rate The amount of additional (marginal) earnings that must be paid explicitly in taxes or implicitly in the form of a reduction in income supplements. Since the marginal tax rate establishes the fraction of an additional dollar earned that an individual is permitted to keep, it is an important determinant of the incentive to work.

Implied forward exchange rate *See* Break-even exchange rate.

Implied repo rate The rate of return from a cash-and-carry transaction implied by the futures price relative to the spot price.

Implied volatility (1) The volatility of an asset that is implicit in the current market price of an option (using a standard Black-Scholes-Merton formula). (2) The standard deviation of changes in the price of the underlying asset that can be inferred from an option's market price in relation to a specific valuation model. (3) The volatility that option traders use to price an option, implied by the price of the option and a particular option-pricing model.

Implied yield A measure of the yield on the underlying bond of a futures contract implied by pricing it as though the underlying will be delivered at the futures expiration.

Import quota A specific limit or maximum quantity (or value) of a good permitted to be imported into a country during a given period.

Imports Goods and services produced by foreigners but purchased by domestic consumers, businesses, and governments.

Income bonds Debentures that stipulate interest payments only if the issuer earns the income to make the payments by specified dates.

Income effect (1) That part of an increase (decrease) in amount consumed that is the result of the consumer's real income (the consumption possibilities available to the consumer) being expanded (contracted) by a reduction (rise) in the price of a good. (2) The known component of the total return for a bond during a period of time if the shape and position of the yield curve did not change.

Income elasticity The percentage change in the quantity of a product demanded divided by the percentage change in consumer income causing the change in quantity demanded. It measures the responsiveness of the demand for a good to a change in income.

Income mobility Movement of individuals and families either up or down income-distribution rankings when comparisons are made at two different points in time. When substantial income mobility is present, one's current position will not be a very good indicator of what one's position will be a few years in the future.

Income statement A financial statement that shows the flow of the firm's sales, expenses, and earnings over a period of time.

Increasing-cost industry An industry for which costs of production rise as output is expanded. Thus, even in the long run, higher market prices will be required to induce the firms to expand the total output in such industries. The long-run market supply curve in such industries will slope upward to the right.

Incremental cash flows The changes or increments to cash flows resulting from a decision or action.

Indenture The legal agreement that lists the obligations of the issuer of a bond to the bondholder, including payment schedules, call provisions, and sinking funds.

Independent With reference to events, the property that the occurrence of one event does not affect the probability of another event occurring.

Independent and identically distributed (IID) With respect to random variables, the property of random variables that are independent of each other but follow the identical probability distribution.

Independent projects Projects whose cash flows are not affected by the acceptance or nonacceptance of other projects.

Independent variable A variable used to explain the dependent variable in a regression; a right-hand-side variable in a regression equation.

Index amortizing swap An interest rate swap in which the notional principal is indexed to the level of interest rates and declines with the level of interest rates according to a predefined scheduled. This type of swap is frequently used to hedge securities that are prepaid as interest rates decline, such as mortgage-backed securities.

Indexing (1) A passive bond portfolio management strategy that seeks to match the composition, and therefore the performance, of a selected market index. (2) An investment strategy in which an investor constructs a portfolio to mirror the performance of a specified index.

Index-linked bond A bond whose interest rate payments and/or redemption value are contractually linked to some specified index (e.g., a commodity price).

Index of leading indicators An index of economic variables that historically has tended to turn down prior to the beginning of a recession and turn up prior to the beginning of a business expansion.

Index option An option in which the underlying is a stock index.

Indifference curve A curve, convex from below, that separates the consumption bundles that are more preferred by an individual from those that are less preferred. The points on the curve represent combinations of goods that are equally preferred by the individual.

Indirect business taxes Taxes that increase the business firm's costs of production and, therefore, the prices charged to consumers. Examples would be sales, excise, and property taxes.

Indirect exchange rate The amount of foreign currency required to purchase one unit of domestic currency.

Industry life cycle analysis An analysis that focuses on the industry's stage of development.

Inferior good A good that has a negative income elasticity, so that, as consumer income rises, the demand for that good falls.

Inflation A continuing rise in the general level of prices of goods and services. The purchasing power of the monetary unit, such as the dollar, declines when inflation is present.

Inflation The amount by which prices increase over time.

Inflationary premium A component of the money interest rate that reflects compensation to the lender for the expected decrease, due to inflation, in the purchasing power of the principal and interest during the course of the loan. It is determined by the expected rate of future inflation.

Information An attribute of a good market that includes providing buyers and sellers with timely, accurate information on the volume and prices of past transactions and on all currently outstanding bids and offers.

Information content (signaling) hypothesis The theory that investors regard dividend changes as signals of management's earnings forecast.

Information ratio (IR) (1) The ratio of excess return over the benchmark to tracking error relative to the benchmark. (2) Statistic used to measure a portfolio's average return in excess of a comparison, benchmark portfolio divided by the standard deviation of this excess return. (3) Mean active return divided by active risk.

Informationally efficient market A more technical term for an efficient capital market that emphasizes the role of information in setting the market price.

Initial margin The amount that an investor must deposit to open a position in futures and some other derivatives; also used to refer to the initial equity required when a stock is purchased using borrowed money.

Initial margin requirement The margin requirement on the first day of a transaction as well as on any day in which additional margin funds must be deposited.

Initial public offering (IPO) A new issue by a firm that has no existing public market.

Innovation The successful introduction and adoption of a new product or process; the economic application of inventions and marketing techniques.

In-sample forecast errors The residuals from a fitted time-series model within the sample period used to fit the model.

Instability in the minimum-variance frontier The characteristic of minimum-variance frontiers that they are sensitive to small changes in inputs.

Insuring The process of setting a minimum level for the future value of a portfolio by taking positions in various derivatives (e.g., options).

Intangible assets Long-term assets with no physical substance whose value is based on rights or advantages accruing to the owner.

Intermediate goods Goods purchased for resale or for use in producing another good or service.

Interest-on-interest Bond income from reinvestment of coupon payments.

Interest rate A rate of return that reflects the relationship between differently dated cash flows; a discount rate.

Interest rate anticipation An active bond portfolio management strategy designed to preserve capital or take advantage of capital gains opportunities by predicting interest rates and their effects on bond prices.

Interest rate call An option in which the holder has the right to make a known interest payment and receive an unknown interest payment.

Interest rate cap or cap A series of call options on an interest rate, with each option expiring at the date on which the floating loan rate will be reset, and with each option having the same exercise rate. A cap in general can have an underlying other than an interest rate.

Interest rate collar (1) The combination of a long position in a cap agreement and a short position in a floor agreement, or vice versa; it is equivalent to a series of range forward positions. (2) A combination of a long cap and a short floor, or a short cap and a long floor. A collar in general can have an underlying other than an interest rate.

Interest rate effect The return on a bond portfolio caused by changes in the term structure of interest rates during a period that affect both bond prices and reinvestment rates.

Interest rate floor or floor A series of put options on an interest rate, with each option expiring at the date on which the floating loan rate will be reset, and with each option having the same exercise rate. A floor in general can have an underlying other than the interest rate.

Interest rate forward *See* Forward rate agreement.

Interest rate option An option in which the underlying is an interest rate.

Interest rate parity (1) An arbitrage process that ensures that the forward discount or premium equals the interest rate differential between two currencies. (2) The relationship that must exist in an efficient market between the spot and forward foreign exchange rates between two countries and the interest rates in those countries. (3) A formula that expresses the equivalence or parity of spot and forward rates, after adjusting for differences in the interest rates.

Interest rate put An option in which the holder has the right to make an unknown interest payment and receive a known interest payment.

Interest rate risk The uncertainty of returns on an investment due to possible changes in interest rates over time.

Interest rate swap (1) A contract to exchange streams of fixed-interest-rate for floating-interest-rate cash flows denominated in the same currency. (2) An agreement calling for the periodic exchange of cash flows, one based on an interest rate that remains fixed for the life of the contract and the other that is linked to a variable-rate index. (3) A swap in which the underlying is an interest rate. Can be viewed as a currency swap in which both currencies are the same and can be created as a combination of currency swaps.

Intergenerational data mining A form of data mining that applies information developed by previous researchers using a dataset to guide current research using the same or a related dataset.

Internal liquidity (solvency) ratios Financial ratios that measure the ability of the firm to meet future short-term financial obligations.

Internal Rate of Return (IRR) (1) The discount rate that equates the present value of a future stream of cash flows to the initial investment. (2) The discount rate at which cash outflows of an investment equal cash inflows. (3) The discount rate that makes net present value equal 0; the discount rate that makes the present value of an investment's costs (outflows) equal to the present value of the investment's benefits (inflows).

International CAPM An equilibrium theory that relates the expected return of an asset to its world market and foreign exchange risks.

International domestic bonds Bonds issued by a foreign firm, denominated in the firm's native currency, and sold within its own country.

International Fisher relation The assertion that the interest rate differential between two countries should equal the expected inflation rate differential over the term of the interest rates.

International Monetary Fund (IMF) An organization set up in 1944 to promote exchange rate stability and to assist member countries facing economic difficulties.

International Securities Market Association (ISMA) An association formed in 1969 to establish uniform trading procedures in the international bond markets. Formerly named AIBD.

International Swaps and Derivatives Association (ISDA) An association of swap dealers formed in 1985 to promote uniform practices in the writing, trading, and settlement procedures of swaps and other derivatives.

Interquartile range The difference between the third and first quartiles of a dataset.

Interval With reference to grouped data, a set of values within which an observation falls.

Interval scale A measurement scale that not only ranks data but also gives assurance that the differences between scale values are equal.

In-the-money option (1) An option that has a positive value if exercised immediately. For example, a call when the strike price is below the current price of the underlying asset, or a put when the strike price is above the current price of the underlying asset. (2) An option that has positive intrinsic value. (3) Options that, if exercised, would result in the value received being worth more than the payment required to exercise.

Intrinsic value (1) The value that would be obtained on an option if it were to be exercised immediately. (2) The portion of a call option's total value equal to the greater of either zero or the difference between the current value of the underlying asset and the exercise price; for a put option, intrinsic value is the greater of either zero or the exercise price less the underlying asset price. For a stock, it is the value derived from fundamental analysis of the stock's expected returns or cash flows.

Invention The creation of a new product or process, often facilitated by the knowledge of engineering and scientific relationships.

Inventory investment Changes in the stock of unsold goods and raw materials held during a period.

Inverse floater A floating-rate note or bond in which the coupon is adjusted to move opposite to a benchmark interest rate.

Investment (1) The purchase, construction, or development of capital resources, including both nonhuman capital and human capital (such as better education). Investment expands the availability of capital resources in an economy. The process of investment is sometimes referred to as capital formation. (2) The current commitment of dollars for a period of time in order to derive future payments that will compensate the investor for the time the funds are committed, the expected rate of inflation, and the uncertainty of future payments.

Investment company (1) A firm that issues (sells) shares, and uses the proceeds to invest in various financial instruments or other assets. (2) A firm that sells shares of the company and uses the proceeds to buy portfolios of stock, bonds, or other financial instruments.

Investment decision process Estimation of value for comparison with market price to determine whether or not to invest.

Investment horizon The time period used for planning and forecasting purposes or the future time at which the investor requires the invested funds.

Investment in human capital Expenditures on training, education, skill development, and health designed to increase human capital and the productivity of an individual.

Investment management company A company separate from the investment company that manages the portfolio and performs administrative functions.

Investment Opportunity Schedule (IOS) A graph of the firm's investment opportunities ranked in order of the projects' rates of return.

Investment strategy A decision by a portfolio manager regarding how he or she will manage the portfolio to meet the goals and objectives of the client. This will include either active or passive management and, if active, what style in terms of top-down or bottom-up or fundamental versus technical.

Invisible hand principle The tendency of market prices to direct individuals pursuing their own interests into productive activities that also promote the economic well-being of the society.

IRR The discount rate which forces the PV of a project's inflows to equal the PV of its costs.

IRR rule An investment decision rule that accepts projects or investments for which the IRR is greater than the opportunity cost of capital.

January effect A frequent empirical anomaly where risk-adjusted stock returns in the month of January are significantly larger than those occurring in any other month of the year.

Jensen measure An absolute measure of a portfolio's risk-adjusted performance, computed as the intercept in a regression equation where the excess returns to a manager's portfolio and the market index are, respectively, the dependent and independent variables.

Joint probability The probability of the joint occurrence of stated events.

***k*th Order autocorrelation** The correlation between observations in a time series separated by *k* periods.

Kurtosis The statistical measure that indicates the peakedness of a distribution.

Labor force participation rate The number of persons in the civilian labor force 16 years of age or over who are either employed or actively seeking employment as a percentage of the total civilian population 16 years of age and over.

Labor union A collective organization of employees who bargain as a unit with employers.

Laffer curve A curve illustrating the relationship between the tax rate and tax revenue. Tax revenue will be low for both very high and very low tax rates. Thus, when tax rates are quite high, a reduction in the tax rate can increase tax revenue.

Lagging indicators A set of economic variables whose values reach peaks and troughs after the aggregate economy.

Later stage With respect to venture capital financing, the stage after commercial manufacturing and sales have begun. Later-stage financing includes second-stage, third-stage, and mezzanine financing.

Law of comparative advantage A principle that states that individuals, firms, regions, or nations can gain by specializing in the production of goods that they produce cheaply (that is, at a low opportunity cost) and exchanging those goods for other desired goods for which they are high-opportunity-cost producers.

Law of demand A principle that states there is an inverse relationship between the price of a good and the amount of it buyers are willing to purchase. As the price of a product increases, other things constant, consumers will purchase less of the product.

Law of diminishing marginal utility The basic economic principle that, as the consumption of a commodity increases, the marginal utility derived from consuming more of the commodity (per unit of time) will eventually decline.

Law of diminishing returns The postulate that, as more and more units of a variable resource are combined with a fixed amount of other resources, employment of additional units of the variable resource will eventually increase output only at a decreasing rate. Once diminishing returns are reached, it will take successively larger amounts of the variable factor to expand output by one unit.

Law of one price The condition in a financial market in which two financial instruments or combinations of financial instruments can sell for only one price. Equivalent to the principle that no arbitrage opportunities are possible.

Law of supply A principle that states there is a direct relationship between the price of a good and the amount of it offered for sale. As the price of a product increases, other things constant, producers will increase the amount of the product supplied to the market.

Leading indicators A set of economic variables whose values reach peaks and troughs in advance of the aggregate economy.

Leading P/E (or forward P/E or prospective P/E) A stock's current price divided by next year's expected earnings.

Lead manager The bank in charge of organizing a syndicated bank credit or a bond issue.

Leasehold A right to occupy land or buildings under a long-term rental contract.

Leasehold improvements Improvements to leased property that become the property of the lessor at the end of the lease.

Legal risk The risk that the legal system will not enforce a contract in case of dispute or fraud.

Leptokurtic Describes a distribution that is more peaked than a normal distribution.

Less-developed countries (LDCs) Low-income countries generally characterized by rapid population growth and an agriculture-household sector that dominates the economy. Sometimes these countries are referred to as developing countries.

Level of significance The probability of a Type I error in testing a hypothesis.

Leverage The relation between the value of the asset position and the amount of equity invested.

Leveraged floating-rate note (or leveraged floater) A floating-rate note or bond in which the coupon is adjusted at a multiple of a benchmark interest rate.

LIBMEAN The average of LIBID and LIBOR.

License The right to use a formula, technique, process, or design.

Licensing A requirement that one obtain permission from the government in order to perform certain business activities or work in various occupations.

Likelihood The probability of an observation, given a particular set of conditions.

Limit down A limit move in the futures market in which the price at which a transaction would be made is at or below the lower limit.

Limit move A condition in the futures markets in which the price at which a transaction would be made is at or beyond the price limits.

Limit order (1) An order to buy or sell a security at a specific price or better (lower for a buy order and higher for a sell order). (2) An order that lasts for a specified time to buy or sell a security when and if it trades at a specified price.

Limit pricing Pricing below average cost to deter entry into an industry.

Limit up A limit move in the futures market in which the price at which a transaction would be made is at or above the upper limit.

Linear association A straight-line relationship, as opposed to a relationship that cannot be graphed as a straight line.

Linear interpolation The estimation of an unknown value on the basis of two known values that bracket it, using a straight line between the two known values.

Linear regression Regression that models the straight-line relationship between the dependent and independent variable(s).

Linear trend A trend in which the dependent variable changes at a constant rate with time.

Liquid Term used to describe an asset that can be quickly converted to cash at a price close to fair market value.

Liquid asset An asset that can be easily and quickly converted to purchasing power without loss of value.

Liquidity (1) The ability to buy or sell an asset quickly and at a reasonable price. (2) The ability to trade a futures contract, either selling a previously purchased contract or purchasing a previously sold contract.

Liquidity premium A premium added to the equilibrium interest rate on a security if that security cannot be converted to cash on short notice and at close to "fair market value."

Liquidity risk (1) Uncertainty due to the ability to buy or sell an investment in the secondary market. (2) The risk that a financial instrument cannot be purchased or sold without a significant concession in price due to the size of the market.

Loanable funds market A general term used to describe the broad market that coordinates the borrowing and lending decisions of business firms and households. Commercial banks, savings and loan associations, the stock and bond markets, and insurance companies are important financial institutions in this market.

Local currency (foreign currency) exposure The sensitivity of the asset return, measured in the asset's local currency, to a movement in the exchange rate.

Locked limit A condition in the futures markets in which a transaction cannot take place because the price would be beyond the limits.

Logit model A qualitative-dependent-variable multiple regression model based on the logistic probability distribution.

Log-linear model With reference to time-series models, a model in which the growth rate of the time series as a function of time is constant.

Log-log regression model A regression that expresses the dependent and independent variables as natural logarithms.

Logrolling The exchange between politicians of political support on one issue for political support on another issue.

London Interbank Bid (LIBID) The rate quoted to a top-quality lender on the London interbank market.

London InterBank Offer Rate (LIBOR) (1) The rate at which international banks lend on the Eurocurrency market. This is the rate quoted to a top-quality borrower. The most common maturities are one month, three months, and six months. There is a LIBOR for the U.S. dollar and a few other major currencies. LIBOR is determined by the British Banking Association in London. *See* also Euribor. (2) The Eurodollar rate at which London banks lend dollars to other London banks; considered to be the best representative rate on a dollar borrowed by a private, high-quality borrower.

Long The buyer of a derivative contract. Also refers to the position of owning a derivative.

Long hedge (1) A hedge involving the purchase of forward or futures contracts in anticipation of a spot purchase. Also known as anticipatory hedge. (2) A long position in a forward or futures contract used to offset the price volatility of a short position in the underlying asset.

Longitudinal data Observations on characteristic(s) of the same observational unit through time.

Long position The buyer of a commodity or security or, for a forward contract, the counterparty who will be the eventual buyer of the underlying asset.

Long run (in production) (1) A time period long enough to allow the firm to vary all factors of production. (2) A time period of sufficient length to enable decision makers to adjust fully to a market change.

Long-term equity anticipatory securities (LEAPS) Options originally created with expirations of several years.

Long-term, high-priority goal A long-term financial investment goal of personal importance that typically includes achieving financial independence, such as being able to retire at a certain age.

Look-ahead bias A bias caused by using information that was unavailable on the test date.

Loss Deficit of sales revenue relative to the opportunity cost of production. Losses are a penalty imposed on those who misuse resources in lower-valued uses as judged by buyers in the market.

Lower bound The lowest possible value of an option.

Lower-priority goal A financial investment goal of lesser personal importance, such as taking a luxurious vacation or buying a car every few years.

Low-load fund A mutual fund that imposes a moderate front-end sales charge when the investor buys the fund, typically about 3 to 4 percent.

Low-regular-dividend-plus-extras The policy of announcing a low, regular dividend that can be retained no matter what, and then when times are good paying a designated "extra" dividend.

M1 (money supply) The sum of (1) currency in circulation (including coins), (2) checkable deposits maintained in depository institutions, and (3) traveler's checks.

M2 (money supply) Equal to M1 plus (1) savings deposits, (2) time deposits (accounts of less than $100,000) held in depository institutions, and (3) money market mutual fund shares.

Macaulay duration (1) A measure of the time flow of cash from a bond where cash flows are weighted by present values discounted by the yield to maturity. (2) The duration before dividing by $1 + y_b$. The term, named for one of the economists who first derived it, is used to distinguish the calculation from modified duration. *See also* Modified duration.

Macroeconomic factor A factor related to the economy, such as the inflation rate, industrial production, or economic sector membership.

Macroeconomic factor model A multifactor model in which the factors are surprises in macroeconomic variables that significantly explain equity returns.

Macroeconomics The branch of economics that focuses on how human behavior affects outcomes in highly aggregated markets, such as the markets for labor or consumer products.

Maintenance margin (1) The minimum margin that an investor must keep on deposit in a margin account at all times. (2) The required proportion that the investor's equity value must be to the total market value of the stock. If the proportion drops below this percent, the investor will receive a margin call.

Maintenance margin requirement The margin requirement on any day other than the first day of a transaction.

Management and advisory firm A firm that provides a range of services from standard banking transactions (savings accounts, personal loans) to advising individual and institutional investors on structuring their portfolios and managing investment funds.

Management effect A combination of the interest rate anticipation effect, the analysis effect, and the trading effect.

Management fee The compensation an investment company pays to the investment management company for its services. The average annual fee is about 0.5 percent of fund assets.

Margin (1) The percent of cost a buyer pays in cash for a security, borrowing the balance from the broker. This introduces leverage, which increases the risk of the transaction. (2) The amount of money that a trader deposits in a margin account. The term is derived from the stock market practice in which an investor borrows a portion of the money required to purchase a certain amount of stock. In futures markets, there is no borrowing so the margin is more of a down payment or performance bond.

Margin account The collateral posted with the futures exchange clearinghouse by an outside counterparty to insure its eventual performance; the initial margin is the deposit required at contract origination while the maintenance margin is the minimum collateral necessary at all times.

Marginal Term used to describe the effects of a change in the current situation. For example, the marginal cost is the cost of producing an additional unit of a product, given the producer's current facility and production rate.

Marginal benefit The maximum price a consumer would be willing to pay for an additional unit. It is the dollar value of the consumer's marginal utility from the additional unit, and thus falls as consumption increases.

Marginal cost The change in total cost required to produce an additional unit of output.

Marginal Cost of Capital (MCC) The cost of obtaining another dollar of new capital; the weighted average cost of the last dollar of new capital raised.

Marginal Cost of Capital (MCC) Schedule A graph that relates the firm's weighted average cost of each dollar of capital to the total amount of new capital raised.

Marginal probability *See* Unconditional probability.

Marginal product The increase in the total product resulting from a unit increase in the employment of a variable input. Mathematically, it is the ratio of the change in total product to the change in the quantity of the variable input.

Marginal propensity to consume (MPC) Additional current consumption divided by additional current disposable income.

Marginal rate of substitution The change in the consumption level of one good that is just sufficient to offset a unit change in the consumption of another good without causing a shift to another indifference curve. At any point on an indifference curve, it will be equal to the slope of the curve at that point.

Marginal revenue (MR) The incremental change in total revenue derived from the sale of one additional unit of a product.

Marginal revenue product (MRP) The change in the total revenue of a firm that results from the employment of one additional unit of a resource. The marginal revenue product of an input is equal to its marginal product multiplied by the marginal revenue of the good or service produced.

Marginal tax rate (MTR) (1) Additional tax liability divided by additional taxable income. It is the percentage of an extra dollar of income that must be paid in taxes. It is the marginal tax rate that is relevant in personal decision making. (2) The part of each additional dollar in income that is paid as tax.

Marginal utility The additional utility received from the consumption of an additional unit of a good.

Margin call A request by an investor's broker for additional capital for a security bought on margin if the investor's equity value declines below the required maintenance margin.

Margin deposit The amount of cash or securities that must be deposited as guarantee on a futures position. The margin is a returnable deposit.

Marked to market The settlement process used to adjust the margin account of a futures contract for daily changes in the price of the underlying asset.

Market (1) An abstract concept that encompasses the trading arrangements of buyers and sellers that underlie the forces of supply and demand. (2) The means through which buyers and sellers are brought together to aid in the transfer of goods and/or services.

Market impact With reference to execution costs, the difference between the actual execution price and the market price that would have prevailed had the manager not sought to trade the security.

Market maker An institution or individual quoting firm bid and ask prices for a security and standing ready to buy or sell the security at those quoted prices. Also called a dealer.

Market, or Beta, risk That part of a project's risk that cannot be eliminated by diversification; it is measured by the project's beta coefficient.

Market order (1) An order to buy (sell) immediately at the best obtainable price. (2) An order to buy or sell a security immediately at the best price available.

Market portfolio The portfolio that includes all risky assets with relative weights equal to their proportional market values.

Market power The ability of a firm that is not a pure monopolist to earn unusually large profits, indicating that it has some monopoly power. Because the firm has few (or weak) competitors, it has a degree of freedom from the discipline of vigorous competition.

Market price of risk The slope of the capital market line, indicating the market risk premium for each unit of market risk.

Market risk The risk associated with interest rates, exchange rates, and equity prices.

Market risk premium (1) The amount of return above the risk-free rate that investors expect from the market in general as compensation for systematic risk. (2) The expected excess return on the market over the risk-free rate.

Market value added (MVA) External management performance measure to compare the market value of the company's debt and equity with the total capital invested in the firm.

Market-value-weighted series An indicator series calculated as the total market value of the securities in the sample.

Marking to market (1) Procedure whereby potential profits and losses on a futures position are realized daily. The daily futures price variation is debited (credited) in cash to the loser (winner) at the end of the day. (2) A procedure used primarily in futures markets in which the parties to a contract settle the amount owed daily. Also known as the daily settlement.

Maturity risk premium (MRP) A premium that reflects interest rate risk.

Maturity strategy A portfolio management strategy employed to reduce the interest rate risk of a bond portfolio by matching the maturity of the portfolio with its investment horizon. For example, if the investment horizon is 10 years, the portfolio manager would construct a portfolio that will mature in 10 years.

Mean absolute deviation With reference to a sample, the mean of the absolute values of deviations from the sample mean.

Mean excess return The average rate of return in excess of the risk-free rate.

Mean rates of return The average of an investment's returns over an extended period of time.

Mean reversion The tendency of a time series to fall when its level is above its mean and rise when its level is below its mean; a mean-reverting time series tends to return to its long-term mean.

Means-tested income transfers Transfers that are limited to persons or families with an income below a certain cutoff point. Eligibility is thus dependent on low-income status.

Mean–variance analysis An approach to portfolio analysis using expected means, variances, and covariances of asset returns.

Measure of central tendency A quantitative measure that specifies where data are centered.

Measure of location A quantitative measure that describes the location or distribution of data; includes not only measures of central tendency but also other measures such as percentiles.

Measurement scales A scheme of measuring differences. The four types of measurement scales are nominal, ordinal, interval, and ratio.

Median The value of the middle item of a set of items that has been sorted into ascending or descending order; the 50th percentile.

Medical savings accounts Special savings accounts that individuals could use for the payment of medical bills or the purchase of a catastrophic (high deductibility) health insurance plan. Unfavorable tax treatment compared to employer-provided health insurance and other regulatory restrictions currently reduce their use.

Medium of exchange An asset that is used to buy and sell goods or services.

Mesokurtic Describes a distribution with kurtosis identical to that of the normal distribution.

Method of comparables An approach to evaluation that involves using a price multiple to evaluate whether an asset is relatively fairly valued, relatively undervalued, or relatively overvalued in relation to a benchmark value of the multiple.

Mezzanine financing With respect to venture capital financing, capital provided to prepare for the step of going public. Also known as bridge financing.

Microeconomics The branch of economics that focuses on how human behavior affects the conduct of affairs within narrowly defined units, such as individual households or business firms.

Middleman A person who buys and sells or who arranges trades. A middleman reduces transaction costs.

Minimum-variance frontier The graph of the set of portfolios that have minimum variance for their level of expected return.

Minimum-variance hedge ratio The hedge ratio that is expected to minimize the variance of the rate of return on the hedged portfolio.

Minimum-variance portfolio The portfolio with the minimum variance for each given level of expected return.

Minimum wage Legislation requiring that workers be paid at least the stated minimum hourly rate of pay.

Mixed factor models Factor models that combine features of more than one type of factor model.

Modal interval With reference to grouped data, the most frequently occurring interval.

Mode The most frequently occurring value in a set of observations.

Model risk The use of an inaccurate pricing model for a particular investment, or the improper use of the right model.

Model specification With reference to regression, the set of variables included in the regression and the regression equation's functional form.

Modified duration (1) Measure of a bond's price sensitivity to interest rate movements. Equal to the duration of a bond divided by one plus its yield to maturity. (2) A measure of Macaulay duration divided by one plus the bond's periodic yield used to approximate the bond's price volatility. (3) An adjustment of the duration for the level of the yield. Contrast with Macaulay duration.

Modified IRR (MIRR) The discount rate at which the present value of a project's cost is equal to the present value of its terminal value, where the terminal value is found as the sum of the future values of the cash inflows, compounded at the firm's cost of capital.

Monetarists A group of economists who believe that (1) monetary instability is the major cause of fluctuations in real GDP and (2) rapid growth of the money supply is the major cause of inflation.

Monetary base The sum of currency in circulation plus bank reserves (vault cash and reserves with the Fed). It reflects the stock of U.S. securities held by the Fed.

Monetary policy The deliberate control of the money supply, and, in some cases, credit conditions, for the purpose of achieving macroeconomic goals.

Money interest rate The percentage of the amount borrowed that must be paid to the lender in addition to the repayment of the principal. It overstates the real cost of borrowing during an inflationary period. When inflation is anticipated, an inflationary premium will be incorporated into this rate. The money interest rate is often referred to as the nominal interest rate.

Money market (1) The market for short-term debt securities with maturities of less than one year. (2) The market for short-term debt instruments (one-year maturity or less).

Money market mutual funds (1) Interest-earning accounts offered by brokerage firms that pool depositors' funds and invest them in highly liquid short-term securities. Since these securities can be quickly converted to cash, depositors are permitted to write checks (which reduce their share holdings) against their accounts. (2) A fund that invests in short-term securities sold in the money market. (Large companies, banks, and other institutions also invest their surplus cash in the money market for short periods of time.) In the entire investment spectrum, these are generally the safest, most stable securities available. They include Treasury bills, certificates of deposit of large banks, and commercial paper (short-term IOUs of large corporations).

Money market yield (or CD equivalent yield) A yield on a basis comparable to the quoted yield on an interest-bearing money market instrument that pays interest on a 360-day basis; the annualized holding period yield, assuming a 360-day year.

Moneyness The relationship between the price of the underlying and an option's exercise price.

Money rate of interest The rate of interest in monetary terms that borrowers pay for borrowed funds. During periods when borrowers and lenders expect inflation, the money rate of interest exceeds the real rate of interest.

Money supply The supply of currency, checking account funds, and traveler's checks. These items are counted as money because they are used as the means of payment for purchases.

Money-weighted rate of return The internal rate of return on a portfolio, taking account of all cash flows.

Money-weighted return A rate of return measure corresponding to the internal rate of return; captures a return on average invested capital.

Monopolistic competition Term often used by economists to describe markets characterized by a large number of sellers that supply differentiated products to a market with low barriers to entry. Essentially, it is an alternative term for a competitive price-searcher market.

Monopoly A market structure characterized by (1) a single seller of a well-defined product for which there are no good substitutes and (2) high barriers to the entry of any other firms into the market for that product.

Monte Carlo simulation A risk analysis technique in which probable future events are simulated on a computer, generating estimated rates of return and risk indexes.

Mortgage bonds Bonds that pledge specific assets such as buildings and equipment. The proceeds from the sale of these assets are used to pay off bondholders in case of bankruptcy.

Moving average The continually recalculating average of security prices for a period, often 200 days, to serve as an indication of the general trend of prices and also as a benchmark price.

Multicollinearity A regression assumption violation that occurs when two or more independent variables (or combinations of independent variables) are highly but not perfectly correlated with each other.

Multifactor model An empirical version of the APT where the investor chooses the exact number and identity of the common risk factors used to describe an asset's risk-return relationship. Risk factors are often designated as macroeconomic variables (e.g., inflation, changes in gross domestic product) or microeconomic variables (e.g., security-specific characteristics like firm size or book-to-market ratios).

Multiple IRRs The situation where a project has two or more IRRs.

Multiple linear regression Linear regression involving two or more independent variables.

Multiple linear regression model A linear regression model with two or more independent variables.

Multiple R The correlation between the actual and forecasted values of the dependent variable in a regression.

Multiplication rule for probabilities The rule that the joint probability of events A and B equals the probability of A given B times the probability of B.

Multivariate distribution A probability distribution that specifies the probabilities for a group of related random variables.

Multivariate normal distribution A probability distribution for a group of random variables that is completely defined by the means and variances of the variables plus all the correlations between pairs of the variables.

Mutual fund (1) An open-end investment company. Also called unit trust in the United Kingdom and some other countries. (2) An investment company that pools money from shareholders and invests in a variety of securities, including stocks, bonds, and money market securities. A mutual fund ordinarily stands ready to buy back (redeem) its shares at their current net asset value, which depends on the market value of the fund's portfolio of securities at the time. Mutual funds generally continuously offer new shares to investors.

Mutually exclusive events Events such that only one can occur at a time.

Mutually exclusive projects A set of projects where only one can be accepted.

National Association of Securities Dealers Automated Quotation (Nasdaq) system An electronic system for providing bid-ask quotes on OTC securities.

National debt The sum of the indebtedness of the federal government in the form of outstanding interest-earning bonds. It reflects the cumulative impact of budget deficits and surpluses.

National income The total income earned by the nationals (citizens) during a period. It is the sum of employee compensation, self-employment income, rents, interest, and corporate profits.

Natural monopoly A market situation in which the average costs of production continually decline with increased output. Therefore, average costs of production will be lowest when a single, large firm produces the entire output demanded.

Natural rate of unemployment The long-run average unemployment rate due to frictional and structural conditions of labor markets. This rate is affected both by dynamic change and by public policy. It is sustainable into the future. The current natural rate of unemployment in the United States is thought to be approximately 5 percent.

Near-term, high-priority goal A short-term financial investment goal of personal importance, such as accumulating funds for making a house down payment or buying a car.

Negative serial correlation Serial correlation in which a positive error for one observation increases the chance of a negative error for another observation, and vice versa.

Negotiated sales An underwriting arrangement wherein the sale of a security issue by an issuing entity (governmental body or a corporation) is done using an investment banking firm that maintains an ongoing relationship with the issuer. The characteristics of the security issue are determined by the issuer in consultation with the investment banker.

Neoclassical growth theory A theory of economic growth that assumes that the marginal productivity of capital declines as more capital is added.

Net asset value The market value of the assets owned by a fund.

Net asset value (NAV) per share The market value of an investment company's assets (securities, cash, and any accrued earnings) after deducting liabilities, divided by the number of shares outstanding.

Net exports Exports minus imports.

Net income of foreigners The income that foreigners earn by contributing labor and capital resources to the production of goods within the borders of a country minus the income the nationals of the country earn abroad.

Net present value (NPV) (1) A measure of the excess cash flows expected from an investment proposal. It is equal to the present value of the cash inflows from an investment proposal, discounted at the required rate of return for the investment, minus the present value of the cash outflows required by the investment, also discounted at the investment's required rate of return. If the derived net present value is a positive value (i.e., there is an excess net present value), the investment should be acquired since it will provide a rate of return above its required returns. (2) The present value of an investment's cash inflows (benefits) minus the present value of its cash outflows (costs).

Net present value (NPV) method A method of ranking investment proposals using the NPV.

Net present value profile A graph showing the relationship between a project's NPV and the firm's cost of capital.

New classical economists Economists who believe there are strong forces pushing a market economy toward full employment equilibrium and that macroeconomic policy is an ineffective tool with which to reduce economic instability.

New issue Common stocks or bonds offered by companies for public sale.

Netting When parties agree to exchange only the net amount owed from one party to the other.

***n* Factorial** For a positive integer *n*, the product of the first *n* positive integers; 0 factorial equals 1 by definition. *n* factorial is written as *n*!.

Node Each value on a binomial tree from which successive moves or outcomes branch.

No-load fund A mutual fund that sells its shares at net asset value without adding sales charges.

Nominal GDP GDP expressed at current prices. It is often called money GDP.

Nominal risk-free interest rate The sum of the real risk-free interest rate and the inflation premium.

Nominal (quoted) risk-free fate, k_{RF} The rate of interest on a security that is free of all risk; k_{RF} is proxied by the T-bill rate or the T-bond rate. k_{RF} includes an inflation premium.

Nominal scale A measurement scale that categorizes data but does not rank them.

Nominal values Values expressed in current dollars.

Nominal yield A bond's yield as measured by its coupon rate.

Nonactivist strategy The maintenance of a steady monetary and fiscal policy during all phases of the business cycle. According to this view, adjusting macro policy in response to current cyclical conditions is likely to increase, rather than reduce, instability.

Nondeliverable forwards (NDFs) Cash-settled forward contracts, used predominately with respect to foreign exchange forwards.

Nonhuman resources The durable, nonhuman inputs that can be used to produce both current and future output. Machines, buildings, land, and raw materials are examples. Investment can increase the supply of nonhuman resources.

Economists often use the term physical capital when referring to nonhuman resources.

Nonlinear relation An association or relationship between variables that cannot be graphed as a straight line.

Nonparametric test A test that is not concerned with a parameter, or that makes minimal assumptions about the population from which a sample comes.

Nonpecuniary job characteristics Working conditions, prestige, variety, location, employee freedom and responsibilities, and other nonwage characteristics of a job that influence how employees evaluate the job.

Nonstationarity With reference to a random variable, the property of having characteristics such as mean and variance that are not constant through time.

Normal backwardation The condition in futures markets in which futures prices are lower than expected spot prices.

Normal (business-cycle-adjusted) earnings per share The earnings per share that a business could achieve currently under mid-cyclical conditions.

Normal distribution A continuous, symmetric probability distribution that is completely described by its mean and its variance.

Normal contango The condition in futures markets in which futures prices are higher than expected spot prices.

Normal good A good that has a positive income elasticity, so that, as consumer income rises, demand for that good rises also.

Normal portfolio A specialized or customized benchmark constructed to evaluate a specific manager's investment style or philosophy.

Normal profit rate Zero economic profit, providing just the competitive rate of return on the capital (and labor) of owners. An above-normal profit rate will draw more entry into the market, while a below-normal rate will cause an exit of investors and capital.

Normative economics Judgments about "what ought to be" in economic matters. Normative economic views cannot be proved false, because they are based on value judgments.

North American Free Trade Agreement (NAFTA) A comprehensive trade agreement between the United States, Mexico, and Canada that went into effect in 1994. Tariff barriers will continue to be phased out under the agreement until 2004.

Notes Intermediate-term debt securities with maturities longer than 1 year but less than 10 years.

Notional principal The principal value of a swap transaction, which is not exchanged but is used as a scale factor to translate interest rate differentials into cash settlement payments.

***n*-Period moving average** The average of the current and immediately prior $n-1$ values of a time series.

NPV rule An investment decision rule that states that an investment should be undertaken if its NPV is positive but not undertaken if its NPV is negative.

Null hypothesis The hypothesis to be tested.

Objective probabilities Probabilities that generally do not vary from person to person; includes a priori and objective probabilities.

Objectives The investor's goals expressed in terms of risk and return and included in the policy statement.

Off-balance sheet asset An item not on the balance sheet that moves to the asset side of the balance sheet when a specified event occurs.

Off-balance sheet liability An item not on the balance sheet that moves to the liability side of balance sheet when a specified event occurs.

Offensive competitive strategy A strategy whereby a firm attempts to use its strengths to affect the competitive forces in the industry and, in so doing, improves the firm's relative position in the industry.

Offer price The price at which a market maker is willing to sell a security (also called ask price).

Official reserves The amount of reserves owned by the central bank of a government in the form of gold, Special Drawing Rights, and foreign cash or marketable securities.

Off-market FRA A contract in which the initial value is intentionally set at a value other than zero and therefore requires a cash payment at the start from one party to the other.

Offsetting A transaction in exchange-listed derivative markets in which a party re-enters the market to close out a position.

Oligopoly A market situation in which a small number of sellers compose the entire industry. It is competition among the few.

One-sided hypothesis test (or one-tailed hypothesis test) A test in which the null hypothesis is rejected only if the evidence indicates that the population parameter is greater than (smaller than) θ_0. The alternative hypothesis also has one side.

Open-end fund An investment company that continuously offers to sell new shares, or redeem them, at prices based on the market value of the assets owned by the fund (net asset value).

Open-end interest The total number of futures or option contracts that have not been closed out by offset or fulfilled delivery.

Open-end investment company The more formal name for a mutual fund, which derives from the fact that it continuously offers new shares to investors and redeems them (buys them back) on demand.

Open market operations The buying and selling of U.S. government securities in the open market by the Federal Reserve.

Operating efficiency ratios Financial ratios intended to indicate how efficiently management is utilizing the firm's assets in terms of dollar sales generated per dollar of assets. Primary examples would be: total asset turnover, fixed asset turnover, or equity turnover.

Operating leverage The use of fixed-production costs in the firm's operating cost structure. The effect of fixed costs is to magnify the effect of a change in sales on operating profits.

Operating profitability ratios Financial ratios intended to indicate how profitable the firm is in terms of the percent of profit generated from sales. Alternative measures would include: operating profit (EBIT)/net sales; pretax profit (EBT)/net sales; and net profit/sales.

Operations risk or operational risk The risk of loss from failures in a company's systems and procedures (for example, due to computer failures or human failures) or events completely outside of the control of organizations (which would include "acts of God" and terrorist actions).

Opportunity cost (1) The highest valued alternative that must be sacrificed as a result of choosing among alternatives. (2) With reference to execution costs, the loss (or gain) incurred as the result of failure or delay in the execution of a trade, or failure to complete a trade in full. (3) The value that investors forgo by choosing a particular course of action; the value of something in its best alternative use.

Opportunity cost of equity capital The implicit rate of return that must be earned by investors to induce them to continue to supply financial capital to the firm.

Opportunity cost of production The total economic cost of producing a good or service. The cost component includes the opportunity cost of all resources, including those owned by the firm. The opportunity cost is equal to the value of the production of other goods sacrificed as the result of producing the good.

Opportunity set The set of assets available for investment.

Optimal dividend policy The dividend policy that strikes a balance between current dividends and future growth and maximizes the firm's stock price.

Optimal portfolio The portfolio on the efficient frontier that has the highest utility for a given investor. It lies at the point of tangency between the efficient frontier and the curve with the investor's highest possible utility.

Optimizer A specialized computer program or a spreadsheet that solves for the portfolio weights that will result in the lowest risk for a specified level of expected return.

Option A financial instrument that gives one party the right, but not the obligation, to buy or sell an underlying asset from or to another party at a fixed price over a specific period of time. Also referred to as contingent claims.

Option-adjusted spread A type of yield spread that considers changes in the term structure and alternative estimates of the volatility of interest rates.

Option contract An agreement that grants the owner the right, but not the obligation, to make a future transaction in an underlying commodity or security at a fixed price and within a predetermined time in the future.

Option premium (or option price or premium) (1) The price of an option. (2) The initial price that the option buyer must pay to the option seller to acquire the contract. (3) The amount of money a buyer pays and seller receives to engage in an option transaction.

Options Clearing Corporation (OCC) A company designed to guarantee, monitor margin accounts, and settle exchange-traded option transactions.

Order-driven market A market without active market makers in which buy-and-sell orders directly confront each other; an auction market.

Ordinal scale A measurement scale that sorts data into categories that are ordered (ranked) with respect to some characteristic.

Ordinary annuity An annuity with a first cash flow that is paid one period from the present.

Ordinary least squares (OLS) An estimation method based on the criterion of minimizing the sum of the squared residuals of a regression.

Orthogonal Uncorrelated; at a right angle.

Other checkable deposits Interest-earning deposits that are also available for checking.

Outcome A possible value of a random variable.

Outliers Small numbers of observations at either extreme (small or large) of a sample.

Out-of-sample forecast errors The differences between actual and predicted value of time series outside the sample period used to fit the model.

Out-of-sample test A test of a strategy or model using a sample outside the time period on which the strategy or model was developed.

Out-of-the-money option (1) An option that has no value if exercised immediately. For example, a call when the strike price is above the current price of the underlying asset, or a put when the strike price is below the current price of the underlying asset. (2) An option that has no intrinsic value. (3) Options that, if exercised, would require the payment of more money than the value received and therefore would not be currently exercised.

Overfunded plan A defined benefit pension plan in which the present value of the pension liabilities is less than market value of the plan's assets.

Overnight A deal from today to the next business day.

Overnight index swap (OIS) A swap in which the floating rate is the cumulative value of a single unit of currency invested at an overnight rate during the settlement period.

Over-the-counter (OTC) A market for securities made up of dealers. It is not an organized exchange, and trading usually takes place by telephone or other electronic means.

Overweighted A condition in which a portfolio, for whatever reason, includes more of a class of securities than the relative market value alone would justify.

Paired comparisons test A statistical test for differences based on paired observations drawn from samples that are dependent on each other.

Paired observations Observations that are dependent on each other.

Pairs arbitrage trade A trade in two closely related stocks involving the short sale of one and the purchase of the other.

Panel data Observations through time on a single characteristic of multiple observational units.

Parameter A descriptive measure computed from or used to describe a population of data, conventionally represented by Greek letters.

Parameter instability The problem or issue of population regression parameters that have changed over time.

Parametric test Any test (or procedure) concerned with parameters or whose validity depends on assumptions concerning the population generating the sample.

Partial regression coefficients (or partial slope coefficients) The slope coefficients in a multiple regression.

Partnership A business firm owned by two or more individuals who possess ownership rights to the firm's profits and are personally liable for the debts of the firm.

Par value The principal amount repaid at maturity of a bond. Also called face value. *See also* Principal.

Par yield curve The yield curve drawn for government coupon bonds of different maturities that trade at, or around, par.

Payback period (1) The length of time required for an investment's net revenues to cover its cost. (2) The time required for the added income from the convertible security relative to the stock to offset the conversion premium.

Payer swaption A swaption that allows the holder to enter into a swap as the fixed-rate payer and floating-rate receiver.

Payment date The date on which a firm actually mails dividend checks.

Payment netting A means of settling payment in which the amount owed by the first party to the second is netted with the amount owed by the second party to the first; only the net difference is paid.

Payoff The value of an option at expiration.

Peak The culmination of a bull market when prices stop rising and begin declining.

Peer group comparison A method of measuring portfolio performance by collecting the returns produced by a representative universe of investors over a specific period of time and displaying them in a simple boxplot format.

Pegged exchange rate regime A system in which a country's exchange rate in relation to a major currency is set at a target value (the peg) but allowed to fluctuate within a small band around the target.

Pegged exchange-rate system A commitment to use monetary and fiscal policy to maintain the exchange-rate value of the domestic currency at a fixed rate or within a narrow band relative to another currency (or bundle of currencies).

P/E ratio *See* Price-earnings ratio.

per capita GDP Income per person. Increases in income per person are vitally important for the achievement of higher living standards.

Percentiles Quantiles that divide a distribution into 100 equal parts.

Perfect collinearity The existence of an exact linear relation between two or more independent variables or combinations of independent variables.

Performance appraisal (1) The assessment of an investment record for evidence of investment skill. (2) The evaluation of risk-adjusted performance; the evaluation of investment skill.

Performance attribution The attribution of investment performance to specific investment decisions (such as asset allocation and country weighting).

Performance guarantee A guarantee from the clearing-house that if one party makes money on a transaction, the clearinghouse ensures it will be paid.

Performance measurement The calculation of returns in a logical and consistent manner.

Performance presentation standards (PPS) A comprehensive set of reporting guidelines created by the Association for Investment Management and Research (AIMR), in an effort to fulfill the call for uniform, accurate, and consistent performance reporting.

Performance shares Stock which is awarded to executives on the basis of the company's performance.

Periodic rate The quoted interest rate per period; the stated annual interest rate divided by the number of compounding periods per year.

Permanent income hypothesis The hypothesis that consumption depends on some measure of long-run expected (permanent) income rather than on current income.

Permutation An ordered listing.

Perpetual bond A bond with no stated maturity.

Perpetuity (1) An investment without any maturity date. It provides returns to its owner indefinitely. (2) A perpetual annuity, or a set of never-ending level sequential cash flows, with the first cash flow occurring one period from now.

Persistent earnings *See* Underlying earnings.

Personal consumption Household spending on consumer goods and services during the current period. Consumption is a flow concept.

Personal income The total income received by domestic households and noncorporate businesses. It is available for consumption, saving, and payment of personal taxes.

Personal trust An amount of money set aside by a grantor and often managed by a third party, the trustee. Often constructed so one party receives income from the trust's investments and another party receives the residual value of the trust after the income beneficiaries' death.

Phillips curve A curve that illustrates the relationship between the rate of change in prices (or money wages) and the rate of unemployment.

Pip The smallest incremental move an exchange rate can make, i.e., the last decimal place in a quote.

Plain-vanilla Refers to a security, especially a bond or a swap, issued with standard features. Sometimes called generic.

Plain vanilla swap An interest rate swap in which one party pays a fixed rate and the other pays a floating rate, with both sets of payments in the same currency.

Platykurtic Describes a distribution that is less peaked than the normal distribution.

Point One percent (1%).

Point estimate A single numerical estimate of an unknown quantity, such as a population parameter.

Policy effect The difference in performance of a bond portfolio from that of a chosen index due to differences in duration, which result from a fund's investment policy.

Policy-ineffectiveness theorem The proposition that any systematic policy will be rendered ineffective once decision makers figure out the policy pattern and adjust their decision making in light of its expected effects. The theorem is a corollary of the theory of rational expectations.

Policy statement A statement in which the investor specifies investment goals, constraints, and risk preferences.

Pooled estimate An estimate of a parameter that involves combining (pooling) observations from two or more samples.

Population All members of a specified group.

Population mean The arithmetic mean value of a population; the arithmetic mean of all the observations or values in the population.

Population standard deviation A measure of dispersion relating to a population in the same unit of measurement as the observations, calculated as the positive square root of the population variance.

Population variance A measure of dispersion relating to a population, calculated as the mean of the squared deviations around the population mean.

Pork-barrel legislation A package of spending projects benefiting local areas at federal expense. The projects typically have costs that exceed benefits, but are intensely desired by the residents of the district getting the benefits without having to pay much of the costs.

Portfolio (1) All the stocks, bonds, or other securities held by an individual or corporation for investment purposes. (2) A group of investments. Ideally, the investments should have different patterns of returns over time.

Portfolio performance attribution The analysis of portfolio performance in terms of the contributions from various sources of risk.

Portfolio possibilities curve A graphical representation of the expected return and risk of all portfolios that can be formed using two assets.

Position trader A trader who typically holds positions open overnight.

Positive economics The scientific study of "what is" among economic relationships.

Positive rate of time preference The desire of consumers for goods now rather than in the future.

Positive serial correlation Serial correlation in which a positive error for one observation increases the chance of a positive error for another observation, and a negative error for one observation increases the chance of a negative error for another observation.

Post-audit A comparison of the actual versus the expected results for a given capital project.

Posterior probability An updated probability that reflects or comes after new information.

Potential credit risk The risk associated with the possibility that a payment due at a later date will not be made.

Potential output The level of output that can be achieved and sustained into the future, given the size of the labor force, expected productivity of labor, and natural rate of unemployment consistent with the efficient operation of the labor market. For periods of time, the actual output may differ from the economy's potential.

Poverty threshold income level The level of money income below which a family is considered to be poor. It differs according to family characteristics (for example, number of family members) and is adjusted when consumer prices change.

Power of a test The probability of correctly rejecting the null—that is, rejecting the null hypothesis when it is false.

Predatory pricing Pricing below average cost to drive competitors out of the industry.

Preferred stock An equity investment that stipulates the dividend payment either as a coupon or a stated dollar amount. The firm's directors may withhold payments.

Pre-investing The strategy of using futures contracts to enter the market without an immediate outlay of cash.

Premium A bond selling at a price above par value due to capital market conditions. *See* also Option premium.

Present (price) value of a basis point (PVBP) The change in the bond price for a 1 basis point change in yield. Also called basis point value (BPV).

Present value (PV) (1) The current worth of future income after it is discounted to reflect the fact that revenues in the future are valued less highly than revenues now. (2) The current worth of a future cash flow. Obtained by discounting the future cash flow at the market-required rate of return. (3) The current (discounted) value of a future cash flow or flows.

Price ceiling A legally established maximum price that sellers may charge for a good or resource.

Price change effect The unknown component of the total return for a bond portfolio during a period of time due to the interest rate effect, sector/quality effect, and residual effect.

Price continuity A feature of a liquid market in which prices change little from one transaction to the next due to the depth of the market.

Price controls Government-mandated prices; they may be either greater or less than the market equilibrium price.

Price discovery A feature of futures markets in which futures prices provide valuable information about the price of the underlying asset.

Price discrimination A practice whereby a seller charges different consumers different prices for the same product or service.

Priced risk Risk that investors require an additional return for bearing.

Price-driven market A market in which dealers (market makers) adjust their quotes continuously to reflect supply and demand; also known as a dealer market.

Price-earnings ratio (P/E ratio) (1) The ratio of the stock market price to the earnings per share. Sometimes called earnings multiplier. (2) The number by which expected earnings per share is multiplied to estimate a stock's value; also called the earnings multiplier.

Price elasticity of demand The percent change in the quantity of a product demanded divided by the percent change in the price causing the change in quantity. Price elasticity of demand indicates the degree of consumer response to variation in price.

Price elasticity of supply The percentage change in quantity supplied, divided by the percentage change in the price causing the change in quantity supplied.

Price floor A legally established minimum price that buyers must pay for a good or resource.

Price limits Limits imposed by a futures exchange on the price change that can occur from one day to the next.

Price momentum A portfolio strategy in which you acquire stocks that have enjoyed above-market stock price increases.

Price multiple The ratio of a stock's market price to some measure of value per share.

Price relative A ratio of an ending price over a beginning price; it is equal to 1 plus the holding period return on the asset.

Price risk The component of interest rate risk due to the uncertainty of the market price of a bond caused by possible changes in market interest rates.

Price searchers Firms that face a downward sloping demand curve for their product. The amount that the firm is able to sell is inversely related to the price that it charges.

Price takers Sellers who must take the market price in order to sell their product. Because each price taker's output is small relative to the total market, price takers can sell all their output at the market price, but they are unable to sell any of their output at a price higher than the market price.

Price-weighted series An indicator series calculated as an arithmetic average of the current prices of the sampled securities.

Primary market (1) Market where financial institutions aid in the sale of new securities. (2) The market in which newly issued securities are sold by their issuers, who receive the proceeds.

Principal (par value) (1) The original value of the debt underlying a bond that is payable at maturity. (2) The amount of funds originally invested in a project or instrument; the face value to be paid at maturity.

Principal-agent problem The incentive problem arising when the purchaser of services (the principal) lacks full information about the circumstances faced by the seller (the agent) and thus cannot know how well the agent performs the purchased services. The agent may to some extent work toward objectives other than those sought by the principal paying for the service.

Principal trade A trade through a broker who guarantees full execution at specified discount/premium to the prevailing price.

Prior probabilities Probabilities reflecting beliefs prior to the arrival of new information.

Private investment The flow of private sector expenditures on durable assets (fixed investment) plus the addition to inventories (inventory investment) during a period. These expenditures enhance our ability to provide consumer benefits in the future.

Privately held government debt The portion of the national debt owed to domestic and foreign investors. It does not include bonds held by agencies of the federal government or the Federal Reserve.

Private placement A new issue sold directly to a small group of investors, usually institutions.

Private property rights Property rights that are exclusively held by an owner, or group of owners, and that can be transferred to others at the owner's discretion.

Probability A number between 0 and 1 describing the chance that a stated event will occur.

Probability density function A function with non-negative values such that probability can be described by areas under the curve graphing the function.

Probability distribution A distribution that specifies the probabilities of a random variable's possible outcomes.

Probability function A function that specifies the probability that the random variable takes on a specific value.

Probit model A qualitative-dependent-variable multiple regression model based on the normal distribution.

Producer surplus The difference between the minimum supply price and the actual sales price. It measures the net gains to producers and resource suppliers from market trade. It is not the same as profit.

Production opportunities The returns available within an economy from investments in productive (cash-generating) assets.

Production possibilities curve A curve that outlines all possible combinations of total output that could be produced, assuming (1) the utilization of a fixed amount of productive resources, (2) full and efficient use of those resources, and (3) a specific state of technical knowledge. The slope of the curve indicates the rate at which one product can be traded off to produce more of the other.

Productivity The average output produced per worker during a specific time period. It is usually measured in terms of output per hour worked.

Profit An excess of sales revenue relative to the opportunity cost of production. The cost component includes the opportunity cost of all resources, including those owned by the firm. Therefore, profit accrues only when the value of the good produced is greater than the value of other goods that could have been produced with those same resources.

Progressive tax A tax in which the average tax rate rises with income. Persons with higher incomes will pay a higher percentage of their income in taxes.

Project cost of capital, k_p The risk-adjusted cost of capital for an individual project.

Promised yield to call (YTC) A bond's yield if held until the first available call date, with reinvestment of all coupon payments at the yield-to-call rate.

Promised yield to maturity (YTM) The most widely used measure of a bond's yield that states the fully compounded rate of return on a bond bought at market price and held to maturity with reinvestment of all coupon payments at the yield to maturity rate.

Property rights The right to use, control, and obtain the benefits from a good or service.

Proportional tax A tax in which the average tax rate is the same at all income levels. Everyone pays the same percentage of income in taxes.

Proprietorship A business firm owned by an individual who possesses the ownership right to the firm's profits and is personally liable for the firm's debts.

Prospective P/E *See* Leading P/E.

Protective put (1) A trading strategy in which a put option is purchased as a supplement to a long position in an underlying asset or portfolio of assets; the most straightforward form of portfolio insurance. (2) An option strategy in which a long position in an asset is combined with a long position in a put.

Pseudo-random numbers Numbers produced by random number generators.

Public bond A long-term, fixed-obligation debt security in a convenient, affordable denomination for sale to individuals and financial institutions.

Public-choice analysis The study of decision making as it affects the formation and operation of collective organizations, such as governments. In general, the principles and methodology of economics are applied to political science topics.

Public goods Jointly consumed goods that are nonexcludable. When consumed by one person, they are also made available to others. National defense, flood control dams, and scientific theories are all public goods.

Purchasing power parity (PPP) A theory stating that the exchange rate between two currencies will exactly reflect the purchasing power of the two currencies.

Pure cash-matched dedicated portfolio A conservative dedicated portfolio management technique aimed at developing a bond portfolio that will provide payments exactly matching the specified liability schedules.

Pure competition A market structure characterized by a large number of small firms producing an identical product in an industry (market area) that permits complete freedom of entry and exit. Also called price-taker markets.

Pure discount instruments Instruments that pay interest as the difference between the amount borrowed and the amount paid back.

Pure factor portfolio A portfolio with sensitivity of 1 to the factor in question and a sensitivity of 0 to all other factors.

Pure play method An approach used for estimating the beta of a project in which a firm (1) identifies several companies whose only business is the project in question, (2) calculates the beta for each firm, and then (3) averages the betas to find an approximation to its own project's beta.

Put An option that gives the holder the right to sell an underlying asset to another party at a fixed price over a specific period of time.

Put-call-forward parity The relationship among puts, calls, and forward contracts.

Put-call parity (1) The theoretical relation between a put and a call option with the same underlying strike price, asset, and expiration. (2) An equation expressing the equivalence (parity) of a portfolio of a call and a bond with a portfolio of a put and the underlying, which leads to the relationship between put and call prices.

Put option (1) A contract giving the right to sell an asset at a specified price, on or before a specified date. (2) Options to sell a firm's common stock within a certain period at a specified price.

Put-call parity The relationship that must exist in an efficient market between the prices for put and call options having the same underlying asset, exercise price, and expiration date.

***p*-Value** The smallest level of significance at which the null hypothesis can be rejected; also called the marginal significance level.

Quadratic optimization A technique that relies on historical correlations in order to construct a portfolio that seeks to minimize tracking error with an index.

Qualitative dependent variables Dummy variables used as dependent variables rather than as independent variables.

Quality financial statements Financial statements that most knowledgeable observers (analysts, portfolio managers) would consider conservatively prepared in terms of sales, expenses, earnings, and asset valuations. The results reported would reflect reasonable estimates and indicate what truly happened during the period and the legitimate value of assets and liabilities on the balance sheet.

Quantile (or fractile) A value at or below which a stated fraction of the data lies.

Quantity theory of money A theory that hypothesizes that a change in the money supply will cause a proportional change in the price level because velocity and real output are unaffected by the quantity of money.

Quanto An option in which the foreign exchange risk in the underlying asset has been removed.

Quartiles Quantiles that divide a distribution into four equal parts.

Quintiles Quantiles that divide a distribution into five equal parts.

Random number An observation drawn from a uniform distribution.

Random number generator An algorithm that produces uniformly distributed random numbers between 0 and 1.

Random variable A quantity whose future outcomes are uncertain.

Random walk A time series in which the value of the series in one period is the value of the series in the previous period plus an unpredictable random error.

Random walk theory (1) The theory that current stock prices already reflect known information about the future. Therefore, the future movement of stock prices will be determined by surprise occurrences. This will cause them to change in a random fashion. (2) A theory stating that all current information is reflected in current security prices and that future price movements are random because they are caused by unexpected news.

Range The difference between the maximum and minimum values in a dataset.

Range forward A trading strategy based on a variation of the put-call parity model where, for the same underlying asset but different exercise prices, a call option is purchased and a put option is sold (or vice versa).

Rate anticipation effect The difference in return because of changing the duration of the portfolio during a period as compared with the portfolio's long-term policy duration.

Rate of unemployment The percentage of persons in the labor force who are unemployed. Mathematically, it is equal to number of persons unemployed/number of persons in the labor force $\times$ 100.

Rating evaluation Performed by a credit rating agency, such as Moody's or Standard & Poor's, to assign a rating to an issue's investment quality.

Rational-expectations hypothesis The hypothesis that economic decision makers weigh all available evidence, including information concerning the probable effects of current and future economic policy, when they form their expectations about future economic events (such as the probable future inflation rate).

Rational ignorance effect Voter ignorance resulting from the fact that people perceive their individual votes as unlikely to be decisive. Therefore, they rationally have little incentive to seek the information needed to cast an informed vote.

Rationing An allocation of a limited supply of a good or resource to users who would like to have more of it. Various criteria, including charging a price, can be utilized to allocate the limited supply. When price performs the rationing function, the good or resource is allocated to those willing to give up the most "other things" in order to obtain ownership rights.

Ratio scales A measurement scale that has all the characteristics of interval measurement scales as well as a true zero point as the origin.

Ratio spread An option strategy in which a long position in a certain number of options is offset by a short position in a certain number of other options on the same underlying, resulting in a risk-free position.

Real balance effect The increase in wealth generated by an increase in the purchasing power of a constant money supply as the price level decreases. This wealth effect leads to an inverse relationship between price (level) and quantity demanded in the goods and services market.

Real earnings Earnings adjusted for differences in the general level of prices across time periods or geographic areas. When real earnings are equal, the same bundle of goods and services can be purchased with the earnings.

Real estate investment trusts (REITs) Investment funds that hold portfolios of real estate investments.

Real exchange rate The exchange rate adjusted by the inflation differential between the two countries.

Real foreign currency risk The risk that real prices of consumption goods might not be identical in different countries. Also known as real exchange rate risk or purchasing power risk.

Real GDP GDP adjusted for changes in the price level.

Real interest rate (1) The interest rate adjusted for expected inflation; it indicates the real cost to the borrower (and yield to the lender) in terms of goods and services. (2) The interest rate adjusted by the inflation rate of the country.

Real risk-free rate of interest, k* The rate of interest that would exist on default-free U.S. Treasury securities if no inflation was expected.

Realized capital gains Capital gains that result when an appreciated asset is sold; realized capital gains are taxable.

Realized yield The expected compounded yield on a bond that is sold before it matures assuming the reinvestment of all cash flows at an explicit rate. Also called horizon yield for the yield realized during an investment horizon period.

Real options Options embedded in a firm's real assets that give managers valuable decision-making flexibility, such as the right to either undertake or abandon an investment project.

Real rate of interest The money rate of interest minus the expected rate of inflation. The real rate of interest indicates the interest premium, in terms of real goods and services, that one must pay for earlier availability.

Real risk-free rate (RRFR) The basic interest rate with no accommodation for inflation or uncertainty. The pure time value of money.

Real values Values that have been adjusted for the effects of inflation.

Receiver swaption A swaption that allows the holder to enter into a swap as the fixed-rate receiver and floating-rate payer.

Recession A downturn in economic activity characterized by declining real GDP and rising unemployment. In an effort to be more precise, many economists define a recession as two consecutive quarters in which there is a decline in real GDP.

Recognition lag The time period after a policy change is needed from a stabilization standpoint but before the need is recognized by policymakers.

Refunding issue Bonds that provide funds to prematurely retire another bond issue. These bonds can be either a junior or senior issue.

Registered bond A bond for which ownership is registered with the issuer. The holder receives interest payments by check directly from the issuer.

Regime With reference to a time series, the underlying model generating the times series.

Registered competitive market makers (RCMMs) Members of an exchange who are allowed to use their memberships to buy or sell for their own account within the specific trading obligations set down by the exchange.

Registered traders Members of the stock exchange who are allowed to use their memberships to buy and sell for their own account, which means they save commissions on their trading but they provide liquidity to the market, and they abide by exchange regulations on how they can trade.

Regression coefficients The intercept and slope coefficient(s) of a regression.

Regressive tax A tax in which the average tax rate falls with income. Persons with higher incomes will pay a lower percentage of their income in taxes.

Regulatory risk The risk associated with the uncertainty of how derivative transactions will be regulated or with changes in regulations.

Reinvestment rate assumption The assumption that cash flows from a project can be reinvested (1) at the cost of capital, if using the NPV method, or (2) at the internal rate of return, if using the IRR method.

Reinvestment rate risk The risk that a decline in interest rates will lead to lower income when bonds mature and funds are reinvested.

Rejection point (or critical value) A value against which a computed test statistic is compared to decide whether to reject or not reject the null hypothesis.

Relative dispersion The amount of dispersion relative to a reference value or benchmark.

Relative frequency With reference to an interval of grouped data, the number of observations in the interval divided by the total number of observations in the sample.

Relative-strength (RS) ratio The ratio of a stock price or an industry index value to a market indicator series, indicating the stock's or the industry's performance relative to the overall market.

Relevant cash flows The specific cash flows that should be considered in a capital budgeting decision.

Rent seeking Actions by individuals and interest groups designed to restructure public policy in a manner that will either directly or indirectly redistribute more income to themselves.

Repeat-purchase item An item purchased often by the same buyer.

Replacement analysis An analysis involving the decision of whether or not to replace an existing asset with a new asset.

Replacement chain (common life) approach A method of comparing projects of unequal lives which assumes that each project can be repeated as many times as necessary to reach a common life span; the NPVs over this life span are then compared, and the project with the higher common life NPV is chosen.

Replacement rate The share of previous earnings replaced by unemployment benefits.

Replacement value The market value of a swap.

Required rate of return The return that compensates investors for their time, the expected rate of inflation, and the uncertainty of the return.

Reserve borrowing capacity The ability to borrow money at a reasonable cost when good investment opportunities arise. Firms often use less debt than specified by the MM optimal capital structure to ensure that they can obtain debt capital later if they need to.

Residual autocorrelations The sample autocorrelations of the residuals.

Residual claimants Individuals who personally receive the excess, if any, of revenues over costs. Residual claimants gain if the firm's costs are reduced or revenues increased.

Residual Dividend Model A model in which the dividend paid is set equal to the actual earnings minus the amount of retained earnings necessary to finance the firm's optimal capital budget.

Residual effect The return on a bond portfolio after taking account of the three prior factors—yield to maturity, interest rate effect, and sector/quality effect.

Resistance level A price at which a technician would expect a substantial increase in the supply of a stock to reverse a rising trend.

Resource An input used to produce economic goods. Land, labor, skills, natural resources, and capital are examples. Throughout history, people have struggled to transform available, but limited, resources into things they would like to have—economic goods.

Resource market 1) A highly aggregated market encompassing all resources (labor, physical capital, land, and entrepreneurship) that contribute to the production of current out-put. The labor market forms the largest component of this market. 2) Markets in which business firms demand factors of production (for example, labor, capital, and natural resources) from household suppliers. The resources are then used to produce goods and services. This market is sometimes called factor markets or input markets.

Resource mobility The ease with which factors of production are able to move among alternative uses. Resources that can easily be transferred to a different use or location are said to be highly mobile. Resources with few alternative uses are immobile.

Restrictive fiscal policy A reduction in government expenditures and/or an increase in tax rates such that the expected size of the budget deficit declines (or the budget surplus increases).

Restrictive monetary policy A shift in monetary policy designed to reduce aggregate demand and place downward pressure on the general level of prices (or the rate of inflation). Bond sales by the Fed, a decline in bank reserves, and a reduction in the growth rate of the money supply are generally indicative of a restrictive monetary policy.

Return prediction studies Studies wherein investigations attempt to predict the time series of future rates of return using public information. An example would be predicting above-average returns for the stock market based on the aggregate dividend yield—e.g., high dividend yield indicates above average future market returns.

Revenue bond A bond that is serviced by the income generated from specific revenue-producing projects of the municipality.

Rho The sensitivity of the option price to the risk-free rate.

Ricardian equivalence The view that a tax reduction financed with government debt will exert no impact on current consumption and aggregate demand because people will fully recognize the higher future taxes implied by the additional debt.

Right-to-work laws Laws that prohibit the union shop, the requirement that employees must join a union as a condition of employment. Each state has the option to adopt (or reject) right-to-work legislation.

Rising trend channel The range defined by security prices as they move progressively higher.

Risk The uncertainty that an investment will earn its expected rate of return.

Risk allocation The decomposition of the risk of a portfolio into the various risk exposures taken by a manager.

Risk-adjusted discount rate The discount rate that applies to a particular risky stream of income; the riskier the project's income stream, the higher the discount rate.

Risk aversion Describes the fact that investors want to minimize risk for the same level of expected return. To take more risk, they require compensation by a risk premium.

Risk budgeting (1) In a portfolio management context, the setting of risk limits for individual managers. (2) The establishment of objectives for individuals, groups, or divisions of an organization that takes into account the allocation of an acceptable level of risk.

Risk-free asset An asset with returns that exhibit zero variance.

Risk governance The setting of overall policies and standards in risk management.

Risk management The process of identifying the level of risk an entity wants, measuring the level of risk the entity currently has, taking actions that bring the actual level of risk to the desired level of risk, and monitoring the new actual level of risk so that it continues to be aligned with the desired level of risk.

Risk-neutral probabilities Weights that are used to compute a binomial option price. They are the probabilities that would apply if a risk-neutral investor valued an option.

Risk-neutral valuation The process by which options and other derivatives are priced by treating investors as though they were risk neutral.

Risk premium (1) The difference between the expected return on an asset and the risk-free interest rate. (2) The increase over the nominal risk-free rate that investors demand as compensation for an investment's uncertainty. (3) The expected return on an investment minus the risk-free rate.

Risky asset An asset with uncertain future returns.

Robust The quality of being relatively unaffected by a violation of assumptions.

Robust standard errors Standard errors of the estimated parameters of a regression that correct for the presence of heteroskedasticity in the regression's error term.

Root mean squared error (RMSE) The square root of the average squared forecast error; used to compare the out-of-sample forecasting performance of forecasting models.

Roy's safety first criterion A criterion asserting that the optimal portfolio is the one that minimizes the probability that portfolio return falls below a threshold level.

RS ratio *See* Relative-strength ratio.

Rule of 70 If a variable grows at a rate of x percent per year, $70/x$ will approximate the number of years required for the variable to double.

Rule of 72 The principle that the approximate number of years necessary for an investment to double is 72 divided by the stated interest rate.

Runs test A test of the weak-form efficient market hypothesis that checks for trends that persist longer in terms of positive or negative price changes than one would expect for a random series.

Safety-first rules Rules for portfolio selection that focus on the risk that portfolio value will fall below some minimum acceptable level over some time horizon.

Samaritan's dilemma General assistance to those with low incomes reduces the opportunity cost of choices that lead to poverty. Thus, there is a conflict between providing income transfers to the poor and discouragement of behavior that increases the incidence of poverty.

Sample A subset of a population.

Sample excess kurtosis A sample measure of the degree of a distribution's peakedness in excess of the normal distribution's peakedness.

Sample kurtosis A sample measure of the degree of a distribution's peakedness.

Sample mean The sum of the sample observations, divided by the sample size.

Sample selection bias Bias introduced by systematically excluding some members of the population according to a particular attribute—for example, the bias introduced when data availability leads to certain observations being excluded from the analysis.

Sample skewness A sample measure of degree of asymmetry of a distribution.

Sample standard deviation The positive square root of the sample variance.

Sample statistic or statistic A quantity computed from or used to describe a sample.

Sample variance A sample measure of the degree of dispersion of a distribution, calculated by dividing the sum of the squared deviations from the sample mean by the sample size (n) minus 1.

Sampling (1) A technique for constructing a passive index portfolio in which the portfolio manager buys a representative sample of stocks that comprise the benchmark index. (2) The process of obtaining a sample.

Sampling distribution The distribution of all distinct possible values that a statistic can assume when computed from samples of the same size randomly drawn from the same population.

Sampling error The difference between the observed value of a statistic and the quantity it is intended to estimate.

Sampling plan The set of rules used to select a sample.

Sandwich spread An option strategy that is equivalent to a short butterfly spread.

Saving The portion of after-tax income that is not spent on consumption. Saving is a "flow" concept.

Savings and loan associations Financial institutions that accept deposits in exchange for shares that pay dividends. Historically, these funds have been channeled into residential mortgage loans. Under banking legislation adopted in 1980, S&Ls are permitted to offer a broad range of services similar to those of commercial banks.

Say's Law The view that production creates its own demand. Demand will always be sufficient to purchase the goods produced because the income payments to the resource suppliers will equal the value of the goods produced.

Scalper A trader who offers to buy or sell futures contracts, holding the position for only a brief period of time. Scalpers attempt to profit by buying at the bid price and selling at the higher ask price.

Scarcity Fundamental concept of economics that indicates that there is less of a good freely available from nature than people would like.

Scatter plot A two-dimensional plot of pairs of observations on two data series.

Scenario analysis A risk management technique involving the examination of the performance of a portfolio under specified situations. Closely related to stress testing.

Scientific thinking Development of a theory from basic postulates and the testing of the implications of that theory as to their consistency with events in the real world. Good theories are consistent with and help explain real-world events. Theories that are inconsistent with the real world are invalid and must be rejected.

Seasoned equity issues New equity shares offered by firms that already have stock outstanding.

Seats Memberships in a derivatives exchange.

Secondary effects Consequences of an economic change that are not immediately identifiable but are felt only with the passage of time.

Secondary market (1) Market where financial institutions aid in the buying and selling of existing securities. (2) The market in which outstanding securities are bought and sold by owners other than the issuers.

Sector/quality effect The return on a bond portfolio caused by changing yield spreads between bonds in different sectors and with different quality ratings.

Sector rotation strategy An active strategy that involves purchasing stocks in specific industries or stocks with specific characteristics (low P/E, growth, value) that are anticipated to rise in value more than the overall market.

Secured (senior) bond A bond backed by a legal claim on specified assets of the issuer.

Security market indicator series An index created as a statistical measure of the performance of an entire market or segment of a market based on a sample of securities from the market or segment of a market.

Security market line (SML) (1) The line that reflects the combination of risk and return of alternative investments. In CAPM risk is measured by systematic risk (beta). (2) The graph of the capital asset pricing model.

Seed stage With reference to venture capital financing, the stage associated with product development and market research.

Semideviation The positive square root of semivariance (sometimes called semistandard deviation).

Semilogarithmic Describes a scale constructed so that equal intervals on the vertical scale represent equal rates of change, and equal intervals on the horizontal scale represent equal amounts of change.

Semistrong-form efficient market hypothesis The belief that security prices fully reflect all publicly available information, including information from security transactions and company, economic, and political news.

Semivariance The average squared deviation below the mean.

Sensitivity analysis A risk analysis technique in which key variables are changed one at a time and the resulting changes in the NPV and IRR are observed.

Separation theorem The proposition that the investment decision, which involves investing in the market portfolio on the capital market line, is separate from the financing decision, which targets a specific point on the CML based on the investor's risk preference.

Serially correlated With reference to regression errors, errors that are correlated across observations.

Serial obligation bond A bond issue that has a series of maturity dates.

Settlement date or payment date The date on which the parties to a swap make payments.

Settlement period The time between settlement dates.

Settlement price (1) The official closing price of a futures contract set by the clearinghouse at the end of the day and used for marking to market. (2) The price determined by the exchange clearinghouse with which futures contract margin accounts are marked to market. (3) The official price, designated by the clearinghouse, from which daily gains and losses will be determined and marked to market.

Settlement risk When settling a contract, the risk that one party could be in the process of paying the counterparty while the counterparty is declaring bankruptcy.

Severance pay Pay by an employer to an employee upon the termination of employment with the firm.

Shareholders' equity Total assets minus total liabilities.

Sharpe ratio (1) The ratio of mean excess return (return minus the risk-free rate) to standard deviation of returns (or excess returns). (2) The average return in excess of the risk-free rate divided by the standard deviation of return; a measure of the average excess return earned per unit of standard deviation of return.

Shirking Working at less than a normal rate of productivity, thus reducing output. Shirking is more likely when workers are not monitored, so that the cost of lower output falls on others.

Short The seller of a derivative contract. Also refers to the position of being short a derivative.

Shortage A condition in which the amount of a good offered for sale by producers is less than the amount demanded by buyers at the existing price. An increase in price would eliminate the shortage.

Shortfall risk The risk that portfolio value will fall below some minimum acceptable level over some time horizon.

Short hedge (1) A hedge involving the sale of forward or futures contracts to cover the risk of a long position in the spot market. (2) A short position in a forward or futures contract used to offset the price volatility of a long position in the underlying asset.

Short run (in production) A time period so short that a firm is unable to vary some of its factors of production. The firm's plant size typically cannot be altered in the short run.

Short sale (1) The sale of a security not owned by the seller at the time of trade. (2) The sale of borrowed securities with the intention of repurchasing them later at a lower price and earning the difference.

Shortsightedness effect Misallocation of resources that results because public-sector action is biased (1) in favor of proposals yielding clearly defined current benefits in exchange for difficult-to-identify future costs and (2) against proposals with clearly identifiable current costs but yielding less concrete and less obvious future benefits.

Shutdown A temporary halt in the operation of a business firm. Because the firm anticipates returning to the market in the future, it does not sell its assets and go out of business. The firm's variable cost is eliminated by the shutdown, but its fixed costs continue.

Signal An action taken by a firm's management which provides clues to investors about how management views the firm's prospects.

Simple interest The interest earned each period on the original investment; interest calculated on the principal only.

Simple random sample A subset of a larger population created in such a way that each element of the population has an equal probability of being selected to the subset.

Simulation trial A complete pass through the steps of a simulation.

Single-payment loan A loan in which the borrower receives a sum of money at the start and pays back the entire amount with interest in a single payment at maturity.

Sinking fund (1) Bond provision that requires the bond to be paid off progressively rather than in full at maturity. (2) Bond provision that requires the issuer to redeem some or all of the bond systematically over the term of the bond rather than in full at maturity.

Skewed Not symmetrical.

Skewness A quantitative measure of skew (lack of symmetry); a synonym of skew.

Small-firm effect A frequent empirical anomaly where risk-adjusted stock returns for companies with low market capitalization (i.e., share price multiplied by number of outstanding shares) are significantly larger than those generated by high market capitalization firms.

Socialism A system of economic organization in which (1) the ownership and control of the basic means of production rest with the state, and (2) resource allocation is determined by centralized planning rather than by market forces.

Soft dollars A form of compensation to a money manager generated when the manager commits the investor to paying higher brokerage fees in exchange for the manager receiving additional services (e.g., stock research) from the broker.

Sovereign risk The risk that a government may default on its debt.

Spearman rank correlation coefficient A measure of correlation applied to ranked data.

Special Drawing Right (SDR) An artificial official reserve asset held on the books of the IMF.

Special-interest issue An issue that generates substantial individual benefits to a small minority while imposing a small individual cost on many other voters. In total, the net cost to the majority might either exceed or fall short of the net benefits to the special-interest group.

Specialist The major market maker on U.S. stock exchanges who acts as a broker or dealer to ensure the liquidity and smooth functions of the secondary stock market.

Special purpose vehicles (SPVs) *See* Enhanced derivatives products companies (EDPC).

Speculative company A firm with a great degree of business and/or financial risk, with commensurate high earnings potential.

Speculative stock A stock that appears to be highly overpriced compared to its reasonable valuation.

Spending phase Phase in the investment life cycle during which individuals' earning years end as they retire. They pay for expenses with income from social security and returns from prior investments and invest to protect against inflation.

Spot price Current market price of an asset. Also called cash price.

Spot rate The required yield for a cash flow to be received at some specific date in the future—for example, the spot rate for a flow to be received in one year, for a cash flow in two years, and so on.

Spread (1) Difference between the ask and the bid quotations. Also refers to a mark-up paid by a given borrower over the market interest rate paid by a top-quality borrower. (2) A trading strategy where long and short positions in two call (or two put) option contracts having the same underlying asset but different exercise prices or expiration dates are combined to create a customized return distribution. (3) An option strategy involving the purchase of one option and sale of another option that is identical to the first in all respects except either exercise price or expiration.

Spurious correlation A correlation that misleadingly points towards associations between variables.

Stand-alone risk The risk an asset would have if it were a firm's only asset and if investors only owned one stock. It is measured by the variability of the asset's expected returns.

Standard deviation (1) A measure of variability equal to the square root of the variance. (2) The positive square root of the variance; a measure of dispersion in the same units as the original data.

Standardized beta With reference to fundamental factor models, the value of the attribute for an asset minus the average value of the attribute across all stocks, divided by the standard deviation of the attribute across all stocks.

Standardizing A transformation that involves subtracting the mean and dividing the result by the standard deviation.

Standard normal distribution (or unit normal distribution) The normal density with mean (μ) equal to 0 and standard deviation (σ) equal to 1.

Stated annual interest rate or quoted interest rate A quoted interest rate that does not account for compounding within the year.

Statement of cash flows A financial statement that shows the effects on the firm's cash flow of income flows and changes in its balance sheet.

Static yield spread Yield spreads that consider a spread over the total term structure.

Statistic A quantity computed from or used to describe a sample of data.

Statistical factor models A multifactor model in which statistical methods are applied to a set of historical returns to determine portfolios that best explain either historical return covariances or variances.

Statistical inference Making forecasts, estimates, or judgments about a larger group from a smaller group actually observed; using a sample statistic to infer the value of an unknown population parameter.

Statistically significant A result indicating that the null hypothesis can be rejected; with reference to an estimated regression coefficient, frequently understood to mean a result indicating that the corresponding population regression coefficient is different from 0.

Statistics The science of describing, analyzing, and drawing conclusions from data; also, a collection of numerical data.

Stock dividend A dividend paid in the form of additional shares rather than in cash.

Stock index arbitrage A trading strategy involving a long position in a stock portfolio and a short position in a stock index futures contract (or vice versa) designed to exploit a mispricing in the futures contract relative to the underlying index.

Stock options The option to buy a specified number of shares of the firm's stock at a designated price. The designated price is generally set so that the options will be quite valuable if the firm's shares increase in price, but of little value if their price falls. Thus, when used to compensate top managers, stock options provide a strong incentive to follow policies that will increase the value of the firm.

Stock repurchase A transaction in which a firm buys back shares of its own stock, thereby decreasing shares outstanding, increasing EPS, and, often, increasing the stock price.

Stock split An action taken by a firm to increase the number of shares outstanding, such as doubling the number of shares outstanding by giving each stockholder two new shares for each one formerly held.

Storage costs or carrying costs The costs of holding an asset, generally a function of the physical characteristics of the underlying asset.

Store of value An asset that will allow people to transfer purchasing power from one period to the next.

Straddle (1) A trading strategy requiring the simultaneous purchase of a call option and a put option having the same exercise price, underlying asset, and expiration date. Variations of this theme include strips, straps, strangles, and chooser options. (2) An option strategy involving the purchase of a put and a call with the same exercise price. A straddle is based on the expectation of high volatility of the underlying.

Straight bond Refers to a plain-vanilla bond with fixed coupon payments and without any optional clauses.

Strangle A variation of a straddle in which the put and call have different exercise prices.

Strap An option strategy involving the purchase of two calls and one put.

Strategic asset allocation The allocation to the major investment asset classes that is determined to be appropriate, given the investor's long-run investment objectives and constraints.

Strategic Business Plan A long-run plan which outlines in broad terms the firm's basic strategy for the next 5 to 10 years.

Stratified random sampling A procedure by which a population is divided into subpopulations (strata) based on one or more classification criteria. Simple random samples are then drawn from each stratum in sizes proportional to the relative size of each stratum in the population. These samples are then pooled.

Stress testing A risk management technique in which the risk manager examines the performance of the portfolio under market conditions involving high risk and usually high correlations across markets. Closely related to scenario analysis.

Stress testing/scenario analysis A set of techniques for estimating losses in extremely unfavorable combinations of events or scenarios.

Strike An action of unionized employees in which they (a) discontinue working for the employer and (b) take steps to prevent other potential workers from offering their services to the employer.

Strike price Price at which an option can be exercised (same as exercise price).

Strip An option strategy involving the purchase of two puts and one call.

Strong-form efficient market hypothesis The belief that security prices fully reflect all information from both public and private sources.

Structural change Economic trend occurring when the economy is undergoing a major change in organization or in how it functions.

Structural unemployment Unemployment due to the structural characteristics of the economy that make it difficult for job seekers to find employment and for employers to hire workers. Although job openings are available, they generally require skills that differ from those of the unemployed workers.

Structured note (1) A bond or note issued with some unusual, often option-like, clause. (2) A bond with an embedded derivative designed to create a payoff distribution that satisfies the needs of a specific investor clientele. (3) A variation of a floating-rate note that has some type of unusual characteristic such as a leverage factor or in which the rate moves opposite to interest rates.

Style analysis An attempt to explain the variability in the observed returns to a security portfolio in terms of the movements in the returns to a series of benchmark portfolios designed to capture the essence of a particular security characteristic such as size, value, and growth.

Style grid A graph used to classify and display the investment style that best defines the nature of a security portfolio.

Subjective probability A probability drawing on personal or subjective judgment.

Subordinate (junior) bonds Debentures that, in case of default, entitle holders to claims on the issuer's assets only after the claims of holders of senior debentures and mortgage bonds are satisfied.

Substitutes Products that serve similar purposes. They are related such that an increase in the price of one will cause an increase in demand for the other (for example, hamburgers and tacos, butter and margarine, Chevrolets and Fords).

Substitution effect That part of an increase (decrease) in amount consumed that is the result of a good being cheaper (more expensive) in relation to other goods because of a reduction (increase) in price.

Sunk cost A cash outlay that has already been incurred and which cannot be recovered regardless of whether the project is accepted or rejected.

Supply shock An unexpected event that temporarily either increases or decreases aggregate supply.

Supply-side economists Modern economists who believe that changes in marginal tax rates exert important effects on aggregate supply.

Support level A price at which a technician would expect a substantial increase in price and volume for a stock to reverse a declining trend that was due to profit taking.

Surplus A condition in which the amount of a good offered for sale by producers is greater than the amount that buyers will purchase at the existing price. A decline in price would eliminate the surplus.

Surprise The actual value of a variable minus its predicted (or expected) value.

Survivorship bias The bias resulting from a test design that fails to account for companies that have gone bankrupt, merged, or are otherwise no longer reported in a database.

Sustainable growth rate A measure of how fast a firm can grow using internal equity and debt financing and a constant capital structure. Equal to retention rate × ROE.

Swap (1) A contract whereby two parties agree to a periodic exchange of cash flows. In certain types of swaps, only the net difference between the amounts owed is exchanged on each payment date. (2) An agreement between two parties to exchange a series of future cash flows.

Swap spread (1) A measure of the risk premium for an interest rate swap, calculated as the difference between the agreement's fixed rate and the yield on a Treasury bond with the same maturity. (2) The difference between the fixed rate on an interest rate swap and the rate on a Treasury note with equivalent maturity; it reflects the general level of credit risk in the market.

Swaption (1) An option to enter into a swap contract at a later date. (2) An option to enter into a swap.

SWOT analysis An examination of a firm's Strength, Weaknesses, Opportunities, and Threats. This analysis helps an analyst evaluate a firm's strategies to exploit its competitive advantages or defend against its weaknesses.

Symmetric information The situation in which investors and managers have identical information about firms' prospects.

Synthetic call The combination of puts, the underlying, and risk-free bonds that replicates a call option.

Synthetic forward contract The combination of the underlying, puts, calls, and risk-free bonds that replicates a forward contract.

Synthetic index fund An index fund position created by combining risk-free bonds and futures on the desired index.

Synthetic put The combination of calls, the underlying, and risk-free bonds that replicates a put option.

Systematic factors Factors that affect the average returns of a large number of different assets.

Systematic risk The variability of returns that is due to macroeconomic factors that affect all risky assets. Because it affects all risky assets, it cannot be eliminated by diversification.

Systematic sampling A procedure of selecting every *k*th member until reaching a sample of the desired size. The sample that results from this procedure should be approximately random.

Tactical asset allocation (1) Short-term adjustments to the long-term asset allocation to reflect views on the current relative attractiveness of asset classes. (2) An investment strategy that adjusts the investor's mix of stocks and bonds by increasing the allocation to the asset class that is relatively undervalued.

Tangible book value per share Common shareholders' equity minus intangible assets from the balance sheet, divided by the number of shares outstanding.

Tap Procedure by which a borrower can keep issuing additional amounts of an old bond at its current market value. This procedure is used for bond issues, notably by the British and French governments, as well as for some short-term debt instruments.

Target capital structure The mix of debt, preferred stock, and common equity with which the firm plans to raise capital.

Target (optimal) Capital Structure The percentages of debt, preferred stock, and common equity that will maximize the firm's stock price.

Target payout ratio The percentage of net income paid out as cash dividends.

Target semideviation The positive square root of target semivariance.

Target semivariance The average squared deviation below a target value.

Tariff A tax levied on goods imported into a country.

Tax base The level or quantity of the economic activity that is taxed (e.g., gallons of gasoline sold per week). Because they make the activity less attractive, higher tax rates reduce the level of the tax base.

Tax incidence The manner in which the burden of a tax is distributed among economic units (consumers, producers, employees, employers, and so on). The actual tax burden does not always fall on those who are statutorily assigned to pay the tax.

Tax rate The per-unit amount of the tax or the percentage rate at which the economic activity is taxed.

Tax risk The uncertainty associated with tax laws.

***t*-Distribution** A symmetrical distribution defined by a single parameter, degrees of freedom, that is largely used to make inferences concerning the mean of a normal distribution whose variance is unknown.

Team production A process of production wherein employees work together under the supervision of the owner or the owner's representative.

Technical analysis (1) A forecasting method for asset prices based solely on information about past prices. (2) Estimation of future security price movements based on past price and volume movements.

Technological advancement The introduction of new techniques or methods that enable production of a greater output per unit of input.

Tenor The original time to maturity on a swap.

Term bond A bond that has a single maturity date.

Terminal price multiple The price multiple for a stock assumed to hold at a stated future time.

Termination date The date of the final payment on a swap; also, the swap's expiration date.

Term structure *See* Yield curve.

Term structure of interest rates The relationship between term to maturity and yield to maturity for a sample of comparable bonds at a given time. Popularly known as the yield curve.

Term to maturity Specifies the date or the number of years before a bond matures or expires.

Test statistic A quantity, calculated based on a sample, whose value is the basis for deciding whether or not to reject the null hypothesis.

Theta The rate at which an option's time value decays.

Third market Over-the-counter trading of securities listed on an exchange.

Tick The minimum price movement for the asset underlying a forward or futures contract; for Treasury bonds, one tick equals 1/32 of 1 percent of par value.

Time-period bias The possibility that when we use a time-series sample, our statistical conclusion may be sensitive to the starting and ending dates of the sample.

Time preferences for consumption The preferences of consumers for current consumption as opposed to savings for future consumption.

Time premium The difference between an option's total market value and its intrinsic value.

Time-series analysis An examination of a firm's performance data over a period of time.

Time-series data Observations of a variable over time.

Time to expiration The time remaining in the life of a derivative, typically expressed in years.

Time value decay The loss in the value of an option resulting from movement of the option price toward its payoff value as the expiration day approaches.

Time value of money The principles governing equivalence relationships between cash flows with different dates.

Time value or speculative value The difference between the market price of the option and its intrinsic value, determined by the uncertainty of the underlying over the remaining life of the option.

Time-weighted rate of return The compound rate of growth of one unit of currency invested in a portfolio during a stated measurement period; a measure of investment performance that is not sensitive to the timing and amount of withdrawals or additions to the portfolio.

Time-weighted return (1) A rate of return measure that captures the rate of return per unit of currency initially invested. (2) The geometric average of (one plus) the holding period yields to an investment portfolio.

Times-interest-earned (TIE) ratio A ratio that measures the firm's ability to meet its annual interest obligations, calculated by dividing earnings before interest and taxes by interest charges. TIE = EBIT/I.

Tombstone (or Tumbstone) Advertisement that states the borrower's name, gives the conditions of an issue, and lists the various banks taking part in the issue.

Top-down With respect to investment approaches, the allocation of money first to categories such as asset classes, countries, or industry followed by the selection of individual securities within category.

Total cost The costs, both explicit and implicit, of all the resources used by the firm. Total cost includes an imputed normal rate of return for the firm's equity capital.

Total fixed cost The sum of the costs that do not vary with output. They will be incurred as long as a firm continues in business and the assets have alternative uses.

Total probability rule for expected value A rule explaining the expected value of a random variable in terms of expected values of the random variable conditional on mutually exclusive and exhaustive scenarios.

Total product The total output of a good that is associated with alternative utilization rates of a variable input.

Total return A return objective in which the investor wants to increase the portfolio value to meet a future need by both capital gains and current income investment.

Total return swap A swap in which one party agrees to pay the total return on a security. Often used as a credit derivative, in which the underlying is a bond.

Total variable cost The sum of those costs that rise as output increases. Examples of variable costs are wages paid to workers and payments for raw materials.

Tournament pay A form of compensation where the top performer (or performers) receives much higher rewards than other competitors, even if the others perform at only a slightly lower level.

Tracking error (1) The standard deviation of the difference in returns between an active investment portfolio and its benchmark portfolio; also called tracking error volatility. (2) The condition in which the performance of a portfolio does not match the performance of an index that serves as the portfolio's benchmark. (3) A synonym for tracking risk and active risk; also, the total return on a portfolio (gross of fees) minus the total return on a benchmark.

Tracking portfolio A portfolio having factor sensitivities that are matched to those of a benchmark or other portfolio.

Tracking risk The standard deviation of the differences between a portfolio's returns and its benchmark's returns; a synonym of active risk.

Trade balance The balance of a country's exports and imports; part of the current account.

Trade deficit The situation when a country's imports of goods and services are greater than its exports.

Trade surplus The situation when a country's exports of goods and services are greater than its imports.

Trading effect The difference in performance of a bond portfolio from that of a chosen index due to short-run changes in the composition of the portfolio.

Trading rule A formula for deciding on current transactions based on historical data.

Trading turnover The percentage of outstanding shares traded during a period of time.

Trailing P/E (or current P/E) A stock's current market price divided by the most recent four quarters of earnings per share.

Tranche Refers to a portion of an issue that is designed for a specific category of investors. French for "slice."

Transaction accounts Accounts, including demand deposits and interest-earning checkable deposits, against which the account holder is permitted to transfer funds for the purpose of making payment to a third party.

Transaction costs (1) The time, effort, and other resources needed to search out, negotiate, and consummate an exchange. (2) The cost of executing a trade. Low costs characterize an operationally efficient market.

Transaction exposure The risk associated with a foreign exchange rate on a specific business transaction such as a purchase or sale.

Translation exposure The risk associated with the conversion of foreign financial statements into domestic currency.

Translation risk Risk arising from the translation of the value of an asset or flow from a foreign currency to the domestic currency.

Treasury bill A negotiable U.S. government security with a maturity of less than one year that pays no periodic interest but yields the difference between its par value and its discounted purchase price.

Treasury bond A U.S. government security with a maturity of more than 10 years that pays interest periodically.

Treasury note A U.S. government security with maturities of 1 to 10 years that pays interest periodically.

Tree diagram A diagram with branches emanating from nodes representing either mutually exclusive chance events or mutually exclusive decisions.

Trend A long-term pattern of movement in a particular direction.

Treynor measure A relative measure of a portfolio's benefit-to-risk ratio, calculated as its average return in excess of the risk-free rate divided by its beta coefficient.

Triangular arbitrage With respect to currencies, an arbitrage involving three currencies only.

Trimmed mean A mean computed after excluding a stated small percentage of the lowest and highest observations.

Trough The culmination of a bear market at which prices stop declining and begin rising.

***t*-Test** A hypothesis test using a statistic (*t*-statistic) that follows a *t*-distribution.

12b-1 plan A fee charged by some funds, named after the SEC rule that permits it. Such fees pay for distribution costs, such as advertising, or for brokers' commissions. The fund's prospectus details any 12b-1 charges that apply.

Two-sided hypothesis test (or two-tailed hypothesis test) A test in which the null hypothesis is rejected in favor of the alternative hypothesis if the evidence indicates that the population parameter is either smaller or larger than a hypothesized value.

Type I error The error of rejecting a true null hypothesis.

Type II error The error of not rejecting a false null hypothesis.

Unanticipated change A change that decision makers could not reasonably foresee. Thus, choices made prior to the event did not take the event into account.

Unanticipated inflation An increase in the general level of prices that was not expected by most decision makers.

Unbiasedness Lack of bias. A desirable property of estimators, an unbiased estimator is one whose expected value (the mean of its sampling distribution) equals the parameter it is intended to estimate.

Unconditional heteroskedasticity Heteroskedasticity of the error term that is not correlated with the values of the independent variable(s) in the regression.

Unconditional probability (or marginal probability) The probability of an event not conditioned on another event.

Uncovered interest rate parity The assertion that expected currency depreciation should offset the interest differential between two countries over the term of the interest rate.

Underfunded plan A defined benefit pension plan in which the present value of the fund's liabilities to employees exceeds the value of the fund's assets.

Underground economy Unreported barter and cash transactions that take place outside recorded market channels. Some are otherwise legal activities undertaken to evade taxes. Others involve illegal activities, such as trafficking in drugs and prostitution.

Underlying (1) Refers to a security on which a derivative contract is written. (2) An asset that trades in a market in which buyers and sellers meet, decide on a price, and the seller then delivers the asset to the buyer and receives payment. The underlying is the asset or other derivative on which a particular derivative is based. The market for the underlying is also referred to as the spot market.

Underweighted A condition in which a portfolio, for whatever reason, includes less of a class of securities that the relative market value alone would justify.

Underlying earnings (or persistent earnings or continuing earnings or core earnings) Earnings excluding nonrecurring components.

Unemployed The term used to describe a person not currently employed who is either (1) actively seeking employment or (2) waiting to begin or return to a job.

Unexpected earnings (earnings surprise) The difference between reported earnings per share and expected earnings per share.

Unitary hedge ratio A hedge ratio equal to 1.

Unit normal distribution *See* Standard normal distribution.

Unit of account The units of measurement used by people to post prices and keep track of revenues and costs.

Unit root A time series that is not covariance stationary is said to have a unit root.

Univariate distribution A distribution that specifies the probabilities for a single random variable.

Unrealized capital gains Capital gains that reflect the price appreciation of currently held unsold assets; taxes on unrealized capital gains can be deferred indefinitely.

Unsecured bonds Bonds that promise payments of interest and principal but pledge no specific assets. Holders have first claim on the issuer's income and unpledged assets. Also known as debentures.

Unsystematic risk Risk that is unique to an asset, derived from its particular characteristics. It can be eliminated in a diversified portfolio.

Unweighted index An indicator series affected equally by the performance of each security in the sample regardless of price or market value. Also referred to as an equal-weighted series.

Unwind The negotiated termination of a forward or futures position before contract maturity.

Uptick An incremental movement upward in a transaction price over the previous transaction price.

Uptick-downtick ratio A ratio of the number of uptick block transactions (indicating buyers) to the number of downtick block transactions (indicating sellers of blocks). An indicator of institutional investor sentiment.

Up transition probability The probability that an asset's value moves up.

User charges Payments that users (consumers) are required to make if they want to receive certain services provided by the government.

Utility The subjective benefit or satisfaction a person expects from a choice or course of action.

Valuation The process of determining the value of an asset or service.

Valuation analysis An active bond portfolio management strategy designed to capitalize on expected price increases in temporarily undervalued issues.

Valuation process Part of the investment decision process in which you estimate the value of a security.

Value The amount for which one can sell something, or the amount one must pay to acquire something.

Value at risk (VaR) (1) A money measure of the minimum loss that is expected over a given period of time with a given probability. (2) A probability-based measure of loss potential for a company, a fund, a portfolio, a transaction, or a strategy over a specified period of time. (3) A money measure of the minimum value of losses expected during a specified time period at a given level of probability.

Value chain The set of transformations to move from raw material to product or service delivery.

Value of marginal product (VMP) The marginal product of a resource multiplied by the selling price of the product it helps to produce. For a price taker firm, marginal revenue product *(MRP)* will be equal to the value marginal product *(VMP)*.

Value stocks Stocks that appear to be undervalued for reasons besides earnings growth potential. These stocks are usually identified based on high dividend yields, low P/E ratios, or low price-to-book ratios.

Variable-rate note A debt security for which the interest rate changes to follow some specified short-term rate, for example, the T-bill rate; see floating rate note.

Variance (1) A measure of variability equal to the sum of the squares of a return's deviation from the mean, divided by the total number of returns. (2) The expected value (the probability-weighted average) of squared deviations from a random variable's expected value.

Variation margin Profits or losses on open positions in futures and option contracts that are paid or collected daily.

Vega The relationship between option price and volatility.

Volatility (1) A measure of the uncertainty about the future price of an asset. Typically measured by the standard deviation of returns on the asset. (2) As used in option pricing, the standard deviation of the continuously compounded returns on the underlying asset.

Warrant An instrument that allows the holder to purchase a specified number of shares of the firm's common stock from the firm at a specified price for a given period of time.

Weak-form efficient market hypothesis The belief that security prices fully reflect all security market information.

Weighted mean An average in which each observation is weighted by an index of its relative importance.

Weighted-average cost of capital A weighted average of the after-tax required rates of return on a company's common stock, preferred stock, and long-term debt, where the weights are the fraction of each source of financing in the company's target capital structure.

White-corrected standard errors A synonym for robust standard errors.

Wholesale Price Index (WPI) A price index defined on a basket of goods produced.

Winsorized mean A mean computed after assigning a stated percent of the lowest values equal to one specified low value, and a stated percent of the highest values equal to one specified high value.

Withholding tax A tax levied by the country of source on income paid.

Working capital management The management of a company's short-term assets (such as inventory) and short-term liabilities (such as money owed to suppliers).

World Bank A supranational organization of several institutions designed to assist developing countries. The International Bank for Reconstruction and Development (IBRD) and the International Finance Corporation (IFC) are the more important members of the World Bank group.

World Trade Organization (WTO) The new name given to GATT in 1994; it is currently responsible for monitoring and enforcing the multilateral trade agreements among the 133 member countries.

Worst-case scenario An analysis in which all of the input variables are set at their worst reasonably forecasted values.

Write-down A reduction in the value of an asset as stated in the balance sheet.

Writer of an option A term used for the person or institution selling an option and therefore granting the right to exercise it to the buyer of the option.

Yankee bonds Bonds sold in the United States and denominated in U.S. dollars but issued by a foreign firm or government.

Yield The promised rate of return on an investment under certain assumptions.

Yield beta A measure of the sensitivity of a bond's yield to a general measure of bond yields in the market that is used to refine the hedge ratio.

Yield curve A curve showing the relationship between yield (interest rate) and maturity for a set of similar securities. For example, the yield curve can be drawn for U.S. Treasuries or for LIBOR. Typically, different yield curves are drawn for zero-coupon bonds (zero-coupon yield curve) and for coupon bonds quoted at par (par yield curve).

Yield illusion The erroneous expectation that a bond will provide its stated yield to maturity without recognizing the implicit reinvestment assumption related to coupon payments.

Yield spread (1) The difference between the promised yields of alternative bond issues or market segments at a given time relative to yields on treasury issues of equal maturity. (2) The difference between the yield on a bond and the yield on a default-free security, usually a government note, of the same maturity. The yield spread is primarily determined by the market's perception of the credit risk on the bond.

Yield to maturity The total yield on a bond obtained by equating the bond's current market value to the discounted cash flows promised by the bond. Also called actuarial yield.

Yield to worst Given a bond with multiple potential maturity dates and prices due to embedded call options, the practice is to calculate a yield to maturity for each of the call dates and prices and select the lowest yield (the most conservative possible yield) as yield to worst.

Zero-cost collar A transaction in which a position in the underlying is protected by buying a put and selling a call with the premium from the sale of the call offsetting the premium from the purchase of the put. It can also be used to protect a floating-rate borrower against interest rate increases with the premium on a long cap offsetting the premium on a short floor.

Zero-coupon bond (1) A bond paying no coupons until final redemption. Such bonds trade at a discount to their face value so that the price differential (face value minus market price) ultimately provides a return to the investor commensurate with current interest rates. (2) A bond that pays its par value at maturity but no periodic interest payments. Its yield is determined by the difference between its par value and its discounted purchase price. Also called original issue discount (OID) bonds.

INDEX

B